HANDBOOK OF
LIFE-SPAN DEVELOPMENT

Karen L. Fingerman, PhD, is the Berner Hanley Professor of Developmental and Family Studies at Purdue University. She is also Director of Purdue's Adult Family Research Center. She has conducted research and published numerous scholarly articles on positive and negative emotions in social relationships. Her current research focuses on middle-aged adults' relationships with their grown children and their aging parents. She was the 1998 recipient of the Springer Award for Early Career Achievement from APA's Division 20 (Adult Development and Aging) and the 1999 recipient of the Margaret Baltes Award for Early Career Achievement in Social and Behavioral Gerontology from the Gerontological Society of America.

Cynthia A. Berg, PhD, is Professor of Psychology at the University of Utah. Her research takes a life-span approach to the examination of how individuals collaborate in close relationships (e.g., parent–child, married couples) to solve everyday problems, especially those surrounding chronic illness (adolescent diabetes, prostate cancer). She is on the Editorial Boards of *Journal of Family Psychology, Journal of Gerontology,* and *Psychology and Aging.* She received the Graduate Student and Postdoctoral Scholar Distinguished Mentor Award from the University of Utah in 2006 and the 2007 Master Mentor Award from APA's Division 20. Her research has been funded by NICHD, NIA, and NIDDK.

Jacqui Smith, PhD, is Professor of Psychology at the University of Michigan. She is also a Research Professor at the Institute for Social Research, where she heads a research group on psychosocial and cognitive aging, and is Co-PI of the NIH-funded Health and Retirement Study (HRS). She currently directs NIH-funded studies of experienced well-being and health in midlife and old age. Before moving to Michigan, she was a Senior Research Scientist at the Max Planck Institute for Human Development in Berlin and she continues to be the Co-Director of the longitudinal Berlin Aging Study (BASE). Her research focuses on questions about age- and death-related changes in well-being and cognition in adulthood and psychosocial functioning in midlife and old age.

Toni C. Antonucci, PhD, is the Elizabeth M. Douvan Collegiate Professor of Psychology and Research Professor of the Institute for Social Research at the University of Michigan. She directs the Life Course Development Program at the Institute for Social Research. She is past President of the Gerontological Society of America; APA's Division of Adult Development and Aging; and the Society for the Study of Human Development. She received the 2001 Master Mentor Award from APA's Division 20, is currently Secretary General-Elect and a Council Member of the International Association of Gerontology. Her research focuses on social relations and health across the life span, including multigenerational studies of the family and comparative studies of social relations in the United States, Europe, and Japan.

HANDBOOK OF
LIFE-SPAN DEVELOPMENT

Karen L. Fingerman, PhD
Cynthia A. Berg, PhD
Jacqui Smith, PhD
Toni C. Antonucci, PhD

SPRINGER PUBLISHING COMPANY
NEW YORK

Springer Publishing Company, LLC
11 West 42nd Street
New York, NY 10036
www.springerpub.com

Acquisitions Editor: Sheri W. Sussman
Production Editor: Gayle Lee
Cover Design: Steven Pisano
Project Manager: Ashita Shah
Composition: Newgen Imaging Systems

ISBN: 978-0-8261-1079-4
E-book ISBN: 978-0-8261-1080-0
10 11 12 13/ 5 4 3 2 1

The author and the publisher of this Work have made every effort to use sources believed to be reliable to provide information that is accurate and compatible with the standards generally accepted at the time of publication. Because medical science is continually advancing, our knowledge base continues to expand. Therefore, as new information becomes available, changes in procedures become necessary. We recommend that the reader always consult current research and specific institutional policies before performing any clinical procedure. The author and publisher shall not be liable for any special, consequential, or exemplary damages resulting, in whole or in part, from the readers' use of, or reliance on, the information contained in this book. The publisher has no responsibility for the persistence or accuracy of URLs for external or third-party Internet Web sites referred to in this publication and does not guarantee that any content on such Web sites is, or will remain, accurate or appropriate.

Library of Congress Cataloging-in-Publication Data

Handbook of life-span development / [edited by] Karen Fingerman ... [et al.].
    p. ; cm.
  Includes bibliographical references.
  ISBN 978-0-8261-1079-4
  1. Developmental psychology—Handbooks, manuals, etc. 2. Developmental psychobiology—Handbooks, manuals, etc. I. Fingerman, Karen L.
  [DNLM: 1. Human Development. BF 713]
  BF713.H36485 2010
  155—dc22   2010031923

Printed in the United States of America by Bang Printing.

To Lily and Bryce, who remind me of the joys and explorations of the early part of the life span, and to Lois, Lou, and Martha, who serve as role models at the other end.—*KF*

To Kiersten and Erik, who have showed me the wonder of life-span development, and Bob, who has been a great collaborator throughout the adult years.—*CB*

CONTENTS

SECTION 2: PHYSICAL AND COGNITIVE

CONTRIBUTORS

Rebecca G. Adams, PhD
Associate Provost for Planning and
  Assessment Professor of Sociology
Department of Sociology
University of North Carolina at Greensboro
Greensboro, North Carolina

Kristine Ajrouch, PhD
Professor
Department of Sociology
Eastern Michigan University
Ypsilanti, Michigan

Carolyn M. Aldwin, PhD
Professor
Department of Human Development and
  Family Sciences
Oregon State University
Corvallis, Oregon

Duane F. Alwin, PhD
McCourtney Professor of Sociology and
  Demography
Director, Center for Life Course and
  Longitudinal Studies
College of the Liberal Arts
Pennsylvania State University
University Park, Pennsylvania

Ramona Fruja Amthor, PhD
Assistant Professor of Education
Department of Education
Bucknell University
Lewisburg, Pennsylvania

Toni C. Antonucci, PhD
Professor, Program Director, and Research
  Professor
Department of Psychology
University of Michigan
Ann Arbor, Michigan

Brendan M. Baird, PhD
Research Associate
Department of Psychology
University of Notre Dame
South Bend, Indiana

Kelly Anne Barnes, PhD
Postdoctoral Research Scholar
Department of Neurology
Washington University School of
  Medicine
St. Louis, Missouri

Cynthia A. Berg, PhD
Associate Professor, Chair
Department of Psychology
University of Utah
Salt Lake City, Utah

Cindy S. Bergeman, PhD
Professor
Department of Psychology
University of Notre Dame
South Bend, Indiana

Kira S. Birditt, PhD
Elizabeth Douvan Research Fellow
Institute for Social Research
University of Michigan
Ann Arbor, Michigan

Rosemary Blieszner, PhD
Alumni Distinguished Professor
Department of Human
  Development
Virginia Polytechnic Institute and
  State University
Blacksburg, Virginia

Marc H. Bornstein, PhD
Senior Investigator
Child and Family Research
Eunice Kennedy Shriver National Institute of
   Child Health and Human Development
Bethesda, Maryland

Robert H. Bradley, PhD
Professor
School of Social and Family Dynamics and
   Department of Psychology
Arizona State University
Tempe, Arizona

Jeanne Brooks-Gunn, PhD
Professor of Pediatrics
College of Physicians and Surgeons
Columbia University
New York, New York

B. Bradford Brown, PhD
Professor
School of Education
University of Wisconsin
Madison, Wisconsin

Maureen Canavan, MPH
PhD Candidate
Division of Chronic Disease Epidemiology,
   School of Public Health
Yale University
New Haven, Connecticut

Susan T. Charles, PhD
Associate Professor
Department of Psychology and Social
   Behavior
University of California-Irvine
Irvine, California

Neil Charness, PhD
William G. Chase Professor of Psychology &
   Associate
Pepper Institute on Aging and Public Policy
Florida State University
Tallahassee, Florida

Jondou J. Chen, M Ed
Graduate Fellow
Human Development, Teachers College
Columbia University
New York, New York

Helena Chui, PhD
Research Associate
Department of Human Development and
   Family Studies
Colorado State University
Fort Collins, Colorado

Pil Chung, MPH
Research Associate
Social and Behavioral Sciences Program
School of Public Health
Yale University
New Haven, Connecticut

Ayse Cici-Gokaltun, MS
PhD Candidate
Department of Psychology
Florida International University
Miami, Florida

Shelia R. Cotten, PhD
Associate Professor
Department of Sociology
University of Alabama at Birmingham
Birmingham, Alabama

Manfred Diehl, PhD
Professor
Department of Human Development and
   Family Studies
Colorado State University
Fort Collins, Colorado

Kristen Fay, MA
Doctoral Research Assistant
Department of Child Development
Tufts University
Medford, Massachusetts

Karen L. Fingerman, PhD
Berner Hanley Professor in Gerontology;
   Acting Director Gerontology Program
Department of Child Development and
   Family Studies
Purdue University
West Lafayette, Indiana

Kristin E. Flegal, MS
Graduate Student
Department of Psychology
University of Michigan
Ann Arbor, Michigan

Lisa Flook, PhD
Scientist
Center for Investigating Healthy
    Minds
University of Wisconsin
Madison, Wisconsin

Mark C. Fox, MS
Graduate Student
Department of Psychology
Florida State University
Tallahassee, Florida

Mary Gauvain, PhD
Professor
Department of Psychology
University of California at Riverside
Riverside, California

Steven J. Gold, PhD
Graduate Program Director
Department of Sociology
Michigan State University
East Lansing, Michigan

Ishtar O. Govia, PhD
Lecturer
Department of Sociology, Psychology,
    and Social Work
The University of the West Indies
Mona, Jamaica

Elizabeth L. Hay, PhD
Research Associate
Department of Human Development and
    Family Studies
Colorado State University
Fort Collins, Colorado

Jutta Heckhausen, PhD
Professor
Department of Psychology
University of California, Irvine
Irvine, California

Christopher Hertzog, PhD
Professor
Department of Psychology
Georgia Institute of Technology
Atlanta, Georgia

Kimberly S. Howard, PhD
Post Doctoral Fellow
National Center for Children and
    Families, Teachers College
Columbia University
New York, New York

Sally I-Chun Kuo, MA
Graduate Student
Institute of Child Development
University of Minnesota
Minneapolis, Minnesota

Frank J. Infurna, MS
Doctoral Candidate
Human Development and Family Studies
The Pennsylvania State University
University Park, Pennsylvania

Sonia S. Issac, MA
Graduate Research Assistant
Department of Child Development
Tufts University
Medford, Massachusetts

James S. Jackson, PhD
Director and Research Professor
Institute for Social Research
University of Michigan
Ann Arbor, Michigan

Ann E. Lambert, MS
Graduate Student
Department of Psychology
University of Utah
Salt Lake City, Utah

Frieder R. Lang, PhD
Professor of Psychology and Gerontology;
    Director of Institute of Psychogerontology
Department of Psychology and Sport Sciences
University of Erlangen-Nuremberg
Erlangen, Bavaria, Germany

Kathleen Leonard, PhD
Post-Doctoral Fellow
Institute for Applied Research in Youth
    Development
Tufts University
Medford, Massachusetts

Richard M. Lerner, PhD
Director of Institute for Applied Research in
  Youth Development
Eliot Pearson Department of Child
  Development
Tufts University
Medford, Massachusetts

Mary J. Levitt, PhD
Professor and Chair
Department of Psychology
Florida International University
Miami, Florida

Becca R. Levy, PhD
Associate Professor of Epidemiology and
  Psychology
Chronic Disease Epidemiology Social and
  Behavioral Sciences Program
School of Public Health
Yale University
New Haven, Connecticut

Jennifer Lodi-Smith, PhD
Adjunct Assistant Professor of Cognition
  and Aging; Postdoctoral Research
  Fellow
School for Behavioral and Brain Sciences;
  Center for Vital Longevity
University of Texas at Dallas
Dallas, Texas

Ting Lu, MS
Graduate Student
Child Development and Family
  Studies
Purdue University
West Lafayette, Indiana

Gloria Luong, MS
Graduate Student
Department of Psychology and Social
  Behavior
University of California, Irvine
Irvine, California

Karen Lutfey, PhD
Director, Center for Patient-Provider
  Relationships
New England Research Institutes
Watertown, MA

Ann S. Masten, PhD
Distinguished McKnight University Professor
Institute of Child Development
University of Minnesota
Minneapolis, Minnesota

Dan P. McAdams, PhD
Chair, Department of Psychology
Professor of Psychology
Professor of Human Development and
  Social Policy
Northwestern University
Evanston, Illinois

Christopher M. McCormick, MA
Graduate Student
Institute of Child Development
University of Minnesota
Minneapolis, Minnesota

Brandi M. McCullough, MA
Clinical Research Coordinator
Department of Neurology
Memory Disorders Program
University of North Carolina at Chapel Hill
Chapel Hill, North Carolina

A. Eve Miller, MS
Graduate Student
Department of Psychology
University of Utah
Salt Lake City, Utah

Ainsley L. Mitchum, MS
Graduate Student
Department of Psychology
Florida State University
Tallahassee, Florida

Jeylan T. Mortimer, PhD
Professor
Department of Sociology
University of Minnesota
Minneapolis, Minnesota

Dan Mroczek, PhD
Professor
Department of Child Development and
  Family Studies
Purdue University
West Lafayette, Indiana

Amy Pennar, MS
Graduate Student
Department of Family and Human
  Development
Arizona State University
Tempe, Arizona

Jonas Persson, PhD
Research Assistant Professor
Department of Psychology
Stockholm University
Stockholm, Sweden

German Posada, PhD
Associate Professor of Developmental Studies
Department of Child Development and
  Family Studies
Purdue University
West Lafayette, Indiana

Rena Repetti, PhD
Professor
Department of Psychology
University of California, Los Angeles
Los Angeles, California

Patricia A. Reuter-Lorenz, PhD
Professor
Department of Psychology
University of Michigan
Ann Arbor, Michigan

Chandra A. Reynolds, PhD
Associate Professor
Department of Psychology
University of California at Riverside
Riverside, California

Margund K. Rohr, MSc
Graduate Student
Department of Psychology and Sport
  Sciences
University of Erlangen-Nuremberg
Erlangen, Bavaria, Germany

Sherrill L. Sellers,
Associate Professor
Department of Family Studies and
  Social Work
Miami University
Oxford, Ohio

Bradley L. Schlaggar, MD, PhD
A. Ernest and Jane G. Stein Associate
  Professor of Developmental
  Neurology
Associate Professor of Radiology,
  Pediatrics, and Anatomy & Neurobiology
Department of Neurology
Washington University School of
  Medicine
St. Louis, Missouri

Yee Lee Shing, PhD
Research Scientist
Department of Lifespan Psychology
Humboldt University
Berlin, Germany

Ellen A. Skinner, PhD
Professor
Psychology Department
Portland State University
Portland, Oregon

Martin J. Sliwinski, PhD
Director, The Gerontology Center Professor
  or Human Development and Family
  Studies
Department of Human Development and
  Family Studies
Pennsylvania State University
University Park, Pennsylvania

Jacqui Smith, PhD
Professor and Research Professor
Department of Psychology
Institute for Social Research
University of Michigan
Ann Arbor, Michigan

Jacqueline Sperling, MA
Graduate Student
Department of Clinical Psychology
University of California, Los Angeles
Los Angeles, California

David L. Strayer, PhD
Professor
Department of Psychology
University of Utah
Salt Lake City, Utah

JoNell Strough, PhD
Professor; Coordinator
Department of Psychology
West Virginia University
Morgantown, West Virginia

Amanda L. Taylor, MS
Graduate Student
Department of Human Development and
   Family Studies
Oregon State University
Corvallis, Oregon

Nicholas Turiano, MA
Graduate Student
Department of Child Development and
   Family Studies
Purdue University
West Lafayette, Indiana

Jason M. Watson, PhD
Assistant Professor
Department of Psychology
Assistant Investigator
The Brain Institute
University of Utah
Salt Lake City, Utah

Bettina Williger, MA
Graduate Student
Department of Psychology and Sport
   Sciences
University of Erlangen-Nuremberg
Erlangen, Bavaria, Germany

Lise M. Youngblade, PhD
Professor and Department Head
Department of Human Development and
   Family Studies
Colorado State University
Fort Collins, Colorado

Melanie J. Zimmer-Gembeck, PhD
Professor
Psychology and Griffith Health Institute
Griffith University
Queensland, Australia

ACKNOWLEDGMENTS

Karen L. Fingerman was supported by R01 AG027769 from the National Institute of Aging.

Cynthia A. Berg was supported by R01 DK-063044 from the National Institute of Diabetes and Digestive and Kidney Diseases.

APPROACHES TO MODELING INTRAINDIVIDUAL AND INTERINDIVIDUAL FACETS OF CHANGE FOR DEVELOPMENTAL RESEARCH

1

Martin J. Sliwinski

The science of human development seeks to understand how individuals change on physical, cognitive, and social dimensions of functioning across the life span. Although many informative developmental studies have relied on cross-sectional comparisons among individuals of different ages, optimal designs for addressing developmental questions must involve the study of intraindividual change across time. Often, the time frame in developmental studies spans years and may be indexed with reference to particular events, such as one's birth, entrance to a particular grade in school, and the onset of puberty, menopause, or retirement. There is also growing interest in the study of short-term change and variability observed across moments or days as means of gaining insight into developmental phenomena (Fleeson & Jolley, 2006; Li et al., 2004). However, it is relatively uncommon for researchers to simultaneously examine both short-term variability and long-term change in the same study. This is unfortunate, because processes that unfold rapidly (e.g., strategy selection, emotion regulation) can be both a cause and consequence of long-term developmental changes in trait-manifesting behavior and health outcomes.

In this chapter, I will discuss the conceptual underpinnings and methodological approaches for linking change processes that operate across different time scales. First, I will discuss important distinctions (i.e., variability vs. change, intraindividual vs. interindividual differences in change) in developmental methodology and how they map onto commonly used analytic approaches. Second, I will explore the utility of different research designs for studying both the intraindividual and interindividual facets of developmental change across different time scales (i.e., over the short-term and long-term). Emphasis will be given to a relatively novel hybrid research design, the measurement burst (Nesselroade, 1991; Sliwinski, 2008). Most longitudinal designs consist of measuring behavior once every several months or years to detect long-term developmental trends. In contrast, measurement-burst designs consist of "bursts" of intensive (e.g., daily) measurements that are repeated over longer intervals (e.g., every several months). Thus, the measurement burst combines elements of intensive short-term measurement designs (e.g., microgenetic, daily diary, experience sampling) with more conventional longitudinal designs that focus on longer-term follow-up. For example, a researcher interested in developmental changes in emotion regulation might examine affective reactivity to daily stress and how characteristics such as personality and chronic stress exposure influence these changes. A measurement-burst approach to this problem could involve repeating a week-long daily diary study every few months to examine longer-term intraindividual changes in patterns of variability and covariation between affect and stress. This type of design affords researchers with the opportunity to pose and address a rich array of questions regarding processes of intraindividual variability and change that operate across very different time intervals.

CROSS-SECTIONAL AND LONGITUDINAL METHODS IN LIFE-SPAN DEVELOPMENT

Developmental research focuses on maturational changes that are part of the normal developmental course of individuals over their life span. This fact emphasizes a design choice that developmental researchers must make—cross-sectional versus longitudinal designs. Cross-sectional designs involve studying groups of individuals of different ages at a single point in time. By comparing the differences among individuals of different ages, cross-sectional designs make indirect inferences regarding how these persons may have or may be expected to change. For example, a cross-sectional approach to studying developmental changes in arithmetic ability might involve comparing a sample of 8-year-old children to a sample of 10 year olds. Longitudinal studies involve studying one group of individuals over a particular time period (e.g., studying how math ability changes over a 2-year period in one sample of 8 year olds). By comparing the same individuals across different points in time, longitudinal studies permit the direct measurement of intraindividual change. Both designs have strengths and weaknesses that influence the validity of inferences researchers can draw from them. In the following section, I describe a few of the more important issues for interpreting results from cross-sectional and longitudinal designs.

One important limitation of cross-sectional designs is their inability to distinguish age-graded developmental changes from cohort effects. Cohort effects refer to differences on developmentally relevant variables that arise from (non-age-related) factors to which each birth cohort is exposed. For example, recent generations have more experience with technology than earlier generations, and this differential exposure could affect computer-based cognitive assessments over and above any developmental (i.e., age) differences in cognitive ability. Generational differences in exposure to environmental hazards (e.g., lead), access to health care, and educational practices are a few other examples that produce cohort effects that may masquerade as maturational effects in cross-sectional designs.

Longitudinal designs must contend with other types of confounds, such as those arising from time-of-measurement effects, reactivity effects, and attrition effects. Time-of-measurement effects threaten the validity of longitudinal studies intended to elucidate maturational effects by confounding common historical exposures with maturational processes. For example, in a recent study, my colleagues and I demonstrated longitudinal increases in negative emotional states and in emotional responses to daily stressors across the adult life span (Sliwinski, Almeida, Smyth, & Stawski, 2009). However, this study spanned certain historical events (e.g., the September 11 World Trade Center attack, initiation of two wars, etc.) that could have resulted in a downturn of emotional well-being in individuals, independent of maturational processes. Reactivity effects result when measurements change as a mere function of previous exposure to the assessment protocol. Retest effects (Ferrer, Salthouse, Stewart, & Schwartz, 2004; Salthouse, 2009) on measures of cognitive performance are a good example of this type of threat to the internal validity of longitudinal development studies. Finally, attrition effects result when the observed effect (e.g., a decrease in well-being) reflects the process by which individuals opt out of longitudinal follow-up. For example, if unhealthy individuals are more likely to drop out of a longitudinal study than are their healthier age peers, the study population may look like it is getting healthier across time when in fact this change reflects nonrandom (selective) attrition. These are just a few examples of threats to the internal validity of cross-sectional and longitudinal studies. There are many excellent scholarly papers (e.g., Schaie & Hofer, 2001) that discuss these and other threats in detail. The remainder of this chapter focuses on longitudinal design issues that have not received as much attention in the literature.

INTRAINDIVIDUAL VARIABILITY AND CHANGE

Nesselroade (1991) distinguished between intraindividual change, which he characterized as "more or less enduring," and intraindividual variability, which he characterized as "changes that are . . . more or less reversible" (p. 215). This characterization distinguishes between variability and change primarily along one dimension—durability. It is often, but not always, the case that durable developmental change manifests over longer time periods and intraindividual variability manifests across a much narrower time interval. In fact, relatively durable developmental changes may occur quite quickly and be observable within a single experimental session (e.g., Siegler & Svetina, 2002), whereas intraindividual variability may transpire over longer intervals (e.g., Sliwinski et al., 2009). For example, adolescents exhibit developmental changes in their ability to engage in formal, abstract reasoning but may, at any given time, revert to less complex forms of reasoning. Advancing age in adulthood has been associated with a trend toward less frequent negative emotional states, but individuals across the adult life span exhibit substantial daily and even momentary fluctuations in their negative mood. These examples distinguish between more or less enduring intraindividual (developmental) changes and transient fluctuations.

Both types of intraindividual dynamics—variability and change—are important for developmental theory. Studying very short-term variability in behavior can provide insight into the current developmental state of a person—this has been shown in the context of skill acquisition in children (e.g., Siegler, 2007), motor development (e.g., Newell, Liu, & Mayer-Kress, 2001), and cognitive aging (e.g., Lovden, Li, Shing, & Lindenberger, 2007). The premise that developmentally relevant change and variability can occur across very different time scales carries two implications. The first is that developmental theories should incorporate temporal as well as functional and structural components. That is, developmental hypotheses must specify not only what types of changes occur but also the time scale over which these changes should occur (e.g., across moments, days, months, or years). The second is that research designs and analytic methods need to provide information regarding variability and change across more than one time scale.

▦ INTRAINDIVIDUAL VERSUS INTERINDIVIDUAL CHANGE

In their seminal chapter on developmental methodology, Baltes and Nesselroade (1979) enumerated five rationales for longitudinal designs:

1. Direct identification of intraindividual change
2. Direct identification of interindividual differences in intraindividual change
3. Analysis of interrelationships in behavioral change
4. Analysis of causes of intraindividual change
5. Analysis of causes of interindividual differences in intraindividual change

The first two rationales pertain to the description of intraindividual developmental change (e.g., the form and timing) and how individuals differ in their patterns and rates of change. In addition to being necessary for describing change, longitudinal studies allow researchers to examine how changes in one variable (e.g., emotion regulation) relate to changes in other variables (e.g., well-being). However, the most important reason for conducting longitudinal studies is to test developmentally relevant hypotheses about the causes of change. In particular, Baltes and Nesseoroade drew a distinction between causes of "intraindividual change" and causes of "interindividual differences in intraindividual change" (i.e., "interindividual change"). The vast majority of longitudinal studies of developmental phenomena have focused exclusively on the fifth rationale—examining causes of interindividual change—such that the study of developmental change has become nearly synonymous with the study of how and why people differ in rates of change. Very few attempts have reflected the fourth rationale for conducting longitudinal developmental research—to identify causes of intraindividual change—and it is not entirely clear that the developmental literature acknowledges the distinction between a cause of intraindividual change (i.e., why people change) and a cause of interindividual differences in change (i.e., why people change differently).

To understand the critical distinction between modeling intraindividual and interindividual change, it is necessary to frame these concepts in a formal analytic approach. Most approaches to modeling longitudinal data have relied on multilevel or growth curve models that represent intraindividual change as a function of a time metric such as time in study, time since birth (i.e., age), time to an event (e.g., dementia diagnosis), or time to death. The descriptive part of this approach usually consists of estimating average rates of change and person-specific deviations from that average. The explanatory part consists of introducing between-person variables to account for those person-specific deviations, that is, to explain the rank order differences among persons in their rates of change. For example, the descriptive part of longitudinal modeling might describe the rate at which infants acquire and use new words, and the explanatory part would include examining how some relatively stable variables (e.g., the mother's vocabulary size) could explain why some infants vocabulary grows at a faster rate than other infants.

To illustrate the approach formally, consider the representation of a simple multilevel model (MLM) for change (Table 1.1). As an example, consider how this approach would be used to model longitudinal changes in levels of self-reported negative affect. This approach consists of a level-1 equation, which represents intraindividual change in affect as a function of changes in chronological age, and

TABLE 1.1

Simple Multilevel Model for Change	
$affect_{ik} = b_{0k} + b_{1k}(age_{ik}) + e_{ik}$	(level 1: intraindividual change)
$b_{0k} = \beta_{00k} + \beta_{01k}(Stress_k) + v_{0k}$	(level 2: interindividual level differences)
$b_{1k} = \beta_{10k} + \beta_{11k}(Stress_k) + v_{1k}$	(level 2: interindividual change)

a set of level-2 equations, which describe interindividual differences in intraindividual change.

The level-1 coefficients, b_{0k} and b_{1k}, represent the intercept and slope (rate of change), and e_{ik} represents the residual for a given person, k, at a particular time, denoted by the index i. This level-1 equation is estimated simultaneously for everyone in the analysis, so that each person has their own person-specific intercept (b_{0k}) and age-slope (b_{1k}). The intercept and slope parameters then function as outcome variables for the level-2 equation. The important difference between the level-1 and the level-2 equations is that the former refers to intraindividual (within-person) processes and the latter refers to interindividual (between-person) processes.

Explanatory modeling typically occurs in the level-2 equations, which are also regression equations. So, for example, a researcher might hypothesize that individuals who are under more stress tend to have higher levels of negative affect and tend to increase more in negative affect over time than their less-stressed age peers. The variable $Stress_k$, which refers to a variable that describes a person's level of stress, functions as a predictor variable in the level-2 equations. Predictor variables added at level 2 can be any variable that provides information about the rank ordering of individuals (i.e., a between-person variable). This can include status variables such as gender or "change" variables such as a slope estimate of change on another variable. The main point is that typical modeling of developmental processes treats change as an outcome and emphasizes explanatory modeling of interindividual or rank order differences among persons in that outcome (Rationale 5).

Identifying predictors of change ($Stress_k$ in this example) in developmental research has become synonymous with explaining between-person differences in rates or amounts of change. By listing them as separate rationales, Baltes and Nesselroade (1979) viewed modeling predictors of intraindividual change and predictors of interindividual differences in change as distinct activities. So, how would this analytic framework differentiate between modeling these two types of predictors? One important limitation of most approaches to modeling developmental change is that our analytic models imply that the change in any individual is solely a function of the passage of time. This is because most level-1 models of intraindividual change only include some index of time, and the inclusion of "explanatory" variables is confined to level 2, the between-person level. My colleagues and I have previously addressed this issue by discussing the utility of "process-based" models which represent intraindividual change as a function not only of the passage of time but also of cognitive, physiological, and psychosocial processes hypothesized to drive intraindividual change (Sliwinski & Buschke, 2004; Sliwinski & Mogle, 2008). Equation 2 (Table 1.2) depicts how one would represent predictors of intraindividual change by including a time-varying variable in the level-1 equation for intraindividual change.

TABLE 1.2

The Multilevel Model for Change with a time-varying predictor

$affect_{ik} = b_{0k} + b_{1k}(age_{ik}) + b_{1k}(Stress_{ik}) + e_{ik}$ (level 1: intraindividual change)

$b_{0k} = \beta_{00k} + \beta_{11k}(Stress_k) + v_{0k}$ (level 2: interindividual level differences)

$b_{1k} = \beta_{10k} + \beta_{11k}(Stress_k) + v_{1k}$ (level 2: interindividual change)

The variable $Stress_{ik}$ represents a predictor of intraindividual change, which must, by definition, be a time-varying variable—it must take on different values for person k across time points (i). Thus, the model in equation 2 is asking whether, for a given person (k), changes in *stress* predict concurrent changes in *affect*. In contrast, predictors of interindividual differences in change are intended to account for the differences among individuals in the magnitude or rate of change and that is why some individuals are changing more or less rapidly than others over time. Contrasting Figures 1.1a and 1.1b clarifies what it means to "explain" intraindividual change (Figure 1.1a) and interindividual differences in intraindividual change (Figure 1.1b). The former focuses on understanding why changes experienced by an individual during one time period differ from changes experienced by the same individual during a different time period. So, in Figure 1.1a an explanation of intraindividual change would entail understanding why the variable y decreases from t1 to t2 and then increases from t2 to t3 by linking those changes to concurrent or previous changes in a predictor variable ($Stress_{ik}$ in equation 2). In contrast, explanations of interindividual differences in intraindividual change focus on between-person differences in variables ($Stress_k$ in equation 2) that can predict why one person changes more (or less) rapidly than another. Thus, the model for intraindividual change (level 1) postulates that a person's affect goes up (or down) as a function of concurrent changes in stress, whereas the model for interindividual change (level 2) postulates that the affect of individuals with higher levels of stress will change more (or less) rapidly than their less-stressed age peers. Thus, intraindividual modeling is concerned with *when* or under what conditions any given individual experiences change and interindividual modeling is concerned with *who* experiences more (or less) change.

A major motivation to conduct longitudinal studies of development is to identify the causes of developmentally relevant change. I have discussed two directions from which to approach this task. The first (and most common) direction involves attempts to understand why individuals change at different rates (Rationale 5) and is, at its core, an essentially between-person (interindividual) approach. The second direction involves taking a within-person (intraindividual) approach by asking how variables are *coupled*, or travel together over time, within individuals (Rationale 4). Although there is little research on the topic, examination of between-person correlates of interindividual differences in change does not necessarily yield information about the correlates of intraindividual change (Sliwinski, Hofer, & Hall, 2003; Sliwinski & Mogle, 2008).

Theorists and methodologists have argued that developmental theories and their predictions must be evaluated at the intraindividual level of analysis (Ford & Lerner, 1992; Wohlwill, 1973). Some have forcefully argued that the analyses of between-person relationships provide no information about how variables are associated within

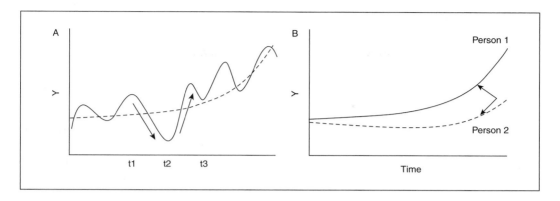

FIGURE 1.1   Panel A illustrates intraindividual change as temporal deviations of an individual from their smoothed trajectory. Panel B illustrates differences in intraindividual change as deviations of individuals from the overall average trajectory.

individuals (Borsboom, Mellenbergh, & van Heerden, 2003), except under a highly restrictive set of assumptions that developmental processes, by their very nature, are unlikely to satisfy (Molenaar, Sinclair, Rovine, Ram, & Corneal, 2009). Most examinations of how variables are coupled within individuals have come from studies involving intensive repeated measurements conducted over a relatively short time period, such as daily diary and experience sampling studies (e.g., Carstensen, Pasupathi, Mayr, & Nesselroade, 2000; Gruhn, Rebucal, Diehl, Lumley, & Labouvie-Vief, 2008; Mroczek & Almeida, 2004; Rocke, Li, & Smith, 2009). These types of studies tend to focus on intraindividual modeling by expressing short-term fluctuations in one variable (e.g., negative affect) as a function of concurrent changes in a predictor variable (e.g., day-to-day minor stressors). With few exceptions (MacDonald, Hultsch, & Dixon, 2003; MacDonald, Hultsch, Strauss, & Dixon, 2003; Sliwinski & Buschke, 1999, 2004), studies of longer-term change have focused almost exclusively on between-person analyses of interindividual differences in intraindividual change and have not attempted to identify predictors of intraindividual changes.

Although many developmental phenomena are most clearly observable over longer time periods (months, years, or even decades), many developmentally relevant processes operate over very short time scales. These include emotion regulation, impulse control, how we allocate attention, and how we select strategies for problem solving. Acceptance that developmentally relevant processes transpire across multiple time scales entails important conceptual and methodological challenges. Conceptually, developmental theories must provide mechanisms that bridge processes operating on different time scales. Methodologically, researchers must endeavor to link measurements of behaviors, cognitions, and emotional states that fluctuate day-to-day or even moment-to-moment to changes that occur over the long term. Measurement-burst designs offer one approach to meeting this challenge because they explicitly incorporate the notion that dynamic processes important for development occur with different cadences. In the next two sections, I will present some examples of how measurement-burst designs can represent and link dynamic processes across different time scales.

DIFFERENT TEMPORAL SCALES OF INTRAINDIVIDUAL VARIABILITY AND CHANGE

Nesselroade (1991) introduced the notion of measurement bursts as a useful design tool to capture the "warp and the woof" of developmental dynamics. This analogy implies that the structure underlying human development consists of interwoven threads that signify longer-term trends (warp) and shorter-term variability (woof) on which those trends are built. Figure 1.2 is a simple elaboration of a figure from Nesselroade's chapter (p. 215) that illustrates the importance of explicitly incorporating time scale in developmental theories, using negative affect as an example. Negative affect is an important outcome variable in research on developmental changes in emotional regulation that exhibits variability and change across different time scales—moment-to-moment variability (e.g., Carstensen et al., 2000; Schneiders et al., 2007; van Eck, Nicolson, & Berkhof, 1998), day-to-day variability (e.g., Eid & Diener, 1999; Kleban, Lawton, Nesselroade, & Parmelee, 1992), and variability across months (Sliwinski et al., 2009). In addition, important developmental theories (e.g., Carstensen, Isaacowitz, & Charles, 1999; Labouvie-Vief, 2003) make predictions about gradual changes in affect that occur across adulthood over the course of years and decades. Bear in mind that negative affect is used only as an example and that many or, perhaps, most other cognitive, psychosocial, and health-related variables also exhibit dynamics across multiple time scales (e.g., cognitive function, physical activity, stress, blood pressure, job satisfaction).

Because most developmental research is traditionally concerned with long-term changes in behavior and individual characteristics that manifest over years or decades, analyses usually focus on smoothed, long-term trends. The dashed line in Figure 1.2 represents such a smoothed trend of a hypothetical individual's long-term

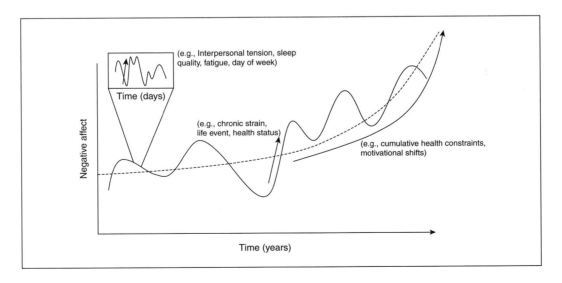

FIGURE 1.2 **This figure illustrates that similar changes in a variable (e.g., negative affect) across different time scales may reflect the operation of very different types of causal influences.**

changes in negative affect. However, in reality we would never expect developmental changes in the negative affect of any individual to be so orderly. If we could measure this person's "real" negative affect continuously, we could also see that over the course of adulthood there are numerous peaks and valleys in their negative affect across months and years, as indicated by the wavy solid line. We could further drill down to examine more local changes that characterize even narrower temporal epochs that span weeks, days, or even moments within a day, as indicated by the boxed wavy line segment in the figure. Thus, an individual's developmental pathway consists of *global* trends (increasing in this figure) and *local* changes restricted to particular segments of the overall developmental path.

Most longitudinal studies tend to focus on variability or change across a single time scale and thereby relegate the dynamics of other time scales to irrelevance or measurement error. These studies are characterized by widely spaced measurements and focus on understanding individual differences around the "average" long-term trajectory of change. For example, studies of how personality and health might influence the rate of developmental changes in self-reports of emotion measure individuals every year or several years (Charles, Reynolds, & Gatz, 2001; Griffin, Mroczek, & Spiro, 2006). Studies of cognitive aging often have retest intervals that span several years or even several decades (e.g., Salthouse, Schroeder, & Ferrer, 2004), with annual assessments considered relatively intensive (e.g., Wilson et al., 2002). While such designs can provide valuable information about rates of change that transpire over long retest intervals, they provide less information about what occurs in the *space between* the changes during which developmentally relevant events and causal influences may operate.

Accurate description of an individual's developmental path would, ideally, consist of continuous measurements obtained over relatively long time periods. Although the possibility of semicontinuous measurement over extended time periods is possible (Pavel et al., 2008), it can be resource-intensive and in many circumstances, unfeasible. The measurement-burst design offers a practical approach to obtaining measurements across widely different time scales (Nesselroade, 1991). The structure of a measurement-burst design consists of intensive measurements obtained within a sequence of discrete temporal epochs. Figure 1.3 depicts such a design that captures variability and change operating over three different time periods—short-term (or state) variability, midterm (or state-of-state) variability, and long-term (global) trends. The descriptors "short term," "midterm," and "long term" are meant to imply relative rather than absolute time scales. In some contexts "short term" might refer to variability across milliseconds (MacDonald, Nyberg, Sandblom, Fischer, & Backman, 2008; Schmiedek, Lovden, & Lindenberger, 2009), and "long term" might refer to trends observed over months (e.g., Sliwinski et al., 2009) or decades (e.g., Schaie, 1989). Another way to conceptualize multiple time scales in developmental research is by identifying "fast" and "slow" change processes (e.g., Newell et al., 2001; Sosnoff & Newell, 2006). What constitutes appropriate short-term (fast) and long-term (slow) time scales will depend on the cadence of both the phenomenon of interest and its causal influences.

Characterizing change across different time scales is critical not only for describing developmental phenomena but also for testing predictions about the antecedents of change. Different types of influences may drive similar changes in a variable across different time scales (see Figure 1.3). Continuing with the

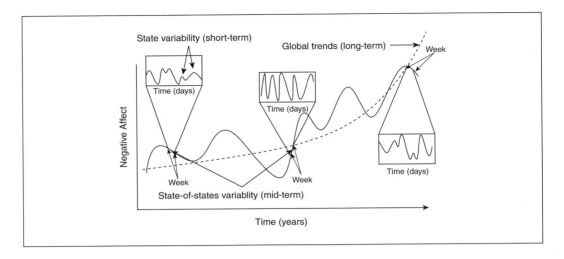

FIGURE 1.3   **This figure illustrates the structure of a measurement-burst design, which allows measurement of intraindividual dynamics across three different time scales.**

example of negative affect, an uptick from one day to the next may result from a recent interpersonal conflict (e.g., Mroczek & Almeida, 2004), whereas an increase of similar magnitude across months may result from the chronic strain of a financial hardship (e.g., Conger et al., 1993). Longer-term global trends might reflect the cumulative effects of health constraints (e.g., Griffin et al., 2006; Lockenhoff & Carstensen, 2004) or gradual shifts in motivational goals (e.g., Carstensen et al., 1999). Thus, an individual's current level of negative affect reflects the joint influence of these change and variability processes that operate across different time scales.

My colleagues and I have conducted measurement-burst studies that provide an example of decomposing variability and change in negative affect across different time scales (Sliwinski et al., 2009). One of the burst studies consisted of six daily assessments repeated every 6 months for a 2-year period in a sample of 116 older adults. During each assessment, individuals reported on their positive and negative mood, stress, and health constraints they experienced on that day. Multilevel modeling (Snidjers & Boskeer, 1999) provides a useful and straightforward approach to analyzing data from multiple time scales. Typically, when MLMs are applied to longitudinal data, they consist of two levels—the within-person (level 1) and the between-person (level 2) levels. However, a measurement-burst design produces a somewhat more complex data structure in which closely repeated measurements are "clustered" into repeated bursts, which are separated by longer time intervals. This data structure can entail three levels—two within-person levels (within-burst, across-burst) and one between-person level. By representing burst data as a three-level MLM one can examine random variation across a fast time scale (within-burst), across a slower time scale (between bursts), as well as across individuals. This approach also permits modeling both local (within-burst) and global (across-burst) trends, as well as allowing for different sets of predictors at different time scales.

TABLE 1.3

Modeling Intraindividual Variability across Two Timescales

$affect_{ijk} = b_{0jk} + e_{ijk}$ (level 1: Daily time scale)

$b_{0jk} = \beta_{00k} + v_{0jk}$ (level 2: biannual 'burst' time scale)

$\beta_{00k} = \gamma_{000} + u_{00k}$ (level 3: between-person variability)

The MLM for measurement-burst data is a simple extension of the MLM described in equations 1 and 2 earlier in this chapter. Instead of a two-level model, with levels 1 and 2 describing intraindividual and interindividual change, respectively, the measurement burst implies a three-level MLM in which the intraindividual part is broken into two components. The level-1 part of this model refers to "fast" intraindividual change and the level-2 part refers to "slow" intraindividual change. Level 3 is now the interindividual or between-person part of the model. The "empty" MLM in Table 1.3 provides a framework for decomposing variability across different time scales (i.e., days and biannual bursts), where $affect_{ijk}$ is the score for day i, burst j, and person k. The parameters in this model estimate the mean level of negative affect for a given person on a given burst averaged across days within that burst (b_{0jk}), for a given person averaged across all days and bursts (β_{00k}), and the grand mean averaged across all days, bursts, and persons (γ_{000}). As noted earlier, most applications of MLMs to repeated measures data consist of two levels: one level (level 1) refers to within-person variability and another level (level 2) refers to between-person variability. In contrast, equation 3 has *two* levels of within-person variability: level 1, which refers to (fast) within-person variability on the daily time scale, and level 2, which refers to (slow) within-person variability on the biannual time scale. Level 3 of this model refers to between-person or stable variability. Fitting a model with no predictors to these data allowed decomposition of the total variance in negative affect into these three components. When we applied this model to our longitudinal data, we found that approximately 53% ($var[e_{ijk}]$ = 3.03), 17% ($var[v_{0jk}]$ = 0.96), and 30% ($var[e_{ijk}]$ = 1.72), corresponded to the daily (fast), biannual (slow), and between-person (stable), respectively (Sliwinski et al., 2009). A conventional single-shot longitudinal design could not have distinguished between the two sources of within-person variability across the slow ($var[v_{0jk}]$) and fast ($var[e_{ijk}]$) time scales.

In contrast, the measurement-burst approach permits analysis of predictors that operate across different time scales. For example, one could examine how stress predicted concurrent changes in negative affect across both daily and biannual time scales, as well as between persons using the MLM in Table 1.4.

TABLE 1.4

Modeling Predictors Across two Timescales

$affect_{ijk} = b_{0jk} + b_{1jk}(Stress_{ijk}) + e_{ijk}$ (level 1: within bursts)

$b_{0jk} = \beta_{00k} + \beta_{01jk}(Stress_{ijk}) + v_{0jk}$ (level 2: across bursts)

$b_{1jk} = \beta_{10k} + \upsilon_{1jk}$

$\beta_{00k} = \gamma_{000} + \gamma_{001jk}(Stress_k) + v_{00k}$ (level 3: between person)

$\beta_{01k} = \gamma_{010} + u_{01k}$

$\beta_{10k} = \gamma_{100} + u_{10k}$

The variable $Stress_{ijk}$ refers to the amount of stress reported by a given person (k) on a given day (i) during a given burst (k). The burst-level stress variable ($Stress_{jk}$) reflects the amount of stress reported by a given person (k) during a given burst (j), averaged across all days within that burst, and $Stress_k$ is the amount of stress for a given person, averaged across all bursts (j) and all days (i). There are two basic approaches to representing a predictor variable at different levels in an MLM.[1] One approach involves within-burst ($Stress_{ijk}-Stress_{jk}$) and within-person ($Stress_{jk}-Stress_k$) centering of the level-1 and level-2 stress variables, respectively. However, this approach would imply that it is the level of stress relative to a person's average stress (or to the person's average stress for a given burst) that predicts negative affect, rather than the absolute level of stress. For example, within-person centering implies that a daily stress score of 0 (i.e., no stress on a particular day) has a different meaning for persons (and bursts) with different average levels of stress. A second option (which we chose) is to use the raw (or grand-mean centered) values to maintain a consistent meaning of the daily-stress values across individuals and bursts. This approach results in the following interpretation of the stress regression coefficients: γ_{100} is the average within-person day-level stress slope, γ_{010} is the difference between the within-person day-level and within-person burst-level slopes, and γ_{001} is the difference between the within-person burst-level and the (between-person) person-level slopes (Snidjers & Boskeer, 1999). The "correct" manner in which to define predictor variables in order to separate influences across different time scales will depend on whether the researcher believes the predictor variable is best scaled in relative or absolute terms.

The parameters b_{1jk} and β_{01jk} reflect the within-person relationships between stress and negative affect across daily and biannual time scales, respectively. At the fast (daily) time scale, a positive association between stress and negative affect would imply that on days when stress is high, negative affect is also high. On the slow (biannual) time scale, a positive association between stress and negative affect would mean that a person's average daily negative affect is higher during bursts when their average daily stress is also high, compared to bursts during which their average daily stress is lower. We fit a model similar to equation 4 to measurement-burst data described in Sliwinski et al. (2009) and demonstrated that within-person variability in stress was positively and significantly associated with negative affect on both time scales. However, variables do not always or even generally operate in the same way across different time scales. For example, Miller, Chen, and Zhou (2007) have shown in a meta-analysis that the relationship between stress and hypothalamic–pituitary–adrenal (HPA) activity depends critically on the timing of the stress—recent upticks in stress are associated with increased HPA activity (fast time scale), but over the long term (slow time scale) chronic stress may result in depressed HPA activity.

Characterizing change across multiple time scales can also help to distinguish effects resulting from short-term reactivity to the assessment procedure from longer-term developmental change. In response to repeated assessments, research participants may become increasingly annoyed, shift response criteria, or become more skilled on performance measures. If change is examined only across one time scale, distinguishing these measurement-induced effects from developmental changes becomes difficult or even impossible. Two examples come from a measurement-burst study conducted

---

[1] A detailed discussion of centering in multilevel models is beyond the scope of this chapter. The interested reader should refer or consult one of the many excellent textbooks on multilevel modeling, such as Hox (2002), Raudenbush and Bryk (2002), or Snidjers and Bosker (1999).

in my laboratory. The first example involves determining whether intraindividual changes in negative affect were attributable to long-term aging-related influences or could be attributed to reactivity to the repeated assessment protocol (e.g., becoming annoyed with the intensive assessment demands). To address this issue, we compared local trends in negative affect within each burst to longer-term across burst trends (Sliwinski et al., 2009). Across bursts, on average, individuals exhibited an increase in negative affect, but within bursts this trend was not present (in fact, there was a slight positive trend). This allowed us to rule out reactivity to repeated assessment as an explanation for across-burst increases in negative affect, because reactivity, if present, should also, and perhaps more strongly, manifest across shorter time scales.

A second example involves retest effects in longitudinal studies of cognitive aging—the improvement in performance on cognitive tests because of repeated test-taking. Although these practice effects dissipate over long durations, positive retest effects may endure for years, which can bias estimates of age-related decline (e.g., Ronnlund, Nyberg, Backman, & Nilsson, 2005; Salthouse, 2009). The measurement burst presents a possible avenue for approaching this problem if one reasonably assumes that across short time scales retest improvement would be most prominent and aging-related decline minimal, and aging-related changes would be easier to observe across longer time scales (Salthouse, 2009). My colleagues and I used data from a measurement-burst design to simultaneously model short-term (within-burst) retest speed up in perceptual speed and long-term (across-burst) aging-related slowing (Sliwinski, Hoffman, & Hofer, 2010). We found that across short time scales (within-bursts), response time is decreasing with each repeated assessment, but across the longer time scales (across-bursts) the asymptotic (i.e., fastest) response time is shifting upward. By modeling change across two time scales, we were able to distinguish short-term practice improvement from long-term aging-related decrements in asymptotic processing speed.

The measurement-burst design can support improved description of developmental phenomena by jointly modeling variability across different time scales. Recognizing that many variables exhibit dynamic properties across different time scales is a necessary first step toward accurately describing development processes. This recognition implies that an individual's current status on any developmentally relevant measure (e.g., behavior, personality, physiology) reflects the confluence of dynamics that operate across very different time scales (e.g., Martin & Hofer, 2004). The inability to tease apart these processes that operate across different cadences is a significant limitation of conventional longitudinal studies consisting of widely spaced single-shot measurements. An important advantage of measurement-burst designs is that they provide an opportunity to distinguish among relatively stable (e.g., trait neuroticism), slow-changing (e.g., diminishing cognitive resources), and more fast-changing dynamic processes (e.g., mood), respectively. In the next section, I will discuss how the measurement burst also permits researchers to test hypotheses that link processes transpiring across different scales.

LINKING INTRAINDIVIDUAL VARIABILITY AND CHANGE ACROSS DIFFERENT TIME SCALES

In the previous section, I described how analysis of data from a measurement-burst design can distinguish variability and change across different time scales. In this section, I describe three ways in which short-term processes may be linked to long-term developmentally relevant change. First, changes observed over a short time scale may *directly* reflect developmental phenomena. A clear example comes from the use of microgenetic designs to study cognitive development in children (Siegler, 2006; Siegler & Crowley, 1991). This approach involves high-frequency observations across relatively short time periods (e.g., days, weeks, or months) that allow a moment-by-moment analysis of change processes, usually associated with learning and cognitive development. The microgenetic approach has mostly been applied to circumstances when the occurrence of change is highly predictable or can be brought under experimental control. For example, Siegler (1995) examined the development of number conversation in children as a function of different feedback conditions. The intensive microgenetic measurement and analysis allowed Siegler to identify and model the source, path, and rate of cognitive change.

Siegler (1997) identified three principles for the study of change that underlie the microgentic approach: (1) measurements should span as much of the period from the beginning of change to the time when behavior has stabilized, (2) the density of measurements should be high relative to the rate of the change, and (3) measurements should be subjected to intensive analysis across the shortest time scale (e.g., momentary, trial-by-trial) to support inferences regarding processes that caused the change. The rationale behind this approach is that only by studying *change as it occurs* can researchers identify underlying mechanisms. However, there are practical challenges to applying this approach to the study of a broad range of developmental phenomena, especially those occurring in adulthood. It may be extremely difficult, inefficient, or even impossible to measure relevant variables at the moment when change is occurring if it is not strongly age-graded or linked to identifiable events and transitional periods (e.g., retirement, menopause, becoming a parent) or if it occurs with a relatively low frequency. That said, designs that better satisfy these principles (e.g., high measurement density) should provide greater insight into developmental processes compared to more conventional designs that consist of few repeated measurements.

In the case of this first example, the measurement processes play a precipitating role in producing developmental gains—children repeatedly exposed to a specific type of math problem will, as a result of this exposure, have an opportunity to learn new strategies and exhibit relatively durable cognitive gains. Other types of developmentally relevant phenomena are less amenable to experimental control and cannot be predicted with a high degree of accuracy. Prominent developmental theories, for example, postulate that certain emotion regulation skills improve with age (e.g., Carstensen et al., 1999), but examining behavior at the "moment" at which this change occurs would be extremely challenging to say the least. Although specific momentary upticks or downturns in negative or positive affect are not themselves developmental changes, their magnitude, patterning, and temporal characteristics are of relevance for developmental theories (Carstensen et al., 2000; Rocke et al., 2009).

The second way in which short-term variability may be linked to long-term change is as an antecedent or early indicator. In general, we cannot expect changes in behaviors, cognitions, or physiology over very short time scales (e.g., moments, days) to represent in either magnitude or form the long-term changes of typical interest to developmental researchers. But measuring the magnitude of short-term variability may provide insight into the long-term processes of interest to developmental researchers (Hultsch & MacDonald, 2004; Nesselroade & Ram, 2004). Increases in intraindividual variability may signify an imminent developmental gain, for example, children's strategies exhibit increased variability associated with exploratory behavior prior to adopting a novel problem strategy (Siegler, 1995). In contrast, increasing behavioral variability may also signify concurrent or imminent neurocognitive impairment (Lovden et al., 2007; MacDonald, Nyberg, & Backman, 2006), decrements in sensorimotor integrity (Newell, Mayer-Kress, & Liu, 2009), and even mortality (Deary & Der, 2005; Eizenman, Nesselroade, Featherman, & Rowe, 1997). Lovden and colleagues (2007) provided compelling demonstration of this point by examining the hypothesis that greater moment-to-moment performance fluctuations at a given time point would predict subsequent declines in mean levels of functioning. Using a bivariate dual change score model (McArdle & Hamagami, 2001), Lovden and colleagues (2007) demonstrated that individuals who exhibited greater increases in momentary reaction time variability also exhibited greater decline on ideational fluency and processing speed during the following 2 years, but that the reverse was not the case. These results replicate and extend earlier findings (MacDonald, Hultsch & Dixon, 2003) that very short-term performance variability covaries with 6-year changes in level of cognitive function. These findings are consistent with predictions from computational models that postulated age-related reductions in the efficiency of dopaminergic neuromodulation (Li, Brehmer, Shing, Werkle-Bergner, & Lindenberger, 2006). As theoretical models become increasingly precise in their mechanistic accounts of developmental change, researchers will find increasingly valuable methodological approaches which allow them to link short time scale processes (mechanisms) to long time scale changes (outcomes).

The earlier examples illustrate how the magnitude of intraindividual *variability* across a short time scale can predict global trends across longer time scales. A third way of linking processes across different time scales involves examining how intraindividual *covariability* changes over time. Most studies of development that focus on intraindividual changes rely on sequences of widely spaced, repeated, single measurements which allow researchers to examine changes in the level of functioning. However, this approach does not provide the opportunity to examine how within-person relationships (i.e., the coupling of variables) across short time scales change across longer time scales. This is an important limitation because it precludes evaluating developmental hypotheses about how within-person processes (e.g., affective responses to stress, the influence of health on well-being) might evolve over time. For example, some evidence suggests that aging adults are better able to regulate their emotions in response to negative events. This prediction has been tested longitudinally, but mostly by examining changes in *level* of negative affect assessed once every several years (e.g., Charles et al., 2001; Griffin et al., 2006). An alternative and potentially more powerful test of this prediction would involve directly assessing daily events and mood states, and then examining whether advancing age is associated with increased or decreased emotional responses to daily stressors. Although a number of studies have examined *age differences* in emotional reactivity to minor stressors using experiencing sampling (Uchino, Berg, Smith, Pearce, & Skinner, 2006) and daily diary methods (Mroczek & Almeida, 2004; Rocke et al., 2009; Stawski, Sliwinski, Almeida, & Smyth, 2008), there is little information on *intraindividual change* in coupling between daily affect and stress. The only way in which change in within-person relationships can be studied is by overlaying intensive measurement protocols on more conventional longitudinal designs. For example, in the study described earlier, my colleagues and I analyzed data from two measurement-burst studies to examine intraindividual variability and change in how the daily coupling between stress and negative affect changed (Sliwinski et al., 2009). Equation 4 described the part of this analysis that separated the within-person relationships between affect and stress into two time scales—daily and biannual. We demonstrated that the average magnitude of the daily stress–affect relationship (b_{1jk} in equation 4) increased within individuals across periods ranging from 2 to 10 years, implying that the average negative emotional responses to daily stressors increases in aging individuals.

In addition to exhibiting long-term trends, the magnitude of coupling between variables may also fluctuate across periods or "epochs," reflecting midterm or "state-of-states" variability. That is, there is a space between the very fast time scales (e.g., moments, days) and slow time scales (e.g., years, decades) in which developmentally relevant variables may operate. There are many types of variables, such as those indexing a person's health status and psychosocial contexts (e.g., available social support, external demands) that are relatively constant during a given brief temporal epoch (e.g., a given week), but may vary considerably across somewhat longer intervals (e.g., weeks and months). Coupling parameters (e.g., the magnitude of negative emotional responses to daily stress) may vary within-persons in accordance with influences that exhibit short-term stability but midterm lability. Figure 1.4 illustrates this point in the context of a measurement-burst design. Data collected in each burst can be thought of as a "mini" daily diary or experience sampling study during

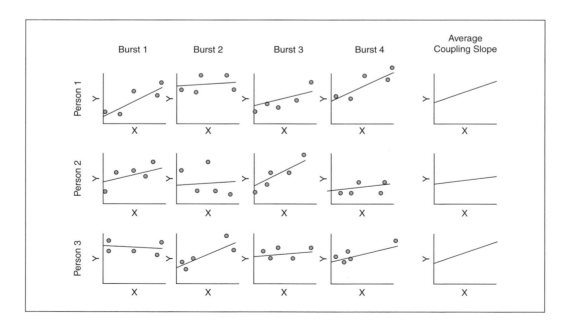

FIGURE 1.4 This figure provides an example of how a measurement-burst approach can distinguish between variability across persons (rows) as well as across time (columns) in short-term relationships as indexed by the coupling between variables.

which the coupling (within-person, across time covariability) between two variables X and Y is examined. Linear models are frequently used to quantify the magnitude of coupling—a common example comes from studies of daily stress and affect, in which the slope relating daily stress (X) to self-reports of negative affect (Y) operationalizes "reactivity" (Bolger & Schilling, 1991). Individuals with steep slopes are more reactive than individuals with shallower slopes because steep slopes imply a greater increase in negative affect for a unit increase in subjective stress.

Assume that the first column in Figure 1.4 represents data from three individuals whose level of stress and mood were assessed each day for 1 week. Person 1 would be the most reactive, with Person 2 being less reactive, and Person 3 hardly showing any reactivity. Multilevel modeling most often emphasizes examination of between-person predictors of individual differences in intraindividual relationships. For example, researchers have attempted to explain individual differences in emotional responses to daily stress by examining between-person variables such as gender or stable personality dispositions (e.g., Mroczek & Almeida, 2004). However, it is possible that the variability observed in the left-most column in Figure 1.4 does not only (or even mostly) reflect stable individual differences in reactivity. Rather, the reasons why Person 1 is more reactive than Person 3 during this week of daily assessments may have more to do with differences in life circumstances than with stable differences in personal characteristics. That is, it may not be the case that Person 1 is generally more reactive than the others, but was more reactive during this week of assessments because of the specific nature of the stressors experienced during the week or other demands or events that have occurred recently but prior to the assessment week. Along these lines, Sliwinski and colleagues (2009) demonstrated that within-person fluctuations across 6-month intervals in the coupling of daily stress and negative affect were predictable by the level of psychological distress experienced by individuals during the month prior to each measurement burst. This finding provides an example of how data from a measurement-burst design can reveal slower time scale processes that create a temporal context for processes that operate across faster time scales.

ANALYTIC AND DESIGN ISSUES

The discussion so far has focused on the merits of measurement-burst designs for modeling change as an intraindividual process, and for distinguishing and linking dynamic processes operating across different time scales. In doing so, I have ignored some of the more thorny issues that confront researchers attempting to design measurement-burst studies. I have discussed some of the practical and feasibility issues related to the implementation of measurement bursts elsewhere (Sliwinski, 2008). In the current discussion, I will focus on the conceptual basis for making principled decisions about the frequency with which repeated measurements should be taken. It is worth noting that this is just as relevant for the design of more conventional longitudinal studies that consist of single-shot measurements, although they become less ignorable in the context of intensive measurement designs.

There is no single answer to the question of "how often do I need to measure Y?" and decisions regarding the optimal frequency and duration of repeated measurements are often based on practical rather than principled basis. For example, longitudinal studies are resource intensive and almost always require funding from grant agencies. The duration of grant awards is usually limited to 5 years or less, which places constraints on the amount of follow-up, although sometimes repeated awards can allow studies to continue for longer durations. However, for the most part, researchers are constrained to frame and test scientifically interesting developmental predictions regarding intraindividual changes that occur within a 5-year period. The critical question then becomes one of how to study developmental processes within a limited time period.

Individuals may decide to maximize the number of subjects in their study to improve the chances of detecting statistically significant average change and individual differences in the amount or rate of change. Also, given that some developmental change especially in adulthood is thought to be subtle or gradual, researchers may also adopt the common sense position that a longer time period between observations will provide a better opportunity for change to occur. As it turns out, it is never a good idea from a design perspective to increase the duration between assessments if that entails obtaining fewer measurements, which would usually be the case. Simulation work by Hertzog and colleagues (Hertzog, Lindenberger, Ghisletta, & von Oertzen, 2006; Hertzog, von Oertzen, Ghisletta, & Lindenberger, 2008) provide convincing demonstrations that power for detecting individual differences in rates of change drops dramatically as the number of measurement occasions decreases. In addition, their power tables indicate that if the cost of adding either another participant or obtaining an additional measurement occasion is equivalent, adding additional occasions is always the better choice (Figure 1, Hertzog et al., 2008).

The work by Hertzog et al. clearly illustrates that improving what they term "growth curve reliability" (GCR) provides a substantial effect on power. The GCR is related to the intraclass correlation and is defined as the variance in y determined by a growth curve model at each time t, divided by the total variance, where σ_{yt}^2 is the variance in y at time t and $\sigma_{\varepsilon y}^2$ is the residual variance, constrained to be equal across time (Table 1.5). Because growth curves that allow variability in rates of change imply that σ_{yt}^2 will vary over time, the GCR is scaled to baseline or $t(0)$. Even modest improvements in GCR can yield dramatic increases in power for detecting variance and covariances of and among rates of change. Conventional single-shot multiwave longitudinal designs require that a single measurement occasion can adequately capture the location of an individual on the variable of interest at a given point in time t. This requirement assumes that there is relatively little intraindividual variability on the variables being measured compared to the expected amount of intraindividual change between measurements. This assumption might be reasonable for research on long-term change in variables that exhibit little variability across short time relative to long time scales. However, it would be highly problematic to rely on

TABLE 1.5

Growth Curve Reliability
$$\mathrm{GCR} = \frac{\left(\sigma_{yt}^2 - \sigma_{\varepsilon t}^2 \right)}{\sigma_{\varepsilon y}^2}$$

a single measurement if interest is on long-term change on any variable that exhibits short-term variability. If a behavior or attribute is highly variable from one day to the next (or from one moment to the next within a given day), then relying on a single measurement point change may provide a relatively poor approximation of a person's level at a given time point.

The measurement-burst designs provide one approach to boosting GCR by averaging across short-term scale variability, which would effectively reduce the magnitude of the error variance. This approach requires a reconceptualization of how to measure an individual's level on any time-varying variables. Rather than thinking of defining an individual's level at a given time by measuring them once, we could define their level for a given temporal epoch by taking a local average of repeated assessments distributed across a short time scale. For example, consider a measurement-burst study consisting of seven daily assessments with bursts repeated every year for 2 years. In this design, we would define a person's level at any burst not by a single measurement but by taking the average of seven measurements within a given burst. Long-term change would not be based on a sequence of individual measurements but on a series of aggregated measurements that signify each person's level during a given narrow temporal epoch or burst. This has the direct result of reducing the error variance, σ_{ey}^2, by a factor proportional to the number of within-burst repeated measurements (n), resulting in an error variance equal to σ_{ey}^2/n. The equation in Table 1.6 illustrates the effect of analyzing long-term change in burst level averages on GCR, where GCR is the reliability as defined in equation 5 and GCR* is the GCR obtained from analyzing intraindividual changes in the average of n observations. Following our example with seven measurements per burst, if GCR is equal to 0.5, the effective GCR* from the measurement burst would be 0.88.

Although increasing the number and frequency of measurements can aid in the identification of correlates of the between-person aspects of change (Rationale 5), the timing of repeated measurements must depend on the cadence of the variable of interest. In general terms, the frequency of repeated measurements must match the dynamic of the changes in the phenomenon under study. Matching the frequency of measurements to the cadence of change is essential for a process-based approach modeling of intraindividual change and to satisfy Baltes and Nesselrode's fourth rationale. The good news is that there is a well-established principle from the signal processing literature that provides guidance for determining measurement frequency. This principle states that measurements should occur with at least twice the frequency as the maximum frequency (f_{max}) of the signal you want to detect, or at a rate of $2f_{max}$. This means that if one hypothesizes that the process of interest varies from day to day, one must measure that process at least twice a day. Or if one is interested in modeling *annual* intraindividual

TABLE 1.6

Growth Curve Reliability in a Measurement-Burst Design
$$GCR^* = \frac{(n \times GCR)}{(1 + [n-1] \times GCR)}$$

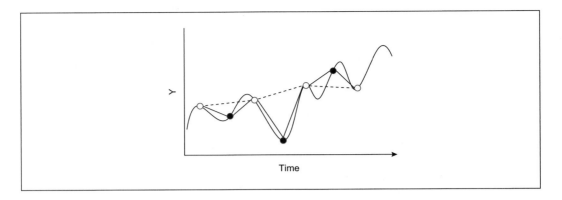

FIGURE 1.5   **This figure illustrates how sampling with insufficient frequency can provide a distorted view, as indicated by the dashed line connecting every second circle, of the actual pattern of variability. Sampling at twice the frequency provided a more accurate description, as indicated by the solid lines connecting each sequential circle.**

change, they must obtain measurements at least every 6 months. This principle runs slightly counter to the intuition that if the interest is in annual change, then obtaining annual measurements would be sufficient. Failure to measure dynamic processes with sufficient frequency can result in aliasing errors, an example of which is provided by Figure 1.5. Aliasing errors occur when measurements of a dynamic process too infrequently to accurately characterize the form of the underlying function. The solid wavy line illustrates a continuous time series representing intraindividual variability for a given individual, with the dotted line connecting low frequency measurements (open circles) of that time series and the solid line connecting high frequency measurements (open and closed circles). The less frequent measurements (indicated by the open circles) provide a distorted picture of the process because they miss critical information about the temporal dynamics of the underlying process, making it impossible to accurately describe or model the causes of the intraindividual change. This leads us to the conclusion that developmental researchers must design studies with far more intensive measurements than is the norm in order to measure the dynamics of developmental processes with adequate frequency to satisfy Baltes and Nesselroade's first and fourth rationales— the modeling of intraindividual change and identification of its causes.

FUTURE DIRECTIONS IN THE METHODOLOGIES TO STUDY LIFE-SPAN DEVELOPMENT

Because most of our longitudinal data comes from studies in which individuals are measured relatively infrequently, there has been little opportunity to understand the timing of developmental changes across any but the longest time scales. Perhaps, our conceptions of the temporal characteristics of developmental changes reflect more the constraints of our research designs than the characteristics of the underlying phenomena. If a researcher is interested in very slow change, obtaining measurements every year or several years may suffice for descriptive purposes. However, we must be careful to measure the mechanisms driving change that operate within the long intervals separating widely spaced repeated measurements.

This chapter presented the rationale for incorporating more intensive measurements into longitudinal developmental designs. However, there are nontrivial barriers to implementing intensive measurement designs that future research needs to address. First, intensive repeated measurement studies are both burdensome to research participants and costly. Development of remote and intensive data-capture technologies, such as the use of smartphones and unobtrusive sensors for collecting behavioral and physiological data, promises to be an exciting and active area of research. Mobile communication technology has become an integral part of daily life. Developmental researchers will have the opportunity to leverage this familiarity and implement intensive data collection protocols in relatively unobtrusive and inexpensive ways. Collecting momentary reports on a person's emotional states and social interactions, and then connecting these behavioral measurements to physiological activity (e.g., hear rate variability) in real time and in ecological valid settings, promise to advance as well as challenge our understanding of human development. However, there is still much work to be done to advance efforts to adapt this technology to provide rigorous tests of developmental hypotheses.

One such challenge is the need to develop measurement instruments that are suitable for repeated and intensive administration. Most measurement scales used in developmental research have been validated for between-person analysis at cross-section; the psychometric properties for within-person (intraindividual) analyses for many widely used scales are unknown. It is also likely that some of the properties we view as psychometrically desirable (e.g., retest stability) for between-person analysis would be less desirable for the study of short-term variability and intraindividual change (Nesselroade, 1991). Measurement scales that are useful for one purpose (e.g., analysis of individual differences) may be far less useful for other purposes (e.g., analysis of intraindividual variability). For example, questionnaires used to assess personality traits, such as neuroticism, may not be suitable to administer on a daily basis. Instead, researchers would need to specify how neuroticism manifests in daily life (e.g., negative affect, increased emotional reactivity, or lability) and develop new measurement tools that can capture the dynamic aspects of what may be a relatively stable trait. Thus, as intensive measurement designs become more common, theorists will be challenged to take a more process-oriented perspective in studying developmental influences on what have been commonly viewed as relatively stable personality and behavioral traits. Additional research is needed to develop and apply approaches for assessing the utility of psychometric scales for intensive measurement designs (e.g., Cranford et al., 2006).

Intensive measurement designs also present numerous challenges as well as opportunities for the analysis of developmental data. Most analytic approaches, even those described in this chapter, impose the same formal model of change and variability on each individual. This approach involves aggregation of individuals into an "average" person and then describing each individual as a deviation from that average. Such aggregation may be necessary for conventional longitudinal studies in which each person has been measured only a few times, but it requires several untenable assumptions (Molenaar, 2004). Intensive measurement designs, such as the measurement burst, can provide dozens or even hundreds of observations for each person, which opens the door for truly individual-level analysis (Boker, Molenaar, &

Nesselroade, 2009; Molenaar et al., 2009). The shifting emphasis to individual-level analysis is long overdue in the study of human development. This shift, which is already taking place, entails a rather drastic change in how researchers frame hypotheses, design studies, measure constructs, and conduct analyses.

This chapter has focused on the importance of measuring developmentally relevant processes that operate very different dynamics. It is highly likely that the more we look for them, the more we will discover that processes transpiring at the daily and even momentary time scales both shape and are shaped by more long-term developmental trends. Our rapidly advancing methodologies challenge theorists to explicitly incorporate the element of time into their mechanistic accounts of developmental processes. Only by specifying the temporal as well as structural and functional elements of human development, can our theories offer a principled basis for making critical design decisions about not only what to measure but also when to measure it.

ACKNOWLEDGMENT

Preparation of this chapter was supported by grants from the National Institute on Aging NIH Grants AG026728 and AG03949.

REFERENCES

Baltes, P. B., & Nesselroade, J. R. (1979). History and rationale of longitudinal research. In J. R. Nesselroade & P. B. Baltes (Eds.), *Longitudinal research in the study of behavior and development* (pp. 1–39). New York: Academic Press.

Boker, S. M., Molenaar, P. C., & Nesselroade, J. R. (2009). Issues in intraindividual variability: Individual differences in equilibria and dynamics over multiple time scales. *Psychology and Aging, 24,* 858–862.

Bolger, N., & Schilling, E. A. (1991). Personality and the problems of everyday life: The role of neuroticism in exposure and reactivity to daily stressors. *Journal of Personality, 59,* 355–386.

Borsboom, D., Mellenbergh, G. J., & van Heerden, J. (2003). The theoretical status of latent variables. *Psychological Review, 110,* 203–219.

Carstensen, L. L., Isaacowitz, D. M., & Charles, S. T. (1999). Taking time seriously. A theory of socioemotional selectivity. *American Psychologist, 54,* 165–181.

Carstensen, L. L., Pasupathi, M., Mayr, U., & Nesselroade, J. R. (2000). Emotional experience in everyday life across the adult life span. *Journal of Personality and Social Psychology, 79,* 644–655.

Charles, S. T., Reynolds, C. A., & Gatz, M. (2001). Age-related differences and change in positive and negative affect over 23 years. *Journal of Personality and Social Psychology, 80,* 136–151.

Conger, R. D., Conger, K. J., Elder, G. H., Lorenz, F. O., Simons, R. L., & Whitbeck, L. B. (1993). Family economic-stress and adjustment of early adolescent girls. *Developmental Psychology, 29,* 206–219.

Cranford, J. A., Shrout, P. E., Iida, M., Rafaeli, E., Yip, T., & Bolger, N. (2006). A procedure for evaluating sensitivity to within-person change: Can mood measures in diary studies detect change reliably? *Personality and Social Psychology Bulletin, 32,* 917–929.

Deary, I. J., & Der, G. (2005). Reaction time explains IQ's association with death. *Psychological Science, 16,* 64–69.

Eid, M., & Diener, E. (1999). Intraindividual variability in affect: Reliability, validity, and personality correlates. *Journal of Personality and Social Psychology, 76,* 662–676.

Eizenman, D. R., Nesselroade, J. R., Featherman, D. L., & Rowe, J. W. (1997). Intraindividual variability in perceived control in an older sample: The MacArthur successful aging studies. *Psycholgy and Aging, 12,* 489–502.

Ferrer, E., Salthouse, T. A., Stewart, W. F., & Schwartz, B. S. (2004). Modeling age and retest processes in longitudinal studies of cognitive abilities. *Psychology and Aging, 19,* 243–259.

Fleeson, W., & Jolley, S. (2006). A proposed theory of the adult development of intraindividual variability in trait-manifesting behavior. In D. Mroczek & T. D. Little (Eds.), *Handbook of personality development* (pp. 41–60). Philadephia: Psychology Press.

Ford, D. H., & Lerner, R. M. (1992). *Developmental systems theory.* Newbury Park, CA: Sage.

Griffin, P. W., Mroczek, D. K., & Spiro, A. (2006). Variability in affective change among aging men: Longitudinal findings from the VA Normative Aging Study. *Journal of Research in Personality, 40,* 942–965.

Gruhn, D., Rebucal, K., Diehl, M., Lumley, M., & Labouvie-Vief, G. (2008). Empathy across the adult lifespan: Longitudinal and experience-sampling findings. *Emotion, 8,* 753–765.

Hertzog, C., Lindenberger, U., Ghisletta, P., & von Oertzen, T. (2006). On the power of multivariate latent growth curve models to detect correlated change. *Psychological Methods, 11,* 244–252.

Hertzog, C., von Oertzen, T., Ghisletta, P., & Lindenberger, U. (2008). Evaluating the power of latent growth curve models to detect individual differences in change. *Structural Equation Modeling—A Multidisciplinary Journal, 15,* 541–563.

Hultsch, D. F., & MacDonald, S. W. (2004). Intraindividual variability in performance as a theoretical window onto cognitive aging. In R. Dixon, L. Backman, & L. Nilsson (Eds.), *New frontiers in cognitive aging* (pp. 65–88). Oxford: Oxford University Press.

Kleban, M. H., Lawton, M. P., Nesselroade, J. R., & Parmelee, P. (1992). The structure of variation in affect among depressed and nondepressed elders. *Journals of Gerontology, 47,* P190–P198.

Labouvie-Vief, G. (2003). Dynamic integration: Affect, cognition, and the self in adulthood. *Current Directions in Psychological Science, 12,* 201–206.

Li, S. C., Brehmer, Y., Shing, Y. L., Werkle-Bergner, M., & Lindenberger, U. (2006). Neuromodulation of associative and organizational plasticity across the life span: Empirical evidence and neuro-computational modeling. *Neuroscience and Biobehavioral Reviews, 30,* 775–790.

Li, S. C., Lindenberger, U., Hommel, B., Aschersleben, G., Prinz, W., & Baltes, P. B. (2004). Transformations in the couplings among intellectual abilities and constituent cognitive processes across the life span. *Psychological Science, 15,* 155–163.

Lockenhoff, C. E., & Carstensen, L. L. (2004). Socioemotional selectivity theory, aging, and health: The increasingly delicate balance between regulating emotions and making tough choices. *Journal of Personality, 72,* 1395–1424.

Lovden, M., Li, S. C., Shing, Y. L., & Lindenberger, U. (2007). Within-person trial-to-trial variability precedes and predicts cognitive decline in old and very old age: Longitudinal data from the Berlin Aging Study. *Neuropsychologia, 45,* 2827–2838.

MacDonald, S. W., Hultsch, D. F., & Dixon, R. A. (2003). Performance variability is related to change in cognition: Evidence from the Victoria Longitudinal Study. *Psychology and Aging, 18,* 510–523.

MacDonald, S. W., Hultsch, D. F., Strauss, E., & Dixon, R. A. (2003). Age-related slowing of digit symbol substitution revisited: What do longitudinal age changes reflect? *Journals of Gerontology: Psychological Sciences, 58,* P187–P194.

MacDonald, S. W., Nyberg, L., & Backman, L. (2006). Intra-individual variability in behavior: Links to brain structure, neurotransmission and neuronal activity. *Trends in Neuroscience, 29,* 474–480.

MacDonald, S. W., Nyberg, L., Sandblom, J., Fischer, H., & Backman, L. (2008). Increased response-time variability is associated with reduced inferior parietal activation during episodic recognition in aging. *Journal of Cognitive Neuroscience, 20,* 779–786.

Martin, M., & Hofer, S. M. (2004). Intraindividual variability, change, and aging: Conceptual and analytical issues. *Gerontology, 50,* 7–11.

McArdle, J., & Hamagami, F. (2001). Latent difference score structural models for linear dynamic analyses with incomplete longitudinal data. In L. Collins & A. G. Sayer (Eds.), *New methods for the analysis of change* (pp. 137–176). Washington, DC: American Psychological Association.

Miller, G. E., Chen, E., & Zhou, E. S. (2007). If it goes up, must it come down? Chronic stress and the hypothalamic–pituitary–adrenocortical axis in humans. *Psychological Bulletin, 133,* 25–45.

Molenaar, P. C. (2004). A manifesto on Psychology as an idiographic science: Bringing the person back into scientific psychology, this time forever. *Measurement, 2,* 201–218.

Molenaar, P. C., Sinclair, K. O., Rovine, M. J., Ram, N., & Corneal, S. E. (2009). Analyzing developmental processes on an individual level using nonstationary time series modeling. *Developmental Psychology, 45,* 260–271.

Mroczek, D. K., & Almeida, D. M. (2004). The effect of daily stress, personality, and age on daily negative affect. *Journal of Personality, 72,* 355–378.

Nesselroade, J. (1991). The warp and woof of the developmental fabric. In R. Downs, L. Liben, & D. Palermo (Eds.), *Visions of aesthetics, the environment, & development: The legacy of Joachim F. Wohwill.* Hillsdale, NJ: Lawrence Erlbaum Associates.

Nesselroade, J., & Ram, N. (2004). Intraindividual variability: What have we learned that will help us understand lives in context. *Research in Human Development, 1,* 9–29.

Newell, K. M., Liu, Y. T., & Mayer-Kress, G. (2001). Time scales in motor learning and development. *Psychological Review, 108,* 57–82.

Newell, K. M., Mayer-Kress, G., & Liu, Y. T. (2009). Aging, time scales, and sensorimotor variability. *Psychology and Aging, 24,* 809–818.

Pavel, M., Jimison, H., Hayes, T., Kaye, J., Dishman, E., Wild, K., et al. (2008). Continuous, unobtrusive monitoring for the assessment of cognitive function. In S. Hofer & D. Alwin (Eds.), *Handbook of cognitive aging: Interdisciplinary perspectives* (pp. 524–543). Thousand Oaks, CA: Sage.

Rocke, C., Li, S. C., & Smith, J. (2009). Intraindividual variability in positive and negative affect over 45 days: Do older adults fluctuate less than young adults? *Psychology and Aging, 24,* 863–878.

Ronnlund, M., Nyberg, L., Backman, L., & Nilsson, L. G. (2005). Stability, growth, and decline in adult life span development of declarative memory: Cross-sectional and longitudinal data from a population-based study. *Psychology and Aging, 20,* 3–18.

Salthouse, T. A. (2009). When does age-related cognitive decline begin? *Neurobiology of Aging, 30,* 507–514.

Salthouse, T. A., Schroeder, D. H., & Ferrer, E. (2004). Estimating retest effects in longitudinal assessments of cognitive functioning in adults between 18 and 60 years of age. *Developmental Psychology, 40,* 813–822.

Schaie, K. W. (1989). Perceptual speed in adulthood: Cross-sectional and longitudinal studies. *Psychology and Aging, 4,* 443–453.

Schaie, K. W., & Hofer, S. M. (2001). Longitudinal studies in aging research. In J. E. Birren & K. W. Schaie (Eds.), *Handbook of the psychology of aging* (5th ed., pp. 53–71). San Diego, CA: Academic Press.

Schmiedek, F., Lovden, M., & Lindenberger, U. (2009). On the relation of mean reaction time and intraindividual reaction time variability. *Psychology and Aging, 24,* 841–857.

Schneiders, J., Nicolson, N. A., Berkhof, J., Feron, F. J., Devries, M. W., & van Os, J. (2007). Mood in daily contexts: Relationship with risk in early adolescence. *Journal of Research on Adolescence, 17,* 697–722.

Siegler, R. S. (1995). How does change occur: A microgenetic study of number conservation. *Cognitive Psychology, 28,* 225–273.

Siegler, R. S. (1997). Concepts and methods for studying cognitive change. In E. Amsel & K. A. Renninger (Eds.), *Change and development: Issues of theory, method and application* (pp. 77–97). Hillsdale, NJ: Erlbaum.

Siegler, R. S. (2006). Microgenetic analyses of learning. In D. Kuhn & R. S. Siegler (Eds.), *Handbookbook of child psychology* (6th ed., Vol. 2: Cognition, perception, and language, pp. 464–510). Hoboken, NJ: Wiley.

Siegler, R. S. (2007). Cognitive variability. *Developmental Science, 10,* 104–109.

Siegler, R. S., & Crowley, K. (1991). The microgenetic method. A direct means for studying cognitive development. *American Psychologist, 46,* 606–620.

Siegler, R. S., & Svetina, M. (2002). A microgenetic/cross-sectional study of matrix completion: Comparing short-term and long-term change. *Child Development, 73,* 793–809.

Sliwinski, M. (2008). Measurement-burst designs for social health research. *Social and Personality Psychology Compass, 2,* 245–261.

Sliwinski, M., Almeida, D. M., Smyth, J., & Stawski, R. S. (2009). Intraindividual change and variability in daily stress processes: Findings from two measurement-burst diary studies. *Psychology and Aging, 24,* 828–840.

Sliwinski, M., & Buschke, H. (1999). Cross-sectional and longitudinal relationships among age, cognition, and processing speed. *Psychology and Aging, 14,* 18–33.

Sliwinski, M., & Buschke, H. (2004). Modeling intraindividual cognitive change in aging adults: Results from the Einstein Aging Studies. *Aging Neuropsychology and Cognition, 11,* 196–211.

Sliwinski, M., Hofer, S. M., & Hall, C. (2003). Correlated and coupled cognitive change in older adults with and without preclinical dementia. *Psychology and Aging, 18,* 672–683.

Sliwinski, M., Hoffman, L., & Hofer, S. (2010). Modeling retest and aging effects in a measurement burst design. In K. M. Newell & P. C. M. Molenaar (Eds.), *Individual pathways of change: Statistical models for analyzing learning and development* (pp. 37–50). Washington, DC: American Psychological Association.

Sliwinski, M., & Mogle, J. A. (2008). The multiple facets of change: Implications for modeling relationships in cognitive aging research. In S. Hofer & D. Alwin (Eds.), *Handbook of cognitive aging: Interdisciplinary perspectives* (pp. 477–491). Thousand Oaks, CA: Sage Publications.

Snidjers, T. A., & Boskeer, R. J. (1999). *Multilevel analysis: An introduction to basic and advanced multilevel modeling.* London: Sage.

Sosnoff, J. J., & Newell, K. M. (2006). The generalization of perceptual-motor intra-individual variability in young and old adults. *Journal of Gerontology: Psychological Sciences, 61,* P304–P310.

Stawski, R. S., Sliwinski, M. J., Almeida, D. M., & Smyth, J. M. (2008). Reported exposure and emotional reactivity to daily stressors: The roles of adult age and global perceived stress. *Psychology and Aging, 23,* 52–61.

Uchino, B. N., Berg, C. A., Smith, T. W., Pearce, G., & Skinner, M. (2006). Age-related differences in ambulatory blood pressure during daily stress: Evidence for greater blood pressure reactivity with age. *Psychology and Aging, 21,* 231–239.

van Eck, M., Nicolson, N. A., & Berkhof, J. (1998). Effects of stressful daily events on mood states: Relationship to global perceived stress. *Journal of Personality and Social Psychology, 75,* 1572–1585.

Wilson, R. S., Beckett, L. A., Barnes, L. L., Schneider, J. A., Bach, J., Evans, D. A., et al. (2002). Individual differences in rates of change in cognitive abilities of older persons. *Psychology and Aging, 17,* 179–193.

Wohlwill, J. F. (1973). *The study of behavioral development.* New York: Academic Press.

THEORIES AND PROCESSES IN LIFE-SPAN SOCIALIZATION

2

Marc H. Bornstein, Jeylan T. Mortimer, Karen Lutfey, and Robert H. Bradley

▨ INTRODUCTION

The stability of human society and all that it entails depend on the current generation socializing the next generation to embrace it, maintain it, promote it, and modify it. Socialization is, therefore, a natural, vital, and central part to lifelong human development. Throughout their short lives, human beings are in the constant business of acquiring different aspects of society, of perfecting, maintaining, or passing them along. We are always learning or teaching. Indeed, no healthy human beings exist outside of society, and individual well-being is linked to enmeshing the self in society. Under these considerations, socialization is not optional but constitutes a human imperative (Bugental & Grusec, 2006). In the main, socialization transpires through interpersonal transactions as people are exposed to and adopt ways of understanding and acting that reflect the norms of their social groups. The ultimate aim in socialization is that people embody societal cognitions and practices (and not simply mimic them), and socialization includes prospects that extend beyond immediate circumstances and guide future action (Valsiner & Lawrence, 1997).

Socialization is a lifelong process, and a life-span perspective on socialization draws attention to the mutually consequential and continuing interplay between individuals and society. Writing from an anthropological perspective, one of the first major figures of socialization, Benedict (1934/1959) observed that "The life-history of the individual is first and foremost an accommodation to the patterns and standards traditionally handed down in his community. From the moment of his birth the customs into which he is born shape his experience and behaviour. By the time he can talk, he is the little creature of his culture, and by the time he is grown and able to take part in its activities, its habits are his habits, its beliefs his beliefs, its impossibilities his impossibilities" (pp. 2–3). To understand socialization, therefore, it is requisite to focus, not only on children's development but also on continuing adult development. That said, socialization operates differently according to the life stage of the socializee, in terms of both the *contexts* in which it occurs and its *contents* or emphases (Bornstein, Bradley, Lutfey, Mortimer, & Pennar, Chapter 32). Socialization occurs in a variety of contexts, from family to peer group to school to work place to nursing home, and context is critical for understanding processes of socialization.

Similarly, the contents of socialization change kaleidoscopically as the developmental requirements of life change. Which characteristics of the individual—which constructs, structures, functions, or processes—are subject to socialization at a given time in a given place will depend on many factors, not the least significant of which are the individual's life stage. People at different stages of the life course take up unique tasks and meet challenges that are specific to their developmental stage (Havighurst,

1972). Broadly speaking, children are socialized in manners and on topics that are qualitatively distinct from adults. Central to many socialization theories are assumptions that, even though socialization and resocialization can occur at any point in the life cycle, childhood is a particularly plastic period when enduring social skills and cultural values are inculcated, and adult–child interactions robustly influence young children vis-à-vis other engagements and later times (Bornstein, 2006). Socialization to maturity places children in learning situations about roles they will occupy in the future, but from which they are currently removed. Accordingly, the contents of what is learned during childhood socialization are often idealized, and young socializees are exposed to a more limited scope of social demands. By contrast, adult socializees must possess the psychological capacities to conduct themselves appropriately in multiple settings that are associated with varied demands. Moreover, the greater social power and influence the mature normally hold in comparison to the immature contribute to a socialization process wherein adults are also usually the active socializers. Socialization occurring in maturity also pertains to roles (such as spouse) in which socializees are incumbent. Many adult roles do not permit or require socializees to first assume the stance of learner; instead, adults must sometimes acquire specific roles while they simultaneously occupy them, as with socialization to marriage, parenthood, or work. Adults may also be subject to resocialization, a mechanism by which society can exert control over socializees who do not exhibit appropriate social competencies. In short, the period in life-span development in which people are located when they are being socialized profoundly influences both the contexts and contents of their socialization experiences.

This chapter on theories and processes in life-span socialization reviews a series of orienting perspectives that are intended to inform the reader about the major dimensions of life-span socialization and to provide an overview of basic principles and processes of life-span socialization. They include definitions of socialization, individual variation and transaction in socialization, socialization indigenous to specific life stages, the contexts and contents of socialization, principal socialization processes, and developmental continuity and stability in socialization. Because this exposition travels across diverse terrain, and marshals myriad examples, we use a common forum of socialization—gender—as a unifying leitmotif. In another chapter in this volume, we discuss specific contexts and contents of socialization at four life-span stages: infancy and early childhood, middle childhood and adolescence, adulthood, and old age (Bornstein et al., Chapter 32). Before beginning these expositions, however, we briefly discuss major moderators of life-span socialization.

▇ MODERATION OF SOCIALIZATION: SOCIAL CLASS, CULTURE, AND TIME

The contexts and contents of socialization are powerfully moderated by social class, culture, and time. A few concrete illustrations will serve to bring home the message of just how limited any monolithic perspective on life-span socialization really is.

Socioeconomic status (SES), conventionally measured by income, occupation, and education, differentiates many facets of socialization (Bornstein & Bradley, 2003). Although socioeconomic groups share important commonalities, SES influences socialization from very early in life. For example, SES moderates when and how parents care for children, the extent to which parents permit children the freedom to

explore, how nurturant or restrictive parents are, which behaviors parents emphasize, and so forth (Bornstein, Hahn, Suwalsky, & Haynes, 2003; Hoff, Laursen, &
Tardif, 2002). SES further influences a wide array of individual psychological orientations by shaping self-concepts, goals, and behaviors, as well as expectations for
future trajectories.

Adolescents' selection of work activities during high school is illustrative.
Adolescents from less advantaged family backgrounds are often less interested
in school and less academically motivated. They seek work during high school to
learn new skills, acquiring human capital through early job experiences (Mortimer,
2003). Their high school work trajectories tend to be more time-consuming, financially rewarding, and stressful, but also involve more advancement opportunities
than those of youth who have greater academic promise on entry to high school. A
different strategy is apparent among adolescents with access to greater resources
that afford higher educational attainment. More advantaged adolescents obtain work
experiences (when and if they do) that are less involving and demanding and that
enable them to participate in extracurricular activities and a diverse array of other
interests besides work. Given these divergent life experiences and orientations of
adolescents, and the varying meanings of their work experience, adolescent employment functions differently in socialization among low- versus high-SES teens.

Adults, too, learn from the modes of successful adaptation to daily life pressures
and situations they encounter in the workplace, and on that basis they generalize to
other situations (Kohn & Schooler, 1983; Schooler et al., 2004). When novice workers
learn that success at work depends on self-directedness and initiative, as in occupations at higher socioeconomic levels, they come to value and enact the same traits
on the job as well as in other settings of their lives. Workers in lower socioeconomic
positions are more likely to become successful in their work when they conform to
rules and regulations established by others. Kohn and Schooler (1983) found that
experiences of self-direction and conformity in the workplace mediate social class
differences across a wide range of outcomes. They influence workers' intellectual flexibility, their goals and values for themselves, their self-esteem and self-confidence,
and their basic orientations (trust or mistrust) toward others as well as their childrearing values. Kohn argued that middle-class parents (those who work in the professional sphere and who have relatively high levels of education) are more likely to
attribute their success to the exercise of autonomy. In contrast, working-class parents (those who work in the nonprofessional arena and who have comparatively low
levels of education) are likely to attribute their success to an ability to carefully follow established rules. Given that parents want their children to be successful, these
views about which contingencies lead to success in their own lives influence the ways
in which parents socialize their children. Specifically, middle-class parents are more
likely to value self-direction in their children, whereas working-class parents are
more likely to value their children following rules. Kohn and his colleagues provided
support for this view with research from a range of societies, including Italy, Japan,
Poland, Ukraine, and the United States (Kohn, Slomczynski, & Schoenbach, 1986;
Kohn et al., 2001). Kohn et al. did not argue that parents want their children only to
conform (if they are working class) or to be autonomous (if middle class); all children
need to be self-directing sometimes and to conform at other times. Kohn's point is
that parents' socioeconomic conditions of life are such that they are more likely to
associate future success either with a greater propensity to act with a greater degree

of autonomy or to follow established rules and to differentially encourage such characteristics in their children as a result.

Culture refers to ways of life shared by members of a population broadly reflecting the psychological, social, and economic adaptation of the people. Culture is the system of shared beliefs, conventions, norms, behaviors, expectations, and symbolic representations that persist over time and prescribe social rules of conduct. Comparative study reveals systematic cultural differences in all domains of socialization. For example, parents from different cultures differ in their opinions about the desirability or necessity of specific competencies to ensure their children's successful adjustment and even in the ages they expect children to attain different milestones or acquire diverse abilities (Bornstein & Lansford, 2009; Goodnow, 2009). After studying developmental timetables in two groups of Australian mothers (Australian born and Lebanese born), Goodnow, Cashmore, Cotton, and Knight (1984) determined that culture shaped parents' expectations of their children's growth more than children's gender or birth order. In another study of the nomadic hunter–gatherer Aka and Ngandu farming cultures in central Africa, Hewlett, Lamb, Shannon, Leyendecker, and Scholmerich (1998) observed that 3- to 4-month-old Aka children experienced more "proximal" relationships with their caregivers (they were more likely to be held and fed) than same-age Ngandu children, who were more likely than Aka children to be left alone, fuss, smile, vocalize, and play. The Aka and Ngandu cultures have similarly high levels of child mortality, equivalently hazardous living conditions, equally healthy children, and comparable maternal workloads, and so these factors do not explain differences in the childhood socialization practices between the two cultures. Culture-specific patterns of socialization are presumably adapted to each specific society's setting and needs. As a result, adults in different cultures structure socialization differently, expose children to different experiences, and interpret the meaning and usefulness of different aspects of socialization differently. Thus, Hewlett et al. (1998) speculated that Aka parents, who frequently move from one location to the next in search of food, are usually less familiar with their home surroundings than are Ngandu parents, who live a comparatively sedentary existence. Aka parents may remain in closer proximity to their children to better protect them in unfamiliar environments. Other stages of the life course are equivalently subject to cultural moderation. Family obligations are typically valued less by adolescents than by their parents across cultures (Phinney, Ong, & Madden, 2000), but Asian American and Mexican American adolescents are socialized more than their European American peers to believe that they should assist parents and siblings throughout the life span and be willing to make sacrifices for the family (Fuligni, Tseng, & Lam, 1999).

We live in the moment, but a principal (and often neglected) component of life-span human development is time (Bronfenbrenner & Morris, 2006). Three main temporal issues occupy socialization science. One concerns stage of life. In our companion chapter, we explore the role of stages of life in life-span socialization in greater detail (Bornstein et al., Chapter 32). For example, adolescence (as opposed to other ontogenetic stages) is often viewed as a period of intensification of gender socialization, that is a time in the life cycle when becoming or being a girl or a boy is particularly stressed by both the individual and the society (Crouter, Manke, & McHale, 1995; Hill & Lynch, 1983; Steinberg & Silk, 2002). A second temporal issue is developmental time, and, in this construal, dynamic questions of individual stability and group continuity in socialization characteristics are posed. We turn to the issue of developmental time in life-span socialization in detail later in this chapter.

A third issue is historical time. A life-span perspective on socialization implies considerations of how the contexts and contents of socialization manifest and change as a reflection of their era (French, 2002). Socialization processes and outcomes vary with historical period, including the attitudes of both socializers and socializees, the conceptualization of life-span stages, demographic changes, and interpersonal dynamics. For example, although gender roles continue to be portrayed in traditional and stereotypic ways in many places, some diachronic changes toward more egalitarian gender-role beliefs are emergent (Huston & Wright, 1998). The roles of "woman," "spouse," "mother," and "worker" are changing as more women work outside the home. In turn, family structure transforms as a result of economic shifts, altering expectations about life styles, family life, and women's responsibilities. The contemporary situation of middle-class and working-class Peruvians has forced men and women to alter their views about gender (Facio & Resett, 2008). Andean and migrant families are traditionally patriarchal. In coastal urban areas, this "macho" family culture still prevails, even among educated Peruvians. The father is the main authority in the household and the last word in decision-making. He chooses rewards and punishments, and his wife is his advisor. However, the behavior of families and adolescents is radically changing as more female adolescents, young adults, and mothers work at home and outside the house. In Argentina, a traditional macho attitude has steadily waned, and the gap between the genders in work, education, and political activity has been narrowing. Although women are highly regarded for their maternal role, contemporary Argentine youth of both genders consider "being capable of caring for children" as important for defining an adult man as it is for defining an adult woman (Facio & Resett, 2008).

Classes, cultures, and times can be understood as created, sustained, and communicated in everyday practices and behavioral routines (Goodnow, Miller, & Kessel, 1995). Socialization transpires through the acquisition of knowledge, skills, attitudes, and through participation in activities (Rogoff, 2003). Whether universal or specific, sanctions, positive or negative, are in place to ensure that each generation socializes in ways so that each following generation acquires appropriate prescribed, and eschews inappropriate proscribed, beliefs and behaviors. All classes, cultures, and times define certain characteristics that their socializees are expected to possess as well as others they must avoid if they are to behave acceptably and adapt successfully (Harkness & Super, 2002). Thus, class, culture, and time constitute important qualifiers of the processes and effects of socialization. Standards and values regarding how socialization should occur vary greatly from one class, culture, or time to another. Looked at a different way, class, culture, and time afford intrinsic and idiosyncratic meaning to socialization. In consequence, even the same content may have a different meaning or a different outcome in different contexts (Bornstein, 1995). Considering class, culture, and time augments our understanding of socialization and points to the importance of meaning in understanding processes of socialization. The study of socialization in different contexts reveals how these moderators transform socialization.

Socialization is not a haphazard process. Over the life span, we are guided along particular paths. Those paths are defined by many factors, including the class, culture, and time in which we live and are expected to function as competent and contributing members of society. Thematicity, the repetition of the same socialization ideas and goals across contexts and contents, has special importance in this connection. Every class, culture, and time is characterized, and distinguished from others, by thoroughgoing, deep-seated, and consistent themes that specify what one needs to know, to think, to feel, and to behave as a functioning member of society as moderated by the class, culture, or time (Quinn & Holland, 1987). Gender socialization illustrates thematicity in the sense that family and various groups in society communicate about gender in convergent ways that come to affect how individuals construct themselves and make sense of their lives. Class, culture, and time prescribe how children of different genders are socialized and by whom, how they are to dress, what behaviors are considered appropriate, and which tasks children of different genders are taught, as well as what roles as adult women and men they will adopt (Best, 2010; Best & Williams, 1997; Whiting & Edwards, 1988). More proximally, parents socialize their young children's gendered beliefs and behaviors and consonantly organize their children's activities and environments inside and outside the family. Peers later reinforce gender standards. Children also engage in more same- than other-gender beliefs and behaviors in part because they are differentially exposed to same-gender models (Crouter et al., 1995). Furthermore, the types of socialization practices directed toward girls and boys in large measure reflect existing opportunities for women and men in a particular class and culture at a particular time. For example, if women in a society are expected to assume primary responsibility for rearing children, socialization processes tend to emphasize the practice of nurturant behaviors in girls more than in boys. If men are expected to take primary responsibility for providing economic subsistence outside of the home, socialization processes tend to emphasize independent and instrumental behaviors in boys more than in girls (Best & Williams, 1997; Hewlett, 1991; Whiting, 1986).

An illustration of how all these forces work in concert was provided by Fredricks and Eccles (2002), who reported that parents who hold stronger stereotypes regarding general differential capabilities of girls and boys in English, math, and sports had specialized expectations regarding their children's abilities in these areas, which in turn related to their children's self-perceptions of their competencies and performance, even when their actual ability levels were controlled. These relations were mediated, in part, by parents' tendencies to provide different experiences for daughters and sons.

Specific patterns of socialization emerge from dynamic and bidirectional interactions with class, culture, and time. A pervading critique of socialization is that theory and research in the field have tended to describe processes that accord with ideals mostly or exclusively appropriate to Western, educated, industrialized, rich, and democratic societies. Admittedly, most is both thought and known about socialization in such circumstances (Henrich, Heine, & Norenzayan, 2010), but that does not equate to idealizing those circumstances. We do not conceive of these populations as normative, we do not accept that their contexts and contents of socialization are universally applicable, nor do we believe that adopting any one group's values is the desired or desirable endpoint of socialization. Thus, the socialization processes we now turn to describe and explicate may be limited by culture, class, or time. However, it may still be that much of what we have to say is more broadly applicable. We believe so.

▦ SOCIALIZATION: DEFINITIONS AND SOCIAL SCIENCE APPROACHES

Broadly construed, socialization encompasses processes in development by which individuals acquire the norms, values, cognitions, practices, language, skills, motives, and roles appropriate to their society and that together help them develop into effective and contributing members of their society (for other definitions, see Bush & Summons, 1981, p. 134; Gecas, 2000, p. 2855; George, 1993, p. 353). Socialization has underpinnings, constituents, and construals that are faithful to a diverse array of the social and behavioral sciences, from anthropology through ethology, psychology, and sociology to zoology. Under functionalist assumptions, socialization serves the interests of the larger society by converting untutored immature members into competent mature members capable of executing their roles and maintaining and advancing the existing social system. Under symbolic interactionist assumptions, actors shape the conditions that influence their subsequent development.

Socialization theory has its roots in philosophical debates of nativists and empiricists on the origins of knowledge and morality, and Descartes, Berkley, Locke, Kant, and James from philosophy as well as Gesell and Watson from early psychology will be familiar figures in this history. Many early scientific views of socialization reflected a psychological perspective grounded in psychoanalytic and behavior theories that viewed socialization as largely the province of parents (especially mothers). For anthropologists and developmental scientists alike, socialization (especially of children) constituted the principal link between societal features and the psychology of adults. Over time, overarching theories of psychoanalysis and behavior socialization yielded to more specific theories faithful to diverse contexts, contents, and ages of socialization (Bornstein et al., Chapter 32; Maccoby, 1992).

▦ INDIVIDUAL VARIATION AND TRANSACTION IN SOCIALIZATION

Ultimately, the influence processes between socializing agents and targets of socialization (socializers and socializees) has come to be understood as lifelong and bidirectional in nature. Continuous reciprocal interchanges obtain between parents and children, between siblings, between peers, between students and teachers, and between workers and supervisors. People are understood as engaged in continuous transactions within their socializing environments, extending beyond their families to include expanded social networks and resources available to individuals, families, and other socializing organizations within their communities. People also actively select, modify, and create their own socialization (Bell, 1968, 1970; Scarr & Kidd, 1983). For example, an experimental study by Anderson, Lytton, and Romney (1986) paired conduct-disordered boys with mothers of conduct-disordered boys and with mothers of normal boys. Conduct-disordered boys elicited negative parenting practices from both sets of mothers. Clearly, in this experimental setting (which controls for shared genetics), characteristics of the child contributed to the type of parenting socialization received. A reciprocal effects model asserts that parenting not only affects children but also that children affect parenting. More generally, the principle of transaction in socialization acknowledges that experiences shape the characteristics of the individual through time and, reciprocally, that the characteristics of an individual shape his or her experiences (Bornstein, 2009; Sameroff, 2009).

People influence which experiences they will be exposed to, and by interpreting and appraising those experiences uniquely, they also (in some degree) determine how those experiences affect them. People bring distinctive characteristics to, and are believed to change as a result of, every interaction. We do not assume that all people (*qua* socializees) are the same, but rather that individuals differ in their capacities for socialization, their abilities to adapt to socialization contexts and contents, their orientations toward being socialized, and so forth. Workers who have greater intellectual flexibility and self-directed orientations tend to choose more complex jobs, which further enhance those very characteristics (Schooler, Mulatu, & Dates, 2004). Adult socialization sometimes reinforces initial propensities, rather than producing entirely new ways of thinking or behaving (Elder & O'Rand, 1995; Lerner & Busch-Rossnagel, 1981). So-called person factors thus constitute an important constellation of variables that moderate socialization. For example, girls and boys differ in their susceptibility to gender socialization: Boys tend to be more resistant to nontraditional gender attitudes and roles than girls are (Bussey & Bandura, 1999; Leaper, 2000). Boys are also more negatively affected than girls by certain socialization experiences, such as single parenthood or divorce (Hetherington, 1993; Needle, Su, & Doherty, 1990) and poverty (Elder & Rockwell, 1979). Likewise, age moderates gender socialization effects. An examination of gender stereotypes among youth of different ages in 25 countries revealed a general developmental pattern of gender stereotype acquisition beginning in early childhood, accelerating during middle childhood, and becoming complete during adolescence (Williams & Best, 1982/1990).

Parents' cognitions and practices as well as those of peers, teachers, and other agents of socialization promote gender-appropriate beliefs and behaviors that come to define "girlhood" and "boyhood"—an illustration of thematicity. However, in parent–child transaction, as we described, children also contribute to their socialization. In this regard, the construct of gender constancy is exemplary. Kohlberg (1966) proposed that children's developing sense of the permanence of categorical gender ("I am a girl and will always be a girl.") critically organizes and motivates learning gender beliefs and behaviors. Indeed, children appear to transit a series of cognitive stages in regard to understanding the nature of gender (Slaby & Frey, 1975)—first identifying their own and others' gender, next accepting that gender remains stable through time, and finally understanding that gender is an immutable characteristic that is not altered by superficial transformations in appearance or activities. A universality of these stages has even been established in cross-cultural research (De Lisi & Gallagher, 1991). Gender socialization, therefore, also entails active construction of the meaning of gender categories that is internal to the socializee. In this respect, research confirms associations between levels of gender constancy and gender socialization in terms of selective attention to same-gender models, same-gender imitation (in activities, clothing, and peer preferences), gender-stereotype knowledge, and heightened responsiveness to gender cues. Children's own developing cognitive structures influence their gender-role orientation and socialization.

Separate from group identification, socializees also differ along multiple key dimensions of socialization, including receptivity, level of engagement, and the like, depending on their genetic endowment and prior experience. Various genotype–environment interactions and correlations have been distinguished that are relevant to an individual-differences perspective on socialization. Interactions emerge when a given experience has different effects on a person depending on the person's traits. "Active" interactions occur when individuals seek out and create socialization experiences and environments (those presumably compatible with their genotypes), and "evocative" interactions occur when people provoke or elicit responses from others. Clausen's (1991) longitudinal research illustrates how active interactions with the environment can influence lifelong socialization outcomes. Adolescents differ in planful competence, a social psychological characteristic that can shape their life-span socialization trajectory. Compared with peers who are not planfully competent, adolescents who are able to rationally and thoughtfully consider educational and career decisions are more likely to elect choices they are happy with in the long term. As a result, these adolescents exhibit greater personality consistency over the life span.

Genetic variation in children can lead to differential susceptibility to socialization (e.g., provided by parents or caregivers), exemplifying reactive personality–environment transactions (Belsky, 2005). Evolutionary reasoning suggests that children vary in their susceptibility to environmental influences, including socialization (Belsky & Pluess, 2009a, 2009b). That is, individuals differ in plasticity, and specific genes might even function like "plasticity factors" rendering some individuals more malleable or susceptible than others to both negative and positive socialization influences (Belsky & Pluess, 2009a, 2009b). Pluess and Belsky (2010) followed a large sample of American children from reasonably diverse backgrounds from 1 month to 11 years with repeated observational assessments of parenting and child care quality as well as teacher report and standardized assessments of children's cognitive–academic and social functioning. Children with histories of certain kinds of temperament proved more susceptible to early rearing effects.

Some types of parenting are more or less effective with children with different temperaments (e.g., Bates, Pettit, Dodge, & Ridge, 1998; Kochanska, 1997). For example, long-term effects of maltreatment are moderated by genetic endowment. Children whose genotype confers high levels of MAOA (monoamine oxidase A, an enzyme that metabolizes neurotransmitters such as serotonin, and thus renders them inactive) are more likely than children without this genetic composition to respond to maltreatment by exhibiting antisocial behaviors (Caspi et al., 2002). Children who are at genetic risk for antisocial behavior (based on the prebirth behavior of their biological mothers) are more likely to elicit coercive parenting from their adoptive parents, a pattern that, in turn, increases children's antisocial behavior (O'Connor, Deater-Deckard, Fulker, Rutter, & Plomin, 1998). Thus, individuals help to construct or evoke their socialization based on their attributes, and individuals differ in the extent to which they are responsive or refractory to socialization processes.

Other individual differences also mediate socialization. Objectively common learning events are not necessarily experienced in the same way by different individuals. The concept of reactive personality–environment transactions means that different socializees likely learn different things from the same experience (Caspi, 1993; Caspi & Roberts, 2001; Shiner & Caspi, 2003). Personal construct theory (Kelly, 1955) long ago asserted that individuals vary in the dimensions along which they construe experience, and self-theory (Epstein, 1990) and personal script theory (Tomkins, 1987) later underscored the role of the individual in interpreting or encoding experienced events. Each person is an active participant in socialization, capable of discovering, maintaining, or transforming the opportunities socialization affords.

It is important to note that individual differences that affect socialization processes are both genetic and biological in origin as well as learned and rooted in experience. Socializees sometimes engage in the socialization process more when they discern a connection between their performance and future valued outcomes. Similarly, being a novice in one socialization context, but having experience in another, influence socialization, including the socializee's compliance with socializers and capacity to fulfill socializers' expectations. Precocious children fulfilling adult roles at home might have trouble completing their homework, exacerbating their struggles to meet teachers' expectations for their student role.

Biography is, therefore, intimately connected to how people respond to socialization opportunities and constraints. The same socialization experience may have different meaning and implications for people who differ in terms of generation, perceptions, temperament, and developmental status. People vary in the extent to which and the ways in which they respond to (even normative) experiences. Putting socialization and group and individual variation together raises the emergent issue of "goodness-of-fit." Whether a person's long-term socialization is favorable or unfavorable depends on the interaction of the person with the environment or, more specifically, the match between them (Lerner, Lewin-Bizan, & Warren, 2011; Thomas & Chess, 1977, 1980). An aging adult with a low activity level, positive mood, and poor adaptability might fit well in a retirement home setting that makes few demands, but such an environment may be a poorer fit for an aging adult with a high activity level, difficult personality, and poorer mood. Moreover, goodness-of-fit is itself a dynamic transactional process. At the end of the day, successful and continuing socialization depends on changing interactions between a person's attributes and the demands of changing socialization experiences and environments. In socialization, experience, environment, and person all have parts to play and none alone constitutes an exclusive or starring determinant.

Reciprocally, the perspectives and contributions of socializers are critical to understanding socialization processes. Socializers' own experiences socializing others helps to shape socialization processes and outcomes. For example, the experiences of attending physicians contribute to socializing future medical students, both in terms of what students learn from their supervisors and how they learn to socialize one another (Becker, Geer, Hughes, & Strauss, 1961; Hafferty, 1991). Practitioners' own experiences with cadavers are critical for teaching new students how to cope adequately with this aspect of medical school. Students know that at some point in their own educational trajectories, their professors have had to become comfortable with dissecting human beings, and so students model that behavior themselves.

There is no reason to expect that socialization operates similarly for every person. Contemporary socialization theory and research are concerned with understanding individual variations, complex transactions, and emergent properties between people and their socialization experiences. One critical individual-difference factor is life stage.

▨ SOCIALIZATION × LIFE STAGE

As we have seen, socializees are active participants in socialization processes. Thus, socializees at different points in the life span bring different competencies and interpretations to their current socialization. Examining socialization in life-span developmental terms is, therefore, vital. Stage is a primary organizing dimension in life-span developmental science, and this metric of development is deeply connected to socialization. Monitoring is a feature of socialization that has received considerable attention. For young children, monitoring involves proximal surveillance, shared activities, and direct supervision by parents themselves or by others; for adolescents, more distal forms of monitoring, such as parent-initiated conversations, cell phones, and imposition of rules, are the norm (Crouter, Helms-Erikson, Updegraff, & McHale, 1999; Laird, Pettit, Mize, Brown, & Lindsey, 1994; Waizenhofer, Buchanan, & Jackson-Newsom, 2004).

With changes in life stage, people's skills and interests develop, and so do the nature of their participation in socialization along with expectations pertaining to their participation. A moment's reflection will confirm that common experiences are interpreted uniquely by children, adolescents, adults, and the aged. How thorough-going age- or stage-related responses or interpretations of the shared environment is sometimes counterintuitive and surprising. For example, teens' brains function differently from those of adults when processing emotional information in the same external stimuli. In a study mapping differences between the verbal reports and brain responses of teens and adults, Yurgelun-Todd (2007) put teenage and adult volunteers in an MRI and monitored how they construed a series of pictures of facial emotions. Adults identified one picture as expressing fear; teenagers interpreted the same picture as indicating shock or anger. When their brain scans were examined, teenagers were found to be using a different part of the brain when reading the images (the amygdala) than adults (the prefrontal cortex). Similarly, as they age, adults experience less negative emotion, pay less attention to negative than to positive emotional stimuli, and are less likely to remember negative than positive emotional materials. Mather et al. (2004) used event-related fMRI in adults to assess whether amygdala activation in response to positive and negative emotional pictures changes with age. Both older and younger adults showed greater activation in the amygdala for emotional than for neutral pictures; however, seeing positive pictures led to greater amygdala activation in older adults than seeing negative pictures, whereas this was not the case for younger adults. Thus, children, adolescents, adults, and the aged do not necessarily encode, organize, interpret, or respond to information in the outside world in the same ways.

Reciprocally, the cast of socializers and their tasks change depending on the socializees' developmental stage. The parent's role in socialization early on is to educate children in beliefs and behaviors that are acceptable for the stage of childhood they occupy as well as prepare children for adaptation to a wider range of life roles and contexts they will encounter as they grow.

However, parents and their infants and young children affect one another reciprocally, and so bidirectional models of early socialization obtain (Corsaro & Eder, 1995; Gecas, 1981, 2000). Parenting approaches affect the responses of the child which, in turn, feed back to affect parental expectations and predilections by confirming and expanding them or, at times, contradicting them. Socialization requires attention to biological and cultural processes involved in caregiver socialization and to the ways in which children and caregivers exert reciprocal influences.

Moreover, the majority of infants and young children throughout the world grow up in family systems where there is more than one significant socializing figure guiding more than one child's socialization at a time. Biological and adoptive mothers and fathers are young children's acknowledged principal caregivers. Parents serve as a source of love, affection, security, protection, advice, and limit setting. However, parents are not the only agents who contribute to the socialization of infants and young children. Brothers and sisters and members of the extended family also contribute. Siblings offer socialization opportunities related to social understanding, conflict management, and differential status (Zukow-Goldring, 2002). Outside the family, peers also have an undeniable socializing effect (Rubin, Coplan, Chen, Bowker, & McDonald, 2011). Peer friendships provide mutual commitment, support, and trust. Moreover, infants and young children are regularly tended by nonparental, nonfamilial care providers (Clarke-Stewart & Allhusen, 2002, 2005). Teachers and nonparental caregivers of infants and young children often act similarly to parents, whereas teachers of older children may be influential in other ways relative to their expertise and access to opportunities (Eccles & Roeser, 2011). In short, many individuals, other than mother and father, socialize infants and young children.

As contexts, peer groups, schools, and work function along with the home in shaping social understanding and social behavior in older children and adolescents. That said, relatively less is known about how these systems influence each other as regards to socialization beyond the fact that there are certain formal structures established for communication between home and school and the fact that parents tend to guide children regarding how to act at school and with respect to peers, teachers, and other adults generally. Older children's friends and the establishments with which they now associate, like school and work, come to hold waxing sway over socialization. Peer influence increases as children grow, helping to structure the transition between early childhood and adulthood. Influence processes between peers differ from those between parents and children. Peer relationships are marked by symmetrical reciprocity and guided by the overarching principle of cooperation, an organizational dynamic that differs from the unilateral authority or power asymmetry that is more characteristic of adult–child relationships. In middle childhood, children develop their own self-socializing goals, which begin to dovetail with peer and teacher expectations and values. Personal goals also reflect experiences in the neighborhood, at work, with media, and with other social agents. As youth transit from early childhood into middle childhood and move forward into adolescence, they become increasingly active in both determining the kinds of socialization experiences they have and how they respond to those experiences. In adolescence, when there is less parental control and monitoring of peers, school experiences, technology and media use play increasingly larger roles in socialization; however, family values, norms, and beliefs continue to shape socialization toward maturity. Adult socialization to family and work often implies that socialization is successful. However, socialization effectiveness cannot always be assumed. When new recruits cannot or do not wish to adapt to the requirements of their socializers, they become alienated and withdrawn, and may even rebel against them. On the one hand, failures of adult socialization may indicate the inability to perform a new role, which is problematic especially if an organization has made a substantial investment in formal training or in informally socializing the neophyte. Little effective socialization to new roles is likely to occur when there are hostile and conflictual relationships between socializers and socializees. On the other hand, such "failures" of socialization may signal that the adult's interests and talents are not a good fit with the initially selected role, leading to new exploration and selection of a role that is more compatible. This kind of process is most evident in the floundering that is frequently observed in the early stages of work careers (Kerckhoff, 2002). Difficulties in socialization following tentative commitments may pave the way for later, more congruent choices that eventuate in a more satisfying career path for the person and greater productivity for the organization.

Taking a broader perspective, adult socialization failures on a large scale may instigate large-scale social change, as whole collectivities develop visions of more fulfilling, moral, or satisfying ways of life, and seek to construct new institutional models to realize their ideals. At a basic level, individuals are often attracted to social movements because of a mismatch between their expectations and ideals for behaviors that were developed in earlier periods of life and new dissatisfying realities that are confronted in the manifold socialization settings of adulthood (McAdam, 1988; Rohlinger & Snow, 2003).

Adulthood heralds changing responsibilities and shifting roles in socialization. The main contexts of socialization in adulthood are family and work, and adulthood is supposedly the fulfillment of past socialization processes in contents of productive and responsible community participation as well as fitting socialization of the succeeding generation. In the past, adulthood would have constituted socialization's culmination and end stage. Today, socialization does not conclude in adulthood. Rather, contemporary biological and social forces have extended longevity to render old age another and new period of life-span socialization.

In general, research on socialization to old age is a topic that lacks the depth and breadth of socialization research for other periods of the life course. Much previous work on socialization in the life span has focused on earlier stages, specific agents of socialization, and key transitions, such as adulthood. Socialization to old age has, by comparison, received less attention. Importantly, however, aging populations, increased longevity, and the increasing range of living arrangements available to elderly people render it a critical topic. Socialization extends beyond maturity, the period normatively conceived of as the culmination of socialization and the home of responsibility for future intergenerational socialization. Today, socialization extends into postadult old age, where the contents and contexts tend to focus on social networks, quality of life, and health care.

Socialization processes in old age have several qualities that distinguish them from other points in the life course, including more agents from more domains of life applicable over a longer period of time. Also, anticipatory socialization for old age occurs over a longer period than for earlier stages and transitions leading up to old age as people develop a sense of the meaning and identities associated with that life stage over many decades. The role of previous experiences and the prominence of family, peer, spousal, and work networks may be greater for this part of the life course relative to younger ages. Furthermore, health is critically salient to old age and in a ways that are not the same for younger groups, and the topic requires tailored attention to understand how it influences socialization.

▨ SOCIALIZATION × CONTEXTS AND CONTENTS

Socialization transpires over the life span via myriad transactions between the person and the physical and social environments in which the person lives. These transactions are multidimensional. They involve many partners and experiences, and they take many forms, including interpersonal contacts and participation in routines, rituals, and institutions; even some solitary activities entail socialization. Many established settings likewise support socialization, including formal institutions such as the school, specialized and intentional arrangements such as apprenticeships, and less formal settings and even incidental opportunities, such as routines and rituals (Serpell & Hatano, 1997).

In this connection, ecological systems theory offers a valuable guide to organizing our understanding of life-span socialization. A wide array of socialization agents, embedded in a wide range of contexts, operate in concert. Socializers in various contexts influence each other and ultimately socializees in both direct and indirect ways. In the view of Bronfenbrenner and Morris (2006), socialization takes place through progressively more complex reciprocal interactions between active, evolving biopsychological socializees and socializers—be they persons, objects, or symbols—in proximal-to-distal contexts. Thus, contexts of socialization are conceived as a series of nested systems, organized hierarchically, from close to the individual to more distant. Accordingly, Bronfenbrenner (cited in Bronfenbrenner & Morris, 2006) differentiated micro-, meso-, exo-, and macro-systems: "A microsystem is a pattern of activities, social roles, and interpersonal relations experienced by the developing person in a given face-to-face setting with particular physical, social, and symbolic features that invite, permit, or inhibit, engagement in sustained, progressively more complex interaction with, and activity in, the immediate environment." The parent–child relationship typifies the microsystem. The mesosystem comprises the linkages and processes that take place between two or more settings containing the developing person. "The exosystem comprises the linkages and processes taking place between two or more settings, at least one of which does not contain the developing person, but in which events occur that indirectly influence processes within the immediate setting in which the developing person lives." Finally, the macrosystem consists of the overarching pattern of micro-, meso-, and exosystems characteristic of a given culture or subculture, with particular reference to the belief systems, bodies of knowledge, material resources, customs, life styles, opportunities, hazards, and life-span options that are embedded in each of these broader systems. Cultural factors that define a society, such as its form of economy, political structure, traditions, and laws, constitute the macrosystem of socialization.

The values, beliefs, and practices considered culturally appropriate are broadly derived from the macrosystem, although their effects are experienced in the microsystem. For example, the greater meaning of gender is communicated through the cultural macrosystem (e.g., perhaps instantiated in power and economic differentials that prevail in a society between women and men) that in turn influences the microsystems that children and youth directly experience at home, in school, and around their neighborhood. This systems conceptualization of socialization contexts by contents reveals that interactions with the environment occur at multiple levels, and all constitute effective stimulants to socialization in life-span development.

The ecological perspective stimulates thinking about life-span socialization from a systemic point of view. In examining socialization, this perspective highlights the different contexts that provide children, adolescents, adults, and aged persons with different physical, cognitive, and social contents.

▦ PROCESSES OF SOCIALIZATION

So far, socialization science has advanced only a handful of general processes by which socialization experiences influence human development—psychodynamic, learning, cognitive, and opportunity. To define and illustrate each concretely, we continue to draw on the domain of gender socialization in childhood. However, these processes apply broadly as they are applicable to diverse contexts and contents of socialization across the life span.

Psychodynamic Socialization, Internalization, and Attachment

Freud (1949) speculated about the special importance of early experiences and early development in socialization, suggesting that the ways parents treat their young offspring establish lifelong personality traits. In Freud's psychosexual stage theory, socializees are characterized as moving through a series of developmental stages. These critical phases define periods in development during which certain experiences—affecting specific types of traits—are of special and lifelong significance (Cohler & Paul, 2002). Although this progression might be retarded or accelerated by experience, inborn (personality) structures—id, ego, and superego—essentially propel children through fixed and universal psychological stages. Freud and his followers in the psychodynamic model posited mechanisms like introjection and identification to account for developmental phenomena like gender socialization. Girls identify with mother and adopt female behaviors, boys with fathers and male behaviors. Mead's (1935) studies of the influence of childrearing patterns on the socialization of gender roles, and Benedict's (1938, 1946) studies of the mechanisms by which cultural customs, beliefs, and knowledge are internalized followed from the putative universality of Freudian psychodynamics.

Bowlby (1969) and successive attachment theorists subsequently proposed that, arising out of their early social experiences with caregivers, young children develop "internal working models" of their caregivers that incorporate both sides of the caregiver–child relationship. These representations are believed to shape the relationships children later establish with others (Sroufe & Fleeson, 1986). Parents remain central in the lives of adolescents even as primary attachment gradually shifts from parents to peers (Fraley & Davis, 1997). Representations of interactions with parents shape individual differences in attachment security in childhood and continue to do so in later ages in relationships with others (Fraley & Shaver, 2000; Mikulincer, Shaver, & Pereg, 2003) so that the qualities of peer attachments and romantic relationships are believed to depend heavily on the quality of relationships with parents (Dekovic & Meeus, 1997). Further along, parents' orientations to their children are asserted to be shaped by their attachment relationships with their own parents, as extensive work in the Adult Attachment Interview (AAI) concludes (George, Kaplan, & Main, 1985). The AAI assesses an adult's model of his or her own relationship with his or her parents. A strong predictive link has emerged between the child's attachment with the mother and the mother's own AAI classification (Smith & Drew, 2002; Van IJzendoorn, 1995). Notably, the correspondence between caregiver and infant attachment classifications is consistently high (Miljkovitch, Pierrehumbert, Bretherton, & Halfon, 2004). Attachment research assumes that, on the basis of repeated experiences of characteristic patterns of interaction, children develop expectations regarding the nature and the nature of social interaction that endure long after children depart their family of origin.

Learning and Imitation

From Watson (1924/1970) to Skinner (1976), attempts have been made to relate learning theories to socialization, and Miller and Dollard (1941) explicitly reformulated psycho-analytic theory in behavior-theoretical terms. Learning theorists interpret socializa-tion as the acquisition of associations that bring information from experience into the individual. Classical, operant, and observational learning all refer to the formation and encoding of information and are thought to constitute species-general rules. From the very beginning of life, human beings make associations and can subsequently make use of what they have learned. Moreover, early simple behavior patterns are asserted to underlie later more complex behavior patterns. For example, a direct avenue of socialization is posited to flow through parents' differential treatment of children. Differential treatment may assume various forms. One type of differential treatment operates through parenting cognitions, for example, the expectations that parents have for, and communicate to, their children. Parents possess different beliefs about (their) girls and boys across a wide array of domains. Mothers of toddlers underestimate their girls' motor skills and overestimate their boys' motor skills even when objective tests show no gender differences in children's motor performance (Mondschein, Adolph, & Tamis-LeMonda, 2000). Later in life, parents convey gender-related expectations about school work. Parents tend to expect boys to do better than girls in science and math (Eccles, Freedman-Doan, Frome, Jacobs, & Yoon, 2000; Tenenbaum & Leaper, 2003), again despite a lack of actual gender differences in performance (Hyde, Lindberg, Linn, Ellis, & Williams, 2008; Tenenbaum & Leaper, 2003). These messages are thought to influence children's self-concepts, motivation, and choices.

A second type of differential treatment occurs through parenting practices, par-enting's direct interactions with children. Parenting practices themselves are of different kinds; some are active, some are passive. Mischel's (1970) social learning perspective called attention to parents' (and others') direct reinforcement of chil-dren's conformity to expected or desired norms, as with respect to gender when, for example, adults compliment a girl when she nurses a doll and a boy when he builds a model airplane. Many family studies indicate that parents treat females and males differently and encourage and reward girls and boys to accept distinctive and often "traditional" gender roles. Gender-differentiated patterns of parent–child interaction in the domain of emotions may contribute to girls learning to express their emo-tions versus boys learning to mute theirs (Eisenberg, Cumberland, & Spinrad, 1998). Children's execution of different behaviors often depends on rewards or injunctions associated with their outcomes.

Understanding the mechanisms of operation of discipline and reward practices has been a primary focus of socialization researchers. Power assertive strategies of discipline include verbal criticism, social isolation, and corporal punishment. In addi-tion to disciplining undesirable actions, parents reinforce desirable ones. Although rewards can detract from an inference of freely chosen action and, therefore, inter-nalization, socializers still use them (Warton & Goodnow, 1995), and they play a major part in some socialization theories. Coercive cycles of interaction tend to develop in problem families through inadvertent use of negative reinforcement, and this sets the stage for exposing children to positive reinforcement for antisocial action from deviant peer groups (Dishion, Andrews, & Crosby, 1995; Patterson, 1980).

Parents too offer children different models for imitation. In one view, children acquire new behaviors without ever performing them overtly and without ever being rewarded, but merely by observing such behaviors being performed by nurturant and powerful parents (Bandura, 1962, 1965). To the extent that mothers, fathers, or other caregivers are important and influential figures in children's lives, often to be emulated or feared, they shape children's impressions of what it means to be a woman or a man, for example, simply by acting like a woman or a man (Bussey & Bandura, 1999). Mothers and fathers traditionally differ in roles and statuses. Imitation is a particularly efficient mechanism for acquiring information of all sorts just by watching or listening. Observational learning is included in the notion of "intent participation," where observation is motivated by the expectation that, at a later time, the observer will be responsible for the action in question (Rogoff, 2003). Intent participation involves more experienced socializers facilitating a socializee's participation and participating along with the socializee, or it may involve direct verbal instruction. Implicit and gradual learning opportunities occur as socializees participate in the activities of their community alongside more experienced socializers; thus, the socialization of routine behaviors and practices is readily observable (Rogoff, 1990). Imitation of the actions of others appears to be virtually automatic in humans (Chartrand & Bargh, 1999). Indeed, so-called "mirror neurons" have been identified in which equivalent brain neural firings occur when an individual carries out an action and when the individual observes that same action being executed by another individual (Gallese, Ferrari, Kohler, & Fogassi, 2002). These brain processes may underlie imitation, which has been observed very early in life (Meltzoff & Moore, 1999). Indeed, it is striking how receptive young children are to "proper" ways of acting or conventional routines, many of which are acquired through observation (e.g., Dunn & Munn, 1985; Emde, Biringen, Clyman, & Oppenheim, 1991). Third-party observation involves attention and listening in (eavesdropping) in anticipation of engaging in a similar activity at a future time (Rogoff, Pardies, Arauz, Correa-Chavez, & Angelillo, 2003).

Children learn from a same-gender model, but also from many same-gender models engaging in the same activity as well as different-gender models engaging in different activities. That is, observational learning and modeling are not necessarily confined to a single model or a specific belief or behavior; instead, socializees may acquire abstract rules and styles. For example, by attending to models of both genders, girls and boys construct more robust ideas of what is gender-appropriate across a range of domains. Thus, a boy may develop the notion of gender-acceptable games based on observations of multiple boys engaging in certain games and girls not participating in those games but in other games. Even if these learning processes are initially externally moderated, they eventually become internalized as children approve or sanction themselves in relation to personal standards of gender conduct (Bussey & Bandura, 1999).

Cognitive Instruction and Scaffolding

Although psychodynamic and learning theorists (in part) depict socializers as molding socializees to function adequately in the society, contemporary evidence (as we have discussed) points to roles for socializers and socializees that do not imply such a unidirectional deterministic orientation. Bandura (1977), for example, moved away from the notion of wholesale incorporation of parental values arguing that children select from diverse sources of information to establish their own standards of behavior, with selection depending on a number of variables including differences in perceived competence between the model and the self, and the degree to which behavior is perceived to arise from one's own efforts rather than being a function of events over which one has no control. Thus, in an instruction and scaffolding view, socialization is an interactive, bidirectional process. Piaget's (1950) cognitive-developmental stage theory identified such collective mechanisms by pointing out that children move from one developmental stage to the next as they learn to cognitively construe their environment with increasing fidelity. Similarly, Vygotsky (1978) viewed the individual as actively engaged with his or her surroundings and emphasized the crucial importance of social interaction with others in development, contending that the more advanced or expert partner (the socializer) influences the behavior (raises the level of performance) of the less advanced or expert partner (the socializee) through their social–cognitive interactions. The difference between the socializee's spontaneous performance without guidance and that observed with socializer guidance is known as the socializee's "zone of proximal development."

Wood, Bruner, and Ross (1976) identified the teaching roles adults adopt in interactions with children under the rubric of "scaffolds." As carpenters would in constructing a building, caregivers sometimes employ temporary aids to support and guide a child's growth. Scaffolding strategies vary depending on the nature and age of the child and the actual activity, and caregivers can vary in the scaffolds they favor. Mothers and fathers tend to scaffold children's learning differently (Power, 1985; Tenenbaum & Leaper, 1998), and they encourage girls' and boys' participation in different learning activities and assign household chores differently in anticipation of expected later gender role differences in adulthood (Goodnow, 1988; Leaper, 2000). Sensitive socializers tailor scaffolds to match their socializees' level of developmental progress, for example, by providing age-appropriate learning experiences as socializees develop. According to scaffolding theory, therefore, socialization occurs mainly in interactive contexts with trusted, more competent partners who do not reward, punish, or correct children so much as to provide circumstances for learning that augment the likelihood of socializees succeeding in their own attempts to learn. This socialization view implies that socializers' enduring influences stem mainly from the nature of the relationships socializers co-construct and continually reconstruct with socializees.

Opportunities

Another important route by which socialization proceeds is through the types of opportunities it provides or promotes (Bussey & Bandura, 1999; Lytton & Romney, 1991). Access to certain settings affords people chances to develop certain conceptions of themselves and to engage in particular activities as well as to receive encouragement for repeating those activities. For example, the availability of feminine-stereotyped toys tends to induce caregiving behaviors (e.g., feeding a doll), whereas the availability of masculine-stereotyped toys tends to generate instrumental behaviors (e.g., constructing a model). Furthermore, stereotyped girls' toys (dolls) provide girls with practice in learning rules, imitating behaviors, and using adults as sources of help for certain outcomes, whereas stereotyped boys' toys (models) refine visual/spatial skills, problem solving, independent learning, self-confidence, and creativity among other outcomes (Martin & Dinella, 2002). To the extent that gender-differentiated material situations become customary in their lives, all features of socializees' gender-related knowledge, expectations, abilities, and activities are likely to be biased. These kinds of creation and control of children's opportunities mean that parents do not need to model, reinforce, or scaffold gendered beliefs or behaviors in children because contexts or implements per se may ordain or elicit desired gendered beliefs or behaviors.

Earlier, we introduced the notion of thematicity, how the same socialization messages may be delivered consistently in different social contexts via different social channels. In the same way, the mechanisms of socialization we have just described often work in concert with one another. Studies of children's household work indicate patterns that are pertinent to such a thematic consideration of gender socialization. First, mothers and fathers typically model a traditional gender-stereotyped division of labor in their own household work (Hilton & Haldeman, 1991). Second, parents tend to allocate gender-typed chores to children. They typically assign childcare and cleaning to daughters and allot maintenance work to sons (Antill, Goodnow, Russell, & Cotton, 1996; Burns & Homel, 1989). In rural agrarian societies, older daughters are usually charged with childcare and older sons with helping outside of the home (Whiting, 1986). Many more boys attend school in the Peruvian highlands because girls are busy with house chores and younger siblings (Pinzas, 2008). Third, mothers teach daughters how to change a baby's diaper, and fathers teach sons how to fix a machine. Parents on outings to museums focus on explanations of scientific content with their boys more than with their girls and so may foster boys' greater interest in and knowledge about science (Crowley, Callanan, Tenenbaum, & Allen, 2001). Fourth, parents further influence gender development in their children by tending to place girls and boys in gender-distinctive contexts (e.g., rooms with certain furnishings; Pomerleau, Bolduc, Malcuit, & Cossette, 1990). Last, children participate actively in culturally organized activities, and in this way gain an understanding of the world they live in and its expectations. Children tend to prefer being delegated with gender-stereotyped chores as many prefer gender-stereotyped clothes (Etaugh & Liss, 1992). As "apprentices" children must learn to think, act, and interact with all of the central characters in their culture to grow up and adapt successfully. Social participation structures a child's reality and experiences in ways that increase the likelihood that the child will develop into a successful member of the society.

Human beings do not develop in isolation. Throughout development, people and their experiences jointly create and regulate their socialization. Traditionally, the socialization mechanisms asserted to convey intergenerational transmission of beliefs and behaviors include identification, conditioning, reinforcement, and modeling, teaching and scaffolding, and the provision of opportunity. It is easy to assume that parents and other adult socializers are responsible for gender-differentiated conduct in children, but it is also the case that daughters elicit more feminine stereotypes (affection) and sons more masculine ones (building). Child/socializee effects on parent/socializer are in play and coexist with parent/socializer effects on children/socializees. Moreover, child characteristics and parent influences interact to consolidate socialization in children. In the end, effects in socialization (as of child gender) run in both directions—parent-to-child and child-to-parent—and this consistency is mutually reinforcing.

CONTINUITY AND STABILITY IN SOCIALIZATION

As a general rule, life-span socialization is interested not only in the status quo of constructs, structures, functions, and processes, but also their developmental dynamics. As discussed earlier, within any group at every age human beings vary dramatically among themselves. With respect to individual differences, it is desirable to distinguish further between consistency/inconsistency within individuals—individual-order consistency (stability/instability)—and consistency/inconsistency in a group—mean-level consistency (continuity/discontinuity). As we use the terms here, then, continuity refers to whether a characteristic displays a mean level at one point in time and that same mean level at a later point across time as a group average, and discontinuity refers to whether a characteristic displays a mean level at one point in time and a different mean level at a later point across time as a group average (the developmental function; Wohlwill, 1973). If parenting socialization showed continuity, mothers and fathers would display some socialization characteristic at the same group mean levels at one point in time and at a second point later in time. Similarly, girls' and boys' level of gender identification would remain consistent. As we use the terms here, stability describes consistency in the relative ranks of individuals in a group with respect to the expression of some characteristic over time, and instability inconsistency in the relative ranks of individuals in a group with respect to the expression of some characteristic over time. It is further desirable to distinguish two types of stability. Homotypic stability describes similarity of rank-order status on an identical characteristic across time (e.g., preference for gender stereotyped play at 12 months and at 36 months), and heterotypic stability describes similarity of rank order status between two related, but not identical, constructs because they presumably share the same underlying process (e.g., preference for gender-stereotyped play at 12 months and gender-related friendship choices at 36 months). Continuity and stability (Hartmann, Pelzel, & Abbott, 2011; Wohlwill, 1973) reflect theoretically and statistically different realms of development (Bornstein, Brown, & Slater, 1996; McCall, 1981), and mean consistency and order consistency are independent and orthogonal constructs. Group *cum* individual patterns can be continuous-and-stable, discontinuous-and-stable, continuous-and-unstable, and discontinuous-and-unstable.

Questions about construct continuity and stability are embedded in conceptions of life-span socialization for several reasons. Continuity provides basic information about the overall developmental course of a given characteristic, insofar as the group of individuals does or does not maintain consistency through time. It is generally assumed, too, that to be meaningful, a characteristic should show substantial stability across time: A major predictor of the expression of a given characteristic at a given age is the expression of that characteristic at an earlier age. Last, consistency affects the environment: Consistent characteristics in socializees likely affect socializers.

Human development is governed by genetic and biological factors in combination with environmental influences and experiences. Consistency could be attributable to genetic or biological factors in the individual, or it might emerge through the individual's transactions with a consistent environment. The life-span perspective specifies that human beings are open systems, and the plastic nature of human functioning ensures that people exhibit both consistency and inconsistency in many characteristics across their life span.

Stage-specific socialization (discussed earlier) assumes that individuals progress from one life stage to the next and experience socialization contexts and contents specific to each stage. Discontinuity, therefore, pervades context as childhood socialization in the family gives way to socialization in the peer group as children grow older (Rubin et al., 2011); later school functions as a major force of socialization for older children and adolescents (Eccles & Roeser, 2011); afterward the work setting assumes priority in socialization, and so on. The "real world" of development, however, embraces no universal, unidirectional, and predictable movements from one context to another. For example, young people leave home to establish an independent residence only to return home again at a subsequent time; move between school and work, and drop out of college for the labor force, only to return to school to acquire additional educational credentials. People remarry following divorce or the death of a spouse and so experience entry to new family roles in ways that differ from that of people entering their first marriages (such as more complex relational structures to which they must adapt with stepchildren and other new relatives). Reconceptualizations of existing roles, as well as the emergence and growth of new roles, are endemic to dynamic life-span socialization.

Although discontinuities appear to be prevalent and pervasive in socialization, they may apply more to socialization stages, contexts, and contents than to socialization processes. Social science has identified only a small universe of possible mechanisms of socialization (reviewed above). Socializees, therefore, are socialized by general processes that appear equally applicable across stages, contexts, and contents. Although variation might be expected in quantitative processes (e.g., the intensity or frequency of rewards and punishments across ages), variation is not predicted for the qualitative nature of socialization mechanisms per se (effort of reward or punishment). Furthermore, even if socialization changes in response to socializee development and situation, it also appears to be stable through time in some nontrivial degree. Holden and Miller (1999) meta-analyzed the existing parenting literature and found that parents' cognitions and practices are relatively consistent across time, parity, and situations, to which van IJzendoorn (1992) added generations. The fact that parenting *qua* socialization is stable (in some degree) implies that socialization cognitions and practices assessed at one point can be assumed to reflect past as well as future parenting *qua* socialization. It also means that indices of socialization can be related systematically to concurrent or future parent and child socialization.

▦ FUTURE ISSUES IN THE STUDY OF LIFE-SPAN THEORIES AND PROCESSES IN SOCIALIZATION

In its most general construal, socialization represents stability for society and the preparation of the person to manage evolving tasks of life. Socialization is both overdetermined and underdetermined in these regards. It is underdetermined in the sense that trajectories and outcomes of socialization alike are both general and specific. This permits the maintenance of necessary and valued ways of living across generations and at the same time allows for individual flexibility and openness, which are essential for innovation and change. A central function of socialization is maintaining society. In a larger sense, then, socialization contributes to the continuity of society by helping to define society and the transmission of society across generations. Through cross-generational transmission, the tenets of society are sustained. Overall system thematicity and redundancy help to ensure these goals; for certain key aims, often essentially the same socialization messages are delivered by multiple agents of socialization, including parents, teachers, religion, media, social groups, and so forth. What is special about human beings, and in many ways the most significant characteristic of our species, is the long period of developmental plasticity, during which mental and social structures emerge in close attunement with their effective environment. This feature, termed neoteny, characterizes a species capable of learning broad and flexible lessons. From this perspective, the relation between environment or experience and socialization in development is neither direct nor unidirectional. Because human beings, and the socialization processes through which development occurs, are plastic and responsive to their conditions, there can be no predetermined course or end point of socialization.

However, socialization is also overdetermined in that the pervasive nature of context ensures that people are enmeshed in certain expectations, activities, and social practices. This dual reality renders socialization a central aspect of normal human development. Specific processes and goals that guide socialization at any point in time are subject to local conditions. Thus, human socialization is inherently accommodating, and as such its contexts and contents vary to best reflect the needs of individuals and their community. The activities that compose socialization are normally targeted toward local solutions, such as solving a particular problem or carrying out a particular practice. The outcomes of socialization are the products of these solutions, and such products are often arrived at in nonlinear and complex ways.

Socialization is composed of many discrete yet related activities in which people engage over a long period of time. Insofar as socializers posses knowledge, investment, and competence, they may assist socializees in ways that add to the individual and common good; but, insofar as socializers do not, they jeopardize socializees individually and society collectively (Bugental & Grusec, 2006). Thus, socializers may benefit or threaten socializees. The effect of socialization for certain goals is often a function of how many different venues promote the same goals and how frequently and over what duration those goals are promoted. Any particular socialization practice is part of a larger menu aimed at promoting specific competencies and behavioral tendencies. In real living systems, elements in the overall package can work unevenly and even to cross purposes, especially in rapidly evolving, multicultural societies.

Contemporary theoreticians and researchers in socialization are concerned with which aspects of socialization affect which aspects of life-span development when and how, and they are also interested to learn the ways in which socializees are socialized as well as the ways socializees affect socializers. The *specificity principle* in socialization science asserts that specific socialization experiences at specific times exert specific effects over specific aspects of socialization in specific people in specific ways (Bornstein, 1989, 2002, 2006). Various agents contribute to socialization, and context determines who tends to socialize and what socializees tend to learn. Contexts are not monolithic entities. Within a given community, for example, social–structural variation in, say, gender relationship depends on people's educational attainment, social class, ethnicity, religious affiliation, as well as other characteristics. The contexts and contents approach that forms the core of our exposition suggests that life-span socialization is best understood within different contexts and for different contents. Class, culture, and time vary in what socialization is important, how socialization is conducted, when people should be socialized, and the like. Systems theory points to constant interaction and mutual influence among elements within the system, with no one element or subsystem achieving hegemony. Thus, models of socialization involve multiple bidirectional and transactional processes. Although socialization is organized by more experienced socializers, socialization processes are reciprocal. They build on the capabilities of the socializee, including the potential for learning, a bias toward social processes and experiences, and the capacity to form strong emotional ties. More generally, the principle of transaction states that people shape and interpret their socialization experiences and environments just as they are shaped by their socialization experiences and environments and people experience socialization differently based on their idiosyncratic attributes. Socialization entails many processes, including observation, imitation, attention regulation, demonstration, instruction, rehearsal, shaping, scaffolding, and guided participation. Several of these practices are deliberate and intentional interventions on the part of socializers, designed to achieve desired goals, and others are less intentional and deliberate. Thus, socializers are exposed to some models deemed worthy of emulation, but they are also exposed to unintended influences of others. Such unintended influences may either be consistent with or counter to the intended goals of socialization. Sometimes the processes used to socialize work well for the person and the society, sometimes they do not. Socializers may be inadvertently exposed to less worthy actions modeled by deviant members of society or by media. Just because a society engages in a particular socialization practice that is designed to promote adaptive functioning within the society does not guarantee adaptive functioning or that the practices in question actually promote well-being.

Socialization is bidirectional. Parenting approaches affect the responses of the child which, in turn, feed back to affect parental expectations and predilections by confirming and expanding them or, at times, contradicting them. Thus, socialization requires attention to biological and cultural processes involved in cognitions and practices and to the ways in which socializee and socializer exert reciprocal influences. There is dynamic asymmetry in socializer and socializee contributions to socialization. In overview, a complex developmental system of primary socialization includes socializees' own capacities and proclivities, socializees' and socializers' multiple social relationships (with one another and others) embedded in multiple developmental contexts (homes, schools, neighborhoods, workplaces, socioeconomic classes, and cultures).

ACKNOWLEDGMENTS

We thank T. Taylor and C. Turek. This study was supported by the Intramural Research Program of the NIH, NICHD.

◼ REFERENCES

Anderson, K. E., Lytton, H., & Romney, D. M. (1986). Mothers' interactions with normal and conduct-disordered boys: Who affects whom? *Developmental Psychology, 22*, 604–609.

Antill, J. K., Goodnow, J. J., Russell, G., & Cotton, S. (1996). The influence of parents and family context on children's involvement in household tasks. *Sex Roles, 34*, 215–236.

Bandura, A. (1962). Social learning through imitation. In M. R. Jones (Ed.), *Nebraska symposium on motivation* (pp. 211–274). Lincoln, NE: University of Nebraska Press.

Bandura, A. (1965). Influence of models' reinforcement contingencies on the acquisition of imitative responses. *Journal of Personality and Social Psychology, 1*, 589–595.

Bandura, A. (1977). *Social learning theory.* Englewood Cliffs, NJ: Prentice Hall.

Bates, J. E., Pettit, G. S., Dodge, K. A., & Ridge, B. (1998). Interaction of temperamental resistance to control and restrictive parenting in the development of externalizing behavior. *Developmental Psychology, 34*, 982–995.

Becker, H. S., Geer, B., Hughes, E. C., & Strauss, A. L. (1961). *Boys in white: Student culture in medical school.* Chicago: University of Chicago Press.

Bell, R. Q. (1968). A reinterpretation of the direction of effects in studies of socialization. *Psychological Review, 75*, 81–95.

Bell, R. Q. (1970). Sleep cycles and skin potential in newborns studied with a simplified observation and recording system. *Psychophysiology, 6*, 778–786.

Belsky, J. (2005). Differential susceptibility to rearing influence: An evolutionary hypothesis and some evidence. In B. J. Ellis & D. F. Bjorklund (Eds.), *Origins of the social mind: Evolutionary psychology and child development* (pp. 139–163). New York: Guilford.

Belsky, J., & Pluess, M. (2009a). The nature (and nurture?) of plasticity in early human development. *Perspectives on Psychological Science, 4*, 345–351.

Belsky, J., & Pluess, M. (2009b). Beyond diathesis stress: Differential susceptibility to environmental influences. *Psychological Bulletin, 135*, 885–908.

Benedict, R. (1934/1959). *Patterns of culture.* Boston: Houghton Mifflin.

Benedict, R. (1938). Continuities and discontinuities in cultural conditioning. *Psychiatry: Journal for the Study of Interpersonal Processes, 2*, 161–167.

Benedict, R. (1946). *The chrysanthemum and the sword: Patterns of Japanese culture.* Boston: Houghton Mifflin.

Best, D. L. (2010). Gender. In M. H. Bornstein (Ed.), *Handbook of cultural developmental science* (pp. 209–237). New York: Psychology Press.

Best, D. L., & Williams, J. E. (1997). Sex, gender, and culture. In J. W. Berry, M. H. Segall, & C. Kagitcibasi (Eds.), *Handbook of cross-cultural psychology: Vol. 3. Social behavior and applications* (2nd ed., pp. 163–212). Boston: Allyn and Bacon.

Bornstein, M. H. (1989). Cross-cultural developmental comparisons: The case of Japanese-American infant and mother activities and interactions. What we know, what we need to know, and why we need to know. *Developmental Review, 9*, 171–204.

Bornstein, M. H. (1995). Form and function: Implications for studies of culture and human development. *Culture and Psychology, 1*, 123–137.

Bornstein, M. H. (2002). Parenting infants. In M. H. Bornstein (Ed.), *Handbook of parenting: Vol. 1. Children and parenting* (2nd ed., pp. 3–43). Mahwah, NJ: Erlbaum.

Bornstein, M. H. (2006). Parenting science and practice. In K. A. Renninger & I. E. Sigel (Vol. Eds.), W. Damon & R. M. Lerner (Eds.), *Handbook of child psychology: Vol. 4. Child psychology in practice* (6th ed., pp. 893–949). Hoboken, NJ: John Wiley & Sons.

Bornstein, M. H. (2009). Toward a model of culture parent child transactions. In A. Sameroff (Ed.), *The transactional model of development: How children and contexts shape each other* (pp. 139–161). Washington, DC: American Psychological Association.

Bornstein, M. H., & Bradley, R. H. (Eds.). (2003). *Socioeconomic status, parenting, and child development.* Mahwah, NJ: Erlbaum.

Bornstein, M. H., Brown, E., & Slater, A. (1996). Patterns of stability and continuity in attention across early infancy. *Journal of Reproductive and Infant Psychology, 14*, 195–206.

Bornstein, M. H., Hahn, C. S., Suwalsky, J. T. D., & Haynes, O. M. (2003). Socioeconomic status, parenting, and child development: The Hollingshead four-factor index of social status and the socioeconomic index of occupations. In M. H. Bornstein & R. H. Bradley (Eds.), *Socioeconomic status, parenting, and child development* (pp. 29–82). Mahwah, NJ: Erlbaum.

Bornstein, M. H., & Lansford, J. E. (2009). Parenting. In M. H. Bornstein (Ed.), *The handbook of cultural developmental science. Part 1. Domains of development across cultures* (pp. 259–277). New York: Taylor & Francis Group.

Bowlby, J. (1969). *Attachment and loss: Vol. I. Attachment.* New York: Basic Books.

Bronfenbrenner, U., & Morris, P. A. (2006). The bioecological model of human development. In R. M. Lerner (Vol. Ed.) & W. Damon (Series Ed.), *Handbook of child psychology: Vol. 1. Theoretical models of human development* (6th ed., pp. 793–828). Hoboken, NJ: Wiley.

Bugental, D. B., & Grusec, J. E. (2006). Socialization processes. In N. Eisenberg (Vol. Ed.), W. Damon, & R. M. Lerner (Series Eds.), *Handbook of child psychology: Vol. 3. Social, emotional, and personality development* (6th ed., pp. 366–428). Hoboken, NJ: John Wiley & Sons.

Burns, A., & Homel, R. (1989). Gender division of tasks by parents and their children. *Psychology of Women Quarterly, 13,* 113–125.

Bush, D. M., & Summons, R. G. (1981). Socialization processes over the life course. In M. Rosenburg & R. H. Turner (Eds.), *Social psychology: Sociological perspectives* (pp. 133–164). New York: Basic Books.

Bussey, K., & Bandura, A. (1999). Social cognitive theory of gender development and differentiation. *Psychological Review, 106,* 676–713.

Caspi, A. (1993). Why maladaptive behaviors persist: Sources of continuity and change across the life course. In D. C. Funder, R. D. Parke, C. Tomlinson-Keasey, & K. Widaman (Eds.), *Studying lives through time: Personality and development* (pp. 343–376). Washington, DC: American Psychological Association.

Caspi, A., McClay, J., Moffitt, T. E., Mill, J., Martin, J., Craig, I. W., et al. (2002). Role of geneotype in the cycle of violence in maltreated children. *Science, 297,* 851–854.

Caspi, A., & Roberts, B. W. (2001). Personality development across the life course: The argument for change and continuity. *Psychological Inquiry, 12,* 49–66.

Chartrand, T. L., & Bargh, J. A. (1999). The chameleon effect: The perception-behavior link and social interactions. *Journal of Personality and Social Psychology, 76,* 893–910.

Clarke-Stewart, K. A., & Allhusen, V. D. (2002). Nonparental caregiving. In M. H. Bornstein (Ed.), *Handbook of parenting Vol. 3 Status and social conditions of parenting* (2nd ed., pp. 215–252). Mahwah, NJ: Erlbaum.

Clarke-Stewart, K. A., & Allhusen, V. D. (2005). *What we know about childcare.* Cambridge, MA: Harvard University Press.

Clausen, J. S. (1991). Adolescent competence and the shaping of the life course. *American Journal of Sociology, 96,* 805–842.

Cohler, B. J., & Paul, S. (2002). Psychoanalysis and parenthood. In M. H. Bornstein (Ed.), *Handbook of parenting: Vol. 3. Being and becoming a parent* (2nd ed., pp. 563–599). Mahwah, NJ: Erlbaum.

Corsaro, W. A., & Eder, D. (1995). The development and socialization of children and adolescents. In K. S. Cook, G. A. Fine, & J. S. House (Eds.), *Sociological perspectives on social psychology* (pp. 421–451). Boston: Allyn & Bacon.

Crouter, A. C., Helms-Erikson, H., Updegraff, K., & McHale, S. M. (1999). Conditions underlying parents' knowledge about children's daily lives in middle childhood: Between- and within-family comparisons. *Child Development, 70,* 246–259.

Crouter, A. C., Manke, B. A., & McHale, S. M. (1995). The family context of gender intensification in early adolescence. *Child Development, 66,* 317–329.

Crowley, K., Callanan, M. A., Tenenbaum, H. R., & Allen, E. (2001). Parents explain more often to boys than to girls during shared scientific thinking. *Psychological Science, 12,* 258–261.

Dekovic, M., & Meeus, W. (1997). Peer relations in adolescence: Effects of parenting and adolescent's self-concept. *Journal of Adolescence, 20,* 163–176.

De Lisi, R., & Gallagher, A. M. (1991). Understanding of gender stability and constancy in Argentinean children. *Merrill Palmer Quarterly, 37,* 483–502.

Dishion, T. J., Andrews, D. W., & Crosby, L. (1995). Antisocial boys and their friends in early adolescence: Relationship characteristics, quality, and interactional process. *Child Development, 66,* 139–151.

Dunn, J., & Munn, P. (1985). Becoming a family member: Family conflict and the development of social understanding in the second year. *Child Development, 56,* 480–492.

Eccles, J. S., Freedman-Doan, C., Frome, P., Jacobs, J., & Yoon, K. S. (2000). Gender-role socialization in the family: A longitudinal approach. In T. Eckes & H. M. Trautner (Eds.), *The developmental social psychology of gender* (pp. 333–360). Mahwah, NJ: Erlbaum.

Eccles, J. S., & Roeser, R. W. (2011). School and community influences on human development. In M. H. Bornstein & M. E. Lamb (Eds.), *Developmental science: An advanced textbook* (6th ed., pp. 566–638). New York: Taylor & Francis Group.

Eisenberg, N., Cumberland, A., & Spinrad, T. L. (1998). Parental socialization of emotion. *Psychology Inquiry, 9*, 241–273.

Elder, G. H., Jr., & O'Rand, A. (1995). Adult lives in a changing society. In K. S. Cook, G. A. Fine, & J. S. House (Eds.), *Sociological perspectives on social psychology* (pp. 452–475). Boston: Allyn and Bacon.

Elder, G. H., Jr., & Rockwell, R. C. (1979). The life-course and human development: An ecological perspective. *International Journal of Behavioral Development, 21*, 1–21.

Emde, R. N., Biringen, Z., Clyman, R. B., & Oppenheim, D. (1991). The moral self of infancy: Affective core and procedural knowledge. *Developmental Review, 11*, 251–270.

Epstein, S. (1990). Cognitive-experiential self-theory. In L. A. Pervin (Ed.), *Handbook of personality: Theory and research* (pp. 165–192). New York: Guilford.

Etaugh, C., & Liss, M. B. (1992). Home, school, and playroom: Training grounds for adult gender roles. *Sex Roles, 26*, 129–147.

Facio, A., & Resett, S. (2008). Argentina. In J. J. Arnett (Ed.), *International encyclopedia of adolescence* (pp. 1–15). New York: Routledge.

Fraley, R. C., & Davis, K. E. (1997). Attachment formation and transfer in you adults' close friendships and romantic relationships. *Personal Relationships, 4*, 131–144.

Fraley, R. C., & Shaver, P. R. (2000). Adult romantic attachment: Theoretical developments, emerging controversies, and unanswered questions. Review of *General Psychology, 4*, 132–154.

Fredricks, J. A., & Eccles, J. S. (2002). Children's competence and value beliefs from childhood through adolescence: Growth trajectories in two male-sex-typed domains. *Developmental Psychology, 38*, 519–533.

French, V. (2002). History of parenting: The ancient Mediterranean world. In M. H. Bornstein (Ed.), *Handbook of parenting: Vol. 2. Biology and ecology of parenting* (2nd ed., pp. 345–376). Mahwah, NJ: Erlbaum.

Freud, S. (1949). *An outline of psychoanalysis*. New York: Norton.

Fuligni, A. J., Tseng, V., & Lam, M. (1999). Attitudes toward family obligations among American adolescents with Asian, Latin American, and European backgrounds. *Child Development, 70*, 1030–1044.

Gallese, V., Ferrari, P., Kohler, E., & Fogassi, L. (2002). The eyes, the hand, and the mind: Behavioral and neurophysiological aspects of social cognition. In M. Bekoff, C. Allen, & G. M. Burghardt (Eds.), *The cognitive animal: Empirical and theoretical perspectives on animal cognition* (pp. 451–461). Cambridge, MA: MIT Press.

Gecas, V. (1981). Contexts of socialization. In M. Rosenberg & R. H. Turner (Eds.), *Social psychology: Sociological perspectives* (pp. 165–199). New York: Basic Books.

Gecas, V. (2000). Socialization. In E. F. Borgatta (Ed.), *Encyclopedia of sociology* (pp. 2855–2864). Detroit, MI: Macmillan.

George, C., Kaplan, N., & Main, M. (1985). The *Berkley Adult Attachment Interview*. Unpublished protocol, University of California, Berkley.

George, L. K. (1993). Sociological perspectives on life transitions. *Annual Review of Sociology, 19*, 353–373.

Goodnow, J. J. (1988). Children's household work: Its nature and functions. *Psychological Bulletin, 103*, 5–26.

Goodnow, J. J. (2009). Culture. In M. H. Bornstein (Ed.), *The handbook of cultural developmental science. Part 1. Domains of development across cultures* (pp. 3–19). New York: Taylor & Francis Group.

Goodnow, J. J., Cashmore, R., Cotton, S., & Knight, R. (1984). Mothers' developmental timetables in two cultural groups. *International Journal of Psychology, 19*, 193–205.

Goodnow, J. J., Miller, P. J., & Kessel, F. (Eds.). (1995). *Cultural practices as contexts for development*. San Francisco: Jossey-Bass.

Hafferty, F. (1991). *Into the valley: Death and the socialization of medical students*. New Haven, CT: Yale University Press.

Harkness, S., & Super, C. M. (2002). Culture and parenting. In M. H. Bornstein (Ed.), *Handbook of parenting: Vol. 2: Biology and ecology of parenting* (2nd ed., pp. 253–280). Mahwah, NJ: Lawrence Erlbaum Associates Publishers.

Hartmann, D. P., Pelzel, K. E., & Abbott. (2011). Design, measurement, and analysis in developmental research. In M. H. Bornstein & M. E. Lamb (Eds.), *Developmental science: An advanced textbook* (6th ed., pp. 107–195). New York: Taylor & Francis Group.

Havighurst, R. J. (1972). *Developmental tasks and education* (3rd ed.). New York: David McKay.

Henrich, J., Heine, S. J., & Norenzayan, A. (2010). The weirdest people in the world? *Behavioral and Brain Sciences, 33,* 61–83.

Hetherington, E. M. (1993). An overview of the Virginia Longitudinal Study of Divorce and Remarriage with a focus on early adolescence. *Journal of Family Psychology, 7,* 39–56.

Hewlett, B. S. (1991). *Intimate fathers: The nature and context of Aka Pygmy paternal infant care.* Ann Arbor, MI: University of Michigan Press.

Hewlett, B. S., Lamb, M. E., Shannon, D., Leyendecker, B., & Scholmerich, A. (1998). Culture and early infancy among central African foragers and farmers. *Developmental Psychology, 34,* 653–651.

Hill, J. P., & Lynch, M. E. (1983). The intensification of gender-related role expectations during early adolescence. In J. Brooks-Gunn & A. C. Petersen (Eds.), *Girls at puberty: Biological and psychosocial perspectives* (pp. 201–228). New York: Plenum.

Hilton, J. M., & Haldeman, V. A. (1991). Gender differences in the performance of household tasks by adults and children in single-parent and two-parent, two-earner families. *Journal of Family Issues, 12,* 114–130.

Hoff, E., Laursen, B., & Tardif, T. (2002). Socioeconomic status and parenting. In M. H. Bornstein (Ed.), *Handbook of parenting: Vol. 2. Biology and ecology of parenting* (2nd ed., pp. 231–252). Mahwah, NJ: Erlbaum.

Holden, G. W., & Miller, P. C. (1999). Enduring and different: A meta-analysis of the similarity in parents' child rearing. *Psychological Bulletin, 125,* 223–254.

Huston, A. C., & Wright, J. C. (1998). Mass media and children's development. In I. E. Sigel & K. A. Renninger (Eds.), *Handbook of child psychology: Vol. 4. Child psychology in practice* (5th ed., pp. 999–1058). New York: Wiley.

Hyde, J. S., Lindberg, S. M., Linn, M. C., Ellis, A. B., & Williams, C. C. (2008). Diversity: Gender similarities characterize math performance. *Science, 321,* 494–495.

Kelly, G. A. (1955). *The psychology of personal constructs* (Vols. 1–2). New York: Norton.

Kerckhoff, A. C. (2002). The transition from school to work. In J. T. Mortimer & R. Larson (Eds.), *The changing adolescent experience: Societal trends and the transition to adulthood* (pp. 52–87). New York: Cambridge University Press.

Kochanska, G. (1997). Multiple pathways to conscience for children with different temperaments: From toddlerhood to age 5. *Developmental Psychology, 33,* 228–240.

Kohlberg, L. A. (1966). A cognitive-developmental analysis of children's sex role concepts and attitudes. In E. E. Maccoby (Ed.), *The development of sex differences* (pp. 82–173). Stanford, CA: Stanford University Press.

Kohn, M. L., & Schooler, C. (1983). *Work and personality: An inquiry into the impact of social stratification.* Norwood, NJ: Ablex.

Kohn, M. L., Slomczynski, K. M., & Schoenbach, C. (1986). Social stratification and the transmission of values in the family: A cross-national assessment. *Sociological Forum, 1,* 73–102.

Kohn, M. L., Zaborowski, W., Janicka, K., Mach, B. W., Khmelko, V., Slomczynski, et al. (2001). Complexity of activities and personality under conditions of radical social change: A comparative analysis of Poland and Ukraine. *Social Psychology Quarterly, 63,* 187–208.

Laird, R. D., Pettit, G. S., Mize, J., Brown, E. G., & Lindsey, E. (1994). Mother child conversations about peers. *Family Relations: Interdisciplinary Journal of Applied Family Studies, 43,* 425–432.

Leaper, C. (2000). Gender, affiliation, assertion, and the interactive context of parent-child play. *Development Psychology, 36,* 381–393.

Lerner, R. M., & Busch-Rossnagel, N. A. (Eds.). (1981). *Individuals as producers of their development: A life-span perspective.* New York: Academic Press.

Lerner, R. M., Lewin-Bizan, S., & Warren. A. E. A. (2011). Concepts and theories of human development. In M. H. Bornstein & M. E. Lamb (Eds.), *Developmental science: An advanced textbook* (6th ed., pp. 3–49). New York: Taylor & Francis Group.

Lytton, H., & Romney, D. M. (1991). Parents' differential socialization of boys and girls: A meta-analysis. *Psychological Bulletin, 109,* 267–296.

Maccoby, E. E. (1992). The role of parents in the socialization of children: A historical overview. *Developmental Psychology, 28,* 1006–1017.

Martin, C. L., & Dinella, L. M. (2002). Children's gender cognitions, the social environment, and sex differences in cognitive domains. In A. McGillicuddy-De Lisi & R. De Lisi (Eds.), *Biology, society, and behavior: The development of sex differences in cognition* (pp. 207–239). Westport, CT: Ablex.

Mather, M., Canli, T., English, T., Whitfield, S., Wais, P., Ochsner, K., et al. (2004). Amygdala responses to emotionally valianced stimuli in older and younger adults. *Psychological Science, 15,* 259–263.

McAdam, D. (1988). *Freedom summer*. Oxford, UK: Oxford University Press.

McCall, R. B. (1981). Nature-nurture and the two realms of development: A proposed integration with respect to mental development. *Child Development, 52*, 1–12.

Mead, M. (1935). *Sex and temperament in three primitive societies*. New York: Morrow.

Meltzoff, A. N., & Moore, K. (1999). Persons and representation: Why infant imitation is important for theories of human development. In J. Nadel & G. Butterworth (Eds.), *Imitation in infancy: Cambridge studies in cognitive perceptual development* (pp. 9–35). New York: Cambridge University Press.

Miljkovitch, R., Pierrehumbert, B., Bretherton, I., & Halfon, O. (2004). Association between parent and child attachment representations. *Attachment & Human Development, 6*, 305–325.

Mikulincer, M., Shaver, P. R., & Pereg, D. (2003). Attachment theory and affect regulation: The dynamics, development, and cognitive consequences of attachment-related strategies. *Motivation and Emotion, 27*, 77–102.

Miller, N. E., & Dollard, J. (1941). *Social learning and imitation*. New Haven, CT: Yale University Press.

Mischel, W. (1970). Sex-typing and socialization. In P. H. Mussen (Ed.), *Carmichael's manual of child psychology* (Vol. 2, pp. 3–72). New York: Wiley.

Mondschein, E. R., Adolph, K. E., & Tamis-LeMonda, C. S. (2000). Gender bias in mothers' expectations about infant crawling. *Journal of Experimental Child Psychology, 77*, 304–316.

Mortimer, J. T. (2003). *Working and growing up in America*. Cambridge, MA: Harvard University Press.

Needle, R. H., Su, S. S., & Doherty, W. J. (1990). Divorce, remarriage, and adolescent substance use: A prospective longitudinal study. *Journal of Marriage and the Family, 52*, 157–169.

O'Connor, T. G., Deater-Deckard, K., Fulker, D., Rutter, M., & Plomin, R. (1998). Genotype-environment correlations in late childhood and early adolescence: Antisocial behavior problems and coercive parenting. *Developmental Psychology, 34*, 970–981.

Patterson, G. R. (1980). Mothers: The unacknowledged victims. *Monographs of the Society for Research in Child Development, 45*, 64.

Phinney, J. S., Ong, A., & Madden, T. (2000). Cultural values and intergenerational value discrepancies in immigrant and non-immigrant families. *Child Development, 71*, 528–539.

Piaget, J. (1950). *The psychology of intelligence*. London: Routledge & Paul.

Pinzas, J. (2008). Peru. In J. J. Arnett (Ed.), *International encyclopedia of adolescence* (pp. 764–773). New York: Routledge.

Pluess, M., & Belsky, J. (2010). Differential susceptibility to parenting and quality child care. *Developmental Psychology, 46*, 379–390.

Pomerleau, A., Bolduc, D., Malcuit, G., & Cossette, L. (1990). Pink or blue: Environmental gender stereotypes in the first two years of life. *Sex Roles, 22*, 359–367.

Power, T. G. (1985). Mother- and father-infant play: A developmental analysis. *Child Development, 56*, 1514–1524.

Quinn, N., & Holland, D. (1987). Culture and cognition. In D. Holland & N. Quinn (Eds.), *Cultural models in language and thought* (pp. 3–42). Cambridge, UK: Cambridge University Press.

Rogoff, B. (1990). *Apprenticeship in thinking: Cognitive development in social context*. New York: Oxford University Press.

Rogoff, B. (2003). *The cultural nature of human development*. Oxford, UK: Oxford University Press.

Rogoff, B., Pardies, R., Arauz, R. M., Correa-Chavez, M., & Angelillo C. (2003). Firsthand learning through intent participation. *Annual Review of Psychology, 54*, 175–203.

Rohlinger, D. A., & Snow, D. A. (2003). Crowds and social movements. In J. Delamater (Ed.), *Handbook of social psychology* (pp. 503–527). New York: Kluwer Academic/Plenum.

Rubin, K. H., Coplan, R., Chen, X., Bowker, J., & McDonald, K. L. (2010). The role of parent-child relationships in child development. In M. H. Bornstein & M. E. Lamb (Eds.), *Developmental science: An advanced textbook* (6th ed., pp. 519–570). New York: Taylor & Francis Group.

Sameroff, A. (Ed.). (2009). *The transactional model of development: How children and contexts shape each other*. Washington, DC: American Psychological Association.

Scarr, S., & Kidd, K. K. (1983). Developmental behavior genetics. In P. H. Mussen (Series Ed.) & M. M. Haith & J. J. Campos (Vol. Eds.), *Handbook of child psychology: Vol. 2. Infancy and developmental psychobiology* (pp. 345–433). New York: Wiley.

Schooler, C., Mulatu, M. S., & Oates, G. (2004). Occupational Self-Direction, intellectual functioning, and self-directed orientation in older workers: Findings and implications for individuals and societies. *American Journal of Sociology, 110*(1), 161–197.

Serpell, R., & Hatano, G. (1997). Education, schooling, and literacy. In J. W. Berry, P. R. Dasen, & T. S. Saraswathi (Eds.), *Handbook of cross-cultural psychology: Vol. 2. Basic processes and human development* (pp. 339–376). Boston: Allyn and Bacon.

Shiner, R., & Caspi, A. (2003). Personality differences in childhood and adolescence: Measurement, development, and consequences. *Journal of Child Psychology and Psychiatry and Allied Disciplines, 44*, 2–32.

Skinner, B. F. (1976). *Walden two.* Englewood Cliffs, NJ: Prentice-Hall.

Slaby, R. G., & Frey, K. S. (1975). Development of gender constancy and selective attention to same-sex models. *Child Development, 52*, 849–856.

Smith, P. K., & Drew, L. M. (2002). Grandparenthood. In M. H. Bornstein (Ed.), *Handbook of parenting Vol. 3 Status and social conditions of parenting* (2nd ed., pp. 141–172). Mahwah, NJ: Erlbaum.

Sroufe, L. A., & Fleeson, J. (1986). Attachment and the construction of relationships. In W. W. Hartup & Z. Rubin (Eds.), *Relationships and development* (pp. 51–71). Hillsdale, NJ: Erlbaum.

Steinberg, L., & Silk, J. S. (2002). Parenting adolescents. In M. H. Bornstein (Ed.), *Handbook of parenting: Vol. 1. Children and parenting* (2nd ed., pp. 103–133). Mahwah, NJ: Erlbaum.

Tenenbaum, H. R., & Leaper, C. (1998). Gender effects on Mexican-descent parents' questions and scaffolding during play: A sequential analysis. *First Language, 18*, 129–147.

Tenenbaum, H. R., & Leaper, C. (2003). Parent-child conversations about science: Socialization of gender inequities. *Developmental Psychology, 39*, 34–47.

Thomas, A., & Chess, S. (1977). *Temperament and development.* New York: Brunner/Mazel.

Thomas, A., & Chess, S. (1980). *Dynamics of psychological development.* New York: Brunner/Mazel.

Tomkins, S. S. (1987). Script theory. In J. Aronoff, A. I. Rabin, & R. A. Zucker (Eds.), *The emergence of personality* (pp. 147–216). New York: Springer.

Valsiner, J., & Lawrence, J. A. (1997). Human development in culture across the life span. In J. W. Berry, P. R. Dasen, & T. S. Saraswathi (Eds.), *Handbook of cross-cultural psychology: Vol. 2. Basic processes and human development* (2nd ed., pp. 69–106). Boston: Allyn and Bacon.

Van IJzendoorn, M. H. (1992). Intergenerational transmission of parenting: A review of studies in nonclinical populations. *Developmental Review, 12*, 76–99.

Van IJzendoorn, M. H. (1995). Adult attachment relations, parental responsiveness, and infant attachment: A meta-analysis on the predictive validity of the Adult Attachment Interview. *Psychological Bulletin, 117*, 387–403.

Vygotsky, L. S. (1978). *Mind in Society: The development of higher mental processes.* Cambridge, MA: Harvard University Press.

Waizenhofer, R. N., Buchanan, C. M., & Jackson-Newsom, J. (2004). Mothers' and fathers' knowledge of adolescents' daily activities: Its sources and its links with adolescent adjustment. *Journal of Family Psychology, 18*, 348–360.

Warton, J. J., & Goodnow, J. J. (1995). Money and children's household jobs: Parents' views of their interconnections. *International Journal of Behavioral Development, 18*, 235–350.

Watson, J. B. (1924/1970). *Behaviorism.* New York: Norton.

Whiting, B. B. (1986). The effect of experience on peer relationships. In E. C. Mueller & C. R. Cooper (Eds.), *Process and outcome in peer relationships* (pp. 79–99). Orlando, FL: Academic Press.

Whiting, B. B., & Edwards, C. P. (1988). *Children of different worlds: The formation of social behavior.* Cambridge, MA: Harvard University Press.

Williams, J. E., & Best, D. L. (1982/1990). *Measuring sex stereotypes: A multination study.* Newbury Park, CA: Sage.

Wohlwill, J. F. (1973). *The study of behavioral development.* Oxford: Academic Press.

Wood, D. J., Bruner, J. S., & Ross, G., (1976). The role of tutoring in problem solving. *Journal of Child Psychology and Psychiatry, 17*, 89–100.

Yurgelun-Todd, D. (2007). Emotional and cognitive changes during adolescence. *Current Opinion in Neurobiology, 17*, 251–257.

Zukow-Goldring, P. (2002). Sibling caregiving. In M. H. Bornstein (Ed.), *Handbook of parenting: Vol. 3. Status and social conditions of parenting* (2nd ed., pp. 253–286). Mahwah, NJ: Erlbaum.

MODELING SUCCESS IN LIFE-SPAN PSYCHOLOGY: THE PRINCIPLES OF SELECTION, OPTIMIZATION, AND COMPENSATION

3

Frieder R. Lang, Margund K. Rohr, and Bettina Williger

This chapter provides an overview on the life-span model selection, optimization, and compensation (SOC) with respect to theory and empirical findings. The chapter begins with a discussion of the meaning structure of success from a life-span perspective and the general nature of development. The discussion of the three SOC principles also addresses critical issues related to the *functionality* of SOC principles, the *coordination* and *sequencing* of SOC, and the *context-dependency* of the mechanisms of SOC. The chapter also reviews three prototypical theoretical specifications of the SOC model with related empirical illustrations: the resource-allocation SOC model, the action-theoretical SOC model, and the context-theoretical SOC model. It is argued that SOC is often reflected in accumulated environmental structures of the developmental context. Such contexts reflect accumulated impacts of SOC principles in human cultures over time. The chapter ends with a discussion of the future potential of the SOC model giving an outlook on open research issues.

▓ INTRODUCTION

In this chapter, we discuss mechanisms and meanings of positive life-span development and success in life. Such reasoning is embedded within a more general perspective on the nature of development (Baltes, 1987; Baltes & Baltes, 1977, 1980, 1990; Heckhausen, 2002; Marsiske, Lang, Baltes, & Baltes, 1995). From this perspective, life success is dynamic, multifaceted, and contingent on specific life-span contexts. In everyday language, success is typically defined as attainment of desired or ideal states, events, or outcomes, such as wealth, health, high social status or eminence (cf., *Merriam-Webster Dictionary; Oxford Advanced Learner's Dictionary*). In a life-span perspective, developmental success goes beyond achievement of desirable outcomes and also reflects human capacities such as loss adaptation and mastery of life challenges. This implies, for example, attainment of goals, compensatory use of resources, adjustment to failure, and coping with loss as well as realization of one's potential. At times, success in life is defined as the deferment of an otherwise unchecked decline or loss. More generally, within a life-span perspective, success involves a contextualized meaning structure. That is, meaning of success always depends on context and on its societal, biological, or personal relevance and impact. This applies to both objective and subjective criteria of success. Even most obvious success indicators such as health or social status may have different implications for success meanings depending on the likelihood, attainability, effectiveness, or stability of such an indicator within a context. Life-span developmental psychology is primarily concerned with the pathways that lead to desirable, achievable, and possibly sustainable outcomes.

According to life-span theory there are three general principles that lead to positive development, mastery, or growth. These principles were described as selection, optimization, and compensation (Baltes, 1987, 1997, 2003; Baltes & Baltes, 1990). *Selection* generally refers to a narrowing of opportunities in life, for example, with respect to goals or life paths. *Optimization* describes the enhancement of resources for producing output, for example, the minimization of costs and the simultaneous maximization of benefits in producing specific behavioral outputs. *Compensation* involves a response to loss or limitations, for example, to protect or stabilize certain behavioral output functions. We elaborate and discuss the model of SOC with respect to three issues: intellectual development across adulthood, life management and motivation, and enhanced person–environment match in later adulthood. Considering the obvious predominance of SOC-related research in adulthood and old age, this chapter will focus on the second half of life, with few exceptions related to adolescence.

Within the past 2 decades more than 120 journal articles and book chapters were published on the model of SOC, not counting publications on other related models of developmental regulation. This wealth of literature on SOC suggests that there has been much progress with respect to an improved understanding of the validity, the strengths, and the caveats of this model. Meanwhile, there exist several theoretical specifications of the SOC model in diverse research fields such as cognitive aging (Baltes, Staudinger, & Lindenberger, 1999; Li, Lindenberger, Freund, & Baltes, 2001; Lindenberger, Marsiske, & Baltes, 2000), life management and self-regulation (Freund, Li, & Baltes, 1999; Freund & Baltes, 2002a, 2007), career development (Abele & Wiese, 2008; Wiese, Freund, & Baltes, 2002), balancing family and work life (Baltes & Heydens-Gahir, 2003; Young, Baltes, & Pratt, 2007), everyday competence in later adulthood (Baltes & Lang, 1997; Lang, Rieckmann, & Baltes, 2002), personal networks and social contact (Lang & Carstensen, 1994; Rohr & Lang, 2009), technological assistance (Lindenberger, Lövdén, Schellenbach, Li, & Krüger, 2008) and person–environment fit (Baltes & Carstensen, 1996, 1999, 2003; Marsiske et al., 1995). For illustrative purposes and reasons of limited space, we highlight three theoretical specifications of the SOC model: (1) the cognitive aging theory on resource allocation, (2) the action-theoretical model of SOC, and (3) context-theoretical considerations on SOC.

Before we give a detailed description of the three main principles of SOC in the second section of this chapter, we begin with a few considerations on the meaning of success in development and the general nature of development in a life-span perspective. Our discussion of the three SOC principles will end with a discussion of a few critical issues related to the *functionality* of SOC principles, the *coordination* and *sequencing* of SOC, and the *context-dependency* of the mechanisms of SOC. *Functionality* is considered with respect to how SOC contributes to adaptive capacities, that is, the resolving or mastering of developmental tasks across adulthood. The *coordination* and *sequencing* is discussed with respect to the interplay of the three principles of SOC according to different theoretical specifications of SOC. Finally, the *context-dependency* refers to the ways in which SOC principles contribute to the match of person and respective environment, and therein to shaping and molding of contexts.

A fourth section of this chapter will illustrate three theoretical specifications of the SOC model with empirical findings related to the resource-allocation model, the action-theoretical SOC model, and the context-theoretical model of SOC. In this vein, we argue that SOC is not only related to individual action but also is often reflected in environmental structures. Such contexts may reflect the accumulated impact of applied SOC principles within human societies and cultures over time (Baltes & Freund, 2003; Marsiske et al., 1995). In this sense, we submit the idea that the enormous success history of modern human societies with respect to technological, medical, and welfare advancements may have contributed importantly to sedimentation of success-related principles within the social organization of developmental opportunities and constraints. We will end this chapter with a discussion of the future potentials of the SOC model giving an outlook on open research issues that we believe need to be addressed.

THE NATURE OF DEVELOPMENT AND THE MEANING OF SUCCESS IN A LIFE-SPAN PERSPECTIVE

Life-span psychology has contributed an integrative perspective on development as a multidimensional, multidirectional, context-specific, and malleable phenomenon that goes beyond more classic conceptions of a linear, unidirectional growth or differentiation (Baltes, 1997; Baltes, Staudinger, & Lindenberger, 1999; Lang & Heckhausen, 2006). We begin with a discussion of the gain–loss dynamic in life span and its powerful implications for understanding life-span success. Some of the fundamental propositions of life-span psychology (e.g., multidimensionality, multidirectionality, plasticity, contextualism) point to the general nature of a gain–loss dynamic across the life span. In this context, we prefer to refer to *life-span success* to capture the potential of the lifelong developmental dynamics of gains and losses. We discuss in what ways the meaning of life-span success is connected to life-span perspectives on human development. These considerations aim at underscoring the idea that success may occur at all phases of the human life span, while there also exist age-related limitations and constraints. Full understanding of life-span success requires consideration of the demands and potentials of each phase in life on its own. There is no period of the human life span that assumes a general superiority over others with respect to its potentials for success in life. In other words, it is never too late for success.

Gain–Loss Dynamics Across the Life Span

A central premise of life-span psychology is that there is no gain in development without a loss and that there is no loss without gain. For example, advancement and progression often involve moving on and *away from* something (i.e., leaving behind something). Moreover, most investments in life (e.g., training of a talent, career decisions) imply that some of the invested resources (e.g., time, physiological functions) are depleted. Considering the finitude of resources and time in life, any investment of a resource in life is one less to be invested in the future. When one succeeds in attaining a desired goal, this typically involves a reduced number of other options, while at the same time other and new options may arise as well. There is an obvious dynamics of gains and losses in any developmental progress. Many gains or losses are unintended, not expected, or just concomitant outcomes. Success is not always a result of willful action. Success in life may result from a prior failure or loss that has evoked the behavior leading to this specific success experience (Baltes, 1997; Smith, 2003). Sometimes a context of loss may even facilitate the development of new behavioral patterns of adaptation or mastery in life. For example, when coping with an undesired loss, such mastery may result in other new opportunities in life (such as helping others with coping). In midlife, adults may feel obligated to take over a caregiver role for their parents, which typically involves the sacrifice of career options. The costs of the caregiver role are considerable, but there also exists potential for gains, for example, finding meaning in caring for a family member, a perceived increase in closeness between care receiver and caregiver, or experiencing personality growth (Farran, Keane-Hagerty, Salloway, Kupferer, & Wilken, 1991; Kinney & Stephens, 1989; Leipold, Schacke, & Zank, 2008; for a review Kramer, 1997). A recent study examined spouses who either cared for the cohabiting impaired partner or not. The results reveal that active caregiving even reduces mortality (Brown et al., 2009). Thus it is often the case that a specific loss delivers an individual from some tasks, duties, or roles, and thus sets the person free for new tasks in life.

We do not mean to say that the experience of loss is a desirable prerequisite of developmental gain. Rather, we argue that it lies in the nature of development that gain and loss often coincide and are interwoven rather than marking opposite ends of one process. In a very few cases, though, human organisms may benefit from loss. For example, acquisition of new roles in a new professional domain often implies that other roles are given up. Promotion in one's career is prototypical for this, but it also pertains to the elaboration and advancement of new skills that often requires the extinction of specific behavioral patterns to learn new ones.

The concept of lifelong gain–loss dynamics is inextricably tied to the concepts of *multidirectionality* and *multidimensionality*. Multidirectionality means that there is not just one single linear direction of change toward growth or toward decline across adulthood, whereas multidimensionality implies that different capacities, skill, and behavioral domains may show specific and unrelated developmental trajectories. Consequently, developmental change typically involves coordination, integration, and balancing of such diverse behavioral domains. Gains and losses may occur at all times, in sequential, alternating, and interdependent patterns within and across domains of functioning. Extended periods of growth may alternate with stagnation or even with phases of loss, and even differently so within specific life domains. To evaluate life-span success, it seems relevant to acknowledge the overall pattern of gains and losses across the life span rather than only domain-specific change. Lifelong gain–loss patterns represent a *gestalt* of life-span success, and thus are more than just the sum of single instances of gain or loss across diverse life domains.

Many empirical illustrations for this pertain to the differentiation of mechanics and pragmatics in intellectual life-span development. There exist robust evidence showing that in midlife and even in old age, many pragmatic abilities related to expertise, wisdom, acculturated capacities, and procedural knowledge may counterbalance losses in more biology-based mechanical capacities (Baltes, Staudinger et al.,

1999; Lindenberger & Baltes, 2000). Such evidence comes from study on the allocation of resources in dual-task paradigms (Huxhold, Li, Schmiedek, & Lindenberger, 2006) as well as from studies with young and older secretaries (e.g., Salthouse, 1984). Clearly, at all times in the life span, individuals seek to maximize sustained gains while minimizing loss. This also involves the need to balance gains against losses. Evidently there are more losses than gains in later adulthood, but the meaning of such gains and losses may differ. In old age, meaningful positive experience may also overrule some of the threats of loss (Carstensen, Fung, & Charles, 2003).

Plasticity implies that human organisms can significantly expand the range of functioning, scope, and efficacy. At all phases of the human life span there exist much behavioral elasticity and malleability, meaning that the human mind can respond in most flexible ways to changing environmental challenges. For example, when brain injury (e.g., a stroke) results in a cerebral lesion and functional loss, other cerebral regions may be activated to take over the lost functions. There also exists enormous plasticity in the *aging* mind. For example, in a classic study using the testing-the-limits paradigm, Kliegl and Baltes (1987) showed that after only a few sessions of memory training using the loci-method, older adults performed as well as untrained young adults. However, there were also clear limits to such plasticity. The training gains of older adults followed an asymptotic trajectory, with no further improvement after 10–15 training sessions. The achieved level of memory performance after more than 30 weeks of training was generally lower as compared with the young adults, who had received intensive training. While behavioral plasticity exists in all phases of the human life span, the limitations of such plasticity become more evident with increasing age. This clearly constrains the potentials for life success across adulthood and old age. However, there is much reason to believe that no level of competence is so low that the individual cannot respond in adaptive ways (Lawton, 1989). For example, in nursing home settings, older residents were found to show adaptive behavioral patterns in response to the affordances in this social environment (Baltes, 1996). Displaying behavioral dependency is one way to maximize one's supportive social encounters in the nursing home setting. This means that very old individuals are capable of generating adaptive responses to contextual demands, even when close to the limits of behavioral plasticity. Obviously, life-span psychology offers a comprehensive perspective on life-span success that applies even to the most extremely constrained contexts of life. In the following, we refer to this idea as the contextualized meaning of success.

Meaning of Success is Contextual

Success depends on meaning. And, there is no sustainable meaning of success in life beyond the prevailing norms, constraints, and challenges of a given culture or society. For example, it is well known that interdependence and autonomy have quite different meanings in collectivistic—as compared to individualistic—societies (Oyserman, Coon, & Kemmelmeier, 2002). While meaning is based on individual conceptions and subjective representations, all meaning is embedded in context. Consequently, sociocultural opportunity structures strongly determine the valence, the relevance, and the impact that is associated with a specific developmental function or outcome. Often, traditional values and cultural norms (co-) determine the individual's desires and strivings. The contextualization of meaning of success may be well illustrated with the famous allegory of roses of the German sociologist Georg Simmel (1897). In his essay, Simmel described a fictitious society, in which the right to breed roses was reserved exclusively to a small privileged group of people. For all other people, it was forbidden to breed roses by law. In this society being able to breed roses constituted a pivotal indication of life success. Obviously, all societies and cultures define the meaning of success in specific and culture-dependent ways. Such definitions of success may even be constitutive for the respective social structure and rules that govern the society. As described in Simmel's tale of roses, personal striving for success implied that more and more individuals in that society attained the right to breed roses. After some time and after a couple of turmoils and revolutions, all members of that society finally were allowed to breed roses. Now, as everyone was breeding roses in more and more differentiated and sophisticated ways, people sensed that breeding roses was only of secondary relevance in their lives, and not a sign of success.

Obviously, it is difficult to perceive normality as success unless one considers historical or ontogenetic dimensions. Success in life is also depending on meanings of change or stability. Stability may involve maintenance or stagnation. Change often relates to meanings of decline or growth. It is part and parcel of life-span psychology to improve understanding of such meaning as it changes in human ontogeny from birth to death. It is not about good or bad, gain or loss, decline or growth, or more or less in life. It is about the deliverance of developmental potentials within specific life-span contexts. Only when a desirable or controllable outcome in life contains meaning, people will perceive this as success. A prototypical example of such meaning contexts is related to aging, and the limitation of resources in life. When it can be shown that some aging outcomes appear desirable while still achievable, there is reason to label such self-generated positive outcomes a life-span success. Even the most adverse situation of an individual's bedridden dependency and need of care may entail adaptive potential for meaning in life. In the next section, we will come back to the role of meaning with respect to the inevitable pressure for selection that characterizes all developmental processes.

To sum up, *success in life* refers to the attainment of meaningful, desirable, and controllable outcomes. The origins and scope of positive outcomes are biologically and culturally defined, and they may also be self-directed. Life-span success results from the lifelong dynamics of gains and losses, that is, a conjoint maximization of gains (approaching desirable outcomes) and the minimization of losses (avoiding undesirable outcomes). The multidirectionality, multidimensionality, plasticity, and contextualization of development point to the general ability of human organisms to co-organize and co-construct desirable outcomes within biological and cultural contexts. Such conceptions of development build on the idea that individuals are capable of intentional self-development and of proactive adaptation to changing life-span contexts. Such a perspective on the individual as coproducer of development (Heckhausen & Schulz, 1999; Lerner & Busch-Rossnagel, 1981) implies that the direction, valence and pace of change in development depend on biology, culture, and psychological mechanisms of self-regulation. With this said, it may appear obvious that reasoning about the potentials of human development leads us to examine the concrete mechanisms and processes that regulate positive and negative life-span outcomes.

▨ THE MODEL OF SOC

In the 1980s, Baltes and Baltes (1980, 1990) suggested a general metatheoretical framework for modeling pathways of life-span success based on three developmental principles: SOC. These three principles conjointly serve to enhance and secure the individual's potentials for positive developmental outcome in response to biological and cultural contexts of ontogeny. Baltes and Baltes (1980) have introduced these principles explicitly for the first time in a seminal book chapter as an adaptive task in the aging process as follows:

> The assumption is that as individuals reach old age, they can maintain or even increase their psychological competence in some classes of behavior, but not in a highly generalized manner as would be true for childhood development. The **adaptive task**, then, for the aging individual is **to select** and **concentrate on those domains which are of high priority** and **involve a convergence** of environmental demands, individual motivations and skills, and biological capacity. (Baltes & Baltes, 1980, p. 59; emphasis added)

According to this early depiction of the idea of selective optimization and compensation, adaptation across adulthood pertained to improving a match between the individual and the environment. Note that this matching refers to both individual self-management (such as motivation and skills) as well as mastering contextual challenges (e.g., environment, biology).

What are the three principles of adaptation across the life span in detail? SOC describe the adaptation of organisms or systems. These principles rest on key prerequisites about the general nature of development across the life span and the respective contextual and evolutionary preconditions of life. We discuss each of the principles in relation to such boundary conditions of developmental contexts across the life span. Table 3.1 gives an overview of the definitions, conditions, and illustrations of the principles of SOC. We argue that the definition of each principle builds on specific premises and assumptions about the context and the nature of development. We define the principles in relation to these contextual prerequisites. We argue that the principles may be derived from specific conditions of development. Moreover, we distinguish between a more general definition of SOC (as it pertains to the life sciences), and the more specific psychological processes of SOC. We begin with a description of each of the three principles before discussing some theoretical issues related to the functionality, coordination, and context-dependency of the SOC principles and model.

Defining the Principles of SOC

Selection is a fundamental mechanism involved in all evolutionary and ontogenetic processes (Carstensen, 2006; Heckhausen, 2002, 2003; Heckhausen & Schulz, 1999; Marsiske et al., 1995). Generally, selection reflects the canalization of life paths (Waddington, 1957), irrespective of whether such canalization is biologically, culturally, or self-determined. The principle of selection is a ubiquitous process in human development, because it is tied to evolutionary and physical conditions of all living systems. In this most general sense, selection occurs because physical time flows in one direction without recurrence. Consequently, selection involves a narrowing of opportunities for alternatives. In a life-span psychology perspective,

TABLE 3.1

Definition, Conditions, and Description of Selection, Optimization, and Compensation in Life-Span Science				
Principle	Contextual Prerequisite	General Description	Psychological Process	Illustrations
Selection	Limitation of resources, finitude of life time, meaning of opportunities	Canalization of pathways and trajectories, emergence of opportunity structures	Implicit or explicit mental organization of choices (tasks or goals); in response to loss (loss-based) or to positive events or outcomes (elective)	Giving direction to efforts or invest-ments, commitment, abandonment, renewal of goals.
Optimization	Amendability of resources, efficiency of resources, plasticity	Improving the function of a system or organism	Enhancing, refining, or strengthening a behavioral function (i.e., resources required for cognitive or physical activity)	Exercise, timing, increasing effort, cognitive motor control, solicit advice or guidance, generate information, and improve opportunities for development
Compensation	Error-proneness (susceptibility to loss or decline), available unused resources, reserve capacity	Replacing or restoring lost or failed functions, balancing failure or loss	Establishing new or restored behavioral functions in response to loss, limits, or failure (i.e., activating or using idle resources)	In response to anticipated loss (like optimization). After failure/loss: disengagement, motivation protection
Source: Adapted from Baltes and Baltes, 1990; Freund and Baltes, 2002a; Marsiske et al., 1995.				

the principle of selection is tied to presuppositions and meaning about its ontoge-netic function.

The presuppositions of selection in development pertain to a meaning of potential developmental trajectories that result from such selection. Meaning is a key concept in the context of selection. In this psychological perspective, we con-tend that selection in life-span development necessarily involves meaning. Selection without meaning is not relevant in a life-span perspective. For example, a selection of two equivalent behavioral options is meaningless, when choosing among such alternatives does not have any consequence. Obviously, in a life-span perspective, the origins and determinants of meaning structures in different phases of life need to be clarified.

Meaning in the philosophy of language refers to the pragmatics and construc-tivism of the human mind and thought (Berger & Luckmann, 1967; Searle, 1979). Meaning in life arises in response to two fundamental challenges of human exis-tence: the limitation of resources (Marsiske et al., 1995) and the finitude of lifetime (Carstensen, 2006). Both challenges not only involve much pressure for selection but they also give reason to selection of an individual pathway or a specific purpose in life. Consequently, such meaningful selection necessarily entails costs and requires availability of psychological resources. Resource-rich individuals, for example, are likely to respond to threats of developmental resources with greater use of adap-tive selection strategies than resource-poor individuals (Baltes & Lang, 1997; Lang et al., 2002). Consequently, we argue that resource-free selection (i.e., selection with-out costs) is not likely to generate adaptive outcomes. For example, when decisions occur arbitrarily, unreflected and without commitment, such decisions may not have any consequences. Not surprisingly, purposelessness or feeling incapable to make use of one's resources reflects depressive states of mind. It is the absence of meaning in such selection that enhances the risk for dysfunctional outcomes or states of mind. Meaningful selection, in contrast, is contingent on states of mental health and depends on available cognitive resources.

Optimization involves the improvement of an output function that operates within an organism or system. Thus, optimization describes minimization of costs and maximization of benefits in producing a specific output. For example, in the economic science, optimization refers to enhancing the efficiency of inputs (e.g., labor, capital, resources) that are required to achieve a desired return. As the efficiency of inputs increases, the costs of the production process decrease. In informational science, optimization refers to catalyzing a flow of information within an integrated system to attain more accurate and faster retrievals. In the life sciences, behavioral functions involve the (physiological, cognitive, mental, social) resources and means required for producing a specific behavioral outcome.

In psychology, optimization of a behavioral function implies that the involved resources are refined to produce more positive outcomes. For example, individuals may train their memory capacities to improve their transactions and tasks of everyday living. They may do this also to enhance their overall mental health and autonomy. In a life-span psychological perspective, optimization involves a more complex issue that also refers to the level, scope, and probability of positive outcomes, including even the possibility of loss (Baltes & Baltes, 1996). Studies examining the ability to delay gratification illustrate optimizing effects in childhood and adolescence. Delay of gratification refers to the ability to postpone immediate fulfillment and pleasure to enlarge future benefits (Shoda, Mischel, & Peake, 1990). In their well-known experiments, Mischel and his colleagues made children choose between one of two desirable objects, a small reward (e.g., one marshmallow) that they would receive immediately or, alternatively, a bigger reward (e.g., two marshmallows) that they would receive later on (e.g., after 30 minutes). In several follow-up studies, researchers revealed even robust long-term effects of such consistent behavioral childhood preferences: Those kids, who delayed the gratification longer, were portrayed more positively by their parents in adolescence (e.g., as being more capable and considerate; Mischel, Shoda, & Peake, 1988; Shoda et al., 1990). Another example is that older people may achieve a relatively high quality in life given the specific life-span conditions. Investing in the maintenance of autonomy in later life, despite age-related constraints, may thus benefit from optimization of one's assistance systems. More generally, optimization pertains to the generation and refinement of developmental resources, including information resources and the generation of contextual opportunities (that create resources for different pathways).

In this sense, optimization constitutes a higher order principle in development that also pertains to the improvement of developmental contexts and environmental resources. Consequently, optimal levels of life quality may differ between various contexts of the life course. Optimization, thus, encompasses the strengthening or refinement of behavioral functions (i.e., resources, means) within age-related contextual opportunities. Optimization involves a balancing of gain–loss dynamics, for example, when individuals improve their knowledge (information resources), generate alternatives before choosing, reflect their own capacities and resources in a life review, or generate time for the decision process. In general, optimization depends on general amenability or renewability, and on the efficiency of means and resources. Some resources or means may not be adequate in achieving specific outputs, and some resources may not be malleable at all. In such cases, any investment in optimization may be dysfunctional.

Compensation refers to a response to loss or limitations. Whenever an output function in an organism or system is limited or lost, other or restored functions are required to produce substitute or comparable output. Compensation, in this context is a fundamental mechanism that results from the error-proneness and the resource limitation of all living systems (Heckhausen, 2003; Marsiske et al., 1995). There are two distinct sources of compensation (Baltes & Baltes, 1996; Dixon & Bäckman, 1995; Marsiske et al., 1995); one is based on internal changes of the system or organism, and a second results from contextual changes in the person–environment fit. Internal sources of compensation result from limitations of resources and means. Whenever individuals choose pathways or invest resources in specific domains, this implies an increased likelihood of confronting limitations or even loss in other behavioral domains, which will have to be compensated. Such self-generated compensation is an inherent and unavoidable component of all positive developmental changes. A second source of compensation results from changes in the person–environment match as a consequence of declining capacities of the person or as a consequence of increases in environmental demands. This context-dependent compensation reflects the adaptive tasks of specific life phases, and requires a restoration or renewal of previous levels of person–environment fit.

How Functional Are SOC in Life-Span Development?

The principles of SOC describe developmental adaptation (Baltes & Baltes, 1990). The three elements of the model involve a set of strategies for resolving or mastering adaptive tasks across adulthood. As individuals grow old, gain–loss dynamics change and limitations multiply with late life, increasing the significance of SOC principles for achieving success, for example, with respect to balancing self-determination and autonomy with increasing needs of interdependency (Baltes, 1996; Lang & Baltes, 1997). A critical issue is what determines the adaptiveness of a behavioral function. To what extent is the adaptiveness of SOC dependent on contextual constraints or on person–environment fit (Lang & Heckhausen, 2006; Marsiske et al., 1995)?

Life-span scholars have referred to the adaptive implementation of SOC principles across the life span with the metaphor of orchestration (Baltes, 1997; Baltes & Freund, 2003). Orchestration, in its literal sense, refers to the process of arranging a piece of music for a larger ensemble of instruments in an orchestra. The process of orchestration aims at bringing the different voices of instruments to sound like one harmonic and integrative piece. With respect to the orchestration of SOC processes, it remains an open question, "what determines such orchestration of the three principles across the life span?" A theoretical perspective on related adaptational processes was formulated, for example, with the dual-process theory of adaptation (Brandtstädter, 2002), as well as with the life-span theory of control (Heckhausen & Schulz, 1995).

In an extensive and control-theoretical elaboration of ideas related to the principles of selection and compensation, Heckhausen and Schulz (1995) argue that individuals strive to enhance their action potentials either by changing the worlds in accordance with their goals (primary control) or by changing themselves and their goals (secondary control). Primary and secondary control are seen as enhancing the individual's motivational resources and general capacity to exert primary control. According to this theory, individuals generally strive for primary control throughout their lives. Whereas primary control encompasses all attempts to modify the environment in accordance with one's goals, necessities, and desires, secondary control refers to the adaptation of one's aims to the external environment and embraces cognitive processes. Primary and secondary control can be evaluated on two dimensions, that is, veridicality and functionality. Adaptive efforts to adapt can be functional or dysfunctional—irrespective of whether the control is illusory or veridical (Heckhausen & Schulz, 1995).

We do not intend to discuss the life-span theory of control in this chapter (for a detailed discussion, see Heckhausen, Chapter 8). Rather, the purpose here is to apply some of the ideas of life-span theory of control, in particular, the distinction of functional versus dysfunctional adaptation in life-span development to the principles of SOC. According to life-span theory of control (Heckhausen, 2002; Heckhausen & Schulz, 1995) strategies of developmental self-regulation (e.g., focusing on unattainable goals, inadequate and exaggerated control perceptions) may become dysfunctional, when they hamper and threaten the individual's developmental potentials in life. Similarly, developmental processes of SOC are defined as protecting the individual's developmental resources. For example, when individuals strive for unrealistic goals and refuse to accept facts that cannot be changed, any further investment will lead to failure or loss (Wrosch, Heckhausen, & Lachman, 2000; Wrosch, Schulz, & Heckhausen, 2004). One implication is that whenever such processes do not serve to protect or improve the individual's ability to generate meaning, efficacy, and purpose in life, it will be dysfunctional or maladaptive.

Consequently, we argue that the adaptive functions of SOC regarding life-span successes depend on the contextual conditions and demands. When there is no meaning of choices in life, selection is arbitrary, and when selection of unrealistic goals occurs, this will lead to failure in the future. When resources are not improvable, optimization is in vain, and when there is no loss, any compensation is premature. When SOC occur in accordance with specific environmental preconditions, they are likely to lead to adaptive behavioral outcomes. It is an open question, though—"what are the mechanisms that ensure adaptive orchestration of SOC principles across the life course?"

In sum, the adaptive function of SOC principles rests on the structure and sequence of developmental constraints and challenges across the life span (Heckhausen, 2002, 2003). However, thus far, there is still a lack of theoretical understanding of how the SOC principles are employed in the process of mastering adaptive developmental tasks.

Is There a Coordination of the Principles of SOC?

The three principles of SOC contribute equally to positive developmental outcomes. Each principle entails a unique lawfulness including causes and consequences. However, such lawfulness may depend on the respective life-span developmental context. For example, in later adulthood the refinement and enhancement of resources may become less salient, whereas selection processes may prevail or even increase

(Carstensen, 2006). Selection pertains to the inevitable limitations of resources and time in life. Optimization refers to the enormous potentials for growth, refinement, and plasticity of human organisms, and compensation results from the indispensable error-proneness in the human evolution and ontogeny. However, in life-span psychology, there is much consensus that the principles are intertwined and reciprocally determined (Marsiske et al., 1995).

Depending on the respective theoretical specifications, the interplay of the three principles may be described in different ways. For example, in resource-theoretical conceptions, allocation of resources assumes some primacy in cognitive adaptation, building on the fact that all demands related to survival of the organism have some priority over other behavioral and cognitive tasks (Baltes, Lindenberger, & Staudinger, 2006; Krampe & Baltes, 2003). In this line of reasoning, any coordination of resources (i.e., optimization) becomes a more central principle in contexts that involve a threat to the survival of the organism.

Action-theoretical perspectives on the SOC principles focus on the developmental regulation of goals across the life span (Freund & Baltes, 2007). In this perspective, depicting goal hierarchies in life is conceived as a primary scope of the adaptational process. Although not explicitly stated in the literature, the principles of (loss-based or elective) selection are typically conceived at the outset of life management processes (Freund et al., 1999). In a contextualistic perspective of the SOC model, not much is known about the interplay of the three principles of SOC (Baltes & Carstensen, 1999; Baltes & Lang, 1997). It is an open question as to what extent the coordination of the three principles of SOC depend on contextual opportunities.

Life-span theory of control (Heckhausen, 2002; Heckhausen & Schulz, 1995) implies a comprehensive conception of how regulatory processes of generating person–environment fit is coordinated and sequentially structured across the life span (see Freund, 2008; Freund & Riediger, 2006). We do not know of any explicit description of how the SOC principles are coordinated or orchestrated across the life span. In the absence of such a coordinative model, we submit a recursive coordination model of the life-span organization and interplay of the principles of SOC that builds on assumptions of control theory. Figure 3.1 illustrates this *recursive SOC coordination model*.

The model suggests that all adaptive efforts typically start with an attempt of optimizing an already existing behavioral function (e.g., "circular reactions" sensu Piaget in early cognitive development). As in control theory, the principle of optimization involves generating, ensuring, or refining alternatives and behavioral flexibility in life review, life management, and life planning. Optimization, thus, refers to a higher order process that regulates the flexibility and functionality of decisional processes across the life span (cf. Heckhausen, 2003).

All optimized behavior functions lead to output related to either success or failure. This implies that optimization refers to resources that are involved in planning or predecision process of generating opportunities and goals across the life span. For example, individuals generally tend to repeat a behavioral function that has lead to success. Optimization often involves a refinement of resources related to maintaining and enhancing one's potentials or existing abilities. Selection, in contrast, gives direction to the individual's potentials or abilities on the basis of goals, decisions, and intentions that reflect prior optimization (success) or compensation (loss or failure).

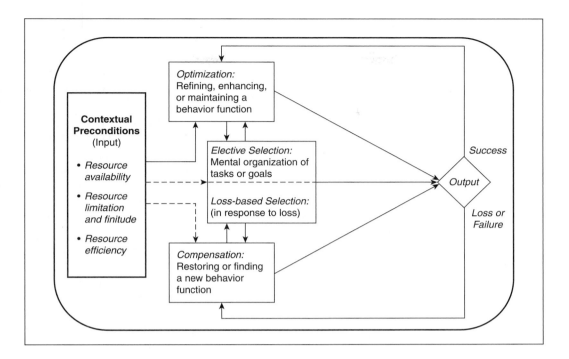

FIGURE 3.1 **Recursive coordination model of the life-span principles of selection, optimization, and compensation. Note: Dotted lines in the figure reflect conditional paths (i.e., depending on context or output).**

The recursive effects of the output on either optimization or compensation depend on whether such outputs are positive or negative. When outputs are positive, the prior behavioral function may be maintained or improved, whereas negative outputs may trigger compensatory functions. This is not to say that success or failure may not also have a recursive effect on selection. However, we argue that the recursive effects of developmental success or failure on selection processes are typically mediated through either an optimization or compensation of behavioral functions.

Selection may occur in the context of optimization (elective selection) or in the context of responding to loss or failure, when new decisions for behavioral functions are required (loss-based selection). Obviously, the developmental principle of (meaningful) selection is embedded in a prior management of resources. Selection relies on the availability of resources, such as time, competence, skills, education, status, or health. When available resources are amendable, elective selection may generally prevail. When there is a threat to the availability of resources, for example, a loss of health, loss-based selection occurs.

Finally, the general principle of compensation is defined as a response to failure and loss. Obviously, compensation may not occur and may not be adequate as long as individuals do not anticipate, perceive, or experience loss. When failure occurs, compensation constitutes an adaptive response, as long as there exist alternative or reserve resources. Consequently, the principle of compensation is triggered when optimization or selection fails. In this context compensation may also serve as a tool for repairing actual or anticipated misfits of person and environment.

In sum, the proposed recursive coordination model of the SOC principles relies on theoretical considerations and empirical findings related to the life-span theory of control (Heckhausen, 2002, 2003). The model transfers control-theoretical considerations to the definitions of the three SOC principles. According to this coordination model, behavioral adaptation consists in the maintenance or improvement of general behavioral functions (optimization) that are directed toward specific desirable outcomes (selection), and that are corrected, balanced, or renewed, when outcomes include loss or failure (compensation). When success occurs, behavioral functions are optimized. When failure or loss occurs, behavioral functions will be restored or substituted. Selection gives direction to either optimizing or compensating functions of behavior.

THEORETICAL SPECIFICATION AND EMPIRICAL ILLUSTRATION OF SOC PRINCIPLES

SOC and the Mind: Allocating and Generating Intellectual Resources

In a well-known classic experiment, Salthouse (1984) investigated the speed assumption of cognitive aging comparing the typing performance of young and old secretaries. The study started from the observation that in a normal everyday context young and old secretaries did not show much difference with respect to the speed and accuracy of typing performance. However, when the young and the old secretaries were experimentally forced to type single letters or one word after the other, strong age differences were observed. Older secretaries in such constrained typing tasks were much slower than young secretaries. The findings suggest that older secretaries made pragmatic use of foresight and anticipation in maintaining a high level of typing performance. One implication is that older secretaries relied on additional pragmatic resources, such as expertise and foresight, to adapt to their decreasing typing performance and speed. This finding has been most influential and fundamental for resource-theoretical conceptions of cognitive aging.

According to such resource-theoretical conceptions of adaptive life-span development, the amount and mixture of available resources change across life span (Riediger, Li, & Lindenberger, 2006). Although old age is not solely characterized by losses, a decrease in overall resources is observable. This reduction in resources demands a directed investment in the realization of selected goals and domains, an optimization of remaining resources, and compensation for the effects of loss. Krampe and Baltes (2003) argue that individual differences in intelligence and expertise reflect human capacity to adapt to changing contexts. More generally, this also relates to creating, managing, and distributing personal resources.

An exemplary approach to issues of cognitive aging that serves to illustrate the balancing of resources involves the dual-task paradigm. Numerous studies demonstrate that older people are less capable in mastering situations that require divided attention or managing dual tasks (Huxhold et al., 2006; Li, Krampe, & Bondar, 2005; Salthouse, Rogan, & Prill, 1984) spanning areas such as navigational and route learning (Lövdén, Schellenbach, Grossman-Hutter, Krüger, & Lindenberger, 2005), dichotomous hearing or auditory tasks (Teasdale, Bard, LaRue, & Fleury, 1993), and verbal communication (Kemper, Herman, & Lian, 2003). According to Li et al. (2001), dual-task conditions mirror the opportunities and limits of compensatory efforts. When confronted with dual tasks, older subjects respond to these limitations by focusing more strongly on one task (*loss-based selection*), in which they show a performance level that compares to that of young adults. However, there are also clear limitations to such compensation, when the task complexity increases or the task context is distracting (Krampe & Baltes, 2003; Li et al., 2001, 2005; Teasdale et al., 1992).

Further illustrations on aging differences of resource allocation relate to research on postural control. For example, age-related losses in sensory and motor functions also affect the capacity to maintain balance and gait and to move steadily. In addition, there are also limitations in postural control based on alterations in accordant brain areas (Lajoie, Teasdale, Bard, & Fleury, 1993). A consequence is a greater need of older people to direct efforts and cognitive resources for good sensori-motor functioning such as balance or walking. It becomes more difficult to chat and stroll at the same time, or to walk on cobbled or icy street as compared with earlier years of adulthood (Krampe & Baltes, 2003; Teasdale et al., 1993). In a dual-task study, Li et al. (2001) demonstrated that younger and older participants invested age-differential efforts while memorizing and walking on a narrow track. Elderly people focused more on balancing their posture and less on memorizing. Moreover, in contrast to young counterparts, older adults more often used walking assistance than a memory aid (Brown, Sleik, Polych, & Gage, 2002; Doumas, Rapp, & Krampe, 2009). Similarly, Fraser, Li, DeMont, and Penhun (2007) compared the performance of young adults, healthy older adults, and older participants who had problems with their balance in a dual-task study. Findings show that young adults and healthy older adults displayed comparable levels of performance. In the group of older adults with impairments of balancing functions, more muscle activity was observed, in response to a dual task including semantic judgment and walking. This pattern may reflect a compensation for the reduced postural control and the related risk of falling. Kemper et al. (2003) examined real-life situation of talking while walking in a laboratory study. Whereas young adults shortened the sentences and reduced their grammatical complexity, older adults slowed down their speech rate. This finding suggests that older participants choose more resource-efficient strategies to master dual-task situations as compared with young adults.

As discussed before, there are also limits to compensation. For example, Huxhold et al. (2006) observed that more complex cognitive tasks in dual-task situations entailed greater difficulty for older adults than for young adults. Lövdén et al. (2005) further investigated the role of task complexity. In a virtual museum task, 16 young and 16 old men had to walk on a treadmill while virtually finding their way through the museum presented in front of them on a flat screen. The task complexity was modulated with the difficulty of the maze and the availability of walking aids. As in previous studies, the cognitive load related to the navigation task hampered older participants more strongly than young adults. These and other studies indicate that older participants can achieve a similar level of performance in one task than young adults, but they do not walk the paths as accurately. Consequently, the effects of task complexity involve not only compensation but also principles related to higher costs of resources required for health-related tasks in old age (Huxhold et al., 2006; Li et al., 2005; Lindenberger et al., 2000; Salthouse et al., 1984; Somberg & Salthouse, 1982).

Finally, we discuss the life-span development of resource allocation with respect to contextual conditions and resource availability. Schaefer, Krampe, Lindenberger, and Baltes (2008) presented children and young adults with a dual-task setting. Children and young adults balanced on a board while doing a working memory task (N-Back task). While young adults performed less well both in the cognitive and in the motor tasks, children showed deficits only in the memorizing task. The findings suggest that children tend to focus more on the motor task, even when instructed to concentrate on the memory task. This reflects a form of adaptive selection because the children invest their (few) resources in balancing and therewith in their protection. In a study by Crossley and Hiscock (1992), young, middle-aged, and old adults tapped with one finger on the desk while concurrently doing nothing, reading silently, speaking, or completing a maze. In this study, linear reductions in the tapping rate occurred across the age groups during the switch task from the single- to the dual-task condition.

In sum, resource theoretical applications of the SOC model point to the over-all resource dependency of the three SOC principles across the life span. When resources are scarce or not available, there are limitations to compensation efforts, while selection occurs, and thus ensures basic behavioral or survival needs of the organism. It is in this resource-theoretical context that selection appears to be less resource-dependent. One reason is that few resources are involved when choices involve hard-wired preferences of the organism in prioritizing survival needs.

Action-Theoretical Considerations on SOC: Life Management Across Adulthood

In action-theoretical concepts, the principles of SOC are related to the motivational processes of self-regulation. In the action-theoretical SOC model (Freund & Baltes, 2002a), the principles of SOC are applied to processes of striving for and achieving goals in life. According to such reasoning, selection is defined as a mental process of delineating goals or tasks (Freund & Baltes, 2002a, 2007). Any decision for one goal or task involves a decisional process, commitment, or abandonment. The developmental meaning of such goals or tasks may originate either from biological or cultural contexts (e.g., degeneration, social norms) or from the individual's mind and thinking. Along with the organization of goals, selection implies a narrowing, focusing, or concentrating of goals or tasks within and across domains of life. Selection, then, is defined as a cognitive process of delineating a goal or task.

In this line of reasoning, response to loss may involve both selection and compensation principles, which are not easy to disentangle in mastery of loss contexts. One implication is that the distinction of two facets of selection—elective and loss-based selection—has proven helpful to describe the two distinct mental processes related to goal delineation in optimizing and in compensating contexts (Baltes, Baltes, Freund, & Lang, 1999): Elective selection pertains to a gain orientation or to a cognitive approach motive, whereas loss-based selection is associated with a loss or avoidance orientation (Freund, 2006). Selection may occur as a consequence of events that entail limitations, such as a health crisis (e.g., receiving a diagnosis of severe chronic disease) or an economic crisis. For example, Ebner, Freund, and Baltes (2006) observed that goal striving of young adults was more growth-oriented (e.g., to become healthy), whereas older adults' goals selection mirrored the prevention of loss and the maintenance of functioning (e.g., do not get sick). This response to the altering availability of resources proved to be adaptive because the focus on prevention was negatively linked with well-being in younger adults and positively with well-being in older adults.

According to the action-theoretical SOC model, optimization involves enhancement of resources needed to achieve a specific (selected) goal or task in life. In this context, optimization involves the acquisition, refinement, coordination, and investment of goal-relevant resources or means (Freund & Baltes, 2007). According to this, any investment toward improved functioning relies on selection toward a specific developmental pathway. In this line of reasoning, there is no optimization without selection. Optimization, in this context also involves the choice of resources that serve as input for a behavioral function in striving for selected goals. The general process of such an orchestration has not yet been integrated in the action-theoretical SOC model.

Finally, compensation in the action-theoretical SOC model refers to the establishment, refinement, coordination, or investment of new resources in response to a loss or limitation (Freund & Baltes, 2002a, 2007). It is not always easy to distinguish optimization from compensation, because the unique feature of compensation is the co-occurrence (or not) of a loss or limitation. Often, though, perceiving a loss or failure remains in the eye of the beholder (e.g., with respect to standards for achieving a goal). Thus, the difference between compensation and optimization relies on a subjective definition of loss, making the distinction difficult to identify or observe. One possible solution is to define a loss as a subjective, conscious representation or anticipation of a loss experience. Considerable individual differences also exist with respect to apperception of loss events in life. One implication is that when relating loss experience to subjective states of mind, compensation may often refer to a maintenance or loss avoidance orientation. In contrast, then, optimization will refer to approach or gain orientations (Freund, 2006, 2008). On this basis, the action-theoretical SOC model allows for a straight integration of an individual difference perspective and personality theories.

A wealth of empirical illustrations exist proving the general significance and usefulness of the action-theoretical SOC framework with respect to diverse sets of life tasks and domains ranging from adolescence to young, middle, and late adulthood. Consequently, the implicit or explicit criteria for adaptive outcomes may differ depending on the respective age period or life phase. In early and middle adulthood, issues of success in life often refer to family, work, or life balance (Abele & Wiese, 2008; Bajor & Baltes, 2003; Wiese, Freund, & Baltes, 2000, 2002), whereas success in later adulthood is more often directed toward issues of autonomy and everyday competence (Baltes & Lang, 1997; Lang et al., 2002), as well as life quality and well-being (Freund & Baltes, 2002a, 2002b). Generally, action-theoretical applications of SOC necessarily begin with a definition of possible success criteria in the respective age groups or life phases under investigation.

In a cross-sectional study with 206 professional young adults in their 30s, Wiese et al. (2000) examined strategies of coordinating work and family activities with respect to the pursuit of career-related and partnership-related goals. Findings of this study suggested that subjective life success was generally associated with self-descriptions of optimization and compensation strategies in everyday life. In this study, selection strategies contributed less importantly to positive outcomes, probably as a consequence of the two preselected life tasks of work and family. In a subsequent 3-year longitudinal study with 80 young professional adults who were in the fourth decade of life, optimization and compensation strategies proved again to be more powerful predictors of subjective well-being and job satisfaction (Wiese et al., 2002). The overall pattern of such findings was also confirmed in a study of Abele and Wiese (2008) with 1,185 young professional adults. Self-reported investment in optimization strategies was associated with subjective success criteria, but unrelated to objective career success. Selection strategies did not contribute substantively to success outcomes in this study. Generally, the effects of self-reported SOC life management strategies proved to be robust above and beyond more stable personality characteristics, such as the Big Five traits. Bajor and Baltes (2003) more explicitly explored the interplay of trait-like personality characteristics, SOC strategies, and job performance in a study with 226 bank employees. In this study, conscientiousness as well as SOC strategies was associated with higher levels of job performance. However, when professional demands were stronger, for example, with respect to involving greater autonomy and responsibility, compensation as well as loss-based selection mediated the positive effects of conscientiousness. This finding suggests that SOC strategies in professional domains may serve as adaptive strategies for making positive use of personality resources (e.g., conscientiousness) for achieving life success.

In a comprehensive review of findings, Freund and Baltes (2000) discuss the application and usefulness of SOC strategies in the context of life management. Generally, research refers to the positive link between growth orientation and variables such as well-being or life satisfaction. However, considering the altering amount of reserves in old age, there must be adjustments in underlying motivational strivings because any persistence in striving for unattainable goals may lead to maladaptation (Freund, 2006; Heckhausen & Tomasik, 2002). For example, when young and old adults are deciding about how much time they spend voluntarily on a sensori-motor task that either involves optimization (e.g., improving one's performance) or compensation (e.g., responding to a loss), older adults spent more time with compensation tasks, whereas young participants showed more persistence in the optimization context (Freund, 2006). There is also evidence suggesting that older adults show less goal interference and more facilitation among goals (Riediger, Freund, & Baltes, 2005).

Overall, the action-theoretical framework of the SOC model has contributed a wealth of insights showing that use of SOC contributes importantly to the adaptive management of life tasks and successful outcomes across the life span. The contexts and demands of different life phases in adolescence, young, middle, and late adulthood were observed to be associated with age-differential patterns of adaptive use of the SOC strategies. For example, in young adulthood, optimization appears to contribute more strongly to positive life outcomes, whereas in later adulthood, compensation with respect to maintenance orientation appears to have more positive effects. Such findings are consistent with the proposed coordination model of SOC strategies. For example, there appear to be no direct paths of resources (i.e., input, see Figure 3.1) on selection strategies, whereas age differences in optimization are observed to be associated with the general availability of resources.

Person–Environment Fit and Contextual Approaches to SOC

Positive developmental outcomes typically involve a convergence of a person and their respective environment. When the individual's capacities and resources match the demands and opportunities of the respective environment, this typically leads to improved adaptation and positive developmental outcomes (Lawton, 1989; Lawton & Nahemow, 1973). In this context, principles of SOC also apply to the emergence of person–environment fit at different phases of the life span. According to this more context-theoretical perspective, the three principles of SOC reflect a proactive molding and shaping of contexts in response to specific opportunity structures (Baltes & Carstensen, 1996; Baltes & Lang, 1997; Marsiske et al., 1995). Two perspectives may be distinguished in such context-theoretical perspectives on the model of SOC. One perspective focuses more on how individuals make use of SOC principles to mold their environments, and a second perspective pertains to the issue of how contexts or societal opportunity structures reflect, initiate, or release principles of SOC, and thus improve positive developmental outcomes across the life span. Understanding and modeling life-span success builds on the idea that success is related to fundamental developmental principles that may not be tied to individual behaviors but are reflected in the social structures and culture that have evolved from the accumulation of individual successes.

First, we discuss the possible influences of proactive personal SOC strategies with regard to enhancing the match between the individual and the social environment. There is considerable evidence indicating the manner in which individuals proactively mold their social environments in accordance with changing preferences and motives across adulthood. One empirical illustration pertains to the regulation of personal networks across adulthood (Antonucci & Akiyama, 1987; Lang, 2001; Lang & Carstensen, 2002). A well-known and robust empirical finding shows that the number of social partners continuously decreases from middle to late adulthood. Such reductions in the size of personal networks reflect reduced functional status, declining mobility and loss of social partners. However, there is convincing evidence that such reductions also mirror changes in social preferences and motivation as well as in strategies of selecting social partners (Carstensen, 2006; Carstensen et al., 2003). Such perspectives appear quite consistent with resource-theoretical and action-theoretical applications of the SOC model.

A second, more contextual approach pertains to the question of what age-specific developmental contexts activate and regulate adaptive responses that serve to enhance improvement of person–environment fit.

In such context-theoretical perspective, *selection* is described with respect to the emergence of opportunity structures that canalize, structure, and sequence the course of life across the life span (Dannefer, 1992; Mayer, 2003). Selection is often expressed in societal, cultural, and technological advancement of a developmental context. According to this, selection implies a historical and biographical dimension as well as the institutionalized pathways of development in a given culture or society. Meaning is derived from the norms, rules, or challenges of societies and environments. Examples are the available educational options, the diversity of social roles, the various career tracks, or technological and engineering advances. It is simply not possible to think of selection outside of societal opportunity structures. The provision of opportunities within the developmental context is a precondition of individual selection of goals and developmental tasks. Clearly, cultures differ with respect to the range and diversity of such institutionalized developmental opportunities provided for each individual in a society.

According to context-theoretical approaches, *optimization* refers not just to growth but also to amplification of resources and constraints (Heckhausen, 2002, 2003; Rohr & Lang, 2009). This implies that optimization involves the expansion or creation of contextual opportunities, for example, related to technological innovation that enhances and refines autonomy and quality of life. Similarly, educational institutions in most cultures provide optimizing contexts that serve to trigger, enhance and extend competence and knowledge, thus, securing and optimizing the intellectual wealth of the individual and the society. Other examples relate to hygiene rules in modern societies and to preventative health protection measures in most modern societies. Such normative constraints in given societies improve and enhance contextual life-span resources (e.g., health). Other illustrative examples of such context-related optimization relate to labor division in modern societies and to pluralism (cf. Mayer, 2003).

In such contextual thinking, the principle of *compensation* involves the restoration and repairing of person–environment misfit. According to this, activating additional internal resources occurs in response to increased demands in the environment, for example, following an actual, perceived, or anticipated loss or failure. In these cases, compensation constitutes a response to losses in response to contextual change. Often, environmental resources (e.g., social support, technical devices) involve compensatory functions, when loss or failure have occurred. Many contexts that serve to assist in compensating for loss or failure bear also developmental risks, when compensatory devices lead to extinction of behavioral functions (e.g., dependency) rather than to maintenance, recovery, or restoration of a prior behavior function.

One prominent empirical illustration pertains to research on the different facets of dependency in nursing homes. In an extensive research program, Margret Baltes and colleagues (Baltes, 1988, 1994, 1996; Baltes & Wahl, 1992, 1996) demonstrated that social interactions between staff and residents of nursing homes implied behavioral scripts that supported dependency rather than independency. Observational studies in nursing homes revealed that dependent behavior of residents was reinforced more positively whereas independent activities were often ignored. For example, when displaying dependent behaviors, the residents received more attention and had more positive social contact with staff. One implication is that adapting to the challenges of nursing home environments involved balancing the costs of increasing dependency against the benefits of receiving social contact and greater attention from nursing home staff. Experimental studies proved that training nursing home staff could change the behavioral patterns and cognitive scripts of staff, and thus, partly reverse such dependency-support scripts (Baltes, Neumann, & Zank, 1994).

Baltes (1994, 1996) suggested that balancing individual competence and weakness in nursing home settings reflect adaptive strategies to the demands and potentials of such environments—and is complemented by the institutional task of negotiating protection and overprotection. According to such considerations, SOC may also serve to improve person–environment fit in nursing home contexts (Volicer & Simard, 2006). Selection, in such contexts pertains to the transitional issues of choosing and entering into a nursing home. This also includes the matching of the resident's preferences and potentials with the opportunities of the respective nursing home. Optimization refers to the process of activation and the enhancement of competence. This typically implies also mutuality and stimulation of social contact in the nursing home environment. The principle of compensation, finally, pertains to the architecture and the caring facilities that serve to counteract those functional losses and mental impairments of residents that may have been responsible for moving into the institution (Baltes, 1988, 1994, 1996; Baltes & Carstensen, 1999).

Generalizing from such considerations to social environments, Baltes and Carstensen (1999) suggested that SOC principles apply to all types of collective social contexts, not only to individual adaptation. According to these considerations, the principles of SOC operate within social systems including the interactions among all agents within such systems. How do partners influence each other, enhance or hinder collectively the developmental outcome? How do persons make use of their respective social contexts to adapt to life tasks? Empirical illustrations come from studies on long-term marriages (Carstensen, Gottman, & Levenson, 1995), collaborative cognition (for a review, see Meegan & Berg, 2002), and studies related to the social context of nutrition and physical activity (Rohr & Lang, 2009). For example, Dixon and Gould (1998) have shown that older couples benefit from recalling a story in the presence of their long-term spouse. Based on their knowledge about the partners' daily (cognitive) performance they managed to complement each other more successfully than was the case in young couples. Baltes and Carstensen (1999) argued that the consideration of interactions can be viewed on the macro- (e.g., institutions), the meso- (e.g., family), and the microlevel (e.g., a couple) and span areas such as goal management or problem solution.

The societal dimension of the SOC principles was supported by a study examining proverbs (Freund & Baltes, 2002b). According to Freund and Baltes, proverbs contain culturally proliferated understanding about how to master daily life. The authors extracted proverbs that mirror SOC principles (e.g., selection: *you can't have your cake and eat it, too;* compensation: *those without a horse walk*) as well as a set of alternatives that where matched regarding criteria such as difficulty and prevalence. In two studies, younger and older adults were presented one proverb reflecting SOC principles and one reflecting alternative life management strategies. Participants indicated which of these proverbs best matched demands of a specific life situation. Findings suggested that proverbs related to the SOC principles were processed faster and were generally preferred at all ages. These findings serve to illustrate that adaptive knowledge related to SOC has accumulated over time and has become part of social norms and social environments in everyday life. This implies that SOC principles can also be found in the organization of modern societies and developmental contexts, which give direction to development (selection); generate, enhance, and provide resources (optimization); and provide service or rebuild resources in case of losses (compensation). Obviously, not much is known about how SOC principles apply to the structure and organization of human environments.

The role of the environment becomes also apparent in technological and engineering advances that provide new potentials for independent living, health, communication, and mobility in aging societies. For example, medical products like hearing aids, binoculars, or pacemakers foster health and even save lives; modern communication and information technologies such as navigational aids, computers, and the internet help to maintain social participation. However, especially from the perspective of users the adoption of modern products and services is linked with a number of costs such as training, personal efforts, or expenses. As a result of such observations, research has focused recently on issues related to improved accessibility, utility, and usability of assistive devices particularly in later adulthood (Charness & Schaie, 2003; Mynatt & Rogers, 2001). This also entails prototypical illustration of how contextual principles of SOC can be applied to improved person–environment fit as it pertains to the engineering of assistive technology in everyday living.

Lindenberger et al. (2008) argued that the demands of technical solutions (e.g., complexity, functional range, adaptability) will contribute to late life adaptation, when such solutions adequately account for age-related change and the enormous heterogeneity of older adults. Based on the principles of SOC, the authors formulate three psychological demands for the engineering of technological innovations. First, assistive technology typically demands the investment of resources, when using the product or service (e.g., training, use of time). Consequently, any assistive device in everyday life should set more resources free than are required or consumed in the process of using the innovative technology (i.e., net resource release). Second, assistive technology should be able to adaptively respond to the user's idiosyncrasy, behavior, and competence (person specificity). For example, when individuals change over time, technical assistance will have to adapt to such changing performance. Third, assistive technology should aim at achieving sustainable effects that imply a balance of risks and benefits of the innovative product or service. To counteract such risks, technical innovations need to be designed so that they support a balance between technical aid and self-initiated processing. For example, an assistive device that bears a risk that important capacities will not be used may also have to include tasks that counteract such disuse effects.

In a focus group study, Melenhorst, Rogers, and Bowhuis (2006) explored motivated choices for using technical innovation in old age. Older adults (aged 65–80 years) considered the use of new and traditional communication media (cell phone, email, telephone, mail, and visit) with respect to various everyday scenarios. Results suggest that older adults are mostly relying on expected benefits, when deciding to use or to not use a new device. Possible costs of use (or nonuse) are less often reflected in this decision process. Such findings are in accordance with predictions of the theory of socioemotional selectivity that emphasize the role of increased preference for positive emotion in later life (Carstensen, 2006).

The role of technical environments for successful life management is not restricted to later adulthood and might be extended to the whole life span. This becomes apparent when considering different kinds of technology that assist users in optimizing work tasks (e.g., a flight simulator) or in acquiring new skills such as a foreign language. Respective empirical results were obtained particularly in the field of computer-assisted learning. For example, O'Byrne, Securro, Jones, and Candle (2006) found that low achieving middle-school students were able to improve their learning efforts by using literacy software supporting their reading and writing abilities within the course of traditional classes. The mechanisms leading to such learning improvements are assumed to be twofold. First, an attractive interaction design (e.g., different media, practical activities) may enhance the learner's motivation. Second, there is a high degree of individualization resulting from the self-directed learning process.

Although the findings have an exploratory and preliminary character, they also point to the direction of potential future research. Considering the role of SOC especially in late life adaptation entails many implications for the engineering and design of age-appropriate technical products and services. Further research should also focus on how technological devices can contribute to the generation of SOC principles in everyday life.

▓ FUTURE DIRECTIONS IN LIFE-SPAN SUCCESS AND THE SOC MODEL

In this chapter, we have reviewed theoretical considerations and empirical evidence on the three principles of SOC with respect to positive or success-related outcomes in life. There is substantive and convincing evidence that the three principles are involved in a large set of positive developmental outcomes across adulthood, and that comprehension and knowledge about such principles contribute to adaptive competence and well-being from early to late adulthood.

The pursuit of goals is part of the evolved human nature. There is even a duality in human existence that seems to struggle between two broad classes of strivings in life, one is related to agency, efficacy, or primary control (Abele & Wiese, 2008; Heckhausen & Schulz, 1995; Lang & Heckhausen, 2001), and another may be related to the pursuit of meaning and communion in life (Bakan, 1966; Carstensen, 2006). The duality in the human mind appears quite fundamental to the understanding of success criteria. For example, Heckhausen and Schulz (1995) claimed in their life-span theory on control that primary control assumes primacy over self-regulatory processes of controlling action. This means, for example, that striving for self-congruence and self-consistency is seen as serving to protect the individual's potential for exerting control over the environment. One implication is that any pursuit of goals that does not serve to enhance the individual's control potentials may not lead to success or positive outcomes. In contrast to this, other theories on life-span success have emphasized the importance of maintaining a sense of meaning in life as a criterion of success (Baltes & Baltes, 1977, 1980, 1990). For example, as people grow old, aging losses may result in complete immobility, need of care, and dependency. Even in this situation, individuals continue to reach goals and experience success in life. With this line of reasoning, success may relate to a mental activity of maintaining meaning in life, even if there is no hope. Obviously, both perspectives on success in life are more complementary rather than contradictory. In the latter view, meaning may be one ultimate purpose in life, and in the former perspective, meaning may constitute the primary force of living. It is important to note, that success in life is not a privilege of one period of life. At all phases in life, there is a potential for success, in terms of meaning and of agency.

There are several open issues in the research on SOC. The first one is related to the relevance and validity of the SOC principles in childhood and early adolescence. Not much is known as to what extent the principles of SOC actually contribute to developmental success in the first decade of life. In this chapter, we reviewed the life-span principles of SOC and three theoretical specifications of these principles with respect to cognitive and intellectual adult development, life management across adulthood, and person–environment fit across adulthood.

It is an open question to what extent these theoretical specifications also apply to childhood. For example, the resource-allocation model of cognitive development may be useful in accounting for some of the ups and downs and progressions and declines in cognitive development as children acquire new skills in coordinating and integrating newly emerging intellectual capacities. In an action-theoretical perspective, the SOC principles may well be applied to improved understanding of how children develop self-regulatory competence in the delay of gratifications and the emergence of success and failures. Contextual specifications of the SOC model may focus on the person–environment transactions from early to late childhood, and how cultural constraints shape the development of specific skills and capacities from across childhood.

A second issue is related to the functionality of the SOC principles. Not much is known about when and how the principles of SOC may lead to dysfunctional or maladaptive outcomes. Future research should more systematically investigate the different conditions, in which selection, optimization, or compensation may not be related to positive outcomes or lead to premature loss, for example, with respect to overcompensation in caregiving contexts, nonselective optimization, and meaningless or premature selection processes.

A third future research issue relates to the organization, sequence, and coordination of the three principles in life-span development. We have suggested a tentative model of how the three principles may depend and interact with each other. However, this tentative model is based on theoretical considerations and awaits empirical investigation. We have presented three different theoretical specifications of the SOC model that are partly overlapping, but that also describe different facets of the SOC principles. In this context, a more precise and operational definition of the processes within the presented three theoretical specifications will be needed before testing the coordinative functions. Not much is known about how contextual changes affect the interplay of the three principles. Although a few longitudinal studies exist, the change of the SOC principles over time in response to changes in the availability, limitations, and efficiency of resources has not yet been systematically addressed.

All together, the life-span model of SOC makes a significant contribution to improved understanding of how individuals adapt and master developmental challenges in life, and how positive developmental outcomes are attained across adulthood. The three principles are known to be associated with general positive outcomes with regard to cognitive and intellectual ontogeny, life management, and improving person–environment over the life span.

■ REFERENCES

Abele, A. E., & Wiese, B. (2008). The nomological network of self-management strategies and career success. *Journal of Occupational and Organizational Psychology, 73,* 490–497.

Antonucci, T. C., & Akiyama, H. (1987). Social networks in adult life and a preliminary examination of the convoy model. *Journal of Gerontology, 42,* 519–527.

Bajor, J. K., & Baltes, B. B. (2003). The relationship between selection optimization with compensation, conscientiousness, motivation, and performance. *Journal of Vocational Behavior, 63,* 347–367.

Bakan, D. (1966). *The duality of human existence: An essay on psychology and religion.* Chicago, IL: Rand McNally.

Baltes, B. B., & Heydens-Gahir, H. A. (2003). Reduction of work-family conflict through the use of selection, optimization, and compensation behaviors. *Journal of Applied Psychology, 88,* 1005–1018.

Baltes, M. M. (1996). *The many faces of dependency in old age.* Cambridge: Cambridge University Press.

Baltes, M. M. (1994). Aging well and institutional living: A paradox? In R. P. Abeles, H. C. Gift, & M. G. Ory (Eds.), *Aging and quality of life* (pp. 185–201). New York: Springer.

Baltes, M. M. (1988). The etiology and maintenance of dependency in the elderly: Three phases of operant research. *Behavior Therapy, 19,* 301–319.

Baltes, M. M., & Baltes, P. B. (1977). The ecopsychological relativity and plasticity of psychological aging: Convergent perspectives of cohort effects and operant psychology. *Zeitschrift für experimentelle und angewandte Psychologie, 24,* 179–197.

Baltes, M. M., & Carstensen, L. L. (2003). The process of successful aging: Selection, optimization, and compensation. In U. M. Staudinger & U. Lindenberger (Eds.), *Understanding human development: Dialogues with lifespan psychology* (pp. 81–104). Dordrecht: Kluwer.

Baltes, M. M., & Carstensen, L. L. (1999). Social-psychological theories and their applications to aging: From individual to collective. In V. L. Bengtson & K. W. Schaie (Eds.), *Handbook of theories of aging* (pp. 209–226). New York: Springer.

Baltes, M. M., & Carstensen, L. L. (1996). The process of successful ageing. *Ageing and Society, 16,* 397–422.

Baltes, M. M., & Lang, F. R. (1997). Everyday functioning and successful aging: The impact of resources. *Psychology and Aging, 12,* 433–443.

Baltes, M. M., Neumann, E.-M., & Zank, S. (1994). Maintenance and rehabilitation of independence in old age: An intervention program for staff. *Psychology and Aging, 9,* 179–188.

Baltes, M. M., & Wahl, H.-W. (1996). Patterns of communication in old age: The dependence-support an independence-ignore Script. *Health Communication, 8,* 217–231.

Baltes, M. M., & Wahl, H.-W. (1992). The dependency-support script in institutions: Generalization to community settings. *Psychology and Aging, 7,* 409–418.

Baltes, P. B. (2003). On the incomplete architecture of human ontogeny: Selection, optimization, and compensation as foundation of developmental theory. In U. M. Staudinger & U. Lindenberger (Eds.), *Understanding human development: Dialogues with lifespan psychology* (pp. 17–43). Dordrecht: Kluwer Academic.

Baltes, P. B. (1997). On the incomplete architecture of human ontogeny: Selection, optimization, and compensation as foundation of developmental theory. *American Psychologist, 52,* 366–380.

Baltes, P. B. (1987). Theoretical propositions of life-span developmental psychology: On the dynamics between growth and decline. *Developmental Psychology, 23,* 611–626.

Baltes, P. B., & Baltes, M. M. (1996). *Selective Optimization with Compensation: Basic Definitions.* Max-Planck-Institute for Human Development and Free University of Berlin: Unpublished internal discussion paper, February 3, 1996, Draft 3.

Baltes, P. B., & Baltes, M. M. (1990). Psychological perspectives on successful aging: The model of selective optimization with compensation. In P. B. Baltes & M. M. Baltes (Eds.), *Successful aging: Perspectives from the behavioral sciences* (pp. 1–34). New York: Cambridge University Press.

Baltes, P. B., & Baltes, M. M. (1980). Plasticity and variability in psychological aging: Methodological and theoretical issues. In G. E. Gurski (Ed.), *Determining the effects of aging on the central nervous system* (pp. 41–66). Berlin: Schering.

Baltes, P. B., Baltes, M. M., Freund, A. M., & Lang, F. R. (1999). *The measurement of selection, optimization, and compensation (SOC) by self-report: Technical report.* Berlin: Max Planck Institute for Human Development.

Baltes, P. B., & Freund, A. M. (2003). Human strengths as the orchestration of wisdom and selective optimization with compensation (SOC). In L. G. Aspinwall & U. M. Staudinger (Eds.), *A psychology of human strengths: Fundamental questions and future directions for a positive psychology* (pp. 23–35). Washington, DC: APA Books.

Baltes, P. B., Lindenberger, U., & Staudinger, U. M. (2006). Lifespan theory in developmental psychology. In R. M. Lerner (Ed.), *Handbook of child psychology* (pp. 569–664). New York: Wiley.

Baltes, P. B., Staudinger, U. M., & Lindenberger, U. (1999). Lifespan psychology: Theory and application to intellectual functioning. *Annual Review of Psychology, 50,* 471–507.

Berger, P., & Luckmann, T. (1967). *The social construction of reality: A treatise in the sociology of knowledge.* Garden City, NY: Anchor Books.

Brandtstädter, J. (2002). Protective self-processes in later life: Maintaining and revising personal goals. In C. v. Hofsten & L. Bäckman (Eds.), *Psychology at the turn of the millenium. Vol. 2: Social, developmental, and clinical perspectives* (pp. 133–152). Hove, UK: Psychology Press.

Brown, L. A., Sleik, R. J., Polych, M. A., & Gage, W. H. (2002). Is the prioritization of postural control altered in conditions of postural threat in younger and older adults? *Journals of Gerontology, 57A*, M785–M792.

Brown, S. L., Smith, D. M., Schulz, R., Kabeto, M. U., Ubel, P. A., Poulin, M., et al. (2009). Caregiving behavior is associated with decreased mortality risk. *Psychological Science, 20*, 488–494.

Carstensen, L. L. (2006). The influence of a sense of time on human development. *Science, 312*, 1913–1915.

Carstensen, L. L., Fung, H. H., & Charles, S. (2003). Socioemotional selectivity theory and the regulation of emotion in the second half of life. *Motivation and Emotion, 27*, 103–123.

Carstensen, L. L., Gottman, J. M., & Levenson, R. W. (1995). Emotional behavior in long-term marriage. *Psychology and Aging, 10*, 140–149.

Charness, N., & Schaie, K. W. (Eds.) (2003). *Impact of technology on successful aging*. New York: Springer.

Crossley, M., & Hiscock, M. (1992). Age-related differences in concurrent-task performance of normal adults: evidence for a decline in processing resources. *Psychology and Aging, 7*, 499–506.

Dannefer, D. (1992). On the conceptualization of context in developmental discourse: Four meanings of context and their implications. In D. L. Featherman, R. M. Lerner, & M. Perlmutter (Eds.), *Life-span development and behavior* (Vol. 11, pp. 83–110). Hillsdale, NJ: Erlbaum.

Dixon, R., & Bäckman, L. (1995). Concepts of compensation: Integrated, differentiated, and janus-faced. In R. Dixon & L. Bäckman (Eds.), *Psychological compensation: Managing losses and promoting gains* (pp. 3–20). Hillsdale, NJ: Erlbaum.

Dixon, R. A., & Gould, O. N. (1998). Younger and older adults collaborating on retelling everyday stories. *Applied Developmental Science, 2*, 160–171.

Doumas, M., Rapp, M. A., & Krampe, R. T. (2009). Working memory and postural control: Adult-age differences in potential for improvement, task-priority and dual-tasking. *Journals of Gerontology, 64B*, P193–P201.

Ebner, N. C., Freund, A. M., & Baltes, P. B. (2006). Developmental changes in personal goal orientation from young to late adulthood: From striving for gains to maintenance and prevention of losses. *Psychology and Aging, 21*, 664–678.

Farran, C. J., Keane-Hagerty, E., Salloway, S., Kupferer, S., & Wilken, C. S. (1991). Finding meaning: An alternative paradigm for Alzheimer's disease family caregivers. *The Gerontologist, 31*, 483–489.

Fraser, S. A., Li, K. Z., DeMont, R. G., & Penhun, V. B. (2007). Effect of balance status and age on muscle activation while walking under divide attention. *Journals of Gerontology, 62B*, P171–P178.

Freund, A. M. (2008). Successful aging as management of resources: The role of selection, optimization, and compensation. *Research on Human Development, 5*, 94–106.

Freund, A. M. (2006). Age-differential motivational consequences of optimization versus compensation focus in younger and older adults. *Psychology and Aging, 21*, 240–252.

Freund, A. M., & Baltes, P. B. (2007). Toward a theory of successful aging: Selection, optimization, and compensation. In R. Fernández-Ballesteros (Ed.), *GeroPsychology. European perspectives for an aging world* (pp. 239–254). Göttingen: Hogrefe.

Freund, A. M., & Baltes, P. B. (2002a). Life-management strategies of selection, optimization, and compensation: Measurement by self-report and construct validity. *Journal of Personality and Social Psychology, 82*, 642–662.

Freund, A. M., & Baltes, P. B. (2002b). The adaptiveness of selection, optimization, and compensation as strategies of life management: Evidence from a preference study on proverbs. *Journals of Gerontology, 57B*, P426–P434.

Freund, A. M., & Baltes, P. B. (2000). The orchestration of selection, optimization, and compensation: An action-theoretical conceptualization of a theory of developmental regulation. In W. J. Perrig & A. Grob (Eds.), *Control of human behaviour, mental processes and consciousness* (pp. 35–58). Mahwah, NJ: Erlbaum.

Freund, A. M., Li, K. Z. H., & Baltes, P. B. (1999). The role of selection, optimization, and compensation in successful aging. In J. Brandtstädter & R. M. Lerner (Eds.), *Action and development: Origins and functions of intentional self-development* (pp. 401–434). Thousand Oaks, CA: Sage.

Freund, A. M., & Riediger, M. (2006). Goals as building blocks of personality and development in adulthood. In D. K. Mroczek & T. D. Little (Eds), *Handbook of personality development* (pp. 353–372). Mahwah, NJ: Lawrence Erlbaum Associates Publishers.

Heckhausen, J. (2003). The future of life-span developmental psychology: Perspectives from control theory. In: U. M. Staudinger & U. Lindenberger (Eds.), *Understanding human development: Lifespan psychology in exchange with other disciplines* (pp. 383–400). Dordrecht, NL: Kluwer.

Heckhausen, J. (2002). *Developmental regulation of life-course transitions: A control theory approach* (pp. 257–280). New York: Cambridge University Press.

Heckhausen, J., & Schulz, R. (1999). Selectivity in life-span development: Biological and societal canalizations and individuals' developmental goals. In J. Brandtstädter & R. Lerner (Eds.), *Action & self-development: Theory and research through the life-span* (pp. 67–103). Thousand Oaks, CA: Sage Publications.

Heckhausen, J., & Schulz, R. (1995). A life-span theory of control. *Psychological Review, 102,* 284–304.

Heckhausen, J., & Tomasik, M. J. (2002). Get an apprenticeship before school is out: How German adolescents adjust vocational aspirations when getting close to a developmental deadline. *Journal of Vocational Behavior, 60,* 199–219.

Huxhold, O., Li, S.-C., Schmiedek, F., & Lindenberger, U. (2006). Dual-tasking postural control: Aging and the effects of cognitive demand in conjunction with focus of attention. *Brain Research Bulletin, 69,* 294–305.

Kemper, S., Herman, R. E., & Lian, C. H. T. (2003). The costs of doing two things at once for young and older adults: Talking while walking, finger tapping, and ignoring speech or noise. *Psychology and Aging, 18,* 181–192.

Kinney, J. M., & Stephens, M. P. (1989). Hassles and uplifts of giving care to a family member with dementia. *Psychology and Aging, 4,* 402–408.

Kliegl, R., & Baltes, P. B. (1987). Theory-guided analysis of mechanisms of development and aging through testing-the-limits and research on expertise. In C. Schooler & K.-W. Schaie (Eds.), *Cognitive functioning and social structure over the life course* (pp. 95–119). Norwood, NJ: Ablex.

Kramer, B. J. (1997). Gain in the caregiving experience: Where are we? What next? *The Gerontologist, 37,* 218–232.

Krampe, R. T., & Baltes, P. B. (2003). Intelligence as adaptive resource development and resource allocation: A new look through the lens of SOC and expertise. In R. J. Sternberg & E. L. Grigorenko (Eds.), *Perspectives on the psychology of abilities, competencies, and expertise* (pp. 31–69). New York: Cambridge University Press.

Lajoie, Y., Teasdale, N., Bard, C., & Fleury, M. (1993). Attentional demands for static and dynamic equilibrium. *Experimental Brain Research, 97,* 139–144.

Lang, F. R. (2001). Regulation of social relationships in later adulthood. *Journals of Gerontology, 56B,* P321–P326.

Lang, F. R., & Baltes, M. M. (1997). Being with people and being alone in late life: Costs and benefits for everyday functioning. *International Journal of Behavioral Development, 21,* 729–746.

Lang, F. R., & Carstensen, L. L. (2002). Time counts: Future time perspective, goals, and social relationships. *Psychology and Aging, 17,* 125–139.

Lang, F. R., & Carstensen, L. L. (1994). Close emotional relationships in late life: Further support for proactive aging in the social domain. *Psychology and Aging, 9,* 315–324.

Lang, F. R., & Heckhausen, J. (2006). Developmental changes of motivation and interpersonal capacities across adulthood: Managing the challenges and constraints of social contexts. In C. Hoare (Ed.), *The Oxford handbook of adult development and learning* (pp. 149–166). Oxford: Oxford University Press.

Lang, F. R., & Heckhausen, J. (2001). Perceived control over development and subjective well-being: Differential benefits across adulthood. *Journal of Personality and Social Psychology, 81,* 509–523.

Lang, F. R., Rieckmann, N., & Baltes, M. M. (2002). Adapting to aging losses: Do resources facilitate strategies of selection, compensation, and optimization in everyday functioning? *Journals of Gerontology, 57B,* P501–P509.

Lawton, M. P. (1989). Behavior-relevant ecological factors. In K. Schaie & K. Schooler (Eds.), *Social structure and aging: Psychological processes* (pp. 57–78). Hillsdale, NJ: Lawrence Erlbaum.

Lawton, M. P., & Nahemow, L. (1973). Ecology and the aging process. In C. Eisdorfer & M. P. Lawton (Eds.), *Psychology of adult development and aging* (pp. 619–675). Washington, DC: APA.

Leipold, B., Schacke, C., & Zank, S. (2008). Personal growth and cognitive complexity in caregivers of patients with dementia. *European Journal of Ageing, 5,* 203–214.

Lerner, R. M., & Busch-Rossnagel, N. A. (1981). Individuals as producers of their development: Conceptual and empirical bases. In R. M. Lerner & N. A. Busch-Rossnagel (Eds.), *Individuals as producers of their development: A life-span perspective* (pp. 1–36). New York: Academic Press.

Li, K. Z. H., Krampe, R. T., & Bondar, A. (2005). An ecological approach to studying aging and dual-task performance. In R. W. Engle, G. Sedek, U. von Hecker, & D. N. McIntosh (Eds.), *Cognitive limitations in aging and psychopathology* (pp. 190–218). New York: Cambridge University Press.

Li, K. Z. H., Lindenberger, U., Freund, A. M., & Baltes, P. B. (2001). Walking while memorizing: Age-related differences in compensatory behavior. *Psychological Science, 12,* 230–237.

Lindenberger, U., & Baltes, P. B. (2000). Lifespan psychology theory. In A. E. Kazdin (Ed.), *Encyclopedia of Psychology* (Vol. 5, pp. 52–57). New York: Oxford University Press.

Lindenberger, U., Lövdén, M., Schellenbach, M., Li, S.-C., & Krüger, A. (2008). Psychological principles of successful aging technologies: A mini-review. *Gerontology, 54,* 59–68.

Lindenberger, U., Marsiske, M., & Baltes, P. B. (2000). Memorizing while walking: Increase in dual-task costs from young adulthood to old age. *Psychology and Aging, 15,* 417–436.

Lövdén, M., Schellenbach, M., Grossman-Hutter, B., Krüger, A., & Lindenberger, U. (2005). Environmental topography and postural control demands shape aging-associated decrements in spatial navigation performance. *Psychology and Aging, 20,* 683–694.

Marsiske, M., Lang, F. R., Baltes, P. B., & Baltes, M. M. (1995). Selective optimization with compensation: Life-span perspectives on successful human development. In R. Dixon & L. Bäckman (Eds.), *Psychological compensation: Managing losses and promoting gains* (pp. 35–79). Hillsdale, NJ: Erlbaum.

Mayer, K. U. (2003). The sociology of life course and lifespan psychology: Diverging or converging pathways? In U. M. Staudinger & U. Lindenberger (Eds.), *Understanding human development: Dialogues with lifespan psychology* (pp. 463–481). Dordrecht: Kluwer Academic Publishers.

Meegan, S. P., & Berg, C. A. (2002). Contexts, functions, forms, and processes of collaborative everyday problem solving in older adulthood. *International Journal of Behavioral Development, 26,* 6–15.

Melenhorst, A.-S., Rogers, W. A., & Bouwhuis, D. G. (2006). Older adults' motivated choice for technological innovation: Evidence for benefit-driven selectivity. *Psychology and Aging, 21,* 190–195.

Mischel, W., Shoda, Y., & Peake, P. K. (1988). The nature of adolescent competencies predicted by preschool delay of gratification. *Journal of Personality and Social Psychology, 54,* 687–696.

Mynatt, E. D., & Rogers, W. A. (2001). Developing technology to support functional independence of older adults. *Ageing International, 27,* 24–42.

O'Byrne, B., Securro, S., Jones, J., & Candle, C. (2006). Making the cut: The impact of an integrated learning system on low achieving middle school students. *Journal of Computer Assisted Learning, 22,* 218–228.

Oyserman, D., Coon, H. M., & Kemmelmeier, M. (2002). Rethinking individualism and collectivism: Evaluation of theoretical assumptions and meta-analyses. *Psychological Bulletin, 128,* 3–72.

Riediger, M., Freund, A. M., & Baltes, P. B. (2005). Managing life through personal goals: Intergoal facilitation and intensity of goal pursuit in younger and older adulthood. *Journals of Gerontology, 60B,* P84–P91.

Riediger, M., Li, S.-C., & Lindenberger, U. (2006). Selection, optimization, and compensation as developmental mechanisms of adaptive resource allocation: Review and preview. In J. E. Birren & K. W. Schaie (Eds.), *The handbooks of aging* (Vol. 2., pp. 289–313). Amsterdam: Elsevier.

Rohr, M. K., & Lang, F. R. (2009). Aging well together—a mini-review. *Gerontology, 55,* 333–343.

Salthouse, T. A. (1984). Effects of age and skill in typing. *Journal of Experimental Psychology, 13,* 345–371.

Salthouse, T. A., Rogan, J. D., & Prill, K. A. (1984). Division of attention: Age differences on a visually presented memory task. *Memory & Cognition, 12,* 613–620.

Schaefer, S., Krampe, R. T., Lindenberger, U., & Baltes, P. B. (2008). Age differences between children and young adults in the dynamics of dual-task-prioritization: Body (balance) versus mind (memory). *Developmental Psychology, 44,* 747–757.

Searle, J. (1979). *Expression and meaning.* Cambridge: Cambridge University Press.

Shoda, Y., Mischel, W., & Peake, P. K. (1990). Predicting adolescent cognitive and self-regulatory competencies from preschool delay of gratification: Identifying diagnostic conditions. *Developmental Psychology, 26,* 978–986.

Simmel, G. (2005/1897). Rosen. Eine soziale Hypothese [Roses. A social hypothesis]. In K. C. Köhnke, C. Jaenichen, & E. Schullerus (Eds.), *Georg Simmel. Anonyme und pseudonyme Veröffentlichungen 1888–1920* [Georg Simmel. Anonymous and pseudonymous publications 1888–1920]. Frankfurt a. M.: Suhrkamp (First published 1897 in: Jugend, 2, 390–392).

Smith, J. (2003). The gain-loss dynamic in lifespan development: Implications for change in self and personality during old and very old age. In U. M. Staudinger & U. Lindenberger (Eds.), *Understanding human development* (pp. 215–241). Boston: Kluwer Academic Publishers.

Somberg, B. L., & Salthouse, T. A. (1982). Divided attention abilities in young and old adults. *Journal of Experimental Psychology: Human Perception and Performance, 8,* 651–663.

Teasdale, N., Bard, C., Dadouchi, F., Fleury, M., LaRue, J., & Stelmach, G. E. (1992). Posture and elderly persons: Evidence for deficits in the central integrative mechanisms. *Advances in Psychology, 87,* 917–931.

Teasdale, N., Bard, C., LaRue, J., & Fleury, M. (1993). On the cognitive penetrability of postural control. *Experimental Aging Research, 19,* 1–13.

Volicer, L., & Simard, J. (2006). Application of SOC Model to care for residents with advanced dementia. In L. Hyer & R. C. Intrieri (Eds.), *Geropsychological interventions in long-term care* (pp. 207–218). New York: Springer Publishing Company.

Waddington, C. H. (1957). *The strategy of the genes.* London: Geo Allen & Unwin.

Wiese, B., Freund, A. M., & Baltes, P. B. (2002). Subjective career success and emotional well-being: Longitudinal predictive power of selection, optimization, and compensation. *Journal of Vocational Behavior, 60,* 321–335.

Wiese, B., Freund, A. M., & Baltes, P. B. (2000). Selection, optimization, and compensation: An action-related approach to work and partnership. *Journal of Vocational Behavior, 57,* 273–300.

Wrosch, C., Schulz, R., & Heckhausen, J. (2004). Health stresses and depressive symptomatology in the elderly: A control-process approach. *Current Directions in Psychological Science, 13,* 17–20.

Wrosch, C., Heckhausen, J., & Lachman, M. E. (2000). Primary and secondary control strategies for managing health and financial stress across adulthood. *Psychology and Aging, 15,* 387–399.

Young, L. M., Baltes, B. B., & Pratt, A. K. (2007). Using selection, optimization, and compensation to reduce job/family stressors: Effective when it matters. *Journal of Business and Psychology, 21,* 511–539.

CHILD–PARENT ATTACHMENT RELATIONSHIPS: A LIFE-SPAN PHENOMENON

4

German Posada and Ting Lu

Based on his research and clinical experience, Bowlby (1946, 1982) proposed that offspring–parent attachment relationships are a central phenomenon in the life of individuals and influence their development in important ways. He described these relationships as characteristic of humans and affirmed that they expand from the cradle to the grave. Their dyadic construction starts in infancy, continues during childhood and adolescence, and endures into adulthood when they continue to be transformed.

Systematic research on such relationships, their continuity, and changes across time is a relatively recent phenomenon. Based on Freud's insights about the relevance of the child–mother relationship, Bowlby (1982) and Ainsworth (1967) put together a theoretical framework that has promoted the study of those relationships. Although attachment as a life-span concept has been proposed by several researchers (e.g., Ainsworth, 1989; Antonucci, 1976; Bowlby, 1979, 1982; Cicirelli, 1983; Troll & Smith, 1976), most research on the topic has been conducted during the period of infancy. More recently, empirical studies on child–parent, mostly child–mother, attachment relationships during childhood and adolescence are increasingly being reported. Research on adult children relationships with their parents from the Bowlby–Ainsworth perspective, however, is practically nonexistent (Magai, 2008). To be sure, there exists an ever-growing amount of information about child–parent attachment relationships beyond infancy using an intraindividual perspective. Yet, substantive research work on actual child–parent exchanges and relational experiences at different points in time in the life of individuals remains to be conducted for attachment to fulfill its promise as a life-span developmental theory.

In this chapter, we briefly review Bowlby and Ainsworth's perspective by presenting key theoretical issues that helped them launch their framework to the forefront and that are relevant to the study of child–parent relationships across the life span. Then, we succinctly review Bowlby's normative developmental model and Ainsworth's work on individual differences, as their propositions constitute the foundations of most research on the issue. Subsequently, we consider research-based conclusions about attachment relationships at different periods of the life span.

We underline the importance of going beyond the view that construes attachment relationships mainly as a stress-reducing system. It is suggested that the attachment system is active in both ordinary and emergency circumstances (Posada et al., 1999; Waters & Cummings, 2000). That is, secure-base relationships are not exclusively or even mainly a relational system to deal with emergencies. Their function importantly touches on sharing daily, not infrequently, positive experiences between the child and the caregiver, as well as on the caregiver's organizing, planning, and supporting a child's (individual's) exchanges with the world. In doing so, we assert the usefulness of studying these relationships from the perspective of the secure-base phenomenon. We also highlight the need to address the study of attachment relationships across the life span using a dyadic perspective. Research on these relationships beyond childhood, during adolescence and adulthood, would benefit from an interactional focus where the context of the relationship is clearly considered and the potential continuities and transformations in dyadic exchanges are explicitly investigated.

▨ SOME KEY ASPECTS OF THE BOWLBY–AINSWORTH PERSPECTIVE

Bowlby was interested in personality development. As a clinician, he was keen to understand the factors that impede individual healthy functioning and, also, those that promote it. Based on his psychoanalytical training and clinical experiences, he realized that child–parent relationships played a key role in what individuals turn out to be. Uncharacteristically, for a psychoanalyst of his day, Bowlby had an inclination to gather and use empirical information to build, test, and contrast his theoretical perspective with that of others. Central characteristics of his theory include the (1) use of observations of children's reactions to separation and loss of attachment figures, (2) role attributed to real-life experiences in the development of attachment, (3) interactional lens employed to explain the formation and maintenance of attachment relationships, and (4) use of the secure-base construct.

Emotional Reaction to Separation and Loss

A point of departure for Bowlby's theory building was a series of observations about children's reaction to separation from, and loss of, important caregiving figures, and the effects that such experiences seemed to have on personality development (Bowlby, Robertson, & Rosenbluth, 1952). Those observations nicely illustrated in Robertson's (1952) film, "A Two-Year-Old Goes to Hospital," pushed Bowlby to search for an explanation to such an emotional response. Why do young children go through the phases of protest, despair, and detachment from parents, if separation is long enough? The answer he provided, namely, the existence of an emotional bond he termed attachment and the rationale elaborated (Bowlby, 1958) offered the basis for his new theoretical perspective, and Ainsworth's innovative studies in Uganda and Baltimore. Further empirical research demonstrated that adults go through a similar emotional reaction when facing the loss of an attachment figure (e.g., Bowlby, 1980; Carr, House, Wortman, Nesse, & Kessler, 2001; Parkes, 1972; Umberson, 2003). This similarity in the response to loss suggests that attachment bonds remain a salient and significant phenomenon throughout an individual's life.

Real-Life Experiences

A central feature of Bowlby's theorizing is the role he attributed to real-life experiences in relationships. On one hand, Bowlby addressed the general tendency to underestimate the richness of mental life during infancy and helped, as other object relations theorists did, recognize the mother and/or other primary caregivers as important players in psychological development. On the other hand, he too was a practicing child psychiatrist who saw children in real families facing separations, suffering losses, and interacting with parents who often experienced real problems of their own. In the context of his clinical work and with the aid of his clinical colleagues (e.g., Lowden and Fairbairn), Bowlby grasped the links that exist between parenting difficulties and both their own experiences of being parented and children's outcomes.

Bowlby agreed that trauma matters and that a child's conceptualization and perspective are as important as objective events are. But based on his experience with children and their families, he disagreed with the idea that most traumatic events are the product of intrapsychic conflict and of fantasy. Bowlby sustained that everyday experiences that are objectively not traumatic can create significant difficulties for children, if they threaten access to attachment figures on a regular basis. Those experiences include significant but routine separations from attachment figures, rejecting behavior from such figures, and threats or implications of abandonment (Bowlby, 1988). According to Bowlby, these experiences are more significant than clinicians appreciated and surprisingly not at all uncommon. Real-life experiences, he considered, are vital sources to understand developmental and personality disorders (Bowlby, 1988), as well as healthy psychological development (Bowlby, 1973). Furthermore, relationship experience provides the raw materials for children's mental representations of attachment relationships, and for the maintenance and change of such representations.

An Interactional Perspective

It is in the context of interactions that infants develop preference for, organize their behavior around, and become attached to their principal caregivers. Attachment relationships are formed through everyday exchanges. Interaction is a central process in attachment relationships construction, maintenance, and elaboration. Much of our understanding of attachment development is built upon Bowlby's insight that attachment behavior and representations depend very much on the cumulative effects of ordinary variations in actual care and family exchanges. The latter typically continue into adolescence and adulthood, although they undergo deep transformations. It is very likely that interaction continues to be key in the maintenance of attachment relationships throughout life.

Bowlby explicitly considered the role played by both offspring and caregiver, in influencing the transactions that occur between them. In addition to his emphasis on infants' learning biases and a propensity to become attached to one or a few primary care figures, as well as the role of an individual's internal working models, Bowlby also highlighted the importance of caregiving behavior complementary to that of the offspring and organized as a caregiving behavioral system. Those infants' biases, he proposed (1982), require an "ordinary expectable caregiving environment" to coalesce into a lasting emotional bond and a working secure-base relationship with a primary caregiver. Bowlby suggested that attachment develops through an extended period of interactions with a caregiver whose behavior provides considerable information about how the attachment secure-base game works. Indeed, subsequent observations of child–caregiver interactions suggest that both members of the dyad are active participants in the formation, continuity, and elaboration of attachment relationships (Ainsworth, 1967; Ainsworth, Blehar, Waters, & Wall, 1978; Pederson & Moran, 1995, 1996; Posada, Carbonell, Alzate, & Plata, 2004).

The Secure-Base Phenomenon

The secure-base phenomenon refers to the apparent purposeful balance between exploring away from an attachment figure and going back to her or him. In describing infant–mother interactions in rural Uganda, Ainsworth (1967) found that infants make little excursions away from their mother exploring their environment; when away from her, they either check by looking back or calling and maintain their exploratory activity, or initiate their return to her. Thus, Ainsworth coined the secure-base construct to capture an infant's behavioral organization during exchanges with his mother and surroundings. Bowlby (1988) placed the secure-base phenomenon at the center of his analysis of the child–parent relationship and hypothesized that trust in a caregiver's availability and response allows children to go out into their world and master it confident that if needed or wanted, they could be back together in close proximity. Indeed, the secure-base phenomenon has been found to be characteristic of human infants when interacting with their mother soon after an infant becomes capable of locomotion, toward the end of the first year (Posada et al., 1995), and during early childhood (Carbonell & Posada, 2009; Posada et al., 1999; Posada, Kaloustian, Richmond, & Moreno, 2007; Symons, Clark, Isaksen, & Marshall, 1998). Although this construct has been useful to describe child–mother interactions during the first years, it should not be limited to that period of time or to that attachment figure. It holds great potential to investigate actual dyadic exchanges, describe transformations in attachment relationships, and facilitate the task of operationalizing the behavioral transactions that occur between members of the dyad during middle childhood, adolescence, and early and later adulthood.

It is important to note here that although returning to an attachment figure has been typically studied in the context of emergency situations and described as going back to a haven of safety when the child is ill, fatigued, or frightened, observations of infants and children indicate that such returns do not exclusively occur under those circumstances. Infants and children go back to attachment figures under ordinary circumstances and for different reasons such as to play near them or with them, show them objects (e.g., toys), or recruit their help in accomplishing or obtaining something they want (Posada et al., 2002). In turn, attachment figures call their children back, check with them, and enjoy joining them in play or in accomplishing tasks in which they are involved, or for affectional exchanges. Going back to an attachment figure in emergency situations is only one, albeit important, reason. Attached individuals enjoy close interactions with their attachment figures in ordinary circumstances (Posada et al., 1999). Those exchanges provide children not only with information about their attachment figures' availability and interactive characteristics but also with a context for other developmental tasks to be accomplished such as mastering their surroundings or learning interactional skills that children can use with their attachment figures and with others in different arenas. Such a context will likely have an impact on achieving other socialization outcomes in which parents are interested, for example, acquisition of norms and rules of good behavior, behavioral and emotional regulation, and the ability to consider others' perspective.

INFANCY

All infants develop an attachment bond to their main caregivers. Yet, this bond does not appear at once and ready-made. It takes time to be constructed and elaborated. Bowlby (1982) proposed that babies go through different phases in the development of attachment during infancy: Orientation and signals with limited discrimination of figure; orientation and signals toward one (or more) discriminated figure(s); and maintenance of proximity to a discriminated figure by means of locomotion as well as signals.

Although from the first days infants show discrimination of their mother's voice and scent, they do not demonstrate a clear preference for any particular caregiver. Based on their behavioral output, it cannot be said that infants are attached to their caregivers (Bowlby, 1982). During the first 2 months or so, infants tend to respond similarly to any individual who interacts with them; anyone responding to their signals and needs would be as effective. In the course of everyday exchanges, infants experience patterns of interaction and care from those looking after him, usually, but not necessarily, the infant's biological parents. These repeated experiences allow children to learn the perceptual and behavioral features of their caregivers and to discriminate them from other individuals. Repeated exposure to patterns of care leads to familiarity with those figures and their interaction routines. Familiarity leads to preference (Waters, Kondo-Ikemura, Posada, & Richters, 1991). The infant continues to be friendly and open, but now distinguishes her or his caregivers from others and responds differently to them. Thus, differential smiling and differential crying toward main caregivers (e.g., infant cries when held by someone other than mother, and stops crying when mother holds him) have been reported as early as 9–10 weeks of age (Ainsworth, 1967).

During these first months, experience—that is, practice—is likely to establish the secure-base game foundations: The baby signals, mother comes close (if not already close) and joins the child in interaction either cooperating with her or his behavior and vocalizations and extending them, or easing the discomfort the infant is experiencing, if necessary. The caregiver expands the child's activities in time and space, and/or restructures the child's behavior and context in ways that the infant is comfortable and/or can re-engage his surroundings. These experiences are likely to provide the behavioral and cognitive substrates for the rapid appearance of the secure-base phenomenon soon after the child develops locomotion.

After locomotion arises, at about 7 months, infants' way of participating becomes more complex; behavior is organized in a goal-oriented manner. Not only do infants orient toward and signal their main caregiver(s) but also they are active in approaching and maintaining proximity by crawling and/or walking. Now they have new means. Their motor behavior is increasingly more integrated and efficient and thus they can use it to achieve their goals for proximity and contact, when the situation requires it (e.g., during play, exploration of a new place, shying away from a visitor coming close, or from a loud noise). Attachment figures are clearly preferred and strangers are treated with caution. The foundations of the secure-base phenomenon are in place and readily observable by 1 year of age in most children from different socioeconomic and cultural contexts (Posada et al., 1995). This, however, does not imply that its development is complete. Although established, it needs to be consolidated and expanded as implementation alternatives are concerned. This important issue, namely, the development of the secure-base phenomenon after the first year has been ignored in research. In brief, the process of attachment development thus far can be succinctly stated as going from interaction to familiarity and preference and to attachment.

Differences in Attachment Relationships

Ainsworth's empirical work is typically tied to the study of dyadic differences in child–parent attachment relationships (Ainsworth, 1967; Ainsworth, Bell, & Stayton, 1971, 1974; Ainsworth & Wittig, 1969; Ainsworth et al., 1978). Her landmark studies in Uganda and Baltimore provide the foundations for most, if not all, subsequent research on the issue (Dixon, 2003). Of course, modifications have been introduced and, yet, a careful read of the literature reveals an inevitable connection to Ainsworth's suggested patterns of attachment organization, if not to her in-depth approach to studying them.

Ainsworth's contributions from her observational studies in Uganda and Baltimore, however, went beyond providing the foundations for research on individual differences and included among others: (1) implementing Bowlby's emphasis on naturalistic observation and empirically accessible constructs; (2) coining the secure-base phenomenon construct to support Bowlby's conceptualization of the child's tie to her or his mother; (3) construing infants' differences in the implementation of the secure-base phenomenon in terms of an insecurity–security dimension; (4) identifying specific patterns of maternal behavior that are associated with individual differences in the infant's ability to use mother as a secure base; (5) coining the sensitivity construct to characterize quality of care; and (6) documenting longitudinally the impact of patterns of maternal care on infants' organization of their secure-base behavior during the first year of life.

Because virtually all infants become attached to their main caregivers, Ainsworth looked at behavior organization associated with different attachment security outcomes. She classified babies into three major groups based on the configuration or patterning of behavior exhibited in the strange situation procedure (Ainsworth et al., 1978). She construed the differences among the groups in terms of security when using mother as a secure base. Two of these groups, avoidant (A) and ambivalent/resistant (C) are considered as consisting of anxiously or insecurely attached infants; the other group, secure (B), consists of securely attached infants.

Specifically, secure infants are able to use their mother as a secure base for exploration in the novel room (Ainsworth et al., 1978). If distressed during separation, they seek proximity and contact with mother during reunion, and contact is effective in promptly reducing stress. If not openly distressed by separation, infants respond to mother with active greeting and interaction during reunion episodes. There is little or no tendency to avoid or to resist and be angry with mother upon reunion. As just mentioned, infants may or may not be distressed during the separation episodes, but when they are, it is clear that they want their mother, even though they may be somewhat consoled by the stranger. Although secure infants tend to affiliate with the stranger in mother's presence, they are clearly more interested in contact and interaction with their mother than with the stranger.

Avoidant infants exhibit little affective sharing with mother and they readily separate to explore toys (Ainsworth et al., 1978). They treat the stranger much as they treat their mothers, and affiliate with the stranger in mother's absence; they show little preference for mother. "A" infants show active avoidance of proximity to, contact, and interaction with mother in reunion episodes. They look, turn, or move away and ignore their mother when she returns. Alternatively, they greet her casually. If there is approach, these infants mix their welcoming with avoidance. If mom picks them up, there is little or no tendency to cling or resist being put down. During separation episodes, avoidant babies are typically not distressed; but if there is distress, it seems to be due to having been left alone for it tends to be alleviated when the stranger returns; there is little or no stranger avoidance.

Resistant babies exhibit poverty of exploration even in preseparation episodes; they seem wary of novel situations and of the stranger (Ainsworth et al., 1978). These infants are likely to be very distressed upon separation and are not easily calmed by the stranger. Upon reunion, babies in group C are not easily calmed by mother's return. They may show proximity seeking and contact mixed with resistance (hitting, squirming, or rejecting toys); alternatively, they may continue to cry and fuss, and show extreme passivity. Babies in this group show no or little tendency to ignore their mother during the reunion episodes. They have also been labeled anxious-ambivalent because upon reunion C infants are likely to seek proximity and contact, but these are not effective in calming them down as shown by their resistance and inability to be soothed. Ainsworth considered that these infants may show general maladaptive behavior in the strange situation, because they tend to be angrier than infants in the other groups.

Main and Solomon (1986, 1990) proposed a fourth classification group "D." Infants in this group often cannot maintain a clear and coherent strategy in their attachment behavior. Because of this, infants in this group are labeled "disorganized/disoriented" and considered to be anxiously attached. This classification is assigned in addition to an alternate best-fitting category of A, B, or C. Infants classified into this group exhibit patterns of behavior that lack a readily observable goal, purpose, or explanation. The most characteristic theme in the list of behaviors is that of disorganization or an observed contradiction in movement pattern. A lack of orientation to the immediate environment is also characteristic of these children.

The validity of the strange situation classification system rests on the demonstration of the association between patterns in the organization of secure-base behavior at home and in the lab (Ainsworth et al., 1978). The significant relation between infants' organization of behavior both at home and in the strange situation is what determines the relevance of the classification system described. Importantly, it is the patterning of behavior, not discrete behaviors, that was found significantly associated in both contexts. For example, in the case of crying, while securely attached infants were found to cry the least at home, they may or may not have cried in the strange situation. By the same token, anxiously attached babies who cried the least (avoidant) or a lot (resistant) in the strange situation were the infants who cried the most at home during both the first and fourth quarter of their first year, and were not distinguishable from each other. Thus, Ainsworth assigned meaning to an infant's behavior in the strange situation based on her findings about different *patterns* of interaction she had observed at home (Ainsworth & Marvin, 1995).

Quality of Care and Differences in Attachment Security

In studying the organization of children secure-base behavior during interactions with their mother, Ainsworth also gathered information about maternal behavior that led her to formulate the hypothesis that the quality of care is important when studying individual differences in infants' attachment security. Findings from her Baltimore study indicated that many aspects of caregiving behavior were significantly related to infant's quality of attachment at 12 months. She collected detailed information on specific classes of maternal behavior such as responsiveness to infant crying, behavior relevant to separation and reunion, close bodily contact, face-to-face interactions, feeding, and behavior relevant to child obedience (e.g., frequency of physical interventions). In addition, she rated mothers on four broader categories of behavior derived from her observations: sensitivity to signals, cooperation with ongoing behavior, acceptance of the child's needs, and accessibility. Each of these categories was found to be highly and significantly related to attachment security in the strange situation.

Those four domains have provided a valuable framework for research on this issue and served as the theoretical foundation for empirical studies investigating the factors that account for individual differences in infants' organization of secure-base behavior. Overall, results indicate that ratings of sensitivity are significantly, if modestly (.24), related to attachment security in middle class samples (see De Wolff & van IJzendoorn, 1997, for a meta-analysis).[1] These findings are noteworthy considering that most studies, subsequent to Ainsworth's, have drastically reduced the window of observation time and situations, and thus, perhaps, the representativeness of the phenomena being observed. Specifically, maternal behavior is observed and scored in contrived situations, once, and for periods usually lasting less than an hour. Low or modest correlations sometimes reflect measurement issues rather than weak effects. Ainsworth's many hours of naturalistic observations throughout the first year afforded a broad sample and a comprehensive evaluation of maternal and child behavior rarely seen in subsequent research. Indeed, the results of more recent studies (Pederson & Moran 1995, 1996; Posada et al., 1999, 2004) that involved observations and measurement strategies more akin to Ainsworth's[2] have yielded comparable results (i.e., correlation coefficients between .40 and .61). Clearly, the issue of effect size in research on maternal care and infant security requires further study with special attention to construct definitions, observational strategies, sampling of behavior, and measurement issues. In the meantime, even small correlations should not be dismissed out of hand in contexts where they can be projected through large numbers of events or interactions to produce important effects.

---

[1] Bowlby postulated that the specific quality of an attachment relationship (i.e., secure or insecure) depends on the particular interaction experiences within a given child–mother dyad. Findings that show different rates of secure and insecure attachment in samples from different socioeconomic and cultural contexts (e.g., Grossmann, Grossmann, Spangler, Suess, & Unzer, 1985; Mikaye, Chen, & Campos, 1985; Valenzuela, 1990, 1997; van IJzendoorn & Kroonenberg, 1988; Vaughn, Egeland, Sroufe, & Waters, 1979), are not inconsistent with the Bowlby–Ainsworth perspective. In fact, if they reflect underlying differences in patterns of early care, they would be an important confirmation of their hypothesis. The key issue is whether the link between early care and infant security (not the proportion of secure versus insecure attachments, or distribution of attachment classifications) is consistent across context and culture.

[2] These new studies have also addressed the criticism of Ainsworth's assessment of maternal sensitivity as mainly consisting of a subjective clinical judgment, by using the maternal behavior Q-sort (Pederson & Moran, 1995) to operationalize and (more) objectively describe and assess maternal sensitivity.

Attachment in Ordinary and Emergency Situations: A Note

Ainsworth's studied the formation of infant–mother attachment bonds in everyday circumstances. She conducted her observations in the home, as infant–mother inter-actions occurred in ordinary situations. Her strange situation offered researchers a window to look into the quality of the infant–mother relationship. The procedure has provided a convenient and economical shortcut that saves hours of observations and logistical complications imposed by long observations of infant–mother inter-actions at home. Yet, because the strange situation places the infant–mother dyad in a mildly stressing situation and because the great majority of research with infants uses this procedure, there is the risk that attachment, or more specifically the attach-ment behavioral system, be construed as a system to deal mainly with emotionally upsetting and emergency situations.

Far from this, we need to keep in mind that although we can indeed see the oper-ation of the attachment behavioral system under such circumstances, this is just half the story. Ainsworth et al. (1978), Pederson and Moran (1995, 1996), and Posada and colleagues (1999, 2002) have illustrated that infant–mother interactions during ordi-nary daily circumstances play a central role in the construction of relationship qual-ity. Thus, for example, well-resolved smooth interactions, maternal initiatives that are enticing to the infant, appropriate physical contact, allowing the child to influ-ence the pace and content of interactions, and consistently responding to the child's initiatives, among others, are key in the formation of attachment relationships that are deemed secure. Infants go back to mother and interact with her because they are frightened, ill, or tired. Also, they go back and look for interactions with their moth-ers because those exchanges are typically the source of pleasant moments that are satisfactory to them (and their mothers) and because caregivers help them negotiate their transactions with their surroundings making those transactions more enjoy-able or easier to navigate.

▪ EARLY CHILDHOOD

Bowlby's last proposed phase in the development of attachment is concerned with the formation of a goal-corrected partnership. By continuously participating in inter-actions with mother and by observing maternal behavior and the factors that influ-ence it, the child begins to conceive of the mother as an individual with her own set of goals and plans to achieve them. Thus, according to Bowlby (1982), at around a child's third year, a partnership begins where the child will increasingly modify his or her behavior and expectations based on those of the attachment figure. Bowlby proposed this phase to acknowledge an increasing sophistication on the child's part when participating in interactions, and recognize changes in the child–mother rela-tionship; changes that index the beginning of a more complex one. He, however, did not elaborate as much about this phase.

The research basis of child–mother attachment relationships during child-hood is not as abundant as that of infancy. There are few observational studies in naturalistic contexts during early childhood (e.g., Posada, Kaloustian, Richmond, et al., 2007; Symons et al., 1998; Vereijken, Riksen-Walraven, & Kondo-Ikemura, 1997). Initially, existing reports built on Ainsworth's individual differences work in infancy by using the taxonomy she proposed and elaborating it to account for developmental transformations in the preschool years. This involved the use of the strange situation procedure and modification of the classification criteria (e.g., Aber & Baker, 1990; Cassidy & Marvin, 1992; Crittenden & Claussen, 2000; Cummings, 1990; Schneider-Rosen, 1990). Studies using new classification systems have typically investigated the associations between individual differences in security and other developmental outcomes (e.g., Campbell et al., 2004; Humber & Moss, 2005; Moss, Bureau, Cyr, Mongeau, & St-Laurent, 2004). Yet, caution is necessary regarding the use of the strange situation at ages for which it was not intended. Cassidy and Marvin (1992) have warned about the importance of studies in which new classification systems are validated against the organization of attachment behavior in real-life settings as Ainsworth did for the procedure during infancy. To underscore the issue, in one such study no significant associations were found for a new coding system to classify preschoolers in the strange situation and secure-base behavior organization at home (Posada, 2006).

Attachment researchers hypothesize that maternal caregiving continues to be a central factor in shaping and maintaining, or changing, the organization of secure-base behavior throughout childhood (e.g., Ainsworth et al., 1974; Bowlby, 1988, 1991; Marvin & Britner, 1999; Posada, Kaloustian, Richmond, et al., 2007; Thompson, 2000; Waters & Cummings, 2000; Waters et al., 1991). Surprisingly, the topic remains relatively unexplored (see George & Solomon, 1989, 2008). It is important to demonstrate the hypothesized association between quality of caregiving and children's security in early childhood to substantiate claims from the theory about the significance of caregivers' concurrent and continuous support (Pianta, Sroufe, & Egeland, 1989; Sroufe, 1979, 1988; Thompson, 2000; Waters et al., 1991). Also, this could help dispel claims about attachment as a theory that gives undue weight to early experience during infancy in determining later attachment outcomes (Breur, 1999; Lewis, 1997). Although experiences during infancy are important and influential in development (Bowlby, 1982; Sroufe, 2002; Sroufe, Egeland, & Kreutzer, 1990; Vereijken et al., 1997), they do not by themselves determine later outcomes (Hamilton, 2000; Waters, Merrick, Treboux, Crowell & Albersheim, 2000; Weinfield, Sroufe, & Egeland, 2000). Ultimately, the study of relations between quality of care and attachment security during childhood and beyond will help build a developmental framework to understand relationships.

Existing research findings do suggest that concurrent sensitive caregiving is an important influence on children's attachment security during early childhood. Thus, maternal interactive behavior observed during relatively short structured intervals (i.e., less than 60 minutes) at home and in laboratory settings (Achermann, Dinneen, & Stevenson-Hinde, 1991; Barnett, Kidwell, & Leung, 1998; Stevenson-Hinde & Shouldice, 1995; Teti & Gelfand, 1997; Teti, Nakagawa, Das Eiden, & Wirth, 1991; Teti, Sakin, Kucera, Corns, & Das Eiden, 1996) has been found to be associated with children's organization of attachment behavior in the expected direction.

Although more scarce, evidence for the concurrent association between quality of maternal care and attachment security with both constructs assessed during long intervals and in ordinary circumstances in naturalistic settings indicates that maternal sensitivity continues to be an important influence on children's security. Thus, Vereijken et al. (1997) reported that sensitivity and security were significantly associated at 14 and 24 months of age. Moreover, the 24-month assessment of sensitivity continued to exert an influence on security at 24 months of age, after controlling for the 14-month sensitivity assessment. Thus, although participation in secure-base relationships early in infancy appears to influence later outcomes, concurrent caregiving input may be equally important for security during the second year. Significant associations between caregiving and attachment security were also obtained in a naturalistic observational study conducted in Colombia for children between 36 and 60 months of age (Posada et al., 1999). Further, in two studies of child–mother interactions with 3- to 5-year olds that involved relatively long observation periods (4–5.5 hours) in naturalistic settings, Posada, Kaloustian, Richmond, et al. (2007) provided evidence on the associations between descriptions of overall quality of maternal care as well as specific domains of maternal care, and preschoolers' organization of secure-base behavior. They found that the quality of secure-base relationships during the preschool years is significantly associated with maternal behavior in interactions that are described as harmonious and cooperative with that of the child and that help create a partnership climate in which the child's activities, signals, and needs are responded to appropriately.

Moreover, because preschoolers are increasingly proficient in exploring their environment and learning from their transactions with it, more physically able, and more cognitively and linguistically sophisticated and capable of participating in give-and-take exchanges with their caregivers and others, changes in caregiving behavior at this age are expected (Ainsworth et al., 1974; George & Solomon, 2008; Sroufe, 1979, 1988; Thompson, 1997, 2000; Waters & Cummings, 2000; Waters et al., 1991). Posada, Kaloustian, Richmond, et al. (2007) investigated age-salient domains of maternal behavior that have been proposed to be important in the relation between caregiving and security outcomes during early childhood. Specifically, those authors studied domains concerned with maternal provision of secure-base base support, supervision, and limit setting. Findings reported provide empirical evidence for significant associations with attachment security.

This set of results suggests that providing appropriate secure-base support for children's explorations from, and retreats to, their mother is important to the consolidation of secure-base behavior during childhood. Further, offering secure-base support is not limited to providing a haven of safety; it also encourages and aids children in their explorations away from mother by enhancing and optimizing their exchanges with their surroundings. Here, again, children were observed going back to their mothers during ordinary circumstances and in situations where no emergency occurred. Preschoolers enjoyed interacting with their mothers, using her assistance, and sharing affective expressions during play. Supervision or monitoring of preschoolers is also suggested as a central domain in mothers' ability to behave as a secure base at this age. At 3–5 years, the child–mother relationship becomes more diverse in part due to children's increased mobility, dexterity, and interest in exploring their environment. To be able to keep track of a child, anticipate problematic situations, intervene when necessary, and enhance a child's experiences, caregivers need to appropriately supervise and monitor their children's whereabouts and activities over longer distances and time intervals. Finally, an important issue in child–mother relationships during the preschool years is concerned with the pro-vision of limits and boundaries around a child's activities (Ainsworth et al., 1974). Results of one of the studies indicated that when mothers set limits and boundar-ies in the context of interactions that respond to the needs of both members of the dyad, children are likely to be confident in their mothers' availability and response (Posada, Kaloustian, Richmond, et al., 2007).

Secure-Base Representations

Secure-base relationships expand from mainly a sensory-motor to a represen-tational form of operation during early childhood. Bowlby (1973) suggested that representational models of relationships are central to personality development because they play a key role in the process through which early infant–parent rela-tionships affect the child's subsequent relations and later child functioning more generally (Cassidy, Kirsh, Scolton, & Parke, 1996). Internal working models during early childhood are presumed to serve as bases that organize early relationship knowledge with primary caregivers and eventually lead to specific and gener-alized information about self, others, and relationships. Since internal working models are believed to integrate and (to some extent) reflect experienced interac-tion patterns between the attached individual and her or his attachment figures(s), the developing working models of self and of attachment figure(s) are complemen-tary. Working models are used to select and shape behavioral and interactional patterns, and guide the active processing of incoming interpersonal information (Bowlby, 1982; Bretherton, 1990, 2005; Bretherton & Munholland, 2008; Bretherton, Ridgeway, & Cassidy, 1990; Cicchetti, Cummings, Greenberg, & Marvin, 1990; Crowell et al., 1996; Fonagy, Steele, & Steele, 1991; George & Solomon, 2008; Ladd, Le Sieur, & Profilet, 1993; Miljkovitch, Pierrehumbert, Bretherton, & Halfon, 2004; Sroufe & Fleeson, 1986).

During infancy, a caregiver's input is essential in building the foundations of infants' attachment-related information and influencing secure-base organization at the behavioral level. For preschoolers, caregiver input is also expected to influence behavior organization as well as the way children structure and represent attach-ment information mentally and verbally. It is through daily occurring transactions with their attachment figures that children construct increasingly complex internal working models of the world and of significant caregivers (Bowlby, 1982, 1973, 1988). Yet, the co-construction process of representation models has barely been studied (e.g., Dubois-Comtois, Cyr, Moss, & St-Laurent, 2008). Further, research on the rela-tions between children's secure-base behavior and their incipient secure-base mental representations is scant. Reports by Bretherton et al. (1990) and Waters, Rodrigues, and Ridgeway (1998) indicate that the two are significantly associated. More recently, Posada and colleagues (Kaloustian & Posada, 2009; Posada, Kaloustian, & Barrig, 2007) corroborated the link between the two. Not much more is known, and we urgently need information on the issue since the study of the development of pre-schoolers' attachment-related representations and their dyadic co-construction is central to our understanding of secure-base relationship expansion from a sensory-motor to a representational modus operandi.

A relatively recent advance concerned with conceptual and methodological innovations (Bretherton et al., 1990; Guttman-Steinmetz, Elliot, Steiner, & Waters,

2003; Waters, Cunliffe, Guttmann-Steinmetz, 2001; Waters et al., 1998) that integrate cognitive psychology (e.g., scripts) and attachment-related concepts (e.g., the
secure-base phenomenon) has made assessments of the organization (not content)
of secure-base information accessible. Based on Bretherton's work (e.g., Bretherton
et al., 1990), Harriet Waters and associates (e.g., Guttman-Steinmetz et al., 2003;
Waters & Rodrigues, 2001; Waters et al., 1998; Waters & Waters, 2006) suggest that
attachment representations could be understood as scripts about secure-base relationships. Using the secure-base phenomenon concept, Waters and colleagues rated
children's narrative responses to attachment-related events in terms of secure-
base scriptedness (Waters et al., 1998). They also designed a word-prompt list task
to assess scripts in adults. This secure base script has an internal order of events
(child is engaged in the environment or the attached dyad is interacting in a warm
manner; an obstacle or conflict is introduced—such as loss of a desired toy or a
minor injury to the attached person; assistance is requested and is offered by the
caregiving member of the dyad; the help is effective in resolving the conflict; the
child is able to go back to activity; or the dyad is able to return to productive interaction) that leads to a typical story.

Such innovations have opened a window for the study of *how* secure-base
knowledge is mentally organized and represented. This is an important area of
inquiry as it allows researchers to begin to detail the structure of attachment representations (a construct that has proven difficult to specify) and tie those representations to specific aspects of experience (see Rodrigues, Zevallos, Turan, &
Green, 2003; Vaughn et al., 2006; Wais et al., 2000). The new assessment strategies
code children's (and adults') attachment-related narratives for secure-base scriptedness. They are valuable as they allow us to address questions about the basic
structure of secure-base knowledge; the relations between caregivers' organization
of secure-base knowledge, the quality of their care, and children's organization
of secure-base behavior; children's cross-time integration of secure-base behavior with secure-base scripted knowledge; and the cross-domain relations between
secure-base behavior and representation and child behavior in peer interactions
and other social contexts.

MIDDLE CHILDHOOD

Child–parent attachment relationships are maintained and elaborated during middle
childhood. Waters et al. (1991) have suggested that with the entrance to school and an
increasing amount of time spent away from home, a restructured parent–child supervision partnership is shaped. As children age, they become increasingly responsible
for maintaining communication and sticking to agreements about whereabouts and
reunion times, facilitating, or not, the parental supervision task. From a Bowlby–
Ainsworth perspective, the goals of the attachment system continue to be both those
of proximity (Ainsworth, 1991) and felt security (Sroufe & Waters, 1977). Yet, interaction strategies are likely to be different in a developmental context that includes
other salient socioemotional (e.g., peers) and sociocultural (e.g., school or work) tasks.
In all likelihood, children become more skillful secure-base users.

Although increasing, empirical research during middle childhood is scant
(Kerns, 2008). Some evidence indicates that 11- to 12-year olds keep using parents

as a haven of safety. Even though children report a decline in utilization of parents in times of stress, they express a strong preference for parents when they are sad or frightened. Existing studies support the notion that maternal availability continues to be important for children and is associated with more adaptive functioning (Kerns, 2008).

As representations are concerned, although the all-encompassing cognitive changes at around 5–7 years of age (Sameroff & Haith, 1996) may hint at reorganization and change in those representations, research on their developmental course is minimal. Bretherton and Munholland (2008) suggest that the integration and generalization of internal working models across different attachment relationships begin during childhood, gradually establishing the foundation for a more generalized attachment representation; yet children continue to have attachment representations that are specific to different types of relationships (e.g., child–mother and child–father) and that are influenced by what transpires in them.

Attachment Relationships as a Context for Development

Information available indicates that the child–parent attachment relationship continues to play a role in children's development. Individual differences in attachment security are found to be associated with other socialization outcomes. Supporting evidence has been presented, among others, by Kerns and colleagues who report data on children's perceptions on parental figures' availability, secure-base use, and associations with children's social competence (e.g., Kerns, 2008; Kerns, Tomich, & Kim, 2006), and by the work of Moss and colleagues (e.g., Moss & St-Laurent, 2001; Moss, Cyr, & Dubois-Comtois, 2004; Moss, Bureau, Beliveau, Zdebik, & Lepine, 2009) who report associations between security and academic engagement (mastery motivation and cognitive engagement; Moss & St-Laurent, 2001) and attachment disorganization and behavior problems (Moss, Rousseau, Parent, St-Laurent, & Saintonge, 1998; Moss et al., 2009).

Still relatively unexplored, middle childhood offers an opportunity to conduct research in different fronts. Information that considers ordinary situations (not exclusively focused on emergencies) is practically nonexistent, despite the fact that parents are likely to play important roles in children's entry and adjustment to school, negotiations of new friendships, academic tasks, and following rules of behavior. Here we have an opportunity to investigate the role that attachment relationships play in offering a context to tackle those tasks. We are not suggesting a direct causal link between attachment security and other socialization outcomes, but an inquiry into the role, if any, that different kinds of attachment relationships play in conjunction with other socialization efforts, for example, direct coaching or teaching on the issue at hand, the input of other family members, school, and peers. Information concerning continuity and change in representations of attachment-related information is also very scarce. This is a fertile ground for researchers to explore important questions concerning what changes, if any, in attachment representations, what the relations between representations and behavior are, and what the links between attachment behavioral organization and representation and other developmental outcomes are (e.g., the formation and maintenance of friendships, self-esteem, perspective taking, etc.).

Parental Caregiving

Attachment relationships are a dyadic phenomenon. Although developmental changes are likely to influence the way children relate to their attachment figures, so are changes in parental input to these relationships. There is very little theoretical or empirical work regarding changes in attachment figures' behavior and representations that accompany children's changes. The study of secure-base support has essentially been ignored after early childhood as research focuses on individuals' attachment representations. A dyadic approach is indispensable to understand the development of child–parent attachment relationships; the study of quality of parental care is necessary to account for the continuity and change between early attachment relationships and attachment in middle childhood and beyond. Existing evidence as to the continuity in the quality of attachment relationships during middle childhood is mixed (Kerns, 2008). An obvious factor to be investigated is that of quality of care. Without such information, it is very difficult to understand those mixed results. It is important to note two issues here. First, changes in the quality of child–parent attachment relationships provide support to the idea that these relationships are an open system susceptible to modifications. Second, changes per se do not question the theory; what is important is to uncover the factors associated with such changes.

It is likely that methodological difficulties are responsible for the scarcity of research on actual relationship exchanges during middle childhood, but certainly that is not the whole story. Although it is true that observation of child–mother interactions after early childhood becomes more complex and difficult and that methodological tools used by researchers switch for the most part to child and maternal reports (substituting for observation of exchanges), this approach (focusing on the intraindividual domain) probably reflects more than just assessment and method strategy obstacles. Perhaps our bias to mainly focus on individuals, when studying developmental issues, can, in part, be responsible for the lack of emphasis on actual relationship experience. Regardless, it is clear that as individuals become more skillful in language use, research focuses less on behavioral interactions, and more on individual perceptions/perspectives of these relationships. This is paradoxical in view of Bowlby's efforts to move the study of attachment relationships beyond the realm of the intrapsychic and highlight the importance of everyday real-life experience in relationships on the organization of internal working models. To be clear, it is not that attachment representations are unimportant; the point here is concerned with the need to understand the development of attachment relationships, a phenomenon that includes two people who contribute to relationship outcomes (e.g., quality of attachment). The lack of information on those everyday exchanges that feed into the relationship is unsettling.

ADOLESCENCE

Bowlby (1982) suggested that attachment relationships are long lasting, and attachment bonds are enduring and not given up voluntarily. Originated in infancy and transformed during childhood, attachment bonds continue to maintain adolescents and their parents together and remain the most significant relationship during adolescence (Collins & Laursen, 2004). Adolescent–parent exchanges are influenced by their relationship history (Hamilton, 2000) by means of cognitive representations (internal working models) and behavioral interaction patterns characteristic of the dyad, as well as contextual characteristics that include developmental tasks faced by both adolescents and their parents (e.g., adolescent autonomy and relationships with peers; parents' professional/work development), who continue to co-construct a mutually regulated relationship system.

Although attachment relationships remain central, they are also transformed. In a developmental context that has been characterized as a period of deep changes (e.g., physical, cognitive, relational, and emotional), these relationships too are likely to exhibit developmental reorganization (Allen, 2008; Collins & Laursen, 2004; Waters et al., 1991). Adolescent–parent attachment relationships are distinctive both cognitively and behaviorally from early attachment relationships (Collins & Laursen, 2004). Adolescents are able to contemplate abstract relationship alternatives which in turn allow them to compare and evaluate relationships with attachment figures and potentially attempt to maintain and/or modify those relationships. Thus, with the acquisition of formal thought, new cognitive capabilities such as the capacity to reflect upon relationships allow the adolescent to put together an integrated and generalized intrapsychic stance toward attachment-related issues (Allen, 2008). Main has argued that such states of mind influence future behavior and expectations regarding self and the other in a relationship (e.g., Main, Kaplan, & Cassidy, 1985). As mentioned before, the making of these states of mind regarding attachment relationships has its beginnings much earlier on (see Bretherton & Munholland, 2008; Bretherton et al., 1990; Waters & Waters, 2006; Waters et al., 1998).

From an interaction perspective, changes have also been hypothesized. Researchers have called attention to adolescents' potential ability to implement the secure-base game from both standpoints: the ability to seek and to provide secure-base support. By participating in attachment relationships, individuals learn not only their own roles (e.g., implementation of secure-base behavior) but also the role the other member of the dyad plays (provision of secure-base support; Sroufe & Fleeson, 1986). Yet, little has been done to explore this in adolescence. Further, inquiry should include the secure-base phenomenon in both stressful circumstances, and dyadic exchanges regarding positive events and everyday issues that are relevant for adolescents. Finally, research on the links between secure-base behavior and secure-base representations is also needed. In a study of adolescent attachment, Allen et al. (2003) investigated the association between attachment states of mind as assessed with the adult attachment interview (AAI, see section on p. 104 for a brief description) and four potential markers of the secure-base phenomenon (i.e., deidealization of mother, perceptions of maternal supportiveness, maternal attunement, and goal-corrected partnership or dyadic relatedness as demonstrated in a problem-solving task). Secure-base markers, assessed via interview, observation, and self-report, were found to explain significant proportions of variance in adolescent attachment security as per the AAI. The results suggest that the secure-base phenomenon remains central to understanding attachment relationships in adolescence, and that adolescent attachment security remains strongly linked to adolescent–mother exchanges (Allen & Land, 1999).

A Context for Further Development

In all likelihood adolescent–parent attachment relationships continue to provide a key context for developmental tasks to be mastered (e.g., formation of intimate friendships, romantic relationships, identity and self-concept, academic issues, and school/work decisions). It is expected that the child–parent relationships of secure as well as insecure adolescents will experience bumps and obstacles, much as they have before, but likely, they will be negotiated differently depending on, among others, their history of previous interactions as well as the quality of their current exchanges, personal characteristics, and concurrent circumstances. Longitudinal studies have documented both continuity in attachment relationships quality from infancy to early adulthood and also lawful discontinuity, with the latter being meaningfully related to changes in the lives of individuals and the family environment (Hamilton, 2000; Waters, Merrick, et al., 2000; Weinfeld et al., 2000). Specifically, evidence supports the notion that negative life events (e.g., loss of a parent, parental divorce, life-threatening illness of parent or child, and parental psychiatric disorder) could bear on the caregiver's availability and responsiveness, which impact child–parent interactions and in turn affect children's security (Waters, Hamilton, & Weinfeld, 2000). The patterning of past interactions, present exchanges, and the ecology of the dyad all seem to play a part in accounting for individual differences in child–parent attachment relationships (Allen & Land, 1999; Hamilton, 2000; Sroufe, Egeland, Carlson, & Collins, 2005; Waters et al., 2000; Weinfeld et al., 2000).

It is in that context that adolescents and parents work out issues of autonomy and connectedness, and negotiate issues of supervision and communication. Security in the relationships with parents helps adolescents navigate various developmental issues they face. For instance, secure adolescents have been found to have higher autonomy (Allen, Hauser, Bell, & O'Connor, 1994), leave home on time (Seiffge-Krenke, 2006), adjust better to new environments such as college and military settings (Larose & Bernier, 2001; Scharf, Mayseless, & Kivenson-Baron, 2004), and have higher capacity for mature intimacy in friendships and romantic relationships (Scharf et al., 2004; Seiffge-Krenke, 2006) than insecure teens. Although there might be overall increases in parent–child conflicts and decreases in proximity during adolescence, teenagers with secure states of mind tend to handle conflicts by engaging in productive problem-solving discussions with parents (e.g., Allen et al., 2003; Kobak, Cole, Ferenz-Gillies, Fleming, & Gamble, 1993), whereas their insecure counterparts are more likely to be overwhelmed by occurring disagreements and withdrawn from the relationship (Allen, 2008; Kobak et al., 1993). Teens who handle conflict with parents by engaging in productive problem-solving discussions that balance autonomy strivings with efforts to preserve the relationship with parents tend to be more autonomous. Discussions may be heated but they are balanced by behaviors that maintain and support the parent–teen relationship. Although most research has been conducted with mothers, more recent research with fathers suggests that similar patterns exist (Allen, 2008).

A Shift of Focus

Although one of Bowlby's key insights was to suggest attachment as a relational outcome tied to interaction experience, the latter is not commonly and/or explicitly considered in research on child–parent attachment relationships during adolescence and adulthood. Research has shifted the focus of attention to intraperson differences concerning states of mind about attachment relationships, or to individual attachment styles (Allen, 2008). The availability of the AAI (George, Kaplan, & Main, 1984,

1996; Main et al., 1985) was a turning point in attachment research as it opened the gate for innumerable studies on the issue. This indeed modified the field and research tendencies. The AAI is a semistructured interview that asks for descriptions of early relationships, attachment-related events, and for an individual's view of how these relationships and events have affected their current personality and functioning. A subject's verbal account is presumed to reflect her or his current state of mind regarding attachment (George et al., 1984; Hesse, 2008). Based on their narrative coherence, individuals are classified into one of four groups: secure-autonomous (individuals' descriptions and evaluations of attachment experiences are coherent and consistent, and their responses are relevant and succinct); dismissing (individuals often unable to recall attachment-related experiences, or use positive terms to describe parents which are unsupported or contradicted in their narrative); preoccupied (interview questions elicit excessive attention to attachment-related memories at the cost of loss of focus on the context); and disorganized (individuals show striking lapse in the monitoring of reasoning during the discussion of traumatic experience; Hesse, 2008). A likely unintended consequence of the AAI accessibility has been a lack of attention to a dyadic perspective and certainly to a dismissal of the behavioral interaction domain in attachment relationships. To date, most research on adolescent attachment relationships conducted within the Bowlby–Ainsworth perspective has focused on the study of individual attachment states of mind.

Significant as attachment representations are as a developmental achievement, specific adolescent–parent attachment relationships continue to exist and be nourished by actual exchanges between members of the dyad. The quality of these exchanges is likely, as it did before, to contribute to individual differences in adolescents' security and to different relationship outcomes. Interestingly, a longitudinal study (Becker-Stoll & Fremmer-Bombik, 1997) showed that infant security was more predictive of observed qualities of autonomy and relatedness in adolescent–mother interactions than of adolescent attachment states of mind. This raises the key issue about the relation between generalized attachment representations and secure-base behavior organization, and about the salience of gathering information on dyadic exchanges. The study of both attachment representations and actual interactions is important.

Furthermore, a dyadic perspective also requires a look at the provision of secure-base support by the caregiver in addition to the implementation of the secure-base game by the adolescent. The dyadic nature of relationships entails the study of each member's contributions. The lack of information in current literature hampers our ability to fully understand adolescence as a period of transformation. An intrapsychic lens typically focuses on changes and continuities within the adolescent as a reason to expect attachment relationships to change or be stable. Equally important is the study of changes in attachment figures' behavior as a secure base, expectations regarding their relationship with their adolescent offspring, and their communication patterns. For example, a key issue to resolve is concerned with the impact of the quality of maternal (or paternal) care on the stability of attachment relationships up to, and during, adolescence (see Belsky & Fearon, 2002; van IJzendoorn, 1996). Empirical evidence illustrates changes in parents' behavior when interacting with their children and adolescents (Shanahan, McHale, Crouter, & Osgood, 2007; Shanahan, McHale, & Osgood, & Crouter, 2007; Whiteman, McHale, & Crouter, 2003). Findings support the notion that parents learn from their experience of parenting and they change the ways they handle conflict from the first to the second child at the same age for both adolescents. Also, a longitudinal study by De Goede, Branje, and Meus (2009) indicates that adolescent–parent interactions change; they become more egalitarian during adolescence. Parents perceived as powerful are viewed as supportive especially in early adolescence, and conflict is not necessarily tied to changes in equality in the relationship. Although these latter findings are based on adolescent perceptions, they illustrate the importance of considering transformations in *both* members of the dyad across time during adolescence. We need to reveal the details of actual dyadic exchanges in adolescent–parent attachment relationships. A relational perspective requires it.

A Brief Note on Meaning

Adolescence has been portrayed as a period during which attachment functions are transferred from parents to peers. Although the salience of peer relationships is indisputable, relationships with both parents and peers are central in adolescents' lives and fulfill different functions. They also have different meaning. The fact that adolescents employ interaction skills and patterns learned by participating in relationships with their parents, when forming relationships with peers, does not necessarily imply a transfer of functions from one type of relationship to the other, nor does it mean transfer of attachment. While adolescents remain active participants in relationships with parents, they too work on building intimate peer relationships that include both secure-base use and secure-base support, but are not exclusively about that. The saliency of peer relationships during adolescence should not be interpreted as a decline of the importance of relationships with parents, nor is it an indication of transferring attachment functions to peers. Theory development and available data indicate that adolescent–parent relationships are better thought of as of being reorganized rather than transferred (Allen, 2008; Collins & Laursen, 2004). How adolescents navigate this process (relation of relationships) needs to be given due attention.

ADULTHOOD

Existing information indicates that attachment bonds with parents remain during adulthood. Neither does an individual's attachment to her or his parents wane in adulthood, nor do parents stop offering secure-base support. Although parents may penetrate fewer aspects of adult children's lives than they did before, most adults maintain a meaningful association with their parents throughout adulthood (Ainsworth, 1989; Umberson, 1992). The existence of an attachment bond can be inferred from the maintained exchanges between adult children and parents, and ultimately from the process of bereavement and grief at parental death. This latter is the single most common cause of bereavement in the United States (Magai, 2008).

In spite of some researchers' use of attachment theory to understand adult children–parent relationships decades ago (e.g., Antonucci, 1976; Cicirelli, 1983; Troll & Smith, 1976), and more recent studies using attachment concepts to understand relationship exchanges between adult children and their parents, particularly in the context of caregiving (see Bradley & Cafferty, 2001, for a review), research from an attachment perspective, however, is still limited at the time. As with adolescents, studies have for the most part focused on adults' states of mind rather than on inter-actions between adult children and their parents (Magai, 2008). A number of empir-ical reports on individual differences in adults' state of mind and their implications for various aspects of adults' lives (e.g., close relationships, marital functioning, and parenting) have been published (e.g., Cohn, Cowan, Cowan, & Pearson, 1992; Fraley & Davis, 1997; Treboux, Crowell, & Waters, 2004).

Relationships with parents, particularly with mothers, remain the, or among the, closest throughout the life span as reported by adults (individuals 21–39, 40–59, and 60–79 years old; Antonucci, Akiyama, & Takahashi, 2004; Umberson, 2003). This was so for samples from Japan and the United States. Results indicated that the adults' relationships with their mothers were the closest through middle age (Antonucci et al., 2004). The finding that this relationship does not appear among the closest ties in later adulthood is probably due to mothers' death (Magai, 2008). In the same vein, findings reported by Bengtson and colleagues (Bengtson, Rosenthal, & Burton, 1996; Silverstein & Bengtson, 1997) indicate that the majority of adults describe themselves as very close to their mothers. Although these reports cannot be taken as defin-itive evidence confirming attachment theory, they do speak to the salience of the offspring–mother relationship during adult years, and are in line of Bowlby's asser-tion that these relationships span from the cradle to the grave.

The Secure-Base Phenomenon in Adulthood

The use of each other as a secure base and the provision of secure-base support in more reciprocal ways may be a useful avenue to study the transformations of the goal-corrected attachment partnership during adulthood. Adult children may seek parents both for emotional or instrumental support during times of stress (e.g., illness, relationship difficulties with significant others, accidents; Cooney & Uhlenberg, 1992; Fingerman, Miller, Birditt, & Zarit, 2009), or simply, to bounce back ideas as to how to proceed in particular situations that they are facing, or communicate and share with them positive events in their lives (e.g., birth of a child, marriage, job success; Fingerman et al., 2009). Despite a general decline in the amount of parental support provided as children grow older, most parental support is responsive to adult children's needs and serves the purpose of provid-ing reassurance and enabling the children to navigate their world more efficiently (Berry, 2008; Cicirelli, 1989; Fingerman et al., 2009). Parents continue to offer and give emotional as well as instrumental support (e.g., help with finances, household tasks, and babysitting), as long as they are reasonably healthy and resourceful (e.g., Cicirelli, 1991; Fingerman et al., 2009; Grundy, 2005; Schoeni & Ross, 2005; Zarit & Eggebeen, 2003).

Similarly, while adult children still receive care from parents in various forms, they may also take on a new role as a provider of secure-base support for their par-ents as they grow old, or in late life. Some researchers have used attachment theory principles to frame adult children's caregiving behaviors toward their aging par-ents. Thus, Cicirelli (1991) proposed that attachment leads to protective behaviors from children to parents, particularly when parents are becoming susceptible to ill-ness and death. Carpenter (2001) found that higher security (as assessed using a dimensional measure of security and anxiety) was associated with the provision of more emotional care and reports of less caregiving burden, while instrumental care was unrelated to attachment dimensions. Carpenter suggests that securely attached adult children may be more willing or comfortable to discuss emotional issues with their parents, and better prepared for the caregiving demands of their aging parents. Not only do secure individuals seem less stressed about caregiving demands from their parents, but also, they are more likely to help parents cope better with their aging process. Steele, Phibbs, and Woods (2004) examined the association between adult daughters' coherence state of mind with their mothers' reunion behaviors in a strange situation. The authors found that even after controlling for severity of dementia, mothers whose daughters had a coherent state of mind (as per the AAI) were more joyful and related better during reunion, for example, they exhibited positive facial expressions, proximity seeking, and responsiveness.

Aging parents may not only provide secure-base support but may also need to seek it within their relationships with their children. Findings about the associations between communication (e.g., Merz & Consedine, 2009) and the search for help from their children by aging parents, and feelings of closeness may be readily understood as part of the evolving nature of the goal-corrected partnership. Having learned the secure base as a context-sensitive system, secure-base use and secure-base support are likely to be implemented in a flexible manner during adulthood depending upon current context and one's own circumstances. Thus, Merz and Consedine (2009) found that attachment quality moderated the association between family support and wellbeing for elderly people. Emotional support had a positive effect, and instrumental support a less negative effect, on the wellbeing for secure individuals. Despite an increase in dependency on others in old age, secure individuals may be more willing to seek help when they need it, and talk about their thoughts and feelings, whereas insecure individuals are more likely to be reluctant to elicit help, feel incompetent when receiving help, or view the provision of support as insufficient or unpredictable.

Although still in its beginning phase, the study of secure-base provision *and* secure-base use between adult children and their parents and their developmental continuities and transformations offers a promising and viable window to investigate adult offspring–parent attachment relationships (for related research on the topic see Silverstein, Conroy, Wang, Giarusso, & Bengtson, 2002). Unfortunately, studies on the developmental course of child–parent attachment relationships during adulthood do not exist to date. Available information typically focuses on individuals' state of mind or representational aspects and includes neither a dyadic perspective nor observations of actual exchanges between adult children and their parents (for research that includes behavioral observation during interactions see Steele et al., 2004). Empirical data is needed, however, to answer basic questions regarding the characteristics of those relationships during adulthood, their course from young to middle and late adulthood, secure-base support and secure-base use as children and parents become older, the usefulness/appropriateness of the infancy classification system in characterizing attachment relationships during adulthood (Bengtson et al., 1996; Carpenter, 2001), the associations, if any, between adult children's caregiving of parents later in life and the quality of their relationship early in adulthood, and the existence of any gender differences (both in child and parent) in the ways attachment relationships are implemented in adulthood (Barnas, Pollina, & Cummings, 1991; Bretherton & Mullohand, 2008). A descriptive account of these relationships would be an important first step. Limited available information severely limits our knowledge and any conclusion at this point in time is, by necessity, tentative.

▧ FUTURE DIRECTIONS IN THE STUDY OF ATTACHMENT ACROSS THE LIFE SPAN

Attachment relationships crafted in infancy and elaborated throughout the life span are characteristic of humans. Evidence gathered so far indicates that they play an important role in relationship, social, and emotional development. Bowlby and Ainsworth provided us with the foundations of a theoretical perspective that has been instrumental in launching a field of studies on attachment and in integrating empirical findings. Much remains to be done, however. Key issues include the need for information on actual child–parent exchanges beyond early childhood and the use of a dyadic lens. Considering the contributions from both children and parents, and changes and continuities in those contributions at different points in time, will allow us to better understand the life course of child–parent attachment relationships. Similarly, investigating the construction and elaboration of attachment-related representations, their change over time, and their relations with actual interactional experiences is necessary. Such studies are likely to illustrate the interplay and transformations between everyday child–parent interactions and individuals' organization of represented information about attachment relationships in both children and parents.

Also, it is important to go beyond the view of attachment relationships as a stress-reducing system, and study their operation and functions during ordinary everyday circumstances. Attachment relationships are built in the context of regular exchanges that include positive nonemergency situations that both children and parents enjoy. As discussed in this chapter, children go back to their attachment figures not only in difficult times but also in ordinary and happy circumstances for affection, to share experiences, or to involve parents who actively participate in the organization of—and support—their offspring's exchanges with the world. This is likely to be the case in infancy, childhood adolescence, as well as in adulthood, although the specific ways at each period are different. Observations of child–parent interactions in everyday exchanges would provide us with a broader view of how attachment relationships unfold throughout life. Finally, we also assert the value and need to study these relationships from the perspective of the secure-base phenomenon, namely, the study of changes and continuities in secure-base use and secure support thorough the life span. This perspective will help us ground, and better account for, the evolving nature of the child–parent partnership through time.

▧ ACKNOWLEDGMENTS

Some of the ideas and data presented were supported by grants from the National Science Foundation (BCS-0645530) and the Kinley Trust.

REFERENCES

Aber, J. L., & Baker, A. J. L. (1990). Security of attachment in toddlerhood: Modifying assessment procedures for joint clinical and research purposes. In M. Greenberg, D. Cicchetti, & E. M. Cummings (Eds.), *Attachment in the preschool years: Theory, research, and intervention* (pp. 427–460). Chicago, IL: University of Chicago Press.

Achermann, J., Dinneen, E., & Stevenson-Hinde, J. (1991). Clearing up at 2.5 years. *British Journal of Developmental Psychology, 9*, 365–376.

Ainsworth, M. D. S. (1967). *Infancy in Uganda: Infant care and the growth of love.* Baltimore, MD: Johns Hopkins University Press.

Ainsworth, M. D. (1989). Attachments beyond infancy. *American Psychologist, 44*, 709–716.

Ainsworth, M. D. S. (1991). Attachment and other affectional bonds across the life cycle. In C. M. Parkes, J. Stevenson-Hinde, & P. Morris (Eds.), *Attachment across the life cycle* (pp. 33–51). London: Routledge.

Ainsworth, M. D. S., Bell, S. M., & Stayton, D. J. (1971). Individual differences in Strange Situation behavior of one-year-olds. In H. R. Schaffer (Ed.), *The origins of human social relations* (pp. 17–57). London: Academic Press.

Ainsworth, M. D. S., Bell, S. M., & Stayton, D. J. (1974). Infant-mother attachment and social development: Socialization as a product of reciprocal responsiveness to signals. In M. P. M. Richards (Ed.), *The integration of a child into a social world* (pp. 99–135). New York: Cambridge University Press.

Ainsworth, M. D. S., Blehar, M. C., Waters, E., & Wall, S. (1978). *Patterns of attachment.* Hillsdale, NJ: Erlbaum.

Ainsworth, M. D. S., & Marvin, R. (1995). On the shaping of attachment theory and research: An interview with Mary D. S. Ainsworth. In E. Waters, B. Vaughn, G. Posada, & K. Kondo-Ikemura (Eds.), *Caregiving, cultural, and cognitive perspectives on secure-base behavior and working models. Monograph of the Society for Research in Child Development, 60*(2–3, Serial No. 244), 3–21.

Ainsworth, M. D. S., & Wittig, B. A. (1969). Attachment and exploratory behavior of one year-olds in a strange situation. In B. M. Foss (Ed.), *Determinants of infant behavior* (Vol. 4, pp. 111–136). London: Methuen.

Allen, J. P. (2008). The attachment system in adolescence. In J. Cassidy & P. Shaver (Eds.), *Handbook of attachment: Theory, research, & clinical applications.* (2nd ed., pp.419–435). New York: Guilford Press.

Allen, J. P., Hauser, S. T., Bell, K. L., & O'Connor, T. G. (1994). Longitudinal assessment of autonomy and relatedness in adolescent-family interactions as predictors of adolescent ego development and self-esteem. *Child Development, 65*, 179–194.

Allen, J. P., & Land, D. (1999). Attachment in adolescence. In J. Cassidy & P. R. Shaver (Eds.), *Handbook of attachment: Theory, research, and clinical applications* (pp. 319–335). New York: Guilford Press.

Allen, J. P., McElhaney, K. B., Land, D. J., Kuperminc, G. P., Moore, C. W., O'Beirne- Kelly, H., et al. (2003). A secure base in adolescence: Markers of attachment security in the mother-adolescent relationship. *Child Development, 74*, 292–307.

Antonucci, T. (1976). Attachment: A life-span concept. *Human Development, 19*, 135–142.

Antonucci, T. C., Akiyama, H., Takahashi, K. (2004). Attachment and close relationships across the life span. *Attachment and Human Development, 6*, 353–370.

Barnas, M. V., Pollina, L., & Cummings, E. M. (1991). Life-span attachment: Relations between attachment and socio-emotional functioning in adult women. *Genetic, Social, and General Psychology Monographs, 117*, 175–202.

Barnett, D., Kidwell, S. L., & Leung, K. H. (1998). Parenting and preschooler attachment among low-income urban African American families. *Child Development, 69*, 1657–1671.

Becker-Stoll, E., & Fremmer-Bombik, E. (1997, April). *Adolescent-mother interaction and attachment: A longitudinal study.* Paper presented at the biennial meetings of the Society for Research in Child Development, Washington, DC.

Belsky, J., & Fearon, R. M. P. (2002). Early attachment security, subsequent maternal sensitivity, and later child development: Does continuity in development depend upon continuity of caregiving? *Attachment and Human Development, 4*, 361–387.

Bengtson, V. L., Rosenthal, C., & Burton, L. (1996). Paradoxes of families and aging. In R. H. Binstock & L. K. George (Eds.), *Handbook of aging and the social sciences* (4th ed., pp. 253–282). San Diego, CA: Academic Press.

Berry, B. (2008). Financial transfers from living parents to adult children: Who is helped and why? *American Journal of Economics and Sociology, 67,* 207–239.

Bowlby, J. (1946). *Forty-four juvenile thieves: Their characters and home-life.* Baillere: Tindall & Cox.

Bowlby, J. (1958). The nature of a child's tie to his mother. *International Journal of Psycho-Analysis, 39,* 350–373.

Bowlby, J. (1969/1982). *Attachment and loss. Vol. I, Attachment.* New York: Basic Books Inc.

Bowlby, J. (1973). *Attachment and loss. Vol. II, Separation.* New York: Basic Books Inc.

Bowlby, J. (1979). *The making and breaking of affectional bonds.* London: Tavistock Publications.

Bowlby, J. (1980). *Attachment and loss. Vol. III, Loss: Sadness and depression.* New York: Basic Books.

Bowlby, J. (1988). *A secure-base.* New York: Basic Books Inc.

Bowlby, J. (1991). Ethological light on psychoanalytical problems. In P. Bateson (Ed.), *Development and integration of behavior* (pp. 301–313). Cambridge: Cambridge University Press.

Bowlby, J., Robertson, J., & Rosenbluth, D. (1952). A two-year-old goes to hospital. *Psychoanalytic Study of the Child, 7,* 82–94.

Bradley, J. M., & Cafferty, T. P. (2001). Attachment among older adults: Current issues and directions for future research. *Attachment and Human Development, 3,* 200–221.

Bretherton, I. (1990). Open communication and internal working models: Their role in the development of attachment relations. In R. A. Thompson (Ed.), *Nebraska Symposium on Motivation: Socioemotional development* (Vol. 36, pp. 57–113). Lincoln: University of Nebraska Press.

Bretherton, I. (2005). In pursuit of the internal working model construct and its relevance to attachment relationships. In K. E. Grossmann, K. Grossmann, & E. Waters (Eds.), *Attachment from infancy to adulthood: The major longitudinal studies* (pp. 13–47). New York: Guilford Publications, Inc.

Bretherton, I., & Munholland, K. (2008). Internal working models in attachment relationships: A construct revisited. In J. Cassidy & P. Shaver (Eds.), *Handbook of attachment: Theory, research, & clinical applications* (2nd ed., pp.102–130). New York: Guilford Press.

Bretherton, I., Ridgeway, D., & Cassidy, J. (1990). Assessing internal working models of the attachment relationship: An attachment story completion task for 3-year-olds. In M. Greenberg, D. Cicchetti, & E. M. Cummings (Eds.), *Attachment in the preschool years: Theory, research, and intervention* (pp. 273–308). Chicago, IL: University of Chicago Press

Breur, J. (1999). *The myth of the first three years.* New York: The Free Press.

Carbonell, O. A., & Posada, G. (2009, April). *Marital adjustment, quality of maternal caregiving and preschoolers' attachment security in Mexican-American families.* Poster presented at the meeting of the Society for Research in Child Development, Denver, CO.

Campbell, S. B., Brownell, C. A., Hungerford, A., Spieker, S. J., Mohan, R., & Blessing, J. (2004). The course of maternal depressive symptoms and maternal sensitivity as predictors of attachment security at 36 months. *Development and Psychopathology, 16,* 231–252.

Carpenter, B. D. (2001). Attachment bonds between adult daughters and their older mothers: Associations with contemporary caregiving. *Journal of Gerontology: Psychological Sciences, 56B,* 257–267.

Carr, D., House, J. S., Wortman, C., Nesse, R., & Kessler, R. C. (2001). Psychological adjustment to sudden and anticipated spousal loss among older widowed persons. *The Journals of Gerontology: Series B: Psychological Sciences and Social Sciences, 56,* 237–248.

Cassidy, J., Kirsh, S. J., Scolton, K. L., & Parke, R. D. (1996). Attachment and representations of peers. *Developmental Psychology, 32,* 892–904.

Cassidy, J., & Marvin, R. S. (1992). *Attachment organization in three- and four-year olds: Coding guidelines.* Unpublished manuscript.

Cicchetti, D., Cummings, E. M., Greenberg, M. T., & Marvin, R. S. (1990). An organizational perspective on attachment beyond infancy. In M. T. Greenberg, D. Cicchetti, & E. M. Cummings (Eds.), *Attachment in the preschool years: Theory, research, and intervention* (pp. 3–49). Chicago, IL: The University of Chicago Press.

Cicirelli, V. G. (1983). Adult's children attachment and helping behavior to elderly parents: A path model. *Journal of Marriage and the Family, 45,* 815–822.

Cicirelli, V. G. (1989). Helping relationships in later life: A reexamination. In J. A. Mancini (Ed.), *Aging parents and adult children* (pp.167–1180). Lexington, MA: D.C. Heath.

Cicirelli, V. G. (1991). Attachment theory in old age: Protection of the attached figure. In K. Pillemer & K. McCartney (Eds.), *Parent-child relations throughout life* (pp. 25–42). Hillsdale, NJ: Erlbaum.

Cohn, D. A., Cowan, P. A., Cowan, C. P., & Pearson, J. (1992). Mothers' and fathers' working models of childhood attachment relationships, parenting styles, and child behavior. *Development and Psychopathology, 4,* 417–431.

Collins, W. A., & Laursen, B. (2004). Parent-adolescent relationships and influences. In R. Lerner & L. Steinberg (Eds.), *The handbook of adolescent psychology* (pp. 331–362). New York: Wiley.

Cooney, T. M., & Uhlenberg, P. (1992). Support from parents over the life course: The adult child's perspective. *Social Forces, 71*, 63–84.

Crittenden, P. M., & Claussen, A. H. (2000). *The organization of attachment relationships.* New York: Cambridge University Press.

Crowell, J. A., Waters, E., Treboux, D., O'Connor, E., Colons-Downs, C., Felder, O., et al. (1996). Discriminant validity of the Adult Attachment Interview. *Child Development, 67*, 2584–2599.

Cummings, E. M. (1990). Classification of attachment on a continuum of felt security: Illustrations from the study of children of depressed parents. In M. T. Greenberg, D. Cicchetti, & E. M. Cummings (Eds.), *Attachment in the preschool years: Theory, research, and intervention* (pp. 311–338). Hillsdale, NJ: Erlbaum.

De Goede, I. H. A., Branje, S. J. T., & Meus, W. H. J. (2009). Developmental changes in adolescents' perceptions of relationships with their parents. *Journal of Youth Adolescence, 38*, 75–88.

De Wolff, M. S., & van IJzendoorn, M. H. (1997). Sensitivity and attachment: A meta-analysis on parental antecedents of infant attachment. *Child Development, 68*, 571–591.

Dixon, W. E. (2003). *Twenty studies that revolutionized child psychology.* Upper Saddle River, NJ: Prentice Hall.

Dubois-Comtois, K., Cyr, C., Moss, E., & St-Laurent, D. (2008). The role of mother-child conversations in the development of attachment representations in childhood. *Enfance, 60*, 140–152.

Fingerman, K., Miller, L., Birditt, K, & Zarit, S. (2009). Giving to the good and the needy: Parental support of grown children. *Journal of Marriage and the Family, 71*, 1220–1233.

Fonagy, P., Steele, H., & Steele, M. (1991). Maternal representations of attachment during pregnancy predict the organization of infant mother attachment at one year of age. *Child Development, 62*, 891–905.

Fraley, R. C., & Davis, K. E. (1997). Attachment formation and transfer in young adults' close friendships and romantic relationships. *Personal Relationships, 4*, 131–144.

George, C., Kaplan, N., & Main, M. (1984, 1996). *Adult Attachment Interview.* Unpublished protocol (3rd ed.). Department of Psychology, University of California, Berkeley, CA.

George, C., & Solomon, J. (1989). Internal working models of caregiving and security of attachment at six. *Infant Mental Health Journal, 10*, 222–237.

George, C., & Solomon, J. (2008). Attachment and caregiving. In J. Cassidy & P. R. Shaver (Eds.), *Handbook of attachment: Theory, research, and clinical applications* (2nd ed., pp. 649–670). New York: The Guilford Press.

Grossmann, K., Grossmann, K. E., Spangler, G., Suess, G., & Unzner, L. (1985). Maternal sensitivity and newborns' orientation responses as related to quality of attachment in Northern Germany. In I. Bretherton & E. Waters (Eds.), *Growing points of attachment theory and research. Monographs of the Society for Research in Child Development, 50*(1–2, Serial No. 209), 233–256.

Grundy, E. (2005). Reciprocity in relationships: Socio-economic and health influences on intergenerational exchanges between third age parents and their adult children in Great Britain. *The British Journal of Sociology, 56*, 233–255.

Guttman-Steinmetz, S., Elliott, M., Steiner, M., & Waters, H. (2003, April). *Co-constructing script-like representations of early secure base experience.* Paper presented at the meeting of the Society for Research in Child Development. Tampa, FLA.

Hamilton, C. (2000). Continuity and discontinuity of attachment from infancy through adolescence. *Child Development, 71*, 690–694.

Hesse, E. (2008). The adult attachment interview: Protocol, method of analysis, and empirical studies. In J. Cassidy & P. R. Shaver (Eds.), *Handbook of attachment: Theory, research, and clinical applications* (2nd ed., pp. 552–598). New York: Guilford Press.

Humber, N., & Moss, E. (2005). The relationship of preschool and early school age attachment to mother-child interaction. *American Journal of Orthopsychiatry, 75*, 128–141.

Kaloustian, G., & Posada, G. (2009, April). *Secure base behavior and representations: Associations with social competence in childhood.* Poster presented at the meeting of the Society for Research in Child Development, Denver, CO.

Kerns, K. A. (2008). Attachment in middle childhood. In J. Cassidy & P. R. Shaver (Eds.), *Handbook of attachment: Theory, research, and clinical applications* (2nd ed., pp. 366–382). New York: The Guilford Press.

Kerns, K. A., Tomich, P. L. & Kim, P. (2006). Normative trends in perceptions of availability and utilization of attachment figures in middle childhood. *Social Development, 15*, 1–22.

Kobak, R. R., Cole, H. E., Ferenz-Gillies, R., Fleming, W., & Gamble, W. (1993). Attachment and emotion regulation during mother-teen problem solving: A control theory analysis. *Child Development, 64*, 231–245.

Ladd, G. W., Le Sieur, K. D., Profilet, S. M. (1993). Direct parental influences on young children's peer relations. In S. Duck (Ed.), *Understanding relationship processes: Learning about relationships* (pp. 152–83). Newbury Park, CA: Sage.

Larose, S., & Bernier, A. (2001). Social support processes: Mediators of attachment state of mind and adjustment in late adolescence. *Attachment & Human Development, 3*, 96–120.

Lewis, M. (1997). *Altering fate: Why the past does not predict the future.* New York: The Guilford Press.

Magai, C. (2008). Attachment in middle and later life. In J. Cassidy & P. R. Shaver (Eds.), *Handbook of attachment: Theory, research, and clinical applications* (2nd ed., pp. 532–551). New York: Guilford Press.

Main, M., Kaplan, N., & Cassidy, J. (1985). Security in infancy, childhood, and adulthood: A move to the level of representation. *Monographs of the Society for Research in Child Development, 50*(1–2), 66–104.

Main, M., & Solomon, J. (1986). Discovery of a new, insecure-disorganized disoriented attachment pattern. In T. B. Brazelton & M. Yogman (Eds.), *Affective development in infancy* (pp. 95–124). Norwood, MA: Ablex.

Main, M., & Solomon, J. (1990). Procedures for identifying infants as disorganized/disoriented during the Ainsworth Strange Situation. In M. T. Greenberg, D. Cicchetti, & E. M. Cummings (Eds.), *Attachment in the preschool years: Theory, research and intervention* (pp. 121–160). Chicago, IL: University of Chicago Press.

Marvin, R. S., & Britner, P. A. (1999). Normative development: The ontogeny of attachment. In J. Cassidy & P. R. Shaver (Eds.), *Handbook of attachment: Theory, research, and clinical applications* (pp. 44–67). New York: Guilford Press.

Merz, E. M., & Consedine, N. (2009). The association of family support and wellbeing in later life depends on adult attachment style. *Attachment and Human Development, 11*, 203–221.

Miljkovitch, R., Pierrehumbert, B., Bretherton, I., & Halfon, O. (2004). Associations between parental and child attachment representations. *Attachment and Human Development, 6*, 305–325.

Miyake, K., Chen, S., Campos, J. J. (1985). Infant temperament, mother's mode of interaction, and attachment in Japan: An interim report. In I. Bretherton & E. Waters (Eds.), *Growing points of attachment theory and research. Monographs of the Society for Research in Child Development, 50*(1–2, Serial No. 209), 276–297.

Moss, E., Bureau, J. F., Beliveau, M. J., Zdebik, M., & Lepine, S. (2009). Links between children's attachment behavior at early school-age, their attachment-related representations, and behavior problems in middle childhood. *International Journal of Behavioral Development, 33*, 155–166.

Moss, E., Bureau, J. F., Cyr, C., Mongeau, C., & St-Laurent, D. (2004). Correlates of attachment at age 3: Construct validity of the preschool attachment classification system. *Developmental Psychology, 40*, 323–334.

Moss, E., Cyr, C., & Dubois-Comtois, K. (2004). Attachment at early school age and developmental risk: Examining family contexts and behavior problems of controlling-caregiving, controlling-punitive, and behaviorally disorganized children. *Developmental Psychology, 40*, 519–532.

Moss, E., Rousseau, D., Parent, S., St-Laurent, D., & Saintonge, J. (1998). Correlates of attachment at school-age: Maternal-reported stress, mother–child interaction and behavior problems. *Child Development, 69*, 1390–1405.

Moss, E., & St. Laurent, D. (2001). Attachment at school age and academic performance. *Developmental Psychology, 37*, 863–874.

Parkes, C. M. (1972). *Studies of grief in adult life.* New York: International Universities Press.

Pederson D. R., & Moran, G. (1995). A categorical description of infant-mother relationships in the home and its relation to Q-sort measures of infant-mother interaction. In E. Waters, B. E. Vaughn, G. Posada, & K. Kondo-Ikemura (Eds.), *Caregiving, cultural, and cognitive perspectives on secure-base behavior and working models: New growing points of attachment theory and research. Monographs of the Society for Research in Child Development, 60*(2–3, Serial No. 244), 111–132.

Pederson, D. R., & Moran, G. (1996). Expressions of the attachment relationship outside of the strange situation. *Child Development, 67*, 915–927.

Pianta, R. C., Sroufe, L. A., & Egeland, M. (1989). Continuity and discontinuity in maternal sensitivity at 6, 24, and 42 months in a high risk sample. *Child Development, 60*, 481–487.

Posada, G. (2006). Assessing attachment security at age three: Q-sort home observations and the MacArthur strange situation adaptation. *Social Development, 15*, 644–658.

Posada, G., Carbonell, O. A., Alzate, G., & Plata, S. J. (2004). Through Colombian lenses: Ethnographic and conventional analyses of maternal care and their associations with secure base behavior. *Developmental Psychology, 40*, 323–333.

Posada, G., Gao, Y., Fang, W., Posada, R., Tascon, M., Schoelmerich, A., et al. (1995). The secure-base phenomenon across cultures: Children's behavior, mothers' preferences, and experts' concepts. In E. Waters, B. Vaughn, G. Posada, & K. Kondo-Ikemura (Eds.), *Caregiving, cultural and cognitive perspectives on secure-base behavior and working models: New growing points of attachment theory and research. Monographs of the Society for Research in Child Development, 60*(2–3, Serial No. 244), 27–48.

Posada, G., Jacobs, A., Carbonell, O. A., Alzate, G., Bustamante, M. R., & Arenas, A. (1999). Maternal care and attachment security in ordinary and emergency contexts. *Developmental Psychology, 35*, 1379–1388.

Posada, G., Jacobs, A., Richmond, M. K., Carbonell, O. A., Alzate, G., Bustamante, M. R., et al. (2002). Maternal caregiving and infant security in two cultures. *Developmental Psychology, 38*, 67–78.

Posada, G., Kaloustian, G., & Barrig, P. (2007, March–April). *The secure base phenomenon in preschoolers: Children behavior and narratives about using mom as a secure base.* Poster presented at the meeting of the Society for Research in Child Development. Boston, MA.

Posada, G., Kaloustian, G., Richmond, M. K., & Moreno, A. (2007). Maternal secure base support and preschoolers' secure base behavior in natural environments. *Attachment and Human Development, 9*, 391–411.

Robertson, J. (1952). *A two-year-old goes to hospital.* New York: University Film Library.

Rodrigues, L., Zevallos, A., Turan, B., & Green, K. (2003, March), Attachment scripts across cultures: Further evidence for a universal secure base script. In H. S. Waters & E. Waters (Eds.), *Script-like representations of secure base experience: Evidence of cross-age, cross-cultural, and behavioral links.* Poster symposium presented at the Biennial Meetings of the Society for Research in Child Development, Tampa, FL.

Sameroff, A. J., & Haith, M. M. (1996). Interpreting developmental transitions. In A. J. Sameroff & M. M. Haith (Eds.), *The five to seven year shift: The age of reason and responsibility* (pp. 3–16). Chicago, IL: University of Chicago Press.

Scharf, M., Mayseless, O., & Kivenson-Baron, I. (2004). Adolescents' attachment representations and developmental tasks in emerging adulthood. *Developmental Psychology, 40*, 430–444.

Schneider-Rosen, K. (1990). The developmental reorganization of attachment relationships: Guidelines for classification beyond infancy. In: M. T. Greenberg, D. Cicchetti, & E. M. Cummings (Eds.), *Attachment in the preschool years: Theory, research, and intervention* (pp. 185–220). Chicago, IL: University of Chicago Press.

Schoeni, R. F., & Ross, K. E. (2005). Material assistance from families during the transition to adulthood. In R. A. Settersten, F. F. Furstenberg, & R. G. Rumbaut (Ed.), *On the frontier of adulthood: Theory, research, and public policy.* Chicago, IL: University of Chicago Press.

Seiffge-Krenke, I. (2006). Leaving home or still in the nest? Parent-child relationships and psychological health as predictors of different leaving home patterns. *Developmental Psychology, 42*, 864–876.

Silverstein, M., & Bengtson, V. L. (1997). Intergenerational solidarity and the structure of adult child-parent relationship in American families. *American Journal of Sociology, 103*, 429–460.

Shanahan, L., McHale, S. M., Crouter, A. C., & Osgood, D. W. (2007). Warmth with mothers and fathers from middle childhood to late adolescence: Within- and between-families comparisons. *Developmental Psychology, 43*, 551–563.

Shanahan, L., McHale, S. M., Osgood, D. W., & Crouter, A. C. (2007). Conflict frequency with mothers and fathers from middle childhood to late adolescence: Within- and between families comparisons. *Developmental Psychology, 43*, 539–550.

Silverstein, M., Conroy, S. J., Wang, H., Giarusso, R., & Bengtson, V. L. (2002). Reciprocity in parent-child relations over the adult life course. *The Journals of Gerontology: Series B: Psychological Sciences and Social Sciences, 57*, 3–13.

Sroufe, L. A. (1979). The coherence of individual development. *American Psychologist, 34*, 834–841.

Sroufe, L. A. (1988). The role of infant-caregiver attachment in development. In J. Belsky & T. Nezworski (Eds.), *Clinical implications of attachment.* Hillsdale, NJ: Lawrence Erlbaum Associates.

Sroufe, L. A. (2002). From infant attachment to promotion of adolescent autonomy: Prospective, longitudinal data on the role of parents in development. In J. G. Borkowski, S. L. Ramey,

M. Bristol-Power (Eds.), *Parenting and the child's world* (pp. 187–202). Mahwah, NJ: Lawrence Erlbaum Associates.

Sroufe, L. A., Egeland, B., Kreutzer, T. (1990). The fate of early experience following developmental change: Longitudinal approaches to individual adaptation in childhood. *Child Development, 61,* 1363–1373.

Sroufe, L. A., & Fleeson, J. (1986). Attachment and the construction of relationships. In W. Hartup & Z. Rubin (Eds.), *Relationships and development* (pp. 51–71). Hillsdale, NJ: Erlbaum.

Sroufe, L. A., & Waters, E. (1977). Attachment as an organizational construct. *Child Development, 48,* 1184–1199.

Sroufe, L. A., Egeland, B., Carlson, E. A., & Collins, W. A. (2005). *The development of the person: The Minnesota study of risk and adaptation from birth to adulthood.* New York: Guilford Publications.

Steele, H., Phibbs, E., & Woods, R. T. (2004). Coherence of mind in daughter caregivers of mothers with dementia: Links with their mothers' joy and relatedness on reunion in a strange situation. *Attachment and Human Development, 6,* 439–450.

Stevenson-Hinde, J., & Shouldice, A. (1995). Maternal interactions and self-reports related to attachment classification at 4.5 years. *Child Development, 66,* 583–596.

Symons, D., Clark, S., Isaksen, G., & Marshall, J. (1998). Stability of Q-sort attachment security from age two to five. *Infant Behavior and Development, 21,* 785–792.

Teti, D. M., & Gelfand, D. M. (1997). The preschool assessment of attachment: Construct validity in a sample of depressed and nondepressed families. *Development and Psychopathology, 9,* 517–536.

Teti, D. M., Nakagawa, M., Das Eiden, R., & Wirth, O. (1991). Security of attachment between preschoolers and their mothers: Relations among social interaction, parenting stress, and mothers' sorts of the attachment Q-Set. *Developmental Psychology, 27,* 440–447.

Teti, D. M., Sakin, J., Kucera, E., Corns, K. M., & Das Eiden, R. (1996). And baby makes four: Predictors of attachment security among preschool-age firstborns during the transition to siblinghood. *Child Development, 67,* 579–596.

Thompson, R. A. (1997). Sensitivity and security: New questions to ponder. *Child Development, 68,* 595–597.

Thompson, R. A. (2000). The legacy of early attachments. *Child Development, 71,* 145–152.

Treboux, D., Crowell, J. A., & Waters, E. (2004). When "new" meets "old": Configurations of adult attachment representations and their implications for marital functioning. *Developmental Psychology, 40,* 295–314.

Troll, L. E., & Smith, J. (1976). Attachment thorough the life span: Some questions about dyadic bonds among adults. *Human Development, 19,* 156–170.

Umberson, D. (1992). Relationships between adult children and their parents: Psychological consequences for both generations. *Journal of Marriage and the Family, 54,* 664–674.

Umberson, D. (2003). *Death of a parent.* New York: Cambridge University Press.

Valenzuela, M. (1990). Attachment in chronically underweight young children. *Child Development, 61,* 1984–1996.

Valenzuela, M. (1997). Maternal sensitivity in a developing society: The context of urban poverty and infant chronic undernutrition. *Developmental Psychology, 33,* 845–855.

van IJzendoorn, M. H. (1996). "Attachment patterns and their outcomes": Commentary. *Human Development, 39,* 224–231.

van IJzendoorn, M. H., Kroonenberg, P. M. (1988). Cross-cultural patterns of attachment: A meta-analysis of the strange situation. *Child Development, 59,* 147–156.

Vaughn, B., Egeland, B., Sroufe, A., & Waters, E. (1979). Individual differences in infant-mother attachment at twelve and eighteen months: Stability and change in families under stress. *Child Development, 50,* 971–975.

Vaughn, B. E., Verissimo, M., Coppola, G., Bost, K. K., Shin, N., McBride, B., et al. (2006). Maternal attachment script representations: Longitudinal stability and associations with stylistic features of maternal narratives. *Attachment and Human Development, 8,* 199–208.

Vereijken, C., Riksen-Walraven, J., & Kondo-Ikemura, K. (1997). Maternal sensitivity and infant attachment security in Japan: A longitudinal study. *International Journal of Behavioral Development, 21,* 35–49.

Wais, D., Rodriguez, L. M., Guttmann-Steinmetz, S., Zevallos, A., Waters, H., Posada, G., et al. (2000, June). *Attachment scripts across cultures.* Poster presented at the 30th Annual Meeting of the Jean Piaget Society, Montreal, QC.

Waters, E., & Cummings, E. M. (2000). A secure base from which to explore close relationships. *Child Development, 71,* 164–172.

Waters, E., Hamilton, C. E., & Weinfield, N. S. (2000). The stability of attachment security from infancy to adolescence and early adulthood: General introduction. *Child Development, 71,* 678–683.

Waters, E., Kondo-Ikemura, K., Posada, G., & Richters, J. E. (1991). Learning to love: Mechanisms and milestones. In M. R. Gunnar & L. A. Sroufe (Eds.), *Self processes and development.* Minnesota symposia on child psychology (Vol. 23, pp. 217–255). Hillsdale, NJ: Erlbaum.

Waters, E., Merrick, S., Treboux, D., Crowell, J., & Albersheim, L. (2000). Attachment security in infancy and early childhood: A twenty-year longitudinal study. *Child Development, 71,* 684–689.

Waters, H. S., & Rodrigues, L. M. (2001). *Are attachment scripts the building blocks of attachment representations? Narrative assessment of representations and the AAI.* Poster presented at the biennial meeting of the Society for Research in Child Development, Minneapolis, MN.

Waters, H. S., Cunliffe, M. A., & Guttmann-Steinmetz, S. (2001). *In search of narrative co-construction.* Paper presented at the Symposium, on Attachment and Early Representation: Integrating Perspectives from Cognitive and Attachment Approaches, at the biennial meeting of the Society for Research in Child Development, Minneapolis, MN.

Waters, H. S., Rodrigues, L. M., & Ridgeway, D. (1998). Cognitive underpinnings of narrative attachment assessment. *Journal of Experimental Child Psychology, 71,* 211–234.

Waters, H. S., & Waters, E. (2006). The attachment working models concept: Among other things, we build script-like representations of secure base experiences. *Attachment and Human Development, 8,* 185–197.

Weinfield, N. S., Sroufe, L. A., & Egeland, B. (2000). Attachment from infancy to early adulthood in a high-risk sample: Continuity, discontinuity, and their correlates. *Child Development, 71,* 695–702.

Whiteman, S. D., McHale, S. M., Crouter, A. C. (2003). What parents learn from experience: The first child as a first draft? *Journal of Marriage and Family, 65,* 608–621.

Zarit, S. H., & Eggebeen, D. J. (2002). Parent-child relationships in adulthood, later years. In M. H. Bornstein (Ed.), *Handbook of parenting: Children and parenting* (Vol. 1, 2nd ed., pp. 135–161). Mahwah, NJ: Lawrence.

DEVELOPMENTAL TASKS ACROSS THE LIFE SPAN

5

Christopher M. McCormick, Sally I-Chun Kuo, and Ann S. Masten

Throughout the life course, the behavior of individuals is judged by self and others as adaptive or maladaptive, successful or unsuccessful, and age-appropriate or not, often by criteria that reflect widely held expectations for age-appropriate and adaptive behavior (Baltes, Reese, & Lipsitt, 1980; Havighurst, 1948/1972; Masten, Burt, & Coatsworth, 2006). An infant is expected to smile and form attachments to caregivers. A toddler is expected to walk and begin to talk. A child of school age is expected to attend school, get along with other children, follow rules, and learn the skills of reading, writing, and mathematics expected for each graded level of learning. Adolescents are expected to adjust to their changing appearance, prepare for adult roles in their society, learn and obey laws of their society, and manage new sexual feelings in culturally acceptable ways. Young adults are expected to establish themselves in adult roles, which often include paid work or higher education, romantic relationships or marriage, and rearing children. In midlife, adults often are expected to contribute to society through civic engagement, mentoring of young people, leadership at work, and helping their own children become established in adult roles. In later life, aging adults are expected to adjust to their changing capabilities or health, retire from work while maintaining meaningful activities, and come to terms with end-of-life transitions. These criteria are grounded in normative developmental and contextual changes over the life course and accrued knowledge about the pathways to adult success in society. In developmental theory, these behavioral criteria for judging how well a person is doing in life have come to be called *developmental tasks*.

In this chapter, we examine the concept of developmental tasks in developmental psychology and the significance of this concept for theory, research, and practice concerned with understanding and promoting positive development. In the first section of the chapter, we discuss the theoretical and historical roots of this idea and its influence on contemporary concepts of development and competence. In the second section, we delineate current perspectives on developmental tasks and the most widely held views about their significance, highlighting research that addresses the most central hypotheses embodied by common tenets of developmental tasks frameworks. In the concluding section, we discuss directions for future research from the developmental tasks perspective, including the need for greater attention to issues of assessment, gender, culture, multiple levels of analysis, and interdisciplinary research.

ROOTS OF DEVELOPMENTAL TASK CONCEPTS

Early Roots

The concept of developmental tasks likely has ancient roots in classical Greek thought, although the concept is usually traced to the 19th century (Masten & Curtis, 2000). The modern concept grew most directly out of 19th century ideas about adaptation, and particularly the ideas of Darwin and Freud (Masten et al., 2006). At that time, the idea of adaptation shifted from a static view of perfect harmony with nature to a dynamic process (Mayr, 1982). The processes of natural selection, which served as the mechanism for evolution, acted through variations in individual adaptation, fitness, and reproductive success. In Freud's structural theory of personality, the job assigned to the *ego* was balancing basic needs and wishes of the unconscious *id* against the demands of social and societal expectations for achievement and proper behavior, resolving conflicts so that the individual could be successful and reasonably content. Freud also delineated issues and tasks that were faced by individuals in the course of their development in his psychosexual stage theory of development. These issues often arose from conflicts between individual drives and fears and the expectations for behavior in family and society, and their resolution spurred healthy development.

Freud's perspective on healthy development also is relevant. In a comment made famous by Erik Erikson (1950/1963), when Freud was asked about "what a person should be able to do well," he reportedly replied, "Lieben und arbeiten" (to love and to work; p. 264–265). Love and work would become central to developmental tasks theory as Freud's stage theory was superseded by Erikson's psychosocial theory of development.

While notions of developmental tasks were evident in Freud's psychosexual theory, it was Erikson who laid the foundation for contemporary developmental task theory (Masten et al., 2006). Erikson's (1950/1963; 1968) conceptualization of psychosocial stages, each with a crisis or issue to be addressed, has clear parallels in the conceptualization of developmental tasks as sociocultural expectations that rise to importance during particular developmental periods. Equally important were Erikson's ideas regarding the longitudinal nature of each issue to be addressed. While Erikson surmised that each of the core issues endured throughout most of the life course, each issue had a particular window of ascendency when it was central to development. At this time, the issue became a "crisis" that required resolution. Identity crisis, for example, was the central issues of adolescence. Erikson also proposed that adaptive responses to the central issue of a psychosocial stage were critical for an individual to do well when future issues needed to be addressed. The central idea that "competence begets competence" in developmental task theory evolved from this fundamental proposition.

The Influence of Robert Havighurst

The first formal delineation of "developmental tasks" in those terms, to our knowledge, dates to a pamphlet originally created around 1948 by Robert Havighurst for a course he was teaching at the University of Chicago that he later developed into a widely disseminated book (Havighurst, 1948/1972). In the preface to the 1972 edition of the book, called *Developmental Tasks and Education*, Havighurst indicated that his use of the concept was influenced by Erikson's theory of psychosocial development. Also in the preface, he described a developmental task as "midway between an individual need and a societal demand" (p. vi). Havighurst also distinguished among tasks that arise primarily from biological maturation or change, those that arise from sociocultural pressures, and those that stem from the values and goals of the individual.

According to Havighurst (1948/1972), each individual, by virtue of being a citizen of a larger society, faces a series of expectations over the life course. He posited that judgments of success by self and society are highly influenced by the degree to which an individual is perceived to be meeting these expectations. Like Freud, Havighurst noted that these tasks reflect a balance of "inner and outer forces" acting upon the individual. Like Erikson, Havighurst proposed a series of tasks to be achieved over the life course, each with a developmentally appropriate age period during which engagement and resolution or mastery is expected: "Living in a modern society is a long series of tasks to learn" (Havighurst, 1948/1972, p. 2). Also like Erikson, Havighurst emphasized the importance of successful achievements in these tasks in regard to both happiness and success in later tasks (versus failure, which leads to unhappiness, disapproval, and difficulties with later tasks; Havighurst, 1948/1972, p. 2). He noted that many of the tasks of early childhood reflect mastery of universal tasks that depend on maturation and experience, such as learning to walk and to talk. Older children, he noted, are expected to learn social roles, skills for playing games, and many other skills needed for achievement in childhood and later in life. Adolescents are expected to adjust to their changing bodies and prepare for adult roles, which they begin to accomplish in early adulthood. By midlife, societies expect adults to be contributing to civic life and launching children they may have had. By the end of this period, physical changes that signal declining fertility, health, or strength often emerge, requiring adjustments of perspective or lifestyle. Mature adults must adapt to issues of aging, such as decreasing strength and declining health, changing family responsibilities, and changes in work life, often including retirement. In addition to describing developmental tasks common to American society across the life span, Havighurst also emphasized the influence of psychological development and culture, as well as biological maturation, on developmental task expectations. Developmental tasks such as developing a career or a philosophy of life were more influenced by personal and cultural motivations and values than the task of learning to walk.

Although primarily interested in education, each of Havighurst's tasks was grounded in the values and expectations that were popular among Americans of his time (Oerter, 1986). In the decades following, many authors contributed to further explication of developmental task theory. The works of Greenspan (1981), Sander (1975), and Sroufe (1979), for example, were important in developing ideas about salient developmental issues confronting children in infancy and early childhood. Hill (1980, 1983) examined the tasks of adolescence. Neugarten (1979) described the expectations that individuals develop about a "normal, expectable life cycle," including a sense of timelines and timetables, evaluating their progress in relation to these expectations ("How am I doing for my age?", p. 888) along with the idea of judging oneself (or others) as "on time" or "off time" (p. 888).

Havighurst and Erikson both drew attention to the idea of developmental tasks beyond childhood and adolescence, discussing issues and expectations across the life span. This more inclusive conceptualization of development tasks was an important building block for life-span developmental psychology. The concept of tasks and their timing became central to theories on life-span developmental psychology, where scholars emphasized the role of context and role transitions for defining the nature and timing of tasks across the life span (Baltes et al., 1980; Elder, 1974/1999, 1998; Perrig-Chiello & Perren, 2005).

Life-Span Developmental Theory

Life-span developmental psychology is centered on assertions that human development occurs from birth to death, proceeds multidimensionally, demonstrates great plasticity, can be described in terms of a ratio of gain to loss, and takes historical and contextual embeddedness into account (Baltes, 1987; Baltes et al., 1980). Similar to the emphasis in Havighurst's perspective on developmental tasks, life-span psychologists distinguish between internal and external influences on development and the role of age, history, and non-normative experiences in relation to biological or cultural influences on development (Baltes, Cornelius, & Nesselroade, 1979; Baltes, Lindenberger, & Staudinger, 1998; Brandtstädter, 1998; Greve & Staudinger, 2006).

Baltes et al. (1980) pointed out that the tasks of adulthood (or the second half of life) are less well delineated by age-graded or developmental stages than are early life tasks and are more influenced by historical and non-normative events. Nonetheless, typical developmental tasks of adulthood and later life continue to be identified in developmental theory and research, often in the context of ascertaining life outcomes of longitudinal cohorts under study (e.g., Elder, 1974/1999; Hawkins, Guo, Hill, Battin-Pearson, & Abbott, 2001; Masten et al., 1995; Masten, Desjardins, McCormick, Kuo, & Long, 2010; Sroufe, Egeland, Carlson, & Collins, 2005; Werner & Smith, 1992, 2001).

Theories of Competence, Resilience, and Self-Efficacy

Another important root of developmental task theory can be traced to Robert White's (1959) theory of competence and the motivation system connected to effective engagement in the environment. White integrated the ego psychology of the neo-Freudians, evolutionary theory, and experimental observations of motivation in animal research to argue that effective adaptation stemmed from a powerful motivation system. This system motivated and rewarded successful engagement and mastery of the environment. The individual was motivated by the anticipation and experienced pleasure in this perceived mastery, yet the cumulative effect on evolution was an increasingly adaptive organism.

White's ideas had a profound influence on developmental theories of the self and self-efficacy, and particularly the work of Susan Harter and Albert Bandura. Harter (1978) extended White's theory of mastery motivation and also developed widely used measures of perceived competence (e.g., Harter's Self-Perception Profile measure; Harter, 1982). Bandura (1977, 1997) extended the concept of self-efficacy, focusing on perceived capacity for adaptive effectiveness, and also developed measures to assess this domain of self-perception. These measures, along with the research based on them by Harter, Bandura, and others, reflect and corroborate a multidimensional and differentiated view of competence and perceived competence, both on the part of investigators and the informants who completed these types of measures, as discussed further in the following section.

The influence of constructs related to competence and developmental tasks was bolstered further by research on competence and resilience in children at risk and the concomitant emergence of developmental psychopathology (Cicchetti, 2006; Luthar, 2006; Masten, 2006; Masten, in press; Masten & Obradović, 2006; Masten et al., 2006; Sroufe & Rutter, 1984). Developmental psychopathology emphasized the importance of understanding pathways to adaptive behavior in addition to the paths to psychopathology and called for the integration of developmental theories about adaptive behavior over the life course. Competence concepts played a central role in the thinking of influential scholars in developmental psychopathology, and assessments of competence and developmental tasks became central to research concerned with the quality of adaptation over time.

The concept of competence was central to the organizational theory of development, as articulated by Alan Sroufe, his collaborators, and his students, who had a profound influence on a generation of research in developmental psychopathology. Waters & Sroufe (1983) asserted that the "key to age-appropriate assessment of competence is to select issues central for each developmental period" (p. 84). They gave examples such as establishing an effective attachment relationship in the first year of life and exploration/individuation later in the toddler years. According to Sroufe and colleagues, assessments of these key issues should show predictive validity for the quality of adaptation with respect to the future salient issues; thus, a secure attachment relationship in infancy, for example, should forecast later success in toddler competencies involving exploration and showing independence or autonomy. In organizational theory, addressing salient developmental issues required the coordinated organization of personal and environmental resources in ways that set the stage for future competence. Broad-based measures of these core issues were predicted to show coherence over time, even though the exact target of measurement would be expected to change (Sroufe, 1979).

Research on resilience gave additional impetus to developmental task theory as investigators began to define competence explicitly in relation to developmental tasks in their longitudinal studies of risk and resilience (Masten, in press; Masten & Powell, 2003). One of the most important contributions of the research on resilience in developmental psychopathology was the attention the investigators brought to defining and measuring competence in terms of developmental task achievement (Masten & Obradović, 2006). Longitudinal research required assessment of competence in a number of studies, and consequently, many of the central tenets of developmental task theory were implicitly or explicitly tested, as discussed further in what follows.

Age-Salient Developmental Tasks

The ideas described earlier from developmental theory and research culminated in the concept of age-salient developmental tasks and efforts to systematically measure how well a person was doing in the context of life course development on the basis of these tasks (Masten & Coatsworth, 1998; Masten et al., 2006; Roisman, Masten, Coatsworth, & Tellegen, 2004). Considerable consistency emerged in identification of key developmental tasks for given periods of development and fundamental tenets emerged. The latter are discussed in the next section.

Table 5.1 provides a list of widely recognized developmental tasks. These are based on prominent conceptual frameworks in developmental social sciences noted previously (e.g., Havighurst, 1948/1972; Sroufe, 1979) and reviews of the literature (e.g., Ford, 1985; Masten & Braswell, 1991; Masten & Coatsworth, 1998; Oerter, 1986). A variety of developmental tasks are listed in the table, both observable (e.g., learning to walk) and internal (e.g., achieving a coherent identity). Some of the tasks are usually viewed as "universal" in the sense that they

TABLE 5.1

Examples of Developmental Tasks Across the Life Span	
Age Period	**Developmental Task**
Infants	Attachment relationship to caregiver
	Learning to sit, crawl, and stand
	Differentiation of self from environment
	Interactive play with caregivers and toys
	Physiological regulation (eating, sleeping)
Toddlers and preschoolers	Learning to walk, run, and climb stairs
	Toilet training
	Functional language
	Self-control and compliance
	Social play
Young school-age children	Attending and behaving properly in school
	Learning to read, write, and calculate
	Getting along with classmates and peers
	Making friends
	Following rules of conduct in society
Adolescents	Academic achievement in secondary school
	Adjusting to pubertal changes
	Close friendships
	Abiding by laws and moral rules of conduct
	Identity exploration and cohesion
	Learning about romantic relationships
Young adults	Establishing work or pursuing higher education
	Behaving appropriately in the work place
	Committed romantic relationships or marriage
	Caring effectively for dependent children
	Maintaining a household
	Establishing financial independence
Middle-aged adults	Maintaining satisfactory work
	Maintaining romantic relationships
	Launching children; adjusting to "empty nest"
	Civic engagement
	Attaining financial security
	Caring for aging parents
	Adaptation to midlife physical changes
Aging adults	Adjusting to changes of aging
	Transitioning to retirement from work
	Adjusting to dependence on others
	Adjusting to death of spouse or close friends
	Coming to terms with mortality
	Settling affairs

are expected in any culture (e.g., learning to talk), whereas others are common but not necessarily universal (e.g., school achievement is not expected in cultures where there is no schooling). It is also worth noting that multiple tasks are readily identified for any broad period of development, although this is perhaps easier in childhood than midlife or late life. As will be discussed further in the following (see tenet 4), the multiplicity or multidimensional nature of developmental tasks and domains implicated by lists of this kind has been investigated and generally corroborated.

A developmental-task list of this kind can be viewed in terms of the criteria for judging whether development is proceeding well. Studies of competence and resilience, for example, require criteria for judging positive adaptation, and measures focused on success or problems in meeting these developmental task expectations have been used to define competence as well as resilience (competence in the context of adversity or risk; see Masten, 2001). Scholars emphasize that these criteria and judgments about whether individuals are doing well in regard to these expectations reflect values and expectations that are deeply embedded in cultural, historical, and political context (Masten & Coatsworth, 1998; Motti-Stefanidi, Berry, Chryssochoou, Sam, & Phinney, in press). Given the inherent bias of such judgments, they argue that some caution is required when such criteria are applied by one group or culture to another. Moreover, efforts have been made to identify competence criteria domains through methods designed to elicit culturally embedded, emic expectations. Developmental task expectations are readily extracted, and some appear to be widely shared across cultures, whereas others are more culturally specific (Boelcke-Stennes, 2001; Durbrow, 1999; Durbrow, Peña, Masten, Sesma, & Williamson, 2001).

Developmental tasks also change as the ways of living and cultures in which individuals live, evolve, and change (Durbrow, 1999; Elder, 1974/1999; Harkness & Super, 1996; Hofer, Noack, & Youniss, 1994; Motti-Stefanidi et al., in press). In the last century, expectations for education and work changed, for example, in societies that shifted from predominantly agrarian to predominantly industrial (Elder, 1974/1999; Elder & Conger, 2000). Arnett (2000) has argued that a confluence of cultural, economic, and societal changes over the last 50–100 years has resulted in a new phase of development for the relatively affluent populations of young people within industrialized countries. *Emerging adulthood,* as Arnett terms this time (2000), falls in between adolescence and the time when young people are expected to take on the responsibilities and expectations of adulthood. Adult developmental tasks are put on hold for a while as young people explore a variety of identities, places, relationships, and possibilities for the future (see Arnett & Tanner, 2006). In the 21st century, as many societies participate and interact in the digital age, with the globalization of cultural interaction that accompanies it, developmental tasks are likely to change as a result of ongoing acculturation processes and changing contexts for human development.

TENETS OF CONTEMPORARY DEVELOPMENTAL TASK THEORY

Although examples of specific developmental tasks and the use of developmental task theory vary in emphasis, there is, nonetheless, an identifiable set of consistent and defining tenets that characterize contemporary developmental task frameworks for understanding development and adaptation across the life span (see Masten et al., 2006; Masten & Obradović, 2006). Seven such tenets are listed in Table 5.2. These are described further in the following sections, along with selected supporting evidence from the empirical literature.

TABLE 5.2

Tenets of Developmental Tasks Theory
1. Developmental tasks emerge and change as a function of development in context
2. Some developmental tasks are universal
3. Some developmental tasks are culturally or contextually specific
4. Developmental tasks include multiple dimensions or domains of behavior
5. Success and failure in age-salient developmental tasks forecasts success and failure in later developmental tasks
6. Success or failure in developmental tasks often has cascading consequences
7. Strategic intervention focused on developmental tasks can promote success and positive cascades while preventing problems and negative cascades

Tenet 1—Developmental Tasks Emerge and Change as a Function of Development in Context

Central tenets of developmental task frameworks for adaptive behavior over the life course derive in large part from common characteristics and features of contemporary developmental systems theory (Gottlieb, Wahlsten, & Lickliter, 1998; Lerner, 2006; Sameroff, 2000; Sroufe, 1997, 2007; Thelen & Smith, 1998) and life-span psychology (e.g., Baltes et al., 1998). Both of these theoretical perspectives assert that the course of individual development is shaped by many processes and interactions within and among individuals and their contexts across many levels (from genes to neural systems to society and even solar effects that influence circadian rhythms). Typically, these approaches make the assumption that developmental tasks emerge from interactions and convergences among biological, cultural, and contextual changes over the life course. Developmental tasks will emerge, become salient, and wane as a function of changes in development and context over the life course. In other words, salient developmental tasks and issues represent expectations based on shared views on development in a particular historical, cultural, or societal context. As a result, developmental tasks have a context of individual and normative development, and prevailing societal and cultural values.

In turn, the developmental significance of a given task will vary as a result of the specific interactions of biological, cultural, and contextual features in an individual's environment. Success in the task of paid work provides an example. In many industrialized cultures (but not all), young children are not expected to work for pay outside the home in formal jobs and, indeed, may be forbidden by law from doing so. At the same time, children may be prepared for work by doing domestic chores, schoolwork, or informal jobs like babysitting. Moreover, in the case of family-owned businesses, exceptions may be allowed by law for children to work on farms or help out in a family restaurant.

In industrialized countries, formal work frequently begins during adolescence, although often in jobs that do not require high levels of skills or training. Work in adolescence and initial types of employment (part-time or apprenticeships) can be viewed as a time when the task of formal work is emerging in many modern societies; then, sometime in early adulthood, work generally becomes a salient developmental task (Masten et al., 2010; Roisman et al., 2004). However, these normative expectations still allow for variability in pathways of work. During late adolescence and early adulthood in the United States, for example, young people follow different work pathways (Mortimer, Vuolo, Staff, Wakefield, & Xie, 2008; Mortimer & Zimmer-Gembeck, 2007). Some move into full time work early, foregoing higher education while others invest in many years of education to prepare for a career. Other youths in adolescence and early adulthood are not especially invested in either education or employment.

At the other end of the formal work time frame, when people decrease their hours or formally retire (signaling that this developmental task has waned in salience), there may be wide variation in timing and patterns of change, as well as traditions and laws. In some contexts or careers, laws require retirement by a certain age, although these rules may change. In the United States, for example, there is a mandatory retirement age for airline pilots, which was changed from age 60 to age 65 in 2007 by the US Congress and signed into law by then President Bush.

Tenet 2—Some Developmental Tasks Are Universal

Although developmental tasks are influenced by historical, developmental, and cultural contexts, some developmental tasks are, nevertheless, expected to be *universal*, as noted earlier. Universal developmental tasks arise from the commonalities in species-typical human development and similarities of contexts and constraints in which they develop. For example, regardless of culture, all children are expected to learn to walk and to communicate with other individuals (unless, of course, there is a significant problem in how the organism is able to function, such as a physical disability).

Presumably, these universal developmental tasks reflect common concepts across culturally diverse societies about human development and important achievements for building future competence. With rapid globalization and widespread use of the Internet, one might expect that the similarity in developmental task expectations would increase.

Tenet 3—Some Developmental Tasks Are Culturally or Contextually Specific

Unusual or unique developmental tasks also occur, probably as a result of atypical confluences of culture and context or beliefs about development in a given geographical or historical setting (Durbrow, 1999; Garcia Coll et al., 1996; Motti-Stefanidi et al., in press). These developmental tasks may arise as a result of specific physical features of a particular environment, a unique distribution of genetic variation based on historical migration patterns, evolution of local customs and cultural traditions, acculturation processes, discrimination, or the interplay of all these influences. The same biological transition (e.g., puberty) may come to be celebrated by developmental-task challenges in very different ways by different cultures. Although many religions and cultures have rites of passage around the time of puberty or early adolescence, there is striking diversity in the nature and timing of the rites of passage that celebrate coming of age or taking on adult roles and responsibilities in different religions or cultural groups. Bar or Bat Mitzvah, for instance, is commonly celebrated in Jewish tradition at the age of 13 with a religious ceremony where the youth demonstrates skills and knowledge of the religion and sacred texts. In pluralistic societies like the United States, these culturally specific tasks expectations are often held by subcultures within the society, while at the same time more broadly experienced accomplishments are also celebrated, such as getting a driver's license or graduating from high school.

Bicultural adaptation has become a topic of considerable interest in contemporary societies with multicultural populations and growing numbers of immigrant youth (see Masten, Liebkind, & Hernandez, in press). Some societies encourage immigrants or cultural subgroups to maintain distinct cultural expectations, languages, and traditions (at least those that do not violate laws), while also supporting the successful engagement in the society's developmental task expectations (e.g., success in school). Other societies encourage assimilation and full adoption of the mainstream society's values in regard to developmental tasks. Conflicts can arise within families and among subcultural constituents of societies as a result of differing beliefs and expectations about developmental tasks and their appropriate timing.

Tenet 4—Developmental Tasks Include Multiple Dimensions or Domains of Behavior

Erikson (1950/1963, 1968) emphasized one particular challenge in each of the stages in his psychosocial stage theory of development, although he also acknowledged that these challenges (e.g., identity) extended beyond the life cycle stage when each challenge was most salient. Current perspectives emphasize the multiplicity of developmental tasks that individuals face at a particular age or period in the life course. Some tasks may be more salient than others, but typically there are multiple tasks and thus multiple criteria by which doing well in life can be judged at any given time in development. Toddlers, for example, are expected to learn how to walk and run, talk, play with toys, identify themselves as a boy or a girl, and begin to show some compliance with parental directives. A toddler who is doing well in life would be expected to show progress in multiple key areas and not just one domain. However, it is widely recognized that individuals vary in how well they may be doing across multiple domains, so that different people may have different profiles of accomplishment with respect to the prevailing developmental tasks for their age or period of development. Thus, it is conceivable that an individual manifests competence in one area (e.g., friendship) while experiencing serious problems in another (e.g., academic or work achievement). A toddler may talk well but manifest an unacceptable degree of aggressive behavior, such as biting other children regularly. An adult may have great work success but not function well at home in the domains of romantic relationships or parenting.

Developmental tasks also reflect the general developmental feature of increasing differentiation over the life course (Dannefer, 2003; Masten et al., 2005). There tend to be more differentiated developmental tasks as children get older and also more options or pathways for manifesting competence. As a result, there is greater diversity in acceptable pathways to achievement as individuals grow older. Throughout much of early life, children follow a fairly limited number of developmental pathways, although these may be gender-differentiated or otherwise limited by discrimination. Within a given context, most children will face the same or highly similar developmental tasks, and be judged based on the similar expectations of success in areas such as academic achievement and social relationships. In adulthood, however, the number of potential pathways an individual may take is larger (i.e., there are more branching pathways). In typical Western or industrialized cultures, for example, it is commonly expected that children will go to school and learn to read; thus, a child who is truant from school and has trouble with reading is not likely to be judged as competent. In adulthood, individuals in these cultures often have the option of deciding among alternative pathways, such as whether or not they want to have children and divide their energies between raising a family and succeeding at work, or forego parenthood in favor of more focused career. In either case, these adults could still be judged and judge themselves as successful members of the society.

Important exceptions to the general similarity of developmental task expectations for children and youth and the expansion of pathways in adulthood are reflected in gender role stereotyping (e.g., Eccles, 1986; Heilman, 2001; Watt & Eccles, 2008) and also in discrimination based on gender, class, ethnicity, or other characteristics (e.g., Schmader, Johns, & Forbes, 2008; Steele, 1997; Quintana & McKown, 2007). In these cases, developmental task expectations are altered by actual or perceived opportunities, obstacles, and prejudice. Indeed, one of the most powerful forms of discrimination may take the form of lower expectations in developmental task domains, potentially leading to lower aspirations and negative developmental cascades. Teachers may hold different expectations based on ethnicity/race or other kinds of labeling. A recent meta-analysis corroborated early meta-analyses indicating that American teachers held varying expectations for students based on their ethnicity (Tenenbaum & Ruck, 2007). Evidence has also suggested that teachers and parents have lower expectations for academic achievement in children with a diagnostic label of "ADHD," despite objective evidence of typical abilities in the academic domain (Eisenberg & Schneider, 2007). These lower expectations may result in differential treatment, which in turn can impair children's self-perceptions of their own abilities and hinder their academic development, serving as the first step in a negative developmental cascade.

The multidimensionality of competence in developmental tasks has been supported in diverse empirical research (Masten et al., 2006). Examples of the evidence include data from factor analyses of widely used measures of adaptive behavior and perceived competence (e.g., Goodman, 2001; Harter, 1982), measurement models in studies using structural equation modeling (e.g., Burt & Roisman, 2010; Masten et al., 1995, 2005, 2010), and analyses to determine implicit models of competence held by laypersons (e.g., Boelcke-Stennes, 2001; Durbrow et al., 2001).

Tenet 5—Success and Failure in Age-Salient Developmental Tasks Forecasts Success and Failure in Later Developmental Tasks

Success in age-salient development tasks reflects not only the skills that are needed for current success, but also those needed to build future success in society (Ford, 1985; Havighurst, 1948/1972; Masten et al., 2006, 2010; Roisman et al., 2004; Sroufe, 1979). This tenet underscores the fundamental proposition that *competence begets competence*. Successful mastery of salient developmental tasks requires the formation and integration of skills and resources to achieve adaptive goals. This process builds adaptive skills and also confidence in the person's capabilities for future success. Conversely, difficulties or failures in salient developmental tasks is concerning to stakeholders (including parents, society, and the self) because it signals some risk for potential difficulties in future task achievements. In addition, there appear to be cumulative and directional effects over time among different domains of function in developmental tasks, over and above any concurrent bidirectional effects. As a result, successes or failures can snowball over time (see tenet 6). Perceived successes may contribute to growing confidence and self-efficacy, whereas perceived failures can contribute to distress and lower self-esteem.

There are two corollaries of this tenet. First, coherence is expected within a developmental task domain over time, in keeping with general developmental principles (Sroufe, 1979). Thus, earlier success or failure in a particular domain (e.g., school achievement or social competence with peers) is expected to show some continuity over time to behavior within the same general domain, although the expectations and assessments in that domain may change in keeping with development. Considerable stability has been observed in major development task domains over long periods of time (Masten et al., 2006). Findings from the Minnesota Study of Risk and Adaptation from Birth to Adulthood (Obradović, van Dulmen, Yates, Carlson, & Egeland, 2006; Sroufe et al., 2005) and the Project Competence Longitudinal Study (Burt, Obradović, Long, & Masten, 2008; Masten & Powell, 2003; Masten et al., 1995, 2005, 2010) provide examples of striking coherence over time within developmental task domains, such as social competence with peers, academic achievement, rule-abiding versus rule-breaking behavior, work, and romantic relationships. On the other hand, both of these longitudinal studies have shown equally impressive "turnaround cases" or resilience, where the life course changes dramatically away from failure toward competence and achievement (Masten, Obradović, & Burt, 2006; Masten et al., 2004; Sroufe et al., 2005).

Second, deeper developmental continuity has been proposed for some domains, where early experience is assumed to have important consequences for later engagement in developmental tasks. The hypothesized significance of secure attachment relationships for later peer friendships and romantic relationships in developmental theories about relationships provides an example (Sroufe & Fleeson, 1986; Sroufe et al., 2005). Good quality relationships between child and caregivers in early development, arising in a context of sensitive and effective parenting, are expected to contribute to the quality of later peer and romantic relationships through a variety of processes. Evidence continues to build in support of this broad hypothesis (Carlson, Sroufe, & Egeland, 2004; Roisman, Madsen, Hennighausen, Sroufe, & Collins 2001; Sroufe, Carlson, Levy, & Egeland, 1999; Sroufe et al., 2005). It has also been hypothesized that high quality parenting is carried forward to parenting in the next generation through developmental task achievements in related domains, such as social competence (e.g., Shaffer, Burt, Obradović, Herbers, & Masten, 2009). This coherence across related domains (e.g., close relationships) over the course of development or generations could be viewed as a form of heterotypic continuity. Spreading consequences across domains also have been discussed in terms of developmental tasks, discussed in the following section.

Tenet 6—Success or Failure in Developmental Tasks Often Has Cascading Consequences

Success or failure in salient developmental tasks is expected to have consequences for the future, and these effects may cascade across time and domains through a variety of processes (Masten & Cicchetti, 2010). Developmental cascades refer to the cumulative consequences of the dynamic interactions in systems across levels of function or domains of function over time, and even across generations. Concurrent, bidirectional influences occurring among domains of developmental tasks (e.g., conduct in the classroom and academic performance) can be carried forward across time, sometimes resulting in the amplification of problems or successes. Alternatively, difficulties in one domain can undermine functions in another domain, as when antisocial behavior in the classroom interferes with learning and academic achievement or academic success alters later work opportunities.

Problems in one domain can have a cumulative directional effect on another domain which in turn alters the odds for success in a third domain. Patterson and colleagues at the Oregon Social Learning Center, for example, proposed such a process in their dual failure model of antisocial behavior (Capaldi, 1992; Patterson, DeBaryshe, & Ramsey, 1989; Patterson, Reid, & Dishion, 1992). Early behavior problems arising in the home context were hypothesized to spread to the school context when the child entered school, disrupting learning, achievement, and teacher and peer relationships. This dual failure was then expected to encourage a drift into deviant peer groups and contribute to depressive symptoms. Data have supported this model, both from these and other investigators (Dodge, Greenberg, Malone, & The Conduct Problems Prevention Research Group, 2008; Obradović, Burt, & Masten, 2010; Patterson & Stoolmiller, 1991).

The cascading effects of economic crisis on families provide another example of cumulative cascade effects across family members and domains of life function. In his classic study of the Great Depression, Elder (1974/1999) observed how the effect of economic distress on parents appeared to undermine parenting with consequences for their children, with effects varying by age, timing, and gender (for both parents and children). More recently, Elder and Conger (2000) examined the cascading effects of economic distress in parents affected by the Iowa farm crisis on their adolescent children, through the effects on the psychological well being and marital relationship of the parents and their parenting.

Recent advances in statistical techniques and computational tools have allowed researchers to examine both within and across domain effects of the attainment of developmental tasks across the life span in a very rigorous way (Masten & Cicchetti, 2010). Through structural equation or growth curve modeling techniques and repeated assessments over time, for example, it is possible to test models of continuity and change across long periods of time and also cascade effects across domains over and above any within time covariation and across-time continuity (e.g., Klimes-Dougan et al., 2010; Masten et al., 2005; Shaffer et al., 2009).

One of the most consistently observed effects in this body of work is the effect that failure to master expectations for socialized (rule-governed) conduct have for future development (Masten et al., 2006; Masten & Cicchetti, 2010). Data consistently suggest that failure to meet developmental expectations for acceptable behavior at school undermines academic achievement and social competence, and is related to increased risk for developing symptoms of psychopathology and other problems in adolescence and adulthood (Burt & Roisman, 2010; Dodge et al., 2008; Obradović et al., 2010; Patterson, Forgatch, & DeGarmo, 2010). These negative effects may have cascading consequences well into adulthood, altering work outcomes, for example (Caspi, Wright, Moffitt, & Silva, 1998; Masten et al., 2010).

Cascade effects across time and developmental task domains have been examined and found in an increasing number of studies. Recent evidence can be found in two special issues of *Development and Psychopathology* on developmental cascades (see Masten & Cicchetti, 2010). The growing evidence of developmental cascade effects has important implications for intervention because it suggests that well timed and targeted interventions could have amplified or what might be termed "multiplier effects" over time.

Tenet 7—Strategic Intervention Focused on Developmental Tasks Can Promote Success and Positive Cascades While Preventing Problems and Negative Cascades

It follows from the tenets discussed previously that developmental tasks can be strategic targets for intervention and prevention effects. Moreover, well-timed and targeted interventions could produce high returns on investment by interrupting negative and facilitating positive cascades. There is, for example, considerable evidence that interventions to promote success in developmental task domains are effective, both for promoting competence and preventing problems (Masten et al., 2006; Masten, Long, Kuo, McCormick, & Desjardins, 2009). There is also growing evidence that prevention experiments show escalating effects over time or produce effects on later emerging, developmental task domains that were not the original focus of the intervention (Hawkins, Catalano, Kosterman, Abbott, & Hill, 1999; Hawkins et al., 2001; Heckman, 2006; Masten & Cicchetti, 2010; Masten et al., 2006, 2009; Patterson et al., 2010; Shonkoff, Boyce, & McEwen, 2009; Tremblay, 2006). Intervening in early life appears to provide a particularly high return on investment, both financially and in terms of developmental task achievement versus failure. Although there may well be effective interventions across the life span for particular problems, the greatest yield on investment generally has been shown for interventions during the earlier years of life (Heckman, 2006, 2007; Heckman & Masterov, 2007; Reynolds & Temple, 2006).

Ground-breaking interventions have demonstrated the potential for capitalizing on the cumulative and cascading nature of developmental tasks to produce results that are both lasting and that spread to positively affect multiple domains, even when the interventions are targeted to one or two salient domains at the time of implementation. PMTO, the parenting intervention developed by Patterson and colleagues at the Oregon Social Learning Center shows cascade effects across domains of child function and across family members (see Patterson et al., 2010). In the Chicago Longitudinal Study on the effects of early prevention, lasting effects have been found over several decades, including higher levels of school achievement in adolescence, enhanced parent participation in the educational process, lower rates of delinquent behavior, and higher rates of consumer skill (Reynolds, 1991, 1994, 1995, 1999, 2000; Reynolds & Temple, 1995, 1998; Temple, Reynolds, & Miedel, 2000). Similarly, the group led by Hawkins and Catalano at the University of Washington implemented a multifaceted intervention focused on reducing delinquency by promoting school engagement and positive social development. They found positive effects that spread across multiple domains of health-risk behavior, mental health, and developmental task achievement over the course of more than 20 years (Catalano & Hawkins, 1996; Hawkins & Weis, 1985; Hawkins, Von Cleve, & Catalano, 1991; Hawkins et al., 1999; Lonczak, Abbot, Hawkins, Kosterman, & Catalano, 2002).

This body of work has provided strong evidence indicating that intervening to alter success in salient developmental tasks of childhood can result in a wide array of positive outcomes in adolescence and adulthood reflecting multiple developmental task domains. These outcomes include reduced rates of aggressive, antisocial, and destructive behavior; better family bonding; lower levels of lifetime violence; higher levels of school engagement and achievement; fewer sexual partners, increased condom use, fewer pregnancies; and lower levels of heavy alcohol use.

FUTURE ISSUES IN THE STUDY OF DEVELOPMENTAL TASKS ACROSS THE LIFE SPAN

Empirical studies pertinent to developmental tasks encompass a large and rapidly growing literature. Only a small fraction of the relevant database to date could be discussed in this chapter. Nonetheless, there are clear issues and directions for future research related to assessment, gender, and culture, as well as the need for better integration of research across the life span, multiple levels of analysis, and disciplines. These issues and future directions are highlighted briefly in the following section.

Assessment

Extensive research now exists on competence (or problems) in developmental tasks, their measurement, and significance. Reviewing this extensive literature is beyond the scope of this chapter (see Masten et al., 2006 for a review of earlier evidence). However, it is time for a thorough review of the data on the variety of available measures and approaches, including their reliability and validity. As mentioned earlier, powerful statistical tools and methods have been applied in longitudinal studies focused on developmental tasks. This work has underscored the multidimensionality, stability, plasticity, predictive significance, and malleability of adaptive behavior in developmental task domains (e.g., Burt et al., 2008; Burt & Roisman, 2010; Chen, Huang, Chang, & Wang, 2010; Masten et al., 1995, 2005, 2010; Obradović et al., 2010; Patterson et al., 2010). Many of these studies use multiple methods and informants to assess developmental task behavior with compelling results. Nonetheless, there is much work to be done. Many different measures and methods have been applied in the effort to assess developmental task achievements or progress, and it would be timely to evaluate this body of work, the various approaches and the evidence, both psychometric and substantive. Moreover, there are numerous issues related to gender and culture, both with respect to assessment and the nature of developmental tasks that need attention.

Gender and Culture

Greater attention to gender differences is needed to explore the role that gender plays in developmental expectations in contemporary society. It is likely that the expectations for young men and for young women differ in significant ways, both within and across cultures, resulting in different measures of success and positive adaptation (Durbrow et al., 2001). Expectations for romantic relationships, marriage, and parenting often differ for males and females within cultures, and these differences also are likely to vary across cultures. Similarly, the differential life expectancies for males and females in many regions of the world could profoundly alter the context of developmental tasks for aging.

An important aspect of developmental tasks, as typically defined, is the culturally embedded nature of these expectations. While some tasks are presumed to be universal, such as walking and talking, most are defined by the ecological context in which a person develops. This reality calls for meaningful attention to sociocultural context in research on developmental tasks. To date, however, there has not been adequate attention to cultural issues in the literature. Much greater attention to cultural issues is needed in future research, particularly given rapid globalization. In addition to having potentially different benchmarks for determining successful adaptation, different cultures may also have different expectations for the timing of developmental task achievement in various domains. In a culture lacking a formal education system, the salience of competence in the world of work may emerge much earlier than in the developed societies, and will likely have different developmental implications for future success.

Attention to cultural issues will require attention to measures as well as concepts. The paucity of culturally informative and international research on developmental tasks is due, in part, to a lack of tools. Greater investment is needed in the development of culturally appropriate research methods and tools to study (and also to compare) developmental tasks within and across more diverse cultural and national contexts.

Additional efforts can be directed at delineating subcultural differences in developmental expectations within a majority or national culture. While there may be broad agreement on some developmental tasks, there are likely to be some tasks that are defined by different expectations in the predominant subculture in which a person is developing (e.g., religious background or neighborhood context). The expectations for judging success in a wealthy suburban community, for example, are likely to differ in some ways from those in a poor urban neighborhood or an agricultural community. These subcultural differences in expectations also result in shifts in timing and salience of particular tasks. In a community where individuals typically graduate from secondary school and continue on to college, the timing of expectations for work achievement and marriage may differ substantially from the expectations in a community where individuals tend to transition from secondary school into full-time employment and/or marriage.

Some individuals navigate multicultural worlds in the course of daily life, characterized in part by different expectations in relation to developmental tasks (Cooper, 1999; Durbrow, 1999; Motti-Stefanidi et al., in press). These individuals may be from a minority culture family in a majority culture community, workplace or school, or they may be new to a community, migrating from rural areas to the city or one country to another. A better understanding of developmental task expectations, both in terms of similarities and differences, might provide important insights for facilitating adaptation and acculturation in increasingly diverse communities.

Research on acculturation and development in immigrant youth is currently a topic of high interest because of the high rates of immigrant youth in many nations (Hernandez, Denton, & Macartney, 2008; Masten et al., in press; Motti-Stefanidi et al., in press). Changes and conflicts in developmental tasks expectations, along with

perceived successes or failures in these tasks, likely play a central role in acculturation (of immigrants and citizens of receiving societies) and the success of immigrant
youth. Much greater attention to concepts and methods will be needed to understand
and promote the adaptation of immigrant youth in diverse communities.

Integrating Research Across the Life Span

Another important issue for future research is a more integrated approach to the life
span. Foundational theory on developmental tasks often has had a life-span perspective (e.g., Baltes et al., 1980; Erikson, 1950/1963, 1968; Havighurst, 1948/1972).
More recent theory and research often has been divided into segments of the life
span, focused on early childhood, youth, middle life or late life, with little cross-
fertilization of ideas to advance more integrative models. By bringing together
researchers interested in different age bands, researchers could begin the challenging process of weaving together a more comprehensive understanding of developmental tasks across the life span. As these efforts progress, it may be important
for researchers to develop a more consistent vocabulary of constructs in relation to
developmental tasks.

Multiple Levels of Analysis

To obtain a more complete understanding of developmental tasks and their roles in
life course development, researchers must also begin to address the lack of knowledge regarding process. Much of the existing literature on developmental tasks provides clear indication that early success and failure are important for future success
and failure. However, it is often the case that little is known about the processes that
may account for these observed effects. That is, many of the studies on developmental tasks provide a "broad strokes" picture of effects that need to be filled in by
studies of finer detail and explanatory processes. More specifically, future research
efforts should seek to uncover *how* and *why* success forecasts success, not only within
a single domain, but also across domains.

Although growing attention has been paid to adopting a multiple-levels-of-anal-
ysis perspective in understanding adaptation and development (Cicchetti & Curtis,
2007; Masten, 2007; Shonkoff et al., 2009), most studies that use the developmental
task frameworks to date have predominantly focused on behavioral levels of analysis. Given the rapidly expanding growth in knowledge of multiple levels in human
function, accompanied by advancements in the tools for studying development
across levels (e.g., genomics, brain imaging, social network analysis, state-space
grid, growth modeling), a much greater emphasis on understanding developmental
tasks across levels is feasible and needed. The processes and dynamics of developmental tasks can be studied at multiple levels, and this task is likely to require
greater collaboration across disciplines. Knowledge gained from a multilevel science on developmental tasks has the potential to elucidate key processes that shape
development and also to guide intervention efforts to promote greater success in
developmental tasks.

Recent interest in executive function (EF) in relation to developmental task
achievement offers an example of promising future directions for multiple-levels
research. Self-regulation skills have been implicated for some time as a promotive

or protective factor for success in developmental tasks in studies of resilience, as well as a risk or vulnerability factor (when these skills are lacking) in studies of psychopathology (Buckner, Mezzacappa, & Beardslee, 2003; Eisenberg et al, 2004, 2005; Masten, 2007; Masten & Coatsworth, 1998). Research on EF in human development has focused on linking behavior to neural function, and understanding the processes that shape EF, including brain development and parenting (Blair, 2002; Blair & Razza, 2007; Carlson, 2005). There is growing interest in the role of prenatal stress, cortisol regulation, inflammation, and other biological processes in the development of EF and self-regulation skills as well (Gunnar & Herrera, in press). Prevention experiments have shown that targeting EF skills results in better school success as well as improved EF function (e.g., Diamond, Barnett, Thomas, & Munro, 2007). Promising studies also indicate that specific EF skills can be trained, with concomitant changes in brain function (e.g., Bierman et al., 2008; Greenberg, 2006; Rueda, Rothbart, McCandliss, Saccomanno, & Posner, 2005). All of this work in diverse ways has the aim of bridging or integrating levels of analysis to understand the development of EF and its role in the promotion, protection, or undermining of success in developmental task achievement.

CONCLUSION

Over the course of the past 40 years, research on developmental tasks has provided considerable insight into the developmental processes that promote and interfere with the development of competence in multiple domains of life. There is some consensus on important developmental tasks, and growing evidence that success or failure in these tasks has repercussions for the future. This work has important implications for prevention theory and design, although there is much work yet to be done. Research on developmental tasks is beginning to provide an evidence base for more effective timing and targeting of interventions. Future research would benefit from greater attention to issues of measurement, gender and culture, as well as processes of change at multiple levels of analysis. In addition, with rising globalization and migration, many societies have a growing stake in the success of immigrants and a growing interest in the issues of acculturation and conflict related to developmental tasks. It is time to integrate the science of developmental tasks across the life span, across disciplines, across levels of analysis, and across cultures and societies.

ACKNOWLEDGMENTS

Preparation of this chapter was supported in part by a grant to Ann Masten from the National Science Foundation (NSF No. 0745643). Any opinions, conclusions, or recommendations expressed in this chapter are those of the authors and do not necessarily reflect the views of NSF.

REFERENCES

Arnett, J. J. (2000). Emerging adulthood: A theory of development from the late teens through the twenties. *American Psychologist, 55*, 469–480.

Arnett, J. J., & Tanner, J. L. (Eds.). (2006). *Emerging adults in America: Coming of age in the 21st century.* Washington, DC: American Psychological Association.

Baltes, P. B. (1987). Theoretical propositions of life-span developmental psychology: On the dynamics between growth and decline. *Developmental Psychology, 23,* 611–626.

Baltes, P. B., Cornelius, S. W., & Nesselroade, J. R. (1979). Cohort effects in developmental psychology. In J. R. Nesselroade & P. B. Baltes (Eds.), *Longitudinal research in the study of behavior and development* (pp. 61–87). New York: Academic Press.

Baltes, P. B., Lindenberger, U., & Staudinger, U. M. (1998). Life span theory in developmental psychology. In R. M. Lerner (Ed.), *Handbook of child psychology: Vol. 1 Theoretical models of human development* (5th ed., pp. 1029–1143). Hoboken, NJ: Wiley.

Baltes, P. B., Reese, H. W., & Lipsitt, L. P. (1980). Life-span developmental psychology. *Annual Review of Psychology, 31,* 65–110.

Bandura, A. (1977). *Social learning theory.* New York: General Learning Press.

Bandura, A. (1997). *Self-efficacy: The exercise of control.* New York: W. H. Freeman.

Bierman, K. L., Domitrovich, C. E., Nix, R. L., Gest, S. D., Welsh, J. A., Greenberg, M. T., et al. (2008). Promoting academic and social-emotional school readiness: The Head Start REDI program. *Child Development, 79,* 1802–1817.

Blair, C. (2002). School readiness: Integrating cognition and emotion in a neurobiological conceptualization of children's functioning at school entry. *American Psychologist, 57,* 111–127.

Blair, C., & Razza, R. P. (2007). Relating effortful control, executive functioning, and false belief understanding to emerging math and literacy ability in kindergarten. *Child Development, 78,* 647–663.

Boelcke-Stennes, K. (2001). *Young adults' criteria of competence: The perspectives of the participants in a 20-year longitudinal study of competence on the criteria of competence of adaptation at age 30.* Unpublished master's thesis, University of Minnesota, Minneapolis, Minnesota.

Brandtstädter, J. (1998). Action perspectives on human development. In R. M. Lerner (Ed.), *Handbook of child psychology: Vol. 1 Theoretical models of human development* (5th ed., pp. 807–863). Hoboken, NJ: Wiley.

Buckner, J. C., Mezzacappa, E., & Beardslee, W. R. (2003). Characteristics of resilient youths living in poverty: The role of self-regulatory processes. *Development and Psychopathology, 15,* 139–162.

Burt, K. B., Obradović, J., Long, J. D., & Masten, A. S. (2008). The interplay of social competence and psychopathology over 20 years: Testing transactional and cascade models. *Child Development, 79,* 359–374.

Burt, K. B., & Roisman, G. I. (2010). Competence and psychopathology: Cascade effects in the NICHD Study of Early Child Care and Youth Development. *Development and Psychopathology, 22,* 557–567.

Capaldi, D. M. (1992). Co-occurrence of conduct problems and depressive symptoms in early adolescent boys: II. A 2-year follow-up at grade 8. *Development and Psychopathology, 4,* 125–144.

Carlson, E. A., Sroufe, L. A., & Egeland, B. (2004). The construction of experience: A longitudinal study of representation and behavior. *Child Development, 75,* 66–83.

Carlson, S. M. (2005). Developmentally sensitive measures of executive function in preschool children. *Developmental Neuropsychology, 28,* 595–616.

Caspi, A., Wright, B. R. E., Moffitt, T. E., & Silva, P. A. (1998). Early failure in the labor market: Childhood and adolescent predictors of unemployment in the transition to adulthood. *American Sociological Review, 63,* 424–451.

Catalano, R. F., & Hawkins, J. D. (1996). The social development model: A theory of antisocial behavior. In J. D. Hawkins (Ed.), *Delinquency and crime: Current theories* (pp. 149–197). New York: Cambridge University Press.

Chen, X., Huang, X., Chang, L., & Wang, L. (2010). Aggression, social competence, and academic achievement in Chinese children: A 5-year longitudinal study. *Development and Psychopathology, 22,* 583–592.

Cicchetti, D. (2006). Development and psychopathology. In D. Cicchetti & D. Cohen (Eds.), *Developmental psychopathology: Vol. 1. Theory and method* (2nd ed., pp. 1–23). Hoboken, NJ: Wiley.

Cicchetti, D., & Curtis, W. J. (2007). Editorial: Multilevel perspectives on pathways to resilient functioning. *Development and Psychopathology, 19,* 627–629.

Cooper, C. R. (1999). Multiple selves, multiple worlds: Cultural perspectives on individuality and connectedness in adolescent development. In A. S. Masten (Ed.), *Cultural processes in child development: The Minnesota symposia on child psychology* (Vol. 29; pp. 25–57). Mahwah, NJ: Lawrence Erlbaum Associates.

Dannefer, D. (2003). Cumulative advantage/disadvantage and the life course: Cross-fertilizing age and social science theory. *Journal of Gerontology, 58B*, S327–S337.

Diamond, A., Barnett, W. S., Thomas, J., & Munro, S. (2007). Preschool program improves cognitive control. *Science, 318*(5855), 1387–1388.

Dodge, K. A., Greenberg, M. T., Malone, P. S., & The Conduct Problems Prevention Research Group. (2008). Testing an idealized dynamic cascade model of the development of serious violence in adolescence. *Child Development, 79*, 1907–1927.

Durbrow, E. H. (1999). Cultural processes in child competence: How rural Caribbean parents evaluate their children. In A. S. Masten (Ed.), *Cultural processes in child development: The Minnesota symposia on child psychology* (Vol. 29., pp. 97–121). Mahwah, NJ: Lawrence Erlbaum Associates.

Durbrow, E. H., Peña, L. F., Masten, A. S., Sesma, A., & Williamson, I. (2001). Mothers' conceptions of child competence in contexts of poverty: The Philippines, St. Vincent, and the United States. *International Journal of Behavioral Development, 25*, 438–443.

Eccles, J. S. (1986). Gender-roles and women's achievement. *Educational Researcher, 15*, 15–19.

Eisenberg, D., & Schneider, H. (2007). Perceptions of academic skills of children diagnosed with ADHD. *Journal of Attention Disorders, 10*, 390–397.

Eisenberg, N., Spinrad, T. L., Fabes, R. A., Reiser, M., Cumberland, A., Shepard, S. A., et al. (2004). The relations of effortful control and impulsivity to children's resiliency and adjustment. *Child Development, 75*, 25–46.

Eisenberg, N., Zhou, Q., Spinrad, T. L., Valiente, C., Fabes, R. A., & Liew, J. (2005). Relations among positive parenting, children's effortful control, and externalizing problems: A three-wave longitudinal study. *Child Development, 76*(5), 1055–1071.

Elder, G. H., Jr. (1974/1999). *Children of the Great Depression: Social change in life experience*. Boulder CO: Westview Press.

Elder, G. H., Jr. (1998). The life course as developmental theory. *Child Development, 69*, 1–12.

Elder, G. H., Jr., & Conger, R. D. (2000). Children of the land: Adversity and success in rural America. Chicago: University of Chicago Press.

Erikson, E. H. (1950/1963). *Childhood and society* (2nd ed.). New York: Norton.

Erikson, E. H. (1968). *Identity, youth and crisis*. New York: Norton.

Ford, M. E. (1985). The concept of competence: Themes and variations. In H. A. Marlowe & R. B. Weinberg (Eds.) *Competence development: Theory and practice in special populations* (pp. 3–49). Springfield, IL: Charles C. Thomas.

Garcia Coll, C., Crnic, K., Lamberty, G., Wasik, B. H., Jenkins, R., Garcia, H. V., et al. (1996). An integrative model for the study of developmental competencies in minority children. *Child Development, 67*, 1891–1914.

Goodman, R. (2001). Psychometric properties of the strengths and difficulties questionnaire. *Journal of the American Academy of Child and Adolescent Psychiatry, 40*, 1337–1345.

Gottlieb, G., Wahlsten, D., & Lickliter, R. (1998). The significance of biology for human development: A developmental psychobiological systems view. In W. Damon & R. M. Lerner (Eds.), *Handbook of child psychology: Vol.1 Theoretical models of human development* (5th ed., pp. 233–273). Hoboken, NJ: Wiley.

Greenberg, M. T. (2006). Promoting resilience in children and youth: Preventive interventions and their interface with neuroscience. *Annuals of the New York Academy of Sciences, 1094*, 139–150.

Greenspan, S. I. (1981). *Psychopathology and adaptation in infant and early childhood: Principles of clinical diagnosis and preventive intervention*. New York: International Universities Press.

Greve, W., & Staudinger, U. M. (2006). Resilience in later adulthood and old age: Resources and potential for successful aging. In D. Cicchetti & D. Cohen (Eds.), *Developmental psychopathology: Vol. 3. Risk, disorder and psychopathology* (2nd ed., pp. 796–840). Hoboken, NJ: Wiley.

Gunnar, M. R., & Herrera, A. M. (in press). The neurobiology of stress and development. In P. D. Zelazo (Ed.), *Oxford Handbook of Developmental Psychology*. New York: Oxford University Press.

Harkness, S., & Super, C. M. (Eds.). (1996). Parents' cultural belief systems: Their origins, expressions, and consequences. New York: Guilford.

Harter, S. (1978). Effectance motivation reconsidered toward a developmental model. *Human Development, 21*, 34–64.

Harter, S. (1982). The perceived competence scale for children. *Child Development, 53*, 87–97.

Havighurst, R. J. (1948/1972). *Developmental tasks and education* (3rd ed.). New York: Longman.

Hawkins, J. D., Catalano, R. F., Kosterman, R., Abbott, R. D., & Hill, K. G. (1999). Preventing adolescent health-risk behaviors by strengthening protection during childhood. *Archives of Pediatrics and Adolescent Medicine, 153*, 226–234.

Hawkins, J. D., Guo, J., Hill, K. G., Battin-Pearson, S., & Abbott, R. D. (2001). Long-term effects of the Seattle Social Development Intervention on school-bonding trajectories. *Applied Developmental Science, 5,* 225–236.

Hawkins, J. D., Von Cleve, E., & Catalano, R. F. (1991). Reducing early childhood aggression: Results of a primary prevention program. *Journal of the American Academy of Child and Adolescent Psychiatry, 30,* 208–217.

Hawkins, J. D., & Weis, J. G. (1985). The social development model: An integrated approach to delinquency prevention. *Journal of Primary Prevention, 6,* 73–97.

Heckman, J. J. (2006). Skill formation and the economics of investing in disadvantaged children. *Science, 312,* 1900–1902.

Heckman, J. J. (2007). The economics, technology, and neuroscience of human capability formation. *Proceedings of the National Academy of Sciences, 104,* 13250–13255.

Heckman, J. J., & Masterov, D. V. (2007). The productivity argument for investing in young children. *Review of Agricultural Economics, 29,* 446–493.

Heilman, M. E. (2001). Description and prescription: How gender stereotypes prevent women's ascent up the organizational ladder. *Journal of Social Issues, 57,* 657–674.

Hernandez, D. J., Denton, N. A., & Macartney, S. E. (2008). Children in immigrant families: Looking to America's future. *Social Policy Report, 22*(3), 1–15.

Hill, J. P. (1980). *Understanding early adolescence: A framework.* Carrboro, NC: Center for Early Adolescence.

Hill, J. P. (1983). Early adolescence: A research agenda. *Journal of Early Adolescence, 3,* 1–21.

Hofer, M., Noack, P., & Youniss, J. (Eds.). (1994). *Psychological responses to social change: Human development in changing environments.* Berlin, Germnay: de Gruyter.

Klimes-Dougan, B. K., Long, J. D., Lee, C. Y. S., Ronsaville, D., Martinez, P., & Gold, P. (2010). Continuity and cascade in offspring of bipolar parents: Longitudinal study of externalizing, internalizing, and thought problems. *Development and Psychopathology, 22,* 849–866.

Lerner, R. M. (2006). Developmental science, developmental systems, and contemporary theories of human development. In W. Damon, & R. M. Lerner (Eds.), *Handbook of child psychology: Vol. 1. Theoretical models of human development* (6th ed., pp. 1–17). Hoboken, NJ: Wiley.

Lonczak, H. S., Abbott, R. F., Hawkins, J. D., Kosterman, R., & Catalano, R. F. (2002). Effects of the Seattle Social Development Project on sexual behavior, pregnancy, birth, and STD outcomes by age 21. *Archives of Pediatrics and Adolescent Medicine, 156,* 438–447.

Luthar, S. S. (2006). Resilience in development: A synthesis of research across five decades. In D. Cicchetti & D. J. Cohen (Eds.), *Developmental psychopathology* (2nd ed., Vol. 3, pp. 739–795). Hoboken, NJ: Wiley.

Masten, A. S. (2001). Ordinary magic: Resilience processes in development. *American Psychologist, 56,* 227–238.

Masten, A. S. (2006). Developmental psychopathology: Pathways to the future. *International Journal of Behavioral Development, 31,* 47–54.

Masten, A. S. (Ed.). (2007). *Multilevel dynamics in developmental psychopathology: The Minnesota Symposia on Child Psychology* (Vol. 34). Mahwah, NJ: Erlbaum.

Masten, A. S. (in press). Risk and resilience in development. In P. D. Zelazo (Ed.), *Oxford Handbook of Developmental Psychology.* New York: Oxford University Press.

Masten, A. S., & Braswell, L. (1991). Developmental psychopathology: An integrative framework. In P. R. Martin (Ed.), *Handbook of behavior therapy and psychological science: An integrative approach* (pp. 35–56). New York: Pergamon Press.

Masten, A. S., Burt, K. B., & Coatsworth, J. D. (2006). Competence and psychopathology in development. In D. Cicchetti & D. J. Cohen (Eds.), *Developmental psychopathology: Vol 3 risk, disorder, and adaptation* (2nd ed., Vol. 3, pp. 696–738). Hoboken, NJ: Wiley

Masten, A. S., Burt, K. B., Roisman, G. I., Obradović, J., Long, J. D., & Tellegen, A. (2004). Resources and resilience in the transition to adulthood: Continuity and change. *Development and Psychopathology, 16,* 1071–1094.

Masten, A. S., & Cicchetti, D. (2010). Editorial: Developmental Cascades. *Development and Psychopathology, 22,* 491–495.

Masten, A. S., Coatsworth, J. D., Neemann, J., Gest, S. D., Tellegen, A., & Garmezy, N. (1995). The structure and coherence of competence from childhood through adolescence. *Child Development, 66,* 1635–1659.

Masten, A. S., & Coatsworth, J. D. (1998). The development of competence in favorable and unfavorable environments: Lessons from research on successful children. *American Psychologist, 53,* 205–220.

Masten, A. S., & Curtis, W. J. (2000). Integrating psychopathology and competence: Pathways toward a comprehensive science of adaptation development. *Development and Psychopathology, 12*, 529–550.

Masten, A. S., Desjardins, C. D., McCormick, C. M., Kuo, S. I-C., & Long, J. D. (2010). The significance of childhood competence and problems for adult success in work: A developmental cascade analysis. *Development and Psychopathology, 22*, 679–694.

Masten, A. S., Liebkind, K., & Hernandez, D. J. (Eds.). (in press). *Capitalizing on migration: The potential of immigrant youth*. New York: Cambridge University Press.

Masten, A. S., Long, J. D., Kuo, S. I. C., McCormick, C. M., & Desjardins, C. D. (2009). Developmental models of strategic intervention. *European Journal of Developmental Science, 3*, 282–291.

Masten, A. S., & Obradović, J. (2006). Competence and resilience in development. *Annals of the New York Academy of Sciences, 1094*, 13–27.

Masten, A. S., Obradović, J., & Burt, K. B. (2006). Resilience in emerging adulthood: Developmental perspectives on continuity and transformation. In J. J. Arnett & J. L. Tanner (Eds.). *Emerging adults in America: Coming of age in the 21st Century* (pp. 173–190). Washington, DC: American Psychological Association Press.

Masten, A. S., & Powell, J. L. (2003). A resilience framework for research, policy, and practice. In S. S. Luthar (Ed.), *Resilience and vulnerabilities: Adaptation in the context of childhood adversities* (pp. 1–25). New York: Cambridge University Press.

Masten, A. S., Roisman, G. I., Long, J. D., Burt, K. B., Obradović, J., Riley, J. R., et al. (2005). Developmental cascades: Linking academic achievement, externalizing and internalizing symptoms over 20 years. *Developmental Psychology, 41*, 733–746.

Mayr, E. (1982). *The growth of biological thought: Diversity, evolution, and inheritance*. Cambridge, MA: Harvard University Press.

Mortimer, J. T., Vuolo, M., Staff, J., Wakefield, S., & Xie, W. (2008). Tracing the timing of "career" acquisition in a contemporary youth cohort. *Work and Occupations, 35*, 44–84.

Mortimer, J. T., & Zimmer-Gembeck, M. J. (2007). Adolescent paid work and career development. In V. B. Skorikov & W. Patton (Eds.), *Career development in childhood and adolescence* (pp. 255–275). Rotterdam, The Netherlands: Sense Publishers.

Motti-Stefanidi, F., Berry, J., Chryssochoou, X., Sam, D. L., & Phinney, J. (in press). Positive immigrant youth adaptation in context: Developmental, acculturation, and social psychological perspectives. In A. S. Masten, K. Liebkind, & D. J. Hernandez (Eds.), *Capitalizing on migration: The potential of immigrant youth*. New York: Cambridge University Press.

Neugarten, B. L. (1979). Time, age, and the life cycle. *The American Journal of Psychiatry, 136*, 887–894.

Obradović, J, Burt, K. B., & Masten, A. S. (2010). Testing a dual cascade model linking competence and symptoms over 20 years from childhood to adulthood. *Journal of Clinical Child & Adolescent Psychology, 39*, 90–102.

Obradović, J., van Dulmen, M. H. M., Yates, T. M., Carlson, E. A., & Egeland, B. (2006). Developmental assessment of competence from early childhood to middle adolescence. *Journal of Adolescence, 29*(6), 857–888.

Oerter, R. (1986). Developmental tasks throughout the life span: A new approach to an old concept. In P. A. Baltes, D. L. Featherman, & R. M. Lerner (Eds.), *Life span development and behavior* (Vol. 7, pp. 233–269). Hillsdale, NJ: Erlbaum.

Patterson, G. R., DeBaryshe, B. D., & Ramsey E. (1989). A developmental perspective on antisocial behavior. *American Psychologist, 44*, 239–335.

Patterson, G. R., Forgatch, M., & DeGarmo, D. (2010). Concerning cascading effects following intervention. *Development and Psychopathology, 22,* 949–970.

Patterson, G. R., Reid, J. B., & Dishion, T. J. (1992). *A social interactional approach, Vol. 4: Antisocial boys*. Eugene, OR: Castaglia.

Patterson, G. R., & Stoolmiller, M. (1991). Replications of a dual failure model for boys' depressed mood. *Journal of Consulting and Clinical Psychology, 59*(4), 491–498.

Perrig-Chiello, P., & Perren, S. (2005). Biographical transitions from a midlife perspective. *Journal of Adult Development, 12*, 169–181.

Quintana, S. M., & McKown, C. (Eds.). (2007). *Handbook of race, racism, and the developing child*. Hoboken, NJ: Wiley.

Reynolds, A. J. (1991). Early schooling of children at risk. *American Educational Research Journal, 28*, 392–422.

Reynolds, A. J. (1994). Effects of a preschool plus follow-on intervention for children at risk. *Developmental Psychology, 30*, 787–804.

Reynolds, A. J. (1995). One year of preschool intervention or two: Does it matter? *Early Childhood Research Quarterly, 10,* 1–31.

Reynolds, A. J. (1999). Schooling and high-risk populations: The Chicago Longitudinal Study [*Special Issue*]. *Journal of School Psychology, 34*(7).

Reynolds, A. J. (2000). *Success in early intervention: The Chicago Child-Parent Centers.* Lincoln, NE: University of Nebraska Press.

Reynolds, A. J., & Temple, J. A. (1995). Quasi-experimental estimates of the effects of a preschool intervention: Psychometric and econometric comparisons. *Evaluation Review, 19,* 347–373.

Reynolds, A. J., & Temple, J. A. (1998). Extended early childhood intervention and school achievement: Age 13 findings from the Chicago Longitudinal Study. *Child Development, 69,* 231–246.

Reynolds, A. J., & Temple, J. A. (2006). Economic benefits of investments in preschool education. In E. Zigler, W. Gilliam., & S. Jones (Eds.), *A vision for universal prekindergarten* (pp. 37–68). New York: Cambridge University Press.

Roisman, G. I., Madsen, S. D., Hennighausen, K. H., Sroufe, L. A., & Collins, W. A. (2001). The coherence of dyadic behavior across parent-child and romantic relationships as mediated by the internalized representation of experience. *Attachment & Human Development, 3,* 156–172.

Roisman, G. I., Masten, A. S., Coatsworth, J. D., & Tellegen, A. (2004). Salient and emerging developmental tasks in the transition to adulthood. *Child Development, 75,* 123–133.

Rueda, M. R., Rothbart, M. K., McCandliss, B. D., Saccomanno, L., & Posner, M. I. (2005). Training, maturation and genetic influences on the development of executive attention. *Proceedings of the National Academy of Science, 102,* 14931–14936.

Sameroff, A. J. (2000). Developmental systems and psychopathology. *Development and Psychopathology, 12,* 297–312.

Sander, L. W. (1975). Infant and caretaking environment: Investigation and conceptualization of adaptive behavior in a system of increasing complexity. In E. J. Anthony (Ed.), *Explorations in child psychiatry* (pp. 129–166). New York: Plenum Press.

Schmader, T., Johns, M., & Forbes, C. (2008). An integrated model of stereotype threat effect on performance. *Psychological Review, 115,* 336–356.

Shaffer, A., Burt, K. B., Obradović, J., Herbers, J. E., & Masten, A. S. (2009). Intergenerational continuity in parenting quality: The mediating role of social competence. *Developmental Psychology, 45,* 1227–1240.

Shonkoff, J. P., Boyce, W. T., & McEwen, B. S. (2009). Neuroscience, molecular biology, and the childhood roots of health disparities. *Journal of the American Medical Association, 301*(21), 2252–2259.

Sroufe, L. A. (1979). The coherence of individual development: Early care, attachment, and subsequent developmental issues. *American Psychologist, 34,* 834–841.

Sroufe, L. A. (1997). Psychopathology as an outcome of development. *Development and Psychopathology, 9,* 251–268.

Sroufe, L. A. (2007). The place of development in developmental psychopathology. In A. Masten (Ed.), *Multilevel dynamics in developmental psychopathology: Pathways to the future. The Minnesota Symposia on Child Psychology* (Vol. 34, pp. 285–299). Mahwah, NJ: Lawrence Erlbaum Associates.

Sroufe, L. A., Carlson, E. A., Levy, A. K., & Egeland, B. (1999). Implications of attachment theory for developmental psychopathology. *Development and Psychopathology, 11,* 1–13.

Sroufe, L. A., Egeland, B., Carlson, E. A., & Collins, W. A. (2005). *The development of the person: The Minnesota Study of Risk and Adaptation from Birth to Adulthood.* New York: Guilford Press.

Sroufe, L. A., & Fleeson, J. (1986). Attachment and the construction of relationships. In W. Hartup & Z. Rubin (Eds.), *Relationships and development* (pp. 51–71). Hillsdale, NJ: Earlbaum.

Sroufe, L. A., & Rutter, M. (1984). The domain of developmental psychopathology. *Child Development, 55,* 17–29.

Steele, C. M. (1997). A threat in the air: How stereotypes shape intellectual identity and performance. *Amerian Psychologist, 52,* 613–629.

Temple, J. A., Reynolds, A. J., & Miedel, W. T. (2000). Can early intervention prevent high school dropout? Evidence from the Chicago Longitudinal Study. *Urban Education, 35,* 31–56.

Tenenbaum, H. R., & Ruck, M. D. (2007). Are teachers' expectations different for racial minority than for European American students? A meta-analysis. *Journal of Eucational Psychology, 99,* 253–273.

Thelen, E., & Smith, L. (1998). Dynamic systems theories. In W. Damon, & R. M. Lerner (Eds.), *Handbook of child psychology: Vol. I. Theoretical models of human development* (5th ed., pp. 563–634). Hoboken, NJ: Wiley.

Tremblay, R. E. (2006). Prevention of youth violence: Why not start at the beginning? *Journal of Abnormal Child Psychology, 34,* 481–497.

Waters, E., & Sroufe, L. A. (1983). Social competence as a developmental construct. *Developmental Review, 3,* 79–97.

Watt, H. M. G., & Eccles, J. S. (Eds.). (2008). *Gender and occupational outcomes: Longitudinal assessments of individual, social, and cultural influences.* Washington, DC: American Psychological Association.

Werner, E. E., & Smith, R. S. (1992). *Overcoming the odds: High risk children from birth to adulthood.* Ithaca, NY: Cornell University Press.

Werner, E. E., & Smith, R. S. (2001). *Journeys from childhood to mid-life: Risk, resilience, and recovery.* Ithaca, NY: Cornell University Press.

White, R. W. (1959). Motivation reconsidered: The concept of competence. *Psychological Review, 66,* 297–333.

CONTINUITY AND DISCONTINUITY IN DEVELOPMENT ACROSS THE LIFE SPAN: A DEVELOPMENTAL SYSTEMS PERSPECTIVE

6

Richard M. Lerner, Kathleen Leonard, Kristen Fay, and Sonia S. Issac

The *raison d'être* of developmental science is that change happens. There are, of course, some (relative) structural and functional constancies across the life span (Lerner, 1984), and part of the work of developmental scientists is to identify and explain both constancy and continuous or discontinuous change (Brim & Kagan, 1980; Lerner, 2002). However, there would be no field of developmental science, and no reference works about life-span human development, if it were not the case that individuals change in quantitative or qualitative ways across the life span (ontogeny), families change across generations, and communities, societies, cultures, and the natural and designed physical ecology change across history.

Moreover, from the perspective of developmental systems theoretical models that, today, are at the cutting-edge of theory in developmental science (Damon, Lerner, Eisenberg, Kuhn, & Siegler, 2008; Lerner, 2002, 2006; Lerner & Overton, 2008; Overton, 2006, 2010), it is not *just* that these changes happen. Critically, ontogenetic, generational, and historical changes are interdependent (Tobach & Greenberg, 1984). Changes at all levels are inextricably fused; that is, changes at one level of organization are products and producers of changes at other levels (Lerner, 1984). At this writing, developmental systems theories provide the major lens through which both the bases and format of developmental change are conceptualized and studied; these models are used to understand whether and why change is continuous or discontinuous or whether and why it varies qualitatively or quantitatively (Overton, 2006, 2010). As such, ideas associated with these theories serve to organize our discussion of continuity and discontinuity across the life span.

Accordingly, after providing definitions of developmental change, we discuss the features of relational, developmental systems theory. We then provide some examples of the use of ideas from developmental systems theory for elucidating mutually influential changes between individuals and contexts. These relations are represented as individual $\leftarrow \rightarrow$ context relations and are termed "developmental regulations"; that is, the basic process of development involves a dynamic interaction across the life span between the changes of the individual on the context and of the context on the individual. The examples we use draw on both "classic" and more recent longitudinal studies of the individual $\leftarrow \rightarrow$ context relations that are involved in shaping diverse developmental trajectories across the life course. Here, we point to the concept of "developmental cascades" (Masten et al., 2005), a term used to depict the changing links among variables from qualitatively different levels of organization within the developmental system. Finally, we discuss the implications of a developmental systems approach for future research and application.

DEFINING DEVELOPMENTAL CHANGE

The fundamental task of a developmental scientist is to study change. Indeed, the goal of developmental science is to describe, explain, and optimize intraindividual change and interindividual differences in intraindividual change across the life span (Baltes, Reese, & Nesselroade, 1977). Within human development, the tasks of the description and explanation of intraindividual, that is, within-person, changes pertain to the issue of continuity–discontinuity.[1]

In seeking to systematically represent the changes that a person goes through across time (i.e., trying to describe intraindividual change), one may ask if the behavior being described takes the same form. If behavior seen at one point in the life span can be represented or depicted in the same way as behavior at another point, then *descriptive continuity* exists. If behavior seen at one point in the life span cannot be represented or depicted in the same way as behavior at another point, then *descriptive discontinuity* exists. In turn, if the variables used to account for developmental processes do not vary from Time 1 to Time 2 in a person's life, *explanatory continuity* exists; if the variables used to account for developmental processes do vary from Time 1 to Time 2 in a person's life, *explanatory discontinuity exists*.

Changes in the description of behavior across a person's life can occur for many reasons. In fact, even the *same* change, despite whether it is descriptively continuous *or* discontinuous, can be explained by many reasons. If the same explanations are used to account for behavior across a person's life, then this means that behavior is interpreted as involving unchanging laws or rules. At just noted, in this case, there is *explanatory continuity*. If, however, different explanations are used to account for behavior across a person's life, then, again, this is *explanatory discontinuity*.

Combinations of Descriptive and Explanatory Change

It is possible to have any combination of descriptive continuity–discontinuity and explanatory continuity–discontinuity. For instance, suppose one were interested in accounting for a person's recreational behavior at different times in his or her life and tried to explain this behavior through the use of motivational ideas. Using this example, there might or might not be changes in the main recreational behaviors (e.g., bicycle riding or aerobic exercises) from childhood to adulthood. There might be descriptive continuity or discontinuity. In either case, however, one might suggest a continuous or a discontinuous explanation.

For instance, it might be argued that recreational behavior—whatever specific form it may take—is always motivated by curiosity. Bike riding in childhood and adulthood, or bike riding in the former period and aerobic exercises in the latter,

---

[1] Interest in interindividual differences in intraindividual change, and whether an individual's location relative to a reference group (e.g., a birth cohort) remains the same or changes across ontogenetic points, pertains to the issue of stability–instability (Lerner, 2002).

may just be determined by the person's curiosity about seeing where the bike ride can take him or her (in the former case) or about learning new exercise regimens (in the latter case). Thus, one would be accounting for behavior based on an explanatory continuous interpretation.

Alternatively, of course, it might be argued that recreational behavior in adulthood is determined not by curiosity motivation but rather by sexual motivation. That is, although curiosity led to bike riding in childhood, the adult goes to aerobic exercise classes to meet possible dating partners. Here, then, one would be accounting for behavior based on an explanatory discontinuous interpretation.

Quantitative Versus Qualitative Changes

Descriptions or explanations of development can involve quantitative or qualitative changes. Descriptively, quantitative changes involve differences in how much (or how many) of something exists. For example, in adolescence, quantitative changes occur in areas such as height and weight because there is an adolescent growth spurt, and these changes are often interpreted as resulting from quantitative increases in the production of growth-stimulating hormones.

In turn, descriptive qualitative changes involve differences in what exists, or in what sort of phenomenon is present. The emergence in adolescence of a drive-state never before present in life, that is, a reproductively mature sexual drive (Freud, 1969), and the emergence in adolescence of new and abstract thought capabilities not present in younger people, that is, formal operations (Piaget 1950, 1970), are instances of changes interpreted as arising from qualitative alterations in the person. It is believed that the person is not just "more of the same"; rather, the individual is seen as having a *new* quality or characteristic.

Explanations of development can also vary in regard to whether one *accounts* for change by positing quantitative changes (e.g., increases in the amounts of growth hormone present in the bloodstream) or by positing new, qualitatively different (emergent) reasons for behaviors. For example, Erikson (1959) proposed that an infant's interactions in his or her social world are predicated on the need to establish a sense of basic trust in the world, whereas an adolescent's social interactions involve the need to establish a sense of identity, or a self-definition, and an adult's social interactions involve efforts to create a sense of generativity.

In other words, it is possible to offer an explanatory discontinuous interpretation of development involving *either* quantitative or qualitative change. For instance, when particular types of explanatory discontinuous qualitative changes are said to be involved in development (those linked to biological or, more specifically, genetic reductionist accounts; e.g., Lorenz, 1965), the critical-periods hypothesis is often raised (e.g., Erikson, 1959, 1968; cf. Lerner, 1984, 2002). Here, development is alleged to be qualitatively different than in prior or subsequent ontogenetic periods because biologically shaped maturational timetables create—independent of any influence of the context within which the individual is embedded—particular times in life when certain phenomena (e.g., imprinting or attachment; Lorenz, 1965) must develop if they are ever to adequately develop. Although no credible evidence exists for the presence of critical periods in human development (e.g., Colombo, 1982; Lerner, 2002), the point of noting this concept is to illustrate the idea that, on the basis of adherence to a particular theory of development (e.g., a predetermined epigenetic, or nature, one), qualitative changes may be believed to characterize ontogeny and, if so, then discontinuous explanations of change are needed.

Accordingly, virtually any statement about the character of intraindividual development involves, explicitly or implicitly, taking a position in regard to three dimensions of change: (1) descriptive continuity–discontinuity, (2) explanatory continuity–discontinuity, and (3) the quantitative versus the qualitative character of one's descriptions and explanations—that is, the quantitative–qualitative dimension pertains to both description and explanation. One may have descriptive quantitative discontinuity coupled with explanatory qualitative continuity, or descriptive qualitative continuity coupled with explanatory quantitative discontinuity, and so forth.

However, the particular couplings that one posits to be involved in human life will depend on the substantive domain of development one is studying (e.g., intelligence, motivation, personality, or peer group relations) and, primarily, on the theory that one uses to frame this domain of development (Lerner, 2002). Accordingly, any particular description or explanation of intraindividual change is the result of a specific theoretical view of development. This idea implies that theory, not data, is the *primary* lens through which one "observes" continuity or discontinuity in development.

Continuity–Discontinuity as a Theoretical Issue

It is, of course, possible to argue that continuity–discontinuity is an empirical issue. This position has a degree of validity. Whether one sees continuity or discontinuity in behavioral development is partially dependent on research data. However, the point is that, because theory determines what variables are studied within a selected domain of human development, the results of research about these variables are not the primary factors determining the existence of continuity or discontinuity.

To illustrate, whether one views infant babbling as continuous or discontinuous with speech depends on one's particular theoretical perspective. Similarly, the events of adolescence may be interpreted as continuations of processes present in earlier ontogenetic periods or as results of processes present only in adolescence. Thus, Davis (1944) explained storm-and-stress behavior in adolescence (behavior that, by the way, was regarded as descriptively discontinuous) by proposing social-learning principles applicable to earlier ontogenetic periods. That is, he used an explanatory continuous idea to account for descriptive changes in the behaviors of children versus adolescents. Hall (1904) coupled descriptive discontinuity with explanatory discontinuity, arguing that the adolescent period recapitulated a distinct portion of phylogeny.

In turn, within the adult and aged portions of the life span, there are decreases, or "losses," in some facets of perceptual–motor and cognitive processing skills (Baltes, Lindenberger, & Staudinger, 2006). One may perceive such losses as involving evidence for the emergence of a new developmental process, one summarized by the term "aging," and thus for qualitative discontinuity. Alternatively, as posited by Baltes (1997; Baltes et al., 2006) and, as agreed on by some developmental scientists (Overton, 2010), one may propose that all of development across the life span involves a common developmental process. Accordingly, as is described by Baltes (1987; Baltes et al., 2006), an integration of processes of gain and loss is present across the life span. As such, there is no new process termed "aging," but only a quantitative change in the gain–loss balance (Riley, 1979).

To take another example, and one that we previously introduced, during childhood a person may be characterized as being (in part) composed of several drives—a hunger drive, a thirst drive, a drive to avoid pain, and perhaps a curiosity drive. With puberty, however, a new drive emerges (or, at least, emerges in a mature form)—the sex drive. With this *emergence*—that is, with the development of a structure or function that cannot be (completely) reduced to a prior form—the adolescent begins to have new feelings, new thoughts, and even new behaviors, which may be interpreted as being a consequence of this new drive (Freud, 1969). The emergence of this new drive is an instance of qualitative discontinuity, given that the sex drive cannot be reduced to hunger and thirst drives, for instance.

Hence, qualitative changes are, by their very nature, discontinuous. A qualitative change, also termed an emergent change (or "epigenetic"; Gottlieb, 1970, 1997), is *always* an instance of discontinuity. Moreover, not only is an emergent change therefore an irreducible change (in that it cannot be construed as a derivative of a prior form), but it is a change characterized by what Werner (1957) termed *gappiness*. Developmental gappiness occurs when there is a lack of an intermediate level between earlier and later levels of development, as seen in the emergence of the sex drive. Gappiness must also be a part of an emergent change. The presence of an intermediate step between what exists at Time 1 and the new quality that emerges at Time 2 would suggest that the new quality at Time 2 could be reduced through reference to the intermediate step. Because we have just seen that an emergent change is defined in terms of its developmental irreducibility to what went before, it is clear that gappiness must also be a characteristic of any emergence.

In sum, then, the characteristics of emergence and gappiness are needed to describe qualitatively discontinuous changes in development; on the other hand, the characteristic of gappiness (abruptness of change) alone seems to suffice for characterizing quantitatively discontinuous changes. Thus, as Werner (1957) stated:

> It seems that discontinuity in terms of qualitative changes can be best defined by two characteristics: "emergence," i.e., the irreducibility of a later stage to an earlier; and "gappiness," i.e., the lack of intermediate stages between earlier and later forms. Quantitative discontinuity on the other hand, appears to be sufficiently defined by the second characteristic.... To facilitate distinction and alleviate confusion, I would suggest substituting "abruptness" for quantitative discontinuity, reserving the term "discontinuity" only for the qualitative aspect of change. (p. 133)

Conclusions

Whether one elects to adopt Werner's (1957) terminology, it is clear that all possible combinations of descriptive and explanatory, qualitative or quantitative, continuity or discontinuity may characterize either portions of, or the entire breadth of, the life span, depending on the theoretical frame brought to the study of a given facet of

development. The embeddedness in theory of the empirical evidence that is generated to rationalize or elucidate such diverse changes is one reason that developmental systems models have become the predominant frame within which to understand
the ways in which this diversity may be instantiated across the levels of organization
that comprise the developmental system. Accordingly, we turn now to an overview of
developmental systems theories and discuss how ideas associated with such models
afford productive and integrative means to describe, explain, and optimize developmental change across the life span.

DEVELOPMENTAL SYSTEMS THEORY AND THE STUDY OF CONTINUITY AND DISCONTINUITY ACROSS THE LIFE SPAN

In developmental systems models, variables nominally associated with either nature
or nurture are, in actuality, fused within a relational, dynamic developmental system
(Garcia Coll, Bearer, & Lerner, 2004; Gottlieb, 1997; Gottlieb, Wahlsten, & Lickliter,
2006; Lerner, 2006; Overton, 2006). Table 6.1 summarizes the features of developmental systems theories.

As described in this table, these theories specify that mutually influential relations between individuals and contexts regulate the course of developmental change
and, because of the temporal nature of this relation (because all levels of organization
within the developmental system are embedded in history and, therefore, all facets
of the system have a change component), the potential for plasticity (for systematic
change in structure or function) exists across the life span (Lerner, 1984, 2006). As
such, within such theories any instance of quantitative or qualitative continuity or
discontinuity may exist within or across periods of the life span, depending on conditions pertinent to the dynamic (mutually influential) relations between individuals
and the multilevel context (ecology) of human development, that is, depending on
the course of individual $\leftarrow \rightarrow$ context relations. Simply, variation in individual $\leftarrow \rightarrow$
context relations can produce intraindividual changes as well as interindividual dif-
ferences in intraindividual change, within and across portions of development.

As envisioned by proponents of relational, developmental systems theories
(Overton, 2006, 2010), the contemporary study of human development involves using
these postmodern, relational models to consider all levels of organization—from the
inner biological through the physical ecological, cultural, and historical—as involved
in mutually influential relationships across the breadth of the entire life course
(Bronfenbrenner & Morris, 2006; Riegel, 1975, 1976). Variations in time and place
constitute vital contexts for systematic changes across all of ontogeny—even into the
10th and 11th decades of life—and, as such, human life is variegated and characterized by intraindividual change and interindividual differences (Baltes, et al., 2006;
Elder, Modell, & Parke, 1993).

In essence, then, because ontogenetic change is embodied in its relation to time
and place (Overton, 2006), contemporary developmental science regards the temporality represented by historical changes as imbued in all levels of organization,
as co-acting integratively, and as providing a potential for this systematic change,
for plasticity, across the life span. In short, the potential for developmental change
across life exists because the basic process of development involves mutually influential relations between an active organism and a changing, multilevel ecology, a

TABLE 6.1

Defining Features of Developmental Systems Theories[a]

A relational metamodel

Predicated on a postmodern philosophical perspective that transcends Cartesian dualism, developmental systems theories are framed by a relational metamodel for human development. There is, then, a rejection of all splits between components of the ecology of human development, for example, between nature- and nurture-based variables, between continuity and discontinuity, or between stability and instability. Systemic syntheses or integrations replace dichotomizations or other reductionist partitions of the developmental system.

The integration of levels of organization

Relational thinking and the rejection of Cartesian splits is associated with the idea that all levels of organization within the ecology of human development are integrated, or fused. These levels range from the biological and physiological through the cultural and historical.

Developmental regulation across ontogeny involves mutually influential individual ←→ context relations

As a consequence of the integration of levels, the regulation of development occurs through mutually influential connections among all levels of the developmental system, ranging from genes and cell physiology through individual mental and behavioral functioning to society, culture, the designed and natural ecology, and, ultimately, history. These mutually influential relations may be represented generically as Level 1 ←→ Level 2 (e.g., Family ←→ Community) and, in the case of ontogeny may be represented as individual ←→ context.

Integrated actions, individual ←→ context relations, are the basic unit of analysis within human development

The character of developmental regulation means that the integration of actions—of the individual on the context and of the multiple levels of the context on the individual (individual ←→ context)—constitute the fundamental unit of analysis in the study of the basic process of human development.

Temporality and plasticity in human development

As a consequence of the fusion of the historical level of analysis—and therefore temporality—within the levels of organization comprising the ecology of human development, the developmental system is characterized by the potential for systematic change, by plasticity. Observed trajectories of intraindividual change may vary across time and place as a consequence of such plasticity.

Plasticity is relative

Developmental regulation may both facilitate and constrain opportunities for change. Thus, change in individual ←→ context relations is not limitless, and the magnitude of plasticity (the probability of change in a developmental trajectory occurring in relation to variation in contextual conditions) may vary across the life span and history. Nevertheless, the potential for plasticity at both individual and contextual levels constitutes a fundamental strength of all human's development.

Intraindividual change, interindividual differences in intraindividual change, and the fundamental substantive significance of diversity

The combinations of variables across the integrated levels of organization within the developmental system that provide the basis of the developmental process will vary at least in part across individuals and groups. This diversity is systematic and lawfully produced by idiographic, group differential, and generic (nomothetic) phenomena. The range of interindividual differences in intraindividual change observed at any point in time is evidence of the plasticity of the developmental system, and makes the study of diversity of fundamental substantive significance for the description, explanation, and optimization of human development.

Optimism, the application of developmental science, and the promotion of positive human development

The potential for and instantiations of plasticity legitimate an optimistic and proactive search for characteristics of individuals and of their ecologies that, together, can be arrayed to promote positive human development across life. Through the application of developmental science in planned attempts (i.e., interventions) to enhance (e.g., through social policies or community-based programs) the character of humans' developmental trajectories, the promotion of positive human development may be achieved by aligning the strengths (operationalized as the potential for positive change) of individuals and contexts.

Multidisciplinarity and the need for change-sensitive methodologies

The integrated levels of organization comprising the developmental system require collaborative analyses by scholars from multiple disciplines. Multidisciplinary knowledge and, ideally, interdisciplinary knowledge is sought. The temporal embeddedness and resulting plasticity of the developmental system requires that research designs, methods of observation and measurement, and procedures for data analysis be change-sensitive and able to integrate trajectories of change at multiple levels of analysis.[b]

---

[a] Based on Lerner (2006).

[b] Representative instances of change-sensitive methodologies may involve (a) innovations in sampling (e.g., theoretically predicated selection of participants and of x-axis divisions, or inverting the x- and y-axis, that is, making time the dependent variable); (b) using measures designed to be sensitive to change; to possess equivalence across temporal levels (age, generation, history), different groups (sex, race, religion), and different contexts (family, community, urban–rural, culture); to provide relational indices (e.g., of person–environment fit); and to provide triangulation across different observational systems (convergent and divergent validation); (c) employing designs that are change-sensitive, such as longitudinal and sequential strategies, person-centered, as compared to variable-centered, analyses ("P" versus "R" approaches); and (d) data analyses that afford multivariate analyses of change, for instance, procedures such as SEM, hierarchical linear modeling (HLM), trajectory analysis, or time series analysis.

relation represented as individual ←→ context (Lerner, 2006). These relations provide the fundamental impetus to systematic and successive changes across the life span (Brandtstädter, 1998; Lerner, 2006; Overton, 1973, 2003).[2]

Developmental Systems Models and Change Across the Life Span

Together, the ideas of developmental systems theories provide several reasons as to why the breadth of the life span and all levels of organization within the ecology of human development must be considered to fully describe, explain, and optimize the course of intraindividual change and of interindividual differences in such change (Baltes et al., 1977, 2006). First, development is seen as a process that begins at conception and continues through the end of life. Developmental processes, conceptualized as involving systematic and successive changes in the organization of relations within and across the levels of organization comprising the ecology of human development (e.g., Bronfenbrenner, 1979; Bronfenbrenner & Morris, 2006; Lerner, 2002, 2006; Overton, 1973, 1978, 2006; Overton & Reese, 1981; Reese & Overton, 1970), may have *both* qualitatively and quantitatively continuous and discontinuous facets of this process. Accordingly, multidirectionality of development (increases, decreases, curvilinearity, smooth or abrupt change, etc.) are all possible forms for a developmental process, and the shape or form of a developmental trajectory for an individual or group is a matter of theory-predicated empirical inquiry (Wohlwill, 1973).

Moreover, because variation in the form of developmental trajectories may occur for different people (e.g., people who vary in regard to age, sex, race, birth cohort), living in different settings, or in different historical eras, developmental process may take a different form at different points in ontogeny, generational time, or history across individuals or groups. Thus, diversity, in regard to within-person changes, as well as in regard to differences between people in within-person change, rises to the level of substantive significance (as opposed to error variance) across the life span. For instance, as explained by Bornstein (1995), in regard to his "specificity principle" of infant development "specific experiences at specific times exert specific effects over specific aspects of infant growth in specific ways" (p. 21). In turn, a similar idea has been advanced by Freund, Nikitin, and Ritter (2009), albeit one focused at the other end of the life span. Underscoring the importance of viewing the developmental process across the breadth of ontogeny, Freund et al. note that a person's development during an historical period of extended life expectancy is likely to have important implications for development during young and middle adulthood.

Accordingly, while it is of course appropriate to study individuals and groups within (as well, of course, as across) ontogenetic "age periods," an age period-specific focus should not be adopted because of the mistaken belief that the developmental process that occurs in childhood or adolescence is somehow a different developmental process than the one that occurs in adulthood and late adulthood. As we have already emphasized, the life-span developmental scientist working from a developmental

---

[2] Because understanding such change requires an integration of information about all these levels, the knowledge base from multiple disciplines needs to be combined to study the nature and bases of change. Indeed, because the contemporary study of human development is embedded within a developmental systems framework, the study of change across the life span is today characterized as the field of developmental science and not as the field of developmental psychology (e.g., Bornstein & Lamb, 2005; Lerner, 2006).

systems theoretical perspective has the task of describing, explaining, and optimizing the form of such change across life. He or she must detail the ways in which changes within one period are derived from changes at earlier periods and affect changes at subsequent periods.

Thus, from a relational, developmental systems perspective, explanations of continuities and discontinuities across life, and of the form (the shape) of the developmental trajectory and of its rate of change, involve a different theoretical frame than the ones that had been dominant in other approaches to the study of development (i.e., the split and reductionist approaches of past eras; e.g., Overton, 1973, 2006, 2010), because they reject as counterfactual the split conceptions, theories, and metatheories that partitioned the sources of development into nature or nurture, or continuity or discontinuity. Rejected as well are "compromise" views that, while admitting that both of these purportedly separate sources of influence were involved in development, used problematic (i.e., additive) conceptions of interaction (conceptualized much as are interaction terms in an analysis of variance or in other instantiations of the General Linear Model; see Gottlieb et al., 2006). These split conceptions are eschewed because scholars using developmental systems models to study life-span development focus on developmental regulations, that is, on mutually influential individual $\longleftrightarrow$ context relations, that link all levels of the ecology of human development within a thoroughly "fused," dynamic, relational system.

To illustrate, these levels of the ecology involve ecological systems within the person (i.e., biosocial influences) or most proximal to him or her (what Bronfenbrenner, 1979, termed the microsystem), extend to the set of contexts within which the individual interacts (the mesosystem; Bronfenbrenner, 1979), and to the systems in the ecology within which components of the mesosystem (e.g., parents) interact (e.g., the work place) that may not directly involve the person but nevertheless may affect him or her. In addition, the ecology includes the macrosystem—the broadest level of the ecology; the macrosystem influences all other systems and includes social policies, major intuitions of society (such as education, health care, and the economy), the designed and natural physical ecology, and, ultimately, history. As we have emphasized, this latter level of organization within the relational, integrated developmental system provides a temporal component for all other facets of the developmental system and creates the potential for systematic change, for plasticity, in the individual $\longleftrightarrow$ context relations.

One recent instantiation of such relational, developmental systems thinking in regard to the dynamics of the person's exchanges with his or her ecology involves the work of Freund and colleagues in regard to the nature of the goals that individuals pursue within their changing context (e.g., Freund, 2007; Nikitin & Freund, 2008). Freund argues that the interplay of different levels of organization is important not only at the level of person, family, and society (or other nested levels) but also for understanding the role of specific constructs—in this case, goals—for development. Extending action theoretical concepts that have tended to view goals as primarily personal constructs, Freund explains that goals are located at multiple levels of the developmental system and that mutually influential relations among these levels need to be assessed to fully understand the nature and role of goals in human development. These levels involve social norms and expectations that inform people about age-related opportunity structures and goal-relevant resources; personal beliefs about the appropriate timing and sequencing of goals; personal goals that are influenced by social norms, personal beliefs, the individual's learning history, and external (e.g., social and physical environment) and internal (e.g., talent) resources; and nonconscious goals and motives that might be particularly influential in times of transitions or in times of routine.

Conclusions

Developmental systems models focus on the changing relations among individuals and contexts that weave together the fabric of the human life span. These changes occur both within and across all of the levels of organization integrated within the ecology of human development. As such, all formats of intraindividual change are possible within or across portions of the life span, depending, as we have explained, on what variables or processes are focused on within a given, theoretically predicated study.

However, the potential for a plethora of formats for change does not (necessarily) result in mindless eclecticism (e.g., "Since anything can happen, then anything that does happen confirms that anything is possible."). When used by developmental scientists whose models specify when, and under what conditions, particular facets of the individual, in relation to specific features of the context, should result in the development of certain characteristics of structure or function, then developmental systems models constitute powerful and integrative conceptual tools for delineating the particular instances of individual $\leftarrow \rightarrow$ context relations that texture and shape the course of development across life. Indeed, in these circumstances, developmental scientists are most likely to use developmental systems models to link together qualitatively different variables—that is, variables from distinct levels of organization within the developmental system—in the theoretical construction and empirical investigation of the life span.

Such links among qualitatively distinct variables have often been conceptualized as developmental "cascades" (e.g., Masten et al., 2005) because they represent the flow of relations across the boundaries of different levels of organization within the ecology of human development. Across the history of the interest in developmental science in the nature of developmental change, there have been several longitudinal studies that illustrate the diversity of instantiations of continuous and discontinuous change that occur in relation to variation in the relations that individuals have with their contexts. More recently, in the present era, when developmental systems models and terminology have come to the forefront of the field; recent longitudinal findings have explicitly focused on the idea of developmental cascades.

In the following section, we discuss some illustrations of this history of longitudinal research. This discussion will enable us to provide some concluding comments about future directions for research pertinent to the continuity and discontinuity of change across the life span.

▓ EMPIRICAL ILLUSTRATIONS OF THE USE OF DEVELOPMENTAL SYSTEMS MODELS FOR STUDYING CONTINUITY AND DISCONTINUITY ACROSS THE LIFE SPAN

We have emphasized that, within developmental systems theories, developmental regulations propel change across the life span. For about the first half of the

20th century, the study of human development (mostly of infants and children) was marked by attempts to *describe* connections among variables, typically within a level but, occasionally, across levels (Bronfenbrenner, 1963; Cairns & Cairns, 2006; Mussen, 1970). However, increasingly since the 1960s, and burgeoning especially within the last 35 years, developmental scientists have sought to *explain* the links among variables, both within and across levels of organization.

A classic example of this interest is the longitudinal work of Kagan and Moss (1962) in regard to the analysis of data from birth to "maturity" (young adulthood) derived from the Fels Longitudinal Study data set. Using this data set, Kagan and Moss (1962) analyzed data across infancy to young adulthood in order to identify which facets of development remained continuous and which facets showed discontinuous change across these portions of the life span. Their interest was in identifying continuity between early portions of development and later life. However, manifesting a central point of this chapter—that the identification of continuity and discontinuity across the life span is primarily a theoretical issue—the interest of Kagan and Moss (1962) in sorting individual change into two categories (continuous or discontinuous) and, more specifically, in demonstrating the connections across developmental periods, is illustrated by their postulation of two types of continuity. This conceptual innovation was required because significant correlations across overtly distinct variables were found across the infancy-to-adult period and, as just noted, Kagan and Moss (1962) were seeking to demonstrate continuity.

Accordingly, Kagan and Moss forwarded the concept of *homotypic continuity* to depict behaviors that may be described identically across the course of life. However, they argued that even when behavior looks different across ontogeny, continuity may exist, *if* the latent (unobserved, explanatory) basis (e.g., the motive) for the two manifestly different behaviors is identical. Kagan and Moss (1962) termed this instance of continuity *heterotypic continuity*. Using this theoretical idea, Kagan and Moss found some instances of homotypic continuity (e.g., high activity levels in infancy and adulthood) and of heterotypic continuity (of a form of a developmental cascade). For example, they related high fear of bodily harm among infant males to high dependency on spouses among adult males, attributing the presence of this descriptively qualitatively discontinuous relation to the qualitatively continuous presence of the same underlying motives.

Bronfenbrenner (1979) also advanced a developmental cascades-like notion. He explained how events in the exosystem of an infant or child (i.e., portions of the social ecology in which the infant does not take part, e.g., the parents work place or the state agency making rules for the availability of home visiting programs for families of adolescent mothers with infants) can nevertheless affect the child's behavior and developmental trajectory. Exemplifying this view, both Elder (1974) and Schaie (1984) used longitudinal data to draw on the links between individuals and features of the historical epoch within which they live to explain individual differences in personality development. However, they did so by drawing on different facets of the concepts of continuity and discontinuity.

Elder (1974) argued that individual differences in development in the adult years of achievement and health, and in degrees of commitments to family values, were influenced by whether a person experienced a qualitatively distinct historical event (e.g., the Great Depression) in his or her childhood or adolescence. Thus, the experience by members of one birth cohort of an individual ←→ context relation that is qualitatively discontinuous from that of another cohort was used by Elder (1974) to account for interindividual differences (across birth cohorts) in intraindividual change.

In turn, Schaie (1984) posited that cohort differences in personality development across the adult and aged years may be explained by quantitative differences across historical eras in the accumulation of life events (such as epidemics, wars, unemployment, inflation, and technological innovations). Accordingly, to account for interindividual differences (again across cohorts) in intraindividual change, Schaie turned to quantitative discontinuities. Accordingly, it is not the nature (quality) of the events per se which explains interindividual differences in intraindividual change in personality. Instead, these differences occur because of quantitative discontinuities across history in the cumulative number of events that comprise the context.

Contextual levels of organization that are more molecular than historical levels are also involved in the individual ←→ context relations affording continuity or discontinuity of development. For example, Simmons and Blyth (e.g., Simmons, Carlton-Ford & Blyth, 1987) illustrated that it is possible to find either continuity or discontinuity in females' self-esteem across early adolescence. Whether one finds continuity or discontinuity depends on the confluence of other individual and contextual changes experienced by the females. For instance, discontinuity (in the direction of a decrement) of self-esteem is most likely when the early adolescent female is experiencing simultaneously the organismic changes associated with menarche and the contextual alterations associated with the transition from elementary school to junior high school.

This sort of empirical association—between a biological characteristic (menarche), a psychological characteristic (self-esteem), and a contextual characteristic (change in school)—not only provides an illustration of the use of the concept of developmental cascades but also underscores the importance of examining multiple levels of organization within the developmental system when assessing continuities and discontinuities in development. The work of Simmons and her colleagues illustrates the idea in developmental systems theory that changes in the relations between the individual and context contribute to development and to the presence of either continuity or discontinuity.

Of course, the inevitability of some association among variables within the ecology of the developmental system would suggest that cascades are commonplace, and thus, potentially marking only small, adventitious, or even trivial associations. However, what makes cascades a powerful concept within developmental science is that they may be used in developmental systems theories of individual ←→ context relations to structure expectations about disparate links among qualitatively distinct variables within the developmental system.

When used to predict patterns of covariation among qualitatively discontinuous variables, ideas about specific developmental cascades enable developmental scientists to avoid capitalizing on the chance or noncausal associations that will arise within the developmental system because the world is ultimately positive manifold within the developmental system, that is, variables across all levels are integrated (Lewin-Bizan, Bowers, & Lerner, 2010). There exist some powerful, recent examples of the theory-predicated, a priori use of the developmental cascades concept.

One instance is provided by Masten et al. (2005), who posited a developmental cascade model to test links among academic competence and externalizing and internalizing symptoms across a 20-year period. Masten et al. proposed a model linking competence and symptoms in a normative, urban school sample of 205 children (initially 8–12 years old). Internalizing and externalizing symptoms and academic competence were assessed by multiple methods at the study outset and after 7, 10, and 20 years. Using structural equation modeling (SEM), Masten et al. confirmed the presence of several hypothesized cascade effects: Externalizing problems evident in childhood appeared to undermine academic competence by adolescence, which subsequently showed a negative effect on internalizing problems in young adulthood. A significant exploratory effect was consistent with internalizing symptoms containing or lowering the net risk for externalizing problems under some conditions. These cascade effects did not differ by gender and were not attributable to effects of IQ, parenting quality, or socioeconomic differences.

Another excellent example of such a theory-based use of the cascade concept is provided by Dodge, Greenberg, and Malone (2008), who tested a model of serious adolescent violence across a span of years from kindergarten through Grade 11. The model included links among the community and family context of the young child, later school behaviors, the peer group, and ultimately adolescent violence. Using as participants 754 children (50% male; 43% African American) from 27 schools at four geographic sites followed annually from kindergarten through Grade 11 (ages 5–18), Dodge et al. found evidence for a complex cascade model: An early social context of disadvantage predicts harsh–inconsistent parenting, which predicts social and cognitive deficits, which predicts conduct problem behavior, which predicts elementary school social and academic failure, which predicts parental withdrawal from supervision and monitoring, which predicts deviant peer associations, which ultimately predicts adolescent violence.

As a final example of the use of a developmental systems-based cascade model, we may note that Lewin-Bizan et al. (2010) used data from the longitudinal 4-H study of positive youth development (PYD) (Lerner et al., 2005) to illustrate the use of such a model in depicting relations between individuals and contexts that promote positive development among adolescents in Grades 5–8 (approximately ages 10–13 years). The model that was tested specified that the social context that parents provide for an adolescent (a context operationalized by two parental behaviors: parental warmth and parental monitoring) provided the resources and the freedom for an adolescent to actively construct goals and engage in goal-exploratory searches, that is, higher levels of these two parenting constructs would positively affect an adolescent's intentional self-regulation. The next step of the cascade linked intentional self-regulation to PYD as a function of one domain "spilling over" to influence another domain. Finally, higher levels of PYD were expected to lead to higher levels of contribution (to self, family, community, and civil society) and to lower levels of depression, delinquency, and risk behaviors. The data confirmed that, as expected, adaptive developmental regulations in adolescence, involving links across time between positive parenting and intentional self-regulation, predicted subsequent scores for PYD and, in turn, PYD positively predicted later youth contribution scores and negatively predicted later youth problem behaviors.

As illustrated by the findings from the Masten et al. (2005), Dodge et al. (2008), and Lewin-Bizan et al. (2010) studies, the developmental system is full of "forks in the road." That is, when particular sets of variables are present at particular times of life, specific roads (trajectories) are more likely to be taken. Some roads will, across decades, lead to positive outcomes and others will eventuate in problematic developments. However, the power of the examples provided by these studies lies in the opportunities they afford for both theory and application. For instance, subsequent studies about the cascades that these researchers discovered might consider what variable or variables need to be added or removed from the sets of individual $\leftarrow \rightarrow$ context relations present at a particular time in life in order to prevent or to promote particular outcomes later in life. Such knowledge could then be used to devise or test intervention models and/or to engage policy discussions. As a consequence, the studying within a developmental systems theoretical framework of continuity–discontinuity—or, more specifically, the study of developmental cascades—can enable developmental scientist to fulfill the tripartite goal of studying change across the life span, that is, describing, explaining, *and* optimizing developmental change.

Indeed, because cascades can be expected to link over time to either positive and/or problematic behaviors, we believe that the core question to ask, in regard to using the developmental cascades notion to structure one's analysis of a developmental (longitudinal) data set, is: What variables, from what levels of organization, at what points (periods) in an individual's life, will lead to what short- and long-term outcomes for the individual and for his/her context? For instance, following the ideas of both Baltes (1997, Baltes et al., 2006) and Brandtstädter (1998, 2006) regarding the nature of individual $\leftarrow \rightarrow$ context relations within the developmental system, we may ask what the person needs to gain or lose at particular times of life in order for adaptive developmental regulations to exist between him/her and his context, as instantiated by positive, healthy development of the individual and benefits for the social context (e.g., the greater presence of social capital; Putnam, 2000). Attempts to answer this question require more nuanced analyses of developmental regulation.

Individual $\leftarrow \rightarrow$ Context Processes in Developmental Change

Insight into the dynamics of this individual $\leftarrow \rightarrow$ context relation has been provided by Cairns and Hood (1983). They discussed five factors that, in the context of the developmental system, may give rise to individual continuity and discontinuity. Cairns and Hood (1983) note that, first, individually specific biological variables may contribute to continuity or discontinuity in an individual's behavior. Such variables include genetic processes that might endure over several developmental periods, hormonal processes, and morphology (Cairns & Hood, 1983). However, they caution that:

> Biological factors are rarely translated directly into differences in social interaction patterns. The linkages between psychobiological processes and social behavior patterns need to be examined at each of the several points in ontogeny. It cannot be safely assumed that biological or genetic-based differences will persist, unmodified by social encounters or interchanges in which the individual engages. (Cairns & Hood, 1983, p. 309)

The second factor that Cairns and Hood (1983) identified as potentially contributing to the continuity–discontinuity of behavior includes the social network in which development occurs. They suggest that, if all other factors are equal, similarities in behavior from one time to the next will be greatest when the social network in which development occurs remains constant. In turn, of course, variation in a person's network (e.g., across developmental transitions, such as ones from elementary school to middle school, from school to work, or from work to retirement) may result in alterations of individual ←→ context relations that may foster discontinuities in behavior across ontogeny.

The third factor Cairns and Hood (1983) identified is behavioral consolidation. For instance, based on social learning, diverse behaviors become part of an integrated behavioral repertoire or sequence. For example, one may learn how to "put together" efficiently all the diverse behaviors involved in creating a Web site, in managing a political campaign, or in hosting a dinner party. Consolidation would, on one level of analysis, represent a discontinuity in development in that new levels of efficiency or of economy of effort may occur. At the same time, consolidation may represent continuity in that components of the past behavioral repertoire remain present in the new one.

The fourth and fifth factors noted by Cairns and Hood (1983) are ones that underscore the potential subtlety and nuances of the links between individuals and contexts that may be involved in continuity and discontinuity. These last points by Cairns and Hood also point to the role of the individual as an active agent in his or her own continuous or discontinuous development (e.g., Lerner, 1982; Lerner & Busch-Rossnagel, 1981). The fourth factor discussed by Cairns and Hood (1983) involves "social evocation and mutual control." Here, individuals contribute to the continuity or discontinuity of their own behavior by virtue of their being involved in a "circular function" (Schneirla, 1957). That is, by virtue of their individual physical and behavioral characteristics, people evoke differential reactions in others, reactions that involve (1) classification of the person-stimulus into categories (e.g., attractive, overweight, male, black) and (2) category-specific feedback to the person (Lerner 1976; see also Kendall, Lerner, & Craighead, 1984). Cairns and Hood (1983) note:

> To the extent that some stimulus properties of the individual remain relatively constant over Time, the social actions contingent upon the actions of others may themselves remain relatively similar. (p. 310)

Finally, Cairns and Hood (1983) describe that individuals may actively promote their own continuity or discontinuity. Especially as self-regulatory competency increases from childhood, across adolescence, and into the adult years, individuals show goal-directed behaviors—they make choices and pursue preferences that may preserve or alter their social network and their social relations, or maintain or change their environmental circumstances (cf. Brandtstädter, 1998, 1999, 2006; Freund, Li, & Baltes, 1999; Gestsdóttir & Lerner, 2008; Heckhausen, 1999).

In short, Cairns and Hood (1983) underscore the idea within developmental systems theory that there are several individual ←→ context relational processes that may maintain continuity or that may foster discontinuity across the life span. The level of plasticity of the individual ←→ context relations that exists across the life span serves, then, as the moderator of whether, and under what individual and contextual conditions, continuity or discontinuity characterizes the features of a person's development. Indeed, because of plasticity and the role of the individual as an active agent in constructing his or her own developmental trajectory, the empirical presence of continuity may not serve in and of itself as evidence against (or for) constancy or change in features of development (Cairns & Hood, 1983; Wohlwill, 1980).

For instance, Baltes (1987; Baltes et al., 2006) and Freund et al. (1999) explain that changes in "molecular" intentional self-regulatory processes may compensate for functional losses in aging and may maintain more "molar" behaviors. For example, an aging professional pianist can still have well-received performances despite slower psychomotor speed if he or she compensates by playing pieces that have slower tempos or that can be played at slower tempos.

Conclusions

The active role of the individual in fostering the continuity or discontinuity of his or her development across the life span, and the role of the plasticity of individual $\leftarrow \rightarrow$ context relations across the life span, combine to change the focus of inquiry about continuity and discontinuity within development from discussions of splits to discussions of integration. However, this change in perspective brings its own challenges. We discuss these new problematics in the final section of this chapter.

▦ CONCLUSIONS: FUTURE ISSUES IN THE STUDY OF CONTINUITY– DISCONTINUITY ACROSS THE LIFE SPAN

Any developmental change may be characterized as being either continuous or discontinuous, and different theories of development proscribe and prescribe the character of the changes that may be involved in human development. Theories that vary in their commitment to nature, to nurture, to nature–nurture interactions, or to the synthetic ideas associated with developmental systems theories may be contrasted, then, in regard to their inclusion of ideas pertinent to qualitative and quantitative, descriptive and explanatory, continuity and discontinuity.

We have noted that developmental systems theories overcome the split concepts of both nature and nurture and of continuity and discontinuity that have characterized past discussions of the features and bases of development across the life span, and that have replaced these categorical ideas with integrative concepts that better depict the dynamics of the relations between individuals and contexts that constitute the fundamental process of development. However, developmental systems theories raise new conceptual and methodological problematics for developmental scientists.

As we have emphasized, at the level of manifest variables, the presence or absence of change across ontogenetic points does not necessarily indicate anything about either the continuity or discontinuity of development. Descriptions of change are independent of explanations and manifest variable constancy does not reveal anything about the potential of changes in individual $\leftarrow \rightarrow$ context relations to actualize any potential of the person for plasticity in his or her structure or function. For instance, constancy in the individual can result from consistency in the demands and/or constraints of the environment within which the individual is functioning and to which the individual must adapt (cf. Wohlwill, 1980).

In addition, the developing individual's progressive ability to be competent in self-regulation means that the individual becomes better able to self-select and shape the context within which he or she interacts and thereby to produce, maintain, or alter the continuity of his or her behavioral repertoire (Baltes, et al., 2006; Brandtstädter, 1998, 1999, 2006; Freund et al., 1999; Gestsdóttir & Lerner, 2008; Heckhausen, 1999; Lerner, 1982; Lerner & Busch-Rossnagel, 1981). Given that the contextual pressures could be changing while such individual production processes are occurring, the maintenance of individual continuity in such a case could be evidence of considerable plasticity and of the use of a discontinuous set of strategies for behavioral management on the part of the individual.

The complexity of the individual ←→ context relational system that creates continuities or discontinuities across the life span means that the developmental scientist must adopt an equally complex approach to developmental research. Consistent with the methodological ideas presented in Table 6.1, the future elucidation of continuities and discontinuities in development will involve the conduct of change-sensitive, multivariate, and multilevel research that longitudinally appraises the dynamics of the individual ←→ context relation. Replacing the simplistic, split questions of the past, the new frame for inquiry about the continuity and discontinuity of human development across the life span must pose integrative and dynamic questions.

That is, (a) to adequately conduct research framed by developmental systems theory; in a manner that is attentive (b) to the plasticity of human development across the life span; and that, as such, remains attentive (c) to the potential that changes may be either continuous or discontinuous, a complex, six-part empirical question must be addressed:

1. What array of individual characteristics (ranging from the diverse genetic, hormonal, and neural characteristics of the person through his or her cognitive, emotional, motivational, and personality attributes to the behaviors in his or her repertoire); in combination with
2. What array of contextual characteristics, ranging from the proximal, or micro- and mesosystem, components of the ecology of human development (Bronfenbrenner & Morris, 2006), such as the family, school, peer group, neighborhood, community, and employment setting, through the distal contextual influences of institutions, policies, and culture, to the designed and natural physical ecology, all changing interdependently across history (Lerner, 2002, 2006); at
3. What points in ontogenetic, family, and historical time (Baltes, et al, 2006; Elder, 1998; Elder & Shanahan, 2006); will foster
4. What instances of continuity and what instances of discontinuity; for
5. What characteristics of human development (e.g., personality); within
6. What portions of the life span?

If this admittedly methodologically complex (and expensive to implement) question is addressed successfully in future research, developmental science will move into a new period of insight into the understanding of development across life. Developmental scientists will be able to specify how to capitalize on the plasticity of individuals and on the resources of their contexts to best maintain or, even better, promote positive, healthy, or valued behaviors. In addition, developmental scientists will be better able to specify what characteristics of the relations between individuals and contexts might be appropriate to change in order to maximize the probability that problem behaviors and development can be reduced or, better, prevented.

Such scientific mastery over the conditions of ontogenetic continuity and discontinuity will enable developmental science to not only better attain its goals of describing and explaining development. In addition, such mastery will also enable developmental scientists to better fulfill their goal of using their scholarship to optimize the course of human development across the breadth of the life span.

ACKNOWLEDGMENT

The writing of this chapter was supported in part by grants from the National 4-H Council, the John Templeton Foundation, the Thrive Foundation for Youth, and the National Science Foundation.

REFERENCES

Baltes, P. B. (1987). Theoretical propositions of life-span developmental psychology: On the dynamics between growth and decline. *Developmental Psychology, 23*, 611–626.

Baltes, P. B. (1997). On the incomplete architecture of human ontogeny: Selection, optimization, and compensation as foundations of developmental theory. *American Psychologist, 52*, 366–380.

Baltes, P. B., Lindenberger, U., & Staudinger, U. M. (2006). Life span theory in developmental psychology. In R. M. Lerner & W. Damon (Eds.), *Theoretical models of human development. Handbook of child psychology* (Vol. 1, 6th ed., pp. 569–664). Hoboken, NJ: Wiley.

Baltes, P. B., Reese, H. W., & Nesselroade, J. R. (1977). *Life-span developmental psychology: Introduction to research methods.* Monterey, CA: Brooks/Cole.

Bornstein, M. H. (1995). Parenting infants. In M. H. Bornstein (Ed.), *Handbook of parenting* (Vol. 1, pp. 3–39). Mahwah, NJ: Lawrence Erlbaum Associates.

Bornstein, M. H., & Lamb, M. E. (Eds.). (2005). *Developmental science: An advanced textbook.* Mahwah, NJ: Lawrence Ealbaum Associates.

Brandtstädter, J. (1998). Action perspectives on human development. In W. Damon, & R. M. Lerner (Eds.), *Theoretical models of human development. Handbook of child psychology* (Vol. 1, 5th ed., pp. 807–863). New York: Wiley.

Brandtstädter, J. (1999). The self in action and development: Cultural, biosocial, and ontogenetic bases of intentional self-development. In J. Brandtstädter & R. M. Lerner (Eds.), *Action and self-development: Theory and research through the life-span* (pp. 37–65). Thousand Oaks, CA: Sage.

Brandtstädter, J. (2006). Action perspectives on human development. In W. Damon & R. M. Lerner (Ed.). *Theoretical models of human development. Handbook of Child Psychology* (Vol 1., 6th ed., pp. 516–568). Hoboken, NJ: Wiley.

Brim, O. G., Jr., & Kagan, J. (Eds.). (1980). *Constancy and change in human development.* Cambridge, MA: Harvard University Press.

Bronfenbrenner, U. (1963). Developmental theory in transition. In H. W. Stevenson (Ed.), *Child psychology. Sixty-second yearbook of the National Society for the Study of Education, Part 1* (pp. 517–542). Chicago: University of Chicago Press.

Bronfenbrenner, U. (1979). *The ecology of human development: Experiments by nature and design.* Cambridge, MA: Harvard University Press.

Bronfenbrenner, U., & Morris, P. A. (2006). The bioecological model of human development. In W. Damon & R. M. Lerner (Eds.), *Theoretical models of human development. Handbook of child psychology* (Vol 1., 6th ed., pp. 793–828). Hoboken, NJ: Wiley.

Cairns, R. B., & Cairns, B. D. (2006). The making of developmental psychology. In W. Damon & R. M. Lerner (Eds.), *Theoretical models of human development. Handbook of child psychology* (Vol 1, 6th ed., pp. 89–165). Hoboken, NJ: Wiley.

Cairns, R. B., & Hood, K. E. (1983). Continuity in social development: A comparative perspective on individual difference prediction. In P. B. Baltes & O. G. Brim, Jr. (Eds.), *Life-span development and behavior* (Vol. 5, pp. 301–358). New York: Academic Press.

Colombo, J. (1982). The critical period concept: Research, methodology, and theoretical issues. *Psychological Bulletin, 91*, 260–275.

Damon, W., Lerner, R. M., Eisenberg, N., Kuhn, D., & Siegler, R. S. (Eds.). (2008). *Child and adolescent development: An advanced course.* Hoboken, NJ: Wiley.

Davis, A. (1944). Socialization and the adolescent personality. In N. B. Henry (Ed.). *Forty-third yearbook of the national society for the study of education* (Vol. 43, Part 1, pp. 198–216). Chicago: University of Chicago Press.

Dodge, K. A., Greenberg, M. T., & Malone, P. S. (2008). Testing an idealized dynamic cascade model of the development of serious violence in adolescence. *Child Development, 79*, 1907–1927.

Elder, G. H. (1974). *Children of the great depression.* Chicago: University of Chicago Press.

Elder, G. H., Jr. (1998). The life course and human development. In W. Damon & R. M. Lerner (Eds.), *Handbook of child psychology. Theoretical models of human development* (Vol 1., 5th ed., pp. 939–991). New York: Wiley.

Elder, G. H., Modell, J., & Parke, R. D. (Eds.) (1993). *Children in time and place: Developmental and historical insights.* New York: Cambridge University Press.

Elder, G. H., Jr., & Shanahan, M. J. (2006). The life course and human development. In W. Damon & R. M. Lerner (Eds.), *Theoretical models of human development. Handbook of child psychology* (Vol 1., 6th ed., pp. 665–715). Hoboken, NJ: Wiley.

Erikson, E. H. (1959). Identity and the life cycle. *Psychological Issues, 1*, 50–100.

Erikson, E. (1968). *Identity, youth, and crisis.* New York: Norton.

Freud, A. (1969). Adolescence as a developmental disturbance. In G. Caplan & S. Lebovici (Eds.), *Adolescence* (pp. 5–10). New York: Basic Books.

Freund, A. M. (2007). Differentiating and integrating levels of goal representation: A life-span perspective. In B. R. Little, K. Salmela-Aro, J. E. Nurmi, & S. D. Phillips (Eds.), *Personal project pursuit: Goals, action, and human flourishing* (pp. 247–270). Mahwah, NJ: Erlbaum.

Freund, A. M., Li, K. Z. H., & Baltes, P. B. (1999). The role of selection, optimization, and compensation in successful aging. In J. Brandtstädter & R. M. Lerner (Eds.), *Action and development: Origins and functions of intentional self-development* (pp. 401–434). Thousand Oaks, CA: Sage.

Freund, A. M., Nikitin, J., & Ritter, J. O. (2009). Psychological consequences of longevity: The increasing importance of self-regulation in old age. *Human Development, 52*, 1–37.

Garcia Coll, C., Bearer, E., & Lerner, R. M. (Eds.). (2004). *Nature and nurture: The complex interplay of genetic and environmental influences on human behavior and development.* Mahwah, NJ: Lawrence Erlbaum Associates.

Gestsdóttir, G., & Lerner, R. M. (2008). Positive development in adolescence: The development and role of intentional self regulation. *Human Development, 51*, 202–224.

Gottlieb, G. (1970). Conceptions of prenatal behavior. In L. R. Aronson, E. Tobach, D. S. Lehrman, & J. S. Rosenblatt (Eds.), *Development and evolution of behavior: Essays in memory of T. C. Schneirla* (pp. 111–137). San Francisco: Freeman.

Gottlieb, G. (1997). *Synthesizing nature-nurture: Prenatal roots of instinctive behavior.* Mahwah, NJ: Erlbaum.

Gottlieb, G., Wahlsten, D., & Lickliter, R. (2006). The significance of biology for human development: A developmental psychobiological systems view. In R. M. Lerner & W. Damon (Eds.), *Handbook of child psychology. Theoretical models of human development* (Vol 1., 6th ed., pp. 210–257). Hoboken, NJ: Wiley.

Hall, G. S. (1904). *Adolescence: Its psychology and its relations to physiology, anthropology, sociology, sex, crime, religion, and education* (Vols. 1 & 2). New York: Appleton.

Heckhausen, J. (1999). *Developmental regulation in adulthood: Age-normative and sociocultural constraints as adaptive challenges.* New York: Cambridge University Press.

Kagan, J., & Moss, H. A. (1962). *Birth to maturity.* New York: Wiley.

Kendall, P. C., Lerner, R. M., & Craighead, W. E. (1984). Human development intervention in childhood psychopathology. *Child Development, 55*, 71–82.

Lerner, R. M. (1976). *Concepts and theories of human development.* Reading, MA: Addison Wesley Publishing Company.

Lerner, R. M. (1982). Children and adolescents as producers of their own development. *Developmental Review, 2*, 342–370.

Lerner, R. M. (1984). *On the nature of human plasticity.* New York: Cambridge University Press.

Lerner, R. M. (2002). *Concepts and theories of human development* (3rd ed.). Mahwah, NJ: Lawrence Erlbaum Associates.

Lerner, R. M., Lerner, J. V., Almerigi, J., Theokas, C., Phelps, E., Gestsdóttir, S., Naudeau, S., Jelicic, H., Alberts, A. E., Ma, L., Smith, L. M., Bobek, D. L., Richman-Raphael, D., Simpson, I., Christiansen, E. D., & von Eye, A. (2005). Positive youth development, participation in community youth development programs, and community contributions of fifth-grade adolescents: Findings from the first wave of the 4-H Study of Positive Youth Development. *Journal of Early Adolescence, 25*(1), 17–71.

Lerner, R. M. (2006). Developmental science, developmental systems, and contemporary theories of human development. In W. Damon & R. M. Lerner (Eds.), *Theoretical models of human development. Handbook of child psychology* (Vol. 1, 6th ed., pp. 1–17). Hoboken, NJ: Wiley.

Lerner, R. M., & Busch-Rossnagel, N. A. (Eds.). (1981). *Individuals as producers of their development: A life-span perspective.* New York: Academic Press.

Lerner, R. M., & Overton, W. F. (2008). Exemplifying the integrations of the relational developmental system: Synthesizing theory, research, and application to promote positive development and social justice. *Journal of Adolescent Research, 23*(3), 245–255.

Lewin-Bizan, S., Bowers, E., & Lerner, R. M. (2010). One good thing leads to another: Cascades of positive youth development among American adolescents. *Development and Psychopathology, 22*(4), 759–770.

Lorenz, K. (1965). *Evolution and modification of behavior*. Chicago: University of Chicago Press.

Masten, A. S., Roisman, G. I., Long, J. D., Burt, K. B., Obradovic, J., Riley, J. R., et al. (2005). Developmental cascades: Linking academic achievement and externalizing and internalizing symptoms over 20 years. *Developmental Psychology, 41*, 733–746.

Mussen, P. H. (Ed.). (1970). *Carmichael's manual of child psychology* (3rd ed.). New York: Wiley.

Nikitin, J., & Freund, A. M. (2008). Hoping to be liked or wishing not to be rejected: Conflict and congruence of social approach and avoidance motivation. *Applied Psychology: An International Review, 57*, 90–111.

Overton, W. F. (1973). On the assumptive base of the nature-nurture controversy: Additive versus interactive conceptions. *Human Development, 16*, 74–89.

Overton, W. F. (1978). Klaus Riegel: Theoretical contribution to concepts of stability and change. *Human Development, 21*, 360–363.

Overton, W. F. (2003). Development across the life span. In R. M. Lerner, M. A. Easterbrooks, & J. Mistry. (Eds.), *Handbook of psychology: Vol. 6. Developmental psychology.* (Vol. 6, pp. 13–42). Editor in chief: I. B. Weiner. Hoboken, NJ: Wiley.

Overton, W. F. (2006). Developmental psychology: Philosophy, concepts, methodology. In W. Damon & R. M. Lerner (Ed.). *Theoretical models of human development. Handbook of child psychology* (Vol. 1, 6th ed., pp. 18–88). Hoboken, NJ: Wiley.

Overton, W. F. (2010). Life-span development: Concepts and issues. In W. R. Overton (Ed.), Cognition, biology, and methods across the life span: Vol. 1, Handbook of life-span development. Editor in chief: R. M. Lerner. Hoboken, NJ: Wiley.

Overton, W., & Reese, H. (1981). Conceptual prerequisites for an understanding of stability-change and continuity-discontinuity. *International Journal of Behavioral Development, 4*, 99–123.

Piaget, J. (1950). *The psychology of intelligence*. New York: Harcourt Brace.

Piaget, J. (1970). Piaget's theory. In P. H. Mussen (Ed.), *Carmichael's manual of child psychology* (Vol. 1, 3rd ed., pp. 703–723). New York: Wiley.

Putnam, R. (2000). *Bowling alone: The collapse and revival of American community*. New York: Simon & Schuster.

Reese, H. W., & Overton, W. F. (1970). Models of development and theories of development. In L. R. Goulet & P. B. Baltes (Eds.), *Life-span developmental psychology: Research and theory* (pp. 115-145). New York: Academic.

Riegel, K. F. (1975). Toward a dialectical theory of human development. *Human Development, 18*, 50–64.

Riegel, K. F. (1976). The dialectics of human development. *American Psychologist, 31*, 689–700.

Riley, M. W. (Ed.). (1979). *Aging from birth to death*. Washington, DC: American Association for the Advancement of Science.

Schaie, K. W. (1984). Midlife influences upon intellectual functioning in old age. *International Journal of Behavioral Development, 7*, 463–468.

Schneirla, T. C. (1957). The concept of development in comparative psychology. In D. B. Harris (Ed.), *The concept of development: An issue in the study of human behavior* (pp. 78–108). Minneapolis, MN: University of Minnesota Press.

Simmons, R. G., & Blyth, D. A. (1987). *Moving into adolescence: The impact of pubertal change and school context*. Hawthorne, NJ: Aldine.

Simmons, R. G., Carlton-Ford, S. L., & Blyth, D. A. (1987). Predicting how a child will cope with the transition to junior high school. In R. M. Lerner & T. T. Foch (Eds.), *Biological-psychosocial interactions in early adolescence* (pp. 325–375). Hillsdale, NJ: Lawrence Erlbaum Associates.

Tobach, E., & Greenberg, G. (1984). The significance of T. C. Schneirla's contribution to the concept of levels of integration. In G. Greenberg & E. Tobach (Eds.), *Behavioral evolution and integrative levels* (pp. 1–7). Hillsdale, NJ: Erlbaum.

Werner, H. (1957). The concept of development from a comparative and organismic point of view. In D. B. Harris (Ed.), *The concept of development* (pp. 125–148). Minneapolis, MN: University of Minnesota Press.

Wohlwill, J. (1980). Cognitive development in childhood. In O. G. Brim, Jr. & J. Kagan (Eds.), *Constancy and change in human development* (pp. 359–444). Cambridge: Harvard University Press.

Wohlwill, J. F. (1973). *The study of behavioral development*. New York: Academic Press.

CONVOYS OF SOCIAL RELATIONS: PAST, PRESENT, AND FUTURE

7

Toni C. Antonucci, Kira S. Birditt, and Kristine Ajrouch

INTRODUCTION

Convoys of social relations constitute an important and ever-present concept for understanding the formation of relationships. Convoys represent social relations as multidimensional and dynamic (Antonucci, 2001; Antonucci, Birditt, & Akiyama, 2009; Kahn & Antonucci, 1980). Over the years, the guiding principles of the convoy model have evolved to account for the complexity inherent to the formation, expression, and association of social relations with health, well-being, and quality of life. In this chapter, we begin with a basic overview of the convoy model. We then incorporate recent, cutting-edge developments that address links between social relations and well-being, and articulate how they both inform and advance the basic tenets of the model. Specifically, we consider advancements in understanding gene–environment interplay, the significance of culture, renewed focus on social networks as a form of social contagion, the emergence of ambivalence as a key theoretical construct, recognition of health disparities as central to population health, and the evolving area of systems science. Finally, we outline how the convoy model provides a valuable lens for understanding the importance of these recent scientific advancements, and consider how they may potentially guide future developments in the scientific study of social relations.

THEORETICAL OVERVIEW OF THE CONVOY MODEL

The convoy model was created to explain the antecedents and far-reaching consequences of social relations. Basic to the model is the incorporation of both life-span developmental and life course organizational perspectives. Antecedent influences are described as personal and situational characteristics which influence social relations, health, and well-being both contemporaneously and longitudinally. Individuals are conceptualized as part of a dynamic network or convoy that moves with them through time, space, and the life course. When functioning optimally, the convoy is an important asset that both protects and socializes individuals. When functioning suboptimally or dysfunctionally, it can put individuals at risk neither protecting them from stress nor helping them cope with the stress they experience. This, in turn, can leave individuals especially vulnerable, threatening both their health and well-being.

The method developed to define a person's social convoy, known as hierarchical mapping (Antonucci, 1986), is made up of three concentric circles, resembling a bulls-eye, with the word "YOU" written in the middle and delineates three levels of closeness and importance. People are instructed that the circles can remain empty or be full. In the inner circle, they are asked to name others so close to them that it would be hard to imagine life without them. They are then asked to think of individuals close and important whom they did not mention in the first circle; those named are then placed in the middle circle. Finally, they are asked whether they have others close enough and important enough to be in their personal network but whom they have not yet mentioned. Those named are placed in the outer circle. The end product results in a convoy of social relations.

The convoy model identifies personal and situational characteristics as defining and shaping the convoy in significant ways. Personal characteristics, which include age, gender, race, religion, education, and occupation, are experienced individually and change as the individual grows and matures. These status characteristics are experienced cumulatively, building on previous events, experiences, and activities. Personal characteristics are experienced intraindividually by the individual over the life span. Thus, one personal characteristic—age—is identified cross-sectionally. An individual who is 5 years old has 5 previous years of experience while a 50-year-old has 50 years of individual, personal experience. The absolute number of years tells us something significant about each of these individuals, and it is also important for understanding how both individuals experience the same event, for example, the loss of a parent, an economic recession, or a life-threatening illness. Previous life-span experiences, individual life periods or stages most certainly differentially influence how current events are experienced.

The life course perspective is illustrated by the inclusion of situational characteristics into the convoy model. Situational characteristics include the groups and organizations to which individuals belong, as well as the demands and expectations of the roles they occupy. These are critically important for understanding the contextual experience of the individual. Examples include being part of a family or company and the expectations associated with roles they have within family or place of employment. Situational characteristics reflect the basic tenets of the life course perspective, that is, incorporating the importance of organizational and historical contexts, group, or cohort perspectives. These factors fundamentally influence the demands and expectations experienced by the individual and may change throughout the life span.

A central element of the convoy model is social relations. Both the personal life-span characteristics and the situational life course characteristics anticipate, shape, and influence the social relations experienced by the individual. As the name convoy implies, these social relations are meant to provide a protective base that leads to better mental and physical health. The convoy model specifically details various aspects of social relations, including social networks, social support, and support satisfaction. Each aspect describes a critical but different aspect of social relations. Social networks refer to the objective structure of support relations, for example, the number of people, age, gender, race, and relationship, with each network member. Social support, on the other hand, refers to the support people exchange in their relationships. Kahn and Antonucci (1980) described three types of support: aid, affect, and affirmation. Aid refers to tangible help, affect refers to emotional support, and affirmation refers to an affirmation by others of your values and beliefs. Optimal social relations create a convoy which provides a protective base that allows individuals to grow and develop and to successfully meet the challenges they face in life.

Evidence has been accumulating in support of the convoy model (Antonucci, 2001). Convoys appear to differ by life stage, with larger, more diverse members during early adulthood and smaller, higher proportions of kin in old age (Ajrouch, Antonucci, & Janevic, 2001).

A cross-sectional examination of convoys (Antonucci, 2008) among people aged 20 to 75+ indicated an 81% overlap in convoy structure. There were age differences in size of network but no differences in sex of network members by age or level of closeness. Convoy composition varied by role relationship with more spouse and children in the inner circle whereas other family and friends were more likely to be in middle and outer circles. Optimal convoys provide practical help but also, and perhaps more importantly, a psychological basis upon which to view the world. This is critical since it has been shown that subjective and perceived support can be far more important than objective and actual support in affecting the health and well-being of the individual (Antonucci, Fuhrer, & Dartigues, 1997; Blazer, 1982).

The pervasive influence of social relations has been documented through associations with mortality and morbidity as well as with ability to cope with stressful situations in adulthood (Berkman & Syme, 1979; Blazer, 1982; Bolger, Foster, Vinokur, & Ng, 1996; Coyne, Rohrbaugh, Shoham, Cranford, Niclas, & Sonnega, 2001; Palinkis, Wingard, & Barret-Connor, 1990; Seeman, Bruce, & McAvay, 1996; Uchino, Holt-Lunstad, Smith, & Bloor, 2004). The significance of social relations to health and well-being is also prominent among children. Classic work by Cochran, Larner, Riley, Gunnarsson, and Henderson (1990) documented the importance of social relations in the lives of children and their mothers in the United States as well as in Sweden, Wales, and West Germany. Their work also demonstrated the importance of social networks on children's school success. More recently, in a nationally representative sample of middle-school Danish children, Due, Lynch, Holstein, and Modvig (2003) found that poor relations with an array of others, including parents, peers, and teachers, were significantly associated with worse health. However, as research in this area has become increasingly sophisticated, evidence suggests that a more nuanced approach is necessary and that all social support under all circumstances does not always lead to "positive" outcomes such as decreased mortality. Walter-Ginzburg, Blumstein, Chetrit, and Modan (2002) found that among the oldest old, people with positive emotional support died sooner, whereas Birditt and Antonucci (2008) found, using longitudinal data, that those with consistently low levels of positive support and increasing levels of negative support were more likely to die. More recently, Antonucci, Birditt, and Webster (2010) have suggested that a more nuanced approach incorporating presence or absence of a chronic illness, relationship type (spouse, child, friend), that is, with spouse, children or friends, as well as positive and negative relationship quality provide the kind of detailed information necessary to more completely understand how social relations affect health. Thus, under "normal" conditions positive relationship quality might lead to increased longevity, better health, and coping. Under conditions of terminal illness, however, positive relationship quality may allow an individual to feel at peace, unwilling to expose relatives to a prolonged illness and, therefore, ready to accept the inevitable. On the other hand, interactions might become more negative when supportive others are constantly reminding the ill person to engage in recommended health behavior changes or insist on strict adherence to medical regimens resulting in longer life but perhaps less pleasant interactions.

In sum, recent advances have made it clear that the association between social relations and health is a complex one. In the following sections we consider the convoy model in relation to six topics, which are currently gaining momentum in the social and behavioral sciences. These are gene–environment interplays, the critical role of culture, social contagion, ambivalence, health disparities, and systems science. Advancements in studies on the interplay between genes and environment point to the critical role social relations play in gene expressions. Attention to culture illuminates the significance of variations in assumptions upon which social relations form and express themselves. Addressing the emergence of both social contagion and ambivalence as key concepts in the scientific study of social relations allows for a critical analysis of how they operate influencing health and well-being. A review of developments in understanding health disparities provides an opportunity to consider the main and buffering effects of social relations on health and well-being status among advantaged and disadvantaged groups. Finally, a consideration of systems science highlights interrelationships between multiple factors that simultaneously operate to influence various outcomes. We suggest that each of these new developments can provide an ever more in-depth illustration of specific aspects of the convoy model across the life span. We believe these newly emerging areas offer new and exciting possibilities that can be incorporated into, and benefit from, the basic tenets of the convoy model. We begin with a consideration of recent developments in genetic science.

Gene–Environment Interplay

With the identification of the human genome many anticipated the articulation of genetic causes of health, illness, disease, and behavior. However, most geneticists now agree that very little is "caused" by genes or at least by genes alone. As the convoy model posits that both personal and situational factors are important determinants of social relations and well-being, geneticists likewise have recognized the fundamental importance of gene–environment interplay including both gene × environment interactions as well as gene–environment correlations.

It is useful to recognize that this latest iteration evolves from both impressive new genetic developments as well as disappointments. The late 20th century saw great advancements in gene identification. Many anticipated the mapping of the human genome as a breakthrough in the discovery of the genetic basis for behavior, disease, and other important human characteristics of interest. We have successfully mapped the human genome, but it has only served to impressively emphasize that there are very few characteristics for which there is one single genetic cause. Rather, geneticists are now convinced that gene expression is considerably more complex, often involving several genes as well as complex interactions with the environment. It is widely agreed that we can no longer afford the luxury of believing that genes are the sole determinants of an outcome. Similarly, while environments can certainly influence outcomes, they, too, are not likely to be the singular causal factor.

Behavioral geneticists and life course epidemiologists both identify environment in the broadest sense including what many psychologists and developmental scientists might identify as social, physical, and/or cultural context. Four different types of interactions are commonly identified (cf., Shanahan & Boardman, 2009) and they include social triggers, social compensation, social control, and social enhancement. Each critically illustrates the importance of both the life-span and life course perspectives. Following, we detail these four because they are instructive for understanding, at an entirely new level, how the convoy model, specifically personal (genes) and situational (environment) characteristics as well as social relations, influence health and well-being.

Social triggers describe a situation where a specific gene or genetic vulnerability is only expressed in the presence of a triggering event. Triggering can be strong or weak. There are many types of triggering events but those most interesting for the convoy model are those involving the context of social interactions to which an individual is exposed. For example, individuals exposed to maltreatment in childhood have a greater tendency toward antisocial behavior as adults especially in the presence of deficiencies in monoamine oxidase A (MAOA), which, metabolizes neurotransmitters. As Caspi et al. (2002) have noted, while childhood maltreatment has long been known to be associated with adult antisocial behavior, it is not true in all cases. Rather, childhood maltreatment plus low levels of MAOA significantly increases the likelihood that the individual will exhibit antisocial behavior as an adult.

A second form of gene × environment interaction, social compensation, serves a protective effect. In this case, an individual might be genetically predisposed to exhibit a certain negative behavior, but is less likely to do so in an enriched or compensating environment. While there is a weak version of social compensation, that is, the absence of distress ensures that people do not exhibit the behavior, the strong effect is more interesting. In this case an individual is prevented from exhibiting a genetically based behavior often associated with a negative outcome because of the environmental context. Shanahan, Erickson, Vaisey, and Smolen (2007) offer the impressive example of individuals with the dopamine D_2 receptor gene (Taq1A), which is usually associated with poor educational achievement. Nevertheless, those with Taq1A who also had a significant teacher–mentor were much more likely to have successful educational achievement, unlike those with Taq1A who had no mentor. While Taq1A is not an "education" gene, it is associated with impulse control, or lack thereof, which, in turn, is associated with problematic classroom behavior and consequently poor academic performance. A teacher–mentor can serve as strong compensation for this genetic vulnerability.

Social control is the third type of gene × environment interaction identified. As the name implies, social environment, that is, situational characteristics such as social norms or structural constraints, inhibit genetically predisposed negative behaviors that might otherwise be expressed by limiting the behavioral choices available. Social control is exhibited at the broader, societal level. An interesting example is evident among people with the aldehyde dehydrogenase 2 (ALDH2) gene. Those with the homozygous gene variant are metabolically less able to process alcohol, resulting in greater impairment when alcohol is ingested. As a result, people with the homozygous form of the ALDH2 have increased motor impairment, hangovers, and so on, and are, therefore, less likely to drink or become alcoholics. By contrast, those with the heterozygous form of the gene are better able to metabolically process alcohol, thus experiencing less impairment when they ingest alcohol. In a fascinating Japanese study, Higuchi et al. (1994) showed an interesting cohort by gene interaction. Those with the homozygous gene refrained from alcohol regardless of cohort, no doubt because of the severe impairments experienced with alcohol. However, those with the heterozygous form of the gene only refrained from alcohol consumption in the earlier cohorts when alcohol was very negatively sanctioned. As that negative sanction loosened in Japan, people with this form of ALDH2 have increased their alcohol intake. Higuchi and colleagues hypothesize that in circumstances of high social control, the differential effect of genetic factors are not evident because all behavior is controlled. When social control is reduced, however, genetic influences become more apparent.

The fourth form of gene × environment interaction, social enhancement, follows logically from the previous three. In this case an enriched environment facilitates the expression of a gene that predisposes the individual toward positive characteristics. In the case of social enhancement, characteristics of the environment make it more likely that the positive expression of some genetically influenced characteristics is maximized. Under normal or nonoptimal conditions an individual might exhibit an average level of a specific physical, cognitive, or social characteristic but under enhancing environmental conditions the individual might achieve higher physical, cognitive, or social skills. Examples include better physical functioning or skills through an exercise program, better cognitive performance through superior education, or improved parenting skills as a result of positive role models or intervention programs. A convoy of social relations might provide encouragement, role models, or environmental norms that emphasize positive behaviors or characteristics.

Since the gene × environment research implies independence between genes and environment, some have also noted the importance of gene–environment correlation. This work suggests that certain genetic characteristics predispose the individual to behave in a specific fashion, which in turn solicits predictable reactions from the environment, thereby reinforcing or encouraging a specific behavior. Building on the assumption that following adult rules is socially undesirable among adolescents, Burt (2008) demonstrated that adolescents with the G-allele in a particular polymorphism (5HT2A-G1438A) were more likely to break rules and were seen as more popular by their peers. Specifically, the polymorphism in question was associated with adolescent's rule-breaking behaviors and through this, with their popularity, such that those with the genetic predisposition for rule-breaking behavior were seen as more likeable by their peers than those without. In other words, as predicted by the theory of the evocative gene–environment correlation, genes appear to predispose individuals not only to specific behaviors but also to the social consequences of those behaviors. The environment is thus not independent of the gene but is instead distinctly influenced by it. Although this work is still in embryonic stages, we mention it because it has implications for the convoy model. Genetically based personal characteristics may influence environmental reactions which may affect the social relations, health, and well-being experienced by the individual. Recent work with centenarians suggests that while there are genetic influences on longevity, these can only manifest under favorable personal and environmental conditions (Perls, 2006). Research on older people's susceptibility to Alzheimer's disease indicates that individuals with the APOE4 gene are more susceptible but only under certain environmental and social conditions (Haan, Shemanski, Jagust, Manolio, & Kuller, 1999). On the other hand, Seeman et al. (2005) found that the presence of the APOE4 allele increased the probability of cognitive decline among those with higher levels of education but had no effect on those with less education. A recent review by Fratiglioni, Paillard-Borg, and Winblad (2004) indicated that an active and socially integrated lifestyle appears to protect against Alzheimer's disease and cognitive decline; it is clear that such work should further identify whether there are differential benefits depending on the presence or absence of specific genes such as the APOE4. In sum, research thus far suggests that gene-environment interplays can operate at any point in the life span and can result in positive or negative effects on health and well-being.

Culture

Culture refers to the values, orientations, and social norms found within a group or society. Given the growing interest in, and need to better understand, social relations within and across global settings, we detail variations in cultural beliefs and values as they apply to social relations, provide a case example of how culture informs relations between young and old, and then illustrate how the convoy model provides a useful framework for delineating universal as well as culturally specific aspects of social relations.

Cross-cultural theorists indicate that cultures vary on several value dimensions, each of which may hold particular significance for social relations including individualism/collectivism, relatedness/separateness, traditional/secular, and self expression/survival (Hofstede, 1980; Inglehart & Welzel, 2005; Markus & Kitayama, 1991; Triandis, Bontempo, Villareal, Asai, & Lucca, 1988). Individualism or separateness involves a concern for the self, personal achievement, freedom of choice, and personal control. Collectivism or relatedness assumes that obligations are to the group or community and the person is considered part of the social unit (Kağitçibaşi, 1996).

Using the World Values Survey, the largest existing study of beliefs and values around the world, Inglehart and Welzel (2005) plotted countries on two value dimensions including traditional/secular and survival/self expression. The study assessed 81 societies, which covers 85% of the world's population. Traditional societies value obedience to god, religion, one's homeland, family, and social conformity while secular rational societies value science and autonomy. Societies that emphasize survival values include constraints on autonomy, stress the importance of economic and physical security, fear of foreigners and other outgroups; they have low levels of subjective well-being, low trust, and traditional gender roles. In contrast, societies that value self-expression emphasize human choice, well-being, and creativity.

These value dimensions are likely to lead to cultural variations in the structure and quality of social relationships. For example, cultures that are individualistic/separate and value self-expression are more likely to maintain relationships that benefit personal goals, invest in children on a psychological rather than economic basis, feel obligated to family but perceive it as voluntary, feel at ease interacting with strangers, and consider individuals as separate, nonoverlapping entities. Individualism is also associated with more direct goal-oriented conversation styles (Kağitçibaşi, 1996; Oyserman, Kemmelmeier, & Coon, 2002). On the other hand, cultures ascribing to collectivism, relatedness, and/or survival tend to believe that group membership is unchangeable and in-group exchanges are based on principals of equality and generosity (Oyserman et al., 2002). They tend to have extended families in which young people provide direct financial help to the elderly, parents prefer sons, parents have more children, and children are valued for old age security. These cultures are more likely to have social interactions with in-group members, engage in indirect communication styles, and are more concerned with partner's feelings.

One case example to illustrate how culture informs social relations across the life span may be found in the work of Suad Joseph, who studies Arab families in Lebanon. Joseph (1993) suggests that contrary to social relations based on Western or U.S. samples where women are found to be more relationally oriented than men, *both* men and women in Lebanese society are socialized to view themselves relationally. Yet, relationships evolve according to an age hierarchy, amounting to what she terms "patriarchal connectivity." Connectivity is not a state of being, but instead refers to an activity or intention meant to facilitate closeness that includes the ability to anticipate the needs of another, answer for others, and shape likes and dislikes in accordance with one another. Joseph elaborates on how language use draws individuals close to one another. As an example, parents often refer to their child using the same titles the child uses to call her/his parent. Mothers may call their child "mama" and fathers may refer to their child as "baba." The connection is intensified when close and important others are referred to as body parts: *eyeyounni* (my eyes) or *elbee* (my heart), or indeed as the very essence of being: *rouhyee* (my soul). Language use establishes an overlapping sense of self, which ties individuals to one another in a fundamental way. She argues that older adults expect to direct the lives of younger members through cultural entitlements that foster relations between youth and elders. Younger members are seen as extensions of older adults, who are expected to serve and comply with the wishes of their elders as expressions of love and loyalty. According to Joseph, in Lebanon, one's sense of self is grounded in social relations that play out as connectivity. Following this logic, an older adult invests her/his well-being in the actions of younger people to whom s/he is connected.

Although theories suggest clear-cut and consistent cultural differences, research demonstrates that aspects of each domain exist within each cultural context. For example, contrary to expectations, a meta-analysis revealed that Americans reported higher collectivism than did the Japanese (Oyserman et al., 2002). Cross-cultural studies have also revealed that the types of relationships beneficial for health and well-being vary by cultural values, norms, and expectations for close relations (van Tilburg, de Jong Gierveld, Lecchini, & Marsiglia, 1998). Thus, it is increasingly clear that cultural expectations about what constitutes support affects an individual's health and well-being. Such findings underscore the need for research on the cultural evaluations of the nature of relationships.

The convoy model provides a useful framework for understanding cultural aspects of social relations. The notion of a social convoy appears to translate extremely well to divergent cultural and national contexts. The hierarchical mapping technique has been used successfully in the United States for children as young as 8 years and among diverse groups including European Americans, African Americans, Arab Americans, and Hispanic Americans (Ajrouch, et al., 2001; Ajrouch, Blandon, & Antonucci, 2005; Ajrouch, 2005; Levitt, Guacci-Franco, & Levitt, 1994). In addition, social convoys have been successfully measured in numerous other countries including Japan (Lansford, Antonucci, Akiyama, & Takahashi, 2005), England—among Bangladeshis (Phillipson, Bernard, Phillips, & Ogg, 2001), France (Antonucci et al.,

1997), and Germany (Minnemann, 1994; Wagner, Schütze, & Lang, 1999). People within various cultural settings and of various ages quite readily identify close and important persons.

Furthermore, the convoy model of social relations has influenced research carried out in various nations around the world (e.g., Chen & Lin, 2008; Guiaux, van Tilburg, & van Groenou, 2007; Haines & Henderson, 2002). Our colleagues (Takahashi et al., 2002) found that while U.S. and Asian cultures are often described as individualistic versus collectivistic, this dichotomy is not universally supported by the literature. They examined convoy structure and support exchanges of parallel samples aged 20–64 years in the two countries, specifically exploring (1) whether the Americans (individualistic culture) were more independent in social relations than the Japanese (collectivist culture) as manifest by the provision of less instrumental support by Americans than by Japanese; (2) whether the Americans (individualistic culture) do not have as strong a desire to maintain harmonious relationships with others as the Japanese (collectivist cultures), as indicated by more positive and less negative quality relationships; and (3) whether Americans (individualistic culture) are not integrated into "ingroups" especially the family, as the Japanese (collectivist culture) are. Their findings indicate that Americans were as collectivist as, if not more collectivist than, the Japanese in approximately half the comparisons examined.

In sum, the universality of convoys is evident in the numerous studies that have used the concept for all ages with children and adults, in multiple sites and various cultures. Convoys are a useful concept easily implemented in cross-cultural and/or cross-national studies. Yet, the structure, quality, and meanings attributed to convoys are also culturally unique. Convoys may form according to various inclusion criteria that may vary by country (e.g., family-focused versus family and friend-focused). In addition, the values and norms upon which social relations operate may differ from one culture to the next. Though the most recent elaborations of convoys allow for a detailed assessment of the nature of social relations regarding structure of networks, support type, and support quality, recent emphasis on the role and importance of culture make it clear that greater specification concerning societal variations (situational characteristics) in social exchanges and/or social interactions is warranted and should be instructive.

Social Contagion

The advent of new social network analysis strategies and the accumulation of longitudinal data regarding social ties has resulted in a relatively new approach to the examination of how behaviors and other health-related phenomena spread across social network members. Social support studies often examine the number of relationships or the amount of support received from those relationships. In contrast, social network studies examine linkages among individuals as predictors of health, which in some ways broaden the examination of social networks. Although social network studies have found associations over time in behaviors and well-being, they often do not examine mechanisms accounting for those effects.

Several studies of adolescent risk behaviors (e.g., drug use, smoking, aggression, sexual behavior, and eating patterns) have found that the best predictor of adolescent behavior is the behavior of their close friends and siblings (Alexander, Piazza, Mekos, & Valente, 2001; Bosari & Carey, 2001; Rende, Slomkowski,

Lloyd-Richardson, & Niaura, 2005; Rodgers & Rowe, 1993). There are several potential reasons for links in social network behaviors including selection effects, socialization, and positive reinforcement. Interestingly, some studies reveal that the
perception of peers rather than actual peer, rather than their actual such effects
(Prinstein & Wang, 2005).

In a series of studies using data from the longitudinal Framingham Heart Study,
Christakis, Fowler, and colleagues have examined reports of adults' friends, neighbors, siblings, and spouses over 30 years and found that happiness, loneliness, obesity,
and smoking spread across social network members; in other words, they argue that
these well-being outcomes are contagious from one network member to the next.
There are several other possible explanations for these findings (e.g., environmental
effects, selection effects) that we discuss in detail later in this section. Interestingly,
these network effects occur irrespective of whether people know each other. In their
study of happiness, Fowler and Christakis (2008) found that happy people tended to
cluster together in networks. Happy people are connected to other happy people with
up to three degrees of separation. In addition, people who are more central in their
networks (e.g., connected to more network members) report more happiness than
people at the periphery of the network. Further, people who have many happy social
network members are more likely to become happy in the future. These effects were
found among friends, spouses, siblings, and neighbors.

Similar to the convoy model finding that having more social network members does not necessarily lead to greater happiness, researchers have found that
the number of social network members also is unrelated to feelings of loneliness.
Individuals can experience profound loneliness in the presence of many others.
Cacioppo, Fowler, and Christakis (2009) examined whether reports of loneliness
spread through social networks. They found that lonely middle-aged adults tended
to have fewer friends in future assessments and that people with more friends were
less likely to feel lonely in subsequent assessments. Lonely people also nominate
fewer friends and are nominated fewer times by others as friends. In addition, people
with lonely friends are more likely to become lonely in the future. Likewise, people
with nonlonely friends are less likely to be lonely in the future. The effects were also
found among spouses and next-door neighbors but not siblings or other neighbors.
Cacioppo et al. (2009) considered this finding as evidence that contagion is not due
to environmental effects. In addition, the effects were found among people with up
to three degrees of separation. Interestingly, loneliness spread more than nonloneli-
ness, unlike which happiness spread more than unhappiness. Furthermore, loneliness spread more among women than men whereas no gender difference occurred
in the spread of happiness.

Evidence of social contagion also emerged when examining the health concerns
of obesity and smoking. In their study of obesity, Christakis and Fowler (2007) found
that individuals who had obese friends, siblings, or spouses were more likely to
become obese in the future. They did not find this effect for neighbors, which they
interpreted as evidence that effects were not due only to environmental factors. They
also found correlations in obesity between individuals with up to three degrees of
separation. Further, friends who nominated one another showed the greatest effects.
They hypothesized several mechanisms that may account for these effects. For example, people may change their perceptions of how normative it is to be overweight or
they may influence one another's eating and exercise habits.

These studies have been criticized by some who propose that there may be three reasons a phenomenon spreads in a network: (1) induction effects in which one member's well-being or behavior induces behavior changes in others through social contagion; (2) homophily effects in which people select similar individuals with whom to associate; and (3) shared environmental factors. In a study of adolescent obesity in the National Longitudinal Study of Adolescent Health (Add Health), Cohen-Cole and Fletcher (2008) found that much of the social network effects found by Christakis and Fowler are actually due to shared environmental factors. When contextual effects were added to the model, much of the social network effects were minimized. In addition, Fletcher and his colleagues found evidence of contagion when examining factors that are clearly not contagious, such as height and acne. Further researchers have noted that the networks in the Framingham Heart study are not complete networks. Participants were asked to record all of their family members but only one friend.

The convoy model, which stresses that networks involve multiple dimensions as well as various levels of closeness and importance, may provide guidance for understanding the phenomenon of social contagion. In addition, the convoy model may be useful as a tool to develop more complex assessments of social networks and identify mechanisms that account for observed effects. According to the model, health and well-being vary as a function of personal factors, situational factors, and social relations (e.g., social network members, relationship quality). We believe it important to consider all of these factors when examining determinants of health. In addition, social relations help us when we experience stress and can provide individuals with a feeling of greater control (Antonucci & Jackson, 1987). These findings suggest that at all ages from childhood to adulthood and concerning factors that may vary by developmental period from loneliness to obesity, social ties influence our life time experiences as well as our own physical and mental health.

Ambivalence

Another possible mechanism to explain links between convoys and health involves the emotional contexts of relationships. Recent research has gone beyond prior studies of only positive or only negative relationships to focus on ambivalence. Ambivalence is defined as the simultaneous experience of positive and negative sentiments regarding an object or relationship. Individuals experience ambivalence when incompatible norms or expectations cause contradictory emotions or beliefs (Merton & Barber, 1963). Ambivalence is most likely to occur in social roles and relationships that involve conflicting norms for behavior such as autonomy and closeness (Connidis & McMullin, 2002). The convoy model recognizes the complexity of social relations, and therefore provides a useful framework for attending to the existence of ambivalence across network ties. The convoy model postulates that although relationships are close they often vary in their positive and negative qualities (Antonucci, 2001). A focus on ambivalence takes this notion one step further with attention to separate measures of individuals' simultaneous feelings of positive and negative sentiments within specific relationships.

A burgeoning parent–child literature has established that the experience of intergenerational ambivalence is common due to conflicting desires for closeness and independence (Luescher & Pillemer, 1998; Pillemer & Suitor, 2002). Much of this research has focused on grown children. Parents report greater ambivalence regarding grown children who have not reached the milestones associated with adulthood (Fingerman, Chen, Hay, Cichy, & Lefkowitz, 2006; Pillemer et al., 2007), whereas children experience greater ambivalence regarding parents with health problems or who may need caregiving. Ambivalence may also be higher at certain points in the life span. Research indicates that older individuals report fewer ambivalent relationships than do younger people (Fingerman, Hay, & Birditt, 2004). Indeed, new longitudinal research shows that there are declines in feelings of ambivalence regarding parents that occur from adolescence to young adulthood which may be indicative of children's greater independence (Tighe, Birditt, & Antonucci, 2009).

In recent work, Ward (2008) examined parents' feelings of ambivalence regarding several children and suggested that parents experience collective ambivalence in which they report feeling highly positive regarding some children and highly negative regarding others. Intergenerational ambivalence also predicts a variety of negative health and well-being outcomes including lower self-rated health, lower quality of life, and greater depressive symptoms (Fingerman, Pitzer, Lefkowitz, Birditt, & Mroczek, 2008; Lowenstein, 2007; Ward, 2008).

Relatively little research has examined ambivalence outside of the intergenerational tie, although there are a few exceptions. Fingerman et al. (2004) used the convoy model of social relations to examine ambivalence across ties that included both family and non–family network members. Ambivalence was defined in this case as nominating a person as simultaneously close and negative. Findings indicated that ambivalence is more common in family ties than in nonfamily ties, perhaps because the latter can more easily be severed.

Studies that link ambivalence across network members with health and well-being have also included both family and nonfamily ties. Birditt and Antonucci (2007) used cluster analyses of positive and negative relationship qualities with spouse, best friend, and child to examine the simultaneous experience of positive and negative sentiments across network ties. They found that people who reported high-quality relations (high positive, low negative) in at least two social ties demonstrated the highest levels of well-being. However, findings were different among married people who either did or did not have a best friend. Among those with poor or ambivalent spousal relationships, having positive relationships with friends that were not also negative, that is, not ambivalent, offset the negative influence of poor or ambivalent relations with spouse on well-being. Overall, these findings show the importance of examining ambivalence in relationships as well as the importance of including multiple relationship types in which people are involved to uncover the complexity of relationship qualities that people experience across network members and throughout their life time.

Uchino and colleagues have also examined ambivalence in network ties. Participants named the 10 most important people in their lives and how helpful or upsetting these people were when they needed different kinds of assistance. Ambivalent network members included those who were rated as both helpful and upsetting. Findings demonstrated that older people who have more ambivalent social network members report more depressive symptoms and have higher heart rate reactivity when they are stressed (Uchino, Holt-Lunstad, Uno, & Flinders, 2001). Further research conducted in a series of laboratory studies showed that when in the presence of an ambivalent friend, people exhibit higher heart rates and also receive less effective and more critical support from those individuals (Holt-Lunstad, Uchino, Smith, & Hicks, 2007). Similarly, in a study of support exchange in the context of positive, negative, or ambivalent relationships, Tighe et al. (2009) found that people generally exchange less support in more negative and ambivalent ties unless individuals report extremely high levels of stress. Indeed, ambivalent relationships may be especially damaging because they are unpredictable (Uchino, 2004).

Ambivalence predicts negative outcomes which makes it particularly important to understand. The convoy model enriches our understanding of ambivalence in social relationships by highlighting the significance of the broader social network. It provides a framework to guide approaches that more specifically measure ambivalent ties, to consider the importance of context and relationship type, and to examine the mechanisms by which ambivalence influences health and well-being. In sum, the convoy model encourages a broadening of the ambivalence concept to not only refer to specific relationships but also recognize the significance of multiple relationships within a network.

Health Disparities

Health disparities refer to gross differences in the prevalence of disease among various populations within a society. The convoy model of social relations provides a useful guiding framework for testing the mediating and moderating role of social relations in the quest to minimize health disparities. Racial/ethnic minorities, socioeconomically disadvantaged individuals and those in some rural and inner city areas are more likely to experience shorter life spans and higher infant mortality as well as health problems and diseases such as cardiovascular disease, cancer, birth defects, asthma, diabetes, stroke, sexually transmitted diseases, mental illness, and obesity (Bulatao & Anderson, 2004; Link & Phelan, 1995; Williams & Collins, 1995; Williams, Yan, Jackson, & Anderson, 1997). Gender disparities are also widely documented with women reporting more illness and disease than men, though men tend to have shorter life expectancies (Barer, 1994; Verbrugge, 1985). In addition, early life experiences reveal health disparities among disadvantaged groups with regard to prenatal care (Kogan, Kotelchuck, Alexander, & Johnson, 1994), infant mortality rates (LaVeist, 2005), and early mortality from diseases in midlife (Haan, Kaplan, & Syme, 1989; Marks, 1996). Links between social relations and health have been clearly demonstrated (Antonucci & Jackson, 1987; Cohen & Syme, 1985; Russell & Cutrona, 1991; Seeman, 1996; Stewart & Hays, 1997), suggesting a potentially critical resource for those in need.

The interplay of social relations with inequality markers provides critical insights into pathways leading to health disparities and potential resources that may alleviate poor health outcomes. According to the mediating hypothesis, the link between an inequality marker such as gender, race/ethnicity, or socioeconomic status (SES) and health may be explained by the fact that those factors differentially influence social relations, which in turn explain variations in health outcomes throughout adulthood. For instance, Kawachi, Kennedy, Lochner, and Prothrow-Stith (1997) found that the relationship between income inequality and mortality was substantially mediated through social relations. Indeed, social relations are thought to vary by SES. Ross and Wu (1995) found, in a national probability sample of adults aged 20–64, that the level of social support increases with education level. Similarly, in a national probability sample of elderly individuals, Krause and Borawski-Clark (1995) found that older adults of higher SES have more contact with friends, provide more support to others, and express greater satisfaction with the support they receive. Another study, however, found that lower levels of education among individuals aged 70–79 were associated with larger social networks and less negative support (Kubzansky, Berkman, Glass, & Seeman, 1998).

Conceptualized as a resource (Ensel & Lin, 1991; Martin, Grünendahl, & Martin, 2001), social relations have also been identified as one of the many psychosocial mechanisms that may moderate health disparities. According to the moderating hypothesis, the quantity and quality of social relations are not necessarily linked to inequality in a systematic way; however, the presence of these resources among individuals in the most vulnerable groups mitigates the negative effects on health and well-being. For instance, Antonucci, Ajrouch, and Janevic (2003) found that the health of less-educated men parallels the advantaged health status of men with higher levels of education in the presence of key social supports. Specifically, social relations exerted a moderating effect such that men, but not women, with less education who have larger networks and greater support from grown children reported better health than lower-educated men who lack such support. These findings suggest that social relations may be a protective factor for the health of men in lower socioeconomic strata. Similarly, social support resources within the family appear to advantage poor children. Sandler (1980) found that inner-city children in kindergarten through third grade, who reported the presence of support resources including multiple older siblings, and a two-parent family, adjusted to negative life events more readily than those lacking such resources.

The convoy model has recently been adapted to focus on an examination of how stress influences health, and interacts with social relations. Stress includes different life events at different points in the life span, such as moving to a new school or residence, breaking up with a girlfriend or boyfriend, or the death of a close family member as well as daily hassles which include minor irritations that occur in daily life involving schoolwork, worries about finances, or work. Social relationships may buffer or exacerbate the effects of stress on health and well-being (Cohen & Wills, 1985). The stress-buffering hypothesis is effectively studied using the convoy model. Social relations may act as a buffer against stress by decreasing the perceived importance of the problem, the stress reaction, or by providing a problem solution (Berkman, Glass, Brissette, & Seeman, 2000). According to Cohen and Wills (1985), emotional support provides a buffer to many types of stressors while instrumental support is effective when the support provided coincides with the stress experienced, such as, financial help in the face of poverty. For example, the detrimental effects of the loss of a spouse may be buffered by emotional support received from friends in old age (Morgan, 1989). These effects can be consistent or inconsistent over time and can lead to accumulating negative or positive effects.

Yet, in some instances, social support may fail to buffer the negative effects of stress and instead link to negative outcomes (Bolger, Zuckerman, & Kessler 2000; Dominguez & Watkins 2003; Hobfoll, Freedy, Lane, & Geller, 1990). Support may be unsolicited and unwanted (Smith & Goodnow, 1999). Support may indicate that one is under great stress, may undermine self-esteem, and furthermore, does not guarantee that help is received (Bolger et al., 2000). In particular, receiving support may incur a cost. Though initially it exerts a positive effect, over time it could lead to feelings of indebtedness to others or fear of being considered a burden (Hobfoll et al., 1990; Newsom & Schulz, 1998). Finally, it may be that various aspects of social relations have positive or negative effects on health and well-being depending on the type and extent of the stressor experienced. Ajrouch, Reisine, Lim, Sohn, and Ismail (2010) found that gradations in stress level indicators among African American caregivers of young children living in high-poverty urban areas react to social support in differing ways. Specifically, social support appeared to help with moderate (as opposed to high) levels of stress in one situation (food insufficiency), but completely buffered the influence of stress on health in another situation (neighborhood disorganization). The convoy model of social relations identifies multiple dimensions through which social relations operate including network structure, support type, and support quality, as well as multiple relationship sources (family, friend). Discerning the complexity of social relations illuminates the various ways through which social relations affect health disparities.

Systems Science

Recently a new approach to scientific inquiry, known as systems science, has emerged that is proving particularly useful. Systems science incorporates a multilevel approach to the study of any phenomenon and, thus, naturally complements the convoy model. Much as the convoy model incorporates personal characteristics, situational characteristics, numerous characteristics of social relations, and well-being within a multifactorial model, systems science offers a theoretical perspective to examine these multiple levels. Systems science benefits from recent methodological developments, including new analytical strategies and techniques, for example, system dynamics, agent-based modeling, and network analysis.

System scientists note the important new developments in computing sciences cyberinfrastructures, informatics superhighway, and computer sciences (Atkins et al., 2003) as critical tools in the exploration of scientific phenomenon. These tools allow the recognition and/or identification of time-delayed influences, nonlinear effects, as well as unintended consequences of intervention. At the substantive level, recent writings outlining the importance of neurons to neighborhoods, cells to society, and genes to geography are illustrative. While each independent, isolated scientist can, without a doubt, make a contribution to any scientific inquiry, new exciting challenges can be addressed by the scientist(s) who takes a systems approach. A systems science approach can move the field forward in both understanding the influences of each element on one another and in considering how to affect change in specific cases, for instance, when an intervention is desirable. A Finnish example, reported by Puska, Pirjo, and Ulla (2002), is both illustrative and impressive because, in essence, the entire town from individuals to community to government were involved and became a supportive and targeted convoy.

A small town in northern Finland had an exceptionally high rate of cardiovascular disease. In fact the province of North Kareila had the highest rate of mortality from heart disease in the world. In 1972, a systems approach, that is, a multilevel intervention, was designed. The intervention included changing dietary norms so that fat intake was reduced while fruit and vegetable consumption was increased, launching an educational campaign to foster healthy life style changes, encouraging health care providers to counsel all their patients and assess their cardiovascular risk factors, engaging community leaders and employers to promote healthy activities, and initiating new laws and policies that penalized unhealthy behaviors and rewarded healthy ones. The results were incredibly impressive with a 75% reduction of cardiovascular mortality. Clearly each intervention would have achieved some improvement, but it is very likely that the systems approach to intervention achieved greater improvement than the sum of each individual intervention would have on its own. Of course, outcomes can be calculated at multiple levels as well, from the individual to the society, for example, number of lives saved, health care costs, family care burden, and amount of work productivity.

On a smaller scale, the recent work of Fogel (2008) on mother–child relations is illustrative. Fogel takes an integrated multiple theoretical perspective, including dynamic systems, to develop a relational-historical approach, which considers individuals and development within the context of developing relationships with people and objects. Fogel focuses on the mother–child developing relationship and emphasizes the importance of the evolving relational system that is part of a dynamic flow of life processes through historical time.

While the strategies may be new, the basic theoretical notion is not. In addition to the convoy model, life-span developmental scientists will recognize similar basic theoretical tenets of systems theory in the work of Bronfenbrenner's bioecological theory (1979), Magnusson's person–context interaction (Magnusson, 1995), Lerner's developmental contextualism (Lerner, 2002), and Thelen's dynamic systems theory, as well as the work of social psychologists such as French's Person-Environment Fit theory, and Blumer's symbolic interactionalism (Blumer, 1986). Nevertheless, new tools make this an exciting and promising development.

FUTURE DIRECTIONS IN THE STUDY OF THE CONVOY MODEL ACROSS THE LIFE SPAN

In this chapter we have elucidated important new developments in the literature and specifically incorporated them into the convoy model. One might consider the above incorporation of gene-environment interplay, culture, social contagion, ambivalence, and health disparities as components of a larger system as exemplified in systems science. We have emphasized the importance of incorporating multiple levels into the examination of an individual's convoy thereby achieving an entirely new level of knowledge. The convoy model was developed to achieve greater understanding by encouraging the broader incorporation of personal and situational factors that influence social relations, including structure, support, and satisfaction, as well as the multiple factors that social relations influence, such as physical and mental health and well-being.

The central concept of the convoy model focuses our attention on the importance of social relations. Conceived of as a multidimensional construct, personal and situational characteristics influence various aspects of social relations both directly and in tandem with one another. In addition, social relations are proposed to have a direct effect on health and well-being, but also may operate through other mechanisms such as self-efficacy, or conversely interact with personal or situational characteristics, as well as with stress to differentially shape such outcomes. By considering the most recent developments in the social and behavioral sciences, we have demonstrated the heuristic value of the convoy model of social relations.

Each area reviewed draws our attention to the importance of considering multiple factors and multiple levels. Attention to the interplay between genes and environment highlights how personal and situational factors operate in tandem with social relations to produce various outcomes. The consideration of culture illustrates the universality of social relations across human groups, but also identifies issues that may need a more particularistic approach. The elaboration of social contagion and ambivalence showcases how attention to multiple factors better specifies the reason why social relations are important for achieving positive well-being outcomes. A focus on health disparities demonstrates the significance of social relations for population-level quality-of-life issues. Finally, a consideration of systems science situates the convoy model within the emerging scientific frameworks that cross multiple disciplines. We believe that future work utilizing the convoy model and incorporating these latest developments in the social sciences are promising and should be especially productive.

ACKNOWLEDGMENTS

This research was supported in part by grants from the National Institute of Mental Health (MH066876) and the National Institute on Aging (AG030569) to T. C. Antonucci and from the National Institute on Aging (K99AG029879) to K. Birditt and from the Doha International Institute of Family Studies and Development to K. J. Ajrouch and T. C. Antonucci. The authors of this research are fully responsible for its content which does not necessarily reflect the views of the National Institute of Mental Health, National Institute of Aging, or Doha International Institute for Family Studies and Development.

REFERENCES

Ajrouch, K. J. (2005). Arab-American immigrant elders' views about social support. *Ageing & Society, 25*(5), 655–673.

Ajrouch, K. J., Antonucci, T. C., & Janevic, M. R. (2001). Social networks among blacks and whites: The interaction between race and age. *The Journals of Gerontology: Series B: Psychological Sciences and Social Sciences, 56B*(2), S112–S118.

Ajrouch, K. J., Blandon, A. Y., & Antonucci, T. C. (2005). Social networks among men and women: The effects of age and socioeconomic status. *The Journals of Gerontology: Series B: Psychological Sciences and Social Sciences, 60B*(6), S311–S317.

Ajrouch, K. J., Reisine, S., Lim, S., Sohn, W., & Ismail, A. (2010). Situational stressors among African-American women living in low-income urban areas: The role of social support. *Women & Health, 50*(2), 159–175.

Alexander, C., Piazza, M., Mekos, D., & Valente, T. (2001). Peers, schools, and adolescent cigarette smoking. *Journal of Adolescent Health, 29,* 22–30.

Antonucci, T. C. (1986). Social support networks: A hierarchical mapping technique. *Generations, X*(4), 10–12.

Antonucci, T. C. (2001). Social relations: An examination of social networks, social support, and sense of control. In K. W. Schaie (Ed.), *Handbook of the psychology of aging* (5th ed., pp. 427–453). San Diego, CA: Academic Press.

Antonucci, T. C. (2008, October). *Convoy model of social relations: Replication and extension.* Paper presented at the Canadian Association of Gerontology 37th Annual Meeting, London, ON.

Antonucci, T. C., Ajrouch, K. J., & Janevic, M. R. (2003). The effect of social relations with children on the education-health link in men and women aged 40 and over. *Social Science and Medicine, 56,* 949–960.

Antonucci, T. C., Birditt, K. S., & Akiyama, H. (2009). Convoys of social relations: An interdisciplinary approach. In V. Bengston, M. Silverstein, N. Putney, & D. Gans (Eds.), *Handbook of theories of aging.* New York: Springer Publishing Company.

Antonucci, T. C., Birditt, K. S., & Webster, N. J. (2010). Social relations and mortality: A more nuanced approach. *Journal of Health Psychology, 15*(5), 649–659.

Antonucci, T. C., Fuhrer, R., & Dartigues, J. (1997). Social relations and depressive symptomatology in a sample of community-dwelling French older adults. *Psychology and Aging, 12*(1), 189–195.

Antonucci, T. C., & Jackson, J. S. (1987). Social support, interpersonal efficacy, and health: A life course perspective. In L. L. Carstensen & B. A. Edelstein (Ed.), *Handbook of clinical gerontology* (pp. 291–311). Elmsford, NY: Pergamon Press.

Atkins, D. E., Droegemeier, K. K., Feldman, S. I., Garcia-Molina, H., Klein, M. L., Messerschmitt, D. G., et al. (2003). Revolutionizing science and engineering through cyberinfrastructure: Report of the National Science Foundation Blue-Ribbon Advisory Panel on Cyberinfrastructure. http://www.communitytechnology.org/nsf_ci_report/. Retrieved on September 1, 2010.

Barer, B. M. (1994). Men and women aging differently. *International Journal of Aging & Human Development, 38*(1), 29–40.

Berkman, L. F., Glass, T., Brissette, I., & Seeman, T. E. (2000). From social integration to health: Durkheim in the new millennium. *Social Science & Medicine, 51*(6), 843–857.

Berkman, L. F., & Syme, S. L. (1979). Social networks, host resistance, and mortality: A nine year follow-up study of the Alameda County residents. *American Journal of Epidemiology, 115,* 684–694.

Birditt, K. S., & Antonucci, T. C. (2007). Relationship quality profiles and well-being among married adults. *Journal of Family Psychology, 21*(4), 595–604.

Birditt, K. S., & Antonucci, T. C. (2008). Life sustaining irritations? Relationship quality and mortality in the context of severe illness. *Social Science & Medicine, 67,* 1291–1299.

Blazer, D. (1982). Social support and mortality in an elderly community population. *American Journal of Epidemiology, 115,* 684–694.

Blumer, C. H. (1986). The effects of perceived truthness of information and repetition on validity estimates. ProQuest Information & Learning. *Dissertation Abstracts International, 46*(8).

Bolger, N., Foster, M., Vinokur, A. D., & Ng, R. (1996). Close relationships and adjustment to a life crises: The case of breast cancer. *Journal of Personality and Social Psychology, 70*(2), 283–294.

Bolger, N., Zuckerman, A., & Kessler, R. C. (2000). Invisible support and adjustment to stress. *Journal of Personality and Social Psychology, 79*(6), 953–961.

Bosari, B., & Carey, K. B. (2001). Peer influences on college drinking: A review of the research. *Journal of Substance Abuse, 13,* 391–424.

Bronfenbrenner, U. (1979). *The ecology of human development: Experiments by nature and design.* Cambridge, MA: Harvard University Press

Bulatao, R. A., & Anderson, N. B., (2004). *Understanding racial and ethnic differences in health and later life.* Washington, DC: National Academic Press.

Burt, S. A. (2008). Genes and popularity: Evidence of an evocative gene-environment correlation. *Psychological Science, 19,* 112–113.

Cacioppo, J. T., Fowler, J. H., & Christakis, N. A. (2009). Alone in the crowd: The structure and spread of loneliness in a large social network. *Journal of Personality and Social Psychology, 97*(6), 977–991.

Caspi, A., McClay, J., Moffitt, T., Mill, J., Martin, J., Craig, I. W., et al. (2002). Role of genotype in the cycle of violence in maltreated children. *Science, 297*(5582), 851–854.

Chen, C., & Lin, H. (2008). Examining Taiwan's paradox of family decline with a household-based convoy. *Social Indicators Research, 87*(2), 287–305.

Christakis, N. A., & Fowler, J. H. (2007). The spread of obesity in a large social network over 32 years. *The New England Journal of Medicine, 357*(4), 370–379.

Cochran, M., Larner, M., Riley, D., Gunnarsson, L., & Henderson, C. R., Jr. (1990). *Extending families: The social networks of parents and their children.* New York: Cambridge University Press.

Cohen, S., & Syme, S. L. (1985). *Social support and health.* San Diego, CA: Academic Press.

Cohen, S., & Wills, T. A. (1985). Stress, social support, and the buffering hypothesis. *Psychological Bulletin, 98*(2), 310–357.

Cohen-Cole, E., & Fletcher, J. M. (2008). Detecting implausible social network effects in acne, height, and headaches: Longitudinal analysis. *British Medical Journal, 337*, 2533–2537.

Connidis, I. A., & McMullin, J. A. (2002). Sociological ambivalence and family ties: A critical perspective. *Journal of Marriage and Family, 64*(3), 558–567.

Coyne, J. C., Rohrbaugh, M. J., Shoham, V., Cranford, J. A., Nicklas, J. M., & Sonnega, J. (2001). Prognostic importance of marital quality for survival of congestive heart failure. *American Journal of Cardiology, 88*, 526–529.

Dominguez, S., & Watkins, C. (2003). Creating networks for survival and mobility: Social capital among African-American and Latin-American low-income mothers. *Social Problems, 50*(1), 111–135.

Due, P., Lynch, J., Holstein, B., & Modvig, J. (2003). Socioeconomic health inequities among a nationally representative sample of Danish adolescents: The role of different types of social relations. *Journal of Epidemiology and Community Health, 57*, 692–698.

Ensel, W. M., & Lin, N. (1991). The life stress paradigm and psychological distress. *Journal of Health and Social Behavior, 32*(4), 321–341.

Fingerman, K. L., Chen, P., Hay, E., Cichy, K. E., & Lefkowitz, E. S. (2006). Ambivalent reactions in the parent and offspring relationship. *The Journals of Gerontology: Series B: Psychological Sciences and Social Sciences, 61B*(3), P152–P160.

Fingerman, K. L., Hay, E. L., & Birditt, K. S. (2004). The best of ties, the worst of ties: Close, problematic, and ambivalent social relationships. *Journal of Marriage and Family, 66*(3), 792–808.

Fingerman, K. L., Pitzer, L., Lefkowitz, E. S., Birditt, K. S., & Mroczek, D. (2008). Ambivalent relationship qualities between adults and their parents: Implications for the well-being of both parties. *The Journals of Gerontology: Series B: Psychological Sciences and Social Sciences, 63B*(6), P362–P371.

Fogel, A. (2008). Relationships that support human development. In A. Fogel, B. J. King, & S. Shanker (Eds.), *Human development in the 21st century: Visionary policy ideas from systems scientists* (pp. 57–64). Cambridge, UK: Cambridge University Press.

Fowler, J. H., & Christakis, N. A. (2008). Dynamic spread of happiness in a large social network: Longitudinal analysis over 20 years in the Framingham Heart Study. *British Medical Journal, 337*, 1–9.

Fratiglioni, L., Paillard-Borg, S., & Winblad, B. (2004). An active and socially integrated lifestyle in late life might protect against dementia. *Lancet Neurology, 8*, 343–353.

Guiaux, M., van Tilburg, T., & van Groenou, M. B. (2007). Changes in contact and support exchange in personal networks after widowhood. *Personal Relationships, 14*(3), 457–473.

Haan, M. N., Kaplan, G. A., & Syme, S. L. (1989). Socioeconomic status and health: Old observations and new thoughts. In J. P. Bunker, D. S. Gomby, & B. H. Kehrer (Eds.), *Pathways to health* (pp. 76–135). Menlo Park, CA: The Henry Kaiser Family Foundation.

Haan, M. N., Shemanski, L., Jagust, W. J., Manolio, T. A., & Kuller, L. (1999). The role of APOE epsilon4 in modulating effects of other risk factors for cognitive decline in elderly persons. *Journal of the American Medical Association, 282*(1), 40–46.

Haines, V. A., & Henderson, L. J. (2002). Targeting social support: A network assessment of the convoy model of social support. *Canadian Journal on Aging, 21*(2), 243–256.

Higuchi, S., Matsushita, S., Imazeki, H., Konoshita, T., Takagi, S., & Kono, H. (1994). Aldehyde dehydrogenase genotypes in Japanese alcoholics. *Lancet, 343*, 741–742.

Hobfoll, S. E., Freedy, J., Lane, C., & Geller, P. (1990). Conservation of social resources: Social support resource theory. *Journal of Social and Personal Relationships, 7*(4), 465–478.

Hofstede, G. H. (1980). *Culture's consequences, international differences in work-related values.* Beverly Hills, CA: Sage Publications.

Holt-Lunstad, J., Uchino, B. N., Smith, T. W., & Hicks, A. (2007). On the importance of relationship quality: The impact of ambivalence in friendships on cardiovascular functioning. *Annals of Behavioral Medicine, 33*(3), 278–290.

Inglehart, R., & Welzel, C., (2005). *Modernization, culture change, and democracy.* New York: Cambridge University Press.

Joseph, S. (1993). Gender and relationality among Arab families in Lebanon. *Feminist Studies, 19*(3), 465–486.

Kağitçibaşi, Ç. (1996). *Family and human development across cultures: A view from the other side.* Hillsdale, NJ: Lawrence Erlbaum Associates, Inc.

Kahn, R. L., & Antonucci, T. C. (1980). Convoys over the life course: Attachment, roles, and social support. In P. B. Baltes & O. Brim (Eds.), *Life-span development and behavior* (Vol. 3). New York: Academic Press. Reprinted 1989 in Joep Munnichs & Gwenyth Uildris (Eds.), *Psychogerontologie* (pp. 81–102). Van Loghum Slaterus.

Kawachi, I., Kennedy, B. P. E., Lochner, K. S. M., & Prothrow-Stith, D. (1997). Social capital, income inequality, and mortality. *American Journal of Public Health, 87*(9), 1491–1498.

Kogan, M. D., Kotelchuck, M., Alexander, G. R., & Johnson, W. E., (1994). Racial disparities reported in prenatal care advice from health care providers. *American Journal of Public Health, 84*(1), 82–88.

Krause, N., & Borawski-Clark, E. (1995). Social class differences in social support among older adults. *The Gerontologist, 35*(4), 498–508.

Kubzansky, L. D., Berkman, L. F., Glass, T. A., & Seeman, T. E. (1998). Is educational attainment associated with shared determinants of health in the elderly? Findings from the MacArthur studies of successful aging. *Psychosomatic Medicine, 60*(5), 578–585.

Lansford, J. E., Antonucci, T. C., Akiyama, H., & Takahashi, K. (2005). A quantitative and qualitative approach to social relationships and well-being in the United States and Japan. *Journal of Comparative Family Studies, 36*(1), 1–22.

LaVeist, T. A. (2005). *Minority populations and health: An introduction to health disparities in the United States.* San Francisco, CA: Jossey-Bass.

Lerner, R. M. (2002). *Concepts and theories of human development* (3rd ed.). Mahwah, NJ: Lawrence Erlbaum Associates.

Levitt, M. J., Guacci-Franco, N., & Levitt, J. L. (1994). Social support and achievement in childhood and early adolescence: A multicultural study. *Journal of Applied Behavioral Development, 15,* 207–222.

Link, B. G., & Phelan, J. C. (1995). Social conditions as fundamental causes of disease. *Journal of Health and Social Behavior, 35*(Extra Issue), 80–94.

Lowenstein, A. (2007). Solidarity-conflict and ambivalence: Testing two conceptual frameworks and their impact on quality of life for older family members. *The Journals of Gerontology: Series B: Psychological Sciences and Social Sciences, 62B*(2), S100–S107.

Luescher, K., & Pillemer, K. (1998). Intergenerational ambivalence: A new approach to the study of parent–child relations in later life. *Journal of Marriage & the Family, 60*(2), 413–425.

Magnusson, D. (1995). Individual development: A holistic, integrated model. In K. Lüscher (Ed.), *Examining lives in context: Perspectives on the ecology of human development* (pp. 19–60). Washington, DC: American Psychological Association.

Marks, N. F. (1996). Socioeconomic status, gender, and health at midlife. *Research in the Sociology of Health Care, 13A,* 135–152.

Markus, H. R., & Kitayama, S. (1991). Culture and the self: Implications for cognition, emotion, and motivation. *Psychological Review, 98*(2), 224–253.

Martin, M., Grünendahl, M., & Martin, P. (2001). Age differences in stress, social resources, and well-being in middle and older age. *The Journals of Gerontology: Series B: Psychological Sciences and Social Sciences, 56B*(4), P214–P222.

Merton, R. K., & Barber, E. (1963). Sociological ambivalence. In E. Tiryakian (Ed.), *Sociological theory: Values and sociocultural change* (pp. 91–120). New York: Free Press.

Minnemann, E. (1994). Geschlechtsspezifische unterschiede der gestaltung sozialer beziehungen im Alter—Ergebnisse einer empirischen untersuchung. *Zeitschrift Für Gerontologie, 27*(1), 33–40.

Morgan, D. L. (1989). Adjusting to widowhood: Do social networks really make it easier? *The Gerontologist, 29,* 101–107.

Newsom, J. T., & Schulz, R. (1998). Caregiving from the recipient's perspective: Negative reactions to being helped. *Health Psychology, 17*(2), 172–181.

Oyserman, D., Kemmelmeier, M., & Coon, H. M. (2002). Cultural psychology, a new look: Reply to Bond (2002), Fiske (2002), Kitayama (2002), and Miller (2002). *Psychological Bulletin, 128*(1), 110–117.

Palinkis, L. A., Wingard, D. L., & Barret-Connor, E. (1990). Chronic illness and depressive symptoms in the elderly: A population-based study. *Journal of Clinical Epidemiology, 43,* 1131–1141.

Perls, T. T. (2006). The different paths to 100. *American Journal of Clinical Nutrition, 83*(2), 484S–487S.

Phillipson, C., Bernard, M., Phillips, J., & Ogg, J. (2001). *Family and community life of older people: Social networks and social support in three urban areas.* London: Routledge.

Pillemer, K., & Suitor, J. J. (2002). Explaining mothers' ambivalence toward their adult children. *Journal of Marriage and Family, 64*(3), 602–613.

Pillemer, K., Suitor, J. J., Mock, S. E., Sabir, M., Pardo, T. B., & Sechrist, J. (2007). Capturing the complexity of intergenerational relations: Exploring ambivalence within later-life families. *Journal of Social Issues, 63*(4), 775–791.

Prinstein, M. J., & Wang, S. S. (2005). False consensus and adolescent peer contagion: Examining discrepancies between perceptions and actual reported levels of friends' deviant and health risk behaviors. *Journal of Abnormal Child Psychology, 33*(3), 293–306.

Puska, P., Pirjo, P., & Ulla, U. (2002). Influencing public nutrition for non-communicable disease prevention: From community intervention to national programme—experiences from Finland. *Public Health Nutrition, 5*(1A), 245–251.

Rende, R., Slomkowski, C., Lloyd-Richardson, E., & Niaura, R. (2005). Sibling effects on substance use in adolescence: Social contagion and genetic relatedness. *Journal of Family Psychology, 19*(4), 611–618.

Rodgers, J. L., & Rowe, D. C. (1993). Social contagion and adolescent sexual behavior: A developmental EMOSA model. *Psychological Review, 100*(3), 479–510.

Ross, C. E., & Wu, C. (1995). The links between education and health. *American Sociological Review, 60*(5), 719–745.

Russell, D. W., & Cutrona, C. E. (1991). Social support, stress, and depressive symptoms among the elderly: Test of a process model. *Psychology and Aging, 6*(2), 190–201.

Sandler, I. N. (1980). Social support resources, stress, and maladjustment of poor children. *American Journal of Community Psychology, 8*(10), 41–52

Seeman, T. E. (1996). Social ties and health: The benefits of social integration. *Annals of Epidemiology, 6*(5), 442–451.

Seeman, T. E., Bruce, M. L., & McAvay, G. J. (1996). Social network characteristics and onset of ADL disability: MacArthur studies of successful aging. *Journal of Gerontology, Social Sciences, 51,* S191–S200.

Seeman, T. E., Huang, J.-H., Bretsky, P., Crimmins, E., Launer, L., & Guralnik, J. M. (2005). Education and APOE-e4 in longitudinal cognitive decline: MacArthur studies of successful aging. *J Gerontol B Psychol Sci Soc Sci, 60*(2), 74–83.

Shanahan, M. J., & Boardman, J. D. (2009). Gene–environment interplay across the life course: Overview and problematics at a new frontier. In J. Z. Giele & G. H. Elder, Jr. (Eds.), *Methods of life course research: Qualitative and quantitative approaches.* Thousand Oaks, CA: Sage.

Shanahan, M. J., Erickson, L. D., Vaisey, S., & Smolen, A. (2007). Helping relationships and genetic propensities: A combinatoric study of DRD2, mentoring, and educational continuation. *Twin Research and Human Genetics, 10*(2), 285.

Smith, J., & Goodnow, J. J. (1999). Unasked-for support and unsolicited advice: Age and the quality of social experience. *Psychology and Aging, 14,* 108–121.

Stewart, A. L., & Hays, R. D. (1997). Conceptual, measurement, and analytical issues in assessing health status in older populations. In T. Hickey, M. A. Speers, & T. R. Prohaska (Eds.), *Public health and aging* (pp. 163–189). Baltimore, MD: Johns Hopkins University Press.

Takahashi, T., Suzuki, M., Kawasaki, Y., Kurokawa, K., Hagino, H., Yamashita, I., et al. (2002). Volumetric magnetic resonance imaging study of the anterior cingulate gyrus in schizotypal disorder. *European Archives of Psychiatry and Clinical Neuroscience, 252*(6), 268–277.

Tighe, L., Birditt, K. S., & Antonucci, T. (2009, April). *It's a love/hate relationship: Adolescents' ambivalence towards their parents.* Poster presented at the annual meeting of the Society for Research on Child Development. Denver, CO.

Triandis, H. C., Bontempo, R., Villareal, M. J., Asai, M., & Lucca, N. (1988). Individualism and collectivism: Cross-cultural perspectives on self-ingroup relationships. *Journal of Personality and Social Psychology, 54*(2), 323–338.

Uchino, B. N., (2004). *Social support and physical health: Understanding the health consequences of relationships.* New Haven, CT: Yale University Press.

Uchino, B. N., Holt-Lunstad, J., Smith, T. W., & Bloor, L. (2004). Heterogeneity in social networks: A comparison of different models linking relationships to psychological outcomes. *Journal of Social and Clinical Psychology, 23,* 123–139.

Uchino, B. N., Holt-Lunstad, J., Uno, D., & Flinders, J. B. (2001). Heterogeneity in the social networks of young and older adults: Prediction of mental health and cardiovascular reactivity during acute stress. *Journal of Behavioral Medicine, 24*(4), 361–382.

Van Tilburg, T., de Jong Gierveld, J., Lecchini, L., & Marsiglia, D. (1998). Social integration and loneliness: A comparative study among older adults in the Netherlands and Tuscany, Italy. *Journal of Social and Personal Relationships, 15,* 740–754.

Verbrugge, L. M. (1985). Women and men: Mortality and health of older people. In E. W. Markson (Ed.), *Growing old in America: New perspectives on old age* (3rd ed., pp. 181–205). New Brunswick, NJ: Transaction Publishers.

Wagner, M., Schütze, Y., & Lang, F. R. (1999). Social relationships in old age. In K. U. Mayer (Ed.), *The Berlin aging study: Aging from 70 to 100* (pp. 282–301). New York, NY: Cambridge University Press.

*Walter-Ginzburg, A., Blumstein, T., Chetrit, A., & Modan, B., (*2002*). Social factors and mortality in the old-old in Israel: The CALAS study. Journal of Gerontology: Social Sciences, 57B,* S308–*S318.*

Ward, R. A. (2008). Multiple parent-adult child relations and well-being in middle and later life. *Journal of Gerontology: Social Sciences, 63B,* S239–S247.

Williams, D. R., & Collins, C. (1995). U.S. socioeconomic and racial differences in health: Patterns and explanations. *Annual Review of Sociology, 21,* 349–386.

Williams, D. R., Yan, Y., Jackson, J. S., & Anderson, N. B. (1997). Racial differences in physical and mental health: Socioeconomic status, stress and discrimination. *Journal of Health Psychology, 2,* 335–351.

AGENCY AND CONTROL STRIVING ACROSS THE LIFE SPAN

8

Jutta Heckhausen

INTRODUCTION

This chapter presents a motivational perspective on life-span development and focuses on agency and control striving (Heckhausen & Heckhausen, 2008c; Heckhausen, Wrosch, & Schulz, 2010). I will discuss the interface of motivation and development from two perspectives: the development of motivation on the one hand and the role of motivation in guiding development on the other. Both perspectives have to take into account the advances and declines in adaptive capacity across the life span. An example of age-related changes in regulatory capacity is the cognitive capacity to self-reflect, which enables the anticipation of feeling competent and powerful after success. Such anticipatory self-reinforcement cannot unfold its motivational dynamic before the cognitive maturity required for self-reflection is attained. Another example reflects age-related challenges to motivational self-regulation: Women moving toward the age of menopause can expect their opportunities for childbearing to decline rapidly in the near future, a phenomenon we refer to as "developmental deadline." As a consequence of the drastically declining opportunities for childbearing, women in the critical age range experience urgency for childbearing and are likely to disengage once they pass the deadline.

This chapter cannot, and will not, attempt to cover the broad and multifacetted field of perceived control, locus of control, and self-efficacy (Skinner, 1996). The topic of perceived control will be addressed only insofar as it is distinguished from control striving and control behavior.

AGENCY AND CONTROL STRIVING ACROSS THE LIFE SPAN

Motivated human action has two basic characteristics, the striving for control of the environment and the organization of behavior into goal engagement and goal disengagement cycles (Heckhausen & Heckhausen, 2008a; Heckhausen et al., 2010). *Control striving*—that is, the striving for direct or primary control of the physical and social environment—is part of the motivational makeup of our species (White, 1959) and beyond, of at least all mammals (see the overview in Heckhausen, 2000; Schneider & Dittrich, 1990). Attaining contingent effects in the environment has its own independent reinforcement value and thus enables the organism to stay focused on bringing about an outcome, while adjusting behavioral means. There are both theoretical and empirical reasons for assuming that a set of basic motivational modules regulate control striving: (1) Mammals and, probably, many other species have a pervasive preference for behavior–event contingencies over event–event contingencies;

organisms are motivated to engage in behaviors that produce contingent effects (e.g., baby smiles, mother vocalizes); (2) Exploration is also a universal motivational system in mammals and engages the organism with the goal of extending its range of control over the external environment; (3) There is much evidence for an asymmetric pattern of affective responses to positive and negative events (Frijda, 1988): organisms soon get used to the positive affect experienced after positive events, whereas the negative emotions elicited by negative events are much longer lasting. This motivates individuals to aspire to new goals rather than resting on their laurels after successes and prevents them from giving up too soon in the face of setbacks.

Human control striving is motivated by an innate preference for a specifically human characteristic; people are motivated by anticipating a positive self-evaluation after achieving a goal. So people are motivated not only by mastering their environment and achieving a goal but also by the expected pride they will feel when achieving success. The latter motivational process of anticipated self-reinforcement is based on the self-concept and entails both positive (i.e., to perceive oneself as highly competent or becoming more competent) and negative incentives (i.e., to perceive oneself as incompetent or loosing competence).

Human action and control striving is organized into *action cycles of goal engagement and goal disengagement* (Heckhausen et al., 2010). Such action cycles start with selecting a goal, then—once a goal has been selected—moving into a phase of goal engagement that leads either to success or failure, followed by a phase of goal disengagement, which concludes the action cycle and can be followed by opening a new action cycle. During each phase, various aspects of action regulation and information processing are adapted to the function of the given action phase, be it goal selection, goal engagement, or disengagement. Perceptions, thoughts, emotions, skills, and activities are coordinated to facilitate either the attainment of goals or disengagement from unattainable or futile goals. During periods of goal engagement, individuals focus on what is important for goal-directed action and ignore irrelevant stimuli. They put key procedures in place, attune their attention and perception to stimuli that trigger or cue behavior, and shield themselves from potential distractions. Expectations of control during goal engagement are optimistic. Motivational research based on a general (not developmental) model of action phases has provided a wealth of empirical evidence for mental and behavioral resources being orchestrated in this way to facilitate goal pursuit (Achtziger & Gollwitzer, 2008; Heckhausen, 2007).

In contrast, goals are deactivated during periods of goal disengagement. Such deactivation is not gradual; on the contrary, goal disengagement is an active process whereby goal-engagement–related commitments are broken down and goal-pursuit–oriented biases are inversed (Wrosch, Scheier, Miller, Schulz, & Carver, 2003). Goal disengagement involves degrading the original goal and enhancing the perceived value and attainability of alternative goals, defending self-esteem against experiences of failure and, more generally, seeking to ensure that disengagement from a particular goal does not undermine motivational resources in the long term (Heckhausen, 1999).

Goal engagement and goal disengagement can be seen as two motivational modes: "go" and "stop." In adaptive behavior, at least, the two modes do not overlap, but discretely focus an organism's cognitive, behavioral, and motivational activities on the efficient investment of resources. After all, it is much more efficient to decide on a goal and pursue it resolutely than to dither between options, squandering resources without attaining the aspired goal. Should a goal prove to be unattainable, or too costly, it makes sense to abandon that goal once and for all, without getting caught up in postdecisional conflicts or clinging half-heartedly to old habits, thus wasting mental, behavioral, and temporal resources that could be put to better use in the pursuit of new, attainable goals. A suitable imagery for this type of adaptive switching between goal engagement and goal disengagement is a lion chasing its prey. The lion will begin the chase at top speed (i.e., goal engagement). As the lion finds itself outrun, it will not slow down gradually but will stop and turn away from its prey abruptly (i.e., goal disengagement) as soon as it becomes clear that its efforts are futile. In this way, the lion will invest effort only as long as the chase is worth it and save its energy for more worthwhile hunts.

EARLY CONTROL STRIVING IN PARENT–CHILD INTERACTIONS: THE CRADLE OF ACTION

Humans and mammals in general seem to be born with a *built-in readiness for primary control striving*, that is, for exerting influence over the environment by one's own behavior. Studies on operant learning have shown that many mammals prefer to control an event by their own behavior over having this event controlled by external factors, regardless of whether the event provides primary reinforcement (e.g., food) or not (for an overview, see White, 1959). Chimpanzees favor objects that can be moved, changed, or made to emit sounds and light (Welker, 1956); rhesus monkeys spend hours solving mechanical puzzles (e.g., bolting mechanisms; Harlow, 1953); and both children and rats prefer response-elicited rewards to receiving the same rewards regardless of their behavior (Singh, 1970).

The first manifestations of control striving in human ontogeny can be observed in newborn babies (Janos & Papousek, 1977; Papousek, 1967). In fact, the ability to engage in operant behavior may develop in the womb. Papousek found that babies just a few days old learned head movements contingent on acoustic signals and milk reinforcement. Even when they were no longer hungry and the milk had lost its reinforcing potential, the babies continued to respond to the acoustic signal with a turn of the head, and showed positive affect when the milk bottle was presented as expected.

Taking a behaviorist perspective, Watson examined how operant learning can be fostered by providing opportunities for experiences of behavior–event contingency in the first months of life (Watson, 1966, 1972). Watson showed that it took only a few sessions of behaviorist training to establish an expectation in the infant for an effect that contingently follows a certain behavior. Confirmation of this expectation elicited intense pleasure when the expected effect occurred. Further studies on what Watson referred to as *generalized contingency awareness* showed transfer effects from one contingency experience to another, interference of noncontingent experiences (Finkelstein & Ramey, 1977; Ramey & Finkelstein, 1978; Rovee & Fagan, 1976; Watson & Ramey, 1972), positive affect in response to behavior-contingent outcomes (Barrett, Morgan, & Maslin-Cole, 1993), and negative affect to noncontingent stimulation that had previously been contingent (DeCasper & Carstens, 1981). In Piagetian terminology, this kind of control striving would be referred to as "secondary circular reactions" (Piaget, 1952): infants repeat activities that have previously produced certain effects time and again and respond to the effects with positive affect.

Human infants are born without the ability to manipulate objects and take months before they can even grab an object, never mind handle the object in a skilled enough way to produce noticeable effects. Does this mean that human infants for the first several months of their lives are deprived from experiencing control of outcomes in the environment? No, because long before infants are able to produce direct effects on their environment, they influence their parents' behavior in everyday interactions. Papousek and Papousek (1967) demonstrated that mother's responses to certain behaviors of their infants show high reliability and low latency and occur without conscious control. Sociobiological approaches to parent–infant interaction have conceptualized such patterns as part of a *natural parenting program* that provides for the basic infant needs of protection, nutrition, emotional warmth, and contingency experience (Keller, 2000).

The mother's greeting response to eye contact with her child is a case in point: The mother's mouth is opened, the eyes opened wide, and the eyebrows raised, whenever the infant gazes at her face. This reaction is automatized and cannot be suppressed. It provides the infant with repeated, reliable contingency experiences that make minimal demands of the infants' competence to initiate action.

Maternal contingency behavior (also known as responsive behavior) seems to be conducive to the formation of generalized contingency expectations as well as to habituation to redundant stimuli (e.g., Lewis & Goldberg, 1969; Papousek & Papousek, 1975, 1987), and to the development of intelligence (Clarke-Stewart, 1973; Clarke-Stewart, VanderStoep, & Killian, 1979). Riksen-Walraven (1978) provided compelling evidence for these relationships in a longitudinal intervention study that trained mothers to either provide more stimulation, or to be more contingently responsive to their infants' behavior, or to do both, provide more stimulation and more responsiveness. Findings showed that enhanced stimulation levels had favorable effects on habituation rate (shorter habituation times) only and did not impact exploratory behavior or contingency learning. When mothers showed heightened responsiveness in their interactions with their children, thus creating a contingent environment, however, there were very favorable effects on both exploratory behavior and the rate of contingency learning.

Another important component of control striving in early social relationships is *exploratory behavior*. We know from extensive experimental and fieldwork in the area of attachment behavior that in the mother–infant attachment system the *mother functions as a secure basis* (Ainsworth & Bell, 1970; Ainsworth, Bell, & Stayton, 1974; Harlow & Harlow, 1966; Harlow & Zimmermann, 1959; Sroufe & Waters, 1976) that enables the offspring to explore the environment and thus make it accessible for primary control striving. Leading researchers in the field concluded from extensive research in this area that infant–mother attachment is based on a need for closeness and also on a balanced system of curiosity and caution that permits exploration, but evades dangers (Ainsworth, 1972; Sroufe, 1977). This dyadic behavioral system facilitates the gradual extension of mobility and autonomy throughout the infant's motor and communicative development. As for interindividual or rather interdyad differences in this regard, a relatively low tendency for maternal interference in the child's exploratory activities (i.e., provision of "floor freedom") has favorable effects on the mother–child bond and was found to be the second strongest predictor of children's intelligence (Ainsworth & Bell, 1970; Stayton, Hogan, & Ainsworth, 1971) after responsiveness (i.e., contingent responses to the child's behavior).

Infants' early experiences of control are thus bound up with their primary social bonds to caregivers, with their striving for autonomy within these relationships, and the restrictions placed on them. At this early age, experiences of control in the domains of achievement, power, and affiliation are not yet separable. Differentiations in control experiences, control striving, and control behavior soon begin to emerge, however, particularly as infants begin to manipulate objects, and as social (affiliation and power/autonomy) and nonsocial motivations (achievement) become distinguishable and, in some cases, collide. Colwyn Trevarthen's observations on the development of intersubjectivity are particularly relevant in this context (Trevarthen, 1980; Trevarthen & Aitken, 2001; Trevarthen & Hubley, 1978). According to Trevarthen children's behavior is driven from birth by two complementary, but sometimes conflicting, motives: First, the motive to have an active influence on objects, and second, the motive to interact with other humans.

Over the first 2 years of life, these two motives for object-related control and social relationships alternate and come into mutual conflict. In their first 3 to 4 months, infants are focused on other humans, particularly the primary caregiver. At about 6 months of age, in what Trevarthen labels the "praxic mode," children begin to play with objects on their own, and to pay the primary caregiver less attention than before (Trevarthen, 1980; Trevarthen & Hubley, 1978). Joint play of mothers and infants at this age goes smoothly, if the mother joins the infant's intention for the activity (see, e.g., Collis & Schaffer, 1975), but infants' get upset when their mother introduces a goal for the activity that is inconsistent with their own. Finally, during the second year, parent–child interactions with objects become more cooperative at a new level of intersubjectivity, which Trevarthen calls "secondary intersubjectivity" (Trevarthen & Hubley, 1978).

Thus, in the course of the second year, the mother–child dyad gains significantly in joint competence. The child adopts challenging action goals proposed by the mother, and both work together to achieve them. Cooperation and persistence in pursuing the shared action goal initially relies on the mother keeping the infant's attention focused on the task at hand, thus providing an external scaffold for volitional action control (Heckhausen, 1987a, 1987b; Kaye, 1977b; Rogoff & Wertsch, 1984; Wood, Bruner, & Ross, 1976). As the child becomes increasingly competent, however, the action goal becomes the focus of the joint interaction.

In sum, the early parent–child interaction is the cradle of action. It is here that the major, universal foundations for individual action regulation are laid: experience of the effectiveness of one's own behavior, feeling comfortable to explore the unknown, setting goals and persist in the face of difficulties, recognizing an attained goal as such, and negotiating with others about goals and action means. At the same time, the significance of early parent–child interactions bears substantial developmental risks. For example, if a mother consistently overchallenges her child and responds negatively to the child's failures to meet her standards, the child will develop low confidence in her own ability and feel discouraged to take up new challenges. Thus, if parental influences are not appropriate to a child's level of development or are otherwise unfavorable, the development of motivation and behavioral regulation may be misdirected, resulting, over time, in maladaptive motivational patterns.

▓ SELF-REINFORCEMENT THROUGH PERCEIVED OWN COMPETENCE: AN ADDED INCENTIVE AND RISK

During the second year, the focus of children's attention gradually shifts to the outcomes of their actions, although they do not yet begin to draw inferences about their competence at this young age. The regulatory demands of focusing on an intended action outcome differ depending on the goal in question with sudden, discrete effects requiring the least representational capacity and volitional self-regulation, and state-related goals of multistep activities (e.g., building a tower of blocks) requiring the most (Heckhausen & Heckhausen, 2008c).

Of the many and diverse incentives for achievement-motivated behavior, three that play a prominent and ubiquitous role in the western industrialized nations, at least, are the exploration of personal competence ("What can I do?"), the emotional and social-cognitive benefits of positive conceptions of personal competence (i.e., self-reinforcement; "This success tells me that I am competent."), and the demonstration of personal competence to others ("This success shows to others that I am competent."). According to achievement motivation theory, individuals are motivated to strive for achievement not only because they enjoy improving their mastery but also, to a large extent, because they anticipate to feel great about having shown themselves to be competent (Heckhausen, 1991). Two emotions play a key role in this motivational scenario, pride and shame. Individuals feel proud about having mastered a relatively difficult task, or feel shame about having failed in a relatively easy task.

Children younger than about 30 months of age show positive affect after success, but they focus on the effects of their actions, not on socially displaying pleasure and triumph about their success (Geppert & Heckhausen, 1990; Heckhausen & Roelofsen, 1962). During the second half of the third year children begin to show the typical pride reaction after success: They raised their eyes from their work, smiled, and gazed triumphantly at the loser. They straightened the upper body, and some of them even threw their arms in the air as if to enlarge their ego. What happens when children fail to attain the goal they set for themselves, for instance in a competitive game of tower building (Heckhausen & Roelofsen, 1962)? The age at which children first show self-evaluative responses to failure ranges between 3 and 4 years depending on the study's experimental set-up (Heckhausen & Heckhausen, 2008c). However, the behavioral pattern of such shame responses is clear: When children lost, they slouched down in their chair, lowered the head, avoided eye contact with the winner, while their hands and eyes remain "glued" to their work. It is intriguing that these postural expressions of pride and shame reflect a close relationship to dominant and submissive behavior (Geppert & Heckhausen, 1990).

Another important behavioral pattern in the early development of motivation is the phenomenon of *wanting-to-do-it-oneself* (Geppert & Küster, 1983). Geppert and Küster studied the relationship between the development of the self-concept and the emergence of self-evaluative responses to success and failure and to offerings of help. Children without any self-concept accepted help without protest, evidently because they were indifferent to who actually executed the action. At the age of about 1½, children who had a rudimentary sense of self started to protest against any interventions of the experimenter. They did not want their goal-directed activity to be interrupted, and were particularly upset when the experimenter tried to take over at the last action step (e.g., last block on tower). Older children older than 2½ years who had a fully developed sense of self as indicated by self-recognition in a mirror, did not mind interruptions, but vehemently protested against offers of help. They often verbally asserted their desire to do the task by themselves. Evidently, offers of help threatened their perceptions that the successful completion of the task was due to their own competence.

Although a focus on self-evaluation can have a wealth of positive consequences, it also makes individuals and their perceptions of their own competence vulnerable to the negative effects of failure. To the extent that the individual sees goal-directed actions as tests of personal competence, he or she is exposed to the risk of negative self-attributions (e.g., low competence, low self-esteem), particularly in social comparison situations with high levels of ego-involvement (Brunstein & Hoyer, 2002). These negative self-attributions can undermine the motivational resources needed for continued control striving, and must be counteracted and compensated by strategies of self-serving interpretation and re-evaluation, conceptualized within the theoretical framework of the life-span theory of control as *compensatory secondary control strategies* (Heckhausen, 1999; Heckhausen & Schulz, 1995). Self-esteem may be protected by compensatory strategies of secondary control such as the following: attributing failure to external factors, thus negating personal responsibility for failure; engaging in "downward" social comparisons with people who are even less successful; and engaging in intraindividual comparisons with domains in which they are personally more competent. So far empirical research has found that simple strategies of self-protection, such as denial or refocusing of attention away from the failure or control loss can be found in children as young as 2 years of age (Heckhausen, 1988); more elaborate cognitive strategies of distraction and reinterpreting the challenging event appear to develop in adolescence (Altshuler & Ruble, 1989; Band & Weisz, 1988; Compas, Worsham, Ey, & Howell, 1996; Heckhausen & Heckhausen, 2008c)

In sum, children enter a fundamentally different phase of motivational development once they realize that action outcomes have implications for their perceptions about their own competence. Anticipated self-reinforcement provides an additional and strong motivational pull for taking up challenges. However, it also bears the risk of self-blame for failure and control loss. Compensatory strategies of secondary control develop throughout childhood, but particularly proliferate during adolescence. A caveat about cultural differences seems appropriate here. Every achievement-related action is characterized by a multitude of incentives residing in the activity itself, the action outcome (reaching an intended goal) and the internal (self-evaluation) and external (other-evaluation and social or material consequences) action-outcome consequences (Heckhausen & Heckhausen, 2008c). Cultures and indeed individuals and their families differ as to which incentives they highlight and how they combine intrinsic and extrinsic incentives for certain actions. In addition, people probably become increasingly savvy with increasing age and experience about what motivates them best and how to facilitate the salience of the personally relevant incentives (Rheinberg, 2008).

COGNITIVE DEVELOPMENT CONTRIBUTES TO ADVANCEMENTS IN MOTIVATED ACTION

We focus here on achievement motivation, because research in this area has developed the most differentiated cognitive models about how goals (i.e., standards of excellence), expectations, perceptions about one's own action resources (i.e., competence and effort), and the combination of causal factors influence incentives and behavior. Cognitive development lays the foundation for these increasingly elaborate conceptions that help the individual decide for goals and interpret success and failure. The constrained space here only allows me to present a summary of research findings that is based on a more elaborate review of the literature (Heckhausen & Heckhausen, 2008c).

The perception of differences in task difficulty is a prerequisite for the formation of standards of excellence. *Task difficulty* and *competence* define each other: the more difficult the task executed, the higher the competence demonstrated. As it turns out, across childhood and adolescence the developing individual switches between focusing on differences in task difficulty and differences in people's competence, depending on what the social context emphasizes. Children first learn to distinguish different degrees of task difficulty at preschool age, and do not start applying social reference norms to evaluate their competence until starting school. At the transition to secondary level schooling, individual reference norms gain in importance, at a time when the youth has to make decisions about which fields of competence to focus on and which to drop. During the last 2 years of high school when preparing for the transition to the adult world and its competitive challenges (e.g., college admission), social reference norms become more dominant than ever.

Causal conceptions of ability and effort are a prerequisite for guiding task choice, behavioral investment, and causal attribution of success and failure. Between preschool age and second or third grade, independent conceptions of effort and ability slowly emerge from a general, optimistic, and failure-resistant conception of competence. The conception of effort seems to be more closely related to children's experience and thus easier to grasp than the conception of ability. With the transition to school, the conception of effort is consolidated—and exposed to the pressures of success and failure in both individual and social comparison. For the first time, ability and effort are set in relation to conceptions of capacity and its limits (How much can I achieve when I apply maximum effort? Can someone else achieve more than I can when we both apply maximum effort?). These developments lay the foundations for the development of more complex causal schemata for the explanation of success and failure, and for realistic and independent assessments of personal capabilities. At the same time, they make children vulnerable to experiences of loss of control and frustration about the limits of their capabilities.

To set realistic yet ambitious levels of aspiration, children must learn to *estimate their probability of success* in a given task, to reason about different components of *perceived personal control*, and to understand the *relation between expecting success and incentive value of success*. It is adaptive to generate broadly realistic, yet optimistic expectancies of success, because it is not usually possible to gauge the exact probability of success, but—in the school setting, at least—it is safe for children to assume that the tasks set are not entirely beyond their capacities, and that it is worth investing effort. Research shows that expectancies of success become increasingly realistic until preadolescence. Interestingly, there are marked individual and cultural differences in how closely children's expectancies of success are related to their actual learning outcomes at school, the major performance domain in childhood and adolescence (Little, 1998). Because the developmental context of the school is determined and controlled by adults for the purposes of cultural instruction, with performance demands being set by adult socialization agents rather than chosen by the students themselves, a strictly realistic approach is not in fact necessary, and might even inhibit goal striving.

In this context, the rich field of *beliefs and perceptions about self-efficacy and control* needs to be addressed, albeit in a brief fashion given the space constraints for this chapter. The two important research traditions investigating people's expectancies about the success of their actions are Bandura's self-efficacy approach (for an overview, see Bandura, 1977, 1986) and the study of control beliefs (for an overview, see Little, 1998; Skinner, 1996; Weisz, 1983). According to Bandura's self-efficacy model, positive beliefs about the efficacy of one's actions in a task situation reinforce effort and persistence, thus increasing the probability of success. The more specific self-efficacy beliefs are to the task at hand, the more accurate the predictions generated by the model.

Seen from the perspective of modern motivation psychology, task-related self-efficacy beliefs are less a source of information about which challenges to address than motivational resources that make individuals more or less confident of success and thus provide them with more or less energy to implement their intentions (i.e., volition) in an ongoing task situation.

Conceptual models of control beliefs, which tend to apply to broader classes of action (e.g., scholastic performance in general), are more general than the construct of self-efficacy beliefs and, at the same time, more differentiated. What control beliefs and self-efficacy beliefs have in common is that they provide volitional resources for action implementation, rather than guiding task selection or goal setting. More recent approaches to children's control beliefs distinguish between beliefs about the contingency between causal factors and outcomes (e.g., the impact of teacher behavior on grades) and beliefs about individual access to causal factors (e.g., ability) (see Skinner et al., 1988; Weisz, 1983).

An individual will consider himself or herself likely to succeed in an activity only if the following two conditions are met: First, success must be dependent on conditions or behaviors that people like me can control. Naive theories or beliefs of this kind are termed contingency beliefs (Weisz, 1983), means-ends beliefs (Skinner et al., 1988), or causality beliefs (Little, 1998). These beliefs address the controllability of certain events (e.g., getting good grades) and the means by which they can be attained (e.g., effort, ability, being on good terms with the teacher).

Second, the person herself must be in the position to control these behaviors (e.g., trying hard) or the presence of the conditions for success (e.g., being the teacher's pet). Conceptions of this kind are referred to as competence beliefs (Weisz, 1983), capacity beliefs (Skinner, 1996), or agency beliefs. They are individuals' beliefs about whether they personally have access to relevant means for bringing about success (e.g., access to personal ability or the support of the teacher).

Numerous studies show that slightly optimistic self-efficacy conceptions and personal control beliefs have a positive effect on subjective well-being and also on achievement and particularly on the development of achievement over time. Optimistic perceptions about the controllability of achievement outcomes and one's own capacities appear to function as a developmental resource (Heckhausen & Heckhausen, 2008c).

After addressing the field of control-related beliefs and perceptions, we finally turn to the development of *causal schemata* for explaining success and failure. When accounting for success and failure in tasks at various difficulty levels, the child has to combine conceptions about their own ability for a given task and the effort they invested in the task. Causal schemata can reflect covariation between effort and ability or at more advanced levels of cognitive development, represent compensatory relations, for example, when high effort can compensate for low ability when mastering moderately difficult tasks. Causal schemata allow the individual to generate conclusions about unknown factors in two ways: They can either attribute known outcomes (e.g., success in a difficult task) to unknown degrees of effort and ability (e.g., both high), or they can predict an outcome, when the main causal factors (primarily ability and effort) are known (e.g., if both effort and ability are low, a failure is likely even for easy tasks). Because they are, in essence, conceptions of the causal significance of effort and ability, causal schemata are highly relevant to the development of achievement-motivated behavior. They also invoke differential emotional responses. For adults, effort is the decisive causal factor in evaluations of others, and ability is the decisive causal factor in self-evaluations. Others are evaluated more highly if they have invested effort, but people tend to see cause for pride in their own achievements if they testify to high ability. In a nutshell, "effort is virtuous, but it's better to have ability" (Nicholls, 1976). Conversely, ability attributions (stable and unchangeable) of failure are problematic, because they imply that future attempts have little chance of success either. In contrast, effort attributions of failure spur the individual to try again, investing more energy and care this time to ensure success.

From the age of about 10 years, ability attributions become decisive for affective self-evaluation (Heckhausen, 1984a, 1984b). At first, this only applies after experiences of success, and not after experiences of failure. It is at this age, as differentiated conceptions of the two causal factors gradually emerge from a global conception of competence, that children also begin to grasp the compensatory relationship between effort and ability (Karabenick & Heller, 1976; Surber, 1980). The more success is attributed to ability, and failure to lack of ability, the more satisfied or dissatisfied they feel with themselves. Attributions focusing on a lack of personal ability pose first developmental risks, because the child may develop a stable conception of lacking ability and become discouraged to take on new challenges (Dweck, 2002). Other people's (e.g., teachers') causal attributions of performance may also involve risks for the development of competence. Excessive praise for mediocre performance can undermine ability attributions; conversely, criticism for failure can be interpreted as indicating that the teacher (mother, friend) had, on the basis of high ability evaluations, expected better outcomes (Meyer, Mittag, & Engler, 1986).

DEVELOPMENT OF INDIVIDUAL DIFFERENCES IN CONTROL STRIVING AND AGENCY

In the past 2 decades, conceptual development in the field of motivation psychology, and indeed psychology in general, has seen a move away from a strictly cognitive focus toward a perspective that also takes affective dynamics into account. The development of individual differences cannot be explained solely in terms of cognitive factors such as levels of aspiration or causal attribution styles, neither can it be clarified by an exclusive focus on how differences in the incentive value of success and failure emerge over socialization. McClelland's comparison of self-attributed (explicit) and implicit (not consciously represented) motives can serve as a useful organizing framework for an overview of research on the development of individual differences in achievement motivation (McClelland, Koestner, & Weinberger, 1989). There is much evidence to indicate that implicit motives (measured by projective tests) and explicit motives (measured by self-report questionnaires) are two independent motive systems that govern different types of behavior and that may be activated in concert or in opposition depending on the situation. Implicit motives are activated by incentives residing in the activity itself (to improve one's performance, to master a challenge) and thus generate motivation for more spontaneous behavior that is not prestructured by the environment: the activity itself is attractive to people high in the achievement motive, independent of its outcomes. Explicit motives, on the other hand, are activated by social incentives (social recognition, reward, status) and thus determine prestructured behavior in socially regulated situations, such as the classroom, where the contingencies for social incentives are transparent (e.g., I have to do my homework carefully to please the teacher and get a good grade).

Individual Differences in Implicit Motives

The foundations for the development of *implicit motives* (e.g., achievement, power, affiliation) are laid in early childhood, before verbal instructions and self-reflection give motivational processes the deliberative character that distinguishes higher cognition (Kuhl, 2008). Although achievement-motivated behavior comprises both cognitive (explicit) and affective (implicit) processes, the preverbal development of individual differences in the incentive value of success and failure is decisive. It is at this early stage that children develop a heightened, probably lifelong, sensitivity to situational conditions that either provide opportunities to develop and optimize their control of the environment (of objects in the case of achievement motive and of other people in the case of the power motive), or that threaten to reduce or restrict that capacity.

Longitudinal studies of the origins and development of implicit motives are scarce, and results have been mixed (Heckhausen & Heckhausen, 2008c). Overall, family and parenting characteristics appear to play a significant role for the development of the achievement and the power motive, but not the affiliation motive (McClelland & Pilon, 1983). Adults with a strong "socialized power motive" had experienced a childhood with a dominant father and a mother who was tolerant of the child's transgression or rules. An adults' egotistic or "personalized power motive" was associated with a childhood dominated by a strong mother figure. Adults with a strong achievement motive had had mothers who insisted on fixed meal times and strict toilet training. Other studies have uncovered the important role of developmental timing in parental mastery challenges (Meyer, 1973a; Reif, 1970; Trudewind, 1975). Developmentally adequate challenges posed by the parents are most conducive for the development of a success-oriented achievement motive.

Individual Differences in Explicit Motives (Goals, Expectancies, Incentives)

As motivation researchers were using the widely accepted risk-taking model of Atkinson (Atkinson, 1957) to explain achievement-related behavior, it soon became clear that achievement-motivated behavior cannot comprehensively be explained by the combination of achievement motive strength with its value and expectancy components and task difficulty alone. Eccles showed, for instance, that the gender differences frequently observed in middle-school and high school students' preferences for certain school subjects cannot be explained by the risk-taking model (Eccles, Wigfield, & Schiefele, 1998). Rather, the choice of subjects and tasks is influenced by the confidence a student has in his or her abilities and by the value of a particular course choice. A wealth of incentives, such as conforming to behavioral norms associated with one's gender and/or self-concept and receiving approval from peers, teachers, and coaches, are thus involved in achievement-related choices. *Eccles and Wigfield's expectancy and value model* (in contrast to Atkinson's expectancy-by-value model) does not assume the "objective" difficulty of a task (in social comparison) to be the decisive motivating factor (according to the risk-taking model, the more difficult a task is, the higher its attraction), but predicts group and individual norms of adolescents' and young adults' to determine the subjective value of an activity (e.g., how desirable it is for a girl to do well in mathematics, sports, essay writing, football, or cheerleading). Another factor that Eccles assumes to influence the value of achievement-related choices is their potential costs (Eccles, 2005). These include the anticipated threat to self-esteem of failure, the possible negative implications of discrepancies from the self-concept or group norms (e.g., if a girl decides to play football), and the opportunity costs incurred by deciding for one activity and against another. Furthermore, in the Eccles and Wigfield model, the expectancy component (i.e., subjective difficulty) is shaped over time by the individual's experiences and preferences. Students who decide against advanced mathematics and physics courses, for example, in favor of literature and theater studies, will soon feel at home in the world of literature and drama, but have little confidence in their mathematics and physics skills.

The Eccles and Wigfield model emphasizes change in individual preferences and achievement-related cognitions over time, and the impact of that change on long-term competence profiles. The model might thus be described as a dynamic, interactive, and inherently developmental psychological approach. The choices an individual makes over time help to shape both subjective and objective influences on achievement-motivated preferences, thus leading—"for better or worse"—to canalized development that increasingly accentuates existing differences between individuals or subgroups.

Concepts of generalized goal orientations (i.e., explicit motives) have come to dominate U.S. research on the development of motivation in the past 20 years. A particularly influential line of research is the *achievement goal approach* (Dweck, 1975; Dweck & Leggett, 1988; Elliot, 2005; Elliot & Church, 1997; Nicholls, 1984). Distinctions are made on two dimensions: learning/mastery goals versus performance/ego goals, on the one hand, and approach goals versus avoidance goals, on the other. The aim of learning or mastery goals is to improve one's competence; the aim or performance or ego goals is to demonstrate one's competence to others and in social comparison. Learning and mastery goals have positive effects on achievement-oriented behavior, but not necessarily on the outcomes attained (Heckhausen & Heckhausen, 2008c). In contrast, a performance goal orientation has been found to have positive or neutral effects on outcomes when conceptions of personal competence are positive, but negative effects when conceptions of personal competence are negative (Harackiewicz & Elliot, 1993) and when the individual feels exposed to public evaluation. Findings also indicate that a combination of learning and performance orientations may be particularly motivating (Elliot, 2005) in the workplace, in sports settings, and even in educational contexts.

Goals can also be distinguished in terms of whether their aim is to approach a desirable action outcome or its consequences or to avoid an undesirable action outcome or its consequences (Elliot, 1999). The approach versus avoidance orientation determines whether performance/ego goals, in particular, are conducive or detrimental to achievement-related behavior (Moller & Elliot, 2006). Goals aiming to minimize displays of incompetence tend to elicit effort avoidance and helplessness responses, especially after failure and when people are exposed to the judgments of others. However, if the assessment of personal competence is favorable, the striving to demonstrate one's competence is conducive to effort, and to choosing ambitious, but attainable levels of aspiration. This conclusion is supported by a host of studies from the United States that found performance-approach goals (i.e., demonstrating one's competence) to be especially conducive to achievement in school and college contexts, whereas mastery-approach goals often seem to have no positive effects on academic achievement (Harackiewicz, Barron, & Elliot, 1998).

AGENCY IN REGULATING ONE'S OWN DEVELOPMENT

After having discussed several major topics regarding the development of motivation in childhood, adolescence, and adulthood, we are, in this following section, moving to the second perspective on the motivation-development interface, a focus on the role of motivation in guiding development. We organize this section according to the life-span theory of control. Other theoretical approaches, such as the selection, optimization, and compensation (SOC) model of Baltes and colleagues (Baltes & Baltes, 1990; Freund & Baltes, 2002; Lang, Rohr, & Williger, Chapter 3) and the dual process model by Brandtstädter and colleagues (Brandtstädter, 2006; Brandtstädter, Wentura, & Rothermund, 1999) are addressing similar phenomena and share some of our theory's concepts (e.g., selection and compensation in the SOC model, action-theoretical concepts in the dual-process model). We have discussed the similarities and differences, benefits, and potential problems of these approaches elsewhere (Haase, Heckhausen, & Wrosch, 2010; Poulin, Haase, & Heckhausen, 2005).

The life-span theory of control provides a comprehensive model for the processes involved in individuals' motivation directed at their own development (Heckhausen, 1999; Heckhausen & Schulz, 1995; Schulz & Heckhausen, 1996; Schulz, Wrosch, & Heckhausen, 2003). Over the past 2 decades, the theory has been elaborated in terms of specific models for goal engagement and disengagement and their sequential organization in action phases (Heckhausen, 1999, 2007; Heckhausen & Schulz, 1993; Schulz et al., 2003). These conceptual and empirical developments were integrated into a comprehensive motivational theory of life-span development (Heckhausen, et al., 2010) that comprises an elaborate set of testable propositions. The theory distinguishes between primary and secondary control striving. *Primary control striving* refers to exerting influence over the environment by one's own behavior. *Secondary control striving*, by contrast, aims at influencing internal, psychological processes, particularly after failure to attain a goal, and includes motivational disengagement from the goal, as well as self-protective strategies such as self-protective social comparisons (i.e., comparison with others inferior to oneself), and causal attributions that avoid self-blame (e.g., attribute to external factors).

Substantial empirical evidence has been collected supporting the theory's central propositions about the functional primacy of primary control striving throughout life and its beneficial consequence for objective and subjective well-being and active capacity, about the increasing importance of secondary control strategies with increasing age, and about the adaptiveness of congruence between goal controllability and goal engagement and disengagement such that goal engagement and disengagement is adjusted to life-course changes in opportunities for goal pursuit and attainability.

Developmental Precursors of Agency in Regulating One's Own Development

With increasing age, partly prompted by their parents, but not least on their own initiative ("wanting to do it oneself") (Geppert & Küster, 1983), children begin to actively strive for independence in their striving for control and mastery. In addition, with the gradual *expansion of the developmental-ecological life space* (Bronfenbrenner & Morris, 1988) from the home to the neighborhood, and later to the school and recreation sites (Eccles, Barber, & Jozefowicz, 1999), children and adolescents are exposed to new and more diverse influences and, at the same time, play an increasingly active role in selecting social contexts and interaction partners. This increasing involvement in the orchestration of opportunities, social relations, and networks—in other words, developmental contexts—is associated with the stabilization and accentuation of conscious and unconscious preferences, values, beliefs, and self-images (Lang & Heckhausen, 2006). Young people's life goals and developmental goals become more individualized, leading to divergent developmental trajectories that become increasingly stable, unique, and irreversible as a result of developmental canalization. This is arguably the reason why individual differences in personality traits increase in their year-to-year stability until midlife when an individual's capacity to determine her own life circumstances and social networks is at its peak (Roberts & DelVecchio, 2000).

Control Striving Reflects Shifts in Gains and Losses Across the Life Span

In modern societies characterized by high levels of social mobility and flexible life choices, individuals play a key role as *producers of their own development* (Brandtstädter & Lerner, 1999; Lerner & Busch-Rossnagel, 1981). However, individuals need to take into account the characteristics of the life course as an action field, including its changing opportunities to attain certain developmental goals (e.g., finish school, enter a career, build a family, reach one's career peak, retire, etc.). For one thing, primary control capacity does not remain stable across the life span, but first increases rapidly in childhood and adolescence, then reaches a peak or plateau in midlife, and finally declines in old age (see inverted U-curve for primary control capacity in Figure 8.1; Heckhausen, 1999; Schulz & Heckhausen, 1996). When asking adults at different age levels about their expectations about developmental change in psychological characteristics, a pattern of predominant developmental gains that decrease with advancing age, and of developmental losses that increase with advancing age, emerges (see Figure 8.2; Heckhausen, Dixon, & Baltes, 1989).

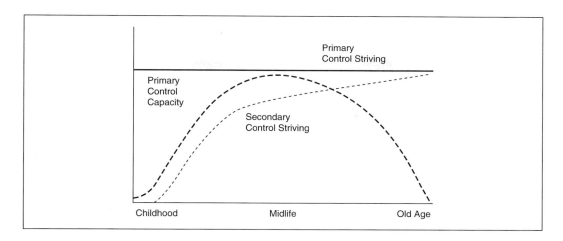

FIGURE 8.1 Hypothetical life-span trajectories for primary control capacity and primary and secondary control striving. *Source:* Adapted from Heckhausen, 1999.

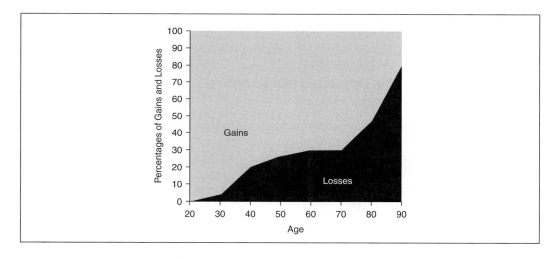

FIGURE 8.2 Gains and losses across the adult life span as expected by adults of various ages. *Source:* Adapted from Heckhausen, Dixon, and Baltes, 1989.

Although *primary control striving* remains a stable source of motivation through-out the life course (see stable line for primary control striving in Figure 8.1), the goals for primary control are typically adjusted to the primary control capacity available at a given point in an individual's life course. On the large scale of the whole adult life span, this means that individuals pursue many growth-oriented goals, but decreas-ingly so at older ages (Ebner, Freund, & Baltes, 2006; Heckhausen, 1997). Analogously, maintenance and loss-preventative goals come increasingly into focus at older ages. In addition to these adjustments of goal content, individuals use other compensatory secondary control strategies to buffer the effects control loss and failure experiences have on their self-confidence and hope for future success (see linearly increasing curve for secondary control strategies in Figure 8.1).

At the level of specific goal pursuit (e.g., having a child, entering a career) developmental goals need to be adjusted to the waxing and waning of control potential at the current age level and social setting (Heckhausen, 2002). Most important life goals are not obtainable at just any time during the life course, but involve a pattern of increasing, peaking, and decreasing opportunity. For example, bearing a child has both biological and social normative age-related constraints. It should not happen before age 18 or so, and typically cannot happen after age 45 or so. In between these onset and deadline age boundaries, opportunities for having a child follow an inverse U trajectory which probably peaks somewhere in the mid- to late 20s for western industrial societies.

Thus, in his/her quest to shape his/her own development and pursue life goals, the individual has to take account of the *constraints and age-graded structures* of both biological maturation and aging (e.g., the "biological clock" and childbearing) and societal institutions (e.g., the age-graded structure of the education system). This age-sequenced structuring of developmental potential provides a framework for developmental regulation (Heckhausen, 1990, 1999). Individuals' movements within this framework, the paths chosen, and the consistency of goal pursuit, depend largely on the direction and effectiveness of individual motivation and its implicit motives and explicit goals.

Developmental Agency is Organized into Phases of Goal Engagement and Disengagement

The *action-phase model of developmental regulation* has been developed in the context of the life-span theory of control to generate specific predictions about the control strategies used to pursue or deactivate goals at different phases in the life span (Heckhausen, 1999, 2002; Heckhausen & Farruggia, 2003; Schulz, et al., 2003; Wrosch, Schulz, & Heckhausen, 2002). The model is based on four major principles: (1) developmental goals function as organizers of developmental regulation; (2) the adaptive developmental principle of congruence between developmental goals and developmental opportunities; (3) the sequence of action phases in a cycle of action directed at a developmental goal—goal selection, goal engagement, and goal disengagement; and (4) radical shifts from goal deliberation and choice to goal engagement and from goal engagement to goal disengagement.

Developmental regulation is directed at goals relating to one's future development and important life-course transitions (Brandtstädter, 2006; Brunstein, Schultheiss, & Maier, 1999; Heckhausen, 1999; Heckhausen & Heckhausen, 2008c; Nurmi, 1992; Nurmi, Salmela-Aro, & Koivisto, 2002). According to our action-phase model of developmental regulation, individuals are most effective in their efforts to influence their own development, if they select their developmental goals in accordance with the current opportunities for goal pursuit. For example, striving for a college degree is most effective during the transition into adulthood, even though a later timing is not unfeasible, but will invoke more costs for competing goal pursuits (e.g., family building).

Another aspect of the organizing characteristic of developmental goals (according to our action-phase model) is that a goal cycle is structured into distinct phases—from the selection of a developmental goal to a phase of active goal pursuit, followed by goal deactivation and finally evaluation of the action outcome. The theory proposes that in order to be most effective, transitions from one phase to the next should be discrete and coherent. This means, for example, that the transition from selecting a goal to investing oneself into pursuing this goal should be rapid and radical. Once a decision for a particular goal is made, there should not be lingering, postdecisional conflict, and distractions by other possible goals. Similarly, once it is clear that a goal that has been pursued for some time is no longer obtainable (e.g., bearing a child after menopausal changes have set in), the individual should shift from goal engagement to goal disengagement.

Developmental deadlines mark the point at which it no longer makes sense to invest resources in goal pursuit, and when the time has come to disengage from that goal (see Figure 8.3). These timing constraints in goal attainability can be anticipated by the individual, and elicit phases of urgent goal striving immediately before the developmental deadline is reached. As soon as the developmental deadline has been passed, however, individuals need to disengage from the now futile goal, and invest their energy in other, more fruitful projects. Developmental deadlines make extraordinary demands of an individual's regulatory capacities; they require a switch from urgent, intensive goal engagement in the immediate run-up to the deadline to goal disengagement and protection of self-esteem as soon as the deadline has been passed. Developmental transitions involving developmental deadlines are thus particularly suitable for testing the potentials and limits of individual developmental regulation.

A series of studies on developmental deadlines for childbearing and romantic partnerships supported key proposals of the action-phase model of developmental regulation (Heckhausen, Wrosch, & Fleeson, 2001; Wrosch & Heckhausen, 1999). Two studies on childbearing showed that overall women tended to adjust their goals regarding childbearing as well as their control strategies to age-graded opportunities, with younger women endorsing childbearing goals and control strategies of goal engagement (Heckhausen et al., 2001). Women in their 40s and 50s did not endorse childbearing goals and reported compensatory secondary control strategies of goal

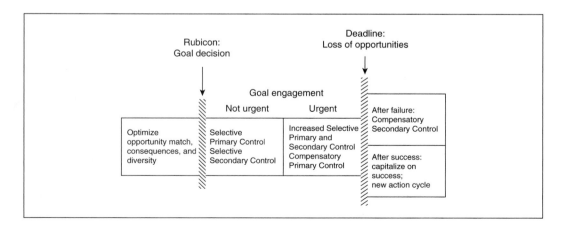

FIGURE 8.3 **Action-phase model of developmental regulation.** *Source:* Adapted from Heckhausen, 1999.

disengagement and self-protection (e.g., "I can lead a happy life without having children." "It is not my fault, if I don't have children."). Moreover, biased information processing was also found, reflecting a focus on child-relevant information in women of childbearing age compared to women at post–child-bearing age. A longitudinal study on partnership goals found that younger adults after a separation were more likely to keep pursuing the goal of finding a romantic partner, whereas people in their mid-50s were more likely to disengage from partnership goals altogether after a separation (Wrosch & Heckhausen, 1999). Moreover, adults who prematurely disengaged from partnership goals, or those who failed to disengage at late midlife, suffered declines in positive affect after an 18-month period following the initial assessment. Thus again it was shown that opportunity-congruent goal engagement and goal disengagement yielded the best developmental outcomes.

Urgent Striving During High Opportunity Phases

Another aspect of the action-phase model of developmental regulation addresses the urgency phase immediately before a developmental deadline is reached. This phase, during which primary control striving is exposed to enormous time pressure, can only be examined in longitudinal studies. Even then, the long time periods involved, and the heterogeneity of developmental trajectories and life-course transitions in adulthood, pose considerable challenges for research. We thus chose a transition involving a developmental deadline that is relatively strictly regulated in Germany, namely the transition from school to vocational training in the dual educational system (on-the-job training combined with general and vocational education at a vocational school). The major challenge of this transition is to find an apprenticeship position, preferably before leaving school. In other countries, such as the United States, the transition from high school to the world of work is far less strictly regulated. Many young people end up "floundering" (Hamilton, 1990) and at risk for downward social mobility (for details on international variation in the school-to-work transition, see Heckhausen, 2002; Heinz, 1999; Paul, 2001). The transition to vocational training is also a challenging and critical step for young people in Germany, however, because the number and quality of apprenticeships (within a single company or at multiple sites; commercial vs. trade apprenticeships) by no means matches the demand. During their final year at school (typically 10th grade), students not wishing to continue their general education have to find an apprenticeship that opens up relatively positive long-term career prospects (Heckhausen & Tomasik, 2002; Tomasik, 2003) given their individual capacities. Navigating between the Scylla and Charybdis of over- and underaspiration under urgency conditions is thus a considerable challenge to developmental regulatory capacities of 16-year-old school leavers.

We investigated students in their final year at four high schools located in lower and lower middle class residential areas in the eastern and western part of Berlin, Germany. Data on students' goals, control strategies, and vocational aspirations were collected twice in ninth grade and five times at 2-month intervals in 10th grade. Findings showed that the adolescents adjusted their vocational aspirations, measured in terms of the social prestige, to their grades (i.e., their educational resources on the labor market). The adolescents even adjusted their ideas of a "dream job" to the apprenticeships they could realistically hope to be offered (Heckhausen & Tomasik,

2002), such that the vision of a dream job did not prevent them from investing in the search for an appropriate position.

Did this strategy of taking into account one's school achievement when selecting vocational aspirations lead to better outcomes? Of course, lower aspirations are easier to attain, but beyond that were well-calibrated students more successful in obtaining a relatively prestigious vocational training position given their school grades. In analyses utilizing the bimonthly data collections during grade 10, we investigated trajectories most likely to result in apprenticeships with relatively high vocational prestige. We found that more promising trajectories would start slightly above one's own achievement level and then adjust downward until an apprenticeship is obtained (Tomasik, Hardy, Haase, & Heckhausen, 2009). Interestingly, youth showing this trajectory of vocational aspirations also were more goal engaged and less disengaged, judging from their ratings of control strategies. Goal engagement with striving for an apprenticeship proved particularly beneficial for girls' success in securing a vocational training position (Haase, Heckhausen, & Köller, 2008).

Conducting a longitudinal study of the transition from high school to college and work in the United States offered a unique opportunity to study the motivational processes that lead to success versus failure under critically different societal conditions. The educational system in the United States differs fundamentally from the German system in that it is integrated until high school graduation, whereas the German system is three-tiered starting at fourth grade (in some of the German states sixth grade). The key difference between institutions of secondary education in the United States and Germany is that the U.S. educational system does not constrain upward mobility by formalized institutional barriers as it does in Germany. To the contrary and particularly in California, the college system provides postsecondary educational opportunities that allows the individual to follow a step-by-step upward mobility from high school or equivalent attainment on an entry test (showing that the student is "capable of benefiting from instruction") to community college and then a transfer to 4-year colleges that lead to a Bachelor degree (Code, 1960). This is not to say that the U.S. high school system does not have its own social inequalities, which are primarily based on the great differences between neighborhoods and make it harder for students from lower-income neighborhoods to take advantage of the institutional opportunities to climb upward in the system.

We tracked a sample of more than a 1,000 high school seniors in the Los Angeles Unified School District longitudinally 1, 2, 3, and 4 years after graduation (Chang, Chen, Greenberger, Dooley, & Heckhausen, 2006; Chang, Greenberger, Chen, Heckhausen, & Farruggia, 2010; Heckhausen & Chang, 2009). It was striking in comparison to the German sample that vocational, and particularly educational, aspirations were high. A large majority of the youth anticipated to complete a Bachelors degree, even if their own senior-year grades were too low to enter a 4-year college right after high school (Heckhausen & Chang, 2009). In an educational system that is more segregated and less permeable as it is in Germany (Hamilton, 1994), such high aspirations would lead to unrealistic choices and failure. However, in this Californian sample the youth with the most ambitious educational expectations actually ultimately succeeded in enrolling in and completing 4-year college degrees (Heckhausen & Chang, 2009). Moreover, those youth with particularly strong and focused goal engagement for attaining a college degree also reported better subjective well-being and mental health after high school graduation.

It was striking in comparison to the German sample that vocational and particularly educational expectations were very high and not calibrated to the actual school performance (Heckhausen, 2010). A large majority of the youth anticipated completing a Bachelors degree or more (i.e., complete graduate school), even if their own senior-year grades were as low as "Cs and lower" (Heckhausen & Chang, 2009). Such high aspirations would lead to unrealistic choices and failure in an educational system, such as the German system, that is more segregated and less permeable (Hamilton, 1994). However, in this Californian sample the youth with the most ambitious educational expectations ultimately succeeded in enrolling in and completing 4-year college degrees, whereas youth with more "realistic" goals ended up with less progress in postsecondary education (e.g., community college or less) (Heckhausen & Chang, 2009). Moreover, those senior high school students with ambitious short-term educational aspirations in terms of planning to enroll in college fared better on the long run, even if they initially did not attain their short-term goals 1 year after high school (Heckhausen, Lessard, & Chang, 2008).

Disengagement With Decline or Loss of Opportunities

An important proposition of our motivational theory is that individuals should disengage from goal pursuits, which are futile. So if opportunities for goal attainment are lost due to developmental change (e.g., "biological clock," aging-related decline), disability or illness, disengaging from the motivational commitment to the goal and withdrawal of effort will preserve behavioral and motivational resources that can be invested in more promising goal pursuits (Heckhausen, 1999; Heckhausen et al., 2010; Miller & Wrosch, 2007; Wrosch, Scheier, Carver, & Schulz, 2003; Wrosch, Scheier, Miller, et al., 2003). In the context of the studies on developmental deadlines, we found evidence that individuals who had passed the deadline for a given life goal were better off in psychological well-being and mental health, if they disengaged from the futile goal, both in terms of conscious goal commitment and with regard to goal-relevant biases in information processing (Heckhausen et al., 2001; Wrosch & Heckhausen, 1999, 2005). Numerous studies indicate that with increasing age (Ebner et al., 2006; Heckhausen, 1997) and under conditions of disability (Boerner, 2004; Evers, Kraaimaat, van Lankveld, Jongen, & Jacobs, 2001; Menec, Chipperfield, & Perry, 1999; Wahl, Becker, & Burmedi, 2004), people disengage from goals that are no longer attainable.

Wrosch and his colleagues conduct an extensive research program on the benefits of goal disengagement under low control conditions. They show that dispositional differences in college students' capacity for goal disengagement under conditions of low controllability are associated with more favorable mental health and well-being (Wrosch, Scheier, Miller, et al., 2003) as well as physical health and diurnal cortisol secretion patterns (Wrosch, Bauer, Miller, & Lupien, 2007). The same is true for a sample of adults who are experiencing a very strong uncontrollable stressor, namely parents of cancer-suffering children (Wrosch, Scheier, Miller, et al., 2003). Very recent work from this group indicates that depressive symptoms experienced during adolescence may prompt an elaboration of the capacity to disengage from unattainable goals and thus can serve to protect against depression on the long run (Miller & Wrosch, 2007; Wrosch & Miller, 2009).

Opportunity-Congruent Goal Engagement and Goal Disengagement in Older Adults With Health Problems

Many older adults face the challenges of acute and chronic health problems. To the extent that these problems are controllable by adaptive health behaviors, they call for intensified primary control. However, over time health problems often become irreversible and thus uncontrollable, especially if they are associated with chronic diseases of old age such as macular degeneration, Parkinson's disease, or dementia. According to the life-span theory of control, primary control striving to overcome acute health problems and to minimize the effects of illness and disease on everyday functioning should be intensified when control opportunities are still present. On the other hand, goal disengagement should occur when control opportunities have been lost and the individual needs to adjust to the new, lowered control capacity (e.g., in terms of mobility, vision, etc.). As summarized in the next paragraphs, several pertinent studies support these predictions.

Health-related primary control striving has beneficial consequences for the psychological well-being and mental health of older adults with health problems (Pakenham, 1999; Wrosch, Schulz, & Heckhausen, 2002; Wrosch, Schulz, Miller, Lupien, & Dunne, 2007) and even helps prevent an increase of chronic and functional health problems over time (Wrosch & Schulz, 2008). Beneficial effects of enhanced primary control has also been shown in an exemplar intervention study, which boosted primary control over the risk of falls by using a combination of physical and occupational therapy tailored to functionally vulnerable older adults' daily activities and home environments (Gitlin, Hauck, Winter, Dennis, & Schulz, 2006; Gitlin, Winter, et al., 2006). Primary control-enhancing interventions improved various aspects of daily functioning (e.g., self-reliant bathing), enhanced self-efficacy, and led to a substantial reduction in fear of falling (Gitlin, Winter, et al., 2006). Moreover, these primary control enhancing interventions also reduced mortality over a 14-month period for the intervention group (1% mortality), but not the control group (10% mortality), and were particularly effective among those with low primary control striving before the intervention (Gitlin, Hauck, et al., 2006).

Wahl, Schilling, and Becker (2007) report that older adults with macular degeneration sharply increase their use of compensatory primary control strategies (seeking help and advice form others) shortly after their initial diagnosis, whereas the use of compensatory secondary control strategies (disengagement, self-protective attributions, and social comparisons) was predicted by the loss of functioning in activities of daily living over longer periods of time.

When controllability of health problems and its consequences on daily functioning is diminished, older adults do better if they adjust their goals for daily functioning (Rothermund & Brandtstädter, 2003) and disengage from overcoming their health problems. Middle-aged and older adults with macular degeneration were found to benefit from a disposition for flexible goal adjustment in terms of having fewer mental health problems, such as social dysfunction and depression (Boerner, 2004). Multiple sclerosis patients' who accepted the reality of their illness and disability reported better health status and mood a year after initial assessment (Evers et al., 2001).

Moreover, patients with uncontrollable health conditions benefit from self-protective strategies such as self-enhancing downward social comparisons (Bailis, Chipperfield, & Perry, 2005; Frieswijk, Buunk, Steverink, & Slaets, 2004) or reappraisal of health problems (Wrosch, Heckhausen, & Lachman, 2000). It also seems to be beneficial, if older adults with health problems that constrain their daily activities replace some lost activities with alternate attractive activities (e.g., listening to music, reading may replace athletic activities) (Duke, Leventhal, Brownlee, & Leventhal, 2002).

Research addressing older adults' use of both primary and secondary control strategies revealed that older adults who predominantly used primary control strategies and those who used a combination of primary and secondary control strategies achieved better physical and psychological well-being compared to older adults who relinquished control or those who failed to used compensatory secondary control (Haynes, Heckhausen, Chipperfield, Perry, & Newall, 2009). Finally, a longitudinal study followed older adults with serious health problems that were either acute and involved some potential for primary control (after heart attack or stroke) or were chronic with little controllability (e.g., arthritis, heart disease) over a period of 9 years. The study was focused on how the older adults dealt with the loss of a specific area of functioning they perceive as the greatest loss associated with their health condition, and specifically investigated which control strategies of goal engagement and goal disengagement and self-protection control strategies were used by the older adults (Hall, Chipperfield, Heckhausen, & Perry, 2010). In accordance with the congruence theorem (i.e., control striving should match controllability) of the life-span theory of control, the use of control strategies associated with goal engagement (e.g., primary control striving) predicted lower mortality for individuals with acute conditions, but poorer physical health for those with chronic conditions and also among the oldest old. In contrast, goal disengagement predicted poorer physical health for those with acute conditions, yet better health for individuals with chronic conditions and the oldest old. Self-protective strategies (positive reappraisal) predicted lower mortality as well as greater health and subjective well-being for those with acute conditions, as well as better physical health for the oldest old.

Overall, the evidence shows that those older adults who flexibly use primary and secondary control strategies in congruence with the degree of controllability of the health condition and its consequences for daily activities fare best both in terms of objective indicators of physical health and functioning and in terms of subjective well-being and mental health.

FUTURE ISSUES IN THE STUDY OF AGENCY AND CONTROL STRIVING ACROSS THE LIFE SPAN

In this final section, I outline a set of research topics that deserve closer attention by future research. A recent article on the motivational theory of life-span development presents a more comprehensive discussion of future research addressing understudied aspects of our theory (Heckhausen et al., 2010). I am considering here a subset of those and some other topics that address the development of motivation.

A first area of future inquiry should focus on the question: How do *divergent developmental pathways* toward adaptive and maladaptive motivational systems of self-regulation come about? Previous research has addressed (at least in part) how strategies of primary and particularly of secondary control develop across childhood and adolescence and are elaborated during adulthood (see review in Heckhausen et al., 2010). Much more can be learned about universal processes here, but the greatest dearth of research concerns the emergence of individual differences. Individual differences can involve various aspects of motivational self-regulation (Heckhausen et al., 2010): (1) the capacity to detect changes in goal attainability that can then lead to goal disengagement and reselection; (2) the capacity to mobilize goal engagement when opportunities for the respective goal open up; (3) persistence in goal engagement in the face of difficulties; (4) the willingness and ability to deactivate and disengage from a goal when opportunities change for the worse; (5) skill and preferences for using certain kinds of self-protective strategies to compensate for a loss or failure of control; and finally (6) the capacity to engage with a new goal after a disengagement from a futile goal. Just to give one example of the kinds of studies needed in this area, here is one addressing the emergence of individual differences in the capacity for goal disengagement. Wrosch and Miller report that adolescents who suffered from depressive symptoms, compared to adolescents without depressive symptoms, were more likely to develop a capacity to disengage from unfeasible goals. Most notably, those who developed a greater capacity for goal disengagement in this way, 18 months later at a follow-up assessment, reported fewer depressive symptoms than comparison peers with less refined capacity for goal disengagement (Wrosch & Miller, 2009).

Another important topic at the interface of motivation and development is the motivational management of *life-course transitions*. During life-course transitions, for example from the exclusive family context into preschool or from college into work life, the individual needs to retool his/her regulatory system for motivated behavior. Transitions typically involve major changes in the way external influences (e.g., the parent, the curriculum of a college major) shape the individual's goal selection, goal engagement, and behavioral investment. The individual thus has to pick up the slack or in some cases (e.g., move from independent living to assisted living) give up some self-regulation. Another aspect of life-course transitions is that they usually involve significant changes in the social context. Transitions may involve a major shift in reference group that metaphorically resembles a move from a big fish in a small pond to a small fish in a big pond. A case in point would be a high-achieving high school graduate moving from an average high school to a highly selective university.

A third promising area of inquiry addresses *how educational institutions influence the development of motivation and self-regulation*. Research about the motivational characteristics of typical classrooms suggests that schools may provide detrimental institutional ecologies for the development of an implicit achievement motive (Heckhausen & Heckhausen, 2008b). One major problem is the dominant emphasis on social comparison for evaluating a student's achievement and the lacking opportunities for the experience of intraindividual improvement of mastery. Another hindrance to stimulating students' implicit achievement striving is the lack of opportunity for self-selected assignments and tests. Here research should address the question of how schools can become more nurturant contexts for the development of achievement motivation. This is not to say that explicit motives and goal setting is of no significance. Indeed, it is of major importance to master developmental challenges in careers and other life domains. Self-regulation should combine implicit and explicit motives (Brunstein & Maier, 2005), and the school context could be a sheltered developmental context to learn managing these two sources of motivational incentives.

A fourth area of inquiry should address dynamic interactions between individuals and their environment in terms of *mutual influences between societal context and individual agent over time* (Roberts & Caspi, 2003). As individuals move into adulthood, they select their social context and relationships, for example, by career choices, mate selection, and selection of friends (Lang & Heckhausen, 2006). An extreme case of environmental selection is migration. A fascinating line of inquiry would address the between-country gradients in primary control potential that motivate people to emigrate from their native environments and launch themselves into the highly risky adventure of immigration. Cross-national studies of subjective well-being suggest that happiness is closely linked to perceptions of greater freedom of choice. Do streams of migration follow the same gradients? Another type of transaction between individual agents and society involves direct active influence of the individual on his/her environments to fit better with his/her motivational preferences. If such active influences are taken by a coherent, sizable, and influential subgroup of the population, it could eventually lead to social change, in normative conceptions as well as ultimately in institutional and legal change. A well-known example from the last century is the student movement in the late 1960s and early 1970s, which had many lasting consequences in society. A recent example is the change in legislation regarding gay individuals' rights to serve in the military, to marry, and to adopt children. During historical phases of sociopolitical change, the dynamic transactional efforts of individuals, coupled with the leverage of the collective, can develop great—albeit rare—powers that transform the societal ecology for life-span development and individual agency far beyond one individual's immediate range of control.

REFERENCES

Achtziger, A., & Gollwitzer, P. M. (2008). Motivation and volition in the course of action. In J. Heckhausen & H. Heckhausen (Eds.), *Motivation and action* (pp. 272–295). New York: Cambridge University Press.

Ainsworth, M. D. S. (1972). Attachment and dependency: A comparison. In J. Gewirtz (Ed.), *Attachment and dependency*. Washington, D.C.: Winston.

Ainsworth, M. D., & Bell, S. M. (1970). Attachment, exploration and separation: Illustrated by the behavior of one-year-olds in a strange situation. *Child Development, 41*(1), 49–67.

Ainsworth, M. D., Bell, S. M., & Stayton, D. F. (1974). Infant mother attachment and social development: Socialization as a product of reciprocal responsiveness to signals. In M.P.M. Richards (Ed.), *The integration of a child into a social world* (pp. 99–135). London: Cambridge University Press.

Altshuler, J. L., & Ruble, D. N. (1989). Developmental changes in children's awareness of strategies for coping with uncontrollable stress. *Child Development, 60*, 1337–1349.

Atkinson, J. W. (1957). Motivational determinants of risk-taking behavior. *Psychological Review, 64*, 359–372.

Bailis, D. S., Chipperfield, J. G., & Perry, R. P. (2005). Optimistic social comparisons of older adults low in primary control: A prospective analysis of hospitalization and mortality. *Health Psychology, 24*, 393–401.

Baltes, P. B., & Baltes, M. M. (1990). Psychological perspectives on successful aging: The model of selective optimization with compensation. In P. B. Baltes & M. M. Baltes (Eds.), *Successful aging: Perspectives from the behavioral sciences* (pp. 1–34). New York: Cambridge University Press.

Band, E. B., & Weisz, J. R. (1988). How to feel better when it feels bad: Children's perspectives on coping with everyday stress. *Developmental Psychology, 24*, 247–253.

Bandura, A. (1977). Self-efficacy: Toward a unifying theory of behavioral change. *Psychological Review, 84*, 191–215.

Bandura, A. (1986). *Social foundations of thought and action: A social cognitive theory*. Englewood Cliffs, NJ: Prentice-Hall.

Barrett, K. C., Morgan, G. A., & Maslin-Cole, C. (1993). Three studies on the development of mastery motivation in infancy and toddlerhood. In D. Messer (Ed.), *Mastery motivation in early childhood: Development, measurement and social processes* (pp. 83–108). London: Routledge.

Boerner, K. (2004). Adaption to disability among middle-aged and older adults: The role of assimilative and accommodative coping. *Journal of Gerontology: Psychological Sciences and Social Sciences, 59*, 35–42.

Brandtstädter, J. (2006). Action perspectives on human development. In R. M. Lerner & W. Damon (Eds.), *Handbook of child psychology. Theoretical models of human development* (Vol. 1, 6th ed., pp. 516–568). Hoboken, NJ: John Wiley & Sons.

Brandtstädter, J., & Lerner, R. (1999). *Action and self-development: Theory and research through the life span*. Thousand Oaks, CA: Sage Publications.

Brandtstädter, J., Wentura, D., & Rothermund, K. (1999). Intentional self-development through adulthood and later life: Tenacious pursuit and flexible adjustment of goals. In J. Brandtstädter & R. M. Lerner (Eds.), *Action and self development: Theory and research through the life span* (pp. 373–400). Thousand Oaks, CA: Sage.

Bronfenbrenner, U., & Morris, P. A. (1988). The ecology of developmental processes. *Handbook of Child Psychology, 5*, 993–1028.

Brunstein, J. C., & Hoyer, S. (2002). Implizites versus explizites Leistungsstreben: Befunde zur Unabhaengigkeit zweier Motvationssysteme [Implicit versus explicit achievement strivings: Empirical evidence of the independence of two motivational systems]. *Zeitschrift fuer Entwicklungspsychologie und Paedagogische Psychologie, 16*, 51–62.

Brunstein, J. C., & Maier, G. W. (2005). Implicit and self-attributed motives to achieve: Two separate but interacting needs. *Journal of Personality and Social Psychology, 89*, 205–222.

Brunstein, J. C., Schultheiss, O. C., & Maier, G. W. (1999). *The pursuit of personal goals: A motivational approach to well-being and life adjustment*. Thousand Oaks, CA: Sage Publications.

Chang, E. S., Chen, C., Greenberger, E., Dooley, D., & Heckhausen, J. (2006). What do they want in life? The life goals of a multi-ethnic, multi-generational sample of high school seniors. *Journal of Youth and Adolescence, 35*, 321–332.

Chang, E. S., Greenberger, E., Chen, C., Heckhausen, J., & Farruggia, S. P. (2010). Non-parental adults as social resources in the transition to adulthood. *Journal of Research on Adolescence, 20*: 1–18.

Clarke-Stewart, K. A. (1973). Interactions between mothers and their young children: Characteristics and consequences. *Monographs of the Society for Research in Child Development, 38*(6–7, Serial No. 153).

Clarke-Stewart, K. A., VanderStoep, L. P., & Killian, G. A. (1979). Analysis and replication of mother-child relations at two years of age. *Child Development, 50*(3), 777–793.

Code (1960). The California master plan for higher education, 66010.1–66010.8 C.F.R.

Collis, G. M., & Schaffer, H. R. (1975). Synchronization of visual attention in mother-infant pairs. *Journal of Child psychology and Psychiatry, 16*, 315–320.

Compas, B. E., Worsham, N. L., Ey, S., & Howell, D. C. (1996). When Mom or Dad has cancer II: Coping, cognitive appraisals, and psychological distress in children of cancer patients. *Health psychology, 15*, 167–175.

DeCasper, A. J., & Carstens, A. A. (1981). Contingencies of stimulation: Effects on learning and emotion in neonates. *Infant Behavior and Development, 4*, 19–35.

Duke, J., Leventhal, H., Brownlee, S., & Leventhal, E. A. (2002). Giving up and replacing activities in response to illness. *Journal of Gerontology Series B: Psychological Sciences and Social Sciences, 57*, P367–P376.

Dweck, C. S. (1975). The role of expectations and attributions in the alleviation of learned helplessness. *Journal of Personality and Social Psychology, 31*, 674–685.

Dweck, C. S. (2002). The development of ability conceptions. In A. Wigfield & J. S. Eccles (Eds.), *Development of achievement motivation* (pp. 57–88). San Diego, CA: Academic Press.

Dweck, C. S., & Leggett, E. I. (1988). A social-cognitive approach to motivation and personality. *Psychological Review, 95*, 256–273.

Ebner, N. C., Freund, A. M., & Baltes, P. B. (2006). Developmental changes in personal goal orientation from young to late adulthood: From striving for gains to maintenance and prevention of losses. *Psychology and Aging, 21*, 664–678.

Eccles, J. S. (2005). Subjective task value and the Eccles et al. model of achievement related choices. In A. J. Elliot & C. S. Dweck (Eds.), *Handbook of competence and motivation* (pp. 105–121). New York: Guilford Press.

Eccles, J. S., Barber, B., & Jozefowicz, D. (1999). Linking gender to educational, occupational and recreational choices: Applying the Eccles model of achievement related choices. In W. B. J. Swann,

J. H. Langlois, & L. A. Gilbert (Eds.), *Sexism and stereotypes in modern society: The gender science of Janet Taylor Spence* (pp. 153–192). Washington, DC: American Psychological Association.

Eccles, J. S., Wigfield, A., & Schiefele, U. (Eds.). (1998). *Motivation to succeed* (5 ed., Vol. 3). Hoboken, NJ: John Wiley & Sons.

Elliot, A. J. (1999). Approach and avoidance motivation and achievement goals. *Educational Psychologist, 34*, 169–189.

Elliot, A. J. (2005). A conceptual history of the achievement goal construct. In A. J. Elliot & C. S. Dweck (Eds.), *Handbook of competence and motivation* (pp. 52–72). New York: Guilford Publications.

Elliot, A. J., & Church, M. (1997). A hierachical model of approach and avoidance achievement motivation. *Journal of Personality and Social Psychology, 72*, 218–232.

Evers, A. W. M., Kraaimaat, F. W., van Lankveld, W., Jongen, P. J. H., Jacobs, J. W. G., & Bijlsma, J. W. J. (2001). Beyond unfavorable thinking: The illness cognition questionnaire for chronic diseases. *Journal of Consulting and Clinical Psychology, 69*, 1026–1036.

Finkelstein, N. W., & Ramey, C. T. (1977). Learning to control the environment in infancy. *Child Development, 48*, 806–819.

Freund, A. M., & Baltes, P. B. (2002). The adaptiveness of selection, optimization, and compensation as strategies of life management: Evidence from a preference study on proverbs. *Journals of Gerontology: Series B: Psychological Sciences and Social Sciences, 57*, 426–434.

Frieswijk, N., Buunk, B. P., Steverink, N., & Slaets, J. P. J. (2004). The effect of social comparison information on the life satisfaction of frail older persons. *Psychology and Aging, 19*, 183–190.

Frijda, N. H. (1988). The laws of emotion. *American Psychologist, 43*, 349–358.

Geppert, U., & Heckhausen, H. (1990). Ontogenese der Emotion [Ontogenesis of emotion]. In K. R. Scherer (Ed.), *Enzyklopädie der Psychologie, Band: Motivation und Emotion* (pp. 115–213). Göttingen: Hogrefe.

Geppert, U., & Küster, U. (1983). The emergence of 'Wanting to do it oneself': A precursor of achievement motivation. *International Journal of Behavioral Development, 3*, 355–369.

Gitlin, L. N., Hauck, W. W., Winter, L., Dennis, M. P., & Schulz, R. (2006). Effect of an in-home occupational and physical therapy intervention on reducing mortality in functionally vulnerable older people: Preliminary findings. *Journal of the American Geriatrics Society, 54*, 950–955.

Gitlin, L. N., Winter, L., Dennis, M. P., Corcoran, M., Schinfeld, S., & Hauck, W. W. (2006). A randomized trial of a multicomponent home intervention to reduce functional difficulties in older adults. *Journal of the American Geriatrics Society, 54*, 809–816.

Hamilton, S. F. (1990). *Apprenticeship for adulthood: Preparing youth for the future.* New York, NY: Free Press.

Hamilton, S. F. (1994). Employment prospects as motivation for school achievement: Links and gaps between school and work in seven countries. In R. K. Silbereisen & E. Todt (Eds.), *Adolescence in context: The interplay of family, school, peers, and work in adjustment* (pp. 267–303). Cambridge, UK: Cambridge University Press.

Haase, C. M., Heckhausen, J., & Köller, O. (2008). Goal engagement in the school-to-work transition: Beneficial for all, particularly for girls. *Journal of Research on Adolescence, 17*, 671–698.

Haase, C. M., Heckhausen, J., & Wrosch, C. (2010). *Goal engagement, goal disengagement and their regulation across the lifespan: A comparison of three models of developmental regulation.* Manuscript submitted for publication, University of California, Berkeley.

Hall, N. C., Chipperfield, J. G., Heckhausen, J., & Perry, R. P. (2010). Control striving in older adults with serious health problems: A 9-year longitudinal study of survival, health, and well-being. *Psychology and Aging, 25*(2), 432–445.

Hamilton, S. F. (1994). Employment prospects as motivation for school achievement: Links and gaps between school and work in seven countries. In R. K. Silbereisen & E. Todt (Eds.), *Adolescence in context: The interplay of family, school, peers, and work in adjustment* (pp. 267–303). Cambridge: Cambridge University Press.

Harackiewicz, J. M., Barron, K. E., & Elliot, A. J. (1998). Rethinking achievement goals: When are they adaptive for college students and why? *Educational Psychology, 33*, 1–21.

Harackiewicz, J. M., & Elliot, A. J. (1993). Achievement goals and intrinsic motivation. *Journal of Personality and Social Psychology, 65*, 904–915.

Harlow, H. F. (1953). Mice, monkeys, men, and motives. *Psychological Review, 60*, 23–32.

Harlow, H. F., & Harlow, M. H. (1966). Learning how to care. *American Scientist, 54*, 244–272.

Harlow, H. F., & Zimmermann, R. (1959). Affectional responses in the infant monkey. *Science, 130*, 421–432.

Haynes, T. L., Heckhausen, J., Chipperfield, J. G., Perry, R. P., & Newall, N. E. (2009). Primary and secondary control strategies: Implications for health and well-being among older adults. *Journal of Social and ClinicalPsychology, 28*, 165–197.

Heckhausen, H. (1984a). Attributionsmuster für Leistungsergebnisse-individuelle Unterschiede, mögliche Arten und deren Genese. In F. E. Weinert & R. H. Kluwe (Eds.), *Metakognition, Motivation und Lernen* (pp. 133–164). Stuttgart: Kohlhammer.

Heckhausen, H. (1984b). Emergent achievement behavior: Some early developments. In J. G. Nicholls (Ed.), *The development of achievement motivation* (Vol. 3, pp. 1–32). Greenwich, CT: JAI Press.

Heckhausen, J. (1987a). Balancing for weaknesses and challenging developmental potential: A longitudinal study of mother-infant dyads in apprenticeship interactions. *Developmental Psychology, 23,* 762–770.

Heckhausen, J. (1987b). How do mothers know? Infants' chronological age or infants' performance as determinants of adaptation in maternal instruction? *Journal of Experimental Child Psychology, 43,* 212–226.

Heckhausen, H. (1991). *Motivation and action.* New York: Springer-Verlag.

Heckhausen, H., & Roelofsen, I. (1962). Anfänge und Entwicklung er Leistungsmotivation: (I) Im Wetteifer des Kleinkindes. *Psychologische Rundschau, 26,* 313–397.

Heckhausen, J. (1988). Becoming aware of one's competence in the second year: Developmental progression within the mother-child dyad. *International Journal of Behavioral Development, 11,* 305–326.

Heckhausen, J. (1990). Erwerb und Funktion normativer Vorstellungen über den Lebenslauf: Ein entwicklungspsychologischer Beitrag zur sozio-psychischen Konstruktion von Biographien [Acquisition and function of normative conceptions about the life course: A developmental psychology approach to the socio-psychological construction of biographies]. *Kölner Zeitschrift für Soziologie und Sozialpsychologie, 31,* 351–373.

Heckhausen, J. (1997). Developmental regulation across adulthood: Primary and secondary control of age-related challenges. *Developmental Psychology, 33,* 176–187.

Heckhausen, J. (1999). *Developmental regulation in adulthood: Age-normative and sociostructural constraints as adaptive challenges.* Cambridge: Cambridge University Press.

Heckhausen, J. (2000). Evolutionary perspectives on human motivation. *American Behavioral Scientist, 43,* 1015–1029.

Heckhausen, J. (2002). Developmental regulation of life-course transitions: A control theory approach. In L. Pulkkinen & A. Caspi (Eds.), *Paths to successful development: Personality in the life course* (pp. 257–280). Cambridge: Cambridge University Press.

Heckhausen, J. (2010). Globalization, social inequality, and individual agency in human development: Social change for better or worse? In R. K. Silbereisen & X. Chen (Eds.), *Social change and human development: Concepts and results* (pp. 148–163). Thousand Oaks, CA: Sage.

Heckhausen, J. (2007). The motivation-volition divide and its resolution in action-phase models of developmental regulation. *Research in Human Development, 4,* 163–180.

Heckhausen, J., & Chang, E. S. (2009). Can ambition help overcome social inequality in the transition to adulthood? Individual agency and societal opportunities in Germany and the United States. *Research in Human Development, 6,* 1–17.

Heckhausen, J., Dixon, R. A., & Baltes, P. B. (1989). Gains and losses in development throughout adulthood as perceived by different adult age groups. *Developmental Psychology, 25,* 109–121.

Heckhausen, J., & Farruggia, S. P. (2003). Developmental regulation across the life span: A control theory approach and implications for secondary education. *British Journal of Educational Psychology, Monograph Series II: Psychological Aspects of Education—Current Trends, 1,* 85–102.

Heckhausen, J., & Heckhausen, H. (2008a). *Motivation and action.* New York: Cambridge University Press.

Heckhausen, J., & Heckhausen, H. (2008b). Motivation and development. In J. Heckhausen & H. Heckhausen (Eds.), *Motivation and action* (pp. 384–443). New York: Cambridge University Press.

Heckhausen, J., & Heckhausen, H. (2008c). Motivation and development. In Heckhausen & H. Heckhausen (Eds.), *Motivation and action.* New York: Cambridge University Press.

Heckhausen, J., Lessard, J., & Chang, E. S. (2008, March). *When hopes for college don't work out right away: Predictors and consequences.* Paper presented at the Bienniel Meeting of the Society for Research on Adolescence, Chicago, IL.

Heckhausen, J., & Schulz, R. (1993). Optimization by selection and compensation: Balancing primary and secondary control in life span development. *International Journal of Behavioral Development, 16,* 287–303.

Heckhausen, J., & Schulz, R. (1995). A life-span theory of control. *Psychological Review, 102,* 284–304.

Heckhausen, J., & Tomasik, M. J. (2002). Get an apprenticeship before school is out: How German adolescents adjust vocational aspirations when getting close to a developmental deadline. *Journal of Vocational Behavior, 60,* 199–219.

Heckhausen, J., Wrosch, C., & Fleeson, W. (2001). Developmental regulation before and after a developmental deadline: The sample case of "biological clock" for child-bearing. *Psychology and Aging, 16*, 400–413.

Heckhausen, J., Wrosch, C., & Schulz, R. (2010). A motivational theory of life-span development. *Psychological Review, 117*, 32–60.

Heinz, W. R. (1999). *From education to work: Cross-national perspectives*. Cambridge, UK: Cambridge University Press.

Janos, O., & Papousek, H. (1977). Acquisition of appetition and palpebral conditioned reflexes by the same infants. *Early Human Development, 1*, 91–97.

Karabenick, J. D., & Heller, K. A. (1976). A developmental study of effort and ability attributions. *Developmental Psychology, 12*, 559–560.

Kaye, K. (1977b). Infants' effects upon their mothers' teaching strategies. In J. C. Glidewell (Ed.), *The social context of learning and development* (pp. 173-206). New York: Gardener.

Keller, H. (2000). Human parent-child relationships from an evolutionary perspective. *American Behavioral Scientist, 43*, 957–969.

Kuhl, J. (2008). Individual differences in self-regulation. In J. Heckhausen & H. Heckhausen (Eds.), *Motivation and action* (pp. 296–322). New York: Cambridge University Press.

Lang, F. R., & Heckhausen, J. (2006). Motivation and interpersonal regulation across adulthood: Managing the challenges and constraints of social contexts. In C. Hoare (Ed.), *Handbook of adult development and learning* (pp. 149–166). New York: Oxford University Press.

Lerner, R. M., & Busch-Rossnagel, N. A. (Eds.). (1981). *Individuals as producers of their development: A life-span perspective*. New York: Academic Press.

Lewis, M., & Goldberg, S. (1969). Perceptual-cognitive development in infancy: A generalized expectancy model as a function of the mother-infant interaction. *Merrill-Palmer Quarterly, 15*, 81–100.

Little, T. D. (1998). Sociocultural influences on the development of children's action-control beliefs. In J. Heckhausen & C. S. Dweck (Eds.), *Motivation and self-regulation across the life span* (pp. 281–315). New York: Cambridge University Press.

McClelland, D. C., Koestner, R., & Weinberger, J. (1989). How do self-attributed and implicit motives differ? *Psychological Review, 96*, 690–702.

McClelland, D. C., & Pilon, D. A. (1983). Sources of adult motives in patterns of parent behavior in early childhood. *Journal of Personality and Social Psychology, 44*, 564–574.

Menec, V. H., Chipperfield, J. G., & Perry, R. P. (1999). Self-perceptions of health: A prospective analysis of mortality, control, and health. *Journals of Gerontology: Series B: Psychological Sciences and Social Sciences, 54B*, 85–93.

Meyer, W.-U. (1973a). *Leistungsmotiv und Ursachenerklärung von Erfolg und Mißerfolg [Achievement motive and causal attribution of success and failure]*. Stuttgart: Klett.

Meyer, W. U., Mittag, W., & Engler, U. (1986). Some effects of praise and blame on perceived ability and affect. *Social Cognition, 4*, 293–308.

Miller, G. E., & Wrosch, C. (2007). You've gotta know when to fold'em: Goal disengagement and systemic inflammation in adolescence. *Psychological Sciences, 18*, 773–777.

Moller, A. C., & Elliot, A. J. (2006). The 2 x 2 achievement goal framework: An overview of empirical research. In A. V. Mitel (Ed.), *Focus on educational psychology research*. New York: Nova Science.

Nicholls, J. G. (1976). Effort is virtuous, but it's better to have ability: Evaluative responses to perceptions of effort and ability. *Journal of Personality and Social Psychology, 10*, 306–315).

Nicholls, J. G. (1984). Achievement motiation: Conceptions of ability, subjective experience, task choice, and performance. *Psychological Review, 91*, 328–346.

Nurmi, J.-E. (1992). Age differences in adult life goals, concerns, and their temporal extension: A life course approach to future-oriented motivation. *International Journal of Behavioral Development, 15*, 487–508.

Nurmi, J.-E., Salmela-Aro, K., & Koivisto, P. (2002). Goal importance and related achievement beliefs and emotions during the transition from vocational school to work: Antecedents and consequences. *Journal of Vocational Behavior, 60*, 241–261.

Pakenham, K. I. (1999). Adjustment to multiple sclerosis: Application of a stress and coping model. *Health Psychology, 18*, 383–392.

Papousek, H. (1967). Experimental studies of appetitional behavior in human newborns and infants. In H. W. Stevenson, E. H. Hess, & H. L. Rheingold (Eds.), *Early behavior: Comparative developmental approaches* (pp. 249–277). New York: Wiley & Sons.

Papousek, H., & Papousek, M. (1975). Cognitive aspects of preverbal social interaction between human infants and adults. *Ciba Foundation Symposium, 33*, 241–269.

Paul, R. (2001). The school-to-work transition: A cross-national perspective. *Journal of Economic Literature, 39*, 34–92.

Poulin, M., Haase, C. M., & Heckhausen, J. (2005). Engagement with and disengagement from goals across the life span: A comparison of two-process models of developmental regulation. In W. Greve, K. Rothermund, & D. Wentura (Eds.), *The adaptive self: Personal continuity and intentional self-development* (pp. 117–135). Göttingen/New York: Hogrefe/Huber Publishers.

Ramey, C., & Finkelstein, N. W. (1978). Contingent stimulation and infant competence. *Journal of Pediatric Psychology, 3*(2), 89–96.

Reif, M. (1970). Leistungsmotivation in Abhängigkeit vom Erziehungsverhalten der Mutter. *Unveröffentlichte Diplomarbeit, Psychologisches Institut der Ruhr-Universität Bochum.*

Rheinberg, F. (2008). Intrinsic motivation and flow. In J. Heckhausen & H. Heckhausen (Eds.), *Motivation and action* (pp. 323–383). New York: Cambridge University Press.

Riksen-Walraven, J. M. (1978). Effect of caregiver behavior on habituation rate and self-efficacy in infants. *International Journal of Behavioral Development, 1*, 105–130.

Roberts, B. W., & Caspi, A. (2003). The cumulative continuity model of personality development: Striking a balance between continuity and change in personality traits across the life course. In U. M. Staudinger & U. Lindenberger (Eds.), *Understanding human development: Dialogues with lifespan psychology* (pp. 183–214). Dordrecht, Netherlands: Kluwer Academic Publishers.

Roberts, B. W., & DelVecchio, W. F. (2000). The rank-order consistency of personality from childhood to old age: A quantitative review of longitudinal studies. *Psychological Bulletin, 126*, 3–25.

Rogoff, B., & Wertsch, J. V. (Eds.). (1984). *Children's learning in the "zone of proximal development". New Directions for Child Development.* San Francisco: Jersey Press.

Rothermund, K., & Brandtstädter, J. (2003). Coping with deficits and losses in later life: From compensatory action to accommodation. *Psychology and Aging, 18*, 896–905.

Rovee, C. K., & Fagan, J. W. (1976). Extended conditioning and 24-hour retention in infants. *Journal of Experimental Child Psychology, 21*, 1–11.

Schneider, K., & Dittrich, W. (1990). Evolution und Funktion von Emotionen [Evolution and the function of emotions]. In K. R. Scherer (Ed.), *Enzyklopädie der Psychologie: Psychologie der Emotionen* (pp. 41–114). Göttingen, Germany: Hogrefe.

Schulz, R., & Heckhausen, J. (1996). A life-span model of successful aging. *American Psychologist, 51*, 702–714.

Schulz, R., Wrosch, C., & Heckhausen, J. (2003). The life-span theory of control: Issues and evidence. In S. H. Zarit, L. I. Pearlin, & K. W. Schaie (Eds.), *Personal control in social and life course contexts: Societal impact on aging* (pp. 233–262). New York: Springer

Singh, D. (1970). Preference for bar-pressing to obtain reward over freeloading in rats and children. *Journal of Comparative and Physiological Psychology, 73*, 320–327.

Skinner, E. A. (1996). A guide to constructs of control. *Journal of Personality and Social Psychology, 71*, 549–570.

Sroufe, L. A. (1977). Wariness of strangers and the study of infant development. *Child Development, 48*(3), 731–746.

Sroufe, L. A., & Waters, E. (1976). The ontogenesis of smiling and laugher: A perspective on the organization of development in infancy. *Psychological Review, 83*, 173–189.

Stayton, D. F., Hogan, R., & Ainsworth, M. D. (1971). Infant obedience and maternal behavior: The origins of socialization reconsidered. *Child Development, 42*(4), 1057–1069.

Surber, C. F. (1980). The development of reversible operations in judgments of ability, effort and performance. *Child Development, 51*, 1018–1029.

Tomasik, M. J. (2003). Adjusting goal aspirations when getting close to a developmental deadline: The role of primary and secondary control strategies. Unpublished unveröffentlichte Diplomarbeit. Freie Universität Berlin.

Tomasik, M. J., Hardy, S., Haase, C. M., & Heckhausen, J. (2008). *Adjustment of vocational aspirations when approaching a developmental deadline.* Germany: University of Jena.

Tomasik, M. J., Hardy, S., Haase, C. M., & Heckhausen, J. (2009). Adaptive adjustment of vocational aspirations among German youths during the transition from school to work. *Journal of Vocational Behavior, 74*, 38–46.

Trevarthen, C. (Ed.). (1980). *The foundations of intersubjectivity: Development of interpersonal and cooperative understading in infants.* In D. Olson (Ed.), *The social foundations of language and thought: Essays in honor of J. S. Bruner* (pp. 316–342). New York; W. W. Norton.

Trevarthen, C., & Aitken, K. J. (2001). Infant intersubjectivity: Research, theory, and clinical applications. *Journal of Child Psychology and Psychiatry and Allied Disciplines, 42*, 3–48.

Trevarthen, C., & Hubley, P. (1978). Secondary intersubjectivity: Confidence, confiding, and acts of meaning in the first year. In Lock, A. (Ed.), *Action, gesture, and symbol: The emergence of language* (pp. 183–229). New York: Academic Press.

Trudewind, C. (1975). *Häusliche Umwelt und Motiventwicklung.* Göttingen: Hogrefe.

Wahl, H.-W., Becker, S., & Burmedi, D. (2004). The role of primary and secondary control in adaptation to age-related vision loss: A study of older adults with macular degeneration. *Psychology and Aging, 19,* 235–239.

Wahl, H.-W., Schilling, O., & Becker, S. (2007). Age-related macular degeneration and change in psychological control: Role of time since diagnosis and functional ability. *Journals of Gerontology Series B: Psychological Sciences and Social Sciences, 62,* P90–P97.

Watson, J. S. (1966). The development and generalization of contingency awareness in early infancy: Some hypotheses. *Merrill-Palmer Quarterly, 12,* 123–135.

Watson, J. S. (1972). Smiling, cooing, and "the Game". *Merrill-Palmer Quarterly, 18,* 55–76.

Watson, J. S., & Ramey, C. (1972). Reactions to response contingent stimulation in early infancy. *Merrill-Palmer Quarterly, 18,* 219–228.

Weisz, J. R. (1983). Can I control it? The pursuit of veridical answers across the life span. In P. B. Baltes & O. G. Brim (Eds.), *Life-span development and behavior* (Vol. 3, pp. 233–300). New York: Academic Press.

Welker, W. L. (1956). Some determinants of play and exploration in chimpanzees. *Journal of Comparative Physiological Psychology, 49,* 84–89.

White, R. W. (1959). Motivation reconsidered: The concept of competence. *Psychological Review, 66,* 297–333.

Wood, D. J., Bruner, J. S., & Ross, G. (1976). The role of tutoring in problem solving. *Journal of Child Psychology and Psychiatry, 17,* 89–100.

Wrosch, C., Bauer, I., Miller, G. E., & Lupien, S. (2007). Regret intensity, diurnal cortisol secretion, and physical health in older individuals: Evidence for directional effects and protective factors. *Psychology and Aging, 22,* 319–330.

Wrosch, C., & Heckhausen, J. (1999). Control processes before and after passing a developmental deadline: Activation and deactivation of intimate relationship goals. *Journal of Personality and Social Psychology, 77,* 415–427.

Wrosch, C., & Heckhausen, J. (2005). Being On-Time or Off-Time: Developmental Deadlines for Regulating One's Own Development. In A.-N. Perret-Clermont (Ed.), *Thinking time: A multidisciplinary perspective on time* (pp. 110–123). Ashland, OH: Hogrefe & Huber Publishers.

Wrosch, C., Heckhausen, J., & Lachman, M. E. (2000). Primary and secondary control strategies for managing health and financial stressacross adulthood. *Psychology and Aging, 15,* 387–399.

Wrosch, C., & Miller, G. E. (2009). Depressive symptoms can be useful: Self-regulatory and emotional benefits of dysphoric mood in adolescence. *Journal of Personality and Social Psychology, 96,* 1181–1190.

Wrosch, C., Scheier, M. F., Carver, C. S., & Schulz, R. (2003). The importance of goal disengagement in adaptive self-regulation: When giving up is beneficial *Self & Identity, 2,* 1–20.

Wrosch, C., Scheier, M. F., Miller, G. E., Schulz, R., & Carver, C. S. (2003). Adaptive self-regulation of unattainable goals: Goal disengagement, goal reengagement, and subjective well-being. *Personality and Social Psychology Bulletin, 29,* 1494–1508.

Wrosch, C., & Schulz, R. (2008). Health engagement control strategies and 2-year changes in older adults' physical health. *Psychological Science, 19,* 536–540.

Wrosch, C., Schulz, R., & Heckhausen, J. (2002). Health stresses and depressive symptomatology in the elderly: The importance of health engagement control strategies. *Health Psychology, 21*(4), 340–348.

Wrosch, C., Schulz, R., Miller, G. E., Lupien, S., & Dunne, E. (2007). Physical health problems, depressive mood and cortisol secretion in old age: Buffer effects of health engagement control strategies. *Health Psychology, 26,* 341–349.

EARLY PRECURSORS OF LATER HEALTH

9

Jacqui Smith and Frank J. Infurna

The proposal that development is a lifelong process from conception to death is fundamental to life course and life-span frameworks in psychology, sociology, economics, biodemography, epidemiology, biology, and the medical sciences. Theorists across disciplines agree that factors in each phase of life are the foundations or precursors for subsequent development and outcomes later in life. In accord with this basic proposition, there is also agreement that it is important to study lives over time and the intersection of multiple levels of influences (biological, social, and psychological). There is less consensus, however, about the relative salience of factors in each life phase, the mechanisms underlying their influence, and the potential to modify or intervene in developmental pathways and trajectories once they are in motion (Baltes, 1997; Elder & Giele, 2009).

In this chapter, we review research about psychological and social precursors of later health from a life course and life-span perspective. The chapter begins with an outline of central etiological and ontogenetic concepts and models derived from life course and life-span theory. We then review research on the effects on later health of five categories of factors. We consider two relatively stable individual difference characteristics, intelligence and personality, and three more dynamic psychosocial factors, namely socioeconomic status (SES) and socioeconomic position (SEP), social environment and social relationships, and non-normative life events and stressors. In separate sections, we review the association of each of these factors with three health outcomes—physical illness, mental health, and longevity. These outcomes were chosen to represent lifelong aspects of health and one end of the life course. In keeping with the life course and life-span perspectives, we report findings from longitudinal studies that have followed individuals for varying lengths of time, some for relatively short periods restricted to early, middle, or late life and others almost lifelong. We conclude with a discussion of research gaps and future directions.

Our review is certainly not comprehensive; for example, there is a growing literature in life course epidemiology on social and environmental determinants of health disparities and late-life health, which we do not cover (e.g., Antonucci & Jackson, 2009; Ben-Shlomo & Kuh, 2002; Berkman, 2009; Marmot, 2006). We also do not consider life course perspectives on the biogenetic and environmental determinants of health and longevity, the role of chance factors in the life course and health, and the inter-relationships between biological, psychological, and social factors (Alwin & Wray, 2005; Finch & Kirkwood, 2000; Mayer, 2009).

▓ CENTRAL CONCEPTS AND MODELS

The core concepts of the life course and life-span frameworks have evolved since the 1960s. At that time, researchers recognized that development and change is not restricted to specific age groups and that processes in all age periods, including old age, are dynamic and cumulative. In part, this recognition was stimulated by previous interest in tracing life biographies of individuals and families. Although there has always been substantial overlap in the central concepts and research principles outlined in life-span and life course theories, disciplines differ in thematic focus, especially in the weight placed on understanding individual versus social contextual processes. Whereas the life course framework takes a macro-level, population and societal view of time-related influences, life-span frameworks focus more on individual-level processes (e.g., Fuller-Iglesias, Smith, & Antonucci, 2009). This difference in emphasis contributes to different research questions.

Researchers who take a life course perspective, for example, ask about (1) the role of time and place in shaping trajectories and how these effects differ by birth cohort and historical period; (2) the accumulation of advantage/disadvantage over time; and (3) the effects of the linked lives of individuals in families, social networks, and communities. Major historical events (e.g., the Great Depression) have the power to transform societies and may differentially affect particular birth cohorts as a function of their age when the event occurred. Status disparities (e.g., in education, SES) are associated with a hierarchy of opportunities and potential exposure to risks that tend to accumulate over the life course. The principle of linked lives refers to the interconnectedness of individuals as they develop and age. Together, these concepts reflect multiple levels of contextual effects.

Researchers from a life-span perspective typically ask about individual differences in intraindividual change and variations in the plasticity (modifiability) of change in different processes (e.g., the aging brain or subjective well-being). Change can occur in different directions (growth, decline), metrics (quantity and quality), and at different rates. There is much variance in capacity of individuals to adapt and change as well as differences in the nature of change with age across functional domains. Life-span researchers develop methods to examine the potential and limits of this within-person variability or plasticity.

Theoretical Models of Trajectories Over Time

Theorists from both the life course and life-span perspectives strive to understand differential trajectories and pathways of lives over time. At first glance, the conceptualization of trajectories over time may appear as a relatively easy task. Each year adds (or subtracts) something to the life of an individual and there is an inevitable sequence of transitions through various age categories (e.g., childhood to adolescence to adulthood to old age). The complexity underlying trajectories become apparent when we ask if status in one period determines status in the next and whether this is true throughout life for all people and all aspects of life and functioning. Figure 9.1 illustrates various proposals about lifelong trajectories.

The first model (A) in Figure 9.1 portrays the idea that influences such as SES or social environment present in each life period primarily have immediate or proximal effects only. The idea is that once the factor is removed, or when the individual moves

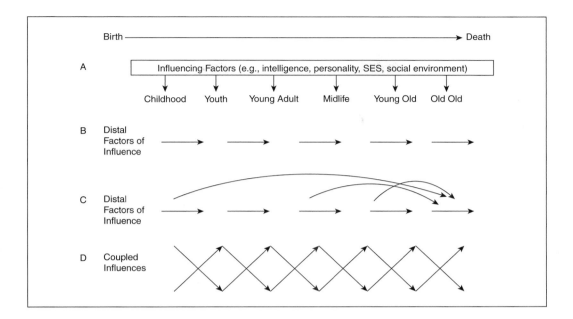

FIGURE 9.1 **Four models of the early life precursors and influences on health over the life course.**

into the next life phase, the effect (whether protective or a risk) on health declines and may return to baseline. All other models in Figure 9.1 illustrate variations of distal effects on later outcomes. The second trajectory (B) is a variation of the basic proposal that childhood factors (or fetal origins; Barker, 1997) establish a cumulative chain of risks or protective factors for all future outcomes. Does childhood education, for example, determine the trajectory of health and illness vulnerability for the rest of life and even set limits on longevity? Some researchers call such a precursor model a "sticky" or social trajectory. Using this model, researchers ask if life events or interventions can break the chain or alleviate the risks and whether there are critical periods in the life course when such interventions are most or least effective.

Trajectory C in Figure 9.1 is an expanded version of the early childhood precursor model. It includes the possibility of factors in early life interacting with those in later life periods thereby modifying the cumulative effects on future health outcomes. Trajectory D portrays the dynamic (transactional) coupling of psychosocial and health trajectories over time. Changes in health status over time affect individual factors (e.g., intelligence or social relationships), perhaps as much as each factor influences health. The extent and direction of dynamic coupling may change with age.

Although the trajectories illustrated in Figure 9.1 commence in childhood, they could commence at any period of the life course. Whereas much contemporary research, especially in the epidemiological literature, focuses on childhood precursors of health in old age, many researchers indeed consider the distal effects of influences associated with other life periods (e.g., adolescence, midlife). The time interval between "early" and "late" also differs with the health outcome of interest. In addition, some models propose latent factors or potential, which are dormant for

TABLE 9.1

Longitudinal Studies Across the Life Span				
Variable	Womb → Childhood	Childhood → Adolescence	Childhood → Midlife	Young Adult → Midlife
Intellectual and cognitive ability			1970 British Cohort study, Aberdeen children	SLS, Swedish 1969 conscription cohort
Personality				
Socioeconomic status	Aberdeen children	Aberdeen children	Dunedin, NLSY	
Social environment and social relationships	Aberdeen children	Aberdeen children, Environmental risk longitudinal twin study	Aberdeen children, Danish Cohort Study, Adverse Childhood Experiences Study	
Non-normative events	Dutch Famine Study, Chinese Famine Study	English Romanian Adoption		

Note. ACL = Americans' Changing Lives Study; BASE = Berlin Aging Study; EPESE = Established Populations for Epidemiologic Studies of

several decades (e.g., epigenetic models, effects of non-normative events) but emerge or increase in salience in old age. In part, the conceptual model selected also depends on the particular influencing factor examined.

The top line of Table 9.1 outlines the multiple time intervals and factors we examine in the chapter and gives examples of longitudinal studies for each factor. Table 9.2 summarizes the constructs typically investigated as precursors of later health over the various time intervals.

INTELLECTUAL AND COGNITIVE ABILITY

Intellectual capacity and functioning are measured traditionally by standardized intelligence tests developed for children and adults. Theoretical models of intelligence typically posit a general factor (g), which encompasses a number of lower level abilities (e.g., reasoning, spatial ability, perceptual speed, memory, verbal ability). Performance on tasks assessing these cognitive abilities (e.g., reaction time, verbal recall, logical reasoning, text comprehension) indicate individual differences in the capacity to learn, comprehend, make decisions, and adapt to changes in the environment. Measures of intelligence were primarily developed to predict early-life education outcomes and occupation selection. As such, individual differences in intelligence are one basis for entry into societal systems associated with different SES levels. As we describe in what follows, there is a longstanding literature on health disparities over the life course associated with SES. Generally, this literature does not consider the unique contribution of intelligence (Ryan & Smith, 2009). Several longitudinal studies, however, have begun to trace the long-term effects of intellectual ability on health and longevity after controls for SES indicators (i.e., Trajectory B in Figure 9.1).

Young Adult → Old Age	Life span: Childhood → Old Age	Midlife → Old Age	Young Old → Old Old
SLS	Nun study, Medical Research Council, UK HALS, Scottish Mental Health Survey, Aberdeen children	SLS	BASE
VA Normative Aging Study	Terman Study, Nun Study	VA Normative Aging Study, HRS, BLSA	Religious Orders Study
ACL, Whitehall Study	Aberdeen children	HRS, Medical Research Council	BASE, EPESE
ACL	Harvard Study, Terman Study	HRS	MacArthur Studies of Successful Aging
	Harvard Study, Dutch Famine Cohort Study, Chinese Famine Study		

the Elderly; HRS = Health and Retirement Study; NLSY = National Longitudinal Survey of Children/Youth; SLS = Seattle Longitudinal Study.

Intelligence and Physical Health

To date, few studies of health and aging in the United States have access to assessments of childhood intelligence or ability assessed during adulthood. One exception is the Seattle Longitudinal Study (SLS: Schaie, 2005), which sampled cohorts from a health maintenance organization and traced longitudinal change in intellectual functioning. Using the medical records of participants in the study, Schaie et al. (2005) have examined the reciprocal and dynamic associations between cognitive ability and health during adulthood: They find that a healthy body facilitates intellectual competence and higher intelligence facilitates the maintenance of health. For example, at each measurement occasion in the longitudinal study, participants with diagnosed cardiovascular diseases (CVD) show lower levels of intellectual functioning and, over time, those participants with more severe manifestations of this illness have a greater risk for cognitive decline. Similar findings are reported in the Berlin Aging Study (BASE), a longitudinal study of participants aged 70 to 100+ (Verhaeghen, Borchelt, & Smith, 2003). Schaie and colleagues also found that participants with higher intellectual ability were more likely to engage in healthy behaviors and to comprehend medication and treatment instructions.

Several large studies in the United Kingdom have traced institutional records of childhood assessments of intelligence and linked these data to adult health records or arranged long-term follow-ups with survivors. Much of this research has come from the nationally mandated Scottish Mental Surveys in 1932 and 1947 of all 11-year-old school children in Scotland (see Deary, Whiteman, Starr, Whalley, & Fox, 2004, for more detail). After compiling impressive data archives, Deary and colleagues (Batty, Deary, & Macintyre, 2007) found that higher intellectual ability at age 5 and 10 is associated with lower prevalence of smoking, obesity, alcoholism, and hypertension at age 30 and midlife and better lung function in old age. These findings are significant

TABLE 9.2

Variables Influencing Health at Different Points Across the Life Span				
Variable	Womb	Birth	Childhood	Adolescence
Intellectual and cognitive ability			Childhood IQ	Cognition
Personality			Conscientious, cheerfulness	
Socioeconomic status		Parent's education, social class at birth	Parent's education, social class at birth	
Social environment and social relationships	In utero alcohol exposure, maternal smoking, maternal nutrition	Birth weight, mother's characteristics	Family history of depression, alcohol abuse, family environment, parental divorce, number of siblings	Parental divorce
Non-normative events	Famine, malnutrition	Deprivation		

after controls for parental SES as well as individual's educational attainments and adult incomes. In the Swedish 1969 Conscription Cohort Study, cognitive ability measured at age 18 had an inverse and graded association with coronary heart disease, and remained significant after controls for poor childhood circumstances, behavioral factors in late adolescence, and adult social circumstances (Hemmingsson, Essen, Melin, Allebeck, & Lundberg, 2007).

Intelligence and Mental Health

Childhood cognitive abilities also show long-term associations with mental health. Two large cohort surveys, Scottish Mental Survey and British 1946 British Cohort Study, found that childhood cognitive ability was an independent predictor of lifetime psychiatric contact over 66 years of follow-up and related to lower prevalence of symptoms of anxiety and depression in adulthood (Walker, McConville, Hunter, Deary, & Whalley, 2002). Each standard deviation decrease in intelligence in the Scottish Mental Survey was associated with a 12% increase in the risk of psychiatric contact (Walker et al., 2002).

Several studies have shown that higher intelligence in early life is protective of cognitive impairment and decline in old age. Whalley et al. (2000), for example, examined the Scottish and Aberdeen cohorts of 1921 and found that early-onset dementia was not associated with lower cognitive ability measured at age 11, but in the Aberdeen sample, lower cognitive ability was associated with late-onset dementia. Participants with lower childhood mental ability in the 1921 and 1936 cohorts of the Scottish Mental Health Surveys experienced greater cognitive decline, whereas those with higher childhood mental ability showed improved performance (Bourne, Fox, Deary, & Whalley, 2007). These findings were replicated in two longitudinal

Young Adulthood	Midlife	Young Old	Old Old	Outcomes
Cognition	Cognition	Cognition	Cognition	Mortality, mental health, physical health
Conscientious, neuroticism, cynicism, emotional content, explanatory style	Cynicism, neuroticism, drinking, smoking, hostility, anxiety, worrying	Conscientious, neuroticism, internal negative affect, hostility, anxiety, worrying	Conscientious, neuroticism	Mortality, mental health, physical health
Education, household income, occupational prestige	Education, household income, occupational prestige	Education, household income, occupational prestige	Education, household income, occupational prestige	Mortality, mental health, physical health
Negative lifetime events	Marriage, social relationships, negative lifetime events, divorce	Social relationships, loneliness, negative lifetime events	Social relationships, loneliness, negative lifetime events, residential status	Mortality, mental health, physical health
Combat exposure, entry into WWII				Mortality, mental health, physical health

surveys in other countries. In the Amsterdam Study of the Elderly, premorbid intelligence predicted incident dementia better than education level, whereas in the Baltimore Longitudinal Study (BLSA), performance on the Benton Visual Retention Test (BVRT) was associated with the risk of Alzheimer's disease up to 15 years later (Kawas et al., 2003; Schmand, Smit, Geerlings, & Lindeboom, 1997).

Intelligence and Mortality

The data archives compiled by Deary and colleagues have also produced compelling evidence that childhood mental ability is predictive of survival into late adulthood (Deary, Batty, Pattie, & Gale, 2008; Deary et al., 2004). They found that childhood intelligence at age 11 is positively associated with survival at age 76, is negatively associated with mortality risk due to lung and stomach cancers, and accounts for later survival after accounting for other identified factors such as personality (Deary et al, 2004; 2008). With more than 55 years of follow-up, children in the lower half of the distribution for intelligence were more than twice as likely to die than those who scored in the upper half (Deary et al, 2008).

Studies of older adults find that higher level and slower rates of cognitive decline are predictive of survival and longevity (e.g., Alwin, McCammon, Wray, & Rodgers, 2008; Anstey, Luszcz, Giles, & Andrews, 2001; Bosworth, Schaie, & Willis, 1999; Maier & Smith, 1999). Lower levels of verbal meaning, spatial, reasoning ability, psychomotor speed, and cognitive impairment were associated with greater mortality risk (Bosworth et al., 1999). Evidence from the SLS suggests that decreases in cognitive performance are a better predictor of subsequent mortality than the level of cognitive performance (Bosworth et al., 1999). Further support from the UK Health and Lifestyle Survey (HALS) shows cognitive change versus cognitive levels as a better predictor of mortality; greater declines between T1 and T2 (5–7 years) on cognitive tasks like simple and choice reaction time mean and variability, memory and visual–spatial reasoning are associated with significantly increased risk of death from all causes up to 14 years later (Shipley, Der, Taylor, & Deary, 2007).

What Underlies the Predictive Effects of Intelligence?

Several factors have been identified as possible mediators between the association of cognitive ability and health outcomes, with educational attainment and adult socio-economic conditions being the primary candidates (see also Ryan & Smith, 2009). In several studies reviewed previously, education attenuated but did not eliminate the effect of childhood intelligence on health factors such as body mass index (BMI) and being overweight, along with unhealthy behaviors like smoking and alcohol consumption (Batty et al., 2007). However, in samples of older adults, education, occupational social class, and smoking did not attenuate the association of intellectual ability and mortality. Educational attainment may have a stronger effect in studies of the intelligence–health association in adulthood, but in longer-term relationships between childhood status and health in old age education appears not to be as critical. In part, this could be due to the effects of selective mortality in this proportion of the population. Correspondingly, SES, health behaviors (smoking, alcohol, and physical activity), and health status attenuated the association between cognition and mortality in the HALS (Shipley, Der, Taylor, & Deary, 2006).

An alternative interpretation is derived from medical and brain science literatures. This literature suggests that intellectual ability is associated with brain development, organization, integrity, and functional efficiency, and that engagement in intellectual activities across the life span contributes to higher brain reserves that buffer cognitive decline (Stern, 2002). It is proposed that individuals with a large cognitive reserve are able to delay normative cognitive decline and pathological brain dysfunction in late life.

PERSONALITY

Personality is the profile of basic tendencies (or dispositions) that predictably distinguish the preferences, feelings, and reactions of individuals across situations and over time. Contemporary research typically characterizes adult personality by five traits: openness to new experience, conscientiousness, extraversion, agreeableness, and neuroticism (e.g., Costa & McCrae, 1985). After age 30, these traits define relatively stable rank order differences between people across situations and over time. Despite this rank order stability, there are age-graded changes in the mean level of each trait and differences in the change directions of each trait (e.g., conscientiousness increases and neuroticism decreases; Caspi, Roberts, & Shiner, 2005). Adult personality is associated with childhood differences in temperament and facets of personality in childhood and old age show similar proximal associations with health (Ozer & Benet-Martinez, 2006; Roberts, Kuncel, Shiner, Caspi, & Goldberg, 2007). Similar to intelligence, Trajectory B in Figure 9.1 is a good representation of the long-term effects of personality on health, but Trajectories C and D also apply.

Personality and Physical Health

The personality traits conscientiousness and neuroticism have strong respective positive and negative associations with physical health and these effects appear to operate indirectly (e.g., via health behaviors or as modifiers of stress reactions). Two life-span prospective cohort studies, the Terman Life Cycle Study and Harvard Study of Adult Development, for example, found conscientiousness in childhood and adolescence is negatively associated with smoking and alcohol abuse in midlife to old age and positively associated with early adult adjustment and maturity of defenses, whereas neuroticism is positively associated with smoking, psychiatric usage, child character, and early adult adjustment (Friedman et al., 1995; Soldz & Vaillant, 1999). Similarly, men with high levels of hostility and anxiety in the VA Normative Aging Study showed increasing levels of physical symptoms from young adulthood to old age compared with male peers who were emotionally stable, educated, nonsmokers, and thin (Aldwin, Spiro, Levenson, & Cupertino, 2001). Additional findings from this longitudinal study indicate that worrying (neuroticism) was most strongly associated with incident coronary heart disease, whereas emotional stability is negatively associated with incidence of hypertension (Kubzansky et al., 1997; Spiro, Aldwin, Ward, & Mroczek, 1995).

Meta-analytic studies (e.g., Bogg & Roberts, 2004) confirm that facets of conscientiousness are negatively associated with risky health behaviors (e.g., excessive consumption of alcohol, risky driving) and that correlations between conscientiousness and health-related behaviors are stronger in childhood and young adulthood (30 years and younger) than in midlife and old age. Individual differences in the experience of negative emotions (e.g., anxiety, sadness) have long been suspected as exacerbating poor health outcomes and hostility is frequently an independent predictor of coronary heart disease (Miller, Smith, Turner, Guijarro, & Hallet, 1996; Smith, 2006).

Personality and Mental Health

Links among facets of personality and mental health, in particular neuroticism and conscientiousness, are seen from adolescence to later life. The Harvard Study of Adult Development found conscientiousness in college was negatively associated with depression, whereas neuroticism was positively associated with depression and psychiatric usage (Soldz & Vaillant, 1999). Similarly, in the Terman Life Cycle Study, mental health problems in adulthood were related to lack of mood permanency in childhood, lower levels of conscientiousness, global attributions, and a tendency to worry (Friedman et al., 1995; Peterson, Seligman, Yurko, Martin, & Friedman, 1998).

Wilson, Schneider, Arnold, Bienias, and Bennet (2007) in the Religious Orders Study found an association between conscientiousness and cognitive impairment, including Alzheimer's disease. High conscientiousness scores (90th percentile) were associated with an 89% reduction in Alzheimer's disease compared to low scores (10th percentile). In addition, conscientiousness was related to a decreased incidence of mild cognitive impairment and reduced cognitive decline.

Personality and Mortality

Conscientiousness, positive explanatory style, and extraversion are associated with reduced risk of mortality, whereas neuroticism, pessimistic explanatory style, cynicism, and hostility are associated with increased risk of mortality. In the Terman

Lifecycle Study, high ratings of conscientiousness at age 11 were associated with an increased chance of survival in middle to old age, whereas cheerfulness and neuroticism were negatively associated with survival (Friedman et al., 1993; 1995). In the Scottish Mental Survey, higher ratings of dependability (conscientiousness) at age 11 uniquely predicted mortality over 55 years of follow-up controlling for childhood intelligence (Deary et al., 2008). Furthermore, explanatory style is related to survival; a pessimistic explanatory style and a high level of global attributions are significantly associated with mortality, whereas positive emotional content has an inverse relationship with mortality risk (Danner, Snowdon, & Friesen, 2001; Peterson et al., 1998).

Neuroticism in young adulthood and midlife has been identified as a unique predictor of mortality in later life in several longitudinal studies. In the UK HALS, a one standard deviation increase in neuroticism is related to a 9% increased risk of mortality from all causes over 21 years after controls for other risk factors; this risk increases to 12% for CVD-related deaths (Shipley, Weiss, Der, Taylor, & Deary, 2007). This was replicated in an 18-year follow-up of participants in the BLSA (Terracciano, Löckenhoff, Zonderman, Ferrucci, & Costa, 2008). In the Religious Orders Study, Wilson and colleagues found that higher baseline neuroticism and negative affect increased an individual's mortality risk (Wilson, Mendes de Leon, Bienias, Evans, & Bennet, 2004). Individuals scoring in the 90th percentile for neuroticism had a doubled risk for mortality (Wilson et al., 2004). Conversely, several of these studies revealed conscientiousness and extraversion to be protective of death (Shipley, Weiss, Der, Taylor, & Deary, 2007; Terracciano et al., 2008; Wilson et al., 2004). Men with high average levels *and* increasing levels of neuroticism in the VA Normative Aging Study had lower chances of survival than those with low baseline levels of neuroticism (Mroczek & Spiro, 2007). These findings from Mroczek and Spiro (2007) demonstrate that the direction of change in personality is equally important as baseline level as a predictor of mortality in later life.

What Underlies the Predictive Effects of Personality?

Several mechanisms have been identified as mediating the personality–health relationship and various distal and dynamic models illustrated in Table 9.2 apply. Caspi et al. (2005), for example, outlined three distinct processes: (1) personality differences may be related to pathogenesis, mechanisms that promote disease, such as greater reactivity in response to stressful experiences, (2) associated with health-promoting or health-damaging behaviors, and (3) they may be related to reactions to illness. In addition, these authors describe how facets of disagreeableness may be most directly linked to disease processes. Facets of low conscientiousness may be more clearly implicated in health-damaging behaviors and facets of neuroticism may contribute to ill health by shaping reactions to illness (Caspi et al., 2005). Smith (2006) suggests four models: That personality is linked to health (1) indirectly via health behavior, (2) indirectly as a modifier of stress that is manifested in a physiological response, (3) bidirectionally, and (4) directly through underlying genetic mechanisms that predispose individuals to particular levels of physiological responsiveness. In part, these models overlap conceptually with those illustrated in Figure 9.1 but do not place the associations in a life course framework.

In midlife and old age, mechanisms underlying specific personality trait effects on health are likely to interact with other personality traits (e.g., conscientiousness paired with neuroticism) and other factors, such as SES, marital status, cognitive status, and social support. Wilson et al. (2004), for example, found the mortality risk for individuals with high levels of neuroticism was halved if they also reported a high conscientiousness score. Furthermore, older individuals who reported being cognitively, socially, and physically engaged in life had a reduced risk of mortality, despite high levels of neuroticism. In addition, in the HALS, occupational social class, education, smoking status, alcohol consumption, physical activity, forced expiratory volume, blood pressure, and BMI completely attenuated the neuroticism–mortality association (Shipley, Weiss, et al., 2007). These findings provide support for bidirectional and dynamic models of predictive associations in later health.

SOCIOECONOMIC STATUS

SES and SEP are associated with health outcomes at all ages of the life course (e.g., Adler, Boyce, Chesney, Folkman, & Syme, 1993; Marmot, 2006). These inequalities in health associated with SES translate into differential prevalence rates, age at illness onset, levels of illness severity, rates of recovery, and disease progression (chronicity). Compared to high SES individuals, those with lower SES experience a higher proportion of their lifetime in poor health (for review, see Ertel, Glymour, & Berkman, 2009). Measures of SES include education, household income, occupational prestige, and parents' occupation and social class. It is important to note that not all measures of SES are equal nor do all measures have similar effects across the life span. For instance, education and income are indicators for different types of resources that have unique direct and indirect effects on different aspects of health (Lantz et al., 2001). With increases in education, individuals gain access to opportunities to earn a higher income and enter higher status occupations. The higher educated also accrue higher levels of brain reserve, knowledge, and cognitive fitness that may translate into health protective effects especially with regard to late-life dementia (e.g., Stern, 2002). Income, on the other hand, is not always highly correlated with education, but is associated with access to health-related resources, better housing, food, and social support (Lantz et al., 2001). Differential effects of SES are observed in childhood and old age, providing supportive evidence for the various proximal, distal, and dynamic models outlined in Figure 9.1.

SES and Physical Health

Individual and neighborhood income, education, and parents' social class are all proximal correlates of physical health at all ages. In addition, childhood social class and circumstances are known to have distal causal effects on later health. Childhood poverty, for example, is related to higher levels of chronic HPA (hypothalamic–pituitary–adrenocortical) axis activity (Evans & Kim, 2007). Living in poor SES conditions, coupled with risky family environment can lead to increases in C-reactive protein and metabolic functioning at later ages (Lehman, Taylor, Kiefe, & Seeman, 2005; Taylor, Lehman, Iefe, & Seeman, 2006). In addition, social class at birth is related to the development of cardiovascular risk factors in young adulthood and the development of coronary heart disease and associated illnesses in midlife (Ertel et al., 2009; Lawlor et al., 2005a; Melchior, Moffitt, Milne, Poulton, & Caspi, 2007).

In some instances, a low childhood socioeconomic circumstance has long-lasting negative influences on adult health, despite upward mobility in the socioeconomic hierarchy as an adult (Poulton et al., 2002). This may indicate lifestyle factors as mediating mechanisms influencing health. Despite such a poor outlook, findings from the Harvard Study of Adult Development and Inner City Cohort show that the health decline of the 25 core-city men who completed 16 or more years of education was no more rapid than that of the college men, regardless of greater differences in parental social class, prestige of college, intelligence test scores, current income, and job status (Vaillant & Mukamal, 2001).

With the transition from childhood to adulthood, health inequalities associated with SES are larger and SES has a greater proximal effect on health (House, Lantz, & Herd, 2005). Empirical evidence has accumulated suggesting a hierarchical health gradient with SES, the so-called social gradient of health, which characterizes adult populations: Every level increase in SES is associated with lower levels of morbidity and mortality (Adler et al., 1993; Marmot, 2006). Supporting evidence comes from the Americans' Changing Lives (ACL), the Whitehall studies, the Health and Retirement Study (HRS), and multiple population surveys of health worldwide. House et al. (2005), for example, found a gradient for compression of morbidity: Individuals possessing the highest income and education had the greatest compression of morbidity, followed by midrange income and education and low income and education groups. Further work from the ACL study shows that education and income depict differential effects on the onset and progression of functional limitations. Several articles show education is a better predictor of onset of functional limitations and health conditions, whereas income is more consequential for the progression and course of health problems (Herd, Goesling, & House, 2007; House et al., 2005). Individuals with high income versus low income are most likely to improve if they have a functional limitation and least likely to cascade into disability (Herd et al., 2007). In addition, individuals with low education and low income are significantly more likely to report severe or moderate functional limitations and lower levels of self-reported health. A similar trend is seen in old age where men and women with less than a high school education had a 1.65 and 1.70 relative risk of incident disability, respectively (Melzer, Izmirlian, Leveille, & Guralnik, 2001).

These findings coupled with results from the Harvard Study of Adult Development and Inner City Cohort illustrate the notion that education and income provide different resources (Vaillant & Mukamal, 2001). SES has the potential to have cumulative disadvantageous (distal) effects across the life span, but educational attainment can buffer the effects of low income on an individuals' health trajectory in later life. Data from the Aberdeen Cohort Study found, for example, that educational attainment attenuated the effect of low childhood SES on cardiovascular risk factors in adulthood (Lawlor et al., 2005a).

SES and Mental Health

SES at various points across the life course has similar consequential effects on mental health outcomes. Family income, parents' education and occupation, in addition to length of life in poverty, are associated with long-term mental health outcomes. Parents' education and social class have proximal effects on childhood cognitive development and intelligence at ages 7, 9, and 11 (Lawlor et al., 2005b). Distal or lasting effects of family income are seen in mental health status in childhood and adulthood. Using data from the National Longitudinal Survey of Children/Youth (NLSY), Korenman, Miller, and Sjaastad (1995) compared respondents living in short-term poverty versus long-term poverty (13 years) and found children in long-term poverty have significantly lower cognitive scores than children living in short-term poverty. Not only does living in poverty have detrimental effects on mental health development but also the length of time lived in poverty may be a stronger predictor. Similarly, parents' education and social class is related to the development of depressive symptoms, cynical hostility, hopelessness, and anxiety in adulthood and midlife (Miech, Caspi, Moffitt, Wright, & Silva, 1999).

Home environment and conduct in adolescence play influential roles in mediating and altering the distal effects poverty has on mental health. The introduction of home environment into the model fit by Korenman et al. (1995) attenuated the effects of long-term poverty on cognition. Similarly, childhood maltreatment (home environment) contributed to the relationship between childhood SES and cardiovascular risk factors at age 32 in the Dunedin Multidisciplinary Health and Development (DMHD) study (Melchior et al., 2007). Behavioral and mental health problems associated with SES attenuated the positive features such as education. This pattern of findings is also evident in the adult epidemiological literature on substance abuse and health.

SES and Mortality

SES not only contributes to physical and mental health but also to greater risks of mortality. Income and educational attainment in childhood and old age have similar distal casual effects on mortality (Bassuk, Berkman, & Amick, 2002; Kuh, Hardy, Langenberg, Richards, & Wadsworth, 2002). In a prospective cohort study of nearly 800,000 people in Norway, childhood SEP significantly predicted deaths from coronary heart disease, stomach and lung cancer in men, and in women similar effects were found for lung cancer, cervical cancer, and coronary heart disease (Næss, Strand, & Smith, 2007). Similarly, parents' occupation and social class during childhood are associated with deaths from CVD and mortality at age 55 (Kuh et al., 2002; Smith & Hart, 2002).

As discussed in relation to physical health, a gradient between income/occupation and mortality has been shown (Adler et al., 1993; Marmot, 2006). The ACL and Whitehall studies have shown empirical support for the income–mortality gradient. In the ACL study, when compared to the highest income group, the risk of mortality was more than doubled for midrange and lowest income groups (Lantz, House, Mero, & Williams, 2005). Furthermore, in the Whitehall Study, lower employment grade was associated with higher mortality risk and this applied to many, although not all causes of death (Marmot, 2006; Smith, Shipley, & Rose, 1990). In a sample of adults aged 65 and older, three measures of SES (education, household income, and occupational prestige) were associated with mortality in men, but only income was significant for women (Bassuk et al., 2002).

What Underlies the Predictive Effects of SES for Later Health?

Our cursory examination of the literature supports various models of distal, proximal, and dynamic effects of SES on health across the life span. It appears that the distal precursory effects of SES operate via multiple pathways, including biological and behavior responses, psychosocial characteristics, education and the home environment (Adler et al., 1993; Korenman et al., 1995; Lantz et al., 2005; Lawlor et al., 2005a). In old age, SES may have specific proximal effects such as through health behaviors, physical activity, and social ties (Bassuk et al., 2002).

Possible mechanisms driving the SES-health causal effects models include risky health behaviors and exposure to traumatic life events. Several studies, including the ACL and Established Populations for Epidemiologic Studies of the Elderly (EPESE) have examined these possible mechanisms. The ACL study found that major health risk behaviors like smoking, alcohol consumption, BMI, and physical activity only explain a modest proportion of the relationship and are not a dominating mediating mechanism between socioeconomic disparities and functional health/limitations and mortality (Lantz et al., 2001). In contrast, the association between education and mortality was attenuated by health behaviors (smoking, alcohol, BMI, number of social ties, physical activity, and regular health care provider) in the Iowa (men and women) and East Boston (men only) cohorts of the EPESE studies (Bassuk et al., 2002). Differences may be due to sample composition: the ACL is composed of individuals aged 25 and older, whereas the EPESE consists of older adults aged 65 and older.

Stress is also an important mechanism driving the SES–health relationship. Stressful life events like financial stress, parental stress, and negative life events are associated with the socioeconomic disparities in relation to health (Lantz et al., 2005; Pearlin, Lieberman, Menaghan, & Mullan, 1981). Living in poverty is stressful and doing so for multiple years can have detrimental cumulative effects on development and health. Risky family environments characterized by conflict and aggression and a cold, unsupportive, or neglectful home or marriage can have direct and indirect effects on health (Cohen, 2004; Kiecolt-Glaser & Newton, 2001; Repetti, Taylor, & Seeman, 2002).

◼ SOCIAL ENVIRONMENT AND SOCIAL RELATIONSHIPS

The social world of individuals plays a critical role in developmental health outcomes across the life span. A myriad of social influences on health have been investigated in multiple disciplines, including constructs ranging from the prenatal and family environment, neighborhoods, social networks and support, to negative life events such as parental loss, divorce, or abuse. Interest in these topics were spurred by developmental and sociological research throughout the 20th century on the effects of impoverished environments, social interaction, socialization, and social isolation (for reviews, see Antonucci, 2001; Berkman, Glass, Brissette, & Seeman, 2000; Cohen, 2004; House, Landis, & Umberson, 1988).

Social Factors and Physical Health

An extensive literature includes reports of positive and negative bidirectional physical health associations with social environments and social relationships in all phases of the life course as well as very long-term distal effects of childhood adversity (i.e. Trajectories B, C, and D in Figure 9.1). In the Coronary Artery Risk Development in

Young Adults (CARDIA) study, for example, a risky family environment characterized by conflict, aggression, and neglect in childhood was associated with higher
levels of C-reactive protein and metabolic functioning in adulthood (Lehman et al.,
2005; Repetti et al., 2002; Taylor et al., 2006). A warm childhood environment is a
significant predictor of physical health at age 65, whereas a risky family environment leads to accumulated risks for mental health disorders, major chronic diseases,
and early mortality (Repetti et al., 2002; Vaillant & Vaillant, 1990). The experience of
negative events in childhood like physical or emotional abuse, violence, and parental divorce are positively related to unhealthy behaviors and poor physical health
in midlife (Felitti et al., 1998; Tucker et al., 1997). Individuals who experienced four
or more categories of adverse childhood experiences compared to those who experienced none had a 4- to 12-fold increase in health risks for alcoholism, drug abuse,
depression, and suicide attempt, in addition to a two to fourfold increase in smoking,
poor self-rated health, ischemic heart disease, cancer, lung and liver disease (Felitti
et al., 1998). Lastly, social isolation in childhood is associated with multiple risk factors for CVD in adulthood, including being overweight and elevated blood pressure
and total cholesterol (Caspi, Harrington, Moffitt, Milne, & Poulton, 2003).

The positive physical health effect experienced by adults who perceive that they
are supported socially and emotionally are well documented (e.g., Antonucci, 2001;
Cohen, 2004; Uchino, Cacioppo, & Kiecolt-Glaser, 1996). It is widely reported, for
example, that married individuals have better health outcomes than those who are
single, divorced, or separated. Some researchers, however, caution that marriage and
social support have positive and negative consequences (Rook, 1987). Negative effects
arise, for example, if there is conflict or strain in the personal relationship (DeLongis
& Lehman, 1989) or if the recipient considers offers of support to be interfering or
critical, or if the support offered indicates that the giver perceives the intended recipient to be incompetent (Kessler, Price, & Wortman, 1985). A stressful marital relationship usually harms the health of both partners over time, but especially wives
(Kiecolt-Glaser & Newton, 2001). Poor marital quality and declines in satisfaction
have been shown to predict increased risk of angina and greater reported physical illness been related to declines in reported health status (Levenson & Gottman,
1985). Poor marital quality and chronic family stress associated with caring for family
members with Alzheimer's disease have also been shown to predict poor immune
function (Kiecolt-Glaser, Dyer, & Shuttleworth, 1988). Negative social relationships
can add wear and tear to the body (Seeman, Singer, Ryff, Dienburg Love, & Levy-
Storms, 2002), whereas social isolation and low frequency of contact leads to greater
risks for developing coronary artery disease, poor physical functioning, and health
status (Bosworth, & Schaie, 1997; Orth-Gomér, Rosengren, & Wilhelmsen, 1993).
Furthermore, social ties can serve as models for "risky" or "unhealthful" behaviors.
Individuals who adopt the less-healthy lifestyle of their social partners and social
networks place their own health at risk (Christakis & Fowler, 2007).

Social Factors and Mental Health

Environmental exposures as early as those in the womb contribute to distal and
proximal influences on mental health in later life. Prenatal exposure to alcohol,
smoking, or cocaine are associated with lower cognitive ability in childhood (Bennett,
Bendersky, & Lewis, 2008) and the risk of developing early and late-onset alcohol

disorders, psychological distress, and somatic distress in young adulthood (Cheung, 2002). Parents who partake in such unhealthy behaviors during pregnancy are more likely to be younger, live in poorer conditions, have poor spousal attributes, and themselves exhibit antisocial behavior and depression (Moffitt & E-Risk Study Team, 2002).

Another indicator of prenatal environment is birth weight. Gestational age and birth weight are inversely related to psychological distress in adulthood and midlife (Cheung, 2002; Wiles, Peters, Leon, & Lewis, 2005). The Aberdeen Birth Cohort Study found that even if born at full term, a birth weight below 5.5 pounds increases the odds of psychological distress in later life (Wiles et al., 2005). Furthermore, empirical studies comparing twins and singletons have shown that birth weight predicts IQ differences; twins within a family with singleton children have lower IQ scores, which could be due to a reduced prenatal growth period and shorter gestations (Ronalds, De Stavola, & Leon, 2005).

Beyond the womb and into childhood, familial influences like maternal age, exposure to parental alcoholism or depression, and the experience of parental divorce influence mental health outcomes. Offspring of mothers 18 years of age and younger are more likely to exhibit disturbed psychological behavior, smoke regularly, consume alcohol, and report poorer levels of school performance, cognitive scores, and reading ability in childhood and into adolescence (Moffitt & E-Risk Study Team, 2002; Shaw, Lawlor, & Najman, 2006). Data from the NLSY reveal that mother's IQ is significantly associated with child's birth weight, which is significantly associated with the child's IQ and the association was attenuated by up to two-thirds after taking into account mother's IQ (Deary, Der, & Shenkin, 2005). Poor familial and home environments have distal consequential effects on mental health. Exposure to familial alcoholism and depression in childhood is associated with the development of alcoholism, depression, sociopathy, and a higher death rate in midlife and old age (Cui & Vaillant, 1996; Rutter & Silberg, 2002). Negative family events such as parental divorce, death of a loved one, job loss, illness, or sexual, physical, or emotional abuse are associated with symptoms of anxiety, depression, and higher mental health scores in midlife and old age (Cui & Vaillant, 1996; Edwards, Holden, Felitti, & Anda, 2003).

In midlife and old age, a strong social network has strong proximal effects on cognitive functioning and psychological well-being. The MacArthur Studies of Successful Aging found that individuals with higher levels of emotional support had better cognitive performance at baseline and 7.5 years later (Seeman, Lusignolo, Albert, & Berkman, 2001). Furthermore, the ACL Study revealed better supportive relationships to be associated with lower levels of psychological distress, whereas strained relationships were associated with higher distress (Umberson, Chen, House, Hopkins, & Slaten, 1996). Fratiglioni, Paillard-Borg, and Winblad (2004) found that active social participation and contact with a supportive social network may protect against cognitive decline to the level of dementia.

Social Factors and Mortality

Across the life course, exposure to negative social environments and social relationships such as parental divorce and a poor social network composition contribute to increased risks for mortality. In the Terman Life Cycle Study, for example, children whose parents divorced before the age of 21 were at a greater risk of mortality

(Friedman et al., 1995). In addition to parental divorce, the Terman Life Cycle Study found that consistently married people lived longer than those who experience marital breakup, in addition to history of divorce being associated with greater risk of mortality, despite remarriage. No mortality differences were seen between individuals who did not marry and those who were consistently married. In old age, social network composition has more proximal effects on longevity. Numerous studies have documented the relationship between social integration and mortality. Poor social network composition, such as social isolation, loneliness, low frequency of contact, and low levels of social integration are associated with increased risk of mortality (for reviews, see Berkman et al., 2000; House et al., 1988).

What Underlies the Predictive Effects of Social Factors?

Families, spouses, and to a lesser extent friends share lifestyles, environments, and exposure to life events. Despite the overall positive health effects of social connection (compared to social isolation), social environments and social relationships can also be detrimental (e.g., especially if the relationship is strained, aspects of health are contagious, or the social group encourages risky health behavior such as lack of exercise, poor eating habits, smoking, and substance abuse). Indeed, recent theories about the social environmental-health relationship suggest psychophysiological mechanisms and indirect effects through health-related behaviors (Cohen, 2004; House et al., 1988; Kiecolt-Glaser & Newton, 2001).

Childhood and adult social environments have similar positive and negative effects on later health. A poor childhood environment has both distal and proximal causal effects on later health. The home environment is important for the development of emotional regulation, social skills, and the ability of the child to mount a successful physiologic/neuroendocrine and/or behavioral response to stress and acquire appropriate emotional and behavioral self-regulatory skills (Berg, Smith, Henry, & Pearce, 2007; Repetti et al., 2002). A poor environment disrupts the child's ability to do so, leading to poor outcomes later in life. In addition, negative life events like parental divorce may lead to unhealthy behaviors (alcohol use, smoking), divorce in midlife, and a greater risk for mortality, whereas parental smoking and alcohol use in utero can have proximal effects in adolescence and lasting effects into adulthood.

A strong social network in adulthood may give individuals encouragement to perform health-promoting behaviors, facilitate coping with life stressors, sustain neuroendocrine functioning, and strengthen the immune system while decreasing allostatic load (Berkman et al., 2000; Seeman et al., 2002; Uchino et al., 1996). Marriage as such provides many protective resources (e.g. Waldron, Hughes, & Brooks, 1996): It is proposed that married individuals are healthier because their spouse monitors their health behaviors, provides care when needed, and acts as a social control by discouraging risky behaviors. Married persons also have access to more material resources than those in single households and a spouse is expected to be a salient source of social and emotional support in times of stress (Antonucci, 2001). Despite the existence of negative aspects associated with marriage, it is argued nevertheless that social isolation and the absence of social support expose an individual to even greater stress (e.g., Berkman et al., 2000; House et al., 1988).

In very old age, social support appears to have more proximal causal effects, in particular due to social losses (e.g., death of spouse, siblings, lifelong friends, and in some cases children). Adapting to the loss of one's close family and social network in late life is a great challenge for many of the very old.

NON-NORMATIVE FACTORS

Non-normative events throughout the life span greatly influence health outcomes in later life. We selected several illustrative non-normative events, namely environmental insults (famine), deprivation in childhood, poor childhood health, and world/cultural events like war. Our specific reason for including this category of factors to consider is the intriguing finding that the effects of non-normative events frequently remain dormant for many years or decades but re-emerge in subsequent life periods of extreme stress or in old age.

Famine has proximal, distal, and dormant effects on later life health. Famine indirectly effects in utero development via the mother's diet or nutrition. Results from the Danish Famine Study reveal that famine exposure during the first 3 months of gestation leads to a greater risk for coronary heart disease, disturbed blood coagulation, glucose intolerance, increased stress responsiveness, obesity, and poorer health ratings in adulthood (Roseboom et al., 2003; Roseboom, de Rooij, & Painter, 2006). In addition, the birth cohort conceived during the peak of the Danish famine exhibited a significant, twofold increased risk of schizophrenia (Susser, Brown, & Matte, 2000). Similarly, the Chinese Famine Study found that individuals conceived or born during famine years were at a greater risk of developing schizophrenia in adulthood and at greater risk of mortality (St. Clair et al., 2005). The Fetal Origins Hypothesis argues that exposure to famine in the womb leads to receipt of fewer nutrients, leading to the child adapting biologically to the poor environment, causing a lower birth weight (Barker, 1997). Biological adaptations in the womb may result in the child being poorly suited for the environment in childhood and at greater risk of poorer health in adulthood.

Early life deprivation has proximal consequential effects on cognitive development in childhood and adolescence. Researchers from the Romanian Adoption Study reported in a slew of articles that early life deprivation is related to poor cognitive development in childhood. At age 4, children that came to the United Kingdom from Romania prior to the age of 6 months had nearly caught up cognitively to the level of the UK children controls (Rutter & ERA Study team, 1998). Despite this catch-up, at age 6 the late-placed Romanian children (post 6 months) exhibited lower cognitive scores and general developmental impairment compared with earlier adopted Romanian children (O'Connor et al., 2000). In addition, at age 6 there was a linear association between length of deprivation and cognitive impairment; 15.4% of the Romanian adoptees compared to 2% of the UK adoptees had cognitive impairment (Rutter, O'Connor, & ERA Study team, 2004). Upon further follow-up, marked adverse effects persisted at age 11 for many of the children who were more than 6 months of age upon arrival into the United Kingdom; however, some catch-up was observed between ages 6 and 11, but only in the bottom 15% of the sample (Beckett et al., 2006).

Poor childhood health has substantial effects on later health. A module in the third wave of the HRS found poor childhood health characterized by extended stays in the hospital, time missed from school because of illness or restriction from sports activity increased the chance of morbidity in later life (cancer, CVD, arthritis; Blackwell, Hayward, & Crimmins, 2001). Similarly, poor childhood health, coupled with a low income environment is associated with an increased risk trajectory for heart attacks (O'Rand & Hamil-Luker, 2005). Finally, childhood serious illness is associated with lower cognitive abilities at age 8 and mortality between ages 9 and 54 (Kuh et al., 2002).

World events such as war alter the course of development. In addition to war resulting in a famine, exposure to and entry into World War II (WWII) has greatly influenced the developmental health outcomes of men. Men with higher combat exposure reported a greater number of posttraumatic stress disorder symptoms and poorer physical health up to 40 years later (Lee, Vaillant, Torrey, & Elder, 1995). In the Stanford-Terman sample, Elder, Shanahan, and Clipp (1994) found that time of entry into WWII significantly affected health outcomes in later life. Individuals with late entry into WWII had a pattern of physical decline (constant poor health, sporadic health problems) and a greater risk of negative trajectories of physical health and mortality (Elder et al., 1994). Some of this effect may be accounted for in part because of work-life disadvantages. Most of the late entries into WWII were married or had a steady job and routine in life, but the onset of the war disrupts it, leading to a different trajectory and outcome in life. Interesting enough, individuals with early entry into the war reported more positive experiences of the war and showed a larger gain in psychological strength and health from adolescence to midlife than did nonveterans (Elder et al., 1994). For some, more military service turned them toward a brighter future, even as it produced a tragic side for others in damaged health or death.

FUTURE DIRECTIONS IN THE STUDY OF PRECURSORS OF LATER HEALTH

In an article in *Science* in 1977, Engel argued for a new perspective on health that evaluated multiple social and psychological factors contributing to illness and being identified as a patient, in addition to biological factors. He acknowledged the difficulties involved in determining the systemic and dynamic nature of a biopsychosocial model but argued that such an approach would eventually lead to understanding why some individuals are more at risk for poor health outcomes than others. Since this seminal article, there have been considerable advances in the investigation of biopsychosocial factors across the life course that contribute to health and longevity, in particular the effects of socioeconomic and racial disparities, marital status, social integration, risky social environments, and individual differences in intelligence and personality. Nevertheless, there remains much to do.

To conclude our review, we outline some of the possible directions that future researchers might take. In particular, we highlight the need for theory development within a life-span and life course perspective, strategies for harvesting archival data and extending existing longitudinal studies, and the application of new techniques in longitudinal data modeling.

To date, attempts to elucidate antecedent factors, possible patterns of trajectories and mechanisms are limited. An ever increasing amount of research focuses on the important role of socioeconomic factors in health disparities across the life course and global comparisons of this association. Indeed, most theory development about the nature of trajectories is derived from researchers interested in SES–health associations. This research is, of course, critical for policy advice and intervention to ensure to the health of nations (Berkman, 2009; Marmot, 2006).

The documentation of cross-national, and cross-decade comparisons of the SES–health association assists in understanding the influence of macro-level societal, cultural, and ecological factors, but what remains is the critical task of understanding the mechanisms at the individual level (behavioral and physiological) and the search for a broader range of precursors across the life course. In addition, information about subgroup differences in vulnerability given their similar exposure to risk in early life (e.g., low education, low income) is often not visible in population comparisons. The identification of subgroups and individuals who defy expectations and risks and live a relatively long healthy life might be a future step that advances the field.

A related aspect that became evident as we delved into the literature is the relatively narrow set of antecedent factors that are currently driving research on early precursors of later health. Future efforts would benefit greatly from exchanges about concepts across disciplinary boundaries, in particular about the etiology of disease and the functions of psychological resources such as intelligence and personality. The disease process may take decades before it manifests as a diagnosed illness and there may be multiple underlying pathways that contribute to a defined onset point (i.e., diagnosis). A clearer understanding of the accumulation and trajectories of these health-related processes would assist in generating hypotheses about the mediational and moderating roles of social, environmental, and psychological factors. In addition, as Smith (2006) comments, the quest to find individual risk factors (e.g., education, social network size, child abuse) may be misguided. Instead, future research could focus on combinations of factors and their interactions. It will also be important to clarify the ways that intelligence and personality contribute to individual differences in adapting to aging, life contexts, and health challenges. Furthermore, it is important to embed theory development about early precursors of health into more general life course and life-span theories about human development.

In addition to broadening the search for important sets of influences, future theoretical work could focus on developing models of the role of time in the onset and progression of illness. Are different illnesses associated with different time trajectories? Are trajectories linear or nonlinear? To what extent are trajectories of different factors in synchrony, relatively independent, or coupled? Theoretical models also need to go hand-in-hand with advances in analysis techniques for longitudinal research.

Finally, future research and advances in understanding will rely on the continued availability of large longitudinal studies tracing not only the health of individuals but also multiple other biopsychosocial factors. Many researchers, especially in European countries, profit by linking archival data to follow-up assessments and national data (e.g., Deary et al., 2004). There is a wealth of information in such archival data, but previous studies often include only a restricted range of factors. For this reason, it is critical to collect extensive retrospective information about early life contexts in ongoing longitudinal studies, in particular those that trace several birth cohorts. These data resources, along with new longitudinal studies, will provide yet another important resource for future researchers and stimulate theory development.

ACKNOWLEDGMENT

Preparation of this article was supported by a Survey Research Center summer internship fellowship from the University of Michigan, Institute for Social Research, awarded to Frank J. Infurna.

REFERENCES

Adler, N. E., Boyce, W. T., Chesney, M. A., Folkman, S., & Syme, S. L. (1993). Socioeconomic inequalities in health: No easy solution. *Journal of the American Medical Association, 269,* 3140–3145.

Aldwin, C. M., Spiro, A. III, Leveson, M. R., & Cupertino, A. P. (2001). Longitudinal findings from the Normative Aging Study: III. Personality, individual health trajectories, and mortality. *Psychology and Aging, 16,* 450–465.

Alwin, D. F., McCammon, R. J., Wray, L. A., & Rodgers, W. L. (2008). Population processes and cognitive aging. In S. M. Hofer & D. F. Alwin (Eds.), *Handbook of cognitive aging: Interdisciplinary perspectives* (pp. 69–89). Thousand Oaks, CA: Sage Publications.

Alwin, D. F., & Wray, L. A. (2005). A life-span developmental perspective on social status and health. *The Journals of Gerontology: Series B: Psychological Sciences and Social Sciences, Special Issues: Health Inequalities Across the Life Course, 60B,* 7–14.

Antonucci, T. C. (2001). Social relations: An examination of social networks, social support, and sense of control. In J. E. Birren & K. W. Schaie (Eds.), *Handbook of the psychology of aging* (5th ed., pp. 427–453). San Diego, CA: Academic Press.

Antonucci, T. C., & Jackson, J. S. (2009). *Annual review of gerontology and geriatrics: Life-course perspectives on late-life health inequalities* (Vol 29). New York: Springer Publishing Company.

Anstey, K. J., Luszcz, M. A., Giles, L. C., & Andrews, G. R. (2001). Demographic, health, cognitive, and sensory variables as predictors of mortality in very old adults. *Psychology and Aging, 16,* 3–11.

Baltes, P. B. (1997). On the incomplete architecture of human ontogeny: Selection, optimization, and compensation as foundation of developmental theory. *American Psychologist, 52,* 366–380.

Barker, D. J. P. (1997). Maternal nutrition, fetal nutrition, and disease in later life. *Nutrition, 13,* 807–813.

Bassuk, S. S., Berkman, L. F., & Amick, B. C. III. (2002). Socioeconomic status and mortality among the elderly: Findings from four US communities. *American Journal of Epidemiology, 155,* 520–533.

Batty, G. D., Deary, I. J., & Macintyre, S. (2007). Childhood IQ in relation to risk factors for premature mortality in middle-aged persons: The Aberdeen Children of the 1950s Study. *Journal of Epidemiology and Community Health, 61,* 241–247.

Beckett, C., Maughan, B., Rutter, M., Castle, J., Colvert, E., Groothues, C., et al. (2006). Do the effects of early severe deprivation on cognition persist into early adolescence? Findings from the English and Romanian Adoptees Study. *Child Development, 77,* 696–711.

Bennett, D. S., Bendersky, M., & Lewis, M. (2008). Children's cognitive ability from 4 to 9 years old as a function of prenatal cocaine exposure, environmental risk, and maternal verbal intelligence. *Developmental Psychology, 44,* 919–928.

Ben-Shlomo, Y., & Kuh, D. (2002). A life course approach to chronic disease epidemiology: Conceptual models, empirical challenges and interdisciplinary perspectives. *International Journal of Epidemiology, 31,* 285–293.

Berg, C. A., Smith, T. W., Henry, N. J. M., & Pearce, G. E. (2007). A developmental approach to psychosocial risk factors and successful aging. In C. M. Aldwin, C. L. Park, & A. Spiro III (Eds.), *Handbook of health psychology and aging* (pp. 30–53). New York: Guilford Press.

Berkman, L. E. (2009). Social epidemiology: Social determinants of health in the United States: Are we losing ground? *Annual Review of Public Health, 30,* 27–41.

Berkman, L. F., Glass, T., Brissette, I., & Seeman, T. E. (2000). From social integration to health: Durkheim in the new millennium. *Social Science & Medicine, 51,* 843–857.

Blackwell, D. L., Hayward, M. D., & Crimmins, E. M. (2001). Does childhood health affect chronic morbidity in later life? *Social Science & Medicine, 52,* 1269–1284.

Bogg, T., & Roberts, B. W. (2004). Conscientiousness and health-related behaviors: A meta-analysis of the leading behavioral contributors to mortality. *Psychological Bulletin, 130,* 887–919.

Bosworth, H. B., & Schaie, K. W. (1997). The relationship of social environment, social networks, and health outcomes in the Seattle Longitudinal study: Two analytical approaches. *Journals of Gerontology, Series B: Psychological Sciences, 52B,* P197–P205.

Bosworth, H. B., Schaie, K. W., & Willis, S. L. (1999). Cognitive and sociodemographic risk factors for mortality in the Seattle Longitudinal Study. *The Journals of Gerontology: Series B: Psychological Sciences and Social Sciences, 54B,* P273–P282.

Bourne, V. J., Fox, H. C., Deary, I. J., & Whalley, L. J. (2007). Does childhood intelligence predict variation in cognitive change in later life? *Personality and Individual Differences, 42,* 1551–1559.

Caspi, A., Harrrington, H., Moffitt, T. E., Milne, B. J., & Poulton, R. (2003). Social isolated children 20 years later: Risk of cardiovascular disease. *Archives of Pediatrics & Adolescent Medicine, 160,* 805–811.

Caspi, A., Roberts, B. W., & Shiner, R. L. (2005). Personality development: Stability and change. *Annual Review of Psychology, 56,* 453–484.

Cheung, Y. B. (2002). Early origins and adult correlates of psychosomatic distress. *Social Science & Medicine, 55,* 937–948.

Christakis, N. A., & Fowler, J. H. (2007). The spread of obesity in a large social network over 32 years. *New England Journal of Medicine, 357,* 370–379.

Cohen, S. (2004). Social relationships and health. *American Psychologist, 59,* 676–684.

Costa, P. T., & McCrae, R. R. (1985). Hypochondriasis, neuroticism, and aging: When are somatic complaints unfounded? *American Psychologist, 40,* 19–28.

Cui, X., & Vaillant, G. E. (1996). Antecedents and consequences of negative life events in adulthood: A longitudinal study. *American Journal of Psychiatry, 153,* 21–26.

Danner, D. D., Snowdon, D. A., & Friesen, W. V. (2001). Positive emotions in early life and longevity: Findings from the Nun Study. *Journal of Personality and Social Psychology, 80,* 804–813.

Deary, I. J., Batty, G. D., Pattie, A., & Gale, C. R. (2008). More intelligent, more dependable children live longer: A 55-year longitudinal study of a representative sample of the Scottish nation. *Psychological Science, 19,* 874–880.

Deary, I. J., Der, G., & Shenkin, S. D. (2005). Does mother's IQ explain the association between birth weight and cognitive ability in childhood? *Intelligence, 33,* 445–454.

Deary, I. J., Whiteman, M. C., Starr, J. M., Whalley, L. J., & Fox, H. C. (2004). The impact of childhood intelligence on later life: Following up the Scottish Mental Surveys of 1932 and 1947. *Journal of Personality and Social Psychology, 86,* 130–147.

DeLongis, A., & Lehman, D. R. (1989). The usefulness of a structured diary approach in studying marital relationships. *Journals of Personality and Social Psychology, 57,* 808–818.

Edwards, V. J., Holden, G. W., Felitti, V. J., & Anda, R. F. (2003). Relationship between multiple forms of childhood maltreatment and adult mental health in community respondents: Results from the Adverse Childhood Experiences Study. *American Journal of Psychiatry, 160,* 1453–1460.

Elder, G. H. Jr., & Giele, J. Z. (2009). *The craft of life course research.* New York: Guilford Press.

Elder, G. H. Jr., Shanahan, M. J., & Clipp, E. C. (1994). When war comes to men's lives: Life-course patterns in family, work, and health. *Psychology and Aging, 9,* 5–16.

Engel, G. L. (1977). The need for a new medical model: A challenge for biomedicine. *Science, 196,* 129–136.

Ertel, K. A., Glymour, M. M., & Berkman, L. F. (2009). Social networks and health: A life course perspective integrating observational and experimental evidence. *Journal of Social and Personal Relationships, 26,* 73–92.

Evans, G. W., & Kim, P. (2007). Childhood poverty and health: Cumulative risk exposure and stress dysregulation. *Psychological Science, 18,* 953–957.

Felitti, V. J., Anda, R. F., Nordenberg, D., Williamson, D. F., Spitz, A. M., Edwards, V., et al. (1998). Relationship of childhood abuse and household dysfunction to many of the leading causes of death in adults: The Adverse Childhood Experiences (ACE) Study. *American Journal of Preventive Medicine, 14,* 245–256.

Finch, C. E., & Kirkwood, T. B. L. (2000). *Chance, development, and aging.* New York: Oxford University Press.

Fratiglioni, L., Paillard-Borg, S., & Winblad, B. (2004). An active and socially integrated lifestyle in late life might protect against dementia. *Lancet Neurology, 3,* 343–353.

Friedman, H. W., Tucker, J. S., Schwartz, J. E., Tomlinson-Keasey, C., Martin, L. R., Wingard, D. L., et al. (1995). Psychosocial and behavioral predictors of longevity: The aging and death of the "termites." *American Psychologist, 50*, 69–78.

Friedman, H. W., Tucker, J. S., Tomlinson-Keasey, C., Schwartz, J. E., Wingard, D. L., & Criqui, M. H. (1993). Does childhood personality predict longevity? *Journal of Personality and Social Psychology, 65*, 176–185.

Fuller-Iglesias, H., Smith, J., & Antonucci, T. C. (2009). Theories of aging from a life-course and life-span perspective: An Overview. In T. C. Antonucci & J. S. Jackson (Eds.), *Annual review of gerontology and geriatrics: Life-course perspectives on late-life health inequalities.* (Vol 29, pp. 3–25). New York: Springer Publishing Company.

Hemmingsson, T., Essen, J. V., Melin, B., Allebeck, P., & Lundberg, I. (2007). The association between cognitive ability measured at ages 18–20 and coronary heart disease in middle age among men: A prospective study using the Swedish 1969 conscription cohort. *Social Science & Medicine, 65*, 1410–1419.

Herd, P., Goesling, B., & House, J. S. (2007). Socioeconomic position and health: The differential effects of education versus income on the onset versus progression of health problems. *Journal of Health and Social Behavior, 48*, 223–238.

House, J. S., Landis, K. R., & Umberson, D. (1988). Social relationships and health. *Science, 241*, 540–545.

House, J. S., Lantz, P. M., & Herd, P. (2005). Continuity and change in the social stratification of aging and health over the life course: Evidence from a nationally representative longitudinal study from 1986 to 2001/2002 (Americans' Changing Lives Study). *Journals of Gerontology, Series B: Psychological Sciences (Special Issue), 60B*, 15–26.

Kawas, C. H., Corrada, M. M., Brookmeyer, R., Morrison, A., Resnick, S. M., Zonderman, A. B., et al. (2003). Visual memory predicts Alzheimer's disease more than a decade before diagnosis. *Neurology, 60*, 1089–1093.

Kessler, R. C., Price, R. H., & Wortman, C. B. (1985). Social factors in psychopathology: Stress, social support, and coping processes. *Annual Review of Psychology, 36*, 531–572.

Kiecolt-Glaser, J. K., Dyer, C. S., & Shuttleworth, E. C. (1988). Upsetting social interactions and distress among Alzheimer's disease family care-givers: A replication and extension. *American Journals of Community Psychology, 16*, 825–837.

Kiecolt-Glaser, J. K., & Newton, T. L. (2001). Marriage and health: His and hers. *Psychological Bulletin, 127*, 472–503.

Korenman, S., Miller, J. E., & Sjaastad, J. E. (1995). Long-term poverty and child development in the United States: Results from the NLSY. *Children and Youth Services Review, 17*, 127–155.

Kubzansky, L. D., Kawachi, I., Spiro, A., Weiss, S. T., Vokonas, P. S., & Sparrow, D. (1997). Is worrying bad for your heart? A prospective study of worry and coronary heart disease in the Normative Aging Study. *Circulation, 95*, 818–824.

Kuh, D., Hardy, R., Langenberg, C., Richards, M., & Wadsworth, M. E. J. (2002). Mortality in adults aged 26–54 years related to socioeconomic conditions in childhood and adulthood: Post War Birth Cohort Study. *British Medical Journal, 325*, 1076–1080.

Lantz, P. M., House, J. S., Mero, R. P., & Williams, D. R. (2005). Stress, life events, and socioeconomic disparities in health: Results from the Americans' Changing Lives Study. *Journal of Health and Social Behavior, 46*, 274–288.

Lantz, P. M., Lynch, J. W., House, J. S., Lepkowski, J. M., Mero, R. P., Musick, M. A., et al. (2001). Socioeconomic disparities in health change in a longitudinal study of US adults: The role of health-risk behaviors. *Social Science & Medicine, 53*, 29–40.

Lawlor, D. A., Batty, G. D., Morton, S. M. B., Clark, H., Macintyre, S., & Leon, D. A. (2005a). Childhood socioeconomic position, educational attainment, and adult cardiovascular risk factors: The Aberdeen Children of the 1950s Cohort Study. *American Journal of Public Health, 95*, 1245–1251.

Lawlor, D. A., Batty, G. D., Morton, S. M. B., Deary, I. J., Macintyre, S., Ronalds, G., et al. (2005b). Early life predictors of childhood intelligence: Evidence from the Aberdeen children of the 1950s study. *Journal of Epidemiology and Community Health, 59*, 656–663.

Lee, K. A., Vaillant, G. E., Torrey, W. C., & Elder, G. H. (1995). A 50-year prospective study of the psychological sequelae of World War II combat. *American Journal of Psychiatry, 152*, 516–522.

Lehman, B. J., Taylor, S. E., Kiefe, C. I., & Seeman, T. E. (2005). Relation of childhood socioeconomic status and family environment to adult metabolic functioning in the CARDIA Study. *Psychosomatic Medicine, 67*, 846–854.

Levenson, R. W., & Gottman, J. M. (1985). Physiological and affective predictors of change in relationship satisfaction. *Journals of Personality and Social Psychology, 49*, 85–94.

Maier, H., & Smith, J. (1999). Psychological predictors of mortality in old age. *Journals of Gerontology: Series B: Psychological Sciences and Social Sciences, 54B*, 44–54.

Marmot, M. (2006). Harveian oration: Health in an unequal world. *The Lancet, 368*, 2081–2094.

Mayer, K. U. (2009). New directions in life course research. *Annual Review of Sociology, 35*, 413–433.

Melchior, M., Moffitt, T. E., Milne, B. J., Poulton, R., & Caspi, A. (2007). Why do children from socioeconomically disadvantaged families suffer from poor health when they reach adulthood? A life-course study. *American Journal of Epidemiology, 166*, 966–974.

Melzer, D., Izmirlian, G., Leveille, S. G., & Guralnik, J. M. (2001). Educational differences in the prevalence of mobility disability in old age: The dynamics of incidence, mortality, and recovery. *Journal of Gerontology: Social Sciences, 56B*, S294–S301.

Miech, R. A., Caspi, A., Moffitt, T. E., Wright, B. R. E., & Silva, P. A. (1999). Low socioeconomic status and mental disorders: A longitudinal study of selection and causation during young adulthood. *The American Journal of Sociology, 104*, 1096–1131.

Miller, T. Q., Smith, T. W., Turner, C. W., Guijarro, M. L., & Hallet, A. J. (1996). A meta-analytic review of research on hostility and physical health. *Psychological Bulletin, 119*, 322–348.

Moffitt, T. E., & The E-Risk Study Team. (2002). Teen-aged mothers in contemporary Britain. *Journal of Child Psychology and Psychiatry, 43*, 727–742.

Mroczek, D. K., & Spiro, A. III. (2007). Personality change influences mortality in older men. *Psychological Science, 18*, 371–376.

Næss, O., Strand, B. H., & Smith, G. D. (2007). Childhood and adulthood socioeconomic position across 20 causes of death: A prospective cohort study of 800,000 Norwegian men and women. *Journal of Epidemiology and Community Health, 61*, 1004–1009.

O'Connor, T. G., Rutter, M., Beckett, C., Keaveney, L., Kreppner, J. M., & The English and Romanian Adoptees Study Team. (2000). The effects of global severe privation on cognitive competence: Extension and longitudinal follow-up. *Child Development, 71*, 376–390.

O'Rand, A. M., & Hamil-Luker, J. (2005). Processes of cumulative adversity: Childhood disadvantage and increased risk of heart attack across the life course. *Journals of Gerontology, Series B: Psychological Sciences and Social Sciences, 60B*, 117–124.

Orth-Gomér, K., Rosengren, A., & Wilhelmsen, L. (1993). Lack of social support and incidence of coronary heart disease in middle-aged Swedish men. *Psychosomatic Medicine, 55*, 37–43.

Ozer, D. J., & Benet-Martínez, V. (2006). Personality and the prediction of consequential outcomes. *Annual Review of Psychology, 57*, 401–421.

Pearlin, L. I., Lieberman, M., Menaghan, E., & Mullan, J. T. (1981). The stress process. *Journal of Health and Social Behavior, 22*, 237–256.

Peterson, C., Seligman, M. E. P., Yurko, K. H., Martin, L. R., & Friedman, H. S. (1998). Catastrophizing and untimely death. *Psychological Science, 9*, 127–130.

Poulton, R., Caspi, A., Milne, B. J., Thomson, W. M., Taylor, A., Sears, M. R., et al. (2002). Association between children's experience of socioeconomic disadvantage and adult health: A life-course study. *The Lancet, 360*, 1640–1645.

Repetti, R. L., Taylor, S. E., & Seeman, T. E. (2002). Risky families: Family social environments and the mental and physical health of offspring. *Psychological Bulletin, 128*, 330–366.

Roberts, B. W., Kuncel, N. R., Shiner, R., Caspi, A., & Goldberg, L. R. (2007). The power of personality: The comparative validity of personality traits, socioeconomic status, and cognitive ability for predicting important life outcomes. *Perspectives on Psychological Science, 2*, 313–345.

Ronalds, G. A., De Stavola, B. L., & Leon, D. A. (2005). The cognitive cost of being a twin: Evidence from comparisons within families in the Aberdeen Children of 1950s Cohort Study. *British Medical Journal, 331*, 1306–1310.

Rook, K. S. (1987). Social support versus companionship: Effects on life stress, loneliness, and evaluations by others. *Journal of Personality and Social Psychology, 52*, 1132–1147.

Roseboom, T. J., van der Meulen, J. H. P., Ravelli, A. C. J., Osmond, C., Barker, D. J. P., & Bleker, O. P. (2003). Perceived health of adults after prenatal exposure to the Dutch famine. *Pediatric and Perinatal Epidemiology, 17*, 391–397.

Roseboom, J., de Rooij, S., & Painter, R. (2006). The Dutch famine and its long-term consequences for adult health. *Early Human Development, 82*, 485–491.

Rutter, M., & Silberg, J. (2002). Gene-environment interplay in relation to emotional and behavioral disturbance. *Annual Review of Psychology, 53*, 463–490.

Rutter, M., & The English and Romanian Adoptees Study Team. (1998). Developmental catch-up, and delay, following adoption after severe global early privation. *Journal of Child Psychology and Psychiatry, 39*, 465–479.

Rutter, M., O'Connor, T. G., & The English and Romanian Adoptees Team. (2004). Are there biological programming effects for psychological development? Findings from a study of Romanian adoptees. *Developmental Psychology, 40*, 81–94.

Ryan, L. H., & Smith, J. (2009). Cognition and health disparities over the life course: Longevity as an example. In T. C. Antonucci & J. S. Jackson (Eds.), *Annual review of gerontology and geriatrics: Life-course perspectives on late-life health inequalities* (Vol. 29, pp. 131–157). New York: Springer Publishing Company.

Schaie, K. W. (2005). *Developmental influences on adult intelligence: The Seattle Longitudinal Study.* New York: Oxford University Press.

Schmand, B., Smit, J. H., Geerlings, M. I., & Lindeboom, J. (1997). The effects of intelligence and education on the development of dementia. A test of the brain reserve hypothesis. *Psychological Medicine, 27*, 1337–1344.

Seeman, T. E., Lusignolo, T. M., Albert, M., & Berkman, L. (2001). Social relationships, social support, and patterns of cognitive aging in healthy, high-functioning older adults: MacArthur Studies of Successful Aging. *Health Psychology, 20*, 243–255.

Seeman, T. E., Singer, B. H., Ryff, C. D., Dienberg Love, G., & Levy-Storms, L. (2002). Social relationships, gender, and allostatic load across two age cohorts. *Psychosomatic Medicine, 64*, 395–406.

Shaw, M., Lawlor, D. A., & Najman, J. M. (2006). Teenage children of teenage mothers: Psychological, behavioural and health outcomes from an Australian prospective longitudinal study. *Social Science & Medicine, 62*, 2526–2539.

Shipley, B. A., Der, G., Taylor, M. D., & Deary, I. J. (2006). Cognition and all-cause mortality across the entire adult age range: Health and lifestyle survey. *Psychosomatic Medicine, 68*, 17–24.

Shipley, B. A., Der, G., Taylor, M. D., & Deary, I. J. (2007). Association between mortality and cognitive change over 7 years in a large representative sample of UK residents. *Psychosomatic Medicine, 69*, 640–650.

Shipley, B. A., Weiss, A., Der, G., Taylor, M. D., & Deary, I. J. (2007). Neuroticism, extraversion, and mortality in the UK Health and Lifestyle Survey: A 21-year prospective cohort study. *Psychosomatic Medicine, 69*, 923–931.

Smith, G. D., & Hart, C. (2002). Life-course socioeconomic and behavioral influences on cardiovascular disease mortality: The Collaborative Study. *American Journal of Public Health, 92*, 1295–1298.

Smith, G. D., Shipley, M. J., & Rose, G. (1990). Magnitude and causes of socioeconomic differentials in mortality: Further evidence from the Whitehall Study. *Journal of Epidemiology and Community Health, 44*, 265–270.

Smith, T. W. (2006). Personality as risk and resilience in physical health. *Current Directions in Psychological Science, 15*, 227–231.

Soldz, S., & Vaillant, G. E. (1999). The big five personality traits and the life course: A 45-year longitudinal study. *Journal of Research in Personality, 33*, 208–232.

Spiro, A. III, Aldwin, C. M., Ward, K. D., & Mroczek, D. K. (1995). Personality and the incidence of hypertension among older men: Longitudinal findings from the Normative Aging Study. *Health Psychology, 14*, 563–569.

St. Clair, D., Xu, M., Wang, P., Yu, Y., Fang, Y., Zhang, F., et al. (2005). Rates of adult schizophrenia following prenatal exposure to the Chinese famine of 1959–1961. *Journal of the American Medical Association, 294*, 557–562.

Stern, Y. (2002). What is cognitive reserve? Theory and research application of the reserve concept. *Journal of the International Neuropsychological Society, 8*, 448–460.

Susser, E., Brown, A., & Matte, T. (2000). Prenatal antecedents of neuropsychiatric disorder over the life course: Collaborative studies of United States birth cohorts. In J. L. Rapoport (Ed.), *Childhood onset of adult psychopathology: Clinical and research advances* (pp. 121–146). Arlington, VA: American Psychiatric Publishing.

Taylor, S. E., Lehman, B. J., Kiefe, C. I., & Seeman, T. E. (2006). Relationship of early life stress and psychological functioning to adult C-reactive protein in the Coronary Artery Risk Development in Young Adults Study. *Biological Psychiatry, 60*, 819–824.

Terracciano, T., Löckenhoff, C. E., Zonderman, A. B., Ferrucci, L., & Costa, P. T. Jr. (2008). Personality predictors of longevity: Activity, emotional stability, and conscientiousness. *Psychosomatic Medicine, 70*, 621–627.

Tucker, J. S., Friedman, H. S., Schwartz, J. E., Criqui, M. H., Tomlinson-Keasey, C., Wingard, D. L., et al. (1997). Parental divorce: Effects on individual behavior and longevity. *Journals of Personality and Social Psychology, 73*, 381–391.

Uchino, B. N., Cacioppo, J. T., & Kiecolt-Glaser, J. K. (1996). The relationship between social support and physiological processes: A review with emphasis on underlying mechanisms and implications for health. *Psychological Bulletin, 119,* 488–531.

Umberson, D., Chen, M. D., House, J. S., & Hopkins, K. (1996). The effect of social relationships on psychological well-being: Are men and women really so different? *American Sociological Review, 61,* 837–857.

Vaillant, G. E., & Mukamal, K. (2001). Successful aging. *American Journal of Psychiatry, 158,* 839–847.

Vaillant, G. E., & Vaillant, C. O. (1990). Natural history of male psychological health, 12: A 45-year study of predictors of successful aging at age 65. *American Journal of Psychiatry, 147,* 31–37.

Verhaeghen, P., Borchelt, M., & Smith, J. (2003). Relation between cardiovascular and metabolic disease and cognition in very old age: Cross-sectional and longitudinal findings from the Berlin Aging Study. *Health Psychology, 22,* 559–569.

Waldron, I., Hughes, M. E., & Brooks, T. L. (1996). Marriage protection and marriage selection: Prospective evidence for reciprocal effects of marital status and health. *Social Science & Medicine, 43,* 113–123.

Walker, N. P., McConville, P. M., Hunter, D., Deary, I. J., & Whalley, L. W. (2002). Childhood mental ability and lifetime psychiatric contact: A 66-year follow-up study of the 1932 Scottish Mental Ability Survey. *Intelligence, 30,* 233–245.

Whalley, L. J., Starr, J. M., Athawes, R., Hunter, D., Pattie, A., & Deary, I. J. (2000). Childhood mental ability and dementia. *Neurology, 55,* 1455–1459.

Wiles, N. J., Peters, T. J., Leon, D. A., & Lewis, G. (2005). Birth weight and psychological distress at age 45–51 years. *British Journal of Psychiatry, 187,* 21–28.

Wilson, R. S., Mendes de Leon, C. F., Bienias, J. L., Evans, D. A., & Bennett, D. A. (2004). Personality and mortality in old age. *Journals of Gerontology, Series B: Psychological Sciences, 59B,* P110–P116.

Wilson, R. S., Schneider, J. A., Arnold, S. E., Bienias, J. L., & Bennett, D. A. (2007). Conscientiousness and the incidence of Alzheimer disease and mild cognitive impairment. *Archives of General Psychiatry, 64,* 1204–1212.

PROBLEM SOLVING ACROSS THE LIFE SPAN

10

Cynthia A. Berg and JoNell Strough

Across the life span, we experience numerous problems to be solved. The following examples illustrate the range of problems considered under the broad label of "problem solving." An infant prior to self-locomotion cannot reach a toy that he or she wishes. A school-aged child must solve an arithmetic problem as well as a problem at recess with a child who prevents him from entering a game of kick ball. An older student must solve a complicated chemistry problem as well as a conflict with a romantic partner. Young adults must solve problems pertaining to achieving career objectives, in addition to interpersonal conflicts within long-term relationships. In midlife and later adulthood, problems may arise as interpersonal relationships with adult children change and individuals deal with changing finances and health.

This array of problems share a common, defining feature—an individual faced with an obstacle to goal-directed behavior applies a strategy to overcome the obstacle and achieve the goal (Siegler & Alibali, 2005). This conceptualization of problem solving has its roots in Piaget's notion of individuals' adaptation to their environment (Piaget, 1952) and has been a central component of intelligence more broadly (Binet & Simon, 1961). That is, successful problem solving involves individuals achieving a better fit between themselves and the demands present in the environment. Given the centrality of adaptation to one's environment in problem solving, diversity in the content of problems individuals face across the life span is not a surprise. As is emphasized in contextualist approaches to intelligence (e.g., Baltes, Dittmann-Kohli, & Dixon, 1984), the contexts or domains of problems change across the life span along with individuals' broader goals and developmental life tasks (Heckhausen, 1997; Roisman, Masten, Coatsworth, & Tellegen, 2004).

We take a broad approach to problem solving across the life span, seeking answers to the question, "What develops across the life span?" Because of diversity in problems and paradigms for examining problem solving, we begin by presenting an organizational framework to provide a guide for our literature review. We then take four domains of problem solving (well-structured, everyday problem solving, social problem solving, collaborative problem solving) and review the literature to address the question, "What Develops?" We highlight features of the problem-solving process that change across the life span. We end by discussing directions for future research to link problem solving to successful adaptation to developmental contexts.

A FRAMEWORK FOR UNDERSTANDING PROBLEM SOLVING ACROSS THE LIFE SPAN

Numerous models of problem solving partition the problem-solving process into a series of discrete stages (Dodge, 1986; Rubin & Krasnor, 1986; Spivack & Shure, 1982).

Individuals first interpret and define the problem (What is the essential problem?). Next, individuals set goals regarding what they want to accomplish in the particular problem-solving situation. After goal setting, individuals generate and explore various strategies for solving the problem, anticipating the outcomes that might be associated with strategy implementation. Finally, individuals implement a strategy and then evaluate the effectiveness with which the strategy dealt with the blocked goal. Models consistent with this general framework have guided research investigating laboratory-based logical problem solving (Halford & Andrews, 2006) and social problem solving (Chang, D'Zurilla, & Sanna, 2004; Crick & Dodge, 1994).

Although this general framework has been influential in guiding research on problem solving, scholars argue that it misses important aspects of the problem-solving process. First, problem solvers may implement plans to prevent problems from occurring (Aspinwall & Taylor, 1997; Berg, Strough, Calderone, Meegan, & Sansone, 1997). Planning to prevent problems may become increasingly important for older adults, especially for social problem solving (Charles, Piazza, Luong, & Almeida, 2009; Sorkin & Rook, 2006). Second, the serial order of these processes has been called into question (Crick & Dodge, 1994; Sansone & Berg, 1993)—problem solvers may continually update their problem definitions and modify goals as they evaluate strategy effectiveness. Third, the process focuses on an "individual" problem solver, missing the inherently social nature of much problem solving (Berg, Meegan, & Deviney, 1998). Problems are frequently defined with other people (Beveridge, Berg, Wiebe, & Palmer, 2006) and solved in collaboration with others (Rogoff, 1998; Strough & Margrett, 2002). Fourth, this framework has been criticized as overly logical and rational, neglecting the fact that much problem solving takes place with cognitive short-cuts (Gigerenzer, 2008; Rivers, Reyna, & Mills, 2008), such as heuristics, that circumvent the critical evaluation of strategy effectiveness in relation to goal attainment. Relatedly, the focus on logical problem solving has obscured the powerful role of affect regulation and emotion in the problem-solving process (Blanchard-Fields, 2007). Most importantly for our treatment of problem solving across the life span, the framework is not a developmental one, as it was developed largely within the information-processing revolution within cognitive psychology (Klahr & Robinson, 1981; Siegler, 1978).

We propose a revision of this framework to facilitate a life-span developmental conceptualization of problem solving (Figure 10.1). We maintain that processes of anticipatory problem solving, problem definition, goal setting, strategy selection, and regulation of affect *may* occur in the problem-solving process depending on the cues that are encoded within the context and accessed in one's memory store and long-term knowledge base. However, these processes may occur in a more recursive fashion rather than a specific linear order. In addition, Figure 10.1 depicts that problem solving may involve more than one problem solver (represented by the two circles reflecting problem-solving processes); pairs, as well as larger groups, may encode cues, select strategies, and regulate affect together. Research on collaborative problem solving (reviewed later) points to the important role of partners' shared knowledge and memories for facilitating collaborative performance (depicted in the shaded area of Figure 10.1).

As outlined in Figure 10.1, our revision of the framework emphasizes that the problem-solving process occurs in proximal contexts (e.g., school, work, family) that change across the life span and that these proximal contexts are bounded by the

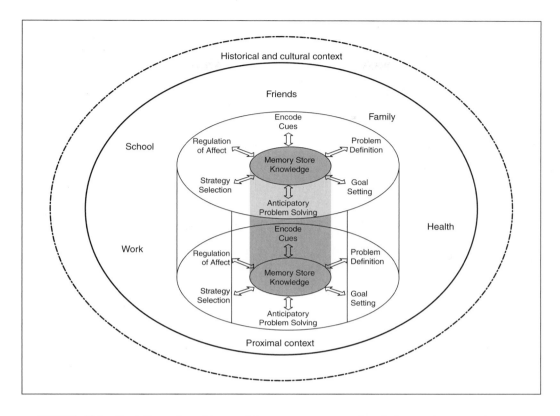

FIGURE 10.1 **Depiction of problem-solving process occurring between two people embedded within a proximal context as well as larger historical and cultural context.**

larger cultural and historical context (Dittmann-Kohli & Baltes, 1984). Consistent with the notion that adaptation at different periods of the life span is organized by different developmental tasks (McCormick, Kuo, & Masten, Chapter 5), we propose that the problem-solving contexts that are most relevant for adaptation vary across the life span. For instance, well-structured problems (e.g., arithmetic problems) occurring within contexts such as school may be more salient and indicative of adaptation for individuals for whom school is a proximal context of development (e.g., children living within a culture and time in history emphasizing compulsory education). Well-structured problem domains also may be salient and indicative of adaptation in adulthood for individuals within specific occupations (e.g., spatial problem solving for architects; Salthouse, Babcock, Skovronek, Mitchell, & Palmon, 1990). The school context may be linked with developmental goals such as autonomy (Hoppmann, Coats, & Blanchard-Fields, 2008) and achievement and learning goals (Grant & Dweck, 2003). Individuals' goals within a specific context may be associated with particular problem-solving cues and strategies. For instance, when a problem is embedded in a school context and achievement goals are salient, problem solvers may attend to cues (e.g., multiple-choice format; an instructor who emphasizes critical individual thought) that communicate that the problem is to be solved alone, via one correct answer using a logical problem-solving process. As individuals' proximal developmental context shifts from school to work, the problem-solving context becomes less structured, more complex, and may be guided by heuristics, biases, and naturalistic decision making (Kahneman & Klein, 2009). Consistent with life-span developmental principles (Baltes, 1987), historical time and birth cohort also have implications for the relevance of problem contexts. The pervasive influence of modern technology (Charness, Fox, & Mitchum, Chapter 13) illustrates how problem contexts may emerge and present new challenges and resources for adaptation to the environment.

Interpersonal relationships present within individuals' proximal developmental contexts also shift in importance across the life span. For example, peer relationships grow in importance across childhood (Larson & Richards, 1991) and the prominence of relationships with same- and other-sex peers undergoes systematic changes from early childhood through later adulthood (Mehta & Strough, 2009). Relationships with friends and romantic partners become especially important in adolescence and emerging adulthood (Roisman et al., 2004). In midlife, familial relationships and relationships with coworkers are important within the proximal contexts of daily life, whereas in later adulthood, relationships with coworkers may recede and family relationships may remain prominent. Characteristics of interpersonal relationships such as whether they are voluntary (e.g., friends) or obligatory (e.g., family) may be associated with emotional cues and social constraints that elicit goals to maintain the relationship or change the behavior of another. In turn, goals may be associated with specific problem-solving strategies such as regulating emotion, collaboration with others, and heuristics that short-cut the logical problem-solving process (Sorkin & Rook, 2006).

Although contexts may provide cues for problem-solving goals and strategies that explain some of the between-person variability across the life span, extensive intraindividual variability in problem solving also exists (Berg & Klaczynski, 2002; Lindenberger & Oertzen, 2006; Siegler, 2006a, 2006b). That is, a single individual will vary in their approach to problems within a domain depending on the specific conditions of the problem (Klaczynski, 2000; Siegler, 2006b). In our review, we highlight both interindividual and intraindividual variability in problem solving across the life span.

REVIEW OF PROBLEM SOLVING ACROSS THE LIFE SPAN

We review research on problem solving from two traditions: well-structured versus ill-structured problems (Wood, 1983). Problems that are "well-structured" are those where problem definitions and goals are well characterized (often constrained by the experimenter through instructions), there are a limited number of strategies available to address the problem, and emotion arousal is muted. Problems that are ill-structured are those where there is great diversity in the ways that people can define the problem, diversity in the goals and strategies to approach the problem, such that there is not a single correct way to solve the problem, and part of the problem approach may be how to avoid the problem and regulate one's emotional reaction. In our review, we focus on well- and ill-structured problems where sufficient research exists across age periods to begin to address the question of "What Develops?" in problem solving.

Well-Structured Problem Solving

Tasks and Methods

A diverse set of well-structured tasks (Tower of Hanoi or London, logical syllogisms, analogical reasoning, scientific reasoning, etc.) have been used to investigate problem solving. In these investigations, the problem solver's goal is constrained by the experimenter; the focus is on individual problem solving and on understanding the development of logical problem solving. Tasks are often age specific and are designed to measure qualitative shifts in the developing person's cognitive structure of logical problem solving, in accord with the influence of Piaget's (1952) theory. During infancy and toddlerhood, studies focus on sensorimotor problem solving (Cohen & Cashon, 2006) such as means–ends problem solving (Chen & Siegler, 2000), deferred imitation (Bauer, 2006), and an understanding of physical objects such as object permanence (Baillargeon, Li, Ng, & Yuan, 2009). During the preschool years, analogical reasoning (Halford & Andrews, 2006), planning problems such as the Tower of Hanoi (Klahr & Robinson, 1981) and planning an efficient route to get items at a grocery store (Gauvain & Rogoff, 1989) are examined. For school-aged children, problem solving on school-based tasks (e.g., arithmetic, Siegler, 1996, 2006a, 2006b), scientific reasoning tasks (e.g., balance scale task, Case, 1985, Siegler, 1981), scientific experimentation (Lehrer & Schauble, 2006), and reasoning more broadly (Halford & Andrews, 2006) are investigated. Across adolescence and adulthood, judgment and reasoning tasks (e.g., Reyna & Rivers, 2008; Weber & Johnson, 2009) as well as tasks more frequently found to reflect tasks of everyday living (e.g., completing tax forms, understanding medication instructions; Allaire & Marsiske, 2002) have been used to investigate logical problem solving.

The age-based segregation of tasks and methods in literature investigating well-structured problem solving makes it challenging to compare problem solving across the life span (see Case & Okamoto, 1996; Siegler, 2006a, for exceptions). For instance, during infancy methods such as habituation (Cohen & Cashon, 2006) and actions on objects (Chen & Siegler, 2000) are used, whereas during the school-aged and adult years verbal justifications (Siegler, 1996) and choosing among alternative answers are examined.

Arithmetic Problem Solving as an Example of Well-Structured Problems

For our review of well-structured problem solving, we examined arithmetic, as it is one of the few tasks that has been extensively studied across the life span. Basic quantitative knowledge may emerge in infancy. Such knowledge has been characterized by Horn and Hofer (1992) as a crystallized ability that is relatively well maintained across the life span. Development of arithmetic problem solving has implications for success in the school context as well as everyday life (e.g., doing price comparisons at the grocery store, Lave, 1989). Further, research on arithmetic problem solving focuses on key issues such as age differences in the ability to adapt strategies to problem features (Lemaire, Arnaud, & Lecacheur, 2004) and intra-individual variability in problem-solving strategies (Siegler, 2006b).

Consistent with research on other well-structured tasks, work on arithmetic problem solving addresses only parts of the problem-solving framework outlined in Figure 10.1. The focus is on the development of strategies, how individuals select strategies in response to problem parameters and adaptively fit those strategies when parameters change. Experimenters typically constrain problem definitions and goals through instructions and the role of affect regulation is only rarely addressed.

Infancy. Research in infancy focuses on a basic understanding of numerosity, ordinality, and addition and subtraction (Geary, 2006). Research on numerosity uses the paradigm of habituation, where infants' abilities to discriminate among new and previously seen objects are assessed (e.g., Starkey & Cooper, 1980; Xu & Spelke, 2000). Results of studies using habituation have been used as evidence that infants discriminate among small sets of items (e.g., two versus three), but not larger sets (four from six) using a perceptual process called subitizing. Research on ordinality uses violation of expectation experiments and suggests that infants may understand rudiments of ordinality (that two is more than one) and simple arithmetic and subtraction (e.g., Wynn, 1990).

Results suggesting infants' abilities to understand aspects of number and simple arithmetic have been replicated across dozens of studies (Geary, 2006). There is disagreement, however, regarding the mechanisms underlying performance. Some view results as evidence for an underlying innate preverbal counting mechanism (Gallistel & Gelman, 1992) that has evolved specifically for quantity representation. Others interpret results as operating off a perceptual process (the displays look different) and not reflecting specific number information.

Preschool and School-Aged Children. An extensive literature exists on preschool and elementary school-aged children's ability to solve single-digit addition and subtraction as well as multiplication problems (Siegler, 1996, 2006a, 2006b). Typically, children are presented with simple arithmetic problems (e.g., 2 + 9) and asked to produce the answer or are presented candidate answers (10, 11, 12) and asked to verify whether the answer is correct or incorrect. For preschool-aged children, problems are presented in a story problem format. The strategies that children use to solve the problems are examined via videotape, from children's self-report, and inferred from reaction time and error analyses of task performance in response to particular aspects of problems presented across many trials. Numerous strategies have been identified such as counting (raising the number of fingers for each addend and counting), sum strategy (counting from 1), min strategy (counting from the larger addend the number of the smaller addend), decomposition (in solving the problem 2 + 9, rounding 9 up to 10 and thinking that the answer is 12–1), retrieval (accessing the answer directly from memory), and guessing. Retrieval strategies are used when the strength of the answer in long-term memory is highly associated with the problem (Shrager & Siegler, 1998).

At all stages of learning, there is extensive intraindividual variability in strategies (Siegler, 2006a, 2006b), a view that contrasts with older views of children's strategy development, where development involved a progression from less sophisticated (e.g., counting) to more sophisticated strategies (e.g., min strategy and then finally retrieval). Even young children (4–8 years) adapt their strategies depending on features of the problems (e.g., using retrieval on easier problems and back-up strategies such as counting on more difficult problems, Siegler, 1996). Although use of optimal strategies such as retrieval increase with age and learning, multiple strategies are used across development, with the discovery of new strategies being an important process of development. The movement from early emerging, less sophisticated "back-up" strategies such as counting to more sophisticated retrieval strategies is dependent on schooling and instruction as well as maturational factors (Geary, Bow-Thomas, Liu, & Siegler, 1996).

Early and Later Adulthood. Consistent with research during childhood, intraindividual variability in strategy use persists into early adulthood. Although retrieval becomes the most frequently used strategy during young adulthood, some adults continue to use back-up strategies (e.g., min counting, decomposition). Hecht (2006) found that for adults who were labeled "not-so-good retrievers" back-up strategies were adaptive, whereas for other adults (labeled "perfectionists") back-up strategies were not needed. Perfectionists have been identified during childhood as well (Siegler, 1988). Hecht's research demonstrates how individual differences may exist in the extent to which intraindividual variability in strategies is adaptive.

Although individual and intraindividual differences in strategies have been investigated, individual differences in goals are not typically considered within the literature on arithmetic problem solving. However, in accord with our problem-solving framework (Figure 10.1), individual differences in goals for accuracy may be present. For example, accuracy goals may be more salient to perfectionists than to "good retrievers" or "not-so-good retrievers." Additional individual differences in strategy selection have been found among those with high math anxiety (Ashcraft & Ridley, 2005), who do not fit their strategies to problem characteristics in the same way and appear to place a greater emphasis on the goal of speed (perhaps as a way to end an experimental session they find aversive) than those without math anxiety. Research on math anxiety reveals how emotion regulation may be involved in problem solving, even for well-structured problems (see Figure 10.1). Moreover, the larger sociohistorical context may affect performance within this domain. For example, some individual differences in math anxiety and expectations about performance may reflect the salience of cultural stereotypes tied to gender or minority group status. When experimental manipulations reduce the salience of such stereotypes, performance may improve (Ben-Zeev, Duncan, & Forbes, 2005; Good & Aronson, 2008).

Individual differences are apparent when younger (typically college-aged, 18–25 years) and older (60 years of age and older) adults are compared. Such comparisons use two-digit multiplication problems to address age differences in the adaptivity of adults' problem-solving strategies to problem conditions (Lemaire et al., 2004; Lemaire & Lecacheur, 2004). For instance, Lemaire et al. (2004) asked adults to estimate answers to 2-by-2 digit multiplication problems (43 × 78). Estimation strategies varied in terms of their efficacy for different types of problems. For instance, for the problem 43 × 78 (answer = 3354) a rounding down strategy (e.g., 40 × 70 = 2800) would be more accurate than rounding up (50 × 80 = 4000), but both would be less accurate than a mixed rounding strategy (rounding down to 40, but up to 80). Older adults, in comparison to younger adults, took more time to complete such problems and were less accurate. Although older and younger adults did not differ in their strategy preferences (all participants preferred rounding down strategies presumably because they were easier to implement), older adults' selected strategies were less optimal in terms of the fit between the strategy and the features of a particular problem (i.e., using rounding down strategies more frequently on problems where rounding down yielded the best estimate). These age-related differences in strategy selection suggest that older adults are less adaptive or less flexible in fitting their strategies to problem characteristics (Lemaire & Lecacheur, 2004).

Similar age-related individual differences are obtained when experimenters attempt to increase the salience of various goals (e.g., instructions to be highly accurate or to be as fast as possible), when individuals are allowed more latitude in strategy selection (e.g., allowed to use the mixed-rounding strategy), and are given additional time to make estimation decisions (Lemaire & Lecacheur, 2004). Older adults' relative lack of flexibility is attributable, in part, to differences in processing speed (Duverne & Lemaire, 2005). However, the reduced flexibility of older adults' strategies to conditions of the problem does not extend to subtraction, where over-learned facts may preserve the ability to flexibly adapt strategies (Arnaud, Lamaire, Allen, & Michel, 2008).

Summary. Across early childhood through late adulthood, individuals use a variety of strategies to solve arithmetic and multiplication problems and they adapt those strategies to fit the constraints of the problem. Age differences are seen in the frequency of retrieval strategies—use of these strategies increases across the life span. Some age differences exist in the ability of individuals to adapt their strategies to fit problem characteristics, with older adults being less flexible. Although researchers typically constrain the goal and definition of the task by asking participants to perform a specific operation often with a specific strategy (e.g., use a rounding-up strategy), individuals at all ages are able to change their strategies in response to goals (e.g., instructions to be more accurate elicit greater back-up strategies such as counting versus instructions to be faster in completing problems elicit more retrieval strategies).

Ill-Structured Problems

In contrast to well-structured problems, ill-structured problems are ones where there are multiple ways to interpret or define the problem and the problems have multiple correct or "good enough" solutions. Such problems are often examined in research on everyday problem solving and social problem solving. Everyday and social problems are problems people encounter on a regular daily basis and are characterized by multiple features (Berg, Skinner, & Ko, 2009; Blanchard-Fields, 2007): (1) they can occur over an extended time frame (e.g., weeks versus the minutes that often characterize well-structured problems), (2) occur in a rich interpersonal context where others may be not only part of the problem but also used for the solution, and (3) explicitly include emotion regulation as part of the problem-solving process. Everyday problems can include both well-structured problems (e.g., how to double a recipe, how much medication to take based on a prescription label) as well as ill-structured ones (e.g., how to get expensive repairs covered by your landlord, how to solve a computer problem at work). We review the work on everyday problem solving and then the literature on social problem solving separately, noting points of overlap between these two literatures.

Everyday Problem Solving

The field of everyday problem solving largely arose within the field of aging as contextualist approaches to intelligence (Baltes et al., 1984) pointed to the changing contexts of intelligence across adulthood from one initially in late adolescence focused within the school context to one that includes adaptation to a variety of contexts (e.g., work, family, and health). Accordingly, there is little research in the field of everyday problem solving present for children younger than early adolescence. However, work within the field of stress and coping examines daily hassles that are similar in content to the types of problems examined in the everyday problem-solving field; the coping responses examined are similar to the problem-solving strategies examined (Seiffge-Krenke, Aunola, & Nurmi, 2009). Both literatures frequently assess problem solving by either presenting individuals with hypothetical everyday problems or stressors or by having individuals describe problems or stressors that they have recently experienced. Thus, we incorporate this work when examining work on everyday problem solving in childhood. In the following section, we review research highlighting some of the key issues addressed within the everyday problem-solving literature over the past decades.

Relation Between Performance on Well-Structured Everyday Problems, Ill-Structured Everyday Problems, and Real-World Adaptation. One important question within the everyday problem-solving literature is whether performance on "well-structured" problems predicts performance on "ill-structured" problems. Allaire and Marsiske (1999, 2002) devised ill-structured everyday analogues of well-structured inductive reasoning, knowledge, declarative memory, and working memory problems. Correlations between the everyday analogues and well-structured problems ranged depending on the specific measure (rs = .13 to .58); correlations between two metrics of performance on ill-structured problems were relatively low (r = .19). Performance on both the ill-structured and well-structured measures contributed to performance on a measure of Instrumental Activities of Daily Living (a measure of the ability to function and complete activities independently in one's environment). These results illustrate the distinctiveness of the measures and suggest that these two dimensions of everyday problem solving are both important for real-world adaptation.

Age-Related Differences in Problem Solving. One metric used to examine age-related differences in everyday problem solving is the number of strategies a person generates when presented with a hypothetical problem (Denney, 1989; Shure & Aberson, 2006). Preschool children who generate more strategies to a problem have higher ego resilience (Arend, Gove, & Sroufe, 1979). Meta-analytic reviews indicate that older adults generate fewer strategies than do younger adults (Thornton & Dumke, 2005), even when problems are designed to be most familiar to older adults (Denney & Pearce, 1989) and when adults are instructed to mention as many strategies as possible (Berg, Meegan, & Klaczynski, 1999; Denney, Tozier, &

Scholtthauer, 1992). These findings have been interpreted to mean that everyday problem solving peaks in midlife (Denney, 1989). However, Berg et al. (1999) found that the smaller number of strategies generated by older adults may reflect their greater experience with everyday problems. Age differences in strategy generation may also be due to the extent to which older adults view generated strategies as effective (Strough, McFall, Flinn, & Schuller, 2008) and their perceived efficacy to solve problems (Artistico, Cervone, & Pezzuti, 2003).

Research has also examined age-related trends in the ability to generate strategies that focus not only on solving the problem but also dealing with emotions and cognitively reappraising the problem to fit better with one's goals and problem-solving capabilities. One benefit to the availability of multiple types of strategies is that if one type fails, other strategies will be available. Spivack and Shure (1982) found that more socially adjusted children were able to generate a greater variety of strategies. Preschool children move from a near exclusive focus on problem-focused strategies to a greater combined use of emotion-focused and cognitive problem analysis (Band & Weisz, 1988). During adolescence, both cognitive and problem-focused strategies increase in frequency with most of the developmental change being situation specific (Seiffge-Krenke et al., 2009). Older adults, compared with younger adults, prefer a mixture of strategies that focus on both addressing the problem as well as regulating one's distressing emotions (Birditt, Fingerman, & Almeida, 2005; Blanchard-Fields, Chen, & Norris, 1997; Blanchard-Fields, Jahnke, & Camp, 1995; Blanchard-Fields, Mienaltowski & Seay, 2007; Watson & Blanchard-Fields, 1998).

Findings regarding age differences in the types of strategies individuals endorse have been interpreted as indicating age-related improvements in everyday problem-solving performance (Blanchard-Fields, 2007), especially for interpersonal problems (as we discuss in more detail in a later section). Because multiple strategies may be effective, measuring the quality of strategies is one challenge that everyday problem solving researchers must face. Strategy quality has been defined as the correlation between individuals' endorsement or generation of strategies and expert judges' ratings of strategy effectiveness (Berg, 1989; Blanchard-Fields et al., 2007; Cornelius & Caspi, 1987), as well as by experts' assessments of strategy effectiveness (Allaire & Marsiske, 2002), researchers' judgments of strategy safety and effectiveness (Denney, 1989), and individuals' perceptions of their strategy effectiveness (Berg et al., 1999). Although few studies compare different methods of assessing strategy quality (cf. Allaire & Marsiske, 2002), different conclusions regarding age trajectories in everyday problem-solving strategies emerge depending on the way in which strategy effectiveness is measured (see Berg et al., 2009 for a review). Older adults typically outperform young adults when their responses are compared to expert judges' responses (Blanchard-Fields et al., 2007; Cornelius & Caspi, 1987) whereas older adults perform worse when the number of strategies is used as the performance metric because they do not generate as many strategies as younger adults (Thornton & Dumke, 2005).

Contextual Specificity of Strategy Selection Across Age. Consistent with the literature investigating well-structured problem solving, the question of age-related differences in the ability of individuals to adapt their strategies to particular features of problems has been of interest. Across childhood and adolescence, individuals show increases in the context specificity of problem-solving strategies (Berg, 1989). Across adulthood, older adults' strategies appear to be more sensitive than those of younger adults to the domain in which a problem is presented (e.g., home, friends, finances), especially when hypothetical problems are used and individuals rate lists of strategies (e.g., Blanchard-Fields et al., 1997). Thus, in contrast to research investigating performance on well-defined problems, older adults may be more likely to adapt their strategies to fit constraints and conditions of the problem.

Summary. The everyday problem-solving literature portrays a different view of problem-solving capabilities across the life span than that depicted by the literature on well-structured arithmetic problems. Age differences are found with respect to the number of strategies individuals generate in response to hypothetical everyday problems with individuals during middle-age able to generate the most strategies. However, the diversity of strategies generated and the ability to fit strategies to conditions of problems may increase throughout the life span. In the everyday problem-solving literature, instrumental problems (dealing with problems at work, school, technology, finances) often are contrasted with more social problems (conflicts with family or friends). We now review research on social problem solving.

Social Problem Solving

Our definition of social problem solving aligns with the conceptualization offered by D'Zurilla, Nezu, and Maydeu-Olivares (2004) as problem solving that occurs in the "real world." Social or interpersonal problems are frequently viewed as a subset of everyday problem solving in the adult development literature (Berg et al., 2009). In everyday life, interpersonal problems may occur in numerous relationships (family, friends, romantic partners, coworkers, acquaintances) and others may not only be the problem but are also often available to the individual as a means of solving the problem (e.g., Berg, Smith et al., 2007; Strough & Margrett, 2002).

To understand the development of social problem solving, we draw from four literatures, each of which investigates the problem-solving process within specific age groups. First, we examine infants' behavioral regulation strategies in response to mild stressors to provide insight as to the early origins of problem solving within a social context. Second, we consider research addressing associations among social information processing and social competence (e.g., Crick & Dodge, 1994). Third, we use research examining the development of conflict resolution skills across childhood and adolescence (see Laursen, Finkelstein, Townsend Betts, 2001; Newcomb & Bagwell, 1995 for reviews) as a demonstration of the intraindividual differences in strategies that occur across development and across relationship contexts. Fourth, we draw from research examining interpersonal everyday problem solving (see Blanchard-Fields, 2007; Thornton & Dumke, 2005 for reviews) to consider adult age differences in problem definitions, goals, and strategies.

Emotion Regulation Strategies in Infancy and Toddlerhood. Young infants are faced with problems and experience distress in response to frustrating events, many of which reflect their dependency and the control others have over their environment. Researchers have used mothers' reports of their infants' behavior in response to frustration as well as a variety of laboratory-based observational tasks to mimic the problems infants face. Such tasks include preventing access to a desirable toy (Crockenberg & Leerkes, 2004), removing a toy (Stifter & Braungart, 1995), restraint of movement (Little & Carter, 2005), maternal separation or unavailability (Ross & Karraker, 1999), and Ainsworth and Bell's (1970) Strange Situation (Diener, Mangelsdorf, McHale, & Frosch, 2002). Together, such studies suggest a developmental progression in that younger infants are more likely than toddlers to use self-soothing behaviors and seek proximity to their mothers, whereas toddlers are relatively more likely to use self-distraction and to employ problem-focused strategies (Karraker, Lake, & Parry, 1994).

Both individual and intraindividual differences are apparent in infancy. Some individual difference characteristics linked to infants' emotion regulation strategies include attachment classification (Diener et al., 2002), temperament (Rothbart, Posner, & Kieras, 2006), and visual attention skills (Morales, Mundy, Crowson, Neal, & Delgado, 2005). Intraindividual differences in strategies are found across situations (Miller, McDonough, Rosenblum, & Sameroff, 2002) and across transient states such as degree of infant fatigue (Ross & Karraker, 1999). Early emotion regulation skills may be linked to later social competence in childhood (Eisenberg et al., 1995; Sallquist et al., 2009).

Social Information Processing. Dodge, Pettit, McClaskey, and Brown (1986) developed naturalistic observations and staged peer group entry and provocation situations to examine children's social information processing. Children's self-reports of their problem interpretations and strategy selection were gathered after children watched videos of peer group entry (joining a game) and ambiguous provocation (one child knocks over a tower of blocks built by another child). Written and auditory vignettes describing hypothetical situations have also been used to assess social information processing and strategy selection (see de Castro, Veerman, Koops, Bosch, & Monshouwer, 2002 for a review), with the content tailored to reflect developmental tasks and contexts of the age group under investigation (e.g., Nas, de Castro, & Koops, 2005; Pettit, Lansford, Malone, Dodge, & Bates, 2010). Teacher report, mother report, peer report (sociometric techniques), and self-report have been used to assess externalizing behaviors (Dodge et al., 1986; Pettit et al., 2010).

Dodge and colleagues' (1986) early research provided a compelling demonstration of links between social information-processing deficits (encoding, interpretation, search and evaluation of potential strategies) and social behavior (enactment of aggressive strategies). A large number of studies now document a link between boys' hostile attributions of other's intent in ambiguous situations and their aggressive behavior (de Castro et al., 2002). Effect sizes are largest when staged provocations are used to assess aggressive strategies and larger when vignettes are presented via audio rather than by actors in videos presumably because watching an actor changes the child's perspective to that of an observer, making it more difficult for the child to imagine the situation happening to them (de Castro et al., 2002). When a greater number of steps of information processing are deficient, the risk of externalizing behavior increases (Lansford et al., 2006). Accordingly, information-processing deficits are considered a proximal process in understanding why more distal individual differences (e.g., gender, race, temperament) are associated with variation in social behavior.

In regards to developmental trajectories, Lansford et al. (2006) found within-person continuity in the number of social information-processing deficits (i.e., encoding cues, making attributions, generating responses, selecting responses) from early to later adolescence (8th to 11th grade), but little continuity from elementary school to adolescence. Moreover, the relation between concurrent information-processing deficits and externalizing behavior became stronger with age through late adolescence, perhaps reflecting that the link between social cognition and behavior becomes stronger with age.

Similar to the framework that guides this Chapter, a central tenet of the social-information processing model (Crick & Dodge, 1994; Dodge, 1986) is the situational or contextual specificity of the problem-solving process. Early work indicated that deficits in social information processing were specific to the situation (e.g., peer entry or provocation). That is, children displayed competence in some settings but not others (Dodge et al., 1986). Recent longitudinal research has examined whether social information-processing deficits within one relationship domain (i.e., peers) predict social deficits (externalizing behavior) across domains (Pettit et al., 2010). Violence in peer relationships shows some evidence of domain specificity, whereas violence in romantic relationships does not.

Research guided by Dodge and colleagues' social information-processing model (Crick & Dodge, 1994; Dodge, 1986) continues to advance our understanding of the cognitive processes underlying social competence. Deficits in social competence are associated with defining ambiguous situations in a more hostile manner and using more aggressive strategies. However, social information processing in one domain does not necessarily translate into other domains nor is there extensive continuity in processing from young childhood through adolescence. Social information-processing deficits of the type examined by Dodge have not been examined in the adult development and aging literature. However, work on hostile personality traits across development does suggest some continuity in hostility in children's temperament from early childhood through adolescence (Raiikkonen, Katainen, Keskivaara, & Keltikangas-Jarvinen 2000) and through young adulthood (Keltikangas-Jarvinen & Heinonen, 2003), which might be suggestive of some continuity in at least some social information processes. One step in Crick and Dodge's (1994) model that has received relatively less emphasis is the step corresponding to clarification of goals. However, the literature on conflict management strategies (reviewed next) suggests that goals are a key element of the problem-solving process.

Conflict Management Strategies Across Childhood, Adolescence, and Early Adulthood. Studies investigating the development of social problem solving in childhood and adolescence focus on strategies used for solving interpersonal conflicts with friends. Learning how to successfully manage interpersonal conflict with peers becomes increasingly important during adolescence, consistent with the high salience of friends during adolescence (Shantz & Hartup, 1992) as well as emerging adulthood (Arnett, 2000). Friends' relative equivalence of status and power are thought to create a context where children learn to use compromise and negotiation strategies to balance self-interest with the interests of others, strategies that are then applied to other relationships later in life such as romantic relationships (Buhrmester, 1996). The voluntary nature of friendships is presumed to promote goals for maintaining the relationship and strategies that serve this goal.

Age-related differences in strategies for resolving actual and hypothetical conflicts are evident when comparing self-reported and observer-reported strategy use across childhood, adolescence, and early adulthood. Based on narrative and meta-analytic reviews of the literature Laursen and colleagues (Laursen & Collins, 1994; Laursen et al., 2001) conclude that coercive strategies (i.e., verbal or physical aggression, commands) decrease across childhood, adolescence, and early adulthood. Among children, coercion is more likely to be employed in actual conflicts than would be expected based on children's endorsement of this strategy when presented with a hypothetical conflict. Thus, hypothetical conflicts may be a less powerful method of detecting age-related decreases in coercive conflict management strategies than actual conflicts. Age-related decreases in coercive strategies could reflect that individuals learn contingencies associated with the use of such strategies in childhood—hostile, coercive strategies result in fewer friends (Rose & Asher, 1999). Importantly, coercive strategies do not completely disappear from individuals' problem-solving repertoires with age. In conflicts with siblings, use of coercive strategies remains stable from childhood through early adulthood reflecting that sibling relationships are obligatory relationships (Laursen et al., 2001).

Negotiation strategies (i.e., talking things out, compromising) increase from childhood through adulthood (Laursen et al., 2001). During adolescence there appears to be a gap between competence (endorsing these strategies when presented with a hypothetical conflict) and performance (using compromise strategies in actual conflicts; Laursen & Collins, 1994). Accordingly, methods that rely upon hypothetical conflicts may provide an inflated estimate of the extent to which adolescents resolve conflicts via negotiation. The competence performance gap in negotiation strategies appears to narrow in early adulthood (Laursen et al., 2001).

Negotiation strategies vary not only according to age but also according to the nature of the interpersonal relationship (Laursen et al., 2001) and individual difference characteristics such as gender (Rose & Rudolph, 2006). Negotiation is more common in conflicts with romantic partners than with friends and is more common in conflicts with friends than acquaintances. On an average, girls are more likely than boys to endorse prosocial strategies such as negotiation.

The differential prevalence of negotiation strategies across relationships is assumed to reflect differences in goals for maintaining these relationships. Specifically, individuals are presumed to have goals for maintaining affiliative ties with friends and romantic partners; such ties are absent in acquaintances (Laursen et al., 2001). Individual differences in the use of negotiation strategies may reflect differences in goals (affiliative goals for relationships may be associated with more negotiation and compromise strategies; Rose & Asher, 1999).

In turn, individual differences in goals may arise from interpretations of features of the situation (e.g., the sex of the person with whom one interacts, the nature of the relationship). For example, intraindividual variability in young men's and women's goals corresponds to whether they interact with a confederate of the same- or other-sex (Pickard & Strough, 2003). Children's self-reported goals vary depending on relationships with specific same-sex classmates (Salmivalli & Peets, 2009) and whether vignettes portray a hypothetical conflict, victimization by peers, or a more benign social interaction (Ojanen, Aunola, & Salmivalli, 2007). Adolescent girls' relatively greater endorsement of negotiation strategies with romantic partners (Feldman &

Gowen, 1998) and their use of prosocial strategies more generally (Rose & Rudolph, 2006) may reflect their participation and socialization within contemporary American culture which views such behaviors as more typical of girls and women (Liben & Bigler, 2002). Thus, goals appear to be a proximal process useful in understanding the variation in social behavior that is often associated with more distal individual difference characteristics such as gender.

In addition to age-related increases in negotiation strategies from childhood through early adulthood, endorsement of passive/avoidant strategies such as withdrawing or disengaging from the conflict also increase as adolescents learn to walk away from conflict (Laursen et al., 2001). Children rarely use this strategy and are more likely to rely on coercion. Individual differences in endorsement of avoidant strategies also are found. Asian-American adolescents are relatively more likely than European-American adolescents to endorse avoidance as a strategy for managing conflict with romantic partners, perhaps as a reflection of exposure to eastern cultural values that emphasize interpersonal harmony (e.g., Feldman & Gowan, 1998).

In sum, research that compares children's, adolescents', and young adults' strategies for managing conflict indicates contextual and individual differences in strategy use. Researchers often suggest that differences in strategies for managing conflict reflect differences in goals. In turn, goals are theorized to correspond to distinguishing characteristics of relationships such as whether the relationship is voluntary or obligatory. Although explanations of strategy variability are often attributed to variability in goals, goals are rarely measured within the literature on conflict management. The utility of investigating links between goals and strategies is evident in research examining social problem solving in adulthood (reviewed next).

Goals and Strategies in Early and Later Adulthood. Within the adult development and aging literature, links between problem-solving strategies and goals are addressed. In line with a contextual approach, some of these studies compare age differences in problem-solving strategies as a function of the problem context such as whether the problem consists of a conflict with a family member or friend, or occurs at work or at school (e.g., Berg, Strough, Calderone, Sansone & Weir, 1998; Cornelius & Caspi, 1987). Researchers use hypothetical problems and either ratings of strategies (e.g., Blanchard-Fields et al., 2007) or strategy generation (e.g., Strough et al., 2008), or ask individuals to describe problems they experienced in their everyday lives and the strategies they used (e.g., Berg et al., 1998).

A handful of studies investigate problem-solving goals and include adolescents, young, middle-aged, and older adults within the same cross-sectional study (Berg et al., 1998; Blanchard-Fields, 1986; Hoppmann et al., 2008; Strough, Berg, & Sansone, 1996). These studies frequently contrast more instrumental domains (e.g., finances, health, and work) with interpersonal domains (e.g., family, friends). When people describe goals for solving their instrumental and interpersonal problems, they often report problem-solving goals that are consistent with developmental tasks (Hoppmann et al., 2008; Strough et al., 1996). For example, Strough et al. (1996) found that pre-adolescents' problem-solving goals were more likely than those of adults to reflect concerns about task improvement—in accord with developmental tasks pertaining to achieving mastery and competence during this developmental period (Veroff & Veroff, 1980). Hoppmann and colleagues found that adolescents and younger adults had the highest proportion of autonomy goals, in accord with their independence tasks (Collins & Steinberg, 2006); whereas older adults had the highest probability of generativity goals, in line with developmental tasks of later life (Erikson, 1968; Lang & Carstensen, 2002). These findings demonstrate how individuals' larger developmental tasks may be reflected in their problem-solving goals.

In addition to the correspondence between goals and developmental tasks, the fit or match between goals and strategies has been more thoroughly investigated within the adult development and aging literature. For example, among older adults who recalled a negative social exchange they had experienced (e.g., receiving unwanted advice), strategies that entailed asserting one's point of view by arguing (conceptually akin to the "coercion" strategy examined in the conflict management literature) were relatively more frequent when the goal was to change the behavior of a partner than when attempting to maintain a harmonious relationship (Sorkin & Rook, 2006). Cognitive distancing (an avoidant strategy) was more frequent when the goal was to maintain the relationship than when the goal was to change the other person. Although the content of goals may differ by age, research indicates that the fit or match between strategies and goals is similar across age groups (Berg, et al., 1998; Hoppmann et al., 2008).

Not only is there some evidence within the adult development and aging literature that goals are systematically related to strategies, but there is also evidence to suggest that goals are useful in understanding the interplay of age and context in strategy selection. For example, in independent studies, Berg et al. (1998) and Hoppmann et al. (2008) each found that goals were a more precise predictor of the strategies individuals reported they used to solve their own everyday problems than the specific context (health, family, friends, finances, work) in which the problem occurred. Berg and colleagues' findings also suggested that the utility of goals over problem context for understanding strategies was more apparent when individuals were directed to describe a problem that had occurred within a specific domain (e.g., family or work) than when individuals were free to select a problem from any domain, perhaps reflecting that domains elicit specific cues regarding goals.

Related to the fit between goals and strategies, there is a growing interest in older adults' goals for avoiding social problems (Charles et al., 2009; Sorkin & Rook, 2006), because of their greater interest in preserving positive emotional affect and close relationship ties (Carstensen & Mikels, 2005; Charles & Carstensen, 2010). Older adults may be better able to solve emotionally salient interpersonal problems (Blanchard-Fields, 2007), in part, because they prioritize emotion regulation goals and may have a decreased tendency to express emotions such as anger (Blanchard-Fields & Coats, 2008; Coats & Blanchard-Fields, 2008). Further, older adults may experience less emotional arousal by engaging more in anticipatory efforts to avoid social problems, but may actually experience greater affective reactivity if their attempts to avoid social problems are unsuccessful (Charles et al., 2009).

Summary. The literature examining social problem solving as it pertains to social competence, conflict management, and negotiation strategies among friends and romantic partners reveals that strategies vary as a function of contexts, goals, and individual difference characteristics (e.g., gender). Age differences in strategies reveal a drop in coercive and aggressive strategies and an increase in negotiation and other affiliative strategies. Older adults may be especially adept at resolving interpersonal conflicts, in part, because of their greater skill at regulating emotions and anticipating and avoiding problems before they occur. Although the interpersonal problem-solving literature examines abilities to resolve interpersonal conflict, the focus has been on how an "individual" solves these problems. We next turn to a review of the collaborative problem-solving literature that addresses how individuals may solve problems in conjunction with another individual.

Collaborative Problem Solving

Research on collaborative problem solving investigates how individuals work together to solve problems that are both well- and ill-structured (Gauvain, 2001; Martin & Wight, 2008; Meegan & Berg, 2002; Rogoff, 1998; Strough & Margrett, 2002). Research on children's collaboration was initiated within the Piagetian and sociocultural views of cognition to understand how adults (e.g., parents, teachers) and peers can scaffold children's performance to optimize their problem solving or spur shifts in children's thinking (see Gauvain & Reynolds, Chapter 11; Rogoff, 1998). Research on adults' collaboration was initiated to understand how adults working together might compensate for individual performance deficits seen in normal aging as well as optimize performance (Baltes & Staudinger, 1996; Dixon & Gould, 1996).

We illustrate the findings in this field by focusing on well- and ill-structured problem-solving tasks (e.g., scientific problem solving, planning tasks, and everyday problems). Three types of designs are frequently used to examine collaboration: (1) explicit comparisons of collaborative performance and individual performance (e.g., Gauvain & Rogoff, 1989; Margrett & Marsiske, 2002), (2) comparing individual differences in collaborative performance across age (e.g., Berg, Smith et al., 2007; Cheng & Strough, 2004; Dixon & Gould, 1998), relationship status of dyads (Margrett & Marsiske, 2002), or interactive communication within the collaborative session (Berg, Johnson, Meegan, & Strough, 2003; Berg, Smith et al., 2007), and (3) comparing the performance of interacting pairs to their dyadic potential as indexed by the combined performance of two individuals who do not interact (the "nominal" pair design, Johansson, Andersson, & Ronnberg, 2000; Strough et al., 2008). The general conclusion from this body of work is that collaborative units can, under certain circumstances, yield better performance than individuals on their own. Collaboration allows individuals to access knowledge and memories that they cannot do independently and thereby boosts performance. Working together, especially within close relationships, may provide individuals with access to a transactive memory or shared knowledge system (see shaded portion of Figure 10.1) that goes beyond the memory and knowledge of either individual (Wegner, Erber, & Raymond, 1991), allowing individuals to cue each other regarding effective strategies and stored memories.

Although much of the literature assumes that collaborators' primary goal is task performance, collaboration involves the coordination of task as well as social demands (Strough, Berg, & Meegan, 2001). However, because collaborative settings also contain social demands, goals may focus on mutual participation (e.g., ensuring consideration of both partners' ideas, making partners feel good about their ideas and getting along) versus controlling the interaction (e.g., getting the partner to pay attention to one's own ideas). Consistent with the framework outlined in Figure 10.1, goals relate to strategies that are used to work with others (interactive strategies involving warm affiliation versus control; Berg, Smith et al., 2007; Kimbler & Margrett, 2009; Strough & Berg, 2000). For instance, when preadolescent classmates were focused on mutual participation goals they employed conversation strategies that were more affiliative in nature (Strough & Berg, 2000). Further, goals mediated the stereotypical gender difference in girls' greater use of affiliative strategies relative to boys (see Rose & Rudolph, 2006 for a comprehensive review of gender differences in strategies for peer interaction).

Children and adolescents use more sophisticated strategies when they interact with adults rather than peers, although peers can be effective under certain circumstances. The enhanced effect of working with adults is that children are able to access their own knowledge that they cannot access alone or use the knowledge and skills of the adult partner (akin to Vygotsky's, 1978, zone of proximal development). For children during the early school years (ages 5–9 years) working on an errand planning task, the greater benefit from collaboration with adults was more pronounced for older children (Radziszewska & Rogoff, 1991). With adults, children engaged in more sophisticated strategies such as moves that involved advance planning (rather than one-step moves) and also engaged in discussions about strategy effectiveness.

Working with a peer on well-structured tasks such as the balance scale task (Tudge, Winterhoff, & Hogan, 1996) or replicating a Lego model (Azmitia, 1992) can be effective if the peer is more competent (Tudge et al., 1996), perhaps due to observation and learning of expert peers' strategies (Azmitia, 1992). Further, collaborative performance is enhanced when preadolescents enter peer collaborative settings with greater expectations concerning enjoyment and affiliation (Strough, Swenson, & Cheng, 2001), which are more likely to occur in same-sex dyads and among classmates with greater friendship. Among young adolescents, peer collaboration can be beneficial when tasks are difficult (Azmitia & Montgomery, 1993), perhaps because greater friendship of collaborators reduces the salience of social problem definitions (Strough et al., 2001) and interpersonal conflict (Swenson & Strough, 2008).

During adulthood, collaboration can be beneficial especially where collaborative partners are familiar, which allows partners to engage in high-level interactive strategies that benefit task performance. Cheng and Strough (2004) found that pairs of same-sex friends outperformed individuals on a composite measure of collaborative performance and made fewer planning mistakes. Kimbler and Margrett (2009) found that the benefit of collaboration was more pronounced among married couples than unacquainted pairs. This enhanced effect for married couples may be due to greater use of shared knowledge or transactive memory in couples (Johansson et al., 2000) and less frequent socializing (Kimbler & Margrett, 2009). Socializing "getting to know you" interactions are more prevalent among unacquainted partners compared to married couples (see also Gould, Kurzman, & Dixon, 1994). The collaborative task performance of married couples is enhanced when dyads interact in ways that are warm and affiliative (Berg et al., 2003) as well as involve "teaching" or "tutoring" episodes (Kimbler & Margrett, 2009). Further, collaborative performance is enhanced when couples adjust the way that they control the task direction as a function of their own and their partner's cognitive abilities (e.g., the more cognitively capable member controls task direction, Berg, Smith et al., 2007).

When a nominal pairs design is used to compare collaborating pairs' performance with their dyadic potential, social interaction may appear to be detrimental, to have no effect, or to be beneficial, depending on the performance metric and qualities of the dyadic relationship (Martin & Wight, 2008). Dyadic potential is indexed by the pooled performance of two people who do not interact, pairs "in name only" (nominal pairs). Strough et al. (2008) found that interacting pairs produced fewer strategies to everyday problems (a measure of fluency of everyday problem-solving performance) than nominal pairs, but there were no differences in the types of strategies generated. Similarly, on more well-structured memory tasks, interacting pairs do not achieve their dyadic potential—interacting pairs remember fewer items than nominal pairs (Johansson et al., 2000), except in the case where older married couples are able to access a transactive memory system. Older married dyads show their collaborative expertise on difficult problem-solving tasks that require the coordination of complex reasoning and memory (Peter-Wight & Martin, in press).

Although much of the research has focused on collaboration within the confines of the laboratory, where pairs were explicitly instructed to work together, there is extensive interest in how naturally occurring pairs and groups may work together in everyday life (Berg, Wiebe et al., 2007; Rogoff, 1998). During the school years, people may choose to work together to complete homework assignments or study for exams. In addition, group projects that require students to work with classmates to complete an assignment are frequently used in elementary, middle, and high school as well as in college. In adulthood, collaboration may be required in some contexts such as at work where teams or committees complete assignments together. Diversity in the contexts in which problems occur and individuals' assessments of their abilities to meet the challenges presented by a given context may be important for understanding the conditions under which collaboration voluntarily occurs in everyday life. In general, people report that they use and prefer self-directed action strategies that focus on solving the problem directly (Berg et al., 1998; Blanchard-Fields et al., 2007). However, when older adults perceive limitations in their own problem-solving abilities in gender-stereotyped contexts, they prefer solving problems collaboratively rather than alone (Strough, Cheng, & Swenson, 2002). For example, older women prefer to solve problems involving household repair collaboratively; whereas men prefer to solve problems with meal preparation collaboratively. Thus, older adults appear to prefer to collaborate when collaboration facilitates compensation. Other features of the problem context such as the greater severity of problems (Strough, McFall, & Schuller, 2010) and the availability of preferred partners such as spouses (among those who are married, Strough, Patrick, Swenson, Cheng, & Barnes, 2003) also may facilitate the occurrence of collaborative everyday problem solving.

In sum, the old adage that "two heads are better than one" appears to hold true in some situations—where children work with partners who are more expert than themselves and when adults work with a familiar partner compared to working alone or with a stranger. There is much left to understand about collaborative problem solving across the life span. Although recent work has emphasized the "social" goals that may be present in the collaborative context, more work is needed to understand how collaborative units coordinate both social and task demands of any given task. Further, although multiple types of relationship partners have been examined in the literature (most especially parent–child, friends, spouses), other existing natural collaborators (most especially siblings and adult child–parent relationships) should be examined to understand the contextual conditions of collaborative problem solving.

▦ FUTURE ISSUES IN THE STUDY OF PROBLEM SOLVING ACROSS THE LIFE SPAN

In this chapter, we reviewed a large body of research that examines problem solving across the life span in both well- and ill-structured domains. Age-related differences appear in many aspects of the problem-solving framework guiding this work: in the ways that individuals define their problems, set goals, the strategies that are used, and the regulation of affect. From early in the life span through middle-adulthood, the picture of what develops across the life span is one of increasing adaptivity and fit of strategies to specific problem-solving conditions and the goals that individuals wish to accomplish. In later adulthood for well-structured problems there is some suggestion of an age-related decrease in the fit between older adults' strategies and the constraints of problems. However, in the ill-structured domain of solving inter-personal problems, compared to younger adults, older adults' strategies appear to fit better with the demands of such problems, which may reflect goals for maintaining personally meaningful relationships and their ability to regulate emotions and mute expression of some emotions. Although we considered a variety of ill- and well-structured problems, there are important domains of problem solving that we did not cover (e.g., problem solving in the domains of health, family interaction and conflict), as work in these areas has not explicitly measured aspects of problem-solving performance. However, the field will benefit by an integration of these related fields. In the following section, we consider two broad directions for future research on problem solving across the life span.

Link Between Problem-Solving Capabilities and Relevant Real-World Adaptation

The definition of problem solving we used emphasizes the process whereby individuals overcome obstacles to goal-directed behavior and adapt to the environment. Our definition makes it crucial to understand how successful problem solving relates to successful adaptation to changing contexts across the life span. Our framework posits that problem solving within certain contexts will be differentially important for predicting adaptation at different points during the life span. Yet, the literature is mostly silent on the link between problem solving and adaptation to relevant environments across age. For instance, given our framework one would predict that problem solving couched in the school context would be less predictive of adaptation for older adults than for school-aged children. This assertion is difficult to assess with the current literature as few studies use similar tasks across the life span and we are aware of no studies that examine problem solving across multiple age periods and at the same time include broad-based measures of adaptation. Even within the confines of a specific problem-solving task such as mental arithmetic, we do not know whether differences in the adaptivity of strategy selection of older adults in response to problem parameters translates into their poorer mathematics performance (a relevant measure of adaptation in the school context) or more broadly their ability to use mathematics in everyday life (e.g., at the grocery store in comparing unit prices, see Lave, 1989). Although some research does include more broad-based measures of adaptation to real-world contexts (e.g., Allaire & Marsiske's, 2002 use of the instrumental activities of daily living, a measure of independent functioning in late life; Dodge's work linking social information processing to social competence), such work typically focuses on only one age group. Addressing the question of whether measures of problem solving are equally relevant for measures of adaptation across the life span will require the development of valid measures of successful adaptation, a task that in itself is a significant undertaking.

One issue important for understanding the development of problem solving across the life span pertains to transitions to and from the contexts most prevalent during a particular age period. What are the consequences of success (or failure) in solving problems that emerge within one developmental context for the success or failure in dealing with the demands of the contexts one encounters later in life? That this question has received relatively little attention within the extant literature is surprising given that one of the earliest theories of life-span human development (Erikson, 1968) highlighted key developmental competencies associated with distinct age periods. Of the research we have reviewed, the research conducted by Dodge, Pettit, and their colleagues comes closest by examining how success or failure with one important task of childhood, acceptance or rejection within the peer group, relates to interpersonal relationships in adulthood. Such work is important in understanding the rigidity or plasticity of developmental trajectories of problem solving and is necessary to advance understanding of what develops in problem solving across the life span.

Mechanisms of Developmental Change

Researchers have begun to address the mechanisms that underlie developmental differences in aspects of the problem-solving process. Such mechanisms may be different for well-structured versus ill-structured problems, although rarely are similar mechanisms examined in these two literatures. For instance, for well-structured problems such as arithmetic problems, one mechanism that may underlie older adults' lower adaptivity of strategies in response to changing problem parameters may be slower processing speed (see Duverne & Lemaire, 2005 for a review). Slower processing speed is a central resource that has been implicated in numerous age differences in cognitive tasks across the life span (Salthouse & Ferrer-Caja, 2003). Across childhood, one mechanism contributing to changes in strategy selection for solving arithmetic problems is thought to be the experience that children have with specific types of problems, especially the experience derived from the school environment (Siegler, 1996).

For ill-structured problems, the mechanisms purported to underlie age differences in strategy selection include emotion regulation skills, greater experience with social situations and contingences, and changes in goals for social problems. The mediating mechanism that has perhaps the greatest evidence for older adults' greater effectiveness in dealing with interpersonal everyday problems is emotion regulation skills (Blanchard-Fields, 2007). Although greater experience has frequently been posited as a factor important for understanding age differences in strategies (Berg et al., 1999; Cornelius & Caspi, 1987), experience is rarely measured in a way that elucidates its role as a mechanism. Researchers have not determined whether the key aspect of experience is the number of times that a person has had a similar problem, global experience or training within the domain (e.g., expertise within a domain like mathematics), or life-long experience such as understanding that confronting one's partner within a close interpersonal relationship may have greater long-term costs than avoiding conflict.

A better understanding of the role of experience may be gained from applying microgenetic designs to examine problem-solving models across time. These designs have been used extensively for well-structured problems (arithmetic, Siegler, 2006a, 2006b). For instance, examining social problem solving in the context of a new social setting where individuals' ability to manage conflict with others is tracked across time might allow for the examination of multiple mechanisms underlying changes in strategies, goal-strategy fit, context specificity of strategies, and individual differences versus intraindividual variability in problem solving. Comparisons across well- and ill-structured problems within the same domain would also be an important contribution to understanding whether the mechanisms of developmental change vary across these two different types of problems (Allaire & Marsiske, 2002).

CONCLUSIONS

To conclude, from infancy through later adulthood, individuals experience a myriad of both well- and ill-structured problems that they must solve in order to adapt to their daily environments. Individuals implement strategies, either on their own or in collaboration with others, that are in large part fit to their goals and reflect the demands of their larger developmental contexts. Building an understanding of "What Develops?" for problem solving across the life span will require researchers to face a number of challenges. Importantly, researchers will need to move beyond the boundaries of the age period under investigation in any given study to think more broadly about developmental precursors and consequences for later periods of development. Although developmental scientists tend to specialize in an age period (e.g., childhood) a greater appreciation and acknowledgment that development occurs across the entire life span will advance our understanding of "What Develops?" In this review, we brought together what we believe are related areas of inquiry (e.g., social problem solving, conflict management) to address one barrier to understanding the development of problem solving across the life span. By highlighting some of the similarities present in what have traditionally been treated as distinct areas of inquiry, our review provides an initial understanding upon which to build future research on the development of problem solving across the life span. The field is armed with an array of interesting tasks and paradigms and is thus well poised to address what develops in problem solving across the life span.

ACKNOWLEDGMENTS

Preparation of this chapter was supported in part by grant R01 DK063044 from the National Institute of Diabetes and Digestive Kidney Diseases. The authors thank Vito Rontino for his assistance in preparing the figure for this chapter and Joseph McFall and Emily Keener for their comments on a draft of this chapter.

REFERENCES

Ainsworth, M. D., & Bell, S. M. (1970). Attachment, exploration, and separation: Illustrated by one-year olds in a strange situation. *Child Development, 41,* 49–67.

Allaire, J. C., & Marsiske, M. (1999). Everyday cognition: Age and intellectual ability correlates. *Psychology and Aging, 14,* 627–644.

Allaire, J. C., & Marsiske, M. (2002). Well- and ill-defined measures of everyday cognition: Relationship to older adults' intellectual ability and functional status. *Psychology & Aging, 17,* 101–115.

Arend, G., Gove, F. L., & Sroufe, L. A. (1979). Continuity of individual adaptation from infancy to kindergarten: A predictive study of ego-resiliency and curiosity in preschooler. *Child Development, 50,* 950–959.

Arnaud, L., Lemaire, P., Allen, P., & Michel, B. F. (2008). Strategic aspects of young, healthy older adults' and Alzheimer patients' arithmetic performance. *Cortex, 44,* 119–130.

Arnett, J. J. (2000). Emerging adulthood: A theory of development from the late teens through the twenties. *American Psychologist, 55,* 469–480.

Artistico, D., Cervone, D., & Pezzuti, L. (2003). Perceived self-efficacy and everyday problem-solving among young and older adults. *Psychology and Aging, 18,* 68–79.

Ashcraft, M. H., & Ridley, K. S. (2005). Math anxiety and its cognitive consequences: A tutorial review. In J. I. D. Campbell (Ed.), *Handbook of mathematical cognition* (pp. 315–327). New York: Psychology Press.

Aspinwall, L. G., & Taylor, S. E. (1997). A stitch in time: Self-regulation and proactive coping. *Psychological Bulletin, 121,* 417–436.

Azmitia, M. (1992). Peer interaction and problem solving: When are two heads better than one? *Child Development, 59,* 87–96.

Azmitia, M., & Montgomery, R. (1993). Friendship, transactive dialogues, and the development of scientific reasoning. *Social Development, 2,* 202–221.

Baillargeon, R., Li, J., Ng, W., & Yuan, S. (2009). An account of infants' physical reasoning. In A. Woodwoard & A. Needham (Eds.), *Learning and the infant mind* (pp. 66–116). New York: Oxford University Press.

Baltes, P. B. (1987). Theoretical propositions of life-span developmental psychology: On the dynamics between growth and decline. *Developmental Psychology, 23,* 611–626.

Baltes, P. B., Dittmann-Kohli, F., & Dixon, R. A. (1984). New perspectives on the development of intelligence in adulthood: Toward a dual-process conception and a model of selective optimization with compensation. In P. B. Baltes & O. G. Brim, Jr. (Eds.), *Life-span development and behavior* (Vol. 6, pp. 33–76). New York: Academic Press.

Baltes, P. B., & Staudinger, U. M. (Eds.). (1996). *Interactive minds: Life-span perspectives on the social foundation of cognition.* New York: Cambridge University Press.

Band, E., & Weisz, J. R. (1988). How to feel better when it feels bad: Children's perspectives on coping with everyday stress. *Developmental Psychology, 24,* 247–253.

Bauer, P. J. (2006). Event memory. In D. Kuhn & R. S. Siegler (Volume Eds.), W. Damon & R. M. Lerner (Series Ed.), *Handbook of child psychology* (pp. 373–425). Hoboken, NJ: Wiley and Sons.

Ben-Zeev, T., Duncan, S., & Forbes, C. (2005). Stereotypes and math performance. In J. I. D. Campbell (Ed.), *Handbook of mathematical cognition* (pp. 235–249). New York: Psychology Press.

Berg, C. A. (1989). Knowledge of strategies for dealing with everyday problems from childhood through adolescence. *Developmental Psychology, 25,* 607–618.

Berg, C. A., Johnson, M. M. S., Meegan, S. P., & Strough, J. (2003). Collaborative problem-solving interaction in young and old married couples. *Discourse Processes, 35,* 33–58.

Berg, C. A., & Klaczynski, P. (2002). Contextual variability in the expression and meaning of intelligence. In R. J. Sternberg & E. L. Grigorenko (Eds.) *The general factor of intelligence: How general is it?* (pp. 381–412). Mahwah, NJ: Lawrence Erlbaum.

Berg, C. A., Meegan, S. P., & Deviney, F. P. (1998). A social contextual model of coping with everyday problems across the life span. *International Journal of Behavioral Development, 22,* 239–261.

Berg, C. A., Meegan, S. P., & Klaczynski, P. (1999). Age and experiential differences in strategy generation and information requests for solving everyday problems. *International Journal of Behavioral Development, 23,* 615–639.

Berg, C. A., Skinner, M., & Ko, K. (2009). An integrative model of everyday problem solving across the adult life span. In M. C. Smith & T. G. Reio (Eds.), *Handbook of research on adult learning and development* (pp. 524–552). Mahwah, NJ: Erlbaum.

Berg, C. A., Smith, T. W., Ko, K., Beveridge, R., Story, N, Henry, N., et al. (2007). Task control and cognitive abilities of self and spouse in collaboration in middle-aged and older couples. *Psychology and Aging, 22*, 420–427.

Berg, C. A., Strough, J., Calderone, K. S., Meegan, S. P., & Sansone, C. (1997). The social context of planning and preventing everyday problems from occurring. In S. L. Friedman & E. K. Scholnick (Eds.), *Why, how, and when do we plan? The developmental psychology of planning* (pp. 209–236). Hillsdale, NJ: Erlbaum.

Berg, C. A., Strough, J., Calderone, K. S., Sansone, C., & Weir, C. (1998). The role of problem definitions in understanding age and context effects on strategies for solving everyday problems. *Psychology and Aging, 13*, 29–44.

Berg, C. A., Wiebe, D. J., Beveridge, R. M., Palmer, D. L., Korbel, C. D., Upchurch, R., et al. (2007). Appraised involvement in coping and emotional adjustment in children with diabetes and their mothers. *Journal of Pediatric Psychology, 32*, 995–1005.

Beveridge, R. M., Berg, C. A., Wiebe, D. J., & Palmer, D. A. (2006). Mother and adolescent representations of illness ownership and stressful events surrounding diabetes. *Journal of Pediatric Psychology, 31*, 818–827.

Binet, A., & Simon, T. (1961). The development of intelligence in children. In J. J. Jenkins & D. G. Paterson (Eds.), *Studies in individual differences: The Search for intelligence* (pp. 81–111). East Norward, CT: Appleton-Century-Crofts.

Birditt, K. S., Fingerman, K. L., & Almeida, D. M. (2005). Age differences in exposure and reactions to interpersonal tensions: A daily diary study. *Psychology and Aging, 20*, 330–340.

Blanchard-Fields, F. (1986). Reasoning on social dilemmas varying in emotional saliency: An adult developmental perspective. *Psychology and Aging, 1*, 325–333.

Blanchard-Fields, F. (2007). Everyday problem solving and emotion: An adult development perspective. *Current Directions in Psychological Science, 16*, 26–31.

Blanchard-Fields, F., & Coats, A. H. (2008). The experience of anger and sadness in everyday problems impacts age differences in emotion regulation. *Developmental Psychology, 44*, 1547–1556.

Blanchard-Fields, F., Chen, Y., & Norris, L. (1997). Everyday problem solving across the life span: Influence of domain specificity and cognitive appraisal. *Psychology and Aging, 12*, 684–693.

Blanchard-Fields, F., Jahnke, H. C., & Camp, C. (1995). Age differences in problem-solving style: The role of emotional salience. *Psychology and Aging, 10*, 173–180.

Blanchard-Fields, F., Mienaltowski, A., & Seay, R. B. (2007). Age differences in everyday problem-solving effectiveness: Older adults select more effective strategies for interpersonal problems. *Journal of Gerontology: Psychological Sciences, 62B*, P61–P64.

Buhrmester, D. (1996). Need fulfillment, interpersonal competence and the developmental contexts of early adolescent friendships. In W. M. Bukowski, A. F. Newcomb, & W. W. Hartup (Eds.) *The company they keep: Friendships and their developmental significance* (pp. 158–185). New York: Cambridge University Press.

Carstensen, L., & Mikels, J. A. (2005). At the intersection of emotion and cognition: Aging and the positivity effect. *Current Directions in Psychological Science, 14*, 117–121.

Case, R. (1985). *Intellectual development*. Orlando, FL: Academic Press.

Case, R., & Okamoto, Y. (1996). The role of central conceptual structures in the development of children's thought. *Monographs of the Society for Research in Child Development, 61*(1–2, Serial No. 246).

Chang, E. C., D'Zurilla, T. J., & Sanna, L. J. (Eds.). (2004). *Social problem solving: Theory, research, and training.* Washington, DC: American Psychological Association.

Charles, S. T., & Carstensen, L. L. (2010). Social and emotional aging. *Annual Review of Psychology, 61*, 383–409.

Charles, S. T., Piazza, J. R., Luong, G., & Almeida, D. M. (2009). Now you see it, now you don't: Age differences in affective reactivity to social tensions. *Psychology and Aging, 24*, 645–653.

Chen, Z., & Siegler, R. S. (2000). Across the great divide: Bridging the gap between understanding of toddlers' and older children's thinking. *Monographs of the Society for Research in Child Development, 65*(2), i–vii, 1–96.

Cheng, S., & Strough, J. (2004). A comparison of collaborative and individual everyday problem solving in young and older adults. *International Journal of Aging and Human Development, 58*, 167–195.

Coats, A. H., & Blanchard-Fields, F. (2008). Emotion regulation in interpersonal problems: The role of cognitive-emotional complexity, emotion regulation goals, and expressivity. *Psychology and Aging, 23*, 39–51.

Cohen, L. B., & Cashon, C. H. (2006). Infant cognition. In D. Kuhn & R. S. Siegler (Volume Eds.), W. Damon & R. M. Lerner (Series Eds.), *Handbook of child psychology* (Vol. 2, pp. 214–251). Hoboken, NJ: John Wiley & Sons.

Collins, A. W., & Steinberg, L. (2006). Adolescent development in interpersonal context. In W. Damon (Series Ed.), N. Eisenberg (Volume Ed.), *Handbook of child psychology: Social, emotional, and personality development* (Vol. 3, 5th ed., pp. 1003–1067). Hoboken, NJ: John Wiley & Sons.

Cornelius, S. W., & Caspi, A. (1987). Everyday problem solving in adulthood and old age. *Psychology and Aging, 2*, 144–153.

Crick, N. R., & Dodge, K. A. (1994). A review and reformulation of social information-processing mechanisms in children's social adjustment. *Psychological Bulleting, 115*, 74–101.

Crockenberg, S. C., & Leerkes, E. M. (2004). Infant and maternal behaviors regulate infant reactivity to novelty at 6 months. *Developmental Psychology, 40*, 1123–1132.

de Castro, B. O., Veerman, J. W., Koops, W., Bosch, J. D., & Monshouwer, H. L. (2002). Hostile attribution of intent and aggressive behavior: A meta analysis. *Child Development, 73*, 916–934.

Denney, N. W. (1989). Everyday problem solving: Methodological issues, research findings, and a model. In L. W. Poon, D. C. Rubin, & B. A. Wilson (Eds.), *Everyday cognition in adulthood and late life* (pp. 330–351). New York: Cambridge University Press.

Denney, N. W., & Pearce, K. A. (1989). A developmental study of practical problem solving in adults. *Psychology and Aging, 4*, 438–442.

Denney, N. W., Tozier, T. L., & Schlotthauer, C. A. (1992). The effect of instructions on age differences in practical problem solving. *Journal of Gerontology: Psychological Sciences, 47*, P142–P145.

Diener, M. L., Mangelsdorf, S. C., McHale, J. L., & Frosch, C. A. (2002). Infants' behavioral strategies with fathers and mothers: Associations with emotional expressions and attachment quality. *Infancy, 3*, 153–174.

Dittmann-Kohli, F., & Baltes, P. B. (1984). Towards an action-theoretical and pragmatic conception of intelligence dfuring adulthood and old age. In C. N. Alexander & E. Langer (Eds.), *Beyond formal operations: Alternative endpoints to human development*. New York: Oxford University Press.

Dixon, R. A., & Gould, O. N. (1996). Adults telling and retelling stories collaboratively. In P. B. Baltes & U. M. Staudinger (Eds.), *Interactive minds: Life-span perspectives on the social foundation of cognition* (pp. 221–241). New York: Cambridge University Press.

Dixon, R. A., & Gould, O. N. (1998). Younger and older adults collaborating on retelling everyday stories. *Applied Developmental Science, 2*, 160–171.

Dodge, K. (1986). A social information processing model of social competence in children. In M. Perlmutter (Eds), *The Minnesota Symposium on Child Psychology* (Vol. 18, pp. 77–125). Hillsdale, NJ: Erlbaum.

Dodge, K. A., Pettit, G. S., McClaskey, C. L., & Brown, M. M. (1986). Social competence in children. *Monographs of the Society for Research in Child Development, 51*(2, Serial No. 213).

Duverne, S., & Lemaire, P. (2005). Aging and mental arithmetic. In J. I. D. Campbell (Ed.), *Handbook of mathematical cognition* (pp. 397–412). New York: Psychology Press.

D'Zurilla, T. J., Nezu, A. M., & Maydeu-Olivares, A. (2004). Social problem solving: Theory and assessment. In E. C. Chang, T. J. D'Zurilla, & L. J. Sanna (Eds.), *Social problem solving* (pp. 11–27). Washington, DC: American Psychological Association.

Eisenberg, N., Fabes, R. A., Murphy, B., Maszk, P., Smith, M., & Karbon, M. (1995). The role of emotionality and regulation in children's social functioning: A longitudinal study. *Child Development, 66*, 1360–1384.

Erikson, E. H. (1968). *Identity: Youth and crisis*. New York: Norton.

Feldman, S. S., & Gowen, L. K. (1998). Conflict negotiation tactics in romantic relationships in high school students. *Journal of Youth and Adolescence, 27*, 691–717.

Gallistel, C. R., & Gelman, R. (1992). Preverbal and verbal counting and computation. *Cognition, 44*, 43–74.

Gauvain, M. (2001). *The social context of cognitive development*. New York: Guilford Press.

Gauvain, M., & Rogoff, B. (1989). Collaborative problem solving and children's planning skills. *Developmental Psychology, 25*, 139–151.

Geary, D. C. (2006). Development of mathematical understanding. In D. Kuhn & R. S. Siegler (Ed.), *Handbook of child psychology: Cognition, perception, and language* (Vol. 2, 6th ed., pp. 777–810). Hoboken, NJ: Wiley.

Geary, D. C., Bow-Thomas, C. C., Liu, F., & Siegler, R. S. (1996). Development of arithmetical competencies in Chinese and American children: Influence of age, language, and schooling. *Child Development, 67*, 2022–2044.

Gigerenzer, G. (2008). Why heuristics work. *Perspectives on Psychological Science, 3,* 20–29.

Good, C., & Aronson, J. (2008). The development of stereotype threat. In C. Wainryb, J. G. Smetana, & E. Turiel (Eds.), *Social development, social inequalities, and social justice* (pp. 155–183). New York: Lawrence Erlbaum.

Gould, O. N., Kurzman, D., & Dixon, R. A. (1994). Communication during prose recall conversations by young and old dyads. *Discourse Processes, 17,* 149–165.

Grant, H., & Dweck, C. S. (2003). Clarifying achievement goals and their impact. *Journal of Personality and Social Psychology, 85,* 541–553.

Halford, G. S., & Andrews, G. (2006). Reasoning and problem solving. In D. Kuhn & R. S. Siegler (Volume Eds.), W. Damon & R. M. Lerner (Series Eds.), *Handbook of child psychology* (Vol. 2, pp. 557–608). Hoboken, NJ: John Wiley & Sons.

Hecht, S. A. (2006). Group differences in adult simple arithmetic: Good retrievers, not-so-good retrievers, and perfectionists. *Memory and Cognition, 34,* 207–216.

Heckhausen, J. (1997). Developmental regulation across adulthood: Primary and secondary control of age-related challenges. *Developmental Psychology, 33,* 176–187.

Hoppmann, C. A., Coats, A. H., & Blanchard-Fields, F. (2008). Goals and everyday problem solving: Examining the link between age-related goals and problem-solving strategy use. *Aging, Neuropsychology, and Cognition, 15,* 401–423.

Horn, J., L., & Hofer, S. M. (1992). Major abilities and development in the adult period. In R. J. Sternberg & C. A. Berg (Eds.), *Intellectual development* (pp. 44–99). Cambridge, MA: Cambridge University Press.

Johansson, O., Andersson, J., & Ronnberg, J. (2000). Do elderly couples have a better prospective memory than other elderly people when they collaborate? *Applied Cognitive Psychology, 14,* 121–133.

Kahneman, D., & Klein, G. (2009). Conditions for intuitive expertise: A failure to disagree. *American Psychologist, 64,* 515–526.

Karraker, K. H., Lake, M. A., & Parry, T. B. (1994). Infant coping with everyday stressful events. *Merrill-Palmer Quarterly, 40,* 171–189.

Keltikangas-Jarvinen, L., & Heinonen, K. (2003). Childhood roots of adulthood hostility: Family factors as predictors of cognitive and affective hostility. *Child Development, 74,* 1751–1768.

Kimbler, K. J., & Margrett, J. A. (2009). Older adults' interactive behaviors during collaboration on everyday problems: Linking process and outcome. *International Journal of Behavioral Development, 33,* 531–542.

Klaczynski, P. A. (2000). Motivated scientific reasoning biases, epistemological beliefs, and theory polarization: A two-process approach to adolescent cognition. *Child Development, 71,* 1347–1366.

Klahr, D., & Robinson, M. (1981). Formal assessment of problem solving and planning processes in children. *Cognitive Psychology, 13,* 113–148.

Lang, F. R., & Carstensen, L. L. (2002). Time counts: Future time perspective, goals and social relationships, *Psychology and Aging, 17,* 125–139.

Lansford, J. E., Malone, P. S., Dodge, K. A., Crozier, J. C., Pettit, G. S., & Bates, J. E. (2006). A 12 year prospective study of patterns of social information processing problems and externalizing behaviors. *Journal of Abnormal Child Psychology, 34,* 715–724.

Larson, R., & Richards, M. (1991). Daily companionship in late childhood and early adolescence: Changing developmental contexts. *Child Development, 62,* 284–300.

Laursen, B., & Collins, W. A. (1994). Interpersonal conflict during adolescence. *Psychological Bulletin, 115,* 197–209.

Laursen B., Finkelstein, B. D., & Townsend Betts, N. (2001). A developmental meta-analysis of peer conflict resolution. *Developmental Review, 21,* 423–449.

Lave, J. (1989). *Cognition in practice.* New York: Cambridge University Press.

Lehrer, R., & Schauble, L. (2006). Scientific thinking and science literacy. In K. A. Renninger & I. Sigel (Volume Eds.) and W. Damon & R. Lerner (Series Eds.), *Handbook of child psychology.* Hoboken, NJ: John Wiley & Sons.

Lemaire, P., Arnaud, L., & Lecacheur, M. (2004). Adults' age-related differences in adaptivity of strategy choices: Evidence from computational estimation. *Psychology and Aging, 19*(3), 467–481.

Lemaire, P., & Lcacheur, M. (2004). Five-rule effects in young and older adults' arithmetic: Further evidence for age-related differences in strategy selection. *Current Psychology Letters, 12,* 2–13.

Liben, L. S., & Bigler, R. S. (2002). The developmental course of gender differentiation: Conceptualizing, measuring, and evaluating constructs and pathways. *Monographs of the Society for Research in Child Development, 67,*(2, Serial No. 269).

Lindenberger, U., & Oertzen, T. (2006). Variability in cognitive aging: From taxonomy to theory. In E. Bialystok & F. I. M. Craik (Eds.), *Lifespan cognition: Mechanisms of change* (pp. 297–314). New York: Oxford University Press.

Little, C., & Carter, A. S. (2005). Negative emotional reactivity and regulation in 12 month olds following emotional challenge: Contributions of maternal-infant emotional availability in a low income sample. *Infant Mental Health Journal, 26*, 354–368.

Margrett, J. A., & Marsiske, M. (2002). Gender differences in older adults' everyday cognitive collaboration. *International Journal of Behavioral Development, 26*, 45–59.

Martin, M., & Wight, M. (2008). Dyadic cognition in old age: Paradigms, findings, and directions. In S. M. Hofer & D. F. Alwin (Eds.), *Handbook of cognitive aging: Interdisciplinary perspectives* (pp. 629–646). Thousand Oaks, CA: Sage.

Meegan, S. P., & Berg, C. A. (2002). Contexts, functions, forms, and processes of collaborative everyday problem solving in older adulthood. *International Journal of Behavioral Development, 26*, 6–15.

Mehta, C. M., & Strough, J. (2009). Sex segregation in friendships and normative contexts across the life span. *Developmental Review, 29*, 201–220.

Miller, A. L., McDonough, S. C., Rosenblum, K. L., & Sameroff, A. J. (2002). Emotion regulation in context: Situational effects on infant and caregiver behavior. *Infancy, 3*, 403–433.

Morales, M., Mundy, P., Crowson, M. M., Neal, A. R., & Delgado, C. E. F. (2005). Individual differences in infant attention skills, joint attention, and emotion regulation behavior. *International Journal of Behavioral Development, 29*, 259–263.

Nas, C. N., de Castro, B. O., & Koops, W. (2005). Social information processing in delinquent adolescents. *Psychology, Crime and Law, 11*, 363–375.

Newcomb, A. F., & Bagwell, C. L. (1995). Children's friendship relations: A meta-analytic review. *Psychological Bulletin, 117*, 306–347.

Ojanen, T., Aunola, K., Salmivalli, C. (2007). Situation specificity of children's social goals: Changing goals according to changing situations? *International Journal of Behavioral Development, 31*, 232–241.

Peter-Wight, M., & Martin, M. (in press). When 2 is better than 1+1: Older spouses' individual and dyadic problem solving. *European Psychologist.*

Pettit, G. D., Lansford, J. E., Malone, P. S., Dodge, K. A., & Bates, J. E. (2010). Domain specificity in relationship history, social information processing, and violent behavior in early adulthood. *Journal of Personality and Social Psychology, 98*, 190–200.

Piaget, J. (1952). *The origins of intelligence in children.* New York: International Universities Press.

Pickard, J., & Strough, J. (2003). Variability in goals as a function of same-sex and other-sex contexts. *Sex Roles, 49*, 643–652.

Radziszewska, B., & Rogoff, B. (1991). Children's guided participation in planning imaginary errands with skilled adult or peer partners. *Developmental Psychology, 27*, 381–389.

Raiikkonen, K., Katainen, S., Keskivaara, P., & Keltikangas-Jarvinen, L. (2000). Temperament, mothering, and hostile attitudes: A 12-year longitudinal study. *Personality and Social Psychology Bulletin, 26*, 3–12.

Reyna, V., & Rivers, S. E. (2008). Current theories of risk and rational decision making. *Developmental Review, 28*, 1–11.

Rivers, S. E., Reyna, V. F., & Mills, B. (2008). Risk taking under the influence: A fuzzy-trace theory of emotion in adolescence. *Developmental Review, 28*, 107–144.

Rogoff, B. (1998). Cognition as a collaborative process. In W. Damon (Ed). *Handbook of child psychology: Cognition, perception, and language* (Vol. 2, pp. 679–744). Hoboken, NJ: John Wiley & Sons.

Roisman, G. I., Masten, A. S., Coatsworth, D. J., & Tellegen, A. (2004). Salient and emerging developmental tasks in the transition to adulthood. *Child Development, 75*, 123–133.

Rose, A. J., & Asher, S. R. (1999). Children's goals and strategies in response to conflicts within a friendship. *Developmental Psychology, 35*, 69–79.

Rose, A. J., & Rudolph, K. (2006). A review of sex differences in peer relationship processes: Potential tradeoffs for the emotional and behavioral development of girls and boys. *Psychological Bulletin, 132*, 98–131.

Ross, C. N., & Karraker, K. H. (1999). Effects of fatigue on infant emotional reactivity and regulation. *Infant Mental Health Journal, 20*, 410–428.

Rothbart, M. K., Posner, M. I., & Kieras, J. (2006). Temperament, attention and the development of emotion regulation. In K. McCartney & D. Phillips (Eds.) *Blackwell handbook of early child development.* Malden, MA: Blackwell.

Rubin, K. H., & Krasnor, I. R. (1986). Social cognitive and social behavioral perspectives on problem solving. In M. Perlmutter (Ed.), *The Minnesota Symposium on Child Psychology* (Vol. 18, pp.
1–68). Hillsdale, NJ: Erlbaum.

Sallquist, J. V., Eisenberg, N., Spinrad, T. L., Reiser, M., Hofer, C., Zhou, Q., et al. (2009). Positive
and negative emotionality: Trajectories across six years and relations with social competence.
Emotion, 9, 15–28.

Salmivalli, C., & Peets, K. (2009). Pre-adolescents peer relational schemas and social goals across
relational contexts *Social Development, 18*, 817–832.

Salthouse, T. A., Babcock, R. L., Skovronek, E., Mitchell, D. R. D., & Palmon, R. (1990). Age and experience effects in spatial visualization. *Developmental Psychology, 26*, 128–136.

Salthouse, T. A., & Ferrer-Caja, E. (2003). What needs to be explained to account for age-related
effects on multiple cognitive variables. *Psychology and Aging, 19*, 91–110.

Sansone, C., & Berg, C. A. (1993). Adapting to the environment across the life span: Different process
or different inputs? *International Journal of Behavioral Development, 16*, 215–241.

Seiffge-Krenke, I., Aunola, K., & Nurmi, J. (2009). Changes in stress perception and coping during
adolescence: The role of situational and personal factors. *Child Development, 80*, 259–279.

Shantz, C. U., & Hartup, W. W. (1992). *Conflict in child and adolescent development.* New York:
Cambridge University Press.

Shrager, J., & Siegler, R. S. (1998). SCADS: A model of children's strategy choices and strategy discoveries. *Psychological Science, 9*, 405–410.

Shure, M. B., & Aberson, B. (2006). Enhancing the process of resilience through effective thinking.
In S. Goldstein & R. B. Brooks (Eds.), *Handbook of resilience in children* (pp. 373–396). New York:
Springer.

Siegler, R. S. (1978). The origins of scientific reasoning. In R. S. Siegler (Ed.), *Children's thinking:
What develops.* Hillsdale, NJ: Erlbaum.

Siegler, R. S. (1981). Developmental sequences within and between concepts. *Monographs of the
Society for Research in Child Development, 46* (Whole No. 189).

Siegler, R. S. (1988). Individual differences in strategy choices: Good students, not-so-good students,
and perfectionists. *Child Development, 59*, 833–851.

Siegler, R. S. (1996). *Emerging minds.* New York: Oxford University Press.

Siegler, R. S. (2006a). Inter- and Intra-individual differences in problem solving across the lifespan.
In Bialystock, E. & Craik, F. I. M. (Eds.), *Life-span cognition:Mechanisms of change* (pp. 285–296).
New York: Oxford University Press.

Siegler, R. S. (2006b). Microgenetic analyses of learning. In D. Kuhn & R. S. Siegler (Volume Eds.),
W. Damon & R. M. Lerner (Series Eds.), *Handbook of child psychology* (Vol. 2, pp. 464–510).
Hoboken, NJ: John Wiley & Sons.

Siegler, R. S., & Alibali, M. W. (2005). *Children's thinking* (4th ed.). Upper Saddle River, NJ: Prentice
Hall.

Sorkin, D. H., & Rook, K. S. (2006). Dealing with negative social exchanges in later life: Coping
responses, goals, and effectiveness. *Psychology and Aging, 21*, 715–725.

Spivack, G., & Shure, M. B. (1982). Interpersonal cognitive problem-solving and clinical theory. In
B. Lahey & A. E. Kazdin (Eds.), *Advances in child clinical psychology* (Vol. 5, pp. 323–372). New
York: Plenum.

Starkey, P., & Cooper, R. G. (1980). Perception of numbers by human infants. *Science, 210*,
1033–1035.

Stifter, C. A., & Baungart, J. M. (1995). The regulation of negative reactivity: Function and development. *Developmental Psychology, 38*, 448–455.

Strough, J., & Berg, C. A. (2000). The role of goals in mediating dyad gender differences in high and
low involvement conversational exchanges. *Developmental Psychology,36*, 117–125.

Strough, J., Berg, C. A., & Meegan, S. P. (2001). Friendship and gender differences in task and social
interpretations of peer collaborative problem solving. *Social Development, 10*, 1–22.

Strough, J., Berg, C. A., & Sansone, C. (1996). Goals for solving everyday problems across the life
span: Age and gender differences in the salience of interpersonal concerns. *Developmental
Psychology, 32*, 1106–1115.

Strough, J., Cheng, S., & Swenson, L. M. (2002). Preferences for collaborative and individual everyday problem solving in later adulthood. *International Journal of Behavioral Development, 26*,
26–35.

Strough, J., & Margrett, J. A. (2002). Overview of the special section on collaborative cognition in
later adulthood. [Special section, J. Strough & J. Margrett (Guest Eds.)] *International Journal of
Behavioral Development, 26*, 2–5.

Strough, J., McFall, J. P., Flinn, J. A., & Schuller, K. L. (2008). Collaborative everyday problem solving among same-gender friends in early and later adulthood. *Psychology and Aging, 23*, 517–530.

Strough, J., McFall, J. P., & Schuller, K. L. (2010). Interpersonal strategies for dealing with hypothetical everyday arthritis problems. *International Journal of Aging and Human Development, 70*, 39–59.

Strough, J., Patrick, J. H., Swenson, L. M., Cheng, S., & Barnes, K. A. (2003). Collaborative everyday problem solving: Interpersonal relationships and problem dimensions. *International Journal of Aging and Human Development, 56*, 43–66.

Strough, J., Swenson, L. M., & Cheng, S. (2001). Friendship, gender, and preadolescents' representations of peer collaboration. *Merrill-Palmer Quarterly, 47*, 475–499.

Swenson, L. M., & Strough, J. (2008). Adolescents' collaboration in the classroom: Do peer relationships or gender matter? *Psychology in the Schools, 45*, 715–728.

Thornton, W. J. L., & Dumke, H. A. (2005). Age differences in everyday problem-solving and decision-making effectiveness: A meta-analytic review. *Psychology and Aging, 20*, 85–99.

Tudge, J. R. H., Winterhoff, P. A., & Hogan, D. M. (1996). The cognitive consequences of collaborative problem solving with and without feedback. *Child Development, 67*, 2892–2909.

Veroff, J., & Veroff, J. B. (1980). *Social incentives: A life span developmental approach.* New York: Academic Press.

Vygotsky, L. S. (1978). *Mind in society: The development of higher psychological processes.* Cambridge, MA: Harvard University Press.

Watson, T. L., & Blanchard-Fields, F. (1998). Thinking with your head and your heart: Age differences in everyday problem-solving strategy preferences. *Aging, Neuropsychology, and Cognition, 5*, 225–240.

Weber, E. U., & Johnson, E. J. (2009). Mindful judgment and decision making. *Annual Review of Psychology, 60*, 53–85.

Wegner, D. M., Erber, R., & Raymond, P. (1991). Transactive memory in close relationships. *Journal of Personality and Social Psychology, 61*, 923–929.

Wood, P. K. (1983). Inquiring systems and problem structure: Implications for cognitive development. *Human Development, 26*, 249–265.

Wynn, K. (1990). Children's understanding of counting. *Cognition, 36*, 155–193.

Xu, F., & Spelke, E. S. (2000). Large-number discrimination in 6-month-old infants. *Cognition, 74*, B1–B11.

THE SOCIOCULTURAL CONTEXT OF COGNITION ACROSS THE LIFE SPAN

11

Mary Gauvain and Chandra A. Reynolds

Human beings live in social and cultural context, and the people, practices, and artifacts in this context make substantial contributions to cognition throughout life. This chapter describes the sociocultural context of human cognition and its development. It begins with a brief historical account of this approach, followed by discussion of the inextricable connection between the sociocultural context and cognitive development and theories that attend to this connection. We then present research that shows how the sociocultural context contributes to human cognition throughout life. Our aim is to describe how experiences generated by the social and cultural context function as mechanisms of cognitive development. We do not consider sociocultural experiences to be the sole mechanisms; biological forces are also important. Human beings have unique biological capabilities and potentials that are activated over development by experiences in the species-specific context or ecological niche. For human beings the ecological niche of psychological development is the sociocultural context.

We view culture as an organized social unit in which members of the group share values, beliefs, and understandings about the world, participate in common practices including symbol systems, and transmit information and ways of living across generations (Goodnow, Miller, & Kessel, 1995). Development in sociocultural context is a dynamic process in which the individual emerges through transactions with others in the culture (Bakhurst, 2007). Individual characteristics including tendencies and constraints of the biological system, such as temperament and certain biological predispositions like some learning disabilities, coordinate with the sociocultural context in ways that yield a unique process of intellectual growth matched to the conditions in which a child lives. Moreover, as the child matures into adulthood, the match of environments to intellectual development may be in part driven by the increasing control individuals have in selecting environments within their sociocultural context (e.g., niche-picking; Scarr & McCartney, 1983). In more general terms, cognitive development is an emergent property of human biology and social and cultural experiences (White, 1996).

Several interrelated sociocultural processes contribute to cognitive development. We emphasize three processes that have received extensive research attention: social interaction, participation in social and cultural practices, and the use of cultural tools or artifacts to support intelligent action (Gauvain, 1995). Examination of this research reveals what has been learned about human cognition at various periods of life when the sociocultural context is taken into account. We conclude with discussion of how this examination provides unique insight into cognitive development over the life course. Future issues for study are also highlighted.

▓ THE SOCIOCULTURAL CONTEXT OF COGNITIVE DEVELOPMENT

A Brief Historical Account

In the late 1800s, some psychologists, most notably Wilhelm Wundt, were interested in the relation between human behavior and culture (Cole, 1996). However, this interest faded rapidly as areas of research that were better suited to experimental study, such as physiological and perceptual psychology, gained prominence. In the early and mid-20th century, the study of culture, at least among western psychologists, was minimal. But in the 1960s, psychologists, including those who studied cognitive development, were once again interested in culture (Cole, Gay, Glick, & Sharp, 1971; Dasen 1977; Greenfield, 1966, 1974; Munroe & Gauvain, 2009). Some of this research, which arose during widespread concern about school failure in western societies, compared the cognitive performance of children in western societies with that of children in nonwestern societies in which there was no formal schooling (Lancy, 1983). Findings raised important questions about human cognition. Assumptions of universality were challenged because children in nonwestern traditional societies did not perform as well as children in western industrial societies on a range of cognitive measures. Yet at the same time, children in nonwestern settings revealed impressive cognitive capabilities reflective of their everyday experiences, such as spatial knowledge, number concepts, and classification skills; and sometimes their expertise surpassed similar behaviors observed among children in western communities (e.g., Greenfield & Childs, 1977; Saxe, 1981; Serpell, 1979). In addition, similar findings were cropping up among anthropologists who reported remarkable cognitive skills among adults in nonwestern communities (Gladwin, 1970; Hutchins, 1983; Lave, 1977).

Researchers offered a number of explanations for the poorer performance of nonwestern children, including unfamiliarity with test materials and forms of discourse used in school (Rogoff, Gauvain, & Ellis, 1984). Yet efforts to control for these factors, for example, using familiar materials, did not eliminate performance differences (e.g., Cole et al., 1971). It appeared that the cultural context is fundamental to the development and expression of human thinking—a realization that introduced new ideas about cognition and its development. First, it indicated that cognitive performance is better on the activities and skills that are practiced and valued in a culture. This was a radical view for a discipline that had grown comfortable with untested assumptions about the universality and generality of cognition. Second, it demonstrated that the more an assessment deviates from the familiar context, the poorer is the performance. This point resonated with research on transfer in which cognitive competence across similar tasks was proving difficult to find. Third, because research with children and adults revealed similar patterns, the connection between culture and cognition is evident throughout life. Because these patterns were identified at the cultural level, what remained to be determined was the source of continuity beyond individual differences. Finally, when taken together, these ideas led to the general conclusion that cognition itself is a contextualized process.

Even though these insights invigorated research on cognitive development, it soon became clear that understanding the connections between context and cognition was a formidable task. Moreover, there was little extant theory to help pave the way, and some conventional research practices, such as separating the social, cognitive, and emotional aspects of development, were proving a hindrance. Some of the difficulty was overcome by ideas put forth by Vygotsky (1962) who viewed cognitive development as a sociocultural or sociohistorical process. For Vygotsky, four interrelated strands of human history contribute to cognitive development (Scribner, 1985). *General cultural history*, or culture, is the social and collective means of human thought and action. It includes material resources or tools that support thinking, socially organized activities and institutions, and symbol systems, including language, that organize and convey thoughts as well as regulate social and individual behavior. *Ontological or individual life history* integrates biological processes responsible for the development of basic mental functions, such as involuntary attention, and sociocultural processes that regulate the development of higher mental functions, such as intentional memory. The *history of a particular learning experience* concerns changes at the microanalytic level during learning. For Vygotsky, much of learning occurs in experiences that are mediated by cultural tools and more skilled cultural members; research on the zone of proximal development focuses on this aspect of history (Vygotsky, 1978). The *history of higher mental functions* is concerned with phylogenesis, in particular how specific mental functions, such as remembering, classifying, and conceptualizing, have changed as they have adapted to the circumstances and environments in which human beings live. This aspect of history is reflected in evolutionary psychology, which provides long-range historical support for the sociocultural context of human cognition.

The Evolutionary Foundation of the Sociocultural Context of Cognition

For evolutionary psychologists, changes in behavior over phylogenesis reflect changes in cognition (Barkow, Cosmides, & Tooby, 1992). Prehominids that could solve critical problems such as finding a mate, hunting for food, and rearing young group members were more likely to reproduce and transmit their genes across generations. Other species characteristics, also crafted by evolution, contributed to the emergence of human intelligence: the social nature of the species; the immaturity of the brain at birth; the protracted developmental course; the formation of emotional ties; and a vast potential for, and flexibility in, learning (Bjorklund & Pellegrini, 2002). Human infants require almost continual care, which provides them with substantial contact with more mature group members at the very time when children have much to learn. These social contacts involve strong emotional ties, a characteristic likely to emerge in early human relationships (Hinde, 1989) and which enhances the potential and motivation for learning (Anderson, 2000; Bretherton, 1992) and provides mental models that guide people in their adult relationships (Thompson, 1998).

Two types of learning account for the development of high levels of intellectual functioning in the individual life course. Some learning involves direct experiences with the world. This type was the focus of much of Piaget's research, especially during the sensorimotor period. The other type of learning, which supports higher-level cognitive processes, is socially mediated. Through social experience, children learn the symbols and tools that are passed across generations, such as language, counting, mnemonic devices, and literacy, which help people address problems of importance and value in the culture. Social mediation occurs in two interrelated ways: through the direct assistance of more experienced cultural members and through the guidance provided by these members, including ancestors, as instantiated in the activities, practices, and artifacts of the culture. Through these social processes, experienced cultural members support and guide children's learning, *and* children learn culturally established and valued ways of carrying out activities and solving problems.

Our human ancestors developed many social-cognitive capabilities to support social learning including the ability to seek, transmit, comprehend, and benefit from the understandings and actions of conspecifics (Hermann, Call, Hernández-Lloreda, Hare, & Tomasello, 2007). Other important skills are the capacity to recognize, communicate, cooperate, and share resources with group members, and the tendency to observe the behaviors of species members (Tomasello, Kruger, & Ratner, 1993). In individual development, these social-cognitive skills, which begin to take shape in early infancy, provide children with access to the thinking of other people and, by extension, the accumulated skills and practices of the culture.

Defining the Sociocultural Context of Cognition Across the Life Span

The sociocultural context of cognition can be defined in different ways. Our definition is rooted in a particular set of theoretical traditions and assumptions, described later, and a practical interest in meshing these ideas with the extensive body of contemporary research on the contextual basis of cognition and its development. We make no claim that what we describe is either the best or most exhaustive way to approach this topic. We simply seek an approach commensurate with current views of culture, human cognition, and psychological development.

The role of the sociocultural context in cognition across the life span is complex and includes three interrelated facets: processes of social interaction, experiences organized by the sociocultural context, and opportunities to learn that are embedded in cultural practices. Although the sociocultural context includes both the settings that give rise to psychological growth and the social-psychological processes that occur in these settings, our interest in process steers our attention toward the social experiences that promote and support human cognition (Gauvain, 2001). These experiences differ across the life span. Whereas learning and socialization are the main foci in childhood and adolescence, the changes in social roles and behaviors that occur with age affect the nature of sociocultural contributions to cognition in the years of maturity. Thus, in early development, we focus on efforts to convey cultural knowledge and ways of behaving to children, such as collaboration in the zone of proximal development (Vygotsky, 1978), scaffolding (Wood & Middleton, 1975), and guided participation (Rogoff, 1990, 1998). Later our attention turns to social processes that are more common among mature cultural members. For instance, formal social arrangements such as leadership and management roles may be helpful for promoting cognitive complexity and improving the maintenance of cognitive skills. In adulthood, less formal social arrangements, such as collaboration and consultation among spouses or adults, may benefit everyday problem solving and memory.

Learning about culture across development is aided by the fact that there are myriad representations and exemplars of mature cultural activities and behaviors for young community members to observe. Both children and adults participate in these activities and behaviors, albeit within the scope of their own capabilities (Gauvain, 1999; Goodnow et al., 1995). These activities and behaviors often involve the use of cultural tools (Cole, 1996). Human beings devise all kinds of tools, both symbolic and material, to support and extend intelligent behavior. Cultures value the tools they use to support intelligent action, pass knowledge of these tools onto new cultural members, and encourage the use of these tools among mature members.

Opportunities to engage in social processes that provide access to, and practice with, the knowledge and skills of the culture are rich sources for learning because they are related to one another over time. That is, people have social experiences that guide them in the development and use of situation-specific cognitive skills, and there is a commonality across the experiences that involve these skills that reflects the coherence of the culture over time and space. This fact increases the opportunities for children and adults to develop and practice valued cognitive skills while at the same time it reduces opportunities to learn and practice skills that are less valued or common in the culture.

Theoretical Perspectives

Several theoretical perspectives inform our understanding of the sociocultural context of human cognition including the sociocultural approach to cognitive development and ecological systems theory. Our thinking, especially in relation to the latter periods of development, is influenced by life-span models, particularly Baltes's selection, optimization, and compensation (SOC) model that emphasizes continual adaptations to biological and social changes (gains and losses) over the life span that affect cognition (Baltes, 1987; Baltes & Baltes, 1980). This view emphasizes the complex, interdependent nature of human development and the environment. In all these theories, the person is viewed as playing an active role in development, and cognition is not seen as an end in itself. Rather, it is the means by which human beings, individually and collectively, carve out and sustain effective ways of living and growing.

Sociocultural Approaches

There are many theories and perspectives that adopt a sociocultural approach (Valsiner & Rosa, 2007). We concentrate on approaches that trace their roots to Vygotsky (1978) because they have had considerable influence on research on cognitive development. The view emphasizes social interactions in which a more experienced person uses the signs and tools of the culture to assist a less experienced partner, or learner, in ways that support the learner's engagement in actions that extend his or her current capabilities. Such interactions are effective when they occur in the region of sensitivity for learning or the zone of proximal development (Vygotsky, 1978). More experienced partners support learning by breaking down an activity into component parts to make it more accessible to the learner, modeling new strategies for solving a problem, encouraging the learner's involvement in the activity, and taking responsibility for more difficult task components so that the learner can concentrate on other aspects. As the learner gains competence, the experienced partner gradually withdraws support and the learner comes to function independently in a more advanced way.

In social interaction, children have the opportunity to learn about themselves, their social partners, and their culture, including the activities and tools that support intelligent action. In this way, social and cultural experiences mediate individual development and transform innate psychological abilities, such as perceptual skills, into more complex, higher-order psychological functions, such as reasoning, that are suited to the needs and interests of the culture. It is not necessary for children to devise the psychological signs and tools that support higher mental functions—they already exist in the culture. However, children need to learn about these signs and tools and how to use them to carry out goal-directed actions. When people learn to use signs and tools to support thinking, such as language, mnemonic devices, literacy, and technology, the fundamental nature of cognition changes. These tools extend intellectual functioning beyond what the individual is capable of doing without these tools. They also connect the individual's thinking and action with other people and, by extension, with the social and cultural history of the community. Thus, over the course of development, the practices and products of culture are embedded in individual psychological experience and they are evident in the ways in which children learn to think about and solve problems alone and with others.

Ecological Systems Theory

Ecological systems theory (Bronfenbrenner and Morris, 2006) stresses the interrelations of the child and various environmental systems, such as the family and the community. It provides a description of the many layers of human social-psychological experience that make up development. In this view, child development is embedded in a set of nested contexts that range from the most immediate settings (the microsystem), such as the family or peer group, to more remote contexts of the child's life, such as the culture's systems of values and rules (exo- and macrosystems). The mesosystem comprises the interrelations among the components of the microsystem (e.g., parents interact with caregivers and teachers). The chronosystem reflects that these systems, as well as the child and the environment, undergo change. The importance of the various systems may change over development, for instance microenvironments may be particularly influential in late adulthood when social and institutional supports are needed to maintain cognitive capacities. Ecological systems theory is useful for conceptualizing the complexity of the sociocultural context of cognition and its development over the life course.

Life-Span Models

The SOC model (Baltes, 1987; Baltes & Baltes, 1980) emphasizes continual adaptations to biological and social changes (gains and losses) that affect cognition and other areas of development over the life span. While losses and gains are present at every age, the SOC model posits that as one ages, losses accumulate more rapidly compared to gains, which may ultimately overwhelm an individual's capacities. Thus, to age successfully, individuals must adapt and reinvest energies toward maximizing or maintaining skills. The model emphasizes the increasing selectivity or adaptation of cognitive abilities with age as well as the duality of life course changes in pragmatic versus mechanic intelligences, that is, crystallized intelligence acquired from culture and experience versus fluid intelligence theorized as fundamentally biological. Pragmatic or crystallized intelligence has a greater capacity to show positive gains into older adulthood whereas mechanics or fluid intelligence peaks earlier and tends to show significant declines with age. As mechanics or fluid capacities are exceeded, individuals may rely more heavily on pragmatic or crystallized intelligence as a buffer or compensatory mechanism. Moreover, individuals may become more selective and choose contexts wherein they can maximize or maintain their skills.

In summary, each of these theoretical approaches provides inroads for addressing aspects of the sociocultural context of human cognition across the life span. Sociocultural approaches describe social processes that mediate psychological functioning and underlie cognition and its development. Ecological systems theory recognizes that cognitive development is embedded in multiple, interacting systems that have unique and mutual patterns of influence on development. The SOC model emphasizes continual adaptations to gains and losses across the life span that may result in the greater selectivity of environments to maximize remaining skills and compensate for losses.

RESEARCH ON THE SOCIOCULTURAL CONTEXT OF COGNITION ACROSS THE LIFE SPAN

In this section we discuss research on the contribution of the sociocultural context to cognition across the life span. Different facets of cognition are discussed at the various age periods because research tends to focus on aspects of development that are important at each age. In infancy we concentrate on attention because of its importance to learning. In early childhood we focus on memory, especially autobiographical memory. In middle childhood we focus on cognitive skills that help children assume more responsible roles in the community, and in adolescence we discuss complex cognitive skills. In early adulthood we examine collaborative cognition, particularly collaborative memory, in middle adulthood the discussion centers on contextual factors that impact intellectual functioning including the social complexity of one's occupation, and in late adulthood we again touch on cognitive collaboration and discuss social engagement, especially how these processes may enhance the maintenance of cognitive abilities.

Infancy: The Sociocultural Context of the Development of Attention

Attention, which involves directing limited cognitive resources toward specific information in the environment, is a vital component of learning in infancy. The development of attention in infancy is deeply entwined with the sociocultural context and this link is clear from the beginning of life. At birth, human babies have perceptual biases that orient them to the social context. These biases make the infant more watchful of human beings relative to other (especially inanimate) stimuli, and, as a result, people are the primary means by which infants learn about the world. Initially, the infant's contributions, which include orienting to certain sights and sounds, are controlled involuntarily by the subcortical system (Johnson & Morton, 1991). These contributions enable young infants to participate, or appear to participate, in social interaction. For instance, when newborns are 30 minutes old they look longer at patterns that are face-like compared to patterns that are not (Mondloch et al., 1999) and 2-day-old babies orient more to the sounds of the human voice than to other sounds (Saffran, Werker, & Werner, 2006). In the second and third months, developing cortical regions replace involuntary pathways and over the next months, the visual and auditory systems are increasingly honed to the faces and sounds of the species and to people in the infant's life (Pascalis, de Haan, & Nelson, 2002; Werker & Vouloumanos, 2001). These initial biases and the tendencies and skills they induce set the stage for the development of attention as a sociocultural process. Other people, principally caregivers, encourage and support the development of attention skills, including how to direct, sustain, and redirect attention and ignore distractions—all of which are pivotal to learning (Gauvain, 2001). Caregivers bring important objects and people to the infant's attention, and they encourage the integration of this information with the culture by providing the labels and categories used to identify and communicate this information. They also convey evaluations of the information that reflect cultural values, which can increase or reduce the infant's interest.

The infant's developing capacity to interact socially contributes to this process. Two-month-old infants will turn their heads to follow another person's line of vision (Scaife & Bruner, 1975), respond to parental overtures by making sounds similar in pitch to the parent's voice (Snow, 1990), and coordinate their behaviors with that of their partners (Murray & Trevarthen, 1985). Once these capabilities are in place, infants begin to engage in interpersonal contact that is focused on the partners or primary intersubjectivity (Trevarthen, 1980). By 2–3 months of age, infants are actively engaged in this process as seen in mutual gaze, sustained social looking time, and face-to-face play. At 4 months of age, infants will switch their gaze and affective response across partners in three-person interactions involving the mother, father, and baby (Fivaz-Depeursinge, Favez, Lavanchy, de Noni, & Frascarolo, 2005). By 6 months of age these capabilities expand into turn-taking routines, as seen in games of anticipation like peek-a-boo (Bruner & Sherwood, 1976). Primary intersubjectivity has consequences for socioemotional development (Trevarthen & Aitken, 2001). Maternal sensitivity to the 6-month-old infant's mental state during intersubjectivity is positively related to security of mother–infant attachment when the infant is 12 months old (Meins, Fernyhough, Fradley, & Tuckey, 2001). Individual differences at 6 months of age in following the gaze of others are related to emotion regulation strategies when children are 2 years old (Morales, Mundy, Crowson, Neal, & Delgado, 2005).

Between 6 and 9 months of age the infants' social-attention skills elaborate into secondary intersubjectivity or joint attention in which infants begin to look in reliable and flexible ways at the objects and people that are the focus of their partner's attention (Bakeman & Adamson, 1984). Joint attention is an active learning process; the infant visually monitors the partner's face and gaze and uses this information to organize his or her attention. Through joint attention, infants learn about objects and people and the labels associated with them (Bruner, 1995; Tomasello, 1988); they also develop a nascent understanding of other people as intentional agents, a chief component of social cognition (Tomasello, 1995). By 12 months of age, another social-attention process, social referencing, appears and infants use information from other people to gauge the emotional states associated with the objects and people that are the focus of attention (Campos & Stenberg, 1981). Infants actively seek this information and if a social partner does not provide it, especially in the presence of unfamiliar or ambiguous stimuli, the infant will seek this information from another person in the setting (Walden & Kim, 2005). Cultural practices, especially early caregiving routines and kin relations, are important in defining these social sources (Martini & Kirkpatrick, 1992; Raeff, 2006).

Information obtained during social referencing is not simply mirrored by the infant; rather the infant uses this information to construct his or her own understanding of the situation. For example, if an infant witnesses a frightened look on the face of the caregiver in response to an unfamiliar object, the infant will not make the same facial expression, but she will move away from or avoid the object (Klinnert, 1984). Infants attend to many forms of social information, but some social cues may be preferred. Combined facial and vocal cues are more effective than either facial or vocal cues alone (Vaish & Staino, 2004). Infants are more attentive to negative emotional displays than to positive or neutral displays (Carver & Vaccaro, 2007), which may be due to inexperience with negative emotional expressions or it may be the first sign of the negativity bias evident in adults (Vaish, Grossman, & Woodward, 2008). Researchers are beginning to understand how brain changes in the first year help infants process social information by regulating attention across multiple sources simultaneously, including cognitive, social, and emotional information (Carver & Cornew, 2009). When infants engage in intersubjectivity and social referencing, they use their developing skills at attention to acquire information about the world from others. Social companions provide structure and guidance as these attention skills unfold, which suggests that these skills emerge from social experience. Other important skills may also emerge from shared attention experiences, for example, differences in joint attention at 12 months of age are related to children's social competence at 30 months even after accounting for infant temperament (Van Hecke et al., 2007).

As infants develop attention skills in social context, their partners convey information about cultural norms and values relative to the objects and people that are the focus of attention (Cowley, Moodley, & Fiori-Cowley, 2004). Cultural variation in these processes attests to the complex interplay of social and cultural factors in the development of attention in infancy. For example, immigrant Chinese mothers of 9–12-month-olds in Britain were more likely to direct the focus of their infant's attention whereas British mothers were more likely to follow the infant's lead (Vigil, 2002). Social interactions may also inform infants and young children about cultural practices related to the use of attention skills. For example, 14- to 20-month-olds living in a traditional Mayan community in Guatemala were observed to attend to two competing events simultaneously whereas same age children in the United States alternated their attention between competing events (Chavajay & Rogoff, 1999). Because social attention processes identify other people as sources of information (Rochat & Striano, 1999), they provide infants with their first experiences with subjective reality (Rochat, 2004). These experiences mark the beginning of the development of the self, which continues into early childhood as memory skills develop.

Early Childhood: The Sociocultural Context of the Development of Event Memory

Between 18 months and 5 years of age, children's cognitive capabilities change enormously. One significant change is in the ability to devise and use symbolic representations, which fundamentally alters how children engage in activities important to learning, including social interaction. Children's emerging competence in understanding and manipulating symbols is seen in improved language and communicative skills (Hoff, 2009), the ability to represent and operate on ideas as in pretend play (Bornstein, Haynes, O'Reilly, & Painter, 1996), and advances in the acquisition and retention of knowledge or memory. Changes in memory in early childhood have great consequence for cognitive development. As Vygotsky (1978) wrote, "memory in early childhood is one of the central psychological functions upon which all other functions are built (p. 50)." Vygotsky was particularly interested in voluntary or intentional memory because it is mediated by other people and cultural artifacts, including stored knowledge. Social processes help children learn the knowledge that is important in their immediate context as well as cultural ways of representing, organizing, and maintaining this knowledge.

There are several facets of memory and many of these undergo change in early childhood (Schneider & Bjorklund, 1998). There are increases in the capacity and speed with which information is processed in short-term memory. Declarative knowledge, which is part of long-term memory, also changes significantly. It includes semantic memory, or world knowledge, and episodic or event memory. Strategies are deliberate behaviors that enhance memory performance and they are especially important for storing and retrieving declarative memories (Harnishfeger & Bjorklund, 1990). In early childhood, the understanding and use of memory strategies expands greatly. Whereas 18-month-olds will use rudimentary strategies to help them find a hidden object (DeLoache & Brown, 1983), with advancing age children's memory strategies become more complex and effective (Schneider & Bjorklund, 1998). The social context is vital to this development. For instance, it is not until late in elementary school that children spontaneously use the strategy of elaboration, or embellishing information to make it more meaningful and easier to remember. Yet even preschoolers can be instructed in this strategy and when reminded to use it, they will do so and it will improve their memory. This behavior is called a production deficiency (Moely, Olson, Halwes, & Flavell, 1969) because children have the capability to use the strategy but they do not use it without being prompted. Note that this implies that memory development is about what children can remember without assistance from others. However, other people and cultural artifacts often support memory and this assistance is especially important in the early years of childhood. Although studying individual memory performance is not without merit, it does not describe the full scope of memory development. In fact, the focus on individual memory performance in the preschool years may be less about memory development in general and more about concerns in industrialized cultures regarding cognitive skills that presage children's performance in school, a setting in which the spontaneous production of memory strategies is needed (Rogoff, 2003).

To illustrate how the sociocultural context contributes to memory development in early childhood, we concentrate on event memory that is autobiographical. Autobiographical memories, which include important events or experiences that have happened to an individual, begin to develop in early childhood and both the content and structure of these memories emerge from social experiences, such as conversations children have with caregivers about the past and as events unfold (Bauer, 2006; Fivush, Reese, & Haden, 2006). The fact that these experiences recount events of personal significance helps children acquire knowledge about themselves, other people, and the world in which they live (Engel & Li, 2004). As such, they contribute to the development of the self, an important achievement of early childhood (Harter, 2006). When these conversations focus on emotional aspects of the memory, they may be especially useful (Bird & Reese, 2008). Such retellings can provide children with a new way of understanding or coping with a difficult or emotional experience such as an asthma attack or an environmental disaster (Bauer, Burch, Van Abbema, & Ackil, 2007; Sales & Fivush, 2005).

The family is a fertile context for the development of autobiographical memory. These memories first appear in conversations with parents when the children are about 2½ years of age (Nelson & Fivush, 2004). The sustained and emotional nature of the family makes it likely that family members have shared experiences, which are often the basis of early autobiographical memories (Fivush, Haden, & Reese, 1996). Differences among family members in age and experience increase the likelihood that processes such as scaffolding (Wood, Wood, & Middleton, 1978) and guided participation (Rogoff, 1990) that support the development of cognitive skills will occur. While much of the conversations that contribute to autobiographical memory focus on unique experiences of the child and the family, parents and other family members also represent the culture. Therefore, cultural conventions of communicating these memories and the values placed on them regulate the structure and content of these exchanges.

Cultural conventions regarding the structure of event memories are seen in research on young children's understanding and use of the narrative form. Narratives are stories that contain a sequence of real or imagined events that include human beings as characters (Engel, 1995). Information about the characters' intentions and the cause and evaluation of the event are also included (Bruner, 1986). Narratives are common in the conversations children have with adults about shared memories and they provide support for memory development (Haden, Ornstein, Eckerman, & Didow, 2001). Children's increasing competence with narratives is evident in the gradual transfer of responsibility for these conversations from parent to child. Early in the child's life, parents assume much of the responsibility for shared reminiscing. By the age of 3, children's contributions increase and their memories, as an index of individual development, begin to endure rather well (Fivush & Hamond, 1989). As children get older, they assume more responsibility, initiate memory conversations, and reframe how events are remembered (Ochs, Taylor, Rudolph, & Smith, 1992). In these conversations children learn how memories are shaped, what memories are important in their family and culture, what they can contribute to creating memories, and what aspects of an event memory are interesting or important to others.

Social and cultural variations reveal the contribution of the sociocultural context to the development of autobiographical memory. Parents differ in the manner and frequency that they talk with their children about the past, which has consequences for memory development (Engel, 1986). Some parents concentrate on facts and practical matters, referred to as a pragmatic or repetitive style (e.g., after a birthday party a mother may ask her son if he ate cake and had fun). Other parents use a more elaborative style in which they encourage their child to create a narrative of the event (e.g., after a birthday party a mother may ask her daughter to describe the treasure hunt). Children whose mothers use an elaborative style have more complete and coherent memories of events, their descriptions include more emotional expression, and they have more self-awareness (Fivush, 2007). They also have earlier first memories when they reach adolescence, which suggests that these conversations have lasting contributions to autobiographical memory (Jack, MacDonald, Reese, & Hayne, 2009). A parent's style of reminiscing is not fixed. Mothers trained in an elaborative style, compared with mothers who were not so trained, engaged in more shared remembering with their young children, and this difference was evident shortly after the training and 1 year later (Reese & Newcombe, 2007).

During shared reminiscing adults communicate cultural values and socialization goals to children. In a study involving mothers and their 3- to 4-year-old children, European American mothers made more reference to, and encouraged more discussion of, their children's thoughts and feelings when they discussed past transgressions, whereas Korean mothers concentrated on social norms (Mullen & Yi, 1995). In other research, when Taiwanese parents of 2-year-old children talked about the child's past transgressions, the parents emphasized proper conduct, respect for others, and the importance of self-control and self-criticism, whereas European American parents understated the child's misdeeds, recast them to show the child's strengths, and encouraged positive self-evaluations regarding the transgressions (Miller, Wiley, Fung, & Liang, 1997). Cultural values and parental reminiscing style may be related. Using a longitudinal design, Wang (2007) compared the reminiscing style of Chinese mothers in China and first-generation immigrant Chinese mothers and multigenerational European American mothers in the United States. She also assessed mothers' values about independence and interdependence and the children's autobiographical memory at three time points when children were between 3 and 4½ years of age. In both cultures, mother's use of elaborations was related to better autobiographical memory in children. However, mothers with greater value orientation to independence, which was higher in European American mothers, were more likely to use an elaborative style. These results suggest that, regardless of culture, elaborative reminiscing by mothers promotes social processes that contribute in positive ways to the development of autobiographical memory. However, this style is more common in cultures that emphasize the development of an independent identity or sense of self.

Children's conversations with more experienced partners as they discuss past events are important contexts of memory development, and these conversations vary across social and cultural settings. Examining conversations as a source of memory development shifts attention away from the view that knowledge is entirely self-constructed and toward the idea that knowledge about the world and the self is rooted in social and cultural experiences (Shweder et al., 2006).

Middle Childhood: The Sociocultural Context of Cognition When Children Reach the Age of Reason and Responsibility

The period of middle childhood begins between 5 and 7 years of age when sweeping changes occur in children's cognitive capabilities, changes that White (1965) identified as the 5-to-7 shift. Examination of children's activities during this period suggests that this shift is universal. Research based on data from over 50 ethnographies revealed that between 5 and 7 years of age children's responsibilities and expectations increase considerably (Rogoff, Sellers, Pirotta, Fox, & White, 1975). As White (1965) pointed out, cultures have long acknowledged these changing cognitive capacities in the behaviors that are expected of children, (e.g., in many religious communities children are not accountable for their behaviors until they reach age 7). Recognition of this change is also evident in theories of development. Piaget saw it as the time when children move from preoperational to concrete operational intelligence; for Margaret Mead it marks the transition from the yard child to the community child.

Contemporary research has confirmed that the capabilities of 5-year-old children in a range of cognitive functions, including reasoning, memory, and problem solving, are different from that of 7-year-old children (Sameroff & Haith, 1996). Changes in the frontal cortex, including myelination, which is related to efficiency, and more streamlined neural connections that enhance knowledge acquisition and organization, underlie many of the cognitive changes of this period (Janowsky & Carper, 1996). In addition, there are changes in children's social and emotional capabilities and experiences.

The breadth of changes at this time coupled with suggestions of universal appearance led scientists in the mid-20th century to view it is a qualitative shift regulated by maturational mechanisms (White, 1996). Over time, this assumption was challenged because the cognitive skills children have before and after age 5 appear to be far more continuous than discontinuous. Also, there is significant variation both within and across social and cultural contexts in children's reasoning and responsibilities during this period. These views do not weaken the claim that children's thinking gets more complex, but they do suggest that understanding these changes requires attention to more than biological mechanisms. As White (1996) wrote,

> ...the imputation of an "age of reason" to the child at age 7 is not an absolute fact about child development but it is a statement of the relationship of the growing child to the society in which he or she lives. What happens to children between 5 and 7 is not the acquisition of an absolute ability to reason; it is an ability to reason with others and to look reasonable in the context of society's demands on the growing child to be cooperative and responsible. (p. 27)

Cognitive changes launched by the 5-to-7 shift introduce an especially intriguing part of the story of development in sociocultural context. As children enter middle childhood, they no longer receive high levels of care and supervision from older individuals. Even though children have engaged in cultural activities and practices since birth, their roles and responsibilities in these settings change and, as a result, they have much to learn. Explicit training in cultural practices, occupations, and ways of thinking take on much importance. In western industrial societies, school begins and children embark on their formal training in culturally valued areas of cognition, such as mathematics. We discuss the development of mathematics skill in middle childhood in relation to the sociocultural context.

For several decades, research has shown substantial differences in children's mathematics achievement across cultures. Most well known are differences between China, Japan, and the United States (Stevenson & Stigler, 1992; Stigler, Gallimore, & Hiebert, 2000). Differences across these countries that reflect social and cultural practices include the amount of time children spend in school, the nature of classroom instruction, beliefs about the basis of individual differences in mathematics performance, and parental involvement in children's mathematics learning (Chen & Uttal, 1988; Pan, Gauvain, Liu, & Cheng, 2006; Stigler et al., 2000). Within cultures, children's mathematics achievement is related to many social factors including variations in school quality and parental support for children's mathematics learning. Pratt, Green, MacVicar, and Bountrogianni (1992) found that fifth graders whose mothers used more effective scaffolding techniques, such as contingent tutoring, showed more improvement in mathematics than children who did not receive such help. This research suggests that parental assistance in mathematics learning that

is responsive to the child's learning needs, as Vygotsky (1978) predicted, is especially useful.

Cross-cultural research has also revealed remarkable competence in mathematics among children who have little experience with school. Researchers have
studied young vendors on the streets of Brazil and asked them to solve mathematics
problems in the form of a familiar commercial transaction or as it would be presented in school (Carraher, Carraher, & Schliemann, 1985; Saxe, 1991). On the familiar commercial transaction, children were correct most of the time, but when the
problems were in the form of a school exercise, performance dropped considerably.
Children used different problem-solving strategies in the two problem situations;
they solved the commercial problem mentally but used pencil and paper to solve the
school-like problem. This research demonstrates how cultural tools, such as mathematical symbols and strategies, mediate this thinking.

Research on early mathematics knowledge also points to the need for better
understanding of the contributions of the sociocultural context. The magnitude of
individual, group, and cultural differences in children's mathematics achievement
in middle childhood, is difficult to reconcile with research on what are likely to be
precursors of this understanding in early childhood such as a basic sense of number
and counting and rudimentary skills at quantitative reasoning (Geary, 2006; Nunes
& Bryant, 1996). Because research on early mathematics knowledge has concentrated
on normative trends and is often guided by assumptions of innateness, there has
been little investigation of the sociocultural contributions to this understanding or to
how it maps onto individual and group differences in older children.

Variations across contexts in how children use and achieve in mathematics in
middle childhood may provide important insights into how the sociocultural context helps steer and support this development. At this point we know that the development of this core cognitive competence is tied to many aspects of the social and
cultural context. When children enter middle childhood they have some basic capabilities to engage in mathematical reasoning, and children use these capabilities to
solve problems even if they do not attend school. For children who attend school,
the social context of the classroom and the home can facilitate mathematical understanding. Cultural contributions to this learning come in many forms and include
symbol systems used to represent mathematics, technology that mediates and supports mathematics, and beliefs about how mathematics is learned and who can learn
it. It is important to stress that the sociocultural processes that support children's
understanding and use of mathematics do more than simply inch the child along in
this development. Rather, they provide children with access to powerful and transformative ways of understanding and operating on the world. At the same time, they
instill in children valued ways of thinking in their community that enable them to
assume many of the responsibilities that are increasingly expected of them.

Adolescence: The Sociocultural Context of Complex
Thinking and Decision Making

Adolescents are at a developmental crossroads. They are beyond the years of childhood, yet they are not quite adults. This in-between status appears to exist worldwide.
In an examination of 175 nonindustrial societies, Schlegel and Barry (1991) found
that 46% of societies identified a period of adolescence for girls and 36% identified a

period of adolescence for boys. In most societies, even where adolescence was not a distinct period, there were behavioral indicators, such as dress, ornamentation, or social segregation with peers, that demarcated societal members who were no longer children yet inexperienced as adults.

There are major changes in cognitive competence during adolescence (Kuhn & Franklin, 2006) and over this period, adolescents gradually engage in the new roles and responsibilities expected by their community. Some new competencies are acquired through interpersonal interactions and relationships, others are learned in formal settings such as school, and others come via the legal system and mass media (Lerner & Steinberg, 2009). Research has shown that understanding cognitive development during adolescence requires an integrated approach that attends to neurological underpinnings, emotional components, and the social and cultural context (Keating, 2004). Neurological development, especially changes in the frontal cortex and increased myelination (Yurgelun-Todd, 2007), enable youth to engage in more complex and abstract reasoning as well as exercise more executive control over cognitive processes and the behavioral expression of these processes. This control is visible in advances in self-regulation, increasing independence from adult authority, and strivings toward personal freedom.

Relations of brain development, cognition, and social experience in adolescence are complex (Steinberg, 2005) and many neurological changes in mid- to late adolescence, such as the pruning of the neural connections that proliferated in early adolescence, are driven by experience (Casey, Getz, & Galvan, 2008). Research using functional magnetic resonance imaging suggests that these cognitive changes are tied to social and emotional changes in internal and external regulatory systems. Grosbras et al. (2007) compared the brain activity of young adolescents who were more resistant to peer influence with that of adolescents who were less resistant. The youths were observed as they watched visual displays of angry hand movements and facial expressions. Adolescents who were more resistant to peer influence showed greater sensitivity to relevant social cues and more engagement of executive control areas of the brain.

Social interaction also supports cognitive development in adolescence. Collaboration is beneficial both with adults and with peers depending on type of activity that is the focus of the interaction. Collaboration with adults is more beneficial when it provides new knowledge, explains knowledge that the youth does not fully comprehend, or offers ideas about how to organize knowledge or behavior. For example, adolescent–mother collaboration about how to manage chronic health problems, such as diabetes, can help youth understand and adhere to the various behavioral regimens that the illness requires (Wiebe et al., 2005). Collaboration with peers is beneficial when it involves the exchange of points of view and promotes sociocognitive conflict (Bearison & Dorval, 2002). For instance, peer discussion about controversial moral issues can create opportunities for youth to consider different moral views and, thereby, helps develop moral reasoning (Kruger, 1992). Sociocognitive conflict among adolescents can also encourage the growth of formal reasoning used in problem solving (Nasir, 2005).

An important area of cognitive development during adolescence is decision making (Jacobs & Klaczynski, 2005). Adolescents need to make many decisions that have great consequence for their physical and mental well-being and sometimes that of others. The mental complexity that comes with formal reasoning can make evaluating and deciding among alternatives and reaching a decision a formidable task for youth. Studies that have examined adolescents' decisions on unfamiliar, hypothetical scenarios have found that by age 15 decision making competence is comparable to that of adults (Reyna & Farley, 2006). But these findings do not tell the whole story. Adolescents have more difficulty making decisions in situations where they have limited knowledge or experience, that are very complex, or the outcomes are uncertain (Fischoff, 2008). Adolescents may be aided in making such decisions by their parents (e.g., parents may help children decide how to make choices important to school achievement; Jacobs & Eccles, 2000, and how to spend their time outside of school; Gauvain & Perez, 2005).

Researchers are interested especially in the decision-making processes that underlie adolescent risk-taking behavior. Adolescents, relative to adults, participate in more risky behaviors such as substance abuse, reckless driving, and unprotected sex (Reyna & Rivers, 2008). Despite impressive cognitive skills, other aspects of brain development that contribute to decision making, such as impulse control, are still maturing (Steinberg, 2007) and contribute to adolescent vulnerability to taking risks. Brain changes during puberty lead to increased efforts to obtain rewards, especially from peers, which means that peers can have enormous influence on risk taking (Steinberg & Monahan, 2007). Gardner and Steinberg (2005) observed adolescents and adults as they participated either alone or with a peer in a computerized driving game that measured risk taking. The task simulated potentially dangerous situations such as driving a car into an intersection after the traffic light has turned yellow. Adolescents, but not adults, who worked with peers took more risks than those who worked alone and, as predicted, this effect was strongest for the youngest participants who were between 13 and 16 years of age. These results indicate that the social context affects how adolescents use their decision-making skills.

Cultural contributions to adolescent cognition are also significant. Not all adolescents, or even adults, in all societies achieve the formal reasoning skills associated with this period (Bond, 1998; Rogoff, 2003). In cultures that do not emphasize analytical skills or in which educational experiences are limited, the complex skills associated with adolescence may occur late in development or be absent (Moshman, 1998). Even in western industrial communities in which analytical skills and educational attainment are highly valued, adolescents and adults are more likely to achieve the capacity for abstract reasoning in their areas of interest or expertise than in other domains. The abstract thinking that has been documented in traditional cultures has been found on tasks of importance to the group, such as negotiating land disputes and navigating on the open seas (Gladwin, 1970; Hutchins, 1980). Similarly, in western industrial cultures, scientific training in such subjects as physics, chemistry, and logic is associated with more complex reasoning skills in these areas of thinking (Kuhn & Franklin, 2006). In short, the type of complex thinking associated with adolescence is not consistent in the performances of an individual or group; rather, it is tied to social and cultural experiences.

Young Adulthood: Collaborative Memory

Young adulthood is a time of achievement where adults apply their knowledge toward the establishment of an occupation and for many the choice of marriage partners (Schaie & Willis, 2000). Social interactions with peers, colleagues, and spouses become increasingly important to decision making in adulthood (Schaie & Willis, 2000). Moreover, in adulthood the problems encountered are less rote and more often ambiguous with multiple possible solutions. While there is theoretical litera-ture on postformal reasoning that suggests the importance of social interactions to the development of adaptive, reflective reasoning (e.g., Labouvie-Vief, 1982), little empirical work has been conducted to illuminate sociocultural processes on post-formal reasoning. However, sociocultural processes are becoming of greater focus in the growing literature on collaborative cognition, focusing on collaborative memory. Collaborative problem solving is reviewed in detail elsewhere in this volume.

Collaborative recall refers to memories about directly shared experiences by all members of a group (Harris, Paterson, & Kemp, 2008). Collaborative recall paradigms typically measure the extent to which group members collaboratively recall details of shared events such as a movie or a word list contrasted with individual level per-formance (e.g., Ekeocha & Brennan, 2008; Meade, Nokes, & Morrow, 2009). Moreover, the collaborative recall of married spouses versus dyads of unacquainted persons may be contrasted (e.g., Gould, Osborn, Krein, & Mortenson, 2002; Ross, Spencer, Blatz, & Restorick, 2008), or those who interact face-to-face versus electronic collab-oration via computer (e.g., Ekeocha & Brennan, 2008).

In general, groups outperform individuals in recall although when "nominal" groups are formed from individual responses the collaborative group results are often poorer in comparison (Harris et al., 2008). This has been referred to as collaborative inhibition, the cause or causes of which are still of some debate. It may be that group processes interfere with individual strategies or that individually proffered recall items may be less likely to be attended to in discussion than items recalled by multi-ple group members (Harris et al., 2008). However, group recall may be more accurate (e.g., fewer false memories; Ross et al., 2008), and of higher quality, (e.g., more central propositions recalled; Ekeocha & Brennan, 2008). Indeed, group collaboration may facilitate *subsequent* individual recall (Ekeocha & Brennan, 2008; Harris et al., 2008), suggesting that socially facilitated processes may benefit individual memory recall.

The relative expertise of group members may enhance recall (Meade et al., 2009). For example, discourse features in dyads with an aviation expert (vs. novices or non-experts) included greater acknowledgment and elaboration of partner contributions in recall of aviation scenes. That is, the expert as the more skilled member of the pair facilitated dyadic recall over other pairings. Indeed recall facilitation rather than inhibition was observed in dyads with experts. Thus, adult cognition may be influ-enced by informal social processes, such as expertise.

Mid-Adulthood: The Sociocultural Context of Occupational Complexity

Middle age (approximately 40 years to 60 or 65 years) is a period when many cog-nitive abilities reach their peak, with the exception of perceptual speed processes that typically decline in young adulthood and crystallized/verbal abilities that often continue to increase into old age (Schaie, 2005). Middle age is also a period when most adults have achieved much social responsibility in their work lives as well as in their family life, including spouses and children (and possibly the care of elderly parents).

For many hours of the day, individuals employed outside the home interact with work colleagues. Social interactions in the workplace shape the environmental complexity for individuals and may support and indeed contribute to intellectual abilities with benefits that may last into older adulthood. Certainly socioeconomic status (SES) has been well studied in terms of the resulting environmental structures that hinder or support intellectual abilities (Schooler & Caplan, 2008). We focus here on the social nature of occupations as supportive of cognitive functioning not only in midlife, but with potentially long-lasting benefits into late adulthood.

Occupational complexity is typically considered in terms of three dimensions: complexity with data, things, and people. In 1977, ratings of occupations along these three dimensions were published in the Dictionary of Occupational Titles (U.S. Department of Labor, 4th ed.). These ratings have been applied to occupational titles in multiple research settings, including predicting late life cognitive outcomes (Andel et al., 2005; Potter, Helms, Burke, Steffens, & Plassman, 2007; Potter, Helms, & Plassman, 2008). Complexity with data ranges from simple comparisons of data to synthesis of data. Complexity with things ranges from handling of tools or objects to setting up machines/equipment (for self or others). Complexity with people ranges from those who simply take instructions and who have no responsibility to those who are in positions of mentorship. Thus, mentorship of other individuals is of greater complexity than taking orders from one's manager.

A lower complexity of work with people in one's lifetime occupation has been shown to be predictive of an increased risk of dementia in Swedish adults from the HARMONY twin study, even when age, gender, and education levels are controlled for in analysis (Andel et al., 2005). Moreover, the co-twin control comparisons within twin pairs were similar to the overall case-control analyses suggesting that genetic factors do not explain the links between complexity and dementia risk. Findings for complexity in people-related occupations and Alzheimer's disease risk have not been confirmed in men who participate in the National Academy of Sciences—National Research Council Twins Registry of World War II veterans (NAS-NRC Twin Registry; Potter et al., 2007), perhaps indicating that occupational complexity of this type of work may have a gender-specific (female) effect (Potter et al., 2007). However, the extent of human (social) interaction and communication in one's primary occupation has been associated with cognitive functioning during retirement in the same NAS-NRC Twin Registry sample of men (Potter et al., 2008). Indeed, the effect of human interaction and communication on cognitive functioning was significant even when the factor capturing "general intellectual demands of the occupation was simultaneously accounted for, suggesting some unique prediction for socially stimulating work environments" (Potter et al., 2008). In addition, the benefits of general intellectual demands were especially favorable to those with lower general intelligence scores in young adulthood. It is worthwhile to note that the general intellectual demands factor included the complexity of work with people. Thus, overall intellectual engagement as well as social engagement each contribute to cognitive health in retirement.

Most recently, complexity with people has been shown to be predictive of cognitive performance and change in middle and older adulthood in twins from the Swedish Adoption/Twin study of Aging (Finkel, Andel, Gatz, & Pedersen, 2009). In particular verbal ability performance improved in middle adulthood for those individuals in people-related occupations with higher complexity. The benefits of complexity with people affected spatial ability into postretirement years, though benefits waned with spatial performance decreasing more rapidly postretirement.

Schooler and colleagues suggest a mutual person–environmental pathway by which occupational complexity contributes to later intellectual functioning, that is, via occupational-self directedness, which features complexity with data and people as well as closeness of supervision at work and routinization of work (see Schooler & Caplan, 2008). Specifically, higher SES and intellectual ability lead to more demanding and self-directing occupations and higher levels of occupational self-directedness. These experiences, in turn, enhance intellectual functioning and magnify the effects of earlier-life SES. In addition, individual difference characteristics of self-directedness and intellectual flexibility are mutually benefited in this manner too.

It is important to note that the benefits of social interaction on cognitive functioning and health may not only result from paid work, they may extend to midlife leisure activities (Carlsen et al., 2008). Moreover, the give-and-take relationships across time between SES and intellectual functioning also play out via the complexity of household work (Caplan & Schooler, 2006; Schooler & Caplan, 2008).

Older Adulthood: The Sociocultural Context of Cognitive Aging

Social and contextual supports may be of even greater importance to maintaining cognitive capacities into older age (65 years and older). Typically accelerating declines are seen for most cognitive abilities after age 65 for spatial, speed, memory, and eventually for verbal skills, though there is much individual variation (Reynolds, 2008, 2009). While genetic factors still play an important role in variation in cognitive abilities, environmental factors gain in prominence. For example, while Alzheimer's disease is strongly heritable (Gatz et al., 2005), there are often marked discordancies in age of onset among identical twins such that one might suggest different disease etiologies may be at play (Gatz et al., 1997). Thus, aspects of the environment may become more salient to the maintenance or decline of cognitive abilities, including the interaction of social factors with genotype (Reynolds, Gatz, Berg, & Pedersen, 2007).

Social-interpersonal contexts, in particular, may become increasing relevance to cognition with age (Meegan & Berg, 2002; Schaie & Willis, 2000). We briefly consider research on cognitive collaboration as a facilitator of memory in older adulthood and more generally on social engagement as a potential protective mechanism in cognitive aging.

Collaborative memory studies of older adults report similar findings to that of young adults: dyadic collaboration produces higher recall than individuals but collaborative inhibition effects are likely if comparing actual dyads to nominal dyads (e.g., Ross, Spencer, Linardatos, Lam, & Perunovic, 2004; Ross et al., 2008). Moreover, not surprisingly, younger dyads often outperform older dyads (Ross et al., 2008). It is yet unclear, however, whether the performance of dyads or groups where members know each other may have advantages over groups of unacquainted individuals (Gagnon & Dixon, 2008; Gould et al., 2002; Harris et al., 2008). The benefits of dyads may lie in the reduction of recall errors (Ross et al., 2004, 2008). For example, in a study of recall of shopping list items and recall of landmarks on a map, fewer false positives were observed in dyadic performance of older adults age compared to nominal groups (Ross et al., 2004). Social processes apparent in collaborative memory contexts may suppress false recall and therefore could be of important benefit to older adults whose memory functioning may be in decline.

In general, social engagement may be important to maintaining cognitive abilities in older age, and indeed offsetting the age at which declines or even dementia occur (see review, Hertzog et al., 2009). The measurement of social engagement takes many forms and includes (1) the number of socially oriented activities that one reports participating in (e.g., church attendance, volunteer work, group memberships); (2) social network size, which often is measured as the number and frequency of contact with friends and relatives; (3) marital status; and (4) perceived isolation or loneliness. Studies of longitudinal cognitive performance, mental status functioning, and even dementia consistently suggest that participation in socially oriented activities predicts long-term benefits to cognitive health and performance (Hertzog et al., 2009). For example, in the Maatsrich Aging Study, a higher number of social activities predicted better memory performance 3 years later while higher performance on attentional, memory, and mental status tasks at baseline predicted a higher number of social activities taken up 3 years later (Bosma et al., 2002). It is important to note that while there appears to be a consistent association between participation in socially oriented activities and cognitive health and performance, the specificity of the association as to cognitive domain (verbal, spatial, speed, memory) is not entirely clear. This may be, in part, due to differences across studies in the classification of items into intellectual versus social activities (see Hertzog et al., 2009). Thus, further work is needed to clarify how general or specific social engagement is related to verbal, spatial, perceptual speed, and memory abilities.

The relations between social network size and cognitive health and performance are less consistent across studies than for social activities (Hertzog et al., 2009). Here, it may be that the number of friends and family that one sees or talks to on a more or less frequent basis must be considered together with perceived quality of the relationships (Fratiglioni, Wang, Ericsson, Maytan, & Winblad, 2000) or global feelings of loneliness and isolation (Wilson et al., 2007). The Honolulu-Asia Aging Study of Japanese-American men found that lower social engagement in older adulthood or declines in engagement from mid- to later adulthood were predictive of dementia risk whereas lower social engagement in mid-adulthood itself was not predictive (Saczynski et al., 2006). This may indicate that reductions in social engagement may be an early symptom of dementia rather than reflect the impact of interpersonal environments on cognitive health (Saczynski et al., 2006). However, it is important to note that measures of social engagement appear to be unrelated to neuropathologies characteristic of Alzheimer disease, indicating that social engagement may be an independent predictor of cognitive health (Bennett, Schneider, Tang, Arnold, & Wilson, 2006; Wilson et al., 2007).

Social engagement in late adulthood may also impact cognitive reserve, such that individuals may maintain cognitive functioning despite the increasing presence of age-associated neural pathologies. In the Rush Memory and Aging Project, baseline social network size moderated the associations between cognitive functioning prior to death and Alzheimer-like neuropathologies measured at autopsy (amyloid plaque load and density of neurofibrillary tangles measured at autopsy; Bennett et al., 2006). Larger social networks mitigated associations between global pathology, tangle density, and decreased cognitive functioning, particularly for memory tasks. These findings held when accounting for health and participation in a variety of leisure activities, including social activities. Although the study is correlative in nature, the findings suggest that social networks reflect the "strength of the neural system" or that other compensatory mechanisms emerging from social experience may mitigate the impact of neuropathology (Bennett et al., 2006).

CONCLUSION

We described the sociocultural context of human cognition across the life span by examining pivotal changes in each developmental period and asking how the social and cultural context is involved in these changes. Our aim was to highlight how the sociocultural context is inherent to all aspects of human cognition and its development. We also tried to show the unique contributions that may result when the sociocultural context is examined in conjunction with cognitive functioning. Two distinct benefits of this inquiry are worth emphasizing.

The first benefit pertains to the conduct of research. Consideration of the sociocultural context introduces questions about the relation between social and cultural experience and cognitive development that other approaches overlook, view as ancillary issues, or consider after the fact, that is, after a study is done and it is difficult to interpret the findings without taking context into account. A second benefit is theoretical and pertains to the nature of cognition itself. Each of the aspects of cognition we discussed could only have arisen from experience in the sociocultural context. For some research, this point is tautological (e.g., in adulthood we focused on collaborative contributions to the maintenance of cognitive functions, which, by definition, reflect experience in the social context). However, in some developmental periods, such as infancy and early childhood, we discussed how individual cognitive functions, such as attention and memory, arise from sociocultural experience. Over the course of development, human beings construct these cognitive processes with other people and with the support and guidance provided by the practices and tools of the culture. In other words, human cognition and the sociocultural context are mutually constituted.

Cognitive change from the vantage point of the sociocultural context reflects two interrelated facets of brain development (Greenough & Black, 1992). Some changes to the brain are experience dependent and emerge from an individual's unique experiences. Other changes are experience expectant and are encountered in the course of species-typical life. We used comparative human research to show how cognitive development in sociocultural context may reveal both experience-expectant and experience-dependent processes. For instance, research suggests that the development of attention relies on assistance from social partners who help young children learn how to deploy and control this valuable cognitive resource. This is a species general, or experience-expectant, feature of cognitive development and full-term human infants are born ready to tap into this social assistance. The fact that the subcortical system offers support for infants in these behaviors before cortical control matures accentuates the critical and indispensible role that the social world plays in the development of attention. Individual differences within and across cultures illustrate the experience-dependent aspects of the development of attention. They also provide information about the range of variation in human attention and the boundaries set by human biology in the development and expression of this cognitive capability. Recall variation in the deployment of attention skills across cultures early in life (e.g., research on divided attention in toddlers in a Mayan community and the United States, showed that children adopt the attention skills of their community; Chavajay & Rogoff, 1999). Research has also shown that biological and emotional changes during adolescence can make decision-making problematic partly because it places high demands on attention (Steinberg, 2007). Considered together, findings such as these may help researchers identify both the potential and the constraints of human attention over the life span.

To this end, there is need for theory to unite findings such as these and integrate them into a comprehensive view of cognitive development. In our view, incorporation of the sociocultural context will be integral to this effort. As we have shown, empirical findings in support of this position are gradually falling into place. However, as our discussion makes clear, the foci of cognitive research tend to differ across the life span and, as a result, tracing any particular cognitive process across development from a sociocultural, or for that matter any vantage point, can be difficult. Theoretical accounts of the sociocultural context of cognitive development across the entire life span are also in short supply. There are some extant theories that attend to the relevant structural features of the sociocultural context of psychological development and these will be useful in this endeavor (Baltes, 1987; Baltes & Baltes, 1980; Bronfenbrenner & Morris, 2006). Yet any such theory (or theories) will need to describe the processes that connect individual cognitive development to the sociocultural context. It is a difficult question indeed as to how the social and culture context becomes embedded in cognitive processes within and across all periods of development.

To conclude, studying cognition in isolation from the sociocultural context not only neglects explanatory power but also ignores the very nature of human cognition and its development. What is needed at this juncture is a theory of cognition that incorporates the sociocultural context as a central and indispensible component across the life span. This theory needs to account for both the structure and the processes produced by the sociocultural context. Such a theory will help guide researchers as they conceptualize the contributions of the sociocultural context to cognition in a way that allows for the dramatic changes in thinking that make up human development.

■ REFERENCES

Andel, R., Crowe, M., Pedersen, N. L., Mortimer, J., Crimmins, E., Johansson, B., et al. (2005). Complexity of work and risk of Alzheimer's disease: A population-based study of Swedish twins. *Journals of Gerontology Series B: Psychological Sciences and Social Sciences, 60*(5), P251–P258.

Anderson, J. R. (2000). *Cognitive psychology and its implications* (5th ed.). New York: Worth.

Bakeman, R., & Adamson, L. B. (1984). Coordinating attention to people and objects in mother-infant and peer-infant interaction. *Child Development, 55*, 1278–1289.

Baltes, P. B. (1987). Theoretical propositions of life-span developmental psychology: On the dynamics between growth and decline. *Developmental Psychology, 23*, 611–626.

Baltes, P. B., & Baltes, M. M. (1980). Plasticity and variability in psychological aging: Methodological and theoretical issues. In G. E. Gurski (Ed.), *Determining the effects of aging on the central nervous system* (pp. 41–66). Berlin: Schering.

Bakhurst, D. (2007). Vygotsky's demons. In H. Daniels, M. Cole, & J. V. Wertsch (Eds.), *The Cambridge companion to Vygotsky* (pp. 50–76). Cambridge: Cambridge University Press.

Barkow, J. H., Cosmides, L., & Tooby, J. (1992). *The adapted mind: Evolutionary psychology and the generation of culture.* New York: Oxford University Press.

Bauer, P. J. (2006). Event memory. In W. Damon & R. M. Lerner (Series Eds.) and D. Kuhn & R. S. Siegler (Vol. Eds.), *Handbook of child psychology: Vol. 2, Cognition, perception, and language* (6th ed., pp. 373–425). New York: Wiley.

Bauer, P. J., Burch, M. M., Van Abbema, D. L., & Ackil, J. K. (2007). Talking about twisters: Relations between mothers' and children's contributions to conversations about a devastating tornado. *Journal of Cognition and Development, 8,* 371–399.

Bearison, D. J., & Dorval, B. (2002). *Collaborative cognition: Children negotiating ways of knowing.* Westport, CT: Ablex Publishing.

Bennett, D. A., Schneider, J. A., Tang, Y., Arnold, S. E., & Wilson, R. S. (2006). The effect of social networks on the relation between Alzheimer's disease pathology and level of cognitive function in old people: A longitudinal cohort study. *Lancet Neurology, 5*(5), 406–412.

Bird, A., & Reese, E. (2008). Autobiographical memory in childhood and the development of a continuous self. In F. Sani (Ed.), *Self continuity: Individual and collective perspectives* (pp. 43–54). New York: Psychology Press.

Bjorklund, D. F., & Pellegrini, A. D. (2002). *The origins of human nature: Evolutionary developmental psychology.* Washington, DC: American Psychological Association.

Bond, T. G. (1998). Fifty years of formal operational research: The empirical evidence. *Archives de Psychologie, 66,* 221–238.

Bornstein, M. H., Haynes, O. M., O'Reilly, A. W., & Painter, K. (1996). Solitary and collaborative pretense play in early childhood: Sources of individual variation in the development of representational competence. *Child Development, 67,* 2910–2929.

Bosma, H., van Boxtel, M. P., Ponds, R. W., Jelicic, M., Houx, P., Metsemakers, J., et al. (2002). Engaged lifestyle and cognitive function in middle and old-aged, non-demented persons: A reciprocal association? *Zeitschrift für Gerontologie und Geriatrie, 35*(6), 575–581.

Bretherton, I. (1992). The origins of attachment theory: John Bowlby and Mary Ainsworth. *Developmental Psychology, 28,* 759–775.

Bronfenbrenner, U., & Morris, P. (2006). The ecology of developmental processes. In W. Damon & R. M. Lerner (Series Eds.) and R. M. Lerner (Vol. Ed.), *Handbook of child psychology: Vol. 1, Theoretical models of human development* (6th ed., pp. 793–828). New York: Wiley.

Bruner, J. S. (1986). *Actual minds, possible worlds.* Cambridge, MA: Harvard University Press.

Bruner, J. S. (1995). From joint attention to the meeting of minds: An introduction. In C. Moore & P. J. Dunham (Eds.), *Joint attention: Its origins and role in development* (pp. 1–14). Hillsdale, NJ: Erlbaum.

Bruner, J. S., & Sherwood, V. (1976). Early rule structure: The case of "peekaboo." In R. Harre (Ed.), *Life sentences* (pp. 55–62). London: Wiley.

Campos, J. J., & Stenberg, C. R. (1981). Perception, appraisal, and emotion: The onset of social referencing. In M. E. Lamb & L. R. Sherrod (Eds.), *Infant social cognition: Empirical and theoretical considerations* (pp. 273–314). Hillsdale, NJ: Erlbaum.

Caplan, L. J., & Schooler, C. (2006). Household work complexity, intellectual functioning, and self-esteem in men and women. *Journal of Marriage and Family, 68*(4), 883–900.

Carlson, M. C., Helms, M. J., Steffens, D. C., Burke, J. R., Potter, G. G., & Plassman, B. L. (2008). Midlife activity predicts risk of dementia in older male twin pairs. *Alzheimer's & Dementia, 4*(5), 324–331.

Carraher, T., Carraher, D. W., & Schliemann, A. D. (1985). Mathematics in the streets and in schools. *British Journal of Developmental Psychology, 3,* 21–29.

Carver, L. J., & Cornew, L. (2009). The development of social information gathering in infancy: A model of neural substrates and developmental mechanisms. In M. de Haan & M. Gunnar (Eds.), *Handbook of developmental social neuroscience* (pp. 122–141). New York: Guilford.

Carver, L. J., & Vaccaro, B. G. (2007). 12-month-old infants allocate neural resources to stimuli associated with negative adult emotion. *Developmental Psychology, 43,* 54–69.

Casey, B. J., Getz, S., & Galvan, A. (2008). The adolescent brain. *Developmental Review, 28,* 62–77.

Chavajay, P., & Rogoff, B. (1999). Cultural variation in management of attention by children and their caregivers. *Developmental Psychology, 35,* 1079–1090.

Chen, C., & Uttal, D. (1988). Cultural values, parents' beliefs, and children's achievement in the United States and China. *Human Development, 31,* 351–358.

Cole, M. (1996). *Cultural psychology: A once and future discipline.* Cambridge, MA: Harvard University Press.

Cole, M., Gay, J., Glick, J., & Sharp, D. W. (1971). *The cultural context of learning and thinking.* New York: Basic Books.

Cowley, S. J., Moodley, S., & Fiori-Cowley, A. (2004). Grounding signs of culture: Primary intersubjectivity in social semiosis. *Mind, Culture, and Activity, 11*, 109–132.

Dasen, P. R. (1977). *Piagetian psychology: Cross-cultural contributions.* New York: Gardner Press.

DeLoache, J. S., & Brown, A. L. (1983). Very young children's memory for the location of objects in a large-scale environment. *Child Development, 54*, 888–897.

Ekeocha, J. O., & Brennan, S. E. (2008). Collaborative recall in face-to-face and electronic groups. *Memory, 16*(3), 245–261.

Engel, S. (1986). *Learning to reminisce: A developmental study of how young children talk about the past.* Unpublished doctoral dissertation, City University of New York Graduate Center, New York.

Engel, S. (1995). *The stories children tell: Making sense of the narratives of childhood.* New York: W. H. Freeman.

Engel, S., & Li, A. (2004). Narratives, gossip, and shared experience: How and what young children know about the lives of others. In J. M. Lucariello, J. A. Hudson, R. Fivush, & P. J. Bauer (Eds.), *The development of the mediated mind: Sociocultural context and cognitive development* (pp. 151–174). Mahwah, NJ: Erlbaum.

Finkel, D., Andel, R., Gatz, M., & Pedersen, N. L. (2009). The role of occupational complexity in trajectories of cognitive aging before and after retirement. *Psychology and Aging, 24*(3), 563–573.

Fischoff, B. (2008). Assessing adolescent decision-making competence. *Developmental Review, 28*, 12–28.

Fivaz-Depeursinge, E., Favez, N., Lavanchy, C., de Noni, S., & Frascarolo, F. (2005). Four-month-olds make triangular bids to father and mother during trilogue play with still-face. *Social Development, 14*, 361–378.

Fivush, R., & Hamond, N. R. (1989). Time and again: Effects of repetition and retention interval on two-year-olds' event recall. *Journal of Experimental Child Psychology, 47*, 259–273.

Fivush, R. (2007). Maternal reminiscing style and children's developing understanding of self and emotion. *Clinical Social Work Journal, 35*, 37–46.

Fivush, R., Haden, C., & Reese, E. (1996). Remembering, recounting, and reminiscing: The development of autobiographical memory in social context. In D. C. Rubin (Ed.), *Remembering our past: Studies in autobiographical memory* (pp. 341–359). Cambridge: Cambridge University Press.

Fivush, R., Reese, E., & Haden, K. (2006). Elaborating on elaborations: Role of maternal reminiscing style in cognitive and socioemotional development. *Child Development, 77*, 1568–1588.

Fratiglioni, L., Wang, H. X., Ericsson, K., Maytan, M., & Winblad, B. (2000). Influence of social network on occurrence of dementia: A community-based longitudinal study. *Lancet, 355*(9212), 1315–1319.

Gagnon, L. M., & Dixon, R. A. (2008). Remembering and retelling stories in individual and collaborative contexts. *Applied Cognitive Psychology, 22*(9), 1275–1297.

Gardner, M., & Steinberg, L. (2005). Peer influence on risk taking, risk preference, and risky decision making in adolescence and adulthood: An experimental study. *Developmental Psychology, 41*, 625–635.

Gatz, M., Fratiglioni, L., Johansson, B., Berg, S., Mortimer, J. A., Reynolds, C. A., et al. (2005). Complete ascertainment of dementia in the Swedish Twin Registry: The HARMONY study. *Neurobiology of Aging, 26*(4), 439–447.

Gatz, M., Pedersen, N. L., Berg, S., Johansson, B., Johansson, K., Mortimer, J. A., et al. (1997). Heritability for Alzheimer's disease: The study of dementia in Swedish twins. *Journals of Gerontology Series A: Biological Sciences and Medical Sciences, 52*(2), M117–M125.

Gauvain, M. (1995). Thinking in niches: Sociocultural influences on cognitive development. *Human Development, 38*, 25–45.

Gauvain, M. (1999). Everyday opportunities for the development of planning skills: Sociocultural and family influences. In A. Göncü (Ed.), *Children's engagement in the world: Sociocultural perspectives* (pp. 173–201). Cambridge: Cambridge University Press.

Gauvain, M. (2001). *The social context of cognitive development.* New York: Guilford.

Gauvain, M., & Perez, S. M. (2005). Parent-child participation in planning children's activities outside of school in European American and Latino families. *Child Development, 76*, 371–383.

Geary, D. C. (2006). Development of mathematical understanding. In W. Damon & R. M. Lerner (Series Eds.) and D. Kuhn & R. S. Siegler (Vol. Eds.), *Handbook of child psychology: Vol. 2, Cognition, perception, and language* (6th ed., pp. 777–810). New York: Wiley.

Gladwin, T. (1970). *East is a big bird.* Cambridge, MA: Harvard University Press.

Goodnow, J. J., Miller, P. J., & Kessel, F. (1995). *Cultural practices as contexts for development.* San Francisco, CA: Jossey-Bass.

Gould, O. N., Osborn, C., Krein, H., & Mortenson, M. (2002). Collaborative recall in married and unacquainted dyads. *International Journal of Behavioral Development, 26*(1), 36–44.

Greenfield, P. M. (1966). On culture and conservation. In J. S. Bruner, R. R. Olver, P. M. Greenfield, et al. (Eds.), *Studies in cognitive growth* (pp. 225–256). New York: Wiley.

Greenfield, P. M. (1974). Comparing dimensional categorization in natural and artificial contexts: A developmental study among the Zinacantecos of Mexico. *Journal of Social Psychology, 93,* 157–171.

Greenfield, P. M., & Childs, C. P. (1977). Understanding sibling concepts: A developmental study of kin terms in Zinacantan. In P. R. Dasen (Ed.), *Piagetian psychology: Cross-cultural contributions* (pp. 335–338). New York: Gardner Press.

Greenough, W. T., & Black, J. E. (1992). Induction of brain structure by experience: Substrates for cognitive development. In M. R. Gunnar & C. A. Nelson (Eds.), *Minnesota symposium on child psychology* (pp. 155–200). Hillsdale, NJ: Erlbaum.

Grosbras, M. H., Jansen, M., Leonard, G., McIntosh, A., Osswalk, K., Poulsen, C., et al. (2007). Neural mechanisms of resistance to peer influence in early adolescence. *The Journal of Neuroscience, 27,* 8040–8045.

Haden, C. A., Ornstein, P. A., Eckerman, C. O., & Didow, S. M. (2001). Mother-child conversational interactions as events unfold: Linkages to subsequent remembering. *Child Development, 72,* 1016–1031.

Harnishfeger, K. K., & Bjorklund, D. F. (1990). Children's strategies: A brief history. In D. F. Bjorklund (Ed.), *Children's strategies: Contemporary views of cognitive development* (pp. 1–22). Hillsdale, NJ: Erlbaum.

Harris, C. B., Paterson, H. M., & Kemp, R. I. (2008). Collaborative recall and collective memory: What happens when we remember together? *Memory, 16*(3), 213–230.

Harter, S. (2006). The self. In W. Damon & R. M. Lerner (Series Eds.) and N. Eisenberg (Vol. Ed.), *Handbook of child psychology. Vol. 3: Social, emotional, and personality development* (6th ed., pp. 505–570). New York: Wiley.

Hermann, E., Call, J., Hernández-Lloreda, M. V., Hare, B., & Tomasello, M. (2007). Human have evolved specialized skills of social cognition: The cultural intelligence hypothesis. *Science, 317,* 1360–1366.

Hertzog, C., Kramer, A. F., Wilson, R. S., & Lindenberger, U. (2009). Enrichment effects on adult cognitive development: Can the functional capacity of older adults be preserved and enhanced? *Psychological Science in the Public Interest, 9*(1), 1–65.

Hinde, R. A. (1989). Ethological and relationships perspectives. In R. Vasta (Ed.), *Annals of child development* (Vol. 6, pp. 251–285). Greenwich, CT: JAI Press.

Hoff, E. (2009). *Language development* (4th ed.). Belmont, CA: Wadsworth.

Hutchins, E. (1980). *Culture and inference: A Trobriand case study.* Cambridge, MA: Harvard University Press.

Hutchins, E. (1983). Understanding Micronesian navigation. In D. Gentner & A. L. Stevens (Eds.), *Mental models* (pp. 191–225). Hillsdale, NJ: Erlbaum.

Jack, F., MacDonald, S., Reese, E., & Hayne, H. (2009). Maternal reminiscing style during early childhood predicts the age of adolescents' earliest memories. *Child Development, 80,* 496–505.

Jacobs, J. E., & Eccles, J. S. (2000). Parents, task values, and real-life achievement-related choices. In C. Sansone & J. M. Harackiewicz (Eds.), *Intrinsic and extrinsic motivation: The search for optimal motivation and performance* (pp. 405–439). San Diego, CA: Academic.

Jacobs, J. E., & Klaczynski, P. A. (2005). *The development of judgment and decision making in children and adolescents.* Mahwah, NJ: Erlbaum.

Janowsky, J. S., & Carper, R. (1996). Is there a neural basis for cognitive transitions in school-age children. In A. J. Sameroff & M. M. Haith (Eds.), *The five to seven year shift: The age of reason and responsibility* (pp. 33–60). Chicago: University of Chicago Press.

Johnson, M. H., & Morton, J. (1991). *Biology and cognitive development: The case of face recognition.* Oxford, UK: Blackwell.

Keating, D. (2004). Cognition and brain development. In R. M. Lerner & L. Steinberg (Eds.), *Handbook of adolescent psychology* (2nd ed., pp. 45–84). Hoboken, NJ: Wiley.

Klinnert, M. D. (1984). The regulation of infant behavior by maternal facial expression. *Infant Behavior and Development, 7,* 447–465.

Kruger, A. C. (1992). The effect of peer and adult-child transactive discussions on moral reasoning. *Merrill-Palmer Quarterly, 38,* 191–211.

Kuhn, D., & Franklin, S. (2006). The second decade: What develops (and how). In W. Damon & L. M. Lerner (Series Eds.) and D. Kuhn & R. S. Siegler (Vol. Eds.), *Handbook of child psychology. Vol. 2: Cognition, perception, and language* (6th ed., pp. 953–993). New York: Wiley.

Labouvie-Vief, G. (1982). Dynamic development and mature autonomy: A theoretical prologue. *Human Development, 25*(3), 161–191.

Lancy, D. F. (1983). *Cross-cultural studies in cognition and mathematics.* New York: Academic Press.

Lave, J. (1977). Cognitive consequences of traditional apprenticeship training in West Africa. *Anthropology and Education Quarterly, 8,* 177–180.

Lerner, R. M., & Steinberg, L. (2009). *Handbook of adolescent psychology. Vol. 2: Contextual influences on adolescent development* (3rd ed.). Hoboken, NJ: Wiley.

Martini, M., & Kirkpatrick, J. (1992). Parenting in Polynesia: A view from the Marquesas. In J. L. Roopnarine & D. B. Carter (Eds.), *Parent-child socialization in diverse cultures* (pp. 199–223). Norwood, NJ: Ablex.

Meade, M. L., Nokes, T. J., & Morrow, D. G. (2009). Expertise promotes facilitation on a collaborative memory task. *Memory, 17*(1), 39–48.

Meegan, S. P., & Berg, C. A. (2002). Contexts, functions, forms, and processes of collaborative everyday problem solving in older adulthood. *International Journal of Behavioral Development, 26*(1), 6–15.

Meins, E., Fernyhough, C., Fradley, E., & Tuckey, M. (2001). Rethinking maternal sensitivity: Mothers' comments on infants' mental processes predict security of attachment at 12 months. *Journal of Child Psychology and Psychiatry, 42,* 637–648.

Miller, P. J., Wiley, A. R., Fung, H., & Liang, C. (1997). Personal storytelling as a medium of socialization in Chinese and American families. *Child Development, 68,* 557–568.

Moely, B. E., Olson, F. A., Halwes, T. G., & Flavell, J. H. (1969). Production deficiency in young children's clustered recall. *Developmental Psychology, 1,* 26–34.

Mondloch, C. J., Lewis, T. L., Budreau, D. R., Maurer, D., Dannemiller, J. D., Stephens, B. R., et al. (1999). Face perception during early infancy. *Psychological Science, 10,* 419–422.

Morales, M., Mundy, P., Crowson, M., Neal, R., & Delgado, C. (2005). Individual differences in infant attention skills, joint attention, and emotion regulation behavior. *International Journal of Behavioral Development, 29,* 259–263.

Moshman, D. (1998). Cognitive development beyond childhood. In W. Damon (Series Ed.), and D. Kuhn & R. S. Siegler (Vol. Eds.), *Handbook of child psychology. Vol. 2: Cognition, perception, and language* (5th ed., pp. 947–978). New York: Wiley.

Mullen, M. K., & Yi, S. (1995). The cultural context of talk about the past: Implications for the development of autobiographical memory. *Cognitive Development, 10,* 407–419.

Munroe, R. L., & Gauvain, M. (2009). The cross-cultural study of children's learning and socialization: A short history. In D. F. Lancy, J. Bock, & S. Gaskins (Eds.), *Anthropological perspectives on learning in childhood.* Lanham, MA: Rowman & Littlefield.

Murray, L., & Trevarthen, C. (1985). Emotional regulation of interactions between two-month-olds and their mothers. In T. M. Field & N. A. Fox (Eds.), *Social perception in infants* (pp. 177–197). Norwood, NJ: Ablex.

Nasir, N. (2005). Individual cognitive structuring and the sociocultural context: Strategy shifts in the game of dominoes. *Journal of the Learning Sciences, 14,* 5–34.

Nelson, K., & Fivush, R. (2004). The emergence of autobiographical memory: A social cultural developmental theory. *Psychological Review, 111,* 486–511.

Nunes, T., & Bryant, P. (1996). *Children doing mathematics.* Oxford, England: Blackwell.

Ochs, E., Taylor, C., Rudolph, D., & Smith, R. (1992). Storytelling as a theory-building activity. *Discourse Processes, 15,* 37–72.

Pan, Y., Gauvain, M., Liu, Z., & Cheng, L. (2006). American and Chinese parental involvement in young children's mathematics learning. *Cognitive Development, 21,* 17–35.

Pascalis, O., de Haan, M., & Nelson, C. A. (2002). Is face processing species-specific during the first year of life? *Science, 5,* 427–434.

Potter, G. G., Helms, M. J., Burke, J. R., Steffens, D. C., & Plassman, B. L. (2007). Job demands and dementia risk among male twin pairs. *Alzheimer's & Dementia, 3*(3), 192–199.

Potter, G. G., Helms, M. J., & Plassman, B. L. (2008). Associations of job demands and intelligence with cognitive performance among men in late life. *Neurology, 70,* 1803–1808.

Pratt, M. W., Green, D., MacVicar, J., & Bountrogianni, M. (1992). The mathematical parent: Parental scaffolding, parenting style, and learning outcomes in long-division mathematics homework. *Journal of Applied Developmental Psychology, 13*(1), 17–34.

Raeff, C. (2006). *Always separate, always connected: Independence and interdependence in cultural contexts of development*. Mahwah, NJ: Erlbaum.

Reese, E., & Newcombe, R. (2007). Training mothers in elaborative reminiscing enhances children's autobiographical memory and narrative. *Child Development, 78*, 1153–1170.

Reyna, V. F., & Farley, F. (2006). Risk and rationality in adolescent decision making: Implications for theory, practice, and public policy. *Psychological Science in the Public Interest, 7*, 1–44.

Reyna, V. F., & Rivers, S. E. (2008). Current theories of risk and rational decision making. *Developmental Review, 28*, 1–11.

Reynolds, C. A. (2008). Genetic and environmental influences on cognitive change. In S. M. Hofer & D. F. Alwin (Eds), *The Handbook on Cognitive Aging: Interdisciplinary Perspectives* (pp. 557–574). Thousand Oaks, CA: Sage.

Reynolds, C. A. (2009). Genetics of brain aging: Twin aging. In L. Squire (Ed), *New Encyclopedia of Neuroscience* (pp. 185–192). London: Elsevier.

Reynolds, C. A., Gatz, M., Berg, S., & Pedersen, N. L. (2007). Genotype-environment interactions: Cognitive aging and social factors. *Twin Research and Human Genetics, 10*(2), 241–254.

Rochat, P., & Striano, T. (1999). Early social cognition: Understanding others in the first months of life. In P. Rochat (Ed.), *Early social cognition: Understanding others in the first months of life* (pp. 3–34). Mahwah, NJ: Erlbaum.

Rochat, P. (2004). Emerging awareness. In G. Bremner & A. Slater (Eds.), *Theories of infant development* (pp. 258–283). Malden, MA: Blackwell Publishing.

Rogoff, B. (1990). *Apprenticeship in thinking: Cognitive development in social context*. New York: Oxford University Press.

Rogoff, B. (1998). Cognition as a collaborative process. In W. Damon (Series Ed.) and D. Kuhn & R. S. Siegler (Vol. Eds.), *Handbook of child psychology: Vol. 2. Cognition, perception, and language* (pp. 679–744). New York: Wiley.

Rogoff, B. (2003). *The cultural nature of human development*. Oxford, UK: Oxford University Press.

Rogoff, B., Gauvain, M., & Ellis, S. (1984). Development viewed in its cultural context. In M. H. Bornstein & M. E. Lamb (Eds.), *Developmental psychology: An advanced textbook* (pp. 533–571). Hillsdale, NJ: Erlbaum.

Rogoff, B., Sellers, M. J., Pirrotta, S., Fox, N., & White, S. H. (1975). Age of assignment of roles and responsibilities to children: A cross-cultural survey. *Human Development, 18*, 353–369.

Ross, M., Spencer, S. J., Blatz, C. W., & Restorick, E. (2008). Collaboration reduces the frequency of false memories in older and younger adults. *Psychology and Aging, 23*(1), 85–92.

Ross, M., Spencer, S. J., Linardatos, L., Lam, K. C. H., & Perunovic, M. (2004). Going shopping and identifying landmarks: Does collaboration improve older people's memory? *Applied Cognitive Psychology, 18*(6), 683–696.

Saczynski, J. S., Pfeifer, L. A., Masaki, K., Korf, E. S., Laurin, D., White, L., et al. (2006). The effect of social engagement on incident dementia: the Honolulu-Asia Aging Study. *American Journal of Epidemiology, 163*(5), 433–440.

Saffran, J. R., Werker, J., & Werner, L. A. (2006). The infant's auditory world. In W. Damon & R. M. Lerner (Series Eds.) and D. Kuhn & R. S. Siegler (Vol. Eds.), *Handbook of child psychology: Vol. 2, Cognition, perception, and language* (6th ed., pp. 58–108). New York: Wiley.

Sales, J. M., & Fivush, R. (2005). Social and emotional functions of mother-child reminiscing about stressful events. *Social Cognition, 23*, 70–90.

Sameroff, A. J., & Haith, M. M. (1996). *The five to seven year shift: The age of reason and responsibility*. Chicago, IL: University of Chicago Press.

Saxe, G. B. (1981). Body parts as numerals: A developmental analysis of enumeration among a village population in Papua New Guinea. *Child Development, 52*, 306–316.

Saxe, G. B. (1991). *Culture and cognitive development: Studies in mathematical understanding*. Hillsdale, NJ: Erlbaum.

Scaife, M., & Bruner, J. S. (1975). The capacity for joint visual attention in the infant. *Nature, 253*, 265–266.

Scarr, S., & McCartney, K. (1983). How people make their own environments: A theory of genotype—environment effects. *Child Development, 54*(2), 424–435.

Schaie, K. W., & Willis, S. L. (Eds.). (2000). *A stage theory model of adult cognitive development revisited*. New York: Springer Publishing Co.

Schaie, K. W. (2005). *Developmental influences on adult intelligence: The Seattle Longitudinal Study*. New York: Oxford University Press.

Schlegel, A., & Barry, H., III. (1991). *Adolescence: An anthropological inquiry*. New York: Free Press.

Schneider, W., & Bjorklund, D. F. (1998). Memory. In W. Damon (Series Ed.) & D. Kuhn & R. S. Siegler (Vol. Eds.), *Handbook of child psychology. Vol. 2: Cognitive, language, and perceptual development* (5th ed., pp. 467–521). New York: Wiley.

Schooler, C., & Caplan, L. J. (Eds.). (2008). *Those who have, get: Social structure, environmental complexity, intellectual functioning, and self-directed orientations in the elderly.* New York: Springer Publishing Co.

Scribner, S. (1985). Vygotsky's uses of history. In J. V. Wertsch (Ed.), *Culture, communication, and cognition: Vygotskian perspectives* (pp. 119–145). Cambridge: Cambridge University Press.

Serpell, R. (1979). *Culture's influence on behavior.* London: Methuen.

Shweder, R. A., Goodnow, J. J., Hatano, G., LeVine, R.A., Markus, H. R., & Miller, P. J. (2006). The cultural psychology of development: One mind, many mentalities. In W. Damon & R. M. Lerner (Series Eds.) and R. M. Lerner (Vol. Ed.), *Handbook of child psychology: Vol. 1, Theoretical models of human development* (6th ed., pp. 716–792). New York: Wiley.

Snow, C. E. (1990). Building memories: The ontogeny of autobiography. In D. Cicchetti & M. Beeghly (Eds.), *The self in transition: Infancy to childhood* (pp. 213–242). Chicago, IL: University of Chicago Press.

Steinberg, L. (2005). Cognitive and affective development in adolescence. *Trends in Cognitive Science, 9*, 69–74.

Steinberg, L. (2007). Risk taking in adolescence: New perspectives from brain and behavioral sciences. *Current Directions in Psychological Science, 16*, 55–59.

Steinberg, L., & Monahan, K. C. (2007). Age differences in resistance to peer influence. *Developmental Psychology, 43*, 1531–1543.

Stevenson, H. W., & Stigler, J. W. (1992). *The learning gap: Why our schools are failing and what we can learn from Japanese and Chinese education.* New York: Summit Books.

Stigler, J. W., Gallimore, R., & Hiebert, J. (2000). Using video surveys to compare classrooms and teaching across cultures: Examples and lessons from the TIMSS video studies. *Educational Psychologist, 35*, 87–100.

Thompson, R. A. (1998). Early sociopersonality development. In N. Eisenberg (Vol. Ed.), *Handbook of child psychology: Vol. 3 Social, emotional, and personality development* (5th ed., pp. 25–104). New York: Wiley.

Tomasello, M. (1995). Joint attention as social cognition. In C. Moore & P. H. Dunham (Eds.), *Joint attention: Its origins and role in development* (pp. 103–130). Hillsdale, NJ: Erlbaum.

Tomasello, M. (1988). The role of joint attentional processes in early language development. *Language Sciences, 10*, 69–88.

Tomasello, M., Kruger, A. C., & Ratner, H. H. (1993). Cultural learning. *Behavioral and Brain Sciences, 16*, 495–511.

Trevarthen, C. (1980). The foundations of intersubjectivity: Development of interpersonal and cooperative understanding in infants. In D. R. Olson (Ed.), *The social foundations of language and thought* (pp. 316–342). New York: Norton.

Trevarthen, C., & Aitken, K. J. (2001). Infant intersubjectivity: Research, theory, and clinical applications. *Journal of Child Psychology and Psychiatry, 42*, 3–48.

Vaish, A., & Staino, T. (2004). Is visual reference necessary? Contributions of facial versus vocal cues in 12-month-olds' social referencing behavior. *Developmental Science, 7*, 261–269.

Vaish, A., Grossman, T., & Woodward, A. (2008). Not all emotions are created equal: The negativity bias in social-emotional development. *Psychological Bulletin, 134*, 383–403.

Valsiner, J., & Rosa, A. (2007). *The Cambridge handbook of sociocultural psychology.* Cambridge: Cambridge University Press.

Van Hecke, A. V., Mundy, P. C., Acra, C. F., Block, J. J., Delgado, C. E. F., Parlade, M. V., et al. (2007). Infant joint attention, temperament, and social competence in preschool children. *Child Development, 78*, 53–69.

Vigil, D. C. (2002). Cultural variations in attention regulation: A comparative analysis of British and Chinese populations. *International Journal of Language and Communicative Disorders, 37*, 433–458.

Vygotsky, L. S. (1962). *Thought and language.* New York: Wiley.

Vygotsky, L. S. (1978). *Mind in society: The development of higher psychological functions.* Cambridge, MA: Harvard University Press.

Walden, T. A., & Kim, G. (2005). Infants' social looking toward mothers and strangers. *International Journal of Behavioral Development, 29*, 356–360.

Wang, Q. (2007). "Remember when you got the big, big bulldozer?" Mother-child reminiscing over time and across cultures. *Social Cognition, 25*, 455–471.

Weibe, D., Berg, C. A., Korbel, C., Palmer, D. L., Beveridge, R., Upchurch, R., et al. (2005). Children's appraisals of maternal involvement in coping with diabetes: Enhancing our understanding of adherence, metabolic control, and quality of life across adolescence. *Journal of Pediatric Psychology, 30,* 167–178.

Werker, J. F., & Vouloumanos, A. (2001). Speech and language processing in infancy: A neurocognitive approach. In C. A. Nelson & M. Luciana (Eds.), *Handbook of developmental cognitive neuroscience* (pp. 269–280). Cambridge, MA: M.I.T. Press.

White, S. H. (1965). Evidence for a hierarchical arrangement of learning processes. *Advances in child development and behavior, 2,* 187–220.

White, S. H. (1996). The child's entry into the "age of reason." In A. J. Sameroff & M. M. Haith (Eds.), *The five to seven year shift: The age of reason and responsibility* (pp. 17–30). Chicago, IL: University of Chicago Press.

Wilson, R. S., Krueger, K. R., Arnold, S. E., Schneider, J. A., Kelly, J. F., Barnes, L. L., et al. (2007). Loneliness and risk of Alzheimer disease. *Archives of General Psychiatry, 64*(2), 234–240.

Wood, D. J., & Middleton, D. (1975). A study of assisted problem solving. *British Journal of Psychology, 66,* 181–191.

Wood, D. J., Wood, H., & Middleton, D. (1978). An experimental evaluation of four face-to-face teaching strategies. *International Journal of Behavioral Development, 2,* 131–147.

Yurgelun-Todd, D. (2007). Emotional and cognitive changes during adolescence. *Current opinion in neurobiology, 17,* 251–257.

MEMORY DEVELOPMENT ACROSS THE LIFE SPAN

12

Christopher Hertzog and Yee Lee Shing

Memory is one of the most widely studied and best understood facets of cognition. Investigations of memory have also played an important role in developmental psychology and have contributed to the evolution of life-span developmental psychology (e.g., Baltes, 1987). We cover the major topics of relevance for understanding the development of memory, acknowledging that our coverage will inevitably be both selective and incomplete.

▧ THEORETICAL CONCEPTS OF MEMORY

We begin with a brief overview of foundational concepts regarding memory and its development. After considering some basic concepts, we then review in detail what is known about memory development across the human life span.

Our perspective, grounded in experimental cognitive psychology, emphasizes memory in terms of how different cognitive processes and procedures affect learning and remembering (e.g., Craik, 2002; Hunt, 2003; Roediger, Rajaram, & Geraci, 2007). For example, remembering information is in large part an outcome of how one attends to that information when it is first encountered. Memory can occur incidentally, as a by-product of attending to and thinking about information, or intentionally, because one has engaged a goal of learning new information.

There are multiple types of memory. The distinction between episodic and semantic memory has special developmental relevance. Semantic memory is defined as declarative knowledge about the world, culture, and one's own environment. It grows during childhood as a function of a child's exposure to information, and it is affected by environmental context, acculturation, social status, and schooling. Knowledge and access to knowledge is well preserved in adulthood. It declines rather late in life, more precociously with pathologies of memory than with normal aging.

Episodic memory is defined as memory for specific instances, events, or episodes in one's life. Some aspects of episodic memory (e.g., recognizing objects such as toys or the faces of adults) seem to develop relatively early in childhood. Other aspects, such as the ability to successfully organize information to facilitate remembering, continue to develop and improve into early adolescence. Unlike semantic memory, performance on at least some kinds of episodic memory tasks begins declining in middle age, with the rate of memory decline accelerating in later life. However, whether specific children or adults show typical or atypical patterns of development depend on a number of factors, and there are reliable individual differences in the rates of memory change in adulthood and old age. A full understanding of memory development, then, requires an appreciation for different ways in which relevant processes—such as the allocation of attention—can influence memory, and how development influences these processes across the life span.

Stages of Memory Processes

The temporal context of learning and remembering is often divided into encoding, storage, and retrieval. Encoding involves perceiving, attending, and comprehending new information. Concentrating on the meaning of new information results in greater memory strength and a higher likelihood of remembering than superficially noticing it, or processing superficial stimulus features (e.g., Craik, 2002). Comprehension (the process of understanding) carries special advantages and benefits for later remembering (Kintsch, 1998).

Memory storage and binding processes integrate information into coherent episodes as a more or less integrated ensemble, preserving them for later access (e.g., Treisman, 1996; Zimmer, Mecklinger, & Lindenberger, 2006). Often, the process of binding includes information about what happens and when it happens; the binding process associates features of events, including how they are interpreted in light of what one already knows, with the temporal context in which events happen (e.g., Polyn, Norman, & Kahana, 2009).

Remembering occurs when previously processed information is retrieved. Retrieval can be incidental (e.g., when perceiving something in the environment reminds us of something else) or intentional (e.g., trying to remember where one put one's keys). Retrieval is not an all-or-none process, in which all elements of an episode are accessed once the episode has been brought to mind. To the contrary, remembering is often reconstructive. One remembers fragments of past events and attempts to reconstruct other aspect of those events by inference or further, guided retrieval attempts (Johnson, 2006). For this reason, and others, individuals are susceptible to a variety of memory errors (Schacter, 2001), such as believing that two different memory fragments they have retrieved are part of the same episode.

Whether information that is available in memory is accessible (can actually be retrieved; Tulving & Pearlstone, 1966) depends on complex interactions involving mechanisms from all three stages of remembering. For example, retrieval is most likely when it is aligned with the type of process used at encoding (transfer-appropriate processing; Morris, Bransford, & Franks, 1977). Retrieval is less likely when encoding results in generalized memory representations, lacking distinctive detail, that are weakly bound to the specific context and contextual cues.

Implicit Versus Explicit Memory

Explicit memory is defined as remembering under the explicit goal of doing so. Implicit memory refers to remembering without intent or awareness, often in the service of some other cognitive processing goal. We have chosen to focus this chapter on explicit memory. Nevertheless, implicit memory is affected by development. It has different patterns of early development, depending on whether it is perceptual or conceptual in nature (Schneider, 2011). In adulthood, implicit memory, whether based on repeated physical features or conceptual features, is relatively spared by aging (see Light, Prull, La Voie, & Healy, 2000). Likewise, procedural memory, remembering how to do things, is relatively spared in old age (e.g., Fraser, Li, & Penhune, 2009), especially if the skill was originally well learned (Krampe & Ericsson, 1996).

LIFE-SPAN THEORIES OF EPISODIC MEMORY DEVELOPMENT

An inverted U-shape function describes many aspects of cognition, including episodic memory (Dempster, 1992; Kail & Salthouse, 1994). As children grow older, their episodic memory improves. In later adulthood episodic memory begins to wane. Nevertheless, old age is not merely the reversal of child development, because different constellations of mechanisms influence cognitive changes at each end of the life span (Baltes, Lindenberger, & Staudinger, 2006; Bialystok & Craik, 2006). Early memory development is influenced by selection and optimization processes that produce individual differences in knowledge relevant for memory encoding and retrieval. Semantic memory development over the life span supports episodic remembering, as discussed in more detail later in the chapter. Individuals gain specific skills and knowledge in domains of interest that they themselves select or those that are selected for them (e.g., Ackerman, 2000). On the other hand, compensatory mechanisms for cognitive loss may be important in old age. Compensation can occur at the neuronal (Park & Reuter-Lorenz, 2009) or behavioral levels (Hertzog, Kramer, Wilson, & Lindenberger, 2009). Compensation can maintain everyday memory functioning in old age, despite decline in underlying memory mechanisms (Bäckman, 1989).

Life-span views embrace the joint influences of multiple factors on memory development, including the important roles of heredity–environment interactions at different stages of the life course (Gottlieb, 1991). Context also plays an important role (Hess, 2005), for example, in terms of history-graded cohort differences in the content relevant knowledge structures (Hultsch, Hertzog, Dixon, & Small, 1998; Schaie, 2005). Moreover, different contexts may be relevant in different ways at different points in the life span (e.g., parental and peer influences on acculturation in childhood, intimate partnership, friendship and occupational-peer networks in adulthood, and family and peer network support structures in old age).

The specific mechanisms that drive developmental changes in memory functioning in childhood and aging have rarely been examined in conjunction (but see Craik & Bialystok, 2006). The life-span theoretical framework of episodic memory development proposed by Lindenberger and colleagues (Shing, Werkle-Bergner, Li, & Lindenberger, 2008; Werkle-Bergner, Müller, Li, Lindenberger, 2006) is an important exception. According to this framework, the ontogeny of episodic memory builds on the interaction between two components: (1) the *strategic component*, involving control operations that aid and regulate memory processes at both encoding and retrieval; and (2) the *associative component*, involving mechanisms that bind memory content into coherent representations.

The two-component framework builds upon neural models that postulate the involvement of prefrontal cortex (PFC) to support the strategic component, mediotemporal lobe (MTL)—particularly the hippocampus—to support the associative component (e.g., Moscovitch, 1992; Simons & Spiers, 2003), and interactions between PFC and MTL regions during encoding and retrieval (Paller & Wagner, 2002). These brain regions undergo substantial alterations across the life span (e.g., Buckner, 2004;

Nelson, 2001). PFC continues to mature well into adolescence, whereas MTL matures earlier in development (e.g., Gogtay et al., 2006; Ofen et al., 2007). In older adults, accelerated decline is observed in both PFC and MTL (e.g., Raz et al., 2005). The life-span framework of episodic memory development postulates that children's difficulties in episodic memory primarily originate from low levels of strategic operations, reflecting the protracted development of the PFC. Deficiencies in episodic memory functioning among older adults, on the other hand, originate from impairments in both strategic and associative components, reflecting senescent changes in the PFC and the MTL.

WORKING MEMORY

Working memory (WM) refers to the ability to flexibly process, transform, and maintain information in a state of heightened accessibility and awareness (Cowan, 1995). Some theorists consider WM to be more or less akin to activation of long-term memory in a state of heightened accessibility (Cowan, 1995; Ericsson & Kintsch, 1995; Unsworth & Engle, 2007). Because WM capacity is an important variable to consider in the context of encoding and retrieval mechanisms, we consider its development first.

The processes relevant to maintaining information in WM can be regarded as a subset of executive functioning or cognitive control. Controlled processing modes are generally conceptualized as requiring attention and effort, and are often (but not always) executed with awareness. Models of WM include multiple executive processes (Shah & Miyake, 1996), such as selection, updating, and resisting interference (Kane & Engle, 2003). Theories of cognitive control have been informed by neuroscience (e.g., Braver, Paxton, Locke, & Barch, 2009). For instance, dopaminergic systems connecting areas of basal ganglia and PFC are involved in goal-directed strategies, pursuit, and the evaluation of reward and punishment (Miller & Cohen, 2001).

The concept of WM capacity has played a critical role in developmental theory about cognitive development in childhood (e.g., Cowan, Nugent, Elliott, Ponomarev, & Saults, 1999; Pascual-Leone, 1970). The ability to retain information for brief periods of time develops early in childhood and shows continuous improvement with age after preschool (e.g., Davidson, Amso, Anderson, & Diamond, 2006; Dempster, 1981; Pascual-Leone, 1970). Recent longitudinal work with participants from age 4 to 23 showed continuous span increases until the age of 18, but no increases thereafter (Schneider, Knopf, & Sodian, 2009). Cowan et al. (1999) found that the average span of apprehension (the amount of information that people can attend to at a single time) increased significantly with age, from childhood to young adulthood, reflecting developmental difference in the short-term storage capacity.

Case's developmental theory proposed that limited WM capacity must be shared between storage and processing functions (e.g., Case, Kurland, & Goldberg, 1982). With increasing age across childhood, the processing function of WM gains more efficiency, resulting in more capacity for storage function and further remembering (for alternatives, see Hitch & Towse, 1995; Pascual-Leone & Baillargeon, 1994). Baddeley's WM model has at least three subcomponents, including the central executive, the visuospatial sketchpad, and the articulatory or phonological loop (Baddeley, 1986). Gathercole, Pickering, Ambridge, and Wearing (2004) suggested that this basic structure of WM is present from 6 years of age, possibly earlier.

WM capacity declines in adulthood, as observed in both cross-sectional (e.g., Salthouse & Babcock, 1991) and longitudinal studies (e.g., Hertzog, Dixon, Hultsch, & MacDonald, 2003). One of the major sources of changes in WM capacity in adulthood appears to be the buildup of proactive interference, where information currently or previously held in memory reduces access to other information (e.g., Lustig, Hasher, & May, 2001; Zeintl & Kliegel, 2007). Older adults are also more susceptible to retroactive interference (where recently processed information reduces access to information learned earlier) in the short lists used in span tasks Hedden & Park, 2003 attributed that effect to confusion about sources (different lists) rather than degraded inhibitory functioning. Oberauer (2005) found that older and younger adults could temporarily disregard information that was designated as irrelevant, reactivating it later as needed, in memory updating tasks. He argued that older adults possessed preserved ability to move information in and out of the focus of WM, but showed difficulties in building and maintaining bindings between different representations in WM.

EPISODIC MEMORY

Episodic memory improves throughout childhood (see Schneider & Pressley, 1997). Figure 12.1 shows longitudinal data of episodic memory performance from children of age 4–12 (Knopf, 1999). Longitudinal and cohort-sequential studies in adulthood show that verbal and visual episodic memory declines in old age, even in individuals who are healthy and show no signs of dementing illness (e.g., Hultsch et al., 1998; Rönnlund, Nyberg, Bäckman, & Nilsson, 2005; Schaie, 2005; Zelinski & Stewart, 1998; see Figure 12.2).

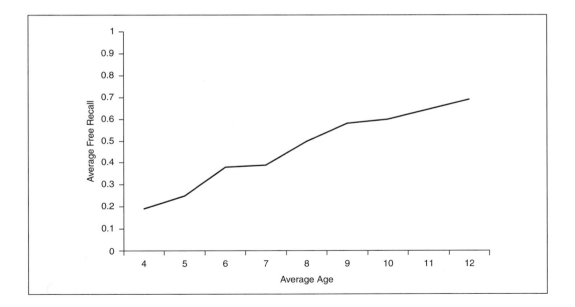

FIGURE 12.1   **Developmental function for free-recall performance based on longitudinal data.** *Source*: **Data adapted with permission from Knopf (1999).**

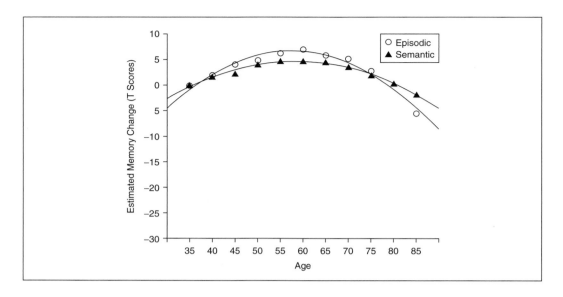

FIGURE 12.2 **Estimated episodic and semantic memory changes across age (T scores) on the basis of longitudinal data.** *Source*: **Data adapted with permission from Rönnlund et al. (2005).**

There are a number of qualifications of these broad generalizations. First, there is at least some evidence of cohort effects on memory performance, such that memory performance may improve for more recently born generations. The magnitude of these effects may be small relative to other types of cognitive ability (e.g., Rönnlund et al., 2005; Schaie, 2005; Zelinski, 2009). Cohort effects imply that historical and contextual events play a role in determining level of function; hence one should not presume that observed cross-sectional age differences in episodic memory are in some sense a pure reflection of ontogenetic aging. Second, the extent of episodic memory decline varies with the type of memory task. For instance, declines in memory for content of narrative texts shows smaller effect sizes of age than paired-associated recall or free recall of word lists (e.g., Hultsch et al., 1998). Third, there are individual differences in memory change in late life, arguing that some individuals experience greater memory decline than others (e.g., Hertzog et al., 2003).

Encoding

Tests of incidental encoding instruct an individual to process information in a certain way. On its surface, this orienting task has nothing to do with memorization per se (e.g., one might be instructed to judge properties of words, such as object size relative to a standard, or its consistency with a concept). Memory for the incidentally encoded information is then evaluated with a surprise memory test. Young children have excellent memory for recent events that have been coded incidentally (Schneider & Pressley, 1997). Memory for incidentally encoded information declines during adulthood (see Kausler, 1994). This contradicts the simple hypothesis that encoding deficits are primarily responsible for aging effects on memory, contrary to the early expectations of levels-of-processing theory (e.g., Craik, 2002), although there has been debate about this issue (e.g., Light, 1991). Age differences in memory following incidental encoding can be reconciled with an encoding deficit by appeal to additional, elaborative encoding by younger adults—in effect, when individuals process information in a manner that enhances or supplements the surface require-ments of the orienting task (e.g., Luo, Hendriks, & Craik, 2007).

Intentional encoding of new information involves strategic or reflective activ-ity that aids the formation of new memory traces. This may take the form of orga-nizing and/or elaborating on the to-be-learned information, often by making use of one's semantic knowledge to relate different features of an episode. For example, memory for new associations is aided by the use of verbal and imagery mediators (e.g., Richardson, 1998).

In the child developmental literature, episodic memory development has been tied to age changes in encoding strategies (Pressley & Hilden, 2006; Schneider & Pressley, 1997). Flavell's (1970) seminal work observed that rehearsal and organiza-tion develop as memory strategies between 5 and 10 years of age. Strategy use is often examined in sort-recall type of memory tasks in which items can be organized into semantic categories. Children's organization of items during study (assessed with sorting tasks) and recall (assessed by clustering like items in the recall sequence) develops rapidly throughout the elementary-school years (see Bjorklund, Dukes, & Brown, 2009; Schneider & Pressley, 1997). Kindergarten and early-grade school children do not spontaneously display strategic organizational behavior. However, when given instructions to use a strategy, they do so, pointing to an initial *production deficiency* of strategy use that can be overcome (Bjorklund et al., 2009). A *utilization deficiency* refers to spontaneous use of strategic behavior (e.g., selective attention) but without major benefits to memory (Bjorklund, Miller, Coyle, & Slawinski, 1997; DeMarie-Dreblow & Miller, 1988), implying inefficient or ineffective use of strategies, possibly due to limitations in WM (Schneider, Kron, Huennerkopf, & Krajewski, 2004) and metamemory (DeMarie, Miller, Ferron, & Cunningham, 2004). Development into young adulthood is characterized by increasing effectiveness of strategy use, which may be related to optimal selection of strategies to match item characteristics. Recent studies reveal that the use of multiple strategies can benefit children's later recall (e.g., DeMarie et al., 2004; Schneider, Kron-Sperl, & Hünnerkopf, 2009; Shin, Bjorklund, & Beck, 2007).

In adulthood, age differences in encoding strategies can reflect production defi-ciencies (Kausler, 1994; Verhaeghen & Marcoen, 1994), with older adults not spontane-ously engaging in effective mnemonic strategies. Craik (1986) posited that successful remembering involves some mixture of externally driven "environmentally support" and internally guided "self-initiated activities." He argued that aging is associated with a decline in self-initiated processing, with older adults relying more on environ-mental support (see also Bäckman, 1989). One way of providing support is to instruct older adults to use mnemonic strategies, which benefits adults' learning (Kausler, 1994; Verhaeghen & Marcoen, 1994; Verhaeghen, Marcoen, & Goossens, 1992).

However, age-related production deficiencies are not an important explanation of aging effects on episodic memory. Dunlosky and Hertzog (2001) used item-level strategy reports to specify age differences in patterns of mediator use. In a paired-associate memory task, participants were instructed to use imagery or any strategy and were asked to report the strategy produced for learning each item. Small age dif-ferences in reported strategy production were only observed when people were not informed about mediational strategies, and this difference did not account for large proportions of variance on older adults' recall. Spontaneous strategy use accounts for a substantial proportion of variance (individual differences) in WM and recall of newly learned associations, but little of the age-related variance in those variables, implying that factors other than a production deficiency are responsible for age differences in memory (e.g., Bailey, Dunlosky, & Hertzog, 2009).

The nature of memory representations created during encoding appears to undergo developmental changes. The fuzzy-trace theory by Brainerd and Reyna (1990) posits that memory representations can be aligned on a continuum ranging from literal, verbatim traces to fuzzy, gist-like traces. Verbatim traces correspond to representations constrained to the surface form of memory content. Gist traces, on the other hand, correspond to generalized representations, such as semantic meaning of memory content. In terms of developmental differences, during the preschool and early elementary-school-years an initial improvement in verbatim memory can be noted. Gist memory, on the other hand, tends to lag behind in development (e.g., Brainerd & Gordon, 1994). Overall, children experience a shift from relying on context-specific to gist-like representations over developmental periods (Brainerd & Reyna, 2004). The higher interference susceptibility of verbatim traces may, thereby, contribute to lower memory performance in younger children. There have also been some suggestions in the adult literature that older adults' self-generated cues are less stable and less distinct than younger adults, contributing to subsequent memory failure (e.g., Mäntylä & Bäckman, 1990), and that they encode general meaning information over specific details in text processing (e.g., Adams, Smith, Nyquist, & Perlmutter, 1997; Stine-Morrow, Miller, & Hertzog, 2006).

Binding and Storage

Binding refers to a set of cognitive processes that associate features within a memory trace or several memory traces among each other (Cohen & Eichenbaum, 1993; Polyn et al., 2009; Zimmer et al., 2006). In one of the few developmental studies that examined binding in childhood, Sluzenski, Newcombe, and Kovacs (2006) showed children and young adults' pictures of animals against arbitrary backgrounds, later testing them on their memory for the animals, the backgrounds, or both. Their results indicate that the quality of binding may progress significantly around 5–6 years of age (see Oakes, Ross-Sheehy, & Luck, 2006 regarding early development of binding in visual short-term memory). Memory for individual features appears to progress at a faster rate during childhood than the trajectory of memory for associations, which may also help to explain preschoolers' difficulty in source monitoring (Sluzenski, Newcombe, & Ottinger, 2004).

Binding may be implicated in greater age-associated impairments in remembering the context and the specific details of memory episodes than in remembering the content itself (see Spencer & Raz, 1995). The *associative deficit hypothesis* postulates that this effect is due, at least in part, to difficulties in binding information into cohesive memory representations. Chalfonte and Johnson (1996) compared age-related differences in memorizing individual features with binding of those features. Older adults' memory for object identity and object color was not worse than younger adults' memory (but feature memory for location was impaired). However, older adults manifested a disproportionate reduction in memory for bound item and location information and bound item and color information. Older adults are disproportionately impaired at encoding and retrieving associations among items, such as associative pairings of two words (Old & Naveh-Benjamin, 2008), relative to the individual words themselves (see also Castel & Craik, 2003).

A recent life span study by Cowan, Naveh-Benjamin, Kilb, and Saults (2006) indicates that memory binding develops early in childhood and declines faster than other aspects of memory. They investigated age differences in the ability to keep the association between a visual object (colored squares) and its spatial location in WM using a change-detection paradigm. Older adults often failed to notice changes in the conjunction of features. The two groups of children (aged 8–10 and 11–12 years) showed lower performance levels than younger adults on both kinds of trials. However, they were not as affected on the feature-conjunction trials as the group of older adults.

Retrieval and Accessibility

Like encoding, retrieval can be viewed as incidental or intentional. Incidental retrieval occurs when environmental cues or mental thoughts activate retrieval of information without explicit goal-directed search for the information. Recognition memory can generically be viewed as involving a passive retrieval process, in which activities or objects in the environment are subjected to comparator processes that match what is perceived to what is known or previously encountered. The phenomenology of recognition has been increasingly important in memory theory. Two-process views of memory retrieval (e.g., Jacoby, 1999) argue that individuals encountering old information experience either recollection (including activation of specific information about the original encounter) or familiarity, recognition of information as something encountered before, but without access to specific details about the encounter. Either type of experience can be illusory—in the Deese–Roediger–McDermott false memory paradigm, individuals report vivid recollection of a semantic category lure that was actually never presented to them (Roediger & McDermott, 1995). Nevertheless, familiarity experiences are more likely to be based on spontaneous retrieval of information that can be misattributed to one source as opposed to another (Dodson & Schacter, 2002).

Incidental retrieval seems in some respects relatively well preserved in adulthood. Older adults fare better on recognition tests than recall tests (e.g., Macht & Buschke, 1983; McDowd & Craik, 1987), especially if the criterion test is "yes/no" recognition that mixes old with new information and simply requires discrimination of each. From a two-process perspective, such outcomes are consistent with the claim that mechanisms supporting familiarity of specific information, such as individual items from a list, are spared by aging (Light et al., 2000). Conversely, older adults show declines in recollection during recognition tests, whether assessed by process-dissociation tasks (e.g., Jennings & Jacoby, 1997) or self-reports of recollection versus familiarity (e.g., Perfect & Dasgupta, 1997). The pattern of adult age deficits in recollection, coupled with relatively intact familiarity, has been demonstrated in a number of studies. For example, Jennings and Jacoby's (1997) repetition-lag paradigm presented people with a series of items at encoding that they would be subsequently asked to recognize from among a set of novel items. During the recognition test, novel items were also repeated at varying lags, and participants were instructed to either exclude (say "no") or include (say "yes") repeated novel items at test. Responding "no" to an exclusion trial required that participants be able to recollect the prior presentation of the item, whereas a "yes" response would likely be a product of context-free familiarity. Jennings and Jacoby's results showed differences in recollection-based processing as a function of age, but they found no age effect on familiarity. Older adults are also more susceptible to familiarity-based memory illusions, such as ironic effects of repetition (Jacoby, 1999), in which repeated lures during a recognition memory test are mistaken for word originally presented during encoding.

Intentional retrieval, on the other hand, involves a goal-directed search for desired information (e.g., "where did I leave my keys?"). It relies on mechanisms of cognitive control, as well as metacognition that influence decisions about whether to stop searching, how to use processes of reconstruction, how to evaluate the products of retrieval, and so on. Cued recall tasks assess externally (experimenter) directed retrieval; self-initiated retrieval may be linked to concepts rather than percepts, and hence its success may hinge on how the desired information is construed at the time retrieval is initiated.

Many recognition memory tasks evoke both incidental and intentional retrieval mechanisms. After having people study paired-associate items, one can test associative memory by asking people to identify intact pairs and reject rearranged pairs (new combinations of unpaired words that were part of the pairs originally studied). Good performance on associative recognition tests of this kind benefit from the use of recollection-based intentional retrieval strategies, such as the use of recall-to-reject strategies in associative recognition tasks (Cohn, Emrich, & Moscovitch, 2008; Light, Patterson, Chung, & Healy, 2004). With this strategy, specific recollection that one element of a rearranged pair was actually paired with a different word when originally studied allows one to reject the rearranged pair as not being part of the original list.

Manipulation of intentional retrieval through memory test formats reveals differential rates of development in children, with smaller age differences being found in recognition memory than in cued or free recall (e.g., Perlmutter & Lange, 1978). Emerging evidence suggests that the development of recollection extends into adolescence, whereas familiarity matures earlier during childhood (e.g., Brainerd & Reyna, 2004; Ghetti & Angelini, 2008). These results support the notion that increasingly efficient inhibitory processes—including deliberate suppression of irrelevant information—contribute to improved memory performance that occurs with age across childhood (e.g., Bjorklund & Harnishfeger, 1990; Harnishfeger & Pope, 1996). Research from eyewitness memory further reveal that memory recall of children until at least 7 years of age is generally low (e.g., Poole & Lindsay, 1995), accompanied by an increase in the number of inaccurate responses. However, with appropriate interview procedure (e.g., motivated to screen out wrong answers by choosing "I don't know"), even young children can enhance the accuracy of their testimony (Roebers & Schneider, 2005).

There are several lines of evidence arguing that self-initiated retrieval becomes less effective as adults get older. Older adults' cued recall differs more from young adults' cued recall, relative to age differences in recognition memory (e.g., Macht & Buschke, 1983). Older adults, under instructions, are equally likely to generate effective mediators at encoding, but they are much less likely to be able to retrieve and report these mediators at test when asked to do so (Dunlosky, Hertzog, & Powell-Moman,

2005). This apparent retrieval deficit appears, in part, to be attributable to a failure to spontaneously use effective retrieval strategies to reconstruct the memory from available evidence (Naveh-Benjamin, Brav, & Levy, 2007).

Access to information during self-initiated retrieval searches depends in part on the extent to which that information has competition for access to retrieval mechanisms. Proactive interference during retrieval is increased in old age (e.g., Ikier, Yang, & Hasher, 2008; Lustig, Konkel, & Jacoby, 2004). The study by Ikier et al. (2008) used word fragment completion for items where one or two competitors had been previously presented that could be relevant completions of the fragment. Only younger adults implemented a controlled retrieval strategy to overcome this interference. Jacoby, Shimizu, Velanova, and Rhodes (2005) showed that older adults engaged in less depth of processing of foils presented at test in the context of words that had been deeply processed at study. The depth of retrieval was revealed by a later recognition test for foils. Jacoby et al. argued that control over retrieval depends on matching test behaviors to benefit from encoding quality.

Automatic inhibition of information at the time of retrieval appears to be intact in older adults (e.g., Holley & McEvoy, 1996), whereas controlled use of inhibition may be affected (Andres, Guerrini, Phillips, & Perfect, 2008). However, not all studies find age-related inhibition deficits during memory retrieval. The list-based method of directed forgetting instructs people to recall information from one of two studied lists, omitting items from the other list. Directed forgetting is relatively intact in older adults (Sego, Golding, & Gottlob, 2006; Zellner & Bäuml, 2006), as it is in older children (Zellner & Bäuml, 2005). When directed forgetting effects are found, they may be due to older adults failing to engage inhibitory strategies when encoding a second list so as to enable effective selective retrieval from the second list, but not the to-be-forgotten first list (Sahakyan, Delaney, & Goodmon, 2008), a problem with strategic processing, not inhibition per se.

Another phenomenon relevant to inhibition is retrieval-induced forgetting, in which retrieving some information from an inter-related set reduces likelihood of retrieving other information in the set. Older adults show similar retrieval-induced forgetting in a task requiring retrieval of exemplars from categories, in which retrieving some members of a category makes it more difficult to retrieve others (Aslan, Bäuml, & Pastötter, 2007). They also show similar part-set cueing effects (Andres, 2009; Marsh, Dolan, Balota, & Roediger, 2004). These studies argue against a general controlled inhibitory deficit concerning memory retrieval, indicating instead that older adults manifest some production deficiencies in retrieval control strategies (Naveh-Benjamin et al., 2007; Sahakyan et al., 2008).

Other phenomena have been used to argue for an increased susceptibility to interference at retrieval as people grow older. The fan effect occurs when a single cue may be associated with multiple targets, which reduces the likelihood of competing targets. Older adults show greater fan effects, in the form of increased errors or slowed response times as the number of elements mapped to a cue increases (Gerard, Zacks, Hasher, & Radvansky, 1991). However, the fan effect may not necessarily reflect interference effects alone. Buchler, Fauce, Light, Reder, and Gottfredson (2009) crossed fan mappings with repetitions of stimuli, using a complicated 5-choice associative recognition test. Repetitions provided both item and associative strengthening for both age groups. Fan-related interference was not greater for older adults, and they showed substantial and equivalent repetition benefits. Buchler et al. argued that older adults manifest a retrieval deficit associated with weak memory strength from a single repetition, as well as a reliance on associative familiarity and item familiarity.

In sum, there is substantial evidence of age-related changes in retrieval effectiveness that may be due to multiple mechanisms. Studies of individual differences in memory and aging also support the hypothesis that age changes in retrieval mechanisms may be responsible for age-related changes in memory performance. Hultsch et al. (1998) and Hertzog et al. (2003) showed that older adults decline longitudinally in world knowledge tests. Such changes suggest reduced or impaired accessibility to knowledge. These changes also correlated highly with changes in WM and episodic memory, possibly implicating age-related problems in retrieval of information as a common influence on rates of episodic and semantic memory change in adulthood.

Encoding-Retrieval Interactions

One reason that it is difficult to separate encoding effects from retrieval effects is that the two sets of processes are interleaved, relying upon one another. Successful remembering requires both kinds of processes. The work by Jacoby et al. (2005) is an important example of encoding-retrieval interactions. The age difference in retrieval depth reported in those studies depends on the nature of encoding at test. Another example is the work on distinctiveness as a means of avoiding source memory errors. Dodson and Schacter (2002) argued that older adults are less likely to use distinctive details that are accessible at test to avoid misattributing what is familiar to the wrong source (see also Jacoby & Rhodes, 2006). Changes in test formats may encourage use of the distinctiveness heuristic, thereby lowering source memory errors. Likewise, the recollection training paradigm of Jennings and Jacoby (2003) trains individuals to avoid effects of repeating lures in a recognition test for items studied on an earlier list. By learning to engage in more effective encoding strategies, older individuals can learn to use recollection of the original words' features at encoding to discriminate them from the repeated lures (see also Lustig & Flegal, 2008).

▨ METAMEMORY AND COGNITIVE CONTROL

Metamemory can be seen as a set of processes that involve self-reflection and evaluation (Wellman, 1983). It provides feedback to control processes on whether current actions are likely to achieve processing goals (Flavell, 1979; Nelson, 1996). Metamemory also involves declarative knowledge—such as knowing different processing strategies—and beliefs about one's own memory capabilities (Hertzog & Hultsch, 2000).

Memory Monitoring

Monitoring can occur with respect to multiple aspects of memory, and can be measured by multiple types of judgments (Nelson & Narens, 1990). Effective monitoring aids the control of learning and remembering. The major question is whether individuals' judgments have good resolution (relative accuracy). Resolution is assessed by within-person correlations of metamemory judgments with memory performance.

Judgments of learning (JOLs) assess monitoring whether information has been sufficiently studied to support later remembering. Schneider, Visé, Lockl, and Nelson (2000) found that JOLs have equal resolution in children from age 5 onward. Moreover, their children showed a delayed-JOL effect, in which the resolution of JOLs after a delay is considerably higher than that of JOLs given immediately after an item is studied (due in large part to the diagnosticity of a retrieval attempt for subsequent test recall). The equivalent resolution of immediate JOLs and delayed-JOLs suggests equivalent item-level monitoring of encoding and retrieval processes. However, Koriat, Ackerman, Lockl, and Schneider (2009) reported an increase from age 7 to age 12 in resolution of children's immediate JOLs, tying it to an age-related increase in reliance on the cue of memorization effort as a basis for making JOLs.

There is evidence that the monitoring of encoding is relatively unimpaired by aging (e.g., Connor, Dunlosky, & Hertzog, 1997; Hertzog, Kidder, Powell-Moman, & Dunlosky, 2002). Connor et al. (1997) also showed that equivalent delayed-JOL effects on resolution for older and younger adults. Recently, Hertzog, Sinclair, and Dunlosky (2010) examined JOLs in an adult cross-sectional sample, showing that JOLs were influenced by both item relatedness (the pre-existing association of word pairs) and the strategy used to encode the word pairs, and that this relationship was invariant over the adult life span.

Feeling of knowing (FOK) judgments assess the ability to forecast correct recognition after cued recall fails. Butterfield, Nelson, and Peck (1988) found a difference favoring younger children over older children in FOK accuracy. Lockl and Schneider (2002) also found no evidence of improved FOK resolution from kindergarten to adulthood. Hence monitoring retrieval appears to develop early in children. In adulthood, there is some controversy regarding the resolution of FOKs. It does not differ for items held in semantic memory (such as facts or world knowledge; e.g., Butterfield et al., 1988), but has been reported to be poorer in old age for FOKs about newly learned information (e.g., Souchay, Moulin, Clarys, Taconnat, & Isingrini, 2007). However, recent studies have indicated age equivalence in episodic FOK resolution in predicting both recognition accuracy and for recollection during the recognition test (Hertzog, Dunlosky, & Sinclair, 2010; MacLaverty & Hertzog, 2009). The discrepancies in the literature have not yet been explained.

In some cases older adults have been found to be falsely confident about the accuracy of their recognition memory. Kelley and Sahakyan (2003) showed that older adults' recognition confidence judgments (CJs) were overconfident about responses to misleading lures in the Jacoby (1999) ironic effects paradigm. Older adults had poorer resolution of CJs for misleading items, but not in a test lacking them (see also Kelley & Rhodes, 2005). Likewise, Dodson, Bawa, and Krueger (2007) found that when older adults made commission errors in source recognition or in cued recall for related items, they tended to be overconfident, relative to younger adults, in the accuracy of their errors. Shing, Werkle-Berger, Li, and Lindenberger (2009) also reported that older adults manifested high-confidence errors in associative recognition, whereas children 10–12 years old did not show such pattern.

Some argue that this kind of "misrecollection" (Dodson et al., 2007) is due to the poor performance of a subset of older adults who manifest low scores on neuropsychological tests of frontal function (Butler, McDaniel, & Dornburg, 2004; Geraci & Roediger, 2007). Similar arguments have been made regarding reported age-related deficits in resolution of episodic FOKs (e.g., Souchay & Isingrini, 2004) and source attributions (Henkel, Johnson, & DeLeonardis, 1998). These phenomena may reflect a failure to engage in controlled search for disconfirming evidence—what can be viewed as a failure of monitoring-guided control.

Monitoring latency or duration of cognitive processes, as opposed to their accuracy, is more influenced by aging. Old and young adults alike are moved by fluent encoding (rapid production of an image) to forecast later remembering in their JOLs, even when such fluency has no effect on actual memory (Robinson, Hertzog, & Dunlosky, 2006). There are also age deficits in monitoring elapsed time during memory task trials, such as in estimating how long it takes to retrieve information (e.g., Craik & Hay, 1999; Hertzog, Touron, & Hines, 2007). Hines, Touron, and Hertzog (2009) showed that older adults were less accurate in estimating recognition retrieval times and this was an apparent cause of lower resolution in their CJs.

Metacognitively Guided Control

Self-regulated learning (Winne, 1996) requires the use of monitoring to optimize learning. For example, self-testing determines how well information has been learned, aiding in the identification of items that need additional study, or a revised study strategy (Dunlosky & Hertzog, 1998).

Children between the ages of 7 and 12 show substantial improvement in the use of monitoring to guide selection of items for study, allocation of effort and study time, and adjustment of strategic behavior (Schneider, 2011). Children above the age of 7 do relatively well in setting thresholds for making or withholding recall responses (Roebers, 2006). In multitrial learning tests, allocation of study time based on JOLs shows developmental improvement from age 7 upward (Dufresne & Kobasigawa, 1989; Koriat et al., 2009). Developmental improvements in strategic regulation of encoding reviewed earlier seem to be accompanied by improvements in what Schneider and colleagues call procedural metamemory—that is, on-line use of monitoring to guide effective control (e.g., Koriat et al., 2009; Roebers & Schneider, 2005).

Older adults have been reported to show deficits in spontaneous self-testing to regulate recall readiness (e.g., Murphy, Schmitt, & Caruso, 1987), although this production deficit was redressed by informing older adults of the self-testing method. Dunlosky and Connor (1997) found that younger adults were more likely than older adults to base subsequent study time allocation on the basis of accurate delayed-JOLs, allocating more time to less well-learned items. However, older adults could have been engaging in extra elaborative rehearsal of recalled items that could be beneficial to their retention. Moreover, Hines et al. (2009) found equivalent influences of recognition memory accuracy and CJs on older and younger adults' next study time allocation, a finding in apparent conflict with Dunlosky and Connor (1997). Older adults have also been found to exhibit similar item selection behaviors, choosing items for study that they have not yet learned over ones they have learned (Dunlosky & Hertzog, 1997). Price, Hertzog, and Dunlosky (2010) found that older adults were similar to younger adults in selecting foreign language vocabulary items for study, although they tended to avoid the most difficult items in restudy. Older adults have also been reported to be flexible in selective learning recall of items designated by experimenters to have higher value (e.g., Castel, Farb, & Craik, 2007). Hence, the evidence is mixed regarding age deficits in metacognitively guided control, possibly indicating that age differences depend on task demands and characteristics of the individuals.

Metamemory Beliefs

Beliefs people have about memory and cognition can play a role in memory development (Hertzog & Hultsch, 2000; Schneider, Korkel, & Weinert, 1987). Young children develop around the age of 4 a theory of mind that accurately reflects the fact that internal thoughts are not accessible to others, including one's parents (Wellman & Gelman, 1992). Later, implicit theories about causes of cognitive success and failure appear to influence how children engage in, react to, and interpret success and failure in testing situations (e.g., Dweck & Leggett, 1988). Metamemory researchers have emphasized the importance of declarative knowledge about strategy effectiveness and its development in guiding self-regulated learning and remembering (Schneider, 2011).

Older adults, like younger adults, believe that episodic memory declines in adulthood (see Hertzog & Hultsch, 2000; e.g., Lineweaver & Hertzog, 1998; Ryan & See, 1993). Although older adults perceive less decline and later decline than younger adults, the fact that they are experiencing late-life effects of aging may make them more vulnerable to negative stereotypes, in terms of stereotype threat (Hess, Auman, & Colcombe, 2003) or implicit activation that harms memory performance (Levy, 1996). Some stereotypes about aging and cognition are positive. Lineweaver, Berger, and Hertzog (2009) showed that reading person descriptions that contain positive stereotypes, such as being active in old age, led younger and older people to predict less memory decline for those persons, relative to persons who had negative attributes. Hertzog, McGuire, Horhota, and Jopp (2010) found that older adults' implicit theory about control over memory was likely to involve lifestyle variables such as exercising the mind and memory, good nutrition, as well as positive motivation. Younger adults rarely mentioned staying active as an influence on memory, instead being more likely to talk about aspects of metacognitive self-regulation.

Older adults typically rate themselves as lower in memory ability and control over memory, and these beliefs often correlate only weakly (about .2) with episodic memory performance in older samples (e.g., Hertzog, Dunlosky, & Robinson, 2009; Lachman, Bandura, & Weaver, 1995). Thus, memory beliefs may not be very accurate. Low memory self-efficacy has been linked to lower memory performance in older adults, as well as less effective strategy use (Berry, 1999). Price et al. (2010) showed that avoidance of difficult items by older adults correlated with memory self-efficacy beliefs. Likewise, lower perceived control over memory is associated with lower levels of strategic encoding behavior in memory tasks (Hertzog, Lineweaver, & McGuire, 1999; Hertzog et al., 2009; Lachman, Andreoletti, & Pearman, 2006). Recently, West, Dark-Freudeman, and Bagwell (2009) showed that a measure of general memory self-concept interacted with a goal-setting manipulation in influencing the amount of older adults' performance improvement on a second exposure to a grocery list. Memory beliefs had no impact on younger adults' performance improvements.

Interventions that target memory self-efficacy and control beliefs have been shown to be effective in raising levels of self-efficacy and control, and in some cases, memory performance (e.g., West, Bagwell, & Dark-Freudeman, 2008). West et al.

(2008) engaged in a comprehensive self-efficacy intervention focusing on mastery experiences, persuasion, and skill-modeling that persisted through training. They found differential benefits of self-efficacy training on strategy use and recall performance on multiple tasks—training benefits were larger and more durable than those seen in earlier studies that implemented more modest belief-restructuring interventions.

Role of Training/Testing Limits in Evaluating Memory Change

Various theories in the field of developmental psychology have emphasized the notion of plasticity, that is, the modifiability of an organism in adapting to changing constraints and opportunities afforded in the developmental context (Baltes, 1987). In this vein, intervention and training studies play an important role in exploring the range and modifiability of cognitive functioning across different age periods (see Hertzog, Kramer et al., 2009, for a recent review). A specific paradigm that plays an important role in episodic memory training studies, particularly in aging, is the *testing-the-limits* procedure (Lindenberger & Baltes, 1995). Its aim is to approximate the upper limits of memory performance potential by providing strategic instruction and extensive practice, often combined with systematic variations in task difficulty.

A robust finding from the testing-the-limits literature is that memory plasticity remains in cognitively healthy older adults (Baltes et al., 2006; Shing, Brehmer, Li, 2008). Instruction and/or practice in a memory technique lead to robust performance improvements in healthy older adults. For example, Kliegl and colleagues (Kliegl, Smith, & Baltes, 1989, 1990) showed that after multiple sessions of training and practice in using the Method-of-Loci strategy, both younger and older adults improved their memory performance. This finding converged with evidence from other intervention studies (e.g., Ball et al., 2002; Derwinger, Neely, Persson, Hill, & Bäckman, 2003; Verhaeghen & Marcoen, 1996; Verhaeghen et al., 1992), indicating continued existence of memory plasticity in old age. Nevertheless, Kliegl et al. (1990) also found that extensive training resulted in a widening of the age difference in memory performance, with all younger adults outperforming older adults after training. Thus, the testing-the-limit paradigm demonstrated age-related differences in upper limits of memory performance (see also comparison to children in Brehmer, Li, Müller, von Oertzen, & Lindenberger, 2007), and these limits are more bounded in very old age (Singer, Lindenberger, & Baltes, 2003).

▓ SEMANTIC MEMORY/KNOWLEDGE

It has long been known that tests of semantic memory show continuous growth in childhood and relative maintenance in adulthood, declining only late in life (e.g., Schaie, 2005). The maintenance of knowledge and knowledge access fueled theoretical distinctions on intelligence throughout the 20th century, as in the fluid-crystallized theory of Cattell (1971) and Horn (e.g., Horn, 1968), and Baltes and colleagues' emphasis on pragmatics versus mechanics from a life-span perspective (e.g., Baltes et al., 2006). Knowledge and expertise can be construed as a return on investment of time and effort (Ericsson & Charness, 1994), as well as an application of fluid intelligence to learning (Ackerman, 2000; Cattell, 1971). This investment that leads to new knowledge structures, characterized by fast and fluent access to and retrieval of information as it is needed for comprehension, evaluation, and inference (Ericsson & Kintsch, 1995).

A large number of developmental studies have demonstrated that the amount of knowledge in a particular domain determines how much new information from the same domain can be stored and retrieved (see reviews by Bjorklund & Schneider, 1996; Chi & Ceci, 1987). As demonstrated in expert studies of various domains including chess, physics, and sport, domain knowledge is a powerful determinant of memory and learning. It increases steadily from infancy to adulthood and contributes to the development of memory competencies (e.g., Schneider & Pressley, 1997). For example, children's recall of categorically related material over the school years can be attributed to age-related increases in the relatively automatic activation of semantic memory relations (e.g., Bjorklund & Harnishfeger, 1987; Hasselhorn, 1995). The importance of interactions among these factors for memory development was highlighted in the "model of good information processing" (see Schneider & Pressley, 1997).

Knowledge and skills learned long ago persist, in at least partially accessible form, for long periods of time. Bahrick (1984) demonstrated that middle-aged adults had some level of recognition vocabulary for Spanish words they had studied years before in high school. Bahrick and colleagues have extended this work to other domains (e.g., Bahrick & Hall, 1991), and formulated the concept of permastore—the idea that once information entered semantic memory it stayed there, with the only issue being whether it could be accessed.

Increasing age appears to be accompanied by changes in both accessibility and the dynamics of accessibility to information held in semantic memory (Craik & Bialystok, 2006). Deliberate search for information in semantic memory according to arbitrary rules, such as word fluency, declines with age (Schaie, 2005). Older adults have difficulty learning and remembering proper names (e.g., James, Fogler, & Tauber, 2008; Seidenberg, Guidotti, & Nielson, 2009), and are generically more susceptible to tip-of-the-tongue effects (Burke, McKay, Worthley, & Wade, 1991; Maylor, 1990). Word finding problems increase with old age, and are particularly associated with some forms of dementia (Laws, Adlington, & Gale, 2007). Even when retrieval from semantic memory is routinely successful, such as in comparative judgments of category typicality or synonym meaning, access is often slowed (e.g., Hertzog, Raskind, & Cannon, 1986), albeit less than slowing of other types of cognitive operations (Hale & Myerson, 1996; Laver & Burke, 1993). Slowed or blocked access is cited by older adults as a cause of loss of control over memory (Hertzog et al., 2010). It could be related to longitudinal changes in world knowledge performance of older adults found in the Victoria Longitudinal Study (Hertzog et al., 2003).

AUTOBIOGRAPHICAL MEMORY

Autobiographical memory refers to memory of past events from one's own life. According to Rubin and colleagues (e.g., Rubin, 2006), autobiographical memories are not single entities but consist of information stored in component processes, with each process occurring in a separate behaviorally and neurally defined system. In this view, the construction and recall of autobiographical memory may involve integrating both episodic and semantic contents (among other domains).

Autobiographical memory research in child development often focuses on childhood amnesia, which refers to the inability to consciously access memories from the earliest years of life. Explanations of childhood amnesia have assumed that early memories are qualitatively different from later memories until the child crosses the so-called "childhood amnesia barrier" (see Bauer, 2006). However, even infants are able to recognize and recall aspects of specific experience and retain these memories over extended period of time (see also Hayne, 2004; Rovee-Collier & Shyi, 1992). Maturation of medial temporal structures shifts the locus of forgetting from the initial phases of memory trace construction to the later phases of trace retrieval (Bauer, 2006). With development, richer and higher-quality traces are more available for retrieval and contribute to an increase in the number of memories that feature autobiographical elements. Furthermore, children begin to verbally communicate past events soon after they begin talking, allowing for rehearsal and reorganization of the memory into a more coherent narrative form (e.g., Fivush, Haden, & Reese, 1996).

At the other end of the life span, the reconstruction of autobiographical memory through episodic and semantic components undergoes changes in aging. Investigations of autobiographical memory recall (e.g., Holland & Rabbitt, 1990; Levine, Svobada, Hay, Winocur, & Moscovitch, 2002) suggest that older adults show greater decline on episodic components of autobiographical memory, but preserved or enhanced recall of semantic components (e.g., Cabeza & St. Jacques, 2007). Another important finding concerning autobiographical memory and aging is the so-called reminiscence bump. In general, regardless of age, we tend to recall recent memories more often than remote memories. Beyond this, middle-aged and older adults experience a peak in the recall of memories of events that occurred when participants were in early adulthood, between approximately 10 and 30 years of age (Rubin, 2000). This reminiscence bump has been repeatedly reported in the literature, although the exact age range of the bump varies across studies (e.g., Chu & Downes, 2000), and the causes of the bump are still a matter of debate.

PROSPECTIVE MEMORY

Prospective memory (PM) is remembering to do something in the future. Perhaps the most salient feature of PM is how contemporary psychological theories interweave other psychological processes such as attention and monitoring (Smith, 2003), motivation, intention formation (e.g., Goschke & Kuhl, 1993), and goal neglect to account for PM successes and failures (see Kliegel, McDaniel, & Einstein, 2008). PM research has also attended to similarities and differences between laboratory tasks assessing PM and PM as it occurs in everyday life. McDaniel and Einstein's (2000) multiprocess view of PM embraces these influences, and more, in a comprehensive account of PM. Two basic types of PM are distinguished in the literature, although these types may blend when discussing prospective remembering in everyday life: event-based and time-based PM. Event-based PM refers to contingent enactment, doing something when environmental circumstances warrant or allow it. Time-based PM involves acting at a specific point in time.

Ceci and Bronfenbrenner (1985) were among the first to evaluate time-based PM in children. In their study, children were instructed to perform future activities after waiting 30 minutes. Children's strategic time monitoring during the waiting period was found to occur less frequently in the laboratory than in the home. In other words, at least when in their familiar environment, children as young as 10 showed relatively well-developed time monitoring for prospective event. In more recent event-based PM studies, results also tend to suggest that, in comparison to retrospective memory, PM skills develop at a relatively early age (e.g., Kurtz-Costes, Schneider, & Rupp, 1995; Kvavilashvili, Messer, & Ebdon, 2001). However, at least modest effect of age was found in a few studies that employed wider age ranges (e.g., Kerns, 2000), calling for the need for more comprehensive investigation.

In adulthood, there is a major discrepancy between studies of PM in the natural ecology and PM in the laboratory. Older adults often do quite well with PM tasks in everyday life, such as remembering to take medications (Park et al. 1999), or remembering to phone the laboratory at a specific time (West, 1988). Older adults often use an organizational system or a routine to support everyday action, rather than relying on remembering their intentions. In laboratory tasks, older adults are clearly impaired in time-based PM (Einstein, Richardson, & Guynn, 1995), and impairments in time monitoring may contribute to this deficit (Park, Hertzog, & Kidder, 1997).

Einstein and McDaniel (1990) created a dual-task laboratory procedure assessing event-based PM. An ongoing activity (e.g., a continuous memory task) is paired with a secondary PM task, for which an occasional primary task event cues a different action (e.g., press a key when an animal name is presented). They found no age-related impairments in event-based PM. A published meta-analysis (Henry, MacLeod, Phillips, & Crawford, 2004) argued that there was a deficit, but a smaller one, for event-based PM relative to time-based PM. Smith and Bayen (2006) localized age deficits in event-based PM to the attentional demands of prospective monitoring during a concurrent task. Age differences are larger in successful PM for cues outside the immediate focus of attention, especially under attentional load (Rendell, McDaniel, Einstein, & Forbes, 2007)—findings broadly consistent with a monitoring deficit. McDaniel, Einstein, Stout, and Morgan (2003) demonstrated that delayed enactment (i.e., when the action must be deferred after detecting the PM cue) is also sensitive to age differences, possibly owing to age deficits in maintaining intentions in WM while performing other actions. Thus, although age differences may be larger in time-based PM, event-based PM differences will be found when additional processing is required to detect a cue or maintain an intention in the face of distraction and intervening events.

INFLUENCES ON LIFE-SPAN MEMORY DEVELOPMENT

We have already mentioned several factors that influence memory development, such as changes in the brain regions envisioned by Lindenberger and colleagues (e.g., Shing et al., 2008) in their life-span theory of memory development. Although space precludes a detailed treatment of other influences, we treat briefly two other aspects: a psychological account of memory development based on the concept of cognitive resources, and the influence of pathological memory change in later life.

Cognitive Resources

By some accounts, basic processing mechanisms can be viewed as resources that can be flexibly allocated in service of achieving cognitive goals. Here, we selectively discuss two basic cognitive resources (i.e., WM and processing speed) that received considerable attention in both fields of cognitive development and aging. WM is a critical resource for encoding information into episodic memory, as well as other higher-order forms of cognition such as inductive reasoning (e.g., Kyllonen & Christal, 1990; Hultsch et al., 1998; Salthouse, 1991). Developmental changes in WM have been cited as a major cause of higher cognitive development in children (Gathercole, 1998) and as a cause of age-related decline in episodic memory (Salthouse & Babcock, 1991; Stine-Morrow et al., 2006). WM changes are highly associated with episodic memory changes in adulthood (Hertzog et al., 2003; Hultsch et al., 1998).

Theories of cognitive development emphasizing the role of processing speed have also been formulated for both ends of the life span (Birren, 1965; Kail & Salthouse, 1994; Salthouse, 1996). For instance, Kail and Park (1994) showed that there is a relationship between processing speed and memory span mediated by articulation rate. In aging, cross-sectional studies have found that between 44 and 80% of cross-sectional age variance in memory task was associated with psychometric tests of perceptual speed (Salthouse, 1996; Verhaeghen & Salthouse, 1997).

However, reduced resource explanations of aging have been challenged on several grounds, including (1) the measurement properties and cognitive constituents of tests of processing speed (e.g., Hertzog, 1989; Lustig, Hasher, & Tonev, 2006); (2) whether one of these information-processing constructs is more basic than the variables they are used to predict (Deary, 2001; Light, 1991); and (3) methodological problems with regression-based estimates of resource-determined age-related variance using cross-sectional data (Hofer, Flaherty, & Hoffman, 2006; Lindenberger & Pötter, 1998). For example, longitudinal data typically show smaller effects of changes in speed and WM on changes in episodic memory performance (Hertzog et al., 2003; Hultsch et al., 1998).

Normal and Pathological Changes in the Central Nervous System

Major memory loss is associated with brain pathologies such as dementia of the Alzheimer's type, frontotemporal dementia, Parkinson's disease, exposure to environmental toxins, and HIV infection. In practice, it can be difficult to separate such effects from normal aging in psychological studies of memory, because of a lack of information about neurological status, neuropsychological evaluation, and postmortem evaluation of brain function. Although memory decline is considered a part of normal aging, it can also be a leading indicator of brain pathology (e.g., Bäckman & Small, 2007). It is reasonable to assume that aging samples mix preclinical and subclinical cases with individuals who have no brain pathology (Sliwinski, Hofer, & Hall, 2003), although some would claim that such partitions are not based on qualitative differences of normal versus pathological, but rather, quantitative differences of amount of age-related pathology, and perhaps age of onset of noticeable symptomatology.

An ongoing issue in clinical memory assessment is whether a category of mild cognitive impairment (MCI) can be differentiated from dementia, on the one hand, and normal aging, on the other. Kral (1958) argued for a category of benign senescent forgetting as distinct from dementia, and that idea continues to have some currency in classifying persons as having MCI (Peterson, 2003). A substantial proportion of persons diagnosed as having MCI (Smith, Peterson, Parisi, & Ivnik, 1996) on the basis of low norm-referenced memory test performance transition to dementia a few years later, which has led some to question the utility of MCI as a separate diagnostic entity.

Individual differences in timing of onset of dementia diagnosis may be due, in part, to cognitive reserve (Stern, 2002). Some individuals begin adulthood with better functional memory, and have more to lose before brain changes can lead to performance impairments (Tucker-Drob, Johnson, & Jones, 2009).

FUTURE ISSUES IN THE STUDY OF LIFE-SPAN MEMORY DEVELOPMENT

Researchers working either in the field of child development or aging have initiated fruitful lines of research to better understand how memory develops and changes within confined age periods. However, little effort has been invested in directly examining and integrating the mechanisms underlying memory changes across the life span. As reviewed earlier, research within separate life periods has addressed whether age-related differences in memory functioning can be accounted for by information-processing constraints or processing resources. In addition to general resource account, there are memory-specific mechanisms that drive memory changes across different age periods. By taking a life-span lens in approaching developmental issues, findings and paradigms in the adult literature could inform new directions in child research, and vice versa. For example, the prominent theory of fuzzy-trace theory has been applied to address changes in false memory in child development (Brainerd & Reyna, 2004) and aging (Dehon, 2006), respectively.

More directly, the inclusion of a life-span sample within the same study helps to elucidate the particular characteristics of episodic memory in children, and vice versa. For example, in the life span study of Brehmer et al. (2007), children and older adults possessed similar levels of baseline performance. However, children gained more from extensive strategy training than older adults, demonstrating life-span differences in developmental plasticity. In the Shing et al. (2008) study, children showed lower hit rates in associative recognition than all other age groups before strategy instruction, but this age pattern was eliminated after instruction and practice. Older adults, on the other hand, showed persistently higher false-alarm rates on rearranged pairs (mostly accompanied with high ratings of confidence, see Shing et al., 2009). Whereas both age groups of the extreme ends of life span show lower memory functioning than younger adults, children and older adults exhibit different patterns of memory problems. By including children and older adults in the same study, one attains a better understanding of what is general and special about the memory performance of each of the two groups. Additional attention to connecting and contrasting development across the full range of the life span could be highly beneficial (e.g., Craik & Bialystok, 2006; Shing et al., 2008).

There are many other questions about memory development that beg for further attention. We highlight a few of them. First, there is a need for better understanding of the development of encoding/retrieval interactions, going beyond focus on either encoding or retrieval as a locus of developmental changes in memory. One important developmental influence may be the role of prior knowledge on effective encoding and subsequent guided retrieval search for the same information. Relative to children, older adults have acquired extensive semantic and rich autobiographical knowledge in the course of their lives. Therefore, it is conceivable that older adults are more likely to process new information and guide remembering in connection to existing representations. On the other hand, children's encoding of new information may rely heavily on the creation of representations that carry a strong novelty value and may be less readily blended with retrieved past experiences. It is possible that older adults' greater susceptibility to interference is in part a consequence of more elaborated and integrated semantic knowledge structures that guide encoding with substantial benefit, but also create more opportunities for retrieval interference (Buchler & Reder, 2007). Whether such effects are less likely during child development, or, alternatively, can be observed under specific encoding conditions (e.g., learning in the classroom) is an interesting and open question.

Second, research on metacognition and metacognitive control has expanded rapidly in the last decade. However, we still do not understand how and whether individuals at different points in the life span spontaneously engage in the kind of top-down self-regulation envisioned by metacognitive theory (effective use of monitoring to achieve self-regulation) as opposed to a more reactive, stimulus driven type of cognitive control. New task paradigms that can explicitly separate reactive versus proactive cognitive control (Braver et al., 2009) are needed in this area.

Finally, an important theme in the cognitive aging literature is the issue of relationships between lifestyle factors and individual variation in aging-related decline. For example, the degree to which an individual is engaged in mentally and physically stimulating activities regularly may be correlated with steepness of cognitive decline. Several rigorous microlongitudinal studies have demonstrated that improvements in cardiovascular fitness impart positive effects on human cognitive abilities, with the largest benefits occurring for executive-control processes (see review by Colcombe & Kramer, 2003). From a life-span perspective, early development is characterized by selection and optimization processes that shape individual differentiation at later stages of life in a cumulative fashion. Neural and behavioral evidence strongly suggests that early interventions targeted toward disadvantaged children are more effective and have higher returns than later remedial interventions (Heckman, 2006; Knudsen, Heckman, Cameron, & Shonkoff, 2006). An important issue for future investigation is to understand the ways in which lifestyle factors such as physical and intellectual activities at early stages of life, including childhood (e.g., Deary, Whalley, & Starr, 2009), can help maintain cognitive competence during adulthood and old age.

▌ REFERENCES

Ackerman, P. L. (2000). Domain-specific knowledge as the 'Dark Matter' of adult intelligence: Gf/Gc, personality, and interest correlates. *Journal of Gerontology: Psychological Sciences, 55B,* 69–84.

Adams, C., Smith, M. C., Nyquist, L., & Perlmutter, M. (1997). Adult age-group differences in recall for literal and interpretive meanings of narrative text. *Journal of Gerontology: Psychological Sciences, 52B,* 187–195.

Andres, P. (2009). Equivalent part set cueing effects in younger and older adults. *European Journal of Cognitive Psychology, 21,* 176–191.

Andres, P., Guerrini, C., Phillips, L., & Perfect, T. (2008). Differential effects of aging on executive and automatic inhibition. *Developmental Neuropsychology, 33,* 101–123.

Aslan, A., Bäuml, K. H., & Pastötter, B. (2007). No inhibitory deficit in older adults' episodic memory. *Psychological Science, 18,* 72–78.

Bäckman, L. (1989). Varieties of memory compensation by older adults in episodic remembering. In L. W. Poon, D. C. Rubin, & B. A. Wilson (Eds.), *Everyday cognition in adulthood and late life* (pp. 509–544). Cambridge, England; Cambridge University Press.

Bäckman, L., & Small, B. J. (2007). Cognitive deficits in preclinical Alzheimer's disease and vascular dementia: Patterns of findings from the Kungsholmen Project. *Physiology & Behavior, 92,* 80–86.

Baddeley, A. (1986). *Working memory.* New York: Oxford University Press.

Bahrick, H. (1984). Semantic memory content in Permastore: 50 years of memory for Spanish learned in School. *Journal of Experimental Psychology: General, 113,* 1–29.

Bahrick, H., & Hall, L. (1991). Preventive and corrective maintenance of access to knowledge. *Applied Cognitive Psychology, 5,* 1–18.

Bailey, H., Dunlosky, J., & Hertzog, C. (2009). Does differential strategy use account for age-related deficits in working memory performance? *Psychology and Aging, 24,* 82–92.

Ball, K., Berch, D. B., Helmers, K. F., Jobe, J. B., Leveck, M. D., Marsiske, M., et al. (2002). Effects of cognitive training interventions with older adults: A randomized controlled trial. *Journal of American Medical Association, 288,* 2271–2281.

Baltes, P. B. (1987). Theoretical propositions of life-span developmental psychology: On the dynamics between growth and decline. *Developmental Psychology, 23,* 611–626.

Baltes, P. B., Lindenberger, U., & Staudinger, U. M. (2006). Lifespan theory in developmental psychology. In W. Damon & R. M. Lerner (Eds.), *Handbook of child psychology: Theoretical models of human development* (Vol. 1, 6th ed., pp. 569–664). New York: Wiley.

Bauer, P. J. (2006). Constructing a past in infancy: A neuro-developmental account. *Trends in Cognitive Sciences, 10*(4), 175–181.

Berry, J. M. (1999). Memory self-efficacy in its social cognitive context. In T. Hess & F. Blanchard-Fields (Eds.), *Social cognition and aging* (pp. 69–96), San Diego, CA: Academic Press.

Bialystok, E., & Craik, F. I. M. (2006). *Lifespan cognition.* Oxford, UK: Oxford University Press.

Birren, J. E. (1965). Age changes in speed of behavior: Its central nature and physiological correlates. In A. T. Welford & J. E. Birren (Eds.), *Behavior, aging, and the nervous system* (pp. 191–216). Springfield, IL: Charles C. Thomas.

Bjorklund, D. F., Dukes, C. H., & Brown, R. D. (2009). The development of memory strategies. In M. L. Courage & N. Cowan (Eds.), *The development of memory in infancy and childhood* (pp. 145–175). Hove, UK: Psychology Press.

Bjorklund, D. F., & Harnishfeger, K. K. (1987). Developmental differences in the mental effort requirements for the use of an organizational strategy in free-recall. *Journal of Experimental Child Psychology, 44,* 109–125.

Bjorklund, D. F., & Harnishfeger, K. K. (1990). The resources construct in cognitive development: Diverse sources of evidence and a theory of inefficient inhibition. *Developmental Review, 10,* 48–71.

Bjorklund, D. F., Miller, P. H., Coyle, T. R., & Slawinski, J. L. (1997). Instructing children to use memory strategies: Evidence of utilization deficiencies in memory training studies. *Developmental Review, 17,* 411–442.

Bjorklund, D. F., & Schneider, W. (1996). The interaction of knowledge, aptitude, and strategies in children's memory performance. In H. W. Reese (Ed.), *Advances in child development and behavior* (Vol. 25, pp. 59–89). San Diego, CA: Academic Press.

Brainerd, C. J., & Gordon, L. L. (1994). Development of verbatim and gist memory for numbers. *Developmental Psychology, 10,* 633–643.

Brainerd, C. J., & Reyna, V. F. (1990). Gist in the grist: Fuzzy-trace theory and the new intuitionism. *Developmental Review, 12,* 164–186.

Brainerd, C. J., & Reyna, V. F. (2004). Fuzzy-trace theory and memory development. *Developmental Review, 24,* 396–439.

Braver, T. S., Paxton, J. L., Locke, H. S., & Barch, D. M. (2009). Flexible neural mechanisms of cognitive control within human prefrontal cortex. *Proceedings of the National Academy of Sciences, 106,* 7351–7356.

Brehmer, Y., Li, S. C., Müller, V., von Oertzen, T., & Lindenberger, U. (2007). Memory plasticity across the lifespan: Uncovering children's latent potential. *Developmental Psychology, 43*, 465–478.

Buchler, N. G., Fauce, P., Light, L. L., Reder, L. M., & Gottfredson, N. (2009). *Associative memory deficits in old age: Dissociating the dual-process contributions of recollection and familiarity.* Unpublished Manuscript.

Buchler, N. G., & Reder, L. M. (2007). Modeling age-related memory deficits: Distinct representations and processes in associative recognition. *Psychology and Aging, 22*, 104–121.

Buckner, R. L. (2004). Memory and executive function in aging and AD: Multiple factors that cause decline and reserve factors that compensate. *Neuron, 44*, 195–208.

Burke, D., McKay, D. M., Worthley, J. S., & Wade, E. (1991). On the tip of the tongue: What causes word finding failures in young and older adults? *Journal of Memory and Language, 30*, 542–579.

Butler, K., McDaniel, M., & Dornburg, C. (2004). Age differences in veridical and false recall are not inevitable: The role of frontal lobe function. *Psychonomic Bulletin & Review, 11*, 921–925.

Butterfield, E., Nelson, T., & Peck, V. (1988). Developmental aspects of the feeling of knowing. *Developmental Psychology, 24*, 654–663.

Cabeza, R., & St. Jacques, P. (2007). Functional neuroimaging of autobiographical memory. *Trends in Cognitive Sciences, 11*(5), 219–227.

Case, R., Kurland, D. M., & Goldberg, J. (1982). Operational efficiency and the growth of short-term memory span. *Journal of Experimental Child Psychology, 33*, 386–404.

Castel, A. D., & Craik, F. I. M. (2003). The effects of aging and divided attention on memory for item and associative information. *Psychology and Aging, 18*, 873–885.

Castel, A. D., Farb, A., & Craik, F. I. M. (2007). Memory for general and specific value information in younger and older adults: Measuring the limits of strategic control. *Memory & Cognition, 35*, 689–700.

Cattell, R. B. (1971). *Abilities: Their structure, growth, and action.* Boston: Houghton Mifflin.

Ceci, S. J., & Bronfenbrenner, U. (1985). 'Don't forget to take the cupcakes out of the oven': Prospective memory, strategic time-monitoring, and context. *Child Development, 56*, 152–164.

Chalfonte, B. L., & Johnson, M. K. (1996). Feature memory and binding in young and older adults. *Memory & Cognition, 24*, 403–416.

Chi, M., & Ceci, S. J. (1987). Context knowledge: Its representation and restructuring in memory development. *Advances in Child Development Research, 20*, 91–146.

Chu, S., & Downes, J. (2000). Long life Proust: The odour-cued autobiographical memory bump. *Cognition, 75*, B41–B50.

Cohen, N. J., & Eichenbaum, H. (1993). *Memory, amnesia, and the hippocampal system.* Cambridge, MA: MIT Press.

Cohn, M., Emrich, S., & Moscovitch, M. (2008). Age-related deficits in associative memory: The influence of impaired strategic retrieval. *Psychology and Aging, 23*, 93–103.

Colcombe, S. J., & Kramer, A. F. (2003). Fitness effects on the cognitive function of older adults: A meta-analytic study. *Psychological Science, 14*, 125–130.

Connor, L., Dunlosky, J., & Hertzog, C. (1997). Age-related differences in absolute but not relative metamemory accuracy. *Psychology and Aging, 12*, 50–71.

Cowan, N. (1995). *Attention and memory: An integrated framework.* New York: Oxford University Press.

Cowan, N., Naveh-Benjamin, M., Kilb, A., & Saults, J. S. (2006). Life-span development of visual working memory: When is feature binding difficult. *Developmental Psychology, 42*, 1089–1102.

Cowan, N., Nugent, L., Elliott, E., Ponomarev, I., & Saults, J. (1999). The role of attention in the development of short-term memory: Age differences in the verbal span of apprehension. *Child Development, 70*, 1082–1097.

Craik, F. I. M. (1986). A functional account of age differences in memory. In F. Klix & H. Hagendorf (Eds.), *Human memory and capabilities: Mechanisms and performances* (pp. 409–422). Amsterdam, Holland: Elsevier.

Craik, F. I. M. (2002). Levels of processing: Past, present, and…future? *Memory, 10*, 305–318.

Craik, F. I. M., & Bialystok, E. (2006). Planning and task management in older adults: Cooking breakfast. *Memory & Cognition, 34*, 1236–1249.

Craik, F. I. M., & Hay, J. (1999). Aging and judgments of duration: Effects of task complexity and method of estimation. *Perception & Psychophysics, 61*, 549–560.

Davidson, M. C., Amso, D., Anderson, L. C., & Diamond, A. (2006). Development of cognitive control and executive functions from 4 to 13 years: Evidence from manipulations of memory, inhibition, and task switching. *Neuropsychologia, 44*, 2037–2078.

Deary, I. J. (2001). Human intelligence differences: Towards a combined experimental-differential approach. *Trends in Cognitive Sciences, 5,* 164–170.

Deary, I. J., Whalley, L. J., & Starr, J. M. (2009). *A lifetime of intelligence: Follow-up studies of the Scottish Mental Surveys of 1932 and 1947.* Washington, DC: American Psychological Association.

Dehon, H. (2006). Variations in processing resources and resistance to false memories in younger and older adults. *Memory, 14,* 692–711.

DeMarie-Dreblow, D., & Miller, P. H. (1988). The development of children's strategies for selective attention: Evidence for a transitional period. *Child Development, 59,* 1504–1513.

DeMarie, D., Miller, P. H., Ferron, J., & Cunningham, W. R. (2004). Path analysis tests of theoretical models of children's memory performance. *Journal of Cognition & Development, 5,* 461–492.

Dempster, F. N. (1981). Memory span: Sources of individual and developmental differences. *Psychological Bulletin, 89,* 63–100.

Dempster, F. N. (1992). The rise and fall of the inhibitory mechanism: Toward a unified theory of cognitive development and aging. *Developmental Review, 12,* 45–75.

Derwinger, A., Neely, A. S., Persson, M., Hill, R. D., & Bäckman, L. (2003). Remembering numbers in old age: Mnemonic training versus self-generated strategy training. *Aging Neuropsychology and Cognition, 10,* 202–214.

Dodson, C. S., Bawa, S., & Krueger, L. E. (2007). Aging, metamemory, and high-confidence errors: A misrecollection account. *Psychology and Aging, 22,* 122–133.

Dodson, C. S., & Schacter, D. L. (2002). Aging and strategic retrieval processes: Reducing false memories with a distinctiveness heuristic. *Psychology and Aging, 17,* 405–415.

Dufresne, A., & Kobasigawa, A. (1989). Children's utilization of study time: Differential and sufficient aspects. *Cognitive Strategy Research, 47,* 274–296.

Dunlosky, J., & Connor, L. (1997). Age differences in the allocation of study time account for age differences in memory performance. *Memory and Cognition, 25,* 691–700.

Dunlosky, J., & Hertzog, C. (1997). Older and younger adults use a functionally identical algorithm to select items for restudy during multi-trial learning. *Journal of Gerontology: Psychological Sciences, 52,* 178–186.

Dunlosky, J., & Hertzog, C. (1998). Aging and deficits in associative memory: What is the role of strategy production? *Psychology and Aging, 13,* 597–607.

Dunlosky, J., & Hertzog, C. (2001). Measuring strategy production during associative learning: The relative utility of concurrent versus retrospective reports. *Memory and Cognition, 29,* 247–253.

Dunlosky, J., Hertzog, C., & Powell-Moman, A. (2005). The contribution of mediator-based deficiencies to age differences in associative learning. *Developmental Psychology, 41,* 389–400.

Dweck, C., & Leggett, E. (1988). A social cognitive approach to motivation and personality. *Psychological Review, 95,* 256–273.

Einstein, G., & McDaniel, M. (1990). Normal aging and prospective memory. *Journal of Experimental Psychology: Learning, Memory, and Cognition, 16,* 717–726.

Einstein, G., Richardson, S., & Guynn, M. (1995). Aging and prospective memory: Examining the influences of self-initiated retrieval-processes. *Journal of Experimental Psychology: Learning, Memory, and Cognition, 21,* 996–1007.

Ericsson, K. A., & Charness, N. (1994). Expert performance: Its structure and acquisition. *American Psychologist, 49,* 725–747.

Ericsson, K. A., & Kintsch, W. (1995). Long-term working memory. *Psychological Review, 102,* 211–245.

Fivush, R., Haden, C., & Reese, E. (1996). Remembering, recounting and reminiscing: The development of autobiographical memory in social context. In D. Rubin (Ed.), *Remembering our past: An overview of autobiographical memory* (pp. 377–397). Cambridge, MA: Cambridge University Press

Flavell, J. H. (1970). Developmental studies of mediated memory. In H. W. Reese & L. P. Lipsitt (Eds.), *Advances in child development and behavior* (Vol. 5, pp. 181–211). New York: Academic Press.

Flavell, J. H. (1979). Metacognition and cognitive monitoring: A new area of cognitive-developmental inquiry. *American Psychologist, 34,* 906–911.

Fraser, S. A., Li, K. Z. H., & Penhune, V. B. (2009). A comparison of motor skill learning and retention in younger and older adults. *Experimental Brain Research, 195,* 419–427.

Gathercole, S. E. (1998). The development of memory. *Journal of Child Psychology and Psychiatry, 29,* 3–27.

Gathercole, S. E., Pickering, S. J., Ambridge, B., & Wearing, H. (2004). The structure of working memory from 4 to 15 years of age. *Developmental Psychology, 40,* 177–190.

Geraci, L., & Roediger, H. (2007). Aging and the misinformation effect: A neuropsychological analy-sis. *Journal of Experimental Psychology: Learning, Memory, and Cognition, 33*, 321–334.

Gerard, L., Zacks, R., Hasher, L., & Radvansky, G. A. (1991). Age deficits in retrieval: The fan effect. *Journal of Gerontology, 46*(4), 131–136.

Ghetti, S., & Angelini, L. (2008). The development of recollection and familiarity in childhood and adolescence: Evidence from the dual-process signal detection model. *Child Development, 79*, 339–358.

Gogtay, N., Nugent, T. F. I., Herman, D. H., Ordonez, A., Greenstein, D., Hayashi, K. M., et al. (2006). Dynamic mapping of normal human hippocampal development. *Hippocampus, 16*, 664–672.

Goschke, T., & Kuhl, J. (1993). Representation of intentions: Persisting activation in memory. *Journal of Experimental Psychology: Learning, Memory, and Cognition, 19*, 1211–1226.

Gottlieb, G. (1991). Experiential canalization of behavioral development: Theory. *Development Psychology, 27*, 4–13.

Hale, S., & Myerson, J. (1996). Experimental evidence for differential slowing in the lexical and non-lexical domains. *Aging, Neuropsychology and Cognition, 3*, 154–165.

Harnishfeger, K. K., & Pope, R. S. (1996). Intending to forget: The development of cognitive inhibi-tion in directed-forgetting. *Journal of Experimental Child Psychology, 62*, 292–315.

Hasselhorn, M. (1995). Beyond production deficiency and utilization inefficiency: Mechanisms of the emergence of strategic categorization in episodic memory tasks. In F. E. Weinert & W. Schneider (Eds.), *Memory performance and competencies: Issues in growth and development* (pp. 141–159). Hillsdale, NJ: Erlbaum.

Hayne, H. (2004). Infant memory development: Implications for childhood amnesia. *Developmental Review, 24*, 33–73.

Heckman, J. J. (2006). Skill formation and the economics of investing in disadvantaged children. *Science, 312*, 1900–1902.

Hedden, T., & Park, D. C. (2003). Contributions of source and inhibitory mechanisms to age-related retroactive interference in verbal working memory. *Journal of Experimental Psychology: General, 132*, 93–112.

Henkel, L. A., Johnson, M. K., & DeLeonardis, D. M. (1998). Aging and source monitoring: Cognitive processes and neuropsychological correlates. *Journal of Experimental Psychology: General, 127*, 251–268.

Henry, J. D., MacLeod, M. S., & Phillips, L. H., & Crawford, J. R. (2004). A meta-analytic review of prospective memory and aging. *Psychology and Aging, 19*, 27–39.

Hertzog, C. (1989). The influence of cognitive slowing on age differences in intelligence. *Developmental Psychology, 25*, 636–651.

Hertzog, C., Dixon, R. A., Hultsch, D. F., & MacDonald, S. W. S. (2003). Latent change models of adult cognition: Are changes in processing speed and working memory associated with changes in episodic memory? *Psychology and Aging, 18*, 755–769.

Hertzog, C., Dunlosky, J., & Robinson, A. E. (2009). *Intellectual abilities and metacognitive beliefs influ-ence spontaneous use of effective encoding strategies.* Unpublished Manuscript.

Hertzog, C., Dunlosky, J., & Sinclair, S. M. (2010). Episodic feeling-of-knowing resolution derives from the quality of original encoding. *Memory & Cognition*.

Hertzog, C., & Hultsch, D. F. (2000). Metacognition in adulthood and aging. In Salthouse, T. & Craik, F. I. M. (Eds.) *Handbook of aging and cognition* (2nd ed., pp. 417–466). Mahwah, NJ: Erlbaum.

Hertzog, C., Kidder, D., Powell-Moman, A., & Dunlosky, J. (2002). Aging and monitoring associative learning: Is monitoring accuracy spared or impaired? *Psychology and Aging, 17*, 209–225.

Hertzog, C., Kramer, A. F., Wilson, R. S., & Lindenberger, U. (2009). Enrichment effects on adult cog-nitive development: Can the functional capacity of older adults be preserved and enhanced? *Psychological Science in the Public Interest, 9*, 1–65.

Hertzog, C., Lineweaver, T. T., & McGuire, C. L. (1999). Beliefs about memory and aging. In F. Blanchard-Fields & T. M. Hess (Eds.), *Social cognition and aging* (pp. 43–68). New York: Academic Press.

Hertzog, C., McGuire, C. L., Horhota, M., & Jopp, D. (2010). Age differences in lay theories about memory control: Older adults believe in "use it or lose it". *International Journal of Aging and Human Development, 70*, 61–87.

Hertzog, C., Raskind, C., & Cannon, C. (1986). Age-related slowing in semantic information process-ing speed: An individual differences analysis. *Journal of Gerontology, 41*, 500–502.

Hertzog, C., Sinclair, S. M., & Dunlosky, J. (2010). Age differences in the monitoring of learn-ing: Cross-sectional evidence of spared resolution across the adult life span. *Developmental Psychology, 46*, 939–948.

Hertzog, C., Touron, D., & Hines, J. (2007). Does a time monitoring deficit contribute to older adults' delayed shift to retrieval during skill acquisition? *Journal of Gerontology, 62B*, 70–76.

Hess, T. M. (2005). Memory and aging in context. *Psychological Bulletin, 131*, 383–406.

Hess, T., Auman, C., & Colcombe, S. (2003). The impact of stereotype threat on age differences in memory performance. *Journal of Gerontology, 58*, 3–11.

Hines, J., Touron, D., & Hertzog, C. (2009). Metacognitive influences on study time allocation in an associative recognition task: An analysis of adult age differences. *Psychology and Aging, 24*, 462–475.

Hitch, G. J., & Towse, J. N. (1995). Working memory: What develops? In F. E. Weinert & W. Schneider (Eds.), *Memory performance and competencies: Issues of growth and development* (pp. 3–21). Mahwah, NJ: Erlbaum.

Hofer, S. M., Flaherty, B. P., & Hoffman, L. (2006). Cross-sectional analysis of time-dependent data: Mean-induced association in age-heterogeneous samples and an alternative method based on sequential narrow age-cohort samples. *Multivariate Behavioral Research, 41*(2), 165–187.

Holland, C., & Rabbitt, P. (1990). Autobiographical and text recall in the elderly: An investigation of a processing resource deficit. *The Quarterly Journal of Experimental Psychology, 42*, 441–470.

Holley, P., & McEvoy, C. (1996). Aging and inhibition of unconsciously processed information: No apparent deficit. *Applied Cognitive Psychology, 10*, 241–256.

Horn, J. L. (1968). Organization of abilities and the development of intelligence. *Psychological Review, 75*, 242–259.

Hultsch, D. F., Hertzog, C., Dixon, R. A., & Small, B. J. (1998). *Memory change in the aged.* Cambridge: Cambridge University Press.

Hunt, R. (2003). Two contributions of distinctive processing to accurate memory. *Journal of Memory and Language, 48*, 811–825.

Ikier, S., Yang, L., & Hasher, L. (2008). Implicit proactive interference, age, and automatic versus controlled retrieval strategies. *Psychological Science, 19*, 456–461.

Jacoby, L. L. (1999). Ironic effects of repetition: Measuring age-related differences in memory. *Journal of Experimental Psychology: Learning, Memory, and Cognition, 25*, 3–22.

Jacoby, L. L., & Rhodes, M. G. (2006). False remembering in the aged. *Current Directions in Psychological Science, 15*, 49–53.

Jacoby, L. L., Shimizu, Y., Velanova, K., & Rhodes, M. (2005). Age differences in depth of retrieval: Memory for foils. *Journal of Memory & Language, 52*, 493–504.

James, L. E., Fogler, J. M., & Tauber, S. K. (2008). Recognition memory measures yield disproportionate effects of aging on learning face-name associations. *Psychology and Aging, 23*, 657–664.

Jennings, J. M., & Jacoby, L. L. (1997). An opposition procedure for detecting age-related deficits in recollection: Telling effects of repetition. *Psychology and Aging, 12*, 352–361.

Jennings, J. M., & Jacoby, L. L. (2003). Improving memory in older adults: Training recollection. *Neuropsychological Rehabilitation, 13*, 417–440.

Johnson, M. K. (2006). Memory and reality. *American Psychologist, 61*, 760–771.

Kail, R. V., & Park, Y. (1994). Processing time, articulation time, and memory span. *Journal of Experimental Child Psychology, 57*, 281–291.

Kail, R. V., & Salthouse, T. A. (1994). Processing speed as a mental-capacity. *Acta Psychologica, 86*, 199–225.

Kane, M. J., & Engle, R. W. (2003). Working memory capacity and the control of attention: The contributions of goal neglect, response competition, and task set to Stroop interference. *Journal of Experimental Psychology: General, 132*, 47–70.

Kausler, D. H. (1994). *Learning and memory in normal aging.* New York: Academic Press.

Kelley, C. M., & Rhodes, M. (2005). Executive processes, memory accuracy, and memory monitoring: An aging and individual difference analysis. *Journal of Memory & Language, 52*, 578–594.

Kelley, C. M., & Sahakyan, L. (2003). Memory, monitoring, and control in the attainment of memory accuracy. *Journal of Memory & Language, 48*, 704–721.

Kerns, K. (2000). The CyberCruiser: An investigation of development of prospective memory in children. *Journal of the International Neuropsychological Society, 6*, 62–70.

Kintsch, W. (1998). *Comprehension: A paradigm for cognition.* New York: Cambridge University Press.

Kliegel, M., McDaniel, M., & Einstein, G. (2008). *Prospective memory: Cognitive, neuroscience, developmental, and applied perspectives.* New York: Lawrence Erlbaum Associates.

Kliegl, R., Smith, J., & Baltes, P. B. (1989). Testing-the-limits and the study of adult age differences in cognitive plasticity of a mnemonic skill. *Developmental Psychology, 25*, 247–256.

Kliegl, R., Smith, J., & Baltes, P. B. (1990). On the locus and process of magnification of age differences during mnemonic training. *Developmental Psychology, 26*, 894–904.

Knopf, M. (1999). Development of memory for texts. In F. E. Weinert & W. Schneider (Eds.), *Individual development from 3 to 12: Findings from the Munich Longitudinal Study* (pp. 106–122). Cambridge, UK: Cambridge University Press.

Knudsen, E. I., Heckman, J., Cameron, J. L., & Shonkoff, J. P. (2006). Economic, neurobiological, and behavioral perspectives on building America's future workforce. *Proceedings of the National Academy of Sciences, 103*(27), 10155–10162.

Koriat, A., Ackermann, R., Lockl, K., & Schneider, W. (2009). The easily learned, easily remembered heuristic in children. *Cognitive Development*.

Kral, V. (1958). Psychiatric observations in an old peoples home. *Journal of Gerontology, 12*, 433–434.

Krampe, R., & Ericsson, K. (1996). Maintaining excellence: Deliberate practice and elite performance in young and older pianists. *Journal of Experimental Psychology: General, 125*, 331–359.

Kurtz-Costes, B., Schneider, W., & Rupp, S. (1995). Is there evidence for intraindividual consistency in performance across memory tasks? New evidence on an old question. In F. E. Weinert & W. Schneider (Eds.), *Memory performance and competencies: Issues in growth and development* (pp. 245–262). Mahwah, NJ: Erlbaum.

Kvavilashvili, L., Messer, D., & Ebdon, P. (2001). Prospective memory in children: The effects of age and task interruption.. *Developmental Psychology, 37*, 418–430.

Kyllonen, P., & Christal, R. (1990). Reasoning ability is (little more than) working memory capacity? *Intelligence, 14*, 389–433.

Lachman, M., Andreoletti, C., & Pearman, A. (2006). Memory control beliefs: How are they related to age, strategy use and memory improvement? *Social Cognition, 24*, 359–385.

Lachman, M., Bandura, M., & Weaver, S. (1995). Assessing memory control beliefs: The memory controllability inventory. *Aging and Cognition, 2*, 67–84.

Laver, G. D., & Burke, D. M. (1993). Why do semantic priming effects increase in old age? A meta-analysis. *Psychology and Aging, 8*, 34–43.

Laws, K., Adlington, R., & Gale, T. (2007). A meta-analytic review of category naming in Alzheimer's disease. *Neuropsychologia, 45*, 2674–2682.

Levine, B., Svoboda, E., Hay, J. F., Winocur, G., & Moscovitch, M. (2002). Aging and autobiographical memory: Dissociating episodic from semantic retrieval. *Psychology and Aging, 17*, 677–689.

Levy, B. (1996). Improving memory in old age through implicit self-stereotyping. *Journal of Personality and Social Psychology, 71*, 1092–1107.

Light, L. L. (1991). Memory and aging: Four hypotheses in search of data. *Annual Review of Psychology, 42*, 333–376.

Light, L. L., Patterson, M. M., Chung, C., & Healy, M. R. (2004). Effects of repetition and response deadline on associative recognition in young and older adults. *Memory & Cognition, 32*, 1182–1193.

Light, L. L., Prull, M. W., La Voie, D. J., & Healy, M. R. (2000). Dual-process theories of memory in old age. In T. J. Perfect & E. A. Maylor (Eds.), *Models of cognitive aging* (pp. 238–300). New York: Oxford University Press.

Lindenberger, U., & Baltes, P. B. (1995). Testing-the-limits and experimental simulation: Two methods to explicate the role of learning in development. *Human Development, 38*, 349–360.

Lindenberger, U., & Pötter, U. (1998). The complex nature of unique and shared effects in hierarchical linear regression: Implications for developmental psychology. *Psychological Methods, 3*, 218–230.

Lineweaver, T., Berger, A., & Hertzog, C. (2009). Expectations about memory change across the life span are impacted by aging stereotypes. *Psychology and Aging, 24*, 169–176.

Lineweaver, T. T., & Hertzog, C. (1998). Adults' efficacy and control beliefs regarding memory and aging: Separating general from personal beliefs. *Aging, Neuropsychology, and Cognition, 5*(4), 264–296.

Lockl, K., & Schneider, W. (2002). Developmental trends in children's feeling-of-knowing judgements. *International Journal of Behavioural Development, 26*, 327–333.

Luo, L., Hendriks, T., & Craik, F. I. M. (2007). Age differences in recollection: Three patterns of enhanced encoding. *Psychology and Aging, 22*, 269–280.

Lustig, C., & Flegal, K. (2008). Targeting latent function: Encouraging effective encoding for successful memory training and transfer. *Psychology and Aging, 23*, 754–764.

Lustig, C., Hasher, L., & May, C. (2001). Working memory span and the role of proactive interference. *Journal of Experimental Psychology: General, 130*, 199–207.

Lustig, C., Hasher, L., & Tonev, S. (2006). Distraction as a determinant of processing speed. *Psychonomic Bulletin & Review, 13*, 619–623.

Lustig, C., Konkel, A., & Jacoby, L. L. (2004). Which route to recovery? Controlled retrieval and accessibility bias in retroactive interference. *Psychological Science, 15*, 729–735.

Macht, M., & Buschke, H. (1983). Age differences in cognitive effort in recall. *The Journal of Gerontology, 38*, 695–700.

MacLaverty, S. N., & Hertzog, C. (2009). Do age-related differences in episodic feeling of knowing accuracy depend on the timing of the judgment? *Memory, 17*, 860–873.

Mäntylä, T., & Bäckman, L. (1990). Encoding variability and age-related retrieval failures. *Psychology and Aging, 5*, 545–550.

Marsh, E., Dolan, P., Balota, D., & Roediger, H. (2004). Part-set cuing effects in younger and older adults. *Psychology and Aging, 19*, 134–144.

Maylor, E. (1990). Recognizing and naming faces: Aging, memory retrieval, and the tip of the tongue state. *Journals of Gerontology, 45*, 215–226.

McDaniel, M. A., & Einstein, G. O. (2000). Strategic and automatic processes in prospective memory retrieval: A multiprocess framework. *Applied Cognitive Psychology, 14*, 127–144.

McDaniel, M. A., Einstein, G. O., Stout, A. C., & Morgan. Z. (2003). Aging and maintaining intentions over delays: Do it or lose it. *Psychology and Aging, 18*, 823–835.

McDowd, J., & Craik, F. (1987). Age differences in recall and recognition. *Journal of Experimental Psychology: Learning, Memory, and Cognition, 13*, 474–479.

Miller, E. K., & Cohen, J. D. (2001). An integrative theory of prefrontal cortex function. *Annual Review of Neuroscience, 24*, 167–202.

Morris, C., Bransford, J., & Franks, J. (1977). Levels of processing versus test-appropriate strategies. *Journal of Verbal Learning and Verbal Behavior, 16*, 519–533.

Moscovitch, M. (1992). Memory and working-with-memory: A component process model based on modules and central systems. *Journal of Cognitive Neuroscience, 4*, 257–267.

Murphy, M., Schmitt, F., & Caruso, M. (1987). Metamemory in older adults: The role of monitoring in serial-recall. *Psychology and Aging, 2*, 331–339.

Naveh-Benjamin, M. (2000). Adult age differences in memory performance: Tests of an associative deficit hypothesis. *Journal of Experimental Psychology: Learning, Memory, and Cognition, 26*, 1170–1187.

Naveh-Benjamin, M., Brav, T. K., & Levy, O. (2007). The associative memory deficit of older adults: The role of strategy utilization. *Psychology and Aging, 22*, 202–208.

Nelson, C. A. (2001). The ontogeny of human memory: A cognitive neuroscience perspective. In M. H. Johnson, Y. Munakata, & R. O. Gilmore (Eds.), *Brain development and cognition: A reader* (pp. 151–178). Oxford, UK: Blackwell Publishing.

Nelson, T. O. (1996). Consciousness and metacognition. *American Psychologist, 51*, 102–116.

Nelson, T. O., & Narens, L. (1990). Metamemory: A theoretical framework and new findings. *The Psychology of learning and motivation, 26*, 125–173.

Oakes, L. M., Ross-Sheehy, S., & Luck, S. J. (2006). Rapid development of feature binding in visual short-term memory. *Psychological Science, 17*(9), 781–787.

Oberauer, K. (2005). Binding and inhibition in working memory: Individual and age differences in short-term recognition. *Journal of Experimental Psychology: General, 134*(3), 368–387.

Ofen, N., Kao, Y. C., Sokol-Hessner, P., Kim, H., Whitfield-Gabrieli, S., & Gabrieli, J. D. E. (2007). Development of the declarative memory system in the human brain. *Nature Neuroscience, 10*, 1198–1205.

Old, S., & Naveh-Benjamin, M. (2008). Differential effects of age on item and associative measures of memory: A meta-analysis. *Psychology and Aging, 23*, 104–118.

Paller, K. A., & Wagner, A. D. (2002). Observing the transformation of experience into memory. *Trends in Cognitive Sciences, 6*, 93–102.

Park, D. C., Hertzog, C., & Kidder, D. (1997). Effect of age on event-based and time-based prospective memory. *Psychology and Aging, 14*, 314–327.

Park, D. C., Hertzog., C., Leventhal, H., Morrell, R. W., Leventhal, E., Birchmore, D., et al. (1999). Medication adherence in rheumatoid arthritis patients: Older is wiser. *Journal of the American Geriatric Society, 47*, 172–183.

Park, D. C., & Reuter-Lorenz, P. (2009). The adaptive brain: Aging and neurocognitive scaffolding. *Annual Review of Psychology, 60*, 173–196.

Pascual-Leone, J. (1970). A mathematical model for the transition rule in Piaget's developmental stages. *Acta Psychologica, 63*, 301–345.

Pascual-Leone, J., & Baillargeon, R. (1994). Developmental measurement of mental attention. *International Journal of Behavioral Development, 17*, 161–200.

Perfect, T. J., & Dasgupta, Z. Z. R. (1997). What underlies the deficit in reported recollective experience in old age? *Memory & Cognition, 25,* 849–858.

Perlmutter, M., & Lange, G. (1978). A developmental analysis of recall-recognition distinctions. In P. A. Ornstein (Ed.), *Memory development in children* (pp. 243–258). Hillsdale, NJ: Erlbaum.

Peterson, R. C. (Ed.). (2003). *Mild cognitive impairment: Aging to Alzheimer's Disease.* New York: Oxford University Press.

Polyn, S. M., Norman, K. A., & Kahana, M. J. (2009). A context maintenance and retrieval model of organizational processes in free recall. *Psychological review, 116,* 129–156.

Poole, D. A., & Lindsay, D. S. (1995). Interviewing preschoolers: Effects of nonsuggestive techniques, parental couching and leading question on reports of nonexperienced events. *Journal of Experimental Child Psychology, 60,* 129–154.

Pressley, M., & Hilden, K. (2006). Cognitive strategies. In W. Damon, R. Lerner, D. Kuhn, & R. Siegler (Eds.), *Handbook of child psychology* (Vol. 2, pp. 511–556). Hoboken, NJ: John Wiley & Sons.

Price, J., Hertzog, C., & Dunlosky, J. (2010). Self-regulated learning in younger and older adults: Does aging affect cognitive control? *Aging, Neuropsychology, and Cognition, 17,* 329–359.

Raz, N., Lindenberger, U., Rodrigue, K. M., Kennedy, K. M., Head, D., Williamson, A., et al. (2005). Regional brain changes in aging healthy adults: General trends, individual differences, and modifiers. *Cerebral Cortex, 15*(11), 1676–1689.

Rendell, P., McDaniel, M., Einstein, G., & Forbes, R. (2007). Age-related effects in prospective memory are modulated by ongoing task complexity and relation to target cue. *Aging, Neuropsychology and Cognition, 14,* 236–256.

Richardson, J. T. E. (1998). The availability and effectiveness of reported mediators in associative learning: A historical review and an experimental investigation. *Psychonomic Bulletin & Review, 5,* 597–614.

Robinson, A., Hertzog, C., & Dunlosky, J. (2006). Aging, encoding fluency and metocognitive monitoring. *Aging, Neuropsychology and Cognition, 13,* 458–478.

Roebers, C. (2006). Developmental progression in children's strategic memory regulation. *Swiss Journal of Psychology, 65,* 193–200.

Roebers, C., & Schneider, W. (2005). The strategic regulation of children's memory performance and suggestibility. *Journal of Experimental Child Psychology, 91,* 24–44.

Roediger, H., & McDermott, K. (1995). Creating false memory: Remembering words not presented in lists. *Journal of Experimental Psychology: Learning, Memory, and Cognition, 21,* 803–814.

Roediger, H., Rajaram, S., & Geraci, L. (2007). Three forms of consciousness in retrieving memories. In P. D. Zelazo, M. Moscovitch, & E. Thompson (Eds.), *The Cambridge handbook of consciousness* (pp. 251–287). New York: Cambridge University Press.

Rönnlund, M., Nyberg, L., Bäckman, L., & Nilsson, L. G. (2005). Stability, growth, and decline in adult life span development of declarative memory: Cross-sectional and longitudinal data from a population-based study. *Psychology and Aging, 20,* 3–18.

Rovee-Collier, C., & Shyi, G. (1992). A functional and cognitive analysis of infant long-term retention. *Developmental Psychology, 31,* 147–169.

Rubin, D. C. (2000). The distribution of early childhood memories. *Memory, 8,* 265–269.

Rubin, D. C. (2006). The basic-systems model of episodic memory. *Perspectives on Psychological Science, 1,* 277–311.

Ryan, A., & See, S. (1993). Age-based beliefs about memory changes for self and others across adulthood. *Journal of Gerontology, 48,* 199–201.

Sahakyan, L., Delaney, P., & Goodmon, L. (2008). Oh, honey, I already forgot that: Strategic control of directed forgetting in older and younger adults. *Psychology and Aging, 23,* 621–633.

Salthouse, T. A. (1991). Mediation of adult age differences in cognition by reductions in working memory and speed of processing. *Psychological Science, 2*(3), 179–183.

Salthouse, T. A. (1996). The processing-speed theory of adult age differences in cognition. *Psychological Review, 103,* 403–428.

Salthouse, T. A., & Babcock, R. (1991). Decomposing adult age differences in working memory. *Developmental Psychology, 27,* 763–776.

Schacter, D. L. (2001). *The seven sins of memory: How the mind forgets and remembers.* Boston, MA: Houghton-Mifflin.

Schaie, K. W. (2005). *Developmental influences on adult intelligence: The Seattle Longitudinal Study.* New York: Oxford University Press.

Schneider, W. (2011). Memory development in childhood. In U. Goswami (Ed.), *The Wiley-Blackwell handbook of childhood cognitive development* (2nd ed., pp. 347–376). West Sussex, UK: Wiley-Blackwell.

Schneider, W., Knopf, M., & Sodian, B. (2009). Verbal memory development from early childhood to early adulthood.. In W. Schneider & M. Bullock (Eds.), *Human development from early childhood to early adulthood: Findings from a 20 year longitudinal study* (pp. 63–90). New York: Psychology Press.

Schneider, W., Korkel, J., & Weinert, F. (1987). The effects of intelligence, self-concept, and attributional style on metamemory and memory behaviour. *International Journal of Behavioral Development, 10*, 281–299.

Schneider, W., Kron, W., Huennerkopf, M., & Krajewski, K. (2004). The development of young children's memory strategies: First findings from the Wuerzburg Longitudinal Memory Study. *Journal of Experimental Child Psychology, 88*, 193–209.

Schneider, W., Kron-Sperl, V., & Hünnerkopf, M. (2009). The development of young children's memory strategies: Evidence from the Würzburg Longitudinal Memory Study. *European Journal of Developmental Psychology, 6*, 70–99.

Schneider, W., & Pressley, M. (1997). *Memory development between two and twenty* (2nd ed.). Mahwah, NJ: Erlbaum.

Schneider, W., Visé, M., Lockl, K., & Nelson, T. O. (2000). Developmental trends in children's memory monitoring: Evidence from a judgment-of-learning task. *Cognitive Development, 15*, 115–134.

Sego, S., Golding, J., & Gottlob, L. (2006). Directed forgetting in older adults using the item and list methods. *Aging, Neuropsychology, and Cognition, 13*, 95–114.

Seidenberg, M., Guidotti, L., & Nielson, K. (2009). Semantic knowledge for famous names in mild cognitive impairment. *Journal of the International Neuropsychological Society, 15*, 9–18.

Shah, P., & Miyake, A. (1996). The separability of working memory resources for spatial thinking and language processing: An individual differences approach. *Journal of Experimental Psychology: General, 125*, 4–27.

Shin, H., Bjorklund, D., & Beck, E. (2007). The adaptive nature of children's overestimation in a strategic memory task. *Cognitive Development, 22*, 197–212.

Shing, Y. L., Brehmer, Y., & Li, S. C. (2008). Cognitive plasticity and training across the lifespan. In O. S. Tan & A. S. H. Seng (Eds.), *Cognitive modifiability in learning and assessment: International perspectives* (pp. 59–82). Singapore: Cengage Learning.

Shing, Y. L., Werkle-Bergner, M., Li, S. C., & Lindenberger, U. (2008). Associative and strategic components of episodic memory: A lifespan dissociation. *Journal of Experimental Psychology: General, 137*, 495–513.

Shing, Y. L., Werkle-Bergner, M., Li, S. C., & Lindenberger, U. (2009). Committing memory errors with high confidence: Older adults do but children don't. *Memory, 17*, 169–179.

Simons, J. S., & Spiers, H. J. (2003). Prefrontal and medial temporal lobe interactions in long-term memory. *Nature Reviews Neuroscience, 4*, 637–648.

Singer, T., Lindenberger, U., & Baltes, P. B. (2003). Plasticity of memory for new learning in very old age: A story of major loss? *Psychology and Aging, 18*, 306–317.

Sliwinski, M., Hofer, S., & Hall, C. (2003). Correlated and coupled cognitive change in older adults with and without preclinical dementia. *Psychology and Aging, 18*, 672–683.

Sluzenski, J., Newcombe, N., & Kovacs, S. L. (2006). Binding, relational memory, and recall of naturalistic events: A developmental perspective. *Journal of Experimental Psychology: Learning, Memory, and Cognition, 32*, 89–100.

Sluzenski, J., Newcombe, N., & Ottinger, W. (2004). Changes in reality monitoring and episodic memory in early childhood. *Developmental Science, 7*, 225–245.

Smith, G. E., Peterson, R. C., Parisi, J. E., & Ivnik, R. J. (1996). Definition, course, and outcome of mild cognitive impairment. *Aging, Neuropsychology, and Cognition, 3*, 141–147.

Smith, R. (2003). The cost of remembering to remember in event-based prospective memory: Investigating the capacity demands of delayed intention performance. *Journal of Experimental Psychology: Learning, Memory, and Cognition, 29*, 347–361.

Smith, R., & Bayen, U. (2006). The source of adult age differences in event-based prospective memory: A multinomial modeling approach. *Journal of Experimental Psychology: Learning, Memory, and Cognition, 32*, 623–635.

Souchay, C., & Isingrini, M. (2004). Age related differences in metacognitive control: Role of executive functioning. *Brain and Cognition, 56*, 89–99.

Souchay, C., Moulin, C. J. A., Clarys, D., Taconnat, L., & Isingrini, M. (2007). Diminished episodic memory awareness in older adults: Evidence from feeling-of-knowing and recollection. *Consciousnes and Cognition, 16*, 769–784.

Spencer, W. D., & Raz, N. (1995). Differential effects of aging on memory for content and context: A meta-analysis. *Psychology and Aging, 10*, 527–539.

Stern, Y. (2002). What is cognitive reserve? Theory and research application of the reserve concept. *Journal of the International Neuropsychological Society, 8*, 448–460.

Stine-Morrow, E., Miller, L., & Hertzog, C. (2006). Aging and self-regulated language processing. *Psychological Bulletin, 132*, 582–606.

Treisman, A. (1996). The binding problem. *Current Opinions in Neurobiology, 6*, 171–178.

Tucker-Drob, E., Johnson, K., & Jones, R. (2009). The cognitive reserve hypothesis: A longitudinal examination of age-associated declines in reasoning and processing speed. *Developmental Psychology, 45*, 431–446.

Tulving, E., & Pearlstone, Z. (1966). Availability versus accessibility of information in memory for words. *Journal of Verbal Learning and Verbal Behavior, 5*, 381–391.

Unsworth, N., & Engle, R. W. (2007). On the division of short-term and working memory: An examination of simple and complex span and their relation to higher order abilities. *Psychological Bulletin, 133*, 1038–1066.

Verhaeghen, P., & Marcoen, A. (1994). Production deficiency hypothesis revisited: Adult age differences in strategy use as a function of processing resources. *Aging and Cognition, 1*, 323–338.

Verhaeghen, P., & Marcoen, A. (1996). On the mechanisms of plasticity in young and older adults after instruction in the method of loci: Evidence for an amplification model. *Psychology and Aging, 11*, 164–178.

Verhaeghen, P., Marcoen, A., & Goossens, L. (1992). Improving memory performance in the aged through mnemonic training: A meta-analytic study. *Psychology and Aging, 7*, 242–251.

Verhaeghen, P., & Salthouse, T. A. (1997). Meta-analyses of age-cognition relations in adulthood: Estimates of linear and non-linear age effect and structural models. *Psychological Bulletin, 122*, 231–249.

Wellman, H. M. (1983). Metamemory revisited. In M. Chi (Ed.), *What is memory development the development of? A look after a decade* (pp. 31–51). Basel, Switzerland: S. Karger.

Wellman, H. M., & Gelman, S. A. (1992). Cognitive development: Foundational theories of core domains. *Annual Review of Psychology, 43*, 337–375.

Werkle-Bergner, M., Müller, V., Li, S. C., & Lindenberger, U. (2006). Cortical EEG correlates of successful memory encoding: Implications for lifespan comparisons. *Neuroscience and Biobehavioral Reviews, 30*, 839–854.

West, R. (1988). Prospective memory and aging. In M. M. Gruneberg, P. E. Morris, R. N. Sykes (Eds.), *Practical aspects of memory: Current research and issues: Clinical and educational implications* (Vol. 2, pp. 119–128). Chichester, UK: Wiley.

West, R. L., Bagwell, D., & Dark-Freudeman, A. (2008). Self-efficacy and memory aging: The impact of a memory intervention based on self-efficacy. *Aging, Neuropsychology, and Cognition, 15*, 302–309.

West, R. L., Dark-Freudeman, A., & Bagwell, D. (2009). Goals-feedback conditions and episodic memory. *Memory, 17*, 233–244.

Winne, P. H. (1996). A metacognitive view of individual differences in self-regulated learning. *Learning and Individual Differences, 8*, 327–353.

Zeintl, M., & Kliegel, M. (2007). The role of inhibitory control in age-related operation span performance. *European Journal of Ageing, 4*, 213–217.

Zelinski, E. (2009). The IMPACT Study: Maintenance of gains after a brain plasticity-based intervention for age-related cognitive decline. *Journal of the American Geriatrics Society, 57*, 168–169.

Zelinski, E., & Stewart, S. (1998). Individual differences in 16-year memory changes. *Psychology and Aging, 13*, 622–630.

Zellner, M., & Bäuml, K. (2005). Intact retrieval inhibition in children's episodic recall. *Memory & Cognition, 33*, 396–404.

Zellner, M., & Bäuml, K. (2006). Inhibitory deficits in older adults: List-method directed forgetting revisited. *Journal of Experimental Psychology: Learning, Memory, and Cognition, 32*, 290–300.

Zimmer, H. D., Mecklinger, A., & Lindenberger, U. (Eds.). (2006). *Handbook of binding and memory: Perspectives from cognitive neuroscience.* Oxford: Oxford University Press.

LIFE-SPAN COGNITION AND INFORMATION TECHNOLOGY

13

Neil Charness, Mark C. Fox, and Ainsley L. Mitchum

The evolution of our species from *homo habilis* (tool-using man) to modern man (*homo sapiens sapiens*: knowing man) was marked by an enlarging brain that enabled us to produce and consume knowledge and to create technologies both to accommodate to our environments as well as to modify them. The recent invention of the microprocessor coupled with the development of clever software has probably created the most powerful cultural tool set yet for augmenting brain function. From a knowledge acquisition perspective, information processing becomes much easier when the information is "at your fingertips" via interconnected computational systems.

Our main goal for this chapter is to trace the impact of technology on life-span development, emphasizing cognitive development. We start first by defining terms. Then we examine the use of some prominent technologies by different age groups/ birth cohorts. Next we discuss knowledge acquisition processes and the role that technology plays in developing cognition, particularly in formal educational environments, focusing on benefits and costs. We end by considering issues likely to affect the study of cognition and technology over the coming years, including measurement issues, intervention issues, cross-generational influences, and trends in human–computer symbiosis.

▪ DEFINITIONS OF TECHNOLOGY AND COGNITION

The *Oxford English Dictionary* gives a number of senses for the word technology, including "practical and industrial arts," but for our purposes we will side with "**d. high-technology** applied *attrib.* to a firm, industry, etc., that produces or utilizes highly advanced and specialized technology, or to the products of such a firm. Also (unhyphened) as *n. phr.* Similarly **low-technology.**" http://dictionary.oed.com/cgi/ entry/50248096?single=1&query_type=word&queryword=technology&first=1&max_ to_show=10. To oversimplify, we can limit discussion of technology by considering mainly information technology, any product or service that depends on a microprocessor chip (e.g., Charness & Boot, 2009). However, in acknowledgment of the critical role that other technologies have played in centuries prior to the 20th, we also briefly mention a few earlier ones that did not involve microprocessors.

Cognition has many definitions as well. We can view it as the set of brain processes responsible for our ability to think and pursue goals, particularly those requiring problem solving. The cognitive system can be seen as a tool that evolved to meet our needs as biological organisms and that was sufficiently powerful that we began to thrive as a species. However, the cognitive system has a limited ability to monitor and reflect on its own states and processes (consciousness). Such self-monitoring improves markedly in childhood (Schneider & Bjorklund, 2003).

It is useful to conceptualize cognition as taking place in an information processing system that consists of multiple processors (perceptual, motor, cognitive), memory systems, and symbol structures (e.g., Anderson, 1983; Card, Moran, & Newell, 1983). The cognitive system is limited in speed and capacity, and these limits change across the life span with development and aging. We start out in life with minimal knowledge and minimal processing ability but great potential for both. Processing speed and memory capacity increase from infancy into young adulthood (e.g., Dempster, 1981; Kail & Salthouse, 1994). Within the psychometric tradition of intelligence measurement, such functions are termed "fluid" abilities (or "mechanics" of intelligence; Baltes, 1987) and contrasted with "crystallized" abilities ("pragmatics"; Baltes, 1987) that depend on acquiring cultural knowledge (Horn, 1982). Abilities that rely on speed of processing and memory capacity peak in early adulthood and then decline.

However, an expanding knowledge base across the adult years ("crystallized" abilities) provides rich data structures (e.g., long-term memory retrieval structures; Ericsson & Kintsch, 1995) that can help skilled older adults bypass the growing limitations that develop on processing speed (Salthouse, 1996), an example of the more general knowledge-search tradeoff (Newell, 1990). An older adult who has been trained to use an efficient algorithm can respond more quickly than a younger adult using a less efficient one when given the problem—"mentally determine the square of 95" (Charness & Campbell, 1988). However, the young adult would be expected to perform much more quickly than the older adult if both practiced a complex cognitive task equally using the same algorithm (Lindenberger, Kliegl, & Baltes, 1992; Touron, Hoyer, & Cerella, 2001). Thus, neural integrity sets limits on information processing efficiency. Similarly, children can be expected to outperform young adults when they possess domain-relevant knowledge that the young adults do not (e.g., knowledge of chess patterns; Chi, 1978; Schneider, Gruber, Gold, & Opwis, 1993) but be surpassed in domains where they have less knowledge, such as number knowledge (Chi, 1978).

TECHNOLOGY'S ROLE IN COGNITIVE DEVELOPMENT

Technology, particularly educational technology, influences cognition primarily through its impact on learning processes. Learning is limited by information processing capabilities of the brain. Until researchers find direct (e.g., chemical) ways to modify the functioning of neurons, humans will always be limited by the rather slow rate (5–10 s/chunk; Simon, 1974) at which new (rote) memories are formed. In the educational context, technology can help address issues of maintaining motivation to learn (the attention issue) and providing information in optimal doses and schedules (Pavlik & Anderson, 2008). However, in a broader developmental context, technology appears to play three broad, overlapping roles.

As seen in Figure 13.1, we postulate three primary roles for technology in cognitive development: substitution, augmentation, and acceleration. Technology can substitute for a missing function or augment an impaired one. Technology can also accelerate the acquisition of culturally important knowledge.

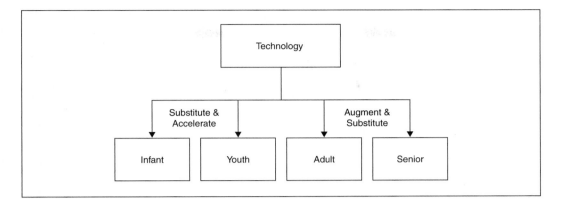

FIGURE 13.1   **Role of technology across the life span.**

Substitution

A good example of the need for substitution is the case of congenital deafness which affects aural language acquisition during its most sensitive time (critical period). A cochlear implant can (partially) substitute for the impaired components in the ear and allow language (particularly spoken language) to develop more normally (Svirsky, Robbins, Kirk, Pisoni, & Miyamoto, 2000). Similarly, at the upper end of the life span, a hearing aid can (partially) substitute for missing hair cells in the cochlea (due perhaps to cumulative noise-induced destruction) allowing an aged person to hear low volume sounds and hence continue to learn important new cultural information through that input modality.

Augmentation

Technology can augment a human capability, allowing the user to exceed biological limits or to repair culturally induced ones. A good example of technology that fits with the former would be a telescope or microscope, allowing a person to resolve visual detail that could not be seen with the unaided eye. A good example of a culturally induced biological weakness is myopia (near-sightedness; Morgan & Rose, 2005). Spectacles, contact lenses, and surgical technology to change the curvature of the cornea enable myopic children and adults to augment their visual capabilities, allowing them to focus successfully on distant objects.

Acceleration

Technology can accelerate the learning process, either directly, by changing the person's biological mechanisms (e.g., through chemical effects on neurons and their supporting cells), or indirectly, by providing efficient access to cultural experiences. Changing a biological mechanism can have direct effects both on a specific information channel, for example, hearing, and on cognitive mechanisms that rely on that channel. For instance, Oakes (2009) makes the argument that visual and memory limitations in the infant are mediators of category boundary development.

Although the efficacy of biological intervention is not yet well understood, it is clear how technology can improve the efficiency of learning. Consider the metabolic cost of hunting down journal articles from library shelves in contrast to searching for them with a computer via databases on the Internet.

Per the Baltes (1987) theoretical framework that stresses the importance of culture for compensating for negative effects of biological aging, these three functions probably assume different weights across the life span. In youth, substitution and acceleration seem central. In old age, augmentation and substitution may play greater roles.

However, there is an old adage that suggests that acceleration carries a risk later in life: "early ripe, early rot." The more modern version of this risk is encapsulated by the term "burnout" applied to children pushed by parents to excel in an activity (e.g., a sport) who tire of, and abandon, the training regimen. When considering the upper end of the life span, some suggest that through vigorous cognitive engagement earlier in life it is possible to build a "reserve capacity" in the brain (Stern, 2006) that will maintain cognition against normative (e.g., biological aging) and non-normative (e.g., diseases such as dementia) influences on development. Thus, given the apparent risk of technology making some processes too easy, we will also discuss potential negative side effects of technology on cognition and other functioning.

We first review some indicators of technology use by different age groups/birth cohorts in order to address the stability versus change question in developmental research: how does technology use change across the life span? Unfortunately, longitudinal data are generally lacking, but there are a number of repeated cross-sectional surveys that can provide first approximation estimates for the trajectory of technology adoption across the life span.

DEMOGRAPHICS OF TECHNOLOGY USE

Figure 13.2 shows cross-sectional population-representative data for adults for three touchstone technology artifacts—the mobile phone, the computer, and the Internet—from the Pew Internet and American Life Project survey for May 2008 (http://www.pewinternet.org/PPF/r/76/dataset_display.asp). There are two features worth noting. First, technology use is uneven across age groups, generally falling off sharply past the decade of the 30s. Second, technology use also varies by product category. In younger cohorts there are minor differences among the three technology items, and use is generally above 80%. Starting with the 65+ cohorts there is a large gap, with mobile phone adoption remaining relatively high (50% or above) until after age 85. However, two landmark technologies of the 20th century, computers and the Internet, are not used by the majority of people in these older cohorts. The drop-off in use by age group past the 30s tends to parallel the drop-off in fluid abilities past the 20s that is seen for intelligence test performance. But, the marked variation in decline by technology type cannot easily be explained simply as an adaptation to normative age-related declines in cognitive abilities in conjunction with the demands of a complex technology artifact.

Because the Pew project has conducted annual surveys that ask the same or similar questions since the beginning of the 21st century, it is also possible to examine how adoption trends vary over time. Given that people will move between age

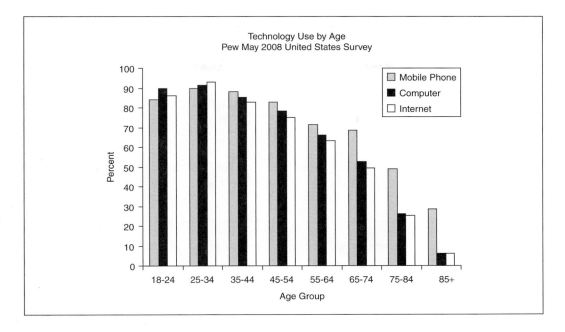

FIGURE 13.2 **Pew Internet and American Life Tracking Survey, May 2008, showing technology use by age group. Questions included: "Do you have a cell phone," "Do you use a computer at your workplace, at school, at home, or anywhere else at least on an occasional basis," and "Do you use the Internet at least occasionally." The survey was administered by phone to a representative sample of U.S. households.**

category cohorts at each (cross-sectional) sampling interval, caution is warranted in interpreting these data as longitudinal trends. Because of the age-related decline in use measured at every point, the lines will probably overestimate use trends within cohorts. Also, current users are probably less likely to become nonusers as they age than are current nonusers to become users. Figure 13.3 shows the trend for Internet use. Again there is wide separation in use between the younger and the older cohorts. The two youngest cohorts have nearly reached asymptote with use at 80–90%. Fifty-year-old cohorts appear to be leveling off at about 70% use, and the 65+ year-old cohorts are leveling off below 40% use.

Unfortunately, there appear to be no recent representative sampling studies of technology use by children and such data depend on querying proxy family members. Data for school-aged children (reported by family member proxies aged 15 and older) are shown in Figure 13.4, based on an October 2003 supplement to the Current Population Survey in the United States concerned with computer and Internet use.

Although computer use rates were remarkably high then, even for preschoolers, hinting at why young generations can help their grandparents with computer issues, Internet use only started to rise to near young adult levels in high school (for comparison see the 2003 use figures for the two youngest cohorts in Figure 13.3).

Frameworks about technology diffusion stress the importance of a multitude of factors, including social ones such as the influence of leading edge adopters (Rogers, 2003). Venkatesh and Davis (2000), building primarily on studies of office technology

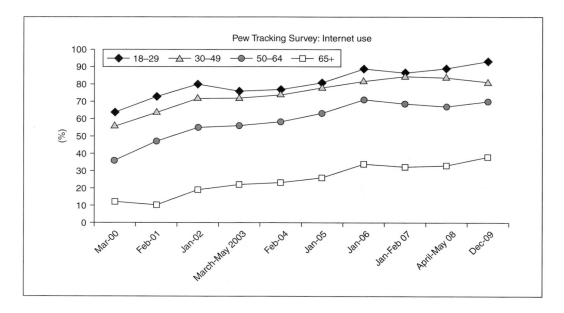

FIGURE 13.3 Pew Internet and American Life Tracking Survey 2000–2010, showing Internet use by age group. The relevant question asked if people went online or used the Internet at least occasionally.

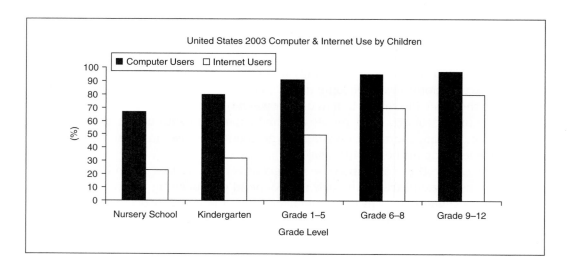

FIGURE 13.4 Computer and Internet use by children in the United States in 2003. Data from the Current Population Survey Supplement. *Source*: Rates of Computer and Internet Use by Children in Nursery School and Students in Kindergarten Through Twelfth Grade: 2003. U.S. Department of Education, Institute of Education Sciences NCES 2005–111rev.

acceptance by adults, have identified perceived usefulness and ease of use as critical factors for intent to use. Charness (2003) argued for access, motivation, ability, design, and training as important mediators of technology adoption at the far end of the life course.

As many surveys have noted with respect to computer technology, education and income are strong predictors of computer and Internet use (Kaiser Family Foundation, 2005; The UCLA Internet report—"Surveying the digital future," 2003; Rainie & Packel, 2001). Cognition is also a strong predictor in adulthood (e.g., as indexed by fluid and crystallized ability measures; Czaja et al., 2006). It is also the case that technology is diffusing through society more quickly over time. For instance, the facsimile (FAX) machine was patented about 150 years before going into widespread use; the telephone took about 50 years; and the Internet became widely used in less than 20 years (Charness, 2008; Charness & Czaja, 2005).

Before we can fully assess the impact of technology on different aspects of cognition across the life span, we need to examine some important assumptions about life-span development. Biological and cultural influences can affect motivation, which is a prerequisite for learning and skill acquisition. Motivational patterns show significant shifts from childhood to adulthood to older adulthood.

LIFE-SPAN PERSPECTIVE ON KNOWLEDGE AND SKILL ACQUISITION

Although philosophers such as Aristotle and John Locke viewed the infant's mind as a blank slate ("tabula rasa") to be written on by experience, this extreme empiricist view is discredited by evidence about the development of neural connections even in the absence of external stimulation (Huberman, Feller, & Chapman, 2008). Nonetheless, it is obvious that the initial year or two of the life span is spent acquiring enormous amounts of information about the (infant's) environment, including the social environment, and particularly its prime communication system: human language, both verbal and nonverbal (e.g., MacWhinney, 1998). Once spoken language is in place, the ability of the culture to educate the child accelerates. In modern literate societies, once written language is mastered, a massive store of human knowledge becomes available. Technology is an important tool in making available information accessible. Gutenberg's printing innovations made possible dissemination of scholarly works to a broader audience. The development of the Internet has had an even greater impact, for example, collaborative development of knowledge sources such as Wikipedia and indexing engines such as Google that make such information sources accessible.

As several life-span theorists have noted (see Part I of this volume), people's motivations vary across the life span. Selective optimization with compensation (SOC) theory (Baltes & Baltes, 1990) suggests that developing organisms attempt to optimize gains and minimize losses in the pursuit of increased adaptive capacity. Early in life humans focus selectively on activities that promote growth, and in early adulthood on those that promote maintenance of achieved function, and then in late adulthood on compensatory activities, particularly for cognitive resources that diminish with adult age. Thus, in early parts of the life span, infants and children are likely to pursue activities that improve their skills and knowledge. Later in life, people will select some activities to protect via higher levels of effort and compensatory strategies, and relinquish others in the face of diminishing biological resources. Socioemotional selectivity theory (Carstensen, Isaacowitz, & Charles, 1999) suggests that information acquisition is a very important goal early in life, whereas attaining emotional satisfaction seems to become more important in the later years. Such frameworks might lead one to predict that children would be much more likely than middle-aged or older adults to be willing to acquire skill at using new technology. As always, individual differences are evident. There are incurious children and highly curious aged adults.

However, both frameworks would predict that people will be driven to acquire new skills in order to adapt to environmental constraints in the service of important goals. Personality and interests will probably influence self-initiated learning characteristics. Social and cultural pressures will dictate other types of learning.

We humans are highly social animals. This poses a dilemma because we have to find a way to balance the conflicts that arise when competing to attain individual goals and cooperating to achieve group goals. Even though, as most parents can testify, infants in need of nutrition or comfort seem to have little ability to accommodate to their parents' needs (e.g., for sleep), it does not take developing infants, particularly irritable ones, too long to learn to reciprocate to achieve goals in order to gain parental attention and favorable communication interactions (e.g., Lowinger, 1999). Those changes represent a shift in focus toward mutuality that benefits both parties. Tomasello and Farrar (1986) show that a mother's language interaction within a period of reciprocal focus of attention (as opposed to parent-directed attention control) is a good indicator of an infant's future vocabulary acquisition.

Particularly during the courtship and pair bonding part of adulthood, communication skills become salient. It is no accident that modern communication tools such as messaging, which is available through phone and computer networks as well as in virtual meeting areas such as personal Web pages (e.g., through Facebook and MySpace), have assumed such an important part of a modern teenager's daily activity (e.g., Schmitt, Dayanim, & Matthias, 2008). Age/cohort differential participation in such activities fits with the hypothesized changing pattern of motivational influences across the life span.

TECHNOLOGY TOOLS FOR COGNITION

We first mention some significant early technologies before restricting discussion to technologies in the 20th and 21st centuries. Efforts to off-load cognitive processes to external aids (augmentation) began with using simple objects as symbols and culminated in the widespread use of calculators, personal computers, and other devices capable of processing information faster and storing it intact longer than the human brain.

The most basic and consequential form of external memory is writing, which is believed to have first appeared in Mesopotamia some 3,000 years ago and to have evolved from a representational form of record keeping that entailed engraving symbols into clay (Schmandt-Besserat, 1992). The impact of writing on civilization as both an external memory aid and nexus for information exchange—especially following Gutenberg's invention of the printing press around 1440—is too great to expound on here, but suffice it to say that our current educational preoccupations with teaching reading, writing, and arithmetic skills effectively owes an enormous debt to written language systems.

Another cognitive aid used in ancient Mesopotamian, Egyptian, and Chinese cultures is the abacus, which eased mathematical operations by absorbing some of the memory load of mental calculation. Computational devices like the abacus were not significantly improved upon for thousands of years until innovators like Wilhelm Schickard, Blaise Pascal, and Gottfried Wilhelm Leibniz attempted to mechanically automatize computation with elaborate machines. Leibniz's Stepped Reckoner was the first mechanical calculator to perform the four arithmetic operations of addition, subtraction, multiplication, and division. In the 19th century, Charles Babbage designed large and elaborate machines to solve polynomial functions (Honeyman & Dwyer, 1993).

The mathematician Alan Turing made a major conceptual advancement in computation in 1936 when he devised a framework for exploring the limits of real-world computation. Turing imagined machines that could processes information when their states were adjusted in response to symbols on long pieces of tape. The tape is fed into these "Turing Machines" with each symbol indicating an adjustment to the machine's state. The meaning of a symbol varies depending on what state the machine is in, meaning that adjustments always depend on both the symbol and the current state. The machines are unbounded by memory constraints as actions are recorded on the strip of tape, which is unlimited in length. Theoretically, such a machine can carry out very complex operations incrementally by making adjustments for every symbol entered. A universal Turing machine can carry out the operations of every such machine and is theoretically more powerful than any realizable computing device (Minsky, 1967).

Achieving the computational power promised by Turing's theoretical model required innovations that allowed for greater computation at faster speeds in smaller devices. By the 1970s hand-held calculators were becoming widely available, soon followed by home computer systems that boasted a wide variety of software applications including those for recreation and education. An early question about this technology when it was still expensive was whether the benefits outweighed the costs.

Costs and Benefits

The decision to adopt a technology depends in part on the perceived costs and benefits. Models of technology acceptance (e.g., Venkatesh & Davis, 2000) suggest that perceived usefulness and perceived ease of use are critical factors in technology adoption in workplace settings (which typically occupy the middle part of the life course). For older adults, perceived benefits are weighted quite heavily in the adoption of technology, sometimes leaving some of the more recent technologies such as e-mail and mobile phones disadvantaged (Melenhorst, Rogers, & Bouwhuis, 2006).

Costs can be parsed into the categories of money and time (including opportunity cost—time spent on one activity cannot be spent on another). In the early part of the life span, unscheduled time is relatively plentiful and money is relatively scarce, hence the child's emphasis on information and skill acquisition, time-intensive processes. The two resources begin to shift positions in young adulthood. People enter the paid labor force full time and increase financial resources accordingly but also have to devote more time to activities such as paid work, building romantic relation-ships, and parenting. Time and money both run out at the end of the life span.

However, one of the most striking changes in adulthood directly affecting time management is that the cost of learning increases strikingly. As an example, older adults take about twice as long in self-paced learning conditions as younger ones for working through tutorials on word processor software, with middle-aged adults fall-ing in between (Charness, Kelley, Bosman, & Mottram, 2001).

From the perspective of the benefit side of the equation, technology can play the role of saving both time and money. When it comes to the human's relatively slow learning rate, any technology promising to accelerate knowledge and skill acquisition is potentially highly beneficial. Technology was thrust into the limelight as a tool to aid cognition a few centuries ago when public education became widespread.

Role of Formal Education in Promoting Cognitive Development

The practice of providing universal public education first emerged in Prussia in the mid-1700s (*Encyclopedia Britannica*: http://search.eb.com/eb/article-47612, accessed 7/21/09). Since that time there has been a growing recognition around the world that countries need skilled work forces to compete effectively in the worldwide economy and that formal education is an effective way to accelerate knowledge and skill acqui-sition to enable children to become productive adults. Thus, it is unsurprising to find technology, from chalkboards to keyboards, being introduced into the classroom in the service of teaching children culturally valued literacy skills, such as reading, writing, and mathematics.

Reading literacy by itself has a significant effect on cognition and brain devel-opment as seen in comparisons of children in the same family who were or were not allowed to attend school (Petersson, Silva, Castro-Caldas, Ingvar, & Reis, 2007). Whether computer technology has helped or hindered the learning process has been much debated (Christmann & Badgett, 2003). For example, strong claims were made that teaching basic programming skills (Papert's Logo system; Papert, 1980) would help children to think more effectively. Evidence in favor of this notion was as lacking as was that for the earlier claim that teaching Latin and Greek would teach a general "mental discipline" (Thorndike, 1924). Thorndike's law of identical elements—that transfer only occurs from one skill to another when there are identical elements in both skills—has proven to be a robust theory about transfer processes (see Singley & Anderson, 1989, for an update).

If one assumes that basic information processing skills—encoding information into symbol structures, reading them from memory, writing them to memory, and transforming them into actions in the world—are already present at birth, school-ing is very unlikely to be teaching students how to think, but rather what to think. That is, education is mainly concerned with how best to induce new symbol struc-tures and programs in the brains of students, particularly programs for acquiring new information: teaching students how to acquire new knowledge without direct instruction. Nonetheless, evidence from the skill acquisition literature makes it clear that cognitive mechanisms such as working memory capacity (Baddeley, 1986) or long-term working memory capacity (Ericsson & Kintsch, 1995) rely on the size of learned symbol structures (chunks, templates, schemas, scripts, retrieval structures) that people can access.

So, the earlier mentioned rise in working memory capacity across the early part of the life span can be attributed to some combination of knowledge acquisition (bigger chunks/symbol structures) coupled with more efficient neural circuits (e.g., through myelination). The negative changes in processing capacity in old age may be driven in part by genetic influences associated with demyelination of neurons with concomitant losses in connectivity (e.g., Finkel, Reynolds, McArdle, Hamagami, & Pedersen, 2009).

Computer Technology and Education

Technology has become a ubiquitous part of modern education, aiming to accelerate learning, starting with the introduction of film and television, followed by microcomputers in the 1970s. However, in spite of the large volume of research examining computer-enhanced learning, there is still much speculation and anecdotal evidence with respect to the efficacy of computers as an educational tool, as well as a significant gap between research and actual implementation in schools (Baylor & Ritchie, 2002). Overall, studies have shown that computer-enhanced instruction benefits student learning, with several meta-analyses showing small to moderate positive gains, ranging from .18 to .33 of a standard deviation, between pre- and post-test measures of student achievement (Christmann & Badgett, 2003; Christmann, Badgett, & Lucking, 1997; Fletcher-Flinn & Gravatt, 1995; Kulik & Kulik, 1991).

However, rapid improvements in both hardware and software have made it difficult for researchers to keep pace with current technology. As microprocessors have become more powerful and significantly less expensive, their potential range of applications has also changed, leaving researchers with a task analogous to hitting a moving target. Just as is the case with computer systems and software, research in educational computing also becomes outdated fairly quickly. Further complicating researchers' task is the blurring of boundaries between different types of computer applications.

Despite the inherent difficulty in systematically evaluating the effectiveness of the use of computers in education, a number of recent trends in educational computing have shown promise. More powerful processors have made it possible to create richer, more complex software that may also include opportunities for online collaboration. Detailed software simulations make experiential learning possible in environments that would otherwise be inaccessible, such as historical events and abstract conceptual systems. While computer simulations may not be effective in teaching new material, they can help deepen students' understanding of previously learned material, as long as activities take place in the broader context of structured learning goals (Winn, 2002).

Since the introduction of personal computers, many have voiced concerns that spending large amounts of time working alone with computers could interfere with students' social development. With the growing popularity of the Internet, the vision of the isolated computer user has given way to concerns that children and teenagers spend too much of their time online engaged in socializing (Subrahmanyam, Greenfield, Kraut, & Gross, 2001; but see also Durkin & Barber, 2002). The popularity of the Internet as a social medium is a trend that is likely to have an impact on how computers are used in educational practice. One promising application is the use of interactive software environments to promote collaborative learning. Collaborative learning has a long history in educational practice (Slavin, 1983), and computer-centered collaborative learning activities have been shown to effectively promote individual learning (Lou, Abrami, & d'Apollonia, 2001). Given that children and teenagers are already comfortable with socializing online, as evidenced by the growing popularity of multiplayer online gaming and social networking sites, online collaborative learning seems a logical next step.

Computer use in education has also been seen as a solution to a common problem in overcrowded public schools: limited access to timely, individualized feedback essential to learning. As discussed later on, cognitive tutoring programs have been shown to be highly effective in mathematics instruction, as well as in other subject areas, because systems are able to adapt to each students' rate of learning (Anderson, Corbett, Koedinger, & Pelletier, 1995). Computers have been seen as having potential as a cognitive support tool, providing scaffolding so students can better develop higher order thinking skills (Lajoie, 2008). For example, allowing students to use computers and calculators to perform simple calculations, may leave more resources for higher order, conceptual reasoning.

In addition to classroom applications, technology has become a part of education in informal settings as well. The success of educational television programs such as *Mister Rogers' Neighborhood, Sesame Street,* and *Blue's Clues* demonstrated the potential for using children's entertainment as an educational tool (Huston & Wright, 1998). As computer and Internet use has started to displace some of the time children spend watching television, the Internet may take up a role as the primary medium for educational entertainment.

If such technology has improved the efficiency of declarative and procedural knowledge transfer (knowing what and knowing how knowledge) to more recently educated students, we should be seeing gains in cognition in younger relative to older adult cohorts. There is evidence for improved cognition, in the so-called Flynn effect, though technology's role is not yet clear.

Flynn Effect

Psychologists have spent more than 2 decades trying to account for Flynn's (1987) observation that IQ test scores in developed countries have increased steadily during the previous century. The Flynn effect has been documented in at least 20 countries and reflects differential increases on tests representing second stratum factors in a three-stratum hierarchical factor structure of intelligence. Fluid ability tests, involving abstract reasoning and novel problem solving, have increased the most; crystallized ability scores, reflecting general knowledge, have increased to a lesser extent; and elementary cognitive task scores, measuring speed of processing, have changed very little (Flynn, 2007). Whether or not technological advancements in the developed world play a significant role is an important question in the context of this chapter as there is little consensus on specific causes of the effect.

Theoretical limitations on the speed at which selection-induced phenotypic change can occur have largely restricted explanations to environmental causes such as education (Teasdale & Owen, 1994) or nutrition (Reynaldo, 1998). Flynn (2007) has argued that increased emphasis on scientific explanations in developed countries impacts the way citizens reason about complex concepts, namely by promoting abstraction skills that allow people to perceive similarities and relationships where differences and disorder are more immediately salient. Flynn and Weiss (2007) propose that characteristics of developing nations such as "urbanization, ratio of adults to children in the home, more liberal parenting styles, emphasis on lateral thinking in schools, [and] more leisure time spent on cognitively demanding activities" might raise scores (p. 210). The contiguity of initial test score increases with adoption of these characteristics within countries lends support to these explanations. For example, Scandinavian countries were some of the first to show improvements and appear to be approaching an asymptote (Teasdale & Owen, 1994), whereas later developing countries such as Kenya are only now beginning to show an effect (Daley, Whatley, Sigman, Espinosa, & Neumann, 2003). These findings suggest that, at the very least, rising IQ scores and technological advancements are two parts of a larger and potentially complex causal relationship.

There has been surprisingly little evidence of technology itself (as defined in this chapter) as a contributor to rising scores. Greenfield (1998) proposed that television and optical displays might have contributed as availability of these devices occurred in tandem with rising scores in many countries. The most compelling evidence for technology as a cause comes from studies implicating older technologies. Barber (2006), for example, found that availability of newspapers and television predicted national achievement of children in math and science across 36 nations even when variance in national wealth was partialled out, implicating availability of media as a potential causal factor. It is possible that more modern media, readily available in developed nations, will be found to have a causal role in the future. More generally, the same author (2005) concluded that cultural complexity, defined by proportion of nonagricultural workers, secondary school enrollment, and literacy, predicted IQ in 81 countries after controlling for a number of confounding variables. It appears that information technology may contribute to rising IQ scores, but it is not yet possible to detect the effects of present-day technologies.

Formal Training of Cognition in Children and Young Adults

First we briefly review training principles that have been espoused since the advent of universal public education. Then we outline their application within computer-based training.

A century ago, the doctrine of formal discipline held that learning in one domain (e.g., Greek literature) would improve skills in another very disparate domain (e.g., music). The notion that learning generalizes between domains has been largely discredited as numerous studies have shown that people have difficulty recognizing and applying previously learned principles in a different but analogically similar context (Gick & Holyoak, 1980). Thus, possibly the most fundamental epistemological discovery of the 20th century is that human abilities adapt specifically to the training context and that practice in one domain seldom generalizes to another. As an example, human expertise tends to be very specific, and its development depends on focused study—deliberate practice—in the context of appropriate goal setting and timely feedback (Ericsson, Charness, Feltovich, & Hoffman, 2006). The importance of training specificity is illustrated by examples of 20th century education and training interventions that either did or did not incorporate the principal. Interventions targeted at improving general cognitive ability (accelerating its development) have had limited success, whereas those targeting specific skills have been more effective.

Large-scale educational intervention programs such as Head Start in the United States grew out of widespread concern that impoverished environments limited the social and educational attainment of low SES children. For better or worse, IQ emerged as the benchmark of program efficacy because it was widely believed to measure general cognitive ability and researchers at the time were optimistic about its malleability (Zigler & Trickett, 1978). Research suggests that these programs are beneficial in many ways, but in many cases have not led to lasting gains in IQ (Barnett, 1995; Nores, Belfled, Barnett, & Schweinhart, 2005; Weikart, Epstein, Schweinhart, & Bond, 1978). However, the treatment condition was sometimes associated with enduring positive outcomes (across age 40), such as higher educational attainment, lower criminal activity, and higher earnings, raising questions about IQ's privileged status as an outcome variable. After all, the tangible outcomes realized by treatment condition children are the ultimate goal of such an intervention. In fact, Nisbett (2005) notes that Head Start's failure to produce enduring gains in IQ has been misconstrued as evidence that intervention programs in general are ineffective. Intensity seems to be very important, as more intensive programs, such as the Abecedarian Project, have produced longer lasting increases that often extend into adulthood (Ramey & Ramey, 1999).

In a National Academies report, Bransford, Brown, and Cocking (1999) outlined the conditions for which technology may help with teaching and learning, including "bringing exciting curricula based on real-world problems into the classroom; providing scaffolds and tools to enhance learning; giving students and teachers more opportunities for feedback, reflection, and revision; building local and global communities that include teachers, administrators, students, parents, practicing scientists, and other interested people; and expanding opportunities for teacher learning" (p. 195). We concentrate here on narrowly focused approaches with a good track record of formal evaluation.

One training technology that has grown out of a better understanding of how humans solve problems and acquire knowledge is model-based training systems. Knowledge structures change qualitatively as skills are developed, and these gradual changes in structure can be emulated with computational models. A computer can monitor the performance of an individual and map it to the model to determine the appropriate feedback or assistance to provide. Incorrect student input (that does not match production rules of the model) activates remediation routines that allow students to recognize and correct errors.

Such tutoring systems have been used in both adolescent and young adult populations. Anderson and his colleagues (Anderson et al., 1995) have designed such tutors with the ACT architecture (Anderson, 1983) that substantially increased the performance and speed of learning in geometry, algebra, LISP (programming), and complex dynamic environments (Fu et al., 2006). In short, computer tutors meet the definition of accelerating skill acquisition.

Formal Training of Cognition in Older Adults

As SOC theory suggests, older adults are the most in need of the support of their culture to help them maintain cognition in the face of biologically mediated declines in some abilities. Technology can help both by substituting for, and remediating, failing functions. See Rogers, Stronge and Fisk (2006) and Czaja and Lee (2007), for recent reviews dealing primarily with substitution functions of technology. There is also a possibility of using technology in a slightly different role: prevention. First we briefly outline trends in adult cognition to indicate what needs to be remediated or prevented.

A variety of theories (e.g., Salthouse, 2010) have been advanced to account for the broad declines seen in so-called fluid abilities (mechanics of intelligence, information processing efficiency) in adulthood, though fewer have addressed the improvements seen in crystallized abilities (knowledge). Trends can be seen in Figure 13.5, based on cross-sectional data from a nonrepresentative adult U.S. sample that was ethnically diverse (Czaja et al., 2006) and focused mostly on age bands of young adults, middle-aged adults, and older adults.

We show scatter-plots to remind the reader of the large individual differences that occur, particularly those in later adulthood, demonstrating the heterogeneity of development. What these plots indicate is the differing patterns for human abilities that rely on knowledge acquisition (Shipley vocabulary) and processing efficiency (alphabet span, a working memory measure). Based on the contrasting positive (vocabulary) and negative (alphabet span) age trends, a worthy goal for technology interventions would be to augment working memory (e.g., providing environmental support; Morrow & Rogers, 2008) and reduce the demands on rapid processing speed. Examples would be automated reminder systems for helping people manage complex pill-taking schedules (Mayhorn, Lanzolla, Wogalter, & Watson, 2005) and audio-based warning systems to alert people to hazards associated with lane changing while driving (Kramer, Cassauvaugh, Horrey, Becic, & Mayhugh, 2007).

An intriguing possibility is to use technology to prevent the development of age-related impairments in cognition by building up cognitive reserves. There have been many attempts to maintain and improve adult cognition, which we will not review given our focus on technology. See the summary by Hertzog, Kramer, Wilson, and Lindenberger (2008). Meta-analysis (Papp, Walsh, & Snyder, 2009) indicates that such interventions have had significant, though modest, effects (effect sizes <0.2).

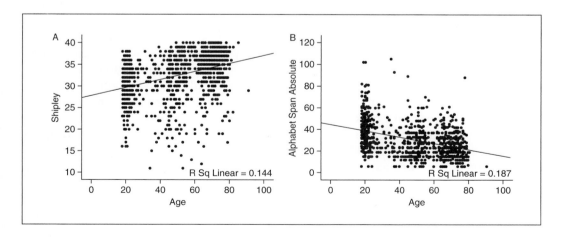

FIGURE 13.5   **CREATE data from project reported in Czaja et al. (2006). Panel A shows the age trend for Shipley vocabulary, a knowledge measure (r = 0.38, n = 1199). Panel B shows the trend for alphabet span, a working memory measure (r = −0.43, n = 1178).**

Given their ubiquity in society today, computer systems are increasingly used in experimental cognitive training programs (e.g., Dahlin, Nyberg, Bäckman, & Neely, 2008). However, deployment of such training programs necessitates training older adults to use computers first (because of low use in current older cohorts per Figure 13.2). This requirement has sparked considerable research into how best to train those at different ability levels (e.g., Hickman, Rogers, & Fisk, 2007; Nair, Czaja, & Sharit, 2007). It has also raised the question of whether learning to use a computer might by itself boost cognition, though a recent Dutch randomized clinical trial found little evidence of cognitive improvement in older adults (Slegers, van Boxtel, & Jolles, 2009).

In summary, the evidence for positive impacts of technology on improving cognition is quite compelling at most points in the life span (e.g., computer tutors for children, adolescents and adults, cognitive interventions in older adults). But, the improvements have tended to be quite specific to the skills or abilities that have been trained rather than generalizing broadly. However, the cost effectiveness of treatments aimed at accelerating cognitive development in youth or remediating cognitive decline in adulthood has not been established.

One of the difficulties with broad-spectrum approaches to remediate declining cognition in adulthood is that the interventions are often multimodal and the "active ingredient" in some of these treatments (training programs) is difficult to identify. To bring such ingredients under tighter experimental control, researchers have turned to video game systems.

Video Games for Cognitive Training

Video gaming is a recreational application of computation that has become increasingly popular since the 1970s. Although parents may decry the many hours that children spend playing games on computer systems, particularly with specialized video game systems, early work suggested that there were some beneficial effects on cognition. Gopher, Weil, and Bereket (1994) were among the first to show benefits of video games, in their case for pilot trainees on early flight performance. However, researchers interested in the psychological effects of gaming on children and adolescents have focused primarily on social consequences such as whether violent video games increase pathological behavior such as excessive aggression, finding effect sizes of around 0.20 (Anderson, 2004; Anderson & Bushman, 2001). However, recent efforts have aimed at determining whether the seemingly high demands that video games make on various motor, perceptual, and cognitive subsystems, may improve performance on cognitive tasks.

Not surprisingly, most research is based on college-age populations, limiting the generalizability of results to other age groups. Green and Bavelier (2003) found that experienced college-age gamers had better selective attention for visual objects in a series of visual search and visual attention tasks. Nongamers showed similar effects after training for 10 hours with an action game requiring a wide field of visual search, but not a control game without this characteristic. The same authors found that experienced gamers and nongamers with training were better able to correctly report how many quickly vanishing objects they were shown (Green & Bavelier, 2006a) and had better visual resolution for identifying objects among distracters with similar properties (Green & Bavelier, 2006b). In both cases, video game training improved nongamer performance.

Feng, Spence, and Pratt (2007) reported that the well-documented difference (about 1 standard deviation) in male and female spatial abilities is smaller among gamers, and male and female nongamers' spatial abilities both improve with training, with females showing greater improvement. Boot, Kramer, Simons, Fabiani, and Gratton (2008) also found that training improved spatial abilities, but found no training effects or differences between gamers and nongamers on several higher-level cognitive tasks involving planning and problem solving, such as Tower of Hanoi and the Raven's Matrices.

In contrast, Basak, Boot, Voss, and Kramer (2008) reported improved older adult performance on executive function tasks such as task switching, working memory, and reasoning, but not visuospatial measures except for mental rotation, after less than 25 hours of training with a real-time strategy video game.

A number of other studies have shown significant benefit in older adults, with some transfer to nonobvious abilities. Clark, Lanphear, and Riddick (1987) demonstrated a benefit for 7 weeks of video game play in older adults (age 57–83) on speeded response in a spatial compatibility task. Dustman, Emmerson, Steinhaus, Shearer, and Dustman (1992) showed benefit for 60–79-year-old adults on response time only, not on other vision, cognition, and affective measures. Goldstein et al. (1997) showed that playing SuperTetris, a spatial reasoning game, benefited response time on a Sternberg task (memory search) but not a Stroop task (inhibitory control) for a sample of 69–90-year-olds. Although well being measures declined in both experimental and control groups at post-test they declined less in the video game group.

One possible explanation for why older, but not younger, adults seemed to benefit on these higher-level cognitive tasks is that they had more to gain from the training. It is well established that older adults tend to perform worse at these types of tasks (Lindenberger & Baltes, 1997), and it is possible that training has greater impact when there is more to be gained.

Recently video game system manufacturers have begun to market video games (e.g., Nintendo's Brain Age) intended to help older adults maintain or improve cognition, though without any research to assess efficacy. Other more research-oriented companies have introduced lengthy (40-hour) computer-based training packages that show significant influences on basic cognitive abilities, particularly on speeded performance tasks, based on rigorous randomized clinical trial testing (Smith et al., 2009). An earlier randomized clinical trial (the ACTIVE trial; Ball et al., 2002) demonstrated modest improvements in the cognitive performance of older adults (e.g., on speeded performance) with relatively short-term computer-based interventions consisting of ten 60–75-minute training sessions.

In general, these results are encouraging, and have shown that there are positive outcomes for some aspects of cognition including somewhat unexpected ones (distal transfer). The hope is that by providing improvements at the ability level (e.g., reasoning, spatial ability, speeded perception) there will be significant transfer to many tasks, not just the trained one, though evidence in favor of this has been weak.

A further concern is that such studies have not demonstrated efficiency. They need to be compared with equivalent amounts of specific training on some critical outcome measures (e.g., compare perceptual speed practice to driving instruction for an outcome variable such as safe driving). There are enough cases of efficacy now in training research that researchers need to begin to demonstrate efficiency, much as the medical research field is beginning to look into comparative effectiveness research, requiring that a drug be superior to the usually prescribed medication, not just to a placebo control condition. Even better would be a focus on cost effectiveness for technology interventions.

Much of the aforementioned research used human experimenters to train older adults in computer use or software use. However, advances in artificial intelligence now permit completely automated training through guided tutoring. The computer becomes both the coach and the conduit for learning.

Technology Coaches

Much of human learning is accomplished in the context of human tutors (parents, teachers, coaches) until the individual becomes knowledgeable enough to pursue learning goals independently. Technology advances have permitted the creation of intelligent tutoring systems that have near-infinite patience and convenient access (e.g., Koedinger, Anderson, Hadley, & Mark, 1997). They operate with models of the learner, rather than in the form of the older practice/drill programs that emphasized rote memorization. In their current state, they still do not have the capability of interacting completely successfully with students through spoken language communication (Litman et al., 2006) but as speech generation and recognition software improves that hurdle may be overcome for some teaching domains.

Although it is not yet clear whether they can be consistently superior to human tutors, such systems can provide learning gains of about one standard deviation (e.g., Graesser, Chipman, Haynes, & Olney, 2005). Thus, they may ultimately be just as effective in terms of student outcomes, and hence may become widespread because they will likely be cost effective. Computer tutors can augment learning over traditional classroom learning today and may substitute for human tutors in the future. Although such tutors have been used mainly with adolescent and young adult populations, they should benefit adults at the upper end of the life span as well.

Given some of the negative changes in cognition with age, having an intelligent coach to augment or substitute for diminishing capabilities, such as working memory, may be a significant factor in maintaining independence. There is considerable interest in having technology coaches that can help with activities of daily living or instrumental activities of daily living in "aware homes" (Mynatt, Melenhorst, Fisk, & Rogers, 2004). Intelligent coaches embedded in these homes can help in preparing foods or managing complex medication schedules. Such coaching systems can augment working memory to enable someone to continue to function independently. Robots such as "nursebot" have already been deployed to nursing home settings to provide advice to older residents (Matthews, 2002).

Negative Impacts of Technology

Technological tools can have both intended and unintended consequences. Although we have portrayed a very positive picture about the benefits of technology for cognition, we would be remiss if we did not mention potential negative effects. Potential drawbacks include displacement of more valuable activities, decay of acquired skills through disuse, as well as side effects such as increases in hyperactivity in children and increases in obesity at all ages, all of which can have negative consequences for cognition.

Infants and Children

Although programs such as *Sesame Street* and *Baby Einstein* effectively capture the attention of infants and young children, research has suggested that they can have a negative impact on children's language development because time spent watching television often displaces opportunities for face-to-face interaction (Zimmerman, Christakis, & Meltzoff, 2007). When studies control for the frequency of adult–child conversation, the relationship between delayed language acquisition and television viewing is reduced (Zimmerman et al., 2009).

Another frequently discussed negative consequence of children's exposure to television, Internet, and computer games is its association with problems in attention and for hyperactivity (Christakis, Zimmerman, DiGiuseppe, & McCarty, 2004; Zimmerman & Christakis, 2007). Although the American Academy of Pediatrics recommends that children younger than 2 should not watch television, recent studies have shown that many children begin watching television regularly as early as 9 months of age and are watching 3.3 hours of television a day by age 3 (Zimmerman et al., 2007).

For school-aged children, as well as for children aged 3–5, viewing educational programs has actually been shown to be beneficial (Anderson, Huston, Schmitt, Linebarger, & Wright, 2001). For this age group, negative effects of television viewing are often more related to the displacement of other activities rather than a direct result of television viewing and are moderated by a number of other factors (e.g., SES, parental education). A similar case has been made for negative effects of video games in terms of taking time from extra-school activities that could be promoting better reading and writing skills (Weiss & Cerankosky, 2010).

However, older children (who have better metacognitive skills) are better able to control their own exposure to television programs by looking away or directing their attention elsewhere (Schmidt, Pempek, Kirkorian, Lund, & Anderson, 2008). For children younger than age 3, it is possible that exposure to television may influence synaptic development and have lifelong consequences on cognitive abilities beyond its already noted negative impact on language development (Christakis & Zimmerman, 2009). While some research suggests a modest relationship between television viewing prior to age 3 and later hyperactivity (Christakis et al., 2004; Miller et al., 2007), with more recent findings suggesting that this effect may be moderated by the type of programming (Zimmerman & Christakis, 2007), other studies have failed to support these findings (Obel et al., 2004). Although the most current research in attention disorders finds that genetic and neurological factors have a far greater influence than environmental factors (Barkley, 1997), the debate about whether media exposure increases children's risk of hyperactivity remains unresolved.

Adolescents and Young Adults

One concern often expressed about substitutive roles for technology is that it potentially weakens either the development or the expression of a skill. The case most often cited is the effect of calculator use on mathematics abilities. A meta-analysis by Ellington (2003) started from the reference point of an earlier set of analyses. Hembree and Dessart (1992; cited in Ellington) showed little or no impact on students' conceptual skills and positive impact on student attitudes toward mathematics. One exception was noted, namely, a negative effect of calculators in Grade 4 on computational skills. The Ellington meta-analysis on students in K-12 education levels showed that outcomes of calculator use depended in part on the form of testing. When calculators were not allowed at test, they showed a very small positive impact ($g = .14$) for operational (e.g., computation) and problem-solving skills. However, when they were allowed during the assessment of student performance, the impacts were uniformly positive (range: $g = .20$ to $.44$ for various skills).

One moderator relevant to our concern with technology was that of calculator type, with stronger positive effects for basic and scientific calculators compared to more complex graphing calculators. (Such a result suggests that time invested in teaching complex calculator use does not pay off in more efficient teaching of mathematics once the calculator is mastered.) As was found in earlier meta-analyses, calculator use evoked more positive attitudes toward mathematics. In summary, contrary to initial concerns that substituting calculators for mental calculation would weaken mathematics skills, the opposite seemed to be the case. Calculator technology had mainly positive effects on student mathematics performance.

However a recent empirical investigation suggests that the issue is not totally resolved. Rittle-Johnson and Kmicikewycz (2008) examined third graders' learning of multiplication problems when they either generated answers or read the answers from a calculator. For memory performance, generating an item is known to be superior to reading it (Slamecka & Graf, 1978). Rittle-Johnson and Kmicikewycz (2008) found an interaction of student ability with condition such that for those with low prior knowledge it was better to generate answers themselves than to read them from a calculator. No differences were observed between generate and read conditions for students with greater prior knowledge (middle, high knowledge levels). Other more subtle impacts of technology are considered next.

Obesity

The prevalence of overweight and obesity among American children and adolescents has increased steadily since the late 1970s and accelerated in the last decade (Adair, 2008). Given that inactivity is associated with weight gain, it would not be surprising if technologies that are assumed to displace physical activities, such as television and video games, contribute to adolescent obesity (Dietz, 1990). Related theories are that television viewing raises caloric intake (Story & Faulkner, 1990; Van den Bulck, 2000) or even decreases metabolic rate (Klesges, Shelton, & Klesges, 1993).

Studies examining the relationship between television viewing and obesity have either found only weak associations between viewing time and obesity-related measurements such as body mass index (BMI; e.g., Dietz & Gortmaker, 1985; Robinson & Killen, 1995), or no relationship at all (Robinson et al., 1993; Van den Bulck, 2000). It is not surprising then that causal evidence (i.e., watching more television causes obesity) has been scarce. One exception is Robinson's (1999) highly cited study of preadolescent children in a randomized experiment evaluating the effects of an intervention program designed to decrease television viewing. Third and fourth graders from two matched schools participated and the schools were randomly assigned to an intervention and no intervention condition. The 6-month program consisted of lessons aimed at motivating children to limit television and video game time, for example, by challenging them to forgo these activities for 10 days. Television viewing (including video game use) was monitored for children in both conditions. The intervention successfully decreased television viewing, and children in the intervention group experienced relative decreases in BMI and other measures of body fat composition. The study both established a causal relationship and demonstrated the feasibility of interventions; however, the sizable decrease in television viewing of about 40% led to only minor decreases in obesity-related measurements (less than 5% difference from the control group), suggesting that the causal influence of television, although real, is probably very minor.

Vandewater, Shim, and Caplovitz (2004) used diaries to record the daily activities of more than 2,800 children between the ages of 1 and 12 for two full 24-hour periods. They found no relationship between minutes of television viewing and weight status, but found complex relationships between weight status and time spent playing video games and using computers. Children with higher BMI played video games for a moderate amount of time compared to children with lower BMI who spent significantly more or less time playing. In contrast, 9- to 12-year-olds with high BMI spent either less or more time using computers than children in this age group with lower BMI. No relationship between BMI and computer use was found for children younger than 9.

It appears that, among adolescents, the relationship between weight status and electronic media use is minor, although very high or low computer use is associated with higher BMI in at least one study. Moreover, causation cannot be inferred from the few relationships observed, because they are only correlational. Electronic media appear to be only a minor contributor among multiple causes of overweight and obesity in adolescents.

Negative Impact of Technology on Older Adults

Classic models of person–environment fit (e.g., Lawton, 1977) postulate the existence of an optimal zone where the challenge posed by the environment is in balance with the capabilities of the person. Too little challenge is thought to lead to boredom, failure to develop, and even potential losses from disuse. One of the challenges faced by those hoping to intervene at the upper end of the life span to make life easier for older adults with waning abilities is that substitutive technology should not accelerate declines in those abilities. Challenging an individual to go beyond their current abilities is a guiding principle in the design of cognitive interventions and education in general (e.g., the notion of scaffolding). However, we found few cases of negative impact of technology in the literature.

Concerns with obesity in the general population also hold for older adults. Shopping on the Internet might be convenient for older adults with mobility impairments but also may lead to less physical activity and increased obesity. Longitudinal research has shown that obesity is a risk factor for dementia in women, though not in men (Whitmer, Gunderson, Barrett-Connor, Quesenberry, & Yaffe, 2005).

However, video game systems are capable of stimulating exercise, and software programs can help track diet. A key feature in the successful deployment of such systems is to ensure that they can attract and hold the interest of older users, taking into account the life-span changes in motivational processes discussed earlier.

FUTURE ISSUES IN THE STUDY OF LIFE-SPAN COGNITION AND INFORMATION TECHNOLOGY

It's easy to predict the future; what's difficult is being right.
—Anonymous

Progress in this challenging research field depends on better measurement tools, better experimental interventions, and better technology. Whereas Moore's law for transistor density (exponential growth: doubling of transistor density every 2 years) can still be counted on to improve microprocessor capabilities for at least the next decade or so, human-related progress on measurement tools and interventions is likely to be slower.

Measurement

Measuring the influence of technology on human development is a difficult task because both humans and technology are changing and likely are having reciprocal influences on each other. For instance, computers have become easier to learn to use as the software interface has improved, making comparisons between computer use now and a decade ago as difficult as comparisons between education levels 50 years ago and today. Successive generations of humans have had different patterns of cognitive strengths and weaknesses as measured by cognitive ability tests (one reason for renorming popular cognitive measurement instruments such as intelligence scales). There are both general increases (e.g., Flynn effect) and cohort-specific patterns of increases and decreases seen for different cognitive abilities (Schaie, 1994). Biological influences (e.g., evolution) are unlikely to be operating over such short time intervals as a generation or two, so such ability changes likely reflect cultural influences.

One of the major difficulties for assessing the influence of technology on development is the absence of both aggregate and fine-grained population data on technology use. Cohort panels are necessary for tracking longitudinal trends in technology use. Even more helpful would be longitudinal studies that could relate use to fine-grained developmental outcomes such as reading achievement in children or instrumental activities of daily living (IADL) competence in older adults. Nonetheless, observational studies cannot provide the best evidence for inferring cause–effect relationships, despite the increasing availability and sophistication of techniques such as latent variable modeling (McArdle, 2009).

Moreover, tools to measure cognition efficiently in a consistent way across the life span need further development. The NIH Toolbox for assessment is a project aimed at providing such instruments (for the age range of 3–85 years; http://www.nihtoolbox.org/default.aspx, accessed 3/8/10). With the development of better tools for measuring cognition, the field can move forward from assessing efficacy of an intervention (rejecting the null for a before-versus-after comparison) to assessing efficiency (comparing treatments) and cost effectiveness (gain per dollar of expenditure).

Interventions

Experimental approaches provide strong cause–effect inference, but most short-term educational interventions with children and even shorter-term cognitive interventions with older adults do not yet provide adequate dose-response curves for assessing the effects of technology on cognition. Knowing more about the dose necessary to achieve long-lasting results is required for evaluating the cost effectiveness of usual versus enhanced technology on cognition.

Cross-Generational Influences

Given the learning advantage that children and young adults have over middle-aged and older adults, it seems likely that technology diffusion will increasingly flow from young to old, the exact opposite of how it probably flowed in prior generations. Recall that aging is a relatively recent phenomenon in human history and "wise elders" for our early ancestors were likely to have been in their 30s and 40s, the decades where people peak in achievement (Roring & Charness, 2007; Simonton, 1988). Cross-generational interaction is increasingly being touted as a means for improving cognition at both ends of the life span (e.g., the use of Experience Corps senior volunteers to tutor children in literacy skills; Rebok, Carlson, & Langbaum, 2007), though evidence for efficiency is lacking at the moment.

Technology Advances

As mentioned at the outset, technology can act on cognition through roles such as substitution, augmentation, and acceleration. There are relatively few technology devices that can aid cognition by substituting for missing cognitive functions, particularly in the early part of the life span, in part because the "hardware" supporting information processing is usually in place (exceptions occur for disorders such as autism) and what is mainly missing is knowledge and information processing efficiency. Also, in a sense, metacognition capability sets limits for whether children can recognize that they need help with cognitive tasks. Technology might be able to provide the necessary scaffolding for augmenting and accelerating both metacognitive capabilities as well as specific cognitive abilities (e.g., instructional design programs to train self-monitoring skills, reading skills). See Bransford et al. (1999), Chapter 9, for suggestions about how to use technology to improve learning and metacognition.

A promising recent focus has been on understanding general mechanisms of learning including the role of tutors. The benefit of this approach is that research findings are less likely to become obsolete before they have an opportunity to impact educational practice. Research in test-enhanced learning and with adaptive tutoring systems (made possible by more powerful microprocessors) has had encouraging results.

With advances in wireless networking, new research will need to evaluate the effect of collaborative learning via Internet connections. Among younger children, research has demonstrated an important role for face-to-face interaction (Zimmerman et al., 2007). Computers are seen as central to promoting better cognition in children, for instance in the one laptop per child (OLPC) movement, despite the lack of evidence for efficiency.

At the far end of the life span, when cognition is failing, either through normative losses in memory functioning or because of dementia, augmentation and substitution may be feasible. Low-cost technology items such as memory wallets (Bourgeois, 1992), or higher-cost technology items such as sophisticated camera-based sensor systems (e.g., Microsoft's SenseCam; Berry et al., 2009) can act as *cognitive coaches* for retrieving episodic memory records for those with severe memory impairments. Such systems currently require a caregiver to organize and annotate photos of recorded events (e.g., memexerciser; http://www.cmu.edu/qolt/Research/projects/cognitive-coach.html). Such coaching systems substitute external memory (environmental support; Craik, 1986) for failing internal memory storage and retrieval processes.

However, much development is still needed before these systems become autonomous and can carry out human-like recognition and categorization processes, become aware of user intent, and provide timely coaching for specific tasks. Advances in artificial intelligence techniques may make more pieces of the process available in the coming decades. Mobile computing devices, particularly the nearly ubiquitous mobile phone, offer a promising platform for delivering cognitive coaching, and such devices have been widely adopted at both ends of the life span.

But, as mentioned earlier, there is a fine line to tread between augmentation and substitution in the early parts of the life span when having mental challenges across a broad variety of domains may prove essential for normal development as well as for later robust aging. Accelerating some skills through technology may cause others to languish. The history of human culture is replete with examples of skills that were deemed valuable in one era but that became obsolete in the next. (How many readers know how to ride a horse versus drive a car?) Nonetheless, basic cognitive skills, such as socializing successfully, are unlikely to go out of fashion (see Cotton, McCullough & Adams, Chapter 25). It is no accident that some of today's most successful technologies are communications related (mobile phone, social networking Web sites).

In the end, technology's influence on cognitive development is limited by human information processing constraints, such as limited attentional capacity (see Watson, Lambert, Miller & Strayer, Chapter 16), and particularly, learning rate for acquiring knowledge. At its best, technology can provide extremely efficient access to information and hence to the opportunity to develop knowledge. Societies, through their institutional structures, vary along dimensions such as who they target for investments that improve cognition (and who they may exclude, such as women and elders) and how skillfully they motivate their members. Technological advances can be seen as increasing the range of opportunities for cognitive growth and maintenance across the life span through acceleration, substitution, and augmentation. Effective technology should enable us to move in the direction of the upper right corner of the cube shown in Figure 13.6, where we achieve more effective cognition sooner in development and maintain cognition at higher levels later in life.

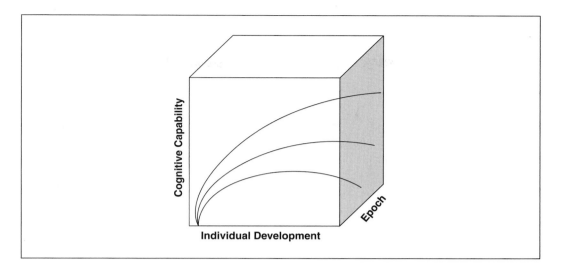

FIGURE 13.6 **Developmental trajectories accelerated and improved across epochs. Technology can be seen as providing a way for people to optimize cognition along a plane extending from the bottom left to the top right edge of the cube. Plotted are three trajectories. The first indicates normative development at this point in time, and two future trajectories represent enhanced cognition due to enhanced technology.**

ACKNOWLEDGMENTS

This research was supported by a grant from NIH/NIA P01 AG17211–10, Project CREATE, to the first author.

REFERENCES

Adair, L. S. (2008). Child and adolescent obesity: Epidemiology and developmental perspectives. *Physiology & Behavior, 94,* 8–16.

Anderson, C. A. (2004). An update on the effects of violent video games. *Journal of Adolescence, 27,* 113–122.

Anderson, J. R. (1983). *The architecture of cognition.* Cambridge, MA: Harvard University Press.

Anderson, C. A., & Bushman, B. J. (2001). Effects of violent video games on aggressive behavior, aggressive cognition, aggressive affect, physiological arousal, and prosocial behavior: A meta-analytic review of the scientific literature. *Psychological Science, 12*(5), 353–359.

Anderson, D. R., Huston, A. C., Schmitt, K. L., Linebarger, D. L., & Wright, J. C. (2001). Early childhood television viewing and adolescent behavior: The recontact study—Introduction. *Monographs of the Society for Research in Child Development, 66*(1), 1-+.

Anderson, J. R., Corbett, A. T., Koedinger, K. R., & Pelletier, R. (1995). Cognitive tutors: Lessons learned. *Journal of the Learning Sciences, 4,* 167–q207.

Baddeley, A. (1986). *Working memory.* New York: Oxford University Press.

Ball, K., Berch, D. B., Helmers, K. F., Jobe, J. B., Leveck, M. D., Marsiske, M., et al. (2002). Effects of cognitive training interventions with older adults: A randomized control trial. *Journal of the American Medical Association, 288,* 2271–2281.

Baltes, P. B. (1987). Theoretical propositions of life-span developmental psychology: On the dynamics between growth and decline. *Developmental Psychology, 231,* 611–626.

Baltes, P. B., & Baltes, M. M. (1990). Psychological perspectives on successful aging: The model of selective optimization with compensation. In P. B. Baltes & M. M. Baltes (Eds.), *Successful aging: Perspectives from the behavioral sciences* (pp. 1–34). New York: Cambridge University Press.

Barber, N. (2006). Is the effect of national wealth on academic achievement mediated by mass media and computers? *Cross-Cultural Research, 40,* 130–151.

Barkley, R. A. (1997). Behavioral inhibition, sustained attention, and executive functions: Constructing a unifying theory of ADHD. *Psychological Bulletin, 121*(1), 65–94.

Barnett, W. S. (1995). Long-term effects of early childhood programs on cognitive and school outcomes. *Future of Children, 5,* 25–50.

Basak, C., Boot, W. R., Voss, M., & Kramer, A. F. (2008). Can training in a real-time strategy videogame attenuate cognitive decline in older adults? *Psychology and Aging, 23,* 765–777.

Baylor, A. L., & Ritchie, D. (2002). What factors facilitate teacher skill, teacher morale, and perceived student learning in technology-using classrooms? *Computers & Education, 39,* 395–414.

Berry, E. L., Hampshire, A., Rowe, J., Hodges, S., Kapur, N., Watson, P., et al. (2009). The neural basis of effective memory therapy in a patient with limbic encephalitis. *Journal of Neurology, Neurosurgery and Psychiatry, 80,* 1202–1205.

Boot, W. R., Kramer, A. F., Simons, D. J., Fabiani, M., & Gratton, G. (2008). The effects of video game playing on attention, memory, and executive control. *Acta Psychologica, 129,* 387–398.

Bourgeois, M. S. (1992). Evaluating memory wallets in conversations with persons with dementia. *Journal of Speech and Hearing Research, 35,* 1344–1357.

Bransford, J. D., Brown, A. L., & Cocking, R. R. (Eds.). (1999). How people learn: Brain, mind, experience, and school. Washington, DC: National Academy Press. Retrieved March 9, 2010, from http://www.nap.edu/openbook.php?record_id=6160&page=R1

Card, S. K., Moran, T. P., & Newell, A. (1983). *The psychology of human-computer interaction.* Hillsdale, NJ: Lawrence Erlbaum Associates.

Carstensen, L. L., Isaacowitz, D. M., & Charles, S. T. (1999). Taking time seriously: A theory of socioemotional selectivity. *American Psychologist, 54,* 165–181

Charness, N. (2003). Access, motivation, ability, design, and training: Necessary conditions for older adult success with technology. In N. Charness & K. W. Schaie (Eds.), *Impact of technology on successful aging* (pp. 15–27). New York: Springer.

Charness, N. (2008). Technology as multiplier effect for an aging work force. In K. W. Schaie & R. Abeles (Eds.), *Social structures and aging individuals: Continuing challenges* (pp. 167–192). New York: Springer.

Charness, N., & Boot, W. R. (2009). Aging and information technology use: Potential and barriers. *Current Directions in Psychological Science, 18,* 253–258.

Charness, N., & Campbell, J. I. D. (1988). Acquiring skill at mental calculation in adulthood: A task decomposition. *Journal of Experimental Psychology: General, 117,* 115–129.

Charness, N., & Czaja, S. J. (2005). Adaptation to new technologies (7.13). In M. L. Johnson (Ed.), *Cambridge handbook on age and ageing* (pp. 662–669). Cambridge: Cambridge University Press.

Charness, N., Kelley, C. L., Bosman, E. A., & Mottram, M. (2001). Word processing training and retraining: Effects of adult age, experience, and interface. *Psychology and Aging, 16,* 110–127.

Chi, M. T. H. (1978). Knowledge structures and memory development. In R. S. Siegler (Ed.), *Children's thinking: What develops?* (pp. 73–96). Hillsdale, NJ: Lawrence Erlbaum Associates.

Christakis, D. A., & Zimmerman, F. J. (2009). Young children and media: Limitations of current knowledge and future directions for research. *American Behavioral Scientist, 52,* 1177–1185.

Christakis, D. A., Zimmerman, F. J., DiGiuseppe, D. L., & McCarty, C. A. (2004). Early television exposure and subsequent attentional problems in children. *Pediatrics, 113*(4), 708–713.

Christmann, E. P., & Badgett, J. L. (2003). A meta-analytic comparison of the effects of computer-assisted instruction on elementary students' academic achievement. *Information Technology in Childhood Education Annual,* 91–104.

Christmann, E. P., Badgett, J., & Lucking, R. (1997). Microcomputer-based computer-assisted instruction within differing subject areas: A statistical deduction. *Journal of Educational Computing Research, 16*(3), 281–296.

Clark, J. E., Lanphear, A. K., & Riddick, C. C. (1987). The effects of videogame playing on the response selection processing of elderly adults. *Journal of Gerontology, 42,* 82–85.

Craik, F. I. M. (1986). A functional account of age differences in memory. In F. Klix & H. Hagendorf (Eds.), *Human memory and cognitive capabilities: Mechanisms and performances* (pp. 409–422). Amsterdam: North-Holland.

Czaja, S. J., Charness, N., Fisk, A. D., Hertzog, C., Nair, S. N., Rogers, W. A., et al. (2006). Factors predicting the use of technology: Findings from the Center for Research and Education on Aging and Technology Enhancement (CREATE). *Psychology and Aging, 21,* 333–352.

Czaja, S. J., & Lee, C. C. (2007). Information technology and older adults. In J. A. Jacko & A. Sears (Eds.), *The human-computer interaction handbook* (2nd ed., pp. 777–792). New York: Erlbaum.

Dahlin, E., Nyberg, L., Bäckman, L., & Neely, A. S. (2008). Plasticity of executive functioning in young and older adults: Immediate training gains, transfer, and long-term maintenance. *Psychology and Aging, 23,* 720–730.

Daley, T. C., Whatley, S. E., Sigman, M. D., Espinosa, M. P., & Neumann, C. (2003). IQ on the rise: The Flynn effect in rural Kenyan children. *Psychological Science, 14,* 215–219.

Dempster, F. N. (1981). Memory span: Sources of individual and developmental differences. *Psychological Bulletin, 89,* 63–100.

Dietz, W. H. (1990). You are what you eat: What you eat is what you are. *Journal of Adolescent Health Care, 11,* 76–81.

Dietz, W. H., & Gortmaker, S. L. (1985). Do we fatten our children at the television set? Obesity and television viewing in children and adolescents. *Pediatrics, 75,* 807–812.

Durkin, K., & Barber, B. (2002). Not so doomed: computer game play and positive adolescent development. *Journal of Applied Developmental Psychology, 23*(4), 373–392.

Dustman, R. E., Emmerson, R. Y., Steinhaus, L. A., Shearer, D. E., & Dustman, T. J. (1992). The effects of videogame playing on neuropsychological performance of elderly individuals. *Journal of Gerontology, 47,* 168–171.

Ellington, A. J. (2003). A meta-analysis of the effects of calculators on students' achievement and attitude levels in precollege mathematics classes. *Journal for Research in Mathematics Education, 34,* 433–463.

Ericsson, K. A., & Kintsch, W. (1995). Long-term working memory. *Psychological Review, 102,* 211–245.

Ericsson, K. A., Charness, N., Feltovich, P., & Hoffman, R. (Eds.) (2006). *Cambridge handbook of expertise and expert performance.* Cambridge: Cambridge University Press.

Feng, J., Spence, I., & Pratt, J. (2007). Playing an action video game reduces gender differences in spatial cognition. *Psychological Science, 18,* 850–855.

Finkel, D., Reynolds, C. A., McArdle, J. J., Hamagami, F., & Pedersen, N. L. (2009). Genetic variance in processing speed drives variation in aging of spatial and memory abilities. *Developmental Psychology, 45,* 820–834.

Fletcher-Flinn, C. M., & Gravatt, B. (1995). The efficacy of computer assisted instruction (CAI): A meta-analysis. *Journal of Educational Computing Research, 12*(3), 219–242.

Flynn, J. R. (1987). Massive IQ gains in 14 nations: What IQ tests really measure. *Psychological Bulletin, 101,* 171–191.

Flynn, J. R. (2007). *What is intelligence? Beyond the Flynn effect.* Cambridge: Cambridge University Press.

Flynn, J. R., & Weiss, L. G. (2007). American IQ gains from 1932 to 2002: The WISC subtests and educational progress. *International Journal of Testing, 7,* 209–224.

Fu, W. T., Bothell, D., Douglas, S., Haimson, C., Sohn, M. H., & Anderson, J. R. (2006). Toward a real-time model-based training system. *Interacting with computers, 18,* 1215–1241.

Gick, M. L., & Holyoak, K. J., (1980). Analogical problem solving. *Cognitive Psychology, 12,* 306–355.

Goldstein, J., Cajko, L., Oosterbroek, M., Michielsen, M., Van Houten, O., & Salvedera, F. (1997). Videogames and the elderly. *Social Behavior and Personality, 25,* 345–352.

Gopher, D., Weil, M., & Bereket, Y. (1994). Transfer of skill from a computer game trainer to flight. *Human Factors, 36,* 387–405

Graesser, A. C., Chipman, P., Haynes, B. C., & Olney, A. (2005). Auto-tutor: An intelligent tutoring system with mixed-initiative dialogue. *IEEE Transactions on Education, 48,* 612–618.

Green, C. S., & Bavelier, D. (2003, May 29). Action video game modifies visual selective attention. *Nature, 423,* 534–537.

Green, C. S., & Bavelier, D. (2006a). Enumeration versus multiple object tracking: The case of action video game players. *Cognition, 101,* 217–245.

Green, C. S., & Bavelier, D. (2006b). Effect of action video games on the spatial distribution of visuospatial attention. *Journal of Experimental Psychology: Human Perception and Performance, 32,* 1465–1478.

Greenfield, P. (1998). The cultural evolution of IQ. In U. Neisser (Ed.), *The rising curve: long-term gains in IQ and related measures* (pp. 81–123). Washington, DC: American Psychological Association.

Hembree, R., & Dessart, D. J. (1992). Research on calculators in mathematics education. In J. T. Fey (Ed.), *Calculators in mathematics education* (pp. 23–32). Reston, VA: National Council of Teachers of Mathematics.

Hertzog, C., Kramer, A. F., Wilson, R. S., & Lindenberger, U. (2008). Enrichment effects on adult cog-
    nitive development: Can the functional capacity of older adults be preserved and enhanced?
    Psychological Science in the Public Interest, 9, 1–65.

Hickman, J. M., Rogers, W. A., & Fisk, A. D. (2007). Training older adults to use new technology.
    Journal of Gerontology: Psychological Science, 62B, 77–84.

Honeyman, J. C., & Dwyer, S. J. (1993). Historical perspective on computer development and glossary
    of terms. *Radiographics, 13*, 145–152.

Horn, J. L. (1982). The theory of fluid and crystallized intelligence in relation to concepts of cogni-
    tive psychology and aging in adulthood. In F. I. M. Craik & S. Trehub (Eds.), *Aging and cognitive
    processes* (pp. 237–278). New York: Plenum Press.

Huberman, A. D., Feller, M. B., & Chapman, B. (2008). Mechanisms underlying development of visual
    maps and receptive fields. *Annual Review of Neuroscience, 31*, 479–509.

Huston, A. C., & Wright, J. C. (1998). Television and the informational and educational needs of chil-
    dren. *Annals of the American Academy of Political and Social Science, 557*, 9–23.

Kail, R., & Salthouse, T. A. (1994). Processing speed as mental capacity. *Acta Psychologica, 86*,
    199–225.

Kaiser Family Foundation (2005). Report #7223: E-health and the elderly: How seniors use the
    Internet for health information. The Henry J. Kaiser Family Foundation, 2400 Sand Hill Road,
    Menlo Park, CA 94025. Retrieved September 25, 2005, from http://www.kff.org/entmedia/7223.
    cfm.

Klesges, R. C., Shelton, M. L., & Klesges, L. M. (1993). Effects of television on metabolic rate: Potential
    implications for childhood obesity. *Pediatrics, 91*, 281–286.

Koedinger, K. R., Anderson, J. R., Hadley, W. H., & Mark, M. A. (1997). Intelligent tutoring goes to
    school in the big city. *International Journal of Artificial Intelligence in Education, 8*, 30–43.

Kramer, A. F., Cassavaugh, N., Horrey, W. J., Becic, E., & Mayhugh, J. L. (2007). Influence of age
    and proximity warning devices on collision avoidance in simulated driving. *Human Factors, 49*,
    935–949.

Kulik, C. L. C., & Kulik, J. A. (1991). Effectiveness of computer based instruction: An updated analy-
    sis. *Computers in Human Behavior, 7*(1–2), 75–94.

Lajoie, S. P. (2008). Metacognition, self-regulation, and self-regulated learning: A rose by any other
    name? *Educational Psychology Review, 20*, 469–475.

Lawton, M. P. (1977). The impact of the environment on aging and behavior. In J. E. Birren &
    K. W. Schaie (Eds.), *Handbook of the psychology of aging* (pp. 276–301). New York: Van Nostrand
    Reinhold.

Lindenberger, U., & Baltes, P. B. (1997). Intellectual functioning in old and very old age: Cross-
    sectional results from the Berlin Aging Study. *Psychology and Aging, 12*, 410–432.

Lindenberger, U., Kliegl, R., & Baltes, P. B. (1992). Professional expertise does not eliminate age
    differences in imagery-based memory performance during adulthood. *Psychology and Aging,
    7*, 585–593.

Litman, D. J., Rose, C. P., Forbes-Riley, K., VanLehn, K., Bhembe, D., & Silliman, S. (2006). Spoken ver-
    sus typed human and computer dialogue tutoring. *International Journal of Artificial Intelligence
    in Education, 16*, 145–170.

Lou, Y., Abrami, P. C., & d'Apollonia, S. (2001). Small group and individual learning with technology:
    A meta-analysis. *Review of Educational Research, 71*, 449–521.

Lowinger, S. (1999). Infant irritability and early mother–infant reciprocity patterns. *Infant and Child
    Development, 8*, 71–84.

MacWhinney, B. (1998). Models of the emergence of language. *Annual Review of Psychology, 49*,
    199–227.

Matthews, J. T. (2002). The Nursebot Project: Developing a personal robotic assistant for frail older
    adults in the community. *Home Health Care Management Practice, 14*, 403–405.

Mayhorn, C. B., Lanzolla, V. R., Wogalter, M. S., & Watson, A. M. (2005). Personal digital assistants
    (PDAs) as medication reminding tools: Exploring age differences in usability. *Gerontechnology,
    4*, 128–140.

McArdle, J. J. (2009). Latent variable modeling of differences and changes with longitudinal data.
    Annual Review of Psychology, 60, 577–605.

Melenhorst, A., Rogers, W. A., & Bouwhuis, D. G. (2006). Older adults' motivated choice for techno-
    logical innovation: Evidence for benefit-driven selectivity. *Psychology and Aging, 21*, 190–195.

Miller, C. J., Marks, D. J., Miller, S. R., Berwid, O. G., Kera, E. C., Santra, A., et al. (2007). Brief report:
    Television viewing and risk for attention problems in preschool children. *Journal of Pediatric
    Psychology, 32*(4), 448–452.

Minsky, M. (1967). *Computation: Finite and infinite machines.* Englewood Cliffs, NJ: Prentice-Hall, Inc.

Morgan, I., & Rose, K. (2005). How genetic is school myopia? *Progress in Retinal and Eye Research, 24*, 1–38.

Morrow, D. G., & Rogers, W. A. (2008). Environmental support: An integrative framework. *Human Factors, 50*, 589–613.

Mynatt, E. D., Melenhorst, A. S., Fisk, A. D., & Rogers, W. A. (2004). Aware technologies for aging in place: Understanding user needs and attitudes. *IEEE Pervasive Computing, 3*, 36–41.

Nair, S. N., Czja, S. J., & Sharit, J. (2007). A multilevel modeling approach to examining individual differences in skill acquisition for a computer-based task. *Journal of Gerontology: Psychological Science, 62B*, 85–96.

Newell, A. (1990). *Unified theories of cognition.* Cambridge, MA: Harvard University Press.

Nisbett, R. E. (2005). Heredity, environment, and race differences in IQ: A commentary on Rushton and Jensen. *Psychology, Public Policy, and Law, 11*, 302–310.

Nores, M., Belfield, C. R., Barnett, W. S., & Schweinhart, L. (2005). Updating the economic impacts of the High/Scope Perry Preschool Program. *Educational Evaluation and Policy Analysis, 27*, 245–261.

Oakes, L. M. (2009). The "Humpty Dumpty Problem" in the study of early cognitive development: Putting the infant back together again. *Perspectives on Psychological Science, 4*, 352–358.

Obel, C., Henriksen, T. B., Dalsgaard, S., Linnet, K. M., Skajaa, E., Thomsen, P. H., et al. (2004). Does children's watching of television cause attention problems? Retesting the hypothesis in a Danish cohort. *Pediatrics, 114*(5), 1372–1373.

Papert S. (1980). *Mindstorms: Children, computers, and powerful ideas.* New York: Basic Books.

Papp, K. V., Walsh, S. J., & Snyder, P. J. (2009). Immediate and delayed effects of cognitive interventions in healthy elderly: A review of current literature and future directions. *Alzheimer's & Dementia, 5*, 50–60.

Pavlik, Jr., P. I., & Anderson, J. R. (2008). Using a model to compute the optimal schedule of practice. *Journal of Experimental Psychology: Applied, 14*, 101–117.

Petersson, K. M., Silva, C., Castro-Caldas, A., Ingvar, M., & Reis, A. (2007). Literacy: A cultural influence on functional left-right differences in the inferior parietal cortex. *European Journal of Neuroscience, 26*, 791–799.

Rainie, L., & Packel, D. (2001). More online, doing more. 16 million newcomers gain Internet access in the last half of 2000 as women, minorities, and families with modest incomes continue to surge online. Retrieved December 29, 2004, from *http://www.pewinternet.org/PPF/r/30/report_display.asp.*

Ramey, S. L., & Ramey, C. T. (1999). Early experience and early intervention for children "at risk" for developmental delay and mental retardation. *Mental Retardation and Developmental Disabilities Research Reviews, 5*, 1–10.

Rebok, G. W., Carlson, M. C., & Langbaum, J. B. S. (2007). Training and maintaining memory abilities in healthy older adults: Traditional and novel approaches. *Journal of Gerontology: Psychological Science, 62B*, 53–61.

Reynaldo, M. (1998). Nutrition and the worldwide rise in IQ scores. In U. Neisser (Ed.), *The Rising Curve: Long-term Gains in IQ and Related Measures* (pp. 183–206). Washington DC: American Psychological Association.

Rittle-Johnson, B., & Kmicikewycz, A. O. (2008). When generating answers benefits arithmetic skill: The importance of prior knowledge. *Journal of Experimental Child Psychology, 101*, 75–81.

Robinson, T. N. (1999). Reducing children's television viewing to prevent obesity: A randomized controlled trial. *Journal of the American Medical Association, 282*, 1561–1567.

Robinson, T. N., & Killen, J. D. (1995). Ethnic and gender differences in the relationships between television viewing and obesity, physical activity, and dietary fat intake. *Journal of Health Education, 26*, S91–S98.

Robinson, T. N., Hammer, L. D., Killen, J. D., Kramer, H. C., Wilson, D. M., Hayward, C., et al. (1993). Does television viewing increase obesity and reduce physical activity? Cross-sectional and longitudinal analyses among adolescent girls. *Pediatrics, 91*, 273–280.

Rogers, E. M. (2003). *Diffusion of innovations* (5th ed.). New York: Free Press.

Rogers, W. A., Stronge, A. J., & Fisk, A. D. (2006). Technology and aging. In R. S. Nickerson (Ed.), *Reviews of human factors and ergonomics* (Vol. 1, pp. 130–171). Santa Monica, CA: Human Factors and Ergonomics Society.

Roring, R. W., & Charness, N. (2007). A multilevel model analysis of expertise in chess across the lifespan. *Psychology and Aging, 22*, 291–299.

Salthouse, T. A. (1996). The processing-speed theory of adult age differences in cognition. *Psychological Review, 103,* 403–428.

Salthouse, T. A. (2010). *Major issues in cognitive aging.* Oxford: Oxford University Press.

Schaie, K. W. (1994). The course of adult intellectual development. *American Psychologist, 49,* 304–313.

Schmandt-Besserat, D. (1992). *Before writing, volume I: From counting to cuneiform.* Austin, TX: University of Texas Press.

Schmidt, M. E., Pempek, T. A., Kirkorian, H. L., Lund, A. F., & Anderson, D. R. (2008). The effects of background television on the toy play behavior of very young children. *Child Development, 79*(4), 1137–1151.

Schmitt, K. L., Dayanim, S., & Matthias, S. (2008). Personal homepage construction as an expression of social development. *Developmental Psychology, 44,* 496–506.

Schneider, W., & Bjorklund, D. (2003). Memory and knowledge development. In J. Valsiner & K. J. Connolly (Eds.), *Handbook of developmental psychology* (pp. 370–403). London: Sage.

Schneider, W., Gruber, H., Gold, A., & Opwis, K. (1993). Chess expertise and memory for chess positions in children and adults. *Journal of Experimental Child Psychology, 56,* 328–349.

Simon, H. A. (1974). How big is a chunk? *Science, 183,* 482–488.

Simonton, D. K. (1988). Age and outstanding achievement: What do we know after a century of research? *Psychological Bulletin, 104,* 251–267.

Singley, M. K., & Anderson, J. R. (1989). *The transfer of cognitive skill.* Cambridge, MA: Harvard University Press.

Slamecka, N. J., & Graf, P. (1978). The generation effect: Delineation of a phenomenon. *Journal of Experimental Psychology: Human Learning and Memory, 4,* 592–604.

Slavin, R. E. (1983). When does collaborative learning increase student achievement? *Psychological Bulletin, 94*(3), 429–445.

Slegers, K., van Boxtel, M. P. J., & Jolles, J. (2009). Effects of computer training and internet usage on cognitive abilities in older adults: a randomized controlled study. *Aging Clinical and Experimental Research, 21,* 43–54.

Smith, G. E., Housen, P., Yaffe, K., Ruff, R., Kennison, R. F., Mahncke, H. W., et al. (2009). A cognitive training program based on principles of brain plasticity: Results from the improvement in memory with plasticity-based adaptive cognitive training (IMPACT) study. *Journal of the American Geriatrics Society, 57,* 594–603.

Stern, Y. (2006). Cognitive reserve and Alzheimer's disease. *Alzheimers Disease and Associated Disorders, 20,* S69–S74.

Story, M., & Faulkner, P. (1990). The prime time diet: A content analysis of eating behavior and food messages in television program content and commercials. *American Journal of Public Health, 80,* 736–740.

Subrahmanyam, K., Greenfield, P., Kraut, R., & Gross, E. (2001). The impact of computer use on children's and adolescents' development. *Journal of Applied Developmental Psychology, 22*(1), 7–30.

Svirsky, M. A., Robbins, A. M., Kirk, K. I., Pisoni, D. B., & Miyamoto, R. T. (2000). Language development in profoundly deaf children with cochlear implants. *Psychological Science, 11,* 153–158.

Teasdale, T. W., & Owen, D. R. (1994). Thirty year secular trend in the cognitive abilities of Danish male school leavers at a high educational level. *Scandinavian Journal of Psychology, 35,* 328–335.

The UCLA Internet report—"Surveying the Digital Future" (2003). UCLA Center for Communication Policy, Box 951586, Los Angeles, CA 90095–1586. Retrieved August 14, 2003, from *http://www. ccp.ucla.edu/pdf/UCLA-Internet-Report-Year-Three.pdf.*

Thorndike, E. L. (1924). Mental discipline in high school studies. *Journal of Educational Psychology, 15,* 1–22, 83–98.

Tomasello M., & Farrar, M. J. (1986). Joint attention and early language. *Child Development, 57,* 1454–1463.

Touron, D. R., Hoyer, W. J., & Cerella, J. (2001). Cognitive skill acquisition and transfer in younger and older adults. *Psychology and Aging, 16,* 555–563.

Vandewater, E. A., Shim, M., & Caplovitz, A. G. (2004). Linking obesity and activity level with children's television and video game use. *Journal of Adolescence, 27,* 71–85.

Van den Bulck, J. (2000). Is television bad for your health? Behavior and body image of the adolescent "couch potato." *Journal of Youth and Adolescence, 29,* 273–288.

Venkatesh, V., & Davis, F. D. (2000). A theoretical extension of the technology acceptance model: Four longitudinal case studies. *Management Science, 46,* 186–204.

Weikart, D. P., Epstein, A. S., Schweinhart, L. J., & Bond, J. T. (1978). *The Ypsilanti Preschool Curriculum Demonstration Project: Preschool years and longitudinal results* (Monographs of the HighScope Educational Research Foundation, 4). Ypsilanti: HighScope Press.

Weiss, R., & Cerankosky, B. C. (2010). Effects of video-game ownership on young boys' academic and behavioral functioning: A randomized, controlled study. *Psychological Science* (Published online Feb. 18), *21*(4), 463–470.

Whitmer, R. A., Gunderson, E. P., Barrett-Connor, E., Quesenberry, E. P. Jr., & Yaffe, K. (2005). Obesity in middle age and future risk of based study dementia: A 27 year longitudinal population. *British Medical Journal, 330,* 1360–1362.

Winn, W. (2002). Current trends in educational technology research: The study of learning environments. *Educational Psychology Review, 14*(3), 331–351.

Zigler, E., & Trickett, P. K. (1978). IQ, social competence, and evaluation of early childhood intervention programs. *American Psychologist, 33,* 789–798.

Zimmerman, F. J., & Christakis, D. A. (2007). Associations between content types of early media exposure and subsequent attentional problems. *Pediatrics, 120*(5), 986–992.

Zimmerman, F. J., Christakis, D. A., & Meltzoff, A. N. (2007). Associations between media viewing and language development in children under age 2 years. *Journal of Pediatrics, 151*(4), 364–368.

Zimmerman, F. J., Gilkerson, J., Richards, J. A., Christakis, D. A., Xu, D. X., Gray, S., et al. (2009). Teaching by listening: The importance of adult-child conversations to language development. *Pediatrics, 124*(1), 342–349.

DEVELOPMENTAL COGNITIVE NEUROSCIENCE: INFANCY TO YOUNG ADULTHOOD

14

Bradley L. Schlaggar and Kelly Anne Barnes

INTRODUCTION

The first 2 decades of human development are marked by amazing changes in sensory, motor, and cognitive functions. Children become increasingly able to focus their attention, to understand and use language, and to form complex social relationships. These abilities, and untold others, emerge and develop at different rates throughout childhood and adolescence. Concurrently, there are dramatic changes in the brain's structure and function. Developmental cognitive neuroscience seeks to understand the neural mechanisms, and changes in these mechanisms, that result in continuity and change in behavior and cognition from infancy to adulthood.

Multiple methods have contributed to our understanding of brain and cognitive development. Much of our knowledge about prenatal and early postnatal development comes from studies of autopsied human brain tissue and from research with animals. In contrast, knowledge about changes in information processing in the developing brain primarily derives from in vivo neuroimaging and neurophysiological studies of children, adolescents, and adults. The application of noninvasive functional and structural neuroimaging methods to pediatric populations that began in the 1990s has allowed for a previously unimaginable look at the brains of typically developing children. Neuroimaging methods such as magnetic resonance imaging (MRI) and neurophysiological measures such as electroencephalography (EEG) allow scientists to probe structural and functional changes in the developing brain with high spatial (~millimeters) and temporal (~milliseconds) resolution. MRI and EEG are noninvasive, safe for use with pediatric subjects, and can be used repeatedly in the same individuals, allowing for longitudinal investigations.

Overview

In this chapter, we will explore what has been learned about development from cognitive neuroscience. This chapter begins by reviewing structural brain development, including research from animal and human models, although we focus primarily on human research. We include a discussion of prenatal brain development with the hope that this section will orient readers outside of the neurosciences to basic principles of neural structure and function. This section ends with a discussion of research that has attempted to account for heterogeneity in cognition by examining the relationship between individual differences in structural brain development and reading ability and intelligence. The next section discusses functional brain development. This section reviews functional MRI (fMRI) studies that examine developmental changes in recruitment of brain regions during cognitive task performance. The chapter ends with a discussion of future directions and general conclusions.

There are several topics that we do not address. First, we focus on studies examining typical development rather than developmental disorders. The study of typical and disordered development can be mutually informative. Indeed, understanding how brain development goes awry can further elucidate mechanisms of typical development (Karmiloff-Smith & Thomas, 2003). Second, we focus on neuroimaging rather than neurophysiology studies that use EEG and task-evoked changes in EEG (i.e., event-related potentials [ERP]). EEG and ERP have important strengths, such as superior temporal resolution relative to fMRI. Nonetheless, a comprehensive review of these topics is beyond the scope of this chapter.

Structural Changes in the Developing Brain

Research on brain development has a long history in neuroscience. In the late 19th century and early 20th century, scientists examined developmental changes in neurons (Ramón y Cajal, DeFelipe, & Jones, 1991) and glial cells (Flechsig, 1920) using histological methods in autopsied brain tissue. Remarkable inferences about development were made from observations of static tissue using cell staining techniques, and many of these insights were subsequently confirmed. A century later, neuroscientists began using modern brain imaging to characterize changes in brain volume and markers of gray and white matter. In this section, we detail several findings about structural brain development that have emerged from this research. We can only present a succinct review of developmental neurobiology in this chapter. The reader is referred to two books, Stiles (2008) and Nelson, De Haan, and Thomas (2006), which provide a thorough discussion of these topics.

Neurogenesis

The adult brain contains approximately 100 billion neurons. Neurogenesis refers to the processes by which these neurons are generated. Neurogenesis occurs prenatally (Bhardwaj et al., 2006) in specific regions of the developing nervous system termed proliferative zones. Genetic and molecular factors exert the greatest influences on neurogenesis (for review see Bystron, Blakemore, & Rakic, 2008). Around embryonic days 31–33 (Bystron, Rakic, Molnar, & Blakemore, 2006), neurogenesis begins when neuroepithelial cells in the ventricular zone begin dividing asymmetrically. This cell division produces one cell that will become a neuron or glial cell and another daughter progenitor cell, which can continue to divide to generate neurons and glia (Gotz & Huttner, 2005). Around gestational weeks 7–8, cell division in the ventricular zone gives rise to the subventricular zone, which is another proliferative zone. Around gestational weeks 25–27, the ventricular zone has reduced in size to a single layer of cells, and this reduction in size is thought to mark the end of neurogenesis in the ventricular zone. Neurogenesis in the subventricular zone continues throughout gestation (Bystron et al., 2008).

Postnatal neurogenesis has been documented in nonhuman primates, with neurons thought to originate in the adult subventricular zone and then migrate to several brain regions, including the olfactory bulb, the dentate gyrus of the hippocampus, and the cerebellum (Gould, 2007). However, the amount of postnatal neurogenesis is far less than the amount of prenatal neurogenesis and the functional significance of postnatal neurogenesis is still debated (Rakic, 2006).

Cortical Layers

Cortical neurons are arranged into distinct layers, which are defined by the presence or absence of cell types and the nature of the axonal and dendritic processes they contain. The adult neocortex is organized into six layers that begin to emerge prenatally. Very soon after the onset of neurogenesis, around embryonic days 31–33, neurons first aggregate in a transient structure termed the preplate. The preplate expands as more neurons migrate to this transient structure. As more neurons migrate to the preplate, the structure becomes heterogeneous, generating the marginal zone and the subplate. Neurons generated in ventricular zone migrate to the preplate, and eventually form the cortical plate between the marginal zone and the subplate. The first neurons arrive in the cortical plate starting approximately at embryonic day 50, although this may happen a few days later in other regions of the developing cortical plate (Bystron et al., 2008). Neurons radially migrate from proliferative zones to the cortical plate along radial glial cells in an "inside-out" sequence (for a review of radial glia development and function see Gotz & Barde, 2005). The earliest born neurons migrate from proliferative zones to the deepest neocortical layer, layer 6, and the latest born neurons migrate to more superficial neocortical layers (e.g., layer 2). The marginal zone ultimately becomes layer 1 of the neocortex (Zecevic & Rakic, 2001). The precise developmental changes in the intermediate and subplate zones are still an active area of investigation (Bystron et al., 2008). However, the subplate appears to be particularly important in the development of connections between the neocortex and other brain regions (e.g., the thalamus, Allendoerfer & Shatz, 1994).

Axonal Growth and Synaptogenesis

Neurons that leave proliferative zones and migrate to their neocortical target locations are not fully developed. Newly migrated neurons have not developed extensive axons and dendrites, the cellular processes that send and receive signals important for information processing. Developing neurons have a unique structure called the growth cone, which helps axons extend to their targets. Growth cones, first identified by Ramon y Cajal, sense chemical cues and respond by moving the axon toward or away from those cues (Luo & O'Leary, 2005). As the axon grows, collateral branches form along the axon and begin to extend toward their targets (Luo & O'Leary, 2005). Axon guidance via growth cones and collateral branching thus results in densely branched axons that reach a large number of targets.

Once axons reach their targets, they begin to form synapses with other neurons. Synaptogenesis changes both the presynaptic axons and the postsynaptic dendrites. The presynaptic axons develop nerve terminals, which can release neurotransmitters, the chemicals used in interneuronal signaling. Postsynaptic dendrites develop specialized regions of their membrane that contain neurotransmitter receptors.

Axonal Pruning and Synapse Elimination

During infancy and early childhood, an overabundance of synapses are formed. At the peak of synaptogenesis, thought to be around age 2 years, there are approximately 40% more synapses in a child's brain than in an adult's brain (Levitt, 2003). While new synapses continue to be formed throughout the life span, starting in the preschool years more synapses are eliminated than are formed. The elimination of synapses is presumed to result in more efficient information processing (Holtmaat & Svoboda, 2009). Two mechanisms, retraction and degeneration, underlie the elimination of axons, dendrites, and synapses over development. These processes can operate on small scales (e.g., affecting single synapses) or large scales (e.g., affecting entire axons; Luo & O'Leary, 2005).

Ocular Dominance Columns

Layers of cortical neurons are organized into columns that share response properties, as originally demonstrated by Mountcastle in the 1950s (for review see, Mountcastle, 1997). Beginning with seminal work by Hubel and Wiesel in the 1960s and 1970s, much has been learned about the development of cortical columns from the study of ocular dominance columns. In adults, neurons projecting from each eye's retina are separate as they pass through the lateral geniculate nucleus of the thalamus and remain separate (i.e., terminate on discrete loci) when they terminate in layer 4 of primary visual cortex in the occipital lobe. This mature organization, termed ocular dominance columns for the alternating columns of projections from each eye, develops postnatally in primates and reaches adult levels of organization around 6 weeks in nonhuman primates (LeVay, Wiesel, & Hubel, 1980).

Both intrinsic (e.g., genetic or molecular factors inherent to particular cortical areas) and extrinsic (e.g., patterned activity from other brain regions) factors shape the development of ocular dominance columns. Intrinsic factors are important in the early cortical patterning that gives rise to adult ocular dominance columns. Molecular cues guide the axons from the lateral geniculate nucleus to layer 4 in primary visual cortex. However, these cues appear to generate a coarse, cortical segregation of inputs from the two eyes (Katz & Crowley, 2002). Extrinsic factors, in the form of patterned activity from the thalamus, refine the developing ocular dominance columns after birth.

To understand the influence of patterned activity on ocular dominance column development, studies have employed a paradigm known as monocular deprivation. In monocular deprivation, an animal's eyelids are sewn shut to deprive one eye of visual input. When monocular deprivation occurs within the first few months of life, ocular dominance column organization changes. The number of cells that respond to stimulation from the sutured eye significantly decreases and the number of cells that respond to stimulation from the open eye significantly increases. Similarly, cortical columns associated with the sutured eye reduce in size, whereas cortical columns associated with the open eye expand. Later in development, however, the effects of monocular deprivation are not seen (LeVay et al., 1980). For instance, a year of monocular deprivation in an adult does not change ocular dominance column organization. This fundamental observation suggests that there is a sensitive period during which patterned activity yields the greatest influence on cortical column organization. Ocular dominance columns show remarkable plasticity during this sensitive period. Indeed, the effects of monocular deprivation are reversible if the sutured eye is reopened within the first 4–5 weeks of life (LeVay et al., 1980).

Cortical Areas

Multiple cortical columns constitute cortical areas. Cortical areas can be defined by their unique function (identified by lesion, neurophysiological, or neuroimaging methods), architectonics (distinctive cellular structure as seen with staining techniques and molecular properties), connectivity, and topography, properties that can be remembered with the acronym FACT (Felleman & Van Essen, 1991). Both intrinsic and extrinsic mechanisms influence the formation of cortical areas (O'Leary & Nakagawa, 2002; O'Leary, Schlaggar, Tuttle, 1994).

One example of how extrinsic factors contribute to cortical area development comes from an examination of input from a subcortical structure called the thalamus. Soon after birth, rodents develop discrete structures in their somatosensory cortex, termed barrels, that represent the whisker field on the rodent's snout. Schlaggar and O'Leary (1991) demonstrated the importance of input from thalamocortical afferents on the formation of barrel cortex. They transplanted a piece of embryonic cortex from the posterior section of the rat's brain, which typically would develop into visual cortex, and grafted it into the presumptive somatosensory cortex of a newborn rat. The grafted piece of cortex developed barrels, demonstrating that extrinsic factors (i.e., thalamic inputs) are important for cortical development, and in particular, for the differentiation of area-specific features.

While much of the early research on cortical area differentiation and development has focused on extrinsic factors such as thalamic input, there is now substantial evidence that intrinsic factors are the first to influence the development of cortical areas (O'Leary & Nakagawa, 2002). Some of these factors, such as genes expressed in the ventricular zone during neurogenesis, are expressed along gradients. For example, the genes *Pax6* and *Emx2* are differentially expressed in the ventricular zone, with *Pax6* expressed more rostrolaterally (toward the front and sides) than caudomedially (toward the back and middle) and *Emx2* expressed more caudomedially than rostrolaterally (O'Leary & Nakagawa, 2002). If the *Pax6* gene is turned off during development, using gene knockout rodents, cortical areas develop atypically, with the more rostral primary motor cortex reducing in size and the more caudal primary visual cortex expanding. In contrast, if the *Emx2* gene is turned off during development, primary visual cortex reduces in size and primary motor cortex expands in size. There is some evidence that these molecular factors may give rise to cortical areas that are optimally sized for the behaviors they support because both increasing and decreasing the size of mouse primary sensory and motor cortex by reducing or enhancing *Emx2* gene expression impaired sensorimotor behaviors (Leingartner et al., 2007). Thus, these studies provide evidence that intrinsic factors (e.g., genes expressed along gradients) influence the development of cortical areas and interact with extrinsic factors to yield sharply bordered cortical areas.

▨ NEUROIMAGING INVESTIGATIONS OF STRUCTURAL BRAIN DEVELOPMENT

Total Brain Volume

Overall brain volume increases rapidly from birth until school age and continues to increase through childhood, albeit at a much slower rate. At term birth, the brain is approximately one fourth to one third of adult volume (Toga, Thompson, & Sowell, 2006). By age 6 years, the brain is approximately 90–95% of adult volume (Giedd, 2004; Reiss, Abrams, Singer, Ross, & Denckla, 1996). By age 10 years, the brain reaches adult volume (Pfefferbaum et al., 1994). Thus, the majority of growth in brain volume occurs during infancy and toddlerhood. Given the evidence that most neurogenesis occurs prenatally, the dramatic growth in postnatal brain volume cannot be the result of the very small amount of postnatal neurogenesis. Rather, increases in total brain volume are thought to result from changes in the number of synapses, dendritic and axonal processes, increasing myelination, and vascularization.

One practical advantage of comparable brain volumes in school-age children and adults is that MRI data from children older than 7 years and MRI data from adults can be registered to a common anatomic frame of reference, without introducing spurious effects in fMRI analyses (Burgund et al., 2002). This is critical because registering subjects to a common anatomic frame of reference is a precursor to conducting direct comparisons (i.e., testing statistically for age-related differences) on MRI data, as done in most of the studies reported in the following section.

Regional Gray Matter Density

Gray matter density, as measured with MRI, is thought to indirectly quantify glia, vasculature, neurons, and their dendritic and synaptic processes (Gogtay et al., 2004). Accordingly, developmental changes in gray matter density could result from changes in any or all of these cells or cellular processes in different neocortical layers. The trajectories of developmental change in gray matter density of different brain areas can be compared to results from histological studies to determine the extent to which developmental change in gray matter density relates to neural changes (e.g., axonal extension or synapse formation that are characterized by an early increase and later decrease).

Gray matter density changes at different rates in different brain regions. Gogtay et al. (2004) followed 13 children and adolescents aged 4–21 years for nearly a decade, and conducted a longitudinal investigation of developmental changes in regional gray matter density. Regions in sensory and motor cortex reached adult-like levels of gray matter density earliest. In contrast, regions outside primary sensory and motor cortex, including lateral prefrontal, lateral parietal, and superior temporal gyrus, underwent a more protracted development, with gray matter density continuing to reduce throughout adolescence. By fitting the data to linear, quadratic, and cubic functions using mixed model regression, the authors quantified the rates of gray matter density change. These trajectories converge reasonably well with histological studies that suggests that synaptogenesis, one of the factors that would contribute to increases in gray matter density, peaks earlier in primary visual and primary auditory cortex than in frontal cortex (Huttenlocher, 1979; Huttenlocher & Dabholkar, 1997; Huttenlocher, de Courten, Garey, & Van der Loos, 1982).

Developmental changes in subcortical gray matter density also proceed at different rates for different regions. For instance, between ages 7–16 years, the lenticular nucleus, which includes the putamen and globus pallidus, and thalamus significantly decrease is size with age (after controlling for total brain volume), whereas the caudate decreases marginally, and decreases in the nucleus accumbens (the ventral portion of the caudate and putamen) were not statistically significant (Sowell, Trauner, Gamst, & Jernigan, 2002). Overall, this body of research indicates that brain regions continue to develop throughout childhood and adolescence and that their development is heterochronous.

Myelination

Approximately 10% of the cells in the nervous system are neurons; the remaining 90% of cells are collectively referred to as glia. In the central nervous system, glial cells called oligodendrocytes wrap axons in myelin, a substance which insulates the neurons. Myelination increases the rate at which action potentials travel along an axon, sometimes leading to a 100-fold increase in conduction speed (Toga et al., 2006). Accordingly, changes in myelination over development can potentially have dramatic effects on information processing in the brain.

Myelination is a progressive process throughout childhood and adolescent development. Myelination is heterochronous, starting at different times and proceeding at different rates for different white matter tracts. Myelination of spinal cord, brainstem, and midbrain axons begins prenatally and reaches adult levels within the first year of life (Yakovlev & Lecours, 1967). Excepting intracortical white matter tracts and the reticular formation, most myelination is complete by age 4 years (Yakovlev & Lecours, 1967). However, intracortical myelination, which begins approximately in the first postnatal year, proceeds linearly throughout childhood and adolescence (Yakovlev & Lecours, 1967). By age 20 years, males are estimated to have approximately 176,000 km of myelinated axons and females are estimated to have approximately 149,000 km of myelinated axons (Marner, Nyengaard, Tang, & Pakkenberg, 2003).

Diffusion tensor imaging (DTI) indirectly quantifies the degree to which axons are myelinated, and allows for a noninvasive examination of developmental changes in myelination over the course of development. DTI quantifies the degree to which water molecules are able to diffuse isotropically (i.e., equally in all directions) in the brain. If axons, particularly myelinated axons, are present, water molecules cannot diffuse freely—their movement is constrained by myelin and diffusion is anisotropic (i.e., to different extents in different directions). However, myelin may not be the only factor that influences anisotropy values. Developmental increases in axonal diameter may also increase anisotropy (Perrin et al., 2008). DTI studies of term infants concur with histological research, and have revealed early maturing white matter (e.g., posterior limb of the internal capsule, Huppi et al., 1998) and late maturing intracortical white matter. DTI studies have consistently documented that cortical anisotropy increases with age prenatally through adulthood (Cascio, Gerig, & Piven, 2007).

Similar to reports of regional variability in the developmental trajectories of cortical and subcortical gray matter density measures, DTI measures for different white matter tracts change at different rates over development. For example, the rate of change in DTI measures in the anterior portions of the corpus callosum were less steep (i.e., continued to change over a longer developmental window) than posterior portions of the corpus callosum (Snook, Paulson, Roy, Phillips, & Beaulieu, 2005).

Functional Network Organization

Resting-state functional connectivity MRI examines correlations in slow, low-frequency (i.e., < ~0.1 Hz) fluctuations in spontaneous brain activity, as measured with the blood oxygenation level–dependent (BOLD[1]) signal. These correlations are thought to reflect the degree to which regions are co-activated (Fair et al., 2007). It is important to note that resting-state functional connectivity MRI is not an index of anatomical connectivity, as there are regions (e.g., in visual cortex) that are functionally connected but not mono-synaptically connected (Vincent et al., 2007).

Resting-state correlations can be examined to identify the organization of functional networks across development. Infant studies suggest that functional network organization is mostly "local," that is, regions are most strongly functionally connected with anatomically proximal regions (Fransson et al., 2007, 2009; Liu, Flax, Guise, Sukul, & Benasich, 2008). Functional network organization changes over childhood and adolescent development. Language used to describe synaptogenesis and synapse elimination provides useful metaphors for thinking about developmental changes in functional connectivity. In this parlance, many local functional connections between anatomically proximal regions "grow down" and functional connectivity becomes weaker with age between these regions. In contrast, many long-range functional connections between anatomically distant regions (e.g., regions in lateral frontal and parietal cortex) "grow up" and become more strongly functionally connected with age (Fair et al., 2007, 2008, 2009). Thus, early data from this method suggests that functional network organization changes from a "local" to a "distributed" organization over childhood and adolescent development.

Despite differences in regional patterns of functional connectivity, both children and adults' functional networks have "small-world" organization. Small-world organization can be determined using methods from a branch of mathematics called graph theory. In this method, brain regions of interest are considered to be functionally connected if the correlation coefficient between brain regions exceeds a particular value (e.g., Pearson's $r > .1$). Small-world networks have high clustering coefficients (where brain regions that are functionally connected to a particular brain region are also functionally connected to each other) and short average path length (where you can get from one brain region to any other by traversing a small number of functional connections). Small-world organization allows for efficient local and distributed processing (Watts & Strogatz, 1998), characterizes adult brain network organization (Sporns & Zwi, 2004), and gives rise to complex dynamics (Sporns, Tononi, & Edelman, 2000). Functional networks in children and adults displayed small world organization, indicated by a high clustering coefficient and a short average path length (Fair et al., 2008, 2009). These findings await independent

---

[1] The BOLD signal is a hemodynamic (i.e., related to blood flow) measure of the ratio of oxygenated to deoxygenated hemoglobin in the brain. Changes in blood flow alter the ratio of oxygenated to deoxygenated hemoglobin, and therefore alter the BOLD signal. It is important to note that while the BOLD signal relates to brain activity, it is not homologous to the firing rates of single neurons, but is more highly correlated with local field potentials and multiunit activity. For a comprehensive review of the physiologic underpinnings of the BOLD signal, see Raichle and Mintun (2006).

replication across a range of ages, although Supekar, Musen, and Menon (2009) have replicated findings of small world organization in children aged 7–9 years and in young adults. Combining resting state functional connectivity MRI and graph theory shows promise as a means to examine functional network organization over development.

Relating Structural and Cognitive Changes Over Development

Understanding the sources of heterogeneity is a fundamental objective of developmental science. Developmental cognitive neuroscientists seek to understand the relationship between individual differences in behavior and cognition and neural measures. Several convergent findings have emerged from these investigations. First, DTI studies have revealed that individual differences in left temporoparietal white matter microstructure are related to reading abilities (for review see Schlaggar & McCandliss, 2007). Correlations between left temporoparietal white matter microstructure and reading ability are seen across a range of reading abilities (Beaulieu et al., 2005; Deutsch et al., 2005; Klingberg et al., 2000; Niogi & McCandliss, 2006). These effects are thought to be localized to portions of the superior corona radiata, a white matter tract that projects from the internal capsule to left motor and premotor regions.

Second, individual differences in intelligence relate to developmental trajectories of gray matter changes, measured using cortical thickness estimates. Shaw et al. (2006) tested whether trajectories of change in cortical thickness in particular brain regions differed across children and adolescents with superior intelligence (IQ = 121–149), high intelligence (IQ = 109–120), and average intelligence (IQ = 83–108). In several regions, including regions in superior frontal gyrus and middle frontal gyrus, trajectories of change in cortical thickness measures were found to relate to differences in IQ. Specifically, children with superior intelligence were found to have initially smaller cortical thickness values, which rapidly increased throughout childhood and then decreased throughout adolescence. Unlike the relationships between reading ability and white matter measures, these effects await independent replication and examination in children with below average intelligence. However, the approach employed by Shaw et al. (2006), relating trajectories of neural change over development to behavioral measures, may be particularly informative (Thomas et al., 2009).

Task-Evoked Recruitment of Multiple Brain Regions Changes Over Development

Over childhood and adolescent development, sensory, motor, cognitive, linguistic, and social processing matures. The developmental trajectories across tasks that tap into these domains vary. For instance, the abilities to initiate, inhibit, or maintain information related to eye movements mature along different trajectories throughout childhood and adolescence (Luna, Garver, Urban, Lazar, & Sweeney, 2004). Performance on tasks that require attentional control and involve manual responses to targets presented in different contexts (e.g., with or without distractors) also reaches adult-like levels at different ages for different tasks (Rueda et al., 2004).

Reliable findings regarding developmental change in the neural correlates of cognitive, linguistic, and social behaviors are hard to come by. It has been 15 years since the first fMRI study examining children was published (Casey et al., 1995), but we still do not understand how task-evoked recruitment of brain regions changes over development. Few areas of research have used comparable tasks across labs, allowing for a synthesis of findings related to the developmental changes in functional brain responses. We highlight one such area in the section entitle Face Processing and Ventral Visual Cortex.

For most of developmental cognitive neuroscience, variability across studies is partly to blame for the slow rate of progress. Task parameters, subject age, control for performance differences, experimental design, and analytic strategy vary widely across studies, precluding the use of meta-analytic techniques to identify reliable effects (Church, Petersen, & Schlaggar, 2010; Palmer, Brown, Petersen, & Schlaggar, 2004). Developmental differences in task performance, particularly accuracy, can have insidious effects on task-evoked responses measured with fMRI because even a single response error can introduce spurious fMRI activation (Murphy & Garavan, 2004). Thus, separately modeling error trials is imperative, and more rigorous measures such as performance matching (Brown et al., 2005; Schlaggar et al., 2002) may further allow age-related effects to be distinguished from performance-related effects. The last three sections highlight approaches that have potential to improve the study of functional brain development. Briefly, the highlighted studies variously employ estimating events of interest relative to baseline (e.g., fixation) rather than employing a subtraction method[2] and performance matching, which collectively ought to reduce confounds and lead to more interpretable data. Accordingly, the titles for the last three sections reflect both a cognitive domain and a methodological issue addressed within the section.

Face Processing and Ventral Visual Cortex

Research in adult lesion and neuroimaging studies and nonhuman primates emphasizes the importance of ventral visual cortex for object coding (Connor, Brincat, & Pasupathy, 2007; Grill-Spector & Malach, 2004). In adults, a region in right mid-fusiform gyrus shows greater responses to pictures or movies of faces relative to other visual stimuli (e.g., other body parts or houses, Kanwisher, McDermott, & Chun, 1997) although right mid-fusiform gyrus is not the only region in ventral visual cortex that provides information that is important for face processing (Haxby et al., 2001). An interesting developmental question is whether the task-evoked response to faces relative to other object categories in right mid-fusiform gyrus differs between children and adults because children display poorer face processing skills (e.g., face recognition, Carey, Diamond, & Woods, 1980) than adults. We review the evidence for developmental changes in right mid-fusiform gyrus activation during face processing. We do not imply that developmental changes in this region are the only, or the

---

[2] The subtraction method assumes that responses (e.g., reaction times or task-evoked BOLD signals in fMRI experiments) can be decomposed into additive stages or processing components which are completed serially (see Posner, 1978) and that a particular stage or processing component can be isolated. The validity of the subtraction method hinges upon several factors including the extent to which processing is serial rather than parallel and does not involve feedback.

most important, changes that underlie the development of face processing. Merely, we highlight this region as it has been probed with comparable paradigms across a wide age range.

Evidence from fMRI studies suggests that the neural correlates of face processing in right mid-fusiform gyrus undergo a protracted development. In the youngest children studied, aged 5–8 years, there were no significant differences in the BOLD response for faces relative to other object categories including fruits and vegetables and manufactured objects (Gathers, Bhatt, Corbly, Farley, & Joseph, 2004; Scherf, Behrmann, Humphreys, & Luna, 2007). Both studies involved a relatively small number of subjects (n = ~11 per group), which raises concerns that null findings within the youngest children could stem from a lack of statistical power[3]. In middle childhood, ages 7–12 years in the following studies, a differential BOLD response was seen in right mid-fusiform gyrus for faces relative to other visual object categories (Gathers et al., 2004; Golarai et al., 2007; Peelen, Glaser, Vuilleumier, & Eliez, 2009, but see Aylward et al., 2005). However, it is unclear whether the magnitude of signal in this region differs between children, adolescents, and adults, as findings are mixed across studies. Data from Golarai et al. (2007) revealed a right mid-fusiform response for both adults and children. In this study there were no significant interactions in right mid-fusiform response amplitudes for age by stimulus type (e.g., faces, objects). By adolescence, ages 12–17 years in the following studies, a reliable response to faces relative to other object categories was seen in right mid-fusiform gyrus, and this response did not differ between adolescents and adults (Golarai et al., 2007; Peelen et al., 2009; Scherf et al., 2007). Thus, the right mid-fusiform response to faces relative to other visual object categories changes with age and reaches adult-like levels by adolescence. Further work is needed to identify the influence of developmental improvements in task performance on age-related changes in ventral visual cortex.

Attentional Processing and Estimating Events of Interest Separately

Models and theories of attention describe the systems that people use to exert control over sensory and motor processes. Understanding the neural changes that give rise to improvements in attentional control is important because children show remarkable improvements in attentional control throughout infancy and into childhood (Rueda et al., 2004). Most models and theories agree that attention can be divided into multiple independent subsystems (Fan, McCandliss, Fossella, Flombaum, & Posner, 2005) that rely on distinct neural mechanisms (Corbetta & Shulman, 2002; Posner & Petersen, 1990). We focus on developmental research that stems from a three subsystem model of attention originally outlined by Posner and Petersen (1990). In this model, alerting, orienting, and executive control are considered distinct attentional subsystems. Understanding how the neural correlates of these subsystems change

---

[3] Statistically reliable effects in young children were found for the face vs. object contrast in other brain regions in ventral visual cortex, including a more posterior region in right fusiform gyrus (Scherf et al., 2007) and left and right occipital cortex (Gathers et al., 2004), which suggests that the studies had enough power to detect some within group effects. See *Statistical Power for Group Comparisons* (this chapter) for a discussion of statistical power in between-groups comparisons.

over development will allow for a more precise assessment of the neural basis of attention in childhood.

Konrad et al. (2005) examined the neural correlates of alerting, reorienting, and executive control of attention in 16 children aged 8–12 years and 16 adults aged 20–34 years using an attention battery (Fan, McCandliss, Sommer, Raz, & Posner, 2002) that combined a cued reaction time task (Posner, 1980) and a Flanker task (Eriksen & Eriksen, 1974). Participants determined whether the middle arrow of five vertical arrows pointed left or right. To assess alerting, trials with a nonspatial warning cue were compared to trials without a warning cue. To assess reorienting, trials with a valid spatial cue were compared to trials with an invalid spatial cue. To assess executive control of attention, trials where the flanking arrows pointed in the same direction as the target were compared to trials where the flanking arrows pointed in the opposite direction as the target. Children showed smaller alerting effects than adults and larger reorienting and executive control effects, indicating that attentional control was immature in the child group. Error trials were omitted from fMRI analyses; no performance matching was conducted.

fMRI data suggested that developmental differences in the neural correlates of attentional processing were task specific (Konrad et al., 2005). For example, developmental differences during the alerting task were seen in anterior cingulate cortex, with adults showing a large positive alerting effect and children failing to show an alerting effect in this region. However, no developmental differences for the reorienting or executive control tasks were reported in the anterior cingulate. For the reorienting task, in a region near right temporoparietal junction, adults showed greater activation than did children, who did not show significant activation in this region. In contrast, children showed greater reorienting effects than adults in a region in left superior frontal gyrus. During the executive attention task, adults showed greater effects than children in regions in left superior parietal cortex and right inferior frontal gyrus, whereas children showed greater effects than adults in another region in left superior frontal gyrus and right superior temporal gyrus. Together, these studies suggest that frontal and parietal regions show developmental differences in the neural correlates of attentional control, but that the precise loci of differences may vary by task.

The conclusions that can be drawn from Konrad and colleagues result in part from the analytic approach they used, which involved estimating the task-evoked responses associated with each event type. These conclusions would have been more difficult to make had the authors used the subtraction method (e.g., cue–no cue in the alerting task) because it would be difficult to determine whether developmental differences were caused by differences in evoked response associated with the task of interest or the lower level task (i.e., the "task B problem," Church et al., 2010; Palmer et al., 2004). Further, Konrad and colleagues' experiment raises an interesting issue for further developmental research. While the neural correlates of alerting, orienting, and executive control are thought to be distinct in adults, it is unknown when this distinction emerges. This issue could be assessed in future research by conducting direct comparisons between attention tasks across development (e.g., testing for task by age group interactions) to identify regions in which developmental differences were task-specific.

Inhibition of Eye Movements and Examining Task-Evoked Timecourses

The neural basis of targeted eye movements, termed saccades, have been studied in a range of human and nonhuman animal systems. There is a rich literature involving lesion, neuroimaging, neuropsychological, behavioral, and electrophysiological studies that have helped inform the development of the neural basis of eye movements (Luna, Velanova, & Geier, 2008).

Velanova, Wheeler, and Luna (2009) examined developmental changes in the neural correlates of inhibiting and executing eye movements using an fMRI design called the mixed block event-related design. This fMRI design allows for separate analysis of sustained BOLD signals (thought to relate to maintaining a task set) and transient BOLD signals (thought to relate to moment-to-moment or online processing). Velanova and colleagues examined sustained and transient signals on the antisaccade task, in which participants view a stimulus that appears briefly in the periphery, inhibit a saccade toward that visual target, and then make a saccade in the opposite direction. Performance on the antisaccade task improved with age over three developmental groups: children (n = 26, 8–12 years), adolescents (n = 25, 13–17 years), and adults (n = 26, 18–27 years). Error trials were modeled separately; no performance matching was conducted.

Velanova et al. (2009) documented changes in sustained and transient signals in frontal and parietal regions. The pattern of developmental change differed across regions and signal type i.e., sustained and transient. In three regions, left anterior prefrontal cortex, right dorsolateral prefrontal cortex, and a region that extended from right anterior supramarginal gyrus into superior temporal gyrus, sustained activation decreased with age (i.e., adults showed smaller sustained activations than adolescents, and adolescents showed smaller sustained activations than children). Children also showed sustained deactivations in regions not recruited by adults, including bilateral precuneus. In three frontal regions, children showed transient activations that were not present in adolescents or adults. Different patterns of developmental change in transient signals were seen in other regions. A right inferior parietal region was not activated by children, was deactivated by adolescents, and was activated by adults. A paracentral region was not activated by children, and was deactivated by adolescents and adults. These patterns of developmental change suggest that the relationship between age and recruitment of a particular brain region is complex. It is overly simplistic to suggest that development is characterized by global increases or decreases in recruitment of brain regions in children relative to adults.

One limitation of the Velanova study is that the relationship between age, performance, and recruitment of brain regions was not explored. It is unclear whether the differences between children, adolescents, and adults related to age or performance. We next discuss a study that has attempted to tease apart age and performance effects on functional activation in the domain of language.

Language and Performance Matching

One of the most remarkable developmental achievements is language acquisition. Understanding the neural mechanisms that give rise to increasingly proficient language production and comprehension is of great interest to neuroscientists, linguists, educators, and parents alike. One of the most studied measures of language processing and production is controlled lexical association, in which participants are presented with a word and are then required to generate another word in response. Controlled lexical association tasks have a long history in cognitive neuroscience, dating back to an early neuroimaging study conducted with positron emission tomography by Petersen, Fox, Posner, Mintun, and Raichle (1988).

To study the neural correlates of language, Brown et al. (2005) examined a large cohort of child, adolescent, and adult subjects during performance of controlled lexical association tasks. Ninety-five subjects aged 7–32 years performed three tasks: (1) verb generation in response to a noun, (2) opposite generation, and (3) rhyme generation. Stimuli were presented both visually and aurally in separate sets, and subjects provided spoken responses. To examine effects of age without the potentially confounding influence of performance, Brown and colleagues generated two cohorts of child and adult subjects, "performance matched" and "performance nonmatched." Performance matched and nonmatched cohorts did not differ along other dimensions such as intelligence or sex. Error trials were modeled separately to further control for performance related effects. We focus on regions showing age-related effects, where activation differed across performance matched cohorts.

Age-related effects were identified in all lobes of the brain. However, the precise nature of the effects varied across regions. Some frontal regions showed increasing activation with age (i.e., they "grew up"), whereas other frontal regions showed decreasing activation with age (i.e., they "grew down"). Similar results were found in parietal cortex, where some regions "grew up" and others "grew down". These results are similar to the findings of Konrad et al. (2005) and Velanova et al. (2009), in that both increases and decreases in activation during task performance with age were found across the brain. However, this study extends previous work by carefully excluding the confounding influence of performance differences between children and adults.

FUTURE DIRECTIONS

Improved experimental design and analytic techniques will improve the ability to integrate findings across labs and lead to a clearer picture of the neural mechanisms of developmental change. Design elements such as performance matching and comparing conditions to a baseline rather than employing subtraction techniques are likely to improve the interpretability of developmental cognitive neuroscience studies (Church et al., 2010; Palmer et al., 2004). In addition, there are many cognitive domains that are ripe for exploration. In this section, we will discuss issues regarding statistical power in group comparisons and point out gaps in the literature.

Statistical Power for Group Comparisons

A major concern in scientific research regards appropriately rejecting the null hypothesis. In most developmental cognitive neuroscience research, the null hypothesis is that different age groups do not differ along some neural index or that age does not vary with such measures. Failing to reject the null hypothesis when it is in fact false (i.e., a Type II error) would thus involve concluding that there are no developmental differences when differences exist.

Power analyses conducted in our lab on fMRI data (using data from Brown et al., 2005) suggests that scans from 20 children and 20 adults would be needed to detect a 0.1% BOLD signal difference between groups with an alpha of .05 and power of .88 (Table 14.1). For rs-fcMRI analyses (using data from Fair et al., 2008), 40 children and 40 adults would be needed to detect a .1 difference in Pearson's r between groups with an alpha of .05 and power of .84 (see Table 14.2). We emphasize that these estimates would depend on the nature of the task-evoked response under investigation (e.g., its magnitude). Thus, the provided tables should be considered as examples tied to particular tasks and designs rather than hard and fast rules.

Conducting MRI research with pediatric populations can be laborious as data is often lost or unusable (e.g., because of subject motion or failure to complete behavioral tasks). Researchers, therefore, must anticipate the amount of data to be lost given the ages studied when designing studies (see Yerys et al., 2009). For example, studies involving 7- to 9-year-old subjects could expect a success rate across an fMRI battery (all of the runs in an fMRI session) to be around 70% (Yerys et al., 2009). If an experimenter wanted fMRI batteries from 20 children aged 7–9 years and 20 adults, then the experimenter would need to scan approximately 30 children aged 7–9 years

TABLE 14.1

A Power Analysis Based on Brown et al. (2005) to Detect a Group Difference of 0.1% BOLD Signal Change in an Event-Related fMRI Paradigm

Percent BOLD Signal Change				
Sample SD	Group 1, n = 20	Group 2, n = 20	Power (α .05)	Power (α .02)
0.05	0.1	0.2	1.0	1.0
0.075	0.1	0.2	0.98	0.97
0.1	**0.1**	**0.2**	**0.88**	**0.79**
0.15	0.1	0.2	0.55	0.41
0.2	0.1	0.2	0.35	0.22
0.25	0.1	0.2	0.24	0.14
Sample SD	Group 1, n = 30	Group 2, n = 30	Power (α .05)	Power (α .02)
0.05	0.1	0.2	1.0	1.0
0.075	0.1	0.2	0.99	0.99
0.1	**0.1**	**0.2**	**0.97**	**0.93**
0.15	0.1	0.2	0.73	0.60
0.2	0.1	0.2	0.49	0.34
0.25	0.1	0.2	0.34	0.21
Sample SD	Group 1, n = 40	Group 2, n = 40	Power (α .05)	Power (α .02)
0.05	0.1	0.2	1.0	1.0
0.075	0.1	0.2	1.0	1.0
0.1	**0.1**	**0.2**	**0.99**	**0.98**
0.15	0.1	0.2	0.84	0.74
0.2	0.1	0.2	0.60	0.46
0.25	0.1	0.2	0.43	0.29

The scenarios are for 20, 30, and 40 subjects with varying standard deviations (SD) bracketed around an expected SD of 0.1.

TABLE 14.2

A Power Analysis Based on Fair et al. (2008) to Detect a Group Difference in Correlation Coefficient of 0.1 in rs-fcMRI				
rs-fcMRI Correlation Coefficient				
Sample SD	Group 1, n = 20	Group 2, n = 20	Power (α .05)	Power (α .02)
0.05	0.1	0.2	1.0	1.0
0.075	0.1	0.2	0.98	0.97
0.1	0.1	0.2	0.88	0.79
0.15	**0.1**	**0.2**	**0.55**	**0.41**
0.2	0.1	0.2	0.35	0.22
0.25	0.1	0.2	0.24	0.14
Sample SD	Group 1, n = 30	Group 2, n = 30	Power (α .05)	Power (α .02)
0.05	0.1	0.2	1.0	1.0
0.075	0.1	0.2	0.99	0.99
0.1	0.1	0.2	0.97	0.93
0.15	**0.1**	**0.2**	**0.73**	**0.60**
0.2	0.1	0.2	0.49	0.34
0.25	0.1	0.2	0.34	0.21
Sample SD	Group 1, n = 40	Group 2, n = 40	Power (α .05)	Power (α .02)
0.05	0.1	0.2	1.0	1.0
0.075	0.1	0.2	1.0	1.0
0.1	0.1	0.2	0.99	0.98
0.15	**0.1**	**0.2**	**0.84**	**0.74**
0.2	0.1	0.2	0.60	0.46
0.25	0.1	0.2	0.43	0.29
Convention follows Table 14.1.				

to account for the expected failure rate. Ignoring children's lower success rates when designing and budgeting a study is costly, yielding either decreased statistical power or unplanned scanning costs.

Gaps in the Literature

Compared with the study of adult cognition, developmental cognitive neuroscience has emphasized different cognitive domains. For instance, there has been a relatively large amount of developmental research on response inhibition and executive attention. Many other aspects of cognitive neuroscience await exploration in development with fMRI. For example, working memory has been heavily investigated in children (Brahmbhatt, McAuley, & Barch, 2008; Bunge & Wright, 2007; Casey et al., 1995; Crone, Wendelken, Donohue, van Leijenhorst, & Bunge, 2006; Kwon, Reiss, & Menon, 2002; Scherf, Sweeney, & Luna, 2006; Thomas et al., 1999), but episodic memory remains relatively understudied (but see Ofen et al., 2007). The relative paucity of investigations of episodic memory is perplexing because understanding the neural mechanisms of learning and memory development may have important implications for educational practice and public policy. Another lopsidedness in the literature surrounds the study of attentional control, where investigations into executive attention greatly outnumber investigations of orienting and alerting. This is not to say that developmental cognitive neuroscience research lags behind its adult peers in all arenas. For example, social cognitive neuroscience is a relatively new area of research that is being actively investigated in adults (Frith & Frith, 2007), children, and adolescents (Burnett & Blakemore, 2009).

The influences of social institutions on brain and cognitive development are beginning to be explored. In one large-scale project, a team of developmental cognitive neuroscientists supported by the John D. and Catherine T. MacArthur Foundation are examining the effects of institutionalization and randomized controlled foster placement on developmental outcomes (Zeanah et al., 2003). Another growing area of research examines the relationship between socioeconomic status and neurological outcomes (Hackman & Farah, 2009). These nascent lines of research will likely have important implications for public policy on human development.

While the majority of pediatric MRI research focuses on school-age children and adolescents, several methods may make pediatric neuroimaging more suitable for younger subjects. Researchers interested in studying task-evoked responses with fMRI can consider employing two methods. First, pediatric subjects can be "trained" to be more still in the scanner using operant conditioning during movie viewing in a mock scanner (i.e., an environment similar to an MRI, but without a magnet). Excessive motion (e.g., > 2 mm) captured by sensors stops the movie, providing prompt feedback about movement (Epstein et al., 2007). Second, researchers can consider acquiring fMRI data during natural sleep. However, this method is only suitable for passive presentation of stimuli or for collection of resting-state functional connectivity MRI. Moving beyond MRI methods, functional near infrared spectroscopy (fNIRS) is a noninvasive optical imaging method that, like fMRI, measures hemodynamic signals in the brain but is more accommodating of subject motion. Currently, fNIRS methods only provide coverage of restricted patches of superficial brain tissue, although researchers are actively pursuing methods to increase coverage (e.g., Zeff, White, Dehghani, Schlaggar, & Culver, 2007). However, these methods are currently being applied to developmental questions (e.g., face processing, Otsuka et al., 2007). Collectively, these methods may allow researchers better access to studying the neural basis of cognitive development in infancy and toddlerhood.

Testing and Refining Theoretical Perspectives

One of the major challenges of developmental cognitive neuroscience is mapping structural and functional changes in the brain to behavioral and cognitive changes during development. Thus, another future direction for developmental cognitive neuroscience is the generation of falsifiable theories that can be tested and refined with further experiments. Johnson (2001) has outlined three theories that have been invoked or implied to explain developing relationships between brain and behavior. Briefly, these theories variously emphasize distinct neural mechanisms of developmental change: intraregional change (the "maturational" account, where changes in a single brain region are used to explain developmental changes), intra- and interregional changes (the "interactive-specialization" account, where changes in a collection of brain regions and the connections between these regions are used to explain developmental change), and performance dependent changes (the "skill-learning account," where different brain regions support behavior at different stages in skill acquisition).

Studies that can assess developmental trajectories will be critical in adjudicating between and testing these theories. In some areas, such as structural brain development and functional network organization, researchers have strived to quantify trajectories of development. This approach has been applied to a lesser extent in functional neuroimaging research (but see Rubia et al., 2006, and Brown et al., 2005). Much has been and can be learned about developmental cognitive neuroscience from between-groups comparisons (e.g., children vs. adults). However, generating the functions or models that characterize development (e.g., using such methods as growth curve modeling) and identifying individual variability in these trajectories remains an essential future direction for the field (Thomas et al., 2009).

Microgenetic designs, where researchers sample behavior across multiple sessions during suspected periods of rapid change and closely observe trial-wise responses (Siegler & Crowley, 1991), may provide a means to test skill-learning hypotheses. Microgenetic studies generally examine development on a much smaller timescale than cross-sectional or longitudinal studies (e.g., days and months vs. months and years). Unlike cross-sectional and longitudinal designs, microgenetic designs have not been used in developmental cognitive neuroscience. Practical constraints are likely at play. Trial-wise estimates of brain activity could be extracted with a slow event-related design, but this design prolongs scan time and could be prohibitive for younger subjects. Microgenetic designs would also involve repeated scanning, which requires scanner time and money. However, under particular circumstances (e.g., a period of rapid change occurring in an age group that could tolerate longer MRI sessions), microgenetic designs could be incorporated into developmental cognitive neuroscience.

CONCLUSIONS

Developmental cognitive neuroscience research has begun to reveal several principles of brain development. First, changes in the brain are widespread during development, affecting all lobes of the brain and the connections between them. These changes affect both intraregional structure and function, and interregional connectivity. Second, neural changes proceed at different rates for different brain regions. Third, functional neuroimaging studies reveal that the neural correlates of cognitive, linguistic, and social processing change with age. However, the precise nature of the relationship between behavioral and cognitive and neural changes is complicated. Integrating the observed structural and functional changes in the developing brain with behavioral and cognitive markers of development remains a great challenge.

ACKNOWLEDGMENT

This work was supported by the National Institutes of Health NS0534250 (BLS) and NS007205–28 (KAB). The authors thank Jessica A. Church, Cynthia Berg, and an anonymous reviewer for their thoughtful comments on this chapter.

REFERENCES

Allendoerfer, K. L., & Shatz, C. J. (1994). The subplate, a transient neocortical structure: Its role in the development of connections between thalamus and cortex. *Annual Review of Neuroscience, 17*, 185–218.

Aylward, E. H., Park, J. E., Field, K. M., Parsons, A. C., Richards, T. L., Cramer, S. C., et al. (2005). Brain activation during face perception: Evidence of a developmental change. *Journal of Cognitive Neuroscience, 17*, 308–319.

Beaulieu, C., Plewes, C., Paulson, L. A., Roy, D., Snook, L., Concha, L., et al. (2005). Imaging brain connectivity in children with diverse reading ability. *NeuroImage, 25*, 1266–1271.

Bhardwaj, R. D., Curtis, M. A., Spalding, K. L., Buchholz, B. A., Fink, D., Bjork-Eriksson, T., et al. (2006). From the cover: Neocortical neurogenesis in humans is restricted to development. *Proceedings of National Academy of Sciences, 103*, 12564–12568.

Brahmbhatt, S. B., McAuley, T., & Barch, D. M. (2008). Functional developmental similarities and differences in the neural correlates of verbal and nonverbal working memory tasks. *Neuropsychologia, 7*, 1020–1031.

Brown, T. T., Lugar, H. M., Coalson, R. S., Miezin, F. M., Petersen, S. E., & Schlaggar, B. L. (2005). Developmental changes in human cerebral functional organization for word generation. *Cerebral Cortex, 15*, 275–290.

Bunge, S. A., & Wright, S. B. (2007). Neurodevelopmental changes in working memory and cognitive control. *Current Opinion in Neurobiology, 17*, 243–250.

Burgund, E. D., Kang, H. C., Kelly, J. E., Buckner, R. L., Snyder, A. Z., Petersen, S. E., et al. (2002). The feasibility of a common stereotactic space for children and adults in fMRI studies of development. *NeuroImage, 17*, 184–200.

Burnett, S., & Blakemore, S. J. (2009). The development of adolescent social cognition. *Annals of the New York Academy of Sciences, 1167*, 51–56.

Bystron, I., Blakemore, C., & Rakic, P. (2008). Development of the human cerebral cortex: Boulder Committee revisited. *Nature Reviews. Neuroscience, 9*, 110–122.

Bystron, I., Rakic, P., Molnar, Z., & Blakemore, C. (2006). The first neurons of the human cerebral cortex. *Nature Neuroscience, 9*, 880–886.

Carey, S., Diamond, R., & Woods, B. (1980). Development of face recognition: A maturational component. *Developmental Psychology, 16*, 257–269.

Cascio, C. J., Gerig, G., & Piven, J. (2007). Diffusion tensor imaging: Application to the study of the developing brain. *Journal of the American Academy of Child and Adolescent Psychiatry, 46*, 213–223.

Casey, B. J., Cohen, J. D., Jezzard, P., Turner, R., Noll, D. C., Trainor, R. J., et al. (1995). Activation of prefrontal cortex in children during a nonspatial working memory task with functional MRI. *NeuroImage, 2*, 221–229.

Church, J. A., Petersen, S. E., & Schlaggar, B. L. (2010). The "Task B" problem and other considerations in developmental functional neuroimaging. *Human Brain Mapping, 31*, 852–862.

Connor, C. E., Brincat, S. L., & Pasupathy, A. (2007). Transformation of shape information in the ventral pathway. *Current Opinion in Neurobiology, 17*, 140–147.

Corbetta, M., & Shulman, G. L. (2002). Control of goal-directed and stimulus-driven attention in the brain. *Nature Reviews Neuroscience, 3*, 201–215.

Crone, E. A., Wendelken, C., Donohue, S., van Leijenhorst, L., & Bunge, S. A. (2006). Neurocognitive development of the ability to manipulate information in working memory. *Proceedings of the National Academy of Sciences, 103*, 9315–9320.

Deutsch, G. K., Dougherty, R. F., Bammer, R., Siok, W. T., Gabrieli, J. D., & Wandell, B. (2005). Children's reading performance is correlated with white matter structure measured by diffusion tensor imaging. *Cortex, 41*, 354–363.

Epstein, J. N., Casey, B. J., Tonev, S. T., Davidson, M., Reiss, A. L., Garrett, A., et al. (2007). Assessment and prevention of head motion during imaging of patients with attention deficit hyperactivity disorder. *Psychiatry Research, 155*, 75–82.

Eriksen, B. A., & Eriksen, C. W. (1974). Effects of noise letters upon the identification of a target letter in a nonsearch task. *Perception and Psychophysics, 16*, 143–149.

Fair, D. A., Cohen, A. L., Dosenbach, N. U., Church, J. A., Miezin, F. M., Barch, D. M., et al. (2008). The maturing architecture of the brain's default network. *Proceedings of the National Academy of Sciences, 105*, 4028–4032.

Fair, D. A., Cohen, A. L., Power, J. D., Dosenbach, N. U. F., Church, J. A., Miezin, F. M., et al. (2009). Functional brain networks develop from a "local to distributed" organization. *PLoS Computational Biology, 5,* e1000381.

Fair, D. A., Dosenbach, N. U. F., Church, J. A., Cohen, A. L., Brahmbhatt, S., Miezin, F. M., et al. (2007). Development of distinct control networks through segregation and integration. *Proceedings of the National Academy of Sciences, 104,* 13507–13512.

Fan, J., McCandliss, B. D., Fossella, J., Flombaum, J. I., & Posner, M. I. (2005). The activation of attentional networks. *NeuroImage, 26,* 471–479.

Fan, J., McCandliss, B. D., Sommer, T., Raz, A., & Posner, M. I. (2002). Testing the efficiency and independence of attentional networks. *Journal of Cognitive Neuroscience, 14,* 340–347.

Felleman, D. J., & Van Essen, D. C. (1991). Distributed hierarchical processing in the primate cerebral cortex. *Cerebral Cortex, 1,* 1–47.

Flechsig, P. E. (1920). *Anatomie des Menschlichen Gehirn und Ruckenmarks, auf Myelogenetischer Grundlage.* Leipzig, Germany: Thieme.

Fransson, P., Skiold, B., Engstrom, M., Hallberg, B., Mosskin, M., Aden, U., et al. (2009). Spontaneous brain activity in the newborn brain during natural sleep: An fMRI study in infants born at full term. *Pediatric Research, 66,* 301–305.

Fransson, P., Skiold, B., Horsch, S., Nordell, A., Blennow, M., Lagercrantz, H., et al. (2007). Resting-state networks in the infant brain. *Proceedings of the National Academy of Sciences, 104,* 15531–15536.

Frith, C. D., & Frith, U. (2007). Social cognition in humans. *Current Biology, 17,* R724–R732.

Gathers, A. D., Bhatt, R., Corbly, C. R., Farley, A. B., & Joseph, J. E. (2004). Developmental shifts in cortical loci for face and object recognition. *Neuroreport, 15,* 1549–1553.

Giedd, J. N. (2004). Structural magnetic resonance imaging of the adolescent brain. *Annals of the New York Academy of Sciences, 1021,* 77–85.

Gogtay, N., Giedd, J. N., Lusk, L., Hayashi, K. M., Greenstein, D., Vaituzis, A. C., et al. (2004). Dynamic mapping of human cortical development during childhood through early adulthood. *Proceedings of the National Academy of Sciences, 101,* 8174–8179.

Golarai, G., Ghahremani, D. G., Whitfield-Gabrieli, S., Reiss, A., Eberhardt, J. L., Gabrieli, J. D., et al. (2007). Differential development of high-level visual cortex correlates with category-specific recognition memory. *Nature Neuroscience, 10,* 512–522.

Gotz, M., & Barde, Y. A. (2005). Radial glial cells defined and major intermediates between embryonic stem cells and CNS neurons. *Neuron, 46,* 369–372.

Gotz, M., & Huttner, W. B. (2005). The cell biology of neurogenesis. *Nature Reviews. Molecular Cell Biology, 6,* 777–788.

Gould, E. (2007). How widespread is adult neurogenesis in mammals? *Nature Reviews. Neuroscience, 8,* 481–488.

Grill-Spector, K., & Malach, R. (2004). The human visual cortex. *Annual Review of Neuroscience, 27,* 649–677.

Hackman, D. A., & Farah, M. J. (2009). Socioeconomic status and the developing brain. *Trends in Cognitive Sciences, 13,* 65–73.

Haxby, J. V., Gobbini, M. I., Furey, M. L., Ishai, A., Schouten, J. L., & Pietrini, P. (2001). Distributed and overlapping representations of faces and objects in ventral temporal cortex. *Science, 293,* 2425–2430.

Holtmaat, A., & Svoboda, K. (2009). Experience-dependent structural synaptic plasticity in the mammalian brain. *Nature Reviews. Neuroscience, 10,* 647–658.

Huppi, P. S., Maier, S. E., Peled, S., Zientara, G. P., Barnes, P. D., Jolesz, F. A., et al. (1998). Microstructural development of human newborn cerebral white matter assessed in vivo by diffusion tensor magnetic resonance imaging. *Pediatric Research, 44,* 584–590.

Huttenlocher, P. R. (1979). Synaptic density in human frontal cortex: Developmental changes and effects of aging. *Brain Research, 163,* 195–205.

Huttenlocher, P. R., & Dabholkar, A. S. (1997). Regional differences in synaptogenesis in human cerebral cortex. *Journal of Comparative Neurology, 387,* 167–178.

Huttenlocher, P. R., de Courten, C., Garey, L. J., & Van der Loos, H. (1982). Synaptogenesis in human visual cortex: Evidence for synapse elimination during normal development. *Neuroscience Letters, 33,* 247–252.

Johnson, M. H. (2001). Functional brain development in humans. *Nature Reviews. Neuroscience, 2,* 475–483.

Kanwisher, N., McDermott, J., & Chun, M. M. (1997). The fusiform face area: A module in human extrastriate cortex specialized for face perception. *Journal of Neuroscience, 17,* 4302–4311.

Karmiloff-Smith, A., & Thomas, M. (2003). What can developmental disorders tell us about the neurocomputational constraints that shape development? The case of Williams syndrome. *Development and Psychopathology, 15*, 969–990.

Katz, L. C., & Crowley, J. C. (2002). Development of cortical circuits: Lessons from ocular dominance columns. *Nature Reviews. Neuroscience, 3*, 34–42.

Klingberg, T., Hedehus, M., Temple, E., Salz, T., Gabrieli, J. D., Moseley, M. E., et al. (2000). Microstructure of temporo-parietal white matter as a basis for reading ability: Evidence from diffusion tensor magnetic resonance imaging. *Neuron, 25*, 493–500.

Konrad, K., Neufang, S., Thiel, C. M., Specht, K., Hanisch, C., Fan, J., et al. (2005). Development of attentional networks: An fMRI study with children and adults. *NeuroImage, 28*, 429–439.

Kwon, H., Reiss, A. L., & Menon, V. (2002). Neural basis of protracted developmental changes in visuo-spatial working memory. *Proceedings of the National Academy of Sciences, 99*, 13336–13341.

Leingartner, A., Thuret, S., Kroll, T. T., Chou, S. J., Leasure, J. L., Gage, F. H., et al. (2007). Cortical area size dictates performance at modality-specific behaviors. *Proceedings of the National Academy of Sciences, 104*, 4153–4158.

LeVay, S., Wiesel, T. N., & Hubel, D. H. (1980). The development of ocular dominance columns in normal and visually deprived monkeys. *Journal of Comparative Neurology, 191*, 1–51.

Levitt, P. (2003). Structural and functional maturation of the developing primate brain. *Journal of Pediatrics, 143*, S35–S45.

Liu, W. C., Flax, J. F., Guise, K. G., Sukul, V., & Benasich, A. A. (2008). Functional connectivity of the sensorimotor area in naturally sleeping infants. *Brain Research, 1223*, 42–49.

Luna, B., Garver, K. E., Urban, T. A., Lazar, N. A., & Sweeney, J. A. (2004). Maturation of cognitive processes from late childhood to adulthood. *Child Development, 75*, 1357–1372.

Luna, B., Velanova, K., & Geier, C. F. (2008). Development of eye-movement control. *Brain and Cognition, 68*, 293–308.

Luo, L., & O'Leary, D. D. (2005). Axon retraction and degeneration in development and disease. *Annual Review of Neuroscience, 28*, 127–156.

Marner, L., Nyengaard, J. R., Tang, Y., & Pakkenberg, B. (2003). Marked loss of myelinated nerve fibers in the human brain with age. *Journal of Comparative Neurology, 462*, 144–152.

Mountcastle, V. B. (1997). The columnar organization of the neocortex. *Brain, 120*(Pt 4), 701–722.

Murphy, K., & Garavan, H. (2004). Artifactual fMRI group and condition differences driven by performance confounds. *NeuroImage, 21*, 219–228.

Nelson, C. A., De Haan, M., & Thomas, K. M. (2006). *Neuroscience of cognitive development: The role of experience and the developing brain.* Hoboken, NJ: Wiley.

Niogi, S. N., & McCandliss, B. D. (2006). Left lateralized white matter microstructure accounts for individual differences in reading ability and disability. *Neuropsychologia, 44*, 2178–2188.

O'Leary, D. D., & Nakagawa, Y. (2002). Patterning centers, regulatory genes and extrinsic mechanisms controlling arealization of the neocortex. *Current Opinion in Neurobiology, 12*, 14–25.

O'Leary, D. D. M., Schlaggar, B. L., & Tuttle, R. (1994). Specification of neocortical areas and thalamocortical connections. *Annual Review of Neuroscience, 17*, 419–439.

Ofen, N., Kao, Y. C., Sokol-Hessner, P., Kim, H., Whitfield-Gabrieli, S., & Gabrieli, J. D. (2007). Development of the declarative memory system in the human brain. *Nature Neuroscience, 10*, 1198–1205.

Otsuka, Y., Nakato, E., Kanazawa, S., Yamaguchi, M. K., Watanabe, S., & Kakigi, R. (2007). Neural activation to upright and inverted faces in infants measured by near infrared spectroscopy. *NeuroImage, 34*, 399–406.

Palmer, E. D., Brown, T. T., Petersen, S. E., & Schlaggar, B. L. (2004). Investigation of the functional neuroanatomy of single word reading and its development. *Scientific Studies of Reading, 8*, 203–223.

Peelen, M. V., Glaser, B., Vuilleumier, P., & Eliez, S. (2009). Differential development of selectivity for faces and bodies in the fusiform gyrus. *Developmental Science, 12*, F16-F25.

Perrin, J. S., Herve, P. Y., Leonard, G., Perron, M., Pike, G. B., Pitiot, A., et al. (2008). Growth of white matter in the adolescent brain: Role of testosterone and androgen receptor. *Journal of Neuroscience, 28*, 9519–9524.

Petersen, S. E., Fox, P. T., Posner, M. I., Mintun, M., & Raichle, M. E. (1988). Positron emission tomographic studies of the cortical anatomy of single-word processing. *Nature, 331*, 585–589.

Pfefferbaum, A., Mathalon, D. H., Sullivan, E. V., Rawles, J. M., Zipursky, R. B., & Lim, K. O. (1994). A quantitative magnetic resonance imaging study of changes in brain morphology from infancy to late adulthood. *Archives of Neurology, 51*, 874–887.

Posner, M. I. (1978). *Chronometric explorations of mind.* Englewood Heights, NJ: Lawrence Erlbaum Associates (reissue 1986).

Posner, M. I. (1980). Orienting of attention. *Quarterly Journal of Experimental Psychology, 32,* 3–25.

Posner, M. I., & Petersen, S. E. (1990). The attention system of the human brain. *Annual Review of Neuroscience, 13,* 25–42.

Raichle, M. E., & Mintun, M. A. (2006). Brain work and brain imaging. *Annual Review of Neuroscience, 29,* 449–476.

Rakic, P. (2006). Neuroscience. No more cortical neurons for you. *Science, 313,* 928–929.

Ramón y Cajal, S., DeFelipe, J., & Jones, E. G. (1991). *Cajal's degeneration and regeneration of the nervous system.* New York: Oxford University Press.

Reiss, A. L., Abrams, M. T., Singer, H. S., Ross, J. L., & Denckla, M. B. (1996). Brain development, gender and IQ in children. A volumetric imaging study. *Brain, 119,* 1763–1774.

Rubia, K., Smith, A. B., Woolley, J., Nosarti, C., Heyman, I., Taylor, E., et al. (2006). Progressive increase of frontostriatal brain activation from childhood to adulthood during event-related tasks of cognitive control. *Human Brain Mapping, 27,* 973–993.

Rueda, M. R., Fan, J., McCandliss, B. D., Halparin, J. D., Gruber, D. B., Lercari, L. P., et al. (2004). Development of attentional networks in childhood. *Neuropsychologia, 42,* 1029–1040.

Scherf, K. S., Behrmann, M., Humphreys, K., & Luna, B. (2007). Visual category-selectivity for faces, places and objects emerges along different developmental trajectories. *Developmental Science, 10,* F15–F30.

Scherf, K. S., Sweeney, J. A., & Luna, B. (2006). Brain basis of developmental change in visuospatial working memory. *Journal of Cognitive Neuroscience, 18,* 1045–1058.

Schlaggar, B. L., Brown, T. T., Lugar, H. M., Visscher, K. M., Miezin, F. M., & Petersen, S. E. (2002). Functional neuroanatomical differences between adults and school-age children in the processing of single words. *Science, 296,* 1476–1479.

Schlaggar, B. L., & McCandliss, B. D. (2007). Development of neural systems for reading. *Annual Review of Neuroscience, 30,* 475–503.

Schlaggar, B. L., & O'Leary, D. D. M. (1991). Potential of visual cortex to develop an array of functional units unique to somatosensory cortex. *Science, 252,* 1556–1560.

Shaw, P., Greenstein, D., Lerch, J., Clasen, L., Lenroot, R., Gogtay, N., et al. (2006). Intellectual ability and cortical development in children and adolescents. *Nature, 440,* 676–679.

Siegler, R. S., & Crowley, K. (1991). The microgenetic method. A direct means for studying cognitive development. *American Psychologist, 46,* 606–620.

Snook, L., Paulson, L. A., Roy, D., Phillips, L., & Beaulieu, C. (2005). Diffusion tensor imaging of neurodevelopment in children and young adults. *NeuroImage, 26,* 1164–1173.

Sowell, E. R., Trauner, D. A., Gamst, A., & Jernigan, T. L. (2002). Development of cortical and subcortical brain structures in childhood and adolescence: A structural MRI study. *Developmental Medicine and Child Neurology, 44,* 4–16.

Sporns, O., Tononi, G., & Edelman, G. M. (2000). Connectivity and complexity: The relationship between neuroanatomy and brain dynamics. *Neural Networks, 13,* 909–922.

Sporns, O., & Zwi, J. D. (2004). The small world of the cerebral cortex. *Neuroinformatics, 2,* 145–162.

Stiles, J. (2008). *The fundamentals of brain development: Integrating nature and nurture.* Cambridge, MA: Harvard University Press.

Supekar, K., Musen, M., & Menon, V. (2009). Development of large-scale functional brain networks in children. *PLoS Biology, 7,* e1000157.

Thomas, K. M., King, S. W., Franzen, P. L., Welsh, T. F., Berkowitz, A. L., Noll, D. C., et al. (1999). A developmental functional MRI study of spatial working memory. *NeuroImage, 10,* 327–338.

Thomas, M. S., Annaz, D., Ansari, D., Scerif, G., Jarrold, C., & Karmiloff-Smith, A. (2009). Using developmental trajectories to understand developmental disorders. *Journal of Speech, Language, and Hearing Research, 52,* 336–358.

Toga, A. W., Thompson, P. M., & Sowell, E. R. (2006). Mapping brain maturation. *Trends in Neurosciences, 29,* 148–159.

Velanova, K., Wheeler, M. E., & Luna, B. (2009). The maturation of task set-related activation supports late developmental improvements in inhibitory control. *Journal of Neuroscience, 29,* 12558–12567.

Vincent, J. L., Patel, G. H., Fox, M. D., Snyder, A. Z., Baker, J. T., Van Essen, D. C., et al. (2007). Intrinsic functional architecture in the anesthetized monkey brain. *Nature, 447,* 46–47.

Watts, D. J., & Strogatz, S. H. (1998). Collective dynamics of 'small-world' networks. *Nature, 393,* 440–442.

Yakovlev, P. I., & Lecours, A. R. (1967). The myelogenetic cycles of regional maturation of the brain. In A. Minkowski (Ed.), *Regional development of the brain in early life* (pp. 3–70). Oxford, UK: Blackwell Scientific.

Yerys, B. E., Jankowski, K. F., Shook, D., Rosenberger, L. R., Barnes, K. A., Berl, M. M., et al. (2009). The fMRI success rate of children and adolescents: Typical development, epilepsy, attention deficit/hyperactivity disorder, and autism spectrum disorders. *Human Brain Mapping, 30,* 3426–3435.

Zeanah, C. H., Nelson, C. A., Fox, N. A., Smyke, A. T., Marshall, P., Parker, S. W., et al. (2003). Designing research to study the effects of institutionalization on brain and behavioral development: The Bucharest Early Intervention Project. *Development and Psychopathology, 15,* 885–907.

Zecevic, N., & Rakic, P. (2001). Development of layer I neurons in the primate cerebral cortex. *Journal of Neuroscience, 21,* 5607–5619.

Zeff, B. W., White, B. R., Dehghani, H., Schlaggar, B. L., & Culver, J. P. (2007). Retinotopic mapping of adult human visual cortex with high-density diffuse optical tomography. *Proceedings of the National Academy of Sciences, 104,* 12169–12174.

COGNITIVE NEUROSCIENCE OF THE AGING MIND AND BRAIN

15

Patricia A. Reuter-Lorenz, Jonas Persson, and Kristin E. Flegal

■ INTRODUCTION

Few aspects of cognition remain untouched by the effects of aging. Some cognitive changes may stem from global alterations in brain functions; others may result from localized decline of specific neural circuits. A neuroscience approach to cognitive aging can help to distinguish between these sources of age-related decline and specify the neural mechanisms that underlie cognitive change. Until the early 1990s, the dominant method for identifying the neural correlates of cognitive aging was to determine the neurological patient population whose cognitive impairments most closely resembled the "normal" elderly profile. The "lesion model" of aging necessarily emphasized deficits and the declining neurocognitive trajectory of older age. The advent of high-resolution neuroimaging methods is radically changing this perspective on aging and giving way to new visions of the aging mind and brain. We are beginning to understand that, while slower and more error prone, older age brings complexly different brain function that is not simply a depleted or reduced version of the younger brain.

We can pursue several valuable and exciting goals by combining cognitive and neural methods to study aging. First, we can deepen our understanding of the mental operations that are most affected by aging by specifying how and when particular mechanisms limit the performance of older adults. Second, we can advance theories of the neural bases of cognitive function more generally. Neurocognitive studies of aging can inform cognitive theories more generally just as studies of patients with focal brain lesions have advanced cognitive psychology: by testing theoretical assumptions and uncovering new phenomena for theories to explain. Finally, and most optimistically, the cognitive neuroscience of aging may provide key insights into ways to combat adverse effects of aging on cognition. There are new indications that the aging brain may engage compensatory processes that reduce performance decline (Reuter-Lorenz & Park, 2010). By identifying what is optimal in older brains, we stand a better chance of promoting the secrets of successful aging.

This chapter summarizes major bodies of evidence linking cognitive changes to their underlying neural substrates, and reviews theories about neurocognitive aging. Because the coverage is broad in scope, the scientific review is selective and the reader is referred to other additional works in each section. We cover five functional domains, each of which has been a major focus of cognitive neuroscience research on aging: perception, attention, working memory, executive control functions, and long-term memory. We then consider pathological aging and theoretical issues in the cognitive neuroscience of aging, and close with an outlook toward future directions in the field. Before turning to our empirical review, we begin with an overview of cortical organization, introduce relevant terminology, and discuss some general challenges entailed in relating brain structure to cognitive function.

■ NEUROANATOMY OVERVIEW

The two cortical hemispheres each contain four major lobes that contribute specific processes to the overall repertoire of human thought and behavior. The occipital lobes at the very back (posterior) of the brain contain the first or primary cortical regions for vision, along with secondary visual and association areas that process the output from primary visual cortex. The basic hierarchy of primary, secondary, and association cortices exists in the temporal lobes for auditory processing and in the parietal lobes, where somatosensory input from different parts of the body is processed. Regions at the junction of occipital, parietal, and temporal cortices integrate input from multiple sensory modalities and can be influenced by goals, emotional-attentional state, and body position in the environment. In the front (anterior) of the brain are the frontal lobes. Their most posterior boundary, adjacent to parietal cortex, is the motor strip, which contains the neural machinery for sending motor commands to the body. In right-handers, Broca's area is located in the left frontal region just anterior to the motor strip and plays a vital role in the planning and programming of language. Other frontal subregions have reciprocal connections to secondary and association cortices of all modalities and to subcortical centers such as thalamus, hippocampus, and amygdala that are involved in emotion and memory. The frontal lobes are therefore thought to reside at the top of the information processing hierarchy where they can modulate (i.e., inhibit or promote) neural operations in other brain regions in accord with an individual's current goals, plans, and intentions.

Under a microscope, the six layers of the neocortex can be seen to vary in thickness and cell density depending on the function of each cortical region. Korbinian Brodmann, a neuroanatomist working at the turn of the last century, classified 52 different subregions of cortex based on cytoarchitecture. Despite their limitations (e.g., Devlin & Poldrack, 2007), Brodmann's numerical classifications are the most widely used reference system in human cognitive neuroscience. Brain areas also can be referred to by the sulci and gyri on which they reside or by their relative location within a particular lobe; toward the side (lateral), middle (medial), top (dorsal), or bottom (ventral).

The brains of older (age 60 and up) and younger (age 18–35) adults differ anatomically. Sulci become more prominent with age, due to cell loss in some regions and the widespread shrinkage of brain tissue itself (Raz et al., 1997; Uylings & de Brabander, 2002). Reduced branching of the spines (dendrites) of neurons contributes to age-related atrophy and presumably affects the quality and efficiency of neuronal communication. Aging also leads to reduced concentration of neurotransmitters, especially dopamine, which contributes to frontal lobe functions, and acetylcholine, which plays an important role in learning and memory (see, e.g., Bäckman & Farde, 2005; Woodruff-Pak, 1997). Intracellular changes and reduced cerebral blood flow compromise the brain's metabolic efficiency. Change in cerebral blood flow (i.e., hemodynamic changes) with age may complicate the interpretation of data from neuroimaging methods, such as positron emission tomography (PET) and functional magnetic resonance imaging (fMRI), both of which rely on blood flow and neural activity. Likewise, aging causes cardiovascular changes that may lead to hypertension and altered capillary structure that may complicate the interpretation of neuroimaging data in aging (Ances et al., 2009; Huettel, Singerman, & McCarthy, 2001). In PET, radioactive water is injected into the blood and the decaying emissions signal blood flow changes that result from localized changes in neural activity. The fMRI technique detects changes in the magnetic properties of blood that result from localized neuronal activity. Several different types of functional neuroimaging results can emerge when comparing younger and older adults. The activation levels can be equivalent, or older adults may show less activation (underactivation) or more activation (overactivation) relative to the younger group (Figure 15.1). Also, recent investigations have examined changes in the functional connectivity of brain regions that occur with increasing age. Observations from such studies indicate age-related alterations in large-scale neurocognitive networks, and that reduced cognitive performance in aging may relate to changes in task-related connectivity (Grady et al., 2009).

Given the brain's structural diversity, it is not surprising that some regions age more than others. Postmortem studies and in vivo cross-sectional structural imaging studies reveal the greatest atrophy in the dorsolateral prefrontal cortex, the striatum, and the cerebellum (Raz et al., 2005). Other regions, such as the primary visual cortex and the entorhinal cortex, seem to be relatively spared in old age. The hippocampus, a region important for long-term memory, shows a more complex pattern of atrophy. Even though volumetric changes of the hippocampus are modest in the absence of Alzheimer's disease (Good et al., 2001; Raz et al., 2004; West, 1993), volume reductions accelerate after the age of 60. Structural MRI research reveals a 2–3% decline in the volume of the hippocampus and parahippocampal gyrus per decade (Raz et al., 2004). Studies using longitudinal measures of regional atrophy indicate that when controlling for individual differences, larger and broader shrinkage estimates are evident, with most association cortices affected to the same degree (Raz, Rodrigue, &

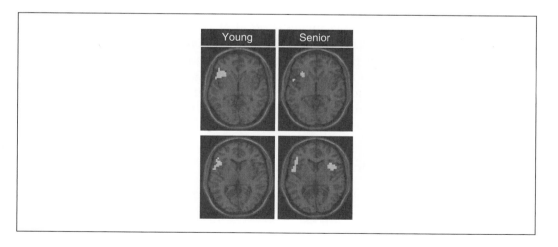

FIGURE 15.1   Activation regions for younger and older adults obtained using fMRI during a verb generation task (*Source*: Adapted from Persson et al. 2004). Activations are superimposed on horizontal slices of a structural magnetic resonance image. The overactivation and underactivation patterns are depicted.

Haacke, 2007). Vascular risk factors could aggravate brain aging and likely underlie some of the observed decline, as both the prefrontal cortex and hippocampus show enhanced vulnerability to hypertension.

Degradation of white matter, which is important for the connectivity between different regions of the brain, has also been related to advancing age (Bartzokis et al., 2004). While the decline in gray matter (i.e., cortical) volume in aging is relatively linear from younger adulthood, the corresponding degradation in white matter tends to be nonlinear, with a plateau in middle-age, and further decline—beyond that of gray matter—in later adulthood (Jernigan et al., 2001; Raz et al., 2004). Neuroimaging studies of healthy adults also suggest an association between age-related decline in white-matter volume and deficits in cognitive performance (Brickman et al., 2006).

The development of diffusion tensor imaging (DTI) has offered a new avenue for understanding the interplay between white-matter integrity, cognitive functioning, and aging, and studies in this field have been accumulating extensively (Madden, Bennett, & Song, 2009). DTI is a form of MRI that measures the directional displacement of water molecules across tissue components, and as a result can examine the properties of white matter. Convergent evidence from DTI studies confirms a role of disconnection among distributed neural systems as a fundamental mechanism for age-related decline in cognitive performance. There also seems to be evidence for an anterior–posterior gradient across studies, showing that age-related reduction in white matter integrity is typically greater in magnitude for anterior regions (e.g., genu of the corpus callosum), although decline is also evident in posterior regions as well (e.g., splenium of the corpus callosum; Madden et al., 2009). In addition, recent observations have found that altered white-matter integrity is related to longitudinal cognitive decline, suggesting that reduced connectivity between brain regions may underlie cognitive deficits in old age (Persson et al., 2006).

But, as the past century of behavioral brain science has shown us, the correspondence between structure and function is not perfect. Physical signs of regional dysfunction may not cause measurable deficits in performance because of functional reorganization, compensatory processes, and strategy changes. Likewise, the neural processes responsible for behavioral or cognitive changes are not easy to identify. Mapping particular cognitive operations onto neural circuitry is difficult because our cognitive theories are imprecise, our behavioral measurements often are highly variable, and our neural measurements can be coarse and indirect. Nevertheless, converging evidence from multiple cognitive neuroscience approaches has significantly advanced our understanding of the neural bases of cognition in younger adults and in older age.

▨ NEUROSCIENCE OF THE AGING MIND

Perceptual Processing

Our senses become less keen with age. Many age-related problems with vision and hearing can be traced to peripheral changes in the eyes and ears that impair the transduction of sensory stimulation into neural signals (see Schneider & Pichora-Fuller, 2000, for a review). Neuroimaging methods can be used to study changes in perceptual representations with age, and to date most researchers have focused on vision. Although volume reductions in occipital cortex are minimal (Raz, 2000), cortical visual functioning may change with age. For example, older adults show a weaker hemodynamic response—the change in cerebral blood flow coupled with neural activity—in primary visual cortex to flashing stimuli such as checker boards (see Madden, Whiting, & Huettel, 2005, for a review). Later processing stages show changes as well. The visual system is organized into two major processing streams, the ventral coursing "what" pathway that codes visual identity, and the dorsal coursing "where" pathway that codes information about spatial location. One of the first functional neuroimaging studies of normal aging examined the distinctiveness of these pathways in older and younger adults using a face-matching task to activate the ventral pathway and a location-matching task to activate the dorsal pathway (Grady et al., 1994). As expected, younger adults selectively activated the appropriate pathway for each task. In contrast, older adults showed less selectivity, activating both pathways regardless of which task they performed. In addition, older adults showed greater activity in regions of prefrontal cortex, suggesting that they may rely on higher-level cognitive processes even for more elementary tasks.

Declining specialization has also been observed *within* the ventral pathway, where there is evidence for special-purpose modules for processing different classes of visual stimuli, such as letters and faces. Using fMRI, areas specialized for letters, faces, and even visual scenes can be localized to specific gyri within a given individual. These regions show selective responsivity or "tuning," with heightened activity levels for their preferred category of input and minimal activity for other categories. Investigations comparing older and younger adults have revealed less visual specialization in older adults (Chee et al., 2006; Devlin & Poldrack, 2007; Park et al., 2004; Voss et al., 2008). That is, in older adults the "face area" is also responsive to letters and places, the "place area" is responsive to faces and letters, and so forth.

Declining specialization may be an example of "dedifferentiation" (Baltes & Lindenberger, 1997), a term that refers to the idea that aging reverses the trend toward increasing specialization or differentiation that characterizes early development. Indeed, dedifferentiation is evident in animal models of neural aging as well. Declining selectivity has been observed in somatosensory cortex of aging rodents where portions of the somatotopic map become less distinct (see Godde, Berkefeld, David-Jurgens, & Dinse, 2002, for a review), and in aging monkeys where visual cortex neurons show degraded selectivity to stimulus orientation and movement direction (Schmolesky, Wang, Pu, & Leventhal, 2000). As perceptual representations become noisier or less distinct in older brains, subsequent processes that utilize these representations may be altered or even compromised (Li, Lindenberger, & Sikström, 2001). Age-related decline in dopamine function has been proposed to play a role in neural dedifferentiation, contributing to poorer cognitive performance in older adults (Bäckman, Nyberg, Lindenberger, Li, & Farde, 2006). An important challenge for future research will be to relate any alterations in early perceptual processes to the integrity of higher-order cognitive processes.

Visual Selective Attention

Attention comes in many varieties that share the property of selecting or facilitating the processing of some representations to the exclusion of others. If perceptual representations become noisier or "blurred" in the older brain, attentional operations may bear an increased processing burden. This seems to be true for the "anterior" attention system, which relies on regions of prefrontal cortex (see Executive Functions, discussed later). In fact, a recent fMRI study found that decreased ventral pathway specificity in older adults coincided with increased prefrontal activation during a working memory task (Payer et al., 2006). To date, however, minimal age-related changes have been documented in the functions of the "posterior" attention system, which involves parietal cortex and the temporal–parietal junction. The posterior system operates at relatively early stages of information processing, where sensory representations are enhanced based on their spatial location or their task relevance more generally (Behrmann, Geng, & Shomstein, 2004). The effects of visual attention can be measured using cues that inform observers of relevant target attributes, such as its color or its location. Evidence suggests that older adults are more susceptible to interference when target and distractor information occupy the same location in space, but not when they are separated (Hartley, 1993) or when the identity of a distractor must be ignored, but not its location (Connelly & Hasher, 1993). These findings are consistent with better preservation of the posterior, than the anterior, attention system with advancing age, although this interpretation is tempered by other reports of visual attention deficits in older adults (Greenwood, 2000).

Behavioral studies of visual attention and aging are surprisingly equivocal in their results, but in general, the similarities between older and younger adults seem to outweigh the differences (see McDowd & Shaw, 2000, for a review). In terms of age-related changes in visual attention, older adults are generally slower and differ from younger adults when attentional strategies are required and when distinguishing targets and distracters is difficult. Neuroimaging measures generally show more activation in older than younger adults as attentional demands increase; however, the locus of increased activation varies due to the conditions of the task, and the functions of such activation increases are not yet well understood (Madden et al., 2005). For example, older adults have been found to activate larger areas of prefrontal cortex than younger adults in a task-switching paradigm, and to demonstrate less selective prefrontal activation, that is, in both switch and nonswitch conditions (DiGirolamo et al., 2001). More parietal activation in older adults than younger adults has also been observed, at times in combination with underactivation in sensory regions (Cabeza et al., 2004). Emerging research findings suggest that age-related increases in fronto-parietal activation may reflect greater engagement of top-down attention in a compensatory manner (Davis, Dennis, Daselaar, Fleck, & Cabeza, 2008; Madden et al., 2007).

Working Memory

Working memory—the capacity to hold information actively in mind for a brief (several seconds) period of time—has been a major focus of behavioral research on aging because this capacity is key to higher-order cognitive abilities, including language comprehension, reasoning, and problem solving. Working memory tasks differ in the amount of "work" they require, with some emphasizing the rote maintenance of several items (i.e., seven or less) and others requiring manipulation or complex processing of the stored contents (e.g., reordering the items; successive updating and deleting contents). Tasks requiring more work place greater burden on executive processes and are more likely to show age differences in performance (see Reuter-Lorenz & Sylvester, 2005, for a review). Although age-related performance differences in rote maintenance tasks are minimal, older adults activate different neural circuitry while performing these tasks compared to their younger counterparts. For maintenance of verbal materials, such as letters, and nonverbal materials, such as faces or objects, older adults seem to rely more on anterior brain regions during these tasks, especially dorsolateral prefrontal cortex (Grady et al., 1998; Reuter-Lorenz et al., 2000; Rypma & D'Esposito, 2000; Rypma, Prabhakaran, Desmond, & Gabrieli, 2001). Greater prefrontal activity for older than younger adults also occurs in working memory tasks that place heavier demands on executive processes, such as task switching (Smith et al., 2001), even when age differences in performance are minimized by making the task easier for the older group.

Finally, fMRI studies using working memory tasks yield pronounced evidence for greater bilateral activation in older adults: young adults show left-lateralized activity for verbal materials and right-lateralized activity for spatial locations, whereas older adults tend to activate regions of both hemispheres in both types of task (Cabeza et al., 2004; Grossman et al., 2002; Reuter-Lorenz et al., 2000). Some regions of additional activation may function in a compensatory manner, because several studies have linked overactivation in older adults to better working memory performance (see Reuter-Lorenz & Sylvester, 2005, for a review). Furthermore, similar sites of additional activation have also been demonstrated in younger adults when they attempt to retain higher memory loads (Cappell, Gmeindl, & Reuter-Lorenz, 2010; Schneider-Garces et al., 2009). The parallels across age groups suggest that additional recruitment is a "natural" response of the brain to higher task demand. For seniors, lower objective loads place higher demands on working memory relative to their younger counterparts.

Executive Functions

Often in daily life, we must hold information in mind while avoiding distraction, or select the appropriate response from several possible alternatives. These aspects of selection and inhibition are executive functions that are the cognitive control processes of prefrontal cortex (Smith & Jonides, 1999). Our ability to select task-relevant stimuli and responses and to inhibit interference declines with age. A classic laboratory test used to study interference effects in working memory is the Brown–Peterson task (Brown, 1958; Peterson & Peterson, 1959). Research participants listen to, and retain, a string of items and then count backward continuously during the retention interval. Then, they try to recall the items. The counting task is disrupting, and memory is comprised. In an early behavioral study, Parkin and Walter (1991) found that older adults performed more poorly on this task than younger adults, and that the greatest deficits occurred in older adults who also were impaired on the Wisconsin Card Sorting Test and on verbal fluency, two neuropsychological measures of frontal function. Likewise, using scalp recordings of electrical brain activity time-locked to the stages of a delayed match-to-sample task, Chao and Knight (1997) found that older adults show a greater response than younger adults to distracting events imposed during a brief retention interval, while also showing a weaker attention-related signal from prefrontal cortex. These electrophysiological results suggest that older brains are less able to suppress responses to interfering information, presumably because executive control functions are compromised with age. This conclusion is supported by more recent fMRI evidence demonstrating that older adults who have a greater neural response to distractors also have poorer memory performance (Gazzaley, Cooney, Rissman, & D'Esposito, 2005).

Interference from prior information, referred to as proactive interference (PI), is also greater in older adults than in younger adults (Lustig, May, & Hasher, 2001). A PET study from our lab linked increased PI in older adults to frontal inhibitory processes that are compromised with age (Jonides et al., 2000). PI was produced in a working memory task by presenting items that were familiar to subjects because they had appeared on a previous trial, but required a "no" response because they were not part of the memory set on the current trial. Even younger adults have a harder time rejecting such familiar items compared with less familiar ones, and when doing so they activate a region of left prefrontal cortex called the inferior frontal gyrus (IFG). Older adults, who show greater interference due to an item's familiarity, demonstrate weaker activation in left IFG, suggesting that they are unable to recruit the frontally mediated process that would help resolve the familiarity-induced interference in favor of selecting the appropriate response.

Age-related difficulties in selecting task-appropriate information have been demonstrated on a variety of experimental paradigms, including the Stroop task, where ink color and color names are put into competition (Milham et al., 2002); go-no-go tasks, where responses must be withheld unexpectedly (Nielson, Langenecker, & Garavan, 2002); and task switching, where the subject shifts between different sets of rules that govern the association between the stimulus and the response (DiGirolamo et al., 2001). In each of these cases, age differences in performance are associated with age differences in prefrontal activation patterns. These neuro-imaging results converge with earlier neuropsychological evidence from behavioral tests of frontal lobe function indicating that prefrontal functions are especially compromised with age (Moscovitch & Wincour, 1995; West, 1996). Furthermore, behavioral performance is related to decline of prefrontal volume as measured from structural MRI. For example, prefrontal volume is negatively correlated with errors caused by an inability to change strategies on the Wisconsin Card Sorting Test (Raz, Gunning-Dixon, Head, Dupuis, & Acker, 1998), and positively correlated with measures of fluid intelligence (Schretlen et al., 2000; Velanova, Lustig, Jacoby, & Buckner, 2007).

There are some indications that it may be possible to compensate for the prefrontal dysfunction that accompanies aging. Of relevance is a study from our lab that examined interference in a verb generation task in which subjects were presented with a noun and instructed to respond with a single verb associated with that noun (Persson et al., 2004). Some nouns had one highly associated response, as in the case of *chair: sit*, and other nouns had several verb associates, as in the case of *ball: hit, throw, catch*. Generating a single verb from among several associates takes longer than when there is just one highly associated response. Moreover, the increased selection demands of the "many" associates condition activates left IFG, in a region that overlaps with the area activated in response to the need to resolve PI in working memory (see aforementioned section). However, the higher selection demand does not disadvantage older more than young adults, indicating an absence of age-related decline on the performance of this task. Using fMRI we found that older adults underactivated left IFG, while showing increased activation of the homologous IFG site in the right hemisphere, a pattern consistent with the possibility that the bilateral activation pattern is compensatory.

Frontally mediated cognitive control processes applied strategically in anticipation of high demand events is referred to as *proactive control* whereas control applied once the event has occurred is called *reactive control* (e.g., Braver, Paxton, Locke, & Barch, 2009). Evidence indicates that older adults are less likely to engage proactive control processes, and tend to rely more on reactive control. Such age-related alterations in top-down control has been shown to influence a variety of performance domains including memory encoding and retrieval (Velanova et al., 2007), processes that are considered more closely in the next section.

Long-Term Memory

Elderly adults frequently complain of poor memory, and cognitive studies show that they are right: memory performance declines with age. Yet, 20th-century psychology has taught us that memory is not a single, unitary entity. There are several dissociable types of memory that are mediated by different neural structures and subsystems. Moreover, certain types of memory show no obvious decline during normal aging. For example, normal older adults often have rich and elaborate autobiographical memories (see, e.g., Maguire & Frith, 2004). They do not forget how to write, ride a bicycle, or get to the nearest grocery store, and vocabulary actually increases throughout life (Park, 2002; Schaie, 1996). Evidence indicates the kinds of memory processes that are most vulnerable to age-related declines are those that involve new learning that is mediated by medial temporal lobe structures (hippocampus, entorhinal cortex, parahippocampal gyrus, and portions of temporal cortex) and interactions with cortical regions, especially prefrontal cortex. Here we consider temporal and prefrontal contributions to aging memory, in turn.

The importance of medial temporal lobe regions for forming new memories has been established by decades of neuropsychological studies and especially by the dramatic anterograde amnesia suffered by patient H.M. (Scoville & Milner, 1957) following the surgical bilateral removal of the medial temporal lobe structures. An association between long-term memory and the hippocampus in old age has also been shown with volumetric studies. Age-related changes in the medial temporal lobe has been found using structural MRI, showing that shrinkage of hippocampal volume over time in older adults is related to worse performance on long-term memory tests (Dickerson et al., 2009; Rodrigue & Raz, 2004).

Functional neuroimaging studies now make it possible to identify the role of the medial temporal lobes in different subprocesses of new learning because the encoding of new memories and their retrieval from long-term memory can be examined separately. When new material is being learned, younger adults typically show activation in hippocampal sites, and the amount of activation during encoding is related to whether an item is later remembered or forgotten. This is usually referred to as the "subsequent memory effect" and has been found for both verbal and nonverbal material (Brewer, Zhao, Desmond, Glover, & Gabrieli, 1998; Otten & Rugg, 2001; see Park & Gutchess, 2005, for a review). Older adults show similar subsequent memory effects as young adults, although they generally show less activation during encoding (Daselaar et al., 2003; Grady et al., 1995; Leshikar, Gutchess, Hebrank, Sutton, & Park, 2010). Gutchess et al. (2005) linked successful encoding in older adults to decreased medial temporal activity in conjunction with increased prefrontal activity, suggesting a compensatory role for prefrontal cortex. In young adults, retrieval of information from memory activates medial temporal lobe regions, and the amount of activation is positively related to the number of recognized items during a recognition test (Nyberg, McIntosh, Houle, Nilsson, & Tulving, 1996). The general finding of age-related equivalence in hippocampal activation during retrieval suggests that poor memory in old age may be related primarily to medial temporal lobe dysfunction during encoding (Daselaar et al., 2003). Recent studies that have shown age differences in medial temporal lobe activity during successful retrieval are as yet equivocal, as recollection-related hippocampal activity in older adults has been associated with both decreases (Daselaar, Fleck, Dobbins, Madden, & Cabeza, 2006) and increases (Morcom, Li, & Rugg, 2007) when compared to young adults.

In addition to reductions in medial temporal lobe volume, atrophy in prefrontal cortex is one of the most significant changes associated with normal brain aging (Raz, 2000). Age-related changes in prefrontal function are implicated in memory declines as well. In neuroimaging studies that examine memory for a particular learning episode (e.g., learning a list of items and subsequently recollecting that list), a typical finding is that left prefrontal regions are activated during the memory encoding phase, and that right prefrontal regions are more activated during memory retrieval (Nyberg, Cabeza, & Tulving, 1996). A pronounced departure from this pattern has been found in older adults. Grady and colleagues (1995), in one of their early reports on face memory, found that older adults did not activate left inferior prefrontal cortex while studying faces and they performed more poorly on a later recognition test. Reduced left frontal activation may reflect inadequate encoding strategies and reduced processing resources, which, in turn, may lead to poor memory in older adults. Age-related decreases in prefrontal activation during encoding have since been replicated in several subsequent studies (see Park & Gutchess, 2005, for a review).

Areas of reduced prefrontal activation during memory encoding in older adults are often accompanied by overactivation of other contralateral prefrontal regions that are not typically activated by young adults. The resulting tendency for bilateral activation in seniors has been found both during memory encoding (Logan, Sanders, Snyder, Morris, & Buckner, 2002; Morcom, Good, Frackowiak, & Rugg, 2003) and retrieval (e.g., Cabeza, Anderson, Locantore, & McIntosh, 2002; Cabeza et al., 1997) tasks. One study (Logan et al., 2002) found that giving subjects a specific encoding strategy (categorizing a word as abstract or concrete) increased the level of prefrontal activity in older adults to that of young adults, but the bilateral activation pattern persisted. This observation suggests that increased bilaterality may be less related to alternative cognitive strategies than to adaptive changes in neural architecture with age (Park & Reuter-Lorenz, 2009). Increased bilaterality in older adults has also been linked to the "subsequent memory effect." For seniors, items that are subsequently remembered are associated with bilateral prefrontal activation during encoding, whereas for young adults this activity is left lateralized (Morcom et al., 2007). Later in this chapter we consider the implications of age-related overactivations and reduced asymmetry in more detail.

NORMAL AND PATHOLOGICAL AGING

As the population is growing older, cognitive disorders such as dementia become increasingly more frequent. The most common type of dementia is Alzheimer's disease (AD) which affects a considerable and increasing segment of the population. Alzheimer's disease is not a part of normal aging, but the risk of the disorder increases with age. About 5% of people between the ages of 65 and 74 have AD, while it affects nearly half of people older than 85 years. The etiology of AD is still incompletely understood, yet it is thought to entail a complex combination of genetic and environmental factors. Despite the lack of a general and effective treatment at present, the discovery of sensitive and accurate markers of early AD would be a major advance as it may allow us, once a treatment is available, to delay or perhaps even prevent the degenerative process before dementia develops. It is therefore of great importance to distinguish between normal aging and cognitive impairments that may represent a transitional stage between normality and dementia.

Alzheimer's disease is characterized by advancing affective, cognitive, and behavioral changes and occurs in a subtle and graded fashion for up to a decade or longer (Braak & Braak, 1994; Buckner, 2004). The pathophysiology of AD appears to be linked to the histopathological changes, which include the presence of neuritic amyloid plaques and neurofibrillary tangles, and loss of synapses (Braak & Braak, 1994). Evidence from postmortem studies, and more recent, neuroimaging studies that can trace the deposition of amyloid (e.g., Dickerson et al., 2009; see Rodrigue, Kennedy, & Park, 2009, for a review) have found that changes in medial temporal lobe structures are highly associated with AD. Not surprisingly, then, memory complaints are one of the earliest cognitive symptoms of AD. Neuropathological studies indicate that the earliest neuronal lesions of AD seem to involve the entorhinal cortex, and later, as the disease progresses, the parahippocampal gyrus and the hippocampus proper are also affected. These regions have extensive projections to other parts of the brain, such as limbic and cortical association areas. Consistent with the histopathological data, volumetric measurements using MRI comparing patients with early probable AD to healthy older adults show that the most specific and sensitive features of AD at this stage are hippocampal and entorhinal cortex atrophy, especially when combined with a reduced volume of the temporal neocortex (Chételat & Baron, 2003). Also, using DTI and volumetric measurements to assess white-matter changes in AD, reduced white-matter integrity and volume have been observed in AD patients compared to controls. Such changes are most pronounced in the splenium of the corpus callosum and the cingulum, a collection of white-matter fibers projecting from the cingulate gyrus to the entorhinal cortex (Bozzali et al., 2002; Chaim et al., 2007; Zhang et al., 2007). Together, these findings suggest that MRI can be used as a potential tool for diagnosing AD.

Functional neuroimaging also reveals brain activation differences between AD patients and normal healthy adults. During resting-state PET experiments of brain metabolism, underactivation in the medial temporal lobes, the posterior cingulate gyrus, and temporal–parietal associative areas have been linked to cognitive deficits (Desgranges et al., 1998; Salmon, Collette, Degueldre, Lemaire, & Franck, 2000). More recently, resting-state assessment of default-mode activation using fMRI has provided evidence for altered patterns of deactivation in AD compared to controls. Greicius, Srivastava, Reiss, and Menon (2004) found that AD patients had decreased resting-state activity in the posterior cingulate and hippocampus, suggesting that disrupted connectivity between these two regions accounts for the posterior cingulate hypometabolism commonly detected in PET studies of early AD.

Moreover, patterns of task-related activation are altered in AD patients, when compared to age-matched healthy subjects. Such changes have been found across task domains (e.g., episodic memory, executive function, attention), and observations include both increased and decreased activation in comparison to normal older adults. During memory encoding and retrieval, decreased activity in the hippocampal formation and the entorhinal cortex has been reported in AD patients (Bäckman et al., 1999; Dickerson et al., 2005). Reduced activation in the prefrontal cortex has also been observed (Kato, Knopman, & Liu, 2001). The inability of patients with AD to recruit frontal regions activated by the normal elderly may reflect dysfunction secondary to changes directly related to AD, such as hippocampal atrophy. Conversely, lateral prefrontal activity has been shown to increase in AD patients relative to age-matched controls during both encoding (Pariente et al., 2005) and retrieval (Bäckman et al., 1999; Grady et al., 2003), suggesting the involvement of compensatory mechanisms. Indeed, a direct relationship between recruitment of additional prefrontal regions by AD patients has been found to relate to task performance. These findings, together with matched concomitant medial temporal lobe dysfunction, have led researchers to suggest that such changes represent compensatory increases as a result of pathology in core circuits (Grady et al., 2003; Pariente et al., 2005). In short, some activation patterns that characterize normal aging become even more pronounced in pathological aging such as AD.

■ THEORETICAL ISSUES IN THE COGNITIVE NEUROSCIENCE OF AGING

Prior to the advent of functional neuroimaging methods in the 1990s, the right hemisphere aging hypothesis was the most prominent neuropsychological theory of aging. This account hypothesized that the right hemisphere aged more rapidly than the left, which in turn led to greater age-related declines on nonverbal, visuospatial tasks than on tasks that rely more heavily on verbal skills. Although reports of greater age-related reductions on nonverbal tasks continue to emerge (Lawrence, Myerson, & Hale, 1998), several direct predictions from the right hemisphere aging hypothesis have yet to receive support. In particular, neither structural nor functional measures of hemispheric integrity have turned up evidence for greater declines in the right hemisphere with advancing age (Daselaar & Cabeza, 2005). Indeed, one of the most striking and consistent results to have emerged from the cognitive neuroscience approach to aging is that older adults rely more heavily on bilateral processing resources from both hemispheres, a result that has been found on matched verbal and spatial tasks, and across cognitive and motor domains (Daselaar & Cabeza, 2005; Reuter-Lorenz & Cappell, 2008; Reuter-Lorenz, Stanczak, & Miller, 1999; Reuter-Lorenz et al., 2000; see Seidler et al., 2010, for a review). This pattern of greater bilateral activation in older adults has been described as HAROLD: "Hemispheric Asymmetry Reduction in OLDer adults" (Cabeza, 2002).

Bilateral activation in older adults falls under the more general rubric of evidence for age-related overactivation. But overactivation need not always involve both hemispheres. Some studies find unique sites of overactivation in older adults with no age differences in the overall pattern of laterality. The more basic question that is at the center of current theoretical debates in the cognitive neuroscience of aging is how to interpret the regions of overactivity that are unique to the older groups

(Park & Reuter-Lorenz, 2009; Persson & Nyberg, 2006; Reuter-Lorenz & Lustig, 2005). Do these overactive sites function in a compensatory manner or are they a sign of impairment, resulting from a breakdown in inhibition between brain areas or a more general process of declining neural specialization (i.e., dedifferentiation)?

The compensation account draws support from findings that age-related overactivation is frequently associated with successful task performance. As reviewed earlier, it has been shown that high-performing older adults exhibit increased activation relative to younger adults in tasks involving top-down visual attention (Madden et al., 2007), working memory (Reuter-Lorenz et al., 2000), executive functions (Persson et al., 2004), and long-term memory (Gutchess et al., 2005). However, another feature of brain aging is decreased neural specialization. As also described earlier in this chapter, this "dedifferentiation" is most prominent in sensory cortices; for example, dorsal and ventral visual processing streams are activated less selectively in older adults (Grady et al., 1994) and the tuning of category-specific regions in ventral visual cortex is degraded (Park et al., 2004). Some researchers have argued that age-related overactivation in brain areas supporting higher cognitive processing (e.g., prefrontal cortex) reflects a similar type of nonselective recruitment, in which case it may be a sign of dysfunction instead of compensation. For example, Logan and colleagues (2002) found that right prefrontal overactivation during verbal memory encoding persisted in older adults even after a deficit in left prefrontal activation was successfully reversed with environmental support.

While there is evidence to support either interpretation of overactivations and reduced asymmetry in older adults, it is likely that compensatory neural processes are a genuine part of normal aging (see Greenwood, 2007; Park & Reuter-Lorenz, 2009, for a more detailed treatment of this topic). Even compensation may have a cost in that neural resources depleted at lower levels of task demand will limit the availability of resources for more demanding neural activity. This has been referred to as CRUNCH: the "Compensation-Related Utilization of Neural Circuits Hypothesis" (Cappell et al., 2010; Reuter-Lorenz & Cappell, 2008). According to this model, age-related decreases in neural efficiency are responsible for overactivation in older brains at levels of task demand that younger brains can meet with fewer resources. Up to a certain point, this additional recruitment is compensatory in supporting successful performance. However, when limited neural resources are exhausted—which occurs at a lower level of objective task demand for older adults than younger adults—overactivation and high performance can no longer be sustained. Also, overactivation may not be specific to normal aging; similar patterns characterize pathological aging due to AD, multiple sclerosis, and in individuals who are sleep deprived (Chee & Choo, 2004; Grady et al., 2003; Staffen et al., 2002). The functional significance of overactivation in the normal aging brain is an important matter for future research.

FUTURE DIRECTIONS IN RESEARCH ON COGNITIVE NEUROSCIENCE AND THE AGING MIND AND BRAIN

Recent research makes evident that multiple factors influence the success with which one meets the challenges of aging. Clearly, the field has moved on from a simple model of global decline to instead center on the relationship between cognitive resources, tasks and compensatory mechanisms late in life. While surviving into old age is undoubtedly accompanied by reductions in aspects of cognition, brain structure, and volume, the plasticity of the brain suggests that compensatory mechanisms may develop to make best use of limited resources to tackle difficult tasks. To better understand the behavioral effects and boundary conditions for compensation for age-related changes in cognition, we need to understand their brain substrates. It has recently been proposed that the aging brain undergoes compensatory changes that either generates new supportive structure (scaffolding) or improves the already existing one (Park & Reuter-Lorenz, 2009). Learning more about how these patterns of scaffolding and compensation develop, and help to maintain cognitive function in old age, is an important goal for future research.

Although compensatory mechanisms associated with old age might help to offset the negative effects of aging, successful aging may rely also on the inherent and differential capacity already available at onset of decline. One increasingly popular notion relates aging success to cognitive reserve, or spare neurocognitive capacity that can be drawn upon to meet mental challenges (e.g., Stern et al., 2005). Cognitive reserve may be influenced by numerous lifestyle factors including physical fitness, diet, education, and social and intellectual engagement throughout adulthood and later life. These factors may influence an enduring capacity for cortical plasticity that in turn permits successful adaptation to neurocognitive aging. While genetics plays an unquestionable role, environmental, cultural, and self-initiated factors clearly contribute to successful aging (see Reuter-Lorenz & Lustig, 2005; Reuter-Lorenz & Mikels, 2006, for reviews). Behavior is indeed influenced by multiple factors and we are becoming much more adept at incorporating multiple levels of analysis in our approach to studying changes in the psychology of aging.

Given that multiple factors contribute to successful aging, an essential and forthcoming task will be to further develop tools by which different kinds of data, such as structural and functional brain images, can be integrated (Casanova et al., 2007). In principle, by adapting such multivariate techniques, it will be feasible to concurrently examine the relation between cognition, brain structure, and brain function while simultaneously taking into consideration influences of genetic and lifestyle factors. Such development would help identifying the risk factors for individual differences in age-related cognitive ability and decline. One area in which such techniques could be useful is to identify genetic risk factors caused by normal aging. For example, recent observations have shown that a specific genetic cluster is linked to episodic memory performance and episodic memory-related brain activity (de Quervain & Papassotiropoulos, 2006). While it remains to be seen if these findings extend to aging, there is already evidence that nondemented older adults with an increased genetic risk for developing dementia have a faster decline in episodic memory (Nilsson et al., 2006) along with altered functional brain activity (Lind et al., 2006).

To fully understand the relationship between various factors that contribute to successful aging, an intraindividual approach (i.e., longitudinal) may be needed. Information about the cognitive and brain correlates of aging is derived mainly from cross-sectional studies. Unlike longitudinal investigations, such studies measure the average rate of aging from correlations with age, and are therefore unable to directly determine rates of change and individual differences therein. Thus, attention needs to be focused on studying the individual as the unit for the observation of developmental change by investigating individual differences across time. Longitudinal measurements have furthered our understanding of individual differences in rate of change in cognition. One of several important future questions, therefore, concerns the basis for intraindividual changes in age-related brain changes.

The current challenges to neurocognitive research on aging are numerous. We have highlighted several in this chapter, including establishing which age-specific activation patterns are linked to compensation versus dysfunction, identifying signs of dysfunction that are transitional stages toward dementia, and determining which neurocognitive strategies characterize successful aging in order to develop effective interventions. There are encouraging signs. New cognitive neuroscience discoveries concerning the possibility for adaptive reorganization and benefits from physical (Colcombe et al., 2004), and cognitive (see Lustig, Shah, Seidler, & Reuter-Lorenz, 2009, for a review) training on the one hand, and improved emotional regulation and well-being on the other (Carstensen & Mikels, 2005), hold promise for revealing positive sides to aging that may have the potential to promote higher quality of life in the later years. Because the brain retains a lifelong capacity for plasticity and adaptive reorganization, an important area for future research involves the neural effects of training and transfer on cognitive for young as well as older adults (e.g. Erickson et al., 2007; Persson & Reuter-Lorenz, 2008). Further research is necessary for identifying the mechanisms of decline, the prospects for improvement, and the constraints on remedial approaches.

ACKNOWLEDGMENTS

This work was supported by National Institute of Health grant AG18286 to the first author. The authors thank the International Max Planck Research School "The Life Course: Evolutionary and Ontogenetic Dynamics" (LIFE) for many rich discussions of life-span development.

REFERENCES

Ances, B. M., Liang, C. L., Leontiev, O., Perthen, J. E., Fleisher, A. S., Lansing, A. E., et al. (2009). Effects of aging on cerebral blood flow, oxygen metabolism, and blood oxygenation level dependent responses to visual stimulation. *Human Brain Mapping, 30*(4), 1120–1132.

Bäckman, L., Andersson, J. L. R., Nyberg, L., Winblad, B., Nordberg, A., & Almkvist, O. (1999). Brain regions associated with episodic retrieval in normal aging and Alzheimer's disease. *Neurology, 52*(9), 1861–1870.

Bäckman, L., & Farde, L. (2005). The role of dopamine systems in cognitive aging. In R. Cabeza, L. Nyberg & A. Park (Eds.), *Cognitive neuroscience of aging* (pp. 58–84). New York: Oxford University Press.

Bäckman, L., Nyberg, L., Lindenberger, U., Li, S. C., & Farde, L. (2006). The correlative triad among aging, dopamine, and cognition: Current status and future prospects. *Neuroscience and Biobehavioral Reviews, 30*(6), 791–807.

Baltes, P. B., & Lindenberger, U. (1997). Emergence of a powerful connection between sensory and cognitive functions across the adult life span: A new window to the study of cognitive aging? *Psychology and Aging, 12*, 12–21.

Bartzokis, G., Sultzer, D., Lu, P. H., Nuechterlein, K. H., Mintz, J., & Cummings, J. L. (2004). Heterogeneous age-related breakdown of white matter structural integrity: Implications for cortical "disconnection" in aging and Alzheimer's disease. *Neurobiology of Aging, 25*(7), 843–851.

Behrmann, M., Geng, J. J., & Shomstein, S. (2004). Parietal cortex and attention. *Current Opinion in Neurobiology, 14*(2), 212–217.

Bozzali, M., Falini, A., Franceschi, M., Cercignani, M., Zuffi, M., Scotti, G., et al. (2002). White matter damage in Alzheimer's disease assessed in vivo using diffusion tensor magnetic resonance imaging. *Journal of Neurology, Neurosurgery, and Psychiatry, 72*, 742–746.

Braak, H., & Braak, E. (1994). Pathology of Alzheimer's disease. In D. B. Calne (Ed.), *Neurodegenerative diseases* (pp. 585–613). Philadelphia, PA: Saunders.

Braver, T. S., Paxton, J. L., Locke, H. S., & Barch, D. M. (2009). Flexible neural mechanisms of cognitive control within human prefrontal cortex. *Proceedings of the National Academy of Sciences in the U S A, 106*(18), 7351–7356.

Brewer, J. B., Zhao, Z., Desmond, J. E., Glover, G. H., & Gabrieli, J. D. E. (1998). Making memories: Brain activity that predicts how well visual experience will be remembered. *Science, 281*, 1185–1187.

Brickman, A. M., Zimmerman, M. E., Paul, R. H., Grieve, S. M., Tate, D. F., Cohen, R. A., et al. (2006). Regional white matter and neuropsychological functioning across the adult lifespan. *Biological Psychiatry, 60*(5), 444–453.

Brown, J. (1958). Some tests of the decay theory of immediate memory. *Quarterly Journal of Experimental Psychology, 10*(1), 12–21.

Buckner, R. L. (2004). Memory and executive function in aging and AD: Multiple factors that cause decline and reserve factors that compensate. *Neuron, 44*, 195–208.

Cabeza, R. (2002). Hemispheric asymmetry reduction in older adults: The HAROLD model. *Psychology and Aging, 17*, 85–100.

Cabeza, R., Anderson, N. D., Locantore, J. K., & McIntosh, A. R. (2002). Aging gracefully: Compensatory brain activity in high-performing older adults. *Neuroimage, 17*, 1394–1402.

Cabeza, R., Daselaar, S. M., Dolcos, F., Prince, S. E., Budde, M., & Nyberg, L. (2004). Task-independent and task-specific age effects on brain activity during working memory, visual attention and episodic retrieval. *Cerebral Cortex, 14*(4), 364–375.

Cabeza, R., Grady, C. L., Nyberg, L., McIntosh, A. R., Tulving, E., Kapur, S., et al. (1997). Age-related differences in neural activity during memory encoding and retrieval: A positron emission tomography study. *Journal of Neuroscience, 17*(1), 391–400.

Cappell, K. A., Gmeindl, L., & Reuter-Lorenz, P. A. (2010). Age differences in prefontal recruitment during verbal working memory maintenance depend on memory load. *Cortex, 46*(4), 462–473.

Carstensen, L. L., & Mikels, J. A. (2005). At the intersection of emotion and cognition: Aging and the positivity effect. *Current Directions in Psychological Science, 14*(3), 117–121.

Casanova, R., Srikanth, R., Baer, A., Laurienti, P. J., Burdette, J. H., Hayasaka, S., et al. (2007). Biological parametric mapping: A statistical toolbox for multimodality brain image analysis. *Neuroimage, 34*(1), 137–143.

Chaim, T. M., Duran, F. L. S., Uchida, R. R., Périco, C. A. M., de Castro, C. C., & Busatto, C. F. (2007). Volumetric reduction of the corpus callosum in Alzheimer's disease in vivo as assessed with voxel-based morphometry. *Psychiatry Research: Neuroimaging, 154*, 59–68.

Chao, L. L., & Knight, R. T. (1997). Prefrontal deficits in attention and inhibitory control with aging. *Cerebral Cortex, 7*(1), 63–69.

Chee, M. W., & Choo, W. C. (2004). Functional imaging of working memory after 24 hr of total sleep deprivation. *Journal of Neuroscience, 24*(19), 4560–4567.

Chee, M. W., Goh, J. O., Venkatraman, V., Tan, J. C., Gutchess, A., Sutton, B., et al. (2006). Age-related changes in object processing and contextual binding revealed using fMR adaptation. *Journal of Cognitive Neuroscience, 18*(4), 495–507.

Chételat, G., & Baron, J. C. (2003). Early diagnosis of Alzheimer's disease: Contribution of structural neuroimaging. *Neuroimage, 18*(2), 525–541.

Colcombe, S. J., Kramer, A. F., Erickson, K. I., Scalf, P., McAuley, E., Cohen, N. J., et al. (2004). Cardiovascular fitness, cortical plasticity, and aging. *Proceedings of the National Academy of Sciences in the U S A, 101*(9), 3316–3321.

Connelly, S. L., & Hasher, L. (1993). Aging and the inhibition of spatial location. *Journal of Experimental Psychology: Human Perception and Performance, 19*(6), 1238–1250.

Daselaar, S. M., & Cabeza, R. (2005). Age-related changes in hemispheric organization. In R. Cabeza, L. Nyberg & A. Park (Eds.), *Cognitive neuroscience of aging* (pp. 325–353). New York: Oxford University Press.

Daselaar, S. M., Fleck, M. S., Dobbins, I. G., Madden, D. J., & Cabeza, R. (2006). Effects of healthy aging on hippocampal and rhinal memory functions: An event-related fMRI study. *Cerebral Cortex, 16*(12), 1771–1782.

Daselaar, S. M., Veltman, D. J., Rombouts, S. A., Raaijmakers, J. G., & Jonker, C. (2003). Neuroanatomical correlates of episodic encoding and retrieval in young and elderly subjects. *Brain, 126*, 43–56.

Davis, S. W., Dennis, N. A., Daselaar, S. M., Fleck, M. S., & Cabeza, R. (2008). Que PASA? The posterior-anterior shift in aging. *Cerebral Cortex, 18*(5), 1201–1209.

de Quervain, D. J., & Papassotiropoulos, A. (2006). Identification of a genetic cluster influencing memory performance and hippocampal activity in humans. *Proceeding of the National Academy of Sciences of the United States of America, 103*(11), 4270–4274.

Desgranges, B., Baron, J. C., de la Sayette, V., Petit-Tabouž, M. C., Benali, K., Landeau, B., et al. (1998). The neural substrates of memory systems impairment in Alzheimer's disease: a PET study of resting brain glucose utilization. *Brain, 121,* 611–631.

Devlin, J. T., & Poldrack, R. A. (2007). In praise of tedious anatomy. *Neuroimage, 37*(4), 1033–1041.

Dickerson, B. C., Bakkour, A., Salat, D. H., Feczko, E., Pacheco, J., Greve, D. N., et al. (2009). The cortical signature of Alzheimer's disease: Regionally specific cortical thinning relates to symptom severity in very mild to mild AD dementia and is detectable in asymptomatic amyloid-positive individuals. *Cerebral Cortex, 19*(3), 497–510.

Dickerson, B. C., Salat, D. H., Greve, D. N., Chua, E. F., Rand-Giovannetti, E., Rentz, D. M., et al. (2005). Increased hippocampal activation in mild cognitive impairment compared to normal aging and AD. *Neurology, 65*(3), 404–411.

DiGirolamo, G. J., Kramer, A. F., Barad, V., Cepeda, N. J., Weissman, D. H., Milham, M. P., et al. (2001). General and task-specific frontal lobe recruitment in older adults during executive processes: A fMRI investigation of task-switching. *Neuroreport, 12,* 2065–2071.

Erickson, K. I., Colcombe, S. J., Wadhwa, R., Bherer, L., Peterson, M. S., Scalf, P. E., et al. (2007). Training-induced plasticity in older adults: effects of training on hemispheric asymmetry. *Neurobiology of Aging, 28*(2), 272–283.

Gazzaley, A., Cooney, J. W., Rissman, J., & D'Esposito, M. (2005). Top-down suppression deficits underlies working memory impairment in normal aging. *Nature Neuroscience, 8*(10), 1298–1300.

Godde, B., Berkefeld, T., David-Jÿrgens, M., & Dinse, H. R. (2002). Age-related changes in primary somatosensory cortex of rats: evidence for parallel degenerative and plastic-adaptive processes. *Neuroscience and Biobehavioral Reviews, 26*(7), 743–752.

Good, C. D., Johnsrude, I. S., Ashburner, J., Henson, R. N. A., Friston, K. J., & Frackowiak, R. S. J. (2001). A voxel-based morphometric study of aging in 465 normal adult human brains. *Neuroimage, 14,* 21–36.

Grady, C. L., Maisog, J. M., Horwitz, B., Ungerleider, L. G., Mentis, M. J., Salerno, J. A., et al. (1994). Age-related changes in cortical blood flow activation during visual processing of faces and location. *Journal of Neuroscience, 14,* 1450–1462.

Grady, C. L., McIntosh, A. R., Beig, S., Keightley, M. L., Burian, H., & Black, S. E. (2003). Evidence from functional neuroimaging of a compensatory prefrontal network in Alzheimer's disease. *Journal of Neuroscience, 23,* 986–993.

Grady, C. L., McIntosh, A. R., Bookstein, F., Horwitz, B., Rapoport, S. I., & Haxby, J. V. (1998). Age-related changes in regional cerebral blood flow during working memory for faces. *Neuroimage, 8,* 409–425.

Grady, C. L., McIntosh, A. R., Horwitz, B., Maisog, J. M., Ungerleider, L. G., Mentis, M. J., et al. (1995). Age-related reductions in human recognition memory due to impaired encoding. *Science, 269,* 218–221.

Grady, C. L., Protzner, A. B., Kovacevic, N., Strother, S. C., Afshin-Pour, B., Wojtowicz, M., et al. (2010). A multivariate analysis of age-related differences in default mode and task-positive networks across multiple cognitive domains. *Cerebral Cortex, 26*(6), 1432–1447.

Greenwood, P. M. (2000). The frontal aging hypothesis evaluated. *Journal of the International Neuropsychological Society, 6*(6), 705–726.

Greenwood, P. M. (2007). Functional plasticity in cognitive aging: Review and hypothesis. *Neuropsychology, 21,* 657–673.

Greicius, M. D., Srivastava, G., Reiss, A. L., & Menon, V. (2004). Default-mode network activity distinguishes Alzheimer's disease from healthy aging: Evidence from functional MRI. *Proceedings of the National Academy of Sciences in the U S A, 101*(13), 4637–4642.

Grossman, M., Cooke, A., DeVita, C., Alsop, D., Detre, J., Chen, W., et al. (2002). Age-related changes in working memory during sentence comprehension: An fMRI study. *Neuroimage, 15,* 302–317.

Gutchess, A. H., Welsh, R. C., Hedden, T., Bangert, A., Minear, M., Liu, L. L., et al. (2005). Aging and the neural correlates of successful picture encoding: Frontal activations compensate for decreased medial-temporal activity. *Journal of Cognitive Neuroscience, 17*(1), 84–96.

Hartley, A. A. (1993). Evidence for the selective preservation of spatial selective attention in old age. *Psychology and Aging, 8*(3), 371–379.

Huettel, S. A., Singerman, J. D., & McCarthy, G. (2001). The effects of aging upon the hemodynamic response measured by functional MRI. *Neuroimage, 13*(1), 161–175.

Jernigan, T. L., Archibald, S. L., Fennema-Notestine, C., Gamst, A. C., Stout, J. C., Bonner, J., et al. (2001). Effects of age on tissues and regions of the cerebrum and cerebellum. *Neurobiology of Aging, 22*, 581–594.

Jonides, J., Marshuetz, C., Smith, E. E., Reuter-Lorenz, P. A., Koeppe, R. A., & Hartley, A. (2000). Age differences in behavior and PET activation reveal differences in interference resolution in verbal working memory. *Journal of Cognitive Neuroscience, 12*(1), 188–196.

Kato, T., Knopman, D., & Liu, H. Y. (2001). Dissociation of regional activation in mild AD during visual encoding—A functional MRI study. *Neurology, 57*(5), 812–816.

Lawrence, B., Myerson, J., & Hale, S. (1998). Differential decline of verbal and visuospatial processing speed across the adult life span. *Aging, Neuropsychology and Cognition, 5*(2), 129–146.

Leshikar, E. D., Gutchess, A. H., Hebrank, A. C., Sutton, B. P., & Park, D. C. (2010). The impact of increased relational encoding demands on frontal and hippocampal function in older adults. *Cortex, 46*(4), 507–521.

Li, S. C., Lindenberger, U., & Sikström, S. (2001). Aging cognition: from neuromodulation to representation. *Trends in Cognitive Sciences, 5*(11), 479–486.

Lind, J., Persson, J., Ingvar, C. M., Larsson, A., Cruts, M., Van Broeckhoven, C., et al. (2006). Reduced functional brain activity response in cognitively intact apolipoprotein E epsilon4 carriers. *Brain, 129*, 1240–1248.

Logan, J. M., Sanders, A. L., Snyder, A. Z., Morris, J. C., & Buckner, R. L. (2002). Under-recruitment and non-selective recruitment: Dissociable neural mechanisms associated with aging. *Neuron, 33*, 827–840.

Lustig, C., May, C. P., & Hasher, L. (2001). Working memory span and the role of proactive interference. *Journal of Experimental Psychology: General, 130*(2), 199–207.

Lustig, C., Shah, P., Seidler, R., & Reuter-Lorenz, P. A. (2009). Aging, training, and the brain: a review and future directions. *Neuropsychology review, 19*(4), 504–522.

Madden, D. J., Bennett, I. J., & Song, A. W. (2009). Cerebral white matter integrity and cognitive aging: Contributions from diffusion tensor imaging. *Neuropsychology review, 19*, 415–435.

Madden, D. J., Spaniol, J., Whiting, W. L., Bucur, B., Provenzale, J. M., Cabeza, R., et al. (2007). Adult age differences in the functional neuroanatomy of visual attention: A combined fMRI and DTI study. *Neurobiology of aging, 28*(3), 459–476.

Madden, D. J., Whiting, W. L., & Huettel, S. A. (2005). Age-related changes in neural activity during visual perception and attention. In R. Cabeza, L. Nyberg, & A. Park (Eds.), *Cognitive neuroscience of aging* (pp. 157–185). New York: Oxford University Press.

Maguire, E. A., & Frith, C. D. (2004). The brain network associated with acquiring semantic knowledge. *Neuroimage, 22*(1), 171–178.

McDowd, J. M., & Shaw, R. J. (2000). Attention and aging: A functional perspective. In F. I. M. Craik & T. A. Salthouse (Eds.), *The handbook of aging and cognition* (pp. 221–292). Mahwah, NJ: Erlbaum.

Milham, M. P., Erickson, K. I., Banich, M. T., Kramer, A. F., Webb, A., Wszalek, T., et al. (2002). Attentional control in the aging brain: Insights from an fMRI study of the Stroop task. *Brain and Cognition, 49*, 277–296.

Morcom, A. M., Good, C. D., Frackowiak, R. S. J., & Rugg, M. D. (2003). Age effects on the neural correlates of successful memory encoding. *Brain, 126*, 213–229.

Morcom, A. M., Li, J., & Rugg, M. D. (2007). Age effects on the neural correlates of episodic retrieval: increased cortical recruitment with matched performance. *Cerebral Cortex, 17*(11), 2491–2506.

Moscovitch, M., & Winocour, G. (1995). Frontal lobes, memory, and aging. *Annual New York Academy of Science, 769*, 119–150.

Nielson, K. A., Langenecker, S. A., & Garavan, H. (2002). Differences in the functional neuroanatomy of inhibitory control across the adult life span. *Psychology and Aging, 17*(1), 56–71.

Nilsson, L. G., Adolfsson, R., Bäckman, L., Cruts, M., Nyberg, L., Small, B. J., et al. (2006). The influence of APOE status on episodic and semantic memory: Data from a population-based study. *Neuropsychology, 20*(6), 645–657.

Nyberg, L., Cabeza, R., & Tulving, E. (1996). PET studies of encoding and retrieval: The HERA model. *Psychonomic Bulletin & Review, 3*(2), 135–148.

Nyberg, L., McIntosh, A. R., Houle, S., Nilsson, L.-G., & Tulving, E. (1996). Activation of medial temporal lobe structures during episodic memory retrieval. *Nature, 380*, 715–717.

Otten, L. J., & Rugg, M. D. (2001). Task-dependency of the neural correlates of episodic encoding as measured by fMRI. *Cerebral Cortex, 11*(12), 1150–1160.

Pariente, J., Cole, S., Henson, R., Clare, L., Kennedy, A., Rossor, M., et al. (2005). Alzheimer's patients engage an alternative network during a memory task. *Annals of Neurology, 58*(6), 870–879.

Park, D. C., Lautenschlager, G., Hedden, T., Davidson, N. S., Smith, A. D., Smith P. K. (2002). Models of visuospatial and verbal memory across the adult life span. *Psychology and Aging, 17*, 299–320.

Park, D. C., & Gutchess, A. H. (2005). Long-term memory and aging: A cognitive neuroscience approach. In R. Cabeza, L. Nyberg, & D. C. Park (Eds.), *Cognitive neuroscience of aging* (pp. 218–245). New York: Oxford University Press.

Park, D. C., Polk, T. A., Park, R., Minear, M., Savage, A., & Smith, M. R. (2004). Aging reduces neural specialization in ventral visual cortex. *Proceedings of the National Academy of Sciences in the U S A, 101*(35), 13091–13095.

Park, D. C., & Reuter-Lorenz, P. (2009). The adaptive brain: Aging and neurocognitive scaffolding. *Annual Review of Psychology, 60,* 173–196.

Parkin, A. J., & Walter, B. M. (1991). Aging, short-term memory, and frontal dysfunction. *Psychobiology, 19,* 175–179.

Payer, D., Marshuetz, C., Sutton, B., Hebrank, A., Welsh, R. C., & Park, D. C. (2006). Decreased neural specialization in old adults on a working memory task. *Neuroreport, 17*(5), 487–491.

Persson, J., & Nyberg, L. (2006). Altered brain activity in healthy seniors: what does it mean? *Progress in Brain Research, 157,* 45–56.

Persson, J., Nyberg, L., Lind, J., Larsson, A., Nilsson, L. G., Ingvar, M., et al. (2006). Structure - function correlates of cognitive decline in aging. *Cerebral Cortex, 16*(7), 907–915.

Persson, J., & Reuter-Lorenz, P. A. (2008). Gaining control: Training executive function and far transfer of the ability to resolve interference. *Psychological Science, 19*(9), 881–888.

Persson, J., Sylvester, C.-Y. C., Nelson, J. K., Welsh, K. M., Jonides, J., & Reuter-Lorenz, P. A. (2004). Selection requirements during verb generation: Differential recruitment in older and younger adults. *Neuroimage, 23,* 1382–1390.

Peterson, L. R., & Peterson, M. J. (1959). Short-term retention of individual verbal items. *Journal of Experimental Psychology, 58*(3), 193–198.

Raz, N. (2000). Aging of the brain and its impact on cognitive performance: Integration of structural and functional findings. In F. I. M. Craik & T. A. Salthouse (Eds.), *Handbook of aging and cognition* (pp. 1–90). Mahwah, NJ: Erlbaum.

Raz, N., Gunning-Dixon, F., Head, D., Rodrigue, K. M., Williamson, A., & Acker, J. D. (2004). Aging, sexual dimorphism, and hemispheric asymmetry of the cerebral cortex: Replicability of regional differences in volume. *Neurobiology of Aging, 25,* 377–396.

Raz, N., Gunning-Dixon, F. M., Head, D., Dupuis, J. H., & Acker, J. D. (1998). Neuroanatomical correlates of cognitive aging: Evidence from structural magnetic resonance imaging. *Neuropsychology, 12,* 95–114.

Raz, N., Gunning-Dixon, F. M., Head, D., Dupuis, J. H., McQuain, J., Briggs, S. D., et al. (1997). Selective aging of the human cerebral cortex observed in vivo: Differential vulnerability of the prefrontal gray matter. *Cerebral Cortex, 7*(3), 268–282.

Raz, N., Lindenberger, U., Rodrigue, K. M., Kennedy, K. M., Head, D., Williamson, A., et al. (2005). Regional brain changes in aging healthy adults: General trends, individual differences and modifiers. *Cerebral Cortex, 15*(11), 1676–1689.

Raz, N., Rodrigue, K. M., & Haacke, E. M. (2007). Brain aging and its modifiers: Insights from in vivo neuromorphometry and susceptibility weighted imaging. *Annals of the New York Academy of Sciences, 1097,* 84–93.

Reuter-Lorenz, P. A., & Cappell, K. (2008). Neurocognitive aging and the compensation hypothesis. *Current Directions in Psychological Science, 17,* 177–182.

Reuter-Lorenz, P. A., Jonides, J., Smith, E. E., Hartley, A., Miller, A., Marschuetz, C., et al. (2000). Age differences in the frontal lateralization of verbal and spatial working memory revealed by PET. *Journal of Cognitive Neuroscience, 12,* 174–187.

Reuter-Lorenz, P. A., & Lustig, C. (2005). Brain aging: Reorganizing discoveries about the aging mind. *Current Opinion in Neurobiology, 15*(2), 245–251.

Reuter-Lorenz, P. A., & Mikels, J. A. (2006). The aging brain: Implications of enduring plasticity for behavioral and cultural change. In P. B. Baltes, P. A. Reuter-Lorenz, & F. Rösler (Eds.), *Lifespan development and the brain: The perspective of biocultural co-constructivism* (pp. 255–276). New York: Cambridge University Press.

Reuter-Lorenz, P. A., & Park, D. (2010). Human neuroscience and the aging mind: A new look at old problems. *Journal of Gerontology: Psychological Sciences, 65B*(4), 405–415.

Reuter-Lorenz, P. A., Stanczak, L., & Miller, A. C. (1999). Neural recruitment and cognitive aging: Two hemispheres are better than one, especially as you age. *Psychological Science, 10*(6), 494–500.

Reuter-Lorenz, P. A., & Sylvester, C.-Y. C. (2005). The cognitive neuroscience of working memory and aging. In R. Cabeza, L. Nyberg, & A. Park (Eds.), *Cognitive neuroscience of aging* (pp. 186–217). New York: Oxford University Press.

Rodrigue, K. M., Kennedy, K. M., & Park, D. C. (2009). Beta-amyloid deposition and the aging brain. *Neuropsychology review, 19*(4), 436–450.

Rodrigue, K. M., & Raz, N. (2004). Shrinkage of the entorhinal cortex over five years predicts memory performance in healthy adults. *Journal of Neuroscience, 24*(4), 956–963.

Rypma, B., & D'Esposito, M. (2000). Isolating the neural mechanisms of age-related changes in human working memory. *Nature Neuroscience, 3*, 509–515.

Rypma, B., Prabhakaran, V., Desmond, J. E., & Gabrieli, J. D. E. (2001). Age difference in prefrontal cortical activity in working memory. *Psychology and Aging, 16*, 371–384.

Salmon, E., Collette, F., Degueldre, C., Lemaire, C., & Franck, G. (2000). Voxel-based analysis of confounding effects of age and dementia severity on cerebral metabolism in Alzheimer's disease. *Human Brain Mapping, 10*, 39–48.

Schaie, K. W. (1996). *Intellectual development in adulthood: The Seattle longitudinal study.* Cambridge: Cambridge University Press.

Schmolesky, M. T., Wang, Y., Pu, M., & Leventhal, A. G. (2000). Degradation of stimulus selectivity of visual cortical cells in senescent rhesus monkeys. *Nature Neuroscience, 3*(4), 384–390.

Schneider-Garces, N. J., Gordon, B. A., Brumback-Peltz, C. R., Shin, E., Lee, Y., Sutton, B. P., et al. (2009). Span, CRUNCH, and beyond: Working memory capacity and the aging brain. *Journal of Cognitive Neuroscience, 22*(4), 655–669.

Schneider, B. A., & Pichora-Fuller, M. K. (2000). Implication of perceptual deterioration for cognitive aging research. In F. I. M. Craik & T. A. Salthouse (Eds.), *The handbook of aging and cognition* (pp. 155–219). Mahwah, NJ: Erlbaum.

Schretlen, D., Pearlson, G. D., Anthony, J. C., Aylward, E. H., Augustine, A. M., Davis, A., et al. (2000). Elucidating the contributions of processing speed, executive ability, and frontal lobe volume to normal age-related differences in fluid intelligence. *Journal of the International Neuropsychological Society, 6*, 52–61.

Scoville, W. B., & Milner, B. (1957). Loss of recent memory after bilateral hippocampal lesions. *Journal of Neurology, Neurosurgery, and Psychiatry, 20*, 11–21.

Seidler, R. D., Bernard, J. A., Burutolu, T. B., Fling, B. W., Gordon, M. T., Gwin, J. T., et al. (2010). Motor control and aging: Links to age-related brain structural, functional, and biochemical effects. *Neuroscience and Biobehavioral Reviews, 34*(5), 721–733.

Smith, E. E., Geva, A., Jonides, J., Miller, A., Reuter-Lorenz, P., & Koeppe, R. A. (2001). The neural basis of task-switching in working memory: Effects of performance and aging. *Proceedings of the National Academy of Sciences in the U S A, 98*(4), 2095–2100.

Smith, E. E., & Jonides, J. (1999). Storage and executive processes in the frontal lobes. *Science, 283*, 1657–1661.

Staffen, W., Mair, A., Zauner, H., Unterrainer, J., Niederhofer, H., Kutzelnigg, A., et al. (2002). Cognitive function and fMRI in patients with multiple sclerosis: evidence for compensatory cortical activation during an attention task. *Brain, 125*, 1275–1282.

Stern, Y., Habeck, C., Moeller, J., Scarmeas, N., Anderson, K. E., Hilton, H. J., et al. (2005). Brain networks associated with cognitive reserve in healthy young and old adults. *Cerebral Cortex, 15*(4), 394–402.

Uylings, H. B. M., & de Brabander, J. M. (2002). Neuronal changes in normal human aging and Alzheimer's disease. *Brain and Cognition, 49*, 268–276.

Velanova, K., Lustig, C., Jacoby, L. L., & Buckner, R. L. (2007). Evidence for frontally-mediated controlled processing differences in older adults. *Cerebral Cortex, 17*(5), 1033–1046.

Voss, M. W., Erickson, K. I., Chaddock, L., Prakash, R. S., Colcombe, S. J., Morris, K. S., et al. (2008). Dedifferentiation in the visual cortex: An fMRI investigation of individual differences in older adults. *Brain Research, 1244*, 121–131.

West, R. L. (1993). Regionally specific loss of neurons in the aging human hippocampus. *Neurobiology of Aging, 14*, 287–293.

West, R. L. (1996). An application of prefrontal cortex function theory to cognitive aging. *Psychological Bulletin, 120*, 272–292.

Woodruff-Pak, D. S. (1997). *The neuropsychology of aging.* Malden, MA: Blackwell.

Zhang, Y., Schuff, N., Jahng, G. H., Bayne, W., Mori, S., Schad, L., et al. (2007). Diffusion tensor imaging of cingulum fibers in mild cognitive impairment and Alzheimer disease. *Neurology, 68*, 13–19.

THE MAGICAL LETTERS *P, F, C,* AND SOMETIMES *U*: THE RISE AND FALL OF EXECUTIVE ATTENTION WITH THE DEVELOPMENT OF PREFRONTAL CORTEX

16

Jason M. Watson, Ann E. Lambert, A. Eve Miller, and David L. Strayer

Just over 50 years ago, in his classic article on the processing capacity of humans, George Miller wrote of being persecuted by the integer seven, plus or minus two (Miller, 1956). To revisit and paraphrase Miller's now-famous opening lines for our purposes, our problem is that we have been persecuted by *letters* rather than *numbers*. Yet, much like Miller's magic number, these letters have followed us around, intruded in our most private data, and assaulted us from the pages of our most public and highly respected journals. Indeed, the persistence with which these letters plague us is far more than a random accident. What letters haunt us? Three of them, and they are in serial order *P, F,* and *C*. When combined, they form the acronym PFC, shorthand notation within cognitive neuroscience for that portion of the brain known as the prefrontal cortex. As with Miller and the number seven, we are convinced there must be something special about these letters, and hence this neural substrate, or else we too are suffering from delusions of persecution.

Before beginning our extended case history of precisely how these three letters have haunted us, given that we were charged by the editors with the task of writing a chapter on the development of attention, we feel compelled to point out straightaway that *age does not cause any observed behavioral difference*. Moreover, this maxim holds true whether it be age-related changes in attention, memory, perception, or any other cognitive domain. At face value, this statement may seem controversial or even inflammatory. This reaction may be particularly true for readers who are new researchers to the field of aging and development and who intend to build their scientific career by observing differences in behavior between children and young adults or between young adults and older adults. However, upon further consideration, what this statement really represents is an ongoing theoretical challenge to a program of psychological research. That is, aging/developmental researchers generally agree that age is merely a proxy for the true underlying cause of cognitive change and that *age must be considered in context*. Despite this common ground, there is considerable debate as to what variable, if any, might adequately capture the common, underlying mechanism associated with age (cf., Baltes & Lindenberger, 1997). In other words, what is the appropriate context in which to consider cognitive aging? Several parties have emerged to advance ostensibly different, but often correlated, "common causes" to explain the age-related changes that have been observed in cognition. For example, researchers comparing young and older adults find that these candidate causes range from the reduced processing speed to the perceptual degradation to the inhibitory dysfunction thought to accompany advanced age, with each theoretical camp often claiming the ability to account for not only their own but also the other's findings (see Hasher & Zacks, 1988; Salthouse, 1996; Schneider & Pichora-Fuller, 2000, for a representative sample).

In the current chapter, our intent is to (1) take a cognitive neuroscience approach, and (2) review the striking symmetry that exists between the well-established biological development of frontal cortex across the life span and the corresponding rise and fall of goal-directed behavior. Although attention is clearly multifaceted and complex, we have elected to use this chapter as an opportunity to have an extended conversation with readers on what we believe to be the particular importance of effective goal maintenance. Indeed, across approximately the past 2 decades, there has been a veritable explosion of research on what Randy Engle and colleagues have referred to as executive attention (Engle, 2002). For our purposes, consistent with Engle, we define executive attention as the ability to effectively maintain task goals in the face of distraction or conflict, thereby exerting cognitive control over the contents of thought and action. And to bring our case history full circle, in virtually every published study on executive attention and goal-directed behavior, we find those pesky but magical letters *P*, *F*, and *C*. Given the widespread use of cognitive neuroscience to more fully develop and test psychological theory, it is entirely appropriate to consider what explanatory traction, if any, might be gained by framing research questions on aging and attention in the context of the biological development of frontal cortex.

From this point of view, in the cognitive neuroscience literature, one observation is clear and stands apart from the rest: *There is an inverted, U-shaped function that characterizes the development of frontal cortex across the life span where not all biological change is strictly loss or gain. If one compares children and young adults, frontal cortex is proliferating, whereas, if one compares young adults against older adults, frontal cortex is diminishing.* In the first section, we briefly review the neurobiological evidence in support of this curvilinear development of frontal cortex across the life span, with particular emphasis on the ubiquitous nature of the inverted, U-shaped function illustrated in Figure 16.1 across a myriad of biological substrates (e.g., myelination, synaptogenesis, metabolism, and brain volume). With the second section, we pay quick tribute to the work of "PFC pioneers" like Alan Baddeley, Patricia Goldman-Rakic, and others who have generated a long, rich history of theoretically inspired research on the neural substrates of executive attention.

We also believe that two, interrelated and testable hypotheses follow from the simple observation that the neurobiological development of frontal cortex is curvilinear: **Hypothesis 1:** *The rise and fall in the development of frontal cortex will be mirrored by increases and decreases in executive attention across the life span for children, young adults, and older adults.* Hence, in the third section, we attempt to harness the full explanatory power of this hypothesis by briefly reviewing executive attention performance in these three age groups across a range of target tasks that vary considerably in their complexity. Specifically, we discuss how children, young adults, and older adults rise and fall in their ability to successfully maintain goals in classic, cognitive psychology lab tasks that manipulate simple stimulus-response

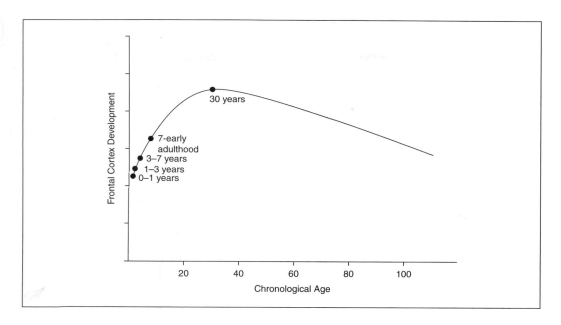

FIGURE 16.1 **The curvilinear development of frontal cortex across the life span.** **Developmental changes have been observed in a variety of dependent measures including myelination, synaptogenesis, dendritic branching, glucose metabolism, blood flow, dopaminergic neurotransmitter function, and brain volume.**

conflict (cf., Simon, 1969; Stroop, 1935). On the opposite extreme, we also review curvilinear patterns that have been observed across age groups in more complicated, applied tasks like driving a motor vehicle where multiple sources of information place stress on the limited-capacity attentional resources that are required for safe driving (cf., Strayer & Drews, 2004). By highlighting executive attention performance in only a small number of behavioral paradigms that vary widely in complexity, we readily acknowledge that our chapter departs from the "data blitz" approach to which many readers of our chapter have likely grown accustomed. To address this potential concern, we refer the interested reader to our References section where other chapters have been cited that provide excellent reviews of additional data/paradigms that have been used to characterize age-related changes in cognition across the life span, including infants (cf., Diamond, 2002; Kramer & Madden, 2008). Our primary point is that the relationship between age and attentional performance tends to be curvilinear, independent of task complexity, and, when considered in context, age might be recast as the progressive and regressive maturation of the PFC in particular.

Hypothesis 2: *The increases and decreases in executive attention across the life span in children, young adults, and older adults will be qualified by individual differences in performance. Executive attention and behavioral performance will be more comparable, independent of age, if/when subsets of individuals across groups have been equated on the observed development of frontal cortex as outlined in* **Hypothesis 1**. In the fourth section, we review the findings that have emerged from the prevailing *zeitgeist* in cognitive psychology of considering individual differences in executive attention strictly in young adults, with particular emphasis on how the work of Randy Engle and colleagues has substantially advanced theory on the brain basis of goal-directed cognition. Furthermore, we consider the merit of extending an individual differences approach to either children or older adults. That is, if only for the ease of statistical comparison, children or older adults are often considered uniform in their behavioral performance. However, it might be possible to equate performance across the life span were one to adequately control for the development or degradation of PFC. To return to an earlier point, such an empirical demonstration would provide strong evidence that age is merely a proxy and does not itself cause cognitive change. Consistent with this argument, recent work suggests that individual differences in the integrity of frontal cortex may contribute to variability in older adult performance in memory tasks that require executive attention (see Roediger & McDaniel, 2007, for a review).

Even so, the promise of individual differences has not yet been fully realized in mainstream research on cognitive aging and development. To this end, in the fifth section, we entertain some pitfalls that might be involved when combining an appreciation of individual differences in the development of PFC with cross-sectional group studies on executive attention in children, young adults, and older adults. Specifically, additional group differences may still exist above and beyond the integrity of PFC such as expertise, processing speed, or even sensory function. In the sixth and final section, to balance these potential pitfalls, we outline an applied cognitive neuroscience approach to conducting psychological research. When guided by this novel approach, we believe several additional, testable hypotheses follow from a frontal account of the biological/cognitive change in executive attention associated with age. We now turn our chapter to a brief review of the curvilinear development of frontal cortex across the life span.

▧ CURVILINEAR DEVELOPMENT OF FRONTAL CORTEX ACROSS THE LIFE SPAN: THE MAGIC LETTER *U*

The frontal lobe refers to the cortex anterior to the central sulcus, and it contains several prominent areas including (1) the primary motor strip that supports gross motor movement, (2) premotor and supplementary motor areas that provide plans for guiding this gross motor movement, and (3) the PFC with its various, specialized subregions (e.g., dorsolateral PFC [DLPFC] that supports goal-directed behavior). The PFC is especially large, accounting for a quarter of all cerebral cortex, and DLPFC in particular is often implicated in higher-order cognition, including a role for executive attention (Diamond, 2002; Kane & Engle, 2002). Across the life span, the frontal lobe houses some of the biggest physiological changes in the brain. Specifically, as shown in Figure 16.1, there is an inverted, U-shaped function that characterizes the development of frontal cortex across the life span such that it gradually builds, then peaks, and eventually declines in terms of both its structural sophistication and its underlying computational power. Although the basic anatomy of the frontal lobe is present at birth, it is far from mature. For example, physiological changes in the frontal lobe during the first few years of life and into adolescence include increased myelination, synaptogenesis, dendritic branching, and glucose metabolism (see

De Luca & Leventer, 2008, for a more extensive discussion of early developmental changes of the brain in each of these structural measures). The other three lobes—parietal, temporal, and occipital—may show similar early developmental trajectories, such as a cortex-wide tendency for increased glucose metabolism from infancy into adolescence (Chugani, Phelps, & Mazziotta, 1987). However, it is noteworthy that the decline in frontal cortex with advanced age across young to middle to old adulthood, including reduced blood flow or loss of neural tissue, is especially dramatic when compared to the other cerebral cortices (Gur, Gur, Obrist, Skolnick, & Reivitch, 1987; Raz et al., 1993; Raz, 2000). Indeed, the decrease in the volume of frontal cortex, particularly in PFC, is apparent by age 30, with the gradual decline progressing at a rate of about 0.2% per year throughout middle age (Buckner, Head, & Lustig, 2006; Raz, 2000; West, 1996).

CONTRIBUTIONS FROM THE PFC PIONEERS

By presenting our frontal lobe hypothesis, we continue a legacy of other cognitive scientists who have sought to draw an association between prefrontal cortex and goal-directed behavior. To give the interested reader some historical perspective, we believe that work connecting the frontal lobe to executive attention has been occurring since at least the mid-19th century. Specifically, in 1848, a man named Phineas Gage was involved in a railroad construction accident that damaged his frontal lobe and forever altered his personality (and ultimately, in hindsight, clinical and scientific interest in the frontal lobe). Prior to his unfortunate accident, Phineas was a conscientious individual with great responsibility as the foreman for a railroad construction company. After the accident, his demeanor changed so drastically that it was said by family and friends that Phineas just "wasn't Phineas anymore." By the same token, post-Phineas, scientific investigation of frontal contributions to complex, higher-order cognition would never be quite the same either. Given that scientific understanding of the role the PFC plays in supporting executive attention has increased exponentially over the past 150 plus years, it is clearly beyond the scope of the current chapter to exhaustively review the empirical or theoretical contributions of every researcher. However, we would be remiss if we failed to briefly acknowledge the seminal work of neuropsychologists like Alexander Luria's studies of executive dysfunction in patients with frontal lobe damage (Luria, 1966). Even so, given that the current authors are cognitive psychologists by training, we will play to our strengths and focus more in-depth, yet admittedly abridged, discussion on what we believe are particularly important milestones from a collection of talented cognitive psychologists and neuroscientists that we affectionately refer to as the "PFC pioneers."

If one were to ask just about any self-respecting cognitive psychologist to list what models of executive attention were among the most influential in his/her field over the last 30 years, the discussion would quite likely begin with Alan Baddeley's research on working memory and the central executive (cf., Baddeley & Hitch, 1974; Baddeley, 1992). In hindsight, Baddeley's model revolutionized the way cognitive psychologists conceived of memory, effectively opening the "black box" of what researchers had been calling *short-term memory* by introducing the concept of a *central executive* that acted as a processor to coordinate the flow of information in various component or slave systems (e.g., the phonological loop or the visuospatial sketchpad). For our purposes, the take-home message was that, according to Baddeley, short-term memory consisted of more cognitive operations than just the *maintenance* or *rehearsal* of information for the sole purpose of transfer into long-term memory. For the sake of comparison and a greater appreciation of the historical context of Baddeley's argument about the *modus operandi* of short-term or working memory, we refer the interested reader to Atkinson and Shiffrin's (1968, 1971) classic modal or "boxes" model of memory. Here the reader will find additional discussion of an equally important but certainly more theoretically limited role of short-term memory acting as a way station into long-term memory. However, to return to our main point, according to Baddeley, one could "work with" or *manipulate* the information stored in short-term memory for other purposes above and beyond transfer into long-term memory by using the attentional processing resources of the central executive (hence, Baddeley's aptly named model of *working memory*).

In our opinion, the novel concept of a central executive that Baddeley pioneered in 1974 would eventually culminate in a wave of models of executive attention that have been developed over approximately the past 15–20 years by both cognitive psychologists and cognitive neuroscientists (e.g., see Braver, Gray, & Burgess, 2007; Cohen, Braver, & O'Reilly, 1998; Cowan, 1995; Dempster, 1992; Diamond, 2002; Duncan, 1995; Engle, 2002; Engle, Kane, & Tuholski, 1999; Fuster, 1989; Miller & Cohen, 2001; Posner & DiGirolamo, 1998; Roberts & Pennington, 1996; Shallice & Burgess, 1996; Smith & Jonides, 1997). Of course, these models differ slightly to considerably in their finer details, and we will reserve more extensive discussion of these models—particularly the influential work of Randy Engle, Jonathan Cohen, Todd Braver, and others on how the PFC supports executive attention—until section IV of this chapter. However, if one were to attempt to synthesize the preceding list of models of executive attention, we believe the spirit of what Baddeley had originally termed the *central executive* would be alive, well, and frequently ascribed to the PFC (leading us to the point where we now claim, only half-jokingly, that these three letters are haunting us). That is, executive attention might well be conceived of as the capacity of Baddeley's central executive to actively maintain task goals, to avoid distraction, and to exert cognitive control over the contents of thought and action. And to return to our ongoing discussion of the magical letters *P, F, C*, and the curvilinear development of this highly specialized neural substrate across the life span as illustrated in Figure 16.1, it is noteworthy that the neuroanatomy of DLPFC seems particularly well suited to support the psychological construct of executive attention. For example, Goldman-Rakic's (1987) landmark work with nonhuman primates demonstrated that the DLPFC is massively interconnected with other cortical and subcortical areas (also see Barbas & Mesulam, 1981, 1985; Nauta, 1964, 1972). Hence, these reciprocal connections between DLPFC and other brain regions may be necessary to successfully implement the complex set of coordinated behaviors captured by the construct of executive attention including goal maintenance, goal updating, and minimizing interference from distracters (see Kane & Engle, 2002; Miller & Cohen, 2001). We now turn our chapter to our third section, a modest review of how the rise and fall of executive attention generally mirrors the curvilinear development of frontal cortex across the life span, independent of task complexity.

▣ THE RISE AND FALL OF EXECUTIVE ATTENTION ACROSS THE LIFE SPAN MIRRORS FRONTAL CORTEX DEVELOPMENT

Having established that the development of frontal cortex is curvilinear, our first hypothesis is the following: *The rise and fall in the development of frontal cortex will be mirrored by increases and decreases in executive attention across the life span for children, young adults, and older adults.* In the current section, to test this hypothesis and to best illustrate its explanatory power, we will restrict our review of curvilinear group differences in executive attention to three target tasks that vary considerably in their complexity and component operations: (1) Simon tasks, (2) divided attention tasks, and (3) driving a motor vehicle. For additional, more direct evidence of the relationship between the integrity of underlying PFC structure and cognitive function across the life span, we refer the interested reader to the thorough, excellent reviews that have been previously written on this topic by both Diamond and Raz (Diamond, 2002; Raz, 2000).

Simon Task

In one version of the classic Simon task (cf., Simon, 1969; Castel, Balota, Hutchison, Logan, & Yap, 2007), participants are asked to push one button with their left hand when they see a left facing arrow (e.g., ←) and to push a different button with their right hand for a right facing arrow (e.g., →). Arrows are presented for an orientation judgment in three different conditions: congruent, neutral, and incongruent. In the congruent condition, arrows are presented on the same side of visual space as they are facing (e.g., ← is presented in the left side of space, a few degrees from a central fixation area). In the neutral condition, arrows are presented centrally. In the incongruent condition, arrows are presented on the opposite side of visual space as they are facing (e.g., ← is presented in the right side of space, again a few degrees from a central fixation area). Typically, participants are instructed to ignore the spatial location of stimuli when making their arrow orientation judgments because spatial cues may mislead them and cause errors. For our purposes, the Simon task is an optimal one because it challenges limited executive attention resources by requiring participants to respond to arrows when spatial cues are incongruent or conflict with the direction of the arrow (e.g., ← presented for a decision in the right side of visual space). Hence, individuals will perform poorer on this task to the extent that reduced executive attention renders them unable to cognitively control stimulus-response conflict or the tendency to use distracting, irrelevant spatial cues when making decisions about the directionality of the arrows. Put somewhat differently, the Simon task might be considered a selective attention task in that it requires individuals to focus mental resources on the task-relevant direction of the arrows while inhibiting the task-irrelevant spatial location of the arrows (Kramer & Madden, 2008). Consistent with these arguments, functional magnetic resonance imaging (fMRI) of the Simon task in young adults revealed increased activity in PFC associated with resolving these interference effects (Peterson et al., 2002).

    To our knowledge, the youngest example of children performing a Simon task comes from Gerardi-Caulton's (2000) study that compared 24-, 30-, and 36-month-old children. In this version of the Simon task, the child had two buttons: one with a star on it and a second with a crescent moon. Stimuli could appear in either the upper left corner, upper right corner, or in the center of the screen. The child's task was to indicate which object appeared on the screen by pressing the corresponding button. Just as with the arrow variant of the Simon task that we described earlier, if the location of the stimulus (e.g., a star presented to the right side) and the corresponding response button were spatially at odds (e.g., a star response button on the left side), this would create stimulus-response conflict that had to be managed in order for the child to respond appropriately. Interestingly, Gerardi-Caulton found that children went from being just above chance on accuracy at 24 months on both the congruent and incongruent trials to over 90% accuracy by 36 months. Moreover, reaction time (RT) also improved from 2800 ms for congruent and 3500 ms for incongruent trials at 24 months to 2050 ms and 2400 ms, respectively, by 36 months. Turning to the other end of the age spectrum, using an arrow variant of the Simon task, Castel et al. (2007) found increased RT and decreased accuracy on incongruent versus congruent trials across young adults to healthy older adults to older adults diagnosed with Alzheimer's disease (AD). Taken together, these studies suggest that as frontal development rises in children and falls with old age and declines further still with dementia, there are corresponding changes in executive attention performance on even relatively simple cognitive tasks like the Simon task that require PFC-mediated goal maintenance to help resolve stimulus-response conflict.

Divided Attention

In contrast to the emphasis placed on selective attention in the Simon task, divided attention experiments require individuals to split their attentional resources between two or more concurrent tasks (Strayer & Drews, 2007). Even so, as complexity increases from selective to divided attention tasks, behavioral performance continues to parallel the rise and fall of frontal cortex development illustrated in Figure 16.1. From a theoretical perspective, divided attention has often been explained in terms of the allotment of limited-capacity resources (Kahneman, 1973; Norman & Bobrow, 1975; Wickens, 1980). The notion is that the processing resources of any system are limited, and there will be performance decrements whenever two or more processes compete for and overload these resources (Norman & Bobrow, 1975). Norman and Bobrow elaborate on this idea by proposing a performance-resource function in which the function is differentiated into data-limited and resource-limited regions. On the one hand, if a task is data-limited, greater allocation of attention will not improve performance. On the other hand, if a task is resource-limited, allocating more attention to the task will improve performance. Thus, when two resource-limited tasks are attempted simultaneously, successful performance on one task will likely come at the expense of the other, yielding classic divided attention costs.

Laboratory task–switching paradigms have been developed to investigate these divided attention costs (Kramer & Madden, 2008). In these paradigms, blocks of trials can either consist of switch trials, requiring a switch of action, or nonswitch trials that do not require an action to be switched. The difference in RT on switch versus nonswitch trials is measured, and the resulting quantity is referred to as a "specific switch cost." Switch costs are thought to tap both the effectiveness of attentional control processes and the efficiency of maintaining dual tasks/goals in working memory (Kramer & Madden, 2008). While both old and young adults show costs of task-switching, it is noteworthy that older adults show larger specific switch costs than younger adults (see Mayr, 2001), and these differences cannot be explained by the reduced processing speed characteristic of those with advanced age (Kramer & Madden, 2008). Laboratory task–switching paradigms have also been used to investigate divided attention costs on the younger end of the age spectrum. Specifically, Crone, Bunge, van der Molen, and Ridderinkhof (2006) investigated task-switching costs for two groups of children (7–10 years and 10–12 years) compared to young adults (20–25 years). They found larger RT costs for children than young adults when participants were required to switch between tasks while repeating responses. Therefore, taken together with Mayr's findings, it appears that a common process may explain both the task-switching improvement observed from childhood to young adults and the task-switching decline observed in old age. Again, as shown in Figure 16.1, these age differences could be explained by a buildup and a reduction in frontally mediated attentional processing resources across the life span (cf., Craik & Byrd, 1982).

Driving

Turning from the lab to an applied setting, driving is another example of a complex divided attention task with multiple embedded goals because it requires drivers to simultaneously scan the visual environment, track their lane, and maintain manual control of a vehicle (Kramer & Madden, 2008). Driving also serves as a good example of how cognitive tasks can transition from an initial classification of data-limited to a classification of resource-limited. That is, the status of a task as data-limited is not necessarily static because with training, a data-limited task can become a resource-limited task. For example, when novice drivers first take the wheel, it is likely that without instruction, they will lack the information (i.e., data) necessary to simply turn on a car. But, given proper information, the novice driver should be able to successfully complete the task. Assuming the information about how to start a car is retained in memory, the behavioral sequence required to complete the task becomes resource-limited rather than data-limited. Moreover, once the basic skill of starting the car is automated, attentional resources become available for additional tasks such as scanning the roadway for potential hazards. In this way, the novice driver becomes an expert as attention-demanding tasks become progressively more automatic (Kramer & Madden, 2008).

These simple sequences, however, pale in comparison to the complexity and diversity of attention-demanding situations that the novice driver may encounter while on the road. For instance, compared to experienced drivers, novices tend to use less effective scan strategies in dangerous driving conditions by looking straight ahead rather than side to side—a scan style that can lead to the failure of the driver to notice merging vehicles or oncoming traffic (Underwood, Crundall, & Chapman, 2007). One explanation for this difference is that novices lack the ability to allocate enough attentional resources to visual search because they have not yet automated preliminary skills such as basic control of the automobile (Underwood et al., 2007).

While this may be partly true, novice driving ability is often confounded with age. In the United States, teenagers can begin to learn to drive as early as age 14 or 15, and by age 16 they are eligible to receive a driver's license. Given that frontal lobe development is not complete until the mid-20s or possibly even age 30, driving performance could also suffer due to a reduced pool of attentional processing resources in the PFC of novice drivers. Consistent with this argument and more generally consistent with the curvilinear development of frontal cortex across the life span as illustrated in Figure 16.1, driving performance fluctuates dramatically across teenagers, middle-aged adults, and older adults. As shown in Figure 16.2, there is a U-shaped function relating driving fatality rates with age such that fatality rates decrease from teenagers to middle-aged adults and then increase steadily in older adults, starting at about age 60 (Figure 16.2 adapted from Insurance Institute for Highway Safety, 2002). This pattern is especially striking in light of the evidence that, with enough practice, data-limited tasks should become well automated. Yet, counter to that prediction, older adult drivers are as susceptible (or more so) to driving related fatality as novice drivers. Older adult drivers are generally more experienced, more likely to wear their seat belts, and have the lowest levels of intoxication of all adults (Strayer & Drews, 2004). Although factors such as lack of experience, greater risk-taking behavior, and greater likelihood of intoxication can partially account for high fatality rates among teenage drivers, it appears that something else must be contributing to the high rates for older adults. We respectfully submit that older adults, at least on the average, may have a reduction in the PFC-mediated executive attention-processing resources that are required to effectively maintain the complex and diverse set of task goals associated with driving.

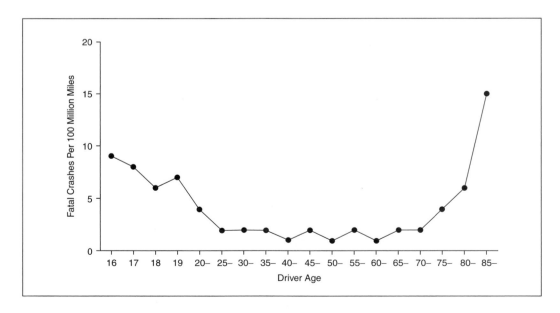

FIGURE 16.2 A U-shaped relationship between age and driving fatality rates. *Source:* Adapted from data reported by the Insurance Institute for Highway Safety (2002).

INDIVIDUAL DIFFERENCES IN PFC-MEDIATED EXECUTIVE ATTENTION

Having established that the rise and fall of executive attention across the life-span mirrors frontal cortex development, our second hypothesis is the following: *The increases and decreases in executive attention across the life span in children, young adults, and older adults will be qualified by individual differences in performance.* That is, it should be possible to equate executive attention performance across the life span were one to adequately control for variability in the development or degradation of PFC. For example, as shown in Figure 16.3, the development of frontal cortex may be typical and well captured by the group average (black line). However, if only for the sake of comparison, for any given individual, the growth of frontal cortex could be accelerated (dotted line), or the degradation could be decelerated (dashed line). In either case, the important point is that individual differences in the precise shape of the inverted, U-shaped function would make it theoretically possible (1) to equate the development of PFC across the life span, and (2) by extension, to potentially equate the executive attention performance of particular individuals drawn from different age groups (e.g., subsets of young and older adults). It is noteworthy that similar arguments have been made elsewhere in the literature, complete with

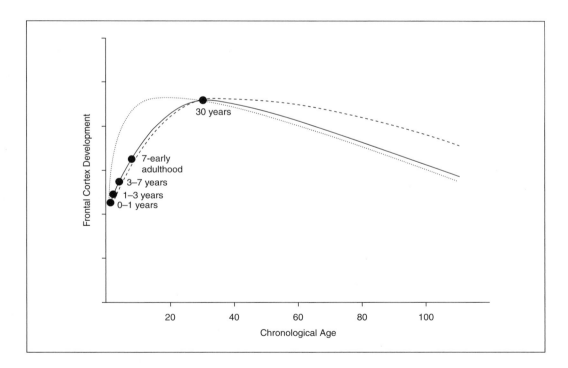

FIGURE 16.3   Individual differences in the curvilinear development of frontal cortex across the life span. The middle black line represents typical or average development with age, as was illustrated previously in Figure 16.1. For the sake of comparison, two additional stylized curves have been depicted. The dotted line represents accelerated growth of frontal cortex, whereas the dashed line represents decelerated degradation.

stylized curves that depict somewhat different developmental trajectories for a given individual based on a variety of factors that might enrich cognition such as mental or physical exercise (cf., Hertzog, Kramer, Wilson, & Lindenberger, 2009). In the current section, to test this individual differences hypothesis and to best illustrate its explanatory power, we begin by briefly reviewing the findings that have emerged from the prevailing *zeitgeist* in cognitive psychology of considering variability in the executive attention performance of young adults.

Individual Differences in Executive Attention in Young Adults

Over the last 20 years, individual differences in the executive attention of young adults have been well investigated by Randy Engle and colleagues. Recently, Kane and Engle (2002) outlined an executive attention framework to synthesize research findings drawn from both cognitive psychology and cognitive neuroscience on the seemingly diverse but related topics of working memory capacity (WMC), generalized fluid intelligence, and PFC function. Central to Kane and Engle's framework is the notion of individual differences in WMC, which for our purposes could be considered the limited pool of executive attention resources in PFC that one has available to effectively maintain task goals, to avoid distraction, and to coordinate intelligent behavior. Referring to models of Duncan (1990, 1993, 1995) and Cohen (Braver & Cohen, 2000; Cohen & Servan-Schreiber, 1992; Miller & Cohen, 2001; O'Reilly, Braver, & Cohen, 1999), Kane and Engle (2002) argued that (1) the PFC evolved in order to maintain and update goal information by biasing information processing in other networked brain areas, and (2) higher-order executive attention may have emerged from these PFC-coordinated interactions.

Typically, individual differences in WMC are measured using an operation span task (OSPAN). In an OSPAN task (cf., La Pointe & Engle, 1990; Turner & Engle, 1989), participants are required to solve math problems followed by a to-be-remembered word—for example, "Is (8/4) + 3 = 4? DOG." After varying numbers of these equation–word pairs, participants are prompted to recall all of the words in each set in serial order. Trials are randomized such that participants cannot predict the set size of upcoming equation–word pairs (where set sizes might range from two to five equation–word pairs). Participants are given points equal to the set size when all of the words in that set are recalled correctly in serial order (i.e., an absolute span score). OSPAN is defined as the sum of points across all of the individual recall periods. Math accuracy may be tracked for the purpose of providing feedback to participants, which intends to keep problem-solving accuracy above 85% and to encourage compliance with the dual-task math/memory instructions that should place a burden on limited-capacity executive attention resources (see Conway et al., 2005, for a guide on administering/scoring of OSPAN tasks).

Engle and colleagues have often relied on structural equation modeling to show that the OSPAN task is a robust measure of one's ability to successfully maintain task goals in the face of distraction, which could be construed as an important element in intelligent behavior. Specifically, they use these models to demonstrate that statistically significant relationships remain between performance on the OSPAN task and performance on measures of fluid intelligence, even after one controls for other sources of variance that might contribute to the OSPAN task such as simple storage of information in the absence of distraction (see Engle & Kane, 2004; Engle, Tuholski,

Laughlin, & Conway, 1999; Kane & Engle, 2002). Thus, one might expect individual differences in OSPAN performance to predict behavior in executive attention tasks that require active maintenance of task goals in the face of potentially interfering information. Consistent with this reasoning, individuals with low OSPAN scores do perform more poorly than individuals with high OSPAN scores in situations where successful performance is dependent on using task goals to minimize interference such as dichotic listening, the antisaccade task, Stroop color naming, and associative false memory paradigms (see Conway, Cowan, & Bunting, 2001; Kane, Bleckley, Conway, & Engle, 2001; Kane & Engle, 2003; Watson, Bunting, Poole, & Conway, 2005, respectively). For example, using the Stroop task where the participants' goal is to name ink colors and to ignore distracting words, Kane and Engle (2003) found that low OSPANs produced more naming errors than high OSPANs in the incongruent condition (i.e., participants with low scores on the OSPAN test were more likely to mistakenly say "red" when the stimulus *RED* was printed in green ink).

Individual Differences in Executive Attention in Older Adults

At about the same time Engle and colleagues began to investigate individual differences in executive attention in young adults via the OSPAN task, Glisky and colleagues were compiling a small battery of standardized neuropsychological tests that they argued could be used to quantify individual differences in both medial temporal and frontal lobe function in healthy older adults (cf., Glisky, Polster, & Routhieaux, 1995). The Glisky battery of tasks was originally intended to assess the nature and extent of cognitive deficits in patients with known or suspected neuropsychological conditions like AD. The battery included the Modified Wisconsin Card Sorting Task (Hart, Kwentus, Wade, &Taylor, 1988), Controlled Oral Word Associations (COWA; Benton & Hamsher, 1976), mental arithmetic from the revised Wechsler Adult Intelligence Scale (WAIS-R; Wechsler, 1981), a selection of tasks from the Wechsler Memory Scale (WMS-R; Wechsler, 1987), and long delayed cued recall from the California Verbal Learning Test (CVLT; Delis, Kramer, Kaplan, & Ober, 1987). For example, the COWA test is a measure of verbal fluency, and participants are given 1 minute to search semantic memory and to generate words that begin with a specific letter (e.g., *F, A,* or *S*). To perform this task successfully and to avoid retrieving redundant items from semantic memory, one must use attentional processing resources to keep track of previously generated items (Balota, Watson, Duchek, & Ferraro, 1999). Glisky et al. (1995) reported two factors that reflected the contribution of different cognitive processes, and by extension, at least two different brain regions, to older adult behavioral performance on this battery of neuropsychological tasks. Specifically, factor analysis revealed that the memory tests in the battery such as the CVLT loaded on one factor and were thought to reflect temporal lobe function. Moreover, the other tests in the battery, including the COWA described briefly earlier, loaded on a different factor and were thought to reflect frontal lobe function (also see Dennis & Cabeza, 2008, for a recent review of neuroimaging evidence suggesting greater recruitment of frontal cortex in better versus poorer performing older adults on certain cognitive tests).

In our opinion, the Glisky frontal battery has rapidly emerged as the "gold standard" for measuring individual differences in frontal function in healthy older adults (see Roediger & McDaniel, 2007), whereas OSPAN or comparable complex span measures of WMC have clearly dominated the literature to this point on individual differences in frontal function in young adults (see Engle, 2002). Consistent with this assertion, until very recently, it has been quite difficult to find instances in the literature where either OSPAN has been used to assess frontal function in older adults or the Glisky battery has been used to assess frontal function in young adults. Indeed, to our knowledge, Chan and McDermott (2007) were the first to implement the Glisky battery with a young adult population and to test the assumption that young adults were uniformly high in frontal lobe function (also see Glisky & Kong, 2008; McCabe, Roediger, McDaniel, & Balota, 2009). Consistent with our second hypothesis, Chan and McDermott observed substantial variability on frontal scores for both young and older adults, demonstrating that young adult frontal function is not uniformly high. Moreover, contrary to the usual age-related declines that have been frequently reported in the memory literature (Balota, Dolan, & Duchek, 2000), Chan and McDermott found that older adults could perform as well as, if not better, than their younger counterparts on episodic memory tests. However, this paradoxical outcome required that the older adults were higher scoring than the young adults in frontal lobe function as indexed by the Glisky frontal battery. When both young and old adults were high in frontal function, age differences in memory were minimized, but they were not completely eliminated (i.e., age and frontal scores were independent contributors to memory performance). Therefore, it would seem that a few caveats are necessary for a strict frontal account of the variability in executive attention that has been observed across the life span.

◼ CAVEATS TO A FRONTAL ACCOUNT OF LIFE-SPAN CHANGES IN EXECUTIVE ATTENTION

Chan and McDermott's (2007) findings nicely illustrate that, although individual differences in frontal lobe function are an important and necessary factor to help explain age-related changes in cognition, other candidate causes are also required. For example, older adults often have diminished processing speed as well as vision or hearing loss (see Salthouse, 1996; Schneider & Pichora-Fuller, 2000). These speed and/or perceptual changes may underlie age-related differences in a variety of higher-order cognitive domains, including those reviewed here on executive attention. Furthermore, as noted by Glisky, Raz, and others, beyond the loss of frontal cortex, there is also age-related degradation in temporal lobe structure and function (Glisky et al., 1995; Raz, 2000). Of course, the challenge in identifying a parsimonious common cause for age-related changes in cognition is somewhat complicated by the notion that tasks such as the OSPAN and those used in the Glisky neuropsychological battery are not process pure and likely map onto a host of brain regions rather than any single region per se (cf., Chan & McDermott, 2007; Jacoby, 1991). As psychologists have found it difficult, if not impossible, to design process-pure tasks, it can be useful to take a broader approach and appeal to alternative accounts of age-related changes in cognition, where appropriate. For example, Chan and McDermott suggested that additional, age-related declines in medial temporal lobe function might explain why high frontal older adults in their study had poorer episodic memory than high frontal young adults (i.e., episodic recall likely requires both intact frontal and medial temporal cortex).

Despite these inherent complexities, we believe the existing literature has supported the fundamental spirit of a frontal account of the variability in executive attention across the life span. For example, with regard to our two core hypotheses, there are cases in which individual differences will complicate the mean-based generality that executive attention is more robust in young adults than in older adults. In these instances, some young adults may have reduced executive attention relative to select older adults, and this may translate into poorer performance on certain, frontally mediated cognitive tests. Clearly, age alone cannot be used to explain these paradoxical patterns, as the usual age-related declines have been turned upside down to demonstrate age-related benefits. And while preliminary evidence suggests that the degradation of PFC should not be considered the sole cause of age-related changes in cognition, particularly in impure tasks (Chan & McDermott, 2007), it still may be possible to gain considerable theoretical traction by framing future research questions/hypotheses on aging and attention in light of the biological development of frontal cortex. To this end, we now turn our chapter to the sixth and final section where we highlight several novel lines of research that follow from a frontal account of the change in executive attention associated with age.

FUTURE ISSUES IN THE STUDY OF LIFE-SPAN EXECUTIVE ATTENTION

As a first step, there may be some utility in conducting either cross-sectional or longitudinal studies of executive attention in children, young adults, and older adults that include both the OSPAN test (and/or comparable complex span measures) and the Glisky frontal battery. A comprehensive study could be particularly useful in determining whether the OSPAN and the Glisky measures capture overlapping or unique aspects of frontal lobe function (cf., McCabe, Roediger, McDaniel, Balota, & Hambrick, 2010). However, as noted earlier, one limitation of this approach is that even the Glisky battery and the OSPAN test, in their traditional formats, should not be considered process-pure measures of executive attention and would be unsuitable for certain populations. For example, children might underperform on either the Glisky battery or the OSPAN test simply because these measures also rely on advanced reading or math skills (as opposed to alternative explanations that might appeal solely to their still-developing frontally mediated executive attention to explain any observed group differences). Therefore, some modification of these two gold standards may be required before undertaking such an ambitious study, especially if it were to involve children.

A second limitation of this sort of combinatorial approach is that it would be indirect and correlational, and hence, assumptions would have to be made regarding the neural locus (or loci) of both shared and unique variance associated with behavioral performance on the Glisky battery and the OSPAN test. It would be tempting to speculate that a correlation between participants' performance on the OSPAN and the Glisky battery would be due to shared recruitment of PFC and individual differences in underlying executive attention. However, in the absence of functional neuroimaging data on these non-process-pure tests that could independently confirm this possibility, this correlation might well be driven by shared recruitment of other brain regions outside of PFC. Furthermore, it is theoretically possible that the unique variance associated with either the OSPAN test or the Glisky frontal battery could be supported at the neural level by different subregions in or near PFC. This is particularly true if one were to acknowledge that executive attention is likely multifaceted and supported by a network of brain areas, including a prominent role for DLPFC in goal maintenance and anterior cingulate cortex (ACC) in conflict monitoring (see Braver et al., 2007; Braver & Ruge, 2006), which will be revisited at the conclusion of this chapter. While we are quick to point out that neuroimaging methods like fMRI ought not to be considered either as a substitute for good cognitive theory or a panacea for problematic cognitive theory (see Balota & Watson, 2000), neuroimaging may still offer leverage in elucidating the neural substrates of different, but complementary, facets of executive attention housed in PFC and in other associated brain areas like the ACC.

As noted by Chan and McDermott (2007), neuroimaging studies that have included component tasks from the Glisky frontal battery have revealed the recruitment of PFC (Cabeza & Nyberg, 2000). For example, in the backward digit span test that is contained within the battery, individuals are asked to memorize and to repeat strings of digits (e.g., 2, 7, 9) in the reverse order of their presentation (e.g., 9, 7, 2), and backward digit span has been shown to broadly recruit both DLPFC and ACC in the executive attention network (Gerton et al., 2004). Although these results are promising and appear to confirm the recruitment of subregions in PFC with the Glisky frontal battery, to our knowledge, comparable neuroimaging studies have not been conducted with the OSPAN test (but see Kane & Engle, 2002, for a convincing argument that the OSPAN test emphasizes goal maintenance and likely recruits at least DLPFC on the basis of converging evidence from behavioral data, neuropsychological patients, computational modeling, and animal models). One reason for this bottleneck may be that, until very recently, traditional versions of the OSPAN test were not particularly scanner friendly, at least with respect to fMRI, which has become the dominant functional imaging technique over the last 15 years (see Raichle, 2006). Specifically, the OSPAN test often requires spoken and/or written responses that could generate movement and degrade the quality of the neuroimaging data that one might obtain (see Culham, 2006, for an overview of how motion affects signal-to-noise ratio in the MR scanner environment). We believe more recent instantiations of the OSPAN test that (1) have been validated against traditional versions of the OSPAN test and/or other comparable complex span measures, and that (2) include slight modifications where both math and recall performance can be assessed using simple button presses on a computer mouse offer the potential for executive attention researchers to more readily adapt the OSPAN test to the MR environment in the near future (cf., Osaka et al., 2003; Smith et al., 2001; Unsworth, Heitz, Schrock, & Engle, 2005).

Venturing Outside the Ivory Tower: Cognitive Psychology Meets the Real World

An alternative, and perhaps more fruitful, approach for future research on life-span executive attention may be to take an applied cognitive neuroscience perspective. That is, rather than attempting to limit our investigation of executive attention to the component processes that may or may not be shared across various laboratory paradigms like the OSPAN test or the Glisky frontal battery, it may be more useful to investigate attention in more naturalistic environments (i.e., the "real world"). Consistent with this idea, Kingstone and colleagues recently implored cognitive psychologists and neuroscientists alike to consider whether their laboratory findings generalized to the real world and what value, if any, they had placed on *cognitive ethology* when structuring their research programs to test cognitive theory on attention (Giesbrecht, Kingstone, Handy, Hopfinger, & Mangun, 2006; Kingstone, Smilek, Ristic, Friesen, & Eastword, 2003). Sympathetic to this point of view, we briefly highlight three lines of ongoing, applied cognitive neuroscience research that is currently being conducted by our laboratory (or by others), each with incremental distance from the "ivory tower," to illustrate the potential that exists for advancing cognitive theory by investigating how executive attention operates in the real world.

Alzheimer's Disease: Beyond Episodic Memory Loss

To bridge the gap between classic, cognitive psychology lab research and the real world, it may be useful to first consider the research being conducted on executive attention with patient populations such as those diagnosed with AD. Although episodic memory loss is the cardinal, clinical symptom of AD (Nebes, 1992), there is increasing evidence that executive attention is also compromised early in the disease (Albert, 2008; Belleville, Chertkow, & Gauthier, 2007; Watson, Balota, & Sergent-Marshall, 2001). Deficits in executive attention are subtle and often overshadowed by an early AD patient's memory loss that may be mediated by extensive neuropathology in the hippocampal formation of the medial temporal lobe (Hyman, Van Hoesen, Damasio, & Barnes, 1984). To further complicate matters and to echo what should now be a familiar story, neuropsychological tests of episodic memory are not pure measures and are sensitive to several other aspects of cognition. Therefore, it can be difficult for clinicians to disentangle memory deficits in early AD from mild deficits in other cognitive domains including executive attention. By using carefully designed experimental procedures to assess different aspects of executive attention, one may gain a richer understanding of the neural mechanisms that contribute to early AD beyond episodic memory loss. For example, to the extent that there are AD-related deficits in PFC-mediated goal maintenance, one might expect AD patients to perform poorly on the OSPAN test. Consistent with this hypothesis, as shown in the left panel of Figure 16.4, our lab recently demonstrated that individuals with a possible prodromal form of AD known as mild cognitive impairment (MCI; see Albert, 2008; Petersen, 2004) have reduced OSPAN scores relative to healthy older adults (Watson, Lambert, Thorgusen, Levy, & Kesner, 2010). Consistent with the spirit of this chapter and the age-related deficits that have been observed in executive attention performance, it is also noteworthy that the healthy older adults in our study, on average, also had reduced OSPAN scores relative to young adults (see McCabe et al., 2010, for additional evidence of age-related declines on other complex span measures comparable to OSPAN). Additional analyses also revealed that these aging/MCI group average deficits were more pronounced for larger than smaller memory set sizes on the OSPAN task. In this way, our OSPAN results are consistent with a growing body of research revealing *intraindividual differences* in behavioral performance across the life span (i.e., within-person change; see MacDonald, Li, & Bäckman, 2009; MacDonald, Nyberg, & Bäckman, 2006; Siegler, 2006; Williams, Hultsch, Strauss, Hunter, & Tannock, 2005, for discussion of the greater intraindividual variability that

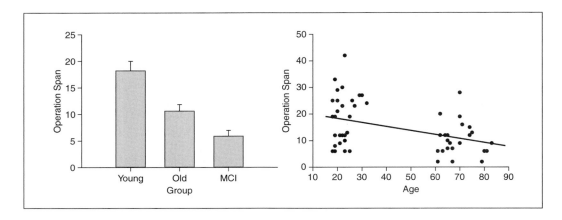

FIGURE 16.4   **OSPAN memory performance in young adults, healthy older adults, and older adults diagnosed with MCI (left panel). Error bars indicate the standard error of the mean. Individual differences in OSPAN memory performance as a function of age (right panel).** *Source:* **Adapted from data reported by Watson et al. (2010).**

has been observed in children, older adults, and various patient populations). More specifically, our results suggest that older adults and MCI patients may experience a transient loss of task goals on the OSPAN test. This is particularly true under situations of high cognitive load that are likely to tax limited-capacity executive attention resources (e.g., trials that require memorizing five words in serial order in the face of concurrent math distraction may be more likely to reveal deficits, as opposed to just memorizing two words while solving math problems). However, as shown in the scatter plot in the right panel of Figure 16.4, these group patterns were qualified by individual differences in executive attention. For example, there were some older adults in our sample who outperformed young adults on the OSPAN test, thereby demonstrating what could cautiously be considered successful aging, at least with regard to preserved ability to maintain task goals in the face of distraction.

Driven to Distraction: Why Cell Phones and Driving Don't Mix

To move the agenda on future issues in the study of life-span executive attention a moderate distance from the ivory tower, let us now consider the growing body of research on driving and cell phone–induced driver distraction (see Strayer & Drews, 2007, for a recent review). As discussed earlier in this chapter, driving is an example of a complex divided attention task with multiple embedded goals that likely requires the use of limited-capacity neural resources in PFC. To more directly address the possible contribution of PFC to driving performance, our lab recently tested 200 young adults in a high-fidelity driving simulator in both single- and dual-task conditions (Watson & Strayer, 2010). The dual-task involved driving while concurrently performing a demanding auditory version of the OSPAN task using a hands-free cell phone. As shown in Figure 16.5, the vast majority of participants showed significant performance decrements in dual-task conditions (compared to single-task conditions for both driving and OSPAN tasks). Borrowing the dual-task logic

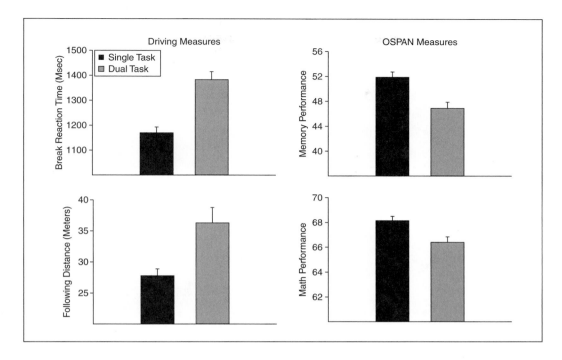

FIGURE 16.5 **Group average performance for single- and dual-task conditions for brake reaction time (upper left panel), following distance (lower left panel), OSPAN memory performance (upper right panel), and OSPAN math performance (lower right panel). Error bars indicate standard error of the mean.** *Source:* **Adapted from data reported by Watson and Strayer (2010).**

developed by Baddeley and colleagues (Baddeley & Hitch, 1974), one implication of this bidirectional interference was that operating a motor vehicle while performing the OSPAN test over the phone placed a competing demand on the limited-capacity attentional resources in PFC that are necessary for the successful maintenance of task goals. That is, cell phones and driving probably don't mix because they both "tie up" or consume limited-capacity executive attention resources in PFC, ultimately increasing brake RTs, lengthening car following distances, diminishing memory span, and reducing math accuracy. In fact, the National Safety Council estimates that 28% of all accidents and fatalities on U.S. highways were caused by drivers using cell phones (National Safety Council, 2010).

Conventional wisdom and cognitive theory both suggest that people cannot multitask without significant performance decrements on one or more constituent tasks (Wickens, 1984). Given the group average findings on driver distraction shown in Figure 16.5, it would seem that the limits on attentional capacity would apply to everyone. However, as shown in Figure 16.6, Watson and Strayer (2010) also noted that 2.5% of the sample showed no noticeable performance decrements when comparing single- and dual-tasks. The idea that some individuals may have extraordinary multitasking abilities does not seem so far-fetched, if one considers well-documented cases of individuals demonstrating extraordinary memory abilities (e.g., Price & Davis, 2008). Consistent with Engle and colleagues, we suggested

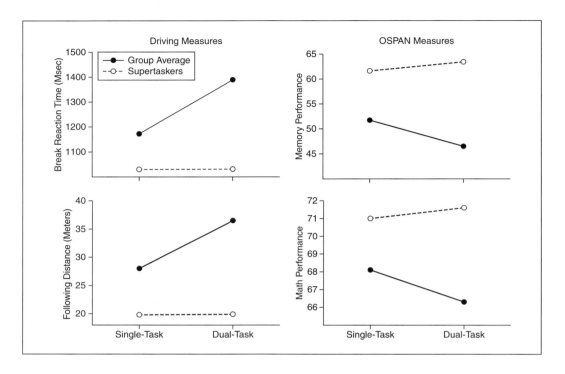

FIGURE 16.6 **Single-task and dual-task performance for the group average and for supertaskers. Brake reaction time (upper left panel), following distance (lower left panel), OSPAN memory performance (upper right panel), and OSPAN math performance (lower right panel).** *Source:* **Adapted from data reported by Watson and Strayer (2010).**

that incorporating an individual differences perspective would significantly improve theoretical understanding of executive attention and performance in both traditional laboratory settings and in more applied contexts. We further argued that individuals who perform significantly better (or worse) than the group average might help to sharpen theoretical understanding of attention and cognitive control in naturalistic settings. As we gain a better understanding of the neural bases of "supertasker" performance, we are likely to gain a better understanding of normal multitasking performance. Clearly, there is something special about these supertaskers. Why can they do something that most of us cannot? We may learn from these very rare individuals that multitasking regions of the brain, particularly in frontal cortex, are different and that there could be a genetic basis for this difference in attention (cf., Parasuraman & Greenwood, 2007). Furthermore, the behavioral characteristics of supertaskers are likely to be important in other domains, beyond combining cell phones and driving, that require coordinating a number of concurrent tasks (e.g., flying a high-performance aircraft). Indeed, as technology spreads, it will be useful to understand the brain's limited-capacity attentional resources in PFC and perhaps to isolate potential behavioral, neural, or genetic markers that predict the extraordinary multitasking ability of supertaskers.

And yet, while future research with these "master multitaskers" offers many exciting possibilities for advancing cognitive theory on executive attention, some caution is certainly warranted (Ophir, Nass, & Wagner, 2009). In particular, some readers may be wondering if they, too, are supertaskers with an exceptional ability to multitask. However, given that supertaskers are at most 2.5% of the population, we suggest that the odds of this are against them. For the sake of comparison, the probability of being a supertasker is about as good as one's chances of flipping a coin and getting five heads (or tails) in a row. The important point is that there are supertaskers in our midst, individuals who seem to violate cognitive scientists' current understanding of executive attention and bottlenecks on limited-capacity attentional resources. And, as an important footnote, alas, we all must acknowledge, however grudgingly, that we are likely not to be counted among these extraordinary, rare, master multitaskers (see Strayer, Watson, & Drews (in press); Watson & Strayer, 2010, for additional details).

Cognition in the Wild: Neural Benefits of Interacting With Nature

Recently, environmental psychologists have shown dual benefits of exposure to nature on mental and physical health (Berman, Jonides, & Kaplan, 2008; Hartig, Evans, Jamner, Davis, & Garling, 2003). According to attention restoration theory (ART; Kaplan, 1995, 2001) interacting with naturalistic environments (e.g., trees, water) improves executive attention and stress levels relative to interacting with urban environments (e.g., skyscrapers, cars). More specifically, Berman et al. (2008) twice demonstrated that interacting with nature improved executive attention in young adults as shown by boosts in memory span on a backward digit span task. Not surprisingly, there is considerable enthusiasm in the popular media and in society at large regarding ART theory and the therapeutic possibility of using something as readily available as nature, with no known side effects, to manage stress and to resolve deficits in executive attention (Berman et al., 2008; Louv, 2008). Although cognitive neuroscience suggests that executive attention is supported by a network of brain regions including a prominent role for PFC and ACC (Braver et al., 2007), it is notable that the neural underpinnings of the benefits of interacting with nature haven't been determined. With respect to practical significance and societal impact, knowledge of these basic brain–behavior relations is essential if one wishes to identify, a priori, those clinical populations (or those behavioral contexts/tests) that are most likely to benefit from interacting with nature. For example, as noted earlier, the neuroimaging of executive attention literature has demonstrated that the backward digit span test used by Berman et al. (2008) is not process pure and recruits both PFC and ACC (Gerton et al., 2004). Hence, presently, it is difficult to determine whether the neural benefits of interacting with nature that have yielded improvements in executive attention will be localized to PFC, ACC, or both (see Kaplan & Berman, 2010, for a review of ART and the diverse tasks/populations where a nature intervention has improved attention).

Although ART clearly does not make strong predictions at the neural level (Kaplan, 2001; Kaplan & Berman, 2010), one possible clue is that interacting with nature has been shown to reduce stress by lowering blood pressure (Hartig et al., 2003). Moreover, neuroimaging evidence indicates a positive correlation between stress levels and neural activity such that as blood pressure rises, ACC activity increases (Gianaros et al., 2005; Uchino, Smith, Birmingham, & Carlisle, in press). In the future, we believe that applied cognitive neuroscientists ought to use the reduction in blood pressure that occurs in response to nature to gain theoretical leverage on neural regions that are most likely to benefit from interacting with nature. Briefly, the logic is that exposure to more stressful urban environments, which contain potentially distracting stimuli (e.g., traffic) will activate ACC and may deplete its limited neural resources. This depletion of neural resources or "cognitive reserve" has implications for current theories of executive attention that include a prominent role for the ACC in detecting environmental sources of conflict (Braver et al., 2007). For example, children with attention deficit disorder (ADD) have diminished ACC activity on behavioral tasks that require detection of conflict (Bush et al., 1999). With regard to our cingulate hypothesis and long-range aspirations of this new area of research on the potential cognitive benefits of interacting with nature, ACC dysfunction in ADD is intriguing, because children with attention deficits have been shown to benefit and to have their attention restored after interacting with nature (Louv, 2008). Returning to the Berman et al. (2008) findings, it may be that the depleting influence of interacting with urban environments carried forward to diminish participants' subsequent performance on the backward digit span test. That is, the digit span test required robust executive attention and limited ACC resources to detect cognitive conflict/stressors (as opposed to directly modulating neural activity related to the maintenance of task goals in PFC, per se, on this non-process-pure test).

We see this new area of research on the neural benefits of interacting with nature as more broadly consistent with the growing list of other approaches that intend to augment cognitive reserve or to replenish the "fountain of youth"—particularly those that have been used with older adults—including mental training, physical exercise, and good nutrition (see Christensen, Anstey, Leach, & Mackinnon, 2008; Hertzog et al., 2009; Kramer et al., 1999; McDaniel, Einstein, & Jacoby, 2008). However, to our knowledge, comparable studies on the potential dual benefits of exposure to nature on mental and physical health have not been conducted with older adults. Similar augmentation techniques, including exposure to nature, have been used successfully with children to improve their cognition, particularly with regard to boosting limited executive attention resources (Davis et al., 2007; Florence, Asbridge, & Veugelers, 2008; Rueda, Rothbart, McCandliss, Saccomanno, & Posner, 2005; Taylor & Kuo, 2009). In this light, one potentially useful study might be to compare the relative benefit of a nature intervention on executive attention in a cross-section of children, young adults, and older adults. Were one to conduct such a study, it would be especially important to select a task that is both suitable for these three populations and highly likely to recruit core brain regions thought to underlie executive attention. One ideal paradigm might be the Go/No-Go task because it is fairly simple in that it variously requires participants to either initiate a response (i.e., Go trials) or withhold a response (i.e., No-Go trials). For our purposes, the Go/No-Go task has at least three advantages. First, neuroimaging studies have shown that the Go/No-Go task recruits both the PFC and the ACC in the executive attention network in a sample of young adults (cf., Braver, Barch, Gray, Molfese, & Snyder, 2001). Second, Go/No-Go performance, especially the ability to inhibit prepotent responding on challenging No-Go trials, has been shown to rise and fall across the life span, perhaps tracking the curvilinear development of frontal cortex as illustrated previously in Figure 16.1 (see Diamond, 2002; Nielson, Langenecker, & Garavan, 2002). Third, a variant of the Go/No-Go task has already proven to be sensitive to the hypothesized benefits of interacting with nature on limited-capacity attentional resources (Berto, 2005).

In the future, it may be useful for applied cognitive neuroscientists to consider to what degree use of various augmentation techniques, including exposure to nature, contributes to individual and/or age differences in the cognitive reserve of core regions of the executive attention network like the PFC or ACC. Regular combined use of exercise, nature, nutrition, and mental training may enhance one's chances of experiencing successful aging across the life span. For example, older adults may be especially likely to benefit from interacting with nature or other interventions given that they tend to under-recruit PFC and may over-recruit and, hence, be at risk for depleting limited-capacity resources in other brain regions, including ACC, while attempting to compensate on tasks that require frontally mediated executive attention (cf., Dennis & Cabeza, 2008; Paxton, Barch, Racine, & Braver, 2008). However, while individual differences in the integrity of the PFC/ACC executive attention network may be critical to understanding many age differences in cognition, it will be important to consider other factors as well. For instance, at the very least, individual differences in the developmental trajectory of the PFC may depend greatly on one's access to and/or affinity for the environmental augmentation techniques listed earlier (e.g., not all individuals would necessarily set aside time or like to take a brisk nature walk or would choose to eat a healthy snack). Indeed, researchers are just beginning to understand the genetic and environmental sources of variability underlying PFC/ACC neural function, and by extension, the mechanisms that contribute to the individual differences observed in executive attention (see Braver, Cole, & Yarkoni, 2010, for a recent review).

▓ SUMMARY AND CONCLUSIONS

To summarize, in the current chapter, we have argued the following: (1) age does not cause any observed behavioral difference, (2) age must be considered in context, (3) age differences in executive attention in children, young adults, and older adults are mirrored by the rise and fall of frontal cortex across the life span, and (4) many of these age differences across the life span are qualified by individual differences in executive attention performance. Although a PFC hypothesis of the development of executive attention is a fairly straightforward and testable idea, complications arose in its explanatory power. However, we believe many of the limitations of the PFC hypothesis can be attributed to the notion that cognitive tests are not process pure and, therefore, do not map onto any single brain region, per se. Finally, we briefly highlighted three lines of applied, cognitive neuroscience research on subtle deficits in executive attention in AD, the neural correlates of driving, and the restoration of attention by nature that are currently being conducted by our laboratory (or by others). In so doing, our intent was to illustrate that there may be substantial theoretical value in venturing outside the ivory tower of classic cognitive psychology to conduct somewhat nontraditional, applied cognitive neuroscience experiments on the brain basis of MCI, driving, and interacting with nature. Essentially, we are advocating the use of controlled laboratory experiments to investigate how attention operates in various naturalistic settings—ranging from neuropsychological clinics, the highway, even to the wilderness. Implementing such a research program may well represent a successive approximation to how attention operates in the real world, if only by attempting to use cognitive theory to better understand and combat real-world problems on dementia, distracted driving, and attentional fatigue. Our primary point is that, in many cases, future researchers of executive attention may find the choice between conducting more traditional, well-controlled, theory-driven laboratory research and more practical, applied research to be a false one because these two kinds of research programs can peacefully, and productively, coexist.

Clearly, some balance is preferred if not required in one's research agenda, because we are not advocating a program of research that forsakes the ivory tower. Quite to the contrary, more traditional laboratory research may be especially useful in analyzing the component processes of impure cognitive tests and in identifying/ isolating the relative contribution of different aspects of executive attention that can be localized to either PFC (goal maintenance) or ACC (conflict monitoring). Consistent with this approach, our lab recently initiated a line of research dedicated to better understanding the dynamic interplay of the PFC and ACC. An as yet unanswered question for future generations of executive attention researchers to ponder and solve is the following: How do the PFC and ACC operate together to coordinate goal maintenance and conflict monitoring, respectively? More specifically, what is the relationship between these two different but complementary aspects of cognitive control (see Braver et al., 2007; Kane, Conway, Hambrick, & Engle, 2007; Miller, Watson, & Strayer, 2010)? In conclusion, we suspect future chapters on the topic of the development of executive attention across the life span will have us complaining about persecution from the magical letters *A*, *C*, and *C*. For now, we respectfully submit for consideration the idea that, similar to *P*, *F*, *C*, and *U*, there is likely something special about these three letters, and by extension, this neural substrate too. Indeed, we feel as though the ACC is only just beginning to haunt us as we attempt to build a more complete theory of how executive attention operates in the laboratory and in the real world. But that is a case history, although growing worse by the moment, best left to another volume.

ACKNOWLEDGMENTS

Authors AEL and AEM made equivalent contributions to this chapter and both should be considered as a second author. Portions of the work reported here were supported by a University of Utah Center on Aging grant to author JMW and a University of Utah Interdisciplinary Research Grant to authors JMW and DLS.

REFERENCES

Albert, M. (2008). The neuropsychology of the development of Alzheimer's disease. In F. I. M. Craik & T. A. Salthouse (Eds.), *Handbook of aging and cognition III* (pp. 97–132). New York: Psychology Press.

Atkinson, R., & Shiffrin, R. (1968). Human memory: A proposed system and its control processes. In K. Spence & J. Spence (Eds.), *The psychology of learning and motivation: II* (pp. 89–195). Orlando, FL: Academic Press.

Atkinson, R., & Shiffrin, R. (1971). The control of short-term memory. *Scientific American, 225*, 82–90.

Baddeley, A. (1992). Is working memory working? The fifteenth Bartlett lecture. *Quarterly Journal of Educational Psychology, 44A*, 1–31.

Baddeley, A. D., & Hitch, G. (1974). Working memory. In G. H. Bower (Ed.), *The psychology of learning and motivation* (Vol. 8, pp. 17–90). New York: Academic Press.

Balota, D. A., Dolan, P. O., & Duchek, J. M. (2000). Memory changes in healthy older adults. In E. Tulving & F. I. M. Craik (Eds.), *The Oxford handbook of memory* (pp. 395–409). Oxford: Oxford University Press.

Balota, D. A., & Watson, J. M. (2000). Methods in cognitive psychology. In A. E. Kazdin (Ed.), *Encyclopedia of psychology* (pp. 158–162). New York: Oxford University Press.

Balota, D., Watson, J. M., Duchek, J., & Ferraro, F. (1999). Cross-modal semantic and homograph priming in healthy young, healthy old, and in Alzheimer's disease individuals. *Journal of the International Neuropsychological Society, 5,* 626–640.

Baltes, P., & Lindenberger, U. (1997). Emergence of a powerful connection between sensory and cognitive functions across the adult life span: A new window to the study of cognitive aging? *Psychology and Aging, 12,* 12–21.

Barbas, H., & Mesulam, M. M. (1981). Organization of afferent input to subdivisions of area 8 in the rhesus monkey. *Journal of Comparative Neurology, 200,* 407–431.

Barbas, H., & Mesulam, M. M. (1985). Cortical afferent input to the principalis region of the rhesus monkey. *Neuroscience, 15,* 619–637.

Belleville, S., Chertkow, H., & Gauthier, S. (2007). Working memory and control of attention in persons with Alzheimer's disease and mild cognitive impairment. *Neuropsychology, 21,* 458–469.

Benton, A. L., & Hamsher, K. (1976). *Multilingual aphasia examination manual.* Iowa City, IA: University of Iowa.

Berman, M., Jonides, J., & Kaplan, S. (2008). The cognitive benefits of interacting with nature. *Psychological Science, 19,* 1207–1212.

Berto, R. (2005). Exposure to restorative environments helps restore attentional capacity. *Journal of Environmental Psychology, 25,* 249–259.

Braver, T. S., Barch, D. M., Gray, J. R., Molfese, D. L., & Snyder, A. (2001). Anterior cingulate cortex and response conflict: Effects of frequency, inhibition, and errors. *Cerebral Cortex, 11,* 825–836.

Braver, T. S., & Cohen, J. D. (2000). On the control of control: The role of dopamine in regulating prefrontal function and working memory. In S. Monsell & J. Driver (Eds.), *Attention and performance XVIII: Control of cognitive processes* (pp. 713–737). Cambridge, MA: MIT Press.

Braver, T. S., Cole, M. W., & Yarkoni, T. (2010). Vive les differences! Individual variation in neural mechanisms of executive control. *Current Opinion in Neurobiology, 20,* 242–250.

Braver, T., Gray, J., & Burgess, G. (2007). Explaining the many varieties of working memory variation: Dual mechanisms of cognitive control. In A. R. A. Conway, C. Jarrold, M. J. Kane, A. Miyake, & J. N. Towse (Eds.), *Variation in working memory* (pp. 76–106). New York: Oxford University Press.

Braver, T., & Ruge, H. (2006). Functional neuroimaging of executive functions. In R. Cabeza & A. Kingstone (Eds.), *Handbook of functional neuroimaging of cognition* (2nd ed., pp. 307–348). Cambridge, MA: MIT Press.

Buckner, R., Head, D., & Lustig, C. (2006). Brain changes in aging: A lifespan perspective. In F. I. M. Craik & E. Bialystock (Eds.), *Lifespan cognition: Mechanisms of change* (pp. 27–42). New York: Oxford University Press.

Bush, G., Frazier, J. A., Rausch, S. L., Seidman, L. J., Whalen, P. J., Jenike, M. A., et al. (1999). Anterior cingulate cortex dysfunction in attention-deficit/hyperactivity disorder as revealed by fMRI and the counting Stroop. *Biological Psychiatry, 45,* 1542–1552.

Cabeza, R., & Nyberg, L. (2000). Neural bases of learning and memory: Functional neuroimaging evidence. *Current Opinion in Neurology, 13,* 415–421.

Castel, A., Balota, D., Hutchison, K., Logan, J., & Yap, M. (2007). Spatial attention and response control in healthy younger and older adults and individuals with Alzheimer's disease: Evidence for disproportionate selection impairments in the Simon task. *Neuropsychology, 21,* 170–182.

Chan, J., & McDermott, K. (2007). The effects of frontal lobe functioning and age on veridical and false recall. *Psychonomic Bulletin & Review, 14,* 606–611.

Christensen, H., Anstey, K., Leach, L., & Mackinnon, A. (2008). Intelligence, education, and the brain reserve hypothesis. In F. I. M. Craik & T. A. Salthouse (Eds.), *The handbook of aging and cognition III* (pp. 133–188). New York: Psychology Press.

Chugani, H., Phelps, M,. & Mazziotta, J. (1987). Positron emission tomography study of human brain functional development. *Annals of Neurology, 22,* 487–497.

Cohen, J. D., Braver, T. S., & O'Reilly, R. C. (1998). A computational approach to prefrontal cortex, cognitive control and schizophrenia: Recent developments and current challenges. In

A. C. Roberts, T. W. Robbins, & L. Weiskrantz (Eds.), *The prefrontal cortex: Executive and cognitive functions* (pp. 195–220). Oxford: Oxford University Press.

Cohen, J. D., & Servan-Schreiber, D. (1992). Context, cortex, and dopamine: A connectionist approach to behavior and biology in schizophrenia. *Psychological Review, 99*, 45–77.

Conway, A., Cowan, N., & Bunting, M. (2001). The cocktail party phenomenon revisited: The importance of working memory capacity. *Psychonomic Bulletin & Review, 8*, 331–335.

Conway, A., Kane, M., Bunting, M., Hambrick, D., Wilhelm, O., & Engle, R. (2005). Working memory span tasks: A methodological review and user's guide. *Psychonomic Bulletin & Review, 12*, 769–786.

Cowan, N. (1995). *Attention and memory: An integrated framework.* New York: Oxford University Press.

Craik, F. I. M., & Byrd, M. (1982). Aging and cognitive deficits: The role of attentional resources. In F. I. M. Craik & S. E. Trehub (Eds.), *Aging and cognitive processes* (pp. 191–211). New York: Plenum.

Crone, E. A., Bunge, S. A., van der Molen, M. W., & Ridderinkhof, K. R. (2006). Switching between tasks and responses: A developmental study. *Developmental Science, 9*, 278–287.

Culham, J. C. (2006). Functional neuroimaging: Experimental design and analysis. In R. Cabeza & A. Kingstone (Eds.), *Handbook of functional neuroimaging of cognition* (2nd ed., pp. 53–82). Cambridge, MA: MIT Press.

Davis, C. L., Tomporowski, P. D., Boyle, C. A., Waller, J. L., Miller, P., Naglieri, J. A., et al. (2007). Effects of aerobic exercise on overweight children's cognitive functioning: A randomized controlled trial. *Research Quarterly for Exercise & Sport, 78*, 510–519.

Delis, D. C., Kramer, J. H., Kaplan, J. H., & Ober, B. (1987). *The California Verbal Learning Test.* San Antonio, TX: Psychological Corp.

De Luca, C. R., & Leventer, R. L. (2008). Developmental trajectories of executive function across the lifespan. In V. Anderson, R. Jacobs, & P. Anderson (Eds.), *Executive functions and the frontal lobes: A lifespan perspective.* London: Psychology Press.

Dempster, F. (1992). The rise and fall of the inhibitory mechanism: Toward a unified theory of cognitive development and aging. *Developmental Review, 12*, 45–75.

Dennis, N. A., & Cabeza, R. (2008). Neuroimaging of healthy cognitive aging. In F. I. M. Craik & T. A. Salthouse (Eds.), *Handbook of aging and cognition III* (pp. 1–54). New York: Psychology Press.

Diamond, A. (2002). Normal development of prefrontal cortex from birth to young adulthood: Cognitive functions, anatomy, and biochemistry. In D. T. Stuss & R. T. Knight (Eds.), *Principles of frontal lobe function* (pp. 466–503). New York: Oxford University Press.

Duncan, J. (1990). Goal weighting and the choice of behavior in a complex world. *Ergonomics, 33*, 1265–1279.

Duncan, J. (1993). Selection of input and goal in the control of behavior. In A. Baddeley & L. Weiskrantz (Eds.), *Attention: Selection, awareness, and control. A tribute to Donald Broadbent* (pp. 53–71). Oxford: Oxford University Press, Clarendon Press.

Duncan, J. (1995). Attention, intelligence, and the frontal lobes. In M. S. Gazzaniga (Ed.), *The cognitive neurosciences* (pp. 721–733). Cambridge, MA: MIT Press.

Engle, R. (2002). Working memory capacity as executive attention. *Current Directions in Psychological Science, 11*, 19–23.

Engle, R. W., & Kane, M. (2004). Executive attention, working memory capacity, and a two-factor theory of cognitive control. In B. Ross (Ed.), *The psychology of learning and motivation* (Vol. 44, pp. 145–199). New York: Elsevier.

Engle, R. W., Kane, M. J., & Tuholski, S. W. (1999). Individual differences in working memory capacity and what they tell us about controlled attention, general fluid intelligence and functions of the prefrontal cortex. In A. Miyake & P. Shah (Eds.), *Models of working memory: Mechanisms of active maintenance and executive control* (pp. 102–134). New York: Cambridge University Press.

Engle, R., Tuholski, S., Laughlin, J., & Conway, A. (1999). Working memory, short-term memory, and general fluid intelligence: A latent-variable approach. *Journal of Experimental Psychology: General, 128*, 309–331.

Florence, M. D., Asbridge, M., & Veugelers, P. J. (2008). Diet quality and academic performance. *Journal of School Health, 78*, 209–215.

Fuster, J. M. (1989). *The prefrontal cortex* (2nd ed.). New York: Raven.

Gerardi-Caulton, G. (2000). Sensitivity to spatial conflict and the development of self-regulation in children 24–36 months of age. *Developmental Science, 3*, 397–404.

Gerton, B. K., Brown, T. T., Meyer-Lindenberg, A., Kohn, P., Holt, J. L., Olsen, R. K., et al. (2004). Shared and distinct neurophysiological components of the digits forward and backward tasks as revealed by functional neuroimaging. *Neuropsychologia, 42*, 1781–1787.

Gianaros, P., Dearbyshire, S., May, J., Siegle, G., Gamalo, M., & Jennings, J. (2005). Anterior cingulate activity correlates with blood pressure during stress. *Psychophysiology, 42*, 627–635.

Giesbrecht, B., Kingstone, A., Handy, T., Hopfinger, J., & Mangun, G. (2006). Functional neuroimaging of attention. In R. Cabeza & A. Kingstone (Eds.), *Handbook of functional neuroimaging of cognition* (2nd ed., pp. 85–111). Cambridge, MA: MIT Press.

Glisky, E. L., & Kong, L. L. (2008). Do young and older adults rely on different processes in source memory tasks? A neuropsychological study. *Journal of Experimental Psychology: Learning, Memory, and Cognition, 34*, 809–822.

Glisky, E., Polster, M., & Routhieaux, B. (1995). Double dissociation between item and source memory. *Neuropsychology, 9*, 229–235.

Goldman-Rakic, P. S. (1987). Circuitry of primate prefrontal cortex and regulation of behavior by representational memory. In F. Plum (Ed.), *Handbook of physiology: The nervous system* (Vol. 5, pp. 373–417). Bethesda, MD: American Physiological Society.

Gur, R. C., Gur, R. E., Obrist, W., Skolnick, B., & Reivitch, M. (1987). Age and regional cerebral blood flow at rest and during cognitive activity. *Archives of General Psychiatry, 44*, 617–621.

Hart, R., Kwentus, J., Wade, J., & Taylor, J. (1988). Modified Wisconsin Sorting Test in elderly normal, depressed and demented patients. *Clinical Neuropsychologist, 2*, 49–56.

Hartig, T., Evans, G., Jamner, L., Davis, D., & Garling, T. (2003). Tracking restoration in natural and urban field settings. *Journal of Environmental Psychology, 23*, 109–123.

Hasher, L., & Zacks, R. (1988). Working memory, comprehension, and aging: A review and a new view. In G. Bower (Ed.), *The psychology of learning and motivation* (Vol. 22, pp. 193–225). New York: Academic Press.

Hertzog, C., Kramer, A. F., Wilson, R. S., & Lindenberger, U. (2009). Enrichment effects on adult cognitive development: Can the functional capacity of older adults be preserved and enhanced? *Psychological Science in the Public Interest, 9*, 1–65.

Hyman, B. T., Van Hoesen, G. W., Damasio, A. R., & Barnes, C. L. (1984). Alzheimer's disease: Cell-specific pathology isolates the hippocampal formation. *Science, 225*, 1168–1170.

Insurance Institute for Highway Safety. (2002). Data on age and driving fatality rates.

Jacoby, L. (1991). A process dissociation framework: Separating automatic from intentional uses of memory. *Journal of Memory and Language, 30*, 513–541.

Kahneman, D. (1973). *Attention and effort*. Englewood Cliffs, NJ: Prentice Hall.

Kane, M. J., Bleckley, K. M., Conway, A. R. A., & Engle, R. W. (2001). A controlled-attention view of working-memory capacity. *Journal of Experimental Psychology: General, 130*, 169–183.

Kane, M. J., Conway, A. R. A., Hambrick, D. Z., & Engle, R. W. (2007). Variation in working memory as variation in executive attention and control. In A. R. A. Conway, C. Jarrold, M. J. Kane, A. Miyake, & J. N. Towse (Eds.), *Variation in working memory*. New York: Oxford University Press.

Kane, M., & Engle, R. (2002). The role of prefrontal cortex in working-memory capacity, executive attention, and general fluid intelligence: An individual-differences perspective. *Psychonomic Bulletin & Review, 9*, 637–671.

Kane, M., & Engle, R. (2003). Working memory capacity and the control of attention: The contributions of goal neglect, response competition, and task set to Stroop interference. *Journal of Experimental Psychology: General, 132*, 47–70.

Kaplan, S. (1995). The restorative benefits of nature: Toward an integrative framework. *Journal of Environmental Psychology, 15*, 169–182.

Kaplan, S. (2001). Meditation, restoration, and the management of mental fatigue. *Environment and Behavior, 33*, 480–506.

Kaplan, S. K., & Berman, M. G. (2010). Directed attention as a common resource for executive functioning and self-regulation. *Perspectives on Psychological Science, 5*, 43–57.

Kingstone, A., Smilek, D., Ristic, J., Friesen, C., & Eastword, J. (2003). Attention, Researchers! It is time to take a look at the real world. *Current Directions in Psychological Science, 12*, 176–180.

Kramer, A., Hahn, S., Cohen, N., Banich, M., McAuley, E., Harrison, C., et al. (1999). Ageing, fitness and neurocognitive function. *Nature, 400*, 418–419.

Kramer, A. F., & Madden, D. J. (2008). Attention. In F. I. M. Craik & T. A. Salthouse (Eds.), *Handbook of aging and cognition III* (pp. 189–249). New York: Psychology Press.

La Pointe, L. B., & Engle, R. W. (1990). Simple and complex word spans as measures of working memory capacity. *Journal of Experimental Psychology: Learning, Memory & Cognition, 16*, 1118–1133.

Louv, R. (2008). *Last child in the woods: Saving our children from nature-deficit disorder.* Chapel Hill, NC: Algonquin Books of Chapel Hill.

Luria, A. (1966). *Higher cortical functions in man.* New York: Basic Books.

MacDonald, S. W., Li, S. C., & Bäckman, L. (2009). Neural underpinnings of within-person variability in cognitive functioning. *Psychology & Aging, 24,* 792–808.

MacDonald, S. W., Nyberg, L., & Bäckman, L. (2006). Intra-individual variability in behavior: Links to brain structure, neurotransmission, and neuronal activity. *Trends in Neurosciences, 29,* 474–480.

Mayr, U. (2001). Age differences in the selection of mental sets: The role of inhibition, stimulus ambiguity, and response-set overlap. *Psychology and Aging, 16,* 96–109.

McCabe, D. P., Roediger, H. L., McDaniel, M. A., & Balota, D. A. (2009). Aging reduces veridical remembering but increases false remembering: Neuropsychological test correlates of remember-know judgments. *Neuropsychologia, 47,* 2164–2173.

McCabe, D. P., Roediger, H. L., McDaniel, M. A., Balota, D. A., & Hambrick, D. Z. (2010). The relationship between working memory capacity and executive functioning.: Evidence for a common executive attention construct. *Neuropsychology, 24,* 222–243.

McDaniel, M., Einstein, G., & Jacoby, L. (2008). New considerations in aging and memory: The glass may be half full. In F. I. M. Craik & T. A. Salthouse (Eds.), *The handbook of aging and cognition III* (pp. 251–310). New York: Psychology Press.

Miller, A. E., Watson, J. M., & Strayer, D. L. (2010). *Individual differences in working memory capacity predict action monitoring and the error-related negativity.* Manuscript in preparation.

Miller, E. K., & Cohen, J. D. (2001). An integrative theory of prefrontal cortex function. *Annual Review of Neuroscience, 24,* 167–202.

Miller, G. (1956). The magical number seven, plus or minus two: Some limits on our capacity for processing information. *Psychological Review, 63,* 81–97.

National Safety Council. (2010). *NSC Estimates 1.6 Million Crashes Caused by Cell Phone use and Texting* (Press release date January 12, 2010. On the web at http://www.nsc.org/).

Nauta, W. J. H. (1964). Some efferent connections of the prefrontal cortex in the monkey. In J. M. Warren & K. Akert (Eds.), *The frontal granular cortex and behavior* (pp. 397–407). New York: McGraw-Hill.

Nauta, W. J. H. (1972). Neural associations of the frontal cortex. *Acta Neurobiologiae Experimentalis, 32,* 125–140.

Nebes, R. (1992). Cognitive dysfunction in Alzheimer's disease. In F. I. M. Craik & T. A. Salthouse (Eds.), *The handbook of aging and cognition* (pp. 373–446). Hillsdale, NJ: Erlbaum.

Nielson, K. A., Langenecker, S. A., & Garavan, H. (2002). Differences in the functional neuroanatomy of inhibitory control across the adult lifespan. *Psychology & Aging, 17,* 56–71.

Norman, D. A., & Bobrow, D. G. (1975). On data-limited and resource-limited processes. *Cognitive Psychology, 7,* 44–64.

Ophir, E., Nass, C. I., & Wagner, A. D. (2009). Cognitive control in media multitaskers. *Proceedings of the National Academy of Sciences, 106,* 15583–15587.

O'Reilly, R. C., Braver, T. S., & Cohen, J. D. (1999). A biologically based computational model of working memory. In A. Miyake & P. Shah (Eds.), *Models of working memory: Mechanisms of active maintenance and executive control* (pp. 375–411). New York: Cambridge University Press.

Osaka, M., Osaka, N., Kondo, H., Morishita, M., Fukuyama, H., Aso, T., et al. (2003). The neural basis of individual differences in working memory capacity: An fMRI study. *NeuroImage, 18,* 789–797.

Parasuraman, R., & Greenwood, P. (2007). Individual differences in attention and working memory: A molecular genetic approach. In A. F. Kramer, D. A. Wiegmann, & A. Kirlik (Eds.), *Attention: From theory to practice* (pp. 59–72). New York: Oxford University Press.

Paxton, J. L., Barch, D. M., Racine, C. A., & Braver, T. S. (2008). Cognitive control, goal maintenance, and prefrontal function in healthy aging. *Cerebral Cortex, 18,* 1010–1028.

Petersen, R. (2004). Mild cognitive impairment. *Journal of Internal Medicine, 256,* 183–194.

Peterson, B., Kane, M., Alexander, G., Lacadie, C., Skudlarski, P., Leung, H., et al. (2002). An event-related functional MRI study comparing interference effects in the Simon and Stroop tasks. *Cognitive Brain Research, 13,* 427–440.

Posner, M. I., & DiGirolamo, G. J. (1998). Executive attention: Conflict, target detection, and cognitive control. In R. Parasuraman (Ed.), *The attentive brain* (pp. 401–423). Cambridge, MA: MIT Press.

Price, J., & Davis, B. (2008). *The woman who can't forget: The extraordinary story of living with the most remarkable memory known to science—A memoir.* New York: Simon & Schuster.

Raichle, M. (2006). Functional neuroimaging: A historical and physiological perspective. In R. Cabeza & A. Kingstone (Eds.), *Handbook of functional neuroimaging of cognition* (2nd ed., pp. 3–20). Cambridge, MA: MIT Press.

Raz, N. (2000). Aging of the brain and its impact on cognitive performance: Integration of structural and functional findings. In F. I. M. Craik & T. A. Salthouse (Eds.), *The handbook of aging and cognition* (2nd ed., pp. 1–90). Mahwah, NJ: Erlbaum.

Raz, N., Torres I. J., Spencer W. D., Baertschie J. C., Millman, D., & Sarpel, G. (1993). Neuroanatomical correlates of age-sensitive and age-invariant cognitive abilities: An in vivo MRI investigation. *Intelligence, 17,* 407–422.

Roberts, R., & Pennington, B. (1996). An interactive framework for examining prefrontal cognitive processes. *Developmental Neuropsychology, 12,* 105–126.

Roediger, H., & McDaniel, M. (2007). Illusory recollection in older adults: Testing Mark Twain's conjecture. In M. Garry & H. Hayne (Eds.), *Do justice and let the sky fall: Elizabeth Loftus and her contributions to science, law, and academic freedom* (pp. 105–136). Hillsdale, NJ: Erlbaum.

Rueda, M. R., Rothbart, M. K., McCandliss, B. D., Saccomanno, L., & Posner, M. I. (2005). Training, maturation, and genetic influences on the development of executive attention. *Proceedings of the National Academy of Sciences, 102,* 14931–14936.

Salthouse, T. (1996). The processing speed theory of adult age differences in cognition. *Psychological Review, 103,* 403–428.

Schneider, B., & Pichora-Fuller, M. (2000). Implications of perceptual deterioration for cognitive aging research. In F. I. M. Craik & T. A. Salthouse (Eds.), *The handbook of aging and cognition* (2nd ed., pp. 155–219). Mahwah, NJ: Erlbaum.

Shallice, T., & Burgess, P. W. (1996). The domain of supervisory processes and temporal organization of behavior. *Philosophical Transactions of the Royal Society of London B., 351,* 1405–1412.

Siegler, R. S. (2006). Inter- and intra-individual differences in problem solving across the lifespan. In E. Bialystok & F. I. M. Craik (Eds.), *Lifespan cognition: Mechanisms of change* (pp. 285–296). Oxford: Oxford University Press.

Simon, J. (1969). Reactions toward the source of stimulation. *Journal of Experimental Psychology, 81,* 174–176.

Smith, E. E., Geva, A., Jonides, J., Miller, A., Reuter-Lorenz, P., & Koeppe, R. A. (2001). The neural basis of task-switching in working memory: Effects of performance and aging. *Proceedings of the National Academy of Sciences, 98,* 2095–2100.

Smith, E., & Jonides, J. (1997). Working memory: A view from neuroimaging. *Cognitive Psychology, 33,* 5–42.

Strayer, D., & Drews, F. (2004). Profiles in driver distraction: Effects of cell phone conversations on younger and older Drivers. *Human Factors, 46,* 640–649.

Strayer, D. L., & Drews, F. A. (2007). Attention. In F. Durso, R. Nickerson, S. Dumais, S. Lewandowsky, & T. Perfect (Eds.), *Handbook of applied cognition II* (pp. 29–54). West Sussex, UK: John Wiley & Sons.

Strayer, D.L., Watson, J.M., & Drews, F.A. (in press). Cognitive distraction while multi-tasking in the automobile. Chapter to appear in B. Ross (Ed.), *The Psychology of Learning and Motivation, Vol. 54,* Elsevier.

Stroop, J. (1935). Studies of interference in serial verbal reactions. *Journal of Experimental Psychology, 18,* 643–662.

Taylor, A. F., & Kuo, F. E. (2009). Children with attention deficits concentrate better after walk in the park. *Journal of Attention Disorders, 12,* 402–409.

Turner, M. L., & Engle, R. W. (1989). Is working memory capacity task dependent? *Journal of Memory and Language, 28,* 127–154.

Uchino, B. N., Smith, T. W., Birmingham, W., & Carlisle, M. C. (in press). Social neuroscientific pathways linking social support to health. In J. Decaty & J. Cacioppo (Eds.), *Handbook of social neuroscience.* New York: Oxford.

Underwood, G., Crundall, D., & Chapman, P. (2007). Driving. In F. Durso, R. Nickerson, S. Dumais, S. Lewandowsky, & T. Perfect (Eds.), *Handbook of applied cognition II* (pp. 391–414). West Sussex, UK: John Wiley & Sons.

Unsworth, N., Heitz, R., Schrock, J., & Engle, R. (2005). An automated version of the operation span task. *Behavior Research Methods, 37,* 498–505.

Watson, J. M., Balota, D. A., & Sergent-Marshall, S. (2001). Semantic, phonological, and hybrid veridical and false memories in healthy older adults and in individuals with dementia of the Alzheimer type. *Neuropsychology, 15,* 254–267.

Watson, J. M., Bunting, M., Poole, B., & Conway, A. (2005). Individual differences in susceptibility to false memory in the Deese-Roediger-McDermott paradigm. *Journal of Experimental Psychology: Learning, Memory, & Cognition, 31,* 76–85.

Watson, J. M., Lambert, A., Thorgusen, S., Levy, J., & Kesner, R. (2010). *Deficits in working memory capacity in persons with amnestic mild cognitive impairment.* Manuscript in preparation.

Watson, J. M., & Strayer, D. L. (2010). Supertaskers: Profiles in extraordinary multi-tasking ability. *Psychonomic Bulletin & Review, 17,* 479–485.

Wechsler, D. (1981). *Wechsler Adult Intelligence Scale—Revised manual.* New York: Psychological Corp.

Wechsler, D. (1987). *Wechsler Memory Scale—Revised Manual.* New York: Psychological Corp.

West, R. (1996). An application of prefrontal cortex function theory to cognitive aging. *Psychological Bulletin, 120,* 272–292.

Wickens, C. D. (1980). The structure of attentional resources. In R. Nickerson (Ed.), *Attention and Performance VIII* (pp. 239–257). Hillsdale, NJ: Erlbaum.

Wickens, C. D. (1984). Processing resources in attention. In R. Parasuraman & R. Davies (Eds.), *Varieties of attention* (pp. 63–101). New York: Academic Press.

Williams, B. R., Hultsch, D. F., Strauss, E. H., Hunter, M. A., & Tannock, R. (2005). Inconsistency in reaction time across the life span. *Neuropsychology, 19,* 88–96.

IMPACT OF EXPLANATORY STYLE AND AGE STEREOTYPES ON HEALTH ACROSS THE LIFE SPAN

17

Becca R. Levy, Pil Chung, and Maureen Canavan

Imagine if every year, along with a medical check-up, we were encouraged to get another check-up—a social-cognitive check-up at which those beliefs that are most likely to affect health were assessed. This check-up would be administered by an expert who could give prescriptions consisting of age-appropriate mental exercises to bolster beneficial beliefs and resist harmful beliefs. Although scientists' findings do not yet support such prescriptions, they are a worthy goal of research.

In this chapter, we will consider how the cognitive and physical health of individuals is influenced across the life span by two frameworks that are used for viewing their world. At first glance, these frameworks share little in common; attributions are defined as causal explanations for an event or behavior, whereas age stereotypes are defined as a set of beliefs about individuals based on their age (we will focus on age stereotypes about older individuals).

In spite of these diverse definitions, the two frameworks have several characteristics in common. Most basically, both are examples of social cognition. As opposed to the traditional study of cognition, which examines how individuals think as isolated beings, social cognition considers how they think as societal beings (Fiske, 2005). The main goal of social cognition is to understand how individuals define situations, themselves, and others, as well as how others define them.

There is evidence that attributions and age stereotypes start to operate before children can speak and continue into old age. Although both of these phenomena can operate unconsciously, they serve as techniques that individuals use to bring order to their world. To that end, both provide readily accessible structures that make it possible to interpret and organize the vast amount of information about the variety of people and situations that are encountered on a daily basis. Because this process tends to eliminate uncertainty from the encounters, there is a compelling and ongoing need to engage in it (Macrae, Milne, & Bodenhausen, 1994). In short, attributions and stereotypes are functional insofar as they make everyday life manageable. But, at the same time, they tend to oversimplify the real world and can cause harm.

For most people, there tends to be a consistency to the attributions and age stereotypes held across the life span. As a result, an understanding of these phenomena provides a basis not only for explaining individuals' attitudes and behaviors in the present but also for predicting them in the future. Both attributions and age stereotypes contribute to either a favorable or unfavorable outlook which corresponds, respectively, to optimistic or pessimistic explanatory styles (which are the types of attributions that will be considered in this chapter), as well as to positive and negative age stereotypes. In general, the favorable perspective has a beneficial effect on cognitive and physical health across the life span, whereas the unfavorable perspective has an adverse effect.

In this chapter, for both attributions and age stereotypes, we will: highlight theoretical underpinnings; present the major findings related to cognitive and physical health across the life span; discuss the stability or instability of both concepts over time; and, finally, provide suggestions for future research.

EXPLANATORY STYLE ACROSS THE LIFE SPAN

Fritz Heider, the Austrian psychologist, suggested that a main feature of social cognition was the way in which individuals explained or "attributed" life events in terms of their dispositions. The perception of causality may be influenced by "the tendency to see the environment as full of hostile or of benevolent intentions directed toward oneself" (Heider, 1958, p. 370). Heider proposed that in order to understand people's actions, it is necessary to know how they rationalize the behaviors of themselves and others (Heider, 1958). The resulting theory of attribution is an attempt to systematically describe how individuals form these rationalizations, and how these rationalizations then influence their behaviors. In addition, it is suggested that attributions for a particular type of behavior or event help to shape future responses to similar situations (Weiner, 1985).

Explanatory style was selected for this chapter because it has been most consistently used in research related to health and functioning over the life span (e.g., Ciarrochi & Heaven, 2008). Explanatory style describes the way that an individual explains the causes of bad events. In its pessimistic form, the bad events are seen as internal, stable, and global; in its optimistic form, the bad events are seen as external, unstable, and specific (Peterson & Seligman, 1984). In this chapter, we will include relevant studies that include all three explanatory-style dimensions, as well as those that include fewer than the three.

The first of these dimensions, location, describes where the attributed cause responsible for a particular outcome is located in relation to the self. This location can be either internal or external. An internal designation indicates that the individual believes the cause of an outcome lies within himself or herself, whereas an external designation indicates that the individual believes the cause lies outside himself or herself (Peterson & Seligman, 1984).

The second dimension, temporality, describes how predictable or fixed the attributed cause is over time. Thus, the temporality of a given attribution can be considered either stable or unstable. A stable designation indicates that the individual believes the cause of an outcome is persistent, whereas an unstable designation indicates that the individual believes the cause is transient (Peterson & Seligman, 1984).

The third attribution dimension, generalizability, describes how applicable the attributed cause is to the varied situations confronted by the individual throughout his or her life. This dimension ranges from global, which denotes that the individual believes the cause of an event is universally applicable, to specific, which denotes that the individual believes the cause of an event applies only to a particular situation (Peterson & Seligman, 1984).

Explanatory Style and Health in Childhood

A debate exists in the child-development literature about the origin of causal perceptions. Some propose that the perception of causality results from an innate cognitive architecture (e.g., Leslie, 1988), whereas others argue that children learn to see causality by observing the world around them (e.g., Cohen, Amsel, Redford, & Casasola, 1998). It is likely that the development of causal perceptions is based on both innate processes and learning.

In a set of experiments designed to partially address this controversy, 7-month-old infants were studied by having them become familiar with a standard animation trial of moving objects on a computer screen, followed by a new animation trial that demonstrated different causal relationships between moving objects. The investigators interpreted the pattern of the infants' looking-times as indicative of their ability to perceive causation in a way that is similar to adults. They concluded that infants can engage in causal perceptions that take into account "subtle and nuanced factors," suggesting that these perceptions are more likely innate than acquired from experience (Newman, Choi, Wynn, & Scholl, 2008, p. 287).

An alternative to this proposed innateness is presented in a study that suggests these causal perceptions, at an older age, are a response to the environment: the explanatory style of 8- to 13-year-olds was thought to be learned from their mothers (Seligman et al., 1984). Further, the children's tendency to use pessimistic explanatory styles was associated with higher levels of current and future depressive symptoms (Seligman et al., 1984).

Several subsequent studies have documented a significant relationship between pessimistic explanatory style and depression in children (Panak & Garber, 1992; Stevens & Prinstein, 2005; Toner & Heaven, 2005). One of these studies followed 11-year-olds over a 1-year period and found that a pessimistic explanatory style was associated with worse school achievement, as well as an increase in depressive symptoms (Nolen-Hoeksema, Girgus, & Seligman, 1986).

Researchers have found that the relationship between explanatory style and school achievement may be due to how children apply temporality (an explanatory-style dimension) to academic life. Children with a maladaptive "helpless style" tend to avoid challenges, show declining academic expectations, and tend to give up after failure, because they attribute such failure to stable factors (e.g., lack of intelligence); but children with an adaptive "mastery-oriented" style tend to seek challenges and continue to strive even after failure, because they attribute academic failure to unstable factors (e.g., lack of effort; Burhans & Dweck, 1995; Licht & Dweck, 1984). The relationship between a mastery orientation and better grades over time has been documented in both the United States and China (Wang & Pomerantz, 2009).

The mechanism that links explanatory style to school achievement in children may involve mental health. A study found that kindergartners with a more helpless style tended to have lower feelings of self-worth and more depressive symptoms 5 years later, according to both self reports and teacher reports (Kistner, Ziegert, Castro, & Robertson, 2001).

Explanatory Style and Health in Younger Adulthood and Midlife

The relationship between explanatory style and academic performance was also found among college students. As an example, a more optimistic explanatory style predicted a higher grade-point average better than traditional measures of academic performance (Schulman, 1999).

Yet, there may be times when an internal attribution (a component of a pessimistic explanatory style) for bad events is adaptive. For instance, among college students, internal attributions for a bad event were found to generate frustration and anger, resulting in improved cognitive performance to overcome the difficulties of a task (Mikulincer, 1988). However, when exposed to several insolvable problems, internal attributors exhibited a decrease in performance, compared to external attributors (Mikulincer, 1988).

Pessimistic explanatory style has been shown to predict depression among young adults in several studies (e.g., Nolen-Hoeksema, Girgus, & Seligman, 1991; Peterson & Seligman, 1984). A mechanism by which pessimistic explanatory style may contribute to depression is through its linkage to weaker social networks. In a study of students over a 4-year period, it was found that those with a more pessimistic explanatory style were less likely to develop and maintain social networks, and showed greater sadness over the course of the research (Ciarrochi & Heaven, 2008).

Research has also examined the relationship of explanatory style to trauma, with the assumption that those who have a more pessimistic explanatory style tend to interpret trauma in a way that makes them more vulnerable to bad outcomes. For instance, a study found that among undergraduates who had suffered a variety of traumatic events, such as being the victim of a violent attack or natural disaster, those with more stable attributions (the pessimistic-explanatory-style component) for the events had significantly more severe posttraumatic-stress-disorder symptoms, even after accounting for depression (Gray, Pumphrey, & Lombardo, 2003).

Most of the previous research on explanatory style and trauma has been conducted in Western countries. To examine whether this framework is useful for understanding trauma experienced in Asian countries, investigators interviewed 264 Sri Lankan tsunami survivors, whose average age was 38, six months following the event (Levy, Slade, & Ranasinghe, 2009). Among those who had been living along the most-affected coastal area, pessimistic explanatory style was significantly associated with worse physical and mental health (Levy, Slade, et al., 2009). For example, individuals who had a pessimistic explanatory style were 30% more likely to have posttraumatic stress disorder, compared to those who did not possess a pessimistic explanatory style (Levy, Slade, et al., 2009). These results suggest that the relationship between a more pessimistic explanatory style and worse mental health may be a universal phenomenon. On the other hand, this study found evidence for culturally specific attributions: 51% of the predominantly Buddhist sample blamed the tsunami on the Buddhist concept of karma (Levy, Slade, et al., 2009).

A life-span approach has been applied to a pair of studies that examine the impact of pessimistic explanatory style on mortality and morbidity. In one of these studies, the investigators matched the explanatory style of teenagers to death information 51–55 years later (Peterson, Seligman, Yurko, Martin, & Friedman, 1998). They found that a tendency to form global attributions (the pessimistic-explanatory-style component of generalizability), or "catastrophizing," predicted lower survival rates—particularly in connection with accidental or violent death, which the authors associated with alienation and risk-taking (Peterson et al., 1998).

In the other longitudinal study, conducted with Harvard graduates, the investigators found that a more pessimistic explanatory style, measured at the age of 25, predicted worse physician-assessed physical health from ages 30–60, after adjusting for baseline physical and emotional health (Peterson, Seligman, & Vaillant, 1988). The strength of the relationship increased over the time period studied. The explanation given for this effect was that pessimistic explanatory style increased a feeling of helplessness, which others have found can contribute to worse health outcomes (Peterson, et al., 1988).

A physiological mechanism by which pessimistic explanatory style may influence health is through the immune system (e.g., Kamen-Siegel, Rodin, Seligman, & Dwyer, 1991). As an example, research has shown that pessimistic explanatory style in college students was inversely correlated with immunoglobin A, which protects against infections (Brennan & Charnetski, 2000).

Explanatory Style and Health in Older Adulthood

In contrast to the explanatory-style research that focuses on academic performance in children and younger adults, the focus for cognitive studies with older adults tends to be on how they assign attributions to memory problems. This shift of focus corresponds to stereotypical views of the old (Levy & Langer, 1994; Löckenhoff et al., 2009). For example, a study showed that when elders evaluate the memory failures of other elders, they tend to attribute these failures to internal and stable causes, such as lack of ability, while they tend to attribute similar failures in younger adults to external and unstable factors, such as an unfair test (Bieman-Copland & Ryan, 1998).

Several studies have found that a pessimistic explanatory style predicts worse physical health among elders (e.g., Kamen-Siegel et al., 1991). For instance, among patients at the Mayo Clinic, those with a more pessimistic explanatory style were found to be at greater risk of mortality 30 years later (Maruta, Robert, Malinchoc, & Offord, 2000).

Less common are studies that focus on the beneficial effects of optimistic explanatory style, but they too are able to explain the operation of pessimistic explanatory style. To illustrate, the explanatory style of men with an average age of 61 was measured at baseline, and their medical condition was followed over the next 10 years (Kubzansky, Sparrow, Vokonas, & Kawachi, 2001). Those who were recorded as having a more optimistic explanatory style, assessed by a 263-item explanatory-style scale, had a significantly lower risk of developing coronary heart disease. The authors surmise that "Because optimistic individuals actively engage in planning and problem solving, they may experience fewer stressors, or they may have more resources with which to deal with stress" (Kubzansky et al., 2001, p. 914). Presumably, individuals with more pessimistic explanatory styles may have more stress because they lack these advantages.

In addition, age attributions or the tendency to blame one's cognitive and physical problems on the aging process, rather than on extenuating circumstances, have been associated with worse health (e.g., Williamson & Fried, 1996). Although age attributions, as such, are not part of explanatory style, they correspond to the internal and stable dimensions of pessimistic explanatory style (Banziger & Derevenstedt, 1982; Erber & Long, 2006). At least a partial explanation for the association of age attributions with worse health may be related to the finding that older individuals who attributed their depression to age were more than four times as likely to believe that it was not important to seek treatment for their depression, compared to older individuals who did not attribute their depression to age (Sarkisian, Lee-Henderson, & Mangione, 2003).

Age attributions have also been explored across cultures and across ages (Levy, Ashman, & Slade, 2009). It was predicted that the tendency to attribute bad health events, such as waking up with aches and pains, to age ("I seem to be getting old") as opposed to extenuating circumstances ("I slept in an uncomfortable position") would be greater among Japanese than Americans. This is because a series of studies found Asians are more likely than Americans to attribute failures to internal factors (Mezulis, Abramson, Hyde, & Hankin, 2004). Therefore, if blaming age for bad health events is an internal attribution, age attributions should be more common among Japanese than Americans. It was also predicted that age attributions would be made more frequently in old age than earlier in life, because of the assumption that they are formed when self-relevant (i.e., in old age). Lastly, it was hypothesized that stronger age attributions would be associated with worse functional health among older participants, after adjusting for relevant covariates (Levy, Ashman, et al., 2009).

As predicted, older individuals in both countries were more likely than younger individuals to make age attributions, with the older Japanese making significantly more age age attributions than the older Americans. Among older Americans, a greater tendency to form age attributions was associated with worse functional health, but there was not a significant association between age attributions and functional health among the older Japanese (Levy, Ashman, et al., 2009). The authors suggest that the different relationships between age attributions and health in these two cultures may be due to the moderating effect of interdependence and to the acceptance of aging as part of the natural life course—both of which are embedded in Japanese culture (Levy, Ashman, et al., 2009; Takagi & Silverstein, 2006).

Explanatory style is able to provide a bridge between earlier-in-life experiences and old age, by interpreting the events of aging and forming a narrative of one's life. As an extreme, but suggestive, example of a life-span process, elders who experienced a trauma in childhood or younger adulthood may replay aspects of it, as they get older, through the flashbacks that characterize posttraumatic stress disorder. In a study of Holocaust survivors, it was found that although most people attributed the bad events they experienced to external causes, 20% attributed these bad events to internal causes—perhaps due to survivors' guilt (Finkelstein & Levy, 2006). Those who formed internal attributions for the traumatic events they had undergone much earlier were less likely to discuss them with others, and they tended to have worse mental and physical health, compared to survivors with external attributions (Finkelstein & Levy, 2006).

Stability and Malleability of Explanatory Style

Existing research has not conclusively answered the question of whether explanatory style is stable or malleable. Indeed, the findings are inconsistent. One study, for instance, found that explanatory style for bad events remained stable across a period of 52 years, while the explanatory style for good events was much more malleable over this same duration (Burns & Seligman, 1989). The current explanatory style of participants, with an average age of 72, was assessed, and they were asked to provide diaries and letters from their youth. These materials were content-analyzed for explanatory styles. The authors suggest that explanatory style for bad events is a trait, because it significantly correlated between the two time points measured decades apart—although inconsistency emerged in the types of events to which the participants applied the explanatory styles (e.g., school and dating in early life, in contrast to health and grandchildren in later life; Burns & Seligman, 1989).

There is some evidence that the stability of explanatory style can be influenced on an institutional level by the social system. A content analysis of East and West Berlin newspapers was published during the 1984 winter Olympics, in which East Germany won 24 medals and West Germany won four medals (Oettingen, 1995). The authors predicted that in spite of the medal count, a pessimistic explanatory style would be found more frequently in East Berlin newspapers, due to the East German government imposing extraordinary control over its citizens, as exemplified by the building of a wall to prevent people from leaving. It was assumed "The differences in political systems of East and West Berlin would be so pervasive and prominent that they would achieve a difference in explanatory style on a cultural level. This would be quite a spectacular product of politics in light of the fact that an individual level explanatory style is very change-resistant" (Oettingen, 1995, p. 216). As expected, a significantly more pessimistic explanatory style was expressed in the newspapers of East Berlin, compared to West Berlin (Oettingen, 1995).

On a short-term basis, the malleability of explanatory style was demonstrated in a series of studies that covered a wide spectrum of target groups. Among the studies is one directed at 11- to 14-year-old girls whose explanatory styles were made more optimistic by teaching them to "identify and evaluate pessimistic thoughts by considering alternatives and examining evidence" (Chaplin et al., 2006, p. 115). Another study focused on employees in an insurance company who were given a training course based on cognitive-behavioral therapy. It led to improvements in explanatory style, as well as in self-esteem and job-related variables (Proudfoot, Corr, Guest, & Dunn, 2009). Although a change of explanatory style was shown within the confines of these studies, the durability of the interventions cannot be gauged beyond the end of their follow-up periods, which were 1 year and three-and-a-half months, respectively (Proudfoot et al., 2009).

The next section covers another concept that influences cognitive and physical health across the life span. Age stereotypes will be considered in life stages that correspond to the ones used for explanatory style.

AGE STEREOTYPES AND HEALTH ACROSS THE LIFE SPAN

Before considering age stereotypes at the level of those who hold them, it is important to acknowledge the role of social institutions in creating and perpetuating them. A particularly flagrant example is the so-called anti-aging industry that sells what are promoted as antidotes to the outward signs of old age, often aimed at those who are middle aged. One of the best known of these items is Botox, for combating wrinkles, which sold close to 2.5 million injection procedures in 2008 ("Cosmetic Surgery National Data Bank Statistics," 2009). Products of this type are made to appear desirable by the industry's marketing campaigns that make aging appear undesirable. The common use of the term "anti-aging" demonstrates "the entrenchment of ageism that such nomenclature does not raise eyebrows or objections" (Calasanti, 2007, p. 338).

The popular acceptance of "anti-aging" reflects the fact that older individuals, unlike the members of several other marginalized groups, do not benefit from political correctness (Levy & Banaji, 2002). There is, then, virtually no societal barrier to the propagation of negative age stereotypes that are internalized by individuals over the life span.

Positive age stereotypes (e.g., *old people are wise*) as well as negative age stereotypes (e.g., *old people are senile*) exist. But it is the negative ones that predominate in Western cultures, both in everyday life and among those held by individuals (Levy, Kasl, & Gill, 2004; Löckenhoff et al., 2009; Nosek et al., 2007).

A theory of age stereotype embodiment has been offered to describe the process by which age stereotypes influence individuals over the life course and affect their health (Levy, 2009). It proposes that stereotypes are assimilated from the surrounding culture and, in old age, contribute to self-definitions. This process empowers the stereotypes to influence health and functioning. The theory is based on four premises stating the conditions that enable the stereotype embodiment to occur. Specifically, age stereotypes: (1) become internalized across the life span, (2) can operate unconsciously, (3) gain salience from self-relevance, and (4) use multiple pathways (Levy, 2009). According to this theory, age stereotypes operate in two directions: top-down (from society to the individual) and over time (from the young child to the elder; Levy, 2009).

Age stereotype embodiment theory is rooted in the idea that the stereotypes are absorbed from popular culture, norms, and everyday interactions, as suggested by three disciplines: sociology (e.g., George Herbert Mead), cultural anthropology (e.g., Margaret Mead), and social psychology (e.g., Gordon Allport). For example, Allport wrote, "A child who adopts prejudice is taking over attitudes and stereotypes from his family or cultural environment" (Allport, 1954, p. 297).

The research findings that support the premises of age stereotype embodiment theory will be reviewed in the following contexts of the life-span stages.

Age Stereotypes and Health in Childhood

There are a number of studies that show infants start to categorize information (e.g., Behl-Chadha, 1996; Quinn, Eimas, & Rosenkrantz, 1993); this is the same process that is involved in forming age stereotypes. For example, an experimenter presented a series of paired images of cats, dogs, and birds to 3- and 4-month-old infants who could differentiate these creatures in a way which suggested an ability to actively categorize natural forms (Quinn et al., 1993).

Among the stereotypes that children assimilate are those that are directed at groups to which they belong in the present or to which they will belong in the future. These can be broadly classified as existing self-stereotypes or anticipatory self-stereotypes. Existing self-stereotypes are held by children who belong to groups that are stigmatized in particular domains or in a more general way. The following cases are illustrative: (1) a decrement in the mathematical performance of girls as young as 5 years was found when their gender was activated (Ambady, Shih, Kim, & Pittinsky, 2001); (2) overweight girls who reported stronger stereotypes about obesity had lower self-worth (Davison, Schmalz, Young, & Birch, 2008); and (3) African American children showed more negative views toward other African American children than toward White children (Williams & Davidson, 2009). In contrast, anticipatory self-stereotypes are held by children in advance of their joining the targeted groups—as is the case of children's stereotypes about the old, which provide the focus for this section of the chapter.

Age stereotypes differ from gender, weight, and race stereotypes in a fundamental way that affects how they operate over the life span. Because children absorb age stereotypes decades before these are self-relevant, they have no perceived need to defend against them; this increases their susceptibility to the stereotypes (Levy, Slade, Kunkel, & Kasl, 2002).

The old is one of the categories about which children are particularly likely to form stereotypes. Children are motivated to understand their social world, so that they pay attention to widely emphasized distinctions made about groups of people. This leads children to form stereotypes about some groups (e.g., the old), but not about others (e.g., right-handed people; Bigler & Liben, 2007). The old as a category meet three criteria that have been formulated to identify groups that are most likely to have negative stereotypes directed against them by children: they are a proportionately smaller cohort than the majority; they are often segregated from the rest of the population (e.g., in leisure activities); and they are frequently labeled as having certain attributes (Bigler & Liben, 2007).

Children pick up the societal attributes assigned to the old in a number of ways. Many of the outlets designed for children, such as television, movies, books, and songs include the age stereotypes of their culture (Donlon, Ashman, & Levy, 2005; Levy, 2009). For example, a popular children's song taught in nursery schools includes the chorus, "I knew an old lady who swallowed a fly, I don't know why she swallowed a fly, perhaps she'll die." The song goes on to describe several other creatures that she ate. Thus, this older person is presented as an object of humor who engages in odd and irrational behavior that might cause her own death.

There are a variety of ways in which it has been established, directly and indirectly, that children assimilate and express the age stereotypes of their culture. In a study of children between the ages of 4 and 7, close to two thirds of the participants indicated that they would prefer not to become old (Burke, 1981–1982). An experiment that examined 10- and 11-year-old children's age stereotypes, expressed in drawings of young and old men and women, found that the drawings of old people were significantly more negative than the drawings of young people (Falchikov, 1990). In another study, when children as young as 5 were asked by an older experimenter in her 70s if two lines of objects of different lengths were of the same length, the participants tended to assume that she was confused and was asking for clarification. In contrast, the children tended to assume an experimenter in her 20s already knew the answer and was testing them (Kwong See & Heller, 2005).

Negative age stereotypes may adversely affect the psychological well-being of children by: increasing their anxiety about the aging of their loved ones and their own eventual aging; impeding social relationships with older individuals; and reducing the likelihood of learning from the experiences of older individuals and having them as role models. Conversely, when children and younger adults hold more positive age stereotypes, it may promote mutually beneficial intergenerational interactions and provide a positive image of future selves to which they might aspire. These effects of positive age stereotypes have been observed in the Deaf American culture (Becker, 1983; Levy & Langer, 1994).

Age Stereotypes and Health in Young Adulthood and Midlife

Compared to children and older adults, those of an age that falls in between gain the most from negative age stereotypes. Younger adults draw on these stereotypes when giving preference to their age group over older adults. The discrimination arising from these negative age stereotypes make younger adults the beneficiaries of limited resources, such as employment and health care (e.g., Butler, 2006). For those given advantages in a social system, there is a tendency to see the advantages as natural and beyond dispute (Jost & Banaji, 1994).

The gain for younger adults derived from negative age stereotyping is also found on a cognitive level. Targeting the old with these stereotypes can lead to enhanced performance in younger adults who benefit from the invidious comparison; the process has been referred to as "stereotype lift" (Walton & Cohen, 2003).

These benefits of negative age stereotypes do not mean they are consciously held. Research conducted with younger adults supports the premise of stereotype embodiment theory that age stereotypes can operate unconsciously. In the first study to document the unconscious operation of age stereotypes in younger adults, it was found that flashing *old* on a computer screen, at a speed that was selected to avoid conscious recognition, resulted in negative traits being judged more quickly than positive traits; the reverse occurred after *young* was flashed on the screen (Perdue & Gurtman, 1990). From these results, the authors concluded that "cognitively categorizing a person as 'old' may create a subset of predominantly negative constructs which are more accessible and more likely to be employed in evaluating that person— and this will tend to perpetuate ageism from the beginning of the social perception process" (Perdue & Gurtman, 1990, p. 213).

Another tool that has been used to assess the way age stereotypes operate unconsciously is the Implicit Association Test (IAT; Greenwald, McGhee, & Schwartz, 1988; Nosek, Greenwald, & Banaji, 2005). The IAT is a reaction-time measure that matches an attitude object (e.g., *young* or *old*) with an evaluative dimension (e.g., *good* or *bad*); the strength of the evaluation is measured by the greater speed at which the pairing occurs. In an analysis based on more than 2.5 million IATs, conducted on the internet, the authors found that implicit views toward the old were more negative than those toward other stigmatized groups, including African Americans and homosexuals. Further, 80% of the participants showed an implicit bias against the old, and only 6% showed an implicit bias in favor of the old (Nosek et al., 2007).

The outward expression of age stereotypes may take the form of a feedback-loop mechanism that reinforces these stereotypes. This occurs when younger adults act toward older adults in ways that are consistent with negative age stereotypes. As a case in point, an assumption about the limited cognitive ability of elders might cause younger adults to speak in an oversimplified manner which, in turn, causes the older adults to act as though they are incompetent, thereby confirming the stereotype (e.g., Giles & Gasiorek, 2010; Ryan, Giles, Bartolucci, & Henwood, 1986).

It is not only other older individuals who are harmed by the negative age stereotypes of younger individuals, for it has been shown that the latter's stereotypes can affect their own health and functioning in later life. Participants, aged 18–39 years, in the Baltimore Longitudinal Study of Aging who expressed more negative age stereotypes at baseline were more than twice as likely to experience a cardiovascular event (e.g., congestive heart failure, heart attacks, and strokes) over the next 38 years, compared to those in the same age group with more positive age stereotypes (Levy, Zonderman, Slade, & Ferrucci, 2009). This effect remained after adjusting for relevant variables, including age and family history of cardiovascular disease.

The detrimental effect of negative age stereotypes can occur even before old age is reached. This was demonstrated by a word-recall experiment, with middle-aged participants (48–62 years), that was designed to compare two ways negative age stereotypes might exert their effect on memory performance (O'Brien & Hummert, 2006). In one condition, the experimenter told the participants that their memory would be compared to individuals under the age of 25, who are stereotypically perceived to have superior memory; therefore, if stereotype threat (Steele & Aronson, 1995) was applicable, memory performance would be adversely affected by the anxiety resulting from the comparison. In the other condition, the experimenter told the participants that their performance would be compared to individuals over the age of 70, who are stereotypically perceived to have inferior memory; therefore, if negative age stereotypes had been internalized, and the participants identified with older individuals, their memory performance would be adversely affected, based on the prediction of previous research (Levy, 1996). The participants who were compared to the older age group had significantly worse word recall than those who were compared to the younger age group. The authors, therefore, concluded, "The results suggest that self-stereotyping, but not stereotype threat, processes were operating in the present investigation" (O'Brien & Hummert, 2006, p. 351).

Age Stereotypes and Health in Older Adulthood

A premise of age stereotype embodiment theory is that as the stereotypes become self-relevant, they will have a greater impact on health and functioning. The self-relevance of old age is generated by the increasing number of reminders from others that the individual is getting old (Levy, 2003). These reminders may be benevolent, such as receiving a social security check, or malevolent, such as loss of job because of age discrimination.

On an interpersonal level, older individuals may be treated with less compassion (Zanardo, De Beni, & Moè, 2006) or more compassion (Fingerman, Miller, & Charles, 2008) compared to younger individuals. For example, younger participants reported that they engaged in less confrontational behavior with older social partners than with younger social partners (Fingerman et al., 2008). To the extent differential treatment is sensed by the older recipient, it is likely to serve as another reminder that old age has been achieved.

The importance of self-relevance to the influence of age stereotypes in later life is suggested by several research findings. First, a number of experimental age-stereotype studies have found an age difference in the stereotypes' impact on outcomes, such that older individuals tend to show effects that are consistent with the stereotypes, whereas younger individuals tend to show either no effects or much weaker effects (e.g., Hess, Auman, Colcombe, & Rahhal, 2003; Levy, 1996; Levy, Ashman, & Dror, 1999–2000). The age-stereotype priming used in the laboratory experiments is thought to be more effective with older participants because it activates their old-age identities, whereas the age-stereotype primes lack self-relevance for the younger participants (Levy, 1996; Levy, 2009). Also, longitudinal studies have found that older individuals' views of old people in general, their age stereotypes, tend to affect the development of how they view their own aging, referred to as "self-perceptions of aging," in later life (Levy, 2008; Levy, Slade, & Kasl, 2002; Rothermund, 2005). For example, in a study of older individuals, it was found that negative age stereotypes at baseline predicted negative self-perceptions of aging expressed in five waves over 18 years (Levy, 2008).

Experiments with age stereotypes show that they are able to induce effects in older individuals that are associated with the aging process. Negative age stereotypes tended to have a detrimental effect, and positive age stereotypes tended to have a beneficial effect, on a wide array of cognitive and physical activities, such as memory performance, will to live, gait, balance, and cardiovascular response to stress (Hausdorff, Levy, & Wei, 1999; Levy, 1996; Levy, Hausdorff, Hencke, & Wei, 2000; Levy & Leifheit-Limson, 2009).

Several experimental studies conducted by other laboratories have replicated and extended Levy's (1996) age-stereotype findings with older individuals (e.g., Hess et al., 2003; Horton, Baker, Pearce, & Deakin, 2008). The authors of a review covering 17 stereotype experiments conducted with older individuals concluded that "stereotypes, whether they are primed implicitly or explicitly, appear to influence older adults' performance on cognitive, physical, physiological, and psychological variables" (Horton et al., 2008, p. 459).

Longitudinal studies conducted with older individuals living in the community have demonstrated that negative age stereotypes predict worse outcomes as diverse as hearing performance and recovery from heart attacks (Levy, Slade, May, & Caracciolo, 2006; Levy, Slade, & Gill, 2006). In addition, a pair of studies that analyzed data from the Ohio Longitudinal Study of Aging and Retirement traced the effect of self-perceptions of aging on older individuals' health over time (Levy, Slade, Kunkel, et al., 2002; Levy et al., 2002b). In one study, participants with more negative self-perceptions of aging at baseline had worse functional health over an 18-year follow-up period than those with more positive self-perceptions of aging (Levy et al., 2002b). In the other study, participants with more negative self-perceptions of aging at baseline lived an average of 7½ years less than those with more positive self-perceptions of aging (Levy, Slade, Kunkel, et al., 2002). The associations in both of these studies remained after controlling for baseline measures of functional health, self-rated health, age, gender, race, and socioeconomic status.

Similar longitudinal results have been found in both Europe and Asia (Kim, 2008; Kotter-Grühn, Kleinspehn-Ammerlahn, Gerstorf, & Smith, 2009; Maier & Smith, 1999). To illustrate, more than 1000 participants in the German Aging Survey, between 40 and 85 years of age, were studied in 1996, and followed up in 2002 (Wurm, Tesch-Römer, & Tomasik, 2007). The investigators found that participants with more negative age stereotypes at baseline tended to report a greater number of physical illnesses at follow-up, compared to those with more positive age stereotypes at baseline. In addition, they found that age stereotypes are a stronger predictor of health than physical illness is of age stereotypes (Wurm et al., 2007).

The self-perception-of-aging measure that was found to predict functional health and survival in the Ohio Longitudinal Study of Aging and Retirement includes the item, "As you get older, you are less useful" (Levy, Slade, Kunkel, et al., 2002; Levy et al., 2002b). The universality of this stereotypical concept was suggested by a Japanese study that showed older individuals who felt less useful had significantly worse self-rated health and mortality over a 6-year period (Okamoto & Tanaka, 2004).

Participants in these longitudinal studies were fully aware of the stereotype measures to which they were responding. However, the laboratory experiments described in the first part of this section were conducted on an unconscious level. Specifically, age-stereotype words were flashed on a computer screen at speeds that were below awareness, followed by participants undertaking a cognitive or physical task (see Levy, 1996, for a full description of the procedure). Moreover, among the outcomes of the laboratory experiments were ones that are not ordinarily under conscious control—such as handwriting (Levy, 2000). Participants who were exposed to the subliminal negative-age-stereotype primes produced handwriting that was rated, compared to the sample produced before exposure, as older and were evaluated as showing a significant increase in *deteriorating, senile,* and *shaky.* In contrast, those exposed to the positive-age-stereotype primes had handwriting that was rated as younger and showing a significant increase in *accomplished, confident,* and *wise* (Levy, 2000).

It is perhaps because unconscious age stereotypes are carried over from earlier in life (Levy, 2009) that individuals aged 60 and above were found to prefer the young rather than the old, at a level below awareness (Nosek et al., 2007). Indeed, the preference was to the same extent as participants in their 20s showed for their own age group (Nosek et al., 2007). This finding, and earlier research relating to the old, suggest that in-group preference, a traditional premise of social cognition (Tajfel, 1978), does not apply to that age group (Levy & Banaji, 2002; Nosek et al., 2007).

The unconscious operation of age stereotypes may have a benefit insofar as they facilitate the activation of positive age stereotypes. It is in their subliminal mode that these stereotypes are most likely to bypass the predominantly held negative age stereotypes (Levy, 1996).

The pathways by which age stereotypes affect older individuals' health and functioning appear to operate along three tracks: psychological, behavioral, and physiological. The psychological pathway includes expectations. This was seen in a study that showed that when the content of older individuals' subliminally primed age stereotypes matched the cognitive or physical outcomes (memory or balance), there was a greater effect than when there was not a match (Levy & Leifheit-Limson, 2009). It seems that his matching effect enabled the age stereotypes to act as more applicable guidelines for reaching the outcomes.

The behavioral pathway includes health practices which tend to suffer from negative age stereotypes that are often based on the assumption that health problems are an inevitable consequence of growing old. As a result of this perceived inevitability, efficacious health practices, such as taking prescribed medications, may be considered futile (Levy & Myers, 2004).

The physiological pathway includes the autonomic nervous system that responds to stress. Subliminal exposure to negative age stereotypes resulted in a heightened cardiovascular stress response, in contrast to the subliminal exposure to positive age stereotypes that resulted in a reduced cardiovascular stress response (Levy et al., 2000). Susceptibility to heart problems can result from repeated elevations of cardiovascular response to stress (Jiang et al., 1996).

An assumption underlying these pathways and age stereotype embodiment theory is that the stereotypes have been internalized and develop into older individuals' self-views (Levy, 2009; Levy, Slade, Kunkel, et al., 2002; Rothermund, 2005). Two alternative explanations for the relationship between age stereotypes and self-views have been considered. One alternative, based on social comparison theory, predicts that negative age stereotypes should lead to more positive self-appraisals. Another alternative is that age stereotypes are a projection of older individuals' self-views. Both of these potential alternative explanations were rejected by an 8-year study (Rothermund, 2005). As summarized, its findings "strongly support the assumption that in the long run, negative age stereotypes have a detrimental effect on the self-views and well-being of elderly people" (Rothermund, 2005, p. 238).

Stability and Malleability of Age Self-Stereotypes

Age stereotypes tend to remain stable over the life span. This stability results, in large part, from their internalization at childhood and reinforcement through-out adulthood. It also follows from stereotype-justification techniques found in all age groups. For instance, those holding negative age stereotypes tend to selectively recall information about elders in order to make it consistent with their stereotypes (Levy, 1996). In this way, age stereotypes can take precedence over actual experience. Hence, if elders who contradict the negative age stereotypes are encountered, they tend to be dismissed as exceptions (Levy & Banaji, 2002).

One way of examining the stability of age stereotypes is to look at them across generations. Whereas countries may differ from each other in the specifics of age stereotypes, younger and older individuals within these cultures report similar age stereotypes. To take an example, the Chinese young and old tend to hold more positive views toward aging than young and old Deaf Americans, who tend to hold more positive views toward aging than young and old hearing Americans (Levy & Langer, 1994). Consistent with this pattern, researchers found a high level of agreement in participants, ranging in age from 20 to 85 years, about positive- and negative-age-stereotype-like characteristics that typify age groups across adulthood; the rankings remained stable at an assessment made 6 months after baseline (Heckhausen, Dixon, & Baltes, 1989).

The stability of age stereotypes has also been found in teenagers. An effort to diminish the negative age stereotypes of high school students did not succeed, even though they were exposed to positive aspects of aging by meeting active community-dwelling "elder heroes" who shared stories about "growing up and growing older" (Klein, Council, & McGuire, 2005, p. 595). The researchers stated that "Ageist attitudes formed in early childhood become difficult to change as children reach adolescence" (Klein et al., 2005, p. 591).

A further demonstration of age-stereotype stability was provided by a study of older individuals recovering from a heart attack over the 7 months following the event (Levy, Slade, May, & Caracciolo, 2006). The recovery process did not appear to affect the positivity of the age stereotypes. The average scores for the age-stereotypes assessments at baseline, 1 month, and 7 months stayed within one point of each other, with a range between 36.1 and 36.9, out of a potential 54 points (Levy et al., 2006). This finding is consistent with a study of German elders that showed positive age stereotypes predicted better subjective health, even after adjusting for serious health events (Wurm, Tomasik, & Tesch-Römer, 2008).

However, the *manifestations* of younger adults' negative age stereotypes, rather than the age stereotypes themselves, have proved to be malleable, at least on a short-term basis. Certified nursing assistants (CNAs) underwent training designed to reduce ageist speech directed at older residents of nursing homes (Williams, Kemper, & Hummert, 2003). Techniques included role playing and listening to recordings of the CNAs' interactions with patients. The training reduced the use of diminutives (e.g., "Honey") and inappropriate collective pronouns (e.g., "Are we ready for our bath?"), and increased the length of utterances and rate of speech. On the emotional tone, the caring dimension remained low, whereas the respect and control dimensions improved, when measured 1 week after the intervention began.

In addition, the laboratory-based, subliminally primed age-stereotype experiments showed that both positive and negative age stereotypes can be activated (for review, see Levy, 2009). This suggests that although the actual age stereotypes held by the participants did not change, the priming caused a change in the dominance of one type of stereotype over the other.

FUTURE ISSUES IN THE STUDY OF AGE STEREOTYPES AND EXPLANATORY STYLE ACROSS THE LIFE SPAN

By examining existing research at the intersection of social cognition, life-span development, and health as it applies to age stereotypes and explanatory style, we can identify issues that would benefit from research in the future.

As a starting point, this research could be directed toward a fuller understanding of how innate and social processes influence age stereotypes and explanatory style. On the one hand, supporting the existence of innate processes, research has found that infants engage in categorization—the precursor to age stereotypes, and causal reasoning—the precursor to explanatory style (Newman et al., 2008; Quinn et al., 1993). On the other hand, studies have shown that the social setting can influence both the operation of age stereotypes and explanatory style from childhood to old age (Levy, 2009; Oettingen, 1995; Seligman et al., 1984). It remains for future research to locate the boundaries of innateness, as well as social setting, and to identify how they work together to shape age stereotypes and explanatory style across the life span.

It would also be helpful for future research to establish the extent to which age stereotypes and explanatory style operate in a consistent way across domains (e.g., cognitive or physical), as opposed to operating differently for specific domains. Much of the research on age stereotypes has measured them as though they operate consistently, but a recent study found the impact of age stereotypes differs by domain (Levy & Leifheit-Limson, 2009). For its part, explanatory style is often measured by combining responses to events occurring in a variety of domains. Yet, research has found that explanatory style may differ across domains (Anderson, Jennings, & Arnoult, 1988; Martin-Krumm, Sarrazin, Peterson, & Famose, 2003). Future studies should address the full range of conditions under which age stereotypes and explanatory style operate in either a universal or domain-specific way, and determine whether these conditions differ across the life span.

Future research is needed to address an inadequately understood area—the pathways that connect the negative age stereotypes and pessimistic explanatory style to functioning and health. There is preliminary evidence that these stereotypes and this explanatory style use psychological, behavioral, and physiological pathways (Ciarrochi & Heaven, 2008; Kamen-Siegel et al., 1991; Levy, 2009; Levy et al., 2000), and that, at least in some cases, they may use the same pathways with the same content. Along the physiological pathway, for instance, a limited ability to cope with stress has been found to follow from both negative age stereotypes and pessimistic explanatory style (Kubzansky et al., 2001; Levy et al., 2000). Future research should aim at identifying the full array of pathways. In addition, it should determine the ways in which these pathways operate—including, whether they act individually or in concert, whether there is an interrelationship between the pathways of age stereotypes and explanatory style, and whether the pathways change over the life span.

Although research has established the importance of unconscious processes in the operation of age stereotype in laboratory experiments involving younger and older adults (e.g., Levy, 1996; Perdue & Gurtman, 1990), children have not been considered. And unconscious processes among all ages for explanatory style have been relatively ignored. It would be highly useful if researchers closed these gaps in explaining the processes by which age stereotypes and explanatory style operate at an unconscious level with respect to different age groups.

The issues presented here for future research have a potential value that extends beyond enhancing our understanding of explanatory style and age stereotypes. They could contribute to interventions across the life span that maximize optimistic explanatory style and positive age stereotypes, and/or minimize pessimistic explanatory style and negative age stereotypes, in order to improve health and well-being. Also, this future research could provide data about the commonality of explanatory style and age stereotypes. Insofar as this relatedness is established, it would point toward a single intervention that applies to both constructs. Perhaps, once we have identified the mutual patterns of explanatory style and age stereotyping, and learned how to modify them to enhance vitality throughout the life span, we can truly provide a comprehensive social-cognitive check-up.

REFERENCES

Allport, G. (1954). *The nature of prejudice*. Cambridge, MA: Addison-Wesley.

Ambady, N., Shih, M., Kim, A., & Pittinsky, T. L. (2001). Stereotype susceptibility in children: Effects of identity activation on quantitative performance. *Psychological Science, 12*, 385–390.

Anderson, C. A., Jennings, D. L., & Arnoult, L. H. (1988). Validity and utility of the attributional style construct at a moderate level of specificity. *Journal of Personality and Social Psychology, 55*, 679–990.

Banziger, G., & Derevenstedt, J. (1982). Achievement attributions by young and old judges as a function of perceived age of stimulus person. *Journal of Gerontology, 37*, 468–474.

Becker, G. (1983). *Growing old in silence*. Berkeley, CA: University of California Press.

Behl-Chadha, G. (1996). Basic-level and superordinate-like categorical representations in infancy. *Cognition, 60*, 343–364.

Bieman-Copland, S., & Ryan, E. (1998). Age-biased interpretation of memory successes and failures in adulthood. *Journal of Gerontology: Psychological Sciences, 53B*, P105–P111.

Bigler, R. S., & Liben, L. S. (2007). Developmental intergroup theory: Explaining and reducing children's social stereotyping and prejudice. *Current Directions in Psychological Science, 16*, 162–166.

Brennan, F. X., & Charnetski, C. J. (2000). Explanatory style and immunoglobulin A (IgA). *Integrative Physiological and Behavioral Science, 35*, 251–255.

Burhans, K. K., & Dweck, C. S. (1995). Helpless in early childhood: The role of contingent worth. *Child Development, 66*, 1719–1738.

Burke, J. L. (1981–1982). Young children's attitudes and perceptions of older adults. *International Journal of Aging and Human Development, 14*, 205–222.

Burns, M. O., & Seligman, M. (1989). Explanatory style across the life span: Evidence for stability over 52 years. *Journal of Personality and Social Psychology, 56,* 471–477.

Butler, R. (2006). *Ageism in America.* New York: International Longevity Center-USA.

Calasanti, T. (2007). Bodacious berry, potency wood and the aging monster: Gender and age relations in anti-aging ads. *Social Forces, 86,* 335–355.

Chaplin, T. M., Gillham, J. E., Reivich, K., Elkon, A. G. L., Samuels, B., Freres, D. R., et al. (2006). Depression prevention for early adolescent girls: A pilot study of all girls versus co-ed groups. *The Journal of Early Adolescence, 26,* 110–126.

Ciarrochi, J., & Heaven, P. C. L. (2008). Learned social hopelessness: The role of explanatory style in predicting social support during adolescence. *Journal of Child Psychology and Psychiatry, 49,* 1279–1286.

Cohen, L. B., Amsel, G., Redford, M. A., & Casasola, M. (Eds.). (1998). *The development of infant causal perception.* East Sussex, UK: Psychology Press.

Cosmetic Surgery National Data Bank Statistics. (2009). American Society for Aesthetic Plastic Surgery.

Davison, K. K., Schmalz, D. L., Young, L. M., & Birch, L. L. (2008). Overweight girls who internalize fat stereotypes report low psychosocial well-being. *Obesity, 16,* S30–S38.

Donlon, M., Ashman, O., & Levy, B. R. (2005). Creating a defense against television's ageism. *Journal of Social Issues, 61,* 307–319.

Erber, J., & Long, B. (2006). Perceptions of forgetful and slow employees: Does age matter? *Journal of Gerontology: Psychological Sciences, 61,* P333–P339.

Falchikov, N. (1990). Youthful ideas about old age: An analysis of children's drawings. *The International Journal of Aging and Human Development, 31,* 79–99.

Fingerman, K. L., Miller, L., & Charles, S. T. (2008). Saving the best for last: How adults treat social partners of different ages. *Psychology and Aging, 23,* 399–409.

Finkelstein, L. E., & Levy, B. R. (2006). Disclosure of holocaust experiences: Reasons, attributions, and health implications. *Journal of Social and Clinical Psychology, 25,* 117–140.

Fiske, S. T. (2005). Social cognition and the normality of prejudgment. In J. Dovidio, P. Glick, & L. Rudman (Eds.), *On the nature of prejudice: Fifty years after Allport* (pp. 36–53). Malden, MA: Backwell.

Giles, H., & Gasiorek, J. (2010). Communication, elderspeak and aging. In K. W. Schaie, S. Willis, R. Knight, B. R. Levy, & B. Park (Eds.), *Handbook of the psychology of aging.* New York: Academic Press.

Gray, M. J., Pumphrey, J. E., & Lombardo, T. W. (2003). The relationship between dispositional pessimistic attributional style versus trauma-specific attributions and PTSD symptoms. *Anxiety Disorders, 17,* 289–303.

Greenwald, A. G., McGhee, D. E., & Schwartz, J. L. K. (1988). Measuring individual differences in implicit cognition: The implicit association test. *Journal of Personality and Social Psychology, 74,* 1464–1480.

Hausdorff, J. M., Levy, B., & Wei, J. Y. (1999). The power of ageism on physical function of older persons: Reversibility of age-related gait changes. *Journal of the American Geriatric Society, 47,* 1346–1349.

Heckhausen, J., Dixon, R. A., & Baltes, P. B. (1989). Gains and losses in development throughout adulthood as perceived by different adult age groups. *Developmental Psychology, 25,* 109–121.

Heider, F. (1958). *The psychology of interpersonal relations.* New York: Wiley.

Hess, T. M., Auman, C., Colcombe, S. J., & Rahhal, T. A. (2003). The impact of stereotype threat on age differences in memory performance. *Journal of Gerontology: Psychological Sciences, 58B,* 3–11.

Horton, S., Baker, J., Pearce, G. W., & Deakin, J. M. (2008). On the malleability of performance: Implications for seniors. *Journal of Applied Gerontology, 27,* 446–465.

Jiang, W., Babyak, M., Krantz, D. S., Waugh, R. A., Coleman, R. E., Hanson, M. M., et al. (1996). Mental stress–induced myocardial ischemia and cardiac events. *Journal of the American Medical Association, 275,* 1651–1656.

Jost, J. T., & Banaji, M. R. (1994). The role of stereotyping in system-justification and the production of false consciousness. *British Journal of Social Psychology, 33,* 1–27.

Kamen-Siegel, L., Rodin, J., Seligman, M. E. P., & Dwyer, J. (1991). Explanatory style and cell-mediated immunity in elderly men and women. *Health Psychology, 10,* 229–235.

Kim, S. H. (2008). Older people's expectations regarding ageing, health-promoting behavior and health status. *Journal of Advanced Nursing, 65,* 84–91.

Kistner, J. A., Ziegert, D. I., Castro, R., & Robertson, B. (2001). Helplessness in early childhood: Prediction of symptoms associated with depression and negative self-worth. *Merrill-Palmer Quarterly, 47,* 336–354.

Klein, D. A., Council, K. J., & McGuire, S. L. (2005). Education to promote positive attitudes about aging. *Educational Gerontology, 31*, 591–601.

Kotter-Grühn, D., Kleinspehn-Ammerlahn, A., Gerstorf, D., & Smith, J. (2009). Self-perceptions of aging predict mortality and change with approaching death: 16-year longitudinal results from the Berlin Aging Study. *Psychology and Aging, 24*, 654–667.

Kubzansky, L., Sparrow, D., Vokonas, P., & Kawachi, I. (2001). Is the glass half empty or half full? A prospective study of optimism and coronary heart disease in the Normative Aging Study. *Psychosomatic Medicine, 63*, 910–916.

Kwong See, S. T., & Heller, R. (Eds.). (2005). *Measuring ageism in children.* Binghamton, NY: Haworth Press.

Leslie, A. M. (Ed.). (1988). *The necessity of illusion: Perception and thought in infancy.* Oxford, UK: Oxford University Press.

Levy, B. (1996). Improving memory in old age by implicit self stereotyping. *Journal of Personality and Social Psychology, 71*, 1092–1107.

Levy, B., Ashman, O., & Dror, I. (1999–2000). To be or not to be: The effects of aging stereotypes on the will to live. *Omega, 40*, 409–420.

Levy, B., & Langer, E. (1994). Aging free from negative stereotypes: Successful memory in China among the American deaf. *Journal of Personality and Social Psychology, 66*, 989–997.

Levy, B. R. (2000). Handwriting as a reflection of aging self-stereotypes. *Journal of Geriatric Psychiatry, 33*, 81–94.

Levy, B. R. (2003). Conscious vs. Unconscious levels of aging self-stereotyping. *Journal of Gerontology: Psychological sciences, 58*, 215–216.

Levy, B. R. (2008). Rigidity as a predictor of older persons' aging stereotypes and aging self-perceptions. *Social Behavior and Personality, 36*, 559–570.

Levy, B. R. (2009). Age-stereotype embodiment: A psychological approach to aging. *Current Directions in Psychological Science, 18*, 332–336.

Levy, B. R., Ashman, O., & Slade, M. D. (2009b). Age attributions and aging health: Contrast between the United States and Japan. *Psychology and Aging, 64*, 335–338.

Levy, B. R., & Banaji, M. (2002). Implicit ageism. In T. Nelson (Ed.), *Ageism: Stereotypes and prejudice against older persons* (pp. 49–75). Cambridge, MA: MIT Press.

Levy, B. R., Hausdorff, J., Hencke, R., & Wei, J. (2000). Reducing cardiovascular stress with positive self-stereotypes of aging. *Journal of Gerontology: Psychological Sciences, 55*, 205–213.

Levy, B. R., Kasl, S., & Gill, T. (2004). Image of aging scale. *Journal of Perceptual and Motor Skills, 99*, 208–210.

Levy, B. R., & Leifheit-Limson, E. (2009). The stereotype-matching effect: Greater influence on functioning when age stereotypes correspond to outcomes. *Psychology and Aging, 24*, 230–233.

Levy, B. R., & Myers, L. M. (2004). Preventive health behaviors influenced by self-perception of aging. *Preventive Medicine, 39*, 625–629.

Levy, B. R., Slade, M., May, J., & Caracciolo, E. (2006). Physical recovery after acute myocardial infarction: Positive age self-stereotypes as a resource. *International Journal of Aging and Human Development, 62*, 285–301.

Levy, B. R., Slade, M. D., & Gill, T. (2006). Hearing decline predicted elders' stereotypes. *Journal of Gerontology: Psychological Sciences, 61*, 82–87.

Levy, B. R., Slade, M. D., & Kasl, S. V. (2002b). Longitudinal benefit of positive self-perceptions of aging on functional health. *Journal of Gerontology: Psychological Sciences, 57*, 409–417.

Levy, B. R., Slade, M. D., Kunkel, S. R., & Kasl, S. V. (2002a). Longevity increased by positive self-perceptions of aging. *Journal of Personality and Social Psychology, 83*, 261–270.

Levy, B. R., Slade, M. D., & Ranasinghe, P. (2009a). Causal thinking after a tsunami save: Karma beliefs, pessimistic explanatory style and health among Sri Lankan survivors. *Journal of Religion and Health, 48*, 38–45.

Levy, B. R., Zonderman, A. B., Slade, M. D., & Ferrucci, L. (2009). Age stereotypes held earlier in life predict cardiovascular events in later life. *Psychological Science, 20*, 296–298.

Licht, B., & Dweck, C. (1984). Determinants of academic achievement: The interaction of children's achievement orientations with skill area. *Developmental Psychology, 20*, 628–636.

Löckenhoff, C. E., De Fruyt, F., Terracciano, A., McCrae, R. R., De Bolle, M., Costa, P. T. J., et al. (2009). Perceptions of aging across 26 cultures and their culture-level associates. *Psychology and Aging, 24*, 941–954.

Macrae, C. N., Milne, A. B., & Bodenhausen, G. V. (1994). Stereotypes as energy-saving devices: A peek inside the cognitive toolbox. *Journal of Personality and Social Psychology, 66*, 37–47.

Maier, H., & Smith, J. (1999). Psychological predictors of mortality in old age. *Journal of Gerontology: Psychological Sciences, 54*, P44–P54.

Martin-Krumm, C. P., Sarrazin, P. G., Peterson, C., & Famose, J. (2003). Explanatory style and resilience after sports failure. *Personality and Individual Differences, 35*, 1685–1695.

Maruta, T., Robert, C. C., Malinchoc, M., & Offord, K. P. (2000). Optimists vs. pessimists: Survival rate among medical patients over a 30-year period. *Mayo Clinic Proceedings, 75*, 140–143.

Mezulis, A. H., Abramson, L. Y., Hyde, J. S., & Hankin, B. L. (2004). Is there a universal positivity bias in attributions? A meta-analytic review of individual, developmental, and cultural differences in the self-serving attributional bias. *Psychological Bulletin, 130*, 711–747.

Mikulincer, M. (1988). Reactance and helplessness following exposure to unsolvable problems: The effects of attributional style. *Journal of Personality and Social Psychology, 54*, 679–686.

Newman, G. E., Choi, H., Wynn, K., & Scholl, B. J. (2008). The origins of causal perception: Evidence from postdictive processing in infancy. *Cognitive Psychology, 57*, 262–291.

Nolen-Hoeksema, S., Girgus, J. S., & Seligman, M. E. (1986). Learned helplessness in children: A longitudinal study of depression, achievement, and explanatory style. *Journal of Personality and Social Psychology, 51*, 435–442.

Nolen-Hoeksema, S., Girgus, J. S., & Seligman, M. E. P. (1991). Sex differences in depression and explanatory style in children. *Journal of Youth and Adolescence, 20*, 233–245.

Nosek, B. A., Greenwald, A. G., & Banaji, M. R. (2005). Understanding and using the implicit association test: II. Methods variables and construct validity. *Personality and Social Psychology Bulletin, 31*, 166–180.

Nosek, B. A., Smyth, F. L., Hansen, J. J., Devos, T., Lindner, N. M., Ranganath, K. A., et al. (2007). Pervasiveness and correlates of implicit attitudes and stereotypes. *European Review of Social Psychology, 18*, 36–88.

O'Brien, L. T., & Hummert, M. L. (2006). Memory performance of late middle-aged adults: Contrasting self-stereotyping and stereotype threat accounts of assimilation to age stereotypes. *Social Cognition, 24*, 338–358.

Oettingen, G. (1995). Explanatory style in the context of culture. In G. M. Buchanan & M. E. P. Seligman (Eds.), *Explanatory style* (pp. 209–224). Hillsdale, NJ: Erlbaum.

Okamoto, K., & Tanaka, Y. (2004). Subjective usefulness and 6-year mortality risks among elderly persons in Japan. *Journal of Gerontology: Psychological Sciences, 59*, 246–249.

Panak, W. F., & Garber, J. (1992). Aggression, rejection, and attributions in the prediction of depression in children. *Development and Psychopathology, 4*, 145–165.

Perdue, C. W., & Gurtman, M. B. (1990). Evidence for the automaticity of ageism. *Journal of Experimental Social Psychology, 26*, 199–216.

Peterson, C., & Seligman, M. E. P. (1984). Causal explanations as a risk factor for depression: Theory and evidence. *Psychological Review, 91*, 347–374.

Peterson, C., Seligman, M. E. P., & Vaillant, G. E. (1988). Pessimistic explanatory style is a risk factor for physical illness: A thirty-five year longitudinal study. *Journal of Personality and Social Psychology, 55*, 23–27.

Peterson, C., Seligman, M. E. P., Yurko, K. H., Martin, L. R., & Friedman, H. S. (1998). Catastrophizing and untimely death. *Psychological Science, 9*, 127–130.

Proudfoot, J. G., Corr, P. J., Guest, D. E., & Dunn, G. (2009). Cognitive-behavioral training to change attributional style improves employee well-being, job satisfaction, productivity and turnover. *Personality and Individual Differences, 46*, 147–153.

Quinn, P. C., Eimas, P. D., & Rosenkrantz, S. L. (1993). Evidence for representations of perceptually similar natural categories by 3-month-old and 4-month-old infants. *Perception, 22*, 463–475.

Rothermund, K. (Ed.). (2005). *Effects of age stereotypes on self-views and adaptation*. Cambridge, MA: Hogrefe & Huber.

Ryan, E. B., Giles, H., Bartolucci, R. Y., & Henwood, K. (1986). Psycholinguistic and social psychological components of communication by and with the elderly. *Language and Communication, 6*, 1–24.

Sarkisian, C. A., Lee-Henderson, M. H., & Mangione, C. M. (2003). Do depressed older adults who attribute depression to "old age" believe it is important to seek care? *Journal of Geriatrics and Internal Medicine, 18*, 1001–1005.

Schulman, P. (1999). Explanatory style and achievement in school and work. In G. M. Buchanan & M. E. P. Seligman (Eds.), *Explanatory Style* (pp. 159–171). Hillsdale, NJ: Lawrence Erlbaum Associates.

Seligman, M. E. P., Kaslow, N. J., Alloy, L. B., Peterson, C., Tanenbaum, R. L., & Abramson, L. Y. (1984). Attributional style and depressive symptoms among children. *Journal of Abnormal Psychology, 93*, 235–238.

Steele, C. M., & Aronson, J. (1995). Stereotype threat and the intellectual test performance of African Americans. *Journal of Personality and Social Psychology, 69*, 797–811.

Stevens, E. A., & Prinstein, M. J. (2005). Peer contagion of depressogenic attributional styles among adolescents: A longitudinal study. *Journal of Abnormal Child Psychology, 33*, 25–37.

Tajfel, H. (1978). *Differentiation between social groups: Studies in the social psychology of intergroup relations*. London, UK: Academic Press.

Takagi, E., & Silverstein, M. (2006). Intergenerational co-residence of the Japanese elderly. *Research on Aging, 28*, 473–492.

Toner, M. A., & Heaven, P. C. L. (2005). Peer-social attributional predictors of socio-emotional adjustment in early adolescence: A two-year longitudinal study. *Personality and Individual Differences, 38*, 579–590.

Walton, G. M., & Cohen, G. L. (2003). Stereotype lift. *Journal of Experimental Social Psychology, 39*, 456–467.

Wang, Q., & Pomerantz, E. M. (2009). Motivational landscape of early adolescence in the United States and China: A longitudinal investigation. *Child Development, 80*, 1272–1287.

Weiner, B. (1985). An attributional theory of achievement motivation and emotion. *Psychological Review, 92*, 548–573.

Williams, K., Kemper, S., & Hummert, M. L. (2003). Improving nursing home communication: An intervention to reduce elderspeak. *The Gerontologist, 43*, 242–247.

Williams, T., & Davidson, D. (2009). Interracial and intra-racial stereotypes and constructive memory in 7- and 9-year old African American children. *Journal of Applied Developmental Psychology, 30*, 366–377.

Williamson, J. D., & Fried, L. P. (1996). Characterization of older adults who attribute functional decrements to "old age". *Journal of the American Geriatrics Society, 44*, 1429–1434.

Wurm, S., Tesch-Römer, C., & Tomasik, M. J. (2007). Longitudinal findings on aging-related cognitions, control beliefs and health in later life. *Journal of Gerontology: Psychological Sciences, 62*, 156–164.

Wurm, S., Tomasik, M., & Tesch-Römer, C. (2008). Serious health events and their impact on changes in subjective health and life satisfaction. *European Journal of Ageing, 5*, 117–127.

Zanardo, F., De Beni, R., & Moè, A. (2006). Influence of other-beliefs on self-beliefs and on everyday memory self-report in the elderly. *Aging Clinical and Experimental Research, 18*, 425–432.

CLOSE RELATIONSHIPS ACROSS THE LIFE SPAN

18

Mary J. Levitt and Ayse Cici-Gokaltun

What are close relationships? How do they develop and change over the life span? How and why do they vary across person, place, and generation? Although the literature on close relationships is voluminous,[1] satisfactory answers to these questions have been elusive, because attempts to address them within a life-span developmental framework have been quite limited. In this chapter, we consider these questions about definition, development, and variation in close relationships, citing relevant literature where possible and indicating gaps to be narrowed through further research. We begin with a consideration of conceptual issues involved in the definition of close relationships. We then review theoretical and empirical work focused specifically on the development of close relationships through the life course, followed by a section addressed to individual, role-based, and cultural variation in this development. Finally, we provide a summary of unresolved issues that afford opportunities for future research.

CONCEPTUAL ISSUES IN THE DEFINITION OF CLOSE RELATIONSHIPS

A scan of the literature on personal relationships suggests that close relationships are typically defined in terms of specific relationship categories linked to social roles, consistent with evolutionary models emphasizing the significance of kinship and mating relationships for survival (Kenrick & Trost, 2004). Empirically, when individuals are asked to nominate persons whom they consider to be close, they typically nominate spouses, romantic partners, children, parents, grandchildren, and/or grandparents (Antonucci, 1986). However, there is wide variation across individuals in the extent to which they consider relationships with specific kin to be close, even though these family members may be closely related to them by role. Thus, researchers generally recognize that close relationships involve dimensions of relatedness in addition to the respective roles that individuals play in each others' lives.

Baumeister and Leary (1995) propose that close relationship formation is motivated by a fundamental "need to belong," whereby humans are innately prepared and universally motivated to seek affectionate, caring relationships as an adaptive means to promote survival. Relations are able to substitute for each other in satisfying this need across role-specific lines and any relationship has the potential to be considered "close." Empirical tests of this proposition are limited, although generally it can

---

[1] It would not be possible to review the exhaustive body of existing work on close relationships within the scope of a single chapter, but a number of comprehensive books on personal relationships have been published in recent years that provide more extensive coverage. These include books authored or edited by Harvey and Weber (2002), Lang and Fingerman (2004), Noller and Feeney (2006), Weiss (2006), and Vangelisti and Perlman (2006).

be said that life-span trends favor this notion. For example, it has been observed that siblings often become closer after the death of a parent or spouse (Gold, 1996) and individuals void of specific relationships (spouse, children, etc.) establish supportive relationships with other relatives or friends (Baumeister & Leary, 1995).

Social exchange theorists focus on the perceived costs and benefits that govern the degree of commitment of individuals within a relationship. Early formulations suggested that equity in the exchange of benefits was important, but such parity is not generally an expectation of close "communal" relationship partners (Clark, 1984). Kelley and his colleagues have elaborated interdependence theory as an extension of social exchange theory, defining relationship closeness in terms of the degree to which the ongoing interactions of individuals are frequent and interdependent (Kelley et al., 1983; Rusbult & Van Lange, 2003). However, relationships perceived as close are sometimes maintained over time and distance, in the absence of frequent interactions.

In the development of attachment theory, Ainsworth initially defined attachment relationships in general terms as enduring affective bonds linking individuals together in space and across time (Ainsworth & Bell, 1970), but attachments have mostly been defined more narrowly as relationships involving the receipt of caregiving (Ainsworth, 1989; Cassidy, 1999). Thus, relationships between adult mates or romantic partners are thought to be attachments only insofar as partners assume the role of nurturing caregiver for each other and relationships of parents to their children may be characterized as attachments only if children assume caregiving roles. However, intergenerational research indicates that care in the form of social support is exchanged normatively from parent to child and child to parent across the life span (Hagestad, 1984) and even infants will engage in nurturing behavior toward their mothers if the mother shows distress (Zahn-Waxler, Radke-Yarrow, Wagner, & Chapman, 1992).

Alternatively, attachment relations have been defined in terms of the likelihood that their loss would result in profound feelings of grief (Antonucci, Akiyama, & Takahashi, 2004; Berman & Sperling, 1994; Levitt, 1991). This definition potentially encompasses a broad range of relationships, including those of parents to children, and seems more suited to extending the attachment concept to a life-span framework. Defining attachments as enduring social bonds that would result in grief if severed is also more consistent with the Baumeister and Leary (1995) formulation of a fundamental need to belong, rather than dependence of the weak on the strong, as the motivational force driving the development of affectively close relationships. Given the significance of social relationships to human survival, the propensity to develop attachments to conspecifics is likely to be an evolutionarily overdetermined phenomenon (Baumeister & Leary, 1995; Levitt, 1991) operative at all phases of the life span.

In the convoy model of life-span social relations (Antonucci, 1986; Antonucci & Birditt, Chapter 7; Kahn & Antonucci, 1980), close attachment relations are viewed as subset of a larger network of relations with whom individuals interact, exchange support, and sometimes engage in conflict throughout their lifetimes. Empirically, the convoy is depicted as a series of three concentric circles, with convoy members arranged hierarchically according to their closeness and importance to the individual, with persons who are "so close and important" that the individual "can't imagine life without them" in the inner circle. Close relationships can then be defined as those in the inner circle of the individual's social convoy.

The location of persons within the convoy is said to be a product of both emotional attachment and social roles, so that inner circle relations are likely to be close to the individual both in the specific role they occupy and in the affective closeness of the relationships (Antonucci, 1986). Empirical data are consistent with this premise. Individuals typically nominate parents, spouses, and children to occupy their inner circles, but these relations are sometimes relegated to outer circles or are not included at all, even though they would be considered close under a definition based entirely on role (Levitt, 2005). Conversely, for some individuals, the inner circle might contain friends or others not typically thought of as closely related by role, but to whom the individual feels a strong emotional tie. Applying the convoy model definition of close relationships as inner circle relations does not settle the issues involved in conceptualizing the meaning of "close relationship," but it provides a means of operationalizing the close relationship construct and tracking changes in relationships over time.

In the next section, we consider the second of our questions, "How do close relations develop and change over the life span?" We focus specifically on life-span developmental theory and research. The reader is referred to Harvey and Wentzel (2006) for an overview of social-psychological theories in this area.

THE DEVELOPMENT OF CLOSE RELATIONSHIPS ACROSS THE LIFE SPAN

In considering theories of close relationship development across the life span, we begin with attachment theory, followed by Takahashi's (1990) affective relationship model, the Kahn and Antonucci (1980) convoy model of social relations, and two related models—Carstensen's (1992, 2006) socioemotional selectivity theory, and Levitt's social expectations model of close relationship development (Levitt, 1991; Levitt, Coffman, Guacci-Franco, & Loveless, 1994). Because both attachment theory and the convoy model are addressed in separate chapters in this volume, our descriptions of these theoretical perspectives are abbreviated.

Attachment Theory

In his seminal formulation of attachment theory, Bowlby (1969/1997) proposed that infants and caregivers are evolutionarily predisposed to engage in interactions promoting infant, and thus, species survival. He viewed the attachment system as regulated by a control parameter functioning analogously to a thermostat, balancing exploratory and attachment behaviors to maintain an appropriate distance between infant and caregiver. Thus, infants explore their surroundings and interact with noncaregivers when secure, but display heightened attachment behavior when their security is threatened. Ainsworth designed the well-known Strange Situation to illustrate this balance of exploratory and attachment behaviors, finding that most infants use their caregivers as a secure base in this situation, exploring freely in the mother's presence and seeking proximity and contact to her following periods of separation and encounters with a stranger (Ainsworth & Bell, 1970).

Bowlby thought of attachment as a life-span phenomenon and Ainsworth wrote an essay on life span attachment in a 1989 issue of *American Psychologist*. Alternative models of life-span attachment were also explored in a special issue of *Human Development* (Antonucci, 1976). For researchers embracing the Bowlby–Ainsworth paradigm, adult orientations toward close relationships are thought to stem from earlier attachment experiences (Crowell, Fraley, & Shaver, 1999). According to Bowlby, these experiences are organized into cognitive–affective "internal working models" that coalesce and guide expectations regarding current and later developing relationships. The relation between infant and primary caregiver is said to be the starting point for the development of attachment representations (Rothbard & Shaver, 1994).

However, this view of the infant–caregiver relationship as a prototype for later relationships poses some problems with respect to conceptualizing the development of close relationships across the life span (Levitt, 2005), because there is little evidence for long-range continuity in attachment orientation and direct links between infant attachment and adult relationships are weak at best. Furthermore, even in infancy, developing individuals interact with multiple figures, other than primary caregivers (Howes, 1999; Lewis, 2005) and infants have been observed to direct attachment behavior toward nonparental adults in their social networks (Levitt, Guacci, & Coffman, 1993). Whether these attachments are formed simultaneously with or secondarily to a primary attachment is an unresolved issue in attachment research and the influence that multiple attachments exert on the development of subsequent relationships remains undefined and largely unexplored (Levitt, 2005; Main, 1999).

Takahashi's Affective Relationship Model

Takahashi (1990, 2004, 2005) has focused on affectively close relationships satisfying the individual's need for emotional interactions with significant others. As in attachment theory, survival needs and security are viewed as important in the development of social bonds. Specific emotion-based needs include the need for proximity, emotional support, reassurance, encouragement and help, sharing information and experience, and giving nurture to another. Specific persons are thought to fulfill specific needs or to provide specific functions, so that individuals draw on divergent sources in seeking to satisfy their emotional needs. Individuals are thought to take an active role in selecting appropriate figures to meet specific needs. The availability and functional appropriateness of figures guides these choices, in the context of cultural expectations related to age and gender.

The individual's affective relationships generally include multiple persons in a hierarchical structure, with focal figures who fill more needs at the top and those who fill fewer needs at the bottom. This affective relationship structure and the relationships comprising it are represented cognitively and, consistent with attachment theory, cognitive representations guide current and future interactions with affective relationship partners.

Takahashi has developed measures assessing figure-function hierarchies from early childhood through old age. These include the Picture Affective Relationships Test (PART) for children and the Affective Relationships Scale (ARS) for adolescents and adults. Based on an extensive body of research employing these measures, she has proposed that affective relationship structures evolve over the life span through several age periods, beginning with the emergence of multiple affective relationships in infancy (with mother, father, grandparents, etc.) that are already differentiated somewhat by the functions they fulfill. The second period involves the rapid expansion of relationships in early childhood. The third, school age, period is characterized by the socialization of affective behaviors in organizational contexts, with age mates becoming increasingly important. In the fourth period, adolescence to young adulthood, an "existential focus" on a primary support figure emerges. Individuals experience subsequent changes in affective relationships in response to major life transitions or age-related changes in emotional needs.

In general, affective relationship structures change throughout the life span as individuals encounter more suitable providers for specific functions, reevaluate their satisfaction with existing figures, or seek to replace figures lost through death, geographic mobility, or other circumstances. However, new experiences are mediated by previous relational experiences, promoting relative stability in the individual's affective structure.

In sum, Takahashi's model shares some aspects of attachment theory, including its ethological grounding and emphasis on emotional security and mental representation. It differs from attachment theory in postulating the presence of multiple close figures, even for infants, who serve a range of functions, and in providing a cohesive account of how affective relationship structures might evolve and change over the life course.

The Convoy Model

The convoy model emerged from and integrated earlier work on social support networks, social roles, and attachment. Kahn and Antonucci (1980) used the term "social convoy" to call attention to the fluid, dynamic nature of personal social networks and the protective function they serve through the life course. The model draws on attachment theory, but broadens its scope to encompass the larger sphere of social relations surrounding the individual from the beginning of life. Convoys are thought to emerge developmentally from a core of attachment relations in infancy, incorporating other significant relationships as the child engages an expanding social environment. In line with attachment theory, supportive interchanges between convoy members are viewed as providing a secure base for efficacious individual functioning (Antonucci et al., 2004; Antonucci & Jackson, 1987).

Although linkages between the substantial literatures on social support and attachment have been addressed infrequently, theoretically there is considerable overlap between the security function of attachment relations and the well-being enhancement function of social support. Asendorpf and Wilpers (2000), for example, reported strong linkages between the perceived supportiveness of mothers, fathers, and peers and the security of college students' attachments to these individuals and, in research based on the convoy model, inner circle relations have been found to provide the highest levels of social support (Levitt, 1991, 2005).

Based on life course theory (Elder, 1998), Kahn and Antonucci framed their developmental analysis in terms of normative and non-normative transitions in personal situations and social roles. Normative role changes, such as school entry, marriage, parenting, and retirement, occur across the life span, confronting the individual with new expectations, demands, and challenges. Non-normative role changes also occur to disrupt the individual's life trajectory. Examples include international migration, sudden disability, or winning the lottery. Normative and non-normative transitions engender the potential for individuals to reconstitute their social convoys as they seek to construct a network adequate to meeting their support needs.

Differences in the structure and function of the social convoy at different life stages and across major life transitions have been found in a number of different cultures (Antonucci et al., 2004; Levitt, 2005). Convoys have been found to increase in size from early childhood to adulthood and, in some cases, to contract in size in old age (Carstensen, 1992; Lang, 2004). Extended family members are more frequently selected as convoy members in middle childhood than before or after, and peer relations become more important in adolescence through early adulthood (Levitt, Guacci-Franco, & Levitt, 1993; Levitt, Weber, & Guacci, 1993).

In general, there appear to be shifts in the proportion of close (inner circle) versus peripheral (outer circle) relations within the convoy across the life span (Levitt, 2005). Drawing on a number of cross-sectional studies employing the concentric circle methodology, Lang (2004) used the pattern of differences observed from age 7 to 103 to develop a hypothetical trajectory in which the number of close inner circle relations remains relatively steady over the life course, declining somewhat from about age 70 through old-old age, whereas peripheral relations show steeper increases until midlife and steeper declines in significance thereafter.

The convoy model is comparable to Takahashi's affective relationship model in emphasizing the developmental significance of multiple relationships, their hierarchical structure, and the functions they serve for the individual. The extent to which specific relations are tied to specific functions is a point of divergence, however, with such specificity being more characteristic of Takahashi's approach.

Socioemotional Selectivity Theory

Carstensen (1992, 2006) has developed a theory of socioemotional selectivity that addresses differences in the extent to which specific relations are viewed as close and important from youth to old age. She proposes that changes in focus from expanded relationship networks in youth to smaller, more intimate networks in later life are related to changes in the balance of motivation to engage in social interaction for purposes of knowledge acquisition about self, others, and the environment versus emotional satisfaction and regulation. Thus, the social worlds of younger individuals tasked with gaining knowledge and achieving independence expand primarily through developing relationships with peers and others outside their close inner circle, whereas an attenuation of knowledge seeking goals and a sense of limited time lead to social contraction and greater investment in emotionally close relationships that provide satisfaction and security in old age (or in other circumstances, such as terminal illness, that shorten one's time perspective).

Lang (2004) has proposed an expanded theory of social motivation as a driving force in shifting patterns of relationships over the life course. Lang endorses the notion advanced by Baumeister and Leary (1995) of an ethologically based need to establish and maintain personal relationships and proposes that motivations to emphasize close emotional relationships shift through the interaction of biologically changing individuals and changing contexts. Following Carstensen, Lang proposes that individuals take an active role in selecting relationships depending on their goals, resources available to pursue them, and the congruence between goals and resources. The two primary types of goals governing relationship selectivity are thought to be goals of belonging (affiliation, intimacy, security, emotion regulation, etc.) and goals of social agency (dominance, achievement, independence, information seeking, etc.).

Reminiscent of the balance between security seeking and exploratory activities discussed by attachment theorists, Lang proposes an inverse relation between belonging and agency motivations, such that the availability of adequate resources and opportunities are associated with enhanced agency goals and a decline in belonging goals, whereas resource limitations (often associated with advanced age) lead to an emphasis on belonging goals and a decline in agency goals. Resources and opportunities change as the individual develops and encounters life transitions and challenges. The ability to shift goal strategies is adaptive, as incongruence between goals and resources leads to personal dissatisfaction and reduced well-being.

Thus, close relationships are considered, in both the convoy model and socioemotional selectivity theory, within the context of the broader network of relations with whom individuals interact over the life course. Levitt's (1991) social expectations model addresses processes through which close relationships develop within the convoy and change over time.

The Social Expectations Model of Close Relationship Development, Continuity, and Change

In general, close inner circle relations are relatively stable within the social convoy across age and time, but changes are known to occur. Relations may become more or less significant through processes that govern relationship continuity or discontinuity, particularly through life transitions that precipitate a realignment of the convoy. In a study of social support following the transition to parenthood, for example, one young mother placed her spouse in the outermost circle of her convoy. Not surprisingly, this couple was subsequently divorced (Levitt, 1991).

Changes in marital relationships after childbirth are probably the best documented of close relationship changes across life transitions (Cowan & Cowan, 2000; Lawrence, Rothman, Cobb, & Bradbury, 2010), but others are known to occur. For example, increased conflict with parents has been reported as children move into adolescence, but emerging adults frequently report feeling closer to their parents following the transition from high school to college or other settings of young adult life (Pipp, Shaver, Jennings, Lamborn, & Fischer, 1985). Very little is known about changes in close relationships across other life transitions. Furthermore, although much has been written about factors that contribute to the stability or fragility of marriage, this issue has rarely been considered within a life-span developmental framework, and even less is known about factors that contribute to change or continuity of other close relationships though the life cycle.

Levitt (1991; Levitt et al., 1994) has proposed a hypothetical model of relationship development, continuity, and change processes applicable across specific relationships and through the life span, as depicted in Figure 18.1. It draws on cognitive expectancy models and incorporates aspects of social exchange and social support conceptualizations. In line with expectancy models in general (e.g. Bowlby, 1969; Lamb & Malkin, 1986; Lewis & Goldberg, 1969), it is proposed that repeated interactions with a relationship partner build expectations about the partner's behavior that have affective consequences, providing a basis for the development of close relationships, beginning in infancy. As social-cognitive abilities expand,

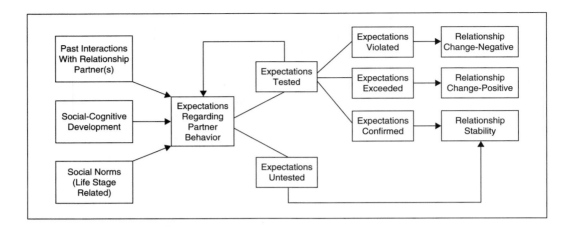

FIGURE 18.1   **Social expectations model of relationship development, continuity, and change.**

interpersonal expectancies are held for extended time periods and are increasingly resistant to change. Social expectations continue to be engendered by direct interactions with relationship partners, but they are also influenced by social norms regarding interpersonal roles. Close relationships are particularly vulnerable during major life transitions, when support needs increase and expectations for support from relationship partners are tested. Relationships may then be enhanced, maintained, or threatened depending on the extent to which the partner exceeds, meets, or violates the individual's expectations. These basic premises are elaborated in the remainder of this section.

Relationship expectations begin as infants develop their first social attachments, displaying preferences for specific persons to whom they seek proximity when stressed. Infants typically direct attachment behaviors preferentially toward their mothers, but this is not always the case, and variations in the selection of attachment figures are yet to be explained (Main, 1999). Bowlby (1969) viewed attachment as an innately driven process, analogous to imprinting in nonhuman species, preparing infants to bond initially to a primary caregiver. Recent work in psychobiology, however, suggests that attachment formation is a more complex process involving "ongoing transactions between the internal features of the developing organism and the specific features of its physical, biological, and social environments" (Lickliter, 2008, p. 400), both prenatally and postnatally. Attachment formation, even in nonhuman species, is thus more experientially influenced than recognized in earlier work. Theoretical and empirical work suggests that contingent or synchronous responding plays a role in attachment formation (Ainsworth, Blehar, Waters, & Wall, 1978; Cairns, 1977; Gewirtz, 1972; Levitt, 1980; Lickliter, 2008). Familiarity is also thought to be a factor in the formation of both infant attachments and adult relationships (Altman & Taylor, 1973; Cairns, 1977; Zajonc, 1968).

Watson's (1972) "game hypothesis" provides a theoretical foundation for examining the role of contingency in attachment formation (Levitt, 1980, 1991; Main, 1999). In presenting infants with mobiles that moved either contingently or noncontingently in relation to the infant's activity, Watson observed that infants displayed intensely positive affect in response to the contingently active mobile.

Noting that contingency experience occurs regularly within social contexts as adults respond to infant overtures, he proposed that social preferences develop as a function of the affective pleasure derived from these contingency "games." Later research by Lewis and his colleagues also indicated that infants display positive emotional responses to contingent events and negative responses when the contingency is withdrawn (Lewis, Alessandri, & Sullivan, 1990). Lamb and Malkin (1986) viewed the positive affective consequences associated with relief of infant distress by contingently responding caregivers as a precursor of attachment.

Levitt (1980) demonstrated experimentally that infants' responses to an approaching adult varied as a function of both familiarization and the presence or absence of prior contingency experience with the adult, although contingency played a larger role in eliciting more positive responses. Levitt and colleagues later demonstrated that infants display attachment behavior preferentially toward individuals in their social networks as a function of their prior responsiveness in free-play and puzzle-solving interactions (Levitt, Guacci, et al., 1993). If contingent responding provides a basis for attachment preferences, it stands to reason that infants must be able to recognize that specific persons are the source of the contingency, an understanding of causality that develops, according to Piaget, at approximately the same time as the emergence of preferential attachment behavior (Levitt & Clark, 1982).

Thus familiarization, contingency experience, and the development of causal understanding are likely candidates with respect to identifying normative processes of attachment formation, although considerable research is needed to gain a full understanding of these processes. Additional questions remain about the processes by which attachments are maintained and those by which new close relationships emerge over time. There is widespread acceptance that some type of representational process is involved, but opinions differ as to the nature of this process and research on this issue has been sparse (Holmes, 2002).

In the social expectations model, expectations are thought to be generated in the course of interactions with relationship partners, beginning in infancy, as inferred from infant distress when mothers fail to respond to them in the Tronick (1989) "still face" paradigm or when contingent events are withdrawn in extinction procedures (Lewis et al., 1990). Research by Rovee-Collier (Rovee-Collier & Gekowski, 1979, Rovee-Collier, Griesler, & Earley, 1985) suggests that even very young infants (age 2–3 months) are able to remember contingent events over brief periods (1–2 weeks). As the capacity to organize and store experience in memory increases, along with communicative abilities, contingently related events may be separated by greater lengths of time, yet still recognized as contingent (Weisz, 1986). Thus, someone who has received support from a friend in a time of crisis may return the favor years later in response to the need of the friend and both parties will recognize the interrelation of these supportive acts.

Antonucci (1990) has suggested that the supportive exchanges of close relationship partners are deposited in a psychological "support bank" and carry with them the implicit assumption that the recipient could be asked for support at a future time, should the provider need it. Emotionally, this implicit expectation regarding the partner's availability to provide support if needed translates into "felt security" as posed by attachment researchers or "interpersonal trust" in Ericksonian (1963) terms and in the writing of some social psychologists (Baumeister & Leary, 1995;

Holmes & Rempel, 1989). Thus, expectations of partner responsiveness grow from experiences of contingent feedback, beginning in infancy and maintained by ongoing interactions with relationship partners and by mental representations that enable them to be maintained over long intervals.

Departing from Bowlby's infant–caregiver prototype model, the social expectations model is based on an exemplar perspective in which categorical information is thought to be represented in terms of multiple exemplars, with new information assimilated to a category in relation to its similarity to an existing exemplar (Smith & Zarate, 1992). From this perspective, expectations regarding new relationships would be based not on experience with a prototypic relationship, but rather on the similarity of the new relationship to specific features of past relationships (Andersen & Chen; 2002; Levitt et al., 1994).

Empirical data consistent with this premise have been accruing in recent years. In a study of children in an Israeli kibbutz, van IJzendoorn, Sagi, and Lambermon (1992), for example, found that infants' security with their nonparental caregivers was more predictive of socioemotional competence in kindergarten than was security with either parent. The highest levels of competence were seen in infants who were secure with both parents and with a nonparental caregiver. Van IJzendoorn and Sagi (1999) proposed that attachment representations integrate experiences with multiple caregivers and that the effects of these representations are specific to the nature of subsequent social encounters.

Andersen and Chen (2002) reviewed evidence to suggest that adult individuals have multiple cognitive–affective representations of "relational selves" based on past relationships with multiple significant others. Different relational selves are triggered through a process of transference, depending on the extent to which new interpersonal encounters share similarities of person and context to existing exemplars. Levitt (2005) has cited additional evidence for specificity in generalizations from earlier to later relationships. Thus, representations of past interactions with a maternal caregiver might be expected to carry over to a mother's relationship with her own child, but not necessarily with her spouse. In this frame, it might be interesting to explore linkages between individuals' representations of their relationship with their opposite sex parent and their spousal relationships.

In addressing the interface of relational self theory and attachment theory, Chen and Andersen (2008) have suggested that attachment working models may reflect internalization of some attachment experiences into a generalized trait-like way of orienting toward relationships that complements relationship-specific generalizations. Creasey and Ladd (2005) found that both generalized attachment representations and relationship-specific representations about a romantic partner seem to operate in partners' behavior in conflict situations. Shaver and Mikulincer (2006) also suggest that individuals have multiple attachment representations that may be invoked in specific social encounters, in addition to global attachment styles. However, the distinction between generalized and specific representations does not resolve the issue with respect to how generalized models are formulated in relation to multiple attachment figures.

Regardless of the specific nature of the representational processes involved, there is widespread consensus that individuals enter new relationships with preexisting expectations based on past relationship experiences (Andersen & Chen, 2002; Blanchard-Fields & Cooper, 2004). It is also known that expectations may change as a result of interactions with a new relationship partner (McNulty & Karney, 2002, 2004). Individuals in the beginning stages of a relationship spend considerable time "getting to know each other" through self-disclosure and they also tend to be highly attentive and responsive to their partners. When the new partner's behavior is clearly inconsistent with the individual's preconceived biases, the individual may accommodate the inconsistency by altering existing expectations. Within the attachment literature, for example, it has been noted that individuals with insecure attachment representations may develop more secure working models within the context of a positive romantic or marriage relationship (Davila, Karney, & Bradbury, 1999; Dinero, Conger, Shaver, Widaman, & Larsen-Rife, 2008). On the other hand, unstable or abusive relationships may result in greater insecurity and more negative representations (Kirkpatrick & Hazan, 1994).

Thus, past interactions with close relationship partners likely play a significant role in formulating the individual's ongoing relationship expectancies. However, as individuals develop the capacity to elaborate and store representations of their close relationships based on social interactions, they also develop the ability to comprehend and integrate culturally defined social norms regarding close relationships. Expectations regarding the behavior of parents and children, husbands and wives, grandparents, siblings, and close relationships in general are defined to some extent by the larger culture and promoted by the interconnected values, attitudes, and behaviors of members of the social convoy within which the relationship is embedded.

Social norms governing the parent–child relationship in the United States are a prime example. Parents are expected to love, protect, and care for their preadult children and experience strong social and legal sanctions for failure to do so. Later in life, adult children are expected to provide care for elderly parents should they become too frail to function independently. This norm is typically followed, even when the child's relationship with the parent has been less than satisfactory (Parrott & Bengtson, 1999; Rossi & Rossi, 1990). Parent care often involves negotiations among siblings, but these often take place in the context of social norms (such as expectations regarding the role of women as caregivers).

Thus, according to the proposed model, children's expectations of love and support from parents may arise both through past supportive interactions with the parent and through the child's awareness that parents are supposed to love their children normatively. This awareness likely plays a role in engendering the defensiveness seen in attachment interviews of adult children who have experienced parental rejection. Similar views regarding the significance of role-based normative expectations in the development of relationship representations have been expressed by Andersen and Chen (2002). Normative role-based expectations are likely to account in large part for cultural variation in close relationships. Generational shifts in the endorsement of role norms have also been cited as a factor in creating intergenerational conflict within families (Luescher & Pillemer, 1998).

Relationship expectations, once established, are resistant to change, because ongoing interactions with the relationship partner are viewed through the biased lens of past experience. The proposed model specifies that close relationships are most likely to change when individuals encounter circumstances that test their expectations. From a life-span perspective, relationship stability is especially vulnerable at times of major life transitions, when support needs are heightened and expectations regarding the provision of support from the partner are tested. Transitions involving role changes may also represent points of vulnerability because expectations associated with the new role and/or conflicting expectations between relationship partners may lead to relationship instability. Examples include conflicting expectations of parents and children that may follow migration to a new country and of marital partners following the transition to childbirth or, in later years, to retirement. In challenging circumstances, relationships may improve when a partner's behavior exceeds expectations, be stable when expectations are met, and be threatened when expectations are violated.

Studies of marital relationship quality across the childbirth transition reported by Levitt et al. (1994) yielded results consistent with the premise that the testing of support expectations is linked to relationship stability versus change. Perceived discrepancies in the emotional and instrumental support expected from the spouse versus that received from the spouse were strong predictors of changes in relationship quality, in both retrospective and prospective analyses. Similar findings emerged from a prospective study of emerging adults prior to and following their high school graduation (Levitt, Silver, Lane, Pierre, & Perez, 2005), with respect to changes in their relationships with their parents. Participants reported, at both time periods, the amount of support received from mother and father, the perceived adequacy of the support (the extent to which the support fell short of, met, or exceeded their expectations), and the perceived closeness of the relationship with each parent. Post-transition relationship closeness was related significantly to both changes in the amount of support provided by each parent and to changes in the extent to which the support was perceived to be adequate. Although not assessing relationship change per se, in research based on the social expectations model, Kelley (1999) found that reported discrepancies in expected and perceived behavior were linked to marital dissatisfaction.

Conflict likely plays an important role in determining relational outcomes at points of vulnerability related to life events, in conjunction with expectancy violations. In general, close relationships are primary sources of support, but they are also frequent sources of negative interaction and conflict (Antonucci, 1990; Antonucci, Akiyama, & Lansford, 1998; Birditt, Jackey, & Antonucci, 2009; Levitt, Silver, & Franco, 1996). Some degree of conflict is healthy in relationships, because it enables partners to clarify and adjust their expectations. However, interactions with excessive or escalating conflict are associated with serious relationship disturbances, including divorce (Gottman, 1994) and severely troubled family relationships (Patterson, 1986). From a social expectations perspective, excessively conflictive encounters typically involve hurtful communications that may violate partner expectations to an irreparable degree. Thus, the capacity to modulate conflict within the bounds tolerable in a given relationship is likely a key to relationship satisfaction and continuity (Levitt, 1991).

In sum, within the proposed model, close relationships are formed through processes of familiarization and contingent feedback, maintained through ongoing interactions and expectations based on past experiences and social norms, and vulnerable to change when expectations are put to the test in the course of challenging life events. In the next section, we address our third and final question regarding close relationships; that is, how and why do close relationships vary across individuals, relational roles, and cultures.

VARIATION IN CLOSE RELATIONSHIPS ACROSS THE LIFE SPAN

Individual variations in close relationships are likely related to variations in personal characteristics and behaviors that feed into ongoing interactions at the microlevel, whereas role-related and cultural variations are more likely related to role-based expectations that are often life stage–related and culture-specific. The literature on individual differences in close relationships is quite extensive, and, as noted previously, much of the life-span literature has been focused on relationship partners in specific role configurations (marital, parent–child, etc.). Much less has been written about cultural variation. We review briefly some of the main issues and findings in these areas in the following sections.

Individual Differences in Close Relationships

Attachment researchers have focused almost exclusively on individual differences. Based on observations of infant behavior in the Strange Situation, Ainsworth and her colleagues initially identified three divergent patterns of attachment behavior. Infants classified as "secure" used the mother as a secure base; they were comfortable exploring in the mother's presence and exhibited attachment behavior toward her when reunited after a separation. "Insecure–avoidant" infants avoided the mother at reunion and "insecure–resistant" infants showed a pattern of ambivalent behavior at reunion, both seeking contact and resisting it. Investigators of adult attachment have developed typologies comparable to those identified by Ainsworth (Crowell et al., 1999).

Although the processes through which these orientations are established, organized, and maintained or altered in the individual's psyche have yet to be fully understood, a substantial body of literature attests to the validity of secure versus insecure attachment classifications in both childhood (Cassidy & Shaver, 1999) and adulthood (Shaver & Mikulincer, 2006). For example, secure attachment orientations are associated with socioemotional competence with peers in childhood (Fagot & Kavanagh, 1990), capacity for romantic intimacy and friendship quality in adolescence (Mayseless & Scharf, 2007), and the regulation of emotion in close relationships in younger and older adults (Magai, Consedine, Gillespie, O'Neal, & Vilker, 2004; Mikulincer & Shaver, 2005; Simpson, Collins, Tran, & Haydon, 2007).

In Takahashi's research, typological variation in affective relationship structures has been defined in terms of the focal figure(s) at the top of the individual's relationship hierarchy who serve the most functions. Takahashi has identified three types of structures, including a family focused type, a friend focused type, and a lone wolf type. She has found these types across age levels and they seem to persist over time within individuals. In studies relating different types of structures to personal well-being, family focused and friend focused individuals appear equally well adjusted and both types are better adjusted than lone wolf types, who receive few emotionally supportive functions and lack a focal figure. However, there do seem to be some advantages or disadvantages to being family or friend focused, depending on the demands of specific contexts. For example, Takahashi reports that emerging adults with friend focused affective relationship structures adapt more readily to the transition to college life (Takahashi, 2005).

Working within the framework of the convoy model, Levitt and colleagues (Levitt et al., 2005) reported similar findings based on cluster analyses of support sources in late childhood and early adolescence. The analyses identified a pattern of support from both close family members and friends, a second pattern of support from both close and extended family members, and a third pattern of more limited support primarily from close family members alone. Participants receiving support from close family in combination with either extended family or friends were better adjusted than were those without multiple sources of support.

Birditt and Antonucci (2007) also employed cluster analyses to develop relationship quality profiles of adults aged 22–79. Analyses revealed varied profiles, ranging from those characterized by high quality relationships across spouse, other family members (mother, father, and/or child), and friends to those with pervasive low quality relationships. Adjustment did not differ overall between those with and without best friends, but among individuals with best friends, profiles including at least two relationships of high quality (family and friend, spouse and friend, family and spouse) were associated with greater well-being. For these individuals, having a high quality best friendship along with a high quality relationship with another family member may have compensated for a poorer relationship with a spouse. For those without best friends, well-being profiles that included good spousal relations were associated with well-being. Older individuals tended to have profiles with higher quality relations, in line with socioemotional selectivity theory (Carstensen, 2006; Charles & Carstensen, 2010).

In general, the identification of meaningful patterns or profiles of close relationships that vary across individuals is clearly a worthwhile pursuit. A related challenge is to understand how varied patterns of relationships evolve in the course of development. As already discussed, experiences with relationship partners are important, but other factors likely enter into divergent types of relationship networks. Temperamental characteristics are a probable source of variation. Simpson, Winterheld, and Chen (2006), for example, focused on the role of basic approach-avoidance tendencies in promoting or hindering the individual's ability to form satisfactory close alliances, concluding that these temperamental dispositions interact with situational forces and partner behaviors to affect ongoing interactions and consequent perceptions of relationship quality. Another important characteristic is the individual's relational competence (Hansson, Daleiden, & Hayslip, Jr., 2004), that is the ability to initiate and sustain relationships and to derive needed support from them.

A number of researchers have also noted that close relationship orientations and behaviors tend to vary by gender, although variability within genders may exceed that observed between genders, and many aspects of close relationships are common across genders (Impett & Peplau, 2006). When differences are found, they tend to be in the direction of women being more invested in intimacy with a broader network of close relations that are more central in their lives (Antonucci et al., 2004).

Numerous additional personal characteristics may feed into the nature of close relationships at the individual level, such as attractiveness or other physical characteristics, social skills, health, and so on. As proposed by Kahn and Antonucci (1980), personal characteristics are likely to interact with situational contexts to govern individual desire for and capacity to acquire and maintain a convoy of close supportive relationships. Situational forces may include such factors as stressful life circumstances, socioeconomic conditions, and the existing organization and functioning of the individual's relationship network.

In sum, individuals vary in meaningful ways with respect to their patterns of relationships and in how these patterns become manifest in personal well-being across the life span. One of the great challenges of therapeutic intervention is to enable individuals lacking in natural sources of social support to establish viable close relationships with supportive partners.

In the next section, we address variation in close relationships as a function of the roles occupied by relationship partners. We also highlight some of the findings regarding how these relationships may evolve over the life span.

Close Relationships as a Function of Relational Role

A significant unresolved challenge of research on close relationships is identifying and categorizing unique versus transcendent properties of relationships across variations in roles. Relationships between parents and children, husbands and wives, and so on, have much in common but also diverge in meaningful ways. In this chapter, so far, we have focused on commonalities, viewing close relationships in general as evolving through social interactions, as governed by social expectations, and as sources of both social support and conflict.

Role differentiation in relationships is likely related to the social norms attached to specific roles that may, in turn, be rooted in biosocial evolution. An example would be the sanctioning of sexual intercourse within marital relationships contrasted with strong prohibitions against this behavior within parent–child relationships. Violations of these norms in the form of platonic marriages and sexual abuse of children by parents suggest that the divide between relational roles is not strictly categorical, however, and may be reflected rather in the degree to which relationship partners generally adhere to normative expectations. In other cases, expectations regarding sexuality associated with specific roles are more ambiguous, as the term "friends with benefits" implies. Another point of differentiation is the degree of caregiving involved in relational roles. Here too, however, relationships likely diverge more in the extent to which they involve expectations for care than in any absolute sense. As already noted, close relationships in general involve mutual support, although support may flow more in one direction than the other, as is typically the case with parents and children.

Thus, in our view, relationships across specific roles are best studied within an overall theoretical framework applicable to close relationships in general, to identify points of articulation between types of relationships with respect to understanding their formation, quality, maintenance, and dissolution. Similar processes are likely to be involved and the fragmentation of research across role-specific lines may hinder this understanding. However, given the existence of a considerable body of role-based literature, in the following sections, we describe briefly some of the literature on life-span changes in relationships within specific role structures, including those of romantic and marital partners, of siblings, and of child, parent, and grandparent generations within the family. Although friendships are often close relationships, peer relationships are addressed elsewhere in this volume and will not be reviewed here (Fingerman, Brown, & Blieszner, Chapter 19).

Romantic and Marital Relationships

There has been an explosion of interest in recent years in the development of romantic relationships. These relationships begin to emerge as early as middle childhood (Carlson & Rose, 2007; Underwood, 2007) and become increasingly important through adolescence and into young adulthood (Furman, 2002). Consistent with the various theoretical perspectives on the development of close relationships, prior family and peer experience play a role in determining the quality of romantic relationships (Crockett & Randall, 2006; Dinero et al., 2008; Furman, 2002; Seiffge-Krenke, Shulman, & Klessinger, 2001; Simpson et al., 2007). Interestingly, Dinero et al. (2008) found that warmer, more positive, less hostile interactions with a romantic partner at age 25 predicted greater attachment security at age 27, but age 25 attachment security did not predict to the quality of romantic interactions at age 27. This finding is consistent with research indicating that a positive marital relationship may foster greater attachment security (Davila et al., 1999) and, more generally, with reports that high quality romantic relationships may have positive developmental consequences (Furman, 2002).

Research on romantic relationships is sometimes framed in terms of love styles, described generally as passionate or companionate, although these general styles have been further differentiated (Bierhoff & Schmohr, 2004). A recent review by Bierhoff and Schmohr (2004) suggests that passionate love declines over time as a function of both age and length of relationship, based on both cross-sectional and longitudinal studies, consistent with socially common beliefs about the nature of love and marriage. Findings with respect to changes in companionate love were less consistent.

Marriages are often the result of romantic involvement, although the extent to which the two are linked varies by culture, as arranged marriages are still common in many societies (Goodwin & Pillay, 2006). Research on marital satisfaction across the life span suggests some prevalence of a U-shaped trajectory for long-term marriages, with satisfaction high in the early years, low through childbearing years, and higher again in the post-childrearing empty nest period, although not all marriages follow this pattern (Anderson, Russell, & Schumm, 1983). An increase in marital satisfaction in later life may coincide with a general trend for older individuals to view their close relations in a positive light, as proposed by socioemotional selectivity theory. Story et al. (2007) found that satisfied older, but not middle age, couples viewed their spouses' interactive behaviors as more positive than did independent observers. However, in a 12-year longitudinal study of negative relationship aspects (the extent to which individuals report that partners make too many demands or get on their nerves), Birditt et al. (2009) found increased negativity in spousal relationships (but not in relations with children or friends) in adults ranging in age from 20 to 93 at the beginning of the study.

Variations in marriages and factors leading to marital longevity versus dissolution have been studied extensively by Gottman (1994). Marriages with frequent negative interactions that are not offset by positive ones are particularly susceptible to dissolution. Marriages appear to be especially vulnerable to divorce within the first few years and, as widely disseminated statistics indicate, approximately half of the marriages in the United States end in divorce (Lawrence et al., 2010). As discussed previously, violations of support expectations are linked to declines in marital relationship quality following the transition to childbirth (Levitt et al., 1994).

Sibling Relationships

Sibling relationships are unique in being, for many individuals, the one relationship that begins in early childhood and persists throughout most of the individual's lifetime. Sibling relationships are often characterized by closeness and conflict, although these relationships vary greatly in the extent to which they are close or conflicted. Consistent with the view that relationships are best studied in context, interactions with parents (Kim, McHale, Osgood, & Crouter, 2006), family emotional climate (Modry-Mandell, Gamble, & Taylor, 2007), and experiences with friends (Kramer & Kowal, 2005) have been reported to contribute to the quality of sibling relationships. Milevsky, Smoot, Leh, and Ruppe (2005) have identified a number of additional contextual factors contributing to sibling relationship quality.

Good sibling relationships in early adolescence and in young adulthood have been found to compensate for poor relations with parents (Milevsky, 2005; Milevsky & Levitt, 2005). Interactions with siblings, particularly the management of conflict, are thought to contribute to the development of emotion regulation across the life span (Bedford & Volling, 2004) and poor sibling relationships in childhood have been linked to depression in adulthood (Waldinger, Vaillant, & Orav, 2007).

Retrospective research with older adults suggests that sibling relations become more distant in the years of marriage and parenting, but closer in relation to later life events, such as loss of parents, retirement, and family illness (Gold, 1996). A short-term longitudinal analysis by White (2001) also found reduced proximity, contact, and support exchange with siblings in young adulthood, whereas supportive exchanges increased in old age. In research based on the convoy model, Guiaux, van Tilburg, and van Groenou (2007) reported increased contact with and support from siblings as a consequence of widowhood. As with other relationships, however, patterns vary across individuals and some sibling relationships show continuity or deterioration in later years, rather than increased closeness (Gold, 1996).

Parents and Children

As the vast literature on attachment, styles of parenting, and other aspects of the parent–child relationship indicate, much more has been written about what Hagestad (1984) referred to as "alpha" (preadult child and parent) dyads than about "omega" (adult child–older parent) dyads, although the literature on both has grown over the past few decades. From a life-span perspective, the trajectory of emotional closeness to parents in the context of increasing personal autonomy has been of interest (Baltes & Silverberg, 1994). Research has converged to suggest that children generally view parents as very close and important relations across the life span, although dependence on parents declines as children mature (Noack & Buhl, 2004).

The transitional periods from late childhood to adolescence and from late adolescence to early adulthood may be important with respect to parent–child relationships. Studies suggest that conflict with parents often increases in adolescence and then declines following the transition to adulthood. In an illustrative study, Pipp et al. (1985) asked college students to draw circles representing their relationship with their parents at stages from infancy to the present time. Students generally depicted greater distance and more conflict in the adolescent period and closer relationships in the present. Prospective studies have confirmed that emerging adults perceive closer relationships with parents in the postadolescent period (Levitt, Silver, & Santos, 2007). However, findings are mixed regarding whether improvements in relationship closeness are linked specifically to emerging adults leaving the parental home (Levitt et al., 2007; Smetana, Metzger, & Campione-Barr, 2004). Increased perceptions of closeness and declines in conflict may be related to the transition to more adult roles (college attendance, full time employment) in late adolescence, whether or not the child remains at home (Levitt et al., 2007; Shaver, Furman, & Buhrmester, 1985).

Parents' transition to old age may represent another point of change in relations with children, particularly if children are called upon to provide care to ailing parents. In general, the literature suggests that children will provide care as a function of parental need, regardless of the quality of the child's attachment or the child's emotional closeness to the parent, although qualitative factors in the relationship may be related to the type of care provided and caregiver satisfaction (Blieszner, 2006; Carpenter, 2001; Rossi & Rossi, 1990). This pattern of findings suggests that both normative expectations regarding filial obligation and relationship quality enter into the caregiving situation. Normative considerations also enter into divisions of responsibility among siblings for care of ailing parents, with daughters being more likely than sons to be primary caregivers (Brody, Litvin, Albert, & Hoffman, 1994).

Middle generation women have often been referred to as the "sandwich generation" (Bengtson, Rosenthal, & Burton, 1995), with responsibility to provide support to both children and parents simultaneously. It is relatively rare for women to be providing active care to both children and parents, as older generation parents do not typically need active caregiving until very late in life, after the younger generation has achieved relative independence. Nevertheless, the "sandwich effect" emerged clearly in a study of perceived reciprocity of support among young adult daughters, their middle aged mothers, and their elderly grandmothers (Levitt, Guacci, & Weber, 1992). Middle generation mothers perceived that they provided more support to both their daughters and their mothers than they received, and these perceptions were affirmed by both the younger and older generations, who reported receiving more support from the middle generation women than they provided to them. In a study of instrumental support provision in a cross-national U.S–U.K. sample of women aged 55–69, Grundy and Henretta (2006) found that most were providing some support to parents or children and about one third were providing support to parents and children simultaneously.

Bengtson and his colleagues have conducted extensive research on adult child–parent relations within the context of an overall focus on intergenerational relationships. Earlier work revealed generally high levels of intergenerational support, similarity in core values, and contact within families, characterized as intergenerational solidarity (Bengtson et al., 1995; Bengtson & Schrader, 1982). Parents provide support to their adult children across the life span, but they differentiate to some extent, providing more support to children with greater needs and to those perceived as more successful (Fingerman, Miller, Birditt, & Zarit, 2009). Providing support on an as-needed basis is consistent with observations regarding communal relationship exchanges (Clark, 1984). According to Fingerman et al. (2009), parents may provide support to more successful children either because these children enhance their own feelings of worth as parents or because successful children may be more likely to reciprocate the support in later years, in line with Antonucci's (1990) notion of a support bank.

Some research has addressed differentiation among families with respect to solidarity. A study of adult child–parent relationship typologies by Silverstein and Bengtson (1997) suggests the presence of five types: tight-knit, sociable, intimate but distant, obligatory, and detached. This promising line of research dovetails with other recent efforts described in this chapter to characterize and explore the correlates and consequences of typological variation in close relationships (Birditt & Antonucci, 2007; Levitt et al., 2005; Takahashi, 2005).

In one of the better known findings from the research of Bengtson and his colleagues, perceptual discrepancies and points of conflict were identified between parent and child generations within families. Older individuals, for example, tend to perceive their relations with their adult children more in terms of emotional closeness, whereas the children view their relations with their parents more in terms of obligation. Also, adult children underestimate, and their parents overestimate, the degree of value consensus in their relationships. Bengtson and Kuypers (1971) attributed this phenomenon to differential expectations and goals associated with life stage differences between parents and children, characterized as differences in developmental stakes. Intergenerational differences (termed "developmental schisms") in relationship perceptions also emerged in studies of older mothers and their middle age daughters by Fingerman (1995, 1996, 1998). A recent study of worry as a significant relationship factor also revealed intergenerational differences related to developmental stage, with children worrying most about their parents' health and elderly parents expressing a variety of concerns (health, safety, finances, relationships, etc.) about their adult children (Hay, Fingerman, & Lefkowitz, 2008). Giarrusso, Feng, and Bengtson (2005) provide an overview of research on the intergenerational stake phenomenon, noting that factors other than parent–child life stage differences may play a role in creating such schisms.

Research on intergenerational solidarity and conflict has been guided recently by a consideration of the coexistence of positive and negative perceptions and emotions in parent–child relationships, characterized as ambivalence (Luescher & Pillemer, 1998). Although close relationships are generally viewed with greater ambivalence than less close relationships (Fingerman, Hay, & Birditt, 2004), much of the work in this area has been focused on intergenerational ties. Luescher and Pillemer (1998) posited that intergenerational ambivalence is related to unresolved issues of dependence and autonomy and conflicting norms and expectations regarding intergenerational relations. Empirical support for this view has been found (Pillemer & Suitor, 2002; Pillemer et al., 2007).

Overall, the literature indicates that parent–child relationships endure throughout life and, like all close relationships, embody varying degrees of closeness, mutual support, conflict, and ambivalence. Significant gaps remain in our knowledge about qualitative features of the parent–child relationship beyond childhood, however. Exemplifying a promising line of research on this issue, Birditt, Miller, Fingerman, and Lefkowitz (2009) have recently examined the extent to which specific tensions are associated with intergenerational ambivalence and lower affective solidarity, in a comprehensive study of adults aged 22–49 and their mothers and fathers. Individual tensions, such as those related to the performance of the child or parent in areas such as housekeeping, job status, handling finances, maintaining health, and child rearing, were of greater concern for the parent generation, suggesting a developmental schism reflecting the parents' goal to foster successful autonomous functioning in their children. Tensions about the relationship itself did not differ in intensity by generation, but these tensions engendered greater ambivalence and were the most detrimental to the affective quality of the relationship.

Another significant gap exists with respect to understanding intergenerational relationships between in-laws. The in-law relationship is unique in that it is an involuntary, yet structurally close relationship ensuing from a marital union to which parents and children must adapt. Studying this adaptive process may facilitate our comprehension of processes involved generally in the development of relationships (Santos & Levitt, 2007). Furthermore, it is important to recognize that intergenerational dynamics within the family are likely to involve in-laws as well as parents and children, with implications for support, marital satisfaction and stability, and grandparent–grandchild relationships.

Grandparents and Grandchildren

Grandparent–grandchild relationships are typically among the closest relationships elicited in social convoy assessments, yet we know relatively little about the socioemotional qualities of these relationships. The significance of this role for grandparents is illustrated in a study by Drew and Smith (2002), who found that losing contact with grandchildren was related to pronounced, long lasting grief, poorer emotional and physical health, and reduced quality of life in grandparents, especially if the loss was through family conflict or divorce.

Several researchers have identified factors that affect grandparent–grandchild relations, including grandparents' age, gender, education, marital status, health, proximity, and relationship with the grandchild's parents (Crosnoe & Elder, 2002; Erber, 2010). Younger grandparents, grandmothers, and grandparents with more education, intact marriages, better health, and geographic proximity are likely to have closer relationships with their grandchildren, as are those related to the grandchild through the child's mother (Erber, 2010). Variations in these factors have been linked to different typologies of relationships, such as those identified by Mueller, Wilhelm, and Elder (2002), who used cluster analysis to yield five types of grandparent–grandchild relationships: influential, supportive, passive, authority-oriented, and detached.

Developmental schisms have also been found in the perceptions of grandchildren and grandparents regarding their relationships. Crosnoe and Elder (2002) found that grandparents of grandchildren transitioning to college viewed their mentoring as more significant than the grandchildren perceived, but this effect was moderated by grandparents' education; that is, if the grandparent had a college education, grandparent and grandchild views of grandparents' mentoring were comparable. Regardless of grandparents' education, the grandchild's entry into college was associated with greater closeness to the grandparent, paralleling findings regarding increased closeness to parents across this transition. It seems likely that this commonality reflects a broader change in relations with close family members ensuing from the child's transition to adult life.

Parallels between parent–child and grandparent–grandchild relationships are most evident when grandparents take on the parenting role and interest in this phenomenon has emerged as the numbers of grandparents raising grandchildren have increased. Reviews by Hayslip and Kaminski (2005 a, b) have addressed a number of issues faced by custodial grandparents and emphasized their need for support in performing this crucial role in the child's life.

General Conclusions Regarding Relational Roles

Our brief review of relationships varying by role suggests that relations with spouses, parents, children, siblings, and grandparents have common elements of emotional closeness, support, and conflict to varying degrees and that all undergo changes through the life span, sometimes ordered by life transitions, such as the child's transition to adulthood or the parent's loss of health in old age, and sometimes by unique circumstances, such as parents abdicating their role to grandparents. The presence of common features and transitions across topologically variant relationships and the oft recognized but largely uninvestigated complex interconnections among these relationships underscores the need to study close relationships in the context of the network of significant relationships affecting the individual's development.

Variations across roles are meaningful, because these likely reflect variations in factors such as developmental timing (developmental stakes), structural position in the family (e.g., parent versus sibling), and culturally defined norms and expectations regarding role performance. The effect of cultural role expectations is illustrated in a study by Yeung and Fung (2007) of elderly parents in Hong Kong showing that parental life satisfaction was related more to emotional support from children than from friends, likely because Chinese culture generally values family commitment (familism) more than American culture, in which late life satisfaction has been related more strongly to support from friends (Antonucci, 1990). At the same time, satisfaction in this sample of Chinese parents was related to instrumental support from a child more for parents higher in familism, reflecting intracultural heterogeneity. In the following section, we explore further the issue of cultural effects on close relationships.

CULTURAL VARIATION IN CLOSE RELATIONSHIPS

At the outset, it should be noted that assessing cultural divergence in social relations is a nearly impossible undertaking, as Gjerde (2004) has observed. First, culture is a rapidly moving target, continually changing in the context of economic, political, and historical forces. Second, individuals within a given cultural group are markedly heterogeneous and there are typically greater differences within, than across, cultures. Third, cultural effects are difficult to categorize and impossible to analyze without the intrusion of researchers' own cultural world views. Fourth, cultural effects at any given time are confounded with those of other contextual variables, such as social class, economic conditions, minority or majority status, migration patterns, and geographic location. Thus, although we might note certain trends or modalities within different cultures that may vary across cultures, we can expect wide variation in the extent to which such trends are manifest at the individual level.

In addition, cross-cultural researchers confront formidable methodological issues. Problems abound with respect to obtaining culturally representative samples, to translating materials, to establishing equivalence in measurement, and to drawing conclusions about the meaning of research findings. Progress in understanding the role of culture in the development of close relationships will likely entail a mix of quantitative and qualitative approaches (Azmitia, Ittel, & Radmacher, 2005; Stanton-Salazar, 2001). Thus, important as the question might be, researchers face daunting challenges in trying to assess culturally divergent and culturally transcendent aspects of close relationships.

With these caveats in mind, we describe some findings regarding culture and close relationships from researchers who have ventured into this difficult area. In general, most of this research has been focused on the issue of personal autonomy versus interdependence and cultures have been characterized as varying on the extent to which they value one or the other, at least at the macrolevel. Western industrialized cultures tend to be viewed as individualistic with an emphasis on self actualization, whereas Eastern cultures and those that are less industrialized tend to be viewed as collectivistic with an emphasis on interdependence (Goodwin & Pillay, 2006; Kagitçibasi, 1996).

Takahashi and her colleagues addressed the individualism–collectivism distinction in a cross-national interview study of close relationships in the United States, considered to be an individualistic culture, and Japan, considered to be a collectivist culture, that included relatively large samples from both countries, ranging in age from 20 to 64 (Takahashi, Ohara, Antonucci, & Akiyama, 2002). They proposed that, if the two cultures could truly be distinguished along an individualism–collectivism divide, those interviewed in the United States would be more independent and less socially connected, less concerned with interpersonal harmony, and less integrated into extended family, having closer relations with nonbiological network members, including spouses and friends, in comparison to those interviewed in Japan. The findings indicated greater complexity across the two cultures than could be captured in terms of individualism versus collectivism. Americans did not seem less connected within their close relationship networks and reported more positive relationships than did the Japanese. They were comparatively less concerned with interpersonal harmony and more likely to report close relationships with friends, but not with spouses. Takahashi et al. concluded that the individualism–collectivism dimension is useful for assessing an aspect of cultural variation, but does not provide a general theoretical model for distinguishing among cultural groups.

Kagitçibasi (1996, 2007) has written extensively on this issue as well, also noting that the individualism–collectivism distinction is too simplistic as a model of cultural divergence. Although economic advancement within a culture tends to promote greater material and geographic independence, she suggests that emotional interdependence is often maintained or increased in the face of socio-economic change.

Other points of cultural divergence have been noted in a review by Goodwin and Pillay (2006), including the extent to which mate selection is voluntary or arranged, the prevalence of different styles of parenting, the ease or difficulty of divorce, and the predominance of extended or nuclear family households. Overall, however, although specific forms of social structure and styles of relating may vary, close relationships appear to be a ubiquitous human phenomenon across cultures (Baumeister & Leary, 1995; Goodwin & Pillay, 2006; Takahashi et al. 2002).

☐ FUTURE ISSUES IN THE STUDY OF CLOSE RELATIONSHIPS ACROSS THE LIFE SPAN

There are extraordinary conceptual and methodological challenges to the study of close relationships that must be resolved if we are to achieve a cohesive analysis of their development across the life span. We have touched on these challenges throughout this chapter, but we summarize them here and offer some suggestions for forwarding the research agenda in this area.

First and foremost, we conclude that understanding the life-long development of close relationships will require unifying theories that are up to the task of organizing the existing literature and directing future research. Given the complexities involved in studying a single dyadic relationship involving two unique individuals and the structures and processes connecting them, along with the fact that dyadic relationships are similarly interconnected within larger units of social structure and process, it is apparent that a systemic, contextualist approach to theory building is required. At present, methodological shortcomings have hampered progress with respect to applying systems theoretical approaches to the study of relationships (Levitt, in press), but as methods for analyzing complex systems become more available, advances in theory construction can be expected.

The adoption of a systems perspective will enable us to unravel another significant question in the study of relationships; that is, what the points of commonality and divergence across relationships are. Some models emphasize the unique properties of relationships, differentiating them by function, whereas others argue for malleability and interchangeability of functions across relationships, although all of the theoretical approaches described in this chapter allow for both in varying degrees. For example, attachment theorists focus on the uniqueness of attachment bonds and emphasize the caregiving function, but they acknowledge the presence of multiple attachments and the potential for later relationships to alter trajectories of security and insecurity grounded in earlier attachments. Theorists accepting the evolutionary universality of a "need to belong" as articulated by Baumeister and Leary (1995) emphasize commonality of function, yet recognize that there are unique qualities to relationships related to the social roles of relationship partners and the cultural norms governing those roles (Levitt, 1991, 2005). The question of interchangeability of relationship functions is theoretically interesting, but it also has important implications for intervention with individuals who have lost or are deficient in relationships vitally needed for support.

Another significant issue in need of theoretical and empirical work is the understanding of representational processes involved in the development of relationships across the life span. Bowlby's conceptualization of working model processes in attachment relationships provided a starting point for consideration of this issue and the proposed social expectations model is an attempt to extend this work, but unresolved questions regarding how multiple attachments are represented and processes of change and continuity in relationship representations remain to be addressed.

The identification of factors leading to change or promoting continuity in relationships is central to understanding close relationships from a life-span developmental viewpoint. Life span theorists commonly refer to life transitions as precipitators of relationship change (Kahn & Antonucci, 1980; Levitt, 1991;

Takahashi, 1990), but more thought is needed to specify processes linking such transitions to relationship outcomes and additional empirical studies of change in relationships across transitional periods are required to bolster the scant body of evidence supporting this view.

There is a compelling need for longitudinal study to address the nature of relationship development over the life course, but implementing such studies will require that the field makes a strong case for investing resources in the study of social relationships. Despite overwhelming evidence of the significance of close relationships for human functioning, however, support for research in this area has been relatively insubstantial compared to that allocated to other areas related to physical and psychological health and well-being.

Advances in identifying significant variations in relationships and in creating meaningful typologies have been noted in this chapter, but far more work remains to be done in this area. The typology developed by attachment theorists (Ainsworth et al., 1978) has had powerful heuristic value and provides a model for the identification of relationship types encompassing a broader range of relationships (Levitt, 2005). The refinement of person-centered methodologies suited to uncovering individual patterns within aggregated datasets (Magnusson, 1997) will enable us to identify meaningful variation in close relationships and to study how specific types of relationships evolve over the life span.

Finally, one of the most challenging areas of future study is the role of culture in close relationships. It is likely that culture affects relationships through its role in conveying norms and expectations (Levitt, 1991). However, as noted, the complexities involved in studying cultural influence are formidable. Nevertheless, existing evidence points to meaningful cultural effects on the nature and development of relationships across the life span and, regardless of the obstacles, we must find a way to approach this issue. Perhaps interdisciplinary efforts incorporating cultural anthropologists in our developmental research are needed.

In sum, despite the availability of a vast literature on relationships, much remains to be accomplished with respect to understanding the development of close relationships across the life span. Advances in theory, methodology, and empirical study are needed and should keep researchers in this area excited and engaged for the foreseeable future.

REFERENCES

Ainsworth, M. D. S. (1989). Attachments beyond infancy. *American Psychologist, 44*, 709–716.

Ainsworth, M. D. S., & Bell, S. M. (1970). Attachment, exploration, and separation: Illustrated by the behavior of one-year-olds in a strange situation. *Child Development, 41*, 49–67.

Ainsworth, M. D. S., Blehar, M. C., Waters, E., & Wall, S. (1978). *Patterns of attachment: A psychological study of the Strange Situation*. Hillsdale, NJ: Erlbaum.

Altman, I., & Taylor, D. A. (1973). *Social penetration: The development of interpersonal relationships*. Oxford: Holt, Rinehart & Winston.

Andersen, S. M., & Chen, S. (2002). The relational self: An interpersonal social-cognitive theory. *Psychological Review, 109*, 619–645.

Anderson, S. A., Russell, C. S., & Schumm, W. R. (1983). Perceived marital quality and family life-cycle categories: A further analysis. *Journal of Marriage & the Family, 45*, 127–139.

Antonucci, T. C. (1976). Attachment: A life span concept. *Human Development, 19*, 135–142.

Antonucci, T. C. (1986). Measuring social support networks: Hierarchical mapping technique. *Generations, Summer*, 10–12.

Antonucci, T. C. (1990). Social supports and social relationships. In R. H. Binstock and L. K. George (Eds.), *The handbook of aging and the social sciences* (3rd ed; pp. 205–226). San Diego, CA: Academic Press.

Antonucci, T. C., Akiyama, H., & Lansford, J. (1998). Negative effects of close social relations. *Family Relations, 47,* 379–384.

Antonucci, T. C., Akiyama, H., & Takahashi, K. (2004). Attachment and close relationships across the life span. *Attachment and Human Development, 6,* 353–370.

Antonucci, T. C., & Jackson, J. S. (1987). Social support, interpersonal efficacy, and health: A life course perspective. In L. L. Carstensen, & B. A. Edelstein (Eds.), *Handbook of clinical gerontology.* (pp. 291–311). Elmsford, NY: Pergamon Press.

Asendorpf, J. B., & Wilpers, S. (2000). Attachment security and available support: Closely linked relationship qualities. *Journal of Social and Personal Relationships, 17,* 115–138.

Azmitia, M., Ittel, A., & Radmacher, K. (2005). Narratives of friendship and self in adolescence. *New Directions for Child and Adolescent Development, Spring*(107), 23–39.

Baltes, M. M., & Silverberg, S. B. (1994). The dynamics between dependency and autonomy: Illustrations across the life span. In Featherman, D. L., Baltes, P. B., Lerner, R. M., & Perlmutter, M. (Eds.) *Life-span development and behavior* (Vol. 12, pp. 41–90). Hillsdale, NJ: Erlbaum.

Baumeister, R. F., & Leary, M. R. (1995). The need to belong: Desire for interpersonal attachments as a fundamental human motivation. *Psychological Bulletin, 117,* 497–529.

Bedford, V. H., & Volling, B. L. (2004). A dynamic ecological systems perspective on emotion regulation development within the sibling relationship context. In F. R. Lang, & K. L. Fingerman (Eds.), *Growing together: Personal relationships across the lifespan* (pp. 76–102). New York: Cambridge University Press.

Bengtson, V. L., & Kuypers, J. A. (1971). Generational difference and the developmental stake. *Aging & Human Development, 2,* 249–260.

Bengtson, V., Rosenthal, C., & Burton, L. (1995). Paradoxes of families and aging. In R. H. Binstock, & L. K. George (Eds.), *Handbook of aging and the social sciences* (pp. 234–259). New York: Academic Press.

Bengtson, V. L., & Schrader, S. S. (1982). Parent-child relations. In D. J. Mangen & W. A. Peterson (Eds.), *Handbook of research instruments in social gerontology* (Vol. 2, pp. 115–185). Minneapolis, MN: University of Minnesota Press.

Berman, W. H., & Sperling, M. B. (1994). Introduction: The structure and function of adult attachment. In M. B. Sperling & W. H. Berman (Eds.), *Attachment in adults: Clinical and developmental perspectives.* New York: Guilford Press.

Bierhoff, H., & Schmohr, M. (2004). Romantic and marital relationships. In F. R. Lang & K. L. Fingerman (Eds.), *Growing together: Personal relationships across the lifespan.* (pp. 103–129). New York: Cambridge University Press.

Birditt, K. S., & Antonucci, T. C. (2007). Relationship quality profiles and well-being among married adults. *Journal of Family Psychology, 21*(4), 595–604.

Birditt, K. S., Jackey, L. M., & Antonucci, T. C. (2009). Longitudinal patterns of negative relationship quality across adulthood. *Journal of Gerontology: Psychological Sciences, 64B,* 55–64.

Birditt, K. S., Miller, L. M., Fingerman, K. L., & Lefkowitz, E. S. (2009). Tensions in the parent and adult child relationship: Links to solidarity and ambivalence. *Psychology and Aging, 24,* 287–295.

Blanchard-Fields, F., & Cooper, C. (2004). Social cognition and social relationships. In F. R. Lang & K. L. Fingerman (Eds.), *Growing together: Personal relationships across the lifespan* (pp. 268–289). New York: Cambridge University Press.

Blieszner, R. (2006). A lifetime of caring: Dimensions and dynamics in late-life close relationships. *Personal Relationships, 13,* 1–18.

Bowlby, J. (1969/1997). *Attachment and loss: Vol. 1 Attachment.* London: Pimlico/Random House.

Brody, E. M., Litvin, S. J., Albert, S. M., & Hoffman, C. J. (1994). Marital status of daughters and patterns of parent care. *Journal of Gerontology: Social Sciences, 49,* S95–S103.

Cairns, R. B. (1977). Beyond social attachment: The dynamics of interactional development. In T. Alloway, P. Pliner, & L. Krames (Eds.), *Attachment behavior.* New York: Plenum.

Carlson, W., & Rose, A. J. (2007). The role of reciprocity in romantic relationships in middle childhood and early adolescence. *Merrill-Palmer Quarterly, 53,* 262–290.

Carpenter, B. D. (2001). Attachment bonds between adult daughters and their older mothers: Associations with contemporary caregiving. *Journals of Gerontology: Psychological Sciences, 56,* P257–P266.

Carstensen, L. L. (1992). Social and emotional patterns in adulthood: Support for socioemotional selectivity theory. *Psychology and Aging, 7*(3), 331–338.

Carstensen, L. L. (2006). The influence of a sense of time on human development. *Science, 312*(5782), 1913–1915.

Cassidy, J. (1999). The nature of the child's ties. In J. Cassidy & P. R. Shaver (Eds.), *Handbook of attachment: Theory, research, and clinical applications* (pp. 3–20). New York: Guilford Press.

Cassidy, J., & Shaver, P. R. (1999). *Handbook of attachment: Theory, research, and clinical applications.* New York: Guilford Press.

Charles, S. T., & Carstensen, L. L. (2010). Social and emotional aging. *Annual Review of Psychology, 61,* 383–409.

Chen, S., & Andersen, S. M. (2008). The relational self in transference: Intrapersonal and interpersonal consequences in everyday social life. In Wood, J. V., Tesser, A., & Holmes, J. G. (Eds.), *The self and social relationships* (pp. 231–253). New York: Psychology Press.

Clark, M. S. (1984). Record keeping in two types of relationships. *Journal of Personality & Social Psychology, 47,* 589–557.

Cowan, C. P., & Cowan, P. A. (2000). *When partners become parents: The big life change for couples.* Mahwah, NJ: Lawrence Erlbaum Associates Publishers.

Creasey, G., & Ladd, A. (2005). Generalized and specific attachment representations: Unique and interactive roles in predicting conflict behaviors in close relationships. *Personality and Social Psychology Bulletin, 31,* 1026–1038.

Crockett, L. J., & Randall, B. A. (2006). Linking adolescent family and peer relationships to the quality of young adult romantic relationships: The mediating role of conflict tactics. *Journal of Social and Personal Relationships, 23,* 761–780.

Crosnoe, R., & Elder, G. H., Jr. (2002). Life course transitions, the generational stake, and grandparent-grandchild relationships. *Journal of Marriage and Family, 64,* 1089–1096.

Crowell, J. A., Fraley, R. C., & Shaver, P. R. (1999). Measurement of individual differences in adolescent and adult attachment. In J. Cassidy & P. R. Shaver (Eds.), *Handbook of attachment: Theory, research, and clinical applications* (pp. 434–465). New York: Guilford.

Davila, J., Karney, B. R., & Bradbury, T. N. (1999). Attachment change processes in the early years of marriage. *Journal of Personality and Social Psychology, 76,* 783–802.

Dinero, R. E., Conger, R. D., Shaver, P. R., Widaman, K. F., & Larsen-Rife, D. (2008). Influence of family of origin and adult romantic partners on romantic attachment security. *Journal of Family Psychology, 22,* 622–632.

Drew, L. M., & Smith, P. K. (2002). Implications for grandparents when they lose contact with their grandchildren: Divorce, family feud, and geographical separation. *Journal of Mental Health and Aging, 8,* 95–119.

Elder, G. H., Jr. (1998). The life course as developmental theory. *Child Development, 69,* 1–12.

Erber, J. T. (2010). *Aging and older adulthood.* Chichester, UK: Wiley-Blackwell.

Erickson, E. H. (1963). *Childhood and society* (2nd ed.). New York: Norton.

Fagot, B. I., & Kavanagh, K. (1990). The prediction of antisocial behavior from avoidant attachment classification. *Child Development, 61,* 864–873.

Fingerman, K. L. (1995). Aging mothers' and their adult daughters' perceptions of conflict behaviors. *Psychology and Aging, 10,* 639–649.

Fingerman, K. L. (1996). Sources of tension in the aging mother and adult daughter relationship. *Psychology and Aging, 11,* 591–606.

Fingerman, K. L. (1998). Tight lips? Aging mothers' and adult daughters' responses to interpersonal tensions in their relationships. *Personal Relationships, 5,* 121–138.

Fingerman, K. L., Hay, E. L., & Birditt, K. S. (2004). The best of ties, the worst of ties: Close, problematic, and ambivalent social relationships. *Journal of Marriage and Family, 66,* 792–808.

Fingerman, K. L., Miller, L. M., Birditt, K. S., & Zarit, S. (2009). Giving to the good and the needy: Parental support of grown children. *Journal of Marriage and Family, 71,* 1220–1233.

Furman, W. (2002). The emerging field of adolescent romantic relationships. *Current Directions in Psychological Science, 11,* 177–180.

Gewirtz, J. L. (Ed.). (1972). *Attachment and dependency.* New York: Halsted Press.

Giarrusso, R., Feng, D., & Bengtson, V. L. (2005). The intergenerational stake over 20 years. In M. Silverstein (Ed.), *Annual review of gerontology and geriatrics* (pp. 55–76). New York: Springer.

Gjerde, P. F. (2004). Culture, power, and experience: Toward a person-centered cultural psychology. *Human Development, 47,* 138–157.

Gold, D. T. (1996). Continuities and discontinuities in sibling relationships across the life span. In V. L. Bengtson (Ed.), *Adulthood and aging: Research on continuities and discontinuities* (pp. 228–243). New York: Springer.

Goodwin, R., & Pillay, U. (2006). Relationships, culture, and social change. In A. L. Vangelisti & D. Perlman (Eds.), *The Cambridge handbook of personal relationships* (pp. 695–708). New York: Cambridge University Press.

Gottman, J. M. (1994). *What predicts divorce? The relationship between marital processes and marital outcomes.* Hillsdale, NJ: Lawrence Erlbaum Associates.

Grundy, E., & Henretta, J. C. (2006). Between elderly parents and adult children: A new look at the intergenerational care provided by the sandwich generation. *Aging & Society, 26,* 707–722.

Guiaux, M., van Tilburg, T., & van Groenou, M. B. (2007). Changes in contact and support exchange in personal networks after widowhood. *Personal Relationships, 14,* 457–473.

Hagestad, G. O. (1984). The continuous bond: A dynamic multigenerational perspective on parent-child relations between adults. In M. Perlmutter (Ed.), *Parent-child relations in child development. The Minnesota Symposium on Child Psychology* (Vol. 17, pp. 129–158).

Hansson, R. O., Daleiden, E. L., & Hayslip, B., Jr. (2004). Relational competence across the life span. In F. R. Lang & K. L. Fingerman (Eds.), *Growing together: Personal relationships across the lifespan* (pp. 317–340). New York: Cambridge University Press.

Harvey, J. H., & Weber, A. L. (2002). *Odyssey of the heart: Close relationships in the 21st century* (2nd ed.). Mahwah, NJ: Erlbaum.

Harvey, J. H., & Wenzel, A. (2006). Theoretical perspectives in the study of close relationships. In A. L. Vangelisti & D. Perlman (Eds.), *The cambridge handbook of personal relationships* (pp. 35–49). New York: Cambridge University Press.

Hay, E. L., Fingerman, K. L., & Lefkowitz, E. S. (2008). The worries adult children and their parents experience for one another. *International Journal of Aging & Human Development, 67,* 101–127.

Hayslip, B., Jr., & Kaminski, P. L. (2005a). Grandparents raising their grandchildren: A review of the literature and suggestions for practice. *The Gerontologist, 45,* 262–269.

Hayslip, B., Jr., & Kaminski, P. L. (2005b). Grandparents raising their grandchildren. *Marriage & Family Review, 37,* 147–169.

Holmes, J. G. (2002). Interpersonal expectations as the building blocks of social cognition: An interdependence theory perspective. *Personal Relationships, 9,* 1–26.

Holmes, J. G., & Rempel, J. K. (1989). Trust in close relationships. In C. Hendrick (Ed.), *Close relationships* (pp. 187–220). Thousand Oaks, CA: Sage.

Howes, C. (1999). Attachment relationships in the context of multiple caregivers. In J. Cassidy & P. R. Shaver (Eds.), *Handbook of attachment* (pp. 671–687). New York: Guilford.

Impett, E. A., & Peplau, L. A. (2006). "His" and "her" relationships? A review of the empirical evidence. In A. L. Vangelisti & D. Perlman (Eds.), *The Cambridge handbook of personal relationships* (pp. 273–291). New York: Cambridge University Press.

Kagitçibasi, Ç. (1996). The autonomous-relational self: A new synthesis. *European Psychologist, 1*(3), 180–186.

Kagitçibasi, Ç. (2007). *Family, self and human development across cultures: Theory and applications* (2nd ed.). Hillsdale, NJ: Erlbaum.

Kahn, R. L., & Antonucci, T. C. (1980). Convoys over the life course: Attachment, roles, and social support. In P. B. Baltes & O. G. Brim (Eds.), *Life span development and behavior* (Vol. 3, pp. 103–123). New York: Academic Press.

Kelley, D. L. (1999). Relational expectancy fulfillment as an explanatory variable for distinguishing couple types. *Human Communication Research, 25,* 420–442.

Kelley, H. H., Berscheid, E., Christensen, A., Harvey, J. H., Huston, T. L, Levinger, G., et al. (1983). *Close relationships.* New York: Freeman.

Kenrick, D. T., & Trost, M. R. (2004). *Evolutionary approaches to relationships.* Philadelphia: Taylor & Francis.

Kim, J., McHale, S. M., Osgood, D. W., & Crouter, A. C. (2006). Longitudinal course and family correlates of sibling relationships from childhood through adolescence. *Child Development, 77,* 1746–1761.

Kirkpatrick, L. A., & Hazan, C. (1994). Attachment styles and close relationships: A four-year prospective study. *Personal Relationships, 1,* 123–142.

Kramer, L., & Kowal, A. K. (2005). Sibling relationship quality from birth to adolescence: The enduring contributions of friends. *Journal of Family Psychology, 19,* 503–511.

Lamb, M. E., & Malkin, C. M. (1986). The development of social expectations in distress-relief sequences: A longitudinal study. *International Journal of Behavioral Development, 9,* 235–249.

Lang, F. R. (2004). Social motivation across the life span. In F. R. Lang & K. L. Fingerman (Eds.), *Growing together: Personal relationships across the lifespan* (pp. 341–367). New York: Cambridge University Press.

Lang, F. R., & Fingerman, K. L. (Eds.). (2004). *Growing together: Personal relationships across the lifespan.* New York: Cambridge University Press.

Lawrence, E., Rothman, A. D., Cobb, R. J., & Bradbury, T. N. (2010). Marital satisfaction across the transition to parenthood: Three eras of research. In M. S. Schulz, M. K. Pruett, P. K. Kerig, & R. D. Parke, R. D. (Eds.), *Strengthening couple relationships for optimal child development: Lessons from research and intervention. Decade of behavior* (pp. 97–114). Washington, DC: American Psychological Association.

Levitt, M. J. (1980). Contingent feedback, familiarization, and infant affect: How a stranger becomes a friend. *Developmental Psychology, 16,* 425–432.

Levitt, M. J. (1991). Attachment and close relationships: A life span perspective. In Gewirtz, J. L., & Kurtines, W. M. (Eds.), *Intersections with attachment* (pp. 183–206). Hillsdale, NJ: Erlbaum.

Levitt, M. J. (2005). Social relations in childhood and adolescence: The convoy model perspective. *Human Development, 48,* 28–47.

Levitt, M. J. (in press). Social networks. In Mayes, L. C. & Lewis, M. (Eds.), *The Environment of human development: A handbook of theory and measurement.* New York: Cambridge University Press.

Levitt, M. J., & Clark, M. C. (1982, April). *Mother-infant reciprocity, causality, and response to contingent feedback.* Paper presented at the meeting of the International Conference on Infant Studies, Austin, TX.

Levitt, M. J., Coffman, S., Guacci-Franco, N., & Loveless, S. C. (1994). Attachment relations and life transitions: An expectancy model. In Sperling, M. B. & Berman, W. H. (Eds.), *Attachment in adults: Clinical and developmental perspectives* (pp. 232–255). New York: Guilford.

Levitt, M. J., Guacci, N., & Coffman, S. (1993). Social networks in infancy: An observational study. *Merrill-Palmer Quarterly, 39,* 233–251.

Levitt, M. J., Guacci-Franco, N., & Levitt, J. L. (1993). Convoys of social support in childhood and early adolescence: Structure and function. *Developmental Psychology, 29,* 811–818.

Levitt, M. J., Guacci, N., & Weber, R. A. (1992). Intergenerational support, relationship quality, and well-being: A bicultural analysis. *Journal of Family Issues, 13,* 465–481.

Levitt, M. J., Silver, M. E., & Franco, N. (1996). Troublesome relationships: A part of human experience. *Journal of Social and Personal Relationships, 13,* 523–536.

Levitt, M. J., Silver, M. E., Lane, J. D., Pierre, F., & Perez, E. (2005, February). *The dynamics of intergenerational relationship change in emerging adulthood.* Paper presented at the Emerging Adulthood Conference, Miami.

Levitt, M. J., Silver, M. E., & Santos, J. D. (2007). Adolescents in transition to adulthood: Parental support, relationship satisfaction, and post-transition adjustment. *Journal of Adult Development, 14,* 53–63.

Levitt, M. J., Weber, R. A., & Guacci, N. (1993). Convoys of social support: An intergenerational analysis. *Psychology and Aging, 8,* 323–326.

Lewis, M. (2005). The child and its family: The social network model. *Human Development, 48,* 8–27.

Lewis, M., Alessandri, S. M., & Sullivan, M. W. (1990). Violation of expectancy, loss of control, and anger expressions in young infants. *Developmental Psychology, 26,* 745–751.

Lewis, M., & Goldberg, S. (1969). Perceptual-cognitive development in infancy: A generalized expectancy model as a function of the mother-infant interaction. *Merrill-Palmer Quarterly, 15,* 81–100.

Lickliter, R. (2008). Theories of attachment: The long and winding road to an integrative developmental science. *Integrative Psychological and Behavioral Science, 42,* 397–405.

Luescher, K., & Pillemer, K. (1998). Intergenerational ambivalence: A new approach to the study of parent-child relations in later life. *Journal of Marriage & the Family, 60,* 413–425.

Magai, C., Consedine, N. S., Gillespie, M., O'Neal, C., & Vilker, R. (2004). The differential roles of early emotion socialization and adult attachment in adult emotional experience: Testing a mediator hypothesis. *Attachment & Human Development, 6,* 389–417.

Magnusson, D. (1997). The logic and implications of a person-oriented approach. In R. B. Cairns, L. R. Bergman, & J. Kagan (Eds.), *Methods and models for studying the individual.* Thousand Oaks, CA: Sage.

Main, M. (1999). Epilogue. Attachment theory: Eighteen points with suggestions for future studies. In J. Cassidy & P. R. Shaver (Eds.), *Handbook of attachment* (pp. 845–888). New York: Guilford.

Mayseless, O., & Scharf, M. (2007). Adolescents' attachment representations and their capacity for intimacy in close relationships. *Journal of Research on Adolescence, 17,* 23–50.

McNulty, J. K., & Karney, B. R. (2002). Expectancy confirmation in appraisals of marital interactions. *Personality and Social Psychology Bulletin, 28,* 764–775.

McNulty, J. K., & Karney, B. R. (2004). Positive expectations in the early years of marriage: Should couples expect the best or brace for the worst? *Journal of Personality and Social Psychology, 86*, 729–743.

Mikulincer, M., & Shaver, P. R. (2005). Attachment theory and emotions in close relationships: Exploring the attachment-related dynamics of emotional reactions to relational events. *Personal Relationships, 12*, 149–168.

Milevsky, A. (2005). Compensatory patterns of sibling support in emerging adulthood: Variations in loneliness, self-esteem, depression and life satisfaction. *Journal of Social and Personal Relationships, 22*, 743–755.

Milevsky, A. M., & Levitt, M. J. (2005). Sibling support in early adolescence: Buffering and compensation across relationships. *European Journal of Developmental Psychology, 2*, 299–320.

Milevsky, A., Smoot, K., Leh, M., & Ruppe, A. (2005). Familial and contextual variables and the nature of sibling relationships in emerging adulthood. *Marriage & Family Review, 37*(4), 123–141.

Modry-Mandell, K. L., Gamble, W. C., & Taylor, A. R. (2007). Family emotional climate and sibling relationship quality: Influences on behavioral problems and adaptation in preschool-aged children. *Journal of Child and Family Studies, 16*, 61–73.

Mueller, M. M., Wilhelm, B., & Elder, G. H., Jr. (2002). Variations in grandparenting. *Research on Aging, 24*, 360–388.

Noack, P., & Buhl, H. M. (2004). Child-parent relationships. In F. R. Lang & K. L. Fingerman (Eds.), *Growing together: Personal relationships across the lifespan* (pp. 45–75). New York: Cambridge University Press.

Noller, P., & Feeney, J. A. (Eds.). (2006). *Close relationships: Functions, forms and processes.* Hove, England: Psychology Press/Taylor & Francis.

Parrott, T. M., & Bengtson, V. L. (1999). The effects of earlier intergenerational affection, normative expectations, and family conflict on contemporary exchanges of help and support. *Research on Aging, 21*, 73–105.

Patterson, G. R. (1986). Performance models for antisocial boys. *American Psychologist, 41*, 432–444.

Pillemer, K., & Suitor, J. J. (2002). Explaining mothers' ambivalence toward their adult children. *Journal of Marriage and Family, 64*, 602–613.

Pillemer, K., Suitor, J. J., Mock, S. E., Sabir, M., Pardo, T. B., & Sechrist, J. (2007). Capturing the complexity of intergenerational relations: Exploring ambivalence within later-life families. *Journal of Social Issues, 63*, 775–791.

Pipp, S., Shaver, P., Jennings, S., Lamborn, S., & Fischer, K. (1985). Adolescents' theories about the development of their relationships with parents. *Journal of Personality and Social Psychology, 48*, 991–1001.

Rossi, A. S., & Rossi, P. H. (1990). *Of human bonding: Parent-child relations across the life course.* New York: Aldine.

Rothbard, J. C., & Shaver, P. R. (1994). Continuity of attachment across the life span. In M. B. Sperling & W. H. Berman (Eds.), *Attachment in adults: Clinical and developmental perspectives* (pp. 31–71). New York: Guilford.

Rovee-Collier, C., & Gekowski, M. J. (1979). The economics of infancy: A review of conjugate reinforcement. In H. W. Reese & L. P. Lipsitt (Eds.), *Advances in child development and behavior* (Vol. 13, pp. 195–258). New York: Academic Press.

Rovee-Collier, C., Griesler, P. C., & Earley, L. A. (1985). Contextual determinants of retrieval in three-month-old infants. *Learning and Motivation, 16*, 139–157.

Rusbult, C. E., & Van Lange, P. A. M. (2003). Interdependence, interaction and relationships. *Annual Review of Psychology, 54*, 351–375.

Santos, J. D., & Levitt, M. J. (2007). Intergenerational relations with in-laws in the context of the social convoy: Theoretical and practical implications. *Journal of Social Issues, 63*, 827–843.

Seiffge-Krenke, I., Shulman, S., & Klessinger, N. (2001). Adolescent precursors of romantic relationships in young adulthood. *Journal of Social and Personal Relationships, 18*, 327–346.

Shaver, P. R., Furman, W., & Buhrmester, D. (1985). Transition to college: Network changes, social skills, and loneliness. In S. Duck & D. Perlman (Eds.), *Understanding personal relationships* (pp. 193–219). London: Sage.

Shaver, P. R., & Mikulincer, M. (2006). Attachment theory, individual psychodynamics, and relationship functioning. In A. L. Vangelisti & D. Perlman (Eds.), *The Cambridge handbook of personal relationships* (pp. 251–271). New York: Cambridge University Press.

Silverstein, M., & Bengtson, V. L. (1997). Intergenerational solidarity and the structure of adult child-parent relationships in American families. *American Journal of Sociology, 103*, 429–460.

Simpson, J. A., Collins, W. A., Tran, S., & Haydon, K. C. (2007). Attachment and the experience and expression of emotions in romantic relationships: A developmental perspective. *Journal of Personality and Social Psychology, 92,* 355–367.

Simpson, J. A., Winterheld, H. A., & Chen, J. Y. (2006). Personality and relationships: A temperament perspective. In A. L. Vangelisti & D. Perlman (Eds.), *The Cambridge handbook of personal relationships* (pp. 231–250). New York: Cambridge University Press.

Smetana, J. G., Metzger, A., & Campione-Barr, N. (2004). African American late adolescents' relationships with parents: Developmental transitions and longitudinal patterns. *Child Development, 75,* 932–947.

Smith, E. R., & Zarate, M. A. (1992). Exemplar-based model of social judgment. *Psychological Review, 99,* 3–21.

Stanton-Salazar, R. D. (2001). *Manufacturing hope and despair: The school and kin support networks of U.S.-Mexican youth.* New York: Teachers College Press.

Story, T. N., Berg, C. A., Smith, T., Beveridge, R., Henry, N. A., & Pearce, G. (2007). Positive sentiment bias in middle and older married couples. *Psychology and Aging, 22,* 719–727.

Takahashi, K. (1990). Affective relationships and their lifelong development. In P. B. Baltes, D. L. Featherman, & R. M. Lerner (Eds.), *Life-span development and behavior* (Vol. 10, pp. 1–27). Hillsdale, NJ: Erlbaum.

Takahashi, K. (2004). Close relationships across the life span: Toward a theory of relationship types. In F. R. Lang & K. L. Fingerman (Eds.), *Growing together: Personal relationships across the lifespan* (pp. 130–158). New York: Cambridge University Press.

Takahashi, K. (2005). Toward a life span theory of close relationships: The Affective Relationships Model. *Human Development, 48,* 48–66.

Takahashi, K., Ohara, N., Antonucci, T. C., & Akiyama, H. (2002). Commonalities and differences in close relationships among the Americans and Japanese: A comparison by the individualism/collectivism concept. *International Journal of Behavioral Development, 26,* 453–465.

Tronick, E. Z. (1989). Emotions and emotional communication in infants. *American Psychologist, 44,* 112–119.

Underwood, M. K. (2007). Girlfriends and boyfriends diverging in middle childhood and coming together in romantic relationships. *Merrill-Palmer Quarterly.Special Issue: Gender and Friendships, 53,* 520–526.

van IJzendoorn, M. H., & Sagi, A. (1999). Cross-cultural patterns of attachment: Universal and contextual dimensions. In J. Cassidy & P. R. Shaver (Eds.), *Handbook of attachment: Theory, research, and clinical applications* (pp. 713–734). New York: Guilford.

van IJzendoorn, M. H., Sagi, A., & Lambermon, M. W. E. (1992). The multiple caretaker paradox: Data from Holland and Israel. In R. C. Pianta (Ed.), *New directions for child development: No. 57. Beyond the parent: The role of other adults in children's lives* (pp. 5–24). San Francisco: Jossey-Bass.

Vangelisti, A. L., & Perlman, D. (Eds.). (2006). *The Cambridge handbook of personal relationships.* New York: Cambridge University Press.

Waldinger, R. J., Vaillant, G. E., & Orav, E. J. (2007). Childhood sibling relationships as a predictor of major depression in adulthood: A 30-year prospective study. *The American Journal of Psychiatry, 164,* 949–954.

Watson, J. S. (1972). Smiling, cooing, and "the game." *Merrill-Palmer Quarterly, 18,* 323–341.

Weiss, R. S. (2006). *Trying to understand close relationships.* Mahwah, NJ: Erlbaum.

Weisz, J. R. (1986). Contingency and control beliefs as predictors of psychotherapy outcomes among children and adolescents. *Journal of Consulting and Clinical Psychology, 54,* 789–795.

White, L. (2001). Sibling relationships over the life course: A panel analysis. *Journal of Marriage & the Family, 63,* 555–568.

Yeung, G. T. Y., & Fung, H. H. (2007). Social support and life satisfaction among Hong Kong Chinese older adults: Family first? *European Journal of Ageing, 4,* 219–227.

Zahn-Waxler, C., Radke-Yarrow, M., Wagner, E., & Chapman, M. (1992). Development of concern for others. *Developmental Psychology, 28,* 126–136.

Zajonc, R. B. (1968). Attitudinal effects of mere exposure. *Journal of Personality and Social Psychology, 9,* 1–27.

INFORMAL TIES ACROSS THE LIFE SPAN: PEERS, CONSEQUENTIAL STRANGERS, AND PEOPLE WE ENCOUNTER IN DAILY LIFE

19

Karen L. Fingerman, B. Bradford Brown, and Rosemary Blieszner

In the early 21st century, an important paper in *Science* presented a methodological innovation to illustrate how psychologists can effectively measure use of time in the United States (Kahneman, Krueger Schkade, Schwartz, & Stone, 2004). The data revealed a finding the authors neglected to highlight, however—U.S. adults spend more time interacting with coworkers, clients, and bosses, than they do with their spouses, children, or other relatives. This pattern is even more evident in research focusing on adolescence; U.S. adolescents spend 30% of their waking hours with peers (Hartup & Stevens, 1997). Even a majority of preschoolers in the United States spend their weekdays with unrelated caregivers, often in group settings with peers (U.S. Department of Education, 2008). Thus, U.S. citizens of all ages spend the majority of their time and energy with social partners normally considered outside the domain of "close ties."

The importance of close relationships has been well documented in developmental theory addressing childhood and adolescence (Bowlby, 1969; Erikson, 1950; Posada & Lu, Chapter 4). Moreover, epidemiological studies document the impact of close ties for health and well-being in adulthood (Berkman, Glass, Brissette, & Seeman, 2000). Close relationships are universal and essential for survival. As such, many repertoires in close ties (i.e., attachment behaviors, sexual intimacy) appear to be innate.

Humans harbor innate capacities that may facilitate interactions with non-intimate social partners as well. Other primates establish relationships in small groups via one-on-one grooming (Dunbar, 1992, 2001), but human language permits communication in the absence of grooming and allows dissemination of information among nonintimates (Christiansen & Kirby, 2003; Pinker, 2004). Indeed, human cognitive abilities to communicate regulations and to devise organizational structures permit the formation of large social groups. Thus, humans are able to establish ties with a wide array of social partners. Nonetheless, such ties do not manifest species-wide behavioral patterns characteristic of close ties (i.e., attachment). Indeed, cultures vary considerably in the balance of time, energy, and functions favored for close family ties versus weaker, nonintimate ties.

In the United States, population density, the structure of work, and advances in communication technology have facilitated a broad array of connections for individuals of all ages. This chapter addresses the wide array of social partners who fall outside the realm of close and intimate partners discussed elsewhere in this volume (e.g., Antonucci, Ajrouch, & Birditt, 2006; Levitt & Cici-Gokaltun, Chapter 18; Posada

& Lu, Chapter 4). We articulate differences and similarities in informal peer ties or peripheral relationships in childhood, adolescence, and adulthood. The following section demonstrates how the definition of weak ties varies at different stages of life. In the "The Functions of Peripheral Ties" section, we lay out perspectives regarding the functions of peripheral ties or peer relationships throughout life. In sections "Peer Ties in Childhood and Adolescence" and "Peripheral Ties in Adulthood and Old Age" we detail information on weak ties in childhood and adolescence and in adulthood and old age, respectively. We close the chapter with recommendations for future research on these understudied relationships.

▥ DEFINITIONS OF NONINTIMATE TIES IN CHILDHOOD AND ADULTHOOD

We focus on social partners people encounter in daily life, but who are not close. People send cards to former neighbors at the holidays, they interact with classmates or clients during the day, run into friends of friends at the local pool, spend time online connecting to an array of like-minded individuals who share their political views, engage in conversation with their barbers, take yoga classes or join little league teams, and grow irritated when a neighbor throws loud parties.

A variety of terms apply to relationships that are not intimate. Social network scholars refer to "core" and "peripheral" relationships. Hundreds of studies have examined "weak ties" (Granovetter, 1973). Researchers have distinguished between "primary" and "secondary" ties (Weiss, 1974; Wireman, 1984). Developmentalists who study childhood and adolescence refer to informal peer relationships. Elsewhere, Fingerman coined the term "consequential strangers" (Fingerman, 2004, 2009) and other researchers have described "sociability in the public realm" (Lofland, 1995). In everyday parlance, people simply use the word "acquaintances." For ease of presentation, we use the terms *weak* or *peripheral* ties to describe these relationships.

In particular, this chapter addresses peripheral relationships outside the family. This is not to say that all family ties are close ties, but rather, the literature across the life span focuses on weak or peer ties outside the family. Moreover, research in early life addresses friendship to a greater extent than weaker peer ties. The delineation of friendship versus weak or peer tie may be ambiguous throughout life, however. To deal with this matter, in the classic paper defining weak ties, Granovetter (1973) stated, "It is sufficient for the present purpose if most of us can agree, on a rough intuitive basis, whether a given tie is strong, weak, or absent" (p. 1361). The subjective delineation of weak and close ties may be further confounded as relationships develop. During formation of close relationships, people often begin with a phase of acquaintanceship (Blieszner & Roberto, 2004). Likewise, amicable dissolution of an intimate relationship may engender formation of a weak one. In sum, definitions of weak ties may be unsatisfying for scholars who prefer precision in terminology and constructs.

Nonetheless, several factors do distinguish close ties from more peripheral ones. In comparison to close ties, weak ties lack strong emotional bonds and stability, are less likely to be part of an insular group, and are more susceptible to status hierarchies (as in school cliques or paid work settings). People are typically committed to, and invested in, their closest ties; these relationships are difficult to replace and tend to remain fairly stable (Marsiglio & Scanzoni, 1995). By contrast, longitudinal studies suggest weak ties are likely to vary over time (Morgan, Neal, & Carder, 1996; Suitor & Keeton, 1997). At any given time, children and adults alike typically have a mix of close, intimate ties and weaker peripheral ties (Hogan, Carrasco, & Wellman, 2007), but the peripheral partners are more likely to change over time.

The nature of weak ties also may vary across the life span. Weak ties may evolve quickly into close ties in childhood; friendships are more easily formed in early life than in adulthood. Moreover, the structure of adolescent peer relationships involves friendships embedded within both cliques and still larger crowds (Brown, 2004). In other words, in adolescence, close ties serve as structural units that bind groups of peripheral ties. Thus, the boundary between close and weak ties (or between peers and friendships) may be fluid in childhood and adolescence (see Bukowski, Parker, & Rubin, 2006). In adulthood, likewise, some weak ties eventually become closer ties, but many social partners remain weak ties, disconnected from closer ones. And in late life, ties that were once close may drift to the periphery. Just as the existence and perceptions of these ties vary across age groups, so too do their functions.

THE FUNCTIONS OF PERIPHERAL TIES

To examine the implications of weak ties, we might consider how these ties are positioned in the social network. The convoy model applies to an understanding of close and weak ties across the life span (Antonucci, Birditt, & Ajrouch, Chapter 7; Kahn & Antonucci, 1980). The model articulates the web and flow of relationships over time by conceiving of the social network as sets of relationships organized from most intimate to least intimate and acknowledging that the degree of intimacy of given relationships might change across the years. The heuristic device used for assessing varying levels of intimacy is a series of concentric circles around the focal person in the center. Studies examining the convoy model have revealed that by age 13, individuals can hierarchically classify their close social partners on the basis of intimacy (Fingerman, Hay, & Birditt, 2004). As an extension of this model, we consider relationship partners who are even less intimate in a more distal outermost circle. Such ties might include a barista who fixes a repeat customer's nonfat latte with extra vanilla syrup each day, children who ride the same school bus (but do not play together), a coworker's sister about whose illness one hears, toddlers who dump sand on one another at the playground, friends of friends on a social networking site, high school students sharing the same lunch period, or the podiatrist who trims an older adult's toe nails. Metaphorically, close relationships are at the center of vision, and peripheral relationships lie in the blurred edges.

Although researchers have elaborated the functions of close ties for individual development, they have given much less consideration to weak ties. Ecological theory expounds that relationships in one milieu affect relationships in another milieu (Bronfenbrenner & Morris, 2006). As such, peripheral relationships affect close relationships and vice versa. Children's relationships with their parents influence their relationships with their peers, their caregivers, and teachers (Bukowski et al., 2006). Literature on work and family describes reciprocal processes between intimate and nonintimate ties in adulthood; workers may return home distressed and withdrawn following unpleasant interactions with coworkers (Repetti, Wang, & Saxbe, 2009). An individual's weaker social partners interact with more intimate partners and vice versa. The effects of different types of ties are more than additive; a synergy of close and peripheral ties constitutes social experience. Although we recognize that peripheral ties affect, interact with, and overlap with close ties, in this chapter, we focus on distinct functions of peripheral ties throughout life. These distinct functions fall under three broader themes: (1) novelty and stimulation, (2) familiarity and stability, and (3) a driving force for developmental outcomes and well-being.

Broadly speaking, weak ties provide novelty, stimulation, and information not available in closer ties. Close social partners often know the same people, share similar backgrounds and values, and have been exposed to similar ideas (Fingerman, 2009). By contrast, peripheral partners may provide connections to distinct social milieus, to new behavioral repertoires, and to wherewithal not available from intimates. Most research on peripheral ties or peer ties has focused on this broad rubric of functions. For middle-class children, peripheral ties provide references to activities such as a gymnastics class for toddlers or an unfamiliar video game in middle childhood. For lower socioeconomic status (SES) families, peripheral ties might provide access to better schools, libraries, and opportunities not available in the immediate milieu (Jarrett, 1999). In young and middle adulthood, weak ties are clearly important for securing employment (Brown & Konrad, 2001; Granovetter, 1973).

Research drawing on the premise that peripheral ties present opportunities for new information has focused on distinct topics at different points in the life span. Related to the function of novelty, studies examining childhood and adolescents suggest peer relationships provide children an opportunity for self-definition, status, and knowledge of their position in social hierarchies not available from parents or family ties (Brown & Larson, 2009; Dodge, 1983). Socioemotional selectivity theory addresses functions of close and peripheral ties in adulthood (Carstensen, Isaacowitz, & Charles, 1999; Charles & Luong, Chapter 21). This theory suggests that motivation to interact with peripheral or close social partners varies as a function of time perspective and goals. Goals for seeking information are most salient when individuals have an open time horizon, as in young adulthood; young adults are motivated to form connections with peripheral partners who can provide novel ideas. By contrast, when individuals have a foreshortened time perspective (as in late life), they wish to spend time with their closest, most emotionally rewarding social partners. Adults may be more inclined to spend time with close partners with increasing age, but nonetheless, peripheral ties remain present in late life. Older adults still need information if they move to a retirement community (Charles & Piazza, 2007; Shippee, 2009) or develop health problems. Thus, as we will discuss, throughout life, peripheral ties are a source of novel information.

Although much developmental theory addresses novel functions peripheral ties may serve, such ties also may ground individuals with a sense of stability. Research on social ties in the public realm suggests that these ties offer a sense of familiarity in unfamiliar territory, as when individuals share adjoining seats at sports events for a season or see one another in a specific setting on a daily basis (Morrill, Snow, & White, 2005). This aspect of peripheral ties has received less attention from a life-span perspective, but tangential evidence supports this premise. Young children clearly benefit from having consistent caregivers in daycare settings (Vandell & Wolfe, 2000). The larger peer network may confer social status, popularity, or a sense of belonging not available from family or dyadic friendships in adolescence

(LaFontana & Cillessen, 2002). In young adulthood, a long commute may be marked by a greeting from the same toll collector each morning. Older adults with disabilities may develop meaningful bonds with paid service providers who assist them (Piercy, 2007).

Research and theory regarding these two overarching themes—novelty and stability—enhance understanding of peripheral relationships across the life span. Different functions have received attention at different stages of life. A common theme in the life span literature suggests that peripheral ties contribute to individual outcomes. The child and adolescence literature focuses on developmental outcomes at a subsequent point in time, whereas the adult development literature typically focuses on psychological or physical well-being (concurrently or at a subsequent point in time).

In childhood, researchers have emphasized the need to acquire social skills and identity in the context of social ties with peers. In adulthood, close ties buffer against detrimental effects of loneliness and serve key social support functions (Antonucci, 2001), but nonintimates further enhance well-being. Studies suggest that social networks containing a mix of different types of relationships—close ones (romantic partner, parent, child) and peripheral ties (coworkers, community organization comembers)—are associated with better well-being (for a review, see Cohen, 2009).

In the remainder of this chapter, we focus on distinct functions nonintimate ties may serve at each stage of the life span. Peer relationships or weak ties may have particular salience and import at different stages of life. Given the bifurcation of the developmental literature and the social world, we consider childhood and adolescence first and then separately address stages of adulthood. Functions that are well-investigated at one stage of life, such as development of self and identity in adolescence, may also occur at other stages of life, but have not necessarily received the same attention from researchers. For example, researchers who study adult relationships have not explicitly examined self and identify functions of peripheral ties, but adults do maintain peripheral ties that enhance distinct aspects of their identity such as hobbies or professional ties (Thoits, 2003). Nonetheless, our review focuses on topics that have received research attention at each stage, beginning with social bonds in infancy through adolescence.

■ PEER TIES IN CHILDHOOD AND ADOLESCENCE

Research examining children's interactions with peers has clearly documented the role of these ties in catalyzing development. Children's developmental stage and predispositions affect the nature of their peer relationships as well. In other words, qualities of children's peer relationships are necessarily constrained by their own cognitive and emotional limitations, but may serve to foster growth in these areas. We address these reciprocal processes from infancy to adolescence.

We discuss novel adults with regard to infancy, but focus primarily on age-peers after that period (as opposed to children's relationships with nonintimate adults such as teachers, coaches, or friends' parents). Throughout childhood and adolescence, children's peers achieve increased prominence in their lives. Whereas the family and close caregivers are the locus of attention in infancy, by late adolescence, youth in the United States manifest considerable interest in friends and peers and devote considerable leisure time to them. The two key questions are (1) At what stage of development are children able to differentiate between close ties (i.e., friendships) and weaker ties? (2) What functions do weak ties serve for young people?

Infancy and Preschool Years

Early cognitive and social abilities permit babies to make distinctions between intimate and nonintimate social contacts prior to the end of the first year. By the 9th month of life, babies react differently to close social partners and strangers by manifesting anxiety with strangers (Mangelsdorf, Shapiro, & Marzolf, 1995). Decades ago, Spitze (1945) observed that infants and very young children fare best when they have a parent (i.e., consistent primary caregiver) in the hospital rather than a succession of nurses or peripheral adults. Infants show clear preferences for their primary caregivers.

Yet, when babies have a stable attachment figure, they may benefit from exposure to less familiar children and adults. For example, high-quality extrafamilial childcare may help children with temperamental tendencies toward inhibition (i.e., fearfulness of novelty) overcome this inhibition (Fox, Henderson, Rubin, Calkins, & Schmidt, 2001). Furthermore, anthropological studies have found that in cultures where babies have frequent exposure to extrafamilial adults, they show greater comfort with nonintimate adults than do babies in cultures that rarely expose children to extrafamilial adults (Briggs, 1970; Tronick, Moreli, & Winn, 1987). Encountering peripheral partners (in the presence of a stable caregiver) may help suppress neophobic responses; babies learn to accept novelty and new people. Nonetheless, it is not clear whether babies conceptualize a hierarchy of social partners. Rather, infants may simply distinguish their primary close ties from others.

During the toddler years, sociability encompasses a wide array of behaviors, including negative and aggressive acts (Williams, Ontai, & Mastergeorge, 2007). Moreover, accumulating evidence suggests toddlers' ability to display appropriate social behaviors with peers (i.e., social competence) is associated with more adept social behavior in the future, whereas poor social behaviors in the toddler yeas are associated with externalizing problems later in childhood (Bukowski et al., 2006; Howes & Phillipsen, 1998; Rubin, Burgess, & Hastings, 2002).

By the time children are in preschool, they evidence clear differentiations between friends and less intimate other children. Friendships involve free choice between children, a degree of reciprocity, and affection. Preschoolers demonstrate supportive behaviors and exclusiveness in their friendships (Sebane, 2003). The ability to differentiate friendships is associated with an increasing diversification in behaviors toward nonfriend peers. Preschool children regulate behavior differently with children whom they do not consider to be friends than they do with their friends. For example, in laboratory settings, preschoolers work hard to find equitable outcomes in situations where they play with many other children without structure from adults. But when dyads comprising young friends play together, they show greater competition and contention (Berndt, Hawkins, & Hoyle, 1986; Hartup, French, Laursen, Johnston, & Ogawa, 1993; Laursen & Collins, 1994).

In sum, in infancy, babies differentiate between strangers and people who care about them. Throughout the preschool years, children increasingly differentiate more and less intimate partners. Manifestations of social skills with peers in the very early years appear to predict subsequent social behaviors in later childhood. Nonetheless, the distinct purposes of weak ties may be limited in scope. Young children can gain similar skills in play and social expertise with friends or siblings as well as with less intimate peers (Goncu, Patt, & Kouba, 2002; Howe, Petrakos, Rinaldi, & LeFebvre, 2004). Exposure to nonfriend peers may facilitate acceptance of novel situations or social partners, however, particularly for children who generally show predispositions toward fearfulness (Fox et al., 2001). In well functioning social milieu, children come to view family members and friends as predictable. Nonintimates, in contrast, provide novelty and unexpected behavioral repertoires. Moreover, negotiating relationships in groups of young children may serve as a precursor to subsequent hierarchies of peer groups that emerge more clearly by adolescence.

Middle Childhood

In early life, contact with peers is necessarily constrained by parental predispositions, socioeconomic position, schedules, and the like (Blieszner & Roberto, 2004). Preschool children cannot seek out play partners on their own. By middle childhood, children in industrialized nations attend school and have some latitude in their selection of social partners. Granted, parents remain a determinant in children's exposure to different types of peer settings; SES and neighborhood set a backdrop for school and extracurricular activities and hence, the types of peers children encounter (Chen, Howard, & Brooks-Gunn, Chapter 31). Parental decisions also may enhance or detract from free time they spend with peers. Nonetheless, in middle childhood, children have the capacity to develop close friendships based on emerging cognitive and emotional developmental gains. Moreover, social organizations involve peer groups, beyond dyadic friendships, and these groups of nonintimates and intimates exert influence on children. Through the 1990s, research focused on the degree to which children were accepted or rejected by the broader group of peers, and more specifically on classifications as popular, rejected, neglected, controversial, or average (Rubin, Bukowski, & Parker, 1998). The influence of weak ties in middle childhood may partially reflect this degree of acceptance children experience in peer groups and in the values peer groups hold.

Research literature going back over half a century has recognized the important role of close friendships in middle childhood. Harry Stack Sullivan (1953) articulated the role of the "chum" or best friendships in children's lives by age 8–10. Likewise, more recent longitudinal research has shown that isolation in first and second grade are associated with internalizing and externalizing symptoms later in development (Laursen, Bukowski, Aunola, & Nurmi, 2007).

With this increased interest in close friendship comes an increasing ability to differentiate peers hierarchically, akin to social convoys of adulthood. The larger peer group, composed of dyadic friends and an outer circle of peers, conveys status and mores for behaviors. Friendships and acceptance are not orthogonal; children who score lower on acceptance via sociometric measures typically have poorer quality friendships than children who score higher on acceptance (Parker & Asher, 1993). Moreover, children who score lower on acceptance may manifest bossiness and negative behaviors in their friendships (Lansford et al., 2006), suggesting that in middle childhood, individual social competence influences qualities of relationships at a dyadic level (in friendships) and at a global diffuse level of the peer group.

Moreover, children interact with other children based on ideas about status, and these interactions may accumulate into beliefs about the self over time; evidence suggests that children who achieve a status as particularly popular or rejected at one point in time will show effects of this status into puberty and even adulthood (Dodge, 1983; Kupersmidt & Coie, 1990; Parker & Asher, 1987). Longitudinal research examining children from kindergarten through fifth grade also reveals that children who suffer rejection or abuse from the larger peer group demonstrate poor school performance and school avoidance (Buhs, Ladd, & Herald, 2006). Of course, persistence in patterns of rejection or popularity and implications of peer acceptance could reflect stable traits within the child, such as a sour demeanor or an easygoing manner, or could reflect the ability to form dyadic friendships.

Studies suggest that peer groups exert influences on development beyond those observed from dyadic friendships, however. For example, groups of peers tend to share similar motivation for academic performance and peer groups appear to socialize children's and young adolescents' achievement in school (Ryan, 2001).

The peer relationships literature in childhood has increasingly focused on individual differences and negative interactions (Bukowski et al., 2006). Thus, recent research on children's peer relationships has documented the effects of being a bully or a victim of bullying. The occurrence of victimization and bullying has been linked to attributes of individual children; children who become either bullies or victims show elevated aggressive tendencies, and victims also manifest social deficits (Camodeca, Goossens, Terwogt, & Schuengel, 2002). Moreover, recent research suggests some children are popular *and* aggressive, suggesting multiple dimensions to social status in childhood (Estell, Farmer, Pearl, Van Acker, & Rodkin, 2008). Likewise, mutual antipathies are evident in middle childhood. An 8-year-old might aptly label partners in such relationships "enemies" (as opposed to "friends"; Abecassis, 2003). It is not clear whether these ties should be classified as peripheral relationships, or whether a distinct category is warranted reflecting the repeated patterns and potentially strong negative impact of these aversive relationships. As we will discuss, these relationships have analogues to peripheral ties in adulthood. When adults list relationships they find purely negative or aversive, they typically list weak ties such as those with coworkers, bosses, neighbors, or other parents (Fingerman et al., 2004). In childhood, these aversive relationships have overt expression and recognition not evident in adulthood.

In sum, research examining peer relationships in middle childhood substantiates the role of peer groups outside of intimate and close friendships. Children of these ages have the capacity to establish close ties and to recognize less close ones. Group structures emerge by middle childhood, and children vary in their experiences of acceptance or rejections by the wider peer group. Research has shown that peer groups also exert influences via shared norms, at least with regard to school achievement.

Adolescence

Most skills and roles peak at some point in adulthood, either in young adulthood (e.g., physical ability, reaction time, working memory), midlife (e.g., generativity, income), or late life (e.g., emotion regulation). For peer relationships, however, adolescence may serve as the apogee, as a function of both developmental imperatives and societal structures that provide opportunities for extended interactions with peers (Brown & Larson, 2009). As young people move into adolescence, peer relationships become more extensive as well as intensive. Over the course of this life stage, individuals spend increasing time with peers and decreasing time with parents and family members (Larson & Richards, 1991). The structure of peer relations grows more elaborate, with individuals learning to navigate dyadic relationships with friends and romantic partners, friendship cliques, and reputation-based crowds (Brown & Larson, 2009). A corresponding shift in intimacy occurs, so that by middle adolescence young people tend to be closer to friends than to parents, and by late adolescence romantic partners supplant friends as an individual's closest relationships (Sharabany, 2000).

The centrality of peer relations in adolescence has prompted most investigators to focus on intimate ties. The literature on friendships is especially extensive, and many other studies have concentrated on romantic affiliations. A smaller cadre of researchers, mostly ethnographers, has examined the dynamics within friendship cliques, but hardly any intentional study of nonintimate peer ties exists. Nevertheless, several strands of research do speak to the importance of nonintimate peer relationships during adolescence.

Part of the elaboration of the peer system in adolescence is the emergence of a status structure. More so than in childhood, adolescents are sensitive to differences in peers' popularity rankings, and the term "popularity" is imbued with different meaning than it had in earlier years. In childhood, popularity refers to how widely liked one is, but in adolescence it measures one's status or degree of influence over peers (Cillessen & Rose, 2005). Curiously, the most popular adolescents are not among the best liked peers, in part because of the relatively high degree of aggression they display toward others (Cillessen & Mayeux, 2004). This aggression changes over the course of adolescence from physical to verbal (comments that belittle others or undermine their peer relationships), and such aggression is often employed to improve or maintain one's status position among peers. The connection between popularity and aggression inspires two forms of nonintimate peer ties that individuals must negotiate during adolescence.

One form captures interactions between two individuals who vary substantially in levels of popularity. Often regarded as bully–victim relationships, they involve one individual verbally or physically aggressing against the other. Investigations of these relationships tend to focus on personality or family background characteristics that make someone a bully or victim (Olweus, 1993). A more fruitful line of inquiry would consider the function of these relationships in the peer social system (Bishop, Bishop, & Bishop, 2003). Often, it appears as if adolescents berate someone of lower status to affirm or enhance their own popularity and to illustrate to associates the costs of not conforming to general peer norms. Merten (1996b), for example, described how a small set of middle school boys, labeled "melvins" by their peers, were teased or physically threatened not only by popular peers but also by classmates who either wanted to gain acceptance by popular youth or at least avoid the negative attention of those youth.

A second form of aggression-inspired nonintimate tie demonstrates that status dynamics can even affect relationships within a popular clique. Normally, adolescents form moderately to very close ties with clique mates, but members of popular friendship groups must constantly be vigilant against threats to their status within the group and the possibility of expulsion from the clique (Adler & Adler, 1995; Finders, 1997; Wiseman, 2002). All group members are viewed as competitors for group status, willing to renounce a friendship or use information obtained through intimate exchanges against the friend if it enhances the person's own status. Thus, intragroup friendships in popular cliques tend to remain guarded and superficial.

Nonintimate peer relationships in adolescence are also influenced by principles of intergroup dynamics. Young people's inclination to become estranged from members of outgroups is well established (e.g., Sherif, Harvey, White, Hood, & Sherif, 1961). In adolescence, however, groups do not form simply on the basis of convenience (e.g., belonging to the same athletic team) or propinquity, as they did in childhood (Rubin, Bukowski, & Parker, 2006). Friendship groups tend to coalesce among individuals with the same or similar crowd affiliations (Brown, Mory, & Kinney, 1994). Crowds reflect different levels of peer status as well as different prototypic identities (Milner, 2004; Kinney, 1993). Because peer status and personal identity are so salient to adolescents, individuals have a vested interest in protecting the reputation of their own group in comparison to other groups, especially if the outgroups espouse a markedly different identity or lifestyle. Stone and Brown (1998) found that adolescents espoused more negative opinions of other crowds than their own crowd, and more negative opinions of crowds that they considered to be very different from their own group than crowds regarded as similar to their group. Navigating the hallways of a school can involve anything from avoiding eye contact or conversation with outcrowd members to avoiding sections of the school where the other group's members hang out (Deyhle, 1986; Eckert, 1989). It is almost as important for adolescents to learn how to interact with nonintimate peers who are members of outgroups (especially if they are rivals for status or project a radically different identity from their own group) as to master more intimate relationships with peers in their own clique or crowd.

The crowd structure and popularity system are instrumental in determining which of one's peers will remain nonintimate associates. Many adolescents face strong pressure from within their own group not to associate with others who are from a rival crowd or who are notably less popular (Eder, 1985; Kinney, 1993). This may also affect the types of extracurricular activities that adolescents pursue, as certain crowds gravitate to, or control, certain extracurricular activities. Merten (1996a) described the strain in social relationships that occurred when a middle school student from the "burnout" crowd somehow was selected for the cheerleading squad, which was normally controlled by popular group members. In many schools, ethnicity is a basis for crowd formation, impeding opportunities for intimate relationships to form across ethnic lines. Crowd dynamics can reinforce patterns of ethnic and racial discrimination (Brown, Herman, Hamm, & Heck, 2008; Foley, 1990). In some cases, however, adolescents will consciously use the crowd structure to avoid forming intimate relationships with peers. Bešić and Kerr (2009) described how socially inhibited youth sometimes adopt a crowd image (e.g., goth, punk) that they know will discourage peers from approaching them so as to avoid the awkwardness they experience in peer social situations.

Young people's concern with status and group affiliation tend to diminish across adolescence (Kinney, 1993), so that by the later years of high school the barriers to forming friendships or romantic relationships across group lines have dissipated. The reasons for these changes are not clear, but they allow adolescents to pursue relationships with peers who previously had been considered too different to become intimate associates. The change also diminishes the impact of nonintimate associates on adolescents' daily activities.

In addition to effects of developmental stage on peripheral relationships in adolescence, contextual differences also influence weak ties. Some communities feature a much stronger status hierarchy and more differentiated peer group system than others (Garner, Bootcheck, Lorr, & Rauch, 2006); the normative dynamics of nonintimate ties that we describe are not experienced by all adolescents.

Face-to-face interactions still dominate adolescent social relationships, but they are being heavily supplemented by Internet-based interactions. Initial studies of adolescents' Internet use focused on instant messaging and involvement in chat rooms. Adults were concerned that Internet modalities of interaction would diminish adolescents' social skills in face-to-face relationships and expose them to sexual predators or other dangerous adults (Kraut et al., 1998). They also worried about the pseudointimacy characteristic of chat room encounters, in which relative strangers known only by their electronic nicknames would become privy to intimate exchanges of information. Nevertheless, the relative anonymity of Internet chat rooms provided adolescents with a new way to explore their identity: projecting an image to nonintimate associates in chat rooms and gauging their reactions before attempting to display the image among one's real-life peers (Subrahmanyam, Greenfield, & Tynes, 2004).

More recently, however, adolescents' involvement in instant messaging and chat rooms has diminished dramatically, replaced by widespread participation in social networking sites such as MySpace or Facebook (Lenhart & Madden, 2007). These sites offer users more control over the people with whom they interact and share information via the Internet. At the same time, they have spawned a new type of nonintimate tie in adolescence, the "Facebook friend." On several social networking sites someone can gain access to a user's profile only if the user declares that person to be a "friend." Yet, the dynamics of popularity have invaded the electronic world, as it is important for adolescents to have sufficient numbers of friends (usually, in the hundreds) to avoid appearing uncool or nerdish. Moreover, most adolescents consider it rather offensive not to respond positively to someone's request to become a friend, or to "defriend" anyone who had been added to one's friend list.

Adolescents tend to accumulate far more Facebook friends than they could possibly maintain intimate ties with in face-to-face interactions, and these friends may be granted access to much more personal information about the adolescent (the contents of the person's Facebook Web page) than they could hope to obtain in everyday encounters (Lenhart & Madden, 2007). In altering the level of information that nonintimate peers have about someone, social networking sites are achieving one of their primary objectives. The original intent of Facebook was to provide a mechanism for students on large university campuses to locate and communicate with each other. Students in these environments often use Facebook as a means of discerning whether a nonintimate peer (a person one meets in class or at a party) has the potential to become a close friend or romantic partner (Yang & Brown, 2009). However, social networking sites have also become effective mechanisms for "cyber-bullying" and disseminating information that can seriously damage someone else's social reputation (Hinduja & Patchin, 2007). Thus, the intergroup rivalries or hostilities existing among nonintimate ties in face-to-face interactions can be seriously magnified through electronic interactions.

In sum, although not as important as the close ties that adolescents form with friends, lovers, and family members, nonintimate relationships are a very significant component of adolescents' social lives. They are instrumental in asserting an individual's group affiliations and social status. They can affect choices of extracurricular pursuits. They may even determine what portions of a school or neighborhood an individual traverses or scrupulously avoids. In many respects, the intensity of adolescents' relationships with intimate associates is replicated in their relationships with nonintimate peers.

Although developmental theory would predict that experiences with weak (or even intimate) ties in adolescence would set the stage for such relationships in adulthood, relatively little research has tracked the effects of earlier social network experiences on adult and old age relationships. Hence, our summary of peripheral ties in adulthood and old age focuses on research investigating those relationships from a more stage-based than developmental conceptual perspective.

▦ PERIPHERAL TIES IN ADULTHOOD AND OLD AGE

The adult development literature deals more explicitly with the notion of weak or peripheral ties than the child or adolescent developmental literature does. Studies have primarily focused on the placement of such ties in the social network and the functions they may serve. Few investigators have examined individual differences at the heart of research in child development, and studies examining reciprocal nominations or group acceptance are absent. Observational approaches are rarely used in the adult development literature outside of studies of marital ties (Story et al., 2007); thus findings regarding interactions between nonintimate adults also are sparse or nonexistent. As such, the notions of social status, popularity, or group norms are not well articulated with regard to the adult social world. Moreover, some of these concepts may not apply to adult development. For example, the concept of "popularity" does not apply to adulthood (many a "nerd" from adolescence has gained widespread acclaim in adulthood as Bill Gates and many workers in the Silicon Valley computing industry can attest).

Instead, the adult development literature has addressed peripheral ties with regard to social network structures and the functions weak ties serve. Several distinct literatures address such functions, including research pertaining to Socioemotional Selectivity Theory, social integration, and sociological constructs including weak ties and network structures (Carstensen et al., 1999; Wenger, 1997).

The adult development literature has clearly articulated the function peripheral ties serve in providing information or novelty. Granovetter's (1973) seminal paper coining the term "weak ties" documented the function of acquaintances in finding jobs. At the time, nepotism and close ties were presumed to carry cachet and resources, but it turned out that people who were farther removed from one's innermost network had access to different social connections and different pockets of information. Because peripheral partners typically do not share the high density of family ties (where everyone knows everyone else), Granovetter argued these persons can serve as bridges to new social partners and provide information leading to new jobs. In the decades since Granovetter published his paper, thousands of studies have confirmed that weak ties diffuse access to information. Many of these studies focused on employment (e.g., Brown & Konrad, 2001), but others covered such diverse topics as taste in music (Lopez-Sintas, Garcia-Alvarez, & Filimon, 2008), political refugees (van Liempt & Doomernik, 2006), and measles prevention in Nepal (Dugger, 2006).

In some situations, rather than merely treating peripheral ties as a source of contacts for job searches or hobbies, adults experience a "stranger on the train" phenomenon and treat strangers as relative intimates at least temporarily for purposes of self-disclosure (Rubin, 1976). This phenomenon is increasingly common online, where people reveal personal information to others whom they barely know (Suler, 2004).

Thus, in some circumstances, peripheral ties may serve functions traditionally associated with intimate ties. Nonetheless, despite such potential overlap in functions, research examining distinct functions of peripheral ties versus intimate ties suggests adults do strongly differentiate among these bonds and derive different benefits from each type.

Research also has documented psychological and physical health benefits of having a mixture of close and peripheral ties. The key characteristic is *variety* in types of partners, not total number of social partners. To illustrate, studies have linked network diversity and well-being across settings. Sörensen et al. (2007) found that ties to family, friends, and groups were associated with increased consumption of fruits and vegetables in an intervention study. Cohen and Lemay (2007) established that lower network variety was associated with more drinking and smoking. Moreover, cultures vary in the emphasis they place on family life, but weak ties appear to enhance close ties for older adults across cultures. Studies from the United States, Israel, and Hong Kong found that older adults who interact with family, friends, and peripheral ties report better physical and psychological well-being and live longer than older adults with less diverse networks comprising only family members (Cheng, Coty, Chan, Fung, & Lee, 2008; Fiori, Antonucci, & Cortina, 2006; Litwin & Laundau, 2000; Litwin & Shiovitz-Ezra, 2006; Wenger, 1997). Thus, networks including weak ties as well as relatives and friends may provide distinct benefits for well-being in late life.

More recent studies of social networks also have looked at links between people in groups. These analyses suggest behaviors and emotions can spread from person to person, such that peripheral social partners may affect adults' health and well-being. For example, research has demonstrated the spread of numerous behaviors and outcomes, including obesity, to peripheral network members (i.e., a friend's friend's friend; Christakis & Fowler, 2007, 2009). The key limitation of these studies, however, is uncertainty about the mechanisms underlying dissemination of behaviors. It is not clear how peripheral ties might exert influences across social networks in adulthood, and this issue warrants greater attention before one can conclude that the observed effects truly do reflect the influence of peripheral ties rather than a shared third factor.

Other researchers have delineated distinct functions that close ties and peripheral ties might serve in adulthood. Over 30 years ago, Weiss (1974) observed that members of Parents Without Partners formed strong friendships, but still missed their spouses. Couples with warm marital ties who had recently moved to a new area missed their friends. He posited that people possess six distinct social needs: intimacy, opportunities to nurture others, confirmation of self-worth, confidence that others will help in times of need, guidance and advice, and a sense of belonging to groups with whom one shares interests and activities. Social partners vary in the functions they fulfill. A grandchild does not provide the confidante role of friendship, and peripheral ties cannot fill needs of intimacy (Russell, Cutrona, Jayne, & Yurko, 1984; Mancini & Blieszner, 1992). Based on this division of functions, peripheral ties are most likely to serve the latter functions, contributing a sense of belonging to salient groups and providing guidance and advice. Weiss's (1974) ideas are compelling, but he did not address developmental changes in partners or relationships. Interest in, and need for, different types of relationships vary across stages of adulthood, and the ebb and flow of interactions in relationships produces changes such that some peripheral ties become intimate over time, whereas some intimate ties may become more peripheral (Antonucci, 2001; Blieszner & Adams, 1998; Fingerman, 2009).

Indeed, the perspectives reviewed thus far with regard to adulthood are adevelopmental in nature and do not address variability in functions that peripheral ties may serve across adulthood. Keeping in mind literature documenting common functions of peripheral ties in adulthood (i.e., spread of information, group belonging, shared activities), we turn next to consider peripheral ties in young adulthood, midlife, and old age.

Young Adulthood

From a developmental perspective, Socioemotional Selectivity Theory suggests younger and older adults may differ in their motivation to pursue contact with persons representing peripheral ties (Charles & Carstensen, 2010). Motivation for interactions with acquaintances are greatest in early adulthood; by late life, individuals selectively cull their social networks to those intimate social partners whom they find most emotionally rewarding (Carstensen et al., 1999). One mechanism underlying differential motivation to pursue peripheral ties is future time perspective. In early life, when the future is open, people have the luxury of time and energy to engage in numerous peripheral ties. When people face a foreshortened time perspective (as in the face of a life-threatening illness or in old age), they wish to spend time with people who are most emotionally rewarding—close friends and family. Because the adult development literature often focuses on late life as an end point, most of the research examining Socioemotional Selectivity Theory has focused on the narrowing of the social network to close relationships when time is curtailed (e.g., Charles & Piazza, 2007; Fung & Carstensen, 2006). Few studies based on this perspective have actually documented the link between acquaintanceship and information seeking in young adulthood, although the sociological literature regarding weak ties suggests that such an association is present.

Although class differences in peripheral ties are evident at all phases of life, completion of education and entrance into the work world make these differences particularly stark in young adulthood. The type of job or career that adults enter influences the types of peripheral ties they encounter. In young adulthood, peripheral liaisons may be both an outcome and an underlying cause of socioeconomic disparities. For example, young adults from higher socioeconomic backgrounds use peripheral ties to secure high-paying jobs that perpetuate their access to powerful peripheral partners

(Wegener, 1991). This is not to say that individuals living in impoverished circum-stances cannot access outside resources via peripheral ties, however. For example, Jarrett (1999) described how poor young African American mothers rely on strong family relationships but also foster peripheral ties to secure tangible and nontangible assets for their children. By connecting to people outside their immediate milieu, women acquire access to resources such as scouting troops, libraries, and private schools for their children. Still, well-off young adults are likely to have greater access to resource-laden ties.

Class differences also may be evident in the negative repercussions of some peripheral partners in young adulthood. As mentioned previously, when adults were asked to list people who annoyed or irritated them, they disproportionately listed peripheral partners. Moreover, young adults reported the greatest number of these types of social partners (Fingerman et al., 2004). Indeed, many studies document the adverse consequences of poor relationships in the work place. For example, low-paid health care aides experience elevated blood pressure on days when they work for unfavorable supervisors compared to days when they work for favorable supervi-sors (Wager, Fieldman, & Hussey, 2003). Although middle-aged and even older adults occupy low wage jobs, young adults are particularly likely to be in low status jobs. Thus, despite the resources peripheral partners may offer, they can also be a source of distress.

Furthermore, peripheral ties also contribute to finding romantic partners and mates. Evolutionary psychologists argue that humans are programmed to establish family ties to perpetuate their gene pool; intimate ties serve important functions in the survival of the species. Humans also must establish relationships outside their immediate gene pool to procreate successfully, and thus, nonintimate ties also may serve important functions in the survival of our species (Fingerman, 2009). Although it is possible to mate with a good friend, acquaintances provide a wider range of potential liaisons for human procreation than intimate ties do.

In sum, in young adulthood, the peripheral network can provide opportunities and resources that establish the place of individuals in the larger society. Scholars have suggested that certain transitions, such as becoming a parent, induce individu-als away from peers and their activities to focus more on the nuclear family (Noller, Feeney, & Peterson, 2001). As individuals accumulate increasing responsibilities through romantic partnership and parenthood, the nature of their peripheral arena may shift toward that found in midlife.

Midlife

Midlife covers a broad age range with few shared developmental markers. Middle age is often defined as beginning around age 40 and ending when adults retire around age 65, but subjective definitions encompass a wider age range (Lachman, 2001) and expressions such as "70 is the new 50" have emerged recently in lay par-lance, suggesting a shift in perception of middle (and old) age. Midlife may be a period of peak social engagement, but much of the focus of social interest at mid-life is with family (Antonucci & Akiyama, 1987; Fingerman & Birditt, 2003). Indeed, by middle adulthood, demands of childrearing and other responsibilities may limit attention devoted to close friendships (Blieszner & Roberto, 2004), but midlife adults typically interact with peripheral partners in a variety of settings based on their jobs, marital status, familial contexts (e.g., via their children's activities or interactions with health care providers for their aging parents), civic engagement, and leisure pursuits.

Given the variety of social contacts individuals encounter at midlife, we speculate that peripheral ties serve many functions. Scholars have argued that secondary (or peripheral) ties provide distinct functions of belongingness and offer opportunities to pursue novel diversions (Weiss, 1974; Wireman, 1984), in addition to providing numerous types of useful information. In midlife, as in earlier stages of life, peripheral ties may contribute to individuals' perceptions of their own social status. In the United States, midlife can be a period of peak accomplishment and success; peripheral ties may confer a sense of respect absent in late life when individuals are more likely to experience ageism. Such ties also may reinforce middle-aged adults' sense of self-definition that emerged from experimenting with identity formation in adolescence and early adulthood (Dunphy, 1969). In midlife, then, peripheral partners may be associated with the multiple roles individuals balance (Thoits, 2003), and may provide a sense of identity coherence and stability.

Late Life

The literature on late-life relationships presents two competing ideas regarding the role of peripheral ties. As mentioned previously, research on social integration finds that older adults who have diverse networks including family ties and community members report better emotional well-being and health than those with a narrower range of network members (Fiori et al., 2006; Litwin & Shiovitz-Ezra, 2006; Wenger, 1997). Moreover, recent findings pertaining to community involvement find that volunteer activities, typically involving contacts with persons representing weak ties, are associated with increased longevity and well-being (Greenfield & Marks, 2004). By contrast, research pertaining to Socioemotional Selectivity Theory suggests older adults harbor less motivation to interact with peripheral partners and benefit emotionally from focusing primarily on their close and intimate social partners (Carstensen, 2006).

It is difficult to reconcile these findings with regard to peripheral ties. An obvious explanation would be that individuals who experience health declines in late life retract from the social world into family ties or loneliness. Such withdrawal would account for findings that network diversity is associated with better health, suggesting that the causal mechanism is changing health, not a change in preference for peripheral ties. But researchers who have investigated network diversity over time have controlled for initial health status and still found that engagement with community, church, volunteerism, and neighbors is associated with better long-term health outcomes. These findings might reflect differences in methodologies. Research examining Socioemotional Selectivity Theory has primarily assessed people's preferences for those with whom they would want to spend time (e.g., a close social partner vs. acquaintance; Carstensen, Isaacowitz, & Charles, 1999), or counted the number of peripheral ties in their subjectively defined social support networks (Lang & Carstensen, 2002). By contrast, the social integration literature specifically asks participants if they have interacted with different types of social partners during a recent time period, often as short as 2 weeks. Thus, it could be that the salience and meaning of close ties does increase for most people as they grow closer to the end of life, but contact with peripheral partners may provide cognitive stimulation, physical activity, and other emotional benefits that late-life adults prefer to sustain as long as possible.

As cognitive and physical changes occur in late life, older adults almost inevitably acquire a new source of peripheral ties that is usually less prevalent in the earlier years: more frequent contact with health care providers and persons supplying aid with household chores and personal needs. Although many family members perform these tasks and services, older adults also come to rely on the expertise offered by numerous professionals as well as the assistance of informal helpers such as church, community, and neighborhood volunteers. Persons comprising these peripheral ties provide a range of services from highly skilled medical assessments and interventions to transportation and help with meals, shopping, and housework to the most intimate of personal care with bathing and grooming. Piercy's research (2000, 2001, 2007) on relationships between families and hired "sitters" for their elderly relatives shows that the older adults, the other family members, and the workers themselves often view the relationships that result from ongoing involvement together as family-like bonds. The sitters still lead separate lives apart from their work time, but growing these peripheral ties into a type of close relationship contributes to satisfaction with the arrangement across the board.

Most older adults and their families would rather rely on such informal ties than engage formal services such as agency personnel or nursing home care. This preference was strong in research on a representative sample of almost 500 older adults living in rural Virginia (Blieszner, Roberto, & Singh, 2002). Although those older adults who had more health and functional limitations were more likely than healthier counterparts to be receiving help from multiple relatives and friends, they nevertheless expressed strong preference for a care arrangement based on informal social connections, as compared to help from formal service providers. It appeared that peripheral ties involving informal helpers were distinct from, and preferred to, the possibility of peripheral ties involving formal service providers. Those who received help only from formal sources typically were able to function more independently and paid for help to sustain their environment (e.g., housekeeping, household repairs), not their person. In these cases, their relationships with their helpers reflected the more typical peripheral ties found across most of adulthood.

An important issue that warrants consideration involves the cursory measurement of peripheral contacts in the social integration literature. The simple presence of an interaction with a peripheral partner is presumed to generate beneficial outcomes without additional data regarding the nature or quality of those interactions. Such measurement is crude in comparison to the in-depth multireporter, multimethod approaches used in the child development literature. As such, the findings may be all the more compelling. Researchers have replicated findings regarding the impact of peripheral ties on well-being (Berkman & Syme, 1979; Cheng et al., 2008; Fiori et al., 2006; Litwin & Shiovitz-Ezra, 2006; Wenger, 1997), suggesting that the association is robust and can be found even with the most rudimentary measurement. Notwithstanding these robust findings, as we discuss in the next section, the ways in which peripheral ties affect older adults warrants increased research attention. It is not clear what the presence of peripheral partners indicates or which functions they serve actually enhance well-being.

▦ DIRECTIONS FOR FUTURE RESEARCH ON
WEAK TIES ACROSS THE LIFE SPAN

As a starting point for investigation, scholars might turn attention to better documenting the array of social ties in individuals' lives. Although we argued that weak ties emerge in childhood, researchers have not examined explicitly differentiated weak and close peer ties. In this chapter, we focused on individual child outcomes and conceptualized group perceptions of a child with regard to overall acceptance or rejection. Instead, researchers might ask how peers interact with children whom they do not consider friends, and moreover, the purposes such interactions might serve for each child. The adult developmental literature has provided attention to differentiating close and peripheral social partners, but has done so in a cursory manner. The presence of such ties in networks is often used as an indicator that peripheral ties affect individuals. The adult development literature sorely neglects reciprocal relationships or processes that might explain such findings.

Indeed, throughout this chapter, we have struggled to reconcile nonequivalent social structures throughout childhood and adulthood. It is not possible to discuss weak ties throughout life because researchers have focused on friends and peers in childhood, and to a lesser extent on weak ties in adulthood. The range of peripheral ties children acquire through their activities, neighborhoods, and schools has been largely overlooked. Children have a wide array of weak ties present in their classes, their activities, and via other family members' connections. Likewise, adults are embedded in an array of weak ties accumulated through paid employment, services, community engagement, schedules, and geographic location. In terms of individual development, the juncture between these two types of social worlds rests in young adulthood. Although theorists argue that interest and motivation for peripheral ties peaks in young adulthood (e.g., Charles & Carstensen, 2010), there is scant research attention to the ascendance and subsequent descent of peer relationships during this period of life. Thus, increased attention to social network patterns from late adolescence throughout adulthood is warranted. We might ask when and why individuals turn their attention from a peer group to a more hierarchically organized social world with intimate ties at the center and peripheral ties on the edges. Formation of enduring romantic liaisons may precipitate this shift, but additional empirical data are necessary to elaborate how and why the social milieu shifts (Milardo, Johnson, & Huston, 1983).

Moreover, given the wide array of technologically assisted social interaction media in which young adults now engage (e.g., Twitter, Facebook, iPhone), collection of naturalistic data is much easier than was previously the case. It remains to be seen, however, whether these social networking technologies facilitate long-term differences in network membership as young and middle-aged adults who currently use them grow older. Systematic investigation of the quality and functions of peripheral ties based on social networking technologies and comparison of those bonds with the quality and function of face-to-face interactions would contribute to enhanced understanding of weak ties.

Future research also might address weak ties in the context of family relationships. The literature, and by extension this chapter, has dealt primarily with nonfamilial relationships when considering weak ties. Yet, family ties also range from weak to intimate. Some in-law relationships are not intimate, and following divorce or remarriage, even previously intimate in-law associations may become weak ties. Aunts and uncles may serve a main role as mentors or they may simply play a bit part at annual holiday gatherings (Milardo, 2010). Likewise, ethnic groups vary in the extent to which nonfamily ties are a locus of social interaction. For example, Latino youth tend to concentrate close peer relationships on siblings and cousins in the extended family network; many of these relationships function like friendships among middle-class (dominant culture) youth in the United States. Elderly African American adults may attribute kinship to, and derive care from, associates who are not actual relatives (Barker, 2002).

Another issue of central importance involves the processes through which weak ties may influence individuals. As Brown, Bakken, Ameringer, and Mahon (2008) pointed out with regard to adolescence, much of the research focuses on outcomes of peer influences, rather than on the processes through which these influences occur. This deficit in the literature is even more pronounced with regard to adults' relationships where self-reported interactions with community members or neighbors are used as proxies for social integration. Experience sampling or diary methodologies may be more appropriate for assessing when and how peripheral ties exert influences on adults' mood or well being.

In this chapter, we have focused primarily on U.S. patterns of friendships and peer interactions. We recognize limitations to this approach and do not mean to imply universality in these patterns. Moreover, although the literature pertaining to adult social ties is primarily based in the United States, studies have examined children's and adolescents' relationships cross-nationally in Europe, Asia, the Middle East, and South America (Chen, French, & Schneider, 2006). Cumulative findings suggest cultural variability in relationship patterns that warrant additional consideration, particularly in adulthood. It seems likely that cultural groups that place a strong emphasis on familialism may harbor disadvantages for weak ties, and vice versa.

Nonetheless, in the 21st century, nonfamilial ties may be increasingly important for individuals' well-being and economic security throughout the industrialized world. Larson, Wilson, Brown, Furstenberg, and Verma (2002) indicated that the ability to interact with a wide array of social partners may be the key imperative for adolescents' future success in adulthood in this century. Throughout young adulthood, peripheral ties confer an array of benefits including access to jobs and mates. Studies have replicated findings regarding benefits of network diversity among adults across cultures and cohorts for older adults as well (Berkman & Syme, 1979; Fiori et al., 2006; Litwin & Shiovitz-Ezra, 2006; Wenger, 1997). These findings suggest that at least in industrialized nations, nonfamilial ties offer complementary benefits to intimate ties. Given the vast research literature pertaining to close and intimate ties, it is surprising that researchers have provided so little attention to the array of peripheral ties that pepper development throughout life.

■ REFERENCES

Abecassis, M. (2003). I hate you just the way you are: Exploring the formation, maintenance, and need for enemies. *New Directions for Child and Adolescent Development, 102,* 5–22.

Adler, P. A., & Adler, P. (1995). Dynamics of inclusion and exclusion in preadolescent cliques. *Social Psychology Quarterly, 58,* 145–162.

Antonucci, T. C. (2001). Social relations: An examination of social networks, social support, and sense of control. In J. E. Birren (Ed.), *Handbook of aging and psychology* (pp. 427–453). San Diego, CA: Academic Press.

Antonucci, T. C., & Akiyama, H. (1987). Social networks in adult life and a preliminary examination of the convoy model. *Journal of Gerontology, 42,* 519–527.

Antonucci, T. C., Ajrouch, K. J., & Birditt, K. S. (2006). Social relations in the third age: Assessing strengths and challenges using the convoy model. In J. B. James & P. Wink (Eds.), *The Crown of life: Dynamics of the early post-retirement period. Annual Review of Gerontology and Geriatrics* (Vol. 26, pp. 193–210).

Barker, J. C. (2002). Neighbors, friends, and other nonkin caregivers of community-living dependent elders. *Journal of Gerontology: Social Sciences, 57,* S158–S167.

Berkman, L. F., & Syme, S. L. (1979). Social networks, host resistance, and mortality: A nine year follow-up study of Alameda County residents. *American Journal of Epidemiology, 109,* 186–204.

Berkman, L. F., Glass, T., Brissette, I., & Seeman, T. E. (2000). From social integration to health: Durkheim in the new millennium. *Social Science and Medicine, 51,* 843–857.

Berndt, T. J., Hawkins, J., & Hoyle, S. G. (1986). Development in friendship from childhood to adolescence. *Child Development, 57,* 1007–1015.

Bešić, N., & Kerr, M. (2009). Punks, goths, and other eye-catching peer crowds: Do they fulfill a function for shy youths? *Journal of Research on Adolescence, 19,* 113–121.

Bishop, J. H., Bishop, M., & Bishop, M. M. (2003). *Peer harassment: A weapon in the struggle for popularity and normative hegemony in American secondary schools* (CAHRS Working Paper #03–19). Ithaca, NY: Cornell University, School of Industrial and Labor Relations, Center for Advanced Human Resource Studies.

Blieszner, R., & Adams, R. G. (1998). Problems with friends in old age. *Journal of Aging Studies, 12,* 223–238.

Blieszner, R., & Roberto, K. A. (2004). Friendships across the lifespan: Reciprocity in individual and relationship development. In F. Lang & K. L. Fingerman (Eds.), *Growing together: Personal relationships across the life span* (pp. 159–182). New York: Cambridge University Press.

Blieszner, R., Roberto, K. A., & Singh, K. (2002). The helping networks of rural elders: Demographic and social psychological influences on service use. *Ageing International, 27,* 89–119.

Bowlby, J. (1969). *Attachment and loss* (Vol. 1). New York: Basic Books.

Briggs, J. (1970). *Never in anger: Portrait of an Eskimo family* (pp. 109–146). Cambridge, MA: Harvard University Press.

Bronfenbrenner, U., & Morris, P. A. (2006). The bioecological model of human development. In W. Damon (Ed.), *Handbook of child psychology* (6th ed., pp. 793–825). New York: Wiley.

Brown, B. B. (2004). Adolescents' relationships with peers. In R. M. Lerner & L. Steinberg (Eds.), *Handbook of adolescent psychology* (2nd ed., pp. 363–394). Hoboken, NJ: John Wiley & Sons Inc.

Brown, B. B., Bakken, J. P., Ameringer, S. W., & Mahon, S. D. (2008). A comprehensive conceptualization of the peer influence process in adolescence. In M. J. Prinstein & K. Dodge (Eds.), *Peer influence processes among youth* (pp. 17–44). New York: Guildford Publications.

Brown, B. B., Herman, M., Hamm, J. V., & Heck, D. (2008). Ethnicity and image: Correlates of minority adolescents' affiliation with individual-based versus ethnically defined peer crowds. *Child Development, 79,* 529–546.

Brown, B. B., & Larson, J. (2009). Peer relationships in adolescence. In R. M. Lerner & L. Steinberg (Eds.), *Handbook of adolescent psychology* (3rd ed., pp. 74–103). New York: Wiley.

Brown, B. B., Mory, M., & Kinney, D. A. (1994). Casting adolescent crowds in relational perspective: Caricature, channel, and context. In R. Montemayor, G. R. Adams, & T. P. Gullotta (Eds.), *Advances in adolescent development: Vol. 6. Personal relationships during adolescence* (pp. 123–167). Newbury Park, CA: Sage.

Brown, D. W., & Konrad, A. M. (2001). Granovetter was right: The importance of weak ties to a contemporary job search. *Group & Organization Management, 26,* 434–462.

Buhs, E. S., Ladd, G. W., & Herald, S. L. (2006). Peer exclusion and victimization: Processes that mediate the relation between peer group rejection and children's classroom engagement and achievement? *Journal of Educational Psychology, 98,* 1–13.

Bukowski, W. M., Parker, J. G., Rubin, K. H. (2006). Peer interactions, relationships, and groups. In W. Damon, N. Eisenberg, R. M. Lerner (Eds.), *Handbook of child psychology: Social, emotional, and personality development* (6th ed., pp. 571–645). Hoboken, NJ: John Wiley & Sons Inc.

Camodeca, M., Goossens, F. A., Terwogt, M. M., & Schuengel, C. (2002). Bullying and victimization among school-age children: Stability and links to proactive and reactive aggression. *Social Development, 11,* 332–345.

Carstensen, L. L. (2006). The influence of a sense of time on human development. *Science, 312,* 1913–1915.

Carstensen, L. L., Issacowitz, D. M., & Charles, S. T. (1999). Taking time seriously: A theory of socioemotional selectivity. *American Psychologist, 54,* 165–181.

Charles, S. T., & Carstensen, L. L. (2010). Social and emotional aging. *Annual Review of Psychology, 61,* 383–409.

Charles, S. T., & Piazza, J. R. (2007). Memories of social interactions: Age differences in emotional intensity. *Psychology and Aging, 22,* 300–309.

Chen, X., French, D. C., & Schneider, B. H. (Eds.). (2006). *Peer relationships in cultural context.* New York: Cambridge University Press.

Cheng, S. T., Coty, K. L., Chan, A. C. M., Fung, E. M., & Lee, J-J. (2008, November). Social network typologies of older adults and associations with psychological well-being in Hong Kong. In H. Fung (Chair), *Self and social regulation across adulthood.* Symposium presented at the Annual Scientific Meeting of the Gerontological Society of America, Baltimore, MD.

Christiansen, M. H., & Kirby, S. (2003). Language evolution: Consensus and controversies. *Trends in Cognitive Sciences, 7,* 300–307.

Christikas, N. A., & Fowler, J. H. (2007). The spread of obesity in a large social network over 32 years. *New England Journal of Medicine, 375,* 370–379.

Christikas, N. A., & Fowler, J. H. (2009). *Connected: The surprising power of social networks and how they shape our lives.* New York: Little, Brown and Company.

Cillessen, A. H. N., & Mayeux, L. (2004). From censure to reinforcement: Developmental changes in the association between aggression and social status. *Child Development, 76,* 147–163.

Cillessen, A. H. N., & Rose, A. J. (2005). Understanding popularity in the peer system. *Current Directions in Psychological Science, 14,* 102–105.

Cohen, S. (2009). Can we improve our physical health by altering our social networks? *Perspectives in Psychological Science, 4,* 375–378.

Cohen, S., & Lemay, E. (2007). Why would social networks be linked to affect and health practices? *Health Psychology, 26,* 410–417.

Deyhle, D. (1986). Break dancing and breaking out: Anglos, Utes, Navajos in a border reservation high school. *Anthropology & Education Quarterly, 17,* 111–127.

Dodge, K. A. (1983). Behavioral antecedents of peer social status. *Child Development, 54,* 1386–1399.

Dugger, C. W. (2006, April 30). Mothers of Nepal vanquish a killer of children. *New York Times.* Retrieved August 4, 2009, from http://www.nytimes.com/2006/04/30/world/asia/30measles. html?scp=1&sq=mothers%20of%20nepal%20vanquish&st=cse

Dunbar, R. I. M. (1992). Neocortex size as a constraint on group size in primates. *Journal of Human Evolution, 20,* 469–493.

Dunbar, R. I. M. (2001). Brains on two legs: Group size and the evolution of intelligence. In F. B. de Wall (Ed.), *Tree of origin: What primate behavior can tell us about human social evolution* (pp. 173–191, 311 pp.). Cambridge, MA: Harvard University Press.

Dunphy, D. C. (1969). *Cliques, crowds, and gangs.* Melbourne: Chesire.

Eckert, P. (1989). *Jocks and burnouts: Social categories and identity in the high school.* New York: Teachers College Press.

Eder, D. (1985). The cycle of popularity: Interpersonal relations among female adolescents. *Sociology of Education, 58,* 154–165.

Erikson, E. H. (1950). *Childhood and society.* New York: W. W. Norton & Company.

Estell, D. B., Farmer, T. W., Pearl, R., Van Acker, R., & Rodkin, P. C. (2008). Social status and aggressive and disruptive behavior in girls: Individual, group, and classroom influences. *Journal of School Psychology, 46,* 193–212.

Finders, M. J. (1997). *Just girls: Hidden literacies and life in junior high.* New York: Teachers College Press.

Fingerman, K. L. (2004). The consequential stranger: Peripheral ties across the life span. In F. Lang & K. L. Fingerman (Eds.), *Growing together: Personal relationships across the life span* (pp. 183–209). New York: Cambridge University Press.

Fingerman, K. L. (2009). Consequential strangers and peripheral partners: The importance of unimportant relationships. *Journal of Family Theory and Review, 1,* 69–82.

Fingerman, K. L., & Birditt, K. S. (2003). Do age differences in close and problematic family ties reflect the pool of available relatives? *Journal of Gerontology: Psychological Sciences, 58,* P80–P87.

Fingerman, K. L., Hay, E. L., & Birditt, K. S. (2004). The best of ties, the worst of ties: Close, problematic, and ambivalent social relationships. *Journal of Marriage and Family, 66,* 792–808.

Fiori, K. L., Antonucci, T. C., & Cortina, K. S. (2006). Social network typologies and mental health among older adults. *Journal of Gerontology: Psychological Sciences, 61B*, P25–P32.

Foley, D. E. (1990). *Learning capitalist culture: Deep in the heart of Tejas.* Philadelphia, PA: University of Pennsylvania Press.

Fox, N. A., Henderson, H. A., Rubin, K. H., Calkins, S. D., & Schmidt, L. A. (2001). Continuity and discontinuity of behavioral inhibition and exuberance: Psychophysiological and behavioral influences across the first four years of life. *Child Development, 72*, 1–21.

Fung, H. H., & Carstensen, L. L. (2006). Goals change when life's fragility is primed: Lessons learned from older adults, the September 11 attacks and SARS. *Social Cognition, 24*, 248–278.

Garner, R., Bootcheck, J., Lorr, M., & Rauch, K. (2006). The adolescent society revisited: Cultures, crowds, climates, and status structures in seven secondary schools. *Journal of Youth and Adolescence, 35*, 1023–1035.

Goncu, A., Patt, M. B., & Kouba, E. (2002). Understanding young children's pretend play in context. In P. K. Smith & C. H. Hart (Eds.), *Blackwell handbook of childhood social development* (pp. 418–437). Malden, MA: Blackwell.

Granovetter, M. S. (1973). The strength of weak ties. *American Journal of Sociology, 78*, 1360–1380.

Greenfield, E. A., & Marks, N. F. (2004). Formal volunteering as a protective factor for older adults psychological well-being. *Journal of Gerontology: Social Sciences, 59*, S258–S264.

Hartup, W. W., & Stevens, N. (1997). Friendship and adaptation in the life course. *Psychological Bulletin, 121*, 355–370.

Hartup, W. W., French, D. C., Laursen, B., Johnston, M. K., & Ogawa, J. R. (1993). Conflict and friendship relations in middle childhood: Behavior in a closed-field situation. *Child Development, 64*, 445–454.

Hinduja, S., & Patchin, J. W. (2007). Offline consequences of online victimization: School violence and delinquency. *Journal of School Violence, 6*, 89–112.

Hogan, B., Carrasco, J. A., & Wellman, B. (2007). Visualizing personal networks: Working with participant-aided sociograms. *Field Methods, 19*, 116–144.

Howe, N., Petrakos, H., Rinaldi, C. M., & LeFebvre, R. (2004). "This is a bad dog, you know": Constructing shared meanings during sibling pretend play. *Child Development, 76*, 783–794.

Howes, C., & Phillipsen, L. (1998). Continuity in children's relations with peers. *Social Development, 7*, 340–349.

Jarrett, R. (1999). Successful parenting in high-risk neighborhoods. *The Future of Children, 9*, 45–50.

Kahn, R. L., & Antonucci, T. C. (1980). Convoys over the life course: Attachment, roles, and social support. In P. B. Baltes & O. Brim (Eds.), *Life-span development and behavior* (Vol. 3). New York: Academic Press. Reprinted 1989 in Joep Munnichs & Gwenyth Uildris (Eds.), *Psychogerontologie* (pp. 81–102). Van Loghum Slaterus.

Kahneman, D., Krueger, A. B., Schkade, D. A., Schwartz, N., & Stone, A. A. (2004). A survey method for characterizing daily life experience: The day reconstruction method. *Science, 306*, 1776–1780.

Kinney, D. (1993). From "nerds" to "normals": Adolescent identity recovery within a changing social system. *Sociology of Education, 66*, 21–40.

Kraut, R., Patterson, M., Lundmark, V., Kiesler, S., Mukophadhyay, T., & Scherlis, W. (1998). Internet paradox: A social technology that reduces social involvement and psychological well-being? *American Psychologist, 53*, 1017–1031.

Kupersmidt, J. B., & Coie, J. D. (1990). Preadolescent peer status and aggression as predictors of externalizing problems in adolescence. *Child Development, 61*, 1350–1362.

Lachman, M. E. (Ed.). (2001). *Handbook of midlife development.* New York: Wiley.

LaFontana, K. M., & Cillessen, A. H. N. (2002). Children's perceptions of popular and unpopular peers: A multimethod assessment. *Developmental Psychology, 38*, 635–647.

Lang, F. R., & Carstensen, L. L. (2002). Time counts: Future time perspective, goals and social relationships. *Psychology and Aging, 17*, 125–139.

Lansford, J. E., Putallaz, M., Grimes, C. L., Schiro-Osman, K. A., Kupersmidt, J. B., & Coie, J. D. (2006). Perceptions of friendship quality and observed behaviors with friends: How do sociometrically rejected, average, and popular girls differ? *Merrill Palmer Quarterly, 52*, 694–720.

Larson, R. W., & Richards, M. H. (1991). Daily companionship in late childhood and early adolescence: Changing developmental contexts. *Child Development, 62*, 284–300.

Larson, R. W., Wilson, S., Brown, B. B., Furstenberg, F. F., & Verma, S. (2002). Changes in adolescents' interpersonal experiences: Are they being prepared for adult relationships in the twenty-first century? *Journal of Research on Adolescence, 12,* 31–68.

Laursen, B., Bukowski, W. M., Aunola, K., & Nurmi, J. E. (2007). Friendship moderates prospective associations between social isolation and adjustment problems in young children. *Child Development, 78,* 1395–1404.

Laursen, B., & Collins, W. A. (1994). Interpersonal conflict during adolescence. *Psychological Bulletin, 115,* 197–209.

Lenhart, A., & Madden, M. (2007). *Social networking sites and teens.* Pew Internet Trust. Retrieved from http://www.pewinternet.org/Reports/2007/Social-Networking-Websites-and-Teens.aspx.

Litwin, H., & Laundau, R. (2000). Social network type and social support among the old-old. *Journal of Aging Studies, 14,* 213–228.

Litwin, H., & Shiovitz-Ezra, S. (2006). Network type and mortality risk in later life. *Gerontologist, 46,* 735–743.

Lofland, L. H. (1995). Social interaction: Continuities and complexities in the study of nonintimate sociality. In K. S. Cook, G. A. Fine, & J. S. House (Eds.), *Sociological perspectives on social psychology* (pp. 176–201). Boston: Allyn & Bacon.

Lopez-Sintas, J., Garcia-Alvarez, M. E., & Filimon, N. (2008). Scale and periodicities of recorded music consumption: Reconciling Bourdieu's theory of taste with facts. *The Sociological Review, 56,* 78–101.

Mancini, J. A., & Blieszner, R. (1992). Social provisions in adulthood: Concept and measurement in close relationships. *Journal of Gerontology: Psychological Sciences, 47,* P14–P20.

Mangelsdorf, S. C., Shapiro, J. R., & Marzolf, D. (1995). Developmental and temperamental differences in emotion regulation in infancy. *Child Development, 66,* 1817–1828.

Marsiglio, W., & Scanzoni, W. H. (1995). *Families and friendships: Applying the sociological imagination.* New York: Harper Collins.

Merten, D. E. (1996a). Burnout as cheerleader: The cultural basis for prestige and privilege in junior high school. *Anthropology and Education Quarterly, 27,* 51–70.

Merten, D. E. (1996b). Visibility and vulnerability: Responses to rejection by nonaggressive junior high school boys. *Journal of Early Adolescence, 16,* 5–26.

Milardo, R. M. (2010). *The forgotten kin: Aunts & uncles.* New York: Cambridge University Press.

Milardo, R. M., Johnson, M. P., & Huston, T. L. (1983). Developing close relationships: Changing patterns of interaction between pair members and social networks. *Journal of Personality and Social Psychology, 44,* 964–976.

Milner, M. (2004). *Freaks, geeks, and cool kids: American teenagers, schools, and the culture of consumption.* New York: Routledge.

Morgan, D. L., Neal, M. B., & Carder, P. (1996). The stability of core and peripheral networks over time. *Social Networks, 19,* 9–25.

Morrill, C., Snow, D. A., & White, C. H. (Eds.). (2005). *Together alone: Personal relationships in public places.* Berkeley, CA: University of California Press.

Noller, P., Feeney, J. A., & Peterson, C. (2001). *Personal relationships across the lifespan.* Philadelphia, PA: Taylor and Francis.

Olweus, D. (1993) *Bullying at school: What we know and what we can do.* Oxford: Blackwell

Parker, J. G., & Asher, S. R. (1987). Peer relations and later personal adjustment: Are low-accepted children at risk? *Psychological Bulletin, 102,* 357–389.

Parker, J. G., & Asher, S. (1993). Friendship and friendship quality in middle childhood: Links with peer group acceptance and feelings of loneliness and social dissatisfaction. *Developmental Psychology, 29,* 611–629.

Piercy, K. W. (2000). When it's more than a job: Relationships between home health workers and their older clients. *Journal of Aging and Health, 12,* 362–387.

Piercy, K. W. (2001). "We couldn't do without them!" The value of close relationships between older adults and their nonfamily caregivers. *Generations, 25*(2), 41–47.

Piercy, K. W. (2007). Successful collaborations between formal and informal care providers: Paul and Patrice's story. *Generations, 31*(3), 72–73.

Pinker, S. (2004). Language as an adaptation to the cognitive niche. In D. T. Kenrick & C. L. Luce (Eds.), *The functional mind: Readings in evolutionary psychology* (pp. 139–156). Auckland, New Zealand: Pearson Education.

Repetti, R. L., Wang, S., & Saxbe, D. (2009). Bringing it all back home: How outside stressors shape families' everyday lives. *Current Directions in Psychological Science, 18,* 106–111.

Rubin, K. H., Bukowski, W., & Parker, J. G. (1998). Peer interactions, relationships, and groups. In N. Eisenberg (Ed.), *Handbook of child psychology: Social, emotional, and personality development* (5th ed., pp. 619–700). New York: Wiley.

Rubin, K. H., Bukowski, W. M., & Parker, J. G. (2006). Peer interactions, relationships, and groups. In W. Damon & R. M. Lerner (Series Eds.) & N. Eisenberg (Vol. Ed.), *Handbook of child psychology: Social, emotional, and personality development* (Vol. 3, 6th ed., pp. 571–645). New York: Wiley.

Rubin, K. H., Burgess, K. B., & Hastings, P. D. (2002). Stability and social-behavioral consequences of toddler's inhibited temperament and parenting. *Child Development, 73*, 483–495.

Rubin, Z. (1976). Naturalistic studies of self disclosure. *Personality and Social Psychology Bulletin, 2*, 260–263.

Russell, D., Cutrona, C. E., Jayne, R., & Yurko, K. (1984). Social and emotional loneliness: An examination of Weiss's typology of loneliness. *Journal of Personality and Social Psychology, 46*, 1313–1321.

Ryan, A. M. (2001). The peer group as a context for the development of young adolescent motivation and achievement. *Child Development, 72*, 1135–1150.

Sebane, A. M. (2003). The friendship features of preschool children: Links with proscial behavior and aggression. *Child Development, 12*, 249–268.

Sharabany, R. (2000). Intimacy in preadolescence and adolescence: Issues in linking parents and peers, theory, culture, and findings. In K. A. Kerns, J. M. Contreras, & A. M. Neal-Barnett (Eds.), *Family and peers: Linking two social worlds* (pp. 227–249). Westport, CT: Praeger.

Sherif, M., Harvey, O. J., White, B. J., Hood, W. R., & Sherif, C. W. (1961). *Intergroup conflict and cooperation: The Robbers Cave experiment.* Norman, OK: University Book Exchange.

Shippee, T. P. (2009). "But I am not moving: Transitions in a continuing care retirement community." *The Gerontologist, 49*, 418–427.

Sörensen, G., Stoddard, A. M., Dubowitz, T., Barbeau, E. M., Bigby, J., Emmons, K. M., et al. (2007). The Influence of social context on changes in fruit and vegetable consumption: Results of the health directions study. *American Journal of Public Health, 97*, 1216–1227.

Spitze, R. A. (1945) Hospitalism: An inquiry into the genesis of psychiatric conditioning in early childhood. *Psychoanalytic studies of the child, 1*, 53–74.

Stone, M., & Brown, B. B. (1998). In the eye of the beholder: Adolescents' perceptions of peer crowd stereotypes. In Rolf E. Muuss & Harriet D. Porton (Eds.), *Adolescent behavior and society: A book of readings* (5th ed., pp. 158–169). New York: McGraw-Hill.

Story, T. N., Berg, C. A., Smith, T., Beveridge, R., & Henry, N. A., Pearce, G. (2007). Age, marital satisfaction, and optimism as predictors of positive sentiment override in middle-aged and older married couples. *Psychology and Aging, 22*, 719–727.

Subrahmanyam, K., Greenfield, P. M., & Tynes, B. (2004). Constructing sexuality and identity in an online teen chat room. *Journal of Applied Developmental Psychology, 25*, 651–666.

Suitor, J., & Keeton, S. (1997). Once a friend, always a friend? Effects of homophily on women's support networks across a decade. *Social Networks, 19*, 51–62.

Suler, J. (2004). The online disinhibition effect. *CyberPsychology & Behavior, 7*, 321–326.

Sullivan, H. S. (1953). *The interpersonal theory of psychiatry.* New York: Norton.

Thoits, P. (2003). Personal agency in the accumulation of multiple role-identities. In P. Burke, T. Owens, R. Serpe, & P. Thoits (Eds.), *Advances in identity theory and research* (pp. 179–194). New York: Kluwer Academic/Plenum Publishers.

Tronick, E. Z., Moreli, G. A., & Winn, S. (1987). Multiple caregiving of Efe (Pygmy) infants. *American Anthropologist, 89*, 96–106.

U.S. Department of Education, National Center for Education Statistics. (2008). *Digest of Education Statistics, 2007* (NCES 2008–022). Retrieved July 1, 2009, from http://nces.ed.gov/fastfacts/display.asp?id=4

van Liempt, I., & Doomernik, J. (2006). Migrant's agency in the smuggling process: The perspectives of smuggled migrants in the Netherlands. *International Migration, 44*, 166–191.

Vandell, D. L., & Wolfe, B. (2000). *Child care quality: Does it matter and does it need to be improved?* University of Wisconsin: Report written for Institute for Research on Poverty. Retrieved March 20, 2010, from http://www.ssc.wisc.edu/irpweb/publications/sr/pdfs/sr78.pdf

Wager, N., Fieldman, G., & Hussey, T. (2003). The effect on ambulatory blood pressure of working under favourably and unfavourably perceived supervisors. *Occupational Environmental Medicine, 60*, 468–474.

Wegener, B. (1991). Job mobility and social ties: Social resources, prior job, and status attainment. *American Sociological Review, 56*, 60–71.

Weiss, R. S. (1974). The provisions of social relationships. In Z. Rubin (Ed.), *Doing unto others* (pp. 17–26). Englewood Cliffs, NJ: Prentice-Hall.

Wenger, G. C. (1997). Social networks and the prediction of elderly people at risk. *Aging and Mental Health, 1*, 311–320.

Williams, S. T., Ontai, L. L., & Mastergeorge, A. M. (2007). Reformulating infant and toddler social competence with peers. *Infant Behavior & Development, 30*, 353–365.

Wireman, P. (1984). *Urban neighborhoods, networks, and families.* Lexington, MA: Lexington Books.

Wiseman, R. (2002). *Queen bees and wannabes: Helping your daughter survive cliques, gossip, boyfriends, and other realities of adolescence.* New York: Crown Publishing.

Yang, C.-C., & Brown, B. B. (2009, April). From Facebook to cell calls: Layers of electronic intimacy in college students' peer relations. In B. B. Brown & Patricia M. Greenfield (Chairs), *Electronic connections: Impact of communication media on adolescents' peer relationships.* Symposium presented at the biennial meetings of the Society for Research in Child Development, Denver, CO.

PERSONALITY TRAIT DEVELOPMENT ACROSS THE LIFE SPAN

20

Jennifer Lodi-Smith, Nicholas Turiano, and Dan Mroczek

Ebenezer Scrooge, the hero of Dickens' *A Christmas Carol*, characterizes personality development by going through a series of experiences transforming him from a man who is a "squeezing, wrenching, grasping, scraping, clutching, covetous, old sinner! Hard and sharp as flint, from which no steel had ever struck a generous fire; secret and self-contained, and solitary as an oyster" to become, "as good a friend, as good a man, as the good old city knew." (Dickens, 1843). This archetypal story of personality change is told over and over every holiday season. However, it takes being haunted by four ghosts in one evening for Scrooge's personality to change. So what does this mean for the everyday person? In the pages that follow, we review the (1) patterns of stability and change in personality traits across the life span, (2) the nonghostly mechanisms underlying personality trait stability and change, and (3) the impact that trait stability and change has on physical health. We hope that this chapter will serve as a primer for scientists interested in beginning to use personality trait variables as tools in developmental research as well as a fulcrum for bringing a few new ideas to scientists already familiar with the development of personality traits.

WHAT ARE PERSONALITY TRAITS?

Personality traits are the characteristic thoughts, feelings, and behaviors unique to a given individual. The most prominent of trait theories is the Big Five (Goldberg, 1993) or Five-Factor Model (McCrae & Costa, 2008). The Big Five personality traits describe the five major traits personality psychologists commonly use to characterize individuals. We list each of these traits below along with a list of subtraits or "facets" of each trait as assessed with the NEO-PI-R measure of the Big Five (Costa & McCrae, 1992). From an empirical standpoint, these facets provide a more nuanced assessment of traits. From a pedagogical standpoint, these facets illustrate the ideas captured by each of the traits.

- **Agreeableness**: trust, straightforwardness, altruism, compliance, modesty, and tender-mindedness
- **Conscientiousness**: competence, order, dutifulness, achievement striving, self-discipline, and deliberation
- **Neuroticism** (often referred to in the reverse as emotional stability): anxiety, angry hostility, depression, self-consciousness, impulsiveness, and vulnerability
- **Extraversion**: warmth, gregariousness, assertiveness, activity, excitement seeking, and positive emotions
- **Openness to experience**: fantasy, aesthetics, feelings, actions, ideas, and values

Each of these traits describes a continuum of thoughts, feelings, and behaviors that is generally descriptive of an individual on a daily basis.

It is important to note at this point that personality traits are not the only important component of an individual's personality. Modern theories of personality characterize individual differences on a number of different domains ranging from traits to goals to life story narratives (McAdams & Pals, 2006; McCrae & Costa, 2008; Roberts, Harms, Smith, Wood, & Webb, 2006). Unfortunately, we cannot do justice to the patterns of development within each domain of personality mentioned previously within one broadly reaching chapter. Indeed, the development of each domain could easily be the topic of its own chapter or even its own book (see McAdams, Chapter 23 for a discussion of narratives and personality development). Instead of briefly addressing the development of the many aspects of global personality, we focus on personality traits in this chapter because we feel that a trait approach to personality lends itself to a discussion of personality development over life span for a number of reasons.

First, childhood temperament and adult personality traits are similar in both their philosophical underpinnings and their scientific substance. Theoretical parallels between temperament and traits draw on the similarity of the behavioral and affective components of both. For example, surgency in childhood characterizes a child who has both positive affect and a positive approach to life and is theoretically quite similar to extraversion. An anxious and irritable child is described as distressed, a concept that is clearly linked to low emotional stability and low agreeableness in adulthood. Similarly, children who are focused and controlled are said to demonstrate effortful control which can be seen in adulthood within conscientious individuals (Caspi, Roberts, & Shiner, 2005). Beyond these theoretical parallels lie a few select longitudinal studies that track the transition from childhood temperament to adult traits. As we review in detail in the following section, these studies provide empirical evidence for the continuity of personality traits across the life span.

Second, personality traits are quickly being recognized as robust predictors of important life outcomes from divorce to mortality (Roberts, Kuncel, Shiner, Caspi, & Goldberg, 2007). Indeed, as we discuss at the end of the chapter, it is not just mean levels of personality traits but change in personality traits that is important for understanding life outcomes such as mortality. Because of the increasing recognition of the importance of personality traits to understanding life outcomes, it is critical for scientists in general to begin to understand the patterns and underlying mechanisms of personality trait development across the life span.

Finally, we will focus on a trait approach to examining personality development from a broad perspective as it has both versatility and depth. Many of the patterns and principles discussed in this chapter can be applied to any of the domains of personality. Thus, by providing a background in personality trait development we are actually providing a framework for understanding the development of the individual as a broader whole.

▨ STABILITY AND CHANGE

Before we can address the patterns of personality trait development over the life span we must first address one of the most frequently debated issues regarding personality trait development. Specifically, scientists studying personality trait development have spent a great deal of effort, time, and research resources addressing the extent to which personality traits are stable and/or change over the life span.

Implicit to this debate is the fundamental assumption that personality traits are, indeed, capable of change. This is not to say that personality traits necessarily change, just that the possibility exists that personality traits can change. In addition, this debate assumes that while personality traits are subject to change in response to one concrete and discrete event such as the change experienced by Scrooge, the more typical pattern of personality trait development over the life span is a gradual and normative shift from childhood to adulthood personality. The extent and details of this general development is the heart of the debate about stability and change in personality trait psychology. To understand this debate and come to some preliminary conclusions about this relative nature of personality trait development over the life span, we address two quantitative ideas: rank-order stability and mean-level change.

Rank-order stability is a quantitative measure of the correlation of a trait at one point in time with the same trait measured at a later time point within the same sample of participants. These test–retest correlations capture the extent to which individuals have consistent personality trait scores relative to other individuals in their sample group over time. For example, if Paul was more conscientious than Jeff when they were in high school together and Paul was still more conscientious than Jeff at their 20th reunion, this would be a demonstration of rank-order stability. However, if, at their 20th reunion, Jeff was now the more conscientious of the two, this would be a demonstration of instability. Meta-analytic evidence regarding the nature of rank-order stability suggests that rank-order stability exists but perfect stability is not present across the life span. Test–retest coefficients vary across the life span with coefficients being the lowest in the first few years of life (.35) and increasing in consistency to be moderate in adolescence (.47) and most consistent in the 50s (.75), as illustrated in Figure 20.1. These findings are invariant across trait, gender, and

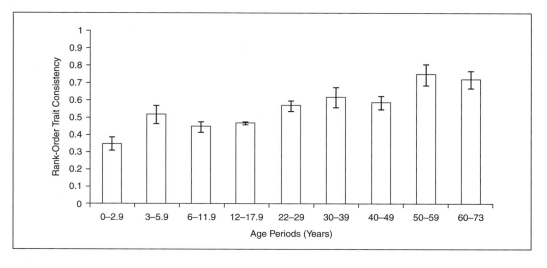

FIGURE 20.1   **Population estimates of rank-order stability across age categories with 95% confidence level estimates.** *Source*: Roberts & DelVecchio, 2000.

method of assessment though, not surprisingly, test–retest coefficients decrease as the interval between assessments increases (Roberts & DelVecchio, 2000).

Mean-level change, on the other hand, is assessed by looking at quantitative net increases or decreases in traits over time. Going back to Paul and Jeff, if both men increased one unit between graduation and their high school reunion, this would demonstrate a normative pattern of mean-level change. However, if Paul increased one unit and Jeff decreased one unit, this would demonstrate a lack of net change over time. A recent meta-analysis of the mean-level patterns of personality development over the life span found that personality traits demonstrate normative patterns of meaningful, mean-level changes throughout adulthood, as shown in Figure 20.2. Specifically, the personality traits of agreeableness, conscientiousness, and the social dominance component of extraversion all increase throughout adulthood and well into old age. Emotional stability shows a similar trajectory until older adulthood when it demonstrates slight declines. Openness to experience, on the other hand, increases through young adulthood into midlife followed by declines during older adulthood. Finally, the social vitality component of extraversion increases through

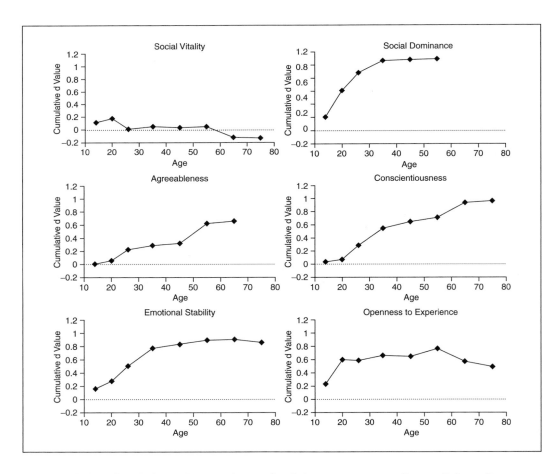

FIGURE 20.2   Population estimates of mean-level change across age. *Source*: Roberts & Mroczek, 2008.

childhood and adolescence, followed by declines during the rest of the life span (Roberts, Walton, & Viechtbauer, 2006).

So which is it? Are personality traits stable over time or do they change? The simple answer to this question is that personality traits are both stable and change. Rank-order stability and mean-level change are not mutually exclusive. If Paul ends high school higher in conscientiousness than Jeff and both men increase one unit on a measure of conscientiousness between the end of high school and their reunion then it is the case that they have demonstrated both stability (Paul is still higher than Jeff) and change (both men have higher scores on the measure of conscientiousness over time). While much more complex than the simple paths of two people over time, this is essentially the story that comes from combining the findings of the two meta-analyses described earlier. Given that these two meta-analyses draw from the same samples of longitudinal data and provide evidence for both stability and change in personality traits the general conclusion is that personality traits can and do change over time but do so in a way that is consistent with the underlying personality of the individual.

Overarching the issues of rank-order and mean-level stability in personality is the concept of individual differences in change. In many ways, the older, simple question of whether personality traits are stable or not has given way to the more subtle and complex perspective that change is an individual difference variable in and of itself. Some people are stable, whereas others are not. This perspective has its origins in the life-span developmental concept of *individual differences in intraindividual change* (Alwin, 1994; Baltes & Nesselroade, 1973; Baltes, Reese & Nesselroade, 1977; Nesselroade, 1988, 1991; Ozer, 1986; Schaie, 1996; Wohlwill, 1973). Over the past 30 years, personality development researchers have rarely focused on individual differences in personality change, focusing instead on aggregate statistical approaches to the question, such as repeated-measures means and correlation coefficients. These approaches have yielded valuable results such as the rank-order stability and mean-level change described earlier.

However, aggregate statistics such as means and correlations do not allow the study of personality stability as an individual differences phenomenon. Rather, they tell if a variable (e.g., a trait or a motive) increases or decreases over time, or if people maintain the same rank-order over time, *in a sample or population*. Repeated-measures means and correlations, as valuable as they are, largely conceal individual differences in stability and change (Aldwin, Spiro, Levenson, & Bossé, 1989; Lamiell, 1981; Mroczek & Spiro, 2003). Do some individuals remain stable and others change? Do some change in one direction, while others change in the opposite direction? Of those who do change, do they change by varying amounts?

Personality psychology is strongly identified with the science of individual differences, yet it is ironic that, until recently, it has largely overlooked the concept of individual differences in stability and change. One major reason why the notion of individual differences in change remained an obscure and mainly theoretical concept for many years was the lack of adequate statistical models to model change well. With the development of such techniques, which include latent growth models as well as the multilevel model for change (McArdle, 1991; Meredith & Tisak, 1990; Muthén & Muthén, 2002; Raudenbush & Bryk, 2001; Rogosa, Brandt, & Zimowski, 1982; Singer & Willett, 2003), investigators have been able to estimate more accurately both overall (sample-level) rates of change as well as individual differences in rate of change. This family of techniques has allowed researchers to confirm that the life-span principle of individual differences in intraindividual change is an empirical fact and no longer a theoretical conjecture with respect to personality traits.

The studies documenting individual differences in rate of change in personality traits are now numerous (Helson, Jones, & Kwan, 2002; Jones, Livson, & Peskin, 2003; Jones & Meredith, 1996; Mroczek & Spiro, 2003; Mroczek, Spiro, & Almeida, 2003; Roberts & Chapman, 2000; Small, Hertzog, Hultsch, & Dixon, 2003). Together, these studies have established that a large number of traits show individual variation in rate of change, including each of the Big Five constructs (Small et al., 2003). Jones et al. (2003) has termed this phenomenon "heterogenous change," meaning that some people change, others do not, and the rate, direction, or pattern of change (e.g., linear, quadratic) varies across people. Put more simply, and as we have argued elsewhere (Mroczek, 2007; Mroczek & Griffin, 2007; Mroczek, Spiro, Almeida, & Pafford, 2006; Mroczek, Spiro & Griffin, 2006;) there is a *range of change.*

So what can we conclude from these findings? Is personality consistent across the life span? Is the Jesuit maxim of "Give me the child until he is seven and I will give you the man" accurate? Or does personality change over time? The short answer to all of these questions is yes. Personality traits demonstrate a substantial level of rank-order consistency while also undergoing normative patterns of mean-level change. People are neither immutable, closed systems nor are they mercurial. Individuals are, themselves, variable in how, when, and why they change over time.

■ LIFE-SPAN DEVELOPMENTAL PATTERNS IN TEMPERAMENT AND TRAITS

Infants and Children

Behavioral differences among infants are apparent from the moment they are born. The earliest scholars to describe temperamental differences between infants (Thomas, Chess, Birch, Hertzig, & Korn, 1963), in addition to providing the now-famous nine-dimension model of temperament (activity level, regularity of behaviors, initial reaction, adaptability, intensity of emotion, mood, distractibility, persistence and attention span, and sensory sensitivity), also stressed the interplay of biological and environmental processes in shaping these features of temperament. This early work on temperament set the foundation for future research on the structure of temperament as well as new questions on the connection between infant temperament and personality in childhood and adulthood. For example, the early nine-dimension model of temperament has more recently been refined into a three-factor higher-order trait structure (surgency, negative affectivity, and effortful control) in infants that more closely resembles the personality structure of older children (Rothbart, Ahadi, Hershey, & Fisher, 2001). Using new instruments, such as the Children's Behavior Questionnaire, work with these three higher-order traits provided convincing evidence that even at young ages of 3, children exhibit traits similar to the Big Five traits measured in adults. However, others remain skeptical of any strong associations between early temperament and later personality (Wachs, McCrae, & Kohnstamm, 2001).

Unfortunately, to date, there is little longitudinal data addressing the link between temperament and personality traits. Researchers who study temperament rarely follow their participants into adolescence or adulthood. Children's families move to other regions or countries and research grants are often not renewed. These and other factors place limits on longitudinal follow-ups often leaving scholars to guess about the extent to which infant and child temperament forms the basis for adolescent and adult personality. However, a couple of notable exceptions in the research provide a picture of the relationship between childhood temperament and adult personality traits.

Longitudinal assessments following over 500 infants into adolescence and beyond (Kagan & Snidman, 2004) found that roughly 20% of infants who showed high reactivity in response to novelty in toys and other unfamiliar stimuli were shy with interviewers and showed biological signs of alarm (emotional reactivity, as it is often referred to in adults) in stressful situations at age 11. At the other end of the continuum, 33% of the calm, easy-going infants grew into composed, sociable preteens or, in the case of some boys, "Clint Eastwood types." In addition, only 7% of the infants who scored on either extreme of reactivity were at the opposite end of reactivity at age 11.

Data from the Dunedin Study, a longitudinal study of over 1,000 children from Dunedin, New Zealand born between 1972 and 1973, provide concrete evidence of the parallels between childhood temperament and adult personality traits. At age 3, the children in the Dunedin Study were clustered into one of five groups: well-adjusted, undercontrolled, confident, reserved, or inhibited. At age 26, these same individuals rated themselves on the personality traits of positive emotionality, negative emotionality, and constraint. The participants who were characterized as well-adjusted at age 3 described themselves as being relatively low on negative emotionality and moderate on both positive emotionality and constraint. As adults, the undercontrolled children, in contrast, described themselves as being high on negative emotionality and somewhat low on positive emotionality and constraint. Confident children later described themselves as being quite high on positive emotionality but low on constraint and moderate on negative emotionality. In contrast, reserved children reported being low on positive emotionality and high on constraint with moderate levels of negative emotionality. Finally, participants who were characterized as inhibited at age 3 reported being quite low on positive emotionality and quite high on negative emotionality and constraint at age 26 (Caspi et al., 2003). Thus, preliminary evidence shows that, in general, early childhood temperament can at least provide a general window into what adult personality will look like.

In addition to specific studies of multiple temperament and trait patterns over time, there is a growing interest in understanding behavioral inhibition (a blend of low extraversion and high fear or anxiety in novel situations) and impulsivity (blend of low conscientiousness and low agreeableness) characteristics in young children. Findings suggest that these two aspects of child temperament predict adult traits (Deal, Halverson, Havill, & Martin, 2005) and children who expressed negative emotionality and fear in experimental settings were less emotionally stable later in life (Putnam, Gartstein, & Rothbart, 2006).

Overall, the data to date suggest that from our earliest days we possess biologically influenced predispositions that, as time passes, change and transform to become adult traits. The ultimate end product often bears some semblance of the early temperamental characteristics, but often does not. For example, while it is impressive that a 45-minute lab observation of 16-week-old infants can inform dispositions 10 years later (Kagan & Snidman, 2004), it would not be prudent to assume that one's early temperament is the sole determinant of later traits. Although 20% of extremely reactive infants turned into extremely reactive adolescents, 80% did not. Although most of these children certainly stayed on the reactive side of the spectrum, some certainly did not. The same is true of the 33% of nonreactive, calm infants who stayed in that extreme: 67% left the extreme and ended up elsewhere along the dimension. Again, most probably stayed on the nonreactive side of the continuum, but clearly there was some change as well. Thus, for some individuals there is a strong positive association between infant temperament, later childhood temperament, and adult personality traits but for others the positive association is less pronounced and for still others there is no association and even, for a very few, a negative relationship between temperament and traits. Understanding when, where, and why consistency is seen over time from childhood to adulthood is an important direction for future research in the field.

Young Adulthood

Young adulthood is a time of increasing consistency in personality traits over time as test–retest correlations are higher in 30-somethings as compared to 20-somethings (.62 vs. .57) and 20-somethings are more consistent than teenagers (.57 vs. .47; Roberts & DelVecchio, 2000). Clearly, young adulthood is a time of growing stability and the establishment of a more concrete personality. As such, young adulthood is characterized by increasing psychological maturity with concomitant normative changes in personality traits from adolescence throughout young adulthood. As captured in the meta-analytic findings described earlier, at the mean level, young adults show normative increases in agreeableness, conscientiousness, and emotional stability while decreasing or remaining unchanged in their extraversion and openness (Roberts et al., 2006).

This distinction of patterns in trait development during young adulthood can be best understood by looking beyond the Five-Factor traits to examine traits at a higher order. Specifically, research suggests that the three traits that increase during young adulthood—agreeableness, conscientiousness, and emotional stability— form one higher-order trait (α) whereas the traits that do not increase during young adulthood—extraversion and openness—form a second higher-order trait (β; Digman, 1997). These two higher-order trait factors capture a unique quality of the developmental process. Specifically, the α factor characterizes the socialization of an individual and captures the person transitioning from reckless youth to a more responsible and mature adulthood. The β factor, on the other hand, describes a more humanistic maturation of independence and freedom of thought characterizing not socialization but instead personal growth toward a unique self set apart from society's presses (Digman, 1997). This higher-order distinction provides a compelling organizing framework for understanding personality trait development in adulthood that, unfortunately, has been overlooked by personality and developmental psychologists during the past decade.

Midlife

Contrary to popular and even scientific opinion, while midlife is characterized by relative trait consistency, personality traits can and do change between age 30 and age 60. Certainly meta-analytic estimates of stability coefficients (.59 to .75) and mean-level change suggest that personality traits are, in general, at their most consistent in midlife (Roberts & DelVecchio, 2000; Roberts et al., 2006), perhaps mirroring the relatively stable lives that many midlife adults experience. However, early in midlife individuals tend to mirror patterns of trait maturation seen in young adulthood with increases on social dominance, conscientiousness, and emotional stability (Roberts et al., 2006), a finding paralleled in recent 10-year longitudinal data (Bleidorn, Kandler, Riemann, Spinath, & Angleitner, 2009). In addition, late midlife is characterized by increasing agreeableness (Roberts et al., 2006). Similarly, curvilinear changes in dominance, independence, and responsibility during midlife suggest that personality traits are by no means fixed, even in the middle years (Helson et al., 2002).

In addition, the notion of individual variability in trait change seems to hold over the life course as some individuals increased, some decreased, and some remained stable on traits such as self-confidence, cognitive commitment, outgoingness, and dependability in a 40-year longitudinal investigation into middle adulthood (Jones & Meredith, 1996) and rates of trait change varies in recent 10-year longitudinal data (Bleidorn et al., 2009). Thus, personality change across midlife is more varied and pervasive than is commonly assumed.

Older Adulthood

Relatively recent investigations have documented personality trait change even during older adulthood, when most researchers thought there was not much possibility for change. While stability estimates remain quite high (.72) in older adulthood (Roberts & DelVecchio, 2000), older adulthood is characterized by increases in conscientiousness and decreases in openness to experience (Roberts et al., 2006). Emotional stability is also malleable in older adulthood as an investigation of men (mostly World War II veterans) from the Normative Aging Study revealed evidence of increasing emotional stability over a 12-year longitudinal investigation (Mroczek & Sprio, 2003). This pattern was paralleled in recent findings from the 12-year Interdisciplinary Study on Adult Development (Allemand, Zimprich, & Martin, 2008). A 6-year investigation into personality change using the reduced NEO-PI personality inventory in older adults provided statistically significant evidence of individual differences in personality change (Small et al., 2003). Thus, while personality change may not be as dramatic in older adulthood as it is in infancy and childhood (e.g., going from the 10th percentile on emotional stability to the 90th percentile) there is evidence that even during the later years subtle changes in personality can occur that are not simply error of measurement.

▨ MECHANISMS OF PERSONALITY TRAIT DEVELOPMENT

If we have done our job well up to this point you should now be asking yourself "but why?" In the pages that follow, we address a number of possible mechanisms underlying both stability and change in personality traits across the life span.

Understanding the patterns of personality trait development is only part of the science of personality development. Now that research has largely established the patterns of personality development over the life span, much of the current work in the personality development literature focuses on the mechanisms of personality development.

Personality, as with almost any individual difference variable, is a result of both biological and environmental processes. While a comprehensive examination of the genetic underpinnings of personality is beyond the scope of this chapter (see Krueger, Johnson, & Kling, 2006 for an excellent review), evidence from research on twins suggests that between 40% and 60% of the variance in personality can be attributed to genetic causes (Krueger et al., 2006). Despite the importance of biological factors to the basic nature of traits, little research examines the influence of biological processes on patterns of temperament or trait development over time. The evidence that does exist suggests that genetics influence the rate of change for α cluster (agreeableness, conscientiousness, and emotional stability) but not β cluster (extraversion and openness) traits in older adulthood (Bleidorn et al., 2009). While the literature on the genetic underpinning of developmental patterns is still in its infancy, scientific understanding of the influence of environment of temperament and traits is much more sophisticated.

One of the primary environmental influences on the development trajectory of childhood temperament is "goodness of fit" (Thomas et al., 1963). If a child has adapted to his or her environment successfully, temperament should remain more consistent over time. Given the environmental setting, some children will need to change while others will not. In either case, early temperamental dispositions may set a certain trajectory of success or failure that, in turn, may or may not change over childhood, adolescence, or adulthood. Empirical evidence supports the idea that how we act and behave as a child (similar to how attachment bond with mother is critical for successful development) may have long lasting effects over the life course (e.g., Caspi et al., 2003).

Specifically, personality is thought to progress from temperament in childhood to traits in adulthood through a process called "developmental elaboration" (Caspi, 1998). Essentially, developmental elaboration captures the mechanisms by which childhood temperament gets reinforced over time to become long-term characteristic traits: learning processes, environmental elicitation, environmental construal, social and temporal comparisons, environmental selection, and environmental manipulation. Temperament influences how an individual learns and is reinforced (learning processes) as well as shaping how an environment responds to an individual (environmental elicitation) and how an individual responds to a given environment (environmental construal). Social and temporal comparisons highlight that children are constantly comparing themselves to others in the process of figuring out who they are as individuals. Finally, temperament influences the experiences children find themselves in (environmental selection) and, once in an environment, children will shape the environment to suit their developing personality (environmental manipulation). All of these processes contribute to the transition of childhood temperament to adult traits. For example, a responsible child will be rewarded for this behavior, be given more responsibility, manage this extra responsibility well, and define the self as responsible relative to peers, all while selecting and manipulating situations that allow for this strength to be noticed and used. This combination of factors will allow the responsible child to grow into a conscientious young adult.

Similar factors contribute to the maintenance of stable personality traits over time in adulthood. For example, the corresponsive principle of personality development states that personality traits facilitate the selection of environments and experiences that serve to bolster those personality traits that lead an individual to select the environment or experience in the first place (Roberts & Wood, 2006). For example, the young woman who is highly open to experience and chooses a career with a lot of travel will likely become increasingly open to experience because of the dictates of her career path.

Fundamental to patterns of trait development in adulthood is that the successful process of establishing and fostering an adult identity in young adulthood helps maintain personality consistency throughout midlife and old age. Specifically, the internalization of the components of identity—values, roles, self-concept, and so on—in adolescence leads to a coherent self in adulthood. From this coherent sense of self, an individual will then make decision to act in certain ways. The greater the internal feeling of self-consistency, the greater the consistency in everyday behaviors and feelings and thus personality traits as everyday experiences are assimilated into the existing identity structure (Roberts & Wood, 2006; Roberts, Wood, & Caspi, 2008).

Within this broad identity framework, the adult roles with which an individual identifies are, arguably, the most central to the establishment of adult identity and, therefore, personality traits. Adult roles influence personality trait development in a number of ways. First, continuity in roles over time creates a stable environment that should facilitate consistency in personality traits. The stable environment affords protection against novel experiences which may lead to challenges to the existing personality structure that must be accommodated thus fostering personality trait change (Roberts & Wood, 2006).

In addition, the social investment principle states that experiences within social roles relate to change in personality traits. Social roles generally affect personality trait change by bringing with them a set of specific behavioral expectations, social values, and life goals (Sarbin, 1967). The incorporation of a given social role into individual identity facilitates commitment to the expectations and values associated with that role and thus subsequent attitudinal, behavioral, and cognitive changes manifested in changing personality traits (Roberts & Wood, 2006). Thus, one of the most promising areas of research regarding the mechanisms for personality trait change is stated in the *social investment hypothesis* that "...investing in social institutions, such as age-graded social roles, is one of the driving mechanisms of personality [trait] development" (Roberts, Wood, & Smith, 2005, p. 173).

Indeed, researchers have long recognized that dynamic transactions between personality and the environment are salient in young adulthood when many individuals are leaving their childhood home, entering college, obtaining occupational stability, and starting a life of their own. Specifically, forming new romantic relationships and having children during young adulthood and early midlife are associated with increases in both conscientiousness and emotional stability (Caspi & Roberts, 1999). Similarly, young adults who formed a relationship during a 4-year period increased on conscientiousness, extraversion, and emotional stability during this same period when compared to those who did not find a partner

(Neyer & Asendorpf, 2001). Social role experiences also influence personality trait development in late midlife and older adulthood with retirement linked to increases in agreeableness and decreases in extraversion (Löckenhoff, Terracciano, & Costa, 2009) and changes in emotional stability over time related to life events, such as death of a spouse (Mroczek & Spiro, 2003).

However, these findings open up a "chicken and egg" issue. Is it the case that young adult personality serves as an active creator of the individual's social relationship (spouse, parent)? Or, rather, is personality the relatively passive recipient of external social forces such as marriage or parenthood? The most likely answer is that the effects are two-way and reciprocal, with personality shaping life choices about social role investment and these very investments reshaping personality in turn. Such a reciprocal process could continue *ad infinitum* and such effects are difficult to study without extensive longitudinal data.

Indeed, research on the etiology of temperament and personality traits clearly points to a system influenced by multiple and diverse factors. Gene-by-environment interactions are fast becoming the norm in understanding personality trait development. For example, findings from the Dunedin study suggest that levels of monoamine oxidase A (MAOA) activity interact with the degree of maltreatment an individual experiences in childhood to predict antisocial behavior in adulthood (Caspi et al., 2002). Understanding the mechanisms underlying both basic patterns of personality trait development and the more complex questions of individual differences in trait development will be an important part of the future personality research from a developmental framework.

▪ OUTCOMES OF PERSONALITY DEVELOPMENT

Central to any discussion of personality development is that childhood temperament has long-term implications for important life outcomes. Extroverted children have better relationships, exhibit greater social competence, and have better social support networks through early adulthood (Shiner, 2000; Shiner, Masten, & Roberts, 2004). Low levels of emotional stability in childhood are linked to poor long-term social functioning (Eisenberg, 2000) whereas high levels of conscientiousness in childhood are clearly related to positive outcomes from better academic performance (Shiner, 2000; Shiner et al., 2004) to less antisocial behavior (Ackerman, Brown, & Izard, 2003; Shiner, 2000). Similarly, agreeableness in childhood predicts later social competence (Graziano, Hair, & French, 1997; Shiner, 2000), better academic achievement and less behavioral problems (Shiner, 2000; Shiner et al., 2004). Clearly, childhood temperament has a robust relationship to important life outcomes at least into young adulthood (for a detailed review see Shiner, 2006).

While longer-term evidence is less prevalent in the literature, teacher ratings of child conscientiousness in the Terman sample predict longevity up to 60 years later (Friedman et al., 1993). Indeed, the relationship of personality traits to important life outcomes ranging from divorce to death is one of the most influential findings to come out of modern personality psychology (Roberts et al., 2007). There is little doubt that both conscientiousness and emotional stability are important predictors of long-term health outcomes (Hampson, Goldberg, Vogt, & Dubanoski, 2007; Mroczek & Spiro, 2007). Recent work also links mean levels of personality traits to the other aspect of health of increasing importance to modern society—cognitive health. Emotionally stable older adults have better self-report and laboratory-based memory function (Meier, Perrig-Chiello, & Perrig, 2002; Neupert, Mroczek, & Spiro, 2008) as well as slower rates of cognitive decline (Perrig-Chiello, Perrig, & Stahelin, 2000). In addition, both emotional stability (Wilson, Barnes, & Bennett, 2003) and conscientiousness (Wilson, Schneider, Arnold, Bienias, & Bennett, 2007) are protective factors in preventing the onset of Alzheimer's disease.

However, the focus of this chapter is on long-term developmental patterns in personality traits. This gives rise to an interesting question. Are normative patterns of personality trait development associated with health, or even longevity? For example, if the normative pattern is to increase in emotional stability as we grow older, and if greater emotional stability is associated with decreased mortality risk, then what happens to that risk when people decline on this trait? Just as importantly, do people who do not show the normative pattern (e.g., those who stay stable or even decrease in emotional stability) show increased mortality risk or other increased health risks? If a personality trait at a given point in time confers a certain mortality risk, but then that trait changes (even if it changes in accordance with a normative pattern), it therefore stands to reason that the mortality and health risk should change as well. Analogously, biological risk factors need not stay static (e.g., high cholesterol can be brought down) and when they do change they alter the resulting health risk. Personality traits should function similarly in their effect on health and mortality, as we hypothesized a number of years ago (Mroczek et al., 2006). Indeed, when we tested this idea empirically, we obtained support for this idea. Those individuals low in emotional stability (low average level), who showed long-term decreases in this trait, died earlier than those without that combination (Mroczek & Spiro, 2007). Moreover the effect was general—results were identical for specific causes of mortality (circulatory, cancer, etc.) as for all-cause mortality. Thus, it is not just mean-level personality traits that predict important life outcomes. Patterns and trajectories of personality trait change are in and of themselves, important for understanding the variables we must be interested in as our society continues to age.

■ FUTURE ISSUES IN THE STUDY OF LIFE-SPAN PERSONALITY DEVELOPMENT

The theory and research summarized in our brief review points to three areas of research on personality trait development—the patterns of personality development, the mechanisms of personality development, and the outcomes of personality development. Throughout our review, personality traits are clearly not static elements. With this in mind, the first area of future research we propose for life-span personality development is to continue the growing trend to not simply treat personality traits as predictors of important outcomes but as outcomes in their own right. Personality traits are part of a life-long system of individual experience that both influence and are influenced by a multitude of experiences. This pattern can come from obvious situations like the one described within our discussion of the correspondence principle where personality traits influence career path decisions and careers subsequently affect the development of personality traits. However, it is our contention that this can come from other areas as well. For example, an emotionally stable person may be able to better cope with pain but, over time, chronic pain may drive decreases in emotional stability.

In addition, we want to point to an area of individual experience that undergoes marked changes throughout the life span but is as yet has been largely unexamined in relation to personality trait development. Specifically, cognitive development is a central focus of developmental psychologists across the life span. Joining the research of cognitive development with the research on personality development could open a new area of understanding the complexities of development in both of these domains. For example, the rate of cognitive growth in childhood may relate to the development of conscientiousness over time. In turn, one of the most marked challenges of the older adult experience is declining cognitive performance (Hultsch, Hertzog, Dixon, & Small, 1999; Park et al., 2002; Rönnlund, Nyberg, Backman, & Nilsson, 2005). These cognitive declines likely facilitate any number of changes in older adults such as increasing conscientiousness because of compensatory strategies implemented to counteract declines such as poor short-term memory performance. In contrast, declines in memory performance may drive individuals and outside observers to report lower levels of conscientiousness. While we review the small selection of studies that do address the relationship of personality traits and cognition, to date, little research investigates the relationship between personality traits and cognitive performance even at the cross-sectional level and the longitudinal research necessary to investigate these likely reciprocal and complex relationships is still in its early stages. Given that cognitive decline is arguably the most important public health issue facing our society today, we believe that developing a systematic program of research in this area is a crucial responsibility of personality psychology in the next decade.

In conclusion, personality variables are very much akin to cognitive functioning variables such as speed of processing or memory. They change over the course of adulthood, but not at a rapid rate. Rapid changes are almost always the result of pathology, such as brain injury (or lacking pathology at least ghostly visitation). Systematic personality trait change, like cognitive change, is not typically observable in short-term studies done over the courses of weeks, months, or even a year or two in length. Like changes in memory, change in personality is slow and is ideally studied over long periods of time. Studies of many years or better, decades, are necessary to observe meaningful changes. Just as memory declines do not occur rapidly from age 30 to 90, neither do personality changes occur quickly. Yet, such change is observable once long-term data are used with multiple measurement occasions and proper modeling such as latent growth or multilevel models for change. We believe that a driving principle of personality development is that the future of understanding personality development lies in studying personality over the life span using sophisticated statistical models in order to fully capture the elegance and nuance of personality development over time.

■ REFERENCES

Ackerman, B. P., Brown, E., & Izard, C. E. (2003). Continuity and change in levels of externalizing behavior in school of children from economically disadvantaged families. *Child Development,* *74*(3), 694–709.

Aldwin, C. M., Spiro, A., Levenson, M. R., & Bossé, R. (1989). Longitudinal findings from the normative aging study: Does mental health change with age?. *Psychology and Aging, 4*(3), 295–306.

Allemand, M., Zimprich, D., & Martin, M. (2008). Long-term correlated change in personality traits in old age. *Psychology and Aging, 23*(3), 545–557.

Alwin, D. F. (1994). Aging, personality, and social change: The stability of individual differences over the adult life span. *Life-span Development and Behavior, 12*, 135–185.

Baltes, P. B., & Nesselroade, J. R. (1973). The developmental analysis of individual differences on multiple measures. In J. R. Nesselroade & H. W. Reese (Eds.), *Life-span Developmental Psychology: Methodological Issues* (pp. 219–251). New York: Academic Press.

Baltes, P. B., Reese, H. W., & Nesselroade, J. R. (1977). *Life-span developmental psychology: Introduction to research methods.* New York: Psychology Press.

Bleidorn, W., Kandler, C., Riemann, R., Spinath, F. M., & Angleitner, A. (2009). Patterns and sources of adult personality development: Growth curve analyses of the NEO PI-R scales in a longitudinal twin study. *Journal of Personality and Social Psychology, 97*(1), 142–155.

Caspi, A. (1998). Personality development across the life course. In N. Eisenberg (Ed.), *Handbook of child psychology: Social, emotional, and personality development* (Vol. 3, 5th ed., pp. 311–388). New York: Wiley.

Caspi, A., Harrington, H. L., Milne, B., Amell, J. W., Theodore, R. F., & Moffitt, T. E. (2003). Children's behavioral styles at age 3 are linked to their adult personality traits at age 26. *Journal of Personality, 71*, 495–514.

Caspi, A., McClay, J., Moffitt, E., Mill, J., Martin, J., Craig, W., et al. (2002). Role of genotype in the cycle of violence in maltreated children. *Science, 297*, 851–854.

Caspi, A., & Roberts, B. W. (1999). Personality change and continuity across the life course. In L. Pervin & O. P. John (Eds.), *Handbook of personality* (2nd ed., pp. 300–326). New York: Guilford Press.

Caspi, A., Roberts, B. W., & Shiner, R. (2005). Personality development. *Annual Review of Psychology, 56*, 453–484.

Costa, P., & McCrae, R. (1992). *Revised NEO Personality Inventory (NEO-PI-R) and NEO Five Factor Inventory (NEO-FFI) professional manual.* Odessa, FL: Psychological Assessment Resources.

Deal, J. E., Halverson, C. F., Havill, V., & Martin, R. (2005). Temperament factors as longitudinal predictors of young adult personality. *Merrill-Palmer Quarterly, 51*(3), 315–334.

Dickens, C. (1843). *A Christmas Carol.* London: Chapman and Hall.

Digman, J. M. (1997). Higher-order factors of the Big Five. *Journal of Personality and Social Psychology, 73*, 1246–1256.

Eisenberg, N. (2000). Emotion, regulation, and moral development. *Annual Review of Psychology, 51*, 665–697.

Friedman, H., Tucker, J. S. J., Tomlison-Keasey, C., Schwartz, J., Wingard, D., & Criqui, M. (1993). Does childhood personality predict longevity? *Journal of Personality and Social Psychology, 65*, 176–185.

Goldberg, L. R. (1993). The structure of phenotypic personality traits. *American Psychologist, 48*, 26–34.

Graziano, W. G., Hair, E. C., & Finch, J. F. (1997). Competitiveness mediates the link between personality and group performance. *Journal of Personality and Social Psychology, 73*, 1394–1408.

Hampson, S. E., Goldberg, L. R., Vogt, T. M., & Dubanoski, J. P. (2007). Mechanisms by which childhood personality traits influence adult health status: Educational attainment and healthy behaviors. *Health Psychology, 26*, 121–125.

Helson, R., Jones, C., & Kwan, V. S. (2002). Personality change over 40 years of adulthood: Hierarchical linear modeling analyses of two longitudinal samples. *Journal of Personality and Social Psychology, 83*, 752–766.

Hultsch, D. F., Hertzog, C., Dixon, R. A., & Small, B. J. (1999). *Memory changes in the aged.* Cambridge: Cambridge University Press.

Jones, C. J., Livson, N., & Peskin, H. (2003). Longitudinal hierarchical linear modeling analyses of California Psychological Inventory data from age 33 to 75: An examination of stability and change in adult personality. *Journal of Personality Assessment, 80*, 294–308.

Jones, C. J., & Meredith, W. (1996). Patterns of personality change across the life span. *Psychology and Aging, 11*, 57–65.

Kagan, J., & Snidman, N. C. (2004). *The long shadow of temperament.* Cambridge: Harvard University Press.

Krueger, R., Johnson, W., & Kling, K. (2006). Behavior genetics and personality development. In D. Mroczek & T. D. Little (Eds.), *Handbook of personality development* (pp. 81–108). Mahwah, NJ: Lawrence Erlbaum.

Lamiell, J. T. (1981). Toward an idiothetic psychology of personality. *American Psychologist, 36*, 276–289.

Löckenhoff, C. E., Terracciano, A., & Costa Jr, P. T. (2009). Five-factor model personality traits and the retirement transition: Longitudinal and cross-sectional associations. *Psychology and Aging, 24*, 722–728.

McAdams, D. P., & Pals, J. L. (2006). A new Big Five: Fundamental principles for an integrative science of personality. *American Psychologist, 61*, 204–217.

McArdle, J. J. (1991). Structural models of developmental theory in psychology. *Annals of theoretical psychology, 7*, 139–160.

McCrae, R. R., & Costa Jr, P. T. (2008). The Five Factor theory of personality. In O. P. John, R. W. Robins, & L. A. Pervin (Eds.), *Handbook of personality, third edition: Theory and research* (3rd ed., pp. 159–181). New York: The Guilford Press.

Meier, B., Perrig-Chiello, P., & Perrig, W. (2002). Personality and memory in old age. *Aging, Neuropsychology, and Cognition, 9*, 135–144.

Meredith, W., & Tisak, J. (1990). Latent curve analysis. *Psychometrika, 55*, 107–122.

Mroczek, D. K. (2007). The analysis of longitudinal data in personality research. In R. W. Robins, R. C. Fraley, & R. F. Krueger (Eds.), *Handbook of research methods in personality psychology* (pp. 543–556). New York: Guilford Press.

Mroczek, D. K., & Griffin, P. (2007). Growth-curve modeling in positive psychology. In A. Ong & M. van Dulmen (Eds.), *Oxford handbook of methods in positive psychology* (pp. 467–476). New York & Oxford: Oxford University Press.

Mroczek, D. K., & Spiro III, A. (2003). Modeling intraindividual change in personality traits: Findings from the Normative Aging Study. *Journals of Gerontology Series B: Psychological Sciences and Social Sciences, 58*, 153–165.

Mroczek, D. K., & Spiro, A. (2007). Personality change influences mortality in older men. *Psychological Science, 18*, 371–376.

Mroczek, D. K., Spiro, A., & Almeida, D. M. (2003). Between-and within-person variation in affect and personality over days and years: How basic and applied approaches can inform one another. *Ageing International, 28*, 260–278.

Mroczek, D. K., Spiro, A., Almeida, D. M., & Pafford, C. (2006). Intraindividual change in personality. In D. Mroczek & T. D. Little (Eds.), *Handbook of personality development*. Mahwah, NJ: Lawrence Elrbaum Associates.

Mroczek, D., Spiro, A., & Griffin, P. (2006). Personality and aging. In J. Birren & K. W. Schaie (Eds.), *Handbook of the psychology of aging* (6th ed., pp. 363–377). San Diego, CA: Elsevier.

Muthén, L. K., & Muthén, B. O. (2002). Mplus 2.02 [Computer software]. Los Angeles: Author.

Nesselroade, J. R. (1988). Some implications of the trait-state distinction for the study of development over the life span: The case of personality. *Life-span Development and Behavior, 8*, 163–189.

Nesselroade, J. R. (1991). Interindividual differences in intraindividual change. In L. M. Collins & J. L. Horn (Eds.), *Best methods for the analysis of change: Recent advances, unanswered questions, future directions* (pp. 92–105). Washington, DC: American Psychological Association.

Neupert, S. D., Mroczek, D. K., & Spiro III, A. (2008). Neuroticism moderates the daily relation between stressors and memory failures. *Psychology and Aging, 23*, 287–296.

Neyer, F. J., & Asendorpf, J. B. (2001). Personality-relationship transaction in young adulthood. *Journal of Personality and Social Psychology, 81*, 1190–1204.

Ozer, D. J. (1986). *Consistency in personality: A methodological framework*. New York: Springer.

Park, D. C., Lautenschlager, G., Hedden, T., Davidson, N. S., Smith, A. D., & Smith, P. K. (2002). Models of visuospatial and verbal memory across the adult life span. *Psychology and Aging, 17*, 299–320.

Perrig-Chiello, P., Perrig, W. J., & Stahelin, H. B. (2000). Differential aspects of memory self-evaluation in old and very old people. *Aging & Mental Health, 4*, 130–135.

Putnam, S. P., Gartstein, M. A., & Rothbart, M. K. (2006). Measurement of fine-grained aspects of toddler temperament: The Early Childhood Behavior Questionnaire. *Infant Behavior and Development, 29*(3), 386–401.

Raudenbush, S. W., & Bryk, A. S. (2001). *Hierarchical linear models: Applications and data analysis methods* (2nd ed.). Thousand Oaks, CA: Sage Publications.

Roberts, B. W., & Chapman, C. N. (2000). Change in dispositional well-being and its relation to role quality: A 30-year longitudinal study. *Journal of Research in Personality, 34*, 26–41.

Roberts, B. W., & DelVecchio, W. F. (2000). The rank-order consistency of personality traits from childhood to old age: A quantitative review of longitudinal studies. *Psychological Bulletin, 126*, 3–25.

Roberts, B., Harms, P., Smith, J., Wood, D., & Webb, M. (2005). Using multiple methods in personality psychology. In E. Diener & M. Eid (Eds.), *Handbook of multimethod measurement in psychology* (pp. 321–355). Washington, DC: American Psychological Association.

Roberts, B. W., Kuncel, N. R., Shiner, R., Caspi, A., & Goldberg, L. R. (2007). The power of personality: The comparative validity of personality traits, socioeconomic status, and cognitive ability for predicting important life outcomes. *Perspectives on Psychological Science, 2,* 313–345.

Roberts, B. W., & Mroczek, D. (2008). Personality trait change in adulthood. *Current Directions in Psychological Science, 17,* 31–35.

Roberts, B. W., Walton, K. E., & Viechtbauer, W. (2006). Patterns of mean-level change in personality traits across the life course: A meta-analysis of longitudinal studies. *Psychological Bulletin, 132,* 1–25.

Roberts, B. W., & Wood, D. (2006). Personality development in the context of the neo-socioanalytic model of personality. In D. Mroczek & T. D. Little (Eds.), *Handbook of personality development* (pp. 11–39). Mahwah, NJ: Lawrence Erlbaum.

Roberts, B. W., Wood, D., & Caspi, A. (2008). The development of personality traits in adulthood. In O. P. John, R. W. Robins, & L. A. Pervin (Eds.), *Handbook of personality: Theory and reasearch* (3rd ed., pp. 375–398). New York: Guilford Press.

Roberts, B. W., Wood, D., & Smith, J. L. (2005). Evaluating Five Factor Theory and social investment perspectives on personality trait development. *Journal of Research in Personality, 39,* 166–184.

Rogosa, D., Brandt, D., & Zimowski, M. (1982). A growth curve approach to the measurement of change. *Psychological Bulletin, 92,* 726–748.

Rönnlund, M., Nyberg, L., Bäckman, L., & Nilsson, L. G. (2005). Stability, growth, and decline in adult life span development of declarative memory: Cross-sectional and longitudinal data from a population-based study. *Psychology and aging, 20,* 3–18.

Rothbart, M. K., Ahadi, S. A., Hershey, K. L., & Fisher, P. (2001). Investigations of temperament at three to seven years: The Children's Behavior Questionnaire. *Child Development, 72,* 1394–1408.

Sarbin, T. R. (1967). On the futility of the proposition that some people be labeled "mentally ill." *Journal of Consulting Psychology, 31,* 447–453.

Schaie, K. W. (1996). *Intellectual development in adulthood: The Seattle Longitudinal Study.* New York: Cambridge University Press.

Shiner, R. L. (2000). Linking childhood personality with adaptation: Evidence for continuity and change across time into late adolescence. *Journal of Personality and Social Psychology, 78,* 310–325.

Shiner, R. L. (2006). Temperament and personality in childhood. In D. Mroczek & T. D. Little (Eds.), *Handbook of personality development* (pp. 213–230). Mahwah, NJ: Erlbaum Associates.

Shiner, R. L., Masten, A. S., & Roberts, J. M. (2004). Childhood personality foreshadows adult personality and life outcomes two decades later. *Journal of Personality, 71,* 1145–1170.

Singer, J. D., & Willett, J. B. (2003). *Applied longitudinal data analysis: Modeling change and event occurrence* (1st ed.). New York: Oxford University Press.

Small, B. J., Hertzog, C., Hultsch, D. F., & Dixon, R. A. (2003). Stability and change in adult personality over 6 years: Findings from the Victoria Longitudinal Study. *Journals of Gerontology Series B: Psychological Sciences and Social Sciences, 58,* 166–176.

Thomas, A., Chess, S., Birch, H., Hertzig, M., & Korn, S. (1963). *Behavioral individuality in early childhood.* New York: New York University Press.

Wachs, T. D., McCrae, R. R., & Kohnstamm, G. A. (2001). *Temperament in context* (1st ed.). New York: Psychology Press.

Wilson, R. S., Schneider, J. A., Arnold, S. E., Bienias, J. L., & Bennett, D. A. (2007). Conscientiousness and the incidence of Alzheimer disease and mild cognitive impairment. *Archives of General Psychiatry, 64,* 1204–1212.

Wilson, R., Barnes, L., & Bennett, D. (2003). Assessment of lifetime participation in cognitively stimulating activities. *Journal of Clinical and Experimental Neuropsychology, 25,* 634–642.

Wohlwill, J. F. (1973). The concept of experience: S or R? *Human Development, 16,* 90–107.

EMOTIONAL EXPERIENCE ACROSS THE LIFE SPAN

21

Susan T. Charles and Gloria Luong

Psychologists have long recognized the interplay between biological and social processes in shaping emotional experiences. Genes provide a biological foundation, and neurobiological pathways necessary to experience and regulate emotions unfold across childhood, adolescence, and into young adulthood. These biological processes, however, are continually shaped by the surrounding environment. Social processes influence future emotional experiences even before an individual is born, and they continue to shape emotional experiences into old age. In the current chapter, we review trajectories of emotional experience commonly observed across the life span. We describe the curvilinear pattern of emotional well-being, with levels decreasing from childhood to adolescence, and then increasing across adulthood. In addition, we discuss how these patterns are related to social processes occurring at each life stage, as well emotion-regulation strategies that are often social in nature. Afterward, the chapter concludes by offering several future research directions for the study of socioemotional processes across human development.

EMOTIONAL EXPERIENCE ACROSS THE LIFE SPAN

Early theorists observed the powerful effects of the environment on emotional experience. In the *Principles of Psychology*, William James began his definition of emotions by stating that objects in the environment provoke characteristic alterations that influence physiological functioning, attitudes, and expression (James, 1890). Although a physiologist and physician by training, James emphasized the role of the environment in determining the physiological arousal necessary for emotional experience. Charles Darwin focused on the social environment when he stated that emotions evolved to meet environmental demands. In *The Expression of Emotions in Man and Animals* (Darwin, 1872/1998), Darwin wrote that emotions provide an evolutionary advantage by communicating information to others.

More than 100 years later, researchers continue to recognize the interdependence between biological and environmental processes for emotional experience. Emotions are biological processes influenced by genetic endowment, yet the environment shapes both genetic expression and physiological development. Environmental influences include a wide range of effects, from nutrition and exposure to toxins to psychosocial factors such as socioeconomic status and social support. In psychology, the environmental effects most often implicated in emotional experiences are arguably social in nature. The importance of social processes for emotional development is underscored by evolutionary theorists, who define social bonds as emotion-regulating events that promote survival of the larger group (Brown & Brown, 2006).

According to one theory, people are motivated to form social bonds for reasons of fitness interdependence, and these bonds are strengthened through shared emotional experiences (Brown & Brown).

Just as evolutionary theorists discuss the role of socioemotional processes for the development of the species, developmental researchers document socioemotional processes critical for individual development (e.g., see review by de Haan & Gunnar, 2009). The current chapter presents the trajectory of emotional experience across the life span. We recognize that a myriad of environmental influences—from nutrition, neighborhood quality, and socioeconomic status—are related to emotional well-being, but we limit our examples of environmental influence to social processes. We further acknowledge that researchers have devoted chapters and entire books to reviewing the literature on emotional development and regulation for specific life stages, including early development (e.g., see review by Calkins & Hill, 2007), adolescence (e.g., see review by de Haan & Gunnar, 2009), early adulthood (e.g., see review by Simpson, Collins, Tran, & Haydon, 2008), and later adulthood (e.g., see review by Charles & Horwitz, 2010). A comprehensive review of these topics is impossible given the scope of the literature. Instead, we provide a broad life-span overview of emotional experience. We discuss individual differences in emotional experience early in life, the social influences that shape these experiences, and how levels of emotional well-being change across adolescence and adulthood.

We begin the current chapter with a brief definition of emotional experience and an introduction into the biological factors considered in the study of emotion. Following, we describe how emotional experience develops across three broadly defined life stages: infancy and childhood, adolescence, and adulthood. For each life stage, we discuss social and physiological processes, and their interactive effects that influence emotional experience. We then chart the course of emotional experience observed for most people, revealing a pattern of emotional well-being that decreases from late childhood to adolescence and then increases throughout adulthood. Finally, we describe how this trajectory of increased well-being in late life continues for the majority of older adults, but for some people interactions between physiological vulnerabilities and environmental demands may tax their ability to sustain emotional well-being over time.

▪ EMOTIONAL EXPERIENCE: DEFINITIONS AND BIOLOGICAL BASES

Researchers have never agreed on a definition of emotion or emotional experience. Most scientists include thoughts, behaviors, and physiology in their definition, but they disagree as to the role each process plays, in the importance of subjective awareness, and in the time course and qualitative nature of an emotional experience. In the current chapter, we focus on the subjective experience of emotion, or affect, that people report when asked how they are feeling. When studying infants, researchers infer these "feelings"—or emotional experiences—from objective behaviors indicating happiness or distress. In infancy and early childhood, these experiences are often classified as temperaments, or fairly consistent pattern of behaviors and emotional expressions. Some temperaments are more often associated with negative emotions (such as high levels of emotionality or an inhibited temperament) and others with more positive emotions (such as high levels of sociability or an uninhibited temperament). When assessing older children and adults, researchers often use self-reports of emotional experience, including happiness, life satisfaction, and overall positive and negative affect. People respond to questions asking about the emotions they have experienced in the prior few days, weeks, the prior month, or "in general." Researchers recognize that these experienced emotions result from multiple influences that interact with one another, including genetic predispositions, physiological processes, and environmental factors (Gross, 2007).

Biological Processes Involved in Emotional Experience

Researchers acknowledge that these emotions include neurobiological processes that vary with age and across different individuals. In this section, we discuss some of the more commonly studied measures related to physiological activity.

When studying emotional reactivity, researchers often focus on the limbic system. The limbic system comprises several structures in the brain involved in a number of functions, including learning, motivation, emotion, and memory. Within this system, researchers often study the activation of the amygdala and the hypothalamus in response to emotional stimuli. When people perceive emotional stimuli, the amygdala sends signals to other areas of the brain that activate a number of processes, including increases in levels of epinephrine and norepinephrine (two neurotransmitters associated with sympathetic nervous system activation) and dopamine (a neurotransmitter implicated in both pleasure and pain). Greater activity in the amygdala has been related to greater emotional reactivity assessed by a variety of biological and psychological measures, including higher basal levels of cortisol (a hormone related to stress), greater withdrawal-related behaviors (e.g., Buss et al., 2003), and greater distress after separation from the parents (Davidson & Fox, 1989).

Researchers also often study the reaction of the hypothalamic–pituitary–adrenal (HPA) axis to stressful experiences. When people perceive a stressful event, the hypothalamus activates a neurobiological response that sends corticotrophin-releasing hormone and vasopressin to the pituitary gland, which releases adrenocorticotropin hormone down to the adrenal gland, and ends with the release of cortisol (see review by Miller, Chen, & Zhou, 2007). Cortisol then passes the blood–brain barrier to the hypothalamus, creating a feedback loop along the axis. Researchers examining emotional reactivity often use levels of cortisol in circulating blood or saliva as an indicator of the HPA response (see review by Dickerson & Kemeny, 2004), and have studied cortisol levels as an indicator of distress among infants (Egliston, McMahon, & Austin, 2007), children (Yim, Quas, Cahill, & Hayakawa, 2010), and adults (see review by Dickerson & Kemeny, 2004).

In addition to studying physiological reactivity to emotional stimuli directly, researchers have been increasingly interested in potential candidate genes related to both emotional reactivity as well as emotional states and predisposition. Candidate genes include those associated with corticotropin-releasing hormone, epinephrine, norepinephrine, oxytocin, and vasopressin (all implicated in emotional reactivity to stress as well as general levels of emotional experience), as well as serotonin, dopamine, and monoamineoxidase A and B (neurotransmitters associated with levels of emotional experience). Researchers have found, for example, that variation in RGS2 is linked to shyness, limbic activation, and anxiety disorders in humans (e.g., Smoller et al., 2008; Yalcin et al., 2004). Serotonin is a neurotransmitter associated with depression, where lower levels of serotonin are associated with greater depressive symptomatology. Serotonin-related genes, such as the 5-HTTLPR have also been implicated in anxiety disorders as well as depressive symptoms (Collier, Arranz, Sham, & Battersby, 1996). Other researchers find associations between allelic variation in oxytocin (OXTR) and a serotonin-related gene (5-HTTLPR) for predicting affiliative behavior (Bakermans-Kranenburg & van Ijzendoorn, 2008); variation in the gene related to an enzyme that breaks down serotonin in the brain (monoamine oxidase A [MAOA]) with aggressive behavior (Popova, 2008); and links between variation in genes related to dopamineric activity and impulsive behavior (Blum et al., 1995).

The Need to Examine Environmental Influences When Studying Genetic Influences

Despite the enthusiasm and growing number of studies examining specific genes implicated in emotional experience and behavior, many researchers call for caution when focusing research on genetically based answers to temperament and other emotional outcomes (Plomin & Davis, 2009). They caution against monogenetic solutions for complex phenomenon that may involve multiple genes and environmental influences. They further stress the need to understand the effects of the environment when studying genetic effects. Plomin and Davis (2009), for example, urge scientists to continue to examine individual genes to understand the role of genetics in psychological phenotypes, but they also note that currently researchers have found only small effects for single genes, generally accounting for about 1% of the variance in the outcome of interest. They further state that studying genes and environment together may reveal more about the powerful role of the environment than the genetic effects. Shanahan and Hofer (2005) also discuss the role of behavioral genetics in identifying specific environments that serve as protective factors, trigger genetic vulnerabilities, or enhance adaptation. Researchers further state that understanding how the environment shapes genetic and physiological processes related to emotional experience at different life stages will allow researchers more insight into consistency and change in emotional experience in childhood, and changes in levels of emotional experience across adulthood (Saudino, 2005).

▓ INFANCY AND CHILDHOOD

Prenatal Social Influences

Infants are born with the innate ability to experience emotions, but nonhuman animal research suggests that the environment is instrumental in shaping these experiences even before birth (e.g., Abe et al., 2007). For example, rats exposed to psychological stress (i.e., watching another rat undergo an electric shock) in the last trimester of gestation give birth to male offspring who later show both heightened HPA axis activity and increased depression-like behavior in response to stressors (Abe et al., 2007). Thus, male rats whose mothers were exposed to psychological stress during pregnancy have stronger physiological reactivity to acute stressors, as indicated by higher levels of cortisol in response to threat.

A growing number of studies using human samples have linked the psychological stress experienced by mothers during pregnancy to adverse physical health outcomes in their offspring (e.g., Davis & Sandman, 2010; Federenko & Wadhwa, 2004), but studying emotional outcomes in infants is more difficult. Researchers discuss the challenges of assessing stress reactivity in infants, including normative levels of cortisol and how to ascertain physiological reactivity (Egliston et al., 2007). Nonetheless, these scientists suggest that this area of inquiry may prosper as they develop more sophisticated methods to study both the level of stress exposure among expectant mothers and levels of emotional reactivity in infants and children. Researchers have documented that among humans, maternal stress is reliably linked to shorter gestational periods and lower birth rates—risk factors for later cognitive and emotional behavior problems (e.g., Zubrick et al., 2000). In recent research, findings have focused directly on emotion-related outcomes among infants (Field et al., 2010). For example, mothers who had high rates of either depressive symptoms or both depressive symptoms and anxiety during their third trimester of pregnancy gave birth to children with higher levels of cortisol and norepinephrine (both related to stress reactivity). They also had lower levels of dopamine and serotonin compared to neonates of mothers who scored high in anxiety alone or mothers scoring low on both depression and anxiety measures (Field et al., 2010).

Emotional Experience in Infants

Researchers often use temperament to gauge emotional experience among infants. Temperament refers to a relatively stable, constitutionally based, set of behaviors and emotional responses that guide reactivity and self-regulation (De Pauw, Mervielde, & Leeuwen, 2009; Rothbart, 2004; Rothbart & Derryberry, 1981). Temperament is assessed by behaviors including soothability, smiling, laughter, physical and vocal activity, and by emotional expressions such as fear, distress, or frustration (Rothbart, 1988). These traits are relatively stable, overlap with temperament and personality traits observed in childhood and adulthood (see review by Caspi, Roberts, & Shiner, 2005), and independently predict problem behavior in childhood (e.g., De Pauw et al., 2009).

Kagan and his colleagues examined the enduring quality of temperament in studies of inhibited and uninhibited children (e.g., Kagan, Snidman, Arcus, & Reznick, 1994). Children classified as inhibited are timid, affectively controlled and easily frightened by novel stimuli. Those who are labeled as uninhibited are highly social, outgoing, and spontaneous. In a series of studies, Kagan and his colleagues followed a sample of children at 4, 14, and 21 months, and at 4, 7, 11, and around 14 years of age (for an in depth review of the study and its findings, see Kagan, Snidman, Kahn, & Towsley, 2007). They found that at 4 months of age, about 20% of the sample was classified as inhibited, as evidenced by their frequent crying, arching backs, and other signs of muscle tension. An additional 40% of the sample was classified as uninhibited, showing minimal crying or fear in response to novel stimuli. The remaining 40% fell in the middle of these two profiles. They also found stability in patterns of uninhibited and inhibited behavior when examining children at 4 months of age and again at 14 months of age (Kagan et al., 1994), a longitudinal pattern replicated in other studies as well (Calkins, Fox, & Marshall, 1996; Moehler et al., 2008).

Early and Later Childhood

Throughout infancy and in early childhood, a gradual integration between emotional and cognitive processes allow for the development of an understanding of emotional experience in self and others (Bell, Greene, & Wolfe, 2010; Rothbart, Posner, & Kieras, 2006). Cognitive development allows children to gain a recognition of their own emotional experiences. Much of the research in emotional processes during early childhood examines how children acquire emotion-related knowledge and skills (e.g., Wang, 2003). As memory develops, children are able to report their health and well-being, such as mood states and emotional experiences (e.g., see related review by Riley, 2004). For example, one study documented that children as young as 5 years can reliably and validly report on their health and well-being, including their experience of positive and negative emotions (Varni, Limbers, & Burwinkle, 2007). When researchers examine emotional behavior in children in their first few years, however, they often focus on temperament, as well as both physiological and environmental correlates to these patterns of change (e.g., Rothbart, Ellis, & Posner, 2004).

Researchers have found some support for consistency in emotional experiences between infancy and throughout young and middle childhood (e.g., Eisenberg, Fabes, Guthrie, & Reiser, 2000). Inhibited children at 4 months of age are also more likely to be rated as shy when they are 15 years old than their uninhibited peers (Kagan et al., 1994, 2007). Children at 8 and 11 years of age who are labeled as inhibited when they were 4 months old smile less, offer fewer spontaneous comments, and are more subdued in response to novel stimuli than are those originally labeled uninhibited (Kagan et al., 2007). Temperamental traits observed in childhood continue to predict behaviors and reactivity into adulthood; one study examined the predictive effects of childhood levels of ill-temper, defined as displays of temper tantrums averaged across behavior assessed at 8, 9, and 10 years of age (Caspi, Bem, & Elder, 1989). Twenty years later, researchers found that men who were ill-tempered as children were rated by judges as being more irritable, undercontrolled, and moody than their peers who had been rated as better-tempered children. In another study, adults in their early 20s who had been classified as having an inhibited temperament during infancy had greater amygdala response to novel stimuli than did same-aged adults who had been rated as having an uninihibited temperament during infancy (Schwartz, Wright, Shin, Kagan, & Rauch, 2003).

Physiology and Emotional Experience in Childhood

Researchers have found consistent differences in physiological reactivity among children who vary in temperament as well. For example, highly inhibited children at 4 months of age show increased brain activity in areas suggesting greater excitability of the amygdala (Kagan & Snidman, 2004). In addition, children displaying signs of inhibited behavior at 4 months of age had greater activation of the right frontal hemisphere compared to the left (Calkins et al., 1996), an asymmetry that has been linked to the experience of greater negative mood and more negative dispositional temperaments. These physiological differences show some stability over time; infants labeled as inhibited at 4 months of age were more likely to be rated as shy at age 11 and have higher levels of morning cortisol than their less shy peers, consistent with the premise that inhibited children exhibit greater activity in the amygdala which causes greater stress reactivity (Schmidt, Fox, Rubin, & Sternberg, 1997). Greater frontal asymmetry is also related to emotion regulation in adulthood. Davidson and colleagues found that greater activity in the left prefrontal cortex was associated with faster recovery after adults viewed negative stimuli (Jackson et al., 2003) and higher levels of psychological well-being (Urry et al., 2004).

Environmental Influences Throughout Childhood

The aforementioned studies point to a great deal of consistency in emotional experience across childhood, but stability in general temperament does not characterize all children. In one study, for example, correlations among observer raters that were taken when children were 14, 18, and 24 months old were low, ranging from 0 to .39 (Saudino, Plomin, & DeFries, 1996). Another study found that about 40% of children originally labeled as "inhibited" were no longer so several years later when they were tested again as preschoolers (Kagan, Reznick, Snidman, Gibbons, & Johnson, 1988). Researchers have turned to environmental influences to explain changes over time, suggesting that how children are treated within the family dynamics as well as other environmental influences unique to the children are mostly likely responsible for these temperament-related changes (Saudino, 2005).

When examining the person most involved in social interactions with infants, researchers often focus on the mother (e.g., Bowlby, 1969). Primary caregivers, most often the mother, influence current and future social, emotional, and physical functioning with effects that remain into adulthood (e.g., Ainsworth & Wittig, 1969; Antonucci, Akiyama, Takahashi, 2004; Bowlby, 1969; Morris, Silk, Steinberg, Myers, & Robinson, 2007; Shaver, Belsky, & Brennan, 2000). In childhood, supportive maternal bonds are related to less internalizing behavior indicative of depression and anxiety (Miljkovitch, Pierrehumbert, & Halfon, 2007) and lower physiological reactivity also consistent with lower levels of anxiety and depressive symptoms (Hane & Fox, 2006).

When children are very young, parents act as external emotion regulators for their children, modeling behavior and guiding the emotion-regulation strategies of their children (Gottman, 2001). The quality of the mother–child relationship influences how children talk about their emotions and regulate their emotional experiences (Waters et al., 2010). For example, researchers observed that inhibited children who had mothers who discouraged shy behavior and were less protective were more likely to become more sociable over time and even lose their status as someone having an inhibited style (Rubin, Burgess, & Hastings, 2002). Conversely, overly critical and protective mothers had infants who were more likely to remain inhibited in childhood. In addition, mothers who attempted to mask the expression of their negative emotions were more likely to have insecurely attached infants at 12 months of age (Pauli-Pott & Mertesacker, 2009).

When mothers experience high levels of emotional distress, the emotional well-being of their children is often affected. Mothers face their own life challenges, including tensions in the home, economic problems, or mental health issues that influence the child. In nonhuman animal studies, for example, mothers who are in unpredictable surroundings are more likely to have children with anxious temperaments (Rosenblum, Forger, Noland, Trost, & Coplan, 2001). In human studies, mothers living in low income areas often report high levels of depression and emotional distress (e.g., Lanzi, Pascoe, Keltner, & Ramey, 1999). Depression both independently and in conjunction with low income is related to higher rates of behavior problems in early childhood (Schoon, Sacker, & Bartley, 2003), middle childhood and into adolescence (Gross, Shaw, & Moilanan, 2008). Thus, the social world of the child is related to social influences on the mother, as well.

As children start interacting with peers, these relationships become another source of both positive and negative emotional experiences. Positive social experiences with friends is related to greater happiness in children (Holder & Coleman, 2009), and concerns about acceptance and social rejection are often sources of distress (e.g., London, Downey, Bonica, & Paltin, 2007). Although definitions of loneliness change with age, children as young as 5 years of age understand the concept of loneliness (Asher & Paquette, 2003). Chronic feelings of loneliness are also associated with negative long-term outcomes. Among 7- and 8-year-olds, for example, children with social anxiety and concerns about social rejection reported higher levels of loneliness than their less socially anxious peers (Weeks, Coplan, & Kingsbury, 2009). These patterns continue throughout elementary and middle school and into high school. For example, lonely children, ranging from 9 to 12 years old, are more likely to be rejected and victimized by their peers, and to become more rejected over a 2-year period (Boivin, Hymel, & Burkowski, 1995). In another study, sixth graders who are anxious and express anger over the possibility of rejection at the beginning of their school year are more likely to report higher levels of anxiety and withdrawal the following spring (London et al., 2007), creating a` vicious cycle that promotes poor social skills and emotional distress. Feelings of loneliness at school at any age is a problem for the child's overall well-being (Asher & Paquette, 2003).

Genetic and Environmental Interactions

Researchers suggest that genetic influences may be largely responsible for the stability in temperamental characteristics, whereas the combination of genetic and environmental influences may be more important for explaining changes in these emotional experiences over time (Ganiban, Saudino, Ulbricht, Neiderhiser, & Reiss, 2008). They emphasize the interactive effects of innate characteristics of the child and environmental influences for determining emotional experiences and behaviors (e.g., Plomin & Davis, 2009). Both nonhuman animal and human models illustrate the need to understand both processes for predicting emotional outcomes. For example, research using Macaque monkeys has found that animals at risk because of allelic variation indicating poor emotional outcomes (e.g., greater aggression or anxiety) fare worse in harsh rearing environments relative to their peers with more resilient gene variations (Stevens, Leckman, Coplan, & Suomi, 2009). In hospitable rearing environments where a nurturing mother is present and the food supply is predictable and available, genetic variation does not predict emotional outcomes. Studies using human samples are consistent with these gene and environmental interactions (e.g., Caspi et al., 2003). For example, researchers found that, unsurprisingly, children exposed to maltreatment had more mental health problems than those who were not (Kim-Cohen et al., 2006). Importantly, there was a gene–environment interaction such that those with a genotype associated with low MAOA activity (a risk factor for conduct disorder and antisocial problems in adulthood; Samochowiec et al., 1999) who were exposed to physical abuse were much more likely to experience mental health problems than their counterparts with high MAOA activity. Other researchers have also acknowledged that understanding these complex person-by-environment interactions and dynamic processes may help to explain childhood maltreatment and resilience (Cicchetti & Toth, 1995; Luthar, Cicchetti, & Becker, 2000)

▧ LATER CHILDHOOD AND ADOLESCENCE

Emotional Well-Being in Later Childhood and Adolescence

Throughout childhood, emotional experiences that were strongly shaped by the actions of the primary caregiver are now increasingly regulated by the individual, such that older children and adolescents play a more active role in regulating their own emotional experiences. Unfortunately, some children enter adolescence at risk for further affective distress: between 1% and 8% of children ranging in age from about 8 to 13 years meet the *DSM-IV* criteria for a depressive disorder, including major depressive episodes, dysthymia, and depression not otherwise specified (Angold, Costello, & Worthman, 1998; Cohen et al., 1993; Hankin et al., 1998; Lefkowitz & Tesiny, 1985); an estimated 12–15% of children 10–13 years old with an anxiety disorder (Cohen et al., 1993); and 11–13% of children ranging from 10 to 13 years of age suffer from separation anxiety (Cohen et al., 1993). In one study, about 13% of children ranging from 9 to 16 years of age developed a psychiatric disorder (e.g., anxiety disorder) during a 3-month study period (Costello, Mustillo, Erkanli, Keeler, & Angold, 2003).

For the majority of children entering adolescence with normative levels of well-being, research suggests that their emotional state usually gets worse before it gets better. In one longitudinal study, 10–14-year-olds completed questionnaires about their emotional states for 1 week via an experience sampling method and again 4 years later when they were 13–18 years old (Larson, Moneta, Richards, & Wilson, 2002). Compared to the preadolescent years, the early teens were associated with less positive emotions, more negative emotions, and greater instability in emotional experiences. These negative emotional experiences seem to peak in magnitude and become more stable at about 15 years of age, when adolescents are typically in 10th grade. Other studies have found that the most dramatic increases in the rates of clinical depression among adolescents occur between 15 and 18 years of age and level off in the later adolescent and early adulthood years (Cohen et al., 1993; Hankin et al., 1998).

Physiology and Emotional Experience in Adolescence

Researchers have examined reasons for this dip in emotional well-being during adolescence, pointing to both physiological and environmental contributing factors. The beginning of adolescence is often associated with puberty, a period of rapid development and hormone surges. Researchers posit that these physiological changes are associated with greater motivations both to experience high-intensity emotional events and to connect more deeply with their peers (Forbes & Dahl, 2010). Although researchers typically believe that by late adolescence emotional experiences become more stable (e.g., Larson et al., 2002), there is evidence to suggest that biological factors related to emotional experience continue to develop during this time. Researchers have found that cortical development continues until around 21 years of age (Giedd, 2004; Gogtay et al., 2004). Cortical development of the frontal lobe is critical for more reasoned emotion-regulation responses (e.g., Davidson, Putnam, & Larson, 2000). The midline limbic structures (i.e., amygdala, cingulate, hypothalamus, hippocampus) are the first areas activated in response to emotional stimuli to produce quick, initial, impulsive reactions. The cortical structures (e.g., prefrontal cortex), however, often downregulate the activity of the limbic system to produce more controlled, restrained responses, or "top down" processing (LeDoux & Armony, 1999), including attentional control, cognitive reappraisal (Ochsner & Gross, 2005), and the inhibition of negative emotional states (Davidson, Jackson, & Kalin, 2000). These findings suggest that the cortical structures may play an important role in the experience, and potentially the regulation, of emotions.

Researchers suggest that the development of these higher pathways may take longer than we once believed. Among postnatal rats, the fiber density (connectivity) between the medial prefrontal cortex and the amygdala continues to develop from the postweaning period through early adulthood (Cunningham, Bhattacharyya, & Benes, 2002). Studies examining brain activation during tasks requiring emotional suppression find that adolescents have less activity in pathways for top-down control mechanisms leading from the prefrontal cortex to the amygdala than do adults (see review by Luna & Sweeney, 2004), suggesting that the limbic-cortical connections may not be fully developed for adolescents. Thus, without a fully formed prefrontal cortex or connections between the limbic and cortical structures, it is possible that adolescents may have difficulty with impulse control, rumination, and emotion regulation when faced with negative life events and daily stressors (see review by Steinberg, 2005).

The physiological correlates to emotional experience become even more complicated when examining patterns across childhood and into adolescence. As we mentioned earlier, temperament in early childhood predicts behavior into adolescence, with inhibited children more likely to be adolescents who are shy (e.g., Kagan et al., 2007). In both childhood and adolescence, inhibited behavior is related to greater activation of the amygdala, consistent with research showing strong correlates between negative emotions (such as anxiety) and hyperactivity of the amygdala (e.g., Davis, 1992). Interestingly, although behaviors in adolescence are predicted by behaviors in childhood, physiological reactivity is not predictive over time. Although physiological reactivity is an important determinant at both ages, different mechanisms are responsible for reactivity in childhood and adolescence. Researchers have posited that perhaps puberty changes the mechanisms responsible for physiological patterns predicting emotion-related experiences (Kagan et al., 2007). Another possibility is that different genes are expressed after puberty that influence the physiological underpinnings of emotional experiences, a premise consistent with the literature showing that the combination of genetic and environmental influences continue to shape emotional experience over time (e.g., Ganiban et al., 2008).

Environmental Factors

During adolescence, many changes to interpersonal relationships occur and create new challenges for adolescents to overcome. For example, peer relationships become increasingly important during this time and adolescents face greater pressure to conform to their peer groups (e.g., Santor, Messervey, & Kusumakar, 2000).

Adolescents also experience greater intimacy in their friendships, which may not only produce high levels of satisfaction but also increase their risk of experiencing interpersonal tensions, rejection, and loss (see review by Compas & Wagner, 1991). In a study by Rudolph and Hammen (1999), adolescents between 13 and 18 years of age reported greater overall stress than preadolescents (8–12 years old), especially interpersonal stressors. The effect was most pronounced among females, with adolescents reporting a greater number of interpersonal stressors with their parents and peers than preadolescents. These findings point to the possibility that the greater number of stressors experienced by adolescents may contribute to increased negative affect during this period. Although the literature has been somewhat mixed, recent studies have shown converging results, with older adolescents reporting more daily and major life stressors than their younger counterparts (Ge, Lorenz, Conger, Elder, & Simons, 1994; Larson & Ham, 1993). An experience sampling study showed that early adolescents reported more daily stressors than preadolescents in peer, school, and family domains (Larson & Ham, 1993). Importantly, the researchers linked these stressors to negative affect, with the experience of multiple daily stressors contributing to greater daily negative affect for young adolescents than for preadolescents. Corroborating these findings, a study of Indian middle-class adolescents and their parents revealed that adolescents' reports of negative affect were associated with school-related stressors (Verma & Larson, 1999). The adolescents also reported experiencing greater variance in both positive and negative emotional states than their parents.

The greater number of stressful events most likely reflects the need to master new skills and the need to undergo a series of social and developmental transitions, such as school transitions, social network development (i.e., with their focus on gaining autonomy from parents and becoming closer to peers), and physical, biological, and sexual maturation (e.g., puberty; Eccles, Wigfield, Harold, & Blumenfeld, 1993). As adolescents develop greater cognitive skills, they also show greater complexity in their thoughts about their own emotions and those of others. Some of these thoughts may aid in emotion regulation, but others might leave people at risk for distress. For example, Nolen-Hoeksema and colleagues posit that females are more prone to depression than males because they are socialized to think about, and dwell on, their negative emotions. Gender differences do not reliably emerge until around the age of 13–15 years and become most exaggerated between the ages of 15 and 18 years (Hankin et al., 1998; Nolen-Hoeksema & Girgus, 1994). Researchers state that poorer coping styles (specifically adopting a ruminative style when reacting to negative events) in conjunction with a greater presence of stressors that emerge in early adolescence may lead to greater depression among females (Ge et al., 1994; Nolen-Hoeksema & Girgus, 1994).

Building on Nolen-Hoeksema and Girgus's (1994) review and others, Hyde, Mezulis, and Abramson (2008) have proposed the ABC (affective, biological, cognitive) model, which integrates previous affective, biological, and cognitive models and explains the emergence of gender differences in depression within a developmental model. The model proposes that preexisting vulnerabilities in affective (e.g., an inhibited temperament), biological (e.g., genetic influences), and cognitive (e.g., rumination) factors interact with stressful life events (e.g., interpersonal stressors) to moderate the existence of depressive symptoms during adolescence. Although the aim of the model is primarily to explain the emergence of gender differences in depression during adolescence, the model may also be generalized to explain predispositions and vulnerabilities to depressive symptoms across the life span.

Given the large number of transitions and developmental cognitive, physical, and psychosocial milestones experienced in adolescence, it is hardly surprising that some researchers have termed adolescence a period of "storm and stress" characterized by conflicts with parents, volatile and intense mood swings, and risky behavior (Hall, 1904). This pattern of emotional experiences and behavior is more common in adolescence but by no means universal for all people (Arnett, 1999; Eccles et al., 1993). Researchers state that environmental factors may be critical for determining whether "storm and stress" occurs during adolescence. Parents continue to play an important role during this time. In one study, adolescents who had friends with conduct problems were less likely to engage in externalizing problem behaviors if they had parents with firm behavioral control (such as enforcing bedtime schedules; Galambos, Barker, & Almeida, 2003). Another study found that parents who emphasized achievement, monitored their children's behavior, and encouraged joint decision-making had adolescents with higher grade point averages and less drug use (Brown, Mounts, Lamborn, & Steinberg, 1993). Eccles and colleagues (1993) have argued that when an adolescent's needs and environment (particularly school environment) are matched, she or he will experience positive psychosocial adjustment.

ADULTHOOD

Emerging adulthood is a term often used to define the period from the late teens to the mid-20s, a time when people no longer consider themselves adolescents but are not ready to define themselves as adults (Arnett, 2000). Although researchers debate about whether this time represents a distinct life period (Bynner, 2005), there is no disputing that much transition and change occurs during these years. For example, the neurological pathways critical for emotion regulation continue to develop into the early 20s, leading to more logical, problem-solving approaches to information (Luna & Sweeney, 2004). In addition, the greatest amount of change in personality traits occurs across the 20s and 30s, including increases in conscientiousness and emotional stability (see review by Roberts, Walton, & Viechtbauer, 2006). The reasons for these personality changes may largely stem from the changing social roles associated with such activities as entry into the workforce and the formation of stable relationships (Roberts, Wood, & Smith, 2005).

Emotional Well-Being: Early and Middle Adulthood

Throughout this period, people report increased emotional well-being compared to what was reported in adolescence. Following people from ages 18 to 25 years, researchers found that depressive symptoms and expressed anger decreased over time and self-esteem increased over this same time period (Galambos, Barker, & Krahn, 2006). Another longitudinal study also found increases in affective well-being; people who began the study when they were, on average, 18 years old showed decreases in negative affect across 23 years (Charles, Reynolds, & Gatz, 2001a). Findings from these longitudinal studies parallel those from cross-sectional studies that include adults ranging in age from the early 20s into their 60s (e.g., Diener & Suh, 1997; Mroczek & Kolarz, 1998; see review by Charles & Carstensen, 2010). In each of these studies, negative affect decreased over time. In contrast, positive affect remained stable in some studies and showed age-related increases in others (see review by Charles & Carstensen, 2010). Ratings of overall life satisfaction are consistent with these results, increasing across adulthood and reaching its peak when people are in their mid-60s (Mroczek & Spiro, 2005). These findings do not appear to be the result of an inability to experience intense emotions; older adults report that they experience emotions with equal intensity as do younger adults on self-reported questionnaires (Lawton, Kleban, Rajagopal, & Dean, 1992), in response to emotional stimuli in the laboratory (Tsai, Levenson, & Carstensen, 2000), and in reports collected from experience sampling techniques (Carstensen, Pasupathi, Mayr, & Nesselroade, 2000). In fact, all the aforementioned studies suggest that the frequency of negative affect declines throughout younger and middle-adulthood, and positive emotions either remain stable or increase in frequency. The result is that the end of middle age (around 60 or 65) is the time when people report highest levels of well-being.

Later Adulthood

After people reach their mid-60s, however, the literature is less consistent regarding the continued trends toward less negative affect. Several studies, for example, found increases in depressive symptoms over time when following people in their 60s (Davey, Halverson, Zonderman, & Costa, 2004) and when comparing people of different age groups in cross-sectional studies (Diener & Suh, 1997; Haynie, Berg, Johansson, Gatz, & Zarit, 2001). Using data from the Berlin Aging Study, researchers found that negative affect was unrelated to age and positive affect decreased with age among people ranging from 70 to 100 years old (Kunzmann, Little, & Smith, 2000). When these researchers controlled for functional health impairments, however, older age was related to less negative affect and higher levels of positive affect (Kunzmann et al., 2000). Other studies find that negative affect is reported with similar frequency when comparing people ranging from their mid-60s to their early 90s (Carstensen et al., 2000), and still others find slight age-related decreases in overall negative affect (Charles et al., 2001a) and depressive symptoms specifically (Kobau, Safran, Zack, Moriarty, & Chapman, 2004). Taken together, the findings indicate that, for some subgroups of older adults, emotional well-being continues to be stable and perhaps increases over time. For other people, however, emotional well-being may decline in later adulthood.

In addition to examining changes in mean levels of positive and negative emotional experiences, researchers have also examined the experience of multiple, co-occurring emotions in what they term "emotional complexity." The ability to recognize the co-occurrence of conflicting emotional states (such as feeling both happy and sad) occurs as early as childhood and is reported by both younger (Larsen, McGraw, & Cacioppo, 2001) and older adults (Ong & Bergeman, 2004). Researchers suggest, however, that these mixed emotional experiences may better define the subjective experiences of older adults than younger adults. For example, researchers have factor-analyzed multiple emotions reported by people five times daily over the course of a week (Carstensen et al., 2000). If people reported the same cluster of positive emotions at one point and a subject of negative emotions at another, for example, then two factors would best describe the organization of their emotional experiences. Results showed that the number of factors that described the combination of emotions they reported experiencing increased with age. Other studies have found that older adults were more likely to report a greater mix of emotions of a similar valence, showing complexity within positive and negative emotional states (Charles, 2005; Ready, Carvalho, & Weinberger, 2008). Thus, emotional well-being increases across adulthood, and for many older adults this trajectory continues into very old age. In addition, their emotional experience may be marked by greater nuances and greater numbers of co-occurring emotional experiences.

Explaining Age Differences in Emotional Well-Being

What is responsible for better emotional functioning across adulthood, and more nuanced emotional experiences? According to socioemotional selectivity theory (Carstensen, Isaacowitz, & Charles, 1999), these age differences in emotional experiences stem from time perspective. According to this theory, the awareness, conscious or not, that all people have about the amount of time remaining in their lives shapes the motivations directing their thoughts and behaviors. When faced with seemingly boundless horizons, as is often true during early adulthood, people prioritize informational goals more so than emotion-related goals. For example, people actively strive to obtain information and knowledge for their future, sometimes at the expense of an emotionally meaningful activity. When the horizon diminishes and people perceive their time as growing shorter, they prioritize emotion-related goals. For this reason, emotionally meaningful activities, and maximizing emotional well-being, increase in importance across adulthood, with the shift in motivational goals and reports of satisfaction following a linear increase with age.

The theoretical model of strength and vulnerability integration (SAVI; Charles & Carstensen, 2010; Charles & Piazza, 2009) predicts that there is a general age-related increase in emotional well-being resulting from the "strengths" of aging, which include time perspective regarding the amount of time one has left to live (as predicted by socioemotional selectivity theory) and the social and emotional experiences and expertise gained from time lived. People's motivation for emotion-related goals increase over time as a result of diminishing time left to live, but their ability to engage in strategies to optimize their well-being reflects information gathered from their social and emotional experiences resulting from time lived. Researchers have discussed the important role that experience plays for learning how to regulate emotions in daily life (e.g., Blanchard-Fields, 2007; Magai, Consedine, Krivoshekova, Kudadjie-Gyamfi, & McPherson, 2006). With this experience, people learn about their environment, but they also learn about themselves. By avoiding the experience of negative arousal, older adults effectively regulate their emotional well-being.

Environmental Influences

As previously discussed, negative emotional experiences are more frequent during late adolescence and young adulthood, whereas emotional well-being generally appears to increase across adulthood. These age differences may be partially due to differences in the social roles and environments normative for each age group. For example, during adolescence and young adulthood, there are many new social roles to master (e.g., school transitions, changes in legal status, exploration of career options, meeting romantic partners, starting families), which may also increase the likelihood of encountering stressful situations. In midlife, career and family goals increase in importance, and are predictive of well-being (e.g., Baruch & Barnett, 1986; Evandrou & Glaser, 2004; Vandewater, Ostrove, & Stewart, 1997). During later life, however, social roles become more predictable (e.g., retirement, grown children have moved out of the home; Elder, 1994). Often, retirement or reduction in work hours among older adults provides more leisure time and greater latitude with which to structure daily routines (Ginn & Fast, 2006; Rosenkoetter, Garris, & Engdahl, 2001). In fact, older age is associated with fewer events overall, which may contribute to decreased negative affect with older age (Charles et al., 2010).

With this greater freedom, people become increasing agentic and are able to control and select into optimal environments (see review by Hawkley & Little, 2002). Researchers have discussed processes of interactional continuity and cumulative continuity that result in people having predictable environments that fit their personality styles (Caspi et al., 1989). Interactional continuity refers to the process whereby people have relatively stable interactional styles, such as stable attachment styles or similar emotional reactions to the same types of events that elicit similar responses from their social partners. Cumulative continuity refers to the process whereby people select similar environments that reinforce their identity and their emotional styles (Caspi et al., 1989). For example, a person who is highly impulsive and enjoys new and exciting experiences may select more high-risk hobbies and careers than a person who is low in impulsivity and prefers predictable and quiet environments.

Both interactional and cumulative continuity have been used to explain interactions between genetic and environmental factors, whereby genetic predispositions partially determine later environments (Caspi et al., 1989). These factors may also explain processes whereby environments become more predictable over time, allowing people to anticipate situations and select those that will maintain or even increase their affective well-being. For the most part, people strive to feel positive emotions and avoid negative emotions and pain—the hedonic principle that is the foundation of many motivational frameworks. People will appraise the world and make decisions taking hedonic goals in mind. Although people often define emotion regulation as actions people do in response to an emotion-eliciting encounter, preselecting situations is also an active emotion-regulation strategy requiring forethought and self-knowledge (Gross, 1998).

Researchers have examined age-related increases in many processes that may lead to increases in well-being. Older adults appraise negative situations more benignly (Charles & Carstensen, 2008), are less likely to report having regrets about events in their lives (Torges, Stewart, & Nolen-Hoeksema, 2008), and remember the past more positively (Kennedy, Mather, & Carstensen, 2004). These strategies all may play a role in the higher levels of emotional well-being reported by older adults, yet some of the most important actions they employ for enhancing their well-being may lie in how they choose and structure their social environment.

The social environment is central to well-being and predicts emotional, cognitive, and physical outcomes (see review by Charles & Carstensen, 2010). People are social animals (Baumeister & Leary, 1995), and social partners are responsible for the majority of stressors (Almeida, 2005) and uplifts (positive events;

Charles et al., 2010) that people experience in their daily lives. Positive emotional ties and interactions are related to higher levels of positive affect, and negative interpersonal exchanges are related to less positive affect and increased levels of depressive symptoms (Newsom, Mahan, Rook, & Krause, 2008; Rook, 1984). One of the most important emotion regulation strategies that people can employ is to surround themselves with people who provide emotional meaning and satisfaction and to limit their exposure to people who cause them distress or who offer little emotional value (Lang & Carstensen, 1994).

Studies of social interactions and social patterns suggest that, with age, people are spending a greater proportion of their time in social interactions with people who provide high levels of emotional fulfillment (Carstensen et al., 1999). This pattern of social activity was first described in the tenets of socioemotional selectivity theory, which posits that social selection is instrumental for the maintenance and, sometimes, increased well-being observed in late life (Carstensen, 2006; Carstensen et al., 1999). Older adults report spending a greater proportion of their time with social partners such as close friends and family members, and they report higher levels of positive affect with these partners than do younger adults (Charles & Piazza, 2007). As people age, they report increasing levels of satisfaction with their family members (Carstensen, 1992). They also report spending less time with casual acquaintances. Over time, the people who are less likely to remain in their social circles are those who were rated as less emotionally fulfilling and important to them (Lang & Carstensen, 2002).

Older adults report less frequent social conflicts than do younger adults (Birditt & Fingerman, 2003; Charles, Piazza, Luong, & Almeida, 2009), an age-related trend that continues when comparing across people in their 60s to their 90s (Charles et al., 2010). Nonetheless, interpersonal conflicts occur at any age. When they do, researchers have found that older adults may respond to, and interpret, these social exchanges in more positive ways than younger adults (e.g., Fung, Yeung, Li, & Lang, 2009). For example, older adults who experience negative social exchanges with their non-kin social partners report an increase in closeness with these social partners over time (Fung et al., 2009). These findings suggest that older adults may be motivated to maintain ties with problematic social partners, possibly because the support and companionship they provide outweigh the costs of occasional negative exchanges.

Older adults are also more likely to engage in strategies that minimize distress and continued conflict when interacting with emotionally close social partners (Birditt & Fingerman, 2005; Birditt, Fingerman, & Almeida, 2005; Blanchard-Fields, 2007; Blanchard-Fields, Mienaltowski, & Seay, 2007; Coats & Blanchard-Fields, 2008). Examples of these passive disengagement strategies include ignoring the situation, avoiding conflict, and doing nothing. When asked what the best strategies are for resolving interpersonal conflicts, older adults recommend these strategies to others (Charles, Carstensen, & McFall, 2001b). When they report having engaged in these strategies, they state their goals for doing so were to primarily preserve harmony in their relationships and to regulate their emotions (Birditt & Fingerman, 2003; Sorkin & Rook, 2006). Their recommendations concur with experts, who agree with older adults that more passive strategies are often the best way of handling tense social interactions with emotionally close others (Blanchard-Fields et al., 2007). Older adults also report greater benefits of using passive strategies when describing the aftermath of such exchanges than when they use more confrontational, active strategies

(Sorkin & Rook, 2006). Older adults who report using more passive strategies with the goal of preserving good will in the relationship report lower levels of emotional distress and higher perceived success in achieving their goal than older adults who report engaging in more active strategies with the intended goals of getting the other person to change (Sorkin & Rook, 2006).

The age differences in the use of more passive strategies may explain why older adults report higher levels of well-being and less emotional reactivity to social stressors compared to younger adults (Birditt et al., 2005). One study examined this question by assessing affective reactivity (i.e., the degree to which affective distress increased in response to an event) in response to two different types of social stressors: an actual argument, and a situation where people could have argued but instead opted for the more passive strategy of letting the situation pass to avoid further disagreement. When people ranging from 25 to 74 years of age reported engaging in an actual argument, age did not predict level of affective reactivity: older adults were just as reactive as were younger adults (Charles et al., 2009). When people reported letting the situation pass, however, older age was associated with less affective reactivity. For younger adults, reactivity was similar across both situations. Therefore, the more passive action was related to less reactivity for older adults and possibly plays an even more important role for emotion regulation in later life.

Recent findings suggest that the more benign social environments reported by older adults may not be the result of actions on the part of the older adults alone. The social input model (Fingerman & Pitzer, 2007) states that people treat older adults in ways that lead to more positive social outcomes. When asked how they would respond to conflicts with either younger or older social partners, people commonly report that they would react to the younger person with more confrontation than they would to an older person (Fingerman, Miller, & Charles, 2008). These actions are partially explained by perceived time left in the relationship: when the time left grows shorter in anticipation of an impending move, people are even more likely to endorse less confrontational styles with their partners regardless of their age. Thus, even younger adults who personally see an expanded horizon for themselves may view a relationship with an older adult as time-limited, and may maximize well-being within this relationship as a result. This same pattern of results is found when younger and older adults are asked about how they would respond to tense interactions with close social partners (Fingerman et al., 2008), as well as how hypothetical younger and older adults would respond to close or casual social partners (Miller, Charles, & Fingerman, 2009). In all of these situations, older social partners are treated with less confrontation, which may, in part, explain why older adults generally experience high levels of well-being.

Change in Physiological Processes

Chronological aging is often related to changes in physiological functioning that also may influence emotional functioning. Some of these changes may have direct effects on patterns of neural activity in response to emotional stimuli. For example, several studies have examined age differences in neural activation in the brain when people view positive, negative, and neutral stimuli. One study examining amygdala activation found that older adults exhibited greater activity for positive stimuli and less activity for negative stimuli than did younger adults (Mather et al.,

2004). Another study also found less activation of the amygdala among older adults than younger adults when viewing negative faces (Iidaka et al., 2002). Similar age differences were found in a study examining activity in the ventromedial prefrontal cortex (an area of the brain associated with emotion regulation). Younger adults exhibited more activity in this area of the brain in response to negative stimuli, whereas older adults exhibited more neural activity in response to positive stimuli (Leclerc & Kensinger, 2008).

This decreased pattern of activity in the amygdala mirrors decreases in other physiological processes as well. For example, researchers have found decreased heart rate and skin conductance level with age when emotions were elicited by film clips (e.g., Tsai et al., 2000) or by relived emotional experiences (Levenson, Carstensen, Friesen, & Ekman, 1991). One study that used emotionally evocative film clips depicting themes relevant to aging (such as the plight of a person with dementia) elicited the same level of physiological activity among older and younger adults and higher self-reported sadness among older adults (Kunzmann & Grühn, 2005). Even when self-reported emotions are similar, however, physiological arousal is often lower among older adults, and researchers have posited that perhaps this attenuated physiological reactivity may make emotions easier to regulate in older age (e.g., Levenson, 2000).

Other studies, the majority using animal models, suggest that decreased flexibility in the aging system may make recovery from emotional arousal more difficult. The glucocorticoid cascade hypothesis, initially used to describe results from animal studies, has expanded to describe factors related to human aging as well (Bakke et al., 2004; see reviews by Björntorp, 2002; Otte et al., 2005). This hypothesis discusses how age influences the physiological response to emotional stimuli. When people experience high levels of negative emotions—either real or perceived—this affective distress causes a chain of chemical reactions that begins with the hypothalamus, travels down the body, and ends with the release of cortisol. Cortisol is a glucocorticoid hormone, which helps to mobilize the body's energy resources during stressful situations (Lovallo & Thomas, 2000). According to the glucocorticoid cascade hypothesis, older age is related to a reduced ability of neurons in the hypothalamus to inhibit this cascading effect, leading to longer periods of activation. This hypothesis is consistent with findings showing that high-affinity receptors responsible for feedback inhibition in the hypothalamus decreases with age (Dodt, Theine, Uthgenannt, Born, & Fehm, 1994; see review by Ferrari, Radaelli, & Centola, 2003). Although this hypothesis needs to be further tested and refined using human samples, studies by Uchino and his colleagues examining the cardiovascular system suggest increased physiological activation in response to stress that may be indicative of poorer downregulation of physiological activity (see review by Uchino, Birmingham, & Berg, 2010). They found that when people experienced stressors in their daily lives, older age was related to greater increases in blood pressure in cross-sectional (Uchino, Uno, Holt-Lunstad, & Flinders, 1999) and longitudinal (Uchino, Holt-Lunstad, Bloor, & Campo, 2005) studies.

Interactions Between Physiological and Environmental Processes

Researchers have found a great deal of variability in patterns of emotional well-being over time (Griffin, Mroczek, & Spiro, 2006). The previous section discussed reasons why affective well-being remains fairly stable or may even increase across adulthood, but this pattern does not continue for everyone. Patterns are even more variable in late life. SAVI posits that when situations occur that elicit low levels of arousal, older adults can employ cognitive strategies (such as appraising the environment as more benign) and will often employ these strategies better than will younger adults (Charles & Piazza, 2009). Their decreased levels of physiological arousal to these types of stressors may even aid their emotion regulation for relatively minor, transient emotional events. When older adults are unable to select into benign environments and unavoidable situations arise that elicit high levels of physiological arousal, SAVI predicts that no age-related benefits in emotion regulation will occur. With prolonged exposure to a distressing situation and no means to escape, older adults may report even poorer emotion-regulation outcomes than younger adults. These chronically stressful situations will change the trajectory of emotional well-being for anyone who encounters them, regardless of age. Because these situations may occur more frequently in late life (e.g., bereavement), however, they may explain why trajectories of affective well-being after the mid-60s and into the 70s are not as predictable as the more positive trajectories of well-being observed earlier in adulthood.

What situations, then, create high levels of sustained arousal that cannot be avoided? These situations include loss of social belonging, where people lose those who provide the most emotional meaning in their lives. These people are often spouses, but they are not limited to this relationship and can encompass family members and close friends as well. Researchers have found that bereavement can have long-term effects on life satisfaction and well-being lasting several years (e.g., Arbuckle & de Vries, 1995; Nolen-Hoeksema, McBride, & Larson, 1997). Another circumstance that may lead to sustained arousal includes accumulated chronic health conditions. These health conditions may increase the number of stressors people encounter in their daily lives, and the combination of decreased ability to regulate physiological arousal coupled with the multiple co-occurring stressors makes them just as vulnerable when coping with daily stressors as are younger adults with similar levels of physical conditions (Piazza, Charles, & Almeida, 2007). Finally, neurological impairment may make emotion regulation difficult, both because older adults are not able to use cognitive strategies as effectively and because they may experience dysregulation of the HPA axis that produces the stress hormone, cortisol, and is so critical for emotion regulation. These neurological impairments include the dementias and Parkinson's disease, conditions associated with high levels of affective distress (Greenwald et al., 1989; Karlsen, Larsen, Tandberg, & Maeland, 1998). These three situations, loss of social belonging, chronic health conditions, and neurological impairment increase in prevalence with age, making subgroups of older adults susceptible to poor emotion regulation.

In addition to these experiences that are encountered in old age that may change the course of affective well-being, SAVI posits that others may have entered old age with vulnerabilities that also place them at risk for continued affective distress. Old age is not a period that people enter in with a clean slate, but one that is built on the foundation laid earlier in life. Researchers have found that older adults who had childhoods that were characterized by emotional neglect or adversity are more likely to report smaller social networks and feeling emotionally isolated from others

(Wilson et al., 2006). Among older adults, those with a history of childhood physical or sexual abuse are more likely to report worse physical and mental health (Draper et al., 2008). In addition, people with high levels of neuroticism do not show the same decreases in negative affect over time observed by their less neurotic peers (Charles et al., 2001a; Griffin et al., 2006). People high in neuroticism also have more fractious social relationships as evidenced by their higher rates of divorce (Roberts, Kuncel, Shiner, Caspi, & Goldberg, 2007), worse physical health (Charles, Gatz, Kato, & Pedersen, 2008), and a greater number of negative life events (e.g., Farmer et al., 2002), which contribute to accumulated stress and adversity later in life. Thus, older adults face greater risk factors with age, which may impede emotional well-being. In sum, SAVI predicts a general age-related increase in emotional well-being as a result of age-related strengths including an increased motivation to regulate emotions (as posited by socioemotional selectivity theory), greater social and emotional experiences and expertise garnered from time lived, and better treatment by social partners (as predicted by social input model). However, age-related vulnerabilities such as less flexibility in physiological systems, which lead to slower reactivity and recovery from arousing situations and an increased prevalence in risk factors associated with poorer well-being (e.g., loss of social belonging) may attenuate age differences in well-being.

▨ FUTURE DIRECTIONS IN RESEARCH ON EMOTIONAL EXPERIENCE ACROSS THE LIFE SPAN

The previous sections highlighted emotional experience across the life span, tracing social and physiological influences before birth and into old age. Although the study of emotion is growing rapidly, many questions about life-span development remain unaddressed. Accurate assessments of emotional well-being and emotional reactivity among infants continue to challenge people studying the effects of prenatal environment on later experiences. In addition, emotional well-being is not often studied among young children, particularly among children who do not yet have the memory capacity to accurately rate their past feelings over the course of several weeks or the prior month. Studying consistency in levels of emotional experience, then, requires clever multimodal assessments to address these concerns. Often, the assessments vary so much between childhood and adolescence that comparisons across modes make studying continuity over time difficult.

Across adulthood, researchers have yet to completely understand the role of physiological reactivity in emotional experiences, and how age-related physiological changes influence emotional experience. In addition, genes continue to express themselves in late life, and continued research examining gene and environmental interactions among adults would greatly enrich our understanding of these interactive processes.

Finally, much of the research reviewed previously was based on Western samples. Much less is known about how these patterns of emotional experience and regulation may vary across cultures. For example, the period known as emerging adulthood (18–25 years) is generally a phenomenon unique to industrialized societies in which young adults have more time to explore their career options and life goals, whereas in less developed countries adolescents and older children may be expected to work and help support the family and do not have the luxury of exploration (Arnett, 1999). Thus, the high levels of depressive symptomatology and negative affect during this age period may be unique to Western cultures. Further research will explore whether the trough in emotional experience during later adolescence and early adulthood is a universal phenomenon. In addition, the age differences in the use of different types of emotion regulation strategies may not be replicated in collectivistic cultures, such as East Asian groups. Passive strategies (e.g., avoidance) may be used by individuals of all ages from collectivistic societies because these cultural groups generally value social harmony and interdependence (Kirkbride, Tang, & Westwood, 1991; Markus & Kitayama, 1991).

In sum, temperamental characteristics observed in infancy and childhood are relatively enduring and are posited to form the basis of later personality traits. How innate qualities unfold throughout the life span, however, is determined by physiological processes but strongly dependent on the environment, particularly the social environment. Throughout life, people ranging from caregivers, peers, and romantic attachments shape emotional experiences. Emotional well-being is among the lowest during adolescence, when social roles and relationships are rapidly changing, but continues to increase throughout adulthood. Older adults increase in their motivations to regulate and more often engage in behaviors and appraisals that allow people to regulate their emotions more effectively than younger adults. Social partners are also motivated to treat older adults more kindly, making their social environments more benign and predictable, as posited by social input model. When people cannot avoid sustained levels of affective distress, however, age differences may be attenuated. Because social relationships so often comprise the situations that elicit intense emotional experiences, social interactions are critically important in determining emotional well-being throughout the life span.

REFERENCES

Abe, H., Hidaka, N., Kawagoe, C., Odagiri, K., Watanabe, Y., Ikeda, T., et al. (2007). Prenatal psychological stress causes higher emotionality, depression-like behavior, and elevated activity in the hypothalamo-pituitary-adrenal axis. *Neuroscience Research, 59,* 145–151.

Ainsworth, M., & Wittig, B. (1969). Attachment and exploratory behavior of one-year-olds in a strange situation. In B. Foss (Ed.), *Determinants of infant behavior* (Vol. 4, pp. 113–136). New York: Barnes & Noble.

Almeida, D. M. (2005). Resilience and vulnerability to daily stressors assessed via diary methods. *Current Directions in Psychological Science, 14,* 64–68.

Angold, A., Costello, E. J., & Worthman, C. M. (1998). Puberty and depression: The role of age, pubertal status, and pubertal timing. *Psychological Medicine, 28,* 51–61.

Antonucci, T. C., Akiyama, H., & Takahashi, K. (2004). Attachment and close relationships across the life span. *Attachment & Human Development, 6,* 353–370.

Arbuckle, N. W., & de Vries, B. (1995). The long-term effects of later life spousal and parental bereavement on personal functioning. *The Gerontologist, 5,* 637–647.

Arnett, J. J. (1999). Adolescent storm and stress, revisited. *American Psychologist, 54,* 371–386.

Arnett, J. J. (2000). Emerging adulthood: A theory of development from the late teens to the early twenties. *American Psychologist, 55,* 469–480.

Asher, S. R., & Paquette, J. A. (2003). Loneliness and peer relations in childhood. *Current Directions in Psychological Science, 12,* 75–78.

Bakermans-Kranenburg, M. J., & van Ijzendoorn, M. H. (2008). Oxytocin receptor (OXTR) and serotonin transporter (5-HTT) genes associated with observed parenting. *Social Cognitive and Affective Neuroscience, 3,* 128–134.

Bakke, M., Tuxen, A., Thomsen, C. E., Bardow, A., Alkjær, T., & Jensen, B. R. (2004). Salivary cortisol level, salivary flow rate, and masticatory muscle activity in response to acute mental stress: A comparison between age and young women. *Gerontology, 50,* 383–392.

Baruch, G. K., & Barnett, R. (1986). Role quality, multiple role involvement, and psychological well-being in midlife women. *Journal of Personality and Social Psychology, 51,* 578–585.

Baumeister, R. F., & Leary, M. R. (1995). The need to belong: Desire for interpersonal attachments as a fundamental human motivation. *Psychological Bulletin, 117,* 497–529.

Bell, M. A., Greene, D. R., & Wolfe, C. D. (2010). Psychobiological mechanisms of cognition—Emotion integration in early development. In S. D. Calkins & M. A. Bell (Eds.), *Child development at the intersection of emotion and cognition* (pp. 115–132). Washington, DC: American Psychological Association.

Birditt, K. S., & Fingerman, K. L. (2003). Age and gender differences in adults' descriptions of emotional reactions to interpersonal problems. *Journals of Gerontology Series B: Psychological Sciences and Social Sciences, 58,* P237–P245.

Birditt, K. S., & Fingerman, K. L. (2005). Do we get better at picking our battles? Age group differences in descriptions of behavioral reactions to interpersonal tensions. *Journals of Gerontology Series B: Psychological Sciences and Social Sciences, 60,* P121–P128.

Birditt, K. S., Fingerman, K. L., & Almeida, D. M. (2005). Age differences in exposure and reactions to interpersonal tensions: A daily diary study. *Psychology and Aging, 20,* 330–340.

Björntorp, P. (2002). Alterations in the ageing corticotropic stress-response axis. In D. Chadwick & J. Goode (Eds.), *Endocrine facets of ageing* (pp. 46–65). Chichester, England: Wiley.

Blanchard-Fields, F. (2007). Everyday problem solving and emotion: An adult developmental perspective. *Current Directions in Psychological Science, 16,* 26–31.

Blanchard-Fields, F., Mienaltowski, A., & Seay, R. B. (2007). Age differences in everyday problem-solving effectiveness: Older adults select more effective strategies for interpersonal problems. *Journals of Gerontology Series B: Psychological Sciences and Social Sciences, 62,* P61–P64.

Blum, K., Sheridan, P. J., Wood, R. C., Braverman, E. R., Chen, T. J., & Comings, D. E. (1995). Dopamine D2 receptor gene variants: Association and linkage studies in impulsive-addictive-compulsive behaviour. *Pharmacogenetics, 5,* 121–141.

Boivin, M., Hymel, S., & Burkowski, W. M. (1995). The roles of social withdrawal, peer rejection, and victimization by peers in predicting loneliness and depressed mood in childhood. *Development and Psychopathology, 7,* 765–785.

Bowlby, J. (1969). Disruption of affectional bonds and its effects on behavior. *Journal of Contemporary Psychotherapy, 2,* 75–86.

Buss, K. A., Malmschadt Schumacher, J. R., Dolski, I., Kalin, N. H., Goldsmith, H. H., & Davidson, R. J. (2003). Right frontal brain activity, cortisol, and withdrawal behavior in 6-month-old infants. *Behavioral Neuroscience, 117,* 11–20.

Brown, S. L., & Brown, M. R. (2006). Selective investment theory: Recasting the functional significance of close relationships. *Psychological Inquiry, 17,* 1–29.

Brown, B. B., Mounts, N., Lamborn, S. D., & Steinberg, L. (1993). Parenting practices and peer group affiliation in adolescence. *Child Development, 64,* 467–482.

Bynner, J. (2005). Rethinking the youth phase of the life course: The case for emerging adulthood. *Journal of Youth Studies, 8,* 367–384.

Calkins, S. D., Fox, N. A., & Marshall, T. R. (1996). Behavioral and physiological antecedents of inhibited and uninhibited behavior. *Child development, 67,* 523–540.

Calkins, S. D., & Hill, A. (2007). Caregiver influences on emerging emotion regulation: Biological and environmental transactions in early development. In J. J. Gross (Ed.), *Handbook of emotion regulation* (pp. 229–248). New York: Guilford.

Carstensen, L. L. (1992). Motivation for social contact across the life span: A theory of socioemotional selectivity. In J. E. Jacobs (Ed.), *Nebraska Symposium on Motivation, 1992: Developmental perspectives on motivation* (pp. 209–254). Lincoln: University of Nebraska Press.

Carstensen, L. L. (2006). The influence of a sense of time on human development. *Science, 312,* 1913–1915.

Carstensen, L. L., Isaacowitz, D. M., & Charles, S. T. (1999). Taking time seriously: A theory of socioemotional selectivity. *American Psychologist, 54,* 165–181.

Carstensen, L. L., Pasupathi, M., Mayr, U., & Nesselroade, J. R. (2000). Emotional experience in everyday life across the adult life span. *Journal of Personality and Social Psychology, 79,* 644–655.

Caspi, A., Bem, D. J., & Elder, G. H., Jr. (1989). Continuities and consequences of interactional styles across the life course. *Journal of personality, 57,* 375–406.

Caspi, A., Roberts, B. W., & Shiner, R. L. (2005). Personality development: Stability and change. *Annual Review of Psychology, 56*, 453–484.

Caspi, A., Sugden, K., Moffitt, T. E., Taylor, A., Craig, I. W., Harrington, H., et al. (2003). Influence of life stress on depression: Moderation by a polymorphism in the 5-HTT gene. *Science, 301*, 386–389.

Charles, S. T. (2005). Viewing injustice: Greater emotion heterogeneity with age. *Psychology and Aging, 20*, 159–164.

Charles, S. T., & Carstensen, L. L. (2010). Social and emotional aging. *Annual Review of Psychology, 61*, 383–409.

Charles, S. T., & Carstensen, L. L. (2008). Unpleasant situations elicit different emotional responses in younger and older adults. *Psychology and Aging, 23*, 495–504.

Charles, S. T., Carstensen, L. L., & McFall, R. M. (2001b). Problem-solving in the nursing home environment: Age and experience differences in emotional reactions and responses. *Journal of Clinical Geropsychology, 7*, 319–330.

Charles, S. T., Gatz, M., Kato, K., & Pedersen, N. L. (2008). Physical health 25 years later: The predictive ability of neuroticism. *Health Psychology, 27*, 369–378.

Charles, S. T., & Horwitz, B. N. (2010). Positive emotions and health: What we know about aging. In C. A. Depp & D. V. Jeste (Eds.), *Successful cognitive and emotional aging* (pp. 55–72). Arlington, VA: American Psychiatric.

Charles, S. T., Luong, G., Almeida, D. M., Ryff, C., Sturm, M., & Love, G. (2010). Fewer ups and downs: Daily stressors mediate age differences in negative affect. *Journals of Gerontology Series B: Psychological Sciences and Social Sciences, 65B*, 279–286.

Charles, S. T., & Piazza, J. R. (2007). Memories of social interactions: Age differences in emotional intensity. *Psychology and Aging, 22*, 300–309.

Charles, S. T., & Piazza, J. R. (2009). Age differences in affective well-being: Context matters. *Social and Personality Psychology Compass, 4*, 82–88.

Charles, S. T., Piazza, J. R., Luong, G., & Almeida, D. M. (2009). Now you see it, now you don't: Age differences in affective reactivity to social tensions. *Psychology and Aging, 24*, 645–653.

Charles, S. T., Reynolds, C. A., & Gatz, M. (2001a). Age-related differences and change in positive affect over 23 years. *Journal of Personality and Social Psychology, 80*, 136–151.

Cicchetti, D., & Toth, S. L. (1995). A developmental psychopathology perspective on child abuse and neglect. *Journal of the American Academy of Child & Adolescent Psychiatry, 34*, 541–565.

Coats, A. H., & Blanchard-Fields, F. (2008). Emotion regulation in interpersonal problems: The role of cognitive-emotional complexity, emotion regulation goals, and expressivity. *Psychology and Aging, 23*, 39–51.

Cohen, P., Cohen, J., Kasen, S., Velez, C. N., Hartmark, C., Johnson, J., et al. (1993). An epidemiological study of disorders in late childhood and adolescence: Age and gender-specific prevalence. *Journal of Child Psychology and Psychiatry, 34*, 851–867.

Collier, D. A., Arranz, M. J., Sham, P., & Battersby, S. (1996). The serotonin transporter is a potential susceptibility factor for bipolar affective disorder. *Neuroreport, 7*, 1675–1679.

Compas, B. E., & Wagner, B. M. (1991). Psychosocial stress during adolescence: Intrapersonal and interpersonal processes. In M. E. Colten & S. Gore (Eds.), *Adolescent stress: Causes and consequences* (pp. 67–86). New York: Aldine de Gruyter.

Costello, E. J., Mustillo, S., Erkanli, A., Keeler, G., & Angold, A. (2003). Prevalence and development of psychiatric disorders in childhood and adolescence. *Archives of General Psychiatry, 60*, 837–844.

Cunningham, M. G., Bhattacharyya, S., & Benes, F. M. (2002). Amygdalo-cortical sprouting continues into early adulthood: Implications for the development of normal and abnormal function during adolescence. *Journal of Comparative Neurology, 453*, 116–130.

Darwin, C. (1872/1998). *The expression of the emotions in man and animals (1872)*. New York: Philosophical Library. 3rd edition (1998) with Introduction. Afterward and Commentary by P. Ekman: London: Harper Collins New York: Oxford University Press.

Davey, A., Halverson, C. F., Jr., Zonderman, A. B., & Costa, P. T. Jr. (2004). Change in depressive symptoms in the Baltimore longitudinal study of aging. *Journals of Gerontology Series B: Psychological Sciences and Social Sciences, 59*, P279–P277.

Davidson, R. J., & Fox, N. A. (1989). Frontal brain asymmetry predicts infants' response to maternal separation. *Journal of Abnormal Psychology, 98*, 127–131.

Davidson, R. J., Jackson, D. C., & Kalin, N. H. (2000). Emotion, plasticity, context, and regulation: Perspectives from affective neuroscience. *Psychological Bulletin, 126*, 890–909.

Davidson, R. J., Putnam, K. M., & Larson, C. L. (2000). Dysfunction in the neural circuitry of emotion regulation—A possible prelude to violence. *Violence, 289,* 591–594.

Davis, E. P., & Sandman, C. A. (2010). The timing of prenatal exposure to maternal cortisol and psychosocial stress is associated with human infant cognitive development. *Child Development, 81,* 131–148.

Davis, M. (1992). The role of the amygdale in fear and anxiety. *Annual Review of Neuroscience, 15,* 353–375.

De Haan, M., & Gunnar, M. R. (2009). The brain in a social environment: Why study development? In M. de Haan & M. R. Gunnar (Eds.), *Handbook of developmental social neuroscience* (pp. 3–12). New York: Guilford.

De Pauw, S. W., Mervielde, I., & Van Leeuwen, K. G. (2009). How are traits related to problem behavior in preschoolers? Similarities and contrasts between temperament and personality. *Journal of Abnormal Child Psychology, 37,* 309–325.

Dickerson, S. S., & Kemeny, M. E. (2004). Acute stressors and cortisol responses: A theoretical integration and synthesis of laboratory research. *Psychological Bulletin, 130,* 355–391.

Diener, E., & Suh, E. (1997). Measuring quality of life: Economic, social, and subjective indicators. *Social Indicators Research, 40,* 189–216.

Dodt, C., Theine, K., Uthgenannt, D., Born, J., & Fehm, H. L. (1994). Basal secretory activity of the hypothalamo-pituitary-adrenocortical axis is enhanced in healthy elderly: An assessment during undisturbed night-time sleep. *European Journal of Endocrinology, 131,* 443–450.

Draper, B., Pfaff, J. J., Pirkis, J., Snowdon, J., Lautenschlager, N. T., Wilson, I., et al. (2008). Long-term effects of childhood abuse on the quality of life and health of older people: Results from the depression and early prevention of suicide in general practice project. *Journal of the American Geriatrics Society, 56,* 262–271.

Eccles, J., Wigfield, A., Harold, R. D., & Blumenfeld, P. (1993). Age and gender differences in children's self- and task perceptions during elementary school. *Child Development, 64,* 830–847.

Egliston, K., McMahon, C., & Austin, M. (2007). Stress in pregnancy and infant HPA axis function: Conceptual and methodological issues relating to the use of salivary cortisol as an outcome measure. *Psychoneuroendocrinology, 32,* 1–13.

Eisenberg, N., Fabes, R. A., Guthrie, I. K., & Reiser, M. (2000). Dispositional emotionality and regulation: Their role in predicting quality of social functioning. *Journal of personality and social psychology, 78,* 136–157.

Elder, G. H. (1994). Time, human agency, and social change: Perspectives on the life course. *Social Psychology Quarterly, 57,* 4–15.

Evandrou, M., & Glaser, K. (2004). Family, work and quality of life: Changing economic and social roles through the lifecourse. *Ageing & Society, 24,* 771–791.

Farmer, A., Redman, K., Harris, T., Mahmood, A., Sadler, S., Pickering, A., et al. (2002). Neuroticism, extraversion, life events and depression: The Cardiff depression study. *The British Journal of Psychiatry, 181,* 118–122.

Federenko, I., & Wadhwa, P. (2004). Women's mental health during pregnancy influences fetal and infant developmental and health outcomes. *CNS Spectrums, 9,* 198–206.

Ferrari, A. U., Radaelli, A., & Centola, M. (2003). Invited review: Aging and the cardiovascular system. *Journal of Applied Physiology, 95,* 2591–2597.

Field, R., Diego, M., Hernandez-Reif, M., Figueiredo, B., Deeds, O., Ascencio, A., et al. (2010). Comorbid depression and anxiety effects on pregnancy and neonatal outcome. *Infant Behavior & Development, 33,* 23–29.

Fingerman, K. L., Miller, L., & Charles, S. (2008). Saving the best for last: How adults treat social partners of different ages. *Psychology and Aging, 23,* 399–409.

Fingerman, K. L., & Pitzer, L. (2007). Socialization in old age. In J. E. Grusec & P. D. Hastings (Eds.), *Handbook of socialization* (pp. 232–255). New York: Guilford Press.

Forbes, E. E., & Dahl, R. E. (2010). Pubertal development and behavior: Hormonal activation of social and motivational tendencies. *Brain and Cognition, 72,* 66–72.

Fung, H. H., Yeung, D. Y., Li, K., & Lang, F. R. (2009). Benefits of negative social exchanges for emotional closeness. *Journal of Gerontology: Psychological Sciences, 64B,* 612–621.

Galambos, N. L., Barker, E. T., & Almeida, D. M. (2003). Parents do matter: Trajectories of change in externalizing and internalizing problems in early adolescence. *Child Development, 74,* 578–594.

Galambos, N. L., Barker, E. T., & Krahn, H. J. (2006). Depression, self-esteem, and anger in emerging adulthood: Seven-year trajectories. *Developmental Psychology, 42,* 350–365.

Ganiban, J. M., Saudino, K. J., Ulbricht, J., Neiderhiser, J. M., & Reiss, D. (2008). Stability and change in temperament during adolescence. *Journal of Personality and Social Psychology, 95,* 222–236.

Ge, X., Lorenz, F. O., Conger, R. D., Elder, Jr., G. H., & Simons, R. L. (1994). Trajectories of stressful life events and depressive symptoms during adolescence. *Developmental Psychology, 30,* 467–483.

Giedd, J. N. (2004). Structural magnetic resonance imaging of the adolescent brain. *Annals of the New York Academy of Sciences, 1021,* 77–85.

Ginn, J., & Fast, J. (2006). Employment and social integration in midlife: Preferred and actual time use across welfare regime types. *Research on Aging, 28,* 669–690.

Gogtay, N., Giedd, J. N., Lusk, L., Hayashi, K. M., Greenstein, D., Vaituzis, A. C., et al. (2004). Dynamic mapping of human cortical development during childhood through early adulthood. *Proceedings of the National Academy of Sciences of the United States of America, 101,* 8174–8179.

Gottman, J. (2001). Meta-emotion, children's emotional intelligence, and buffering children from marital conflict. In C. D. Ryff & B. H. Singer (Eds.), *Emotion, social relationships, and health: Series in affective science* (pp. 23–40). New York: Oxford University Press.

Greenwald, B. S., Kramer-Ginsberg, E., Marin, D. B., Laitman, L. B., Hermann, C. K., Mohs, R. C., et al. (1989). Dementia with coexistent major depression. *American Journal of Psychiatry, 146,* 1472–1478.

Griffin, P. W., Mroczek, D. K., & Spiro, A. (2006). Variability in affective change among aging men: Longitudinal findings form the VA normative aging study. *Journal of Research in Personality, 40,* 942–965.

Gross, J. J. (1998). The emerging field of emotion regulation: An integrative review. *Review of General Psychology, 2,* 271–299.

Gross, J. J. (Ed.). (2007). *Handbook of emotion regulation.* New York: Guilford Press.

Gross, H. E., Shaw, D. S., & Moilanen, K. L. (2008). Reciprocal associations between boys' externalizing problems and mothers' depressive symptoms. *Journal of Abnormal Child Psychology, 36,* 693–709.

Hall, G. S. (1904). *Adolescence: Its psychology and its relations to physiology, anthropology, sociology, sex, crime, religion, and education* (Vols. 1 & 2). New York: Appleton-Century-Crofts.

Hane, A., & Fox, N. (2006). Ordinary variations in maternal caregiving influence human infants' stress reactivity. *Psychological Science, 17,* 550–556.

Hankin, B. L., Abramson, L. Y., Moffitt, T. E., Silva, P. A., McGee, R., & Angell, K. E. (1998). Development of depression from preadolescence to young adulthood: Emerging gender differences in a 10-year longitudinal study. *Journal of Abnormal Psychology, 107,* 128–140.

Hawkley, P. H., & Little, T. D. (2002). Evolutionary and developmental perspectives on the agentic self. In D. Cervone & W. Mischel (Eds.), *Advances in personality science* (pp. 177–195). New York: Guilford Press.

Haynie, D. A., Berg, S., Johansson, B., Gatz, M., & Zarit, S. H. (2001). Symptoms of depression in the oldest old: A longitudinal study. *Journals of Gerontology Series B: Psychological Sciences and Social Sciences, 56,* P111–P118.

Holder, M. D., & Coleman, B. (2009). The contribution of social relationships to children's happiness. *Journal of Happiness Studies, 10,* 329–349.

Hyde, J. S., Mezulis, A. H., & Abramson, A. Y. (2008). The ABCs of depression: Integrating affective, biological, and cognitive models to explain the emergence of gender difference in depression. *Psychological Review, 115,* 291–313.

Iidaka, T., Okada, T., Murata, T., Omori, M., Kosaka, H., Sadato, N., et al. (2002). Age-related differences in the medial temporal lobe responses to emotional faces as revealed by fMRI. *Hippocampus, 12,* 352–362.

Jackson, D. C., Mueller, C. J., Dolski, I., Dalton, K. M., Nitschke, J. B., Urry, H. L., et al. (2003). Now you feel it, now you don't: Frontal brain electrical asymmetry and individual differences in emotion regulation. *Psychological Science, 14,* 612–617.

James, W. (1890). *Principles of psychology.* New York: Henry Holt and Company.

Kagan, J., Reznick, J. S., Snidman, N., Gibbons, J., & Johnson, M. O. (1988). Childhood derivatives of inhibition and lack of inhibition to the unfamiliar. *Child Development, 59,* 1580–1589.

Kagan, J., & Snidman, N. (2004). *The long shadow of temperament.* Cambridge: Belknap Press/Harvard University Press.

Kagan, J., Snidman, N., Arcus, D., & Reznick, J. S. (1994). *Galen's prophecy: Temperament in human nature.* New York: Basic Books.

Kagan, J., Snidman, N., Kahn, V., & Towsley, S. (2007). The preservation of two infant temperaments into adolescence. *Monographs of the Society for Research in Child Development, 72,* 1–75.

Karlsen, K. H., Larsen, J. P., Tandberg, E., & Maeland, J. G. (1998). Quality of life measurements in patients with Parkinson's disease: A community-based study. *European Journal of Neurology, 5,* 443–450.

Kennedy, Q., Mather, M., & Carstensen, L. L. (2004). The role of motivation in the age-related positive bias in autobiographical memory. *Psychological Science, 15,* 208–214.

Kim-Cohen, J., Caspi, A., Taylor, A., Williams, B., Newcombe, R., Craig, I.W., et al. (2006). MAOA, maltreatment, and gene-environment interaction predicting children's mental health: New evidence and a meta-analysis. *Molecular Psychiatry, 11,* 903–913.

Kirkbride, P. S., Tang, S. F. Y., & Westwood, R. I. (1991). Chinese conflict preferences and negotiating behaviour: Cultural and psychological influences. *Organization Studies, 12,* 365–386.

Kobau, R., Safran, M. A., Zack, M. M., Moriarty, D. G., & Chapman, D. (2004). Sad, blue, or depressed days, health behaviors and health-related quality of life, Behavioral Risk Factor Surveillance System, 1995–2000. *Health Quality of Life Outcomes, 2,* 40.

Kunzmann, U., & Grühn, D. (2005). Age differences in emotional reactivity: The sample case of sadness. *Psychology and Aging, 20,* 47–59.

Kunzmann, U., Little, T. D., & Smith, J. (2000). Is age-related stability of subjective well-being a paradox? Cross-sectional and longitudinal evidence from the Berlin aging study. *Psychology and Aging, 15,* 511–526.

Lang, F. R., & Carstensen, L. L. (1994). Close emotional relationships in late life: Further support for proactive aging in the social domain. *Psychology and Aging, 9,* 315–324.

Lang, F. R., & Carstensen, L. L. (2002). Time counts: Future time perspective, goals, and social relationships. *Psychology and Aging, 17,* 125–139.

Lanzi, R., Pascoe, J., Keltner, B., & Ramey, S (1999). Correlates of depressive symptoms in a national Head Start program sample. *Archives of Pediatrics and Adolescent Medicine, 153,* 8, 801–807.

Larsen, J. T., McGraw, A. P., & Cacioppo, J. T. (2001). Can people feel happy and sad at the same time? *Journal of Personality and Social Psychology, 81,* 684–696.

Larson, R., & Ham, M. (1993). Stress and "storm and stress" in early adolescence: The relationship of negative events with dysphoric affect. *Developmental Psychology, 29,* 130–140.

Larson, R. W., Moneta, G., Richards, M. H., & Wilson, S. (2002). Continuity, stability, and change in daily emotional experiences across adolescence. *Child Development, 73,* 1151–1165.

Lawton, M. P., Kleban, M. H., Rajagopal, D., & Dean, J. (1992). Dimensions of affective experience in three age groups. *Psychology and Aging, 7,* 171–184.

Leclerc, C. M., & Kensinger, E. A. (2008). Age-related differences in medial prefrontal activation in response to emotional images. *Cognitive, Affective, and Behavioral Neuroscience, 8,* 153–164.

LeDoux, J., & Armony, J. (1999). Can neurobiology tell us anything about human feelings? In D. Kahneman, E. Diener, & N. Shwwartz (Eds.), *Well-being: The foundations of hedonic psychology* (pp. 489–499). New York: Russel Sage Foundation.

Lefkowitz, M. M., & Tesiny, E. P. (1985). Depression in children: Prevalence and correlates. *Journal of Consulting and Clinical Psychology, 53,* 647–656.

Levenson, R. W. (2000). Expressive, physiological, and subjective changes in emotion across adulthood. In S. H. Qualls & N. Abeles (Eds.), *Psychology and the aging revolution: How we adapt to longer life* (pp. 123–140). Washington, DC: American Psychological Association.

Levenson, R. W., Carstensen, L. L., Friesen, W. V., & Ekman, P. (1991). Emotion, physiology, and expression in old age. *Psychology and Aging, 6,* 28–35.

London, B., Downey, G., Bonica, C., & Paltin, I. (2007). Social causes and consequences of rejection sensitivity. *Journal of Research on Adolescence, 17,* 481–506.

Lovallo, W. R., & Thomas, T. L. (2000). Stress hormones in psychophysiological research: Emotional, behavioral, and cognitive implications. In J. Cacioppo, L. Tassinary, & G. Berntson (Eds.), *The handbook of psychophysiology* (pp. 342–367). New York: Cambridge University Press.

Luna, B., & Sweeney, J. A. (2004). The emergence of collaborative brain function: FMRI studies of the development of response inhibition. *Annals of the New York Academy of Science, 1021,* 296–309.

Luthar, S. S., Cicchetti, D., & Becker, B. (2000). The construct of resilience: A critical evaluation and guidelines for future work. *Child Development, 71,* 543–562.

Magai, C., Consedine, N. S., Krivoshekova, Y. S., Kudadjie-Gyamfi, E., & McPherson, R. (2006). Emotion experience and expression across the adult life span: Insights from a multimodal assessment study. *Psychology and Aging, 21,* 303–317.

Markus, H. R., & Kitayama, S. (1991). Culture and the self: Implications for cognition, emotion, and motivation. *Psychological Review, 98,* 224–253.

Mather, M., Canli, T., English, T., Whitfield, S., Wais, P., Ochsner, K., et al. (2004). Amygdala responses to emotionally valenced stimuli in older and younger adults. *Psychological Science, 15,* 259–263.

Miljkovitch, R., Pierrehumbert, B., & Halfon, O. (2007). Three-year-olds' attachment play narratives and their associations with internalizing problems. *Clinical Psychology & Psychotherapy, 14*, 249–257.

Miller, L. M., Charles, S. T., & Fingerman, K. L. (2009). Perceptions of social transgressions in adulthood. *Journals of Gerontology: Psychological Sciences, 64B*, 551–559.

Miller, G. E., Chen, E., & Zhou, E. S. (2007). If it goes up, must it come down? Chronic stress and the hypothalamic-pituitary-adrenocortical axis in humans. *Psychological Bulletin, 133*, 25–45.

Moehler, E., Kagan, J., Oelkers-Ax, R., Brunner, R., Poustka, L., Haffner, J., et al. (2008). Infant predictors of behavioural inhibition. *The British Journal of Developmental Psychology, 26*, 145–150.

Morris, A. S., Silk, J. S., Steinberg, L., Myers, S. S., & Robinson, L. R. (2007). The role of the family context in the development of emotion regulation. *Social Development, 16*, 361–388.

Mroczek, D. K., & Kolarz, C. M. (1998). The effect of age on positive and negative affect: A developmental perspective on happiness. *Journal of Personality and Social Psychology, 75*, 1333–1349.

Mroczek, D. K., & Spiro, A., III. (2005). Change in life satisfaction during adulthood: Findings from the Veterans Affairs Normative Aging study. *Journal of Personality and Social Psychology, 88*, 189–202.

Newsom, J. T., Mahan, T. L., Rook, K. S., & Krause, N. (2008). Stable negative social exchanges and health. *Health Psychology, 27*, 78–86.

Nolen-Hoeksema, S., & Girgus, J. S. (1994). The emergence of gender differences in depression during adolescence. *Psychological Bulletin, 115*, 424–443.

Nolen-Hoeksema, S., McBride, A., & Larson, J. (1997). Rumination and psychological distress among bereaved partners. *Journal of Personality and Social Psychology, 72*, 855–862.

Ochsner, K. N., & Gross, J. J. (2005). The cognitive control of emotion. *Trends in Cognitive Sciences, 9*, 242–249.

Ong, A. D., & Bergeman, C. S. (2004). The complexity of emotions in later life. *Journals of Gerontology Series B: Psychological Sciences and Social Sciences, 59*, P117–P122.

Otte, C., Hart, S., Neylan, T., Marmar, C. R., Yaffe, K., & Mohr, D. C. (2005). A meta-analysis of cortisol response to challenge in human aging: Importance of gender. *Psychoneuroendocrinology, 30*, 80–91.

Pauli-Pott, U., & Mertesacker, B. (2009). Affect expression in mother-infant interaction and subsequent attachment development. *Infant Behavior and Development, 32*, 208–215.

Piazza, J. R., Charles, S. T., & Almeida, D. M. (2007). Living with chronic health conditions: Age differences in affective well-being. *Journals of Gerontology Series B: Psychological Sciences and Social Sciences, 62*, P313–P321.

Plomin, R., & Davis, O. S. P. (2009). The future of genetics in psychology and psychiatry: Microarrays, genome-wide association, and non-coding RNA. *Journal of Child Psychology and Psychiatry, 50*, 63–71.

Popova, N. K. (2008). From gene to aggressive behavior: The role of brain serotonin. *Neuroscience and Behavioral Physiology, 38*, 471–475.

Ready, R. E., Carvalho, J. O., & Weinberger, M. I. (2008). Emotional complexity in younger, midlife, and older adults. *Psychology and Aging, 23*, 928–933.

Riley, A. W. (2004). Evidence that school-age children can self-report on their health. *Ambulatory Pediatrics, 4*, 371–376.

Roberts, B. W., Kuncel, N. R., Shiner, R., Caspi, A., & Goldberg, L. R. (2007). The power of personality: The comparative validity of personality traits, socioeconomic status, and cognitive ability for predicting important life outcomes. *Perspectives on Psychological Science, 2*, 313–345.

Roberts, B. W., Walton, K. E., & Viechtbauer, W. (2006). Patterns of mean-level change in personality traits across the life course: A meta-analysis of longitudinal studies. *Psychological Bulletin, 132*, 1–25.

Roberts, B. W., Wood, D., & Smith, J. L. (2005). Evaluating five factor theory and social investment perspectives on personality trait development. *Journal of Research in Personality, 39*, 166–184.

Rook, K. S. (1984). The negative side of social interaction: Impact on psychological well-being. *Journal of Personality and Social Psychology, 46*, 1097–1108.

Rosenblum, L. A., Forger, C., Noland, S., Trost, R. C., & Coplan, J. D. (2001). Response of adolescent bonnet macaques to an acute fear stimulus as a function of early rearing conditions. *Developmental Psychobiology, 39*, 40–45.

Rosenkoetter, M. M., Garris, J. M., & Engdahl, R. A. (2001). Postretirement use of time: Implications for preretirement planning and postretirement management. *Activities, Adaptation, & Aging, 25*, 1–18.

Rothbart, M. K. (1988). Temperament and the development of inhibited approach. *Child Development, 59,* 1241–1250.

Rothbart, M. K. (2004). Temperament and the pursuit of an integrated developmental psychology. *Merrill-Palmer Quarterly. Special Issue: 50th Anniversary Issue: Part II The Maturing of the Human Developmental Sciences: Appraising Past, Present, and Prospective Agendas, 50,* 492–505.

Rothbart, M. K., & Derryberry, D. (1981). Development of individual differences in temperament. In M. E. Lamb & A. L. Brown (Eds.), *Advances in developmental psychology* (Vol. 1, pp. 37–86). Hillsdale, NJ: Erlbaum.

Rothbart, M. K., Ellis, L. K., & Posner, M. (2004). Temperament and self-regulation. In R. F. Baumeister & K. D. Vohs (Eds.), *Handbook of self-regulation: Research, theory, and applications* (pp. 357–372). New York: Guilford.

Rothbart, M. K., Posner, M. I., & Kieras, J. (2006). Temperament, attention, and the development of self-regulation. In K. McCartney & D. Phillips (Eds.), *Blackwell handbook of early childhood development* (pp. 338–357). Malden: Blackwell.

Rubin, K. H., Burgess, K. B., & Hastings, P. D. (2002). Stability and social-behavioral consequences of toddlers' inhibited temperament and parenting behaviors. *Child Development, 73,* 483–495.

Rudolph, K. D., & Hammen, C. (1999). Age and gender as determinants of stress exposure, generation, and reactions in youngsters: A transactional perspective. *Child Development, 70,* 660–677.

Samochowiec, J., Lesch, K., Rottmann, M., Smolka, M., Syagailo, Y. V., Okladnova, O., et al. (1999). Association of a regulatory polymorphism in the promoter region of the monoamine oxidase A gene with antisocial alcoholism. *Psychiatry Research, 86,* 67–72.

Santor, D. A., Messervey, D., & Kusumakar, V. (2000). Measuring peer pressure, popularity, and conformity in adolescent boys and girls: Predicting school performance, sexual attitudes, and substance use. *Journal of Youth and Adolescence, 29,* 163–182.

Saudino, K. J. (2005). Special article: Behavioral genetics and child temperament. *Journal of Developmental and Behavioral Pediatrics, 26,* 214–223.

Saudino, K. J., Plomin, R., DeFries, J. C. (1996). Tester-rated temperament at 14, 20, and 24 months: Environmental change and genetic continuity. *British Journal of Developmental Psychology, 14,* 129–144.

Schmidt, L. A., Fox, N. A., Rubin, K. H., & Sternberg, E. M. (1997). Behavioral and neuroendocrine responses in shy children. *Developmental psychobiology, 30,* 127–140.

Schoon, I., Sacker, A., & Bartley, M. (2003). Socio-economic adversity and psychosocial adjustment: A developmental-contextual perspective. *Social Science & Medicine, 57,* 1001–1015.

Schwartz, C. E., Wright, C. I., Shin, L. M., Kagan, J., & Rauch, S. L. (2003). Inhibited and uninhibited infants "grown up": Adult amygdalar response to novelty. *Science, 300,* 1952–1953.

Shanahan, M. J., & Hofer, S. M. (2005). Social context in gene--environment interactions: Retrospect and prospect. *Journals of Gerontology Series B: Psychological Sciences and Social Sciences, 60,* 65–76.

Shaver, P. R., Belsky, J., & Brennan, K. A. (2000). The adult attachment interview and self-reports of romantic attachment: Associations across domains and methods. *Personal Relationships, 7,* 25–43.

Simpson, J. A., Collins, W. A., Tran, S., & Haydon, K. C. (2008). Developmental antecedents of emotion in romantic relationships. In J. P. Forgas & J. Fitness (Eds.), *Cognitive, affective, and motivational processes* (pp. 185–202). New York: Psychology Press.

Smoller, J. W., Paulus, M. P., Fagerness, J. A., Purcell, S., Yamaki, L. H., Hirshfeld-Becker, D., et al. (2008). Influence of RGS2 on anxiety-related temperament, personality, and brain function. *Archives of General Psychiatry, 65,* 298–308.

Sorkin, D. H., & Rook, K. S. (2006). Dealing with negative social exchanges in later life: Coping responses, goals, and effectiveness. *Psychology and Aging, 21,* 715–725.

Steinberg, L. (2005). Cognitive and affective development in adolescence. *Trends in Cognitive Sciences, 9,* 69–74.

Stevens, H., Leckman, J., Coplan, J., & Suomi, S. (2009). Risk and resilience: Early manipulation of Macaque social experience and persistent behavioral and neurophysiological outcomes. *Journal of the American Academy of Child and Adolescent Psychiatry, 48,* 114–127.

Torges, C. M., Stewart, A. J., & Nolen-Hoeksema, S. (2008). Regret resolution, aging, and adapting to loss. *Psychology and Aging, 23,* 169–180.

Tsai, J. L., Levenson, R. W., & Carstensen, L. L. (2000). Autonomic, subjective, and expressive responses to emotional films in older and younger Chinese Americans and European Americans. *Psychology and Aging, 15,* 684–693.

Uchino, B. N., Birmingham, W., & Berg, C. A. (2010). Are older adults less or more physiologically reactive? A meta-analysis of age-related differences in cardiovascular reactivity to laboratory tasks. *Journal of Gerontology: Psychological Sciences, 65B*, 154–162.

Uchino, B. N., Hold-Lunstad, J., Bloor, L. E., & Campo, R. A. (2005). Aging and cardiovascular reactivity to stress: Longitudinal evidence for changes in stress reactivity. *Psychology and Aging, 20*, 134–143.

Uchino, B. N., Uno, D., Hold-Lunstad, J., & Flinders, J. (1999). Age-related differences in cardiovascular reactivity during acute psychological stress in men and women. *Journal of Gerontology Series B: Psychological Sciences and Social Sciences, 54B*, P339–P346.

Urry, H. L., Nitschke, J. B., Dolski, I., Jackson, D. C., Dalton, K. M., Mueller, C. J., et al. (2004). Making a life worth living: Neural correlates of well-being. *Psychological Science, 15*, 367–372.

Varni, J. W., Limbers, C. A., & Burwinkle, T. M. (2007). How young can children reliably and validly self-report their health-related quality of life?: An analysis of 8,591 children across age subgroups with the PedsQL 4.0 Generic Core scales. *Health and Quality of Life Outcomes, 5*, 1.

Vandewater, E. A., Ostrove, J. M., & Stewart, A. J. (1997). Predicting women's well-being in midlife: The importance of personality development and social role involvements. *Journal of Personality and Social Psychology, 72*, 1147–1160.

Verma, S., & Larson, R. (1999). Are adolescents more emotional? A study of the daily emotions of middle class Indian adolescents. *Psychology and Developing Societies, 11*, 179–194.

Wang, Q. (2003). Emotion situation knowledge in American and Chinese preschool children and adults. *Cognition and Emotion, 17*, 725–746.

Waters, S. F., Virmani, E. A., Thompson, R. A., Meyer, S., Raikes, H. A., & Jochem, R. (2010). Emotion regulation and attachment: Unpacking two constructs and their association. *Journal of Psychopathology and Behavioral Assessment, 32*, 37–47.

Weeks, M., Coplan, R. J., & Kingsbury, A. (2009). The correlates and consequences of early appearing social anxiety in young children. *Journal of Anxiety Disorders, 23*, 965–972.

Wilson, R. S., Krueger, K. R., Arnold, S. E., Barnes, L. L., Mendes de Leon, C., Bienias, J. L., et al. (2006). Childhood adversity and psychosocial adjustment in old age. *American Journal of Geriatric Psychiatry, 14*, 307–315.

Yalcin, B., Willis-Owen, S. A. G., Fullerton, J., Meesaq, A., Deacon, R. M., Rawlins, J. N. P., et al. (2004). Genetic dissection of a behavioral quantitative trait locus shows that Rgs2 modulates anxiety in mice. *Nature Genetics, 36*, 1197–1202.

Yim, I. S., Quas, J. A., Cahill, L., & Hayakawa, C. M. (2010). Children's and adults' salivary cortisol responses to an identical psychosocial laboratory stressor. *Psychoneuroendocrinology, 35*, 241–248.

Zubrick, S. R., Kurinczuk, J. J., McDermott, B. M. C., McKelvey, R. S., Silburn, S. R., & Davies, L. C. (2000). Fetal growth and subsequent mental health problems in children aged 4 to 13 years. *Developmental Medicine & Child Neurology, 42*, 14–20.

COPING AND SELF-REGULATION ACROSS THE LIFE SPAN

22

Carolyn M. Aldwin, Ellen A. Skinner,
Melanie J. Zimmer-Gembeck, and Amanda L. Taylor

Both coping and self-regulation have become very popular constructs, studied by researchers concerned with different life stages, from infancy through very late life. However, child and adult developmentalists have had differing emphases and theoretical roots, which have resulted in interesting similarities and discrepancies in their conceptions of coping and self-regulation. We have recently completed comprehensive surveys of how coping and self-regulation change across the life span (Aldwin, Yancura, & Boeninger, 2010; Skinner & Zimmer-Gembeck, 2009), and three interesting cross-cutting themes emerged. These are control and accommodation as complementary coping processes; the embeddedness of coping in social relationships, especially dyadic relationships; and the adaptive processes of energy regulation. The purpose of this chapter is to investigate these three important themes in greater depth. We will show how the differences in treatment of these ideas in the fields of child and adult development can extend our understanding of adaptation across the life span. Coping and self-regulation from a life-span perspective have relevance for a number of fields, including childhood trauma (Walsh, Fortier, & DiLillo, 2010) and the burgeoning resilience literature (Luthar, in press; Masten & Wright, 2009). However, our focus will be restricted to those studies that focus on more general coping and self-regulation processes. Thus, we will briefly discuss the similarities and differences between *regulation* (which figures prominently in the child development literature) and *coping* (studied extensively in both the child and the adult development literatures), and then the importance of our three themes for understanding the development of coping and regulation across the life span.

OVERLAP AND DIFFERENCES BETWEEN REGULATION AND COPING

The child development literature often focuses on regulation, which in general, refers to how children learn to guide, modulate, or manage their own behavior, emotion, or attention, when dominant responses do not serve. Early work on regulation examined behavioral self-regulation, defined as "learning to wait before acting, self-monitoring, and acquiring the ability to organize segments of behavior sequentially" (National Research Council, 2000, p. 103). Current work on behavioral regulation focuses on both "don't regulation" or inhibiting a dominant response (e.g., delay of gratification; Metcalfe & Mischel, 1999) and "do regulation" or compliance with requests for nondominant responses (Kochanska, Coy, & Murray, 2005; for a review, see McClelland, Ponitz, Messersmith, & Tominey, 2010). Behavioral regulation can be contrasted with emotion regulation, defined as "initiating, maintaining, modulating, or changing the occurrence, intensity, or duration of internal feeling states and emotion-related physiological processes, often in the service of accomplishing one's goals" (Eisenberg & Zhou, 2000, p. 167). Most recently, research has focused on the regulation of attention, including its temperamental and neurological basis (Rueda & Rothbart, 2009). The literatures on all forms of regulation have burgeoned and, although they represent largely distinct lines of work, all have as a common theme the important role that the intentional initiation and inhibition of action components (i.e., behavior, emotion, and attention) play in adaptation to environmental demands.

In contrast, adult developmentalists who study adaptation have focused more on the role of coping. While there are several competing definitions of coping, we have chosen to focus on coping *processes*, or behaviors and cognitions that individuals use to cope with particular stressful episodes. Coping processes include efforts to both manage the problem and the attendant negative emotions. Personal goals, beliefs, and characteristics, as well as the environmental context, influence the use of coping strategies. Coping is multidimensional and flexible in that individuals tailor their multiple efforts to fit the demands of particular situations, and recursive, in that they observe the outcomes of their actions, judge whether or not they are achieving their goals in the situation, and modify their strategies accordingly. When coping is viewed from this perspective, its overlap with processes of self-regulation becomes more apparent.

Some of the biggest strides in integrating conceptualizations of coping and regulation have been made in the study of the development of coping during childhood and adolescence. From this perspective, coping can actually be defined as "regulation under stress" (Compas, O'Connor-Smith, Saltzman, Thomsen, Wadsworth, 2001; Eisenberg, Fabes, & Gutherie, 1997; Skinner, 1999; Skinner & Zimmer-Gembeck, 2007, 2009). Coping describes how people mobilize, modulate, manage, and coordinate multiple aspects of the self under stress (or fail to do so). In contrast to most work on regulation, which focuses on efforts to manage a specific feature (e.g., *emotion* regulation or *attention* regulation), coping is an organizational construct and involves the regulation of all the aspects of self that are influenced by stress, including physiology, emotion, behavior, cognition, motivation, and attention, as well as attempts to influence the environment, including the actions, thoughts, and emotions of others, in dealing with stressful situations, whether actual or anticipated (Aspinwall & Taylor, 1997). Understanding how coping develops can be informed by studying not only the development of action regulation in all its facets (attentional, behavioral, emotional, etc.), but also how they are coordinated with each other over the course of a coping episode, and how they become more integrated over development.

Thus, there is much overlap between work on self-regulation and coping, and the goal of this chapter is to explicitly explore that overlap as a means to advance our understanding of both. We identified three aspects of coping and self-regulation, which have particularly interesting differences in their conceptions in the child and adult developmental literatures, including issues of control versus accommodation, the social embeddedness of coping, and processes of energy regulation. Each of these issues will be addressed in the following sections. They can be seen as part of a general movement in the field to go beyond traditional conceptualizations of coping that focus almost exclusively on interindividual differences and that privilege solo efforts aimed at bringing the environment in line with one's wishes through effort and determination. We are attempting to move toward a consideration of coping as encompassing a profile of adaptive processes, including accommodation, enacted as parts of dyads and social groups, which are malleable over the short-run, and have the potential to develop over the long term.

PRIMARY CONTROL, SECONDARY CONTROL, AND ACCOMMODATION

For more than 25 years, the constructs of *primary* and *secondary control* have captured the imagination of researchers studying coping and regulation (Heckhausen & Schulz, 1995; Morling & Evered, 2006). When the ideas were first introduced by Rothbaum, Weisz, and Snyder (1982), the field was dominated by theories of perceived control, as conveyed in concepts like locus of control, learned helplessness, self-efficacy, and causal attributions. Rothbaum et al. bundled these constructs together into "primary control," which focuses on effecting changes in the external environment, and "relinquished control," which focuses on helplessness, and then contrasted them with "secondary control."

Over time, however, two different conceptualizations of "secondary control" have evolved (Morling & Evered, 2006). "Control-focused" definitions posit that secondary control "targets the self and attempts to achieve changes directly within the individual" (Heckhausen & Schulz, 1995, p. 285). According to this perspective, secondary control is "secondary" in two ways: It is less adaptive than primary control, and it is also secondary in a temporal sense, in that it is employed only after attempts at primary control have been exhausted.

In contrast, "fit-focused" definitions of secondary control highlight "fitting in" and "going with the flow." This set of adaptive processes de-emphasizes attempts to change or influence anything (self or world), but instead refers to adjusting the preferences of the self to fit with current conditions in the world. From this perspective, processes of fit are not secondary to primary control strategies; they represent an alternative equally important set of adaptive processes. Since "fit-focused" constructs do not reflect control and are not secondary, it has been suggested that they should no longer be referred to as "secondary control" (Morling & Evered, 2006; Skinner, 2007). Instead, terms like "accommodation" or "fit" have been suggested (Brandtstädter & Renner, 1990).

Primary control, relinquishment of control, secondary control, and accommodation have all been used to describe coping resources, coping strategies, and forms of regulation. However, different facets have been emphasized at different ages, and child versus adult developmentalists have come to markedly different conclusions about their relative importance and functioning. The critique and integration of work from different developmental periods may provide a clearer and more comprehensive perspective on the roles of control and accommodation in stress, coping, and resilience across the life span.

Primary Control

The role of primary control in coping is relatively well understood; it has been the target of multiple theories and decades of research (Elliot & Dweck, 2005; Skinner, 1996). Having a sense of control and feeling efficacious shape the coping process

(Dweck, 1999; Folkman, 1984). Individuals who have high levels of self-efficacy tend to appraise stressful events as challenges and they cope constructively. Regulation is action-oriented and focused on generating strategies, exerting effort, and using outcomes (even failures) as information to shape subsequent strategies. This pattern of regulation and coping is more likely to actually solve problems, and when problems are not solvable, to nevertheless lead to gains in knowledge and skills. Such episodes contribute to increases in actual competence and to decreases in the probability of future stressful encounters, which in the long run, reinforce a sense of control (e.g., Schmitz & Skinner, 1993).

Processes of "relinquishment of control," or helplessness, have also been studied closely (Peterson, Maier, & Seligman, 1993). Individuals who feel incompetent or that desired outcomes are based on causes they cannot influence (like powerful others, chance, luck, or fate) are particularly vulnerable to encounters with setbacks or failure. Their regulation loses focus, with energy and concentration sapped by self-doubt and worry; as a result, they lose access to their own best skills (Dweck, 1999). Coping includes passivity, confusion, escape, and help avoidance. This pattern of coping and regulation interferes with effectiveness, sidetracking the development of actual competencies, and making future stressors more likely. Cumulatively, these experiences can further cement feelings of helplessness (e.g., Nolen-Hoeksema, Girgus, & Seligman, 1986).

Development of Primary Control

The bulk of the work in this area examines individual differences. However, small strands of research examine the development of perceived control (e.g., Flammer, 1995; Skinner, 1995; Skinner, Zimmer-Gembeck, & Connell, 1998). Perceived control (the sense of personal force or that "I can do it") seems to be helpful in dealing with stress, beginning in infancy, when it blunts the physiological consequences of painful events (Amat, Paul, Zarza, Watkins, & Maier, 2007), all the way to old age, when it bolsters life satisfaction and well-being (Lachman & Prenda-Firth, 2004; Skaff, 2007).

Some of the benefits of control are conferred through the kinds of coping they shape. However, the actual ways of coping that are promoted by a sense of control change significantly with age. Some examples can illustrate the general idea. In earliest infancy, expectations of control prompt increases in exertion and efforts to reproduce desired events (Papousek & Papousek, 1980). For toddlers, control expectations may also lead to repeated requests to caregivers to produce desired outcomes (Heckhausen, 1982). During preschool age, children try out a variety of concrete actions when they expect control (Heckhausen, 1984). In middle childhood, this behavioral problem-solving gives way to cognitive problem-solving and consultation with adults to guide active attempts (Dweck, 1999). Adolescence may bring planning into the action repertoire, and later preventative action and proactive avoidance of problems (Aspinwall & Taylor, 1997; Zimmer-Gembeck & Skinner, 2008). Adulthood contains a wide variety of primary control strategies, which include effort exertion, problem-solving, and information seeking, which are among the most common strategies of coping (Skinner, Edge, Altman, & Sherwood, 2003).

At the same time, developmental differences mark how control experiences are interpreted and translated into future expectancies (Flammer, 1995; Skinner, 1995).

For example, by age 2, children usually want to "do it myself!" for a success to "count" toward a feeling of efficacy (Heckhausen, 1984). During the elementary school years, children begin to understand that efforts are not enough for feelings of competence; one also needs to reach a certain standard of performance (Stipek & McIver, 1989). By late childhood, the level of performance is compared to peers, with self-evaluations potentially declining (Ruble, 1983). Beginning in early adolescence with the differentiation of effort and ability, feelings of competence require success on normatively difficult tasks (Nicholls, 1978). Throughout the life span, efforts to protect a sense of control while these developments unfold may lead to coping strategies that have maladaptive consequences, such as refusing to try hard or devaluing domains in which control is difficult to exert (e.g., Covington & Omelich, 1979).

Secondary Control

Control-focused definitions of secondary control draw attention to control efforts aimed, not at the context, but at the self. When dealing with stressful events, individuals want not only to change external events (primary control) but also to regulate facets of the self that might aid in achieving primary control. The function of these secondary control efforts is "to minimize losses in, maintain, and expand existing levels of primary control" (Heckhausen & Schulz, 1995, p. 284). Although theorists have not carefully distinguished between *beliefs* and *strategies* of secondary control, it is reasonable to assume that (following primary control distinctions) secondary control *beliefs* involve feelings of efficacy in deploying and modifying aspects of the self needed to exert primary control, such as behavior, volition, and motivation. A sense of secondary control entails confidence and optimism about being able to "get myself" to do what is needed to produce desired and prevent undesired outcomes. The opposite would likely be a sense of helplessness with respect to "getting myself" to do what is required. If so, then these beliefs reflect a sense of self-regulatory or coping efficacy.

In contrast, secondary control *strategies* typically refer to actions, most of which have been studied as ways of coping and forms of self-regulation. Some of these actions can be considered "back-up" strategies, used after initial attempts have failed (Thompson et al., 1998). For example, people can increase the attractiveness of the blocked goal, shift resources from other activities to the implementation of the blocked goal, narrow focus toward the goal, and construct new strategies or means; strategies may also include changing the self by developing new competencies or accessing the resources of others through "proxy" control (Bandura, 1997; Brandtstädter & Renner, 1990; Heckhausen & Schulz, 1995).

Other secondary control strategies refer to means of suspending current efforts without giving up on the goal. For example, people can attempt to create alternative "secondary" routes, through information search, consultation, and other attempts to find out more about possible contingencies. They could also employ mental activities such as extending deadlines, waiting for the right moment, or bolstering optimism (e.g., Brim, 1992). These strategies involve continued commitment to the goal, combined with a focus on action readiness and monitoring conditions for when they are likely to be favorable for control efforts (Brandtstädter & Rothermund, 2002).

Another kind of secondary control strategy come into play when it is no longer possible to "fix" the chosen target, such as when dealing with an irrevocable loss or an inevitable negative outcome: People can shift their goals toward outcomes they can more feasibly control. For example, in the case of a terminal illness, people can shift their focus from finding a cure to influencing the symptoms, course, or treatment of the illness, and its effects on others (Thompson, Sobolew-Shubin, Galbraith, Schwankovsky, & Cruzen, 1993). Also referred to as "consequence-related control" (Thompson, Nanni, & Levine, 1994), this includes turning efforts toward the self, attempting to influence one's own emotions or reactions; many of these activities are also studied as emotion regulation (Gross, 1998). These secondary control strategies, as well as confidence in one's capacity to enact them (i.e., secondary control beliefs or coping self-efficacy), are directly related to increasing the probability that future attempts to exert control will be successful. Hence, they produce many of the same benefits as primary control, and serve to create control experiences even in "low control" circumstances.

Development of Secondary Control

Because of the confusion surrounding the construct of secondary control (Morling & Evered, 2006), very little research has targeted its development. The most focused set of studies examines the level and functions of different kinds of secondary control across the adult life span (Schulz, Wrosch, & Heckhausen, 2003). These researchers suggested that declining levels of direct primary control (based on developmental losses, societal constraints, and previous life choices) normatively result in the increasing use and benefits of compensatory strategies (e.g., help-seeking) and secondary control strategies.

It seems clear that the study of the development of "secondary control" would benefit from exploiting the almost complete overlap between these concepts and work on coping self-efficacy and the development of self-regulation. Because secondary control encompasses individuals' attempts to target the self as an object of change, by definition secondary control refers to self-regulation. If secondary control is activated when primary control efforts fail, then secondary control by definition refers to coping (Folkman, 1984). This suggests that research on the development of behavioral and emotional self-regulation during infancy, childhood, and adolescence could provide a map to the development of secondary control.

For example, research relevant to secondary control can be found in the study of self-regulated learning during childhood and adolescence, which targets the use of adaptive help-seeking (Newman, 2000) and other strategies students employ to organize and guide their behavior so that they can learn effectively (Zimmerman & Schunk, 2001). The capacity for self-regulated learning is considered to emerge in middle childhood when the development of metacognitive capacities and executive functions allow children to intentionally deploy behaviors, such as practice, studying, note-taking, and homework planning, in ways that contribute to future achievement outcomes (e.g., Paris & Newman, 1990). Many of the strategies studied in self-regulated learning are also considered ways of coping (Eisenberg, Valiente, & Sulik, 2009).

Work on the development of emotion-focused coping may be particularly relevant to the study of secondary control strategies. The emergence of intentional emotion-focused coping during toddlerhood can be traced to neurological developments accompanied by supportive social interactions between parent and child in stressful situations (Kopp, 2009). Between the ages of 6 and 9, there is a dramatic increase in emotion-focused coping (Compas, Worsham, & Ey, 1992). Children develop the ability to verbalize and differentiate their feelings, are also more differentiated in the type of emotion-focus strategies they use, and thus are better able to self-regulate. In middle childhood, the development of language and symbolic reasoning allows the child to develop more cognitively oriented problem- and emotion-focused coping (Compas et al., 2001), and they are better able to judge the controllability of the environment and tailor their coping strategies accordingly. They may also become more adept at inhibiting actions (Losoya, Eisenberg, & Fabes, 1998). Taken together, these developments should facilitate improved secondary control coping.

Fit-Focused Accommodative Processes

One of the most exciting ideas to emerge from discussions of primary and secondary control is that "control" is not the only adaptive process important to dealing with stress. In addition to changing the world to achieve the goals of the self (as in primary control), it is often adaptive to flexibly adjust goals to accommodate current options, priorities, resources, and constraints. These accommodative processes have been at the core of fit-focused definitions of secondary control (Morling & Evered, 2006). They were originally called secondary control because it was assumed that they came into play only when primary control efforts failed. However, since that time, many theorists have argued that "going with the flow" can be a preferred mode of adaptation, employed as a first step when stress is encountered. Attempts to "fit in," "roll with the punches," or "bend" in the face of adversity can be used as primary coping strategies any time that attempts to change the world would be inappropriate, upset relationships, consume too many resources, or threaten other goals that are more important.

Although no comprehensive list of accommodative processes has been compiled, in general, they involve processes that allow people to dissolve commitments to previously important goals and find satisfaction in the current state of affairs (Brandtstädter & Rothermund, 2002). The aim is to recruit genuine acceptance, gracious acquiescence, or willing assent, and not just a state of resignation or grudging compliance (Skinner, 2007). Examples of such strategies include downward social comparison, sour grapes, distraction, and focus on the positive (Connor-Smith, Compas, Wadsworth, Thomsen, & Saltzman, 2000). Other researchers have suggested that these processes can be boosted through deference, taking the larger perspective, listening to others, empathy, compassion, gratitude, humility, trust, self-discipline, and willpower (Greve & Strobl, 2004).

In early models of assimilation (primary control) and accommodation, researchers argued that primary control and accommodation were *not* opposites, but instead were two complementary processes of adaptation (Brandtstädter & Renner, 1990). Primary control referred to "tenacious goal pursuit" and its opposite was helplessness. In contrast, accommodation referred to flexible goal adjustment, and its opposite was "rigid perseveration." Psychometric analyses have confirmed this hypothesized structure, revealing two distinguishable bipolar dimensions that are positively related to each other (Brandtstädter & Renner, 1990). Subsequent research on fit-focused constructs has also shown that they are positively related to primary control (Morling & Evered, 2006).

As the opposite of accommodation, rigid perseveration involves inflexible fixation on a specific goal no matter what the costs to self or others. Some processes that may contribute to perseveration are making unattainable goals more attractive, dwelling on losses and "might-have-beens," upward social comparison or envy, and stubborn insistence about the feasibility of an unattainable goal. The way of coping within this family that has been studied the most closely is rumination, which refers to involuntary engagement with the distressing features of negative life events (e.g., Connor-Smith et al., 2000; Nolen-Hoeksma, Wisco, & Lyubomirsky, 2008). Such perseveration invokes and amplifies negative mood as well as capturing attention and occupying working memory capacity, thus interfering with constructive problem-solving and priority setting (Nolen-Hoeksma et al., 2008).

The capacity to accommodate or "let go," that is, to disengage from previously held goals or activities, seems particularly important when dealing with extremely stressful events (such as traumatic loss) or serious normative losses, such as in very old age. In accounts of accommodative processes, some researchers assert that these processes operate outside of conscious awareness and cannot be intentionally deployed (Brandtstädter & Rothermund, 2002). However, accommodative ways of coping, such as distraction, focus on the positive, and cognitive reappraisal, are included in coping interventions designed for children, youth, and adults, suggesting that at least some of them can be taught and acquired.

Development of Accommodation

Although consideration of accommodation and its benefits appear most frequently in discussions about cultural differences in control preferences and the challenges of successful aging, accommodative processes also play a big role in the lives of young children. The capacity for "committed compliance" is considered the desired end-state for the development of self-regulation in early childhood (Kochanska, 2002). Willing compliance involves easily going along with the requests and demands of adults as well as with standard rules and routines. The normative development of these early forms of accommodation is based in temperamental factors and requires the emergence of cognitive and linguistic skills within a supportive set of social relationships (Kochanska, Aksan, & Carlson, 2005). Compared to discussions about adulthood and aging, which debate the merits of accommodation (e.g., Gould, 1999; Heckhausen & Schulz, 1995), discussions about childhood clearly recognize that the capacity to defer one's current impulses and desires in service of larger goals is a critical capacity to develop and one that underlies effective coping (Bronson, 2000).

SOCIAL EMBEDDEDNESS OF COPING AND SELF-REGULATION

Early models of coping focused on individual attempts to deal with stress—sometimes referred to as "heroic" effort models (Dunahoo, Hobfoll, Monnier, Hulsizer, & Johnson, 1998). However, there is a growing recognition that coping efforts are inextricably embedded in social relationships and higher-order social contexts of demands, resources, supports, and hindrances (Cutrona & Gardner, 2006; Revenson & Pranikoff, 2005). Historically, research on adulthood has tended to acknowledge the social nature of coping by focusing on social support—how family and friends in informal social support networks assist individuals with their problems. More recent programs of research have expanded this conception to the realization that problems generally affect more than one person, and have started explicitly examining "dyadic coping" that involves how couples (and other dyads) seek to deal with problems that affect them jointly (Berg, personal communication, March, 2009).

Research on coping during childhood has traditionally considered the social dimension as part of the "socialization" of emotion and coping by parents. More recently, developmental analyses have revealed that self-reliant coping emerges from social interactions with more competent partners, and looks at support-seeking as a strategy that becomes more differentiated and selective across childhood and adolescence. In recent reviews of the development of coping, support-seeking has emerged as an "all-purpose" coping strategy, commonly called upon to deal with all kinds of stressors from childhood to old age (Aldwin, 2007; Skinner & Zimmer-Gembeck, 2007).

People assist each other with coping and regulation in multiple ways, such as giving direct assistance, giving advice, providing protection against stress, soothing emotional reactions, creating an environment that makes coping easier, or modeling new appraisal and coping strategies (e.g., Thoits, 1986). Different areas of study tend to focus on only one of these processes within one age group, and sometimes limit their focus to a particular stressor (e.g., divorce, illness, or conflict). Other researchers attend to the broader social context or to particular people (e.g., Tolan & Grant, 2009).

Nevertheless, all these lines of work make clear the critical importance of social partners, relationships, families, and social contexts. In general, coping and regulation benefit from relationships that are warm, responsive, and autonomy supportive. Also beneficial are families who are cohesive, communicative, structured, and consistent, and contexts that are challenging but not chronically overwhelming. Unsupportive social relationships and contexts are ones that are neglectful, dismissive, coercive, controlling, overbearing, intrusive, inconsistent, or otherwise not attuned to the needs of the person doing the coping. These social coping resources and liabilities seem to exert an impact on all phases of the stress and coping process, including threat appraisals, distress reactions, ways of coping, experiences of coping efficacy, and recovery from setbacks.

As mentioned earlier, researchers interested in the social embeddedness of coping have turned their attention to the "particular ways that couples potentially interact as they deal with stressors" (Berg & Upchurch, 2007, p. 920). Compared to other studies of social resources for coping, such studies of dyadic coping (Berg & Upchurch, 2007; Bodenmann, Pihet, & Kayser, 2006) seek to more explicitly examine the strategies used by each member of a dyad, and draw attention to how stressors can impact upon one or both members, as well as their extended social networks. One critical task has been to examine how congruence or balance between the coping beliefs and strategies of two members in a close dyad might have implications for mental health and other outcomes.

Another task has been to more directly examine coping at the dyadic level rather than considering each individual and their differences or similarities. New terminology emerges from this literature such as collective coping congruence, collective ineffective coping (Berg & Upchurch, 2007), and supportive, common, delegated, hostile, ambivalent, or superficial dyadic coping (Bodenmann et al., 2006). This terminology has been used primarily in research on married couples coping with health problems (Berg & Upchurch, 2007), with some exceptions (e.g., Bodenmann et al., 2006), but the notion of dyadic coping has implications for identifying the social processes involved in stress and coping for other stressors and during all life stages.

Infancy, Toddlerhood, and Childhood

Caregivers, especially sensitive and responsive ones, are an integral part of infants' reactions to stress, influencing not just how they respond but whether they even experience an event as physiologically stressful (Gunnar & Quevedo, 2007). In fact, during infancy, caregivers carry out many of the responses that typically qualify as "coping" (Holodynski & Friedlmeier, 2006; Sroufe, 1996). Lewis and Ramsay (1999) proposed four primary ways the environment can assist infants to manage stress. Other people can: (1) protect against stress; (2) soothe reactions to stressors; (3) promote individual resources such as self-competence and well-being that aid coping and promote resilience; and (4) promote positive mental representations of others and the self that can assist in times of stress (see Berg & Upchurch, 2007; Kliewer et al., 2006 for similar descriptions of the roles of the social context in coping). Even children as young as 15–18 months of age can have complex cognitive representations and schemas (Lewis & Ramsay, 1999; Stipek, Gralinski, & Kopp, 1990).

A primary task of parents of young children is to respond sensitively and appropriately to their distress. Although evidence is mixed about whether parents' attempts at soothing infant distress can change stress reactivity in the short term (e.g., reduce future bouts of crying or cortisol responses; e.g., Lewis & Ramsay, 1999), a few studies have shown that sensitive responsiveness can lead to reduced physiological responding to normative stressors (such as inoculations) over a period of months, especially for infants with difficult temperaments (Gunnar & Quevado, 2007). At the same time, it is clear that temperament itself plays a significant role in the emotional displays, coping, and regulation of infants and young children (Compas et al., 2001; Fox & Calkins, 2003; Lewis & Ramsay, 1999; Rueda & Rothbart, 2009), as do aspects of attention and attention regulation (Kopp, 2002).

Beginning in the middle of the first year of life, children often rely on their parents for direct assistance with coping and regulation (Grolnick, Bridges, & Connell, 1996; Holodynski & Friedlmeier, 2006), and as social references for how to respond to novel and potentially distressing situations (Diamond & Aspinwall, 2003). Between 6 and 18 months of age children become increasingly likely to engage in other directed regulatory behavior (Gianino & Tronick, 1998) by directly seeking the aid of caregivers to help them regulate their own responses to stressful events (Braungart-Rieker & Stifter, 1996). According to Barrett and Campos (1991), early in the second half of the first year infants develop the ability to direct their facial responses in ways that elicit support or direct the instrumental actions of others, and parents or others respond in a coregulatory pattern. Other adaptive strategies for support-seeking and assistance with regulation also emerge around this time, such as seeking eye contact with caregivers when soothing or other forms of assistance are desired.

The importance of toddler signals and caregivers' responses in early interactions is illustrated in the research on attachment, stress, and regulation. The emotional sensitivity of the caregiver to children's distress, including soothing and coping assistance, are used as markers of the attachment status of the parent–child relationship, reflecting the history of parental responsiveness and child security. Hence, many studies of infant or toddler attachment have focused on the child's response to parental soothing upon reunion after a stressor. Because secure attachments have been associated with dampened stress cortisol (i.e., stress reactivity) among toddlers (Gunnar & Quevedo, 2007), parents' responses to infant distress are considered an important part of a child's coping resources and as parents' "social regulation" of young children (Gunnar & Vasquez, 2006, p. 533). Others have referred to this process as "coregulation," which is believed to be a necessary precursor of the development of children's own self-regulation (Mikulincer, Shaver, & Horesch, 2006).

Early harsh family environments often deplete parental capacities to soothe, protect, and promote resources and positive cognitive representations. Environments, such as those without sufficient financial resources or that involve high conflict or maltreatment of children, have been linked to poor coping and regulatory behaviors in young children both concurrently and over time (Cicchetti & Rogosch, 2009; Propper & Moore, 2006). Such environments may have greater impact on some children than others. Harsh parenting or low resource environments seem to interact with children's genetic risk (Propper & Moore, 2006) and their temperamental emotionality (Propper & Moore, 2006; Valiente, Fabes, Eisenberg, & Spinrad, 2004) to reduce vulnerable children's capacities for regulation and constructive coping even further.

Early Childhood to Adolescence

In the toddler and early childhood years, children begin to be able to reliably control their own coping behavior voluntarily (Bronson, 2000; Kopp, 2009), and cognition, social relations, emotion, and self-understanding increase in capacity and integration (Sameroff & Haith, 1996). High-quality parenting is essential for these accumulated foundations and parents continue to be resources for coping and regulation under stress (Fabes, Leonard, Kupanoff, & Martin, 2001; Newman, 2000; Valiente et al., 2004). Other individuals such as teachers, peers, and siblings can take on important roles in these processes (Seiffge-Krenke, 1995; Zimmer-Gembeck & Locke, 2007).

An important task for more knowledgeable and experienced social partners has been referred to as the "coping socialization" of children and adolescents (Kliewer et al., 2006). Socialization has been defined as "an adult-initiated process by which young persons, through education, training, and imitation, acquire their culture and their habits and values congruent with adaptation to that culture" (Baumrind, 1996, p. 408). Similar perspectives can be found in studies of emotional socialization, which focus on parental expressivity and emotion coaching (Cole, Teti, & Zahn-Waxler, 2003; Valiente et al., 2004).

As part of the socialization process, adult caregivers can scaffold how children manage their emotional arousal and coping responses via direct instruction, coaching, and modeling of coping behaviors, as well as by filtering the specific events to which children are exposed (Kliewer et al., 2006; Power, 2004). Research has examined associations between coping used by parents and their children's ways of coping in response to chronic medical conditions (Kliewer & Lewis, 1995), acute stressors (Koplik, Lamping, & Reznikoff, 1992) and everyday problems (Kliewer, Fearnow, & Miller, 1996). Although findings are not always consistent, parental coping behaviors seem to be at least moderately related to children's coping, with overt parental coping responses likely being the most readily modeled by children. Evidence suggests that children's use of avoidant coping is positively associated with maternal expression of emotion, maternal disengagement and denial, and negatively associated with maternal use of cognitive restructuring (Kliewer et al., 1996). Further, parents who actively cope with their own stressors, for example, by reframing situations to focus on the positive and using social support, tend to have children who are more likely to approach rather than avoid dealing with problems.

By adolescence and into adulthood, coping is an organized pattern of responding using both self-reliance and social resources. Adolescents and adults employ a wider range of coping strategies than children, and it is this increasing flexibility and organization of their responses that is likely to be most adaptive (Zimmer-Gembeck & Skinner, 2008). New close relationships form and can be new bases of security for tackling life's challenges (Feeney, 2004) and provide helpful collaborators (Berg et al., 2007; Gagnon & Dixon, 2008). Such close intimate relationships are supportive and satisfying partly because they are buffers, supports, helpers, protectors, and places of security and safety in times of difficulty. These are the experiences that make up what is often referred to as intimacy, commitment, and reliable alliance, and are some of the key elements of good quality relationships (Berscheid, Snyder, & Omoto, 1989).

Dyadic Coping in Adult Couples

There is a growing literature on dyadic coping with stress in adulthood, although much of what is known comes from studies of middle-aged and older adult couples coping with health problems (Berg & Upchurch, 2007). Theory and research on dyadic coping acknowledges that an integral part of close relationships is *joint* coping with the same objectively stressful event, in which each member of the dyad not only engages in the process of coping with stress, but also perceives and interprets the behaviors of the other (Berg & Upchurch, 2007). For example, one member may believe that the other is supportive either emotionally or instrumentally, collaborative, controlling, or uninvolved (Berg, Meegan, & Deviney, 1998; Bodenmann et al., 2006; Coyne & Smith, 1991).

When both members of the dyad are considered, there can be a match or mismatch in perceptions, appraisals, and coping responses, and the collective pattern or joint perception may be more important than either person's particular appraisals or ways of coping independently. For example, a collective dyadic pattern of ineffective coping may be more detrimental to stress reduction and future functioning than a couple with one partner who compensates for the other's intermittent or persistent ineffective responses. Moreover, the overall adaptive dyadic pattern of coping has been more strongly associated with positive adjustment than congruence in coping between partners (Revenson, 2003), unless that congruence indicates mutual collaboration (Badr, 2004; see also Gagnon & Dixon, 2008, for a study on the benefits of collaborative cognition).

A recent model of dyadic coping highlights the temporal patterning of coping within each partner and between partners, and acknowledges the influence of individual factors (e.g., cognitive functioning), the stressor (e.g., type of medical condition), the broader sociocultural context (e.g., gender and race/ethnicity), other features of the relationship (e.g., marital quality), and the interactions between all of these elements (e.g., different cultural groups have different prevalence of illness; Berg & Upchurch, 2007). Despite these complexities, some tentative conclusions about dyadic coping can be made. First, threat appraisals can be examined as dyadic or group level phenomena (Hobfoll, 1998). In fact, studies indicate that, compared to individual stress appraisals, stress appraisals at the dyadic level may be more relevant to understanding coping responses as well as health and relationship outcomes (Figueiras & Weinman, 2003; Heijmans, de Ridder, & Bensing, 1999).

Second, dyadic coping seems to serve both a stress-coping function and a relationship function (Bodenmann, 2005). Regarding the stress-coping function, lower distress and better individual health have been found to be associated with constructive dyadic coping, such as support provision, stress communication, supportive coping (e.g., direct assistance, advice, help with cognitive reframing when one dyad member is most affected by the stressor), and common dyadic coping (e.g., joint problem-solving, information sharing, discussing feelings, relaxing together; Badr, 2004; Coyne & Smith, 1991; Cutrona & Gardner, 2006). Bodenmann (1995) also found that negative dyadic coping, in which support is provided unwillingly, superficially, or with hostility, adds to distress and problems.

Although it is challenging methodologically to disentangle dyadic coping from assessments of marital satisfaction or other relationship qualities, there is also evidence that dyadic coping serves a relationship function. It is a significant correlate of relationship qualities such as conflict, quarreling, intimacy, tenderness, and togetherness; such associations have been found concurrently (Bodenmann, 2005; Wright & Aquilino, 1998) and longitudinally (see Cutrona & Gardner, 2006 for a review). For example, in a longitudinal study of 90 married Swiss couples assessed four times Bodenmann et al. (2006) found that partners who reported more positive and less negative dyadic coping had higher concurrent marital quality assessed as not quarreling, tenderness, and togetherness over a 2-year period. In this study, dyadic coping, whether positive or negative, at one time point was *not* associated with later marital quality. However, Bodenmann and Cina (2006; cited in Cutrona & Gardner, 2006) reported a longitudinal association between positive dyadic coping and subsequent relationship quality, suggesting that further research on the effects of dyadic coping on marital quality is warranted.

Aging and Later Life

As suggested previously, dyadic coping does not occur in isolation from a range of individual and contextual factors, such as the typical behaviors, temperament, and coping histories of each partner; the type of stressor and the characteristics of the stressor such as level of threat, perceived controllability, chronicity, and novelty; relationship history; and the sociocultural context (Berg & Upchurch, 2007; Cutrona & Gardner, 2006). Of all of these, length of relationship and age may be particularly and directly important to dyadic coping. Long-term relationships are often of higher quality and more satisfying, so may have better foundations for dyadic coping (Berg & Upchurch, 2007; Carstensen, Gottman, & Levenson, 1995) and collaboration (Dixon, 1999).

Although often confounded with relationship length, age may also be important. Young couples may not have the same histories of stress experience and coping, and they may be experiencing a significant stressor together for the first time. This may cause more distress and challenges to the coping and regulation of each member and for dyadic coping (Revenson, 2003; Revenson & Pranikoff, 2005). With experience and age, a division of coping strategies may occur, such that younger couples have been found to be more congruent in their coping, whereas among older couples, coping is more complementary.

Overall, with age and as relationships progress, individual members become more accustomed to dyadic stressors and more familiar with partners' reactions and needs. As described by Dixon (1999) in his work on collaborative cognition, older couples and those in longer term relationships are better at communicating and at pooling their resources to compensate for individual deficits when faced with demanding cognitive-based tasks. Research has shown that using collaboration allows older married couples to perform better on challenging cognitive tasks when compared to other same-aged pairs; older married couples also performed as well as younger couples (Dixon & Gould, 1998). However, as Cutrona and Gardner (2006) eloquently described, some failures at dyadic coping are normal for everyone when stress is high and resources fall short. Most interesting to consider is how others can provide mismatched responses even when trying their best. Miller, Green, and Bales (1999) give compelling examples of parents' responses to children's impending medical procedures that may be intuitively appealing and easily enacted, but may not have the best short- or long-term outcomes for children. "Our goal should not be 'perfect dyadic coping' but multiple opportunities for redemption" (Cutrona & Gardner, 2006, p. 513).

In late life, coping and regulation can be challenged by new and significant stressors, as well as by changes to dyadic coping resources. Although there are many stressors that are more prevalent in older than younger persons (e.g., medical problems), the loss of a partner is one of the most significant stressful life events associated with getting older. Not only does it come with emotional distress, but also widowhood usually is accompanied by losses of important coping resources that are not easily replaced (Ha, Carr, Utz, & Nesse, 2006). Although couple relationships may be the most important coping resources for many people, particularly males (Gurung, Taylor, & Seeman, 2003), many individuals rely on parents and friends for large portions of their lives. This is partly due to the high incidence of divorce and relationship breakdown, the extended age period without marrying or making a life-long commitment to a partner, and the high number of older persons who are living without a spouse or a partner.

Although no research has yet addressed the topic of the development of dyadic coping processes in other relationships after the death of a spouse or long-term partner, one of the adaptations to widowhood is the increasing flow of support from child to the widowed parent, particularly for women with less education (Ha et al., 2006). Research also shows that social networks may decline in size with increasing age, but the availability of social support does not (Gurung et al., 2003). For many people who are dealing with significant life transitions, new sources of support do seem to fill the gap (Gurung et al., 2003), but it is quite likely that the development of new dyadic coping resources is an adaptive process that does not occur quickly or easily.

There is evidence in the adult literature that the impact of social support (and its disruption) may change with age, but the evidence is not always consistent. In general, studies have found that social support has a stronger impact in late life (Knoll & Schwarzer, 2002). For example, Adams and Jackson (2000) found that the effects of contact with friends and family had a stronger effect on subjective well-being for the older participants than for younger or middle-aged participants. In contrast, however, bereavement may have greater effects on morbidity and mortality in midlife than in late life, even controlling for spousal similarities in health behavior habits (Johnson, Backlund, Sorlie, & Loveless, 2000).

There are also likely to be *negative* effects of social support, including in late life (Rook, Mavandadi, Sorkin, & Zettel, 2007). For example, providing large amounts of social support to chronically ill individuals can result in greater manifestations of disability (Seeman, Bruce, & McAvay, 1996) and may contribute to disability onset and progression, especially in older adults (Mendes de Leon, Gold, Glass, Kaplan, & George, 2001) and older men (Avlund, Lund, Holstein, & Due, 2004). Over-protection may threaten feelings of autonomy and independence and erode confidence in one's own ability to provide self-care (Coyne, Wortman, & Lehman, 1988). This finding is particularly true for instrumental support (Newsom, 1999). In general, emotional support from adult children is associated with higher levels of social well-being in later life, but provision of information, especially if unsolicited, can have weaker and/or negative effects. However, these findings may vary by type of health outcome and disease progression. For example, Zautra and Manne (1992) found that over-protectiveness by husbands in earlier stages of their wives' rheumatoid arthritis led to increased distress, but to more positive outcomes at later stages. Baltes (1996) has argued strongly that over-protective support greatly diminishes the quality of life for older adults.

Nonetheless, the positive aspects of social support in general outweigh the negative. Complementary social support allows older couples to compensate for individual deficits, whether physical or cognitive, and may allow them to better manage the resources they do have. As we shall see, energy management, is an important adaptive strategy throughout the life span, but may be particularly important in late life.

ENERGY MANAGEMENT ACROSS THE LIFE SPAN

Ecological biologists study the biomechanics of movement with an eye toward understanding the relationship between energy expended and energy gained. For example, if a leopard or other hunter expends more caloric energy in catching prey than it takes in, over the long term, the animal is not likely to survive. More experienced hunters expend the minimum amount of energy necessary to catch their prey and thus are more successful. In modern humans, the direct relationship between energy expended and calories consumed is less relevant to understanding the process of adaptation (except vis-à-vis obesity). However, the issue of relative efficiency in coping with stress is potentially an important issue, one that has not received much scientific attention. There have been discussions of coping effort, which is generally operationalized simply as the total number of coping strategies used, as well as their frequency or intensity of use. In general, when stress is higher, the coping efforts are greater (Aldwin, 2007). This is important to remember, because all too often studies simply correlate coping scores with outcomes, and find that all coping is related to distress. However, one must take into account the stressfulness of the situation to determine the true relationship between coping and outcomes.

The more interesting question is, "what is the appropriate level of effort for a given problem?" An early study by Aldwin and Revenson (1987) found a complicated interaction between coping effort level and coping efficacy. The best mental health was seen among individuals who expended minimal coping effort but thought that those efforts were efficacious. In contrast, individuals who expended minimal effort but who felt they were ineffective had the most distress. Similarly, a study by Coyne, Aldwin, and Lazarus (1981) found that chronically depressed individuals used more coping strategies, rather than fewer, contrary to what learned helplessness theory would predict. Presumably depressed individuals either did not know which strategies "worked" in any given situation, or used strategies ineffectively, and expended more energy in coping.

Issues of energy and its management have surfaced in theories of self-regulation and intrinsic motivation, as well as in theories of coping. On the one hand, there are theories that focus on resource depletion. Certainly Hobfoll (1998) has been a major proponent of the idea that coping with stress requires the utilization of resources; under chronic stress, one runs the risk of simply running out of resources. This view is consistent with theories of self-regulation that emphasize how the exercise of self-control depletes ego resources, thus interfering with subsequent activities that require energy (Baumeister, Bratslavsky, Muraven, & Tice, 1998). From this perspective, coping drains energy resources.

In contrast, theories of intrinsic motivation argue that self-regulatory activities that are performed autonomously, that is, willingly and with authentic assent, do not deplete ego energy (Moller, Deci, & Ryan, 2006). In fact, when individuals deal with demands in ways that meet their fundamental psychological needs, this kind of coping can actually replenish energy stores and enhance subjective vitality. This perspective is consistent with the notion of stress-related growth (SRG), sometimes called posttraumatic growth (PTG; Tedeschi & Calhoun, 2004). Theories of SRG posit the somewhat startling notion that individuals can increase their resources through coping with stress—at least in the long term. These resources include a greater sense of mastery and self-esteem, better coping skills, closer community ties, greater clarity in values, and sometimes an increased sense of spirituality.

One possibility which incorporates both of these perspectives is that the most adaptive coping profile may be one in which expenditure of the minimal amount of energy needed to be effective is combined with ways of coping that are rejuvenating, and thus refill energy reserves. Such a profile likely involves actively creating a balance among ways of coping—balancing approach with avoidance (Roth & Cohen, 1986), control with accommodation (Brandtstädter & Rothermund, 2002), and self-reliance with reliance on others and reciprocity. Moreover, the capacity to manage one's energy, like all regulatory capacities, should develop with age.

Theories that focus on the balance among ways of coping rather than on specific coping strategies are rare, but several promising perspectives can be identified. One theory, which may provide valuable insights into this process, is Stroebe and Schut's (1999) Dual Process model of coping. Although approach and avoidance are generally seen as opposite coping styles, the Dual Process model suggests they can be seen as alternating strategies. Ideally, individuals use approach (i.e., problem-focused) coping when the environmental conditions permit and when the individual has enough skills and/or energy to attempt to modify the environment, and switch to avoidant (i.e., emotion-focused or accommodative) coping when energy flags or the situation is not amenable to problem-solving efforts. By alternating between these modes, individuals can expend energy when it might be more efficacious, and yet conserve energy for future efforts. Aldwin et al. (in press) argued that this is a potential framework for understanding self-regulatory and energy management strategies across the life span.

A second important dual-process framework focuses on the balance between control and accommodation, or between goal pursuit and goal adjustment, in negotiating conflicting demands (Brandtstädter & Rothermund, 2002). Instead of seeing control and accommodation as competing processes, this perspective views them as complementary. As discussed in previous sections, neither is seen as "primary" and both are seen as adaptive. As explained by Brandtstädter and Rothermund, "well-being and self-esteem depend not only on perceived control over future developmental outcomes, but also on the readiness to accept one's past (which is unalterable) and to disengage without regret from counterfactual life paths that were desired but have never been accomplished... Wisdom seems to imply an integration of technical knowledge concerning the efficient pursuit of personal goals with an experience-based sensitivity as to which goals are feasible and worth pursuing and which should be given up for the sake of other, more valuable ones" (2002, pp. 118–119).

A third perspective which focuses on energetic resources is a motivational theory of coping that explicitly incorporates the idea of constructive coping as a process of engagement that leads to the development of coping resources—specifically, skills and competencies, supportive relationships, and clarity of priorities (Skinner et al., 2003). Constructive families of coping allow people to coordinate their actions with the contingencies available in the environment (through problem-solving and information seeking), to coordinate their reliance on others with available social resources (through support-seeking and self-reliance), and to coordinate their preferences with available options (through negotiation and accommodation). Maladaptive families of coping are ones that lead people to give up too soon (helplessness and escape), to persist too long (perseveration), to fight when it is not productive (opposition), or to rely on others too much (delegation) or too little (social isolation).

Infancy and Childhood

In infancy, regulation of energy expenditure is critical, because very young infants lack sufficient body fat for sustained activity, and much of their energy is used in physical development. Murphy and Moriarty (1976) documented the ways in which even very young infants regulate stimulation, mainly by gaze aversion, fussing, or simply going to sleep. They also found that toddlers and young children are capable of bursts of energy, but similar bouts of effort and rest, or approach and avoidance, can be seen, especially when they are trying to master a new task.

Adolescents and young adults often have seemingly unlimited energy. They may exhibit "unrealistic" control expectations (Zuckerman, Knee, Kieffer, Rawsthorne, & Bruce, 1996), leading them to waste a lot of energy trying to control situations which may not be amenable to control. Because they are faced with many new challenges and often do not as yet have "mature" coping repertoires, they actually report more daily stressors than middle-aged or older adults, which Aldwin and Levenson (2001) interpreted as showing a lack of efficient coping ability.

One of the most important ways that children and adolescents manage the energy they use to cope is by relying on other people. Finding a balance between reliance on others and reliance on the self in coping with stress is an important life-long task. As mentioned previously, at the youngest ages infants and small children count on adult caregivers to perform many of their "coping" actions. In fact, as is made clear by work on attachment, seeking support from caregivers is the most frequently used strategy for coping with problems and distress for young children. Although support-seeking remains a central coping strategy, infants and children become steadily more self-reliant in dealing with stressors, and support-seeking decreases during childhood (ages 7–12), and then levels off during adolescence (Zimmer-Gembeck & Skinner, 2009). During middle and late childhood, children and adolescents still report that they frequently rely on support from others, including parents, friends, and romantic partners, when they are distressed (Frydenberg & Lewis, 2000).

At the same time, older children and adolescents show more differentiated and selective use of support-seeking than younger children (Zimmer-Gembeck & Skinner, 2009). A shift in the network of support seems to start in late childhood and early adolescence, when support-seeking from adults begins to decline and adolescents increasingly rely on support from others, particularly peers. Adolescents do seem to continue to rely on adults selectively: for guidance and to deal with uncontrollable stressors. This is part of a larger trend in which, as youth develop, they increasingly structure their own responses, including to whom they turn for support (Diamond & Aspinwall, 2003). Young people may continue to seek help and information from adults, and this might even increase with age. At the same time, there are decreases in other forms of support seeking from adults and increases in emotional self-regulation and emotional support-seeking from peers.

Overall, children take an increasingly active role in managing their social coping resources by turning to others whom they perceive will be of most assistance for particular stressors and their particular goals or needs. Although no study has been conducted on age changes in the importance of processes involved in dyadic coping, this suggests that young people become more aware of the dyadic aspects of coping, such as the mutuality of the dyad, as they get older. By adolescence, most young people have developed a sophisticated map of their social resources in times of stress.

Adulthood and Aging

Young adulthood is characterized by increasing emotional maturity, which can be defined as better regulation of both one's self and one's social relations. Better self and social regulation presumably entails more efficient use of energy resources. Aldwin and Levenson (2005) identified several facets of emotional maturity that emerge in young adulthood. First, there is increasing emotional stability and mastery (Roberts, Caspi, & Moffit, 2001), which may be the *sine qua non* for efficient use of coping strategies. Second, Arnett (2000) found that the hallmark of becoming an adult was accepting increasing responsibility for one's own actions, which is a necessary prerequisite for learning from one's mistakes and thus SRG. A related facet is the ability to accept critical feedback, especially from mentors but also from peers, which can increase one's self-knowledge and also sets the stage for learning and development. Arnett also found that the ability to self-generate goals, as well as goal-directed behavior, may also be necessary for efficient adaptation. Goals allow one to direct and focus energy and attention, providing a more cohesive and efficient adaptive framework. This new-found autonomy, however, is necessarily accompanied by an ability to work as a team member and engage in reciprocity, submerging one's own goals when necessary for the good of the larger group. Thus, emotional maturity entails a kind of dialectic between autonomy and accepting responsibility for one's own actions, on the one hand, and being able to accept (constructive) criticism and work in a group setting. The hypothesis that the ability to navigate this dialectic is important to coping in an efficient way, as it allows one to set goals and prioritize, but learn to work with others to achieve larger social goals, which are not necessarily amenable solely to individual effort.

With age, energy stores may become limited, and middle-aged and older adults may need to develop more efficient coping strategies, which allow them to expend less energy. Surprisingly, daily stressors decrease from midlife to late life, despite the increase in health problems, suggesting an increase in coping efficiency in an effort to conserve energy resources (Aldwin, Sutton, Chiara, & Spiro, 1996). Both Aldwin (2007) and Skinner and Edge (1998) have suggested that the decrease in problem-focused coping seen in later life may actually index greater efficiency rather than an increase in passivity with age. Johnson and Barer's (1993) qualitative study of coping in very late life suggests that elders may engage in more routinization in an attempt to avoid stress and to conserve energy. Boeninger, Shiraishi, Aldwin, and Spiro (2009) found that individuals may use appraisal processes to avoid perceiving situations as stressful.

The elderly also have to strive to find a balance between self-reliance and reliance on others as their action resources diminish. Recent views of support have focused on its reciprocity (George, 2006; Schwarzer & Knoll, 2007). It is the rare individual who is only the recipient of social support; most individuals have a long history of providing and receiving support from family members, friends, and close colleagues. Antonucci (1985) describes this as a type of support bank in which individuals "make deposits" with the expectation that this will offset future support received. Further, reciprocity may play out over time with individuals alternating between sequences of social support provision over receiving. Schwarzer and Knoll (2007) found that there was a strong association between providing support at Time 1 and receiving support at a 6-month follow-up. Further, there may be differences in the types of support exchanged. For example, van Tilburg (1998) found that older adults received more instrumental support from family and friends over a 4-year period, but also provided more emotional support as a way of maintaining reciprocity.

FUTURE DIRECTIONS IN THE STUDY OF LIFE-SPAN COPING

This chapter has focused on some key issues that may serve to further integrate conceptions of coping and regulation across the life span. In doing so, we have identified gaps in the current literature which may be germane for future studies of coping. In terms of primary control, key questions for developmental researchers include more systematic inquiry into: (1) the kinds of coping promoted by a sense of control at different ages; (2) how developmental changes in the processes of perceiving control lead to shifts in coping; and (3) the way that coping experiences shape expectations of control at different ages. Especially important is information about how social contexts and task conditions promote a sense of control that is resilient to repeated developmental changes and exposure to failures and losses.

For secondary control, important next steps for theorists are to clarify both overarching definitions and criteria for distinguishing beliefs and strategies. To what extent is secondary control simply reflective of coping self-efficacy and self-control? Moreover, now that secondary control has been differentiated from accommodation, research can focus on the balance between tenacious goal pursuit and flexible goal adjustment when dealing with obstacles and setbacks. Wrosch (in press) has conducted several studies demonstrating that accommodative processes have both psychological and physical benefits, especially in late life. Thus, understanding how accommodative coping develops is a particularly important next step for future study. This research can benefit from considering previous work on the development of accommodative coping during childhood, on the development of willing compliance (which focuses on both temperamental and social factors), and on the development of autonomous self-regulation (e.g., Ryan & Connell, 1989).

Similarly, future research is needed to examine the development of dyadic coping, and its changing impact on health and well-being across the life span. Such research might be most revealing of developmental processes if it is focused on studying individuals at times of transition, such as following relationship loss or during the formation of new close relationships. To our knowledge, little empirical work has been done on precisely how social networks influence stress appraisals. Work by Christakis and Fowler (2009) on the importance of social networks for moods and political attitudes might form a basis for future work in this area.

Finally, work on the importance of energy regulation for coping efforts potentially would be highly significant, but at this point there are a number of methodological and conceptual difficulties, which first must be addressed. Much of the work on coping processes takes place in a field setting and relies upon self-report data. While there have been attempts to investigate the importance of self-efficacy (e.g., Aldwin et al., 1996), to date, all of the work has relied on self report, and developing more objective measures of coping efficacy is an important first step. Further, there are also difficulties in judging what the "appropriate" level of energy expenditure is. A critical task is to determine how to judge whether an individual has expended insufficient effort, has engaged in perseverance, or is perseverating on a problem.

Research on energy regulation would likely benefit from models of coping and self-regulation which consider ways of dealing with demands that potentially generate energetic resources as well as deplete them. Some of the value of positive emotions and close relationships as well as laughter and fun even when coping with traumatic events may be explained by their powers of rejuvenation. Especially useful may be theories that incorporate the notion of profiles of coping and "balance"—between engagement and disengagement, between fighting and "going with the flow," and between reliance on self and others. The capacity to find and (re)achieve balance is likely a developmental process that depends on social partners, groups, and contexts, and is practiced through coping episodes themselves.

In summary, we believe that effective coping and self-regulation are critical to the maintenance of both mental and physical health at all stages of the life span. However, many issues remain in the conceptualization and measurement of these constructs in age-appropriate ways. Current investigations have yielded extensive and sometimes counter-intuitive insights into the adaptive process, and future research should add to our rich understanding of these processes and their effects on mental and physical health.

REFERENCES

Adams, V. H., & Jackson, J. S. (2000). The contribution of hope to the quality of life among aging African Americans: 1980–1992. *International Journal of Aging and Human Development, 50,* 279–297.

Aldwin, C. M. (2007). *Stress, coping, and development: An integrative approach* (2nd ed.). New York: Guilford.

Aldwin, C. M., & Levenson, M. R. (2001). Stress, coping, and health at mid-life: A developmental perspective. In M. E. Lachman (Ed.), *The handbook of midlife development* (pp. 188–214). New York: Wiley.

Aldwin, C. M., & Levenson, M. R. (2005). Military service and emotional maturation: The Chelsea Pensioners. In K. W. Warner & G. Elder, Jr. (Eds.), *Historical influences on lives and aging* (pp. 255–281). New York: Plenum.

Aldwin, C., & Revenson, T. (1987). Does coping help? A re-examination of the relationship between coping and mental health. *Journal of Personality & Social Psychology, 53,* 337–348.

Aldwin, C. M., Sutton, K. J., Chiara, G., & Spiro, A. III. (1996). Age differences in stress, coping, and appraisal: Findings from the Normative Aging Study. *Journals of Gerontology: Psychological Sciences, 51B,* P179–P188.

Aldwin, C. M., Yancura, L. A., & Boeninger, D. (2010). Coping across the lifespan. In A. Freund & M. Lamb (Eds.), *Handbook of lifespan developmental psychology* (Vol. 2) (pp. 298–340). New York: John Wiley.

Amat, J., Paul, E., Zarza, C., Watkins, L. R., & Maier, S. F. (2007). Previous experience with behavioral control over stress blocks the behavioral and dorsal raphe nucleus activating effects of later uncontrollable stress: Role of the ventral medial prefrontal cortex. *The Journal of Neuroscience, 26,* 13264–13272.

Antonucci, T. C. (1985). Personal characteristics, social networks, and social behavior. In R. H. Binstock & E. Shanas (Eds.), *Handbook of aging and the social sciences* (2nd ed.). New York: Van Nostrand Reinhold.

Arnett, J. J. (2000). Emerging adulthood: A theory of development from the late teens through the twenties. *American Psychologist, 55,* 469–480.

Aspinwall, L. G., & Taylor, S. E. (1997). A stitch in time: Self-regulation and proactive coping. *Psychological Bulletin, 121,* 417–436.

Avlund, K., Lund, R., Holstein, B. E., & Due, P. (2004). Social relations as determinant of onset of disability in aging. *Archives of Gerontology and Geriatrics, 38,* 85–99.

Badr, H. (2004). Coping in marital dyads: A contextual perspective on the role of gender and health. *Personal Relationships, 11,* 197–211.

Baltes, M. M. (1996). *The many faces of dependency in old age.* New York: Cambridge University Press.

Bandura, A. (1997). *Self-efficacy: The exercise of control.* New York: W. H. Freeman.

Barrett, K. C., & Campos, J. J. (1991). A diacritical function approach to emotions and coping. In E. M. Cummings, A. L. Greene, & K. H. Karraker (Eds.), *Life-span developmental psychology: Perspectives on stress and coping* (pp. 21–41). Hillsdale, NJ: Erlbaum.

Baumeister, R. F., Bratslavsky, E., Muraven, M., & Tice, D. M. (1998). Ego depletion: Is the active self a limited resource? *Journal of Personality & Social Psychology, 74,* 1252–1265.

Baumrind, D. (1996). The discipline controversy revisited. *Family Relations, 45,* 405–414.

Berscheid, E., Snyder, M., & Omoto, A. M. (1989). The relationship closeness inventory: Assessing the closeness of interpersonal relationships. *Journal of Personality & Social Psychology, 57,* 792–807.

Berg, C. A., Smith, T. W., Ko, K. J., Henry, N. J. M., Florsheim, P., Pearce, G. et al. (2007). Task control and cognitive abilities of self and spouse in collaboration in middle-aged and older couples. *Psychology and Aging, 22,* 420–427.

Berg, C. A., & Upchurch, R. (2007). A developmental-contextual model of couples coping with chronic illness across the adult life span. *Psychological Bulletin, 133,* 920–954.

Berg, C. A., Meegan, S. P., & Deviney, F. P. (1998). A social contextual model of coping with every-day problems across the life span. *International Journal of Behavioral Development, 22,* 239–261.

Bodenmann, G., & Cina, A. (2006). Stress and coping among stable-satisfied, stable-distressed, and separated/divorced Swiss couples: A 5-year prospective longitudinal study. *Journal of Divorce and Remarriage, 44,* 71–89.

Bodenmann, G. (1995). A systemic-transactional conceptualization of stress and coping in couples. *Swiss Journal of Psychology, 54,* 34–49.

Bodenmann, G., Pihet, S., & Kayser, K. (2006). The relationship between dyadic coping and marital quality: A 2-year longitudinal study. *Journal of Family Psychology, 20,* 485–493.

Boeninger, D. K., Shiraishi, R. W., Aldwin, C. M., & Spiro, A. III. (2009). Why do older men report lower stress ratings? Findings from the Normative Aging Study. *International Journal of Aging & Human Development, 68,* 149–170.

Brandtstädter, J., & Renner, G. (1990). Tenacious goal pursuit and flexible goal adjustment: Explication and age-related analysis of assimilative and accommodative strategies of coping. *Psychology and Aging, 5,* 58–67.

Brandtstädter, J., & Rothermund, K. (2002). The life-course dynamics of goal pursuit and goal adjust-ment: A two-process framework. *Developmental Review, 22,* 117–150.

Braungart-Rieker, J. M., & Stifter, C. A. (1996). Infants' responses to frustrating situations: Continuity and change in reactivity and regulation. *Child Development, 67,* 1767–1779.

Brim, O. G. (1992). *Ambition: How we manage success and failure throughout our lives.* New York: Basic Books.

Bronson, M. B. (2000). *Self-regulation in early childhood: Nature and nurture.* New York: Guilford Press.

Carstensen, L. L., Gottman, J. M., & Levenson, R. W. (1995). Emotional behavior in long-term mar-riage. *Psychology and Aging, 10,* 140–149.

Christakis, N. A., & Fowler, J. H. (2009). *Connected: The surprising power of our social networks and how they shape our lives.* New York: Little, Brown & Company.

Cicchetti, D., & Rogosch, F. A. (2009). Adaptive coping under conditions of extreme stress: Multi-level influences on the determinants of resilience in maltreated children. In E. A. Skinner & M. J. Zimmer-Gembeck (Eds.), *Perspective on children's coping with stress as regulation of emotion, cognition and behavior. New directions in child and adolescent development series.* San Francisco: Jossey-Bass.

Cole, P. M., Teti, L. O., & Zahn-Waxler, C. (2003). Mutual emotion regulation and the stability of con-duct problems between preschool and early school age. *Development and Psychopathology, 15,* 1–18.

Compas, B. E., Worsham, N. L., & Ey, S. (1992). Conceptual and developmental issues in children's coping with stress. In A. M. La Greca, L. J. Siegel, J. L. Wallander, & C. E. Walker (Eds.), *Stress and coping in child health* (pp. 7–24). New York: Guilford Press.

Compas, B., O'Connor-Smith, J. K., Saltzman, S., Thomsen, A. H., & Wadsworth, M. E. (2001). Coping with stress during childhood and adolescence: Problems, progress, and potential in theory and research. *Psychological Bulletin, 127,* 87–127.

Connor-Smith, J. K., Compas, B. E., Wadsworth, M. E., Thomsen, A. H., & Saltzman, H. (2000). Responses to stress in adolescence: Measurement of coping and involuntary stress responses. *Journal of Counseling and Clinical Psychology, 68,* 976–992.

Covington, M. V., & Omelich, C. L. (1979). Effort: The double-edged sword in school achievement. *Journal of Educational Psychology, 71,* 169–182.

Coyne, J., Aldwin, C., & Lazarus, R. (1981). Depression and coping in stressful episodes. *Journal of Abnormal Psychology, 90,* 439–447.

Coyne, J. C., & Smith, D. A. F. (1991). Couples coping with myocardial infarction: Contextual perspec-tives on patient self-efficacy. *Journal of Personality & Social Psychology, 61,* 404–412.

Coyne, J. C., Wortman, C. B., & Lehman, D. R. (1988). The other side of support: Emotional overin-volvement and miscarried helping. In B. H. Gottlieb (Ed.), *Marshaling social support* (pp. 305–330). Thousand Oaks, CA: Sage.

Cutrona, C. E., & Gardner, K. A. (2006). Stress in couples: The process of dyadic coping. In A. L. Vangelisti & D. Perlman (Eds.), *The Cambridge handbook of personal relationships* (pp. 501–515). New York: Cambridge University Press.

Diamond, L. M., & Aspinwall, L. G. (2003). Emotion regulation across the life span: An integrative perspective emphasizing self-regulation, positive affect, and dyadic processes. *Motivation and Emotions, 27,* 125–156.

Dixon, R. A. (1999). Exploring cognition in interactive situations: The aging of N+1 minds. In T. M. Hess & F. Blanchard-Fields (Eds.), *Social cognition and aging* (pp. 267–290). San Diego, CA: Academic Press.

Dixon, R. A., & Gould, O. N. (1998). Younger and older adults collaborating on retelling everyday stories. *Applied Developmental Science, 2,* 160–171.

Dunahoo, C. L., Hobfoll, S. E., Monnier, J., Hulsizer, M. R., & Johnson, R. (1998). There's more than rugged individualism in coping. Part 1: Even the Lone Ranger had Tonto. *Anxiety, Stress, and Coping, 11,* 137–165.

Dweck, C. S. (1999). *Self-theories: Their role in motivation, personality, and development.* Philadelphia: Psychology Press.

Eisenberg, N., Valiente, C., & Sulik, M. (2009). How the study of regulation can inform the study of coping. In E. A. Skinner & M. J. Zimmer-Gembeck (Eds.), *Coping and the development of regulation, New directions in child and adolescent development.* San Francisco: Jossey-Bass.

Eisenberg, N., Fabes, R. A., & Guthrie, I. K. (1997). Coping with stress: The roles of regulation and development. In S. A. Wolchik, & I. N. Sandler (Eds.), *Handbook of children's coping: Linking theory and intervention* (pp. 41–70). New York: Plenum Press.

Eisenberg, N., & Zhou, Q. (2000). Regulation from a developmental perspective. *Psychological Inquiry, 11,* 167–171.

Elliot, A. J., & Dweck, C. S. (Eds.). (2005). *Handbook of competence and motivation.* New York: Guilford.

Fabes, R. A., Leonard, S. A., Kupanoff, K., & Martin, C. L. (2001). Parental coping with children's negative emotions: Relations with children's emotional and social responding. *Child Development, 72,* 907–920.

Feeney, J. A. (2004). Adult attachment and relationship functioning under stressful conditions: Understanding partners' responses to conflict and challenge. In W. S. Rholes & J. A. Simpson (Eds.), *Adult attachment: Theory, research, and clinical implications* (pp. 339–364). New York: Guilford Publications.

Figueiras, M. J., & Weinman, J. (2003). Do congruent patient and spouse perceptions of myocardial infarction predict recovery? *Psychology and Health, 18,* 201–216.

Flammer, A. (1995). Developmental analysis of control beliefs. In A. Bandura (Ed.), *Self-efficacy in changing societies* (pp. 69–113). New York: Cambridge University Press.

Folkman, S. (1984). Personal control and stress and coping processes: A theoretical analysis. *Journal of Personality & Social Psychology, 46*(4), 839–852.

Fox, N. A., & Calkins, S. D. (2003). The development of self-control of emotion: Intrinsic and extrinsic influences. *Motivation and Emotion, 27,* 7–26.

Frydenberg, E., & Lewis, R. (2000). Teaching coping to adolescents: When and to whom? *American Educational Research Journal, 37,* 727–745.

Gagnon, L. M., & Dixon, R. A. (2008). Remembering and retelling stories in individual and collaborative contexts. *Applied Cognitive Psychology, 22,* 1275–1297.

George, L. K. (2006). Perceived quality of life. In R. H. Binstock & L. K. George (Eds.), *Handbook of aging and the social sciences* (6th ed.). San Diego, CA: Elsevier.

Gianino, A., & Tronick, E. Z. (1988). The mutual regulation model: The infant's self and interactive regulation and coping and defensive capacities. In T. M. Field, P. M. McCabe, & P. M. Schneiderman (Eds.), *Stress and coping across development.* Hillsdale, NJ: Erlbaum.

Gould, S. J. (1999). A critique of Heckhuasen and Schulz's (1995) life-span theory of control from a cross-cultural perspective. *Psychological Review, 106,* 597–604.

Greve, W., & Strobl, R. (2004). Social and individual coping with threats: Outlines of an interdisciplinary perspective. *Review of General Psychology, 8,* 194–207.

Grolnick, W. S., Bridges, L. J., & Connell, J. P. (1996). Emotion regulation in two-year-olds: Strategies and emotional expression in four contexts. *Child Development, 67,* 928–941.

Gross, J. (1998). The emerging field of emotion regulation: An integrative review. *Review of General Psychology, 2,* 271–299.

Gunnar, M. R., & Quevedo, K. (2007). The neurobiology of stress and development. *Annual Review of Psychology, 58,* 11.1–11.29.

Gunnar, M. R., & Vazquez, D. (2006). Stress neurobiology and developmental psychopathology. In D. Cicchetti & D. J. Cohen (Eds.), *Developmental psychopathology* (Vol. 2, 2nd ed., pp. 533–577). Hoboken, NJ: Wiley.

Gurung, R. A. R., Taylor, S. E., & Seeman, T. E. (2003). Accounting for changes in social support among married older adults: Insights from the MacArthur Studies of Successful Aging. *Psychology and Aging, 18,* 487–496.

Ha, J., Carr, D., Utz, R. L., & Nesse, R. (2006). Older adults' perceptions of intergenerational support after widowhood: How do men and women differ? *Journal of Family Issues, 27*, 3–30.

Heckhausen, H. (1982). The development of achievement motivation. In W. W. Hartup (Ed.), *Review of child development research,* (Vol. 6, pp. 600–668). Chicago: University of Chicago Press.

Heckhausen, H. (1984). Emergent achievement behavior: Some early developments. In M. Haehr (Ed.), *Advances in motivation and achievement* (pp. 1–32). Greenwich, CT: JAI Press.

Heckhausen, J., & Schulz, R. (1995). A life-span theory of control. *Psychological Review, 102*, 284–304.

Heijmans, M., de Ridder, D., & Bensing, J. (1999). Dissimilarity in patients' and spouses' representations of chronic illness: Exploration of relations to patient adaptation. *Psychology and Health, 14*, 451–466.

Hobfoll, S. E. (1998). *Stress, culture, and community: The psychology and philosophy of stress.* New York: Plenum Press.

Holodynski, M., & Friedlmeier, W. (2006). *Development of emotions and emotion regulation.* New York: Springer.

Johnson, C. I., & Barer, B. M. (1993). Coping and a sense of control among the oldest old: An exploratory analysis. *Journal of Aging Studies, 7*, 67–80.

Johnson, N. J., Backlund, E., Sorlie, P. D., & Loveless C. A. (2000). Marital status and mortality: The national longitudinal mortality study. *Annals of Epidemiology, 10*(4), 224–238.

Kliewer, W., Fearnow, M. D., & Miller, P. A. (1996). Coping socialization in middle childhood: Tests of maternal and paternal influences. *Child Development, 67*, 2339–2357.

Kliewer, W., & Lewis, H. (1995). Family influences on coping processes in children and adolescents with sickle cell disease. *Journal of Pediatric Psychology, 20*, 511–525.

Kliewer, W., Parrish, K. A., Taylor, K. W., Jackson, K., Walker, J. M., & Shivy, V. A. (2006). Socialization of coping with community violence: Influences of caregiver coaching, modeling, and family context. *Child Development, 77*, 605–623.

Knoll, N., & Schwarzer, R. (2002). Gender and age differences in social support: A study on East German refugees. In G. Weidner, M. Kopp, & M. Kristenson (Eds.), *Heart disease: Environment, stress, and gender. NATO Science Series, Series I: Life and Behavioural Sciences* (Vol. 327). Amsterdam, The Netherlands: IOS Press.

Kochanska, G. (2002). Committed compliance, moral self, and internalization: A mediational model. *Developmental Psychology, 38*, 339–351.

Kochanska, G., Aksan, N., & Carlson (2005). Temperament, relationships, and young children's receptive cooperation with their parents. *Developmental Psychology, 41*, 648–660.

Kochanska, G., Coy, K. T., & Murray, K. T. (2005). The development of self-regulation in the first four years of life. *Child Development, 72*, 1091–1111.

Koplik, E. K., Lamping, D. L., & Reznikoff, M. (1992). The relationship of mother-child coping styles and mothers' presence on children's response to dental stress. *Journal of Psychology: Interdisciplinary and Applied, 126*, 79–92.

Kopp, C. B. (2002). Commentary: The codevelopments of attention and emotion regulation. *Infancy, 3*, 199–208.

Kopp, C. B. (2009). Emotion focused coping in young children: Self and self-regulatory processes. In E. A. Skinner & M. J. Zimmer-Gembeck (Eds.), *Perspective on children's coping with stress as regulation of emotion, cognition and behavior. New directions in child and adolescent development series.* San Francisco: Jossey-Bass.

Lachman, M. E., & Prenda-Firth, K. M. (2004). The adaptive value of feeling in control during midlife. In O. G. Brim, Jr., C. D. Ryff, & R. C. Kessler (Eds.), *How healthy are we? A national study of well-being at midlife* (pp. 320–349). Chicago: The University of Chicago Press.

Lewis, M., & Ramsay, D. (1999). Environments and stress reduction. In M. Lewis & D. Ramsay (Eds.), *Soothing & stress* (pp. 171–192). Mahwah, NJ: Erlbaum.

Losoya, S., Eisenberg, N., & Fabes, R. A. (1998). Developmental issues in the study of coping. *International Journal of Behavioral Development, 22*, 287–313.

Luthar, S. S. (in press). Resilience in development: A synthesis of research across five decades. In D. Cicchetti & D. J. Cohen (Eds.), *Developmental psychopathology: Risk, disorder, and adaptation* (Vol. 3, 2nd ed). New York: Wiley.

Masten, A. S., &Wright, M. O. (2009). Resilience over the lifespan: Developmental perspectives on resistance, recovery, and transformation. In J. W. Reich (Eds.), *Handbook of adult resilience* (pp. 213–237). New York: Guilford.

McClelland, M. M., Ponitz, C. C., Messersmith, E. E., & Tominey, S. (2010). Self-regulation: The integration of cognition and emotion (pp. 509–553). In R. Lerner (Series Ed.) & W. Overton (Vol. Ed.), *Handbook of life-span development.* Hoboken, NJ: Wiley and Sons.

Mendes de Leon, C. F., Gold, D. T., Glass, T. A., Kaplan, L., & George, L. K. (2001). Disability as a function of social networks and support in elderly African Americans and Whites: The Duke EPESE 1986–1992. *Journals of Gerontology: Psychological Sciences, 56B*, 179–190.

Metcalfe, J., & Mischel, W. (1999). A hot/cool-system analysis of delay of gratification: Dynamics of willpower. *Psychological Review, 106*, 3–19.

Mikulincer, M., Shaver, P. R., & Horesch, N. (2006). Attachment bases of emotion regulation and posttraumatic adjustment. In D. K. Snyder, J. A. Simpson, & J. N. Hughes (Eds.), *Emotion regulation in couples and families* (pp. 77–99). Washington, DC: American Psychological Association.

Miller, S. M., Green, V. A., & Bales, C. B. (1999). What you don't know can hurt you: A cognitive-social framework for understanding children's responses to stress. In M. Lewis & D. Ramsay (Eds.), *Soothing & stress* (pp. 257–292). Mahwah, NJ: Erlbaum.

Moller, A., Deci, E. L., & Ryan, R. M. (2006). Choice and ego-depletion: The moderating role of autonomy. *Personality & Social Psychology Bulletin, 32*, 1024–1036.

Morling, B., & Evered, S. (2006). Secondary control reviewed and defined. *Psychological Bulletin, 132*, 269–296.

Murphy, L., & Moriarty, A. (1976). *Vulnerability, coping, and growth: From infancy to adolescence*. New Haven, CT: Yale University Press.

National Research Council [NRC]. (2000). *From neurons to neighborhoods*. Washington, DC: National Academies Press.

Newman, R. S. (2000). Social influences on the development of children's adaptive help seeking: The role of parents, teachers, and peers. *Developmental Review, 20*, 350–404.

Newsom, J. T. (1999). Another side to caregiving: Negative reactions to being helped. *Current Directions in Psychological Science, 8*, 183–187.

Nicholls, J. G. (1978). The development of the concepts of effort and ability, perceptions of academic attainment, and the understanding that difficult tasks require more ability. *Child Development, 49*, 800–814.

Nolen-Hoeksma, S., Girgus, J. S., & Seligman, M. E. P. (1986). Learned helplessness in children: A longitudinal study of depression, achievement, and explanatory style. *Journal of Personality & Social Psychology, 51*(2), 435–442.

Nolen-Hoeksma, S., Wisco, B., & Lyubomirsky, S. (2008). Rethinking rumination. *Perspectives on Psychological Science, 3*, 400–424.

Papousek, H., & Papousek, M. (1980). Early ontogeny of human social interaction: Its biological roots and social dimensions. In M. von Cranach, K. Foppa, W. Lepenies, & D. Ploog (Eds.), *Human ethology: Claims and limits of a new discipline*. Cambridge: Cambridge University.

Paris, S. G., & Newman, R. S. (1990). Developmental aspects of self-regulated learning. *Educational Psychologist, 25*, 87–102.

Peterson, C., Maier, S. F., & Seligman, M. E. P. (1993). *Learned helplessness: A theory for the age of personal control*. New York: Oxford University Press.

Power, T. G. (2004). Stress and coping in childhood: The parents' role. *Parenting: Science and Practice, 4*, 271–317.

Propper, C., & Moore, G. A. (2006). The influence of parenting on infant emotionality: A multi-level psychobiological perspective. *Developmental Review, 26*, 427–460.

Revenson, T. A. (2003). Scenes from a marriage: Examining support, coping, and gender within the context of chronic illness. In J. Suls & K. A. Wallston (Eds.), *Social psychological foundations of health and illness* (pp. 530–559). Malden, MA: Blackwell.

Revenson, T. A., & Pranikoff, J. R. (2005). A contextual approach to treatment decision making among breast cancer survivors. *Health Psychology, 24*, S93–S98.

Roberts, B. W., Caspi, A., & Moffitt, T. E. (2001). The kids are alright: Growth and stability in personality development from adolescence to adulthood. *Journal of Personality & Social Psychology, 81*, 670–683.

Rook, K. S., Mavandadi, S., Sorkin, D. H., & Zettel, L. A. (2007). Optimizing social relationships as a resource for health and well-being in later life. In C. M. Aldwin, C. L. Park, & A. Spiro III (Eds.), *Handbook of health psychology & aging* (pp. 267–285). New York: Guilford.

Roth, S., & Cohen, L. (1986). Approach, avoidance, and coping with stress. *American Psychologist, 41*, 813–819.

Rothbaum, F., Weisz, J. R., & Snyder, S. S. (1982). Changing the world and changing the self: A two-process model of perceived control. *Journal of Personality & Social Psychology, 42*, 5–37.

Ruble, D. (1983). The development of social comparison processes and their role in achievement-related self-socialization. In E. T. Higgins, D. N. Ruble, & W. W. Hartup (Eds.), *Social cognition and social development: A sociocultural perspective* (pp. 134–157). New York: Cambridge University Press.

Rueda, M. R., & Rothbart, M. K. (2009). Temperament, coping, and development. In E. A. Skinner & M. J. Zimmer-Gembeck (Eds.), *Perspective on children's coping with stress as regulation of emotion, cognition and behavior. New directions in child and adolescent development series.* San Francisco: Jossey-Bass.

Ryan, R. M., & Connell, P. (1989). Perceived locus of causality and internalization: Examining reasons for acting in two domains. *Journal of Personality & Social Psychology, 57,* 749–761.

Sameroff, A. J., & Haith, M. M. (1996). *The five to seven year shift: The age of reason and responsibility.* Chicago: University of Chicago Press.

Schmitz, B., & Skinner, E. (1993). Perceived control, effort, and academic performance: Interindividual, intraindividual, and multivariate time-series analyses. *Journal of Personality & Social Psychology, 64,* 1010–1028.

Schulz, R., Wrosch, C., & Heckhausen, J. (2003). The life-span theory of control: Issues and evidence. In S. H. Zarit, L. I. Pearlin, & K. W. Schaie (Eds.), *Personal control in social and life course contexts* (pp. 233–262). New York: Springer.

Schwarzer, R., & Knoll, N. (2007). Functional roles of social support within the stress and coping process: A theoretical and empirical overview. *International Journal of Psychology, 42,* 243–252.

Seeman, T. E., Bruce, M. L., & McAvay, G. J. (1996). Social network characteristics and onset of ADL disability: MacArthur studies of successful aging. *Journal of Gerontology, 51B,* 5191–5200.

Seiffge-Krenke, I. (1995). *Stress, coping, and relationships in adolescence.* Hillsdale, NJ: Erlbaum.

Skaff, M. M. (2007). Sense of control and health: A dynamic duo in the aging process. In C. M. Aldwin, C. L. Park, & A. Spiro III (Eds.), *Handbook of Health Psychology & Aging* (pp. 186–209). New York: Guilford.

Skinner, E. A. (1995). *Perceived control, motivation, and coping.* Newbury Park, CA: Sage.

Skinner, E. A. (1996). A guide to constructs of control. *Journal of Personality & Social Psychology, 71,* 549–570.

Skinner, E. A. (1999). Action regulation, coping, and development. In J. B. Brandtstädter & R. M. Lerner (Eds.), *Action and self-development* (pp. 465–503). Thousand Oaks, CA: Sage.

Skinner, E. A. (2007). Secondary control critiqued: Is it secondary? Is it control? Commentary on Morling and Evered, 2006. *Psychological Bulletin, 133,* 911–916.

Skinner, E. A., Edge, K., Altman, J., & Sherwood, H. (2003). Searching for the structure of coping: A review and critique of category systems for classifying ways of coping. *Psychological Bulletin, 129,* 216–269.

Skinner, E., & Edge, K. (1998). Reflections on coping and development across the lifespan. *International Journal of Behavioral Development, 22,* 357–366.

Skinner, E. A., Zimmer-Gembeck, M. J., & Connell, J. P. (1998). Individual differences and the development of perceived control. *Monographs of the Society for Research in Child Development, 63*(2–3), 1–220.

Skinner, E. A., & Zimmer-Gembeck, M. J. (2007). The development of coping. *Annual Review of Psychology, 58,* 119–144.

Skinner, E. A., & Zimmer-Gembeck, M. J. (2009). Challenges to the developmental study of coping. In E. A. Skinner & M. J. Zimmer-Gembeck (Eds.), *Coping and the development of regulation, New Directions in Child and Adolescent Development.* San Francisco: Jossey-Bass.

Sroufe, L. A. (1996). *Emotional development: The organization of emotional life in the early years.* New York: Cambridge University Press.

Stipek, D. J., Gralinski, J. H., & Kopp, C. B. (1990). Self-concept development in the toddler years. *Developmental Psychology, 26,* 972–977.

Stipek, D. J., & MacIver, D. (1989). Developmental change in children's assessment of intellectual competence. *Child Development, 60,* 521–538.

Stroebe, M., & Schut, H. (1999). The dual process model of coping with bereavement: Rationale and description. *Death Studies, 23,* 197–224.

Tedeschi, R. G., & Calhoun, L. G. (2004). Posttraumatic growth: Conceptual foundations and empirical evidence. *Psychological Inquiry, 15,* 1–18.

Thoits, P. (1986). Social support as coping assistance. *Journal of Consulting and Clinical Psychology, 54,* 416–423.

Thompson, S. C., Sobolew-Shubin, A., Galbraith, M. E., Schwankovsky, L., & Cruzen, D. (1993). Maintaining perceptions of control: Finding perceived control in low-control circumstances. *Journal of Personality & Social Psychology, 64,* 293–304.

Thompson, S. C., Thomas, C., Rickbaugh, C. A., Tantamjarik, P., Otsuki, T., Pan, D., et al. (1998). Primary and secondary control over age-related changes in physical appearance. *Journal of Personality, 66*, 583–605.

Thompson, S., Nanni, C., & Levine, A. (1994). Primary versus secondary and central versus consequence-related control in HIV-positive men. *Journal of Personality & Social Psychology, 67*, 540–547.

Tolan, P., & Grant, K. (2009). How social and cultural contexts shape the development of coping: Youth in he inner-city as an example. In E. A. Skinner & M. J. Zimmer-Gembeck (Eds.), *Coping and the development of regulation, New Directions in Child and Adolescent Development*. San Francisco: Jossey-Bass.

Valiente, C., Fabes, R. A., Eisenberg, N., & Spinrad, T. L. (2004). The relations of parental expressivity and support to children's coping with daily stress. *Journal of Family Psychology, 18*, 97–106.

Van Tilburg, T. (1998). Loosing and gaining in old age: Changes in personal network size and social support in a four year longitudinal study. *Journals of Gerontology, Series B: Psychological Sciences and Social Sciences, 53B*, S313–S323.

Walsh, K., Fortier, M. A., & DiLillo, D. (2010). Adult coping with childhood sexual abuse: A theoretical and empirical review. *Aggression and Violent Behavior, 15*, 1–13.

Wright, D. L., & Aquilino, W. S. (1998). Influence of emotional support exchange in marriage on caregiving wives' burden and marital satisfaction. *Family Relations, 47*, 195–204.

Wrosch, C. (in press). Self-regulation of unattainable goals and pathways to quality of life. In S. Folkman (Ed.), *Oxford handbook of stress, health, & coping*. London: Oxford University.

Zautra, A. J., & Manne, S. J. (1992). Coping with rheumatoid arthritis: A review of a decade of research. *Annals of Behavioral Medicine, 14*, 31–39.

Zimmer-Gembeck, M. J., & Locke, E. M. (2007). The socialization of adolescent coping: Relationships at home and school. *Journal of Adolescence, 30*, 1–16.

Zimmer-Gembeck, M. J., & Skinner, E. A. (2008). Adolescents' coping with stress: Development and diversity. *Prevention Researcher, 15*, 3–7.

Zimmer-Gembeck, M. J., & Skinner, E. A. (2009). *The development of coping across childhood and adolescence: An integrative review and critique of research*. Manuscript submitted for publication.

Zimmerman, B. J., & Schunk, D. H. (Eds.). (2001). *Self-regulated learning and academic performance: Theoretical perspectives*. Malweh, NJ: Erlbaum.

Zuckerman, M., Knee, C. R., Kieffer, S. C., Rawsthorne, L., & Bruce, L. M. (1996). Beliefs in realistic and unrealistic control: Assessment and implications. *Journal of Personality, 64*, 435–464.

LIFE NARRATIVES

23

Dan P. McAdams

It is a truth increasingly acknowledged among psychologists in the 21st century that a modern young adult in possession of childhood memories and aspirations for the future must be in want of a good life story.

With apologies to Jane Austen (1813/1980), my first sentence plays with a form she made famous in the opening words of *Pride and Prejudice,* to convey a double message regarding the psychology of life narratives. The first part of the message is a historical observation. The idea that lives may be rendered into stories, and that such a rendering may bring profit to a life, is an ancient insight. But it took psychology a very long time to see the wisdom in this very old idea. In the 1980s and 1990s, psychological scientists and practitioners finally began to turn their attention to the role of stories in human life (e.g., Bruner, 1986; McAdams, 1985; Sarbin, 1986; White & Epston, 1990). The result today is a rapidly expanding literature on the psychology of life narratives, spanning cognitive neuroscience and cognitive psychology (Conway & Pleydell-Pearce, 2000; Roser & Gazzaniga, 2004), developmental psychology (Bohn & Berntsen, 2008; Fivush & Haden, 2003), life-span and life course studies (McAdams, 2005; Pasupathi, 2001), social and personality psychology (McAdams, 2008; McLean, Pasupathi, & Pals, 2007), cultural psychology (Hammack, 2008; Wang, 2006), industrial–organizational psychology (Gabriel, 2000), and psychotherapy practice (Angus & McLeod, 2004; Singer, 2005). Narrative approaches have also come to inform the disciplines of sociology and criminology (Maruna & Ramsden, 2004), family and marital studies (Pratt & Fiese, 2004), communication studies (Shotter & Gergen, 1989), public health (Crossley, 2001), and a range of other fields that focus their attention on the stories people tell about their lives, their relationships, and their social worlds (Josselson & Lieblich, 1993; McAdams, Josselson, & Lieblich, 2006).

The second part of the message is a developmental claim—that beginning at a certain point in the human life span, many people become authors of their own lives, constructing internalized and evolving narratives of the self to provide their lives with some semblance of meaning and purpose. It is this developmental claim that forms the thesis of the current chapter. In what follows I will draw on research and theory from a number of different disciplines to trace the development of the life story, from its precursors in infancy and childhood to its construction, elaboration, and possible diminution across the adult life span.

We do not begin life as authors of our own stories, and for many of us who journey into advanced old age we may not end life in that role either. But in the great and long middle of the human life span, we create stories out of our lives and we endeavor to live our lives within the confines of our evolving narrative frames. We work on our stories. The work proceeds intermittently, in fits and starts, sometimes consciously and often unconsciously, in response to normative developmental demands, off-time surprises and unexpected life changes, and the constantly evolving social ecology of everyday life. In the great and long middle of the human life span, we make meaning out of our lives by making narratives.

WHAT IS A LIFE NARRATIVE?

A life narrative is simply a story that a person formulates about his or her life. The story may refer to a particular episode or event in a person's life, or it may encompass a broader time frame such as an extended period or chapter in one's life, or even one's entire life course (Conway & Pleydell-Pearce, 2000). The story may be about events from the remembered past (Singer & Salovey, 1993) or about what the person imagines will happen in the future (Bauer & McAdams, 2004a). The story may be told to others in the course of everyday events, as when good friends get together to share tales about last weekend (Pasupathi, 2006). Or the story may be told in a more formal context, such as psychotherapy and counseling (Lieblich, McAdams, & Josselson, 2004) or in the course of a research interview. Importantly, the story *does not need to be told* to exist as a story in the mind of the narrator. Indeed, researchers often distinguish between the public or manifest narrative accounts provided by a person and the private or latent stories about life that most all people are presumably walking around with, even if they never tell these stories to anybody else. Some research methods, such as intensive life story interviews (McAdams, 1993), are designed to encourage participants to make clear, explicit, and manifest something that may have hitherto existed in a more inchoate and implicit form.

Life narratives resemble other kinds of narratives in many ways. Like fairy tales, modern novels, television sitcoms, and many other familiar story forms, life narratives typically feature main characters who, equipped with desires and beliefs, set out to attain some kind of goal or end state and who, along the way, often confront obstacles or complications in goal pursuit. As Bruner (1986) puts it, stories are almost always about the "vicissitudes of human intention" organized in time (p. 17). A story begins when a human or human-like character intends to do something. The plot unfolds over time as the character's goal-directed activity plays itself out across successive scenes, typically reaching a climax or high point in the story and eventually ending with some form of resolution. The story may express a theme or suggest a moral, message, or insight. The story holds the attention of the listener or audience by building suspense and by eliciting some kind of emotional response, be it gentle amusement, sadness, excitement, or horror. Whether or not the story is literally true—in the sense of corresponding precisely to what may have happened in a particular time and place—is typically less important than the extent to which the story engages the emotions or expresses a compelling meaning. Indeed, veracity may be irrelevant for many kinds of stories. As Bruner (1986) emphasizes, stories seek verisimilitude (lifelikeness) over veracity (correspondence to objective facts); that is, a story should express something true about life, about why people do what they do, about the human condition or the nature of human society, or about how people live with each other, and live with themselves, even if the events in the story never literally happened.

Stories about life are the same, to a point. Whether telling about the day I met my wife or recalling a vivid childhood memory, I provide an account of how a human character, equipped with desires and beliefs, aimed to achieve some sort of end over time. What may make the story worth telling is something likely to engage the listener's (and teller's) emotions—how she resisted my initial entreaties because she thought I was a fool or how I was thrilled when my father came home for Christmas and then horrified when he said he would never return. But is my story true? Because life narratives are about actual lives, the teller is more obligated than, say, a novelist to stick to the actual facts. Audiences expect life narratives to have credibility. If I tell you that I was born to a rich family and that I was a star athlete in high school, I am lying, and sooner or later you will probably see through the lie. If I tell you that my dream for the future is to become president of the United States, you are likely to be suspicious, for at age 55 I have yet to run for any public office. Indeed, social life as we know it—in families, among friends, in professional organizations, in civic communities, and so on—depends on some degree of credibility and attention to objective reality when it comes to the telling of life narratives.

At the same time, audiences give tellers substantial literary license, depending on social, cultural, and discursive norms. In casual talk, then, audiences expect tellers to embellish a little bit, to highlight the best parts of the event (as reconstructed from the past or imagined in the future), and to ignore aspects that get in the way of a good story. Audiences also expect stories to conform to the demand characteristics of particular social settings. People tell certain kinds of life narratives in a job interview, and those are not likely to be the same stores they tell on a first date, or when hanging out with old friends. Furthermore, we know that tellers have a great deal of discretion in *choosing* what to tell. From the countless possibilities that might be chosen, why choose to tell the story of one Christmas afternoon? Why not talk about one's first kiss, hitting a game-winning home run at age 15, graduation from high school, the first day of kindergarten, or a pleasant afternoon at the beach? Even though people expect life narratives to be credibly based on reality, therefore, storytellers still enjoy a great deal of freedom in the way they reconstruct the past and imagine the future, what they decide to reveal and conceal, and what they determine to be the meaning and significance of the stories they tell about their lives. Life narratives, then, are *psychosocial constructions* (McAdams, 1996). Based on the objective data of one's life as lived, life narratives nonetheless reflect the constructive and imaginative powers of an author who lives and tells within a particular social world.

Constructing and telling life narratives fulfill many psychological functions. For example, sharing personal stories with others may build social relationships and help to establish intimacy between people (Alea & Bluck, 2003). Life storytelling may serve therapeutic functions (Lieblich et al., 2004). For example, recounting and making narrative sense of stressful events in one's life may help the teller cope with those events, leading to enhanced psychological functioning and even better physical health (Pals, 2006; Pennebaker, 1997). Storytelling may be an especially powerful means of coping with personal trauma. Clinicians and researchers have shown how people who have experienced profound losses and setbacks may eventually come to terms with these especially negative events in their lives by casting them into coherent narratives that aim to wrench meaning or solace out of suffering (Neimeyer, 2001; Tedeschi & Calhoun, 1995).

A developmentally critical function of life narrative is *integration* (McAdams, 1985). To integrate is to bring disparate things together into a coherent and meaningful whole. In my *life story model of identity*, I have argued that beginning in late adolescence and young adulthood, people living in modern societies typically seek to put their lives together into broad and integrative stories as they construct what Erikson (1963) called ego identity (McAdams, 1985, 2008). We may conceive of the construction and elaboration of an integrative life story as the process of formulating a *narrative identity* (McAdams, 2008; McLean et al., 2007; Singer, 2004). Narrative identity is the broad life story that a person begins to work on in late adolescence and young adulthood to provide his or her life with a sense of unity, purpose, and meaning in the adult world. The story develops in the head of the narrator—an internalized and evolving story of how the person came to be who he or she is today and where the person is heading in the future. As a selective reconstruction of the past and imagined projection into the future, narrative identity is much more than the little stories about life that people tell on this occasion and that. It is, instead, the big story—*the* big life story that I am working on, developing inside my head but constructed, reconstructed, refined, edited, and continuously worked over in social relationships and in the context of my expanding social world. As this chapter's opening sentence suggests, narrative identity emerges as the central storytelling task at a particular point in human development—when a modern young adult, in possession of childhood memories and aspirations for the future, finds that he or she is "in want of a good life story." But how do we get to this developmentally critical juncture in the human life span? And what happens then?

▪ THE DEVELOPMENT OF STORYTELLING AND THE EMERGENCE NARRATIVE IDENTITY

Stories are accounts of the vicissitudes of human *intention* organized in time (Bruner, 1986). In virtually all intelligible stories, humans or human-like characters act to accomplish intentions upon a social landscape, generating a sequence of actions and reactions extended as a plot in time. Human intentionality is at the heart of narrative, and therefore the development of intentionality is of prime importance in establishing the mental conditions necessary for storytelling and story comprehension. Research on imitation and attention suggests that by the end of the first year of life human infants recognize that other human beings are intentional agents who act in a goal-directed manner (Kuhlmeier, Wynn, & Bloom, 2003). They implicitly understand that a story's characters act in accord with goals.

The second year of life marks the emergence of a storytelling, autobiographical self. By 24 months of age, toddlers have consolidated a sense of themselves as agentic and appropriating subjects in the social world who are, at the same time, the objects of others' observations (as well as their own). The 2-year-old self is a reflexive, duplex, I-Me configuration: A subjective I that observes (and begins to construct) an objective Me. Among those elements of experience that the I begins to attribute to the Me are autobiographical events. Howe and Courage (1997) argue that children begin to encode, collect, and narrate autobiographical memories around the ages 2–3—*my* little stories about what happened to *me*, stories the I constructs and remembers about the Me.

With development and experience in the preschool years, the storytelling, autobiographical self becomes more sophisticated and effective. The burgeoning research literature on children's *theory of mind* shows that in the third and fourth years of life most children come to understand that intentional human behavior is motivated by internal desires and beliefs. Interpreting the actions of others (and oneself) in terms of their predisposing desires and beliefs is a form of mind reading, according to Baron-Cohen (1995), a competency that is critical for effective social interaction. By the time children enter kindergarten, mind reading seems natural and easy. To most school children, it makes intuitive sense that a girl should eat an ice-cream cone because "she wants to" (desire) or that a boy should look for a cookie in the cookie jar because "he believes the cookies are there." But autistic children often find mind reading to be extraordinarily difficult, as if they never developed this intuitive sense about what aspects of mind are involved in the making of motivated human behavior. Characterized by what Baron-Cohen (1995) calls *mindblindness*, children with autism do not understand people as intentional characters, or do so only to a limited degree. Their lack of understanding applies to the self as well, suggesting that at the heart of severe autism may reside a disturbing dysfunction in "I-ness," and a corresponding inability to formulate and convey sensible narratives of the self (Bruner, 1994).

Autobiographical memory and self-storytelling develop in a social context. Parents typically encourage children to talk about their personal experiences as soon as children are verbally able to do so (Fivush & Nelson, 2004). Early on, parents may take the lead in stimulating the child's recollection and telling of the past by reminding the child of recent events, such as this morning's breakfast or yesterday's visit to the doctor. Taking advantage of this initial conversational scaffolding provided by adults, the young child soon begins to take more initiative in sharing personal events. By the age of 3 years, children are actively engaged in co-constructing their past experience in conversations with adults. By the end of the preschool years, they are able to give a relatively coherent account of their past experiences, independent of adult guidance. Yet individual differences in how parents converse with their children appear to have strong impacts on the development of the storytelling self. For example, mothers tend to encourage daughters, more than sons, to share *emotional* experiences, including especially memories of negative events that produce sadness (Fivush & Kuebli, 1997). Early on, girls use more emotion words than boys in their autobiographical recollections. When mothers consistently engage their children in an elaborative conversational pattern, asking children to reflect and elaborate upon their personal experiences, children develop richer autobiographical memories and tell more detailed stories about themselves. Conversely, a more constricted style of conversation on the part of mothers is associated with less articulated personal narratives in children (Reese & Farrant, 2003). Research also suggests that mothers of securely attached children tend to use more elaborative and evaluative strategies when reminiscing with their children, compared with mothers of insecurely attached children. Securely attached children may in turn be more responsive than insecurely attached children in the conversations they have with their mothers about personal events (Reese, 2002).

By the time children are able to generate their own narrative accounts of personal memories, they also exhibit a good understanding of the canonical features of stories themselves. Five-year-olds typically know that stories are set in a particular time and place and involve characters that act upon their desires and beliefs over time. They expect stories to evoke suspense and curiosity and will dismiss as "boring" a narrative that fails to live up to these emotional conventions (Brewer & Lichtenstein, 1982). They expect stories to conform to a conventional *story grammar*

(Mandler, 1984), or generic script concerning what kinds of events can occur and in what order. In a simple, goal-directed episode, for example, an initiating event may prompt the protagonist to attempt some kind of action, which will result in some kind of consequence, which in turn will be followed by the protagonist's reaction to the consequence (Mandler, 1984). Stories are expected to have definite beginnings, middles, and endings. The ending is supposed to provide a resolution to the plot complications that developed over the course of the story. If a story does not conform to conventions such as these, children may find it confusing and difficult to remember, or they may recall it later with a more canonical structure than it originally had.

As children move through the elementary school years, they come to narrate their own personal experiences in ways that conform to their implicit understandings of how good stories should be structured and what they should include. Importantly, they begin to internalize their culture's norms and expectations concerning what the story of an *entire human life* should contain. As they learn that a telling of a single life typically begins, say, with an account of birth and typically includes, say, early experiences in the family, eventual moves out of the family, getting a job, getting married, and so on, they acquire what Habermas and Bluck (2000) term a *cultural concept of biography*. Cultural norms define conventional phases of the life course and suggest what kinds of causal explanations make sense in telling a life. As children learn the culture's biographical conventions, they begin to see how single events in their own lives—remembered from the past and imagined for the future—might be sequenced and linked together to create their own life story.

Still, it is not until adolescence, according to Habermas and Bluck (2000), that individuals craft causal narratives to explain how different events are linked together in the context of a biography. What Habermas and Bluck (2000) call *causal coherence* in life narratives is exhibited in the increasing effort across the adolescent years to provide narrative accounts of one's life that explain how one event caused, led up to, transformed, or in some way was/is meaningfully related to other events in one's life. An adolescent girl may explain, for example, why she rejects her parents' liberal political values, or why she feels shy around boys, or how it came to be that her junior year in high school represented a turning point in her understanding of herself in terms of personal experiences from the past that she has selected and reconstrued to make a coherent personal narrative. She will explain how one event led to another, which led to another, and so on. She will likely share her account with others and monitor the feedback she receives to determine whether her attempt at causal coherence makes sense (McLean, 2005; Thorne, 2000). Furthermore, she may now identify an overarching theme, value, or principle that integrates many different episodes in her life and conveys the gist of who she is and what her biography is all about—a cognitive operation that Habermas and Bluck (2000) call *thematic coherence*. In their analyses of life-narrative accounts produced between the ages of 8 and 20 years, Habermas and Paha (2001) and Habermas and de Silveira (2008) show that causal and thematic coherence are relatively rare in autobiographical accounts from late childhood and early adolescence but increase substantially through the teenage years and into early adulthood.

Cognitive development, then, sets the stage for narrative identity. But as Erikson (1963) emphasized, socioemotional and cultural factors also play important roles in moving the identity agenda forward in the teens and 20s. In modern societies, teachers, parents, peers, and the media all urge the adolescent to begin thinking about who he or she *really* is and what he or she wants to *become* as an adult. Social and cultural forces tell the young person that it will soon be time to *get a life* (Habermas & Bluck, 2000). Of course, even children know vaguely that they will become adults someday, and they may wonder what they will be when they grow up. In early adolescence, these wonderings may begin to take narrative form in fantasies, diaries, web postings, and other self-expressions. Elkind (1981) described these early drafts of narrative identity as *personal fables*. Often grandiose and breathless, these tales of personal greatness and personal tragedy (I will write the great American novel; I will play shortstop for the New York Yankees; I will save the world, or maybe destroy it; I will find the perfect love, and my lover will save me; nobody will ever understand how deep and unique my life has been and will be) may spell out a coherent story of life, but it is typically one that is wildly unrealistic. This is (usually) okay, Elkind suggested, putting grossly paranoid and destructive ideation aside. Narrative identity needs to start somewhere. As they mature into later adolescence and beyond, the authors of personal fables edit, revise, and often start the whole thing over, so as to compose life narratives that are better grounded in reality, reflecting a keener understanding of social constraints and a more astute appraisal of personal skills, values, gifts, and past experiences (Elkind, 1981; McAdams, 1985).

Even though most people ultimately abandon their personal fables, narrative identity never completely descends into literal realism. If they are to inspire and integrate, the stories we tell ourselves about who we are and how we came to be must retain their mythic qualities. Like personal fables, they are acts of imagination that creatively select, embellish, shape, and (yes, it is true) distort the past so that it connects causally and thematically to an imaginatively rendered and anticipated future, all in the service of making meaning (McLean et al., 2007; Singer, 2004). The task of constructing a narrative identity requires people to assume a role that is more like a novelist than a secretary. The job is to tell a good story rather than to report exactly what happened at the meeting. Still, facts are important. A person's narrative identity should be based on the facts of his or her life as they are generally understood in a social community, for credibility is a cardinal criterion of maturity in identity and in social life (McAdams, 1985). Those facts are part of the material—the psycho-literary resources—with which the author works to craft a self-defining narrative. But all by themselves, facts are devoid of social and personal meaning. A fact of my life may be that I lost a limb in the Iraq War. What do I make of that fact? Marshalling all the resources at my disposal and working within a social community that privileges some kinds of narratives and discourages others, I decide if my loss signals tragedy, irony, romance, redemption, a return to God, a recommitment to family, a loss of faith, or whatever. There are many narrative possibilities. But not an infinite number. In narrative identity, the storyteller can work only with the material at hand. Narrative identity draws upon the powers of imagination and integration to shape those materials into a good story, empowered and constrained as the storyteller is by the physical, biological, psychological, ideological, economic, historical, and cultural realities in play (Hammack, 2008; McAdams, 2006; Rosenwald & Ochberg, 1992).

Narrative identity emerges during a period of the life course that will forever retain a special salience in autobiographical memory. One of the most well-documented findings in cognitive psychology is the tendency for older adults (say, older than 50 years) to recall a disproportionate number of life events from the emerging adulthood years (roughly age 15 to 30). What is called the *memory bump* represents a dramatic departure from the linear forgetting curve that one might expect to prevail for autobiographical recollections (Conway & Pleydell-Pearce, 2000; Fitzgerald, 1988). This is to say, that people tend to recall fewer and fewer events as they go back further and further in time. I remember yesterday better than the day before. I remember what happened in the year 2007 better than what happened in 2003. The research shows that this general trend holds, except for memories of what happened in my emerging adulthood years. For those years, I likely hold many more memories, especially highly emotional memories, than the linear temporal trend predicts. Researchers have proposed many different reasons for the memory bump, such as the possibility that this period in the life course simply happens to contain a disproportionate number of objectively momentous life events, such as leaving home, first job, first sexual relationships, and so on. But the memory bump may also reflect the developmental emergence of narrative identity. As the storytelling I begins to author a narrative of the Me, it invests personal experiences with special meaning and salience. I remember so much about my emerging adulthood years because, in part, that was when I began to put my life together into a story.

NARRATING SUFFERING, PERSONAL GROWTH, AND SELF-TRANSFORMATION

Life stories contain accounts of high points, low points, turning points, and other emotionally charged events (Singer & Salovey, 1993; Tomkins, 1987). Positive events entail emotions such as joy, excitement, and love; negative events are about experiences of distress, sadness, fear, anxiety, anger, guilt, shame, and the like. In his script theory of personality, Tomkins (1987) suggested that people tend to organize emotionally positive and negative scenes in their life stories in correspondingly different ways. Scenes built around the positive affects of joy and excitement tend to be construed and organized as *variants*, Tomkins argued. People accentuate variation in their positive scenes, and in so doing their stories affirm the notion that people can be happy in many different ways. By contrast, scenes built around negative affects tend to be construed and organized as *analogs*. People accentuate the similarities among their negative events, perceiving common patterns and repetitive sequences, as if to suggest that unhappiness tends to happen in the same old way, over and over again. Positive scenes in narrative identity feel like this: "Wow! This is cool!" For negative scenes, it is more like, "Oh no! Here we go again."

There are many reasons to believe that emotionally positive and negative events present correspondingly different challenges and fulfill different functions in life stories (Pals, 2006). At a general level, many theories in psychological science link positive emotions to a behavioral approach system in the brain, designed to regulate reward-seeking activities. By contrast, negative emotions may signal avoidance behaviors in response to threat or uncertainty, regulated by a behavioral inhibition system. In her mobilization–minimization theory, Taylor (1991) underscored the asymmetrical effects of positive and negative events. Negative (adverse or threatening) events evoke strong and rapid physiological, cognitive, emotional, and social responses, Taylor argued. The organism mobilizes resources to cope with and ultimately minimize the adverse effect of a negative event. Negative events produce more cognitive activity in general and more efforts to engage in causal reasoning, compared with positive events. At the level of the life story, negative events seem to *demand an explanation*. They challenge the storyteller to make narrative sense of the bad thing that happened—to explain why it happened and perhaps why it may not happen again, to explore the consequences of the negative event for later development in the story.

Many researchers and clinicians believe that the cognitive processing of negative events leads to insight and positive consequences for psychological well-being and health. Pennebaker's (1997) landmark studies show that writing about (and presumably working through) negative events in life produces positive effects on health and well-being. Whether reviewing and analyzing positive life events produces the same kinds of effects remains an open question (Burton & King, 2004), but at least one study suggests that extensively processing positive events may lead to *reduced* well-being (Lyubomirsky, Sousa, & Dickerhoff, 2006). It may be better simply to *savor* positive life story scenes, to re-experience the positive emotions involved rather than trying to make cognitive sense of them (Burton & King, 2004). Negative scenes, however, seem to demand more storytelling work. In recent years, narrative research has examined the nature of that work: How do people process negative events in their life stories? And what are the psychological consequences of telling different kinds of stories about personal suffering and adversity?

When it comes to life storytelling, there are many ways to narrate negative events. Perhaps the most common response is to *discount* the event in some way. The most extreme examples of discounting fall under the rubrics of repression, denial, and dissociation. Some stories are so bad that they simply cannot be told—cannot be told to others and, in many cases, cannot really be told to the self. Freeman (1993) argued that some traumatic and especially shameful experiences in life cannot be incorporated into narrative identity because the narrator (and perhaps the narrator's audience as well) lacks the world assumptions, cognitive constructs, or experiential categories needed to make the story make sense. Less extreme are examples of what Taylor (1983) called *positive illusions*. People may simply overlook the negative aspects of life events and exaggerate the potentially positive meanings: "I may be sick, but I am not nearly as sick as my good friend's wife." "God is testing my resolve, and I will rise to the challenge." Bonnano (2004) showed that many people experience surprisingly little angst and turmoil when stricken with harsh misfortunes in life. People often show *resilience* in the face of adversity, Bonanno argued. Rather than ruminate over the bad things that happen in their lives, they put it all behind them and move forward.

In many situations, however, people cannot or choose not to discount negative life events. Instead, they try to make meaning out the suffering they are currently experiencing, or experienced once upon a time. For example, McLean and Thorne (2003) showed that adolescents often find it necessary to discern lessons learned or insights gained in self-defining memories that involve conflict with others. Pals (2006) argued that autobiographical reasoning about negative events ideally involves a two-step process. In the first step, the narrator explores the negative experience in depth, thinking long and hard about what the experience feels or felt like, how it came to be, what it may lead to, and what role the negative event may play in one's overall understanding of self. In the second step, the narrator articulates and commits the self to a positive resolution of the event. Pals (2006) warned that one should not pass lightly over Step One. When it comes to narrative identity, Pals suggested, the unexamined life lacks depth and meaning.

Consistent with Pals (2006), a number of studies have shown that exploring negative life events in detail is associated with psychological maturity. For example, King and her colleagues have conducted a series of intriguing studies wherein they ask people who have faced daunting life challenges to tell stories about "what might have been" had their lives developed in either a more positive or more expected direction (see King & Hicks, 2006, for an overview). In one study, mothers of infants with Down Syndrome reflected upon what their lives might have been like had they given birth to babies not afflicted with Downs. Those mothers who were able to articulate detailed and thoughtful accounts, suggesting a great deal of exploration and meaning-making in their processing of this negative life event, tended to score higher on Loevinger's (1976) measure of ego development than did mothers who discounted what might have been (King, Scollon, Ramsey, & Williams, 2000).

In a study of how midlife women respond to divorce, the elaboration of loss in narrative accounts interacted with time since divorce to predict ego development (King & Raspin, 2004). Among women who had been divorced for an extended period of time, vivid and highly elaborate accounts of the married life they had lost were associated with higher ego development at the time of their life telling, and narrative elaboration predicted increases in ego development measured 2 years later. In a methodologically similar study, King and Smith (2005) found that the extent to which gay and lesbian individuals explored what might have been had their lives followed a more conventional (heterosexual) course predicted high levels of ego development at the time of their life-narrative accounts and increases in ego development 2 years later.

Narrative studies of life transitions have also shown that self-exploration and elaboration are associated with higher levels of ego development. Bauer and McAdams (2004b) examined narrative accounts from people who had undergone major life changes in either work or religion. People high in ego development tended to construct accounts of these difficult transitions that emphasized learning, growth, and positive personal transformation. The extent to which personal narratives emphasizing self-exploration, transformation, and integration are positively correlated with ego development has also been documented in studies of life goals (Bauer & McAdams, 2004a) and narrative accounts of life's high points, low points, and turning points (Bauer, McAdams, & Sakaeda, 2005). In another study linking development to narrative processing, McLean and Pratt (2006) found that young adults who used more elaborated and sophisticated forms of meaning-making in narrating turning points in their lives tended also to score higher on an overall identity maturity index. Analyzing data from the Mills Longitudinal Study, Pals (2006) found that the extent to which women at age 52 explored the ramifications of negative life events mediated the relationship between age-21 coping style and age-61 psychosocial maturity. Women who in early adulthood scored high on self-report scales assessing an open and nondefensive coping style constructed more elaborate and exploratory narrative accounts of difficult life events at age 52, and narrative exploration at age 52 predicted (and accounted for the relationship of coping openness to) clinical ratings of maturity at age 61.

If the first step in making narrative sense of negative life events is exploring and elaborating upon their nature and impact, Step Two involves constructing a positive meaning or resolution (Pals, 2006). This can be done in many ways. The narrator may derive from the event a particular lesson ("I learned I should never criticize my sister") or a more general insight about life ("I realized how important it is to cherish every moment"; McLean & Thorne, 2003). The narrator may show how the negative event ultimately made it possible for very positive events to occur later on or how it turned the person's life in a positive direction (McAdams, Reynolds, Lewis, Patten, & Bowman, 2001). The positive turn in life may involve a move toward activities that are of deep intrinsic interest for the person, serving to reconnect the person to what he or she feels to be the "true" or authentic self. Or the positive turn may enhance intimacy and consolidate social relationships (King & Smith, 2005; Woike & Matic, 2004). When narrators are able to derive positive or redemptive meanings from negative life events, they may feel that they have now fully worked through the event and attained a sense of narrative closure (King & Hicks, 2006; Pals, 2006).

Numerous studies have shown that deriving positive meanings from negative events is associated with life satisfaction and indicators of emotional well-being. In their studies of mothers of Down Syndrome children, divorced women, and gay and lesbian adults who reflect on what might have been in life, King and colleagues demonstrated that attaining a sense of closure regarding negative experiences from the past and/or lost possible selves predicts self-reported psychological well-being (see King & Hicks, 2006, for an overview). Bauer and colleagues documented strong correlations between well-being and the extent to which people underscore intrinsic motivations in their narrations of difficult life scenes and life transitions (Bauer & McAdams, 2004a, 2004b; Bauer et al., 2005). Bauer and colleagues also provided evidence to suggest that positive associations between age and psychological well-being across the adult life course may be partly accounted for by the fact that older people tend to emphasize themes of intrinsic motivation and growth in their narrative accounts of significant life scenes. McAdams et al. (2001) showed that the number of redemption sequences—scenes in which bad events lead to good outcomes—that a person includes in his or her life story predicts psychological well-being above and beyond the effect of a generally optimistic narrative style. In her analysis of longitudinal data from the Mills study, Pals (2006) found that coherent positive resolutions of difficult life events at age 51 predicted life satisfaction at age 61 and were associated with increasing ego resiliency between young adulthood and midlife.

Finding positive meanings in negative events is the central theme that runs through my own conception of *the redemptive self* (McAdams, 2006). In a series of nomothetic and idiographic studies conducted over the past 15 years, my colleagues and I have consistently found that midlife American adults who score especially high on self-report measures of generativity—suggesting a strong commitment to promoting the well-being of future generations and improving the world in which they live (Erikson, 1963)—tend to see their own lives as narratives of redemption (Mansfield & McAdams, 1996; McAdams, 2006; McAdams & Bowman, 2001; McAdams, Diamond, de St. Aubin, & Mansfield, 1997; McAdams et al., 2001). Compared with their less generative American counterparts, highly generative adults tend to construct life stories that feature redemption sequences, in which the protagonist is delivered from suffering to an enhanced status or state. In addition, highly generative American adults are more likely than their less generative peers to construct life stories in which the protagonist (1) enjoys a special advantage or blessing early in life; (2) expresses sensitivity to the suffering of others or societal injustice as a child; (3) establishes a clear and strong value system in adolescence that remains a source of unwavering conviction through the adult years; (4) experiences significant conflicts between desires for agency/power and desires for communion/love; and (5) looks to achieve goals to benefit society in the future. Taken together, these themes articulate a general script or narrative prototype that many highly generative American adults employ to make sense of their own lives. For highly productive and caring midlife American adults, the redemptive self is a narrative model of *the good life*.

The redemptive self is a life story prototype that serves to support the generative efforts of midlife men and women. Their redemptive life narratives tell how generative adults seek to give back to society in gratitude for the early advantages and blessings they feel they have received. In every life, generativity is tough and frustrating work, as every parent or community volunteer knows. But if an adult constructs a narrative identity in which the protagonist's suffering in the short run often gives way to reward later on, he or she may be better able to sustain the conviction that seemingly thankless investments today will pay off for future generations. Redemptive life stories support the kind of life strivings that a highly generative man or woman in the midlife years is likely to set forth. They also confer a *moral legitimacy* to life, a life-narrative function that Taylor (1989) and MacIntyre (1981) identify as central to the making of a modern identity. Certain kinds of life narratives exemplify what a society deems to be a good and worthy life. Indeed, virtually all life narratives assume some kind of moral stance in the world. Narrators operate from a moral perspective and seek to affirm the moral goodness of their identity quests. Taylor (1989) writes that "in order to make minimal sense of our lives, in order to have an identity, we need an orientation to the good," and "we see that this sense of the good has to be woven into my understanding of my life as an unfolding story" (p. 47).

CULTURE AND NARRATIVE

The conception of the redemptive self brings to attention the crucial role of culture in the construction of narrative identity over the life span. The kinds of life stories that highly generative American adults tend to tell reprise quintessentially American cultural themes—themes that carry a powerful moral cachet. Indeed, the stories of highly generative American adults may say as much about the cultural values that situate the story and the teller as they do about the storytellers themselves. The life story themes expressed by highly generative American adults recapture and couch in a psychological language especially cherished, as well as hotly contested, ideas in American cultural history—ideas that appear prominently in spiritual accounts of the 17th-century Puritans, Benjamin Franklin's 18th-century autobiography, slave narratives and Horatio Alger stories from the 19th century, and the literature of self-help and American entrepreneurship from more recent times (McAdams, 2006). Evolving from the Puritans to Emerson to Oprah, the redemptive self has morphed into many different storied forms in the past 300 years as Americans have sought to narrate their lives as redemptive tales of atonement, emancipation, recovery, self-fulfillment, and upward social mobility. The stories speak of heroic individual protagonists—the *chosen people*—whose *manifest destiny* is to make a positive difference in a dangerous world, even when the world does not wish to be redeemed. The stories translate a deep and abiding script of *American exceptionalism* into the many contemporary narratives of success, recovery, development, liberation, and self-actualization that so pervade American talk, talk shows, therapy sessions, sermons, and commencement speeches. It is as if especially generative American adults, whose lives are dedicated to making the world a better place for future generations, are, for better and sometimes for worse, the most ardent narrators of a general life story format as American as apple pie and the Super Bowl.

Different kinds of narrative identities make sense in different kinds of cultures. In Erikson's (1958) classic study of Martin Luther's identity formation, the stories that young man Luther constructed to make sense of his own life—stories about physical encounters with devils and saints—made all kinds of cultural sense in 16th-century Christian Germany, but they strike the modern secular ear as somewhat odd. A member of a rural Indian village may account for his feelings of tranquility this morning as resulting from the cool and dispassionate *food* he ate last night (Shweder & Much, 1987). His story will make sense to his peers in the village, but it will not fit expectations for life-narrative accounts in contemporary Berlin. Furthermore, within modern societies different groups are given different narrative opportunities and face different narrative constraints. Especially relevant here are gender, race, and class divisions in modern society. The feminist author Carolyn Heilbrun (1988) remarked that many women have traditionally "been deprived of the narratives, or the texts, plots, or examples, by which they might assume power over—take control of—their own lives" (p. 17). The historical and contemporary life experiences of many African Americans do not always coalesce nicely into the kind of life-narrative forms most valued by the white majority in the United States (Boyd-Franklin, 1989). Narrative identity, therefore, reflects gender and class divisions and the patterns of economic, political, and cultural hegemony that prevail at a given point in a society's history (Franz & Stewart, 1994; Gregg, 2006; Rosenwald & Ochberg, 1992).

With respect to cultural effects, researchers have noted strong differences in autobiographical memory and narrative identity between East Asian and North American societies. For example, North American adults typically report an earlier age of first memory and have longer and more detailed memories of childhood than do Chinese, Japanese, and Korean adults (Leichtman, Wang, & Pillemer, 2003). In addition, several studies have noted that North Americans' personal memories tend to be more self-focused than are the memories of East Asians (e.g., Wang, 2001, 2006). The differences are consistent with the well-known argument that certain Eastern societies tend to emphasize interdependent construals of the self whereas Western societies emphasize independent self-conceptions (Markus & Kitayama, 1991). From an early age, Westerners are encouraged to think about their own individual exploits and to tell stories about them. In a more collectivist culture that inculcates interdependent self-construals, by contrast, children may be encouraged to cultivate a listening role over a telling role and to construct narratives of the self that prioritize other people and social contexts.

Wang and Conway (2004) asked European American and Chinese midlife adults to recall 20 autobiographical memories. Americans provided more memories of individual experiences and one-time events, and they focused their attention on their own roles and emotions in the events. In contrast, Chinese adults were more inclined to recall memories of social and historical events, and they placed a greater emphasis on social interactions and significant others in their stories. Chinese also more frequently drew upon past events to convey moral messages than did Americans. Wang and Conway (2004) suggested that personal narratives and life stories fulfill both self-expressive and self-directive functions. Euro-Americans may prioritize self-expressive functions, viewing personal narratives as vehicles for articulating the breadth, depth, and uniqueness of the inner self. By contrast, Chinese may prioritize the self-directive function, viewing personal narratives as guides for good social conduct. Confucian traditions and values place a great deal of emphasis on history and respect for the past. Individuals are encouraged to learn from their own past experiences and from the experiences of others, including their ancestors. From a Confucian perspective, the highest purpose in life is *ren*—a blending of benevolence, moral vitality, and sensitive concern for others. One method for promoting ren is to scrutinize one's autobiographical past for mistakes in social conduct. Another method is to reflect upon historical events to understand one's appropriate position in the social world. It should not be surprising, then, that personal narratives imbued with a Confucian ethic should draw upon both individual and historical events to derive directions for life.

■ CONTINUITY AND CHANGE IN ADULTHOOD

Narrative identity emerges as a central psychosocial problem in late adolescence and young adulthood, corresponding roughly to what Erikson (1963) originally identified as the stage of *identity versus role confusion*. The problem of constructing a story for one's life, however, should not be expected to fade away quickly once the individual resolves an identity "stage." The common reading of Erikson's (1963) theory to suggest that identity is a well-demarcated stage to be explored and resolved in adolescence and early adulthood is, from the standpoint of narrative theory and recent life course research in psychology and sociology (e.g., Arnett, 2000), an increasingly misleading reading of how modern people live and think about their lives. More accurate, it now appears, is this view: *Once narrative identity enters the developmental scene, it remains a project to be worked on for much of the rest of the life course.* Into and through the midlife years, adults continue to refashion their narrative understandings of themselves, incorporating developmentally on-time and off-time events, expected and unexpected life transitions, gains and losses, and their changing perspectives on who they were, are, and may be into their ongoing, self-defining life stories (Birren, Kenyon, Ruth, Shroots, & Svendson, 1996). Adults continue to come to terms with society and social life through narrative. The autobiographical, storytelling self continues to make narrative sense of life, and its efforts may even improve with age.

The lion's share of empirical research on narrative identity in adulthood has examined (1) relations between particular themes and forms in life narratives on the one hand and personality variables (such as traits, motives, and defenses) on the other, (2) life-narrative predictors of psychological well-being and mental health, (3) variations in the ways that people make narrative sense of suffering and negative events in life, (4) the interpersonal and social functions of and effects on life storytelling, (5) uses of narrative in therapy, and (6) the cultural shaping of narrative identity (McAdams, 2008). To date, there exist few longitudinal studies of life stories, and no long-term efforts to trace continuity and change in narrative identity over decades of adult development. Nonetheless, the fact that researchers have tended to collect life-narrative data from adults of many different ages, rather than focusing on the proverbial college student, provides an opportunity to consider a few suggestive developmental trends.

Because a person's life is always a work in progress and because narrative identity, therefore, may incorporate new experiences over time, theorists have typically proposed that life stories should change markedly over time (e.g., Gergen, 1991). Yet, if narrative identity is assumed to provide life with some degree of unity and purpose, then one would expect that life stories should also show some longitudinal continuity. But how might continuity and change be assessed? By determining the extent to which a person "tells the same story" from Time 1 to Time 2? If yes, does "same story" mean identifying the same key events in a life? Showing the same kinds of narrative themes? Exhibiting the same sorts of causal or thematic connections? In a 3-year longitudinal study that asked college students to recall and describe 10 key scenes in their life stories on three different occasions, McAdams et al. (2006) found that only 28% of the episodic memories described at Time 1 were repeated 3 months later (Time 2), and 22% of the original (Time 1) memories were chosen and described again 3 years after the original assessment (Time 3). Despite change in manifest content of stories, however, McAdams et al. (2006) also documented noteworthy longitudinal consistencies (in the correlation range of 0.35–0.60) in certain emotional and motivational qualities in the stories and in the level of narrative complexity. Furthermore, over the 3-year period, students' life-narrative accounts became more complex, and they incorporated a greater number of themes suggesting personal growth and integration.

Cross-sectional studies suggest that up through middle age, older adults tend to construct more complex and coherent life narratives than do younger adults and adolescents (Baddeley & Singer 2007). One process through which this developmental difference is shown is *autobiographical reasoning,* which is the tendency to draw summary conclusions about the self from autobiographical episodes (McLean et al. 2007). Autobiographical reasoning tends to give a life narrative greater causal and thematic coherence (Habermas & Bluck, 2000). Pasupathi and Mansour (2006) found that autobiographical reasoning in narrative accounts of life turning points increases with age up to midlife. Middle-aged adults showed a more interpretive and psychologically sophisticated approach to life storytelling, compared with younger people. Bluck and Gluck (2004) asked adolescents (age 15–20), younger adults (age 30–40), and older adults (age 60 and more) to recount personal experiences in which they demonstrated wisdom. Younger and older adults were more likely than the adolescents to narrate wisdom scenes in ways that connected the experiences to larger life themes or philosophies, yet another manifestation of autobiographical reasoning.

Singer, Rexhaj, and Baddeley (2007) found that adults older than 50 years narrated self-defining memories that expressed a more positive narrative tone and greater integrative meaning compared with college students. Findings like these dovetail with Pennebaker and Stone's (2003) demonstration, based on laboratory studies of language use and analyses of published fiction, that adults use more positive and fewer negative affect words, and demonstrate greater levels of cognitive complexity, as they age. The findings are also consistent with research on autobiographical recollections showing a positivity memory bias among older adults (e.g., Kennedy, Mather, & Carstensen, 2004). At the same time, evidence suggests that older adults tend to recall more general, as opposed to specific, event memories, tending to skip over the details and focus mainly on the memory's emotional gist (Baddeley & Singer, 2007). In our later years, narrative identity may become warmer and fuzzier.

Counselors who work with the elderly sometimes employ the method of *life review* to encourage older adults to relive and reflect upon past events (Butler, 1963). In life review, older adults are encouraged to mine their autobiographical memory for specific events that seem to have meaning and value. Life review therapists teach their clients how to reminisce productively about these events and to reflect upon their meaning. Some studies suggest that life review can improve life satisfaction and relieve symptoms of depression and anxiety among older adults (Serrano, Latorre, Gatz, & Montanes, 2004). Even without undergoing formal training or assistance in life review, however, older adults may draw increasingly on reminiscences as the years go by. Positive memory biases among older people may give narrative identity a softer glow in the later years. The increasing tendency with age to recall more generalized memories may also simplify life stories in old age (Singer et al, 2007).

FUTURE DIRECTIONS IN THE STUDY OF LIFE NARRATIVES ACROSS THE LIFE SPAN

The psychological study of life narratives has made substantial advances in the past few years as developmentally oriented researchers have examined how people tell stories about their lives across the human life span. An organizing construct for this literature is narrative identity, defined as the internalized and evolving story of the self that people begin to work on in the emerging adulthood years to provide their lives with some degree of unity and purpose. Researchers have explored the nature and manifestations of life storytelling, the origins of narrative identity in children's autobiographical stories, the cognitive skills required to construct narrative identity, the different ways in which adults narrate suffering and transformation in their lives, continuity and change in narrative identity over the adult life span, and the relationships between narrative and culture. The research has opened up a host of new questions about narrative, identity, and development. In this last section, I will briefly raise five of these questions as potential sources for future research.

How Do We Get from Children's Stories to Narrative Identity?

A number of theorists argue that narrative identity emerges in the late-adolescent and young-adult years, when individuals living in modern societies are challenged to create a story for their lives that explains how they came to be who they are and where their lives may be going, while justifying their commitments to particular adult roles (Giddens, 1991; Hammack, 2008; McAdams, 1985; McLean et al., 2007; Singer, 2005). A handful of studies have shown that certain cognitive skills required for the construction of narrative identity do not come online until the adolescent years (Elkind, 1981; Habermas & Bluck, 2000). But researchers have yet to document in detail the step-by-step process whereby young people come to take on the task of constructing a full life story. McLean et al. (2007) have suggested that small stories about the self, situated in particular life events, eventually become organized into larger life narratives as people repeatedly tell their stories to each other, receive feedback on their tellings, and gradually edit their accounts to express a broader and clearer understanding of themselves, their past, and their goals for the future. Selves create stories, which create new selves, which create new stories, and so on, over developmental time. Charting this kind of process in the adolescent and young-adult years remains an exciting challenge for future research.

What Developmental Trends May Be Detected in Narrative Identity During the Adult Years?

Cross-sectional studies have begun to explore age differences in the structure and content of life stories. For example, Pasupathi and Mansour (2006) have shown that midlife adults tend to engage in more causal autobiographical reasoning in their life stories than do younger adults. Older adults tend to express more positive and more general memories about life events, compared with younger adults (Singer et al., 2007). The cross-sectional studies are suggestive of important developmental trends, but in the absence of longitudinal studies, research in this area cannot really distinguish true developmental findings from (equally interesting) cohort effects. Of course, longitudinal studies are daunting projects, especially given the labor-intensive nature of research on life narratives. But until investigators obtain life-narrative accounts from the same individuals on successive occasions, ideally spread out over many years, research will be unable to offer more than intriguing suggestions regarding developmental trends in narrative identity across the adult life span.

How Do Life Narratives Relate to Other Features of Psychological Functioning?

The current chapter focuses mainly on the developmental dimensions of life narratives. Outside this purview, however, a growing literature has examined how life narratives relate to mental health, personality traits, human motives and goals, and a host of other psychological and social factors (McAdams, 2008). In this regard, McAdams and Pals (2006) have proposed an ambitious model of psychological individuality that decomposes human personality into three layers—dispositional traits, characteristic adaptations (such as motives and goals), and integrative life stories (see also Hooker & McAdams, 2003). In this model, narrative identity is viewed to be an integral part of personality itself, of equal standing with such well-worn concepts as dispositional personality traits. The model provides a framework for making sense of the growing number of studies that examine how the structure and content of life narratives connect to the panoply of psychological factors and features that distinguish one person from another, including those factors that speak directly to psychopathology and, on the other end of the spectrum, to superior social and moral functioning (e.g., Adler & McAdams, 2007; Lodi-Smith, Geise, Robins, & Roberts, 2009; McAdams et al., 2004, 2008; Raggatt, 2006; Sheldon, 2004; Walker & Frimer, 2007). A challenge for the future is to integrate findings like these—from personality, social, and clinical psychology—within a life-span developmental context.

How Do People Use Their Life Narratives?

Whereas researchers have focused most attention on the structure and content of life stories themselves, little research has examined how people draw upon their life narratives in everyday life, and how that process might change over the life span. Alea and Bluck (2003) and Pasupathi (2006) have shown how sharing personal narratives promotes interpersonal relationships and consolidates intimacy, especially among young people. Serrano et al. (2004) have shown how life review can promote wellness in older people. But beyond these scattered findings, researchers know very little about the conditions under which people call upon their autobiographical memories or dreams for the future to inform their own behavior, to shape their decisions, to provide advice to others, and so on. Of special interest in this regard is the use of life narratives in families—how, for example, parents use stories for the purposes of socializing their children, how children react to the life-narrative accounts provided by their parents, and how inter-generational storytelling affects the development of people at all ages (Pratt & Fiese, 2004).

How Does Culture Influence Life Narratives?

Many narrative researchers suggest that life narratives are as much a reflection of a person's cultural context as they are a reflection of the person (e.g., Cohler & Hammack, 2006; Gregg, 2006; McAdams, 2006; Rosenwald & Ochberg, 1992). A number of studies have examined how East Asian and Euro-American adults differ in the ways they tell stories about their lives (e.g., Wang, 2006). But more nuanced and detailed examinations are needed, especially those that might go beyond a simple East versus West distinction. Hammack (2008) and McAdams (2006) have provided models for how cultural studies of life narratives might proceed. In *The Redemptive Self: Stories Americans Live By*, I draw upon quantitative studies of life-narrative interviews, published autobiographies, classic works of fiction, and a wide range of historical and contemporary sources—from 19th-century slave narratives to Hollywood movies—to develop a cultural portrait of a one particular kind of narrative identity that has traditionally enjoyed great favor in American society (McAdams, 2006). On a more limited scale, Hammack (2008) has developed contrasting portraits of Israeli and Palestinian national origin myths, and shown how they play themselves out in the private lives of young Israelis and Palestinians today. Over the life span, human beings come to terms with their culture through life narrative. The examination of culture's relationships with narrative identity over the life span is arguably the most challenging and most promising arena for future research on life narratives.

ACKNOWLEDGMENT

I thank Keith Cox and Brad Olson for help in developing the arguments in this chapter. The preparation of this chapter was supported by a grant from the Foley Family Foundation to establish the Foley Center for the Study of Lives at Northwestern University.

REFERENCES

Adler, J., & McAdams, D. P. (2007). The narrative reconstruction of psychotherapy. *Narrative Inquiry, 17,* 179–202.

Alea, N., & Bluck, S. (2003). Why are you telling me that? A conceptual model of the social function of autobiographical memory. *Memory, 11,* 165–178.

Angus, L. E., & McLeod, J. (Eds.). (2004). *The handbook of narrative and psychotherapy: Practice, theory, and research.* London: Sage.

Arnett, J. J. (2000). Emerging adulthood: A theory of development from the late teens through the twenties. *American Psychologist, 55,* 469–480.

Austen, J. (1813/1980). *Pride and prejudice.* Franklin Center, PA: The Franklin Library.

Baddeley, J., & Singer, J. A. (2007). Charting the life story's path: Narrative identity across the life span. In J. Clandinin (Ed.), *Handbook of narrative research methods* (pp. 177–202). Thousand Oaks, CA: Sage.

Baron-Cohen, S. (1995). *Mindblindness: An essay on autism and theory of mind.* Cambridge, MA: MIT Press.

Bauer, J. J., & McAdams, D. P. (2004a). Growth goals, maturity, and well-being. *Developmental Psychology, 40,* 114–127.

Bauer, J. J., & McAdams, D. P. (2004b). Personal growth in adults' stories of life transitions. *Journal of Personality, 72,* 573–602.

Bauer, J. J., McAdams, D. P., & Sakaeda, A. (2005). Interpreting the good life: Growth memories in the lives of mature, happy people. *Journal of Personality and Social Psychology, 88,* 203–217.

Birren, J., Kenyon, G., Ruth, J. E., Shroots, J. J. F., & Svendson, J. (Eds.). (1996). *Aging and biography: Explorations in adult development.* New York: Springer.

Bluck, S., & Gluck, J. (2004). Making things better and learning a lesson: Experiencing wisdom across the lifespan. *Journal of Personality, 72,* 543–572.

Bohn, A., & Berntsen, D. (2008). Life story development in childhood: The development of life story abilities and the acquisition of cultural life scripts from late middle childhood to adolescence. *Developmental Psychology, 44,* 1135–1147.

Bonanno, G. A. (2004). Loss, trauma, and human resilience: Have we underestimated the human capacity to thrive after extremely aversive events? *American Psychologist, 59,* 20–28.

Boyd-Franklin, N. (1989). *Black families in therapy: A multisystems approach.* New York: Guilford Press.

Brewer, W. F., & Lichtenstein, E. H. (1982). Stories are to entertain: A structural-affect theory of stories. *Journal of Pragmatics, 6,* 473–486.

Bruner, J. S. (1986). *Actual minds, possible worlds.* Cambridge, MA: Harvard University Press.

Bruner, J. S. (1994). The "remembered" self. In U. Neisser and R. Fivush (Eds.), *The remembering self* (pp. 41–54). New York: Cambridge University Press.

Burton, C. M., & King, L. A. (2004). The health benefits of writing about intensely positive experiences. *Journal of Research in Personality, 38,* 150–163.

Butler, R. N. (1963). The life review: An interpretation of reminiscence in old age. *Psychiatry, 26,* 65–76.

Cohler, B. J., & Hammack, P. (2006). Making a gay identity: Life story and the construction of a coherent self. In D. P. McAdams, R. Josselson, & A. Libelich (Eds.), *Identity and story: Creating self in narrative* (pp. 151–172). Washington, DC: American Psychological Association Press.

Conway, M. A., & Pleydell-Pearce, C. W. (2000). The construction of autobiographical memories in the self-memory system. *Psychological Review, 107,* 261–288.

Crossley, M. L. (2001). Sense of place and its import for life transitions: The case of HIV-positive individuals. In D. P. McAdams, R. Josselson, & A. Lieblich (Eds.), *Turns in the road: Narrative studies of lives in transition* (pp. 279–296). Washington, DC: American Psychological Association Press.

Elkind, D. (1981). *Children and adolescents (3rd ed.).* New York: Oxford University Press.

Erikson, E. H. (1958). *Young man Luther.* New York: Norton.

Erikson, E. H. (1963). *Childhood and society (2nd ed.).* New York: Norton.

Fitzgerald, J. M. (1988). Vivid memories and the reminiscence phenomenon: The role of a self-narrative. *Human Development, 31,* 261–273.

Fivush, R., & Haden, C. (Eds.). (2003). *Autobiographical memory and the construction of a narrative self.* Mahwah, NJ: Erlbaum.

Fivush, R., & Kuebli, J. (1997). Making everyday events emotional: The construal of emotion in parent-child conversations about the past. In N. L. Stein, P. A. Ornstein, B. Tversky, & C. Brainerd (Eds.), *Memory for everyday and emotional events* (pp. 239–266). Mahwah, NJ: Erlbaum.

Fivush, R., & Nelson, K. (2004). Culture and language in the emergence of autobiographical memory. *Psychological Science, 15,* 573–577.

Franz, C., & Stewart, A. J. (Eds.). (1994). *Women creating lives: Identity, resilience, resistance.* Boulder, CO: Westview Press.

Freeman, M. (1993). *Rewriting the self: History, memory, narrative.* London: Routledge.

Gabriel, Y. (2000). *Storytelling in organizations: Facts, fictions, and fantasies.* New York: Oxford University Press.

Gergen, K. J. (1991). *The saturated self: Dilemmas of identity in contemporary life.* New York: Basic Books.

Giddens, A. (1991). *Modernity and self-identity: Self and society in the late modern age.* Stanford, CA: Stanford University Press.

Gregg, G. (2006). The raw and the bland: A structural model of narrative identity. In D. P. McAdams, R. Josselson, & A. Lieblich (Eds.), *Identity and story: Creating self in narrative* (pp. 89–108). Washington, DC: American Psychological Association Press.

Habermas, T., & Bluck, S. (2000). Getting a life: The emergence of the life story in adolescence. *Psychological Bulletin, 126,* 748–769.

Habermas, T., & de Silveira, C. (2008). The development of global coherence in life narratives across adolescence: Temporal, causal, and thematic aspects. *Developmental Psychology, 44,* 707–721.

Habermas, T., & Paha, C. (2001). The development of coherence in adolescents' life narratives. *Narrative Inquiry, 11,* 35–54.

Hammack, P. L. (2008). Narrative and the cultural psychology of identity. *Personality and Social Psychology Review, 12,* 222–247.

Heilbrun, C. (1988). *Writing a woman's life.* New York: Norton.

Hooker, K. S., & McAdams, D. P. (2003). Personality reconsidered: A new agenda for aging research. *Journal of Gerontology: Psychological Sciences and Social Sciences, 58B,* P296–P304.

Howe, M. L., & Courage, M. L. (1997). The emergence and early development of autobiographical memory. *Psychological Review, 104,* 499–523.

Josselson, R., & Lieblich, A. (Eds.). (1993). *The narrative study of lives.* Thousand Oaks, CA: Sage.

Kennedy, Q., Mather, M., & Carstensen, L. L. (2004). The role of motivation in age-related positivity effect in autobiographical memory. *Psychological Science, 15,* 208–214.

King, L. A., & Hicks, J. A. (2006). Narrating the self in the past and future: Implications for maturity. *Research in Human Development, 3,* 121–138.

King, L. A., & Raspin, C. (2004). Lost and found possible selves, subjective well-being, and ego development in divorced women. *Journal of Personality, 72,* 602–632.

King, L. A., Scollon, C. K., Ramsey, C., & Williams, T. (2000). Stories of life transition: Subjective well-being and ego development in parents of children with Down Syndrome. *Journal of Research in Personality, 34,* 509–536.

King, L. A., & Smith, S. N. (2005). Happy, mature, and gay: Intimacy, power, and difficult times in coming out stories. *Journal of Research in Personality, 39,* 278–298.

Kuhlmeier, V., Wynn, K., & Bloom, D. (2003). Attribution of dispositional states by 12-month olds. *Psychological Science, 14,* 402–408.

Leichtman, M. D., Wang, Q., & Pillemer, D. B. (2003). Cultural variations in interdependence: Lessons from Korea, China, India, and the United States. In R. Fivush & C. Haden (Eds.), *Autobiographical memory and the construction of a narrative self* (pp. 73–97). Mahwah, NJ: Erlbaum.

Lieblich, A., McAdams, D. P., & Josselson, R. (Eds.). (2004). *Healing plots: The narrative basis of psychotherapy.* Washington, DC: American Psychological Association Press.

Lodi-Smith, J., Geise, A., Robins, R. W., & Roberts, B. W. (2009). Narrating personality change. *Journal of Personality and Social Psychology, 96,* 679–689.

Loevinger, J. (1976). *Ego development.* San Francisco: Jossey-Bass.

Lyubomirsky, S., Sousa, L., & Dickerhoff, R. (2006). The costs and benefits of writing, talking, and thinking about life's triumphs and defeats. *Journal of Personality and Social Psychology, 90,* 692–708.

MacIntyre, A. (1981). *After virtue.* Notre Dame, IN: University of Notre Dame Press.

Mandler, J. M. (1984). *Stories, scripts, and scenes: Aspects of schema theory.* Hillsdale, NJ: Erblaum.

Mansfield, E. D., & McAdams, D. P. (1996). Generativity and themes of agency and communion in adult autobiography. *Personality and Social Psychology Bulletin, 22,* 721–731.

Markus, H., & Kitayama, S. (1991). Culture and the self: Implications for cognition, emotion, and motivation. *Psychological Review, 98,* 224–253.

Maruna, S., & Ramsden, D. (2004). Living to tell the tale: Redemption narratives, shame management, and offender rehabilitation. In A. Lieblich, D. P. McAdams, & R. Josselson (Eds.),

Healing plots: The narrative basis of psychotherapy (pp. 129–149). Washington, DC: American Psychological Association Press.

McAdams, D. P. (1985). *Power, intimacy, and the life story: Personological inquiries into identity.* Homewood, IL: Dorsey Press.

McAdams, D. P. (1993). *The stories we live by.* New York: Morrow.

McAdams, D. P. (1996). Personality, modernity, and the storied self: A contemporary framework for studying persons. *Psychological Inquiry, 7,* 295–321.

McAdams, D. P. (2005). Studying lives in time: A narrative approach. In R. Levy, P. Ghisletta, J. M. Legoff, D. Spini, & E. Widmer (Eds.), *Towards an interdisciplinary perspective on the life course: Advances in life course research* (Vol. 10, pp. 237–258). London: Elsevier.

McAdams, D. P. (2006). *The redemptive self: Stories Americans live by.* New York: Oxford University Press.

McAdams, D. P. (2008). Personal narratives and the life story. In O. John, R. Robins, & L. Pervin (Eds.), *Handbook of personality: Theory and research* (3rd ed., pp. 241–261). New York: Guilford Press.

McAdams, D. P., Albaugh, M., Farber, E., Daniels, J., Logan, R. L., & Olson, B. (2008). Family metaphors and moral intuitions: How conservatives and liberals narrate their lives. *Journal of Personality and Social Psychology, 95,* 978–990.

McAdams, D. P., Anyidoho, N. A., Brown, C., Huang, Y. T., Kaplan, B., & Machado, M. A. (2004). Traits and stories: Links between dispositional and narrative features of personality. *Journal of Personality, 72,* 761–784.

McAdams, D. P., Bauer, J. J., Sakaeda, A. R., Anyidoho, N. A., Machado, M. A., Magrino-Failla, K., et al. (2006). Continuity and change In the life story: A longitudinal study of autobiographical memories in emerging adulthood. *Journal of Personality, 74,* 1371–1400.

McAdams, D. P., & Bowman, P. J. (2001). Turning points in life: Redemption and contamination. In D. P. McAdams, R. Josselson, & A. Lieblich (Eds.), *Turns in the road: Narrative studies of lives in transition* (pp. 3–34). Washington, DC: American Psychological Association Press.

McAdams, D. P., Diamond, A., de St. Aubin, E., & Mansfield, E. D. (1997). Stories of commitment: The psychosocial construction of generative lives. *Journal of Personality and Social Psychology, 72,* 678–694.

McAdams, D. P., Josselson, R., & Lieblich, A. (Eds.). (2006). *Identity and story: Creating self in narrative.* Washington, DC: American Psychological Association Press.

McAdams, D. P., & Pals, J. L. (2006). A new Big Five: Fundamental principles for an integrative science of personality. *American Psychologist, 61,* 204–217.

McAdams, D. P., Reynolds, J., Lewis, M., Patten, A., & Bowman, P. J. (2001). When bad things turn good and good things turn bad: Sequences of redemption and contamination in life narrative, and their relation to psychosocial adaptation in midlife adults and in students. *Personality and Social Psychology Bulletin, 27,* 472–483.

McLean, K. C. (2005). Late adolescent identity development: Narrative meaning making and memory telling. *Developmental Psychology, 41,* 683–691.

McLean, K. C., Pasupathi, M., & Pals, J. L. (2007). Selves creating stories creating selves: A process model of self-development. *Personality and Social Psychology Review, 11,* 262–278.

McLean, K. C., & Pratt, M. W. (2006). Life's little (and big) lessons: Identity statuses and meaning-making in the turning point narratives of emerging adults. *Developmental Psychology, 42,* 714–722.

McLean, K. C., & Thorne, A. (2003). Late adolescents' self-defining memories about relationships. *Developmental Psychology, 39,* 635–645.

Neimeyer, R. A. (Ed.). (2001). *Memory Reconstruction and the Experience of Loss.* Washington, DC: American Psychological Association Press.

Pals, J. L. (2006). Authoring a second chance in life: Emotion and transformational processing in narrative identity. *Research in Human Development, 3,* 101–120.

Pasupathi, M. (2001). The social construction of the personal past and its implications for adult development. *Psychological Bulletin, 127,* 651–672.

Pasupathi, M. (2006). Silk from sows' ears: Collaborative construction of everyday selves in everyday stories. In D. P. McAdams, R. Josselson, & A. Lieblich (Eds.), *Identity and story: Creating self in narrative* (pp. 129–150). Washington, DC: American Psychological Association Press.

Pasupathi, M., & Mansour, E. (2006). Adult age differences in autobiographical reasoning in narratives. *Developmental Psychology, 42,* 798–808.

Pennebaker, J. (1997). Writing about emotional experiences as a therapeutic process. *Psychological Science, 8,* 162–166.

Pennebaker, J. W., & Stone, L. D. (2003). Words of wisdom: Language use over the life span. *Journal of Personality and Social Psychology, 85,* 291–301.

Pratt, M., & Fiese, B. (Eds.). (2004). *Family stories and the life course: Across time and generations.* Mahwah, NJ: Erlbaum.

Raggatt, P. (2006). Putting the five-factor model in context: Evidence linking big five traits and narrative identity. *Journal of Personality, 74,* 1321–1348.

Reese, E. (2002). Social factors in the development of autobiographical memory: The state of the art. *Social Development, 11,* 124–142.

Reese, E., & Farrant, K. (2003). Social origins of reminiscing. In R. Fivush & C. A. Haden (Eds.), *Autobiographical memory and the construction of a narrative self* (pp. 29–48). Mahwah, NJ: Erlbaum.

Rosenwald, G. C., & Ochberg, R. L. (Eds.). (1992). *Storied lives: The cultural politics of self-understanding.* New Haven, CT: Yale University Press.

Roser, M., & Gazzaniga, M. S. (2004). Automatic brains – interpretive minds. *Current Directions in Psychological Science, 13,* 56–60.

Sarbin, T. (Ed.). (1986). *Narrative psychology: The storied nature of human conduct.* New York: Praeger.

Serrano, J. P., Latorre, J. M., Gatz, M., & Montanes, J. (2004). Life review therapy using autobiographical retrieval practice for older adults with depressive symptomatology. *Psychology and Aging, 19,* 272–277.

Sheldon, K. M. (2004). *Optimal human functioning: An integrated multi-level perspective.* Mahwah, NJ: Erlbaum.

Shotter, J., & Gergen, K. (Eds.). (1989). *Texts of identity.* London: Sage.

Shweder, R. A., & Much, N. C. (1987). Determinants of meaning: Discourse and moral socialization. In W. M. Kurtines & J. L. Gewirtz (Eds.), *Moral development through social interaction* (pp. 197–244). New York: Wiley.

Singer, J. A. (2004). Narrative identity and meaning making across the adult lifespan: An introduction. *Journal of Personality, 72,* 437–459.

Singer, J. A. (2005). *Personality and psychotherapy: Treating the whole person.* New York: Guilford Press.

Singer, J. A., Rexhaj, B., & Baddeley, J. (2007). Older, wiser, and happier? Comparing older adults' and college students' self-defining memories. *Memory, 15,* 886–898.

Singer, J. A., & Salovey, P. (1993). *The remembered self.* New York: The Free Press.

Taylor, C. (1989). *Sources of the self: The making of the modern identity.* Cambridge, MA: Harvard University Press.

Taylor, S. E. (1983). Adjustment to threatening events: A theory of cognitive adaptation. *American Psychologist, 38,* 624–630.

Taylor, S. E. (1991). Asymmetrical effects of positive and negative events: The mobilization-minimization hypothesis. *Psychological Bulletin, 110,* 67–85.

Tedeschi, R. G., & Calhoun, L. G. (1995). *Trauma and Transformation: Growing in the Aftermath of Suffering.* Thousand Oaks, CA: Sage.

Thorne, A. (2000). Personal memory telling and personality development. *Personality and Social Psychology Review, 4,* 45–56.

Tomkins, S. S. (1987). Script theory. In J. Aronoff, A. I. Rabin, & R. A. Zucker (Eds.), *The emergence of personality* (pp. 147–216). New York: Springer.

Walker, L. J., & Frimer, J. A. (2007). Moral personality of brave and caring exemplars. *Journal of Personality and Social Psychology, 93,* 845–860.

Wang, Q. (2001). Culture effects on adults' earliest recollections and self-descriptions: Implications for the relation between memory and the self. *Journal of Personality and Social Psychology, 81,* 220–233.

Wang, Q. (2006). Earliest recollections of self and others in European American and Taiwanese young adults. *Psychological Science, 17,* 708–714.

Wang, Q., & Conway, M. A. (2004). The stories we keep: Autobiographical memory in American and Chinese middle-aged adults. *Journal of Personality, 72,* 911–938.

White, M., & Epston, M. (1990). *Narrative means to therapeutic ends.* New York: Norton.

Woike, B. A., & Matic, D. (2004). Cognitive complexity in response to traumatic experiences. *Journal of Personality, 72,* 633–657.

THE DEVELOPMENT OF SELF-REPRESENTATIONS ACROSS THE LIFE SPAN

24

Manfred Diehl, Lise M. Youngblade, Elizabeth L. Hay, and Helena Chui

This chapter focuses on the development of *self-representations* across the life span. The main questions addressed in this chapter are as follows: How do individuals develop an understanding of their own person and what are the developmental milestones in this process? How does the content and structural organization of self-representations change across the life span? How is individuals' development of self-representations linked to basic developmental processes in cognitive and social–emotional functioning? Are there qualitative differences in the organization and the functions of self-representations at different parts of the life span? What role do different social and cultural contexts play in the development of self-representations across the life span?

These questions will be addressed within the meta-theoretical framework of life-span developmental psychology (Baltes, 1987; Baltes, Lindenberger, & Staudinger, 2006) and from a perspective that conceives individuals as producers of their own development (Brandstädter & Lerner, 1999). These perspectives are chosen as guiding frameworks for several reasons. First, self-representations constitute what James (1890/1981) defined as the *self-concept*, the Me-self, the self as object, or the self as known. As defined by James, the self-concept represents the complete collection of self-representations a person has formed from the early beginnings of self-awareness, reflecting his or her significant experiences (Thompson, 2006). Thus, some theorists have referred to the self-concept as a person's theory about and understanding of the self (Epstein, 1973, 1991).

Second, since the mid-1980s theory and research have conceptualized the self-concept as a contextualized and dynamic *knowledge structure* with adaptive and self-regulatory functions (Brandstädter & Greve, 1994; Higgins, 1996; Markus & Wurf, 1987). This knowledge structure includes general and context-specific information of a person's traits, beliefs, and values, and also autobiographical information that is encoded as episodic (i.e., memories of actual events) and semantic memories (i.e., attributional information). Also, as a knowledge structure, the self-concept is actively involved in the processing of self-relevant information (Campbell et al., 1996). For example, as a dynamic knowledge structure, self-representations are subject to corrections and reevaluations based on a person's stage of development and ongoing experiences. Such corrections and reevaluations reflect cognitive processes like assimilation, accommodation, and immunization and indicate the individual's active involvement in protecting the self-concept (Brandstädter & Greve, 1994; Greve & Wentura, 2003; Markus & Wurf, 1987; Thompson, 2006). Assimilation is taking place when individuals transform situational circumstances to fit their existing self-concept, whereas accommodation is taking place when the self-concept is reconfigured to fit more closely with situational demands (Brandstädter & Greve, 1994). Immunizing processes are involved when self-relevant cognitions are defended against discrepant evidence (Greve & Wentura, 2003). In addition, self-representations are *contextualized representations* of the self and reflect that the self-concept is both a cognitive *and* a social construction (Harter, 2006). That is, from the very beginning an individual's self-representations emerge in the context of and are shaped by social relationships (e.g., interactions with caregivers in young children; interactions with peers in adolescence; Bretherton, 1993; Harter, 1999; Selman, 1980).

Third, life-span psychologists have emphasized that the self-concept gives individuals a sense of continuity and permanence, allows them to distinguish themselves and their developmental history from others, and gives their experiences meaning within a larger biography (Brandstädter & Greve, 1994; Markus & Herzog, 1991). In this sense, the term "self-concept" has a certain affinity to the construct of identity which also refers to an individual's knowledge and beliefs about the own person (Whitbourne & Connolly, 1999). All of these aspects indicate that self-representations are actively constructed and reconstructed, exemplifying the active involvement of the person in the formation and continuity of his or her self-concept. Thus, taken together, these reasons illustrate that self-representations are an integral part of the developing person that play a multifaceted role in human development.

For purposes of terminological clarity, it is important to provide a working definition of the key construct. Specifically, in this chapter the terms *self-representations* and *self-concept* are used interchangeably to refer to those attributes that are (1) part of a person's self-understanding and self-knowledge; (2) the focus of self-awareness and self-reflection; and (3) consciously acknowledged by the person through language or other means of communication (see also Harter, 1999). Other synonyms frequently used in the literature are "self-conceptions," "self-definitions," "self-descriptions," "self-perceptions," or "self-understanding." This terminological clarification is necessary to distinguish self-representations from related but distinct constructs such as self-esteem, self-worth, or self-evaluation. Although self-representations may contain evaluative aspects, they tend to be primarily descriptive in nature and reflect an individual's understanding of the own person. In contrast, individuals' statements in terms of self-esteem or self-worth are primarily and explicitly evaluative in nature and tend to require a social or temporal comparison.

This chapter has three major parts. The first major part focuses on the development of self-representations in childhood and adolescence. Specifically, this section describes the developmental milestones from early childhood to late adolescence, the part of the life span for which the greatest amount of research exists. The second major part addresses the development of self-representations across the adult years, describing findings that cover the life span from early adulthood to late life. The third major section focuses on several key issues in the study of self-representations across the life span. These issues address to what extent and under what circumstances self-representations may serve as risk or resilience factors, what role social and cultural contexts play vis-à-vis self-representations, and whether psychosocial interventions can optimize the adaptive function of self-representations. This section also identifies the major gaps in our current knowledge and outlines future directions for the study of self-representations.

ORGANIZING STRUCTURE

Any attempt at reviewing the development of self-representations across the life span is confronted with the challenge of how to organize the large body of research that has accumulated on this topic. In particular, the challenge consists in establishing an organizing structure or framework that permits the description of developmental changes during childhood, adolescence, and across the adult life span along several crucial dimensions without neglecting the qualitative subtleties that characterize the observed changes. Thus, to meet this challenge, we adopt, as much as possible, a *tripartite structure* to organize the available empirical research.

This tripartite structure extends the organizational structures of previous handbook chapters on the development of self-representations (see Diehl, 2006; Harter, 2006) and represents a hybrid that facilitates the review of findings across the entire life span. Specifically, findings are first presented in terms of the *normative developmental features* that characterize individuals' self-representations during a given age period. This description focuses not only on the content and structure/organization of the self-representations but also discusses their valence and accuracy, associations with behavioral outcomes, and the role that basic cognitive and social–emotional processes and others play in the emergence and expression of self-representations.

Second, this description is followed by a discussion of the *normative developmental challenges* (i.e., risks and opportunities) that characterize the emergence of qualitatively different levels of self-concept development. Addressing the potential risks and opportunities associated with advances in development has been a tradition in life-span psychology (Baltes et al., 2006) and has been particularly emphasized in Erikson's (1950, 1959) life-span theory of human development. Moreover, the notion that development is associated with challenges and liabilities is also reflected in neo-Piagetian approaches to cognitive and social–emotional development (Fischer, 1980; Fischer & Canfield, 1986; Harter, 1999, 2006). The discussion of challenges or liabilities is particularly important with regard to the development of self-representations in childhood and adolescence because the emergence of new insights about the self is linked to advances in cognitive and social–emotional development and has profound consequences for children's and adolescents' relationships with others (Harter, 2006). However, in the transition from one developmental level to the next, lack of cognitive control (Fischer, 1980) often results in an uncertainty that keeps the final outcome open and creates a tension between possible failure and possible success (Erikson, 1959). Uncertainty and challenge usually dissipate as the newly acquired skills become integrated into an individual's cognitions and behavioral repertoire, thus leading to the anticipated normative outcomes.

Third, the last part of the tripartite structure focuses on *individual differences* in self-concept development and discusses the factors and contexts that contribute to the emergence of individual differences in self-representations. In terms of this focus, the evidence that can be presented is much richer for the early life span than for the adult years, reflecting that the overwhelming amount of research has focused on the development of self-representations in childhood and adolescence (Damon & Hart, 1988; Harter, 1999, 2006).

▣ DEVELOPMENT OF SELF-REPRESENTATIONS IN CHILDHOOD

Several reviews of the development of self-representations in childhood and adolescence have been published over the years (Damon & Hart, 1988; Harter, 1998, 1999), with the most recent one provided by Harter (2006). Overall, these reviews give a more comprehensive and detailed account of the early developmental milestones in self-concept development than is possible in this chapter. Thus, interested readers are referred to these sources for additional information. In the following, we will review the research regarding the development of self-representations in childhood, covering the age periods from infancy to late childhood.

Infancy, Toddlerhood, and Early Childhood

Although it is well established that children's *representational sense of self* emerges between 15 and 18 months of age in the form of featural self-recognition (Damon & Hart, 1988; Lewis & Brooks-Gunn, 1979), several authors have pointed out that featural self-recognition is preceded by *pre-representational* forms of self-awareness (Thompson, 2006). These pre-representational forms of self-awareness are most prominently displayed from about 9 to 15 months of age and are linked to the emergence of perceptual abilities that permit the distinction between self and others, advances in locomotion resulting in increased intentionality of the infant's behavior, and cognitive advances (e.g., social referencing, the emergence of intentional communicative efforts) suggesting that the infant can distinguish between self and others (Carpenter, Nagell, & Tomasello, 1998; Thompson, 2006). These pre-representational forms of self-awareness together with the emergence of language provide the scaffold upon which featural self-recognition as the earliest form of conscious self-representation builds.

Because young children's ability to describe their self-representations in words is limited, researchers have used *nonverbal feature recognition tasks* to examine toddlers' and young children's self-recognition abilities (Lewis & Brooks-Gunn, 1979). These studies have shown that between 15 and 18 months of age, toddlers reliably show evidence of self-recognition when placed before a mirror after their noses have been surreptitiously marked with a spot of rouge. That is, toddlers reliably touch their own noses rather than the noses of the mirror image, indicating that they are capable of self-recognition. Additional signs of self-awareness and emerging self-understanding are that toddlers start to show self-referent emotions like embarrassment and increased awareness of standards of appearance and behavior (Lewis, 2000). In addition, between age 2 and 3 toddlers show (1) an increase in self-referential verbalizations, as indicated by the use of personal pronouns (e.g., "Me big!"), (2) increased verbal labeling of internal experiences, such as self-referential emotions (Barrett, Zahn-Waxler, & Cole, 1993; Bretherton, Fritz, Zahn-Waxler, & Ridgeway, 1986), and (3) assertions of competence, independence, and ownership (Fasig, 2000; Thompson, 2006).

As toddlers develop into young children, the emergence of language skills permits them to create verbal self-representations. These verbal self-representations have specific characteristics and reflect the child's level of cognitive development. In terms of the *content*, the verbal self-representations of 3- to 4-year-olds refer to observable features and behaviors, such as physical attributes ("I am a boy."), activity-related skills and preferences ("I can run really fast." "I like my dog."), social attributes ("I have an older brother."), and to a lesser extent psychological attributes ("I'm always happy."). Overall, self-representations at this age are directly tied to behavior and represent categorical identifications (Damon & Hart, 1988; Harter, 2006). In terms of their *organization* and *valence*, the self-representations at this age are isolated from each other, lack coherence, and tend to be unrealistically positive (Harter, 1999, 2006). Fischer (1980) labeled these kinds of self-representations "single representations" because the cognitive limitations at this age make it impossible for the child to integrate single representations into a coherent self-concept. The cognitive limitations of early childhood are also reflected in the fact that children's self-descriptions tend to vastly overestimate their actual abilities and tend to reflect a certain "grandiosity," which Kohut (1977) referred to as "egocentric grandiosity." Harter (2006) emphasized that it is important to keep in mind "that these apparent distortions are normative in that they reflect cognitive limitations rather than conscious efforts to deceive the listener" (p. 514).

In terms of *contextual influences*, it has been shown that self-development during this age period greatly benefits from the interactions of the young child with the different socializing agents, in particular the parents and close caregivers (Fonagy, 2002). Interactions with close others, especially if they are warm and sensitive, facilitate language acquisition and the development of perspective-taking skills and are instrumental in laying the foundation for the emergence of autobiographical memory (Bretherton, 1993; Fivush, 1993; Fonagy, 2002; Nelson, 1993). Although the young child's narrative tends to be heavily co-constructed by the parents and close caregivers, it nevertheless builds the scaffold upon which the child continues to form a more elaborate personal story as his or her language and cognitive skills continue to develop (Fivush & Haden, 2003). Moreover, the emotional quality of the interaction also lays the foundation for a secure attachment bond and the development of a secure internal working model of self and others (Bretherton, 1993). This internal working model tends to get more elaborate as cognitive and emotional skills develop.

Although the acquisition of language skills and increasingly complex social interactions lead to the demise of infantile amnesia during the third year of life (Thompson, 2006), children's self-representations at that age show several *normative limitations* (Harter, 2006). First, young children's self-representations tend to be unrealistically positive. In part this is due to 3- and 4-year-olds' inability to engage in social comparisons for self-evaluation purposes (Pomerantz, Ruble, Frey, & Greulich, 1995) because their thinking is at the pre-operational level of cognitive development (Piaget, 1960). A hallmark of pre-operational thinking is that children cannot hold two dimensions in mind simultaneously for comparison, which is a prerequisite for social comparison (Thompson, 2006). Second, for the same reasons young children are also not able to distinguish between their actual and ideal self-attributes. Thus, without that discriminative ability they tend to believe that their ideal self is their actual self, resulting in an overly positive self-view (Carroll & Steward, 1984). Third, young children are also limited in their perspective-taking ability (Case, 1992; Selman, 1980). Thus, they are limited in understanding the views and opinions of others and therefore cannot incorporate these views in an evaluation of the self (Pomerantz et al., 1995). Although all of these aspects highlight young children's cognitive limitations, Harter (2006) points out that they may serve a protective function, making it easy for children at this age to maintain positive perceptions of the self. Such positive perceptions, in turn, may serve as motivating forces that can drive further development.

Factors that contribute to individual differences in self-concept development during this age period are mostly related to the behavior of the key *socializing agents*, namely the behavior of the parents and close caregivers (Harter, 2006; Thompson, 2006). In particular, parents' and caregivers' behavior has profound effects on the child's cognitive and social–emotional development and a large body of research has documented the positive effects that sensitive care, emotional availability, and cognitive stimulation have on children's self-development (Thompson, 2006). Attachment theory describes the development of internal working models of self and other (Bowlby, 1988; Bretherton & Munholland, 1999) and elaborates on the conditions that the socializing agents need to provide for the development of a positive self-view. Specifically, parents who treat their infant and toddler in a loving and sensitive way, who are emotionally available, and who support the child's striving for mastery and independence create a developmental context that results in a secure attachment bond (Biringen, 2000; Bretherton, 2000). In turn, a securely attached child develops an internal working model of the self as being loved, valued, and competent. In contrast, a context in which the needs of the child are ignored or rejected very likely leads to the development of an insecure attachment bond. The internal working model that an insecurely child develops tends to be characterized by feelings of rejection, unworthiness, and incompetence (Beeghly & Cicchetti, 1994). Empirical support for the critical importance of the attachment bond and the socializing context in infancy and early childhood is provided by research on the effects of neglect and abuse on children's development. Overall, findings from this research indicate that the stories of neglected and abused children tend to have more negative self-representations and more negative maternal representations than the narratives of children who have not been maltreated (Toth, Cicchetti, Macfie, & Emde, 1997). Similarly, maltreated children have also been found to display more incoherent self-representations and impoverished descriptions of internal states and feelings compared with children with no known history of neglect or abuse (Harter, 2006).

In summary, the self-representations in toddlerhood and early childhood build the foundation for further developments in middle childhood. Although children's self-views at this age are characterized by a number of cognitive limitations, a positive and nurturing socializing context provides the scaffold for the development of a positive internal working model of self and others. This working model is further elaborated by cognitive and social–emotional advances in middle childhood.

Middle Childhood

Middle childhood represents the period from about 5 to 7 or 8 years of age; thus, it covers the transition into elementary school. Typical self-representations during middle childhood show several cognitive advances compared with early childhood. First, in terms of content, children start to put attributes or behaviors that fall into the same category together (e.g., describing several competencies together;

Case, 1985). This is an advance over the earlier compartmentalized self-descriptions. Second, in middle childhood, children start to incorporate opposites into their self-representations, but they do so in a rather rigid and rudimentary way. For example, although they can acknowledge having two or more emotions of the same valence and emotions of opposing valence, overall the representations of positive and negative emotions are still kept mostly separate from each other and are typically seen as incompatible (Harter, 2006). Third, because of the fact that opposites are still mostly kept separate, children's overall self-representations tend to be still very positive and tend to display a lingering sense of grandiosity.

In terms of influences of the socializing environment, this age period shows great improvements in children's *perspective-taking skills* (Case, 1992; Higgins, 1991; Selman, 1980). This means that children gain a better understanding that other people, especially their parents and teachers, have particular viewpoints toward them and that they are the subject of their evaluations. Because of this understanding, the viewpoints of others start to function as "self-guides" (Higgins, 1991) as the child incorporates the expectations of the socializing agents into his or her self-representations. In interactions with significant others, children in middle childhood also show the ability to engage in basic temporal comparisons (Suls & Sanders, 1982) and in rudimentary social comparisons (Frey & Ruble, 1985; Ruble & Frey, 1991). The comparison processes, however, are fairly simplistic, are mostly oriented on age norms rather than on specific behaviors, and are not used for critical self-evaluation (Harter, 2006; Thompson, 2006). Overall, the child's comparisons still suffer from a personal positivity bias and, hence, may serve a motivating or emotionally protective function. Thus, although there are some clear advances in 5- to 8-year-olds self-representations in terms of linking attributes in simple ways, overall children during this age period still lack the ability to develop an overall coherent self-concept and the ability to critically evaluate their self-representations (Harter, 1999, 2006).

During middle childhood, the factors that contribute to individual differences in self-representations are a continuation of the influences that were already at work during infancy and early childhood. That is, the socializing environment that significant others create in terms of warmth, acceptance, nurturance, and predictability will affect the nature and coherence of 5- to 8-year-olds' self-representations (Thompson, 1999). For example, Cassidy (1988) showed that compared with insecurely attached 6-year-olds, securely attached children had more positive self-representations and were able to point out negative attributes, thus showing a more realistic representation of their self. Other research has shown that children's perspective-taking ability is also influenced by the socializing environment and that different contexts are associated with different kinds of self-representations. For example, children who live in neglectful or abusive families tend to be more likely to hold negative and dissociated self-representations (Fischer & Ayoub, 1994). In addition, they often tend to be confused about how others may view them, resulting in the introjections of incoherent and fragmented values and insecurity in the evaluation of the self (Harter, 2006).

In summary, although the cognitive changes of middle childhood result in advances in self-concept development, the self-representations of 5- to 8-year-olds continue to have limitations. Although perspective-taking ability and language skills greatly influence children's self-understanding, allowing them to engage in rudimentary temporal and social comparisons, their ability to engage in realistic self-evaluation remains underdeveloped. Thus, further changes and advances wait for the age period of late childhood.

Late Childhood

Late childhood refers to the age period from 8 to 11 years. During this age period children's self-representations focus on attributes that describe traits, competencies, and increasingly interpersonal characteristics (Harter, 1999, 2006). From a cognitive developmental perspective describing the self in terms of traits and competencies reflects the child's new ability to connect specific behaviors and characteristics to form higher order generalizations (Fischer, 1980; Siegler, 1991). For example, competencies in specific educational subjects lead 8- to 11-year-olds to the formation of the trait concept "intelligent" or "smart." Similarly, interpersonal attributes (e.g., being likeable, being popular) become more and more incorporated into children's self-representations, indicating that relations with others become increasingly salient for children's self-concept. Finally, in late childhood, children also integrate both positive and negative emotions into their self-representations (Donaldson & Westerman, 1986) and recognize that the same person is capable of experiencing both (Fischer, Shaver, & Carnochan, 1990).

During late childhood, children also gain an understanding that they are increasingly evaluated by others (e.g., teachers or peers; Thompson, 2006). Most children understand that these others compare their behavior, skills, and competencies against those of other children with the purpose of communicating standards of quality and conduct (Harter, 2006). This general observation leads children to use social comparison processes for *self-evaluation purposes,* which is another major development during this age period. Thus, overall, the advances in self-concept development during late childhood are related to the emergence of three major cognitive skills: (1) the ability to use social comparison for the purpose of self-evaluation (Suls & Sanders, 1982); (2) the ability to distinguish between one's actual and ideal self (Thompson, 2006); and (3) improved perspective-taking skills (Case, 1992; Fischer, 1980). Taken together, the cognitive advances result in less positive, more realistic, and sustainable self-representations (Harter, 1999, 2006).

Individual differences in 8- to 11-year-olds' self-representations and self-evaluations have been investigated in terms of their associations with parenting behavior and parenting styles (Lamborn, Mounts, Steinberg, & Dornbush, 1991). Overall, this research has revealed that certain parenting behaviors and styles are more likely to result in positive self-representations and self-evaluations than others (see Harter, 2006). Specifically, findings from this research have shown that children with positive self-representations and high self-esteem were more likely to have parents who engaged in the following behaviors. First, parents were accepting, were affectionate, and actively involved in their child's activities. Second, they preferred disciplinary practices that were non-coercive and age appropriate. Third, they enforced rules consistently and encouraged their child to adopt high standards of behavior and, fourth, they involved their child in family decisions in a democratic way. Thus, in combination with findings discussed earlier in terms of the importance of attachment relations and parental support, this empirical evidence shows that socializing agents, such as parents and teachers, have a great deal of influence on children's self-representations and self-evaluations (Lamborn et al., 1991). This influence continues to be important as relationships with peers and individuals out-side the family increase in frequency and importance over the course of adolescence (Wigfield, Eccles, MacIver, Reuman, & Midgley, 1991).

DEVELOPMENT OF SELF-REPRESENTATIONS DURING ADOLESCENCE

Adolescence is a particularly important age period in the development of self-representations for several reasons. First, puberty brings a number of physical changes that challenge individuals' self-understanding and require that these changes are incorporated into the overall self-concept (Graber, 1996; Rosenberg, 1986; Williams & Currie, 2000). Second, cognitive advances result in greater introspection and self-reflection and permit a greater differentiation of self-representations (Fischer, 1980). At different stages of adolescence, however, this differentiation can also create problems (Harter & Monsour, 1992). Third, adolescents have improved social skills, have greater awareness of how they are perceived by others, and increasingly form their own network of friends and social interaction partners. Overall, these changes occur over three fairly distinct periods that are usually referred to as early (age 11–13), middle (age 14–16), and late adolescence (age 16–18).

Self-Representations in Early Adolescence

The salient content of young adolescents' self-representations focuses on com-petencies (e.g., scholastic or athletic abilities), interpersonal attributes and social skills, and affective states (Harter, 1999, 2006; Wigfield et al., 1991). Several authors have described how during adolescence there is a proliferation of selves that vary as a function of social roles and contexts (Hart, 1988; Harter, Bresnick, Bouchey, & Whitesell, 1997; Smollar & Youniss, 1985). Thus, young adolescents start to describe themselves increasingly in differentiated and context-specific ways and their self-representations are indicative of what Fischer (1980) called "single abstractions" (e.g., cheerful, outgoing, depressed, or reserved). That is, although early adolescents' self-representations show a higher order integration of attributes (e.g., multiple specific attributes are integrated into concepts such as "emotional" or "intelligent") and also the acknowledgement of positive and negative attributes, these representa-tions are still highly compartmentalized (Harter & Monsour, 1992; Higgins, 1991). This compartmentalization is shown by the fact that in early adolescence single abstractions are not compared with one another and, hence, potential contradictions are not detected. For example, several studies by Harter and colleagues have shown that although young adolescents included opposing and potentially conflicting attri-butes in their self-descriptions, they usually did not experience any contradictions or any conflicts when talking about the opposing attributes (Harter & Monsour, 1992; Harter et al., 1997). Thus, although young adolescents have an understanding of mul-tiple selves, this understanding is rather rudimentary and undeveloped. The same applies to the social comparisons that young adolescents make (Harter, 2006).

In terms of normative developmental challenges, several authors have pointed out that young adolescents still engage to some extent in all-or-none thinking and are overly sensitive to what others might think about them (Wigfield et al., 1991). This often results in great volatility of their self-evaluations which led Rosenberg

(1986) to coin the term "barometric self." These aspects of early adolescents' self-representations also have important contextual or ecological correlates. For example, early adolescence brings the transition from elementary school to middle or junior high school, which represents a new social setting with new rules and new peers (Eccles & Midgley, 1989; Wigfield et al., 1991). Eccles and Midgley (1989) pointed out that the climate in middle or junior high school tends to be characterized by new and different educational practices (e.g., public posting of grades; grouping by ability level) that often result in stronger social comparisons and different attributions with regard to the self. For example, some of these practices may challenge young adolescents' self-understanding (e.g., poor performance may not be attributed to lack of effort anymore but to lack of ability). Moreover, challenges to early adolescents' self-concept and self-esteem may also come from their interactions with peers, especially if they are the subject of peer rejection, humiliation, or bullying (Harter, 2006; Harter, Low, & Whitesell, 2003).

The heightened self-consciousness and introspectiveness that is typical for adolescence widens the individual differences in young adolescents' self-representations (Harter, 1999, 2006). Other factors that contribute to individual differences in self-concept and self-esteem are mostly related to the quality of adolescents' relationships with parents and peers. In particular, young adolescents who have positive and unconditional parental support and also have favorable relationships with peers tend to report more positive self-evaluations than adolescents for whom this is not the case (Roberts, Seidman, & Pedersen, 2000). On the other hand, some studies have shown that highly conditional relationships with parents and peers tend to be associated with more inauthentic self-representations and more unstable and fragile self-esteem (Harter, Marold, Whitesell, & Cobbs, 1996) that may also carry over into middle adolescence and may jeopardize successful development during this age period (see Harter, 2006).

Self-Representations in Middle Adolescence

Middle adolescence (age 14–16) sees further differentiation of the attributes associated with different social roles, relational contexts, and newly emerging roles (Harter, 2006). This increasing differentiation is in part due to advances in cognitive development but also due to greater introspection and preoccupation with the self and with what others might think of the self. An advance in self-understanding that takes place in middle adolescence is reflected in the combination of single abstractions into abstract mappings (Fischer, 1980). However, although single abstractions are now combined into abstract mappings that reflect adolescents' self-understanding within a role or across roles, adolescents at this stage of development cannot yet integrate contradictions or opposites into a coherent self-concept. Harter and her colleagues (Harter & Monsour, 1992; Harter et al., 1997) showed that this lack of integration often results in the experience of psychological conflict, confusion, and distress. Thus, in middle adolescence individuals are often concerned about the attributes that define their true self and confusion and intrapsychic conflict may arise when the role-specific multiple selves are very discrepant and when the individual lacks the cognitive ability to reconcile opposites and contradictions. Harter (2006) described a prototypical adolescent who agonized over whether she was an extrovert or an introvert. This adolescent stated: "Am I just acting like an extrovert, am I just trying to impress them, when really I'm an introvert? So which am I, responsible or irresponsible? How can the same person be both?" (Harter, 2006, p. 541). There is also evidence suggesting that this challenge of achieving a coherent and internally consistent self-concept is exacerbated for ethnic minority youth as they must bridge "multiple worlds" (Cooper, Jackson, Azmitia, Lopez, & Dunbar, 1995).

In addition to being more introspective, adolescents during this period are also very preoccupied with the views and opinions of others, especially the views of their peers. Several authors have described this preoccupation as "gazing intently into the social mirror" (Harter, 2006) or as "imaginary audience" (Elkind, 1967). Thus, it is very important for adolescents between the age of 14 and 16 to understand what significant others think of the self and to figure out how they can reconcile expectations in different social roles or the expectations of parents and peers. Higgins (1991) observed that adolescents often struggle with this challenge and may develop conflicting self-guides—a finding that is consistent with results provided by Harter and her colleagues (Harter & Monsour, 1992).

Consistent with this struggle to define and understand one's true self is the observation that middle adolescence often is associated with a *decline in self-esteem* (Harter, 2006; Kling, Hyde, Showers, & Buswell, 1999; Rosenberg, 1986). Decline in self-esteem is often linked to adolescents' concerns regarding their physical appearance and their body image (Williams & Currie, 2000), but is also greatly influenced by the quality of their relations with parents and peers (Harter et al., 1996; Usmiani & Daniluk, 1997). For example, adolescent girls who strongly endorse a feminine gender orientation and who try to meet cultural standards with regard to physical appearance seem to be particularly prone to declines in self-esteem and possibly symptoms of depression. Indeed, several authors have argued that these self-processes in middle adolescence may be at the root of the considerable gender differences in depression that are observed across the adult years (Harter, 1999; Kling et al., 1999; Nolen-Hoeksema & Girgus, 1994). On the other hand, it has been shown that a supportive relationship with parents and mutually accepting relationships with peers can play a protective role against the decline of self-esteem (Harter et al., 1996; Moretti & Higgins, 1990). In particular, support and unconditional regard from parents and peers allow the adolescent to find his or her own voice and to develop an understanding that it is appropriate to act and feel differently in different social contexts and interpersonal relations (Harter, 2006; Harter et al., 1996). The development of this understanding and the formation of an integrated self-concept take on a new meaning during the period of late adolescence.

Self-Representations in Late Adolescence

In late adolescence and into early adulthood the attributes that characterize individuals' self-representations increasingly reflect personal beliefs, values, and moral standards that have been internalized or are based on personal experiences (Damon & Hart, 1988; Harter, 2006). In addition, self-representations in late adolescence tend to be more realistic in terms of strengths and weaknesses, and less concerned with the expectations and opinions of others (Harter & Monsour, 1992). Also, compared with the previous developmental stage, late adolescence sees the meaningful integration of single abstractions into higher order abstractions (Case, 1985), the emergence of future possible selves (Markus & Nurius, 1986), and the linkage of self-attributes with goals and strivings (Harter, 2006). Contradicting and opposing self-attributes are acknowledged and reconciled in a cognitively advanced way, thus resulting in most instances in the resolution of the psychological conflict that was a hallmark of middle adolescence (Harter & Monsour, 1992; Harter et al., 1997). Higgins (1991) described the development in later adolescence as a process during which the adolescent and young adult actively selects among alternative "self-guides" that will direct his or her behavior and actions for the years to come. In summary, developmental changes in self-representations in late adolescence suggest that cognitive and social–emotional advances result in the creation of a personal identity (Erikson, 1982) that lays the foundation for the developmental tasks of early adulthood.

Evidence from longitudinal studies also suggests that late adolescents' global sense of self-worth and self-esteem improve compared with middle adolescence (O'Malley & Bachman, 1983; Block & Robins, 1993; Rosenberg, 1986). Reasons for this overall increase in self-esteem are (a) generally smaller discrepancies between adolescents' ideal and real self; (b) gains in personal autonomy and greater independence when making decisions; and (c) increased role-taking ability resulting in improved understanding of the motives and attitudes of others (Harter, 2006; Block & Robins, 1993). Specifically, later adolescence is often accompanied by the recognition that others, including one's parents, have favorable attitudes toward the self and that these others make important contributions to one's life.

Although self-concept development in late adolescence tends to be mostly positive, there are also some risks for maladaptive self-processes and less favorable outcomes. Rosenberg (1986), for example, pointed out that older adolescents' self-representations are still characterized by a certain degree of uncertainty and that this uncertainty can result in a more unstable sense of self-worth. Similarly, Harter's research group (Harter, 1999) has shown that maladaptive self-processes can be observed if adolescents are preoccupied with meeting impossible cultural standards, such as standards of physical attractiveness or social acceptance. For example, in female adolescents a preoccupation with the cultural standards of physical attractiveness tends to be associated with lower self-esteem and the risk of developing eating disorders. Similarly, in male adolescents, chronic rejection and humiliation by peers increases the risk for acting out behavior and possibly violent actions, as has been the case in a number of shootings at high schools and colleges (Harter et al., 2003).

In summary, late adolescence (age 16–18) is an age period during which a number of positive changes occur in terms of self-concept development. These changes and consolidations lay the foundation for self and social–emotional development in adulthood and influence how the developmental tasks of adulthood are represented and approached. To what extent self-representations continue to develop across adulthood and what is known about self-concept development in adulthood is the focus of the next section of this chapter.

■ DEVELOPMENT OF SELF-REPRESENTATIONS IN ADULTHOOD

Compared with the extensive literature on the development of self-representations in childhood and adolescence, research on self-concept development in adulthood is more limited. Moreover, because chronological age tends to lose its primacy as the dimension along which self-concept development can be mapped, it is not possible to describe the development of self-representations in adulthood in the same age-structured way as it was done for childhood and adolescence. This also means that questions related to *normative* self-concept development in adulthood are much more difficult to answer. Thus, although self-representations have increasingly been implicated in successful adult development (Brandtstädter & Greve, 1994; Greve & Wentura, 2003; Labouvie-Vief, Chiodo, Goguen, Diehl, & Orwoll, 1995; Markus & Herzog, 1991), it is more difficult to paint a comprehensive picture of self-concept development throughout the adult years.

This difficulty is due to several reasons and is reflected in a slightly different organizational structure for this part of the chapter. First, like for adult personality development in general, the commonly held assumptions regarding self-concept development were for a long time biased in favor of notions of stability and continuity and it was believed that self-concept development was completed by early adulthood. This assumption was, to some extent, also supported by theorizing and research on identity development (Kroger, 2000). Only fairly recent theoretical developments have led to a revisiting of this position (Diehl, 2006). Second, there are few theories that have focused on adult self-concept development and most of the studies on self-representations have been conducted with college-aged young adults. It was not until the early 1990s that several theorists explored the role of self-representations in middle and later adulthood (Brandtstädter & Greve, 1994; Cross & Markus, 1991; Filipp & Klauer, 1986; Ryff, 1991) and developed propositions that focused on self-representations as a potential force in adult development. Third, there are few longitudinal studies that have examined changes in adults' self-representations over longer periods of time and over the major stages of the adult life span (e.g., from early adulthood to midlife and old age). Although a few studies exist that have followed young adults through college and beyond, longitudinal studies are particularly absent with regard to self-concept development in midlife and later adulthood. Fourth, the lack of a coherent picture in terms of self-concept development across the adult life span is also due to the fact that quite disparate theoretical approaches have been used to study adults' self-representations. For example, although there is an extensive literature on the role of *possible selves* in adulthood (Hooker, 1999), this literature is not systematically linked to other bodies of research that have examined the role of self-representations in the context of adaptation and well-being.

Given this less than optimal situation, the following sections will first review findings from cross-sectional studies conducted with adult samples followed by a review of longitudinal research. We will close this part of the chapter by reviewing studies that have examined the role of the structural organization of adults' self-representations in the context of coping with challenging developmental tasks or stressful events.

Findings From Cross-Sectional, Age-Comparative Studies

As already stated earlier, the commonly held assumptions regarding self-concept development in adulthood are biased in favor of stability and continuity, because the development of self-representations was thought for a long time as being completed by early adulthood. McCrae and Costa (2003), however, offered a perspective that leaves room for both stability and change of adults' self-representations. Building on the notion that people's self-conceptions draw on multiple dimensions of behavior, McCrae and Costa (2003) proposed that adults' self-representations may remain stable as they relate to their (relatively) stable personality characteristics (i.e., traits). However, self-representations that are related to roles and relationships may change over time as these roles and relationships change. This more differentiated view is supported by results from several studies. This view is also consistent with existing theorizing about adults' identity development which assumes that salient identities are relatively stable but can change in response to significant life events (Diehl, 1999; Whitbourne & Connolly, 1999) or in the context of striving toward relevant goals (Gollwitzer, Bayer, Scherer, & Seifert, 1999).

Age Differences in Role- or Domain-Specific Self-Representations

Although adults' self-representations are theoretically conceived as being role or domain specific, research that has applied such a perspective has been the exception rather than the rule (see Diehl, Hastings, & Stanton, 2001). Mueller, Wonderlich, and Dugan (1986) examined age differences in the self-schemas of young and older adults. In particular, they asked college students and elderly adults to select from a large set of descriptors those attributes that were self-descriptive. They found no age differences in the *number* of attributes that were judged as self-descriptive, suggesting that older adults' self-representations were as rich as young adults' self-descriptions. However, there were some interesting age differences with regard to other aspects of the self-schemas. For example, although both young and older adults endorsed more positive than negative attributes (i.e., positivity bias), this tendency was significantly more pronounced for older adults. In addition, older adults' self-representations were also more varied and included both "elderly" traits (e.g., mature, experienced, tolerant, slow, anxious, cranky) as well as "young" traits (e.g., active, ambitious, confident, inconsiderate), as judged by independent raters. Thus, Mueller et al. (1986) suggested that older adults' self-schemas were reflective of life experiences that permitted them to incorporate both young and elderly attributes.

McCrae and Costa (1988) examined the spontaneous self-representations of adults who ranged in age from 32 to 84 years. Adults in this sample described themselves primarily in terms of their major life roles, personal dispositions, and their day-to-day activities. Significant differences between younger and older adults were found in that younger adults were more likely to describe themselves in terms of family roles, personal relationships, personality traits, and routine tasks, whereas older adults were more likely to mention age, health status, life circumstances, interests, hobbies, and beliefs as part of their spontaneous self-representations. Thus, McCrae and Costa's (1988) study suggests that there are significant age-related differences in adults' spontaneous self-representations. A similar study by George and Okun (1985), however, found no significant age differences in the content of the self-definitions of three adult age groups.

Diehl, Owen, and Youngblade (2004) employed the method developed by Harter and Monsour (1992) to examine the role-specific self-representations of adults, ranging in age from 20 to 88 years. Specifically, adults provided, separately for each of five role-specific self-representations (e.g., self with family, self with close friend, self with colleagues, self with significant other, self with a disliked person), up to six attributes that described their own self in the respective role. These self-descriptors were then categorized as to whether they represented an agency- or communion-related attribute (Guisinger & Blatt, 1994) and age and sex differences were examined. Findings showed that young and middle-aged adults included significantly more agency attributes in their self-representations than older adults, and men included more agency attributes than women. In contrast, older adults included significantly more communion attributes in their self-representations than young adults (Figure 24.1), and women listed significantly more communion attributes than men. As hypothesized, the correlation between age and the number of agency words was negative, whereas the correlation between age and the number of communion words was positive.

Finally, using a sample of adults ranging in age from 70 to 103 years, Freund and Smith (1999a) addressed several questions with regard to the content and function of spontaneous self-definitions in late adulthood. Consistent with McCrae and Costa's (1988) results, Freund and Smith (1999a) found that older adults included a broad spectrum of life domains in their self-definitions, reflecting an activity-oriented lifestyle. Statements about life review and personality traits also played an important role in these older adults' self-representations, indicating that they were not exclusively activity oriented, but also engaged in self-reflection about their lives. Health proved to be an important aspect of participants' self-definition. Overall, there were more similarities than differences between the old (70–84 years) and the very old (85–103 years) with regard to the content of their self-definitions. Of 24 content categories only five revealed statistically significant age differences. The multifacetedness of older adults' self-definitions was significantly associated with emotional well-being. However, multifacetedness did not moderate the negative impact of physical and sensory impairments on well-being.

In summary, a number of studies have documented age differences in adults' spontaneous self-representations. These age differences have been shown with different measurement approaches and different samples of adults. These findings

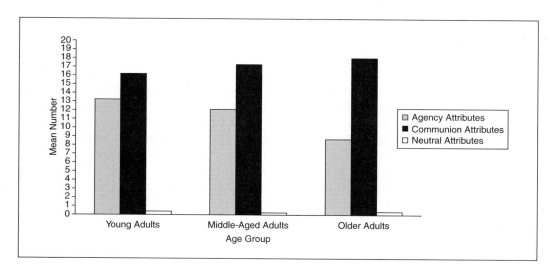

FIGURE 24.1   **Mean number of agency- and communion-related attributes across age groups.**

suggest that the observed age differences may reflect age-period-specific conceptions of the own person and may, at least in part, be related to age-associated changes in social roles and relationships (McCrae & Costa, 2003). Further evidence for this notion and for the notion that age differences in self-representations may be reflective of age-specific developmental tasks is provided by research on adults' possible selves.

Age Differences in Possible Selves

Whereas research on age differences in current self-representations is still somewhat tentative, findings on age differences in possible selves in adulthood are more solidly established (Hooker, 1999). In contrast to current self-conceptions, *possible selves* refer to individuals' representations of future selves (Markus & Nurius, 1986). These future selves can include positive representations of the self, so-called *hoped-for-selves*, or they can include negative representations of one's person, so-called *feared selves*. Hooker (1999) pointed out that the construct of possible selves has been of particular interest to life-span psychologists because they view possible selves as being potentially sensitive to changes in the major developmental contexts of the adult life span (e.g., family, work, health, leisure). Similarly, Markus and Herzog (1991) stated that "aging requires casting away some possible selves and provides opportunities for the creation of new ones" (p. 117).

Cross and Markus (1991) were among the first to document age differences in possible selves across the adult life span. Specifically, they showed that young and middle-aged adults reported significantly more hoped-for-selves in the family and occupation domain than older adults. In contrast, older adults reported more hoped-for-selves in the physical health and leisure domain. With regard to feared selves, all age groups mentioned possible selves related to physical health most often; however, older adults reported significantly more physical health- and lifestyle-related feared selves than the younger age groups. In contrast, older adults reported fewer feared selves in the family domain. Cross and Markus (1991) also found that adults who scored low in life satisfaction reported different possible selves than those who scored high in life satisfaction, suggesting that possible selves are not only indicative of individuals' developmental position in adulthood but also indicative of their perceived discrepancies between actual and ideal self-representations.

The findings of Cross and Markus (1991) have been further corroborated by research by Hooker (1999) and Smith and Freund (2002). In a series of studies, Hooker and her colleagues showed that across the adult life span, health-related possible selves become increasingly incorporated into adults' self-representations (Hooker & Kaus, 1994). The increasing salience of health-related self-representations is of importance because of how they may motivate individuals to change their health behaviors so that psychological and physical well-being can be maintained for as long as possible (Hooker, 1999).

Smith and Freund (2002) examined possible selves in a German sample of old and very old adults (age range 70 to 103 years). They found that young-olds generated significantly more hoped-for-selves than the old-old age group; there were no age differences in the number of feared selves. Participants' possible selves were predominantly related to personal characteristics, health, and social relationships and were reflective of gain motives (e.g., "I would like to become a grandfather"). Over a

4-year follow-up period, health became the most frequently mentioned domain for hoped-for-selves.

Ryff (1991) examined the possible selves of young, middle-aged, and older adults with regard to six dimensions of psychological well-being (i.e., self-acceptance, positive relations with others, autonomy, environmental mastery, purpose in life, and personal growth). Findings showed that young and middle-aged adults expected continued improvement in the future for most of these dimensions. In contrast, older adults expected either decline for most aspects of well-being (i.e., environmental mastery, personal growth, purpose in life, positive relations with others) or no change (i.e., autonomy, self-acceptance). The future expectations of older adults were consistently lower than the expectations of the two younger age groups. Although this finding may sound discouraging with regard to older adults' possible selves, Ryff (1991) also found that age was positively associated with a closer fit between ideal and actual self-representations. This suggests that middle-aged and older adults may adjust their ideal self-representations in response to perceived age-related changes in their actual abilities. This may be a very effective accommodative strategy for maintaining high self-esteem and a sense of agency as individuals grow older (see Brandtstädter & Greve, 1994; Greve & Wentura, 2003).

In summary, research on possible selves in adulthood has documented fairly consistent age differences with regard to the domains of adults' hoped-for and feared selves. Moreover, findings on possible selves related to psychological well-being have yielded age differences that are consistent with research on normative conceptions of gains and losses across the adult life span (see Heckhausen, Dixon, & Baltes, 1989). Although these patterns of age differences are suggestive of age-related changes, data from longitudinal studies are required to draw conclusions about developmental changes in self-representations across the adult life span.

Findings from Longitudinal Studies

Stability and Change in Self-Representations

The short-term malleability of self-representations in response to different feedback conditions or different social comparison targets has been well documented in the social psychological literature (for a review, see Kernis & Goldman, 2003) and in the experience sampling literature (Savin-Williams & Demo, 1984). However, long-term longitudinal studies elaborating the developmental antecedents, correlates, and consequences of self-concept variability and/or stability in adulthood are relatively scarce. To date, only a few longitudinal studies exist, providing us with a relatively tentative description of how adults' self-representations may change or may stay the same over the course of adulthood. Moreover, these studies tend to be limited to particular age periods, such as early or late adulthood, thus making generalizations across the whole adult life span difficult.

Mortimer, Finch, and Kumka (1982) analyzed panel data from male college students over a 14-year period and assessed four types of stability (i.e., structural invariance, normative, level, and ipsative stability; see Caspi & Roberts, 2001) with regard to the four self-concept dimensions of well-being, sociability, competence, and unconventionality. Mortimer et al. (1982) found support for the structural invariance of the observed variables (i.e., items) to the latent factors of the multidimensional self-concept. The covariances among the latent factors were moderate to high over time, suggesting that the structure of the self-concept remained relatively invariant over the 14-year period in early adulthood. Stability coefficients were in excess of 0.60 over the 4 years in college and stayed in the same range over the 10 years after graduation, suggesting a considerable amount of normative or rank-order stability. In terms of level stability, participants' scores on well-being and competence declined significantly over the 4 years in college, followed by subsequent increases over the 10-year period after graduation. Scores for sociability and unconventionality showed significant declines over the whole 14-year period, suggesting that the young men increasingly committed to their careers and social relationships and settled into their roles as young adults. Thus, whereas the pattern of individual differences (i.e., normative stability) among participants was mostly preserved, the mean levels of scores on different dimensions of the self-concept shifted significantly upward or downward over the 14-year period, suggesting that more attention should be paid to changes in level rather than changes in rank order.

In terms of ipsative stability, Mortimer et al. (1982) found that the intraindividual ordering of the four self-concept dimensions was quite consistent over time. To understand stability and change in self-concept in more detail, Mortimer et al. (1982) also examined the reciprocal relations between self-representations and life events for the dimension of personal competence. They found that men who maintained a strong sense of personal competence over the decade after graduation differed in a number of ways from those who changed significantly. Participants who maintained a strong sense of personal competence had more positive relationships with their parents; were less likely to experience occupational insecurity (e.g., unemployment or subemployment); were more likely to achieve high income and work autonomy; and were more likely to have good social support and high marital satisfaction. These findings suggest that stability in young adults' self-representations of personal competence were to a good extent related to stability in the social circumstances in the family and professional domain, underscoring the importance of these two life domains for the successful transition into adulthood (Arnett, 2004).

Filipp and Klauer (1986) used a standardized method and unstructured spontaneous self-descriptions to assess the stability of self-representations over a 4-year period in German men from five birth cohorts. With regard to the standardized assessment, these investigators found support for the structural invariance of the rating scales and for high normative stability of three self-concept dimensions (i.e., efficiency, competence, social integration). Indeed, the correlation coefficients obtained in this study were very similar in size to the stability coefficients obtained by Mortimer et al. (1982). In contrast to Mortimer et al. (1982), however, this study failed to find any significant changes in mean level over the 4-year period.

With regard to the stability of the unstructured self-descriptions, Filipp and Klauer (1986) found that although the mean *number* of self-descriptive statements was fairly stable over time, the index of normative stability was rather modest. Moreover, there was considerable change in the *content* of spontaneous self-descriptions as indicated by increases in the reference to (a) social roles; (b) ideological, religious, or political attitudes; (c) physical appearance and body features; and (d) sociability and social relations. Significant decreases were found in reference to emotionality, autonomy, and independence. Overall, this study showed a decrease in the diversification of self-descriptive statements across content domains. In general, the findings from this study suggest that free-response formats may be more sensitive to change in adults' self-representations over time than standardized rating methods, and that the properties of the measurement procedure need to be taken into account in the assessment of the temporal stability of self-representations.

Troll and Skaff (1997) examined the continuity in self-attributes in a sample of very old individuals (age 85 and older) over a 28-month period. Although respondents expressed a great deal of continuity in self-attributes, they also reported that they had changed. The majority of reported changes were in the areas of personality, physical health, and lifestyle adjustments. Most of the perceived changes in personality were described as being positive (e.g., "I'm more tolerant." "I'm calmer."), whereas most of the changes in physical health and lifestyle were seen as negative or constraining. Perceptions of continuity were not significantly related to subjective health or affect balance in this sample of very old individuals.

Two studies have examined the temporal stability of adults' self-representations over shorter time frames. Freund and Smith (1999b) examined the temporal stability of spontaneous self-definitions in a sample of German adults (age 69–92 years, *M* age = 78.9 years) over an 8-week period. They found low intraindividual stability for a free-response format and a card-sorting task and low interindividual stability, suggesting that older adults' spontaneous self-representations exhibited low consistency over a short period of time.

Diehl, Jacobs, and Hastings (2006) investigated the temporal stability of role-specific self-representations (i.e., self with family, self with a friend, etc.) in a sample of adults (age range 20–88 years) over a 4-week period. Respondents spontaneously generated a list of up to 20 self-descriptors and rated each descriptor in terms of how characteristic it was of them in each of the five roles. In general, adults' role-specific self-representations exhibited a great deal of temporal stability, with mean stability coefficients ranging from 0.75 to 0.80. However, there were significant differences in stability between self-representations. Across age groups, the self with family and self with significant other were significantly less stable than the real me representation. Significant age differences in stability were found for several self-representations. For example, middle-aged adults' self with family and self with significant other representations were significantly more stable than young and older adults' self-representations in these roles. Temporal stability was significantly related to a measure of personal authenticity; the more authentic adults were in a particular role, the more stable their self-representations were in this role.

In summary, findings from longitudinal studies are less than conclusive. On one hand there are findings from long-term studies in early adulthood showing high normative and ipsative stability but also significant changes in level stability (Mortimer et al., 1982). Although some of these findings were replicated in a sample of middle-aged and older adults, this study failed to find significant changes in level stability (Filipp & Klauer, 1986). Moreover, the latter study also documented that the obtained results varied by measurement approach, suggesting that findings with standardized rating scales may be biased in favor of stability, whereas free-response measures may be more sensitive to change (see also Diehl et al., 2006; Freund & Smith, 1999b).

Stability and Change in Possible Selves

Only few studies have examined the temporal stability of adults' possible selves. Thus, most theorizing on the development of possible selves in adulthood is guided by the implicit assumption that the age differences that have been documented in cross-sectional, age-comparative studies may be reflective of age-related changes. Whether and to what extent this assumption is justified is currently not known.

One of the studies that have examined longitudinal changes in possible selves was reported by Smith and Freund (2002). This study documented a high degree of intraindividual change over the 4-year observation period. Across all domains, a total of 66% of the participants changed their number of hoped-for-selves and 70% changed the number of feared selves. In contrast, analyses at the domain level indicated more stability than change. The largest number of changes occurred in the domains of personal characteristics and health. In the domain of personal characteristics there was a tendency to relinquish hopes and fears rather than to add any. In the domain of health, however, more participants added than gave up hoped-for-self-representations.

Another interesting finding from this study was related to the motivational orientations of the changes in possible selves. Smith and Freund (2002) distinguished three motivational orientations that they referred to as improvement, maintenance, or avoidance of loss. With regard to hoped-for-selves, the majority of participants reported the motivational orientation of improvement over time (i.e., to attain something). Over time, however, an increasing number of older adults mentioned the maintenance orientation as their motivation for hoped-for-selves, and the observed changes differed by age/cohort group. In particular, compared with participants older than 80 years, more individuals in the 70- to 79-age range added the maintenance orientation. For feared selves, the motivational orientation of avoidance of loss (e.g., losing one's independence) was highly stable over time.

These findings on the role of possible selves in late life were recently complemented by a study by Hoppmann, Gerstorf, Smith, and Klumb (2007). These researchers used a subsample of the Berlin Aging Study ($N = 83$, M age = 81 years) and a time-sampling approach to investigate the associations between possible selves and daily activities in three behavioral domains (i.e., health, everyday cognition, and social relations), and how these associations were related to subjective and objective indicators of successful aging. Overall, this study showed that hoped-for-selves in the health and social relations domains were associated with a greater likelihood of performing daily activities in those domains. Results also showed that individuals who engaged in daily activities related to hoped-for-selves reported higher concurrent positive affect and were less likely to die over a 10-year follow-up. Thus, findings from this study underscore the motivational importance of hoped-for-selves and document the long-term effects of daily activities that were linked to older adults' hoped-for-selves.

Two other studies examined continuity and change in possible selves. Frazier, Hooker, Johnson, and Kaus (2000) investigated continuity and change in the possible selves of older adults (M age = 77 years) in the domains of health, physical functioning, independence/dependence, family, and lifestyle. They showed that continuity was the norm for most domains over a 5-year period. Specifically, continuity was significantly greater than change for hoped-for-selves in the independence, physical, and lifestyle domains, and for feared selves in the family domain. These findings suggest that in later life certain domains of self-representations may be best characterized by preservation.

Preservation of self-representations, however, is not the whole story. Frazier et al. (2000) also found some evidence for changes in possible selves. Intraindividual change was generally in the emergent direction (i.e., possible self not present at Time 1 but present at Time 2), with possible selves related to health and physical functioning becoming more important and more prevalent over time. Most participants showed a high degree of balance between their hoped-for and feared selves in the five domains over the 5-year period.

Morfei, Hooker, Fiese, and Cordeiro (2001) examined the possible selves of young adults in the parenting domain over a 3-year period. They found that 70% of the mothers and 54% of the fathers reported the same hoped-for-selves as parents, showing a good deal of continuity. In contrast, feared parenting selves showed less continuity (54% of the mothers, 29% of the fathers) over the 3-year period. There were significant gender differences in continuity, with fathers reporting significantly less continuity for both hoped-for and feared parenting selves.

Taken together, findings from these two studies showed that there is continuity in adults' possible selves, but that the amount of continuity varies across different parts of the adult life span. In both studies and related to different behavioral domains, adults' possible selves also exhibited change and appeared to be responsive to age-related changes in the different domains of functioning. How the structural organization of individuals' self-representations plays a role in coping with age-related challenges and in adaptation and psychological well-being will be reviewed next.

Self-Concept Structure and Adaptation in Adulthood

Although the structural organization of self-representations has been the focus of theorizing for a long time (James, 1890/1981; Lecky, 1945; Rogers, 1959), empirical work examining the structural organization of self-conceptions from a *developmental perspective* is rather scarce (cf. Showers & Zeigler-Hill, 2003). Studying the structural organization of self-knowledge is rooted in the assumption that different structures are associated with different ways of processing self-related information which are, in turn, associated with either adaptive or maladaptive behavior (Campbell, Assanand, & DiPaula, 2000; Showers & Zeigler-Hill, 2003). Thus, focusing on structural features of the self-concept goes beyond the simple examination of content and tries to elucidate how structural features, such as complexity, compartmentalization, or incoherence, may moderate the effects of stressful events on individuals' adjustment and well-being (Campbell et al., 2000; Showers & Zeigler-Hill, 2003). In the following, we focus on self-complexity, self-compartmentalization, and self-concept incoherence (SCI) as the most frequently studied self-concept structures and review the existing literature on age differences and age-related changes in these structural organizations.

Self-Complexity

Linville (1987) introduced the term *self-complexity* to refer to the number and independence of different self-aspects (e.g., "Me as a parent," or "Me as a researcher").

Individuals who have a greater number of self-aspects and maintain greater distinctions among their self-aspects show greater self-complexity. Thus, a highly complex individual has many self-aspects that do not overlap in their attribute content. The basic assumption is that self-concept complexity moderates the negative effects of stressful events on physical and mental well-being, because when one self-aspect is challenged or thwarted, then the individual with a greater number of and more distinct self-aspects has other ones to draw on for compensation and counterbalance.

Self-Compartmentalization

The concept of *self-compartmentalization* (Showers, 1992) builds on Linville's notion of self-complexity, but also includes the valences that are associated with each self-representation. According to this model, individuals' self-representations can be organized in an *evaluatively compartmentalized* or *evaluatively integrated* way. In an evaluatively compartmentalized organization positive and negative knowledge about the self is organized into separate self-aspects so that each self-aspect contains primarily positive or primarily negative information. In contrast, in an evaluatively integrated organization positive as well as negative attributes are represented within self-aspects, suggesting that the individual acknowledges the coexistence of both positive and negative self-knowledge.

Self-Concept Incoherence

The construct of *SCI* draws on theorizing in clinical, social, and developmental psychology and refers to the extent to which persons' self-representations are different across social roles or contexts (Block, 1961; Donahue, Robins, Roberts, & John, 1993; Harter & Monsour, 1992).[1] To assess SCI, individuals rate a set of personal attributes with regard to how characteristic each attribute is for a given social role or context. These ratings are used to calculate separately for each person the degree of non-overlap as an index of SCI. Although the emergence of multiple selves in late adolescence is generally seen as the result of cognitive advances (Harter & Monsour, 1992) and as indication of a higher level of adaptive competence, to date, findings from a number of studies suggest that the SCI index is a measure of a divided and fragmented self-concept and is associated with poorer developmental outcomes (Bigler, Neimeyer, & Brown, 2001; Diehl et al., 2001; Donahue et al., 1993).

In summary, different structural organizations of self-representations have been described in an attempt to understand the dynamic nature of the human self-concept and how adults' self-representations may serve as a psychological resource (Brandtstädter & Greve, 1994). Although a considerable body of empirical research has emerged from these efforts (see Campbell et al., 2000; Rafaeli-Mor & Steinberg, 2002; Showers & Zeigler-Hill, 2003), only a limited number of studies have examined how certain self-structures develop across the adult life span.

---

[1] Previous publications have used the term "self-concept differentiation (SCD)" rather than the term "self-concept incoherence (SCI)." We prefer the latter term over the former because numerous studies have shown that the index of SCD as used in our research is a measure of a divided and fragmented self rather than a measure of a differentiated and specialized self (Donahue et al., 1993). Using the term "incoherence" also helps to avoid misunderstandings related to the cognitive developmental literature in which the term "differentiation" tends to be used to describe more elaborated and efficient cognitive schemata.

Empirical Findings

Although some initial studies provided support for Linville's complexity hypothesis, the overall empirical results regarding the stress-buffering effect of *self-complexity* have been rather mixed (Koch & Shepperd, 2004; Rafaeli-Mor & Steinberg, 2002). Rafaeli-Mor and Steinberg's (2002) review of the literature, for example, found little support for self-complexity as a stress buffer. Instead, these authors showed that self-complexity served more often as a moderator of positive, uplifting events. Koch and Shepperd's (2004) literature review arrived at similar conclusions. Based on these reviews, more recent studies have investigated the effects of number of self-aspects and distinctness of self-aspects separately and have shown that it is mostly the number of self-aspects that moderates the relationship between stress and well-being (Rothermund & Meiniger, 2004). Also, because all of these studies have been conducted with young adults (i.e., college students), currently little is known about the potential stress-moderating effect of self-complexity in other age groups and across the adult life span.

With regard to *self-compartmentalization,* several studies have shown that positive and negative compartmentalization of self-knowledge is an effective strategy of dealing with short-lived stress (Showers, 1992; Showers & Kling, 1996). From a developmental perspective two studies are of particular importance because they either adopted a longitudinal design (Showers, Abramson, & Hogan, 1998) or addressed the role of self-compartmentalization in the context of a life transition (Showers & Ryff, 1996). Showers et al. (1998) conducted a prospective study in which they followed a sample of college students over a 2-year period. Findings from this study showed that compartmentalization was associated with less negative mood when stress was short-lived, suggesting that self-compartmentalization was a strategy of first resort. However, participants who were confronted with stress over an extended period of time did not benefit from compartmentalization and showed higher levels of negative mood compared with individuals who structured their self-knowledge in an integrated way (Showers et al., 1998).

How self-concept structure moderated the stressful effects of a life transition (i.e., residential relocation) was examined by Showers and Ryff (1996) in a sample of older women. They found that high evaluative compartmentalization was associated with lower levels of depressive symptoms and greater well-being when the relocation was associated with improvements in positively evaluated domains of the self. However, if the relocation resulted in a loss in a positive domain, then compartmentalization was associated with higher levels of depression and lower well-being. Thus, this study replicated findings from earlier laboratory studies in a real-life setting and showed that the self-concept structure moderated the stress associated with a life transition in old age (see also Kling, Ryff, & Essex, 1997).

In terms of *SCI* only a small number of studies have been conducted with adults. Using a sample of young, middle-aged, and older adults, Diehl et al. (2001) found a U-shaped relationship between age and the index of SCI derived from adults' role-specific self-representations. That means from early adulthood to middle age, SCI, on average, went down, reaching its lowest level in middle adulthood. Conversely, from late middle age to old age, SCI increased again, showing a positive association with age for this part of the adult life span. Additional analyses showed that age moderated the effect of SCI on measures of emotional adjustment and psychological well-being

(Figure 24.2). As can be seen in panel A of Figure 24.2, the slope of the regression line representing the association between SCI and positive psychological well-being was significantly steeper for older adults than for younger adults. The same association is shown in panel B with regard to negative psychological well-being. In combination, these findings suggest that the negative effect of SCI on psychological well-being differed across age groups and was most pronounced in older adults. To say it differently, SCI was associated with significantly poorer psychological well-being in older adults than in younger adults. Thus, having a coherent self-concept may represent an important psychological resource in late life when adults are at risk for experiencing losses and are challenged by physical and/or psychological declines (Brandtstädter & Greve, 1994; Showers & Ryff, 1996).

Donahue et al. (1993, Study 2) used data from the Mills Longitudinal Study to examine the precursors of SCI in a sample of middle-aged women. They found that SCI at age 52 showed significant positive correlations with measures of neuroticism and anxiety at ages 21, 27, and 43, and negative correlations with measures of well-being, self-realization, socialization, good impression, and overall emotional adjustment over this time span. Moreover, the bivariate correlations tended to increase over this age range, suggesting that SCI had a lasting effect in the lives of these middle-aged women. Donahue et al. (1993) also examined the relations between SCI and role involvement, role satisfaction, and role changes from age 21 to 43. Although they found no support for the hypothesis that occupying a larger number of roles resulted in increased SCI, they found significant negative correlations with role satisfaction and significant positive correlations with the number of experienced role changes. Specifically, women who had many role changes in early adulthood, such as marriage, divorce, and job-related changes, tended to have higher levels of SCI in their 50s. Obviously, the correlational nature of these data cannot address whether high SCI was a cause or a consequence of the role-related events and the poorer psychological adjustment in these middle-aged women. Nevertheless, these findings suggest that a coherent self-concept is important for psychological adjustment in adulthood and that high SCI seems to be indicative of a fragmented and divided self.

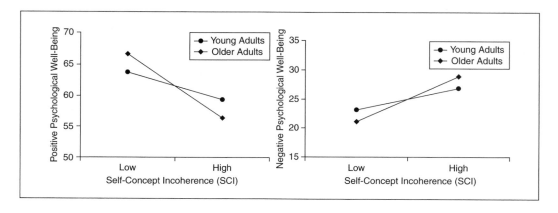

FIGURE 24.2 Interaction of self-concept incoherence and age for positive (panel A) and negative (panel B) psychological well-being. *Source:* Reprinted with permission from Diehl et al., 2001.

In summary, there is convincing evidence that different self-concept structures are associated with different psychological outcomes (Campbell et al., 2000; Showers & Zeigler-Hill, 2003; 2007). Although most of these studies have been limited to the age period of young adulthood, some findings suggest that self-concept structure serves as a moderator of stress at later stages of the adult life span as well (Diehl et al., 2001; Donahue et al., 1993; Kling et al., 1997; Showers & Ryff, 1996). From a developmental point of view, long-term longitudinal studies are needed to examine intraindividual changes and interindividual differences in intraindividual changes in self-concept structure over longer and different periods of the adult life span.

Self-Representations and Coping With Stress or Changes in Performance

Examination of the dynamic nature of adults' self-representations has also resulted in several studies on how the organization of self-representations and related processes may play out in the context of coping with stress or when dealing with age-related changes in performance. Specifically, Greve and Wentura (2003) reported findings from three studies examining whether processes of *self-concept immunization* would protect adults' (age range 18–85 years) self-representations against perceived negative changes. Similar to biological immunization, self-immunization refers to a process by which a self-threatening situation or perceived change is consciously acknowledged (e.g., "My memory for remembering a shopping list has gotten worse") and is responded to by flexibly adjusting the self-defining importance of the situation or the perceived change. As Greve and Wentura (2003) stated, self-immunization results in a stabilization of the person's self-concept on a more general (trait) level "by reducing the diagnosticity of deficient or decreased skills while heightening the diagnosticity of those skills that are currently perceived as sufficiently positive or well developed" (p. 41). Overall, these investigators found for several behavioral domains (e.g., memory, intelligence, independence, physical fitness, communication) that self-immunization helped to stabilize adults' self-concept by adjusting the diagnosticity/importance of a skill that was perceived as either poor or having changed in a negative direction. Thus, they concluded that documentation of self-immunization over such a broad age range and across various behavioral domains provided support for the hypothesis that self-immunization assists realistic self-assessment and self-concept stabilization. Both of these aspects are particularly important in late life when functional declines tend to become normative.

Drawing on the basic assumption that self-concept structures are associated with specific ways of processing self-relevant information and, hence, with adaptive or maladaptive behavior, several recently published studies have examined the effects of self-compartmentalization and SCI using daily diary methods. Aside from the fact that daily diary studies have a number of desirable methodological characteristics (e.g., minimization of recall bias), these studies permitted the examination of the effects of self-structures on the variability of other behaviors. For example, Zeigler-Hill and Showers (2007) conducted two daily diary studies with young adults examining the effect of evaluative self-compartmentalization and evaluative self-integration on state self-esteem in response to positive and negative daily events. In both studies, evaluative integration was associated with more stable self-esteem than evaluative compartmentalization in individuals with generally high self-esteem. In addition, analyses of self-esteem reactivity showed that the reactivity of state self-esteem to daily events was greater for compartmentalized individuals than for individuals with integrative self-concept structures. In summary, individuals with compartmentalized self-structures seemed more vulnerable to shifts in self-evaluations in response to daily events than individuals with integrated self-structures (see also Showers & Zeigler-Hill, 2007).

Findings that are mostly consistent with Showers and Zeigler-Hill's work have been reported by Diehl and Hay (2007). In a 30-day diary study with adults ranging in age from 18 to 89 years, these researchers built on the cross-sectional findings that greater SCI tends to be associated with poorer adjustment and tried to address how SCI exerts its effects on individuals' physical and psychological health. Overall, the investigators hypothesized that a higher level of SCI would result in a greater perturbation of the person-environment fit when a person experiences a stressful event. They also assumed that this greater perturbation in person-environment fit would be observable as greater intraindividual variability (IIV) in behavior, such as greater fluctuations in positive and negative affect or more frequent and/or intense physical symptoms. Thus, it was expected that a person with a higher SCI score would react to a stressful event with a greater deviation from his or her own average level of functioning (i.e., greater IIV) compared with a person with a lower SCI score. This increased IIV may underlie the documented negative associations between SCI and indicators of physical and psychological well-being and, over time, may put the person at greater risk for experiencing poorer physical and psychological health.

The investigators' assumptions were mostly supported by the study's findings (see Diehl & Hay, 2007). For example, as can be seen in Figure 24.3, this study found a significant positive association between SCI and IIV in negative affect before and after controlling for individuals' average level of stress (Diehl & Hay, 2010). That

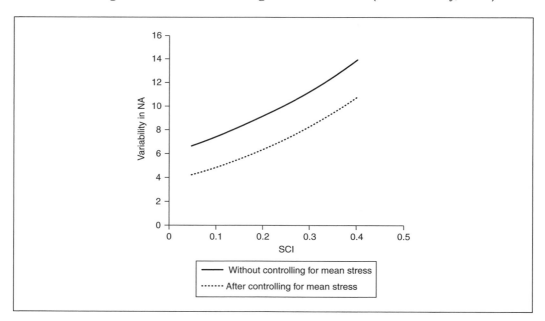

FIGURE 24.3   Intraindividual variability in negative affect as a function of SCI before and after controlling for average level of daily stress. *Source*: Reprinted with permission from Diehl & Hay, 2010.

means, adults with an incoherent self-concept showed greater fluctuations in negative affect than adults who had a more coherent self-concept. Interestingly, analyses with data from a second study sample showed that this effect of SCI was more pronounced in adult cancer survivors, suggesting that a coherent self-concept represents a particularly important psychological resource in individuals coping with a serious illness.

In addition to examining the effect of SCI, Diehl and Hay (2007) also examined the effect of the valence of adults' daily self-representations on their affective states. Multilevel analyses showed that on days when individuals endorsed negative self-attributes more strongly, they also showed significantly higher levels of negative affect. On the other hand, on days when individuals endorsed positive self-attributes more strongly, they tended to show significantly lower levels of negative affect. Findings also showed that the Daily Stress X Negative Self-Attributes interaction was significant, indicating that when individuals endorsed negative self-attributes more strongly, daily stressors had a greater impact on their daily negative affect (Figure 24.4).

In summary, in combination with other short-term longitudinal studies (e.g., Showers et al., 1998), findings from these daily diary studies help to shed further light on the ways in which the structural organization of self-representations is associated with variability in behavior that may underlie the observed negative outcomes of an incoherent or compartmentalized self-concept. Taken together, the findings are consistent with Showers and Zeigler-Hill's (2007) observation that integrated and coherent self-structures have certain characteristics, including greater temporal and situational stability, greater realism, and less extreme self-views, that may contribute to greater resilience when individuals' adaptive capacity is challenged by life stress. Thus, there is increasing support for the notion that self-representations may serve

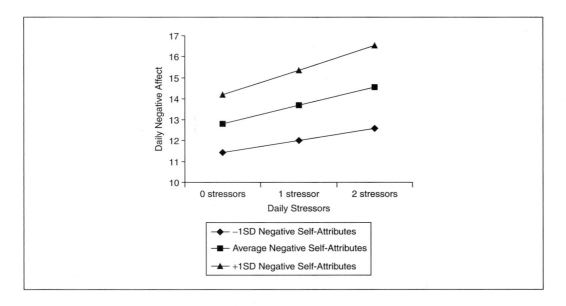

FIGURE 24.4   **Interaction of stressors and negative self-attributes for daily negative affect.**
Source: Reprinted with permission from Diehl & Hay, 2007.

as a psychological resource both in terms of specific processes (Greve & Wentura, 2003) as well as their structural organization (Diehl & Hay, 2007). However, despite this accumulating evidence there still remain a number of key issues that warrant further investigation across the life span.

FUTURE DIRECTIONS IN THE STUDY OF SELF-REPRESENTATIONS ACROSS THE LIFE SPAN

The attempt to describe the development of self-representations across the entire life span is clearly a challenging task. This is the case because research has not addressed the development of self-representations with equal intensity and sophistication for each major segment of the life span. In a similar vein, starting with early adulthood chronological age tends to be a rather imperfect and uninformative parameter for mapping out self-concept development. Thus, starting in early adulthood, other factors, such as social-contextual and interpersonal variables, assume greater importance for fostering or hindering the development of self-representations. In the following, we will discuss several key issues that are of importance for gaining a better understanding of the role of self-representations across the life span and in particular across the adult years.

First, although there is evidence in the childhood literature regarding the effects of the social environment and caregivers' behavior on the development of children's self-understanding and social–emotional development (Harter, 2006), little longitudinal research exists examining the long-term effects of sensitive parenting and attachment styles on individuals' self-concept. Thus, although it is in general assumed that a secure attachment style will also result in greater self-confidence and more clearly defined self-representations later in life, little is known about the extent to which critical life events or relationship experiences later in life may have the potential to challenge a person's self-understanding. Even less is known about how such later events and experiences may interact with early childhood experiences and processes in ways that may result in discontinuity and perhaps maladaptive outcomes. This gap in knowledge seems to be particularly important for the developmental period of emerging adulthood as cultural guidelines for this developmental stage are rather tentative (Arnett, 2004). Indeed, young adults are often challenged in areas such as identity formation, self-regulation, and commitment to personally meaningful social roles and it is important to understand how they negotiate these challenges and how they create continuity in terms of their self-understanding and their self-representations (see Shulman, Feldman, Blatt, Cohen, & Mahler, 2005) so that they can serve as the foundation for self-development in midlife and late adulthood.

Second, another key issue that has not been addressed sufficiently is the role that *social and cultural contexts* play in the development and maintenance of self-representations across the life span. Although some research exists that has examined self-concept consistency and stability across relationship contexts and within social roles for different ethnic groups (English & Chen, 2007), from a developmental perspective such investigations can only be the beginning of exploring the role of cultural and social factors more systematically and comprehensively. As most Western societies have become multicultural societies and as different cohorts of individuals encounter greater ethnic diversity in their lives (Angel & Angel, 2006), it becomes important to understand to what extent individuals' self-representations are shaped by specific cultural and social factors (Markus & Kitayama, 1991). Gaining a better understanding of the role of cultural and social influences on self-representations and their development across the life span also has the potential to inform research on how self-related processes, such as self-esteem, authenticity, or ethnic identity, play a role in long-term psychological well-being and adjustment.

Third, based on the proposition that social roles, interpersonal contexts, and critical life events are the major shaping forces for individuals' self-representations in adulthood, another key issue refers to the limited empirical knowledge that is available to support this basic notion. For example, there are only few longitudinal studies that have focused on how changes in adults' basic social roles (e.g., as a parent, spouse/partner, professional) are associated with changes in self-representations. There is, however, evidence from research showing that following a certain social clock and assuming specific social roles shaped women's personality development with regard to characteristics such as responsibility and masculinity versus nurturance and femininity (Helson, Mitchell, & Moane, 1984). In a similar way, it seems reasonable to assume that normative and non-normative changes in adults' social roles should have lasting effects on their self-representations and should influence how self-representations change over time (Diehl, 1999). For example, it would be interesting to gain a deeper understanding of how individuals' self-representations in the role as a parent change as their children grow up and become adults themselves (Fingerman, Pitzer, Lefkowitz, Birditt, & Mroczek, 2008). Such knowledge seems particularly important given that the stability of nuclear families has eroded through high divorce rates and because of a greater variety of alternative living arrangements (Bumpass & Lu, 2000). However, even in stable families the development of the parent–child relationship over the life span can be expected to result in redefined and reconstructed self-representations that very likely influence how parents and children communicate and interact with each other (Ryff, Lee, Essex, & Schmutte, 1994; Ryff & Seltzer, 1996). More systematic research is needed to address this issue across adults' basic social roles in the domains of family, work, leisure, and in other important self-defining domains.

On a more fundamental level it is also important to gain a better understanding of how adults' self-representations change as a function of *normal aging-related changes* and how the awareness of one's own aging process may translate into revised and readjusted self-representations to provide self-concept and self-esteem stability (Brandtstädter & Greve, 1994; Diehl & Wahl, 2010; Greve & Wentura, 2003). For example, using data from an 8-year longitudinal study, Rothermund and Brandtstädter (2003) showed that as participants aged their evaluation of the typical old person (i.e., age stereotype) became increasingly more positive, suggesting that the earlier held age stereotype was gradually assimilated to support their self-view. This assimilative process became increasingly important with advancing age. Furthermore, Rothermund and Brandtstädter (2003) showed that participants who scored high on flexible goal adjustment were more capable in protecting their self-representations from negative age stereotypes than individuals who scored low on this variable. In summary, more systematic longitudinal studies are needed examining how and to what extent adaptive reorganizations of self-representations take place across the life span, and under what conditions such reorganizations are assimilative, accommodative, or immunizing in nature.

A fourth key issue builds on the dynamic and contextualized nature of self-representations and raises the question whether psychosocial interventions can be developed to optimize the adaptive functions of self-representations. For example, can findings from studies showing that certain self-concept structures are associated with more adaptive behavior be used to develop training programs so individuals can benefit in a deliberate manner from their self-representations. Few authors have addressed this issue to date. However, Showers and Zeigler-Hill (2007) pointed to several studies providing preliminary evidence that psychological counseling resulted in more integrated thinking about the self. Thus, there is some evidence that maladaptive structural organizations of self-representations may be amenable to psychosocial interventions. However, more systematic research is needed to develop evidence-based interventions.

A last key issue is related to the fact that research on the role of self-representations in the context of psychological well-being and development has almost exclusively been correlational in nature. Although, recent developments in assessing the role of self-representations via experience sampling and daily diary methods, in combination with the use of advanced multivariate statistical methods, has allowed researchers to get a better handle on the directionality of effects (Diehl & Hay, 2007; Zeigler-Hill & Showers, 2007), additional research is still needed to address issues of causality and underlying psychological mechanisms. For example, at this point fairly little is known about whether certain self-concept structures are causally related to certain health-compromising behaviors, such as rumination, prolonged self-doubt and self-criticism, or volatility in self-esteem. Knowledge about such behaviors, however, would be needed to address possible underlying psychological mechanisms and to elaborate possible pathways from behavior to physical and psychological health (Gruenewald, Kemeny, Aziz, & Fahey, 2004; Segerstrom & Roach, 2008). Thus, it would be ideal if intensive repeated measurement studies on the functions of self-representations would be complemented by laboratory studies that examine specific behaviors of individuals with identified self-concept structures in controlled situations, such as induced failure situations or specific induced mood states. Such studies, especially if they are conducted over a diverse age range or in a longitudinal fashion, hold the promise to elucidate the role of self-representations and related psychological mechanisms in a more conclusive way, and may help in the development of effective intervention approaches.

In conclusion, although self-concept development has been much more extensively studied for the age periods of childhood and adolescence (Harter, 2006), over the past two decades, research on the role of self-representations in adult development and aging has made great progress and it has become possible to draw a first outline of self-concept development across the life span. Overall, there is growing consensus among theorists and investigators alike that individuals' self-representations form a knowledge structure that is centrally implicated in adaptive and maladaptive development (Brandtstädter & Greve, 1994; Markus & Herzog, 1991). Future research will help us to further elucidate the role of self-representations as a dynamic and contextualized knowledge structure that integrates individuals' experiences across time and life stages and, hence, will inform us about their role as a fundamental building block of successful human development.

▩ ACKNOWLEDGMENT

The writing of this chapter and the presented research were supported by grant R01 AG21147 from the National Institute on Aging.

▩ REFERENCES

Angel, R. J., & Angel, J. L. (2006). Diversity and aging in the United States. In R. H. Binstock & L. K. George (Eds.), *Handbook of aging and the social sciences* (6th ed., pp. 94–110). San Diego, CA: Academic Press.

Arnett, J. J. (2004). *Emerging adulthood: The winding road from the late teens through the twenties.* New York: Oxford University Press.

Baltes, P. B. (1987). Theoretical propositions of life-span developmental psychology: On the dynamics between growth and decline. *Developmental Psychology, 23,* 611–626.

Baltes, P. B., Lindenberger, U., & Staudinger, U. M. (2006). Life span theory in developmental psychology. In W. Damon (Series Ed.) & R. M. Lerner (Vol. Ed.), *Handbook of child psychology: Vol. 1. Theoretical models of human development* (6th ed., pp. 569–664). New York: Wiley.

Barrett, K., Zahn-Waxler, C., & Cole, P. (1993). Avoiders versus amenders: Implications for the investigation of guilt and shame during toddlerhood? *Cognition and Emotion, 7,* 481–505.

Beeghly, M., & Cicchetti, D. (1994). Child maltreatment, attachment, and the self-system: Emergence of an internal state lexicon at high social risk. *Development and Psychopathology, 6,* 5–30.

Bigler, M., Neimeyer, G. J., & Brown, E. (2001). The divided self revisited: Effects of self-concept clarity and self-concept differentiation on psychological adjustment. *Journal of Social and Clinical Psychology, 20,* 396–415.

Biringen, Z. (2000). Emotional availability: Conceptualization and research findings. *American Journal of Orthopsychiatry, 70,* 104–114.

Block, J. (1961). Ego-identity, role variability, and adjustment. *Journal of Consulting and Clinical Psychology, 25,* 392–397.

Block, J. H., & Robins, R. W. (1993). A longitudinal study of consistency and change in self-esteem from early adolescence to early adulthood. *Child Development, 64,* 909–923.

Bowlby, J. (1988). *A secure base: Parent-child attachment and healthy human development.* New York: Basic Books.

Brandtstädter, J., & Greve, W. (1994). The aging self: Stabilizing and protective processes. *Developmental Review, 14,* 52–80.

Brandtstädter, J., & Lerner, R. M. (Eds.). (1999). *Action and development: Theory and research through the life span.* Thousand Oaks, CA: Sage.

Bretherton, I. (1993). From dialogue to internal working models: The co-construction of self in relationships. In C. A. Nelson (Ed.), *Minnesota Symposia on Child Psychology: Vol. 26. Memory and affect in development* (pp. 237–363). Hillsdale, NJ: Erlbaum.

Bretherton, I. (2000). Emotional availability: An attachment perspective. *Attachment and Human Development, 2,* 233–241.

Bretherton, I., Fritz, J., Zahn-Waxler, C., & Ridgeway, D. (1986). Learning to talk about emotions: A functionalist perspective. *Child Development, 57,* 529–548.

Bretherton, I., & Munholland, K. (1999). Internal working models in attachment relationships: A construct revisited. In J. Cassidy & P. Shaver (Eds.), *Handbook of attachment* (pp. 89–111). New York: Guilford Press.

Bumpass, L., & Lu, H. H. (2000). Trends in cohabitation and implications for children's family contexts in the United States. *Population Studies, 54,* 29–41.

Campbell, J. D., Assanand, S., & DiPaula, A. (2000). Structural features of the self-concept and adjustment. In A. Tesser, R. B. Felson, & J. M. Suls (Eds.), *Psychological perspectives on self and identity* (pp. 67–87). Washington, DC: American Psychological Association.

Campbell, J. D., Trapnell, P. D., Heine, S. J., Katz, I. M., Lavallee, L. F., & Lehman, D. R. (1996). Self-concept clarity: Measurement, personality correlates, and cultural boundaries. *Journal of Personality and Social Psychology, 70,* 141–156.

Carpenter, M., Nagell, K., & Tomasello, M. (1998). Social cognition, joint attention, and communicative competence from 9 to 15 months of age. *Monographs of the Society for Research in Child Development, 63*(4, Serial No. 255).

Carroll, J. J., & Steward, M. S. (1984). The role of cognitive development in children's understanding of their own feelings. *Child Development, 55*, 1486–1492.

Case, R. (1985). *Intellectual development: Birth to adulthood.* New York: Academic Press.

Case, R. (1992). *The mind's staircase.* Hillsdale, NJ: Erlbaum.

Caspi, A., & Roberts, B. W. (2001). Personality development across the life course: The argument for change and continuity. *Psychological Inquiry, 12*, 49–66.

Cassidy, J. (1988). Child-mother attachment and the self in 6-year-olds. *Child Development, 59*, 121–134.

Cooper, C. R., Jackson, J. F., Azmitia, M., Lopez, E., & Dunbar, N. (1995). Bridging students' multiple worlds: African American and Latino youth in academic outreach programs. In R. F. Marcias & R. G. Garcia-Ramos (Eds.), *Changing schools changing students: An anthology of research on language minorities* (pp. 211–234). Santa Barbara, CA: University of California Linguistic Minority Research Institute.

Cross, S., & Markus, H. (1991). Possible selves across the life span. *Human Development, 34*, 230–255.

Damon, W., & Hart, D. (1988). *Self-understanding in childhood and adolescence.* New York: Cambridge University Press.

Diehl, M. (1999). Self-development in adulthood and aging: The role of critical life events. In C. D. Ryff & V. W. Marshall (Eds.), *The self and society in aging processes* (pp. 150–183). New York: Springer Publishing.

Diehl, M. (2006). Development of self-representations in adulthood. In D. K. Mroczek & T. D. Little (Eds.), *Handbook of personality development* (pp. 373–398). Mahwah, NJ: Erlbaum.

Diehl, M., & Hay, E. L. (2007). Contextualized self-representations in adulthood. *Journal of Personality, 75*, 1255–1283.

Diehl, M., & Hay, E. L. (2010). Risk and resilience factors in coping with daily stress in adulthood: The role of age, self-concept incoherence, and personal control. *Developmental Psychology, 46*, 1132–1146.

Diehl, M., Hastings, C. T., & Stanton, J. M. (2001). Self-concept differentiation across the adult life span. *Psychology and Aging, 16*, 643–654.

Diehl, M., Jacobs, L., & Hastings, C. T. (2006). Temporal stability and authenticity of self-representations in adulthood. *Journal of Adult Development, 13*, 10–22.

Diehl, M., Owen, S. K., & Youngblade, L. M. (2004). Agency and communion attributes in adults' spontaneous self-representations. *International Journal of Behavioral Development, 28*, 1–15.

Diehl, M., & Wahl, H. W. (2010). Awareness of age-related change: Examination of a (mostly) unexplored concept. *Journal of Gerontology: Psychological Sciences and Social Sciences, 65B(3)*, 340–350.

Donahue, E. M., Robins, R. W., Roberts, B. W., & John, O. P. (1993). The divided self: Concurrent and longitudinal effects of psychological adjustment and social roles on self-concept differentiation. *Journal of Personality and Social Psychology, 64*, 834–846.

Donaldson, S. K., & Westerman, M. A. (1986). Development of children's understandings of ambivalence and causal theories of emotion. *Developmental Psychology, 22*, 655–662.

Eccles, J. P., & Midgley, C. (1989). State/environment fit: Developmentally appropriate classrooms for early adolescents. In R. Ames & C. Ames (Eds.), *Research on motivation in education* (Vol. 3, pp. 139–181). New York: Academic Press.

Elkind, D. (1967). Egocentrism in adolescence. *Child Development, 38*, 1025–1034.

English, T., & Chen, S. (2007). Culture and self-concept stability: Consistency across and within contexts among Asian Americans and European Americans. *Journal of Personality and Social Psychology, 93*, 478–490.

Epstein, S. (1973). The self-concept revisited or a theory of a theory. *American Psychologist, 28*, 405–416.

Epstein, S. (1991). Cognitive-experiential self-theory: Implications for developmental psychology. In M. Gunnar & L. A. Sroufe (Eds.), *Minnesota Symposium on Child Development: Vol. 23. Self-processes and development* (pp. 111–137). Hillsdale, NJ: Erlbaum.

Erikson, E. H. (1950). *Childhood and society.* New York: Norton.

Erikson, E. H. (1959). Identity and the life cycle. *Psychological Issues, 1*, 18–164.

Erikson, E. H. (1982). *The life cycle completed.* New York: Norton.

Fasig, L. G. (2000). Toddler's understanding of ownership: Implications for self-concept development. *Social Development, 9*, 370–382.

Filipp, S. H., & Klauer, T. (1986). Conceptions of self over the life span: Reflections on the dialectics of change. In M. M. Baltes & P. B. Baltes (Eds.), *The psychology of control and aging* (pp. 167–205). Hillsdale, NJ: Erlbaum.

Fingerman, K. L., Pitzer, L., Lefkowitz, E. S., Birditt, K. S., & Mroczek, D. (2008). Ambivalent relationship qualities between adults and their parents: Implications for the well-being of both parties. *Journal of Gerontology: Psychological Sciences and Social Sciences, 63B,* P362–P371.

Fischer, K. W. (1980). A theory of cognitive development: The control and construction of hierarchies of skills. *Psychological Review, 87,* 477–531.

Fischer, K. W., & Ayoub, C. (1994). Affective splitting and dissociation in normal and maltreated children: Developmental pathways for self in relationships. In D. Cicchetti & S. Toth (Eds.), *Rochester Symposium on Developmental Psychopathology: Vol. 5. Disorders and dysfunctions of the self* (pp. 149–222). Rochester, NY: University of Rochester Press.

Fischer, K. W., & Canfield, R. (1986). The ambiguity of stage and structure in behavior: Person and environment in the development of psychological structure. In I. Levin (Ed.), *Stage and structure: Reopening the debate* (pp. 246–267). New York: Plenum.

Fischer, K. W., Shaver, P., & Carnochan, P. (1990). How emotions develop and how they organize development. *Cognition and Emotion, 4,* 81–127.

Fivush, R. (1993). Emotional content of parent-child conversations about the past. In C. Nelson (Ed.), *Minnesota Symposia on Child Psychology: Vol. 23. Memory and affect in development* (pp. 39–77). Hillsdale, NJ: Erlbaum.

Fivush, R., & Haden, C. A. (Eds.). (2003). *Autobiographical memory and the construction of a narrative self: Developmental and cultural perspectives.* Mahwah, NJ: Erlbaum.

Fonagy, P. (2002). Understanding of mental states, mother-infant interaction, and the development of the self. In J. M. Maldonado-Duran (Ed.), *Infant and toddler mental health: Models of clinical intervention with infants and their families* (pp. 58–72). Washington, DC: American Psychiatric Publishing.

Frazier, L. D., Hooker, K., Johnson, P. M., & Kaus, C. R. (2000). Continuity and change in possible selves in later life: A 5-year longitudinal study. *Basic and Applied Social Psychology, 22,* 237–243.

Freund, A. M., & Smith, J. (1999a). Content and function of the self-definition in old and very old age. *Journal of Gerontology: Psychological Sciences and Social Sciences, 54B,* P55–P67.

Freund, A. M., & Smith, J. (1999b). Temporal stability of older persons' spontaneous self-definition. *Experimental Aging Research, 25,* 95–107.

Frey, K. S., & Ruble, D. N. (1985). What children say when the teacher is not around: Conflicting goals in social comparison and performance assessment in the classroom. *Journal of Personality and Social Psychology, 48,* 550–562.

George, L. K., & Okun, M. A. (1985). Self-concept content. In E. Palmore, E. W. Busse, G. L. Maddox, J. B. Nowlin, & I. C. Siegler (Eds.), *Normal aging III* (pp. 267–282). Durham, NC: Duke University Press.

Gollwitzer, P. M., Bayer, U., Scherer, M., & Seifert, A. E. (1999). A motivational-volitional perspective on identity development. In J. Brandtstädter & R. M. Lerner (Eds.), *Action and self-development: Theory and research through the life span* (pp. 283–314). Thousand Oaks, CA: Sage.

Graber, J. A. (Ed.). (1996). *Transitions through adolescence: Interpersonal domains and context.* Mahwah, NJ: Erlbaum.

Greve, W., & Wentura, D. (2003). Immunizing the self: Self-concept stabilization through reality-adaptive self-definitions. *Personality and Social Psychology Bulletin, 29,* 39–50.

Gruenewald, T. L., Kemeny, M. E., Aziz, N., & Fahey, J. L. (2004). Acute threat to the social self: Shame, social self-esteem, and cortisol activity. *Psychosomatic Medicine, 66,* 915–924.

Guisinger, S., & Blatt, S. (1994). Individuality and relatedness. *American Psychologist, 49,* 104–111.

Hart, D. (1988). The adolescent self-concept in social context. In D. K. Lapsley & F. C. Power (Eds.), *Self, ego, and identity* (pp. 71–90). New York: Springer-Verlag.

Harter, S. (1998). The development of self-representations. In W. Damon (Series Ed.) & N. Eisenberg (Vol. Ed.), *Handbook of child psychology: Vol. 3. Social, emotional, and personality development* (5th ed., pp. 553–617). New York: Wiley.

Harter, S. (1999). *The construction of the self: A developmental perspective.* New York: Guilford.

Harter, S. (2006). The self. In W. Damon, R. M. Lerner (Series Eds.) & N. Eisenberg (Vol. Ed.), *Handbook of child psychology: Vol. 3. Social, emotional, and personality development* (6th ed., pp. 505–570). Hoboken, NJ: Wiley.

Harter, S., Bresnick, S., Bouchey, H. A., & Whitesell, N. R. (1997). The development of multiple role-related selves during adolescence. *Development and Psychopathology, 9,* 835–854.

Harter, S., Low, S., & Whitesell, N. R. (2003). What have we learned from Columbine: The impact of the self-system on suicidal and violent ideation among adolescents. *Journal of Youth Violence, 2,* 3–26.

Harter, S., Marold, D. B., Whitesell, N. R., & Cobbs, G. (1996). A model of the effects of parent and peer support on adolescent false self behavior. *Child Development, 55,* 1969–1982.

Harter, S., & Monsour, A. (1992). Developmental analysis of conflict caused by opposing attributes in the adolescent self-portrait. *Developmental Psychology, 28,* 251–260.

Heckhausen, J., Dixon, R. A., & Baltes, P. B. (1989). Gains and losses in development throughout adulthood as perceived by different adult age groups. *Developmental Psychology, 25,* 109–121.

Helson, R., Mitchell, V., & Moane, G. (1984). Personality and patterns of adherence and nonadherence to the social clock. *Journal of Personality and Social Psychology, 46,* 1079–1096.

Higgins, E. T. (1991). Development of self-regulatory and self-evaluative processes: Costs, benefits, and tradeoffs. In M. R. Gunnar & L. A. Sroufe (Eds.), *Minnesota Symposia on Child Development: Vol. 23. Self processes and development* (pp. 125–166). Hillsdale, NJ: Erlbaum.

Higgins, E. T. (1996). The "self digest": Self-knowledge serving self-regulatory functions. *Journal of Personality and Social Psychology, 71,* 1062–1083.

Hooker, K. (1999). Possible selves in adulthood: Incorporating teleonomic relevance into studies of the self. In T. Hess & F. Blanchard-Fields (Eds.), *Social cognition and aging* (pp. 97–121). San Diego, CA: Academic Press.

Hooker, K., & Kaus, C. R. (1994). Health-related possible selves in young and middle adulthood. *Psychology and Aging, 9,* 126–133.

Hoppmann, C. A., Gerstorf, D., Smith, J., & Klumb, P. L. (2007). Linking possible selves and behavior: Do domain-specific hopes and fears translate into daily activities in very old age? *Journal of Gerontology: Psychological Sciences and Social Sciences, 62B,* P104–P111.

James, W. (1890/1981). *The principles of psychology* (Vol. 1). Cambridge, MA: Harvard University Press. (Original work published in 1890).

Kernis, M. H., & Goldman, B. M. (2003). Stability and variability in self-concept and self-esteem. In M. R. Leary & J. P. Tangney (Eds.), *Handbook of self and identity* (pp. 106–127). New York: Guilford.

Kling, K. C., Hyde, J. S., Showers, C. J., & Buswell, B. N. (1999). Gender differences in self-esteem: A meta-analysis. *Psychological Bulletin, 125,* 470–500.

Kling, K. C., Ryff, C. D., & Essex, M. J. (1997). Adaptive changes in the self-concept during a life transition. *Personality and Social Psychology Bulletin, 23,* 981–990.

Koch, E. J., & Shepperd, J. A. (2004). Is self-complexity linked to better coping? A review of the literature. *Journal of Personality, 72,* 727–760.

Kohut, H. (1977). *The restoration of the self.* New York: International Universities Press.

Kroger, J. (2000). *Identity development: Adolescence through adulthood.* Thousand Oaks, CA: Sage.

Labouvie-Vief, G., Chiodo, L.M., Goguen, L.A., Diehl, M., & Orwoll, L. (1995). Representations of self across the life span. *Psychology and Aging, 10,* 404–415.

Lamborn, S. D., Mounts, N. S., Steinberg, L., & Dornbush, S. M. (1991). Patterns of competence and adjustment among adolescents from authoritative, authoritarian, indulgent and neglectful families. *Child Development, 62,* 1049–1065.

Lecky, P. (1945). *Self-consistency: A theory of personality.* New York: Anchor Books.

Lewis, M. (2000). Self-conscious emotions: Embarrassment, pride, shame, and guilt. In M. Lewis & J. Haviland-Jones (Eds.), *Handbook of emotions* (pp. 563–573). New York: Guilford.

Lewis, M., & Brooks-Gunn, J. (1979). *Social cognition and the acquisition of self.* New York: Plenum.

Linville, P. W. (1987). Self-complexity as a cognitive buffer against stress-related illness and depression. *Journal of Personality and Social Psychology, 52,* 663–676.

Markus, H. R., & Herzog, R. A. (1991). The role of the self-concept in aging. In K. W. Schaie (Ed.), *Annual review of gerontology and geriatrics* (Vol. 11, pp. 110–143). New York: Springer.

Markus, H. R., & Kitayama, S. (1991). Culture and the self: Implications for cognition, emotion, and motivation. *Psychological Review, 98,* 224–253.

Markus, H. R., & Nurius, P. (1986). Possible selves. *American Psychologist, 41,* 954–969.

Markus, H. R., & Wurf, E. (1987). The dynamic self-concept: A social psychological perspective. *Annual Review of Psychology, 38,* 299–337.

McCrae, R. R., & Costa, P. T., Jr. (1988). Age, personality, and the spontaneous self-concept. *Journal of Gerontology, 43,* S177–S185.

McCrae, R. R., & Costa, P. T., Jr. (2003). *Personality in adulthood: A five-factor theory perspective* (2nd ed.). New York: Guilford.

Morfei, M. Z., Hooker, K., Fiese, B. H., & Cordeiro, A. M. (2001). Continuity and change in parenting possible selves: A longitudinal follow-up. *Basic and Applied Social Psychology, 23,* 217–223.

Moretti, M. M., & Higgins, E. T. (1990). The development of self-esteem vulnerabilities: Social and cognitive factors in developmental psychopathology. In R. J. Sternberg & J. Kolligian (Eds.), *Competence considered* (pp. 286–314). New Haven, CT: Yale University Press.

Mortimer, J. T., Finch, M. D., & D. Kumka (1982). Persistence and change in development: The multidimensional self-concept. In P. B. Baltes & O. G. Brim, Jr. (Eds.), *Life-span development and behavior* (Vol. 4, pp. 263–313). New York: Academic Press.

Mueller, J. H., Wonderlich, S., & Dugan, K. (1986). Self-referent processing of age-specific material. *Psychology and Aging, 1,* 293–299.

Nelson, K. (1993). Events, narratives, memory: What develops. In C.A. Nelson (Ed.), *Minnesota Symposia on Child Psychology: Vol. 26. Memory and affect in development* (pp. 1–24). Hillsdale, NJ: Erlbaum.

Nolen-Hoeksema, S., & Girgus, J. S. (1994). The emergence of gender differences in depression during adolescence. *Psychological Bulletin, 115,* 424–443.

O'Malley, P., & Bachman, J. (1983). Self-esteem: Change and stability between 13 and 23. *Developmental Psychology, 19,* 257–268.

Piaget, J. (1960). *The psychology of intelligence.* Patterson , NJ: Littlefield-Adams.

Pomerantz, E. V., Ruble, D. N., Frey, K. S., & Greulich, F. (1995). Meeting goals and confronting conflict: Children's changing perceptions of social comparison. *Child Development, 66,* 723–738.

Rafaeli-Mor, E., & Steinberg, J. (2002). Self-complexity and well-being: A review and research synthesis. *Personality and Social Psychology Review, 6,* 31–58.

Roberts, A., Seidman, E., & Pedersen, S. (2000). Perceived family and peer transactions and self-esteem among urban early adolescents. *Journal of Early Adolescence, 20,* 68–92.

Rogers, C. (1959). A theory of therapy, personality, and interpersonal relationships, as developed in the client-centered framework. In S. Koch (Ed.), *Psychology: A study of science. Vol. 3. Formulations of the person and the social context* (pp. 184–256). New York: McGraw-Hill.

Rosenberg, M. (1986). Self-concept from middle childhood through adolescence. In J. Suls & A. G. Greenwald (Eds.), *Psychological perspectives on the self* (Vol. 3, pp. 107–135). Hillsdale, NJ: Erlbaum.

Rothermund, K., & Brandtstädter, J. (2003). Age stereotypes and self-views in later life: Evaluating rival assumptions. *International Journal of Behavioral Development, 27,* 549–554.

Rothermund, K., & Meiniger, C. (2004). Stress-buffering effects of self-complexity: Reduced affective spillover or self-regulatory processes? *Self and Identity, 3,* 263–281.

Ruble, D. N., & Frey, K. S. (1991). Changing patterns of comparative behavior as skills are acquired: A functional model of self-evaluation. In J. Suls & T. A. Wills (Eds.), *Social comparison: Contemporary theory and research* (pp. 70–112). Hillsdale, NJ: Erlbaum.

Ryff, C. D. (1991). Possible selves in adulthood and old age: A tale of shifting horizons. *Psychology and Aging, 6,* 286–295.

Ryff, C. D., Lee, Y. H., Essex, M. J., & Schmutte, P. S. (1994). My children and me: Midlife evaluations of grown children and of self. *Psychology and Aging, 9,* 195–205.

Ryff, C. D., & Seltzer, M. M. (Eds.). (1996). *The parental experience in midlife.* Chicago, IL: University of Chicago Press.

Savin-Williams, R. C., & Demo, D. H. (1984). Developmental change and stability in adolescent self-concept. *Developmental Psychology, 20,* 1100–1110.

Segerstrom, S. C., & Roach, A. R. (2008). On the physical health benefits of self-enhancement. In E. C. Chang (Eds.), *Self-criticism and self-enhancement: Theory, research, and clinical implications* (pp. 37–54). Washington, DC: American Psychological Association.

Selman, R. L. (1980). *The growth of interpersonal understanding.* New York: Academic Press.

Showers, C. J. (1992). Compartmentalization of positive and negative self-knowledge: Keeping bad apples out of the bunch. *Journal of Personality and Social Psychology, 62,* 1036–1049.

Showers, C. J., Abramson, L. Y., & Hogan, M. E. (1998). The dynamic self: How the content and structure of the self-concept change with mood. *Journal of Personality and Social Psychology, 75,* 478–493.

Showers, C. J., & Kling, K. C. (1996). Organization of self-knowledge: Implications for recovery from sad mood. *Journal of Personality and Social Psychology, 70,* 578–590.

Showers, C. J., & Ryff, C. D. (1996). Self-differentiation and well-being in a life transition. *Personality and Social Psychology Bulletin, 22,* 448–460.

Showers, C. J., & Zeigler-Hill, V. (2003). Organization of self-knowledge: Features, functions, and flexibility. In M. R. Leary & J. P. Tangney (Eds.), *Handbook of self and identity* (pp. 47–67). New York: Guilford.

Showers, C. J., & Zeigler-Hill, V. (2007). Compartmentalization and integration: The evaluative organization of contextualized selves. *Journal of Personality, 75,* 1181–1204.

Shulman, S., Feldman, B., Blatt, S. J., Cohen, O., & Mahler, A. (2005). Emerging adulthood: Age-related tasks and underlying self processes. *Journal of Adolescent Research, 20,* 577–603.

Siegler, R. S. (1991). *Children's thinking* (2nd ed.). Englewood Cliffs, NJ: Prentice-Hall.

Smith, J., & Freund, A. M. (2002). The dynamics of possible selves in old age. *Journal of Gerontology: Psychological Sciences and Social Sciences, 57B,* P492–P500.

Smollar, J., & Youniss, J. (1985). Adolescent self-concept development. In R. L. Leahy (Ed.), *The development of self* (pp. 247–266). New York: Academic Press.

Suls, J., & Sanders, G. (1982). Self-evaluation via social comparison: A developmental analysis. In L. Wheeler (Ed.), *Review of personality and social psychology* (Vol. 3, pp. 67–89). Beverly Hills, CA: Sage.

Thompson, R. A. (1999). Early attachment and later development. In J. Cassidy & P. R. Shaver (Eds.), *Handbook of attachment: Theory, research, and clinical applications* (pp.265–286). New York: Guilford.

Thompson, R. A. (2006). The development of the person: Social understanding, relationships, conscience, self. In W. Damon, R. M. Lerner (Series Eds.) & N. Eisenberg (Vol. Ed.), *Handbook of child psychology: Vol. 3. Social, emotional, and personality development* (6th ed., pp. 24–98). Hoboken, NJ: Wiley.

Toth, S. L., Cicchetti, D., Macfie, J., & Emde, R. N. (1997). Representations of self and others in the narratives of neglected, physically abused, and sexually abused preschoolers. *Development and Psychopathology, 9,* 781–796.

Troll, L. E., & Skaff, M. M. (1997). Perceived continuity of self in very old age. *Psychology and Aging, 12,* 162–169.

Usmiani, S., & Daniluk, J. (1997). Mothers and their adolescent daughters: Relationship between self-esteem, gender role identity, and body image. *Journal of Youth and Adolescence, 26,* 45–62.

Whitbourne, S. K., & Connolly, L. A. (1999). The developing self in midlife. In S. L. Willis & J. D. Reid (Eds.), *Life in the middle: Psychological and social development in middle age* (pp. 25–45). San Diego, CA: Academic Press.

Wigfield, A., Eccles, J. S., MacIver, D., Reuman, D. A., & Midgley, C. (1991). Transitions during early adolescence: Changes in children's domain-specific self-perceptions and general self-esteem across the transition to junior high school. *Developmental Psychology, 27,* 552–565.

Williams, J. M., & Currie, C. (2000). Self-esteem and physical development in early adolescence: Pubertal timing and body image. *Journal of Early Adolescence, 20,* 129–149.

Zeigler-Hill, V., & Showers, C. J. (2007). Self-structure and self-esteem stability: The hidden vulnerability of compartmentalization. *Personality and Social Psychology Bulletin, 33,* 143–159.

TECHNOLOGICAL INFLUENCES ON SOCIAL TIES ACROSS THE LIFE SPAN

25

Shelia R. Cotten, Brandi M. McCullough, and Rebecca G. Adams

INTRODUCTION

Keeping in contact with our friends and family members, which is vital for relationship maintenance, has never been easier. We can telephone, text, e-mail, instant message, comment on their Facebook wall or blog, and so forth. We know who is calling us and we can monitor the locations of those with whom we have network ties and their activities based upon their status updates on social networking sites (SNSs) and Twitter. The range of ways that we can communicate and maintain contact with our social ties has never been greater.

Over the past decade, the range of information and communication technologies (ICTs) available and people's use of them have changed dramatically. The purpose of this chapter is to synthesize the current literature on the range of ICTs that have proliferated in the past decade, examine how these ICTs vary in use across life-span groups, discuss how they are used to help individuals maintain social ties, and note areas where further research is needed. In so doing, we discuss the theoretical challenges of studying this topic, describe the range of ICTs now in use, and provide examples of research on how people of different ages use technology to maintain social ties.

We focus on ICTs as they are used most often by individuals and how they assist individuals in maintaining and enhancing their social relationships. Although the Internet has been around for 40 years and the computer for several decades longer, in the past decade or so there have been dramatic increases in a range of applications that utilize computer or Internet technologies. For instance, blogs came into existence in 1997, MySpace was created in 2003, Facebook began in 2004, and Twitter was initiated in 2006. As of 2008, 74% of households had computers and 91% of adults reported using e-mail. In 2009, 85% of adults and 75% of those between 12 and 17 years of age used mobile phones. All of these ICTs and related applications greatly enhance the ability to communicate with others and to maintain social ties. As will be discussed later in this chapter, however, their use often varies across life span groups.

KEY IDEAS IN STUDYING ICTS AND RELATIONSHIPS

Understanding technological influences on social ties across the life span is particularly challenging in the context of rapid technological and social change. Throughout the 1990s and early 2000s, researchers debated whether it was possible to form or at least to maintain "real" relationships through online interaction. Now the use of the Internet and other ICTs to form and maintain social relationships is taken for granted and the definitions of terms for various types of social ties terms have evolved. For example, the word "friend" now has different meanings given the proliferation of SNSs. Although "friends" on SNSs are often those with whom participants have strong social ties, they are increasingly casual acquaintances or friends of friends whom individuals have rarely if ever met (i.e., similar to what Granovetter [1973] called "weak ties"). Fingerman (2009) coined the term "consequential strangers" to refer to the myriad casual connections that individuals in today's society now have, some of which are a direct result of ICT use. These consequential strangers have a variety of types of impact on our lives and our relationships, in ways that we often do not even consider. The terms "friend," "family member," "coworker," "romantic partner," and "neighbor" no longer capture all possible types of social ties and knowing how far one person lives from his or her relationship partner is no longer a good predictor of how frequently they interact. The use of ICTs allows individuals to mitigate distance and to be in constant interaction or at least to be continuously available (Baron, 2008).

A Framework for Studying ICTs and Relationships

Adams and Stevenson (2004) introduced a synthetic dynamic framework for the study of a lifetime of relationships mediated by technology based on four social theories, including two that address aging (i.e., individual development and life course theories) and two that address group development and change (i.e., family development and network change theories). This synthetic model was developed to guide and encourage studies designed to answer the questions: "'How do changes in the life course and developmental stages of individuals affect their use of technology?' and 'How, in turn, does the use of this technology change the structure and development of individuals?' (p. 383)." The model distinguishes between the sociological and psychological aspects of age (Blieszner & Adams, 1992) and between individual change and group change and, in their chapter, Adams and Stevenson outline research questions accordingly.

Although as is illustrated by the examples of studies described in the remainder of this chapter, research on how people of different ages use technologies to mediate their social ties has become more plentiful since Adams and Stevenson developed this synthetic model and outlined some research questions derived from it, most of this recent research is not designed to distinguish between the effects of the sociological and psychological aspects of aging or between individual change and changes to groups. Furthermore, because cohorts defined by their access to technological innovations span shorter time periods than they did previously (Adams, 1998), developmental differences between adjacent cohorts are not as large as they once were and the methodological challenge of separating out age, period, and cohort effects is even greater than in the past. Often by the time a carefully designed study has been conceived and executed, the technological context has altered and a new cohort has been defined. So although the framework Adams and Stevenson outlined in 2004 raises important and interesting theoretical questions, it is not surprising that apparently no one has developed studies inspired by it because of the practical challenges doing so would pose.

At the time Adams and Stevenson (2004) developed this model, they attributed the relative lack of theoretically driven scholarship on how people of different ages use technologies to mediate their social ties, not only to the lack of the application of dynamic theories of aging and group development and change, but also to the state of theory on the formation and maintenance of social relationships. They describe how despite the recognition that intimacy can exist at a distance (e.g., Litwak & Szelenyi, 1969; Rosenmayr, 1977), some interest in communities based on beliefs and interests rather than on shared territory (e.g., Craven & Wellman, 1974; Effrat, 1974; Webber, 1973), and some interest in long-distance and virtual relationships (e.g., Cuba & Hummon, 1993; Rohlfing, 1995), most quantitative and qualitative research on social ties was based on the assumption that they were formed and maintained primarily, if not exclusively, through face-to-face interaction. From the perspective of these early personal relationship theories, the main questions were not how technology supported relationship development or supplemented face-to-face interaction, but whether it was possible for relationships to be formed and maintained without the latter and how inferior computer-mediated communication was in comparison with it (Adams, 1998).

As of this writing, scholars are beginning to revisit theories and concepts and to revise them to reflect current technological possibilities for long-distance relationships. For example, as Johnson, Haigh, Craig, and Becker (2009, p. 631) observe, "previous research on relational closeness has either presupposed or privileged face-to-face contact (e.g., Berscheid, Snyder, & Omoto, 1989) or has not distinguished between long-distance and geographically-close relationships (e.g., Fehr, 2004; Monsour, 1992)." In their research, they explore the concept of relational closeness by comparing how geographically close and long-distance friends define closeness in their relationships and assess prior methods of defining and measuring relational closeness in light of these differences.

Similarly, in another reconsideration of an existing concept in light of recent technological developments, Quan-Haase and Wellman (2004) discuss the concept of social capital. They point out that there are two complementary uses of the "social capital" concept: social contact and civic engagement. Both of these uses of the term are relevant to our understanding of personal relationships, the first as a direct measure of relationship process and the second as an indicator of opportunities to develop social ties. In a similar vein, Shah, Kwak, and Holbert (2001) explore the relationship between Internet use and the individual-level production of social capital. Although the size of associations they report is generally small, their data suggest that informational uses of the Internet are positively related to individual differences in the production of social capital, whereas social-recreational uses are negatively related to these civic indicators. Their research thus suggests that social-recreational use of the Internet might lead to fewer opportunities to establish new social ties through civic engagement. These studies represent just a few of those adding to our theoretical understanding of how technology is changing not only personal relationships but the relevant theories and concepts useful in studying them.

Although some early studies examining the social impacts of Internet use reported negative effects on various aspects of relationships and well-being, such as increased loneliness and social isolation, Internet addiction, stress, and depression (Griffiths, 1999; Kandel, 1998; Kraut et al., 1998; Nie & Erbring, 2000; Scherer, 1996) and, as recently as 2005, Nie and colleagues continued to suggest that the use of ICTs was associated with declines in social interaction and engagement, the majority of more recent research reveals positive social effects. These studies show that use of the Internet decreases loneliness, feelings of isolation, and depression among individuals by allowing them to seek new relationships or continue existing relationships (Cotten, 2008; Morgan & Cotten, 2003; Parks & Floyd, 1996). Some of this change from negative to positive perspectives and findings is probably because technology is less mediated now than it was in the recent past. Now that ICTs do not restrict users to communication mainly by typed text, richer and more complex communication is possible and computer-mediated exchanges are more similar to face-to-face ones.

Weaknesses in Existing Literature on ICTs and Relationships

The dynamic and dramatic nature of these technology developments over the past decade has resulted in a discrepancy between the rate of social change and the amount of time needed to produce scholarship. In particular, lags exist in research examining the impacts of particular technologies, the effects of technology on certain types of relationships, and oftentimes reliance on small studies and atheoretical research designs to study relevant phenomena quickly before they evolve into new forms or cease their current functions. As noted earlier, weaknesses also exist in three specific areas: (1) an overemphasis on the importance of face-to-face contact for maintaining social relationships; (2) a lack of a detailed examination of how the interrelationships among geographical proximity, emotional closeness, and ICT usage help maintain relationships; and (3) an abundance of studies focusing on the use of ICTs to enhance social capital, without clear conceptualization and operationalization of social capital. Finally, we note that the majority of work in this area examining differences across the life span in ICT usage has been primarily descriptive in nature and has focused on young adults and adults. Although the Pew Internet & American Life Project reports are common standards for noting the latest usage statistics, they are almost exclusively descriptive in nature and they often do not include youth, especially those younger than 12 years of age, in their surveys. Although it is important to know the percentages of different age groups that use specific ICTs, this does not help us to determine the specific processes through which ICT usage impacts social relationships and network ties. Further explanatory research in this area is clearly warranted.

We turn now to a discussion of the range of ICTs currently available and used in significant numbers by different groups across the life span. In this section, we note key differences in usage by different age groups.

RANGE OF ICTs

There is no doubt that the use of technology, and ICTs more specifically, has resulted in a transformation in our society. Adams and Stevenson (2004) outlined the developments in transportation and communication technologies during the past 200 years, describing how the barriers to the formation and maintenance of social ties had gradually been lowered, first with the development of the Pony Express, the postal system, the telegraph, and telephones; then with the invention of steamships, locomotives, automobiles, and airplanes; and finally with the growth of the Internet. The rate of change in technologies, specifically ICTs, and individuals using them has escalated in the past decade.

Individuals are using ICTs to find information and keep in contact with others in ways that were not envisioned even a few decades ago. Over the past 40 years since the Internet began in 1969 as ARPANET, there has been explosive growth in individuals using computers, the Internet, and associated technologies (Castells, 2001). Although individuals often use the terms Internet and World Wide Web (WWW) interchangeably, they are actually two different entities. The Internet is the large infrastructure that contains the WWW and allows individuals to connect to the WWW, whereas the WWW is the compilation of all the Web sites around the world taken together.

COMPUTERS AND THE INTERNET

In 1985, less than 9% of U.S. households had computers; by 2001, this percentage had escalated to 57%. As of 2008, 73.7% of individuals reported using computers (Hale, Cotten, Drentea, & Goldner, 2010). Among youth aged between 8 and 18 years, 93% reported having a computer at home (Rideout, Foehr, & Roberts, 2010). Laptops are increasing in use, particularly among youth, with netbooks (a type of mini-laptop) surging in popularity in 2009. A third of youth aged 8–18 years report owning their own laptop, with the percentages rising among older youth age groups (Rideout et al., 2010). Though individuals use computers for a variety of purposes, accessing the Internet is a main reason they do so.

The Internet was originally invented to facilitate the exchange of information between government scientists in the United States during the Cold War; however, it is now used extensively by a majority of individuals in the United States. Recent reports indicate that 74% of individuals have "gone online" and this rate is even higher among younger aged persons (Table 25.1; Jones & Fox, 2009). More than 80% of those aged 44 years or younger report going online. Approximately 84% of those between the ages of 8 and 18 years report having Internet access at home (vs. only 59% having high-speed wireless Internet access at home), whereas 70% of those between the ages of 8 and 18 years go online on a typical day (Rideout et al., 2010).

TABLE 25.1

Age Group[a]	ICT Usage (%)				
	Go Online	E-mail[b]	Instant Messaging[b]	Social Networking Sites[b]	Read Blogs[b]
12–17	93	73	68	65	49
18–32	87	94	59	67	43
33–44	82	93	38	36	34
45–54	79	90	28	20	27
55–63	70	90	23	29	25
64–72	56	91	25	11	23
73+	31	79	18	4	15

ICT Usage By Age Group

[a] To date, Pew has not collected data on ICT usage among those younger than 12 years of age.
[b] Percentages are for those who go online only.
ICT, information and communication technology.
Source: Data from Jones & Fox, 2009; www.pewinternet.org

Over 90% of those 12–17 and 18–29 years old go online (Lenhart, Purcell, Smith, & Zickuhr, 2010). Children 10 years old and younger spend less time using computers than do older-aged youth (Rideout et al., 2010). For many, "the Internet is a central and indispensable element" in their lives (Lenhart et al., 2010, p. 5).

ICT APPLICATIONS

Applications that allow individuals to communicate online have seen tremendous growth in popularity and usage. Research (Jones & Fox, 2009; Morgan & Cotten, 2003; Palfrey & Gasser, 2008) shows that communication is a main use of the Internet. An asynchronous form of communication, e-mail has been used extensively by individuals to maintain contact with others and disseminate information. Among Internet users, 91% of adults in the United States report using e-mail (Jones & Fox, 2009). Individuals aged 12–17 years are least likely to use e-mail (see Table 25.1). Youth aged 8–18 years spend fewer than 10 minutes per day, and children aged 8–10 years spend only 2 minutes per day using e-mail (Rideout et al., 2010).

In contrast to e-mail, instant messaging (IM), another form of electronic communication, is synchronous in that individuals involved in the exchanges are both online and present simultaneously during the exchanges. Thus, the textual exchanges occur more in "real time," in contrast to someone retrieving their e-mail and at some later time deciding to respond to it. IM operates within other software programs as a feature of those programs, allows individuals to see which of their network members are online, and affords users the opportunity to send private messages instantly from one person to another via computer. Fewer than 40% of online adults report using IM (Jones & Fox, 2009). Sixty-eight percent of online teens aged 12–17 years report using IM; however, fewer than 25% of those online aged 64 years and older use IM (see Table 25.1; Jones & Fox, 2009). Among youth 11–18 years old, most report spending about 14 minutes per day using IM, although the levels among those 8–10 years old are much lower (Rideout et al., 2010). Youth use IM more frequently, though increasingly this use is integrated in SNSs and other ICTs.

A variety of technology applications besides e-mail and IM, such as social networking and video-sharing sites, online communities, Skype, virtual worlds, dating sites, blogs, and Twitter (a micro-blogging platform), have been developed and seen record growth in recent years. One of the most discussed ICTs in recent years has been SNSs. According to recent research, approximately 35% of those who are online use SNSs. Usage levels, however, are much higher among those aged 32 years and younger (see Table 25.1; Jones & Fox, 2009). Almost three fourths of online teens and those aged 18–29 years report using SNSs, whereas only 47% of online adults report using these sites (Lenhart et al., 2010). In a recent study of those aged 8–18 years, 18% of those 8–10 years old, 42% of those 11–14 years old, and 53% of those 15–18 years old reported using SNSs on a typical day; although SNS usage represents the largest proportion of recreational time spent online among these groups, average time spent for each group was fewer than 30 minutes per day (Rideout et al., 2010).

Although there are hundreds of SNSs and more being created every day, the two that have received the most attention and the most research to date are MySpace and Facebook. MySpace started as a way for bands and musicians to expand their networks of appeal. Although both Facebook and MySpace were originally developed for younger age cohorts, both have now proliferated across the age spectrum. In particular, the fastest growing group going on Facebook currently is individuals aged 55 years and older (Inside Facebook, 2009a). The median age of Facebook users is 33 years (Fox, Zickuhr, & Smith, 2009).

MySpace was founded in 2003 and Facebook was initiated a year later. Both SNSs allow users to make connections with others online, post materials on the sites, and easily communicate with their friends. MySpace saw tremendous growth in its early years; however, in 2008 Facebook became the most popular SNS when measured by the number of members (Inside Facebook, 2009a). As of late 2009, there were 98.1 million Facebook users, the slight majority of whom were females (56.1%; Inside Facebook, 2009b), and Facebook was the most often used SNS among online adults (Lenhart et al., 2010). Although almost one third of individuals living in the United States are Facebook participants, there are still those nonusers who are either disenfranchised, essentially lacking Internet access, or are conscientious objectors (Boyd, 2007). At any rate, SNSs have had a profound impact on civil society in that regardless of whether they participate, almost everyone knows about them (Boyd, 2007).

Although not as interactive as SNSs, video-sharing sites, such as YouTube and Hulu, have also become popular in recent years. These sites allow individuals to upload/post, comment, and rate videos. Users typically have to register on the sites before they can post to the site. According to data from comScore (comScore, 2010), 86.5% of Internet users in the United States viewed videos online in December 2009, Google accounted for almost 40% of videos watched (and this was a result of them owning YouTube), and the average length of videos watched was 4 minutes.

In 2009, video sharing was more popular among adults than was SNS usage. Sixty-two percent of adults watched videos online compared with only 46% who used SNSs (Madden, 2009). Almost all young adults (18–29 years old) watch content on these sites, with more than a third doing so on a typical day. Among those 8–18 years old, 81% report that they have watch a video online at some point; however, the average time spent on a typical day for this activity is low—fewer than 20 minutes (Rideout et al., 2010). It is anticipated that online video sharing and video viewing will continue to increase as more and more content is becoming available for viewing via these sites and others.

Blogs are another type of ICT that facilitate the exchange of information, opinions, and communication in today's society. John Barger coined the term web log in 1997 to refer to an online Web site where individuals could post links and comments about things (Blood, 2000). Web logs, referred to as blogs since 1999, were originally likely to be primarily a list of links with commentary and personal asides by individuals (Blood, 2000). They have now become much more interactive and journalistic in design and are often updated frequently by the blog owner and those who read the blog. Blogs became more common once *Blogger* was released in 1999, as this free form interface allowed users to create blogs without having to know how to program a webpage (www.blogger.com). There are over 100 million blogs and over 100,000 new blogs being created each day around the world (Sifry, 2007; Technorati, 2009). Approximately a third of online adults report reading blogs, but far fewer (11%) report creating them (Jones & Fox, 2009). About 10% of adults who use the Internet maintain a blog or online journal (Lenhart et al., 2010). Although the differences between age groups are not equal, there is a monotonic decrease in reports of reading and creating blogs across cohorts as they age. Among students in 7th–12th grade, 49% report having read a blog, but only 28% have written a blog (Rideout et al., 2010). Recent data suggest that the rates of teens and young adults who blog has been declining since 2006, yet has been increasing among older age groups (Lenhart et al., 2010).

A specific form of blogging, known as micro-blogging, has developed in the past few years. Microblogs allow users to post short postings and encourages users to post frequently. Twitter, the most recognized and most discussed of the microblogs, began in 2006 but the number of its users increased dramatically in 2008–2009 (www.twitter.com). The developers of Twitter began the site as a way for people to stay in touch with others but it is currently more often used for professional purposes (www.twitter.com; Miller, 2009). Individuals can post messages of up to 140 characters in length, which are known as tweets; they can "follow" others and be "followed" by others who are on Twitter. Following allows participants to see the micro-blog postings of those whom they follow. In essence, Twitter allows for the creation of a social network of people who are interested in hearing what individuals think is useful or interesting to post. Some would suggest that this occurs in almost real time, as new tweets are constantly posted and available to view. Twitter can be accessed by the main Web site or through a variety of applications designed to link tweets with posts on SNSs, blogs, and so on.

When Twitter began, many people simply reported what they were doing rather than posting specific information that others might find useful. The types of posts are much more diverse currently and many are using Twitter to promote themselves or their organizations and to relay information that they find useful in specific domains (Miller, 2009).

Unlike SNSs, Twitter initially became popular with middle-aged groups. Individuals aged between 35 and 54 years represented the largest group on Twitter as of July 2009. However, a Pew Internet & American Life Project report (Lenhart et al., 2010) found that those 18–24 years old were more likely to report using Twitter or another status-updating site than were older age groups. This finding is likely due to the question wording, as they asked about Twitter or "another status-updating site"; youth are more likely to use Facebook and other SNSs as status-updating sites, thus inflating this response level. ComScore reports that those aged between 12 and 17 years and between 18 and 24 years are the fastest growing age groups on Twitter (Lipsman, 2009), which is in contrast to recent media reports that suggest that "teens don't tweet" (Miller, 2009). September 2009 data reveal that only 8% of 12–17 years old report using Twitter, with use being higher as youth age and among females (Lenhart et al., 2010). Growth in Twitter usage has been dramatic in the past year: usage has increased 27-fold (Lipsman, 2009). Fox et al. (2009) report that 19% of individuals in the United States use Twitter or another status-updating service currently, with SNS users, Internet-enabled mobile phone users, and individuals younger than 44 years leading the growth in status updating.

An additional outgrowth of the increased use of the Internet is the proliferation of online dating sites. Although personal advertisements have been in existence for hundreds of years, online personals and dating sites expedite meetings for dating and mating. There are an estimated 1,400 online dating sites operating in North America (Homer, 2009). A 2006 Pew Internet & American Life Project report (Madden & Lenhart, 2006) found that almost a third of U.S. adults reported that they knew someone who had used a dating Web site at some point, and 15% reported knowing someone who had been in a long-term relationship with someone they met online.

Madden and Lenhart (2006) also reported that 11% of all Internet users and 37% of singles who are looking for someone to date have utilized online dating sites. New research finds that individuals who have known others who have used online dating sites are more likely to use them to find potential mates (Sautter, Tippett, & Morgan, 2010). This same study reports that those who are Internet daters are more likely to have higher computer literacy, have others in their social networks who have used online dating sites, and view Internet dating in more positive terms than are single Internet users in general (Sautter et al., 2010).

Online dating sites typically request that individuals post the following information describing themselves and what they desire in a dating or mating partner when completing a profile: location, age, race, gender, physical characteristics, smoking and drinking status, and other descriptive information about themselves or desired others (Fiore, 2004). These sites also typically include a messaging system so that members can contact others who appear to match their desired qualifications.

Online mating and dating sites are often different than other types of SNSs in that they typically do not have common forums where individuals can make posts for large numbers of people to read or see. As Fiore (2004, p. 26) notes, "Most traditional online dating sites facilitate narrow-purpose community. They offer tools for finding people to date and communicating with them, but they tend not to provide tools for communicating in a broader context or establishing ties outside of a dating context." Even with this caveat, Madden and Lenhart (2006) note that most U.S. adults who are Internet users who are looking for others to date have used the Internet to help them find others for dating and mating. Given the increasing percentage of individuals utilizing ICTs and the decreasing stigma of online dating sites, we anticipate that the use of these sites will continue to proliferate in the coming years.

Playing games online has also increased in popularity in recent years (Rideout et al., 2010). In particular, massively multiplayer online games (MMOGs), such as World of Warcraft, have become highly popular among young people (Palfrey & Gasser, 2008). Approximately 38% of all adults, 74% of adult gamers, and 76% of teen-aged gamers play games on desktop or laptop computers (Lenhart, Jones, & Macgill, 2008). Among those 8–18 years old, over half of all gaming occurs on portable devices (Rideout et al., 2010). The numbers are smaller for those who play games on mobile phones, Blackberries, and other handheld devices (13% of all adults, 25% of adult gamers, 62% of teen-aged gamers; Lenhart et al., 2008); and, middle school students are similar to teen-aged gamers (64% report playing games on their mobile phones at least every few months; Cotten, Anderson, & Tufekci, 2009). Youth aged 8–18 years report spending an average of 1 hour and 13 minutes playing video games on a typical day; however, boys spent significantly more time playing games than did girls (Rideout et al., 2010). These numbers are expected to rise as mobile devices are increasingly becoming integrated with gaming and Internet systems (Cotten et al., 2009; Rideout et al., 2010).

Free online phone calling software has also been developed in the past few years; this software allows users to talk to others via computers and some gaming systems, and has increased access to long-distance communication. Skype, the most popular of these types of software, became available in 2002 (www.skype.com; About Skype, 2009) and accounts for 8% of global international telephone calls being made. According to the Skype Web site, up to 20 million users have been online at the same time during peak hours.

■ MOBILE OR CELL PHONE USAGE

In addition to the ICTs and related applications noted earlier, mobile or cell phone usage has proliferated in the past few years. Although telephones were initially developed to facilitate organization efficiency and reduce isolation among rural families (Goggin, 2006), telephones of today are more advanced and provide a range of options for individuals. Many mobile phones in today's society allow users to do things that previously could only be done with computers and access to the Internet. In particular, wireless technology, miniaturization, ability to access the Internet, and more affordable pricing plans have led to a majority of individuals in the United States having access to and using mobile or cell phones (Cotten et al., 2009).

The percentage of adults who own mobile phones has increased in recent years, from 65% in 2004 to 85% in 2009 (Lenhart, 2009b). Harris Interactive (2008) estimates slightly higher percentages of adults who have a mobile phone (i.e., 89%). Thirty-one percent of 8- to 10-year-olds, 69% of 11- to 14-year-olds, and 85% of 15- to 18-year-olds report owning a mobile phone (Rideout et al., 2010). In another study, among 12- to 17-year-olds, 75% report owning mobile phones, whereas the rate is even higher among those 18–29 years (93%) (Lenhart et al., 2010). Cotten and colleagues (2009) found in a study of middle school students that mobile phone use and ownership was also high. Nearly 61% of middle school students reported owning mobile phones, whereas around three fourths reported using a mobile phone. Seventy-one percent of those between the ages of 12 and 17 years reported owning a mobile phone, ranging from a low of 52% for those between 12 and13 years old to a high of 84% for those 17 years old (Lenhart, 2009b). Research suggests that increasing percentages of U.S. adults report that they only own mobile phones (thus, no landlines). As of 2008, 14% of U.S. adults had mobile phones only and this is more common among younger age cohorts as the statistics for the following age ranges show: 18–29 years—49%; 30–39 years—22%; 40–49 years—13%; 50–64 years—11%; 65 years and older—6% (Harris Interactive, 2008).

Goggin (2006) notes that the most prominent feature of new mobile phones is text messaging. Text messaging, also known as short message service (SMS), has become increasingly popular among younger age cohorts. Recent studies show that 71% of those aged between 12 and 17 years, 85% of those aged between 18 and 29 years, 65% of those aged between 30 and 49 years, 38% of those aged between 50 and 64 years, and 11% of those aged 65 years and older report sending text messages (Horrigan, 2008; Lenhart, 2009b). Among middle school students, 54% report using text messaging at least every few months (Cotten et al., 2009). Among those 8–18 years old, 46% report texting on a typical day, and among 7th–12th graders, most spend on average an hour and a half per day sending and receiving texts (Rideout et al., 2010). Of those between 12 and 17 years old, older teens are more likely to use mobile phones and to use text messaging (Lenhart, 2009). Some research suggests that college students prefer text messaging over e-mail communication (Junco & Cole-Avent, 2008).

As the prior two sections have illustrated, there are a range of ICTs and related applications. This review has not been exhaustive but has merely tried to highlight the research that is most discussed and relevant for understanding social ties and social relationships. In sum, the range of ICTs and related applications has increased dramatically in recent years, as has the number of people using them. The availability of these ICTs and applications greatly enhances the ability for those on the right side of the digital divide to communicate with others, find information, acquire a variety of social and professional resources, and maintain social ties.

USE OF TECHNOLOGY IN RELATIONSHIPS ACROSS THE LIFE SPAN

Despite the difficulty in documenting how the use of technology to form and maintain social ties varies across social and developmental age, let alone by period and cohort, people at different stages of the life course (social ages) and at different levels of maturity (developmental ages) do indeed use technology in different ways, use different types of technologies, and use technology to mediate relationships in different ways. Much literature exists documenting the digital divide between socioeconomic groups, with the less advantaged having less access to ICTs and access to less variety of ICTs (Davison & Cotten, 2009; DiMaggio, Hargittai, Celeste, & Shafer, 2004; Hargittai & Shafer, 2006). As is documented in the review of the literature that follows, however, studies comparing the use of technology by different age groups are less common and are mostly descriptive in nature. Later we describe the literature on how people of different ages use technology to form and maintain relationships and thereby provide some insight into how developmental and age-related social structural barriers might create an age-based digital divide.

Childhood

When babies are born their digital lives have already begun. They are exposed to digital information in at least four places: their parental home, obstetrician's office, hospital (if born at a hospital or mother is cared for in hospital), and pediatrician or health care provider's office (Palfrey & Gasser, 2008). They are already interacting with technology or being integrated into society through the use of technology (e.g., by ultrasounds, monitoring devices), and also through their parents' use of ICTs to distribute ultrasound pictures, latest reports on prenatal visits, birth announcements, birth pictures, and so on.

Children also live rich digital lives and, unlike babies, use ICTs themselves to form and maintain social ties (Livingstone, 2003). The worlds of play for children have become much more digitized during the past 10 years. A plethora of organizations (e.g., governmental, nonprofits, museums, educational) have developed Web sites that now offer preschoolers (and older youth too) opportunities to play games, watch videos, and interact with cartoon characters and other children (see, e.g., www.disney.com; www.pbskids.org; Marsh et al., 2005; Montgomery, 2000). In addition, the American Library Association hosts a Web site that provides links to hundreds of Web sites that have been reviewed and been deemed appropriate for children (see: http://www.ala.org/greatsites). Montgomery (2000) suggests, however, that commercially oriented Web sites tend to overshadow the educational ones. Children's television shows routinely encourage children and parents to visit the shows' Web sites to find out more about the shows and for other activities associated with the television shows. In addition, marketers target parents of preschoolers with laptops, cell phones, MP3 players, and so on, which are toys but sometimes also educational in nature.

Unfortunately, however, we know little about how children of preschool age and younger use ICTs and how the use of them affects their social relationships. Most of the research examining children has focused on those school-aged and older. A recent Kaiser Family Foundation study (Rideout et al., 2010) reports that those 8–10 years old are exposed to close to 8 hours of media per day on average, and they spend over 5 hours per day using media. Although most of this time is spent watching television (3:41 hours), 46 minutes is spent with computers and an hour with video games. On average, those between the ages of 8 and 10 years spend approximately 5 minutes per day using SNSs, 17 minutes playing games, 8 minutes watching videos on Web sites, 3 minutes IM, 2 minutes on e-mail, and 3 minutes with graphics or photos on the computer (Rideout et al., 2010). We are aware of no data that document blog usage among children. Over 60% of those 8–10 years old report owning an iPod/MP3 player, 65% a handheld video game player, 31% a mobile phone, and 17% a laptop computer (Rideout et al., 2010). As these percentages illustrate, the ICTs owned most often by this age group are those primarily for entertainment purposes, rather than for communication and relationship enhancement.

Although they are technically "digital natives" because of the time period in which they were born and the pervasive nature of technology in their environments, children of preschool age are still being socialized as to what is socially appropriate and how to exist in structured environments. As Livingstone (2003) concludes, the body of research on children's use of the Internet, and we would add on ICTs in general, is still small and mainly addresses potential opportunities and dangers of technology use. In addition, the majority of this research is descriptive in nature and does not examine the effects of this ICT use on social relationships. Although we recognize that babies and especially children are affected by ICTs through their own use and use by their elders, their worlds are more geographically constrained and perhaps as a result most of the research on how technology mediates social ties focuses on adolescents and adults.

Adolescence and Young Adulthood

Researchers and media personnel often refer to youth of today as digital natives, born into a digital world where ICTs are already pervasive. Most researchers consider youth born around 1980 and afterwards to be part of the digital-native generation (Palfrey & Gasser, 2008). When the average digital native was born, e-mail had been around for 22 years, personal computers were 15 years old, video games had been around for more than 40 years, commercial cell phones had been in existence for over a decade, and the WWW had already been created by Tim Berners-Lee (Rainie, 2009).

Among digital natives, most use a variety of ICTs, they are constantly connected, and they have the skills to effectively utilize and navigate these technologies. They did not have to relearn how to do things with ICTs, as did digital immigrants and older generations. Youth are comfortable with technology and use many ICTs and related applications at very high levels compared with older age groups (Cotten et al., 2009; Ito et al., 2008; Jones & Fox, 2009; Lenhart et al., 2010; Smith, Salaway, & Caruso, 2009).

Digital natives are different than are older cohorts in that they do almost everything differently than do older age cohorts, including writing, studying, interacting, maintaining social networks and relationships, and working (Palfrey & Gasser, 2008). Each of these activities is mediated by digital natives' use of ICTs and related applications. For digital natives, they have never known another way to interact, study, work, and so forth because these technologies existed in their world when they entered it (Ito et al., 2008; Montgomery, 2007; Palfrey & Gasser, 2008).

"They are joined by a set of common practices, including the amount of time they spend using digital technologies, their tendency to multitask, their tendency to express themselves and relate to one another in ways mediated by digital technologies, and their pattern of using the technologies to access and use information and create new knowledge and art forms" (Palfrey & Gasser, 2008, p. 4). Online communities, SNSs, and other ICTs that facilitate online interactions represent areas where youth are socialized as to what is appropriate behavior and how to act in different situations, as well as being a space where their identity can develop (Ito et al., 2008; Montgomery, 2007; Palfrey & Gasser, 2008). They can experiment with their status, develop identities, and learn how to interpret social cues.

The majority of research on youth and ICTs has focused on ICT usage patterns and how this varies by different sociodemographic groups (Cotten et al., 2009; Jones & Fox, 2009; Lenhart, 2009b; Lenhart, Arafeh, Smith, & Macgill, 2008; Lenhart et al., 2010; Ling & Yttri, 2006; Roberts & Foher, 2008). Increasingly, research is also focusing on SNS usage among youth (Ellison, Steinfeld, & Lampe, 2007; Hargittai, 2007; Tufekci, 2008). Less research has examined the effects of ICT usage on social relationships, social capital, health outcomes, and education (for exceptions, see Cotten, 2008; Ito et al., 2008; Pasek, More, & Hargittai, 2009; Quan-Haase, 2007).

The lives of digital natives are intertwined with technologies. Most have never known a life without them (Ito et al., 2008; Palfrey & Gasser, 2008). Digital natives use a multitude of ICTs and ICT applications to help them maintain social ties. Few youth use ICTs and applications to form new relationships; rather they use them to maintain their existing ties and relationships (Ito et al., 2008). Given that they often do not differentiate between online and offline worlds (Palfrey & Gasser, 2008), they do not think of one key technology as being critical to maintaining social ties. Rather, they utilize the milieu of ICTs and applications that are pervasive in their social worlds. For younger youth, these tend to be IM and e-mail, with increasing numbers using mobile phones and texting as they move into the teenage years, particularly the high school years (Jones & Fox, 2009; Lenhart, 2009b). SNS usage is also high among these groups, although teens have shown a slight decline in their likelihood of using SNSs to connect with friends (Lenhart et al., 2010). Teens and young adults' use of blogs has been declining in recent years (Lenhart et al., 2010), perhaps as a result of their increasing use of SNSs and mobile phones and their desire for more immediate forms of contact and communication.

With this constant connectivity we see the nature of relationships being changed. "Online friendships are based on many of the same things as traditional friendships—shared interests, frequent interactions—but they nonetheless have a very different tenor: They are often fleeting; they are easy to enter into and easy to leave, without so much as a goodbye; and they are also perhaps enduring in ways we have yet to understand" (Palfrey & Gasser, 2008, p. 5). Digital natives don't remember a time when individuals wrote letters out by hand and mailed them to others. They live most of their lives online and often don't distinguish between interactions mediated by technology and those that are not (Ito et al., 2008). The changing nature of social relationships is second nature to digital natives.

As noted earlier, youth use ICTs at extremely high levels compared with other age groups (Cotten et al., 2009; Ito et al., 2008; Jones & Fox, 2009; Smith et al., 2009). Technology is such a part of their lives that for many they could not fathom an existence without its use. They utilize it to form, maintain, and end social relationships with both strong and weak social network ties (Ito et al., 2008; Palfrey & Gasser, 2008).

Family

Although youth are digital natives, the majority of their older adult family members do not use technology as much as they do and are not as proficient or as technologically savvy as they are. Thus, though it would be easier for youth to manage their relationships with their family members through the use of a range of ICTs that they commonly use, for many this possibility is not an option. This is particularly the case for SNS usage as older age groups are less likely to participate in these sites (Jones & Fox, 2009).

Many family members, however, are using mobile phones, which represents an important way that youth maintain relationships with these family members. Phone calls are more often used than are text messages (a preferred means of communication for youth) with older family members, as older age groups are less likely to use text messaging than are youth (Horrigan, 2008; Lenhart, 2009b).

Friends and Romantic Partners

Youth live much of their lives online; thus, for them it is natural to form, maintain, and change relationships via technological mechanisms (Palfrey and Gasser, 2008). For youth, maintaining and even ending relationships are done primarily through the use of ICTs whether it is via SNSs, texting, calls, e-mails, or other ICT applications. For younger youth, the ICTs most frequently used tend to be IM and e-mail, with increasing numbers using mobile phones and texting as they move into the teenage years, particularly the high school years (Jones & Fox, 2009; Lenhart, 2009; Lenhart et al., 2010). Texting for high school and young adults is a key way they maintain contact with their friends and romantic partners (Ito et al., 2008; Lenhart, 2009). SNSs are also used by online teens to maintain contact with friends (91%), make plans (72%), and make new friends (49%) (Lenhart, 2009a).

Some researchers suggest that the nature of online friendships is similar to traditional friendships; however, they tend to be less long-lasting and easier to enter and exit than offline friendships (Palfrey and Gasser, 2008). Although they at times form relationships online first, most research suggests that youth use ICTs to help them maintain existing relationships with friends rather than as a mechanism to meet new friends (Ito et al., 2008).

As we have noted earlier, for digital natives the world isn't divided into "online" and "offline" segments. Youth constantly use the tools at hand, whether they are ICTs or others, to help them maintain their relationships with their friends and romantic partners.

Gaps in Literature on Youth, Social Ties, and Technology

Ito and colleagues note that in the United States there is a lack of research on how youth ICT practices are "embedded in a broader social and cultural ecology" (2008, p. 6). We suggest that additional research is needed which follows youth over time as they more fully integrate different aspects of ICTs into their lives, education, and work experiences. Research is also needed that examines the interrelationships among ICT use, social ties, and social and health effects of ICT usage. We know little about the psychological and physiological aspects of such high levels of technology usage and what happens when ways of interacting change because of changing technologies. Is Google really making us stupid, as one highly circulated media report recently suggested (Carr, 2008)? Only studies that follow youth from very early ages will be able to distinguish how this usage affects these outcomes.

In addition, we know little about how ICT use changes over time as individuals move into and out of specific social roles. For example, what happens when the 22-year-old college graduate enters his or her first full-time job and the norms of ICT use are different? What are the effects on self-concept, social relationships, and perceptions of self-efficacy when companies have a "no texting" policy and youth can no longer be "constantly available" or when companies monitor Facebook, e-mail, and other ICT usage?

We must also not ignore that there are multiple layers of the digital divide (Davison & Cotten, 2009; Hargittai & Hinnant, 2008) that affect how youth use ICTs and their effects. Although youth are most often thought of as digital natives, there are important segments of youth who have minimal access to ICTs, or if they do have access they do not have the skills and abilities to use the ICTs to enhance their social ties.

As ICTs and related applications continue to evolve, so must our study of these technologies. Although it is important to illustrate changing trends in use and sociodemographic variation over time, we must go beyond simply documenting patterns so that we can begin to better understand the variety of effects of ICTs across the life course.

Midlife

Researchers typically refer to those who are currently in midlife as "digital immigrants" (Palfrey & Gasser, 2008). Unlike their children, who were born into digital culture, middle-aged ICT users were adults before ICTs became pervasive in our society. Nonetheless, out of necessity, they have learned new technologies as adults—first e-mail, chat rooms, cell phones, and text messaging and more recently SNSs and Twitter. They are recognizable by "the lame jokes and warnings about urban myths that they still forward to large cc: lists" (Palfrey & Gasser, 2008, p. 4). Like immigrants from one country to another, they sometimes feel like strangers in a strange land.

The literature relevant to understanding the role of ICTs in shaping personal relationships during midlife does not comprise a coherent whole. Rather than defining midlife in terms of the responsibilities facing people (committed relationship, children, or a steady job) or in terms of their maturity (approach to generativity, depth of personal insights, feelings of competence) researchers of midlife have arbitrarily focused on people of a certain age, typically some subset of people between the ages of 18 and 64 years (Adams & Blieszner, 1996). This vast age span includes young adults and those in the early stages of old age as well as middle-aged ones, all of whom are likely to have differing responsibilities and developmental characteristics. Even defining this period of life more narrowly to include only those between the ages of 33 years and 64 years means that three of the cohorts included in Table 25.1 would comprise midlife—Gen Xers, younger boomers, and older boomers. We know these three cohorts have had very different experiences with technology over their life courses. As reported in this table, their varying experiences result in different usage rates, with monotonic decreases in going online (from 87% among those 33–44 years old to 79% among those 55–63 years old), e-mailing (from 94% among those 33–44 years old to 90% among those 55–63 years old), IM (from 38% among those 33–44 years old to 23% among those 55–63 years old), and blogging (from 34% among those 33–44 years old to 25% among those 55–63 years old) across these three "midlife" cohorts. The one exception to this monotonic pattern is that 29% of those between 55 and 63 years old use SNSs whereas only 20% of those between the ages of 45 and 54 years do.

As Adams and Stevenson stated in 2004, what reports they could find on research on the impact of ICTs on midlife personal relationships were in the various literatures on the types of activities in which adults are involved such as education, work, and leisure rather than in the literatures on different types of relationships such as family, friend, and romantic ones. With a few exceptions (e.g., Ellison, Heino, & Gibbs, 2006), we found this statement remains true and, furthermore as discussed earlier, this type of research does not treat midlife conceptually but happens to focus on activities in which middle-aged people (and others) are involved. For example, Kamarade and Burchell (2004) recently studied whether telecommuting was a friendly or isolating form of work and Yardi, Golder, and Brzozowski (2009) examined blogging at work. Similarly, Kavanaugh, and Patternson (2001) studied the impact of computer use on community involvement, and Boase, Horrigan, Wellman, and Rainie (2006) reported that people use the Internet to put their networks into motion when they need help with important issues in their lives and those who use the Internet are more likely to get the help they need than non-Internet users. Although the studies of how ICTs shape family, friend, and romantic relationships often include midlife adults in the samples, the reports on the data do not often compare findings across age groups. For these reasons, we know very little about the impact of ICTs on midlife social ties and there are therefore virtually unlimited opportunities for research on this age group.

Older Adulthood

Just as the terms "digital natives" and "digital immigrants" have been used to describe younger and middle-aged ICT users, respectively, there are also nicknames describing older adults' use of technology. Internet users within this cohort have been referred to as "cyberseniors" (McMellon & Schiffman, 2000, 2002), "mature users" (Fox, 2004), and "silver surfers" (Selwyn, 2004). Conversely, those who do not participate in Internet use have been deemed members of the "gray gap" (Fox et al., 2001) and the "informational blackhole" (Norris, 2001). Regardless of which label is most apt, it is more accurate to think of older adults' relationships to ICTs as along a continuum, in that this cohort is not simply made up of users versus nonusers (Selwyn, 2004).

There are varying degrees of use of specific ICTs among older adults, as is also the case among younger cohorts. As Czaja and Barr predicted two decades ago (1989), the technological revolution and the graying of the population have ushered in a need for society to take the relationship of older adults and technology into careful consideration.

Although the use of technology among older adults has risen within the past decade, there is still a smaller percentage of seniors using the Internet as compared with younger age groups (see Table 25.1; Fox, 2004; Jones & Fox, 2009; Millward, 2003). Even within their own cohort, there are age differences in rates of use, with those in advanced years reporting that they hardly ever use the Internet (33%) more frequently than do their younger counterparts (Millward, 2003). This age group is the least likely to use ICTs, despite their great potential to become ICT users and to gain from using these technologies (Blit-Cohen & Litwin, 2004; Cotten, 2009).

Many older adults report no interest in going online (Fox, 2004), although this "lack of interest" might more accurately be a fear of technology (Millward, 2003). Rather than reporting a lack of computer skills, many seniors portray an ambivalent attitude toward Internet technology, choosing to opt out of online participation altogether (Millward, 2003). Other nonusers do not see the relevance of Internet technology for their day to day lives (Selwyn, 2004) and feel as if they are not missing out on anything in choosing to abstain from its use (Fox et al., 2001).

A senior's desire to become technologically capable is not necessarily enough, however, to transition the individual into becoming a proficient cyber-participant. Barriers to ICT usage among older adults relate to physical and cognitive factors, personal factors (including technology attitudes, such as computer anxiety), ICT usability factors (such as small fonts, color choices, graphics, etc.), organizational factors (such as access and assistance), and environmental factors related to where individuals use the technology (Becker, 2004; Fox, 2004; Laguna & Babcock, 1997; Morrell, Dailey, Feldman, Mayhorn, & Echt, 2004; Namazi & McClintic, 2003).

In a small study of Alabama older adults, Cotten and Anderson (2006) found that barriers to ICT use include the following: perceptions of the technologies being too complicated for them, no perceived need for them, and concerns about scams and identity theft. Melenhorst, Rogers, and Bouwhuis (2006) note that older adults are willing to learn and to use technologies if the benefits of using the technologies are made clear to them. Barriers such as a lack of IT knowledge and physical or cognitive impairments continue to prevent seniors from becoming users (Fox, 2004). Access to Internet technology is becoming less of a barrier for senior users, whereas usability is a more critical issue for the older adult (Millward, 2003). Providing computer and Internet training is absolutely necessary in integrating the oldest cohort into a technologically advanced society (Blit-Cohen & Litwin, 2004; Cotten, 2009; Fox, 2004; Millward, 2003). After receiving adequate training, older adults' negative perceptions of ICTs often change as they begin to embrace the online world; they often become just as enthusiastic and devoted as younger ICT users (Fox et al., 2001; Fox, 2004; White, McConnell, Clipp, Bynum, & Teague, 1999). Research does suggest, however, that although the lag in older adults' adaptation of technology is sure to lessen in future generations, it will not altogether disappear (Charness & Boot, 2009).

Older adults are typically motivated to become Internet users because they associate ICTs with modern society and realize their usefulness (Cotten, 2009; White & Weatherall, 2000). The Internet allows this cohort to adapt to old age by providing them an opportunity to interact with the world outside their homes without ever having to exit through the front door (McMellon & Schiffman, 2000, 2002). Some of the negative effects of aging, such as decreased social interactions and increased loneliness, can be mediated through the use of technology (McMellon & Schiffman, 2000). Essentially, older adults' participation in cyberspace can enable them to maintain a sense of continuity in personal relationships, social activity (Cody, Dunn, Hoppin, & Wendt, 1999; McMellon & Schiffman, 2002), information seeking, and mental stimulation (Millward, 2003).

Cognitive and physical impairments as well as overall frailty often prohibit older adults from becoming proficient computer and Internet users (Hutchinson, Eastman, & Tirrito, 1997). As Charness and Boot (2009) point out, the model of older adult-friendly technology is one that provides training while allowing for impaired cognitive or physical abilities. Time constraints as a result of caregiving responsibilities are another cited reason for lower rates of usage among seniors (White et al., 2002). This population, however, is more likely to become involved with ICTs if provided with proper training (Bradley & Poppen, 2003; Cotten, 2009; McConatha, McConatha, & Dermigny, 1994; Morrell, Mayhorn, & Bennett, 2000; Swindell, 2001; White et al., 2002) and modified equipment (Czaja & Barr, 1989; Hutchinson et al., 1997; White et al., 1999). Computer and technology manufacturers need to consider this population when designing products (Czaja & Barr, 1989; White et al., 1999), especially considering that many older adults are interested in becoming users (Hutchinson et al., 1997).

Seniors who are isolated and homebound often become less lonely over time after becoming involved in online activity (Barnett & Adkins, 2001; Blit-Cohen & Litwin, 2004; Bradley & Poppen, 2003; McMellon & Schiffman, 2002; Swindell, 2001; White et al., 1999; White et al., 2002). Overall, the Internet has the potential to enrich older adults' lives, allowing them to build and maintain social networks, and enabling them to extend their lives past the confines of their homes or care domiciles (Barnett & Adkins, 2001; Blit-Cohen & Litwin, 2004; McConatha et al., 1994; McMellon & Schiffman, 2002; Swindell, 2001).

Family

Some older adults report online activity as being a means through which they can become closer to their families (Karavidas, Lim, & Katsikas, 2005; McMellon & Schiffman, 2002). Communicating with family often ranks as being of the highest benefit for online participation for older adults (Fox et al., 2001). Having geographically distant adult children often acts as a motivator for seniors to get online. As Climo (2001) reported, dispersed families often use the Internet as a primary vehicle through which they sustain generational bonds.

Friends

Older adults often use ICTs to maintain friendships that have extended over the life course. The Internet enables this population to maintain a friendship network through the use of e-mail, IM, and chatting online (Karavidas et al., 2005). For those with limited mobility, the online world may become a crucial aspect of their environment (McMellon & Schiffman, 2002), enabling them to stay connected to life-long friends via e-mail (Barnett & Adkins, 2001). Cody and others (1999) found that having satisfying contacts with friends prompted a greater use of e-mail. Furthermore, there is a gender effect in using the Internet to maintain social ties, with older women being more likely than older men to use the Internet to connect with friends (Millward, 2003).

Not only do older adults use ICTs to maintain existing friendships, but they also use them to develop new ties. Older adults involved in a computer training program in China found supportive peer relationships they had not formerly had as a result of their involvement (Xie, 2007). Similarly, Czaja and Barr (1989) reported that older adults were able to form new friendships through the use of e-mail networks and support groups. As shown with a group of previously unacquainted quilters (Barnett & Adkins, 2001), a common interest may be a catalyst by which a large online network is formed. Friendships that are formed online may eventually go offline as well (Kanayama, 2003; McMellon & Schiffman, 2002). Overall, ICTs can help older adults build supportive friendships that provide companionship (Kanayama, 2003) at a time when decreased social engagement is a normative experience.

Gaps in Literature on Older Adults, Social Ties, and Technology

Over 5 years ago, Adams and Stevenson (2004) documented a lack of literature on older adults' use of technology. Since that time, there have been multiple studies conducted on the topic, with some even documenting how technology mediates older adults' personal relationships, but there are still gaps in the literature. For instance, little is known about how older adults might use technology to develop and maintain romantic relationships. Research tells us that older adults primarily use ICTs for e-mail and information seeking (Fox, 2004); however, there is still more to learn about seniors' online dating patterns. Are "silver surfers" open to exploring the online world for this domain of life? And if so, what are the outcomes? Might older adults capitalize on a wider pool of potential romantic partners if they use ICTs?

Although Jones and Fox (2009; see Table 25.1) found that 15% of those 64 years and older used SNSs, much still remains to be learned about how this age group interacts with ICTs to mediate their personal relationships. Is this demographic group beginning to use these sites as a way to connect with family and friends? We simply do not know, because only sparse data are available, as evidenced by those 65 and older not even being represented on Facebook's recent graph on the site's usage (Inside Facebook, 2009b). Likewise, little is known about older adults' use of blogging. Although we do know that almost 40% of those 64 and older who go online are blog readers, and that 12% are bloggers, we know little of how these usage trends might impact older adults' social relationships.

We also know little about how ICT use helps mediate the effects of social isolation and isolation from place among older adults. Because of declining mobility, older adults are less likely to be able to travel as extensively as perhaps they did in their younger years. Using the Internet, in particular, offers the potential for individuals to "visit" places through the computer that they are no longer physically capable of visiting in person (Cotten, 2009). How these activities affect older adults' social connections, sense of isolation, and quality of life remains to be determined.

Lastly, there is still more conclusive research needed on the relationship of ICTs to older adults' well-being. Although multiple studies have documented a connection between the two (Cody et al., 1999; Karavidas et al., 2005; McConatha et al., 1994; McMellon & Schiffman, 2002; White et al., 1999; Wright, 2000; Xie, 2007), at least one has demonstrated the contrary (Dickinson & Gregor, 2006). Barriers to consistent findings on the topic include the lack of a systematic definition of well-being and a misattribution of the effects of computer-training programs to computer use itself rather than to the social connections and interactions that are a result of the training programs (Cotten, 2009; Dickinson & Gregor, 2006). In sum, we need to continue to explore how older adults use ICTs and how this might influence their well-being.

▦ THE FUTURE OF RESEARCH ON THE IMPACT OF TECHNOLOGY ON CLOSE RELATIONSHIPS ACROSS THE LIFE SPAN

Studying the impact of technology on social ties across the life span represents theoretical and methodological challenges. These challenges include the need to revisit concepts developed when scholars assumed that face-to-face contact was necessary for the formation and maintenance of social ties (Adams, 1998) and to apply theories of aging, group development, and network change to content (Adams & Stevenson, 2004) that is changing so quickly it is almost impossible to study. Longitudinal studies are needed that simultaneously follow multiple cohorts of individuals as they make transitions from one stage of the life course to another or achieve a new phase of developmental maturity. Such studies would be an improvement over current crosssectional studies, especially those that do not compare findings across age groups, and would allow for the development of an understanding of both social and developmental age, period, and cohort effects on the ways in which the use of technology mediates the formation, maintenance, and erosion of personal relationships. New approaches to study design and implementation will be necessary to allow researchers to capture a sufficient number of cross-sectional snapshots of the social landscape to illustrate the complexities of its evolution.

As in most bodies of literature, the focus of research on the use of the technology and the establishment and evolution of social ties in specific age groups is dictated by the particular developmental and social challenges facing them. As discussed in this chapter, the research on children's use of ICTs focuses on its dangers; the comparable work on adolescents addresses their experimentation regarding their status, identity, and the interpretation of social cues; the sparse examinations of ICT use in midlife are conducted in the context of work, education, and leisure activities; and the literature on later adulthood focuses on the developmental and physical challenges the use of ICTs pose and the ways their use can reduce loneliness and improve quality of life. In-depth studies of these topics and others across all age groups would allow for a more meaningful assessment of how the relationships between technology use and the constellation of social ties change over the life course.

As we noted in earlier sections of this chapter, there are inherent digital divide issues that must also be considered when one is studying the impacts of technology usage on social ties across the life course. Within each of the groups discussed in this chapter, there are those who are on the wrong side of the digital divide. Research shows that those with lower levels of education and income are less likely to have ICT access and to be skilled in the effective use of ICTs (Davison & Cotten, 2009; DiMaggio et al., 2004). As our review of the literature on ICT use by people of different ages shows, developmental and age-based social factors can also inhibit or facilitate patterns of usage. As Table 25.1 illustrates, just as different levels of use occur across socioeconomic groups, different levels of use occur across age groups. Researchers must also consider how age factors into digital divide issues, as usage patterns (and probably effects) vary dramatically depending upon the specific type of ICT and the age group being examined.

When Adams and Stevenson wrote their 2004 chapter, the importance of ICTs for personal relationships was just beginning to be apparent. Some still viewed the topic as trivial or merely of transitory importance. Considering the current pervasiveness of ICT use, it should now be clear that studying ICT use is central to understanding not only personal relationships, but everyday life as a whole, not only now, but for the foreseeable future. One can only imagine what life will be like when digital natives comprise the entire population and cohorts are defined by when they first have access to as-yet-to-be-imagined innovations in ICTs. Between now and then, researchers will need to be vigilant and work quickly if they are to record the evolution of the ways we relate to each other as ICTs change.

▨ REFERENCES

About Skype. (2009). Retrieved February 15, 2010, from http://about.skype.com/

Adams, R. G. (1998). The demise of territorial determinism: Online friendships. In R. G. Adams & G. Allan (Eds.), *Placing friendship in context* (pp. 153–182). Cambridge: Cambridge University Press.

Adams, R. G., & Blieszner, R. (1996). Midlife friendship patterns. In N. Vanzetti & S. Duck (Eds.), *A lifetime of relationships* (pp. 336–363). Monterey, CA: Brooks/Cole.

Adams, R., & Stevenson, M. (2004). A lifetime of relationships mediated by technology. In F. Lang and K. Fingerman (Eds.), *Growing together: Personal relationships across the life span* (pp. 368–393). New York: Cambridge University Press.

Barnett, K., & Adkins, B. (2001). Computers: Community for aging women in Australia. *Women and Environments, 50–51,* 23–25.

Baron, N. (2008). *Always on: Language in an online and mobile world.* New York: Oxford University Press.

Becker, S. A. (2004). A study of Web usability for older adults seeking online health resources. *ACM Transactions on Computer-Human Interaction, 11*(4), 387–406.

Berscheid, E., Snyder, M., & Omoto, A. (1989). The relationship closeness inventory: Assessing the closeness of interpersonal relationships. *Journal of Personality and Social Psychology, 57,* 792–807.

Blieszner, R., & Adams, R. G. (1992). Adult *friendship.* Newbury Park: Sage.

Blit-Cohen, E., & Litwin, H. (2004). Elder participation in cyberspace: A qualitative analysis of Israeli retirees. *Journal of Aging Studies, 18,* 385–398.

Blood, R. (2000). Weblogs: A history and perspective. In *Rebecca's pocket.* Retrieved August 20, 2007, from http://www.rebeccablood.net/essays/weblog_history.html

Boase, J., Horrigan, J. B., Wellman, B., & Rainie, L. (2006). *The strength of Internet ties: The Internet and email aid users in maintaining their social networks and provide pathways to help when people face big decisions, pew internet and American life project,* Washington, D.C. Retrieved January from http://www.pewinternet.org/. Accessed October 10, 2010.

Boyd, D. (2007). Why youth (heart) social network sites: The role of networked publics in teenage social life. In D. Buckingham (Ed.), *MacArthur Foundation series on digital learning—Youth, identity, and digital media volume.* Cambridge, MA: MIT Press.

Bradley, N., & Poppen, W. (2003). Assistive technology, computers and Internet may decrease sense of isolation for homebound elderly and disabled persons. *Technology and Disability, 15*(1), 19–25.

Carr, N. (2008). Is Google making us stupid? *The Atlantic.* Retrieved December 4, 2009, from http://www.theatlantic.com/doc/200807/google

Castells, M. (2001). *The Internet galaxy: Reflections on the Internet, business, and society.* New York: Oxford University Press.

Charness, N. & Boot, W. R. (2009). Aging and information technology use: Potential and barriers. *Current Directions in Psychological Science, 18,* 253–258.

Climo, J. J. (2001). Images of aging in virtual reality: The Internet and the community of affect. *Generations, 25,* 64–68.

Cody, M. J., Dunn, D., Hoppin, S., & Wendt, P. (1999). Silver surfers: Training and evaluating Internet use among older adult learners. *Communication Education, 48,* 269–286.

comScore. (2010). *U.S. online video market ascent as Americans watch 33 billion videos in December.* Retrieved from www.comscore.com. Accessed October 10, 2010.

Cotten, S. R. (2008). Students' technology usage and the impacts on well-being. In R. Junco & D. M. Timm (Eds.), *New directions for student services: Using emerging technologies to enhance student engagement, 124* (pp. 55–70). San-Francisco: Jossey-Bass.

Cotten, S. R. (2009, November). *Using ICTs to enhance quality of life among older adults: Preliminary results from a randomized controlled trial.* Paper presented at the annual meeting of the Gerontological Society of America, Atlanta, GA.

Cotten, S. R., & Anderson, W. (2006, June). *Use of IT among older adults in Alabama.* Paper presented for the Center for Aging's IT and Quality of Life among Older Adults Steering Committee, University of Alabama-Birmingham.

Cotten, S. R., Anderson, W., & Tufekci, Z. (2009). Old wine in a new technology or a different type of digital divide? *New Media & Society, 11*(7), 1163–1186.

Craven, P., & Wellman, B. (1974). The network city. In M. P. Effrat (Ed.), *The community: Approaches and applications.* Glencoe, IL: The Free Press.

Cuba, L., & Hummon, D. M. (1993). Constructing a sense of home: Place affiliation and migration across the life cycle. *Sociological Forum, 8,* 547–572.

Czaja, S. J., & Barr, R. A. (1989). Technology and the everyday life of older adults. *The Annals of the American Academy of Political and Social Science, 503,* 127–137.

Davison, E., & Cotten, S. R. (2009). Connection disparities: The importance of broadband connections in understanding today's digital divide. In E. Ferro, Y. Dwivedi, J. Gil-Garcia, & M. D. Williams (Eds.), *Overcoming digital divides: Constructing an equitable and competitive information society* (pp. 346–358). Hershey, PA: IGI Global Publishers.

Dickinson, A., & Gregor, P. (2006). Computer use has no demonstrated impact on the well-being of older adults. *International Journal of Human-Computer Studies, 64,* 744–753.

DiMaggio, P., Hargittai, E., Celeste, C., & Shafer, S. (2004). Digital inequality: From unequal access to differentiated use. In K. Neckerman (Ed.), *Social inequality* (pp. 355–400). New York: Russell Sage Foundation.

Effrat, M. P. (1974). Approaches to community: Conflicts and complementaries. In M. P. Effrat (Ed.), *The community: Approaches and applications.* Glencoe, IL: The Free Press.

Ellison, N., Heino, R., & Gibbs, J. (2006). Managing impressions online: Self-presentation processes in the online dating environment. *Journal of Computer-Mediated Communication, 11*(2), Article 2. Retrieved December 17, 2009, from http://jcmc.indiana.edu/vol11/issue2/ellison.html

Ellison, N. B., Steinfield, C., & Lampe, C. (2007). The benefits of Facebook "friends": Social capital and college students' use of online social network sites. *Journal of Computer-Mediated Communication, 12*(4), 1143–1168.

Fehr, B. (2004). Intimacy expectations in same-sex friendships: A prototype interaction-pattern model. *Journal of Personality and Social Psychology, 86,* 265–284.

Fingerman, K. L. (2009). Consequential strangers and peripheral partners: The importance of unimportant relationships. *Journal of Family Theory and Review, 1,* 69–82.

Fiore, A. R. T. (2004). *Romantic regression: An analysis of behavior in online dating systems.* Unpublished master's thesis, Massachusetts Institute of Technology. Retrieved December 2, 2009, from http://people.ischool.berkeley.edu/~atf/fiore_thesis_final.pdf

Fox, S. (2004). *Older Americans and the Internet.* Retrieved September 23, 2006, from Pew Internet and American Life Project: http://www.pewinternet.org/pdfs/PIP_Seniors_Online_2004.pdf

Fox, S., Rainie, L., Larsen, E., Horrigan, J., Lenhart, A., Spooner, T., et al. (2001). *Wired seniors: A fervent few, inspired by family ties.* Retrieved December 17, 2009, from Pew Internet and American Life Project: http://www.pewinternet.org/~/media//Files/Reports/2001/PIP_Wired_Seniors_Report.pdf.pdf

Fox, S., Zickuhr, K., & Smith, A. (2009). *Twitter and status updating.* Retrieved October 25, 2009, from Pew Internet and American Life Project: http://www.pewinternet.org/Reports/2009/17-Twitter-and-Status-Updating-Fall-2009.aspx

Goggin, G. (2006). Making voice portable: The early history of the cell phone. In G. Goggin (Ed.), *Cell phone culture.* New York: Routledge.

Granovetter, M. S. (1973). The strength of weak ties. *American Journal of Sociology, 78,* 1360–1380.

Griffiths, M. (1999). Internet addiction: Fact or fiction? *The Psychologist, 12,* 246–250.

Hale, T., Cotten, S. R., Drentea, P., & Goldner, M. (2010). Rural-urban differences in general and health-related Internet use. *American Behavioral Scientist, 20*, 1–22.

Hargittai, E. (2007). Whose space? Differences among users and non-users of social network sites. *Journal of Computer-Mediated Communication, 13*(5), 276–297.

Hargittai, E., & Hinnant, A. (2008). Digital inequality: Differences in young adults' use of the Internet. *Communication Research, 35*(5), 602–621.

Hargittai, E., & Shafer, S. (2006). Differences in actual and perceived online skills: The role of gender. *Social Science Quarterly, 87*(2), 432–448.

Harris Interactive. (2008, April). *Cell phone usage continues to increase.* Retrieved September 8, 2009, from http://www.harrisinteractive.com/harris_poll/index.asp?PID=890

Homer, T. (2009). *Current online dating and dating services facts & statistics.* Retrieved September 8, 2009, from Dating Sites Reviews: http://www.datingsitesreviews.com/staticpages/index.php?page=Online-Dating-Industry-Facts-Statistics

Horrigan, J. (2008). *Mobile access to data and information.* Retrieved September 8, 2009, from Pew Internet & American Life Project: http://www.pewinternet.org/Reports/2008/Mobile-Access-to-Data-and-Information/Methodology.aspx?r=1

Hutchinson, D., Eastman, C., & Tirrito, T. (1997). Designing user interfaces for older adults. *Educational Gerontology, 23*, 497–513.

Inside Facebook. (2009a). *New study shows how different generations use Facebook.* Retrieved December 4, 2009, from http://www.insidefacebook.com/2009/07/30/new-study-shows-how-different-generations-use-facebook/

Inside Facebook. (2009b). *November data on Facebook's US growth by age and gender: Young men following the women.* Retrieved December 5, 2009, from http://www.insidefacebook.com/2009/12/03/november-data-on-facebook%E2%80%99s-us-growth-by-age-and-gender-young-men-following-the-women/

Ito, M., Horst, H., Bittanti, M., Boyd, D., Herr-Stephenson, B., Lange, P., et al. (2008). Living and learning with new media: Summary of findings from the digital youth project. *The John D. and Catherine T. MacArthur foundation reports on digital media and learning.* Retrieved December 12, 2008, from www.macfound.org

Johnson, A. J., Haigh, M. M., Craig, E. A., & Becker, J. A. H. (2009). Relational closeness: Comparing undergraduate college students' geographically close and long-distance friendships. *Personal Relationships, 16*(4), 631–646.

Jones, S., & Fox, S. (2009). *Generations online in 2009.* Retrieved September 8, 2009, from the Pew Internet & American Life Project: http://www.pewinternet.org/Reports/2009/Generations-Online-in-2009.aspx

Junco, R., & Cole-Avent, G. A. (2008). An introduction to technologies commonly used by college students. In R. Junco and D. M. Timm (Eds.), *Using emerging technologies to enhance student engagement: New directions for student services, Number 124* (pp. 3–17). San Francisco: Jossey-Bass.

Kamarade, D., & Burchell, B. (2004). Teleworking and participatory capital: Is teleworking an isolating or community-friendly form of work? *European Sociological Review, 20*(4), 345–361.

Kanayama, T. (2003). Ethnographic research on the experience of Japanese elderly people online. *New Media & Society, 5*(2), 267–288.

Kandel, J. J. (1998). Internet addiction on campus: The vulnerability of college students. *CyberPsychology & Behavior, 1*, 11–18.

Kavanaugh, A. L. & Patterson, S. J. (2001). The impact of community computer networks on social capital and community involvement. *American Behavioral Scientist, 45*, 3, 496–509.

Karavidas, M., Lim, N. K., & Katsikas, S. L. (2005). The effects of computers on older adult users. *Computers in Human Behavior, 21*, 697–711.

Kavanaugh, A.L. & Patterson, S.J. (2001). The impact of community computer networks on social capital and community involvement. *American Behavioral Scientist, 45, 3*, 496–509.

Kraut, R. E., Patterson, M., Lundmark, V., Kiesler, S., Mukhopadhyay, T., & Scherlis, W. (1998). Internet paradox: A social technology that reduces social involvement and psychological well-being? *American Psychologist, 53*, 1017–1032.

Laguna, K., & Babcock, R. L. (1997). Computer anxiety in young and older adults: Implications for human–computer interactions in older populations. *Computers in Human Behavior, 13*(3), 317–326.

Lenhart, A. (2009a). *Adults and social network websites.* Retrieved February 15, 2010, from the Pew Internet & American Life Project: http://www.pewinternet.org/Reports/2009/Adults-and-Social-Network-Websites.aspx?r=1

Lenhart, A. (2009b). *Teens and mobile phones over the past five years: Pew Internet looks back.* Retrieved September 8, 2009, from the Pew Internet & American Life Project: http://www.pewinternet.org/Reports/2009/14--Teens-and-Mobile-Phones-Data-Memo.aspx

Lenhart, A., Arafeh, S., Smith, A., & Macgill, A. (2008). *Writing, technology and teens.* Retrieved April 26, 2008, from the Pew Internet & American Life Project: http://www.pewinternet.org/Reports/2008/Writing-Technology-and-Teens.aspx

Lenhart, A., Jones, S., & Macgill, A. (2008). *Adults and video games.* Retrieved September 8, 2009, from the Pew Internet & American Life Project: http://www.pewinternet.org/Reports/2008/Adults-and-Video-Games.aspx

Lenhart, A., Purcell, K., Smith, A., & Zickuhr, K. (2010). *Social media & mobile Internet use among teens and young adults.* Retrieved February 8, 2010, from the Pew Internet & American Life Project: http://www.pewinternet.org/Reports/2010/Social-Media-and-Young-Adults.aspx

Ling, R., & Yttri, B. (2006). Control, emancipation, and status: the mobile telephone in teens' parental and peer relationship. In R. Kraut, M. Brynin, & S. Kiesler (Eds.), *Computer, phones, and the Internet: Domesticating information technology* (pp. 219–234). New York: Oxford University Press.

Lipsman, A. (2009). *What Ashton vs. CNN foretold about the changing demographics of Twitter.* Retrieved September 2, 2009, from http://blog.comscore.com/2009/09/changing_demographics_of_twitter.html

Litwak, E., & Szelenyi, I. (1969). Primary group structure and their functions: Kin, neighbors, and friends. *American Sociological Review, 34*(4), 465–481.

Livingstone, S. (2003). Children's use of the Internet: Reflections on the emerging research agenda. *New Media & Society, 5,* 147.

Madden, M. (2009). *The audience for online video-sharing sites shoots up.* Retrieved February 15, 2010, from the Pew Internet & American Life Project: http://www.pewinternet.org/Reports/2009/13--The-Audience-for-Online-VideoSharing-Sites-Shoots-Up.aspx

Madden, M., & Lenhart, A. (2006). *Online dating.* Retrieved December 2, 2009, from the Pew Internet & American Life Project: http://www.pewinternet.org/Reports/2006/Online-Dating.aspx?r=1

Marsh, J., Brooks, G., Hughes, J., Ritchie, L., Roberts, S., & Wright, K. (2005). *Digital beginnings: Young children's use of popular culture, media and new technologies.* Retrieved March 4, 2010, from http://www.esmeefairbairn.org.uk/docs/DigitalBeginningsReport.pdf

McConatha, D., McConatha, J. T., & Dermigny, R. (1994). The use of interactive computer services to enhance the quality of life for long-term care residents. *The Gerontologist, 34*(4), 553–556.

McMellon, C. A., & Schiffman, L. G. (2002a). Cybersenior empowerment: How some older individuals are taking control of their lives. *Journal of Applied Gerontology, 21*(2), 157–175.

McMellon, C. A., & Schiffman, L. G. (2000). Cybersenior mobility: Why some older consumers may be adopting the Internet. *Advances in Consumer Research, 27,* 139–144.

Melenhorst, A. S., Rogers, W. A., & Bouwhuis, D. G. (2006). Older adults' motivated choice for technological innovation: Evidence for benefit-driven selectivity. *Psychology & Aging, 21*(1), 190–195.

Miller, C. C. (2009). Who's driving Twitter's popularity? Not teens. *The New York Times.* Retrieved September 2, 2009, from http://www.nytimes.com/2009/08/26/technology/internet/26twitter.html?_r=4

Millward, P. (2003). The "grey digital divide": Perception, exclusion and barrier of access to the Internet for older people. *First Monday, 8*(7). Retrieved December 4, 2009, from http://firstmonday.org/issues/issue8_7/millward/index.html

Monsour, M. (1992). Meanings of intimacy in cross- and same-sex friendships. *Journal of Social and Personal Relationships, 9,* 277–295.

Montgomery, K. C. (2000). Media culture in the new millennium: Mapping the digital landscape. *The Future of Children, 10*(2), 145–167.

Montgomery, K. C. (2007). *Generation digital.* Cambridge, MA: MIT Press.

Morgan, C., & Cotten, S. R. (2003). The relationship between Internet activities and depressive symptoms in a sample of college freshmen. *Cyberpsychology and Behavior, 6*(2), 133–142.

Morrell, R. W., Dailey, S. R., Feldman, C., Mayhorn, C. B., & Echt, K. V. (2004). *Older adults and information technology: A compendium of scientific research and web site accessibility guidelines.* Bethesda, MD: National Institute on Aging.

Morrell, R. W., Mayhorn, C. B., & Bennett, J. (2000). Survey of World Wide Web use in middle-aged and older adults. *Human factors, 42,* 175–182.

Namazi, K. H., & McClintic, M. (2003). Computer use among elder persons in long-term care facilities. *Educational Gerontology, 29,* 535–550.

Nie, N. H., & Erbring, L. (2000). Internet society: A preliminary report. *IT & Society, 1,* 275–283.

Nie, N. H., Stepanikova, I., Pals, H., Zheng, L., & He, X. (2005). *Ten years after the birth of the Internet: How do Americans use the Internet in their daily lives?* Stanford, CA: Stanford University, Stanford Institute for the Quantitative Study of Society.

Norris, P. (2001). *Digital divide: Civic engagement, information poverty and the Internet in democratic societies.* Cambridge: Cambridge University Press.

Palfrey, J., & Gasser, U. (2008). *Born digital: Understanding the first generation of digital natives.* New York: Basic Books.

Parks, M., & Floyd, K. (1996). Making friends in cyberspace. *Journal of Communication, 46,* 80–96.

Pasek, J., More, E., & Hargittai, E. (2009). Facebook and academic performance: Reconciling a media sensation with data. *First Monday, 14*(5), 4. Retrieved June 22, 2009, from http://firstmonday.org/htbin/cgiwrap/bin/ojs/index.php/fm/article/viewArticle/2498/2181

Quan-Haase, A. (2007). "University students" local and distant social ties: Using and integrating modes of communication on campus. *Information, Communication & Society, 10*(5), 671–693.

Quan-Haase, A., & Wellman, B. (2004). How does the Internet affect social capital? In M. Huysman & V. Wulf (Eds.), *Social capital and information technology* (pp. 113–132). Cambridge, MA: Massachusetts Institute of Technology.

Rainie, L. (2009, January). Teens and the Internet. From the *Pew Internet & American Life Project.* Paper presented at the Consumer Electronics Show—Kids@Play Summit.

Rideout, V., Foehr, U. G., & Roberts, D. F. (2010). *Generation M², media in the lives of 8- to 18-year olds.* Kaiser Family Foundation. Retrieved January 30, 2010, from www.kff.org/entmedia/upload/8010.pdf

Roberts, D. F., & Foher, U. G. (2008). Trends in media use. *The future of children, 18*(1), 11–37.

Rohlfing, M. E. (1995). "Doesn't anybody stay in one place anymore?" An exploration of an under-studied phenomenon of long-distance relationships. In J. T. Wood & S. Duck (Eds.), *Understudied relationships: Off the beaten track.* Newbury Park, CA: Sage.

Rosenmayr, L. (1977). The family: A source of hope for the elderly? In E. Shanas & M. B. Sussman (Eds.), *Family, bureaucracy, and the elderly* (pp. 132–157). Durham, NC: Duke University Press.

Sautter, J. M., Tippett, R. M., & Morgan, P. (2010). Social demography of Internet dating. *Social Science Quarterly, 91*(2), 554–575.

Scherer, K. (1996). College life online: Health and unhealthy Internet use. *Journal of College Student Development, 38,* 655–665.

Selwyn, N. (2004). The information aged: A qualitative study of older adults' use of information and communications technology. *Journal of Ageing Studies, 18*(4), 369–384.

Shah, D. V., Kwak, N., & Holbert, R. L. (2001). "Connecting" and "disconnecting" with civic life: Patterns of Internet use and the production of social capital. *Political Communication, 18*(2), 141–162.

Sifry, D. (2007). *The state of the blogosphere.* Retrieved September 2, 2009, from http://www.sifry.com/alerts/archives/000493.html

Smith, S. D., Salaway, G., & Caruso, J. (2009). *The ECAR study of undergraduate students and information technology, Volume 6.* Retrieved October 10, 2009, from www.educause.edu/ecar

Swindell, R. (2001). Technology and the over 65? Get a life. *Social Alternatives, 20*(1), 17.

Technorati. (2009). *State of the Blogosphere 2008.* Retrieved September 2, 2009, from http://technorati.com/blogging/state-of-the-blogosphere-2008/

Tufekci, Z. (2008). Grooming, gossip, Facebook, and Myspace. *Information, Communication & Society, 11*(4), 544–564.

Webber, M. M. (1973). Urbanization and communications. In G. Gerbner, L. P. Gross, & W. H. Melody (Eds.), *Communications, technology, and social policy.* New York: John Wiley & Sons.

White, H., McConnell, E., Clipp, E., Branch, L. G., Sloane, R., Pieper, C., et al. (2002). A randomized controlled trial of the psychosocial impact of providing internet training and access to older adults. *Aging and Mental Health, 6*(3), 213–221.

White, H., McConnell, E., Clipp, E., Bynum, L., & Teague, C. (1999). Surfing the net in later life: A review of the literature and pilot study of computer use and quality of life. *The Journal of Applied Gerontology, 18*(3), 358–378.

White, J., & Weatherall, A. (2000). A grounded theory analysis of older adults and information technology. *Educational Gerontology, 26,* 371–386.

Wright, K. (2000). Computer-Mediated Social Support, Older Adults, and Coping. *Journal of Communication, Summer,* 100–118.

Yardi, S., Golder, S. A., & Brzozowski, M. J. (2009). Blogging at work and the corporate attention economy. *Proceedings of the 27th International Conference on Human Factors in Computing Systems, USA,* 2071–2080.

Xie, B. (2007). Older Chinese, the Internet, and well-being. *Care Management Journals, 8*(1), 33–38.

DEMOGRAPHIC TRANSITIONS AND LIFE-SPAN DEVELOPMENT

26

Duane F. Alwin

INTRODUCTION

There is hardly any issue facing modern social and behavioral science that is not informed by the knowledge of *population processes* and the conceptual apparatus provided by the science of demography. The concept of a *population* is basic to modern social and behavioral science. Viewed from a statistical perspective, we refer to "the population" as the universe of generalization, providing a philosophical grounding for drawing inferences from a sample to something broader to provide external validity for our conclusions (Kaplan, 1964). Viewed from a *demographic perspective*, the concept of population has substantive meaning—since demography is the study of an area's population: its size, its composition, *and its change.* Thus, from a scientific point of view, it is not only important to understand the nature of the relevant population when generalizing about the nature of human behavior and the factors shaping it, it is perhaps even more important to understand *the nature of the population processes* that provide the background for understanding the nature of the phenomenon of interest and how it may have changed over the course of history.

This chapter focuses primarily on the population processes that produce change— those macro-level processes that affect change in the population and its characteristics, principally fertility, migration, morbidity, and mortality. *These are the phenomena that organize human life and around which human lives are constructed.* Consequently, modern demography has increasingly focused on other aspects of society that are *affected* by population processes and which can be better informed by taking the study of population into account. One such area is the study of human development, carried out primarily by life-span psychologists, but an area increasingly studied by social scientists as well (e.g., see Alwin & Wray, 2005).

The focus of this chapter is on the interplay between population processes and human life-span development from a social and historical perspective. In the first part of the chapter, I review *three* major "demographic transitions" that have affected the nature of life-span development over the course of time: (1) what is known as the first "demographic transition," when beginning in the early 19th century, Western society changed from high to low rates of fertility, (2) changes over the last half of the 20th century in the nature of the family/household, what Ron Lesthaeghe (1983, 1995) has named the "2nd demographic transition," involving changes in cultural values with respect to the nature of the family formation, which includes a wide range

Note: The author is the inaugural holder of the Tracy Winfree and Ted H. McCourtney Professorship in Sociology and Demography at Pennsylvania State University, where he directs the Center for Life Course and Longitudinal Research. The author acknowledges the assistance of Alyson Otto in the preparation of this chapter.

of attitudinal and behavioral changes, and the status/role of women (Lupri, 1983), and (3) the transition in the age structure of the population occasioned by declines in mortality rates and increased life expectancy resulting in the phenomenon of population aging. After reviewing these three key aspects of population processes and population change, I then summarize what is known about the impacts they have had on the nature of the life-span and human development, focusing on the historical changes in the nature of childhood, adolescence, adulthood, and old age.

■ POPULATION PROCESSES

As noted in the foregoing, in the following sections of this chapter, I refer to three major demographic transitions that are relevant to the study of life-span development—fertility declines that occurred over the past two centuries, the transition to new family forms and normative structures governing those changes, and the transition to new population age structures that will dominate the future of society.

Fertility Decline

The family is a unit of social organization that is highly relevant to the study of life-span human development because this is the locus of many important social functions, including the care and nurture of children, the provision of social supports for family members, the production of well-being and happiness, as well as economic production associated with the household. There are a number of demographic issues that are linked to the understanding of life-span development—one such issue, which is the focus of this section, is the change in the nature of modern family (and ultimately life-span development) linked to fertility and fertility decline. Population processes are linked in critical ways to families and their functioning, because *families* are the principal means by which societies reproduce themselves biologically, in addition to the transmission of values and norms required for the reproduction of social institutions.

   In most Western societies, the current demographic issues related to fertility have to do with the emergence over the past few decades of extremely low levels (i.e., below replacement) of fertility (e.g., Booth & Crouter, 2005), a topic that is gaining widespread public attention (see, e.g., Economist, 2009). Birth rates have reached an all-time low throughout the industrialized world, with many Western countries now experiencing levels of fertility that are below replacement (Bongaarts, 2002; Davis, 1986), and with most developing nations moving in the same direction (Dorius, 2008). In this regard, the United States is somewhat of an exception, compared with its European counterparts, with overall fertility at about the level (2.1 children per woman) required for replacement of the aging population (Morgan & Hagewen, 2005, p. 3). To the naïve observer, this fertility transition was of relatively recent origins, with fertility rates falling from the high post–World War II levels associated with the Baby Boom. Fertility declines have, however, occurred throughout most of the past century and well before, so the post–Baby Boom readjustments to lower birth rates were not so much "revolutionary" as they were a continuation of a rather long-term trend toward lower levels of fertility beginning more than two centuries ago (Teitelbaum & Winter, 1985). What has been known to demographers as the "demographic transition" (and now perhaps we should call it the "first demographic transition") has been defined as "the decline in mortality and fertility from the high rates characteristic of premodern and low-income societies to the low rates characteristic of modern and high-income societies" (Casterline, 2003, p. 210). This transition is of central concern to the subfield of demography; however, despite vast efforts to arrive at an explanation of these patterns, there is little agreement on its causes (see Casterline, 2003; Mason, 1997).

In a classic statement on this issue, Davis (1963) elaborated upon the strains creased natural fertility increases in the context of northern and western European and Japanese societies. In this Western context, the overpopulation of the household created by these natural demographic forces created a situation in which "regardless of nationality, language, and religion, each industrializing nation tended to postpone marriage, to increase celibacy, to resort to abortion, to practice contraception in some form, and to emigrate overseas" (Davis, 1963, p. 351). There were naturally many differences across national contexts, but the overall response to declining mortality rates, argued Davis, was a strain produced by larger cohorts of younger generations and consequent increments in household size that created the pressures for changes in reproductive behavior. Mason's (1997, p. 449) analysis is probably the most convincing to date, emphasizing the role of mortality declines as a necessary condition for fertility transitions, but not a sufficient one. Rather she emphasizes the fact that fertility transitions "occur under a variety of institutional, cultural, and environmental conditions" (p. 449), including the family and society's readjustment high birth rates, through antinatalist and birth-prevention policies that deal with their inability to accommodate more children.

The 2nd Demographic Transition

In addition to the fertility declines associated with the fertility transition mentioned earlier, and the changes in the nature of economic production that accompanied them, across the last one-half of the past century, the United States and other western nations have experienced unique demographic and social changes in the nature and functioning of family life. Lesthaeghe (1983, 1995) and his colleagues (Lesthaeghe & Meekers, 1986; Lesthaeghe & Neidert, 2006; Lesthaeghe & Surkyn, 1988) have named this the "2nd demographic transition." Patterns of marriage formation have undergone revolutionary changes in the past several decades, suggesting an increased flexibility in the emerging norms about marriage and union formation. The practice of cohabitation before (or instead) of marriage has grown increasingly acceptable, especially in the Scandinavian countries, and there has been a monumental increase in post–World War II rates of marital dissolution through divorce. Although divorce has become increasingly easy to obtain throughout the western nations (with the exception of Ireland, where the Catholic Church still strongly influences divorce legislation), rates of divorce in the United States over the past few decades have systematically increased to the point that they are the highest in Western industrialized countries (see Cherlin, 1992).

Changes in patterns of fertility, nuptiality, and divorce have been accompanied by changes in the gender-based division of labor, and there are several indications of significant shifts in the greater acceptance of nonfamilial roles for women. Perhaps the most dramatic of these is the pervasive changes in women's labor-force participation—changes that are not simply due to shifting patterns of fertility, marriage, and divorce. There has been a steadily increasing trend toward employment in the paid labor force by married women, especially those with young children. This has occurred in virtually every country in Western Europe, as well as in North America, although in Europe the changes are mainly seen in part-time employment (Rosenfeld & Birkelund, 1995).

Research over the past three decades in Australia, the Netherlands, Germany, Great Britain, and the United States shows that, in part as a consequence to changes in women's employment, attitudes and beliefs have become steadfastly more supportive of women's dual family and work roles (see, e.g., Alwin & Scott, 1996; Alwin, Scott, & Braun, 1996; Bolzendahl & Myers, 2004; Brewster & Padavic, 2000; Evans, 1995; Lee, Alwin, & Tufiş, 2007; Mason & Jensen, 1995; Mason & Lu, 1988; Neve, 1995; Scott, Alwin, & Braun, 1996; Thornton & Young-DeMarco, 2000). Changes in beliefs and attitudes have been experienced to a greater extent among educated women, those with labor-force experience, and those with nonfundamentalist religious orientations (see, e.g., Thornton, Alwin, & Camburn, 1983). These changes have occurred for both women and men, although changes for men have lagged behind those of women.

Accompanying the trends toward smaller and more egalitarian families is the growth of several alternative family forms and living arrangements (e.g., Goldscheider & Waite, 1991). Single-parent families, temporary partnerships, or same-sex relationships represent the main variation in new family forms, and substantial shifts have occurred in residential norms, with dramatic increases in persons living alone. However, despite the increased acceptability of alternative family forms and approval of divorce as a way out of unsuccessful marriages, conjugal unions continue to be the predominant family form as we move into the 21st century, and except for those choosing cohabitation, marriage is the persistent preference of the vast majority of individuals (Scott, Braun, & Alwin, 1993).

Although not everyone agrees on the causes of these changes, many point to the women's movement, the sexual revolution, the changing demography of the household, and the growing economic independence of women in modern life, all of which reinforce the notion that there are cultural changes in family-linked values of individualism. "At the heart of the matter," Lesthaeghe (1995, p. 58) argues, "is the articulation of individual autonomy and individuals' right to choose." Writing explicitly about fertility changes in Western Europe early on, Lesthaeghe (1983) made the argument for the importance of understanding the cultural underpinnings of changes in demographic conditions that appear to be related to a number of aspects of family change. Lesthaeghe (1983, 1995) encouraged a view of family change, emphasizing the role, not only of economic models of decision-making characteristic of previous literature, but changes in institutional arrangements reflecting cultural dynamics. He argued that changes in fertility in the European setting "can be viewed as manifestations of a cultural dimension that had already emerged at the time of the demographic transition in Europe" (p. 411). Economic theories of rational choice have a certain amount of appeal, but without understanding economic rationality within the context of sociological factors, especially the tendency toward the secularization of religion and the rise of humanistic ideational structures emphasizing individual freedom of choice, it would be difficult to fully understand the nature of fertility declines. Lesthaeghe (1983, 1995) pointed to the Enlightenment near the end of the 18th century, which he refers to as one of the most important ideational legacies of Western history, as redefining the position of the individual relative to society, "legitimizing the principle of individual freedom of choice" (p. 413). It is important, therefore, to consider the exogenous role of cultural factors in promoting social change, which helped bring about lower fertility via the shift toward the importance of "secular individualism" or the "rationality of the individual rather than the group" (Lesthaeghe, 1983, p. 415). And, against these economic, cultural, and political changes, one can not only see declining fertility as a reflection of the greater emphasis on individualism, but other changes in the family (e.g., the legitimation of nonmarital cohabitation, rising ages of first marriage, voluntary childlessness, sexual freedom, rises in divorce, and the demand for abortion) can be seen as part of the larger picture of social change in the direction of religious secularization and the rise of individualism (Lesthaeghe & Surkyn, 1988).

Thus, the issues facing individuals during the first and second demographic transitions were very different. Whereas in the first demographic transition persons face issues of fertility control and finding mechanisms for avoiding large numbers of births and/or births at younger and old ages, the issue in the second demographic is not one of fertility control, but of delaying parenthood, or avoiding it altogether. It is interesting to note that nearly 70 years ago Schumpeter (1988/1942) predicted that under modern conditions parenthood would be regarded as too heavy a personal sacrifice to make. For individuals and couples in the modern context it is "a matter of postponing or eschewing parenthood altogether because of more pressing competing goals such as prolonging education, achieving more stable income positions, increased consumerism associated with self-expressive orientations, finding a suitable companion and realizing a more fulfilled partnership, keeping an open future, and the like" (Lesthaeghe & Neidert, 2006, p. 1).

The Longevity Revolution

At some point over the next decade, the human species will reach a watershed moment—people over 60 will outnumber children, for the first time in human history (Waite, 2005). As I noted earlier, fertility rates have declined in recent decades to replacement levels in most of the western industrialized world (and below replacement in some parts of Europe; Morgan, 1996, 2003; Morgan & Hagewen, 2005), and many believe that declining mortality rates are causally linked to the other changes in family and household.

In preindustrial societies, both birthrates and death rates remained high and populations remained stable. In traditional societies, the social structure and cultural values helped maintain high fertility and reinforce the motivation to produce as many children as possible. Large numbers of children were advantageous because they contribute labor as children and as young adults; they bolster the family's political and economic position; they ensure survival of the lineage; they undertake necessary religious services for ancestors; and they care for parents in old age (Caldwell, 1976). With industrialization and technological advances, mortality rates tended to fall whereas birth rates remained high for a while and the population tended to grow. And then at some point in advanced industrial societies, birthrates began to fall in line with death rates. After industrialization, the costs of having children are high, in terms of the need for parents to invest heavily in their development, with less possibility of an economic or social return on the investment, and the motivation to have children is substantially less (Caldwell, 1982). After the mid-19th century, with improvements in sanitation, nutrition, income, and medical technology, older age mortality began to decline. There are several hypotheses about the processes involved—Finch and Crimmins (2004), for example, argue that because of substantially less exposure to infectious disease in childhood, levels of serum inflammatory proteins (e.g., C-reactive protein), which contribute to the risk of heart attack, stroke, and cancer, have declined in older populations.

Technological advances and scientific discoveries over the past century and more have resulted in a near doubling of life expectancy in developed regions of the world—increases estimated to be roughly 3 months per year since 1840 in most industrial societies (Oeppen & Vaupel, 2002). Population aging is a demographic fact, yet virtually all research on individual aging was conducted in a different era, under a different demographic regime, in which life expectancy was much lower. The pace of population aging is remarkable and allows little doubt that it is a global phenomenon (Gavrilov & Heuveline, 2003; Hayward & Zhang, 2001; United Nations, 2002).

CONSEQUENCES FOR LIFE-SPAN DEVELOPMENT

To understand the implications of the historical changes in demographic phenomena discussed earlier in this part of the chapter, I focus on four stages in the life cycle: *childhood, youth* or *adolescence, adulthood* (and middle age), and *old age* (what is sometimes called "the third age"), focusing on *how these demographic changes have altered the nature of people's lives*. To organize this discussion, I introduce what we consider to be a *life-span developmental perspective* in which we consider these phases as the life cycle in the context of historical and demographic change, but also as distinct phases that have been independently (e.g., the transition to adulthood), but as an interconnected whole.

First, however, it is useful to introduce some terminology that will be helpful in understanding the import of this scheme. The distinction between biographic and historical time is straightforward and I need not spend time on this, except to note that variations occurring with biographic time—variation in life cycle and life course—can interact in important ways with those events occurring in historical time. Variations in human experiences that occur in biographic time are often confused in part because they are confounded in time. I prefer to think of the biologically driven stages or phases of the life span—that is, the stages of the life cycle—in a much broader time metric and life-course events and transitions as more narrowly construed within the social constructions derived from them. In other words, variations in "life courses," that is differences in the social pathways from one life stage to another, for example, the transition from adolescence to adulthood, occur with a much narrow definition of time, than the much longer view of time considered over the entire life span (Alwin, 2010).

The Life Course

One theoretical framework that motivates the present chapter is that of the *life course*—defined by trajectories of events and transitions, for example, role sequences, which extend across the life span, but which are concentrated at certain transition points between life stages (Alwin, 2010; Elder, 1975, 1985, 1995, 1997a, 1997b, 1999, 2000; Elder & Johnson, 2003; Elder, Johnson, & Crosnoe, 2003; Elder & O'Rand, 1996; Elder & Shanahan, 2006; O'Rand & Krecker, 1990). The life-course perspective can be viewed as embedded within a larger, more all-encompassing *life-span developmental perspective* (Alwin, 2010; Alwin & Wray, 2005). The life-course framework has become a mainstay for demographers, since most notable events occurring between birth and death are *demographically relevant*, for example, transitions to preschool and school, leaving the parental home, marriage, marriage dissolution by divorce or widowhood, migration, labor-force entry and exit. Clearly, demographers have contributed to the study of the life course through (1) the focus of demography on the life course (e.g., Rindfuss, 1991; van Wissen & Dykstra, 1999; Willekens, 1999); (2) the measurement of life histories in the study of the life course (e.g., Belli, Stafford, & Alwin, 2009; Freedman, Thornton, Camburn, Alwin, & Young-DeMarco, 1988); and (3) the statistical analysis of the life course using demographic statistical tools, such as event history models, event-centered growth modeling strategies, and latent class models of life pathways (e.g., Alwin & Campbell, 2001; Alwin, Hofer, & McCammon, 2006; Macmillan & Eliason, 2003; Teachman, 1983).

Childhood

Childhood marks the beginning of the life span and the family provides the institutional base for the care of most children. The nature of childhood is a subject that is of great interest to historians, as well as social and behavioral scientists. Indeed, there has been quite a lot written in recent years about changes in the European family going back over the past three or four centuries. Although many of the family's institutional functions have remained the same over such lengthy spans of time—for example, the family has continued to be the *primary* agent for the care and nurture of children—the nature of parent–child relationships have experienced some significant changes (French, 2002; Vinovskis, 1987), One needs to exact a certain degree of care in approaching the historical literature on the nature of the family and parent–child interactions, as historians often lack a direct empirical portal into the past. History is always written from the point of view of the present and of the writer. There is often a tendency to perceive different periods of time in terms of an evolution of stages, whereas in fact the temporal continuities and discontinuities may not be driven by any such evolutionary mechanisms (Thornton, 2001, 2005). We nonetheless find a great deal of value in what historians of the family have to say about historical contrasts in parental practices because it alerts us to the potential for change in the environments in which children and parents interact and some of the explanations for that change (see Hernandez, 1993).

History of Childhood

In his classic historical study of conceptions of childhood, Philippe Ariès (1962) suggested that the development of the idea of the individuality of children, the acceptance of their inherent worth, and the emergence of an awareness of the innocence and purity of childhood all reflect a "privileged age" of 19th-century childhood (see Sommerville, 1982, p. 160). This shift in the perceived nature of children, Ariès argued, was in part a consequence of the changing demography of childhood. With declines in rates of infant mortality, children became more valuable, and this brought increased emotional commitment to children and interest in their development, at least among the elite classes in many parts of Europe and North America, and, theoretically at least, diffused to the working and peasant classes as well (Alwin, 1988, 1996a; Schlumbohm, 1980; Stone, 1977). Not everyone agrees with the Ariès (1962) thesis. For example, Pollock's (1983) examination of diaries among the educated classes of England across the 16th through 19th centuries casts considerable doubt on the assumption of maternal indifference to children during that period. And others (e.g., Shorter, 1975) have argued that the harsh treatment of children persisted into the 18th and 19th centuries among all social classes in Western Europe.

One does not have to look very far back to see some changes in parental orientations to children and the recognition of this fact should help signify that the potential for change in parental practices over long spans of time can be great. Wrigley (1989) performed a content analysis of child-rearing manuals published in America over the 20th century and found that the professional advice of child experts has changed from a preoccupation with such things as nutrition and toilet-training toward a greater emphasis on the need for cognitive development. And using survey data from a number of different sources over the 20th century, Alwin (1984, 1986, 1988, 1989b, 1996b) has shown that significant changes have occurred in Western countries in the values they emphasize in raising their children. Research results indicate a fairly clear pattern of increasing preferences for an emphasis that stresses the autonomy of children and a decline in the valuation of obedience. Over the periods and settings studied parental orientations to children had changed from a concentration on fitting children into society to one of providing for children in a way that would enhance their development (see Alwin, 2001, for a review).

Looking back even farther, the historical literature has suggested that there have been major changes in the role of parents in the socialization of children from medieval times onward, although admittedly such arguments must be considered in light of the difficulties of drawing any conclusions about what family life was like in past centuries. I already mentioned one of the most highly cited works on the history of childhood in which Ariès (1962) argued that during the Medieval period the boundaries between the household and the rest of society were relatively less rigidly defined as they are in their modern Western counterparts and this had major implications for the parental responsibility in the socialization of children. Relationships within the nuclear family were not necessarily closer than those outside and there was greater reliance on neighbors, relatives, and friends in the monitoring of children's behavior (see also Stone, 1977; Vinovskis, 1987). This may have been a consequence of the lack of privacy as much as anything else, but it clearly suggests differences in the nature of childhood.

With regard to parenting practices, some argue that the history of childhood since the Industrial Revolution is a nightmare from which we have only begun to awaken, referring to past periods in which children were subjected to exploitation, abuse, abandonment, and murder (DeMause, 1974). Life in an industrialized society was very difficult for children of the working classes, given their likely involvement in the labor force. By contrast, the lives of children of the elite classes were comfortable and relatively isolated from the ravages of working-class life. Some of these class differences can also be followed into the 19th and 20th centuries. In the American case, Zelizer (1985), for example, has argued that the "economically useful" child of 19th century industrialized society was eventually replaced by the "economically worthless," but "emotionally priceless" child of the 20th century. She contrasts these two views of childhood, as expressed in a variety of historical public documents in American society (child labor legislation, life insurance for children, compensation for the death of children, and patterns of adoption and foster care). The value conflicts inherent in the portraits Zelizer (1985) presents reflect important class differences. Working class children were those exploited by the industrial economy and to some extent by the circumstances of their own families. But middle-class reforms against child labor eventually denied them access to income from jobs in factories and stores. According to Zelizer, the children of the elite and business classes were rarely involved in paid labor and were removed from public environments of day-to-day life. The promulgation of the "sentimentalized" view of children by middle-class reformers thus conflicted with working-class strategies to obtain optimal economic well-being for the family through the labor-force involvement of their children (see Cunningham, 1991).

Fertility Declines and the Nature of Childhood[1]

A link between macro-level fertility declines and patterns of child socialization is posited by Caldwell (1976, 1982) in his theory of "wealth flows." He argues that the fundamental issue in the transition from high- to low-fertility regimes is "the *direction and magnitude of intergenerational wealth flows* or the net balance of the two flows—one from the parents to children and the other from children to parents—over the period from when people become parents until they die" (1976, p. 344; italics in original). In primitive and traditional societies, youngsters are economically advantageous because they contribute to labor as children and as young adults; they bolster the family's political and economic position; they ensure survival of the lineage; they undertake necessary religious services for ancestors; and they care for parents in old age. In such societies—especially where agriculture is the main mode of economic production—the net flow of intergenerational investment is from child to parent, and therefore high fertility is the rational choice. Caldwell emphasizes that in traditional societies the social structure—embodied in the nature of parent–child relationships—and the cultural values help maintain high fertility and reinforce the motivation to produce as many children as possible. In such societies, then, childrearing emphasizes loyalty, obligation, obedience, and commitment to family members.

In societies with an industrial mode of production, the balance of wealth flow changes: the net flow is toward children, and low or no fertility is rational. When the costs of having children are high, in terms of the need for parents to invest heavily in their development, with little possibility of an economic or social return, the motivation to have children is substantially less. Under such conditions, the need for loyalty and obedience in children is not as great, and it becomes much more important to teach independence and individual responsibility. In industrial societies, with

---

[1] See Alwin (1996b) for an extended discussion of the transition from an emphasis on childbearing to an emphasis on child rearing.

the expanding role of educational institutions in the socialization of children, the emphasis is on child development and children's autonomy. It is no accident, then, that researchers have identified education as a key component in the movement from high to low fertility regimes (Caldwell, 1982).

These themes are also emphasized in what must be the earliest discussion in American sociology of the linkage between fertility decline and a focus on the concern with the techniques of childrearing—the Lynds' famous *Middletown* study (Lynd & Lynd, 1929, pp. 131–152). To the Lynds, declining rates of fertility in the early 20th century, along with the technological shifts from an agrarian to an industrial economy, were critical factors in understanding the conditions of family life that shaped parental orientations to children. This theme is present in early research and scholarship concerning the "value of children" (see Bulatao, 1982; Hoffman, 1987) and "child quality" (see Blake, 1989), and in life-course analysis of parenting (Hogan, 1987; Rossi, 1987). Hoffman's (1987) research, based on a cross-sectional study of the value of children and childrearing goals in eight countries, concluded that people who "saw children as satisfying economic needs were more likely to want obedient than independent children," and where the value of children was viewed more in terms of noneconomic needs, independence and related traits were preferred over obedience (p. 140).

Adolescence

Positioned as a recognized life stage (or phase) between childhood and adulthood, adolescence is typically defined as a period between puberty and adulthood, beginning with the teen years and terminating at the age that "legal age of majority" is reached. The latter is largely a Western concept, and the legal age of majority may be different across regions, countries, states, and cultures. Still, a literature has emerged on the theme of a "youthful" status between childhood and when the society considers persons to be adults, and the transition to adulthood has become a thriving area of research in life-course studies. The current literature emphasizes that there is increasing variability in pathways to adult roles through historical time and that developmental processes are highly sensitive to transition behaviors (Shanahan, 2000). Accounts of such processes typically examine the active efforts of young people to shape their biographies or the socially structured opportunities and limitations that define pathways into adulthood. By joining these concepts, Shanahan (2000) suggests new lines of inquiry that focus on the interplay between agency and social structures in the shaping of lives.

History of Adolescence

Historical accounts often stress the fact that in traditional society individuals were not free of the constraints of the family and the locale, and were not able to exercise much control over the ways their lives developed. Although there may be some distortion of the extent to which young individuals struck out on their own, the idea that adolescence is a period in which the individual exerts a great deal of agency is relatively new (Shanahan, 2000, p. 670). There is plenty of evidence for the existence of a period of adolescence in the modern context, and Elder (1980) develops an interesting argument regarding social changes in the definition of adolescence. In a society characterized by a lengthy youthful stage in which the individual experiences a great deal of independence and a period of flexibility and openness to change, it may be reasonable to speak about the "impressionable years." On the other hand, in a society characterized by a rather abrupt transition from childhood to adulthood, with fewer choices open to the individual, there may not be such a youthful stage during which the individual is preoccupied with the pursuit of identity and autonomy (Kett, 1977; Shanahan, 2000). Elder's (1980; Elder, Caspi, & Burton, 1988) argument illustrates the great value of recent theorizing with respect to the consideration of the interaction of social change and life-span development, and his recent collaborative project on the implications of a changing society for children's growth and development is a landmark accomplishment (Elder, Modell, & Parke, 1993). From an historical perspective the life-course period of youth can be quite malleable. Modell (1989, p. 26) argues that the transformation in the transition to adulthood in American society over the 20th century "underlines much of the enlarged *salience* of the youthful life course... [reinforcing the view that]...the way one grows up is closely related to what one becomes."

The Impressionable Years

How open are young people to change, relative to other times in their lives? Developmental psychologists have argued that youth, at least in Western culture, does appear to represent a time of susceptibility to change. In the words of Erik Erikson (1988, p. 21) "to enter history, each generation of youth must find an identity consonant with its own childhood and consonant with an ideological promise in the perceptible historical process." During youth the tables are turned, continues Erikson: "No longer is it merely for the old to teach the young the meaning of life... it is the young who, by their responses and actions, tell the old whether life as represented by the old and presented to the young has meaning; and it is the young who carry in them the power to confirm those who confirm them and, joining the issues, to renew and to regeneration, or to reform and to rebel."

Thus, youth is a stage that represents an intersection of life history with social history, and developmentally, it is a time when individuals confirm their own identities within an historical context. It is also the case that developmental trajectories and stages of the life cycle for children interact in significant ways with historical period. For example, Elder's (1980) argument, mentioned above, has a more general applicability to the issues being addressed here. He suggests that in a society characterized by a lengthy youthful stage in which the individual experiences a great deal of independence and a period of flexibility and openness to change, it may be reasonable to theorize about the lifelong impact of youthful socialization experiences (see Alwin, 1994; Alwin, Cohen, & Newcomb, 1991).

One of the classic studies in sociology that illustrates these points was carried out in the 1930s and 1940s by Theodore Newcomb at Bennington College, then a newly formed women's college in southwestern Vermont. The young women who attended Bennington at that time came primarily from conservative backgrounds. By contrast, the faculty members were notably *progressive* in their economic and political views. Newcomb observed that the longer the young women stayed at Bennington, the more their political and economic views changed in the direction of the more liberal faculty. He concluded that young adulthood is constituted in terms of a period of openness to identity formation and change and that the individual's immediate environment plays a powerful role in shaping their views (Newcomb, 1943). It is now commonplace to assume that an individual's reference groups mediate and interpret the influences of social and political events (see Alwin et al., 1991). Newcomb's (1943) theoretical insights into the processes by which responses to social change are shaped by the individual's immediate environment have since become standard social psychological perspectives on human development.

There is also some additional indirect evidence to support the conclusion that youth is a particularly impressionable time when peoples' experiences are highly salient. When older adults are asked in laboratory settings to provide autobiographical memories from their lives without restrictions to the content or time period, they show a preponderance of memories for events that occurred during their adolescence and early adulthood (Rubin, 1999). In addition, when people are asked in surveys to report the most important event or change in the past half-century, there is often a heightened tendency to report things that occurred when they were young, say 10–30 years old (Schuman & Scott, 1989; Scott & Zac, 1993). Thus, there is some tangible support for the idea that *in the modern world* youth is a particularly impressionable period, insofar as memories of youthful experiences often seem to be the most salient.

Transition to Adulthood

The transition from being an adolescent to an adult has long been of interest to students of human development. Defined in terms of age (see Rindfuss, 1991), early adulthood extends from roughly ages 18 to 30, although this is clearly arbitrary. The life-course transitions experienced by individuals in most industrialized societies in this period focus on the domains of school, marriage, work, migration, and family, and the role shifts these events imply This is one of the most dense periods across the life span, in that individuals are experiencing a period of multiple transitions; stated differently, they are demographically dense. The sequence of roles or activities experienced by young adults can be similar or quite diverse, and these sequences may or may not occur in a socially mandated order (see Settersten, 2003). The transitions may be clear-cut, or they may be ambiguous as to whether the transition has even occurred, and Rindfuss (1991) talks about an increase in the diversity of the order in which young adults transition through life events that are typical of their experiences. In contrast to other periods of the life course, the young adult years represent a highly dense period involving multiple transitions. What is normative is *not* the pattern followed in making the transition, but the heterogeneity in the life experiences of individuals during this phase (Rindfuss, 1991). It is not clear when a particular behavior (or pattern of behavior) is considered "normative," in that there is both a multiplicity of norms, as well as an entire range of novel experiences. For example, for children growing up in the past few decades, divorce is an example. With the current divorce rates, we might begin to consider experiencing parental divorce and living in a "step family" as a normative trajectory for children. At the same time, Rindfuss (1991) considers that the United States is now characterized by its substantial diversity in the sequences of roles in the family and work/ school spheres, and these events are found in greater concentration in the young adult years, such as migration, childbearing, marriage, and changes in employment. The young adult years may be viewed as a chaotic, or anomic, time in one's life. Order refers to a sequence of roles that is expected because of the norms, values, and preferences of a society. Disorder, likewise, refers to an unexpected or undesirable sequence of roles in a segment of the life course (Rindfuss, 1991). Rindfuss (1991) suggests that disorder that occurred in early adulthood could have lasting effects into old age, especially for men and less so for women (footnote 7, p. 509), but that we do not have a great deal of knowledge of the outcomes of order and disorder. Rindfuss (1991) notices, for example, that both marital fertility and unmarried women's fertility rates have risen for every age group between 1974 and 1987 but the latter has risen faster than those for the former. Then, he points out the reasons of fertility increase as changing relationships between marriage and fertility, structural changes (e.g., childcare services), and declines in the fertility-inhibiting effects of singlehood.

Social Pathways and the Life Course

There are several ways in which demographers have furthered the study of life-span development through their focus on the life-course framework, including the development of event history models, the development of event-centered models of within-person change, and the examination of role configurations over time. One of the most important contributions to the study of the demography of the life course is Macmillan and Eliason's (2003) investigation of the normative social pathways that are followed by young people in modern society. Their study is perhaps one of the most unique studies to date of the social pathways to adulthood using data from the United States. Their analysis provides an overtime snapshot of the interplay of probabilistic pathways of social roles that characterize the life course. They simultaneously describe the timing of social roles, their probabilistic ordering, and the general diversity that exists in the structure of the life course, resulting in a description of the following *three* latent life paths during the transition to adulthood in contemporary U.S. society: (1) *Latent Life Path I*: school—work—marriage—children; (2) *Latent Life Path II*: school—work—children—marriage; and (3) *Latent Life Path III*: school—children—marriage—work. I mention the Macmillan and Elison (2003) results in depth here because their work offers a powerful framework both for conceptualizing and empirically modeling the life course as a series of transitions and trajectories. It builds on a strong sociological literature (the life-course framework discussed earlier) that has produced a lot of ideas, but which has not come forth with a set of methodological tools for modeling these aspects of the life course— transitions and trajectories. Their work also provides that set of tools—latent class analysis—and as such it may represent a major step forward in the empirical analysis of role transitions. Their proposed approach provides an analytic framework for formally modeling role configurations over time—what they call *life paths*—and assessing a number of empirical issues (e.g., heterogeneity and density) that have been addressed by the literature.

The Macmillan and Eliason (2003) investigation is not without limitations. First, it studies a narrow range of cohorts, persons born in 1962 and 1963, in a particular place. Although this is a useful baseline, clearly one of the principles of the life-course perspective is that how lives unfold is conditioned by time and place. Greater emphasis should be given to this aspect of the design when generalizations are made about the transition to adulthood in Western societies. We know for example that access to schooling has undergone dramatic changes in the half century prior to the birth of these cohorts in ways that would have dramatically altered the paths of role configurations. Certainly these are issues that will confront other "life path" modelers who will examine the historical changes in the population probabilities and conditional probabilities. Second, the Macmillan–Eliason framework presents a highly descriptive model—taking information about what role people are occupying at 2-year intervals and linking them over time—that is focused on role configurations and life pathways. What is absent in this presentation are two kinds of variables that capture what we might (for lack of a better term) refer to as "human development." One of these is *resources* that account for what "latent life path" a person is likely to occupy. Describing the patterns separately for race and gender give some life to this set of issues, but there are other types of resources, some material, some cognitive, some experiential, that condition the likelihood of following one or another life path. What is left unstated here is how the latent class approach can be modified to essentially incorporate "explanatory" factors (or predictors) which might be used in a larger framework that focuses not simply on describing life pathways, but also on accounting for them. This would in fact be very Elder-esque in the way in which he studied the *Children of the Great Depression*—he explicitly asked about how different levels of resources conditioned the pathways people followed through the Depression years (Elder, 1974). The second class of variables that is "left out" of this framework is what might be called "developmental outcomes"—that is, outcomes that occur to individuals as a consequence of following a particular pathway, for example, economic well-being, psychological well-being, attitudes, etc. My point in stressing the omission of these variables from the picture is not intended as a criticism, but as a challenge for the future application of this approach. People who want to follow this approach are going to need to know how to incorporate both "explanatory" factors as well as "outcome" factors to make full use of the advantages of the latent class approach.

Adulthood

Adulthood is roughly considered to span the age range from 30 onward, and includes what we typically call "midlife," although at some point across the life span of adulthood this term is eclipsed by additional life phases recently called the "third age" and "old age," which come into play after the age of retirement. For present purposes I consider adulthood to range to age 65, and the "third age" to commence from that point onward. "Old age" in the modern context is somewhat difficult to define, although some efforts have made a distinction in which those age 85+ are referred to as the "oldest old" (Suzman, Willis, & Manton, 1992). Because of different rates of biological aging, and because chronological age is an imprecise measure of biological aging, such arbitrary categorizations are often heuristically valuable, but operationally worthless. Rather than assume some type of homogeneity of experience associated with age, it is better to employ the life-course conceptualization that focuses on the age at which persons make transitions from work and the ages associated with the outcomes of health and longevity.

Traditional Views

Becoming an adult is a life cycle transition that is indicated by multiple markers (Hogan & Astone, 1986). It involves the passage through several objective statuses, typically assumed to involve the completion of schooling, the establishment of a residence apart from the parental home, the achievement of economic self-sufficiency, marriage and/or cohabitation with a spouse or partner, the legal status of emancipation, the ability to vote and serve in the military, for most, the entry into full- or part-time productive work, and for many, a phase of sexual reproduction (Mortimer & Aronson, 2000). Achieving adult status and the reproductive years are often thought to complete the "cycle of life," although modern views on human development extend well beyond these traditional notions of the life cycle.

The concept of "life cycle" has a very precise meaning in the biological sciences—the life cycle of humans includes the prolonged dependence on adults, generally monogamous and private pursuit of sex, concealed ovulation, and menopause among females, and this is what makes us distinctive from other mammals (Diamond, 1992). In the social sciences the concept of "life cycle" refers not simply to biological characteristics and changes in the organism, but also to the socially constructed, age-related sequence of stages individuals pass through beginning with birth and ending with death (Hogan, 2000). Historically "life cycle" refers to a fixed sequence of irreversible stages, tied specifically to sexual reproduction. An adult then produces gametes (sex cells) and fertilization of an egg begins the process over again with the development of a new individual (O'Rand & Krecker, 1990, p. 242). In recent discussions, old age is typically included as a postreproductive life stage.

The life cycle concept's emphasis on reproduction and generation within the framework of a population has retained considerable interest among demographers. Hogan (2000), one contemporary proponent of the utility of the life cycle concept, argues, for example, that the life cycle concept links individual aging, the organization of roles in society, reproduction, and through the notion of age-succession (cohort replacement) societal innovation and change. Underlying the sociological conception of life cycle is the recognition that humans are biological organisms that are born, mature, and die. As with other biological organisms, reproduction is a key feature of human maturation, ensuring the persistence of the species (Hogan, 2000, p. 1623), but there is an important element of social construction that is ignored by biological perspectives.

There seems to be a variety of opinion on the value of the life cycle concept, and the distinctiveness of the concept of "life cycle" has all but been lost in the social and behavioral sciences. As O'Rand and Krecker (1990, p. 248) note "the terms *aging* and *life cycle* have often been treated as synonymous" in the field of individual aging research. The principle model of *life cycle* that predominated at the end of the 19th century "referred to the unilinear series of changes (transformations) in form undergone by organisms in their development over time from early stages to equivalent stages in the succeeding generation." The irreducible properties of the life cycle, therefore, were successive forms (stages), irreversible development (maturation), and the reproduction of form (generation). These elements of the life cycle defined the linkage between time and variation over the life span.

In the 1940s, Glick (1947, 1967) introduced the idea of a "family life cycle," suggesting that families progress through a sequence of stages, from courtship to the death of one's spouse (see also Duvall, 1977; Hill, 1970). This concept has been roundly criticized, especially by those who introduced the life-course concept into the social and behavioral sciences, but despite this alternative theorizing about family-related life events, the concept of *family life cycle* appears to be alive and well in some sectors of demographic research.

In stark contrast, for many developmental scientists the term "life cycle" is problematic, partly because there is more to the human life cycle than biological development. Furthermore, the theories of the "family life cycle" adapted these ideas, construing family life as a fixed sequence of discrete states: "courtship, engagement, marriage, birth of the first child, birth of the last child, children's transition in school, departure of the eldest and youngest child from the home, and marital dissolution through the death of one spouse" (Elder, 1997b, p. 945). These models seem too deterministic and leave little or no room for deviation. Sociologists have adopted in their place the more sophisticated and flexible "life-course" perspective. As Settersten (2003, p. 16) notes these family life cycle models are "largely inappropriate in contemporary times: marriage and parenting are often independent of one another; family size has shrunk; a period of cohabitation may occur before marriage; nontraditional family forms are prevalent, divorce occurs in record numbers, children return to the nest, and the joint survival time of spouses has lengthened."

Parenthood

Like other aspects of the life course, *parenthood* is both a biological and social status. Viewed within a biological life cycle framework parenthood can be seen as a natural outcome of reproduction and regeneration. Viewed from a social and cultural perspective the situation of parenthood conveys certain rights, responsibilities, obligations, and associated expectations regarding the care and nurture of children. Although the role of parenthood viewed biologically has important consequences for children—particularly in the transmission of genetic information and predispositions that may have developmental consequences—our focus here is primarily on parenthood as a social and cultural phenomenon. A central theme of the contemporary literature is that what parents want for their children, and what they believe is the best approach to achieving their goals through their parenting practices will depend not only upon a host of parental and child characteristics but upon a number of historical, economic, demographic, cultural, ecological, and structural variables that shape parental approaches to child-rearing (see Seltzer & Ryff, 1994, for a review).

It is interesting to note that nearly 70 years ago Schumpeter (1988/1942) predicted that under modern conditions parenthood would be regarded as too heavy a personal sacrifice to make. Still, most people in modern industrialized societies will become parents at some point in their lives. Although we recognize there may be some universal consequences that derive from the parent–child relationship, we must also indicate at the outset that the meaning of parenthood is quite diverse even within the same historical period and in the same society. The rights and obligations of parenthood depend on a host of parental and child characteristics. For example, what it means to be a *mother* versus what it means to be a *father* are generally quite different things in virtually all cultural settings. Also, what parents may try to achieve in parenting a newborn infant is something quite different from what they may aspire to in parenting an adolescent. The demands arising both from the parent–child relationship and from the social context in which the parental role is enacted are quite different across these life stages.

Many discussions of human parenting begin with the assumption that there are species-level universals that affect the nature of human parenting—*what parents do to their children and when and how they do it*. An extreme version of such a view would suggest that what parents do with respect to raising their young are determined largely by biological factors (instincts) and cultural variations in how parents approach developmental issues are irrelevant or relatively less important to the course of that development (Corter & Fleming, 2002). Support for this view comes from well-documented species-related patterns of parental behaviors that humans hold in common with other primates. These consist, for example, of patterns of feeding, grooming, protection, and extended periods of intensive nurturance and investment in child care (Altmann, 1987). There are also some striking contrasts between humans and other species and considerable variation among primates (Bard, 2002). Although there are substantial investments by parents in the care and nurture of offspring among most primates, mainly by the mother, it is also the case among a great many species individuals other than the biological mother and father interact with children in significant ways (McKenna, 1987). This may be true in some human cultures as well, and we know that parental time investments vary considerably by culture (Bjorklund, Yunger, & Pellegrini, 2002; Draper & Harpending, 1987).

This chapter raises the question of whether changes in the lives of adults have an effect on their ability to parent. There are several traditions of thought in Western behavioral science regarding processes that are candidates to be considered as universal developmental processes that are intimately linked to parenting practices, including attachment theory, object-relations theory, ego development theory, symbolic interaction theory, moral development theory, and psychoanalytic theories of psychosexual development. I do not discuss these further except to note that it has long been believed that one of the most basic and universal features of human life is the close and immediate attachment between the infant child and its parents, especially the mother. The period of infancy is believed by most modern experts to be a time of special sensitivity in which children play an active part in their own development. The intense mutual interaction between one or more parents during this period is thought to be critical (Bornstein, 2002, p. 7). Early theories of attachment went a long way toward organizing our knowledge about the importance of parental responsiveness to the early development, arguing that the critical factor is maternal deprivation. Deprivation during infancy, it was argued, would contribute to affective problems in later childhood, adolescence, and adult life. The alternative view is that, although infancy is an important period of development, humans exhibit an amazing ability to adapt to their surroundings and early experiences may be altered or supplanted by later ones (Kagan, 1984).

Transitions From Work

One of the most predictable events in the life span of most persons is the fact that at some point they will withdraw from the occupational realm, wherein they have some type of labor-force status. Although it is inadequate in many ways, the term "retirement" is what is often used to describe the transition from an active role in the productive labor force to the status of not being actively engaged in the labor force. Over the past two decades, policy makers have worried that the continued popularity of early retirement, increasing life expectancy, and the changing age composition of the population may place significant strain on contemporary pension and health care systems unless workers remain in the labor force longer than they currently do. On the other hand, some posit that recent demographic and economic trends will force older workers to work beyond their desired retirement ages, and that current employers will not be prepared for either opportunities or challenges that older workers may bring, especially as the Baby Boom cohorts reach retirement age. Because of population aging, increasing uncertainty regarding the solvency of the Social Security system, and the recent impact of economic downturns on the adequacy of private pensions, retirement policies in the United States are increasingly likely to be the subject of public debate; thus, there is an urgent need to understand the critical precursors of retirement decisions.

Understandably, the study of retirement behavior has historically been viewed as the province of economists and other social scientists (e.g., Hanushek & Maritato, 1996). To date, the literature on health and transitions out of paid work generally focuses on two issues—the economic and health antecedents of the transitions (particularly to retirement) and the consequences of the transitions for health and economic well-being. According to existing literature, people retire when income and assets allow them to; or they retire when their physical health begins to fail and they can no longer work. Certainly, physical health is crucial to a person's functioning in daily life, including working for pay; however, other domains of health and functioning—such as cognitive functioning and psychological well-being—may also play a part. The focus on physical health alone is often due to the lack of data on other domains of health, and new data sources are now available that include measures within these expanded conceptual domains, and there is a high priority on understanding the precursors of transitions in and out of the labor force in older age.

The Third Age

As I noted earlier, the monotonic and irreversible declines in fertility and mortality rates associated with the first demographic transition have lead to the inevitable second-order growth in the proportion of elderly people in modern day populations. Increasingly, individuals are considered to have entered the "third age" in their lives. This term came from France, where in the 1970s and 1980s in conjunction with "Universities of the Third Age," designed for the enrichment of the lives of pensioners, made reference to a *new* life stage (Laslett, 1989; Moen & Spencer, 2006). The third age is viewed "as distinct from both the second age [adulthood] and the fourth age [old age]" (Moen & Spencer, 2006, p. 128), and the emergence of this new life stage between the traditional age of retirement and what many consider to be "old age" challenges many of our preconceptions about the "expected" life course. This is a new area for research, inasmuch as the traditional blueprints for how persons pattern their lives are diverging from the ways in which future cohorts will develop their later life choices.

Old Age

Population aging is a defining issue for this century, and it is doubtful that current research literatures will be adequate to address this challenge, since so little is known about the aging of populations beyond the past few decades. As the proportion of the world's population in the older age ranges continues to increase, there is a need for new and improved information about the factors that contribute to health and longevity—a need to reconcile current bodies of knowledge with the changing experiences of an aging population. Historical demographers (e.g., Kertzer & Laslett, 1995; Laslett, 1995) argue that one place to begin is with the available knowledge we have of the history of old age. Biodemographers (e.g., Carey, 2003) argue that another is the study of the biology and demography of longevity in nonhuman species.

The History of Old Age

Although the study of old age and old people is a burgeoning industry in all contemporary industrialized countries, due in part to increases in population aging, this has not always been the case, and for most present-day populations we know little about the experience of old age in past societies. This is in part because of lack of good demographic data, but also because of the phenomenon itself, and, in general, historical demographers can tell us little about the lives and social roles of the elderly population over the past several centuries. Because women did not bear many children after they reached the age of 40, coupled with lower life expectancies characteristic of past societies, there was no differentiation between adulthood and old age (Haber, 1983). Thus, the historical meaning of the human life span has undergone dramatic change, and consequently, those who research human development have changed the focus of research.

From a biographical point of view the concept of the *life span*—the length of life for an individual organism—draws attention to the biological limits on development and signals the temporal scope of inquiry. A life-span developmental perspective, thus, focuses on the processes and experiences occurring throughout the entire life span, from birth to death. What happens between birth and death is the focus of studies of human development in psychology, sociology, and related fields, and historically the study of aging has been viewed as synonymous with the study of human development after some arbitrary point in the life span. The "life-span developmental" perspective is a somewhat broader framework, as it considers "aging" to begin at the beginning. Life-span perspectives conceptualize human development and aging as multidimensional and multidirectional processes of growth involving both gains and losses. Human development and/or aging are embedded in multiple contexts and are conceived in terms of dynamic processes in which the ontogeny of development interacts with the social environment, a set of interconnected social settings, embedded in a multilayered social and cultural context. The uniqueness of individual biographies and the diversity of life patterns have encouraged a more radical approach to human development within the social sciences.

There are two relatively new developments in the study of old age. First, David Kertzer and Peter Laslett's (1995) monumental work on *aging in the past* initiated a new subfield of historical family studies that focuses on the historical demography of old age. Hardly two decades old, the study of the history of old age has produced a number of new findings and approaches. Technological advances and scientific discoveries over the past century and more have resulted in a near doubling of life expectancy in developed regions of the world—increases estimated to be roughly 3 months per year since 1840 in most industrial societies (Oeppen & Vaupel, 2002). Population aging is a demographic fact, yet virtually all research on individual aging was conducted in a different era, under a different demographic regime, in which life expectancy was much lower. The pace of population aging is remarkable and allows little doubt that it is a global phenomenon (Gavrilov & Heuveline, 2003; Hayward & Zhang, 2001; United Nations, 2002). As the proportion of the world's population in the older age ranges continues to increase, there is a need for new and improved information about the factors that contribute to health and longevity—a need to reconcile current bodies of knowledge with the changing experiences of an aging population.

Life span, aging, and mortality present some of the most profound puzzles in modern human science. Despite our deep interest in mortality, little is known about why some individuals live to middle age and others to extreme old age (Vaupel, Manton, & Stallard, 1979; Weiss, 1990; Wilmoth, 1998). A second new development is on population processes involved in longevity is the work of James Carey (2003) and his colleagues that focuses on a biological and demographic framework for understanding the key factors that govern the aging of populations. Carey's (2003) recent research presents the results of a long-term study of the determinants of longevity using data from the life tables of five million Mediterranean fruit flies, one of the most comprehensive sets of data available on a single species. Carey (2003) interprets the fruit fly data within the context of aging processes in general and especially with respect to human aging. Several themes emerge from this type of research: the suggestion that there are no species-specific life-span limits, the context-specific nature of the mortality rate, and the biodemographic linkages between longevity and reproduction. The study of human longevity is now only in its infancy, since we have not have population data on humans through the end of their life spans.

The Future of Old Age

In the modern context, the aging of the population will substantially increase the number of elderly persons with physical and cognitive disability in need of long-term care over the next several decades. We will have unprecedented numbers of people living longer, but more often living with chronic disease and disability, both physical and cognitive. The study of disability is, thus, an increasing focus of studies of aging, and new formulations, such as the concept of "disability-free life expectancy" (see e.g., Crimmins & Saito, 2001).

One measure of aging is to employ measures from the cognitive literature. It is typically assumed that "cognitive decline" typically occurs with aging, and that regardless of one's "cognitive reserve," there is an inevitable process of neurological decline, resulting in many cases in dementia (i.e., the inability to function in society). Current literature indicates that cognitive impairment in older age is largely unpreventable, and that dementia, particularly due to Alzheimer's Disease, will increase in prevalence in the coming years (Brookmeyer & Gray, 2000; Brookmeyer, Gray, & Kawas, 1998; Evans et al., 1992). To cite one study team, "the prevalence of AD in the next 50 years is projected to nearly quadruple, which means that 1 in every 45

Americans will be affected by the disease" (Kawas & Brookmeyer, 2001, p. 1160). The population sciences are central to our understanding of the future health and well-being of an aging population, particularly where the boundaries of traditional demographic approaches are being redrawn. Until recently, a behavioral and social research program by National Institute on Aging emphasized narrow approaches to the demography and economics of aging; but the mounting evidence that broader approaches are necessary has encouraged a more expansive view: narrowly bounded demographic and economic approaches are not sufficient to generate the much-needed information on the consequences of population aging (for an alternative view, see Suzman, 2005).

FUTURE DIRECTIONS IN THE STUDY OF DEMOGRAPHY ACROSS THE LIFE SPAN

In this chapter, I have argued that to understand the nature of human life-span development one needs to know the demographic context of that development. The understanding of population processes, involving fertility, mortality, and migration are essential to understanding the challenges presented by the life course at each of several phases in the overall life span. At the same time, a demographic perspective is hardly enough. I conclude the chapter with the observation that determining variation in health and longevity requires not only a demographic approach, but an interdisciplinary perspective, one that includes the integration of the population sciences with the developmental, biomedical and policy sciences. Key mechanisms linking population characteristics to health and longevity include developmental or biological (including genetic) influences and society-level policies or institutional arrangements that shape the life course of health and well-being.

Future research in the area of human development will increasingly focus on the integration of the *population* and *developmental* sciences. In contrast to many related social, economic, and biological sciences, where structural concepts are dominant, a unique feature of both population and developmental perspectives is their focus on the processes and mechanisms of change. As the human sciences traditionally concerned with the geographical concept of population (e.g., size, composition, and change) as well as factors that shape those features, demography has evolved to emphasize processes at both micro- and macro-social levels. Demographic processes—such as fertility, migration, population aging, disease and its transmission, and mortality—that organize human life and around which human lives are constructed, affect society in fundamental ways. As a modern science, demography has begun to explore other aspects of society that are affected by *population processes* and which can be better informed by taking the study of population into account. As a discipline, demography produces theoretical insights and empirical findings about human well-being, by employing core population concepts, macro- and micro-unit data and measures, and unique quantitative science methodologies (e.g., life tables, cohort analysis, and event history analysis). Demographers increasingly found that using theories and models of human development can improve population projections (DeJong, 2003).

In addition to the value of the demographic approach, the life-span developmental perspective laid out earlier argues that developmental science is indispensable to understanding the challenges of an aging society. To be sure, developmental science has pioneered methodological literatures that focus on the measurement of human traits (e.g., factor analysis, item response theories) and change (e.g., growth modeling); the influences of social context (e.g., multilevel modeling); and the examination of relative impacts of theoretically relevant determinants (e.g., structural equation models and path analysis). Developmental scientists, who are increasingly exposed to the core concepts, knowledge, and techniques of population science, see the need to understand the relationship of human development to differences in population composition and vital rate phenomena. In turn, population scientists have been turning to the emerging models of individual development and quantitative approaches to the study of change and stability in individual and environmental influences on demographic phenomena (DeJong, 2003). Looking to the future, research and scholarship necessary to fully understand process at both micro- and macro-social levels will require a transdisciplinary integration. Preparation of scientists for such future cross-disciplinary work is necessary to meet the future challenges of knowledge development in the study of health, disability, functional status, and population well-being.

REFERENCES

Altmann, J. (1987). Life span aspects of reproduction and parental care in anthropoid primates. In J. B. Lancaster, J. Altmann, A. S. Rossi, & L. R. Sherrod (Eds.), *Parenting across the life span: Biosocial dimensions* (pp. 15–29). New York, NY: Aldine de Gruyter. Alwin, D. F. (1984). Trends in parental socialization values: Detroit, 1958 to 1983. *American Journal of Sociology, 90*, 359–382.

Alwin, D.F. (1984). Trends in parental socialization values: Detroit, 1958 to 1983. *American Journal of Sociology, 90*, 359–382.

Alwin, D. F. (1986). Religion and parental child-rearing orientations: Evidence of a Catholic-Protestant convergence. *American Journal of Sociology, 92*, 412–440.

Alwin, D. F. (1988). From obedience to autonomy: Changes in traits desired in children. *Public Opinion Quarterly, 52*, 33–52.

Alwin, D. F. (1989a). Cohort replacement and parental socialization values. *Journal of Marriage and the Family, 52*, 347–360.

Alwin, D. F. (1989b). Changes in qualities valued in children in the United States, 1964 to 1984. *Social Science Research, 18*, 195–236.

Alwin, D. F. (1994). Aging, personality, and social change: The stability of individual differences over the adult life span. In D. L. Featherman, R. M. Lerner, & M. Perlmutter (Eds.), *Life span development and behavior* (Vol. 12, pp. 135–185). Hillsdale, NJ: Lawrence Erlbaum Associates, Inc.

Alwin, D. F. (1996a). Parental socialization in historical perspective. In C. Ryff & M. M. Seltzer (Eds.), *The parental experience at midlife* (pp. 105–167). Chicago: University of Chicago Press.

Alwin, D. F. (1996b). From childbearing to childrearing: The link between declines in fertility and changes in the socialization of Children. In J. B. Casterline, R. D. Lee, and K. A. Foote (Eds.), *Fertility in the United States: New patterns, new theories* (pp. 176–196). New York: Population Council.

Alwin, D. F. (2001). Parental values, beliefs, and behavior: A review and promulga for research into the new century. In S. J. Hofferth & T. J. Owens (Eds.), *Children at the millenium: Where have we come from, where are we going?* (pp. 97–139). New York: JAI Press.

Alwin, D. F. (2010). Integrating varieties of life course concepts. Paper presented at the 105th annual meetings of the American Sociological Association, August 15, 2010, Atlanta, GA. Available from the Center for Life Course and Longitudinal Research, College of the Liberal Arts, Pennsylvania State University.

Alwin, D. F., & Campbell, R. T. (2001). Quantitative approaches: Longitudinal methods in the study of human development and aging. In R. H. Binstock & L. K. George (Eds.), *Handbook of aging and the social sciences* (5th ed., pp. 22–43). New York: Academic Press.

Alwin, D. F., Cohen, R. L., & Newcomb, T. M. (1991). *Political attitudes over the life span: The Bennington women after fifth years*. Madison, WI: University of Wisconsin Press.

Alwin, D. F., Hofer, S. M., & McCammon, R. J. (2006). Modeling the effects of time: Integrating demographic and developmental perspectives. In R. H. Binstock & L. K. George (Eds.), *Handbook of aging and the social sciences* (6th ed., pp. 20–38). New York: Academic Press.

Alwin, D. F., & Scott, J. L. (1996). Attitude change: Its measurement and interpretation using longitudinal surveys. In B. Taylor & K. Thomson (Eds.), *Understanding change in social attitudes*. Aldershot, UK: Dartmouth Publishing Co. Ltd.

Alwin, D. F., Scott, J. L., & Braun, M. (1996, August). *Sex-role attitude change in the United States: National trends and cross-national comparisons*. Biannual meetings of the Research Committee on Social Stratification, International Sociological Association. Ann Arbor, MI.

Alwin, D. F. & Wray, L. A. (2005). A life-span developmental perspective on social status and health [Special issue II]. *Journals of Gerontology, 60B*, 7–14.

Ariès, P. (1962). *Centuries of childhood: A social history of family life*. New York: Knopf.

Bard, K. A. (2002). Primate parenting. In M. Bornstein (Ed.), *Handbook of parenting*. (Vol. 2, pp. 99–140). Mahwah, NJ: Lawrence Erlbaum Associates.

Belli, R. F, Stafford, F. P., & Alwin, D. F. (2009). *Calendar and time diary methods in life course research*. Thousand Oaks, CA: Sage Publications.

Bjorklund, D. F., Yunger, J. L. & Pellegrini, A. D. (2002). The evolution of parenting and evolutionary approaches to childrearing. In M. Bornstein (Ed.), *Handbook of parenting*. (Vol. 2, pp. 3–30). Mahwah, NJ: Lawrence Erlbaum Associates.

Blake, J. (1989). *Family size and achievement*. Berkeley, CA: University of California Press.

Bolzendahl, C. L., & Myers, D. J. (2004). Feminist attitudes and support for gender equality: Opinion change in women and men, 1974–1998. *Social Forces, 83*, 759–789.

Bongaarts, J. (2002). The end of fertility transition in the developed world. *Population and Development Review, 28*, 419–444.

Booth, A., & Crouter, A. C. (2005). *The new population problem: Why families in developed countries are shrinking and what it means*. Mahwah, NJ: Lawrence Erlbaum Associates.

Bornstein, M. H. (2002). *Handbook of parenting* (Vols. 1–-5). Mahwah, NJ: Lawrence Erlbaum.

Brewster, K. L. & Padavic, I. (2000). Change in gender-ideology, 1977–1996: The contributions of intracohort change and population turnover. *Journal of Marriage and the Family, 62*, 477–487.

Brookmeyer, R., & Gray, S. (2000). Methods for projecting the incidence and prevalence of chronic diseases in ageing populations: application to Alzheimer's disease. *Statistics in Medicine, 19*, 1481–1493.

Brookmeyer, R., Gray, S., & Kawas, C. (1998). Projections of Alzheimer's disease in the United States and the public health impact of delaying disease onset. *American Journal of Public Health, 88*, 1337–1342.

Bulatao, R. (1982). *On the nature of the transition in the value of children*. Honolulu: East-West Center.

Caldwell, J. C. (1976). Toward a restatement of demographic transition theory. *Population and Development Review, 2*, 321–366.

Caldwell, J. C. (1982). *Theory of fertility decline*. New York: Academic Press.

Carey, J. R. (2003). *Longevity—The biology and demography of life span*. Princeton, NJ: Princeton University Press.

Casterline, J. (2003). Demographic transition. In P. Demeny & G. McNicoll (Eds.), *Enclyclopedia of population* (pp. 210–216). New York, NY: Macmillan Reference USA.

Cherlin, A. (1992). *Marriage, divorce, remarriage*. Cambridge, MA: Harvard University Press.

Corter, C. M., & Fleming, A. S. (2002). Psychobiology of maternal behavior in human beings. In M. Bornstein (Ed.), *Handbook of parenting*. (Vol. 2, pp. 141–181). Mahwah, NJ: Lawrence Erlbaum Associates.

Crimmins, E. M., & Saito, Y. (2001). Trends in healthy life expectancy in the United States, 1970–1990: Gender, racial, and educational differences. *Social Science and Medicine, 52*, 1629–1641.

Cunningham, H. (1991). *The children of the poor: Representations of childhood since the seventeenth century*. Cambridge, MA: Blackwell.

Davis, K. (1963). The theory of change and response in modern demographic history. *Population Index, 29*, 345–366.

Davis, K. (1986). Low fertility in evolutionary perspective. In K. Davis, M. Bernstam, & R. Ricardo-Campbell (Eds.), *Below-replacement fertility in industrialized societies*. Cambridge, UK: Cambridge University Press.

DeJong, G. F. (2003). Paradigms for graduate training in population studies. *PAA Affairs, Spring*, 3–4.

DeMause, L. (1974). The evolution of childhood. In L. DeMause (Ed.), *The history of childhood*. New York: Psychohistory Press.

Diamond, J. (1992). *The third chimpanzee: The evolution and future of the human animal*. New York, NY: Harper Collins Publishers.

Dorius, S. (2008). Global demographic convergence? A reconsideration of changing intercountry inequality in fertility. *Population and Development Review, 34*, 519–537.

Draper, P., Harpending, H. (1987). Parent investment and the child's environment. In J. B. Lancaster, J. Altmann, A. S. Rossi, & L. R. Sherrod (Eds.), *Parenting across the life span: Biosocial dimensions* (pp. 207–235). New York, NY: Aldine de Gruyter.

Duvall, E. M. (1977). *Marriage and family development* (5th ed.). Philadelphia: J.B. Lippincott.

Economist. (2009, October 29). Go forth and multiply a lot less—Lower fertility is changing the world for the better. *The Economist Newspaper*.

Elder, G. H., Jr. (1974). *Children of the Great Depression: Social change in life experience*. Chicago, IL: University of Chicago Press.

Elder, G. H., Jr. (1975). Age differentiation and the life course. *Annual Review of Sociology, 1*, 165–190.

Elder, G. H., Jr. (1980). Adolescence in historical perspective. In J. Adelson (Ed.), *Handbook of adolescent psychology* (pp. 3–46). New York: John Wiley & Sons.

Elder, G. H., Jr. (1985). Perspectives on the life course. In G.H. Elder Jr. (Ed.), *Life course dynamics: Trajectories and transitions, 1968–1980* (pp. 23–49). Ithaca: Cornell University Press.

Elder, G. H., Jr. (1995). The life course paradigm. In P. Moen, G. H. Elder Jr., & K. Lüscher (Eds.), *Examining lives in context: Perspectives on the ecology of human development* (pp. 101–139). Washington, DC: American Psychological Association.

Elder, G. H., Jr. (1997a). *The life course as developmental theory*. Presidential address, Society for Research on Child Development, Washington, DC, April 5, 1997.

Elder, G. H., Jr. (1997b). The life course and human development. In R.M. Lerner (Ed.), *Handbook of child psychology: Vol. 1. Theoretical models of human development* (pp. 939–991). New York: John Wiley.

Elder, G. H., Jr. (1999). *The life course and aging: Some reflections*. Distinguished Scholar Lecture, Section on Aging and Life Course, Annual meetings of the American Sociological Association, August 10, 1999.

Elder, G. H., Jr. (2000). The life course. In E. F. Borgatta & R. J. V. Montgomery (Eds.), *Encyclopedia of sociology* (2nd ed., vol. 3, pp. 1614–1622). New York: Macmillan Reference USA.

Elder, G. H., Jr., Caspi, A., & Burton, L. M. (1988). Adolescent transitions in developmental perspective: Sociological and historical insights. In M. Gunnar (Ed.), *Minnesota Symposium on Child Psychology* (pp. 151–179). Hillsdale, NJ: Lawrence Erlbaum Associates.

Elder, G. H., Jr., & Johnson, M. K. (2003). The life course and aging: Challenges, lessons, and new directions. In R. A. Settersten Jr. (Ed.), *Invitation to the life course: Toward new understandings of later life* (pp. 49–81). Amityville, NY: Baywood Publishing Co. Inc.

Elder, G. H., Jr., Johnson, M. K., & Crosnoe, R. (2003). The emergence and development of life course theory. In J. T. Mortimer & M. J. Shanahan (Eds.), *Handbook of the life course* (pp. 3–19). New York: Kluwer Academic/Plenum Publishers.

Elder, G. H., Jr., Modell, J., & Parke, R. D. (Eds.). (1993). *Children in time and place*. Cambridge: Cambridge University Press.

Elder, G. H., Jr., & O'Rand, A. M. (1996). Adult lives in a changing society. In K. S. Cook, G. A. Fine, and J. S. House (Eds.), *Sociological perspectives on social psychology* (pp. 452–475). Boston: Allyn and Bacon.

Elder, G. H., Jr., & Shanahan, M. J. (2006). The life course and human development. In W. Damon and R. M. Lerner (Eds.), *Handbook of child psychology: Vol. 1. Theoretical models of human development* (6th ed., pp. 665–715). New York, NY: John Wiley & Sons, Inc.

Erikson, E. H. (1988). Youth, fidelity and diversity. *Daedalus, 117*, 1–24.

Evans, M. D. R. (1995). Norms on women's employment over the life course: Australia, 1989–93. *Worldwide Attitudes, 1995.11.06*, 1–8.

Evans, D. A., Scherr, P. A., Cook, N. R., Albert, M. S., Funkenstein, H. H., Beckett, L. A., et al. (1992). The impact of Alzheimer's disease in the United States population. In R. M. Suzman, D. P. Willis, & K. G. Manton (Eds.), *The oldest old* (pp. 283–299). New York, NY: Oxford University Press.

Finch, C. E., & Crimmins, E. M. (2004). Inflamatory exposure and historical changes in human life-spans. *Science, 305*, 1736–1739.

Freedman, D., Thornton, A., Camburn, D., Alwin, D. F., & Young-DeMarco, L. (1988). The life history calendar: A technique for collecting retrospective data. In C. C. Clogg (Ed.), *Sociological methodology* (pp. 37–68). Washington, DC: American Sociological Association.

French, V. (2002). History of parenting: The ancient Mediterranean world. In M. H. Bornstein (Ed.), *Handbook of parenting: Biology and ecology of parenting* (2nd ed., Vol. 2). Mahwah, NJ: Lawrence Erlbaum.

Gavrilov, L. A., & Heuveline, P. (2003). Aging of population. In P. Demeny & G. McNicoll (Eds.), *The encyclopedia of population* (Vol. 1, pp. 32–37). New York: Macmillan Reference USA.

Glick, P. C. (1947). The family life cycle. *American Sociological Review, 12,* 164–174.

Glick, P. C. (1967). Updating the life cycle of the family. *Journal of Marriage and the Family, 39,* 5–13.

Goldscheider, F. K., & Waite, L. J. (1991). *New families, no families? The transformation of the American home.* Berkeley, CA: University of California Press.

Haber, C. (1983). *Beyond sixty-five.* Cambridge, UK: Cambridge University Press.

Hanushek, E. A. & Maritato, N. L. (Eds.). (1996). *Assessing knowledge of retirement behavior.* Panel on Retirement Income Modeling. Committee on Statistics. Commisson on Behavioral and Social Sciences and Education. National Research Council. Washington, DC: National Academy Press.

Hayward, M. D., & Zhang, Z. (2001). Demography of aging: A century of global change, 1950–2050. In R. H. Binstock & L. K. George (Eds.), *Handbook of aging and the social sciences* (5th ed., pp. 69–85). New York: Academic Press.

Hernandez, D. J. (1993). *America's children: Resources from family, government and the economy.* New York: Russell Sage Foundation.

Hill, R. (1970). *Family development in three generations.* Cambridge, MA: Schenkman.

Hoffman, L. W. (1987). The value of children to parents and childrearing patterns. *Social Behaviour, 2,* 123–141.

Hogan, D. P. (1987). Demographic trends in human fertility and parenting across the life span. In J. B. Lancaster, J. Altmann, A. S. Rossi, & L. R. Sherrod (Eds.), *Parenting across the life span: Biosocial dimensions* (pp. 315–349). New York, NY: Aldine de Gruyter.

Hogan, D. P. (2000). Life cycle. In E. F. Borgatta & R. J. V. Montgomery (Eds.), *Encyclopedia of sociology* (2nd ed., vol. 3, pp. 1623–1627). New York: Macmillan Reference USA.

Hogan, D. P., & Astone, N. M. (1986). The transition to adulthood. *Annual Review of Sociology, 12,* 109–130.

Kagan, J. (1984). *The nature of the child.* New York: Basic Books.

Kaplan, A. (1964). *The conduct of inquiry.* San Francisco: Chandler.

Kawas, C. H, & Brookmeyer, R. (2001). Editorial—Aging and the public health: Effects of dementia. *The New England Journal of Medicine, 344,* 1160–1161.

Kertzer, D. I., & Laslett, P. (Eds.). (1995). *Aging in the past: Demography, society, and old age.* Berkeley, CA: University of California Press.

Kett, J. F. (1977). *Rites of passage: Adolescence in America, 1790 to the present.* New York: Basic Books.

Laslett, P. (1989). *A fresh map of life: The emergence of the third age.* Cambridge, MA: Harvard University Press.

Laslett, P. (Eds.). (1995). Necessary knowledge: Age and aging in the societies of the past. In D. I. Kertzer & P. Laslett (Eds.). *Aging in the past: Demography, society, and old age* (pp. 3–77). Berkeley, CA: University of California Press.

Lee, K. S., Alwin, D. F., & Tufiş, P. A. (2007). Beliefs about women's labour in the reunified Germany, 1991–2004. *European Sociological Review, 23,* 487–503.

Lesthaeghe, R. (1983). A century of demographic and cultural change in Western Europe: An exploration of underlying dimensions. *Population and Development Review, 9,* 411–435.

Lesthaeghe, R. (1995). The second demographic transition in western countries: An interpretation. In K. OMason & A.-M. Jensen (Eds.), *Gender and family change in industrialized countries* (pp. 17–62). Oxford: Clarendon Press.

Lesthaeghe, R., & Meekers, D. (1986). Value change and the dimensions of familism in the European community. *European Journal of Population, 2,* 225–268.

Lesthaeghe, R. &, Neidert, L. (2006). The second demographic transition in the United States: Exception or textbook example? *Population and Development Review, 32,* 669–698.

Lesthaeghe, R., & Surkyn, J. (1988). Cultural dynamics and economic theories of fertility change. *Population and Development Review, 11,* 1–45.

Lupri, E. (1983). *The changing position of women in family and society: A cross-national comparison.* Leiden: E.J. Brill.

Lynd, R. S. & Lynd, H. M. (1929). *Middletown: A study in comtemporary American culture.* New York: Harcourt-Brace.

Macmillan, R., & Eliason, S. R. (2003). Characterizing the life course as role configurations and pathways: A latent structure approach. In J. T. Mortimer & M. Shanahan (Eds.), *Handbook of the life course* (pp. 529–554). New York: Kluwer Academic/Plenum Publishers.

Mason, K. O. (1997). Explaining fertility transitions. *Demography, 34*, 443–454.

Mason, K. O., & Jensen, A-M. (1995). *Gender and family change in industrialized countries*. Oxford, UK: Clarendon Press Oxford.

Mason, K. O., & Lu, Y.-H. (1988). Attitudes toward women's familial roles: Changes in the United States, 1977–1985. *Gender and Society, 2*, 39–57.

McKenna, J. J. (1987). Parental supplements and surrogates among primates: Cross-species and cross-cultural comparisons. In J. B. Lancaster, J. Altmann, A. S. Rossi, & L. R. Sherrod (Eds.), *Parenting across the life span: Biosocial dimensions* (pp. 143–184). New York, NY: Aldine de Gruyter.

Modell, J. (1989). *Into one's own: From youth to adulthood in the United States 1920–1975*. Berkeley: The University of California Press.

Moen, P., & Spencer, D. (2006). Converging divergences in age, gender, health, and well-being: Strategic selection in the third age. In R. H. Binstock & L. K. George (Eds.), *Handbook of aging and the social sciences*. New York, NY: Academic Press.

Morgan, S. P. (1996). Characteristic features of modern American fertility. In J. B. Casterline, R. D. Lee, & K. A. Foote (Eds.), *Fertility in the United States: New patterns and new theories*. New York, NY: The Population Council. [A supplement to *Population Development Review*, vol. 22, 1996.]

Morgan, S. P. (2003, May). *Is low fertility a 21st century crisis?* Presidential address at the annual meeting of the Population Association of America, Minneapolis, MN.

Morgan, S. P., & Hagewen, K. (2005). Is very low fertility inevitable in America? Insights and forecasts from an integration model of fertility. In A. Booth & A. C. Crouter (Eds.), *The new population problem—Why families in developed countries are shrinking and what it means* (pp. 3–28). Mahwah, NJ: Lawrence Erlbaum Associates, Inc.

Mortimer, J. T., & Aronson, P. (2000). Adulthood. In E. F. Borgatta & R. Motgomery (Eds.), *Encyclopedia of sociology* (2nd ed., Vol. 1, pp. 25–41). New York: Macmillan.

Neve, R. (1995). Changes in attitudes toward women's emancipation in the Netherlands over two decades: Unraveling a trend. *Social Science Research, 24*, 167–187.

Newcomb, T. M. (1943). *Personality and social change: Attitude formation in a student community*. New York, NY: Dryden Press.

Oeppen, J., & Vaupel, J. W. (2002). Broken limits to life expectancy. *Science, 296*, 1029–1031.

O'Rand, A. M., & Krecker, M. L. (1990). Concepts of the life cycle: Their history, meanings, and uses in the social sciences. In W. R. Scott and J. R. Blake (Eds.), *Annual review of sociology* (Vol. 16, pp. 241–262). Palo Alto, CA: Annual Reviews Inc.

Pollock, L. A. (1983). *Forgotten children: Parent--child relations from 1500 to 1900*. Cambridge: Cambridge University Press.

Rindfuss, R. R. (1991). The young adult years: Diversity, structural change and fertility. *Demography, 28*, 493–512.

Rosenfeld, R. A. & Birkelund, G. E. (1995). Women's part time work: A cross-national comparison. *European Sociological Review, 11*, 111–134.

Rossi, A. S. (1987). Parenthood in transition: From lineage to child to self-orientation. In J. B. Lancaster, J. Altmann, A. S. Rossi, & L. R. Sherrod (Eds.), *Parenting across the life span: Biosocial dimensions* (pp. 31–81). New York, NY: Aldine de Gruyter.

Rubin, D. C. (1999). Autobiographical memory and aging: Distributions of memories across the life-span and their implications for survey research. In N. Schwarz, D. Park, B. Knäuper, & S. Sudman (Eds.), *Cognition, aging, and self-reports* (pp. 163–183). Washington, DC: Taylor & Francis.

Schlumbohm, J. (1980). "Traditional" collectivity and "Modern" individuality: Some questions and suggestions for the historical study of socialization: The examples of the German lower and upper bourgeoisie around 1800. *Social History, 5*, 71–103.

Schuman, H., & Scott, J. L. (1989). Generations and collective memories. *American Sociological Review, 54*, 359–381.

Schumpeter, J. (1988). Decomposition. *Population and Development Review, 14*, 499–506. [Originally published in *Capitalism, socialism, and democracy*. (1942). New York: Harper & Row.]

Scott, J. L., Alwin, D. F. & Braun, M. (1996). Generational changes in gender role attitudes: Britain in cross-national perspective. *Sociology, 30*, 471–492.

Scott, J. L., Braun, M., & Alwin, D. F. (1993). The family way. In R. Jowell, L. Brook & L. Dowds (Eds.), *International social attitudes: The 10th BSA report*. Brookfield, VT: Dartmouth Publishing Company, Ltd.

Scott, J. L., & Zac, L. (1993). Collective memories in the United States and Britain. *Public Opinion Quarterly, 57*, 315–331.

Seltzer, M. M., & Ryff, C. D. (1994). Parenting across the life span: The normative and nonnormative cases. In D. L. Featherman, R. M. Lerner, & M. Perlmutter (Eds.), *Life span development and behavior* (Vol. 12, pp. 2–40). Hillsdale, NJ: Lawrence Erlbaum Associates, Inc.

Settersten, R. A., Jr. (2003). Propositions and controversies in life-course scholarship. In R. A. Settersten Jr. (Ed.), *Invitation to the life course: Toward new understandings of later life* (pp. 15–45). Amityville, NY: Baywood Publishing Co. Inc.

Shanahan, M. J. (2000). Pathways to adulthood in changing societies: Variability and mechanisms in life course perspective. *Annual Review of Sociology, 26,* 667–692.

Shorter, E. (1975). *The making of the modern family.* New York: Basic Books.

Stone, L. (1977). *The family, sex and marriage in England, 1500–1800.* New York: Oxford University Press.

Sommerville, J. (1982). *The rise and fall of childhood.* Beverly Hills, CA: SAGE Publications.

Suzman, R. M. (2005). Research on population aging at NIA: Retrospect and prospect. In L. J. Waite (Ed.), *Aging, health, and public policy: Demographic and economic perspectives* (pp. 239–264). New York: Population Council.

Suzman, R. M., Willis, D. P., & Manton, K. P. (1992). *The oldest old.* New York, NY: Oxford University Press.

Teachman, J. (1983). Analyzing social processes: Life tables and proportional hazards models. *Social Science Research, 12,* 263–301.

Teitelbaum, M. S. & Winter, J. M. (1985). *The fear of population decline.* Orlando, FL: Academic Press.

Thornton, A. (2001). The developmental paradigm, reading history sideways, and family change. *Demography, 38,* 449–465.

Thornton, A. (2005). *Reading history sideways—The fallacy and enduring impact of the developmental paradign on family life.* Chicago: University of Chicago Press.

Thornton, A., Alwin, D. F., & Camburn, D. (1983).Causes and consequences of sex-role attitudes and attitude change. *American Sociological Review, 48,* 211–227.

Thornton, A., & Young-DeMarco, L. (2001). Four decades of trends in attitudes toward family issues in the U.S.: 1960s through 1990s. *Journal of Marriage and Family, 63,* 1009–1037.

United Nations. (2002). *World population ageing: 1950–2050.* Population Division, Department of Economic and Social Affairs. New York, NY: United Nations Publications.

van Wissen, L. J. G., & Dykstra, P. A. (Eds.). (1999). *Population issues: An interdisciplinary focus.* New York: Kluwer Academic/Plenum Publishers.

Vaupel, J. W., Manton, K. G., & Stallard, E. (1979). The impact of heterogeneity in individual frailty on the dynamics of mortality. *Demography, 16,* 439–454.

Vinovskis, M. A. (1987). Historical perspectives on the development of the family and parent-child interactions. In J. B. Lancaster, J. Altmann, A. S. Rossi & L. Sherrod (Eds.), *Parenting acros the life span—Biosocial dimensions.* New York: Aldine de Gruyter.

Waite, L. J. (2005). Aging, health, and public policy: Demographic and economic perspectives. New York: Population Council.

Weiss, K. M. (1990). The biodemography of variation in human frailty. *Demography, 27,* 185–206.

Willekens, F. J. (1999). The life course: Models and analysis. In L. J. G. van Wissen and P. A. Dykstra (Eds.), *Population issues: An interdisciplinary focus* (pp. 23–51). New York: Kluwer Academic/Plenum Publishers.

Wilmoth, J. (1998). The future of human longevity: A demographer's perspective. *Science, 280,* 395–397.

Wrigley, J. (1989). Do young children need intellectual stimulation? Experts' advice to parents, 1900–1985. *History of Education Quarterly, 29,* 41–75.

Zelizer, V. A. (1985). Pricing the priceless child: The changing social value of children. New York: Basic Books

LIFE-SPAN DEVELOPMENTAL BEHAVIOR GENETICS

27

Brendan M. Baird and Cindy S. Bergeman

A central tenet of life-span psychology is that development can occur at any time during a person's life, from conception to death, and does not necessarily proceed toward a specific end state (Baltes, Reese, & Lipsitt, 1980). In other words, a person does not stop developing once he or she reaches a certain age or attains a certain level of maturity. Instead, behavior is continually subjected to forces that bring about both stability and change. As a result, development is often largely independent of biological age and is capable of proceeding indefinitely. In some cases, changes that occur during one period may be caused by the same factors that bring about changes during other periods, whereas in other cases, development that occurs in different periods may be due to processes that are entirely distinct from one another (Baltes, Reese, & Nesselroade, 1977). Another tenet of life-span psychology is that development occurs within, and is affected by, the cultural and historical contexts in which individuals live. Furthermore, these contextual factors change over time and their influences can vary both across different aspects of behavior and across different developmental periods (Baltes et al., 1980). The challenges for researchers, therefore, are to examine the patterns of development that occur during different periods of the life course, to discover the forces underlying those changes, and to identify the relationships among them.

Information about the factors that contribute to successful development, as well as the mechanisms through which these processes take place, is critical for understanding individual differences in life trajectories (Smith, 2009). In this chapter, we present the theoretical and methodological foundations of the behavioral genetic approach to studying development across the life span. We begin by providing an overview of basic behavior genetic methodologies, including a description of different genetically informative research designs, such as twin, family, and adoption studies. We then discuss how these basic designs can be extended in ways that may help researchers find answers to complex questions about developmental processes. To illustrate the utility of behavior genetic designs, we review several examples of research on the heritability of cognitive abilities during different parts of the life span. This review is not intended to be exhaustive, but rather to demonstrate how behavioral genetics studies can inform theories not only in childhood and adolescence, but in midlife and later life as well. Finally, we conclude with a discussion of the ways in which developmental scientists and behavioral geneticists can join forces to the benefit of both fields. In particular, studies of the interplay between genetic and environmental influences across the life span, as well as the surge in efforts to identify genetic markers for complex behavioral traits, offer a number of exciting opportunities to advance the field of life-span psychology.

▦ INTRODUCTION TO BEHAVIORAL GENETICS

Behavioral genetics is a social science metatheory, rooted in the biology of sexual reproduction, which provides a set of research methodologies for investigating the influences of genes and environments on behavior (Plomin, DeFries, & McClearn, 1980). The goal of behavioral genetics research is to determine the extent to which individual differences in a trait or characteristic, called a *phenotype*, are the result of variation in people's genetic makeup, called a *genotype*. Although there are many single-gene disorders, there is no example of a behavioral phenotype that is governed by a single gene. Instead, the complexities of behavior are due to combinations of genes, each having a small effect, and environmental influences. The gene action works through the regulation of proteins that interact in physiological systems. In addition to influencing individual differences in a behavior, genes can also influence the developmental trajectories of that behavior. For example, if cognitive ability is an inherited trait, then changes that occur across the life span, and the rate at which those changes occur, may also be under genetic influence. This is a topic that we will cover in more detail later.

In quantitative or statistical genetics, phenotypic variance in a population of individuals is broken down into components that are attributable to genetic and environmental sources of influence. *Heritability* is a descriptive statistic that is used to estimate the proportion of variance in a phenotype that is the result of genotypic differences between people. In other words, the more a trait varies from person to person because of differences in those people's genes, the higher the heritability of that trait. Heritability can be further divided into *additive genetic variance*, which is the extent to which there is a linear relation among the alternate forms of a gene, called *alleles*, and *nonadditive genetic variance*, which is the extent to which there are interactions between alleles. Interactions that take place at a single locus are called *dominance*, whereas an interaction that takes place between alleles at different loci is called *epistasis*. For simplicity, in most studies these two types of nonadditive effects are combined. The proportion of phenotypic variance that is not due to genotypic differences between people is attributed to environmental influences. Just as is the case with heritability, variance due to environmental influences can be broken down into more specific components. The component of environmental variance that leads to similarities among relatives is called *shared, common,* or *between-family variance*, whereas the component of environmental variance that makes relatives different from one another is called *nonshared, specific,* or *within-family variance*. Because of their ability to differentiate specific types of environmental influences, behavioral genetics studies can provide compelling evidence regarding the role that environments play in human development.

An area of particular interest to life-span researchers is the interface between genes and environments (Belsky & Pluess, 2009). *Genotype–environment (GE) interactions* occur when individuals with certain genetic propensities are more sensitive to specific aspects of the environment (Bergeman & Plomin, 1989). In other words, the impact that the environment has on behavioral development is due, at least in part, to a person's genetic predispositions. Rutter (2006) calls these inherited factors "susceptibility" genes, because they may make certain individuals more sensitive than others to particular environmental effects. For example, Cadoret and colleagues found evidence of GE interactions in the development of conduct disorder, adult antisocial behavior, and aggression (Cadoret, Cain, & Crowe, 1983; Cadoret, Yates, Troughton, Woodworth, & Stewart, 1995). Although it is often difficult to identify GE interactions (Wahlsten, 1990), particularly in research on cognitive abilities, genetic influences on effects of socioeconomic status (SES; Turkheimer, Haley, Waldron, D'Onofrio, & Gottesman, 2003) and parental education (Rowe, Jacobson, & van den Oord, 1999) on intelligence have been reported.

Recent reports of interactions between genetic markers and environmental experiences in the development of psychiatric disorders have led to renewed interest in this area. Specifically, Caspi et al. (2003) reported a relationship between a specific gene polymorphism (in the 5-HTT serotonin transporter gene) and life stress on depression, a finding that has been replicated in several studies (Eley et al., 2004; Kendler, Kuhn, Virtum, Prescott, & Riley, 2005). In contrast, a recent meta-analysis of results from 14 studies suggested that there is no evidence of an effect of the 5-HTT genotype in concert with stressful life events affecting an elevated risk of depression (Risch et al., 2009). In fact, Eaves (2008), using a series of simulated models, suggests that the results supporting a GE interaction may be spurious, rather than definitive, and possibly due to problems in measurement (e.g., the way in which interview data are transformed into a psychiatric diagnosis) or genotyping error. Although the results of this simulation study do not preclude the influence of specific genes on psychiatric outcomes that is conditional on exposure to environmental risk, more research is needed (Caspi et al., 2003).

Another area of interest to life-span researchers is the association between genetic variation and environmental differences, called *genotype-environment correlation* (Plomin, DeFries, & Loehlin, 1977). *Passive* GE correlation occurs when children "inherit" environments that are correlated with their genetic propensities because they share both family environment and genes with their parents (e.g., parents with higher intelligence are more likely to read to their children and provide them with education-oriented toys). *Reactive*, or *evocative*, GE correlations are due to exposures that derive from people reacting differently to individuals with different genotypes (e.g., students are chosen to participate in a gifted and talented program at their school because of their intellectual ability). Finally, *active* GE correlation describes the situation in which children seek out or even create environments for themselves that are correlated with their genetic propensities (e.g., individuals with higher intellectual ability choose a profession that stimulates their cognitive ability or enhances opportunities for learning). It is important to point out that the various components of genetic and environmental influence can only be estimated with specific types of data, so researchers must consider their goals for a particular study when choosing a research design.

GENETICALLY INFORMATIVE RESEARCH DESIGNS

Because the purpose of behavioral genetics research is to estimate the extent to which behavior is influenced by heritable and environmental influences, the prototypical behavioral genetic study includes samples that come from groups of individuals who are (a) of varying levels of genetic relatedness and (b) are exposed to environments that are of varying levels of similarity. In this section we describe each of the three major research designs in behavioral genetics. For each design, we start by describing the basic features in detail; we then discuss the strengths and weaknesses, and point out how those problems may be addressed. Finally, we describe how each design can be extended in ways that are useful for testing hypotheses about life-span development. We refer readers to Neale and Cardon (1992) for information about specific methods of analyzing data from genetically informative designs.

Family Design

In family studies, information about a behavior of interest is collected from individuals who are in the same family but who have varying degrees of genetic relatedness, such as children, parents, brothers and sisters, aunts and uncles, grandparents, and cousins. Because the number of genes that are shared by various family members is specified in quantitative genetic theory, the heritability of a behavior can be estimated from the extent to which different sets of relatives are similar to one another. If a particular behavior is heritable, then first-degree relatives who share a lot of the same genes, such as siblings and their parents, should behave in ways that are more similar to one another than second-degree relatives who only share a few of the same genes, such as cousins and their grandparents. On the other hand, if a behavior is not heritable, then closely related individuals should be no more similar to one another than distantly related individuals. In a similar way, the family design allows researchers to estimate the effects of environmental influences by comparing family members living in the same household with family members who live in different households. If a behavior is influenced by environmental factors, then people who live together should be more similar to one another than people who do not live together. These basic comparisons can provide a great deal of information about the origins of individual differences.

In behavioral genetics research, family studies are valuable for at least two reasons. First, they can be used to estimate the upper limit of additive genetic effects, which by definition must be less than or equal to twice the phenotypic correlation between first-degree relatives. It is important to keep in mind that in most cases, the true additive genetic effect will be lower than this estimate because of the fact that shared environments can also make first-degree relatives similar to one another. The second reason that family studies are valuable is they provide a comparison against research that is based on other genetically informative designs. As we will discuss in more detail later, because twins and adoptees may be fundamentally different than other people, results from studies based on twin and adoption designs may not generalize to the broader population. Therefore, family studies offer a great way to test the external validity of findings from behavioral genetics research.

In spite of these strengths, family studies also have some notable limitations. First, the effects of heredity and shared environment are inherently confounded in the basic family design. This is because genetic relatedness between two people is correlated positively with the likelihood that those individuals live in the same household. For example, siblings share more of the same genes than do first cousins, but because siblings are also likely to live together whereas cousins are not, they tend to share more of the same environments. This means that it is often impossible for researchers to rule out the possibility that phenotypic similarities among first-degree relatives are caused by shared environmental effects. Thus, the combined effects of shared genes and shared environments, which both contribute to family resemblance, are referred to as *familiality*. Another limitation of family studies is that heritability estimates can become inflated when spouses are more similar to one another than would be expected by chance (see Buss, 1984, 1985; Plomin et al., 1980). This phenomenon, called *assortative mating*, leads to a significant correlation between parental phenotypes and to an increase in the similarity between any one parent and his or her offspring. When this happens, researchers can use the mid-parent score, which is simply the mean of the two parents' scores on the trait, to account for non-random mating in their analyses.

Fortunately, these limitations can also be addressed by adding more complex relationships to the basic family design. For instance, blended family households, which often include half-siblings and step-siblings, allow researchers to compare brothers and sisters who have varying degrees of genetic relatedness. Similarly, multiple-generation households, in which grandparents, parents, and children all live together and are exposed to the same environments, can be compared with families in which multiple generations do not live together. Finally, the family design can also be useful for testing hypotheses about life-span development (Loehlin, 1992; Plomin, 1986). For example, it might be interesting to know whether age plays a role in determining similarity between members of the same family. This can be examined by comparing pairs of family members who are of the same level of genetic relatedness but who vary in age similarity. If age has an influence on similarity, then (1) parents and children should be less similar to one another than siblings, (2) siblings of very different ages should be less similar than siblings of similar ages, and (3) siblings of similar ages should be less similar than fraternal twins, who are the exact same age, even though all these pairs of relatives share approximately half of their genes (Loehlin, 1992). With additional modifications, the basic family design can be even more powerful when it is combined with other types of studies.

Twin Design

In twin studies, researchers take advantage of the naturally occurring phenomenon in which a single pregnancy produces multiple offspring through one of two different biological processes. Twins that result from the division of a single egg, called *monozygotic* (MZ) or *identical* twins, share all of the same hereditary influences, whereas twins that result from the fertilization of two eggs, called *dizygotic* (DZ) or *fraternal* twins, share roughly half of the hereditary influences that are due to additive genetic effects and roughly a quarter of the hereditary influences that are due to nonadditive effects. This means that fraternal twins are, on average, no more alike than any other pair of full siblings, whereas identical twins are exactly alike in their genetic makeup. Because of these fundamental differences in the genetic relatedness of MZ and DZ twins, researchers can estimate the heritability of a behavior by comparing the level of similarity between twins of one type to the level of similarity between twins of the other type. For instance, if a behavior is entirely accounted for by additive genetic influences, then we would expect the correlation between MZ twins to be 1.0 and the correlation between DZ twins to be 0.5. If a behavior is completely tied to shared environmental influences, then MZ and DZ correlations would be equivalent. Finally, if nonshared environmental influences account for all the phenotypic variance, then MZ and DZ correlations would both be equal to zero.

There are both practical and empirical benefits to using the twin design in behavioral genetics research. First, twins are relatively common, occurring in roughly 1 out of every 85 live births (Plomin et al., 1980); therefore, it is relatively easy to find eligible participants. Second, a multitude of twin studies have been initiated in several different countries, many of which include a number of different age groups, so a great deal of data already exist (Bergeman & Ong, 2007; Boomsma, Busjahn, & Peltonen, 2002). Third, unlike the family design, twin studies provide researchers the opportunity to estimate both additive and nonadditive genetic influences. Fourth, because fraternal twins can be either the same sex or opposite sex, researchers can compare twins that are the same gender with those that are different genders. Finally, because twins are the same age at the same time, they are likely to share more of the same family environment than regular siblings. Unlike regular siblings, twins are raised by parents who are of the same age, the same level of parenting experience, and who have the same amount of financial resources. According to the *equal environments assumption*, this is just as true for DZ twins as it is for MZ twins, making it possible to separate the impact of heritability from shared environmental influences, something which cannot be done in the basic family design.

In spite of these advantages, twin studies also present some notable challenges. First, although it may seem simple, it is often difficult for researchers to correctly identify the type of each pair of twins that is included in a sample. Inaccurate *zygosity determination* can lead to lower estimates of heritability because mistakenly identifying MZ twins as DZ will produce higher correlations among the group of DZ twins, and mistakenly identifying DZ twins as MZ will produce lower correlations among the group of MZ twins. As costs have become more affordable, this problem has been lessened by new DNA technology that allows for accurate zygosity diagnosis. Another challenge involved in using the twin design is the potential for violations of the *equal environments assumption*. Recall that to differentiate heritability from shared environment, the degree of environmental similarity for fraternal twins must be equivalent to that of identical twins. When this is not the case, the greater phenotypic similarity between identical twins is due at least partially to greater environmental similarity. A final concern about the twin design relates to the extent to which twins are representative of the general population. Although twin births occur in all racial and ethnic groups, at all ages of motherhood, and across every level of SES, twins themselves may be inherently different than singletons. For instance, the birth weight of twins is usually around 30% lower than for the average singleton (MacGillivray, Campbell, & Thompson, 1988) and twins tend to display slower language development and receive lower scores on tests of verbal abilities (Deary, Pattie, Wilson, & Whalley, 2005). Fortunately, many of these differences may be limited to childhood and do not seem to affect other individual differences, such as personality traits (Johnson, Krueger, Bouchard, & McGue, 2002). Nevertheless, researchers must be cautious when generalizing results from twin studies.

An extension of the basic twin design, called the *children-of-twins design*, includes features of traditional family studies (Nance, 1976). Among other things, this type of design has been used to study the etiology of child birth weight (D'Onofrio et al., 2003) and nonverbal intelligence (Rose, Harris, Christian, & Nance, 1979). In contrast to the families of non-twin siblings, offspring of an MZ twin share half of their genes with the parent's co-twin, but do not share the same household environment as the co-twin. In other words, the twin aunt or twin uncle is related genetically in the same way that a parent would be, but is related only socially as an aunt or uncle. As a result, the two sets of children from MZ twins are related genetically to each other as half-siblings, but are reared socially as first cousins. Finally, assuming the absence of assortative mating, the children will share neither genes nor household environments with the spouse of the twin aunt or twin uncle. Comparisons among these extended family relationships may provide information about the intergenerational transmission of genetic and environmental influences on behavior (see Eaves, Silberg, & Maes, 2005).

The basic twin design can be used to test hypotheses about life-span development in a number of ways. The simplest of these is to conduct cross-sectional analyses of heritability across different age groups. If a sample of MZ and DZ twins contains participants of varying ages, then age can be added to a model of twin similarity (Plomin, 1986). For instance, this can be done using a multiple regression that predicts Twin 1's score from Twin 2's score (twin similarity), along with the Twin 2 × age interaction (age differences in twin similarity), the Twin 2 × zygosity interaction (heritability), and the Twin 2 × zygosity × age interaction (age differences in heritability). Because this type of analysis requires very large samples, it is perhaps better to conduct it in a meta-analysis that combines results from multiple twin studies. Nevertheless, a drawback to these approaches is that it is impossible to rule out cohort differences as the cause of cross-sectional differences in heritability (Schaie, 1975). Thus, the cohort-sequential design, in which multiple birth cohorts are measured at different time points, must be used to separate age-related differences in heritability from cohort differences. Finally, longitudinal studies of twins can be used to estimate the heritability of changes in behavior over time. This can be done using simple difference scores across two time points or with more complex, latent-variable growth models of data from multiple time points (McArdle, 1986; McArdle & Hamagami, 2003; Neale, Boker, Bergeman, & Maes, 2006). We will return to the issues of age differences in heritability and heritability of age changes when we discuss developmental genetics theory in detail.

Adoption Design

The third type of genetically informative research design involves studying adopted children and their adoptive and biological families. The adoption design provides a way for researchers to completely disentangle the relationship between shared environment and shared heredity. This is because adoption creates situations in which genetically related individuals are reared in environments that are completely unshared. For example, the biological siblings of children given up for adoption share roughly half of their genes, but share no common environmental influences. Therefore, individuals who are genetically related, but who are reared in uncorrelated environments, can only be similar to one another because of influences that are due to heredity. At the same time, adoption also creates situations in which family members who share the same environment are completely unrelated, genetically. For instance, although the adoptive siblings of adopted children share the all of the same between-family environmental influences, they share none of the same genes. This means that unrelated individuals who are reared in the same family can only be similar to one another because of effects that are due to the shared environment.

Studies that are based on the adoption design are some of the most compelling in all of behavior genetics because of their ability to provide unambiguous evidence for genetic influences on behavior. As mentioned before, the major strength of this type of research is that it can be used to distinguish heritable and environmental sources of familiality. Whereas in the family design, genetic relatedness is positively correlated with between-family environments, in the adoption design, those factors are uncorrelated, as long as children are placed into adoptive families at random. Although quite rare in practice, extensions of the basic adoption design which include MZ and DZ twins reared apart are particularly powerful in this regard. Two notable adoption studies that include twins are the Minnesota Study of Twins Reared Apart and the Swedish Adoption/Twin Study of Aging (SATSA).

Adoption studies can be particularly useful for studying life-span development because of their ability to separate effects of familiality that are due to heredity and shared environment. As adopted children age, it is possible to compare their development with the development of their adoptive and biological family members. If a trait is environmentally influenced, then adopted children should develop in ways that resemble their adoptive parents and siblings, whereas if a trait is genetically influenced genetically, they should begin to resemble their biological relatives over time. Unfortunately, only a small number of longitudinal adoption studies exist. For example, the Minnesota/Texas Adoption Research Project includes waves of data collection that occurred when the adopted children were between 4 and 12 years of age, at adolescence, and during young adulthood. This type of study offers a unique perspective on the interplay of genetic and environmental influences on development among genetically unrelated family members.

Although adoption studies have unique advantages, there is some concern that participants in adoption studies may not be representative of the general population. For instance, stereotypes of birth parents who give their children up for adoption are that they must have lower intelligence or less income than average. This perception may be due, at least in part, to the fact that birth parents tend to be young, but their own parents are often representative of normative SES (Petrill, Plomin, DeFries, & Hewitt, 2003). Similarly, it is possible that parents who are willing to adopt a child may be different than those who are not and this difference may affect their methods of childrearing. If either of these is true, then results from adoption studies may not generalize to the broader population. A second concern in adoption studies is with the possibility of non-random pairings of adoptees with adoptive families, called *selective placement*. Adoption agencies may place children with an adoptive family that resembles their birth family in some way, possibly leading to a correlation between the child's rearing environment and his or her genetic makeup. For example, a child whose birth parents have above average IQ may be adopted by parents that are also intelligent. As a result, the child may end up resembling his or her biological parents because of the stimulating rearing environment provided by the adoptive parents. In other words, if the trait under investigation is genetically influenced, then selective placement will increase the resemblance between adoptees and their adoptive parents, and to the extent that the trait is environmentally influenced, it will lead to stronger correlations between adoptees and their biological parents. A final concern about adoption studies is that it is becoming increasingly difficult to find participants. Perhaps because of increases in the availability of abortion and the ability of single mothers to raise their children on their own, adoption is less common than it used to be. As a result, only a handful of adoption studies remain active today.

DEVELOPMENTAL BEHAVIOR GENETICS

Developmental behavior genetics merges developmental science with behavioral genetic theories and methodologies. Research questions that are of particular interest in developmental genetics concern how genes turn on and off across development and whether there are changes in the extent to which genetic and environmental factors are important during various segments of the life course. A common misconception is that if a particular behavior is heritable, then it must also be stable. In truth, characteristics that exhibit longitudinal stability are not necessarily influenced by genetic factors, and traits that show strong heritability are not necessarily stable (Bergeman & Plomin, 1996). Research has indicated that the influence of a given combination of genes may show continuous effects across the life span, or new genes may come into play at particular developmental stages (Hahn, Hewitt, Henderson, & Benno, 1990). Similarly, the effects of the environment may be uniform over time, or the quality of environmental influences may vary across the life span. Given the complexity of these phenomena, behavioral geneticists have developed research designs and analytic strategies that can be used to test whether genetic and environmental influences on a trait during childhood or adolescence are the same ones that impact individual differences in that trait during adulthood or old age.

There are two general hypotheses that have been put forth to portray possible changes in the relative influences of genetic and environmental factors across the life span. First, as the number of life experiences that an individual has increases, the impact of the environment (especially environmental influences of the nonshared type) should play an increasingly important role in determining the course of development (Baltes et al., 1980; McCartney, Harris, & Bernieri, 1990). According to this perspective, as a person experiences a greater diversity of environmental opportunities, his or her behavior will increasingly be shaped by the environment and the role of hereditary influences will decrease. For example, someone's career success is shaped by educational opportunities and other learning experiences that occur during childhood and adolescence, and by the professional relationships, social conditions, and economic markets a person is exposed to during young adulthood. Thus, as one ages, the accumulation of these diverse experiences will shape behavior increasingly and override genetic influences.

On the other hand, some developmental geneticists have suggested that when heritability changes with development, it typically increases (Plomin, 1986). Some characteristics, like personality traits and cognitive abilities, are not fully developed until late adolescence or early adulthood, so environmental influences may be most prominent at early ages and genetic influences may be more prominent in adulthood. In addition, Scarr and McCartney (1983) argued that with continued development, individuals gain increasing control over their environment and, as part of this process, they become more active in selecting environments that support or even promote their inherited tendencies. Under this scenario, individuals who have a genetic predisposition toward high intelligence may be more likely to benefit from learning opportunities, seek higher educational attainment, marry someone with a similar outlook on life, select an occupation or engage in hobbies that facilitate intellectual growth, and/or associate with friends, family, and coworkers who also participate in novel experiences or enjoy exchanging ideas. Although this view weaves a tapestry of both genetic and environmental influence, Scarr and McCartney argue that it is the genetic propensity that "drives" the environmental experience.

To date, the empirical support for either of these competing hypotheses is lacking because the majority of research in this area is based on cross-sectional designs, which compare subjects of different ages within a single sample, or that include meta-analyses of results across studies focusing on different age groups. Unfortunately, like any cross-sectional design, these approaches do not assess the extent to which the contributions of genes and environment *change* with development; rather, this research only provides information about *age differences* in genetic and environmental factors. As a result, the comparison of individuals in different age groups may reflect cohort differences rather than the developmental processes that occur as people age. That is, the uniqueness associated with specific cohorts or factors related to historical change (e.g., advances in technology, education, or medicine) may contribute to different estimates of genetic and environmental influence on attributes of interest. This occurs because heritability is a population-specific parameter, and parameter estimates from quantitative genetic analyses can change when genetic and environmental sources of variation change (see Bergeman, 1997).

When reviewing behavioral genetic research, it is important to keep in mind that estimates of heritability and environmentality are static, because they are typically based on findings from a specific population at a single point in time. Different estimates of the relative role of genetic and environmental influences can be obtained from samples of subjects who have vastly different experiences because of their birth cohort, SES, culture, or other factors that contribute to differential experience. Traditionally, the variance due to age is controlled statistically in behavioral genetic analyses or removed by selecting participants from narrow age bands because age effects cannot be assigned to either a genetic or an environmental component of variance (see McGue & Bouchard, 1984, for details). Researchers must be cautious when generalizing results beyond the age or cohort of the samples used in a single study, because without a longitudinal design, there is no way to disentangle effects that are due to development (age change) from those that are due to experience (age differences).

Longitudinal behavioral genetic designs can be used to assess the etiology of continuity and change in genetic and environmental influences over time. In this type of study, age-to-age genetic correlations indicate the extent to which latent genetic effects at one age are correlated with genetic effects at another age. For example, a genetic correlation of 1.0 would mean that the same genetic factors contribute to phenotypic variance at both ages, whereas a genetic correlation of zero would imply that completely different sets of genetic factors affect individual differences on the trait at the two ages. In other words, the genetic correlation reflects the extent to which genetic effects on individual differences "overlap" at two ages, regardless of their relative contribution to phenotypic variance. Developmental changes in heritability do not necessarily implicate molecular mechanisms of change—heritability can increase from one age to another, even if the same genes are being actively transcribed at both ages, simply because environmental variance decreases over time. Finally, heritability can remain the same for a particular trait at two ages, even when a completely different set of genes is being transcribed. When combined with information about genetic and environmental influences at each measurement occasion, genetic and environmental correlations indicate the extent to which phenotypic stability for a particular trait is mediated genetically and/or environmentally, and provide standardized measures of the genetic and environmental contributions to age-to-age phenotypic resemblance. Because longitudinal behavioral genetic designs can explicitly differentiate these effects, they are crucial in the study of stability or change in genetic and environmental effects on attributes associated with intellectual abilities.

Developmental Genetics of Cognitive Functioning

Individual differences in cognitive functioning are among the most widely studied phenotypes in behavioral genetics. Research in this area encompasses many aspects of general and specific cognitive abilities, including fluid and crystallized intelligence, long-term and working memory, language comprehension and production, and scholastic aptitude. In this section, we review research on the heritability of cognitive abilities across the life span. Rather than attempting to cover the entire literature on cognitive development, we chose to focus on research that exemplifies the various methodologies in developmental behavior genetics. The studies included in this review are based on the designs described in the previous sections and were conducted for the purpose of studying cognitive development during specific periods of the life span. For the sake of presentation, this section is organized around the major developmental periods of (1) infancy and childhood, (2) adolescence and young adulthood, and (3) middle and late adulthood. We do not mean to suggest that these periods are somehow distinct or that cognitive development is segmented. Instead, as can be seen in many of the studies described later, processes that influence the development of cognitive functioning during childhood may persist throughout the life span.

Infancy and Childhood

The pace of cognitive development during early childhood is faster than at any other developmental period. For this reason, a great deal of behavioral genetic research has focused on the heritability of spurts and lags in cognitive development during this time. The Louisville Twin Study (LTS) is one of the longest-running and most comprehensive studies of child development. Among other things, the LTS has been used to investigate individual differences in physical characteristics, such as height (Wilson, 1976) and eye color (Matheny & Dolan, 1975), and personality traits, such as attachment style (Finkel, Wille, & Matheny, 1998) and temperament (Phillips & Matheny, 1997). The sample includes several hundred pairs of infant twins who were first tested at 3 months of age. Following the initial assessment, the children were assessed every 3 months until they were a year old, and then every 6 months during the ages of 2 and 3 and every 12 months thereafter until the age of 9 years (Wilson, 1983). Measures of cognitive abilities were collected at each assessment and these data have been used to study synchronies in intellectual development over time. For instance, Wilson (1983) found that the difference between within-pair correlations for MZ and DZ twins increased with age. Specifically, during the first 2 years of life, the MZ and DZ twins were equally similar, but after the age of 2, correlations between MZ twins were significantly higher than those between DZ twins. Furthermore, Wilson (1974, 1978) found that age-to-age changes in cognitive abilities were more concordant among MZ twins than DZ twins, suggesting that, in addition to having an influence on levels of cognitive abilities, genetic factors may also be responsible for changes in cognitive ability during childhood.

In a similar study, Plomin and colleagues (1993) used data from the MacArthur Longitudinal Twin Study to investigate the extent to which genes mediate the changes in cognitive ability that occur from 14 to 20 months of age. Several aspects of cognitive functioning were assessed through observational measures and parental reports of object categorization, spatial memory, and language comprehension. Heritability estimates for scores on the Bailey Mental Development Index (MDI) and for parent reports of expressive and receptive language increased over time, whereas the heritability of spatial memory and object categorization decreased and were nonsignificant at 20 months of age. In contrast, estimates of common environmental influences on parent reports of language abilities were significant at 14 months, but decreased substantially over time. Results from model-fitting analyses of the longitudinal data indicated that genetic and shared environmental influences contributed to continuity in scores on the MDI and measures of language abilities. Nonshared environmental influences contributed to change in all the measures, whereas genetic influences contributed to changes in the MDI and in the measure of expressive language. This study was one of the first to demonstrate how traits that are heritable are not always stable, and how traits that change can be under the influence of genes.

More recently, Bartels, Rietveld, van Baal, and Boomsma (2002) examined changes in the etiology of cognitive ability during middle childhood in a longitudinal study of twins from the Netherlands Twin Registry. These researchers found that the best fitting model for their data was one that included a common factor for genetic influences, a common factor with additional age-specific factors for shared environmental influences, and age-specific factors for nonshared environmental influences. This means that the genes that influenced IQ when the twins were 5 years old continued to have an influence as the children got older, all the way through the age of 12. In contrast, some of the shared environmental factors had a continuous influence and others were unique to each age, whereas nonshared environmental influences were unique at every age. Bartels et al. (2002) also found that the percentage of age-to-age covariance that was accounted for by additive genetic effects increased as the twins got older, indicating that genes contributed mostly to stability in cognitive functioning over time. In contrast, the percentage of age-to-age covariance accounted for by environmental effects decreased with age. Overall, this pattern of findings supports the view that genetic influences contribute to continuity in IQ whereas environmental influences primarily contribute to change.

Finally, Bishop and colleagues (2003) used longitudinal data from the Longitudinal Twin Study and the Colorado Adoption Project (a combined adoption-family design) to investigate continuity and change in general cognitive ability among MZ and DZ twins, as well as adoptive and non-adoptive siblings, between the ages of 1 and 12 years. They found that heritability estimates were significant at each age, ranging from 0.43 at age 3 to 0.74 at age 10, and tended to increase as the children got older. They also found that the component of heritability at each age that was newly emerging increased during early childhood. For example, in a structural equation model of age-to-age genetic correlations, almost 60% of the genetic variance at age 7 was accounted for by a factor that was unique to that age. After the age of 7, however, almost all of the genetic variance in cognitive abilities was attributable to a genetic factor that was common to every age. This pattern of changing heritability suggests that genes contribute to change in cognitive ability in early childhood and to continuity in middle childhood. In contrast, effects of shared environment were modest at age 3 (0.30) and at age 4 (0.22) but were otherwise negligible, and these influences remained relatively constant throughout childhood, with no new effects arising at any age. Finally, the influence of nonshared environment was relatively stable over time, ranging from 0.23 to 0.41, and this source of variance was unique at nearly every age. In other words, the nonshared environmental influences that emerged at one age were entirely different from those that influenced cognitive ability the year before. For most ages, nonshared environments contributed to changes in general cognitive ability.

The picture of cognitive development that is captured in these studies provides strong evidence of the role that genes play in shaping the course of intellectual functioning in childhood. For the most part, heritability increased with age and genetic influences contributed to stability in cognitive abilities over time. At the same time, it is clear that the transition into formal education introduces a number of important environmental opportunities that contribute to individual differences among school-aged children. This is evident in the findings that most nonshared environmental influences are age specific and contribute to age-related changes. Finally, shared environmental influences appear to be highest in early childhood, the time in life when parents and members of the immediate family provide most of the childrearing, but then gradually decrease as children begin to spend more and more time outside the home. Unfortunately, much less is known about potential gene–environment interactions that may unfold during this period. For instance, it may be the case that children are selected into peer groups on the basis of heritable characteristics or that social relationships affect certain genotypes differently than others. Nevertheless, genetic and environmental influences are likely to continue having an impact on cognitive abilities as children move into young adulthood.

Adolescence and Young Adulthood

An important question concerning adolescent cognitive development is whether genetic influences that are present in childhood persist into young adulthood or whether new genes come into play, such as those that regulate physical development during puberty. If the first scenario is true, then the genes that regulate cognitive functioning in childhood should continue to influence cognitive abilities in the teenaged years. On the other hand, if new genes come into play during adolescence, then genetic influences on cognitive functioning should become more age specific and show less age-to-age genetic transmission than they do during early childhood. Another question is whether nonshared environmental influences begin to carry over from one age to another, perhaps because of the structure of educational experiences or an increasing stabilization of social networks, or whether they continue to show patterns of unique, age-specific innovation, as was the case during preadolescence. To test these hypotheses, researchers often rely upon longitudinal studies of child development that follow the same sample of participants through adolescence.

In a parent–offspring study from the Colorado Adoption Project, Plomin, Fulker, Corley, and DeFries (1997) compared the similarities between adopted children and their adoptive and biological parents to the similarities between a matched-control sample of non-adopted children and their biological parents. The children were assessed annually between the ages of 1 and 4 years, and again at ages 7, 12, and 16 years. The biological parents (mostly mothers) were assessed when the mothers were in their third trimester of pregnancy, whereas the adoptive parents and control parents were assessed twice, once when the children were under a year old and again when the children were 7 years old. Correlations between adopted children and their adoptive parents were low during early childhood and tended to decline as the children got older, whereas correlations between adopted children and their biological parents were modest in early childhood and continually increased from early to late adolescence. In other words, adopted children became less like their adoptive parents and more like their biological parents over time, and this pattern of increasing resemblance to biological parents was similar to that found in the control families. Finally, model-fitting analyses of data collected when the children were 16 years of age resulted in a heritability estimate of 0.56 for general cognitive ability and showed that shared environmental influences on general and specific cognitive abilities were negligible. These findings suggest that genes are increasingly important for cognitive development during adolescence and that shared environments have little to no effect, but they do not provide a way of examining the role of non-shared environments.

To address this limitation, Petrill and colleagues (2004) used sibling data from the Colorado Adoption Project to compare the similarities between adopted children and their adoptive siblings to the similarities between non-adopted children and their biological siblings. Same-age correlations between biological siblings were significant at every age, whereas adoptive siblings showed significant resemblance at only ages 3 and 9 years. This suggests a consistent genetic influence throughout adolescence and modest influence of shared environments in childhood. Biological siblings were also more similar than adoptive siblings across different measurement occasions, indicating that genes have an influence on age-to-age stability of cognitive functioning in adolescence. Model-fitting analyses showed that genetic influences were due to a common factor that contributed to stability, whereas shared environmental influences had no significant effects on either stability or change over time. Nonshared environmental effects were consistently age specific, which means that they contributed mostly to changes in cognitive ability. These findings, along with the results from the parent–offspring study, support the predictions that genetic influences on childhood cognitive functioning continue to play a role during adolescence and that environmental influences encountered outside the home are more influential than those encountered within it.

In another recent study, Hoekstra, Bartels, and Boomsma (2007) used longitudinal data from the Netherlands Twin Registry to examine the development of verbal and nonverbal IQ from age 5 through the age of 18. They also examined the extent to which genetic influences are responsible for the phenotypic overlap between specific cognitive abilities and tested whether this genetic correlation increases with age. With regards to changes in heritability, genetic contributions to variance in verbal ability at ages 12 ($h^2 = 0.80$) and 18 ($h^2 = 0.84$) were significantly higher than at ages 5 ($h^2 = 0.46$), 7 ($h^2 = 0.39$), and 10 ($h^2 = 0.56$), but the heritability of nonverbal ability at age 18 (h^2 = 0.74) was not significantly different from estimates at any of the younger ages. With regards to the etiology of cognitive development, genetic influences on both traits were attributable to age-to-age transmission effects that contributed to stability over time, whereas all effects of nonshared environments were age specific. Shared environmental influences, on the other hand, were found only for verbal abilities and these effects were attributable to both a common factor (at ages 5, 7, and 10) and to age-specific factors (at ages 5, 7, 10, and 12). No significant effects of shared environments were found at age 18. Finally, all of the covariance between verbal and nonverbal abilities was accounted for by genetic influences, and the genetic correlations at ages 12 (r_g = 0.76) and 18 (r_g = 0.73) were significantly higher than at age 10 (r_g = 0.57). It is apparent from these findings that genes contribute to both the stability of cognitive functioning and to the phenotypic associations between specific abilities during adolescence.

The development of cognitive ability during adolescence is increasingly under the influence of genetic factors. Most of the evidence supported the prediction of an increase in heritability during adolescence. In the Petrill et al. (2004) study, heritability was stable through age 9, but in Hoekstra et al. (2007) and Plomin et al. (1997), heritability was significantly higher among teenagers than among younger children. Furthermore, it appears that genetic effects begin to carry over from year to year, such that most of the heritability in cognitive functioning during young adulthood is associated with genetic effects that emerged in early adolescence. In contrast, rather than stabilizing over time, new influences of nonshared environments continue to emerge from one year to the next, whereas effects of shared environments, which tend to be modest during early childhood, become almost nonexistent by the late teenage years. These findings may also provide some insight into the patterns of genetic influence that can be expected during adulthood. For instance, because the biological parents in the Plomin et al. (1997) study were assessed much later in life than were their adolescent children, the correlations between teenagers and their biological parents may indicate that genes underlying cognitive abilities in adolescence continue to be manifested in adulthood. On the other hand, perhaps the effects of nonshared environments begin to outweigh genetic influences, once young adults move out of their parents' homes, begin their careers, and have families of their own.

Middle Age and Late Adulthood

Although the pace of development in adulthood may be somewhat slower than it is during childhood, the magnitude of the changes that take place and the complexity of process underlying those changes make it equally interesting. First, it is often the case that phenotypic variance increases with age, meaning that individual differences become more pronounced in adulthood. Second, there is considerable evidence of age-related declines in cognitive abilities in later adulthood, so behavioral genetic research can be useful for identifying potential causes of those changes. Finally, compared with earlier periods of the life span, there have been relatively few large-scale behavioral genetic studies of middle age and later adulthood. This is unfortunate because there are both theoretical and empirical reasons to expect that genes will continue having an influence on cognitive ability during adulthood (McGue, Bouchard, Iacono, & Lykken, 1993; Plomin, 1986). On the one hand, cognitive abilities related to fluid intelligence may decline over the life span, whereas those related to crystallized intelligence may remain stable or even increase over the life span (Cattell, 1971; Horn & Donaldson, 1976). On the other hand, it is quite possible that new genetic influences may emerge during adulthood. In particular, cognitive functioning in late life may be influenced genes that underlie abnormal development, such as those associated with Alzheimer's disease. If this is true, then some genetic factors should remain influential throughout the life span and other genetic factors that do not appear in childhood should begin to emerge in later life.

In contrast, if the research on adolescence and young adulthood generalizes to middle and late adulthood, then the relative influences of shared environments should continue to decline. By the time most people reach middle age, they have been out of their household of origin for many years and share very few experiences in common with their biological relatives. According to life-span theories of development, the timing of important life experiences also becomes less age-graded over the life span (Baltes et al., 1980). The ages at which people get married, have children, retire, or become widowed can vary a great deal from person to person. Therefore, it is unlikely that any new effects of shared environments would emerge. Instead, non-shared environmental influences should become more prevalent in adulthood, as the opportunity for unique experiences increases and the opportunity for shared experiences decreases. It may also be the case that effects of nonshared environments gradually cumulate over time, resulting in greater influence in late life than at other ages. Finally, according to theories of optimal aging (Baltes, 1987), older adults are faced with the challenge of compensating for normative declines in mental and physical functioning. Therefore, it may be during this period of the life span that non-shared environments exert their greatest influence.

Some of the strongest tests of genetic influences on cognitive ability in adulthood come from a series of studies on the SATSA, in which MZ and DZ twins reared together are compared with MZ and DZ twins reared apart (Finkel, Pedersen, Plomin, & McClearn, 1998; Pedersen, Plomin, Nesselroade, & McClearn, 1992; Plomin, Pedersen, Lichtenstein, & McClearn, 1994; Reynolds, Finkel, Gatz, & Pedersen, 2002; Reynolds, Finkel, McArdle, Gatz, Berg, & Pedersen, 2005). In the first of these, Pedersen and colleagues (1992) analyzed data from over 300 pairs of twins who were at an average age of 65 years, and found that genetic factors accounted for 81% of the total variance in general intelligence (operationalized as the first principal component of scores on measures of specific cognitive abilities). This suggests that the heritability of IQ in adulthood may actually be higher than it is during earlier periods of the life span. Nonshared environmental influences accounted for the remaining 19% of total variance and shared rearing environment had no significant effects on general intelligence. Finally, a cross-sectional test of age effects revealed no significant differences in the amount of variance explained by genetic and environmental sources across middle and late adulthood.

In a follow-up study, Plomin and colleagues (1994) analyzed longitudinal data that were collected 3 years after the initial assessment. They found that heritability was around 0.80 at both time points. They also found that the longitudinal phenotypic stability was 0.93, indicating that IQ is highly stable in adulthood, and that the genetic contribution to phenotypic stability was 0.83, which suggests that almost all of the stability in adult IQ can be attributed to genetic influences. Finally, the genetic correlation across the two assessments was 0.99, indicating that no new genetic influences emerged over time. All of the environmental sources of variance were of the nonshared variety and accounted for roughly 20% of the total variance in general cognitive ability. This means that being reared in the same household during childhood does not contribute to similarity between twins later in life, whereas unique experiences that make twins different do contribute to individual differences in adulthood.

Additional follow-ups on the SATSA twins allowed researchers to conduct more sophisticated studies of cognitive development in adulthood. With data from a third assessment, Finkel, Pedersen, Plomin, and McClearn (1998) used cross-sequential analyses to examine age changes and cohort differences in sources of phenotypic variance over time (although see Widaman, 1998, for a critique). They found that genetic variance did not differ significantly across cohorts, but estimates of heritability declined from about 0.80 in the younger cohorts to about 0.60 in the older cohorts because of longitudinal increases in environmental variance in the older cohorts. In contrast to the Plomin et al. (1994) study, they also found significant longitudinal decreases in genetic sources of variance, particularly among the older cohorts. These findings were replicated in a study by Reynolds and colleagues (2005) that included data from a fourth wave of assessments, collected roughly 13 years after the initial assessment. Using latent growth curve modeling of the first principal component, these researchers found that genetic influences accounted for 91% of the variance in intercepts and 43% of the variance in quadratic change, whereas nonshared environmental influences accounted for 99% of the variance in linear change and 57% of variance in quadratic change. Influences of shared and correlated environments did not account for any of the variance in intercepts or slopes. Finally, in this study, genetic variance in general intelligence increased from age 50 to age 60, but declined thereafter, whereas nonshared environmental variance decreased from age 50 to age 60, but increased thereafter.

A number of researchers have argued that declines in genetic variance over time during late adulthood may indicate the presence of effects due to terminal decline, a phenomenon in which cognitive abilities steadily decrease as individuals approach the end of their lives. Although the probability that a person will experience terminal decline may have genetic influences, such as a predisposition to certain forms of cancer, it is also likely that nonshared environmental factors, such as exposure to air pollution, play a role in determining the timing of its onset. Reynolds, Finkel, Gatz, and Pedersen (2002) found support for this hypothesis in the SATSA. They analyzed data on levels (intercepts) and rates of change (slopes) in three specific cognitive abilities (fluid intelligence, recognition memory, and perceptual speed), as well as covariation in those parameters with two factors that are known to predict late-life declines in cognitive ability (education level and pulmonary function). Among adults older than 65 years, genetic effects were most influential in accounting for phenotypic associations between the covariates and the intercepts of cognitive abilities, whereas nonshared environmental influences contributed to associations between the covariates and rates of change in cognitive abilities. Taken together, these findings suggest that the timing of terminal decline is a stochastic phenomenon, primarily under the influence of factors in the external environment, and contributes to decreases in the heritability of cognitive ability in old age.

Overall, existing evidence indicates that genetic influences on cognitive abilities tend to decline during older adulthood and that nonshared environmental influences tend to increase. Whereas in the Plomin et al. (1994) study, there were no changes in heritability over time, Finkel et al. (1998) and Reynolds et al. (2005) found that genetic influences decreased among people older than 60 years. Nevertheless, the decline in heritability during later adulthood should not overshadow the fact that genetic influences on cognitive ability remain highly significant throughout old age. In a study of 240 pairs of twins older than 80 years, McClearn and colleagues (1997) found heritability estimates above 0.50 for measures of general intelligence, verbal ability, processing speed, and memory. McGue and Christensen (2001) conducted a similar study with data from the Longitudinal Study of Aging Danish Twins (LSADT), and found significant heritability for scores on the Mini-Mental State Examination ($h^2 = 0.49$) and for composite scores of specific cognitive abilities ($h^2 = 0.54$). They also showed that genetic influences on cognitive functioning in late life are not due to genetic influences on dementia. Finally, in a longitudinal analysis of four LSADT waves, McGue and Christensen (2002) found that heritability estimates were stable across each year of the study (roughly 0.50), whereas individual differences in linear change were almost entirely accounted for by environmental influences. Thus, genetic influences remain substantial throughout adulthood.

Finally, it is worth noting that some of the strongest genetic influences on cognitive functioning during later life may be those associated with health-related outcomes. For example, there is growing evidence that risk factors for premature mortality are heritable. To the extent that diseases with later-life onsets, such as cardiovascular disease, Parkinson's, or Alzheimer's, contribute to individual differences in cognitive behavior, it is important to consider research on the heritability of health and longevity in old age as well (for a review, see Braungart-Rieker & Bergeman, 1999). Recent research on families and siblings of the oldest adults has shown that being genetically related to someone who has lived to an extreme old age increases expected longevity and vitality (Perls & Terry, 2003; Wilcox, Wilcox, Hsueh, & Suzuki, 2006). In contrast, many health-related attributes that are heritable also show associations with cognitive decline. For example, research on serum lipid and lipoprotein parameters show strong linkages with cognitive functioning in later life (Reynolds, Gatz, Prince, Berg, & Pedersen, 2010). Of primary interest has been the significant relationship between high cholesterol levels in midlife and cognitive decrements in later life (Anstey, Lupnicki, & Low, 2008). In addition, the Apolipoprotein E gene, involved in cholesterol transport in the blood, is associated with late-onset Alzheimer's disease (Condor et al., 1993). The different alleles appear to act in a dose-related fashion to increase risk and decrease age-of-onset, with the E4 allele. Although we have provided only a sampling of the work on health and cognitive functioning, this is an area of active research in life-span genetics.

Summary

From the preceding review, it is evident that behavioral genetics research has made tremendous contributions to our understanding of individual differences in cognitive functioning. Clearly, a substantial amount of phenotypic variance in general and specific cognitive abilities can be attributed to genetic differences among people. This work also provides some of the most compelling evidence for the importance of environmental factors, which sometimes account for more than half of the total variance. The use of genetically informative designs in developmental research has also provided a great deal of insight into the processes that underlie stability and change in cognitive functioning across the life span. Although we chose to focus on the field of cognitive abilities for this chapter, it is important to point out that behavioral genetics has already contributed a great deal to the study of other individual differences, such as temperament and personality development. We believe that genetically informative designs will continue to hold great promise for developmental research, especially with the emergence of innovations in measurement techniques, multivariate analysis, and longitudinal modeling. The challenge, however, will be to determine the best ways of integrating behavioral genetics and life-span developmental psychology.

FUTURE ISSUES IN LIFE-SPAN DEVELOPMENTAL BEHAVIOR GENETICS

For the remainder of the chapter, we will be focusing on current controversies, imminent challenges, and potential opportunities in life-span developmental genetics. First, we briefly discuss an ongoing debate over the relevance of developmental genetics research for theories in developmental science. In particular, we describe the conceptual distinctions between the two approaches and explain how much of the disagreement stems from three fundamental differences in the types of questions that they address. Second, we identify two areas of research that hold great promise for advancing the field of life-span developmental behavior genetics: molecular genetics and GE interactions. Finally, we close the chapter by offering some ideas about strategies for capitalizing upon those opportunities.

Developmental Genetics Versus Developmental Science

A chapter on life-span genetics would not be complete without a discussion of the ongoing controversy between researchers using behavioral genetic approaches to study development and developmental scientists (see Griffiths & Tabery, 2008, for more details). Both sides agree that genes and environments are important for the development of behavior, but they disagree as to how genes and environments combine to produce behavior. Developmental scientists argue that it is the continuous interplay between genes and environment that makes each individual unique. The focus is on "how genes cause development, rather than how much development genes cause" (Griffiths & Tabery 2008, p. 335), where the latter is the type of question addressed by behavioral genetic research. Thus, the developmental science approach focuses on the dynamic interaction between genes and environment on individual development, whereas developmental behavioral geneticists assess the etiology of individual differences in developmental processes. These are both important questions in their own right, but they focus on different levels of analysis and require different methods of research.

The controversy can be traced to three conceptual differences between the two approaches—specifically the meanings of "reaction range," gene–environment interaction, and gene or gene action. Griffiths and Tabery describe each of these in much more detail and provide explanations for the historical and ideological differences. In brief, the *norm of reaction,* or *reaction range,* as initially defined (Dobzhansky, 1955) was a hypothetical entity that incorporated not only manifest variation, but potential

unexpressed variation as well. Developmental behavioral geneticists saw this as limiting the scientific usefulness of this concept, because any given genotype would
never be exposed to the full range of possible environments, so it would be impossible
to fully capture the norm of reaction (Turkheimer, Goldsmith, & Gottesman, 1995).
Reaction range, the term redefined by this group, could be used to estimate the linear
relation between genetic predispositions and phenotypic expressions within some
range of environmental circumstances to better understand the genetic potential of
the system. Gottlieb (1995) on the other hand believed that understanding behavioral development meant understanding the causal structure, even though there
were parts that would never be realized, and could not be estimated. In contrast,
he believed that the realized reaction range confounded the causal structure of the
system with the particular environmental exposures found in existing populations.

Gene–environment interaction from a behavioral genetic perspective generally
focuses on the interaction of genotypic and environmental sources of variation in
the population. That is, G X E is a third component of variance that results from the
product of particular genetic propensities and exposures to specific environmental
circumstances. Developmental scientists, on the other hand, emphasize the importance of the bidirectional gene–environment co-action in individual development
(Gottlieb, 2003). That is, the focus is on the causal–mechanical interaction between
genes and the environment during individual development. From this perspective,
gene–environment interaction is a property of causal networks of material entities.
Behavioral geneticists coined the term *interactionism* to describe this view; the perspective that "environmental and genetic threads in the fabric of behavior are so
tightly interwoven that they are indistinguishable" (Plomin et al., 1977, p. 309), and to
distinguish it from the population concept. Interestingly, although results vary from
trait to trait, behavioral geneticists regularly identify main effects for genes and environment, but fail to find a high level of interaction between genes and environment.

The final area of disagreement is the miscommunication regarding ways to conceptualize genes and gene action. The *gene* has always been defined as the basic
unit of heredity, but behavioral geneticists more typically conceptualize genes in the
Mendelian sense, as intervening variables in the genetic analysis of phenotypes (i.e.,
this conception allowed prediction of the phenotypes of offspring from the phenotypes of parents). Even when linked with a more molecular conceptualization, when
a "gene" is found for a trait of interest, what we often know is that there is something
about a particular locus that makes a heritable difference in the disease, or attribute, phenotype. Developmental scientists conceptualize genes as determinants of the
value of a developmental parameter in the context of a larger developmental system.
Although some recent research (e.g., Suomi, 2003) has begun to tie specific sequences
in the genome to the parameters of developmental models, genes were discussed
historically as hypothetical determinants of development, because they could not be
accessed or manipulated as easily, or as directly, as could the environment.

In general, traditional behavioral geneticists highlight the practical value of the
conclusions that can result from variation that is actually observed in a population,
whereas developmental scientists maintain that the contributory understanding of
potential variation, even if it is not normally found in nature, is equally, if not more,
important (Griffiths & Tabery, 2008). Although proponents of these different views
of genetic and environmental influences on development often talk past one another,
both contribute to an important, albeit different, understanding of the etiology of

continuity and change in behavioral development. Finding that genetic factors contribute to individual differences in intelligence, for example, is not in opposition to such developmental concepts as embeddedness or plasticity. Attributing individual differences to genetic or environmental components of variance does not put constraints on what could be, the result is probabilistic, not deterministic. Unfortunately, little research is available that tests these different approaches to understanding development across the life span. Because much of the evidence is indirect, models that include specific gene expression with measures of life experiences are one way to begin to bridge the gap between these two perspectives (Gottlieb, 2003). To be useful, future research must take advantage of new molecular techniques and incorporate a more complex understanding of the environment.

Molecular Genetics

As has been overviewed in this chapter, behavioral genetic research from family, twin, and adoption designs has provided unequivocal evidence for the importance of genetic influences on IQ and related abilities. Beyond signifying the importance of heritability, studies of this type can be used to structure developmental questions about genetic continuity and change, explore correlations and interactions between genotypes and environments, and answer multivariate questions about genetic heterogeneity and comorbidity. Recent research in behavioral genetics has extended this traditional approach, which has focused primarily on components of variance, in ways that can begin to identify the underlying genetic mechanisms by which heredity influences behavioral characteristics. This information, in turn, can be used to investigate developmental pathways between genes and behavior (Plomin, DeFries, Craig, & McGuffin, 2003). As previously mentioned, the search is not for single genes that importantly impact the behaviors and abilities highlighted in this chapter, but rather the goal is to find a confluence of genetic (and environmental) factors that contribute to cognitive ability.

One approach to research in this area is to identify *quantitative trait loci* (QTL), which refers to genes of assorted effect sizes that contribute to continuous variation in a phenotype (Plomin et al., 2003). In the early 1990s it was suggested that integrating quantitative and molecular genetics would revolutionize research on the etiology of intelligence, by identifying genes that importantly contribute to individual differences in IQ (Plomin & Neiderhiser, 1991). Instead this progress has been slow (not just for intelligence, but for all complex traits), likely because heritability for complex traits involves more QTLs, of much smaller size, than originally expected (Plomin, Kennedy, & Craig, 2006). For example, it was thought that it would be possible to identify genes that would account for at least 1% of the variation in intelligence, but effect sizes have been much smaller, and most studies are under powered to find these effects. This does not mean, however, that this is not a fruitful endeavor. The identification of each QTL provides an additional portal into the relation between genes and behavior.

To overcome the limitation of small effect sizes, researchers have recommended the use of combinations, or sets, of QTLs as a multivariate indicator of genetic risk (Plomin & Crabbe, 2000). Although each QTL is likely to have a small effect, by aggregating several QTLs it may be possible to reach an effect size that will facilitate identification of genes of importance. An example of a study of this type was conducted using longitudinal cognitive data from more than 7,000 thousand twins (Harlaar, Butscher, Meaburn, Craig, & Plomin, 2005) from the Twins Early Development Study (Trouton, Spinath, & Plomin, 2002). At 7 years of age, a QTL set (which was composed of five DNA single-nucleotide polymorphisms, referred to as "snips" [SNPs]) was associated with general cognitive ability (assessed by a composite of four cognitive measures administered via telephone). The composite measure of "g" at 7 years yielded a heritability of 0.43 (with a 95% confidence interval of 0.36–0.51; Harlaar, Hayiou-Thomas, & Plomin, 2005). The SNP set tested in this study was more strongly associated with verbal than nonverbal ability and with reading more than mathematics performance. Because these children were also assessed at ages 2, 3, and 4 on measures of cognitive and language development, it was possible to test developmental questions using this methodology. Analyses of this type suggested that this QTL set significantly correlated with intelligence as early as 2 years of age in this sample, further suggesting genetic continuity in the development of intellectual ability. Although research of this type has been slow to develop, it offers a promising pathway by which the links between strands of DNA that code for proteins and the complexities of intellectual behavior can be understood.

This chapter covers a portion of the behavioral genetic research across the life span and much of this work has generated more questions than answers. In fact, the research in this area has led to the conclusion that development of complex traits is due to the dynamic interrelation between genes and environment working in tandem. The next step is to focus on how genes affect behaviors of interest and how these genetic influences unfold with development. Advances in molecular genetics, however, will make it increasingly possible to identify specific genes responsible for the heritability of behavior. Many of the studies described have banked subject's DNA for future studies, are conducting candidate gene searches, or have done entire genome scans. The allure of molecular genetics, however, should not detract from the need for more quantitative genetics research that can guide the search for genes. Such quantitative genetic research is likely to be most helpful in understanding nurture rather than nature, and especially the interface between them.

So, how can we integrate behavioral genetics and life-span developmental psychology? On the whole, both perspectives focus on similar questions, and draw from the same portfolio of measures; the primary difference between these approaches is the types of subjects that are included in the studies. Adding genetically informative data to theoretically rich developmental studies will increase the types of questions that can be answered. For example, in studies of children and parents, having moms and dads complete measures about themselves, and not just their children, adding information from multiple children in the family, taking advantage of blended families and including twins or adoptees when available, would add an additional layer of explanation. In addition, results of cross-sectional behavior genetic studies have indicated that there may be some important etiological differences at various points in the life span. Therefore, longitudinal studies should be focused on continuity and change across transition periods. One particularly interesting example might be the transition to school, which typically occurs between ages 6 and 7. Much of the behavioral genetic research indicates that this is a time of marked change in genetic influences on intelligence (Davis, Hayworth, & Plomin, 2009). Finally, assessment techniques that incorporate frequent measurements, combined with genetically informative designs, provide an opportunity to disentangle the dynamic pattern of genetic and environmental influences on the etiology of stability and change in behavioral phenotypes. It is at the intersection of these multiple approaches that we will realize the complexities and intricacies of human development.

REFERENCES

Anstey, K. J., Lipnicki D. M., & Low, L. F. (2008). Cholesterol as a risk factor for dementia and cognitive decline: A systematic review of prospective studies with meta-analysis. *American Journal of Geriatric Psychiatry, 16*, 343–354.

Baltes, P. B. (1987). Theoretical propositions of life-span developmental psychology: On the dynamics between growth and decline. *Developmental Psychology, 23*, 611–626.

Baltes, P. B., Reese, H. W., & Lipsitt, L. P. (1980). Life-span developmental psychology. *Annual Review of Psychology, 31*, 65–110.

Baltes, P. B., Reese, H. W., & Nesselroade, J. R. (1977). *Life-span developmental psychology: Introduction to research methods*. Belmont, CA: Wadsworth.

Bartels, M., Rietveld, M. J. H., van Baal, G. C. M., & Boomsma, D. I. (2002). Genetic and environmental influences on the development of intelligence. *Behavior Genetics, 32*, 237–249.

Belsky, J., & Pluess, M. (2009). Beyond diathesis stress: Differential susceptibility to environmental influences. *Psychological Bulletin, 135*, 885–908.

Bergeman, C. S. (1997). *Aging: Genetic and environmental influences*. Thousand Oaks, CA: Sage.

Bergeman, C. S., & Ong, A. (2007). Behavioral genetics. In J. E. Birren (Ed.), *Encyclopedia of Gerontology, 2nd ed.* (pp. 149–159). Oxford: Elsevier.

Bergeman, C. S., & Plomin, R. (1989). Genotype-environment interaction. In M. Bornstein & J. Bruner (Eds.), *Interaction in human development.* (pp. 157–171). Hillsdale, NJ: Lawrence Erlbaum Associates.

Bergeman, C. S., & Plomin, R. (1996). Behavioral genetics. In J.E. Birren (Ed.), *Encyclopedia of Gerontology* (pp. 163–172). Orlando, FL: Academic Press.

Bishop, E. G., Cherny, S. S., Corley, R., Plomin, R., DeFries, J. C., & Hewitt, J. K. (2003). Development genetic analysis of general cognitive ability from 1 to 12 years in a sample of adoptees, biological siblings, and twins. *Intelligence, 31*, 31–49.

Boomsma, D., Busjahn, A., & Peltonen, I. (2002). Classical twin studies and beyond. *Nature Reviews Genetics, 3*, 872–882.

Braungart-Rieker, J., & Bergeman, C.S. (1999). Behavioral genetics and health across the lifespan. In T. Whitman, T. Merluzzi, & R. White (Eds.), *Psychology and medicine* (pp. 47–65). Hillsdale, NJ: Erlbaum.

Buss, D. M. (1984). Marital assortment for personality dispositions: Assessment with three different data sources. *Behavior Genetics, 14*, 111–123.

Buss, D. M. (1985). Human mate selection. *American Scientist, 73*, 47–51.

Cadoret, R. J., Cain, C. A., & Crowe, R. R. (1983). Evidence for gene-environment interaction in the development of adolescent antisocial behavior. *Behavior Genetics, 13*, 301–310.

Cadoret, R. J., Yates, W. R., Troughton, E. Woodworth, G. & Stewart. M. A. (1995) Genetic-environmental interaction in the genesis of aggressivity and conduct disorders. *Archives of General Psychiatry, 52*, 916–924.

Caspi, A., Sugden, K., Moffitt, T. E., Taylor, A., Craig, I. W., Harrington, H., et al. (2003). Influence of life stress on depression: Moderated by a polymorphism in the 5-HTT gene. *Science, 301*, 386–389.

Cattell, R. B. (1971). *Abilities: Their structure, growth, and action*. Boston: Houghton Mifflin.

Condor, E. H., Saunders, A. M., Strittmatter, W. J., Schmechel, D. E., Gaskel, P. C., Small, G. W., et al. (1993). Gene dose of apolipoprotein E type 4 allele and the risk of Alzheimer's disease in late onset families. *Science, 261*, 921–923.

Davis, O. S. P., Haworth, C. M. A., & Plomin, R. (2009). Dramatic increase in heritability of cognitive development from early to middle childhood: An 8-year longitudinal study of 8,700 pairs of twins. *Psychological Science, 20*, 1301–1308.

Deary, I. J., Pattie, A., Wilson, V., & Whalley, L. J. (2005). The cognitive cost of being a twin: Two whole-population surveys. *Twin Research and Human Genetics, 8*, 376–383.

Dobzhansky, T. (1955). *Evolution, genetics, and man*. New York: Wiley.

D'Onofrio, B. M., Turkheimer, E. N., Eaves, L. J., Corey, L. A., Berg, K., Solaas, M. H., et al. (2003). The role of the children of twins design in elucidating causal relations between parent characteristics and child outcomes. *Journal of Child Psychology and Psychiatry, 44,* 1130–1144.

Eaves, L. J. (2008). Genotype X environment interaction in psychopathology: Fact or artifact? *Twin Research and Human Genetics, 9,* 1–8.

Eaves, L. J., Silberg, J. L., & Maes, H. H. (2005). Revisiting the children of twins: Can they be used to resolve the environmental effects of dyadic parental treatment on child behavior? *Twin Research and Human Genetics, 8,* 283–290.

Eley, T. C., Sugdern, K., Corsico, A., Gregory, A. M., Sham, P., McGuffin, P., et al. (2004). Gene-environment interaction analysis of serotonin system markers with adolescent depression. *Molecular Psychiatry, 9,* 908–915.

Finkel, D., Pedersen, N. L., Plomin, R., & McClearn, G. E. (1998). Longitudinal and cross-sectional twin data on cognitive abilities in adulthood: The Swedish Adoption/Twin Study of Aging. *Developmental Psychology, 34,* 1400–1413.

Finkel, D., Wille, D., & Matheny, A. P., Jr. (1998). Preliminary results from a twin study of infant-caregiver attachment. *Behavior Genetics, 28,* 1–8.

Gottlieb, G. (1995). Some conceptual deficiencies in 'developmental' behavior genetics. *Human Development, 38,* 131–141.

Gottlieb, G. (2003). On making behavioral genetics truly developmental. *Human Development, 46,* 337–355.

Griffiths, P. E., & Tabery, J. (2008). Behavioral genetics and development: Historical and conceptual causes of controversy. *New Ideas in Psychology, 26,* 332–352.

Hahn, M., Hewitt, J. K., Henderson, N. D., & Benno, R. (1990). *Developmental behavior genetics: Neural, biometrical, and evolutionary approaches.* New York: Oxford University Press.

Harlaar, N., Butscher, L., Meaburn, E., Craig, I. W., & Plomin, R. (2005). A behavioral genomic analysis of DNA markers associated with general cognitive ability in 7-year-olds. *Journal of Child Psychology and Psychiatry, 46,* 1097–1107.

Harlaar, N., Hayiou-Thomas, M. E., & Plomin, R. (2005). Reading and general cognitive ability: A multivariate analysis of 7-year-old twins. *Scientific Studies of Reading, 9,* 197–218.

Hoekstra, R. A., Bartels, M., & Boomsma, D. I. (2007). Longitudinal genetic study of verbal and non-verbal IQ from early childhood to young adulthood. *Learning and Individual Differences, 17,* 97–114.

Horn, J. L., & Donaldson, G. (1976). On the myth of intellectual decline in adulthood. *American Psychologist, 31,* 701–719.

Johnson, W., Krueger, R. F., Bouchard, T. J., Jr., & McGue, M. (2002). The personalities of twins: Just ordinary folks. *Twin Research, 5,* 125–131.

Kendler, K. S., Kuhn, J. W., Virtum, B. S., Prescott, C. A., & Riley, B. (2005). The interaction of stressful life events and a serotonin transporter polymorphism in the prediction of episodes of major depression: A replication. *Archives of General Psychiatry, 62,* 529–535.

Loehlin, J. C. (1992). *Genes and environment in personality development.* Newbury Park, CA: Sage.

MacGillivray, I., Campbell, D. M., & Thompson, B. (1988). *Twinning and twins.* Chichester, UK: John Wiley & Sons.

Matheny, A. P., & Dolan, A. B. (1975). Changes in eye color during early-childhood - Sex and genetic differences. *Annals of Human Biology, 2,* 191–196.

McArdle, J. J. (1986). Latent variable growth within behavior genetic models. *Behavior Genetics, 16,* 163–200.

McArdle, J. J., & Hamagami, F. (2003). Structural equation models for evaluating dynamic concepts within longitudinal twin analyses. *Behavior Genetics, 33,* 137–159.

McCartney, K., Harris, M. J., & Bernieri, F. (1990). Growing up and growing apart: A developmental meta-analysis of twin studies. *Psychological Bulletin, 107,* 226–237.

McClearn, G. E., Johansson, B., Berg, S., Pedersen, N. L., Ahern, F., Petrill, S. A., et al. (1997). Substantial genetic influence on cognitive abilities in twins 80 or more years old. *Science, 276,* 1560–1563.

McGue, M., & Bouchard, T. J. (1984). Adjustment of twin data for the effects of age and sex. *Behavior Genetics, 14,* 325–343.

McGue, M., Bouchard, T. J., Jr., Iacono, W. G., & Lykken, D. T. (1993). Behavioral genetics of cognitive ability: A life-span perspective. In R. Plomin & G.E. McClearn (Eds.), *Nature, nurture, & psychology* (pp. 59–76). Washington, DC: American Psychological Association.

McGue, M., & Christensen, K. (2001). The heritability of cognitive functioning in very old adults: Evidence from Danish twins aged 75 years and older. *Psychology and Aging, 16,* 272–280.

McGue, M., & Christensen, K. (2002). The heritability of level and rate-of-change in cognitive functioning in Danish twins aged 70 years and older. *Experimental Aging Research, 28,* 435–451.

Nance, W.E., & Corey, L.A. (1976). Genetic models for the analysis of data from the families of identical twins. *Genetics, 83,* 811–826.

Neale, M. C., Boker, S. M., Bergeman, C. S., & Maes, H. H. (2006). The utility of genetically informative data in the study of development. In C. S. Bergeman & S. M. Boker (Eds.), *Methodological Issues in aging research* (pp. 269–327). Mahwah, NJ: Erlbaum.

Neale, M. C., & Cardon, L. R. (1992). *Methodology for genetic studies of twins and families.* Dordrecht, The Netherlands: Kluwer Academic Publishers.

Pedersen, N. L., Plomin, R., Nesselroade, J. R., & McClearn, G. E. (1992). A quantitative genetic analysis of cognitive abilities during the second half of the life span. *Psychological Science, 3,* 346–353.

Perls, T., & Terry, D. (2003). Genetics of exceptional longevity. *Experimental Gerontology, 38,* 725–730.

Petrill, S. A., Lipton, P. A., Hewitt, J. K., Plomin, R., Cherny, S. S., Corley, R., et al. (2004). Genetic and environmental contributions to general cognitive ability through the first 16 years of life. *Developmental Psychology, 40,* 805–812.

Petrill, S. A., Plomin, R., DeFries, J. C., & Hewitt, J. K. (2003). *Nature, nurture, and the transition to early adolescence.* New York: Oxford University Press.

Phillips, K., & Matheny, A. P., Jr. (1997). Evidence for genetic influence on both cross-situation and situation-specific components of behavior. *Journal of Personality and Social Psychology, 73,* 129–138.

Plomin, R. (1986). *Development, genes, and psychology.* Hillsdale, NJ: Erlbaum.

Plomin, R., & Crabbe, J. C. (2000). DNA. *Psychological Bulletin, 126,* 806–828.

Plomin, R., DeFries, J. C., Craig, I. W., & McGuffin, P. (2003). *Behavioral genetics in the postgenomic era.* Washington, DC: American Psychological Association.

Plomin, R., DeFries, J. C., & Loehlin, J. C. (1977). Genotype-environment interaction and correlation in the analysis of human behavior. *Psychological Bulletin, 84,* 309–322.

Plomin, R., DeFries, J. C., & McClearn, G. E. (1980). *Behavioral genetics: A primer.* San Francisco: W.H. Freeman & Company.

Plomin, R., Fulker, D. W., Corley, R., & DeFries, J. C. (1997). Nature, nurture, and cognitive development from 1 to 16 years: A parent-offspring adoption study. *Psychological Science, 8,* 442–447.

Plomin, R., Kagan, J., Emde, R. N., Reznick, J. S., Braungart, J. M., Robinson, J., et al. (1993). Genetic change and continuity from fourteen to twenty months: The MacArthur Longitudinal Twin Study. *Child Development, 64,* 1354–1376.

Plomin, R., Kennedy, J. K. J., & Craig, I. W. (2006). The quest for quantitative trait loci associated with intelligence. *Intelligence, 34,* 513–526.

Plomin, R., & Neiderhiser, J. M. (1991). Quantitative genetics, molecular genetics, and intelligence. *Intelligence, 15,* 369–387.

Plomin, R., Pedersen, N. L., Lichtenstein, P., & McClearn, G. E. (1994). Variability and stability in cognitive abilities are largely genetic later in life. *Behavior Genetics, 24,* 207–215.

Reynolds, C. A., Finkel, D., Gatz, M., & Pedersen, N. L. (2002). Sources of influence on the rate of cognitive change over time in Swedish twins: An application of latent growth models. *Experimental Aging Research, 28,* 407–433.

Reynolds, C. A., Finkel, D., McArdle, J. J., Gatz, M., Berg, S., & Pedersen, N. L. (2005). Quantitative genetic analysis of latent growth curve models of cognitive abilities in adulthood. *Developmental Psychology, 41,* 3–16.

Reynolds, C. A., Gatz, M., Prince, J. A., Berg, S., & Pedersen, N. L. (2010). Serum lipid levels and cognitive change in later life. *Journal of the Geriatric Society, 58,* 501–509.

Risch, N., Herrell, R., Lehner, T., Liang, K. Y., Eaves, L., Hoh, J., et al. (2009). Interaction between the serotonin transporter gene (5-HTTLPR), stressful life events, and risk of depression. *Journal of the American Medical Association, 301,* 2462–2471.

Rose, R. J., Harris, E. L., Christian, J. C., & Nance, W. E. (1979). Genetic variance in nonverbal intelligence: Data from the kinships of identical twins. *Science, 205,* 1153–1155.

Rowe, D. C., Jacobson, K. C., & van den Oord, E. J. (1999). Genetic and environmental influences on vocabulary IQ: Parental education level as moderator. *Child Development, 70,* 1151–1162.

Rutter, M. (2006). *Genes and behavior: Nature-nurture interplay explained.* Malden, MA: Blackwell.

Scarr, S., & McCartney, K. (1983). How people make their own environments: A theory of genotype-environment effects. *Child Development, 54,* 424–435.

Schaie, K. W. (1975). Research strategy in developmental human behavior genetics. In K. W. Schaie, V. E. Anderson, G. E. McClearn, & J. Money (Eds.), *Developmental human behavior genetics: Nature-nurture redefined* (pp. 205–219). Lexington, MA: Lexington Books.

Smith, G. T. (2009). Why do different individuals progress along different life trajectories? *Perspectives on Psychological Science, 4,* 415–421.

Suomi, S. J. (2003). How gene-environment interactions can influence emotional development in rhesus monkeys. In C. Garcia-Coll, E. L. Bearer, & R. M. Lerner (Eds.), *Nature and nurture: The complex interplay of genetic and environmental differences on human behavior and development.* (pp. 35–51). Mahwah, NJ: Erlbaum.

Trouton, A., Spinath, F. M., & Plomin, R. (2002). Twins Early Development Study (TEDS): A multivariate, longitudinal genetic investigation of language, cognition and behavior problems in childhood. *Twin Research, 5,* 444–448.

Turkheimer, E., Goldsmith, H. H., & Gottesman, I. I. (1995). Commentary. *Human Development, 38,* 142–153.

Turkheimer, E., Haley, A., Waldron, M., D'Onofrio, B., & Gottesman, I.I. (2003). Socioeconomic status modifies heritability of IQ in young children. *Psychological Science, 14,* 623–628.

Wahlsten, D. (1990). Insensitivity of the analysis of variance to heredity–environment interaction. *Behavioral and Brain Sciences, 13,* 109–161.

Widaman, K. F. (1998). Ruminations on aging changes in mental abilities and their heritability: Comment on Finkel, Pedersen, Plomin, and McClearn. *Developmental Psychology, 34,* 1414–1416.

Wilcox, D. C., Wilcox, B. J., Hsueh, W. C., & Suzuki, M. (2006). Genetic determinants of exceptional human longevity: Insights from the Okinawa Centenarian Study. *Age, 28,* 313–332.

Wilson, R. S. (1974). Twins: Mental development in the preschool years. *Developmental Psychology, 10,* 580–588.

Wilson, R. S. (1976). Concordance in physical growth for monozygotic and dizygotic twins. *Annals of Human Biology, 3,* 1–10.

Wilson, R. S. (1978). Synchronies in mental development: An epigenetic perspective. *Science, 202,* 939–948.

Wilson, R. S. (1983). The Louisville Twin Study: Developmental synchronies in behavior. *Child Development, 54,* 298–316.

SOCIAL INEQUALITIES

28

Ishtar O. Govia, James S. Jackson, and Sherrill L. Sellers

INTRODUCTION

Social inequalities are important in human development because both intra- and interindividual change and consistency across the life span are affected and contextualized by disparities among social groups. The increasing trend to integrate life-span and life course perspectives in human development research (Antonucci & Jackson, 2010) addresses directly an enhanced appreciation of social determinants of change and consistency throughout an individual's life. Increasing calls have been made to ensure that both life-span (based largely in psychology) and life course (based largely in sociology) perspectives are used in framing research questions, developing research designs, and conducting appropriate analyses (Shanahan & Porfelli, 2002). We see these integrations as especially pertinent in the study of health disparities, a rapidly evolving area of research requiring examinations of intra- and interindividual consistency and change.

Although these integration efforts support a notion of the importance of social context in development, much of the theory and research on how social inequalities function as a major context for development has not been brought together in a comprehensive manner. This is likely because of the interdisciplinary nature of scholarship on social inequalities, the few theories that address social inequalities as an overarching concept with specific inequalities as subtopics, a dearth of empirical studies that test specific hypotheses about the mechanisms through which social inequalities affect health and well-being, and the reality that the methodology to explore the role of social inequalities in relation to change throughout the life span is still in its early stages. The aim of this chapter is to briefly synthesize some of this work and to contribute to an understanding of how social inequalities affect life course and life-span development.

The topic of social inequalities in life-span development requires a focus on, and synthesis of, the roles of situations and contexts in addition to the traditional emphasis of person-level psychological variables, such as cognition, emotion, and motivation, that are at the core of individual life-span development (Baltes, 1987). Because life-span development "does not assume unidirectional or cumulative change functions from birth to death, but instead envisions human development as multi-linear and discontinuous" (Baltes, Reese, & Lipsitt, 1980, p. 72), understanding the role of social inequalities in how people change and remain constant makes an already complex field even more so. Yet, without striving to capture this complexity in the development of research questions, research designs, and the conduct of studies and analyses, we fail to truly understand the dynamism involved in human growth.

This chapter uses groups within the United States as the focus for a discussion on group-based social inequalities throughout an individual's life. In doing so, it is not the intention to assume that the treatment of, and issues involved in, understanding social inequalities across the life course are transferable from one country to another (Henrich, Heine, & Norenzayan, 2010). In fact, it is clear that the United States has peculiarities in the issues it faces—it is among the top four Organisation for Economic Co-Operation and Development (OECD) countries with the largest income inequality (OECD, 2008) and, among industrialized countries, it is the country that demonstrates the greatest financially influenced barriers in both access to health care and the quality of health care received (Schoen et al., 2007). However, we examine social inequalities in the individual life span by focusing on the United States using an n of 1 (Jackson, 2002) for two main reasons.

First, preliminary national comparisons suggest some commonalities in the relationships between social inequalities and health and well-being (e.g., Olafsdottir, 2007). These include individual-level factors, such as perceptions (e.g., dissatisfaction with health care) and behaviors (e.g. poor health behaviors), as well as systems-level factors, such as health policies (Blendon, Schoen, DesRoches, Osborn, & Zapert, 2003).

Second, focusing on the United States facilitates exploring the heterogeneity of social inequalities in one national context. For example, research suggests that within individual nations, social inequalities are intricately linked to disparities in health based upon racial and ethnic group categorization, gender, sexuality, age, ability, citizenship, geographic residence, and other social category memberships. And in the specific case of the United States, empirical research has increasingly revealed that the relationships between social inequalities has to be examined among subgroups separately, instead of examining Americans as one uniform population group (Blendon et al., 2007).

This chapter focuses mainly on racial and ethnic group health disparities. We selected this emphasis to demonstrate the complexity of the relationships involved. Attending to racial and ethnic group disparities, and highlighting a few group comparisons in-depth, facilitates exploration of how intersections of social identities (Cole, 2009) are implicated in the role that social inequalities play over life course and across life-span development. For example, studies that explore within-group variables among Blacks and Whites[1] (e.g., residence in rural vs. urban areas or in affluent vs. high-poverty areas) suggest that these group comparisons may help unearth more nuanced information about the connections between identities and health and well-being outcomes, than do examinations that concentrate simply on intergroup variables (Blendon et al., 2007).

Finally, this chapter focuses on negative health outcomes (physical and psychiatric health disorders). We appreciate that disparities in health and well-being can also be conceptualized within a positive psychology framework (Franklin & Jackson, 1990), with outcomes related to psychological well-being, such as happiness and life satisfaction. However, this latter framework tends to be applied infrequently in examining the role of social inequalities in life course and individual life-span development. While this is a promising area for future study, we are interested in

---

[1] Throughout this chapter, we use Whites to describe non-Hispanic Whites and Blacks to describe non-Hispanic Blacks. We use Black and African American interchangeably.

synthesizing existing research on disparities, and in so doing, illuminate directions for more refined examinations in these and other likely areas of research in social inequalities and life course and life-span development.

WHAT ARE SOCIAL INEQUALITIES?

In recent decades, there has been an increased focus on the role that social inequalities play in development across the individual life span, and how this in turn translates to group-based disparities (Adler & Stewart, 2010). For example, the 2008 Public Broadcasting Service documentary series, *Unnatural causes: Is inequality making us sick?* (Adelman, 2008) marshals data, expert testimony, and stories of individuals and families to highlight how racial and socioeconomic inequalities are intricately implicated in inter- and intragroup differences in health-related outcomes. But what exactly are social inequalities?

Social inequalities refer to disproportionate allocations or possessions of economic and social resources among groups (Adler & Stewart, 2010). Some of the key individual, group, and structural domains in which these disparities occur include, but are not limited to, race, ethnicity, gender, sexual orientation, class, age, geographical location (country, rural vs. urban setting, affluent vs. high-poverty concentration environment), and citizenship. Social inequalities concern the power dynamics that are ingrained in how these identities and locations translate to differential interindividual and intergroup outcomes. Furthermore, while objective positioning as defined by measureable outcomes are crucial elements of social inequalities, subjective location within hierarchies and power structures are also critical components to understanding how these inequalities translate to inter- and intragroup differences and similarities in outcomes (Griffin & Jackson, 2009).

STRUCTURAL INEQUALITIES

One of the clearest ways in which social inequalities manifest is in indicators of structural inequalities, such as household income, and unemployment rates (Adler & Stewart, 2010). For example, while the median household income for all families in the United States increased from 1968 to 2007, the disparities between Whites and Blacks remained constant (Dillahunt, Miller, Prokosch, Huezo, & Muhammad, 2010). In 1968, the median household income for Blacks ($27,995) was just a few thousand dollars more than half of the median household income for Whites ($46,678). In 2007, this increased to $40,143 for Blacks and $69,937 for Whites. As the data show, the Black/White disparity in median household income has, in fact, grown.

Racial and ethnic disparities are also present in the 2008–2009 unemployment rates (Dillahunt et al., 2010). While the economic crisis has ensured that unemployment rates increased steadily across racial and ethnic groups from December 2008 through December 2009, Blacks were the most disadvantaged—both in terms of initial higher rate (11.9%) and final estimates (16.2%). Comparatively, in December 2008, unemployment was 6.6% for Whites and 9.2% for Latino/Hispanic; and in December 2009, 9.0% and 12.9% for Whites and Latinos/Hispanics respectively. Blacks historically experience the most disadvantages in unemployment, and the current economic crisis is no exception to this trend (Muhammad, Davis, Lui, & Leondar-Wright, 2004).

This brief overview of two key indicators of structural inequalities suggests the sobering reality of the interlocking nature of social inequalities (Adler & Stewart, 2010). If an individual's development occurs within comparatively and objectively limited circumstances, these conditions will inevitably affect the possibilities and norms for maturation. Indeed, this interlocked nature of social inequalities translates into physical and psychological disparities in development across the life course and over the individual life span.

HEALTH STATUS INEQUALITIES AND HEALTH DISPARITIES

Large disparities in all-cause and specific-cause death rates exist among racial and ethnic groups. In addition, disparities exist in health care. This section reviews some of the trend data available on these disparities using national databases. Mortality reflects one of the most visible areas of health disparities. Infant mortality rates, for example, show that while there has been an overall decline from 1995 to 2005, Black mothers consistently have higher rates than mothers from any other racial/ethnic group (Mathews & MacDorman, 2008). In 2005, for example, Black mothers had rates of 13.63 infant deaths per 1,000 live births, while the corresponding 2005 infant death rates per 1,000 live births were 8.30, 8.06, 5.76, 5.53, 4.89, 4.68, and 4.42, for Puerto Rican, American Indian or Alaska native, White, Mexican, Central and South American, American Asian or Pacific Islander, and Cuban mothers, respectively. The large difference between Black and White mothers is consistent from 1995 through 2005, with the rates for Black mothers more than double that of White mothers in both 1995 (14.65 compared to 6.28 deaths per 1,000 live births) and 2005 (13.63 compared to 5.76 deaths per 1,000 live births).

Pregnancy-related mortality risk of death has also been consistently approximately four times higher for Black women than for White women over the past 5 decades (Tucker, Berg, Callaghan, & Hsia, 2007). The numbers of pregnancy-related deaths per 100,000 live births, called the pregnancy-related mortality ratios, are also lower for Hispanic, Asian/Pacific Islander, and American Indian/Alaska native women, than for Black women (Anonymous, 2001).

On the other end of the life span, mortality data show that Black men and women continue to be worse off than their peers from other racial and ethnic groups. Age-adjusted mortality rates at 65 and older demonstrate that for Black men and women the mortality is 5,248 per 100,000 compared to rates of 4,696 for White, 3,340 for Hispanic, and 2,699 for Asian/Pacific Islander men and women respectively (Centers for Disease Control and Prevention/National Center for Health Statistics [CDC/NCHS], 2007a). However, the disadvantage that Black men and women have across the life span ceases to exist in the mortalities for those 85 and older. For persons in this group, mortalities are highest for White (14,001), followed by Black (12,863), Hispanic (9,277), and then Asian/Pacific Islander (8,528) persons (CDC/NCHS, 2007a).

Similar declines in racial group differences at older ages occur in life expectancy. The data from 1976, 1986, 1996, and 2006 show that, for the total U.S. population, life expectancy at birth, at age 65, and at age 85 have all increased steadily in the 10-year increments (CDC/NCHS, 2007b). However, at each of the 4 years, the life expectancy for Black males and females has been consistently higher than for White males and females (CDC/NCHS, 2007b). The reasons for the declines in racial group differences remain a source of some debate, with arguments focusing on age misreporting and changes in the methodology used to calculate estimates versus the likelihood of better health among the Black women and men who survive to the oldest ages (Manton, Stallard, & Wing, 1991; Preston, Elo, Rosenwaike, & Hill, 1996). The main point, however, remains; mortality data show that Black men and women continue to be worse off than their peers in other racial and ethnic groups.

Other areas in which Black men and women experience negative outcomes in relation to their White peers, and often in relation to peers from other racial and ethnic groups, are acute and chronic illness health status, and poor health behaviors (smoking, lack of vigorous physical health activity, heavy alcohol use, drug use). These disadvantages that Black men and women experience appear to be intricately tied to their structural difficulties. Those who experience the most structural disadvantage tend to rely on poor health behaviors to cope with the chronic stressors that are intertwined with these disadvantaged statuses (Krueger & Chang, 2008).

In short, the data on morbidity and mortality, acute and chronic illness statuses, and poor health behavior and lifestyles, suggest that, with the exception of mortality and life expectancy at the oldest ages (and to some extent the youngest ages), across the life span, Blacks more than any other racial or ethnic group in the United States are the most consistently disadvantaged—particularly relative to Whites (Jackson, Govia, & Sellers, 2010).

In contrast to physical health outcomes, prevalence rates for major psychiatric disorders reveal very few, if any, Black/White disparities favoring persons from White backgrounds. Household surveys of mental disorder prevalence estimates since the 1980s all reveal equivalent, or higher, rates for Whites in comparison to Blacks (Breslau, Kendler, Su, Gaxiola-Aguilar, & Kessler, 2005; Jackson et al., 2004; Kessler et al., 1994, 2003; Riolo, Nguyen, Greden, & King, 2005; Somervell, Leaf, Weissman, Blazer, & Bruce, 1989; Weissman & Myers, 1980).

These data suggest that social inequalities do not follow a uniform trajectory across racial and ethnic groups in their effects on physical and mental health outcomes. While social conditions are intricately linked with development throughout the life course, the links are complex. Social inequalities do not simply cause adverse health outcomes, but instead are the functions of dynamic cycles of growth and stagnation and their interrelationships with inequalities at each stage in the lifecycle (Crimmins, Hayward, & Seeman, 2004; Whitfield & Hayward, 2003).

A FRAMEWORK OF HEALTH AND WELL-BEING OVER THE LIFE COURSE AMONG DISPARATE GROUPS

Racial and ethnic group disparities exist in both physical and mental well-being. Among populations with equal access to health care, minorities do worse than nonminorities when it comes to the quality health care they receive, and Blacks again demonstrate very strong negative disparities (Copeland, 2005). Health Care utilization patterns differ significantly among groups, and clearly there is a role of health care systems and the legal and regulatory climate in contributing to these differences

(Institute of Medicine Committee on Understanding and Eliminating Racial and Ethnic Disparities in Health Care [IOM], 2002).

As noted earlier, many racial and ethnic groups, especially Blacks, are at disproportionate risk for negative health outcomes over the life course when compared to Whites (Sellers, Govia, & Jackson, 2009). As we have outlined, a number of factors may contribute to these disparities, ranging from biological dispositions to dietary habits, to a failure to receive adequate health care (IOM, 2002). The specific mechanisms, however, that produce these differential outcomes are less clear (Antonucci & Jackson, 2010). Given complex sociohistorical contexts it may be less useful to compare between racial and ethnic groups than within groups in uncovering specific mechanisms. For example, Black/White comparisons may be less illuminating than the examination of various intragroup social and cultural factors as possible sources of risk and resilience for Black men, women, and children (Jackson & Govia, 2009; Sellers et al., 2009).

It is important to continue to develop a life course framework within which the nature of the economic, social, and health circumstances of racial and ethnic group members over their life spans can be explained and understood in the context of historical and current structural disadvantage and blocked mobility opportunities (Antonucci & Jackson, 2010). This framework contextualizes individual and group experiences by birth cohort, period events, and individual aging processes (Jackson & Govia, 2009). For example, Blacks and other underrepresented racial and ethnic minorities arrive in adulthood and older ages with extensive histories of disease, ill health, and varied individual adaptive reactions to their poor health (Anderson, Bulatao, & Cohen, 2004). The available cohort data over the last few decades for cause-specific mortality and morbidity, as reviewed earlier, across the life course indicates that there are accumulated deficits that perhaps place Black, Latino, and Native American middle-aged and older people at greater risk than comparable chronologically aged Whites (Antonucci & Jackson, 2010). Similarly, the fact that Blacks actually outlive their White counterparts in the very older ages suggests possible selection factors at work that may result in hardier older Blacks (Jackson, Govia, et al., 2010). These selection factors may act on successive cohorts of Blacks in a "sandwich-like" manner leaving alternate cohorts of middle-aged and older Blacks of relative wellness and good functional ability. The cohort experiences of Blacks undoubtedly play a major role in the nature of their health experiences over the life course in terms of the quality of health care from birth, exposure to risk factors, and the presence of exogenous environmental factors. Another contributing factor is the stressor role of prejudice and discrimination across the life course and over the individual life span, even though it may differ in form and intensity as a function of birth cohort, period, and age (Jackson, Govia, et al., 2010).

The role of socioeconomic status (SES) has been touted as a major risk factor and implicated in the effects of other risk factors in mortality and morbidity (Adler & Stewart, 2010; Williams, Mohammed, Leavell, & Collins, 2010). Impressive evidence exists that SES plays a major role in a wide variety of diseases such that increasing SES is associated with better health and lowered morbidity (Adler & Stewart, 2010). These effects have been shown at both the individual and ecological levels on blood pressure, general mortality, cancer, cardiovascular heart diseases, cerebrovascular disease, diabetes, and obesity. The effects of SES on the health of Black Americans require additional research (Adler & Stewart, 2010; Williams et al., 2010).

Contemporary cohorts of Blacks and members of other race and ethnic groups being born today are at considerable risk. For example, studies reveal that Black Americans are most likely to spend the majority of their childhoods in low income, single female-only–headed households. Poverty in turn places Black Americans at risk for inadequate diets, fewer educational opportunities, greater exposure to crime, and limited opportunities for occupational advancement (Jackson, 2000). Even for those born into middle-class homes, wealth differentials between Blacks and Whites in this society are huge. Thus, in the face of severe structural, social, and psychological constraints, studies that address the coping skills, capacity, and adaptability of racial and ethnic groups at different points in the life course are particularly important (Antonucci & Jackson, 2010).

It is possible that the most important racial and ethnic group effects are in the form of interactions with other structural or cultural factors (e.g., religion, SES, and world views; Sellers et al., 2009). As described later, Blacks and other disadvantaged groups may utilize, over the individual life span, different mechanisms than Whites to maintain levels of productivity, physical and mental health, and effective functioning (Jackson & Knight, 2006).

We have consistently suggested the need to develop better national policies directed to the growing U.S. ethnic and racial minority populations (Antonucci & Jackson, 2010; Sellers et al., 2009). Similarly, we have proposed that these policies must be responsive to life course and family considerations in order to address the health and well-being of racial and ethnic minority populations, especially Blacks and Latinos (e.g., Antonucci & Jackson, 2010). As we suggest in this chapter we believe that a life course/life-span framework is required to explore how sociohistorical context influences and interacts with individual and group resources to both impede and facilitate the quality of life and health of successive cohorts of Blacks over the group life course, and in the nature of their individual human development experiences over their life spans (Baltes, 1987). For example, relationships between environmental factors, such as high crime rates, high noise and pollution levels and social isolation, and negative health factors (e.g., asthma, hypertension, etc.) affect all members of families and communities and contribute to poorer health among younger and older Blacks (Anderson et al., 2004). A life course perspective clarifies that both current younger and older cohorts of racial and ethnic group minorities have been, and are being, exposed to the conditions that will influence profoundly their social, psychological, and health statuses from childhood to adulthood and older ages in the years and decades to come (Baltes, 1987; Sellers et al., 2009).

Human development and the life course are the central concerns in any approach to understanding ostensible racial and ethnic group effects in physical and mental health statuses and service use. Racial and ethnic groups have divergent life experiences because of sociostructural, socioeconomic, and cultural reasons (Antonucci & Jackson, 2010). These different experiences will have significant influences, both positive and negative, on individual, family, and group well-being and health at all stages of the life course, ultimately influencing the adjustment to major late-life transitions (e.g., loss of spouse, retirement, and disability, etc.). Figure 28.1 provides an illustration of one perspective on the group life course and within this context the intraindividual life spans of individuals who share group characteristics and identities. In this figure, advantaged and disadvantaged groups are represented by the large ovals over the life course. The slope and size of the differences between groups

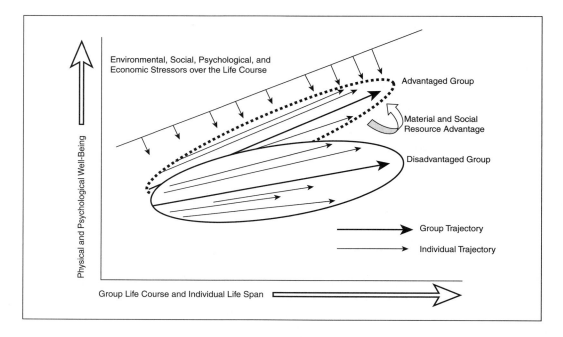

FIGURE 28.1 **Group life course and individual life spans of members of advantaged and disadvantaged groups.**

(represented by the large arrows within the ovals) are determined by historical period and cohort experiences. Thus, if Whites represent the advantaged group and American Blacks represent the disadvantaged group, then during earlier periods of U.S. history these group tendencies would have even larger slope differences and less overlap in the general group life course than today, as well as in the overlap in experiences of individuals within the groups. Over time the figure illustrates the continuing effects of environmental, social, and economic experiences that influence individuals and families within each of the groups.

We hypothesize that the more advantaged group is advantaged because of greater material, social, and economic resources, which permits each individual within the group to better withstand the negative consequences of life experiences. Because of the greater material and economic and social resources available to members of the advantaged group, these individual life spans will be more tightly bunched around the more positive central tendency of the group. We also hypothesize that based upon individual resilience factors some members of disadvantaged groups fare better than others, and thus there will be greater individual variation around the central trajectory tendencies of the group.

This life course/life-span perspective illustrated in Figure 28.1 provides the overarching scientific framework for understanding the influence of racial and ethnic categories. This influence can be best understood from the sociohistorical and current circumstances that different groups with well-defined physical characteristics encounter, and how "own-" and "other-group" attitudes and behaviors toward members who belong to these categories affect the general group trajectories over the life course within which individual life spans (Jackson & Sellers, 2001). While some genetic and biological factors may vary with the group categorization (e.g., sickle cell anemia), for example, we believe that the fundamental nature of the experiences of being a member of an advantaged or disadvantaged racial or ethnic group derives from self- and other- and societal-definitions, and continuing favored treatment or, conversely, discrimination and maltreatment (Antonucci & Jackson, 2010).

It is not completely understood how racial and ethnic group categorizations fit in models of health, human development, and life course and life-span development, but the conceptualization represented in Figure 28.1 may help move closer to comprehending the ways that group life course trajectories influence the observed nature of individual life spans of persons who share group characteristics and common treatment (either valued or devalued) in a society.

▇ THEORIES, MODELS, AND FRAMEWORKS FOR SOCIAL INEQUALITIES

Several different perspectives have been used in sociological, public health, and epidemiological research for indirect and direct explorations of the role of social inequalities in the life course and in life-span development. In this section we review three main theories, models, or frameworks that we believe speak most directly to racial and ethnic health disparities.

The first of these is the stress process model (Pearlin, 1999; Pearlin, Menaghan, Lieberman, & Mullan, 1981). This model specifies that acute and chronic stressors affect health via different mechanisms. The model has often been used to examine the role of chronic stressors among disadvantaged populations, under the assumption that objectively assessed or perceived chronic stressors such as discrimination based upon race or color categorization can, over time, strain the individual's psychological capacities. Discrimination and perceived racism as a class of stressors have been shown to have health and mental health effects among racial and ethnic minorities (Brondolo et al., 2008; Guyll, Matthews, & Bromberger, 2001; Krieger, 2000; Krieger & Sidney, 1996; Ong, Fuller-Rowell, & Burrow, 2009). Discrimination both operates in the context of, and shapes, health over the individual and group life course.

The law of small effects (LSE) in race and ethnic group-related health outcomes (Jackson, 2004; Jackson, Govia, et al., 2010) is a second perspective that is helpful in understanding how social inequalities affect individual life-span development. This conceptual framework suggests that there is no one single factor that produces observed health disparities among racial and ethnic groups in the United States. Instead, it suggests that it is likely a group of small differences that accumulate over the life course to produce observed differences in adulthood and older ages among different racial and ethnic groups. Some candidates include gene/gene and gene/environment interactions, discrimination and perceived racism (stress process), life course selection, cultural factors, behavioral differences, SES, and institutional arrangement (Adler & Stewart, 2010).

The LSE perspective works in tandem with theories about accumulated treatment differences. Specifically, it is consistent with the weathering hypothesis, which suggests that early exposure to chronic stressors and high-level coping efforts to deal with these strains have a cumulative negative impact on health (Geronimus, Hicken, Keene, & Bound, 2006; Taylor, 2008; Thomas, Geronimus, Hicken, Keene, &

Bound, 2006). It is also consistent with the allostatic load framework, which similarly suggests that strains and acute stressors experienced cumulatively affect various biological systems (Geronimus et al., 2006; Green & Darity, 2010; McEwen & Seeman, 1999; Peek et al., 2010; Seeman, Epel, Gruenewald, Karlamangla, & McEwen, 2010). The third type of perspective with which the LSE works in tandem is an appreciation of the role of social and psychological factors (e.g., John Henryism, self-efficacy, mastery, self-system blame). Finally, the LSE also considers how culturally and environmentally mediated behavioral coping strategies affect health. While these ideas cannot be easily parsed to determine their individual contributions, the LSE approach presupposes that different perspectives will be more pertinent at some points in the life course versus others, or for some persons rather than others over their individual life spans.

This brings us to the third framework that facilitates a careful exploration of racial and ethnic group health disparities. Intersectionality theory and research provides some useful premises to help with understanding the ways in which social inequalities contextualize individual life-span development. Research methodology has been catching up with theoretical work in the past few years (Bowleg, 2008; Cole, 2009; Sen, Iyer, & Mukherjee, 2009; Warner, 2008) to reveal how the different social identities that an individual holds are implicated in different psychological and health outcomes. Intersectionality theory does not presume that these identities are hierarchically ordered. Neither does it assume commonality in the outcomes for individuals who share specific social identities.

One of the principal ways in which intersectionality theory and research can be used in understanding how social inequalities contextualize and affect development across the individual life span is by considering the subjective identities that arise from specific intergenerational positioning, time periods, and generational cohorts. These identities can be considered social locations that function in much the same way as the identities that are traditionally explored with intersectionality theory (racial and ethnic group membership, gender, sexuality, age).

Disciplines such as public health, epidemiology, and sociology contribute substantially to the empirical research focused on the role of social inequalities in how people change or remain consistent throughout their individual life spans. Suggestions have been made recently to develop theoretical frameworks that center race and culture in discussions about biological and social functioning and how these in turn affect health across the life span (Griffin & Jackson, 2009; Jackson & Govia, 2009).

We now turn to a description of a conceptual life course/life-span framework that while drawing from the stress process model, the LSE, and intersectionality frameworks, centers upon race and ethnicity. We envision the articulation of this conceptual framework as an important early step in the development of a comprehensive theory of the role of racial and ethnic group inequalities in life course and individual life-span development.

▩ A CULTURE-BASED EXAMPLE: THE CASE OF BLACK/WHITE PHYSICAL VERSUS PSYCHIATRIC HEALTH DISPARITIES

The differences between physical and mental health disparities by race and ethnicity are not straightforward (Jackson & Knight, 2006). These differences lead some to speculate that understanding psychiatric disparities will gain a prominent place in the health disparities literature (e.g., Cohen, 2002). Why do Blacks do worse than Whites in physical disorders but have positive disparities in mental health disorders? While most theoretical formulations about disparities remain silent or static about the fundamental causes (Phelan, Link, Diez-Roux, Kawachi, & Levin, 2004), we have begun a program of research that involves the development of a theoretical framework (Figure 28.2) and empirical research that attempts to capture the dynamism and complexity of the role of social inequalities in producing the physical health disadvantage/psychiatric health advantage across the life course that Blacks demonstrate when compared to Whites (Jackson & Knight, 2006; Jackson, Knight, & Rafferty, 2010).

We suggest that one route by which these differences may be mediated is through behaviors used over the life course by some racial and ethnic groups to cope with the psychological consequences of chronically stressful life conditions (Kershaw et al., 2010). These behaviors are, in turn, nuanced by gender, culture, and environments that are differentially stressful, such as neighborhoods (Diez Roux & Mair, 2010). These environments facilitate different environmental opportunities or affordances (e.g., food, service, jobs; e.g., Morland, Wing, Diez Roux, & Poole, 2002), and offer a distinct menu of coping resources (fast food outlets, liquor stores, illegal drug distributors) that are linked to specific health behaviors (Diez Roux & Mair, 2010; Moore, Diez Roux, Nettleton, Jacobs, & Franco, 2009). The environmental affordances are shaped by factors such as noise, poverty, and urban density. And these in turn influence stressors, such as lack of jobs and financial resources that can also carry some of the effects of environment into physical disorders (Adler & Stewart, 2010).

Behavioral coping strategies in the face of chronic stressful conditions, that may be effective in "preserving" Black mental health, may simultaneously contribute, along with structural inequalities and stressful life conditions, to observed physical health disparities in morbidity and mortality over the life course among some racial and ethnic groups (Jackson & Knight, 2006; Jackson, Hudson, et al., 2010). Black men and women are understood to possess effective coping strategies to deal with stressful conditions of life; strategies that are learned early in their lives and that are environmentally mediated. These behaviors are not "merely" hedonic; instead, they reflect adaptive responses to maladaptive environments. However, the behaviors contribute, along with poor living conditions, lack of resources, and environmentally produced chronic stress, over the life course, to negative racial disparities in physical health morbidity and mortality.

We hypothesize that stress-related precursors of serious mental health problems are more available to consciousness than are those of physical health problems (Jackson & Knight, 2006). This psychological awareness motivates individuals to behavioral action. The relationship between behavioral coping strategies and physical health disparities may, in turn, be mediated by the stress response network (Dallman, 2003; Dallman, Akana, et al., 2003; Dallman, Pecoraro, et al., 2003; Kershaw et al., 2010). The effectiveness of the behaviors may occur via the chronic stress-response network. Specifically, the behaviors (smoking, drinking alcohol, over eating, etc.) may impede the biological cascade of stress response to mental disorders, resulting in positive mental disorder disparities for Blacks in comparison to Whites. For example, research suggests that people eat comfort food to reduce activity in the chronic stress-response network (Cannetti, Bachar, & Berry, 2002;

Dallman, Pecoraro, et al., 2003). We propose that other behaviors, such as smoking, alcohol, and drug use have similar, immediate, effects to reduce activation of the stress-response network.

It is hypothesized that the activation of the stress-response network occurs through the hypothalamic–pituitary–adrenal (HPA) axis and related hormonal systems. Under chronic stress, negative feedback breakdown and there is continued release of corticotropin-releasing factor (CRF) and cortisol. The long-term chronic activation of HPA axis may be related to etiology of some mental disorders (Barden, 2004; McEwen, 2007; Stokes & Sikes, 1991; Young et al., 2004). In terms of the HPA axis and poor health behaviors, comfort foods (high in fats and carbohydrates) may aid in shutdown of stress response by inhibiting release of CRF (Dallman, Akana, et al., 2003; Dallman, Pecoraro, et al., 2003). Similarly, alcohol, nicotine, and drug use stimulate release of dopamine and β-endorphins, and in so doing aid in the shutdown of stress response and lead to feelings of relaxation and calm (e.g., Akil & Cicero, 1986). Paradoxically these drugs may also further activate the HPA axis—thus individuals may be psychologically released from stress, but they are not physically released from the effects of stress (Dallman, Akana, et al., 2003; Dallman, Pecoraro, et al., 2003). In short, we hypothesize that poor health behaviors through their actions on the HPA axis and other brain hormones actually interfere with the cascade of neural and hormonal events that ordinarily would lead, over time, to mental disorders.

In sum, stressors act as a mediator of the effects of environment on physical health disorders. Poor health behaviors (smoking, overeating, using alcohol and drugs) then become the mechanism that links stressors and physical health disorders. Mental health disorders (major depression, anxiety, post-traumatic stress disorder) and physical health disorders are conceptualized to be distinct, yet intricately linked, health outcomes (Figure 28.2).

▓ FUTURE DIRECTIONS IN THE STUDY OF SOCIAL INEQUALITIES ACROSS THE LIFE SPAN

In thinking about the role of social inequalities in how people change and remain consistent throughout their life spans, the research we synthesized, and our presentation of a developing theoretical framework, suggests that the future main issues and directions can be summarized in four main areas.

Perhaps the most pressing issue is the development of sound theory and theoretically guided empirical studies. Along these lines, one of the most exciting directions in the study of social inequalities over the individual life span is to move from a conceptual framework to a theoretical one regarding the influence of racial and ethnic group memberships and to develop a series of propositions and testable hypotheses.

A related issue is that there are few theoretically guided, empirical tests of longitudinal or multilevel models of how social inequalities affect individual life-span development. With a few exceptions, such as studies that attempt to capture the ways in which contexts affect intelligence in infancy and early childhood, or nutrition, there are few studies that integrate an appreciation of social inequalities (Antonucci & Jackson, 2010). Yet, several analytic techniques have been developed in recent years, such as age-period-cohort analysis (Keyes, Utz, Robinson, & Li, 2010; Yang & Land, 2008; Yang, Schulhofer-Wohl, Fu, & Land, 2008), multilevel structural equation

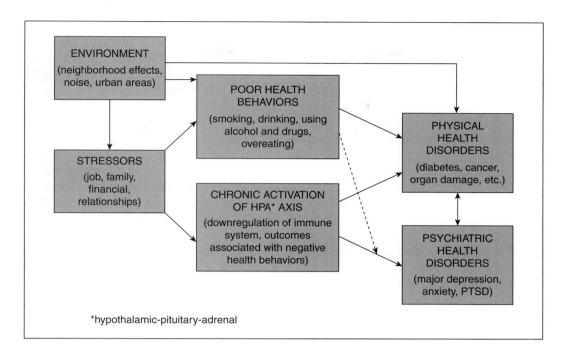

FIGURE 28.2 **Possible interrelationships among environment, stressors, negative health behaviors, and physical and mental health disorders.** *Source:* Jackson & Knight, 2006.

modeling (Bovaird, 2007), and latent change score models (Ferrer & McArdle, 2010) that can facilitate such analysis.

It is now a matter of ensuring that these techniques can be applied to existing data and that future data collections pay careful attention to the data requirements for these analytic possibilities during the conceptualization and design phases of the research projects. It is also necessary to push these analytic techniques even further in order to accurately capture the complexity of lived experience. One example of this is adding gender interactions as predictors of health outcomes to APC models (Jackson, Hudson, et al., 2010). This example suggests that a crucial next step for examinations of social inequalities in life-span development is the employment of multilevel modeling to capture the interrelationships between social inequalities and life-span development—not just for one disparate group, but within and across disparities, such as age, gender, class, and citizenship, for example.

The second main issue is that there are few theoretically guided empirical tests of intra- and intergenerational processes that are implicit in models of social inequalities in development across the life course. Generational processes are implicit in ideas about the heredity of certain physical and mental health disorders (Braun, 2004). They are also implicit in ideas about the cyclical nature of poverty and health behaviors that are intricately linked with environmental factors, such as teenage pregnancy (Adler & Stewart, 2010). Yet, few studies have empirically tested these inter- and intragenerational processes, and even fewer have tested them using analytic approaches that account for the nonindependence of the data in dyads, triads, and larger social groups. These processes and dynamics need to be explored even more urgently given the shifts in demographic compositions contributing to the coming aging society that are expected within the next several decades (Rowe & Berkman, 2009). These demographic shifts will contribute to changes in intergenerational dynamics, and consequently, health implications of these changed intergenerational dynamics must be explored (Antonucci & Jackson, 2010).

The third main issue is that in-depth examinations of groups within specific countries are needed. These types of examinations will shed light on conundrums that still exist in the health disparities literature, such as why ethnic disparities that disadvantage Blacks and other minorities exist for psychological distress and depressive symptoms, but are reversed for more serious mental and psychiatric disorders (Jackson & Knight, 2006). Other issues that these in-depth examinations can highlight include how self versus other constructions of racial group membership affect health outcomes, and similarities and differences between racism and discrimination and other stressors.

Finally, more cross-national comparisons are needed so that we can learn more about how social inequalities function and contextualize and inform the development of individuals in other countries and continents throughout the individual life span (e.g., Jackson & Antonucci, 2005).

CONCLUSIONS

In sum, in the United States, the Black and other racial and ethnic minority group life experiences, perhaps more so than in the majority population, illuminate the continuities and discontinuities of a life course/life-span perspective on health and well-being. For example, from birth to death, Blacks in the United States are at greater risk than the general population for debilitating social, psychological, and material conditions that negatively influence the quality of individual and family life; resulting in greater fetal death rates, premature deaths, greater homicide statistics in adolescence and midlife, and greater risk of death from chronic health conditions early in old age (Antonucci & Jackson, 2010). However, as we represent in Figure 28.1, not all Blacks and other individuals and families within disadvantaged groups are born into, or live under, such circumstances throughout their lives. For example, though its relative proportions wax and wane (Jackson, 2000), there exists a sizeable Black middle-class, and some Blacks in the United States can look forward to relatively comfortable styles of living over their life spans. This SES heterogeneity, however, is intertwined with categorical group membership and consequent chronic experiences of racial and ethnic group discrimination and mobility barriers (Williams et al., 2010).

The life course and life-span perspective we have advocated here suggests the need to consider these human development, historical context, and structural position factors that influence the health and well-being of present and future cohorts of Blacks and other racial and ethnic group individuals. Different birth cohorts, historical and current environmental events, and individual differences in development and aging processes interact with one another to affect physical and mental well-being. Racial and ethnic group memberships play a critical role, and, as the example (Figure 28.2) in this chapter suggests, cultural resources can provide important coping and adaptive and maladaptive mechanisms to alleviate the distinct socioeconomic and psychological disadvantages of categorical racial and ethnic group membership (Jackson, 1993; Jackson & Knight, 2006).

The unique social history and the nature of their group and individual developmental experiences, however, continue to place new cohorts of racial and ethnic minority group Americans from birth to death at disproportionate risk for poor physical and psychological well-being (Antonucci & Jackson, 2010). This is illustrated by the continuing disproportionate rates of mortality, poor physical living conditions, numbers of women and children in poverty, joblessness, and unemployment over the individual and group life course (Jackson, 2000; Sellers et al, 2009). Without significant interventions sensitive to the cultural, sociohistorical, and intersectional nature of the life course, and an understanding of the interlocking nature of social inequalities on individual life-span development, the future health and well-being of many individuals from these populations remains at risk (Antonucci & Jackson, 2010).

▓ REFERENCES

Adelman, L. (Writer). (2008). Unnatural causes: Is inequality making us sick? In L. Adelman, L. M. Smith, & C. Herbes-Sommers (Producer). USA: California Newsreel.

Adler, N. E., & Stewart, J. (2010). Health disparities across the lifespan: Meaning, methods, and mechanisms. *Annals of the New York Academy of Sciences, 1186,* 5–23.

Akil, H., & Cicero, T. J. (1986). Overview of the endogenous opioid systems: Anatomical, biochemical, and functional issues. In R. J. Rodgers & S. J. Cooper (Eds.), *Endorphins, opiates and behavioural processes* (pp. 1–23). Chichester, UK: John Wiley and Sons Ltd.

Anderson, N. B., Bulatao, R. A., & Cohen, B. (Eds.). (2004). *Critical perspectives on racial and ethnic differences in health in late life.* Washington, DC: The National Academies Press.

Anonymous. (2001). Pregnancy-related deaths among Hispanic, Asian/Pacific islander, and American Indian/Alaska Native women—United States, 1991–1997. *MMWR. Morbidity and Mortality Weekly Report, 50*(18), 361–364.

Antonucci, T. C., & Jackson, J. S. (2010). Introduction: Life course perspectives on late life health inequalities. *Annual Review of Gerontology and Geriatrics, 29, 2009,* xvii–xxxi.

Baltes, P. B. (1987). Theoretical propositions of life-span developmental psychology: On the dynamics between growth and decline. *Developmental Psychology, 23,* 611–626.

Baltes, P. B., Reese, H. W., & Lipsitt, L. P. (1980). Life-span developmental psychology. *Annual Review of Psychology, 31,* 65–110.

Barden, N. (2004). Implication of the hypothalamic-pituitary-adrenal axis in the physiopathology of depression. *Journal of Psychiatry and Neuroscience, 29,* 185–193.

Blendon, R. J., Buhr, T., Cassidy, E. F., Perez, D. J., Hunt, K. A., Fleischfresser, C., et al. (2007). Disparities in health: Perspectives of a multi-ethnic, multi-racial America. *Health Affairs, 26,* 1437–1447.

Blendon, R. J., Schoen, C., DesRoches, C., Osborn, R., & Zapert, K. (2003). Common concerns amid diverse systems: Health care experiences in five countries. *Health Affairs, 22,* 106–121.

Bovaird, J. A. (2007). Multilevel structural equation models for contextual factors. In T. D. Little, J. A. Bovaird, & N. A. Card (Eds.), *Modeling contextual effects in longitudinal studies* (pp. 149–182). Mahwah, NJ: Lawrence Erlbaum Associates.

Bowleg, L. (2008). When Black + lesbian + woman ≠ Black lesbian woman: The methodological challenges of qualitative and quantitative intersectionality research. *Sex Roles, 59,* 312.

Breslau, J., Kendler, K., Su, M., Gaxiola-Aguilar, S., & Kessler, R. (2005). Lifetime risk and persistence of psychiatric disorders across ethnic groups in the United States. *Psychological Medicine, 35,* 317–327.

Brondolo, E., Libby, D. J., Denton, E.-G., Thompson, S., Beatty, D. L., Schwartz, J., et al. (2008). Racism and ambulatory blood pressure in a community sample. *Psychosomatic Medicine, 70,* 49–56.

Cannetti, L., Bachar, E., & Berry, E. M. (2002). Food and emotion. *Behavioral Processes, 60,* 157–164.

CDC/NCHS. (2007a). *Health Data Interactive [Mortality by underlying cause, ages 18+: US/State, 2001–2006],* Retrieved March 10, 2010, from the Centers for Disease Control and Prevention National Center for Health Statistics Web site http://www.cdc.gov/nchs/hdi.htm.

CDC/NCHS. (2007b). *Health Data Interactive [Life expectancy at birth, 65, and 85 years of age, US, selected years 1900–2006],* Retrieved March 10, 2010, from the Centers for Disease Control and Prevention National Center for Health Statistics Web site http://www.cdc.gov/nchs/hdi.htm.

Cohen, C. I. (2002). Economic grand rounds: Social inequality and health: Will psychiatry assume center stage? *Psychiatric Services, 53,* 937–939.

Cole, E. R. (2009). Intersectionality and research in psychology. *American Psychologist, 64,* 170–180.

Copeland, V. C. (2005). African Americans: Disparities in health care access and utilization. *Health and Social Work, 30,* 265–270.

Crimmins, E. M., Hayward, M. D., & Seeman, T. (2004). Race/ethnicity, socioeconomic status and health. In N. B. Anderson, R. A. Bulatao, & B. Cohen (Eds.), *Critical perspectives on racial and ethnic differences in health in later life* (pp. 310–352). Washington, DC: The National Academies Press.

Dallman, M. F. (2003). Stress by any other name...? *Hormones and Behavior, 43,* 18–20.

Dallman, M. F., Akana, S. F., Laugero, K. D., Gomez, F., Manalo, S., Bell, M. E., et al. (2003). A spoonful of sugar: Feedback signals of energy stores and corticosterone regulate responses to chronic stress. *Physiology & Behavior, 79,* 3–12.

Dallman, M. F., Pecoraro, N., Akana, S. F., Fleur, S. E. l., Gomez, F., Houshyar, H., et al. (2003). Chronic stress and obesity: A new view of "comfort food." *Proceedings of the National Academy of Sciences of the United States of America, 100,* 11696–11701.

Dillahunt, A., Miller, B., Prokosch, M., Huezo, J., & Muhammad, D. (2010). *State of the dream 2010: Drained: Jobless and foreclosed in communities of color.* Boston, MA: United for a Fair Economy.

Diez Roux, A. V., & Mair, C. (2010). Neighborhoods and health. *Annals of the New York Academy of Sciences, 1186,* 125–145.

Ferrer, E., & McArdle, J. J. (2010). Longitudinal modeling of developmental changes in psychological research. *Current Directions in Psychological Science, 19,* 149–154.

Franklin, A. J., & Jackson, J. S. (1990). Factors contributing to positive mental health among Black Americans. In D. Smith-Ruiz (Ed.), *Handbook of black mental health and mental disorder among black Americans* (pp. 291–307). Westport, CT: Greenwood Press.

Geronimus, A. T., Hicken, M., Keene, D., & Bound, J. (2006). "Weathering" and age patterns of allostatic load scores among Blacks and Whites in the United States. *American Journal of Public Health, 96,* 826–833.

Green, T. L., & Darity, W. A., Jr. (2010). Under the skin: Using theories from biology and the social sciences to explore the mechanisms behind the Black-White health gap. *American Journal of Public Health, 100,* S36–S40.

Griffin, T. M., & Jackson, J. S. (2009). Racial differences. In I. B. Weiner & W. E. Craighead (Eds.), *The Corsini encyclopedia of psychology* (4th ed., pp. 1411–1413). Wiley: New York.

Guyll, M., Matthews, K. A., & Bromberger, J. T. (2001). Discrimination and unfair treatment: Relationship to cardiovascular reactivity among African American and European American women. *Health Psychology, 20,* 315–325.

Henrich, J., Heine, S., & Norenzayan, A. (2010). The weirdest people in the world? *Behavioral and Brain Sciences, 33,* 61–135.

Institute of Medicine Committee on Understanding and Eliminating Racial and Ethnic Disparities in Health Care. (2002). *Unequal treatment: Confronting racial and ethnic disparities in health care.* Washington, DC: National Research Council.

Jackson, J. S. (1993). Racial influences on adult development and aging. In R. Kastenbaum (Ed.), *The encyclopedia of adult development* (pp. 18–26). Phoenix, AZ: Oryx Press.

Jackson, J. S. (Ed.). (2000). *New directions: African Americans in a diversifying nation.* Washington, DC: National Policy Association.

Jackson, J. S. (2002). Conceptual and methodological linkages in cross-cultural groups and cross-national aging research. *Journal of Social Issues, 58,* 825–835.

Jackson, J. S. (2004). Discussion: Genetic explanation for health disparities: What is at stake? In E. Singer & T. C. Antonucci (Eds.), *Proceedings of the Conference on Genetics and Health Disparities* (pp. 20–21). Ann Arbor, MI: Institute for Social Research, University of Michigan.

Jackson, J. S., & Antonucci, T. C. (2005). Physical and mental health consequences of aging in place and aging out of place among black Caribbean immigrants. *Research in Human Development, 2,* 229–244.

Jackson, J. S., & Govia, I. O. (2009). Quality of life for ethnic and racial minority elders in the 21st century: Setting a research agenda. In G. Cavanaugh & P. Sanford (Eds.), *Diversity and aging.* Washington, DC: AARP.

Jackson, J. S., Govia, I. O., & Sellers, S. L. (2010). Racial and ethnic influences over the life course. In R. H. Binstock & L. K. George (Eds.), *Handbook of aging and the social sciences* (7th ed., pp. 91–103). Philadelphia, PA: Elsevier Inc.

Jackson, J. S., Hudson, D., Kershaw, K. N., Mezuk, B., Rafferty, J., & Tuttle, K. K. (2010). Discrimination, chronic stress, and mortality among black Americans: A life course framework. In R. G. Rogers & E. M. Crimmins (Eds.), *International handbook of adult mortality*. New York: Springer.

Jackson, J. S., & Knight, K. M. (2006). Race and self-regulatory health behaviors: The role of the stress response and the HPA Axis in physical and mental health disparities. In K. W. Schaie & L. L. Carstensen (Eds.), *Social structures, aging, and self-regulation in the elderly* (pp. 189–239). New York: Springer Publishing Co.

Jackson, J. S., Knight, K. M., & Rafferty, J. A. (2010). Race and unhealthy behaviors: Chronic stress, the HPA Axis, and physical and mental health disparities over the life course. *American Journal of Public Health, 100*, 933–939.

Jackson, J. S., & Sellers, S. L. (2001). Health and the elderly. In R. L. Braithwaite & S. E. Taylor (Eds.), *Health issues in the black community* (pp. 81–96). San Francisco, CA: Jossey-Bass.

Jackson, J. S., Torres, M., Caldwell, C. H., Neighbors, H. W., Nesse, R. M., Taylor, R. J., et al. (2004). The National Survey of American Life: A study of racial, ethnic and cultural influences on mental disorders and mental health. *International Journal of Methods in Psychiatric Research, 13*, 196–207.

Kershaw, K. N., Mezuk, B., Abdou, C. M., Rafferty, J. A., & Jackson, J. S. (2010). Socioeconomic position, health behaviors, and C-reactive protein: A moderated-mediation analysis. *Health Psychology, 29*, 307–316.

Kessler, R. C., McGonagle, K. A., Zhao, S., Nelson, C. B., Hughes, M., Eshleman, S., et al. (1994). Lifetime and 12-month prevalence of DSM-III-R psychiatric disorders in the United States: Results from the National Comorbidity Survey. *Archives of General Psychiatry, 51*, 8–19.

Kessler, R. C., Berglund, P., Demler, O., Jin, R., Koretz, D., Merikangas, K. R., et al. (2003). The epidemiology of major depressive disorder: Results from the National Comorbidity Survey Replication (NCS-R). *Journal of the American Medical Association, 289*, 3095–3105.

Keyes, K. M., Utz, R. L., Robinson, W., & Li, G. (2010). What is a cohort effect? Comparison of three statistical methods for modeling cohort effects in obesity prevalence in the United States, 1971–2006. *Social Science & Medicine, 70*, 1100–1108.

Krieger, N. (2000). Discrimination and health. In L. F. Berkman & I. Kawachi (Eds.), *Social epidemiology* (pp. 36–75). New York: Oxford University Press.

Krieger, N., & Sidney, S. (1996). Racial discrimination and blood pressure: The CARDIA study of young Black and White adults. *American Journal of Public Health, 86*, 1370–1378.

Krueger, P. M., & Chang, V. W. (2008). Being poor and coping with stress: Health behaviors and the risk of death. *American Journal of Public Health, 98*, 889–896.

Manton, K. G., Stallard, E., & Wing, S. (1991). Analyses of black and white differentials in the age trajectory of mortality in two closed cohort studies. *Statistics in Medicine, 10*, 1043–1059.

Mathews, T. J., & MacDorman, M. F. (2008). Infant mortality statistics from the 2005 period linked birth/infant death data set. *National Vital Statistics Reports, 57*, 1–32.

McEwen, B. S. (2007). Physiology and neurobiology of stress and adaptation: Central role of the brain. *Physiological Reviews, 87*, 873–904.

McEwen, B. S., & Seeman, T. (1999). Protective and damaging effects of mediators of stress: Elaborating and testing the concepts of allostasis and allostatic load. *Annals of the New York Academy of Sciences, 896*, 30–47.

Moore, L. V., Diez Roux, A. V., Nettleton, J. A., Jacobs, D. R., & Franco, M. (2009). Fast-food consumption, diet quality, and neighborhood exposure to fast food: The multi-ethnic study of atherosclerosis. *American Journal of Epidemiology, 170*, 29–36.

Morland, K., Wing, S., Diez Roux, A., & Poole, C. (2002). Neighborhood characteristics associated with the location of food stores and food service places. *American Journal of Preventive Medicine, 22*, 23–29.

Muhammad, D., Davis, A., Lui, M. & Leondar-Wright, B. (2004). *The state of the dream 2004:Enduring disparities in black and white*. Boston, MA: United for a Fair Economy.

OECD. (2008). *Growing unequal? Income distribution and poverty in OECD countries*. Paris, France: Organisation for Economic Co-Operation and Development.

Olafsdottir, S. (2007). Fundamental causes of health disparities: Stratification, the welfare state, and health in the United States and Iceland. *Journal of Health and Social Behavior, 48*, 239–253.

Ong, A. D., Fuller-Rowell, T., & Burrow, A. L. (2009). Racial discrimination and the stress process. *Journal of Personality and Social Psychology, 96*, 1259–1271.

Pearlin, L. I. (1999). The stress process revisited: Reflections on concepts and their interrelationships. In C. S. Aneshensel & J. C. Phelan (Eds.), *Handbook of sociology of mental health* (pp. 395–415). Dordrecht Netherlands: Kluwer Academic Publishers.

Pearlin, L. I., Menaghan, E. G., Lieberman, M. A., & Mullan, J. T. (1981). The stress process. *Journal of Health and Social Behavior, 22*, 337–356.

Peek, M. K., Cutchin, M. P., Salinas, J. J., Sheffield, K. M., Eschbach, K., Stowe, R. P., et al. (2010). Allostatic load among non-Hispanic Whites, non-Hispanic Blacks, and people of Mexican origin: Effects of ethnicity, nativity, and acculturation. *American Journal of Public Health, 100*, 940–946.

Phelan, J. C., Link, B. G., Diez-Roux, A. V., Kawachi, I., & Levin, B. (2004). "Fundamental causes" of social inequalities in mortality: A test of the theory. *Journal of Health and Social Behavior, 45*, 265–285.

Preston, S. H., Elo, I. T., Rosenwaike, I., & Hill, M. (1996). African-American mortality at older ages: Results of a matching study. *Demography, 33*, 193–209.

Riolo, S. A., Nguyen, T. A., Greden, J. F., & King, C. A. (2005). Prevalence of depression by race/ethnicity: Findings from the National Health and Nutrition Examination Survey III. *American Journal of Public Health, 95*, 998–1000.

Rowe, J. & Berkman, L. (2009). Investing over the life-course: A winning strategy. *The Huffington Post*, June 23, 2009. http://www.huffingtonpost.com/john-rowe/investing-over-the-life-c_b_210391.html

Schoen, C., Osborn, R., Doty, M. M., Bishop, M., Peugh, J., & Murukutla, N. (2007). Toward higher-performance health systems: Adults' health care experiences in seven countries, 2007. *Health Affairs, 26*, w717–w734.

Seeman, T., Epel, E., Gruenewald, T., Karlamangla, A., & McEwen, B. S. (2010). Socio-economic differentials in peripheral biology: Cumulative allostatic load. *Annals of the New York Academy of Sciences, 1186*, 223–239.

Sellers, S. L., Govia, I. O., & Jackson, J. S. (2009). Health and Black older adults: Insights from a life-course perspective. In R. L. Braithwaite, S. E. Taylor, & H. M. Treadwell (Eds.), *Health issues in the Black community* (3rd ed., pp. 95–116). San Francisco, CA: Jossey-Bass.

Sen, G., Iyer, A., & Mukherjee, C. (2009). A methodology to analyse the intersections of social inequalities in health. *Journal of Human Development and Capabilities: A Multi-Disciplinary Journal for People-Centered Development, 10*, 397–415.

Shanahan, M. J., & Porfelli, E. (2002). Integrating the life course and life-span: Formulating research questions with dual points of entry. *Journal of Vocational Behavior, 61*, 398–406.

Somervell, P. D., Leaf, P. J., Weissman, M. M., Blazer, D. G., & Bruce, M. L. (1989). The prevalence of major depression in black and white adults in five United States communities. *American Journal of Epidemiology and Community Health, 130*, 725–735.

Stokes, P. E., & Sikes, C. R. (1991). Hypothalamic-pituitary-adrenal axis in psychiatric disorders. *Annual Review of Medicine, 42*, 519–531.

Taylor, M. G. (2008). Timing, accumulation, and the Black/White disability gap in later life: A test of weathering. *Research on Aging, 30*, 226–250.

Thomas, N. M., Geronimus, A. T., Hicken, M., Keene, D., & Bound, J. (2006). What's missing from the weathering hypothesis? Geronimus et al. respond. *American Journal of Public Health, 96*, 955–956.

Tucker, M. J., Berg, C. J., Callaghan, W. M., & Hsia, J. (2007). The Black-White disparity in pregnancy-related mortality from 5 conditions: Differences in prevalence and case-fatality rates. *American Journal of Public Health, 97*, 247–251.

Warner, L. R. (2008). A best practices guide to intersectional approaches in psychological research. *Sex Roles, 59*, 454.

Weissman, M. M., & Myers, J. K. (1980). Psychiatric disorders in a U.S. community: The application of research diagnostic criteria to a resurveyed community sample. *Acta Psychiatrica Scandinavica, 62*, 99–111.

Whitfield, K. E., & Hayward, M. D. (2003). The landscape of health disparities among older adults. *Public Policy and Aging Report, 13*, 1–7.

Williams, D. R., Mohammed, S. A., Leavell, J., & Collins, C. (2010). Race, socioeconomic status, and health: Complexities, ongoing challenges, and research opportunities. *Annals of the New York Academy of Sciences, 1186*, 69–101.

Yang, Y., & Land, K. C. (2008). Age-period-cohort analysis of repeated cross-section surveys: Fixed or random effects? *Sociological Methods Research, 36*, 297–326.

Yang, Y., Schulhofer-Wohl, S., Fu, W. J., & Land, K. C. (2008). The intrinsic estimator for age-period-cohort analysis: What it is and how to use it. *American Journal of Sociology, 113*, 1697–1736.

Young, E. A., Altemus, M., Lopez, J. F., Kocsis, J. H., Schatzberg, A. F., deBattista, C., et al. (2004). HPA axis activation in major depression and response to fluoxetine: A pilot study. *Psychoneuroendocrinology, 29*, 1198–1204.

FAMILY INFLUENCES ON DEVELOPMENT ACROSS THE LIFE SPAN

29

Rena Repetti, Lisa Flook, and Jacqueline Sperling

The subject of this chapter seems impossibly broad. The family influences all aspects of development—biological, social, emotional, and cognitive—and its forces are exerted through vastly different means—genes, intimate relationships, material factors, routines, cultural values, and practices. Not only are the effects of experiences in the family observed across the life span but those consequences also unfold over varying timeframes; they can be felt in the short term or many years in the future. Given that it is not feasible for a single chapter to cover each of these topics comprehensively, we approach our task by identifying broad life-stage categories and highlighting the aspects of development that are most prominently addressed in the research literature on each phase. We found that investigations of family influence tend to focus on health outcomes, as well as social and emotional well-being and adjustment; much of the research is geared toward identifying the family characteristics that predict *adaptive* versus *maladaptive* outcomes.

Of course, the manifestations of adaptive or maladaptive outcomes within a particular domain change over the life span. For example, during the prenatal period we cover birth weight and preterm birth, whereas later discussions of physical maturation and health refer to topics like pubertal timing, risky sexual behaviors and substance abuse, mental health, and physical disease. There is an emphasis on social and emotional development in our chapter, beginning with the regulation of arousal and stress response systems during infancy, moving to the growth of moral conscience, self-control, and compliance in the toddler years, and advancing to the formation of relationships with peers and the understanding of emotions during childhood. Our discussion of social development in the adolescent period includes the establishment of an identity outside of the family and the formation of romantic relationships. In adulthood and older ages, we consider educational and occupational attainments and relationships with spouse and children.

By necessity, our chapter must leave much territory uncovered; to cite one example, grapples with morality certainly do not end with the toddler years, yet our discussion of the family's influence on moral development does. Extremes of family environments that we know have significant effects on development, such as poverty and child abuse, are mentioned but are not discussed at any length. In addition, the research we review focuses almost exclusively on nuclear families (parents and their offspring) living in the United States. Space constraints did not allow us to delve into special issues that are relevant to groups of families that are either prevalent or increasing in U.S. society, such as those headed by immigrants, single parents, or same-sex parents. Although a single chapter cannot possibly provide encyclopedic coverage of all family influences on every facet of development at each stage in life, we encourage readers to use the reference list, which includes more comprehensive summaries of the different substantive research literatures, as a resource for further detail. In addition, many excellent chapters in this volume provide greater depth by focusing on specific aspects of development.

SOCIAL ECOLOGY, RECIPROCAL INFLUENCES, AND GENES

There are a number of important elements of family influence that are relevant to all stages of development. We mention three of them before beginning our journey through the life span: the larger social contexts in which families are embedded, the bidirectional nature of influence processes within the family, and the roles played by genes.

The term *family* is generally used to refer to related individuals living under one roof. However, it is much easier to draw the boundaries that define a single family than those that define the family's influences. As Bronfenbrenner's ecological systems theory describes (Bronfenbrenner, 1989), the different settings that affect human development are interrelated. In a sense, a family carries multiple social contexts with it; the effects of other settings—such as school, daycare, and neighborhood—are part of the family's larger social ecology and, therefore, are part of its influence. In addition, social class, cultural values, customs, and laws are intertwined with variations in home environments and parenting behavior. For instance, in the United States, infants in middle-class families are typically provided with more opportunities for variety in daily stimulation, more appropriate play materials, and more total stimulation. Compared to lower socioeconomic status (SES) mothers, mothers from the middle-class talk to their infants more, and in more sophisticated ways, which is probably why babies from higher SES families produce more sounds in the first months of life (Bornstein, 1995). Virtually all aspects of parenting are informed by cultural practices, such as when and how parents care for infants, the extent to which infants are encouraged to explore, how nurturing or restrictive parents are, and the role played by others, such as grandparents and siblings. Perhaps the influence of the family can be most readily seen in how different cultural practices and expectations relate to when babies sit, stand, crawl, and walk, and when and how they sleep, eat, and play (Bornstein, 1995). Although this chapter focuses on direct experiences within the family, it is critical to recognize, first, that those experiences are shaped by the larger social context in which the household exists and, second, that experiences outside of the home can indirectly reflect the family's influence.

Of course, individuals are far from passive inhabitants of their social environments. Even during infancy, crying and other signs of distress signal to caregivers that babies need attention. Those behaviors motivate adults to approach and soothe; smiling encourages others to stay near (Bornstein, 1995). Behavior geneticists argue that by eliciting particular kinds of responses (e.g., smiles versus harshness) from others, children shape their relationships with parents and other family members. In a sense, they help to "evoke" the very social environments that will influence their development (Grusec & Davidov, 2007). Although the influences of parenting practices and relationships on development are often framed as a one-way street, it is important to bear in mind that the reality is a reciprocal process. An individual's traits, behaviors, attitudes, and emotions all contribute to the family social environment.

Genetic inheritance represents the first and most enduring influence of the biological family on development. Genes exert their power on development regardless of the presence of the parent in the child's life; even in the case of sperm donors, there is a parental influence through the passage of genes. Our chapter cannot possibly do justice to current knowledge about the biological family's contribution to development through genetic inheritance. Instead, we emphasize here that genes do not act in a vacuum; they can only be expressed in an environment. Beginning with the prenatal environment, the family's influence is shaped through gene–environment interactions. Research within the last decade suggests that many effects of the family environment are modified by genetically based differences between children. For instance, a longitudinal study found that insensitive parenting during infancy predicted less controlled and more aggressive behavior when the children were 3 years old, but only among children with a particular allele of a gene involved with dopamine (D4) receptors in the limbic area of the brain; insensitive parenting did not predict externalizing behavior in the absence of that allele (Bakermans-Kranenburg & van IJzendoorn, 2006). In a study of young adults, those who described a more adverse early family environment (some conflict, moderate household chaos, and/or cold, unaffectionate, and distant behaviors) also reported more symptoms of depression. However, the most depressive symptoms were reported by those who both described the risky early family environment and carried a particular allelic variation of the serotonin transporter gene *5-HTTLPR* (Taylor et al., 2006). Studies like these suggest that genes and the family rearing environment interact to produce a developmental outcome down the road.

PRENATAL PERIOD

The first environment in which genes are expressed is the prenatal environment. Studies of major diseases, such as schizophrenia, point to the powerful role that prenatal factors, such as infection, nutritional deficiency, and obstetric complications, play in shaping gene expression. Because the mother provides the world in which the fetus grows, whatever she eats, drinks, and breathes directly affects the quality of that environment. Maternal characteristics, behaviors, and emotions represent other mechanisms through which mothers influence fetal development. Fathers and other family members may also contribute through their impact on the mother's experience of stress and social support during pregnancy.

Some maternal characteristics, such as race and age, are associated with pregnancy outcomes that are important in predicting children's later development. Advanced maternal age is associated with pregnancy complications and, in the United States, rates of preterm delivery, infant mortality, and low birth weight are higher among African Americans than among women in other racial and ethnic groups (Dunkel-Schetter, 2009; Savitz & Dunkel-Schetter, 2007). These pregnancy outcomes are important because children born preterm or at low birth weight tend to have poorer educational outcomes and lower scores on measures of cognitive functioning, as well as increased rates of attention-deficit hyperactivity disorder and other behavioral problems (Bhutta, Cleves, Casey, Cradock, & Anand, 2002). Preterm infants are also at risk for adverse health outcomes including respiratory, gastrointestinal, immune, central nervous system, and sensory problems (Behrman & Butler, 2006; Dunkel-Schetter, 2009).

Drug use during pregnancy, particularly high levels of alcohol consumption, cocaine use, or cigarette smoking, is associated with adverse birth outcomes. For example, smoking is related to placental abruption, reduced birth weight, and infant mortality, and consumption of large amounts of alcohol has adverse effects on fetal development, including risk for preterm birth (Savitz & Dunkel-Schetter, 2007). Fetal alcohol syndrome is associated with mental retardation that persists through life; environmental and educational interventions do not appear to have strong compensatory effects on the later intellectual development of affected children (Spohr, Wilms, & Steinhausen, 1993). In general, unfavorable health behaviors tend to cluster among pregnant women. For instance, substance abuse may co-occur with a poor diet and a lack of physical activity. Moreover, some maternal behavioral influences on pregnancy outcomes are associated with the pregnant woman's socioeconomic conditions. For example, smoking during pregnancy is linked to lower SES (Savitz & Dunkel-Schetter, 2007). It is therefore difficult to distinguish the effects of maternal behaviors, like the use of substances, from the effects of other life circumstances on prenatal development and birth outcomes.

A woman's experience of chronic or catastrophic stress during pregnancy can increase the risk of preterm birth. In particular, women who experience domestic or personal violence during pregnancy are at risk for adverse birth outcomes, including low birth weight (Savitz & Dunkel-Schetter, 2007). Homelessness, especially the percent of one's lifetime spent homeless, predicts preterm birth, even after controlling for birth weight and other factors, such as substance use, ethnicity, income, and medical risk (Dunkel-Schetter, 2009). The effects of stress on pregnancy may be mediated by increased levels of catecholamines and cortisol, or by altered immune function leading to increased susceptibility to infection or inflammation. Any of these responses would change the fetal environment and could precipitate the onset of preterm labor. In addition, risky behaviors, such as substance use, may be used as a way of coping with stress (Savitz & Dunkel-Schetter, 2007).

The experience of depression or anxiety during pregnancy also predicts preterm birth and low birth weight. Although the factors that link maternal emotions to pregnancy outcomes are not yet understood, health behaviors such as diet and nutrition, substance use, sleep, and inactivity are good candidates for further study (Savitz & Dunkel-Schetter, 2007). The emotional experiences of pregnant women may also reflect an influence of other family members. In one study, women's appraisals of the effectiveness of the support that they received from their partners predicted their level of anxiety during pregnancy; women who reported more effective support from their partners experienced less anxiety (Rini, Dunkel-Schetter, Hobel, Glynn, & Sandman, 2006). Thus, social support in the family may indirectly affect development during the prenatal period. Although observational studies indicate that prenatal maternal social support is linked with birth weight or fetal growth, intervention trials have not supported the expectation that provision of additional social support to high-risk women would reduce rates of low birth weight. It may be that many of the women in these studies required more support than the programs provided in order to overcome the deficits in their social environments (Savitz & Dunkel-Schetter, 2007).

▨ INFANCY

Once a baby is born, its caregivers replace many of the functions of the womb. Not only are infants completely dependent on their parents for physical survival, but families also provide their experience of the world during a period of intense development. Infancy covers the period from birth to the emergence of language between 18 and 24 months. It is the stage of greatest physical and nervous system development. We see enormous change in the areas of perception, cognition, and motor coordination as well as in the regulation of sleep cycles, emotions, and social behavior. All of these developments are shaped by the infant's social environment. Through social interaction and play, babies acquire information by listening, watching, and imitating parents, siblings, and others (Bornstein, 1995).

The formation of attachments to the individuals who have been consistently available to provide care and nurturance during the first months of life is particularly important. Those relationships play a critical role in the infant's cognitive, social, and emotional development (Bornstein, 1995). According to attachment theory, "secure trust" in the protection provided by caregivers enhances an infant's willingness to be socialized (Laible & Thompson, 2007). Behaviors like maternal attentiveness, speaking, affectionate touching, rocking, holding, and smiling during the early months of life facilitate the development of "secure trust" in the infant. They also predict more advanced cognitive and language development later in the toddler years (Bornstein, 1995). On the opposite end of the spectrum, early social deprivation, such as limited face-to-face interactions, results in cognitive and social impairments, as seen in studies of babies reared in Romanian orphanages during the Communist regime (Zeanah et al., 2003). Infants also look to family members and other caregivers for emotional cues and are influenced by both positive and negative facial expressions and vocal characteristics. This may explain why infants of depressed mothers show deficits in social referencing skills. When responses to the baby's cries and other signals are prompt and appropriate the infant experiences social partners as reliable and comforting, a message that later carries over to relationships outside of the family (Bornstein, 1995). According to attachment theory, the mental representations of relationships that infants form based on a history of sensitive parental care influence how they experience subsequent relationships (Laible & Thompson, 2007).

The family provides the environment in which a baby's physiological, emotional, and behavioral arousal is experienced. Infants need others to help them regulate that arousal; caregivers soothe infants to alleviate their distress and reinforce their positive emotions. As a result, babies gradually acquire the ability to self-regulate their emotions and to express negative emotion in an appropriate way (Grusec & Davidov, 2007). However, the development of self-regulation suffers when the infant's social world is not reliable and responsive. One of the ways that the family influences the growth of self-regulation is through an impact on infant brain development. Early experiences with caregivers are linked to the development of neurotransmitter systems that control many of the brain's regulatory functions. Three monoamines—dopamine, norepinephrine, and serotonin—comprise the "diffuse modulatory systems" in the brain that regulate arousal and mood as well as motor control, memory, motivation, attention, and learning. Studies of rats and nonhuman primates show an association between early social experiences and neurobiological changes in these neurotransmitter systems. Although research with humans is much more limited, the findings are consistent in linking adverse early family environments with the development of differences in children's neurotransmitter profiles (Repetti, Taylor, & Saxbe, 2007). For example, evidence points to differences in the serotonin neurotransmitter system of children who have been maltreated or abused compared to nonabused children (Kaufman et al., 1998).

Parents and the family environment determine the frequency and timing of social challenges during infancy. These experiences help to shape the development of biological stress response systems. For example, harsh and insensitive parenting appears to be linked to greater reactivity of the hypothalamic–pituitary–adrenal (HPA) axis, one of the primary systems involved in responses to stress (Repetti et al., 2007). Infants who are exposed to corporal punishment at home show greater reactivity to stress as measured by cortisol, the hormone that is released into the blood stream when the HPA axis is activated (Bugental, Martorell, & Barazza, 2003). A mother's insensitivity to her child during play predicts increases in the child's cortisol during free play (Spangler, Schieche, Ilg, & Ackermann, 1994) and infant attachment patterns moderate babies' cortisol responses in stressful circumstances (Gunnar & Donzella, 2002).

To summarize, the family's influence during infancy extends to cognitive, social, and emotional aspects of development. Infants' experiences in the family also seem to shape their ability to modulate emotional and physiological reactivity and the development of systems that regulate those responses, with implications for later physical and mental health (Repetti et al., 2007; Repetti, Taylor, & Seeman, 2002).

■ TODDLERS AND PRESCHOOLERS

During the period between infancy and early childhood, toddlers venture from the close-knit bond with their parents into the larger social world which includes relationships with other family members, peers, nonfamilial caregivers, neighbors, and others outside the family. The process of becoming a member of society involves the development of a sense of self separate from the mother, the ability to function outside of the immediate care of parents, the first stirrings of moral conscience, and the development of relationships with peers. The family plays a role in each of those major developmental tasks beginning when children are toddlers and continuing through the preschool years.

Sometime during the second year of life, toddlers recognize themselves in the mirror, begin to label themselves by names, and use personal pronouns, such as "I" and "me." By the age of 3 or 4 years, they construct a gender identity: children are certain about their own gender and have formed one of the most stable self-categorizations they will make in their lifetimes. Through interactions with family members and by observing the world around them, they learn about gender roles and develop gender-based preferences and meanings. For example, parents' emotional reactions can direct toddlers toward gender-typed behavior. Parents have been observed becoming more involved and excited when playing with their toddlers using same-gender toys, and such toys, in turn, elicit gender-typed play (Edwards & Liu, 2002).

Just as toddlers develop a sense of themselves as separate individuals, they also begin to function autonomously. This requires the development of self-control over impulses and the capacity to comply with standards for proper and desirable behavior. As demands for mature behavior increase during the second year of life, toddlers are expected to modulate their behavior in accordance with caregiver commands; compliance with those expectations increases from toddler to preschool to school years. The control strategies used by parents relates to the development of compliance in toddlers. For example, mothers' use of guidance and nonassertive methods of control is associated with better compliance in toddlers whereas power assertive techniques and physical punishment are associated with toddler defiance (Edwards, 1995).

During this stage of development, children also learn to regulate their behavior and emotions without adult supervision and other external controls. They internalize standards of conduct for behavior and experience empathy as well as feelings of guilt and shame. The standards and values that form the basis of a moral conscience are conveyed and enforced in the context of family relationships (Kochanska & Thompson, 1997). Toddlers are more likely to show empathy and attempt to help someone in pain if their mothers demonstrate concern for others. In comparison, toddlers who are abused at home are not only less likely to show concern when a peer is in distress, they may even react with fear or aggression and anger toward the victim (Edwards & Liu, 2002). Thus, the modeling of social behavior in the family appears to play an important role in the early development of moral conscience. The social and emotional climate in the family, as well as the security of attachment to the mother, also play a role in the way that toddlers and preschoolers self-regulate other emotions and in how they understand emotions in others. More anger and aggression at home or less secure attachments have been linked with greater emotional reactivity, less competent coping, and less accuracy in recognizing emotions depicted in facial expressions (Repetti et al., 2002).

One of the major developmental tasks of the toddler and preschool years is the formation of sustainable relationships. Attachment theory proposes that early caregivers, especially mothers, play a critical role in how children join an ever-widening array of social networks. The quality of early family relationships influences children's emotional security and their "internal working models" of relationships which, consequently, shape their affective responses to others, communication styles, and social skills (Edwards, 1995; Ladd & Pettit, 2002). Although differences in personality and temperament also play an important role, children with secure attachments to parents develop more positive expectations about others and are more socially competent during the preschool years. They are more likely to form friendships, to have large support networks, and to garner acceptance from peers (Ladd & Pettit, 2002). Not surprisingly, toddlers and preschoolers growing up in families marked by conflict and aggression or with parents who are less responsive and sensitive are less able to effectively resolve conflicts, are more aggressive, and demonstrate fewer social skills with their peers (Repetti et al., 2002).

Parents can also exert a direct impact on their children's peer networks. Toddlers' social ties are more likely to extend beyond the family when their parents actively initiate informal peer contacts. During the preschool years, the children who have more consistent play companions are better liked by their classmates, display more prosocial behavior, and develop more harmonious ties with peers. In addition, when they become involved in the process of arranging informal play activities, these children master the skills needed to initiate and manage their own interactions with peers. The supervision of their children's ongoing interactions, activities, and relationships with peers is another common mode of direct parental influence, one that benefits toddlers more than preschoolers (Ladd & Pettit, 2002).

With their first steps, toddlers begin the gradual process of moving away from their parents and toward greater autonomy and ties to people outside of the family. Between infancy and kindergarten, children's initial forays into the outside world are guided by experiences in the family. The sense of self they launch, the stance they adopt toward society's expectations of them, the moral conscience they begin to develop, and the relationships they forge with peers during those early years are shaped by their early attachments and the attitudes and behavior of their parents.

■ MIDDLE CHILDHOOD

Middle childhood covers roughly the ages of 5 to adolescence, a relatively long period of development marked by dramatic changes in physical maturity, cognitive abilities, and social relationships (Collins, Madsen, & Susman-Stillman, 2002). During these years, children spend more time engaged in activities outside of the home, particularly in the school setting, and gradually transition from more adult-directed activities to more self-directed activities. Healthy development during middle childhood is marked by increasing levels of self-control, such that children are able to regulate and modulate their emotional and behavioral responses to meet environmental demands and engage in goal-oriented activity. Although they play an increasingly active role in selecting and shaping their immediate environments, children are still largely influenced by their parents and family during this period.

Parents may directly influence their child through the nature of parent–child interactions and parenting practices such as monitoring and discipline. Children may also be influenced indirectly through behavior modeled by parents, marital interactions, and the emotional climate of the family. Behaviors and social patterns that children learn in the home have far-reaching implications for their functioning in multiple domains outside of the home, including school performance and interactions with peers and adults.

Parent Socialization of Emotion and Social Competence

The socialization of emotion, defined as the shaping of children's understanding, experience, expression, and regulation of emotion (Eisenberg, Cumberland, & Spinrad, 1998), takes place within the context of the family. Children learn to understand their own and other's emotions, display emotions in a socially and culturally age-appropriate manner, and inhibit or modulate experience and expression of emotion in order to achieve goals in a socially acceptable manner. Parents' own coping with frustration and distress influences children's regulation of their emotions (Kliewer, Fearnow, & Miller, 1996). For example, children of parents who express less positive emotion and more negative emotion show less constructive coping in response to stress (Valiente, Fabes, Eisenberg, & Spinrad, 2004).

We know that positive, accepting, secure parent–child relationships seem to enhance children's capacities for forming and maintaining positive relationships with others (e.g., Contreras, Kerns, Weimer, Gentzler, & Tomich, 2000). Studies have linked parental warmth and involvement to child displays of prosocial behavior and low levels of child aggression at home and at school (Pettit, Bates, & Dodge, 1993; Rothbaum, Rosen, Pott, & Beatty, 1995). Involved parents may also encourage positive peer relationships by providing opportunities for social contact (Parke & Buriel, 2006). Direct parent supervision and guidance with peers facilitate social competence among younger children, whereas offering advice or consultation about difficult social situations is helpful for older children (O'Neil & Parke, 2000).

Another mechanism that links parenting to children's social competence is reflected in the skills that children learn and practice at home; parents have an impact by modeling, eliciting, and reinforcing social behavior. Through these experiences, children learn strategies for relating to peers and resolving conflicts. Children's construals of the parent–child relationship and parenting practices may be another pathway by which parenting influences children's social behavior. Research suggests that children form an internal working model or schema of interpersonal relationships that incorporate behaviors, feelings, and expectancies of reactions from others (Bowlby, 1988; Dodge, 1993). In fact, children's perceptions of parenting predict social competence to a greater degree than parents' own reports of their parenting behavior (Domitrovich & Bierman, 2001).

Whether through the acquisition of social skills and behaviors or by the development of internal models of how relationships work, we know that disciplinary practices in the home are associated with children's social behavior outside of the home. High levels of coercive and punitive discipline promote child aggression and are associated with low levels of child prosocial behavior (Pinderhughes, Dodge, Bates, Pettit, & Zelli, 2000). For example, parenting practices that involve high levels of punitive interactions are associated with elevated rates of oppositional, aggressive, hyperactive, and internalizing behaviors in kindergarten children (Stormshak, Bierman, McMahon, Lengua, & CPPRG, 2000). In addition, ineffective maternal discipline, characterized by threats and ridicule directed toward the child, predicts an increase in child conduct problems (Snyder, Cramer, Afrank, & Patterson, 2005). Parents' ineffective disciplinary practices have been found to increase the likelihood of behavior problems and academic failure by maintaining and reinforcing antisocial tendencies (Vuchinich, Bank, & Patterson, 1992).

Parenting Dimensions and Parent Mental Health

A well-documented finding in the child-rearing literature is that authoritative parenting, characterized by firm limit-setting, warmth, and responsiveness, is conducive to positive child outcomes. This type of parenting is contrasted with authoritarian and permissive styles of parenting that are overly controlling or provide too little support and structure. Authoritative parenting is considered beneficial to positive social, emotional, and cognitive outcomes in children. Examples of these outcomes include peer acceptance, school success, self-esteem, and responsibility-taking, all of which predict success later in life. This research is primarily based on studies of middle-class Caucasian families (Baumrind, 1989), and therefore is limited in generalizability to families from low SES or ethnically diverse backgrounds. However, across cultures perceived parental acceptance–rejection accounts for approximately 26% of the variation in children's self-reported psychological adjustment (Khaleque & Rohner, 2002).

Parenting behavior and attitudes that are centered on parental concerns, rather than attunement to individual child characteristics and needs, are consistently associated with less positive child outcomes. Insensitive parenting in middle childhood is a risk factor for long-term difficulties in child adjustment. Parent mental health is a factor that influences child development not only through genetic heritability, but also by potentially compromising parenting quality and practices. Maternal depression is tied to parenting practices that are associated with development of poor emotion regulation in children. Women who are depressed tend to show less responsiveness and attunement to their children and therefore are often less able to appropriately meet their children's needs (Arsenio, Sesin, & Siegel, 2004; Goodman & Gotlib, 1999). Given that women who are depressed experience deficits in their own emotion regulation, they may not be able to model or teach their children adaptive ways of coping. Hence, maternal depression is linked to deficits in parenting behavior that are associated with compromised psychosocial and cognitive functioning in children (Burke, 2003).

Alterations in biological stress reactivity via the HPA axis have also been observed in children of depressed mothers (Lupien, King, Meaney, & McEwen, 2000; Pendry & Adam, 2007). Disturbances in the HPA system in the context of chronic stress, indicated by either hyper- or hypocortisolism, are associated with poor physical and mental health (McEwen, 1998). Early experiences are believed to have long-lasting effects on the reactivity and regulation of stress-sensitive physiological systems that are closely tied to regions of the brain active in attention and emotion regulation (Blair, Granger, & Razza, 2005; Shonkoff & Phillips, 2000). Consequently, disruptions in sensitive parenting, such as those that occur with maternal depression, may deplete a developing child's internal and physiological resources for meeting environmental demands and thereby render children vulnerable to a wide range of health and behavioral problems.

The bulk of research on parenting has typically focused on mothers as caregivers; but fathers are also involved in child rearing, particularly with older children and sons (Wood & Repetti, 2004). Early research on the role of fathers focused primarily on the impact of an absent father. Children in father-absent families tend to have fewer economic and socioemotional resources and show more behavioral problems (McLanahan & Carlson, 2002). However, sheer quantity of involvement is less important than the quality of father's involvement. A close relationship with a non-residential father who is responsive has been associated with gains in children's academic achievement and reductions in behavioral problems (Amato & Gilbreth, 1999). One way that fathers shape their children's social behavior is by their responses to difficult emotions. Fathers who accept and assist their children with sadness and anger and who employ emotion and problem-focused coping strategies in response to distress have children who are more socially competent and show less aggressive and disruptive behavior (Gottman, Katz, & Hooven, 1997; Parke & O'Neil, 1999).

Marital Relationship and Conflict

The overall quality of the marital relationship is related to parenting, with higher marital quality associated with better parenting and, in turn, more positive child adjustment (Coiro & Emery, 1998). Marital conflict has adverse consequences for children's psychological health, social functioning, and school performance (Davies, Winter, & Cicchetti, 2006; Margolin, Oliver, & Medina, 2001; Troxel & Matthews, 2004). For example, marital conflict and parental disagreement over child rearing practices have been linked to children's antisocial tendencies and poor relationships with peers (Gonzales, Pitts, Hill, & Roosa, 2000). Unlike marital conflict that involves physical aggression, hostility, or threat, marital disagreements expressed through calm discussion and supportive problem-solving are significantly less likely to evoke distress responses from children (Cummings, Goeke-Morey, & Papp, 2003).

Aggressive marital conflict may impact children's behavioral, cognitive, and emotional adjustment via modeling aggressive behaviors, negative cognitive representations of aggressive marital conflict, and disruptions in children's sense of emotional security (Davies, Woitach, Winter, & Cummings, 2008). Aggression between parents may also disrupt relationships with children and parenting practices. For example, negative affect elicited in the marital dyad may spill over into parent–child interactions contributing to more irritable and punitive discipline practices (Erel & Burman, 1995). Parents may use similar harsh and coercive strategies in reaction to child misbehaviors, thereby reinforcing aggressive exchanges with their children and contributing to problems with aggression among offspring (Buehler & Gerard, 2002; Patterson & Fisher, 2002). Some research suggests that a general social climate of anger and aggression in the home is even more potent for the development of child behavior problems than is discord in the marital or parent–child relationship per se (Jaycox & Repetti, 1993).

Siblings

Siblings also influence child development by changing the family structure and relationship dynamics. Research has documented the potential for positive as well as negative effects associated with the presence of siblings. For example, there may be disruptions in the parent–child relationship with the birth of new siblings. In particular, there appears to be more of a negative impact in terms of behavior problems and academic adjustment on older children from families with limited financial resources (Demo & Cox, 2000). On the other hand, brothers and sisters allow children to practice skills and interaction styles that they have learned or observed. Older siblings act as tutors and supervisors of younger siblings during social interactions and may extend or limit opportunities for social contact outside of the family. Thus, the prosocial or deviant interests and activities of siblings contribute to the relative positive or negative influence that brothers and sisters have on each other (Parke & Buriel, 2006).

Other Family Influences

Although most of the psychological literature focuses on social dimensions of the family environment (e.g., parental discipline strategies, relationship quality), material and other aspects are also important. For instance, children may learn about work and responsibilities by contributing to household chores (Lee, Schneider, & Waite, 2003). A key finding of the large-scale National Longitudinal Survey of Youth was that less learning stimulation (e.g., books in the home, parent reading with child) was associated with more behavior problems among children in every ethnic group from early childhood through adolescence, controlling for family demographics, parental responsiveness, and level of spanking. Thus, objects in the home, such as books, and parents' efforts to provide learning opportunities for their children should also be considered in explaining potential causes and maintenance of behavior problems as well as other aspects of development (Bradley, Corwyn, Burchinal, McAdoo, & Garcia-Coll, 2001).

Children engage in different ways with their family as they grow older. Interactions with parents become less frequent whereas interactions with others outside the home, especially peers, increase. Some scholars have reasoned that the influence of certain aspects of the home environment may therefore decline over the course of middle childhood. A longitudinal study of children between ages 8 and 13 found that the association between parental responsiveness and children's competence weakened as children got older (Gottfried, Fleming, & Gottfried, 1998). Undoubtedly, the influence of the family depends on, and interacts with, the broader sociocultural context in which it is situated, such that the norms and mores of a society shape family socialization processes and how behaviors are expressed (Collins, Maccoby, Steinberg, Hetherington, & Bornstein, 2000). A limitation of research to date is that the degree to which links between parent–child relationships and social and emotional development during middle childhood reflect the effects of the current environment, or the longer history of interactions between parent and child, is not well understood (Collins et al., 2002). Overall, research on 5- to 12-year-old children clearly indicates that the family exerts a powerful influence on children's development and sets the stage for the transition into adolescence.

ADOLESCENCE

During adolescence, children's social, emotional, cognitive, and physical characteristics develop to more closely resemble adults (Beveridge & Berg, 2007). With these changes come a less hierarchical parent–child relationship (Steinberg & Morris, 2001). Teenagers strive to develop more autonomy and their own identities, and they want to take a greater part in family decision making (Beveridge & Berg, 2007). It once was thought that a teen's assertion of autonomy engendered family discord. However, there is not so much an increase in the frequency of conflict between parents and adolescents as there is an increase in the intensity of conflicts; abstract thought and other cognitive developments help teens make better arguments (Windle et al., 2008). To maintain positive relationships, parents must find a balance between granting independence and providing guidance at the same time as adolescents explore ways of asserting their own opinions while respecting their parents' perspectives (Beveridge & Berg, 2007).

Although peers play an increasingly important role in adolescents' lives, the family continues to have a significant impact on their development (Steinberg & Morris, 2001). Discussed in the following sections are four important areas of development that are influenced by the family during this period: sexuality, substance use, academic achievement, and mental health.

Pubertal Development, Romantic Relationships, and Sexual Behavior

Physical development (puberty), sexual attitudes and behavior, and the formation of romantic relationships are all part of the development of sexuality during adolescence, and all are influenced by the family. During puberty, secondary sexual characteristics (e.g., breast, pubic hair, testicular and menarche development) emerge as well as changes in height and weight (Coleman & Coleman, 2002). While the sequence of developmental changes is similar for most adolescents, the timing of development varies (Belsky et al., 2007). Early pubertal onset is associated with higher rates of depression and anxiety in females (Steinberg & Morris, 2001). Research has shown that early-maturing females have higher rates of body dissatisfaction and eating disorders, and that these differences persist even after their peers have reached puberty (Mendle, Turkheimer, & Emery, 2007). While genetic factors account for the majority of variance in pubertal timing, environmental factors, such as psychosocial stressors, are also important (Eaves et al., 2004). Evolutionary theories postulate that certain psychosocial stressors are linked to early pubertal development. According to this perspective, when females cannot depend on others for support it is adaptive to begin reproduction earlier. With more offspring, there is a greater probability that some will survive (Belsky et al., 2007; Saxbe & Repetti, 2009). Consistent with this line of reasoning, family characteristics that are stressful for children and convey a lack of support, such as discord, parent psychopathology, and father absence, are associated with earlier pubertal onset among daughters (Ellis & Garber, 2000). Marital conflict and marital dissatisfaction have been associated with early pubertal onset in both girls and boys (Kim & Smith, 1998; Saxbe & Repetti, 2009), and harsh and controlling parenting predicts daughters' earlier pubertal onset whereas sensitive and warm parenting have been associated with later pubertal onset in girls (Belsky et al., 2007). Girls living in households with step-fathers also begin puberty earlier than girls living with their biological fathers (Ellis & Garber, 2000). Some have speculated that the presence of unrelated males in the home may shape females' pubertal development more than the absence of biological fathers.

At the same time that their bodies are developing secondary sex characteristics, children begin socializing with the opposite sex, dating, and exploring sexuality. Although genes influence one's sexual orientation (Mustanski, Chivers, & Bailey, 2002), family social processes can shape the quality of romantic relationship patterns. In particular, early attachment experiences with parents may influence expectations for romantic relationships. Anxiously attached teens report more fears of rejection and abandonment in their dating life than their securely attached peers; those with avoidant caregiver attachments express greater discomfort with intimacy and have trouble forming close bonds with partners. In contrast, securely attached adolescents are more likely to be involved in supportive romantic relationships (Tracy, Shaver, Albino, & Cooper, 2003).

National survey data indicate that almost half of high school students have engaged in sexual intercourse, and 39% of this group had not worn contraceptives during their most recent sexual activity (Eaton et al., 2008). What role does the family play in adolescents' risk for sexually transmitted diseases and teen pregnancy? Parental monitoring and control and parent–adolescent relationship quality and communication have received the most attention as factors that influence risky sexual behavior. More parental monitoring, defined as supervision of adolescents' social activities, is associated with less sexual activity. Not permitting any social freedom, however, predicts increases in risky sexual behavior (Kotchick, Shaffer, Forehand, & Miller, 2001). In this situation, adolescents may be rebelling against their parents' over-control and seeking an extreme form of independence. Positive parent–adolescent relationships and communication between the dyad are associated with lower levels of risky sexual behavior (Kotchick et al., 2001; Miller, Benson, & Galbraith, 2001). Frequent, positive, and open communication with adolescents exposes them to parents' values about sex and they, in turn, are less likely to engage in risky sexual behavior (Kotchick et al., 2001; Miller et al., 2001).

Adolescents with a history of sexual abuse by family members are at risk for early sexual behavior and teen pregnancy (Kotchick et al., 2001). Victims of sexual abuse often develop depressive symptoms, low self-esteem, low self-worth, post-traumatic stress disorder, and lack of assertiveness. These psychological outcomes may make adolescents less able to defend themselves and reject unwanted sexual advances (Steel & Herlitz, 2005).

In sum, as adolescents mature, close and positive relationships with their parents pave the way for more secure romantic relationships and lower rates of risky sexual behavior.

Substance Use

Family relationships and communication during adolescence also influence other risky behaviors, such as substance abuse. The effects can be far reaching because drug use in adolescence is associated with substance abuse later in life, as well as a host of other negative outcomes such as poor academic performance, failure to complete high school, criminal behavior, premature commencement of and problems with adult roles (e.g., job or marriage instability), physical health problems, loneliness, and psychopathology (Newcomb, 1997). High levels of discord in the family may be linked to substance use because family conflict interferes with the development of effective emotion regulation; teens may use substances to help them cope with difficult emotions and stressful home environments (Repetti et al., 2002). Evidence suggests that these adolescents often disengage from their families and are likely to befriend peers who are delinquent and facilitate drug use (Westling, Andrews, Hampson, & Peterson, 2008; Wills & Yaeger, 2003). Some research indicates that changes in parenting practices during preadolescence can lead to reductions in risky behaviors more than 2 years later. Participants were randomly assigned either to a family-centered preventive intervention program designed to delay the initiation of risk behaviors (alcohol and marijuana use and sexual activity), the Strong African American Families (SAAF) program, or to a control condition. Findings showed that the SAAF program improved parents' communication and monitoring of children and that it reduced risk behaviors among children at genetic risk. At long-term follow-up, youth with a genetic vulnerability factor (those with the short allele on the serotonin transporter gene *5-HTTLPR*) who were randomly assigned to the control group initiated significantly more risk behaviors than did youth in the other three groups (i.e., those at genetic risk whose families were assigned to the SAAF program, and those who were not at genetic risk, regardless of whether they were assigned to the control or intervention group; Brody, Beach, Philibert, Chen, & McBride Murry, 2009).

The attitudes and behaviors regarding substances that teens are exposed to at home also have an impact on their drug use. Family members who abuse drugs model that behavior and make drugs more available, increasing the risk of substance abuse (Denton & Kampfe, 1994). Siblings appear to be even more influential than parents in shaping substance use behaviors (Slomkowski, Rende, Novak,

Lloyd-Richardson, & Niaura, 2005). A national study of adolescent sibling pairs (i.e., monzygotic twins, dyzygotic twins, full-siblings, half-siblings, and unrelated siblings) revealed that even after controlling for genetic relatedness, parent smoking, and peer smoking, social connectedness to one's siblings moderated the shared environment effect of a sibling who smoked cigarettes. Teens were more likely to initiate cigarette smoking or increase their smoking frequency if they had close ties with their siblings who smoked (Slomkowski et al., 2005). Family members, however, can model positive drug-related behaviors too. For example, parents who openly express disapproval of drug use have adolescent offspring who are less likely to use drugs (Burrow-Sanchez, 2006).

Academic Achievement

Family environments that foster learning have longstanding effects on children's academic achievement. A longitudinal study that followed 6-month-olds and their parents until the children reached 19 years of age found that family influences begin in early development and create a pathway to academic achievement (Jimerson, Egeland, Sroufe, & Carlson, 2000). One of the ways that parents influence their children's educational attainment is through involvement in school. Even after controlling for multiple child and family characteristics (e.g., child cognitive abilities, gender, and race, and parent employment status, marital status, education, and income), parental involvement with children's education predicted lower rates of high school dropout and more years of education. For example, a child whose parents were involved at school by participating in school activities, communicating with teachers, and/or helping in the classroom for at least 3 years before high school had a 63% less likelihood of dropping out of high school than their peers who had fewer than 3 years of parental involvement before high school (Barnard, 2004). In addition to parents, siblings also can play a role in adolescent academic performance. Longitudinal research revealed that adolescents who spent time teaching their younger siblings demonstrated growth in their own language and overall academic achievement 2 years later (Smith, 1993). Taking the time to teach one's younger siblings rehearses and reinforces the material.

Mental Health

The stressors that many children experience during adolescence can be exacerbated by living in an unsupportive or high conflict home. Such an environment can act as a breeding ground for depression in a vulnerable teen (Sander & McCarty, 2005). Several of the risk factors for suicide, the third leading cause of death for adolescents (Centers for Disease Control, 2007), are linked to daily life at home, such as poor communication and poor problem-solving in families (Perkins & Hartless, 2002; Prinstein, Boergers, Spirito, Little, & Grapentine, 2000). Using a proportional hazards model that controlled for adolescent individual characteristics, researchers found that certain kinds of experiences in the family, such as insecure caregiver attachment, parent alcohol abuse, and exposure to sexual abuse, predicted adolescent suicide ideation (Fergusson, Woodward, & Horwood, 2000). Once adolescent mental health and stressful life events exposure were added to the model, however, the links between these factors and suicide ideation no longer were significant (Fergusson et al., 2000).

Family members do not necessarily cause adolescent suicide, but they can intensify teens' depression, and adolescent depression typically mediates the association between family risk factors and suicide (Prinstein et al., 2000).

Raising adolescents is no simple task; parents must relinquish some control while also continuing to keep a close eye on their children. Teens' past experiences with their family guide their exploration of sexuality, romantic relationships, and substance use. Parents strive to prepare their adolescents with sufficient independence and maturity to embrace their transition to emerging adulthood.

▩ EMERGING ADULTHOOD

In the United States, the emerging adult years, from approximately age 18–25, are considered to be distinct from adolescence and full adulthood (Arnett, 2007). Young adults' lives are less structured by their families and schools as compared to earlier periods, and are usually not yet shaped by new family roles and long-term employment. Emerging adults subjectively report feeling like neither adolescents nor adults, but somewhere in between, on their way to adulthood (Arnett, 2004).

Identity exploration, which begins during adolescence, becomes a prominent theme during the emerging adult years. Young adults are actively engaged in exploring their talents and abilities and making consequential decisions about their work and personal lives. Although there is considerable individual variability in the timing, duration, and sequencing of life-course transitions, a defining feature of this period is frequent changes in multiple life spheres including relationships and work. A tension exists between emerging adults' need for autonomy and continued dependency. Parents' acceptance and support of their child's independence facilitates identity exploration and commitment during these years, whereas parental anxiety around separation hinders growth in these areas (Bartle-Haring, Brucker, & Hock, 2002).

In contemporary industrialized society, the time it takes to reach full-fledged adulthood has increased. As a result, young adults may reside with parents for a longer time, an arrangement that poses certain challenges in terms of emotional boundaries, privacy, and parental intrusiveness. Leaving home, on the other hand, may promote individuation and the opportunity to establish a more adult-like relationship with parents (Arnett, 2004). Regardless, parents' provision of emotional and economic support enables many emerging adults to increase their education and explore career options (Semyonov & Lewin-Epstein, 2001).

Earlier parent–child relationships shape socioemotional outcomes in the early adult years. Reciprocity, associated with an authoritative parenting style, in the earlier parent–child relationship predicts better adjustment to college and higher academic achievement (Wintre & Yaffe, 2000). The parent–child relationship also influences the central task of forming intimate relationships in emerging adulthood. Involved and nurturing parenting earlier in life predict warm and supportive behavior toward romantic partners in emerging adults (Conger, Cui, Bryant, & Elder, 2000). Parental divorce and family conflict, on the other hand, negatively affect intimacy and security in emerging adults' romantic relationships. Depression and other mental health problems common among emerging adults have also been linked to parental divorce in childhood.

Emotional closeness and conflict between parents and emerging adult children are in part influenced by the nature of the parent–adolescent relationship. However, the influence of earlier relationship patterns is attenuated as children move further into adulthood (Aquilino, 1997, 2006). As a result of the transitions and exploration during this phase of life, emerging adults begin to relate to family members in new ways. They endorse a sense of obligation to support, assist, and respect their families (Fuligni & Pedersen, 2002). As emerging adults mature, they recognize their parents as individual beings apart from their parental role. The influence of siblings is seen in emerging adult's greater sense of well-being (i.e., higher self-esteem and life satisfaction) associated with perceived sibling support, which also appears to offset low parental and peer support (Milevsky, 2005). Most of the research on this group has focused on middle-class and Caucasian samples and, therefore, less is known about variability related to SES and ethnicity.

ADULTHOOD

By the adult years, there are potentially three streams of family influence. One represents the continuing developmental pressures exerted by past experiences in the family, which are evident in health, achievements, and relationships long after the individual has moved out of the home. The second represents the consequences of new family relationships—the adult's current experiences in the roles of spouse and parent. The third source of influence comes from present relationships with elderly parents, adult siblings, and others in the family of origin.

Childhood Experiences

Having grown up in a home marked by overt conflict—including recurrent episodes of anger and aggression—or one in which relationships were cold, unsupportive, and neglectful has damaging effects that can be observed in the mental and physical health of adults (Repetti et al., 2002). This includes an increased risk of psychiatric disorder (Johnson, Cohen, Kasen, Smailes, & Brook, 2001). Even physical growth seems to suffer. In one representative sample of a British birth cohort, exposure to family conflict at age 7 predicted less height attainment at age 33 (24% of the adults exposed to conflict were in the lowest fifth percentile of height distribution; Montgomery, Bartley, & Wilkinson, 1997). Physical health in adulthood fares no better. A number of longitudinal studies indicate that severe dissension or maltreatment during childhood, or even just a more negative relationship with parents, are associated with higher rates of illness and disease during the adult years (Lundberg, 1993; Russek & Schwartz, 1997; Walker et al., 1999). The elevated risk for serious health problems are also observed in studies that control for other risk factors, such as alcohol use, cigarette smoking, and being overweight (Shaffer, Duszynski, & Thomas, 1982). According to the risky families model, the health effects result from an accumulation of disruptions to the physiological stress response systems, as well as deficits in the emotion processing, social competence, and behavioral self-regulation that resulted from growing up in a family that was abusive, conflictual, or failed to provide adequate nurturing. The bulk of the damage to physical health may derive from allostatic load; repeated social challenges in the early family environment may have disrupted basic homeostatic processes that are critical to the maintenance of health and resulted in dysregulated responses to stress (Repetti et al., 2002).

The same risky family characteristics that predict poor health are also associated with lower status on a number of indicators of adult life success, such as educational attainment (in years), income, and occupational status (Power & Hertzman, 1997). A home life in childhood and adolescence characterized by harmonious marital interactions and strong attachments to both mother and father is associated with higher career aspirations and greater likelihood of adult employment in prestigious occupations. In general, warm, supportive relationships with one's parents, and, in some cases, one's siblings, facilitate a more secure sense of identity, higher levels of aspirations and expectations, increased career self-efficacy, and a sense of commitment to one's career choice (Whiston & Keller; 2004). Of course, a family's financial resources and the role models and knowledge it provides also influence achievements observed in adulthood (Schulenberg, Vondracek, & Crouter, 1984). However, these kinds of material and social advantages may not overcome the emotional costs associated with growing up in an aggressive or neglectful family. Even after controlling for childhood social class and neighborhood of residence, and a history of parental arrest and alcohol/drug problem, adults with documented histories of abuse or neglect are less likely to have completed high school or to be employed in managerial or professional occupations (Widom & White, 1997).

Because children first learn about relationships in their families, it is not surprising that longitudinal studies also find a more troubled and conflictual home in childhood and less closeness to parents predict relationships with friends and family in midlife that are less connected and a generally more avoidant attachment style (based on attitudes and feelings about closeness, intimacy, and interdependence in relationships; Graves, Wang, Mead, Johnson, & Klag, 1998; Klohnen & Bera, 1998). If parents were jealous, moody, critical, domineering, or quick to anger, their grown children are more likely to have marriages that are less harmonious and more discordant (Amato & Booth, 2001). Having experienced or witnessed violence in one's family of origin appears to increase the likelihood of experiencing abuse in future intimate relationships (Kwong, Bartholomew, Henderson, & Trinke, 2003) and some studies, though not all, find evidence of intergenerational transmission of child physical abuse (Ertem, Leventhal, & Dobbs, 2000).

The Marital and Parental Role in Adulthood

Although not everyone marries or has children, when a new household is created through marriage and parenthood, those relationships have a profound influence on development during the adult years. Being married seems to confer a number of advantages for individual health and well-being, including lower rates of morbidity and mortality, greater life satisfaction, happiness, and lower risk for depression (Holt-Lunstad, Birmingham, & Jones, 2008). The quality of the spousal relationship also matters because an unhappy marriage compromises physical and mental health. Divorce, extramarital affairs, and a husband's use of physical aggression, in particular, lead to increases in depressive symptoms among women (Christian-Herman, O'Leary, & Avery-Leaf, 2001). At the same time that divorce can create the kind of turmoil from which some never fully recover, others adjust relatively quickly and benefit from the ending of a highly conflicted or violent marriage (Amato, 2000). In general, lower levels of marital satisfaction are associated with declines in psychological well-being—an association that may be especially true for women (Dehle & Weiss, 1998). Negative dimensions of marital functioning—especially conflict, hostility, and a lack of support—also have both direct and indirect effects on physical health. Those effects are mediated by increasing risks for depression, by influencing health behaviors (such as greater alcohol use) and through physiological mechanisms—particularly the cardiovascular, endocrine, and immune systems. Although being married appears to have more benefits for men's health than for women's, the negative effects of marital conflict appear to be greater for the health of wives compared to husbands (Kiecolt-Glaser & Newton, 2001; Robles & Kiecolt-Glaser, 2003).

The closeness and intimacy of a marital relationship means that a spouse's stressful experiences also have an impact on health and well-being of his or her partner. For instance, recent evidence suggests that a spouse's mood and physiology can have a contagious effect, such that the couple's negative moods and stress hormones begin to sync up over the course of a day, particularly if their marriage is unhappy (Saxbe & Repetti, 2010). Even something as minor as daily worries about work can influence physiological stress indicators in a spouse (Slatcher, Robles, Repetti, & Fellows, in press). In extreme cases, such as living with a depressed spouse, daily interactions can become burdensome and lead to significant personal distress, including more depressed mood in the nondepressed partner (Benazon & Coyne, 2000). A husband's or a wife's job loss or prolonged unemployment can degrade the quality of the couple relationship as well as the spouse's mental health and increase the risk of divorce (Howe, Levy, & Caplan, 2004; Strom, 2003).

Just as marriage exerts a powerful influence over adult health and well-being, so does the experience of becoming a parent and rearing children. Although many would argue that parenthood is one of the most positive, important, and meaningful roles that anyone can fulfill, the quality of that experience varies over time and among individuals (Heinicke, 2002). Parenting that is demanding and stressful, or marked by daily arguments and hassles, contributes to significant declines in adult well-being (Crnic & Low, 2002). Of course, relationships with children continue to exert an influence on well-being and development throughout the life span. Watching children emerge into adulthood is a source of great fulfillment and pride for many parents; however, when offsprings struggle in their adult years, parents may experience doubts and regrets about their performance as parents. The personal and social adjustment that offspring experience as young adults has an impact on parents' evaluations of themselves, including their ratings of self-acceptance and depression (Ryff, Schmutte, & Lee, 1996).

Relationships With the Family of Origin

The relationship between adult children and their older parents is a two-way street where the roles of provider and recipient of support switch depending on the needs and resources of each generation at any given point. For example, it is common for adult offspring to continue to receive routine help from their older parents in the form of advice, assistance with childcare or household tasks, and more rarely, monetary transfers (Zarit & Eggebeen, 2002). The role that elderly parents play in providing assistance to their adult children and grandchildren is discussed in greater detail in the next section. However, when older parents become widowed, develop health problems, or their cognitive functioning declines, parent–child relationships often change. The amount of help needed can range from minimal to extensive around-the-clock care. Adult daughters often enjoy feeling appreciated for the assistance that they provide for their aging parents, especially if the parents are relatively healthy (Fingerman, 2000). The provision of long-term assistance, however, can place significant strain on adult offspring; if they are employed, they often find it difficult to manage job responsibilities, their social and leisure activities are restricted, and they face increased conflict with their own spouses and other family members. It can be especially stressful to care for a parent who is cognitively impaired, such as one with a dementing illness like Alzheimer's disease or with a mental disorder. When long-term care is provided by an adult child, the caregiver is most likely a daughter. Although they often receive some form of assistance from siblings, the relationship between caregiving daughters and their siblings can be quite stressful. Ultimately, the burden of providing long-term care for a disabled elderly parent can exceed the caregiver's physical, emotional, and financial resources. In the United States, adult children who assume that role are at an increased risk of depression and other types of emotional distress; they also face greater vulnerability to health problems and increased mortality (Mancini & Blieszner, 1989; Zarit & Eggebeen, 2002).

◼ OLDER ADULTHOOD

With recent increases in longevity, older adulthood currently starts later in life and continues longer than before (Zarit & Eggebeen, 2002). This period of development now typically begins at retirement or after age 65, and retirement decisions are often based on family circumstances. For example, spouses may plan their retirements to start at the same time (Szinovacz & Ekerdt, 1995); women rarely retire after their husbands, perhaps because their continued employment could threaten their husbands' traditional role as family breadwinner and place a strain on the marital relationship (Szinovacz & DeViney, 2000). Early retirement is more likely when there are strong relational ties to the family and members want to enjoy more time together. Those who are not as close with their families may choose to remain in the workforce longer to maintain regular social contacts. Financial responsibility for other family members also delays retirement (Szinovacz, DeViney, & Davey, 2001).

Providers and Recipients of Care

Increases in life expectancy have expanded the period when older adults typically spend time caring for and receiving care from family members. Parental assistance to adult children is routine: older adults report offering an average of 1.22 hours of support (e.g., financial, emotional, childcare, or household care support) each week to one of their adult children (Logan & Spitz, 1996). Relationship quality between older adults and their grown children improves the more independent the adult children become and the less assistance they need. Parents of adult offspring who have yet to meet social expectations of independence often experience distress and a sense of personal failure because they feel responsible for this delay (Pillemer & Suitor, 2002). Although older parents may experience a mixture of positive and negative feelings about relationships with adult offspring, there is less ambivalence if the adult offspring are in marriages in which they are highly invested, and when they rate their relationships with their parents as being very important in their lives (Fingerman, Chen, Hay, Cichy, & Lefkowitz, 2006).

Early research suggested that older adults who took on caregiving roles for grandchildren experienced declines in physical and mental health (Hughes, Waite, LaPierre, & Luo, 2007). However, whether or not health declines depends on the degree of caregiving demands and the available resources. A cross-sectional study of adults over the age of 50 found that, after controlling for a number of factors (including age, gender, ethnicity, employment status, income, education, and marital status), caregiving of grandchildren was not associated with a decline in health and actually was associated with some health benefits (Hughes et al., 2007). A national longitudinal survey of elderly married individuals found that those who provided 14 or more hours of care each week to a spouse had lower rates of mortality than those who did not provide any care—a mortality difference that persisted even after controlling for the elderly caregiver's age, gender, health, education, and other demographic variables (Brown et al., 2009). Being able to care for others (e.g., assisting others financially, emotionally, or physically) boosts self-esteem and feelings of independence which, in turn, improve life satisfaction. Across five countries, researchers found that elderly adults who provided more care for their adult children than they received reported the highest level of life satisfaction (Lowenstein, Katz, & Gur-Yish, 2007).

Increases in life expectancy have directed researchers' attention to the quality of caregiving not only of grandchildren and adult children but also of caregiving experienced by elderly people (Schiamberg & Gans, 2000). As discussed previously, the responsibility of caregiving typically falls on adult children, and the quality of that care shapes the older parent's life satisfaction. When physical needs were controlled, for example, the elderly people who perceived having more emotional support from their adult children reported higher levels of life satisfaction than those who perceived less emotional support (Lowenstein et al., 2007). Older adults who do not have any children and never marry are more likely to receive care from their siblings (Van Volkom, 2006). Elderly people who reported satisfaction with the degree of contact with their siblings had better mental and physical health and overall life satisfaction (McCamish-Svensson, Samuelsson, Hagberg, Svensson, & Dehlin, 1999).

A longer life span means increased caregiving demands. With this change also comes an increase in reports of elder abuse (Schiamberg & Gans, 2000). Although it is a rare occurrence—only 2.7 out of every 1,000 older adults are victims of abuse (Hajjar & Duthie, 2001)—the effects of elder abuse can be serious, including physical injury, depression, and stress, all of which predict early mortality. Researchers speculate that premature mortality is linked to abuse victims' chronic stress and loss of social support from their children (Baker, 2007).

Death of Family Members and Suicide

The loss of friends and family is a normative experience after the age of 65. Ten percent of those over this age have a living parent; the limited research that is available suggests that older adult offspring tend to distance themselves emotionally in order to prepare for the loss of an elderly parent (Moss & Moss, 1995). The death of an adult child, in contrast, usually is unexpected and often leaves parents plagued with distress and guilt over their own survival. Not only do grieving parents lose a primary source of social support, but they also lose the identity that they gained from the parental role. Mourning the loss of a spouse is associated with a decline in both physical and mental health. One study examined elderly pairs of twins who were married. During the months directly following the death of a spouse, widowers and widows were at greater risk for death compared to the twins whose spouses were living; this effect held even after controlling for smoking status, excessive alcohol use, education, body mass index, and chronic diseases (Lichtenstein, Gatz, & Berg, 1998). Because individual identities are often tied to relationships with loved ones, the death of family members not only leads to changes in roles in order to manage the gap left by the deceased, but also to changes in self-concept (Moss & Moss, 1995).

Old age marks a period of multiple losses—not only of loved ones but also of independence and health, which places many at risk for depression (Waern, Rubenowitz, & Wilhelmson, 2003). Consequently, suicide rates are highest among the elderly. Loneliness is a strong predictor of geriatric suicide; those who take their life in old age are more likely to have lived alone (Conwell, 2001), lost or divorced a spouse, or experienced family discord (Cattell, 2000). It is believed that these risk factors predict suicide because of their association with depression (Waern et al., 2003). Marriage, on the other hand, acts as a protective factor, perhaps due to the social support that a spouse provides (Moorman, Booth, & Fingerman, 2006).

It is important to bear in mind that the older adult years are often filled with many joys associated with grandparenthood, postretirement leisure time, and increased life span. No longer concerned with their offspring's emergence into adulthood, older adults can invest in strengthening ties with their adult children (Fingerman, 2000). In fact, older people report fewer interpersonal tensions in their daily lives and they seem to be better able to regulate their responses to problems compared with younger adults (Birditt, Fingerman, & Almedia, 2005). As the expected life span increases, researchers should focus more on how the family influences elderly people as they continue to age.

FUTURE ISSUES IN THE STUDY OF FAMILY INFLUENCES ACROSS THE LIFE SPAN

This chapter took us from fetal development, when the family's influence is expressed through genes and the prenatal environment, to old age, when influence processes can range from the lingering effects of early experiences in the family of origin to the current impact of relationships with adult offspring and spouse. Although the topic of family influence is addressed by different disciplines using a wide variety of designs and methods, there were some commonalities in the diverse literatures we reviewed. Because of a disproportionate focus on mothers, there is a relative scarcity of research on fathers and siblings that may have resulted in an unwarranted discounting of the roles that they play in development. Another similarity across different fields is that most studies are conducted in North America and, although there has been increased focus on minority populations in developmental studies, there remains an overrepresentation of middle-class White families in the literatures we reviewed. Consequently, there is much that we do not understand about how family influence processes vary across cultures or even across subgroups within the United States and Canada. Attachment theory stands out in our review because it is the one model that is used in the study of family influence at many life stages. However, no true life-span perspective is currently represented in any of the research literatures we reviewed. A life-span perspective opens the door to cross-fertilization of ideas and integration of findings across what are now separate literatures. A goal for family scholars is to begin the process of synthesizing theory, knowledge, and methods across different stages of development and research traditions.

Scholars working from an integrative life-span approach will face several major challenges. First, the family's influence over even a single aspect of development is expressed in different ways over a lifetime. For instance, emotion regulation could be manifested in the frequency and intensity of crying during infancy, the ability to recognize facial expressions among toddlers and preschoolers, coping strategies adopted during the elementary school years, risky sexual behaviors and substance abuse in adolescence, and depression or anxiety in adulthood. Emotion regulation also has a profound impact on social competence; the family's influence on the experience, control, and expression of emotions may be expressed in the way that interactions and relationships with peers, romantic partners, spouses, and offspring are managed at different points through life. The other chapters in this volume reviewing different facets of human development over the life span offer family researchers valuable guideposts that could help steer the process of synthesis.

A second challenge is presented by the fact that most families provide a fairly consistent type of environment that persists over many years; the developmental consequences therefore cumulate, making it difficult to specify the timing of effects. An apparent influence of early family events and conditions may be explained to some unknown degree by continuities in the home environment. As an example, consider the impact of parenting on the quality of peer relationships in adolescence. How much do sensitive and responsive parents in early childhood contribute to the ability to form and maintain relationships during the teen years? To address that question, it is critical to understand how early experiences are reflected in the quality of parenting provided by the same mother and father years later and the extent to which the stability of experience in the family accounts for associations between early parenting and outcomes assessed afterward. Intervention studies that create discontinuities in parenting practices or other aspects of family life discriminate the effects of early conditions from the effects of current conditions in the family much better than correlational studies do.

Because of correlations between family influence processes, a third challenge for researchers is disentangling the different streams of family influence. Individuals and subsystems within the family share traits and characteristics; a child with one caring and sensitive parent is more likely to have a second parent and siblings with nurturing traits than is a child with an abusive parent. In addition, parents who are angry and aggressive with each other are more likely to behave in a similar manner with their children (Margolin, Gordis, & Oliver, 2004). To complicate matters further, genetic predispositions account for some of the observed associations between family environments and outcomes in biological offspring. Family social environments are to some degree shaped by parents' heritable characteristics. When genes contributing to those traits are passed on to offspring and influence their development, the result is a gene–environment correlation that fuels what may appear to be an effect of the home environment on development. Special research designs such as adoption studies and experimental interventions that modify the family environment (like the Brody et al., 2009, SAAF program described earlier) help to overcome this obstacle.

Ecological systems theory, mentioned at the start of this chapter, highlights another source of correlation among family influences. For instance, social class shapes not only the materials that are found in the family's home, but also child rearing values and practices. Compared to lower SES parents, those with higher education and incomes typically provide more books in the home, emphasize educational endeavors, and can provide more assistance with homework, all of which contribute to better academic outcomes in children. Moreover, the family's impact is magnified by characteristics of other settings that affect child development and are correlated with family SES, such as the quality of schools, the social and material resources in neighborhoods, and the attitudes and behaviors of peers. In short, because of correlations between genes, the kinds of experiences and relationships that children have at home, and the broader social context in which families exist, the isolation and identification of different sources of family influence will continue to be a challenging task for researchers for some time.

We conclude our chapter where we began: family influences on development are pervasive and multifaceted. Investigators face the challenges of determining how developmental consequences are manifested at different points in the life span, identifying when effects of the family are observed, and decoding the components of family life that are potent for different outcomes. More long-term longitudinal designs and intervention studies, as well as more attention to cross-cultural perspectives, fathers, and siblings will advance the next generation of research. As knowledge from different disciplines continues to accumulate, a life-span perspective could be the thread that weaves together the bits and pieces of information about family influences.

ACKNOWLEDGMENTS

Rena Repetti and Jacqueline Sperling thank the Alfred P. Sloan Foundation and the UCLA Center on the Everyday Lives of Families for supporting their work on this chapter. We appreciate helpful comments from Shu-wen Wang, Richard Slatcher, Leah Dickenson, and Delana Parker on an earlier draft of this chapter.

REFERENCES

Amato, P. R. (2000). The consequences of divorce for adults and children. *Journal of Marriage and Family, 62*(4), 1269–1287.

Amato, P. R., & Booth, A. (2001). The legacy of parents' marital discord: Consequences for children's marital quality. *Journal of Personality and Social Psychology, 81*(4), 627–638.

Amato, P. R., & Gilbreth, J. G. (1999). Nonresident fathers and children's well-being: A meta-analysis. *Journal of Marriage and the Family, 61,* 557–573.

Aquilino, W. S. (1997). From adolescent to young adult: A prospective study of parent-child relations during the transition to adulthood. *Journal of Marriage & the Family, 59*(3), 670–686.

Aquilino, W. S. (2006). Family relationships and support systems in emerging adulthood. In J. J. Arnett & J. L. Tanner (Eds.), *Emerging adults in America: Coming of age in the 21st century* (pp. 193–217). Washington, DC: American Psychological Association.

Arnett, J. J. (2004). *Emerging adulthood: The winding road from the late teens through the twenties.* New York: Oxford University Press.

Arnett, J. J. (2007). Socialization in emerging adulthood: From the family to the wider world, from socialization to self-socialization. In J. E. Grusec & P. D. Hastings (Eds.), *Handbook of socialization: Theory and research* (pp. 208–231). New York: Guilford Press.

Arsenio, W. F., Sesin, M., & Siegel, L. (2004). Emotion-related abilities and depressive symptoms in Latina mothers and their children. *Development and Psychopathology, 16*(1), 95–112.

Baker, M. W. (2007). Elder mistreatment: Risk, vulnerability, and early mortality. *Journal of the American Psychiatric Nurses Association, 12*, 313–321.

Bakermans-Kranenburg, M. J., & van IJzendoorn, M. H. (2006). Gene-environment interaction of the dopamine D4 receptor (DRD4) and observed maternal insensitivity predicting externalizing behavior in preschoolers. *Developmental Psychobiology, 48*(5), 406–409.

Barnard, W. M. (2004). Parental involvement in elementary school and educational attainment. *Children and Youth Services Review, 26*, 39–62.

Bartle-Haring, S., Brucker, P., & Hock, E. (2002). The impact of parental separation anxiety on identity development in late adolescence and early adulthood. *Journal of Adolescent Research, 17*(5), 439–450.

Baumrind, D. (1989). Rearing competent children. In W. Damon (Ed.), *Child development today and tomorrow* (pp. 349–378). San Francisco: Jossey-Bass.

Behrman, R. E., & Butler, A. S. (Eds.). (2006). *Preterm birth: Causes, consequences and prevention.* Washington, DC: National Academy Press.

Belsky, J., Steinberg, L. D., Houts, R. M., Friedman, S. L., DeHart, G., Cauffman, E., et al. (2007). Family rearing antecedents of pubertal timing. *Child Development, 78*, 1302–1321.

Benazon, N. R., & Coyne, J. C. (2000). Living with a depressed spouse. *Journal of Family Psychology, 14*(1), 71–79.

Beveridge, R. M., & Berg, C. A. (2007). Parent-Adolescent collaboration: An interpersonal model for understanding optimal interactions. *Clinical Child and Family Psychology Review, 10*, 25–52.

Bhutta, A. T., Cleves, M. A., Casey, P. H., Cradock, M. M., & Anand, K. J. S. (2002). Cognitive and behavioral outcomes of school-aged children who were born preterm. *Journal of the American Medical Association, 288*(6), 728–737.

Birditt, K. S., Fingerman, K. L., & Almeida, D. M. (2005). Age differences in exposure and reactions to interpersonal tensions: A daily diary study. *Psychology and Aging, 20*, 330–340.

Blair, C., Granger, D., & Razza, R. P. (2005). Cortisol reactivity is positively related to executive function in preschool children attending head start. *Child Development, 76*(3), 554–567.

Bornstein, M. H. (1995). Parenting infants. In M. H. Bornstein (Ed.), *Handbook of parenting: Volume I, children and parenting* (pp. 3–39). Mahwah, NJ: Lawrence Erlbaum Associates.

Bowlby, J. (1988). *A secure base: Parent-child attachment and healthy human development.* New York: Basic Books.

Bradley, R. H., Corwyn, R. F., Burchinal, M., McAdoo, H. P., & García Coll, C. (2001). The home environments of children in the united states part II: Relations with behavioral development through age thirteen. *Child Development, 72*(6), 1868–1886.

Brody, G. H., Beach, S. R. H., Philibert, R. A., Chen, Y., & Mc Bride Murry, V. (2009). Prevention effects moderate the association of 5-HTTLPR and youth risk behavior initiation: Gene x environment hypotheses tested via a randomized prevention design. *Child Development, 80*, 645–661.

Bronfenbrenner, U. (1989). Ecological systems theory. *Annals of Child Development, 6*, 187–249.

Brown, S. L., Smith, D. M., Schulz, R., Kabeto, M. U., Ubel, P. A., Poulin, M., et al. (2009). Caregiving behavior is associated with decreased mortality risk. *Psychological Science, 20*, 488–494.

Buehler, C., & Gerard, J. M. (2002). Marital conflict, ineffective parenting, and children's and adolescents' maladjustment. *Journal of Marriage and Family, 64*(1), 78–92.

Bugental, D. B., Martorell, G. A., & Barraza, V. (2003). The hormonal costs of subtle forms of infant maltreatment. *Hormones and Behavior, 43*, 237–244.

Burke, L. (2003). The impact of maternal depression on familial relationships. *International Review of Psychiatry, 15*(3), 243–255.

Burrow-Sanchez, J. (2006). Understanding adolescent substance abuse: Prevalence, risk factors, and clinical implications. *Journal of Counseling & Development, 84*, 283–290.

Cattell, H. (2000). Suicide in the elderly. *Advances in Psychiatric Treatment, 6*, 102–108.

Centers for Disease Control. (2007). Suicide trends among youths and young adults aged 10–24 years—United States, 1990–2004. *Morbidity and Mortality Weekly Report, 56*, 905–908.

Christian-Herman, J. L., O'Leary, K. D., & Avery-Leaf, S. (2001). The impact of sever negative events in marriage on depression. *Journal of Social and Clinical Psychology, 20*(1), 24–40.

Coiro, M. J., & Emery, R. E. (1998). Do marriage problems affect fathering more than mothering? A quantitative and qualitative review. *Clinical Child and Family Psychology Review, 1*(1), 23–40.

Coleman, L., & Coleman, J. (2002). The measurement of puberty: A review. *Journal of Adolescence, 25*, 535–550.

Collins, W. A., Maccoby, E. E., Steinberg, L., Hetherington, E. M., & Bornstein, M. H. (2000). Contemporary research on parenting: The case for nature and nurture. *American Psychologist, 55*(2), 218–232.

Collins, W. A., Madsen, S. D., & Susman-Stillman, A. (2002). Parenting during middle childhood. In M. H. Bornstein (Ed.), *Handbook of parenting: Children and parenting* (Vol. 1, 2nd ed., pp. 73–101). Mahwah, NJ: Lawrence Erlbaum Associates.

Conger, R. D., Cui, M., Bryant, C. M., & Elder, G. H., Jr. (2000). Competence in early adult romantic relationships: A developmental perspective on family influences. *Journal of Personality and Social Psychology, 79*(2), 224–237.

Contreras, J. M., Kerns, K. A., Weimer, B. L., Gentzler, A. L., & Tomich, P. L. (2000). Emotion regulation as a mediator of associations between mother-child attachment and peer relationships in middle childhood. *Journal of Family Psychology, 14*(1), 111–124.

Conwell, Y. (2001). Suicide in later life: A review and recommendations for prevention. *Suicide and life-threatening behavior, 31*, 32–47.

Crnic, K., & Low, C. (2002). Everyday stresses and parenting. In M. H. Bornstein (Ed.), *Handbook of parenting* (2nd ed., pp. 243–268). Mahwah, NJ: Lawrence Erlbaum Associates.

Cummings, E. M., Goeke-Morey, M. C., & Papp, L. M. (2003). Children's responses to everyday marital conflict tactics in the home. *Child Development, 74*(6), 1918–1929.

Davies, P. T., Winter, M. A., & Cicchetti, D. (2006). The implications of emotional security theory for understanding and treating childhood psychopathology. *Development and Psychopathology, 18*(3), 707–735.

Davies, P. T., Woitach, M. J., Winter, M. A., & Cummings, E. M. (2008). Children's insecure representations of the interparental relationship and their school adjustment: The mediating role of attention difficulties. *Child Development, 79*(5), 1570–1582.

Dehle, C., & Weiss, R. L. (1998). Sex differences in prospective associations between marital quality and depressed mood. *Journal of Marriage and the Family, 60*(4), 1002–1011.

Demo, H., & Cox, M. J. (2000). Families with young children: A review of research in the 1990s. *Journal of Marriage and the Family, 62*(4), 876–895.

Denton, R. E., & Kampfe, C. M. (1994). The relationship between family variables and adolescent substance abuse: A literature review. *Adolescence, 29*, 475–495.

Dodge, K. A. (1993). Social-cognitive mechanisms in the development of conduct disorder and depression. *Annual Review of Psychology, 44*, 559–584.

Domitrovich, C. E., & Bierman, K. L. (2001). Parenting practices and child social adjustment: Multiple pathways of influence. *Merrill-Palmer Quarterly, 47*(2), 235–263.

Dunkel-Schetter, C. (2009). Stress processes in pregnancy and preterm birth. *Current Directions in Psychological Science, 18*(4), 205–209.

Eaton, D. K., Kann, L., Kinchen, S., Shanklin, S., Ross, J., Hawkins, J., et al. (2008). Youth risk behavior surveillance—United States, 2007. *Morbidity and Mortality Weekly Report, 57*, 1–131.

Eaves, L., Silberg, J., Foley, D., Bulik, C., Maes, H., Erkanli, A., et al. (2004). Genetic and environmental influences on the relative timing of pubertal change. *Twin Research, 7*, 471–481.

Edwards, C. P. (1995). Parenting toddlers. In M. H. Bornstein (Ed.), *Handbook of parenting* (pp. 41–63). Mahwah, NJ: Lawrence Erlbaum Associates.

Edwards, C. P., & Liu, W. (2002). Parenting toddlers. In M. H. Bornstein (Ed.), *Handbook of parenting* (2nd ed., pp. 45–72). Mahwah, NJ: Lawrence Erlbaum Associates.

Eisenberg, N., Cumberland, A., & Spinrad, T. L. (1998). Parental socialization of emotion. *Psychological Inquiry, 9*(4), 241–273.

Ellis, B. J., & Garber, J. (2000). Psychosocial antecedents of variation in girls' pubertal timing. *Child Development, 71*(2), 485–501.

Erel, O., & Burman, B. (1995). Interrelatedness of marital relations and parent-child relations: A meta-analytic review. *Psychological Bulletin, 118*(1), 108–132.

Ertem, I. O., Leventhal, J. M., & Dobbs, S. (2000). Intergenerational continuity of child physical abuse: How good is the evidence? *The Lancet, 356*, 814–819.

Fergusson, D. M., Woodward, L. J., & Horwood, L. J. (2000). Risk factors and life processes associated with the onset of suicidal behavior during adolescence and early adulthood. *Psychological Medicine, 30*, 23–39.

Fingerman, K. (2000). "We had a nice little chat": Age and generational differences in mothers' and daughters' descriptions of enjoyable visits. *The Journals of Gerontology Series B: Psychological Sciences and Social Sciences, 55*, 95–106.

Fingerman, K. L., Chen, P., Hay, E., Cichy, K. E., & Lefkowitz, E. S. (2006). Ambivalent reactions in the parent and offspring relationship. *Journal of Gerontology: Psychological Sciences, 61B*, 152–160.

Fuligni, A. J., & Pedersen, S. (2002). Family obligation and the transition to young adulthood. *Developmental Psychology, 38*(5), 856–868.

Gonzales, N.A., Pitts, S.C., Hill, N.E. & Roosa, M.W. (2000). A mediational model of the impact of interparental conflict on child adjustment in a multiethnic, low-income sample. *Journal of Family Psychology, 14*(3), 365–379.

Goodman, S. H., & Gotlib, I. H. (1999). Risk for psychopathology in the children of depressed mothers: A developmental model for understanding mechanisms of transmission. *Psychological Review, 106*(3), 458–490.

Gottfried, A. E., Fleming, J. S., & Gottfried, A. W. (1998). Role of cognitively stimulating home environment in children's academic intrinsic motivation: A longitudinal study. *Child Development, 69*(5), 1448–1460.

Gottman, J. M., Katz, L. F., & Hooven, C. (1997). *Meta-emotion: How families communicate emotionally.* Hillsdale, NJ: Lawrence Erlbaum Associates.

Graves, P. L., Wang, N. Y., Mead, L. A., Johnson, J. V., & Klag, M. J. (1998). Youthful precursors of midlife social support. *Journal of Personality and Social Psychology, 74*, 1329–1336.

Grusec, J. E., & Davidov, M. (2007). Socialization in the family: The roles of parents. In J. E. Grusec & M. Davidov (Eds.), *Handbook of socialization: Theory and research* (pp. 284–308). New York: The Guilford Press.

Gunnar, M. R., & Donzella, B. (2002). Social regulation of the cortisol levels in early human development. *Psychoneuroendocrinology, 27*, 199–220.

Hajjar, I., & Duthie, E. (2001). Prevalence of elder abuse in the United States: A comparative report between the national and Wisconsin data. *Wisconsin Medical Journal, 100*, 22–26.

Heinicke, C. M. (2002). The transition to parenting. In M. H. Bornstein (Ed.), *Handbook of parenting* (2nd ed., pp. 363–388). Mahwah, NJ: Lawrence Erlbaum Associates.

Holt-Lunstad, J., Birmingham, W., & Jones, B. Q. (2008). Is there something unique about marriage? The relative impact of marital status, relationship quality, and network social support on ambulatory blood pressure and mental health. *Annals of Behavioral Medicine, 35*(2), 239–244.

Howe, G. W., Levy, M. L., & Caplan, R. D. (2004). Job loss and depressive symptoms in couples: Common stressors, stress transmission, or relationship disruption? *Journal of Family Psychology, 18*, 639–650.

Hughes, M. E., Waite, L. J., LaPierre, T. A., & Luo, Y. (2007). All in the family: The impact of caring of grandchildren on grandparents' health. *Journal of Gerontology: Social Sciences, 62B*, S108–S109.

Jaycox, L. H., & Repetti, R. L. (1993). Conflict in families and the psychological adjustment of preadolescent children. *Journal of Family Psychology, 7*, 344–355.

Jimerson, S., Egeland, B., Sroufe, A., & Carlson, B. (2000). A prospective longitudinal study of high school dropouts examining multiple predictors across development. *Journal of School Psychology, 38*, 525–549.

Johnson, J. G., Cohen, P., Kasen, S., Smailes, E., & Brook, J. S. (2001). Association of maladaptive parental behavior with psychiatric disorder among parents and their offspring. *Archives of General Psychiatry, 58*, 453–460.

Kaufman, J., Birmaher, B., Perel, J., Stull, S., Brent, D., Trubnick, L., et al. (1998). Serotonergic functioning in depressed abused children: Clinical and familial correlates. *Biological Psychology, 44*, 973–981.

Khaleque, A., & Rohner, R. P. (2002). Perceived parental acceptance-rejection and psychological adjustment: A meta-analysis of cross-cultural and intracultural studies. *Journal of Marriage and Family, 64*(1), 54–64.

Kiecolt-Glaser, J. K., & Newton, T. L. (2001). Marriage and health: His and hers. *Psychological Bulletin, 127*(4), 472–503.

Kim, K., & Smith, P. K. (1998). Retrospective survey of parental marital relations and child development. *International Journal of Behavioral Development, 22*, 729–751.

Kliewer, W., Fearnow, M. D., & Miller, P. A. (1996). Coping socialization in middle childhood: Tests of maternal and paternal influences. *Child Development, 67*(5), 2339–2357.

Klohnen, E. C., & Bera, S. (1998). Behavioral and experiential patterns of avoidantly and securely attached women across adulthood: A 31-year longitudinal perspective. *Journal of Personality and Social Psychology, 74*(1), 211–223.

Kochanska, G., & Thompson, R. A. (1997). The emergence and development of conscience in toddlerhood and early childhood. In J. E. Grusec & L. Kuczynski (Eds.), *Parenting and children's internalization of values: A contemporary theory* (pp. 53–77). New York: Wiley.

Kotchick, B. A., Shaffer, A., Forehand, R., & Miller, K. S. (2001). Adolescent sexual risk behavior: A multi-system perspective. *Clinical Psychology Review, 21*, 493–519.

Kwong, M. J., Bartholomew, K., Henderson, A. J. Z., & Trinke, S. J. (2003). The intergenerational transmission of relationship violence. *Journal of Family Psychology, 17*(3), 288–301.

Ladd, G. W., & Pettit, G. S. (2002). Parenting and the development of children's peer relationships. In M. H. Bornstein (Ed.), *Handbook of parenting* (2nd ed., pp. 269–310). Mahwah, NJ: Lawrence Erlbaum Associates.

Laible, D. J., & Thompson, R. A. (2007). Early socialization: A relational perspective. In J. Grusec & P. Hastings (Eds.), *Handbook of socialization* (Rev. Ed., pp. 181–207). New York: Guilford.

Lee, Y., Schneider, B., & Waite, L. J. (2003). Children and housework: Some unanswered questions. In K. B. Rosier & D. A. Kinney (Eds.), *Sociological studies of children and youth* (Vol. 9., pp. 105–125). New York: Elsevier Science.

Lichtenstein, P., Gatz, M., & Berg, S. (1998). A twin study of mortality after spousal bereavement. *Psychological Medicine, 28*, 635–643.

Logan, J., & Spitze, G. (1996). *Family ties: Enduring relations between parents and their grown children.* Philadelphia: Temple University Press.

Lowenstein, A., Katz, R., & Gur-Yaish, N. (2007). Reciprocity in parent-child exchange and life satisfaction among elderly: A cross-national perspective. *Journal of Social Issues, 63*, 865–883.

Lundberg, O. (1993). The impact of childhood living conditions on illness and mortality in adulthood. *Social Science Medicine, 36*, 1047–1052.

Lupien, S. J., King, S., Meaney, M. J., & McEwen, B. S. (2000). Child's stress hormone levels correlate with mother's socioeconomic status and depressive state. *Biological Psychiatry, 48*(10), 976–980.

Mancini, J. A., & Blieszner, R. (1989). Aging parents and adult children: Research themes in intergenerational relations. *Journal of Marriage and the Family, 51*(2), 275–290.

Margolin, G., Gordis, E. B., & Oliver, P. H. (2004). Links between marital and parent-child interactions: Moderating role of husband-to-wife aggression. *Development and Psychopathology, 16*, 753–771.

Margolin, G., Oliver, P. H., & Medina, A. M. (2001). Conceptual issues in understanding the relation between interparental conflict and child adjustment: Integrating developmental psychopathology and risk/resilience perspectives. In J. H. Grych & F. D. Fincham (Eds.), *Interparental conflict and child development: Theory, research, and applications* (pp. 9–38). New York: Cambridge University Press.

McCamish-Svensson, C., Samuelsson, G., Hagberg, B., Svensson, T., & Dehlin, O. (1999). Social relationships and health as predictors of life satisfaction in advanced old age: Results from a Swedish longitudinal study. *International Journal of Aging and Human Development, 48*, 301–324.

McEwen, B. S. (1998). Stress, adaptation, and disease: Allostasis and allostatic load. In S. M. McCann, J. M. Lipton, E. M. Sternberg, G. P. Chrousos, & P. W. Gold (Eds.), *International congress of the society for neuroimmunomodulation* (pp. 33–44). New York: New York Academy of Sciences.

McLanahan, S. S., & Carlson, M. J. (2002). Welfare reform, fertility, and father involvement. *The Future of Children, 12*(1), 147–165.

Mendle, J., Turkheimer, E., & Emery, R. E. (2007). Detrimental psychological outcomes associated with early pubertal timing in adolescent girls. *Developmental Review, 27*, 151–171.

Milevsky, A. (2005). Compensatory patterns of sibling support in emerging adulthood: Variations in loneliness, self-esteem, depression and life satisfaction. *Journal of Social and Personal Relationships, 22*(6), 743–755.

Miller, B. C., Benson, B., & Galbraith, K. A. (2001). Family relationships and adolescent pregnancy risk: A research synthesis. *Developmental Review, 21*, 1–38.

Montgomery, S. M., Bartley, M. J., & Wilkinson, R. G. (1997). Family conflict and slow growth. *Archives of Disease in Childhood, 77*, 326–330.

Moorman, S. M., Booth, A., & Fingerman, K. L. (2006). Women's romantic relationships after widowhood. *Journal of Family Issues, 27*, 1281–1304.

Moss, M. S., & Moss, S. Z. (1995). Death and bereavement. In R. Blieszner & V. H. Bedford (Eds.), *Aging and the family* (pp. 422–439). Westport, CT: Greenwood Publishing Group.

Mustanski, B. S., Chivers, M. L., & Bailey, J. M. (2002). A critical review of recent biological research on human sexual orientation. *Annual Review of Sex Research, 13,* 89–140.

Newcomb, M. D. (1997). Psychosocial predictors and consequences of drug use: A developmental perspective within a prospective study. *Journal of Addictive Diseases, 16,* 51–88.

O'Neil, R., & Parke, R. D. (2000). Family-peer relationships: The role of emotion regulation, cognitive understanding, and attentional processes as mediating processes. In K. A. Kerns, J. M. Contreras, & A. M. Neal-Barnett (Eds.), *Family and peers: Linking two social worlds* (pp. 195–225). Westport, CT: Praeger Publishers/Greenwood Publishing Group.

Parke, R. D., & Buriel, R. (2006). Socialization in the family: Ethnic and ecological perspectives. In N. Eisenberg, W. Damon, & R. M. Lerner (Eds.), *Handbook of child psychology: Social, emotional, and personality development* (Vol. 3, 6th ed., pp. 429–504). Hoboken, NJ: John Wiley & Sons.

Parke, R. D., & O'Neil, R. (1999). Social relationships across contexts: Family-peer linkages. In W. A. Collins & B. Laursen (Eds.), *Minnesota symposium on child psychology., Oct 1996, MN, US* (pp. 211–239). Mahwah, NJ: Lawrence Erlbaum Associates.

Patterson, G. R., & Fisher, P. A. (2002). Recent developments in our understanding of parenting: Bidirectional effects, causal models, and the search for parsimony. In M. H. Bornstein (Ed.), *Handbook of parenting: Practical issues in parenting* (Vol. 5, 2nd ed., pp. 59–88). Mahwah, NJ: Lawrence Erlbaum Associates.

Pendry, P., & Adam, E. K. (2007). Associations between parents' marital functioning, maternal parenting quality, maternal emotion and child cortisol levels. *International Journal of Behavioral Development, 31*(3), 218–231.

Perkins, D. F., & Hartless, G. (2002). An ecological risk-factor examination of suicide ideation and behavior of adolescents. *Journal of Adolescent Research, 17,* 3–26.

Pettit, G. S., Bates, J. E., & Dodge, K. A. (1993). Family interaction patterns and children's conduct problems at home and school: A longitudinal perspective. *School Psychology Review, 22*(3), 403–420.

Pillemer, K., & Suitor, J. J. (2002). Explaining mothers' ambivalence toward their adult children. *Journal of Marriage & Family, 64,* 602–613.

Pinderhughes, E. E., Dodge, K. A., Bates, J. E., Pettit, G. S., & Zelli, A. (2000). Discipline responses: Influences of parents' socioeconomic status, ethnicity, beliefs about parenting, stress, and cognitive-emotional processes. *Journal of Family Psychology. Special Issue: Cultural Variation in Families, 14*(3), 380–400.

Power, C., & Hertzman, C. (1997). Social and biological pathways linking early life and adult disease. *British Medical Bulletin, 53,* 210–221.

Prinstein, M. J., Boergers, J., Spirito, A., Little, T., & Grapentine, W. L. (2000). Peer functioning, family dysfunction, and psychological symptoms in a risk factor model for adolescent inpatients' suicidal ideation severity. *Journal of Clinical Child Psychology, 29,* 392–405.

Repetti, R. L., Taylor, S. E., & Saxbe, D. (2007). The influence of early socialization experiences on the development of biological systems. In J. Grusec & P. Hastings (Eds.), *Handbook of socialization: Theory and research* (pp. 124–152). New York: Guilford Publications.

Repetti, R. L., Taylor, S. E., & Seeman, T. E. (2002). Risky families: Family social environments and the mental and physical health of offspring. *Psychological Bulletin, 128*(2), 330–366.

Rini, C., Dunkel-Schetter, C., Hobel, C. J., Glynn, L. M., & Sandman, C. A. (2006). Effective social support: Antecedents and consequences of partner support during pregnancy. *Personal Relationships, 13,* 207–229.

Robles, T. F. & Kiecolt-Glaser (2003). The physiology of marriage: *Pathways to health. Physiology & Behavior, 79,* 409–416.

Rothbaum, F., Rosen, K. S., Pott, M., & Beatty, M. (1995). Early parent-child relationships and later problem behavior: A longitudinal study. *Merrill-Palmer Quarterly, 41*(2), 133–151.

Russek, L. G., & Schwartz, G. E. (1997). Feelings of parental caring can predict health status in midlife: A 35-year follow-up of the Harvard Mastery of Stress study. *Journal of Behavioral Medicine, 20,* 1–13.

Ryff, C. D., Schmutte, P. S., & Lee, Y. H. (1996). How children turn out: Implications for parental self-evaluation. In C. D. Ryff & M. M. Seltzer (Eds.), *The parental experience in midlife* (pp. 383–422). Chicago: University of Chicago Press.

Sander, J. B., & McCarty, C. A. (2005). Youth depression in the family context: Familial risk factors and models of treatment. *Clinical Child & Family Psychology Review, 8,* 203–219.

Savitz, D., & Dunkel-Schetter, C. (2007). Behavioral and psychosocial contributors to preterm birth. In R. E. Behrman & A. S. Butler (Eds.), *Preterm birth: Causes, consequences and prevention* (pp. 87–123). Washington, DC: National Academy Press.

Saxbe, D., & Repetti, R. L. (2009). Brief report: Fathers' and mothers' marital relationship predicts daughters' pubertal development two years later. *Journal of Adolescence, 32*(2), 415–423.

Saxbe, D., & Repetti, R. L. (2010). For better or worse? Coregulation of couples' cortisol levels and mood states. *Journal of Personality and Social Psychology, 98*(1), 92–103.

Schiamberg, L. B., & Gans, D. (2000). Elder abuse by adult children: An applied ecological framework for understanding contextual risk factors and the intergenerational character of quality of life. *International Journal of Aging and Human Development, 50*, 329–359.

Schulenberg, J. E., Vondracek, F. W., & Crouter, A. C. (1984). The influence of the family on vocational development. *Journal of Marriage and the Family, 46*(1), 129–143.

Semyonov, M., & Lewin-Epstein, N. (2001). Impact of parental transfers on living standards of married children. *Social Indicators Research, 54*(2), 115–137.

Shaffer, J. W., Duszynski, K. R., & Thomas, C. B. (1982). Family attitudes in youth as a possible precursor of cancer among physicians: A search for explanatory mechanisms. *Journal of Behavioral Medicine, 5*, 143–163.

Shonkoff, J. P., & Phillips, D. A. (Eds.). (2000). *From neurons to neighborhoods: The science of early childhood development.* Washington, DC: National Academy Press.

Slatcher, R. B., Robles, T. F., Repetti, R. L., & Fellows, M. D. in press. *Momentary work worries, marital disclosure and salivary cortisol among parents of young children.* Psychosomatic Medicine.

Slomkowski, C., Rende, R., Novak, S., Lloyd-Richardson, E., & Niaura, R. (2005). Siblings effects on smoking in adolescence: Evidence for social influence from a genetically informative design. *Society for the Study of Addiction, 100*, 430–438.

Smith, T. E. (1993). Growth in academic achievement and teaching younger siblings. *Social Psychology Quarterly, 56*, 77–85.

Snyder, J., Cramer, A., Afrank, J., & Patterson, G. R. (2005). The contributions of ineffective discipline and parental hostile attributions of child misbehavior to the development of conduct problems at home and school. *Developmental Psychology, 41*(1), 30–41.

Spangler, G., Schieche, M., Ilg, U., & Ackermann, C. (1994). Maternal sensitivity as an external organizer for biobehavioral regulation in infancy. *Developmental Psychobiology, 27*(7), 425–437.

Spohr, H. L., Willms, J., & Steinhausen, H. C. (1993). Prenatal alcohol exposure and long-term developmental consequences. *The Lancet, 341*(8850), 907–910.

Steel, J. L., & Herlitz, C. A. (2005). The association between childhood and adolescent sexual abuse and proxies for sexual risk behavior: A random sample of the general population of Sweden. *Child Abuse & Neglect, 29*, 1141–1153.

Steinberg, L., & Morris, A. S. (2001). Adolescent development. *Annual Review of Psychology, 52*, 83–110.

Stormshak, E. A., Bierman, K. L., McMahon, R. J., Lengua, L. J., & Conduct Problems Prevention Research Group. (2000). Parenting practices and child disruptive behavior problems in early elementary school. *Journal of Clinical Child Psychology, 29*(1), 17–29.

Strom, S. (2003). Unemployment and families: A review of research. *Social Service Review, 77*, 399–430.

Szinovacz, M. E., & DeViney, S. (2000). Marital characteristics and retirement decisions. *Research on Aging, 22*, 470–498.

Szinovacz, M. E., DeViney, S., & Davey, A. (2001). Influences of family obligations and relationships on retirement: Variations by gender, race, and marital status. *Journals of Gerontology: Series B: Psychological Sciences and Social Science, 56*, 20–27.

Szinovacz, M. E., & Ekerdt, D. J. (1995). Families and retirement. In R. Blieszner & V. H. Bedford (Eds.), *Aging and the family* (pp. 375–400). Westport, CT: Greenwood Publishing Group.

Taylor, S. E., Way, B. M., Welch, W. T., Hilmert, C. J., Lehman, B. J., & Eisenberger, N. I. (2006). Early family environment, current adversity, and the serotonin transporter promoter polymorphism, and depressive symptomatology. *Biological Psychiatry, 60*, 671–676.

Tracy, J. L., Shaver, P. L., Albino, A. W., & Cooper, M. L. (2003). Attachment styles and adolescent sexuality. In P. Florsheim (Ed.), *Adolescent romantic relations and sexual behavior: Theory, research, and practical implications* (pp. 137–160). Hillsdale, NJ: Lawrence Earlbaum.

Troxel, W. M., & Matthews, K. A. (2004). What are the costs of marital conflict and dissolution to children's physical health? *Clinical Child and Family Psychology Review, 7*(1), 29–57.

Valiente, C., Fabes, R. A., Eisenberg, N., & Spinrad, T. L. (2004). The relations of parental expressivity and support to children's coping with daily stress. *Journal of Family Psychology, 18*(1), 97–106.

Van Volkom, M. (2006). Sibling relationships in middle and older adulthood. *Marriage & Family Review, 40,* 151–170.

Vuchinich, S., Bank, L., & Patterson, G. R. (1992). Parenting, peers, and the stability of antisocial behavior in preadolescent boys. *Developmental Psychology, 28*(3), 510–521.

Waern, M., Rubenowitz, E., & Wilhelmson, K. (2003). Predictors of suicide in the old elderly. *Gerontology, 49,* 328–334.

Walker, E. A., Gelfand, A., Katon, W. J., Koss, M. P., Von Korff, M., Bernstein, D., et al. (1999). Adult health status of women with histories of childhood abuse and neglect. *The American Journal of Medicine, 107*(4), 332–339.

Westling, E., Andrews, J. A., Hampson, S. E., & Peterson, M. (2008). Pubertal timing and substance use: The effects of gender, parental monitoring and deviant peers. *Journal of Adolescent Health, 42,* 555–563.

Whiston, S. C., & Keller, B. K. (2004). The influences of the family of origin on career development: A review and analysis. *The Counseling Psychologist, 32*(4), 493–568.

Widom, C. S., & White, H. R. (1997). Problem behaviours in abused and neglected children grown up: Prevalence and co-occurrence of substance abuse, crime, and violence. *Criminal Behaviour and Mental Health, 7,* 287–310.

Wills, T. A., & Yaeger, A. M. (2003). Family factors and adolescent substance use: Models and mechanisms. *Current Directions in Psychological Science, 12,* 222–226.

Windle, M., Spear, L. P., Fuligni, A. J., Angold, A., Brown, J. D., Pine, D., et al. (2008). Transitions into underage and problem drinking: Developmental processes and mechanisms between 10 and 15 years of age. *Pediatrics, 121,* 273–289.

Wintre, M. G., & Yaffe, M. (2000). First-year students' adjustment to university life as a function of relationships with parents. *Journal of Adolescent Research, 15*(1), 9–37.

Wood, J. J., & Repetti, R. L. (2004). What gets dad involved? A longitudinal study of change in parental child caregiving involvement. *Journal of Family Psychology, 18,* 237–249.

Zarit, S. H., & Eggebeen, D. J. (2002). Parent-child relationships in adulthood and later years. In M. H. Bornstein (Ed.), *Handbook of parenting* (2nd ed., pp. 135–164). Mahwah, NJ: Lawrence Erlbaum Associates.

Zeanah, C. H., Nelson, C. A., Fox, N. A., Smyke, A. T., Marshall, P., Parker, S. W., et al. (2003). Designing research to study the effects of institutionalization on brain and behavioral development: The Bucharest Early Intervention Project. *Development and Psychopathology, 15,* 885–907.

LIFE-SPAN DEVELOPMENT AND INTERNATIONAL MIGRATION

30

Steven J. Gold and Ramona Fruja Amthor

This chapter concerns how life-span development is transformed when individuals, families, and groups move from one national location to another. While biological, physiological, and psychological processes are clearly important, they are the province of other disciplines. As Sigelman and Shaffer (1995) explain, among the multidisciplinary contributions to understanding life-span development, sociology offers an exploration of the "the exosystem," the nature of society and the individual's interaction with it. As sociologists, therefore, we concentrate here upon the collective impact of social, economic cultural, social psychological, political, and familial forces that shape the life-span development of international migrants.

Most sociologists believe that social structures are far more powerful in determining lives than are individual choices (Mayer, 2004). Therefore, considering "immigrants," generically, and the life span is an immensely complex endeavor that is shaped not just by individuals, but also varies according to many social factors including historical context, demographics, economic and legislative factors, legal status (documented vs. undocumented), human and social capital, and gender. The impact of immigration on development across the life span is thus an interplay between the personal characteristics of the immigrant and the social and institutional characteristics of the host society.

Sociological and historical literature on immigration has traditionally stressed the assimilationist model, whereby immigrants were assumed to cope with the new environment by abandoning inured outlooks and practices in favor of those of the host society. Hence, the value of pre-migration social practices and resources to life in the host society was either ignored or denigrated (Foner, Rumbaut, & Gold, 2000). Scholars further assumed it would take immigrants several generations to adapt to the social practices and institutional patterns of the host society (Gordon, 1964; Park, 1950). Accordingly, immigrants and their American-born children resided in enclaves, isolated rural communities and urban villages, were expected to take years or even generations to cast off the mores and cultural practices of the country of origin.

However, since the 1970s, students of international migration have increasingly attended to the positive effects of migrants' social and cultural practices in the new setting. Consequently, they have noted that incorporation takes place much more rapidly, with immigrant children and the second generation becoming fully immersed in the culture and language of the host society (Portes & Rumbaut, 2006). Research reveals that immigrants possess various social and cultural means that allow them to survive, compete and even succeed in points of settlement. For example, immigrants' work ethic, value for education, strong families, health practices, low rates of criminality, communal solidarity, entrepreneurial propensity, and minimal dependence on public assistance have been identified as valuable resources for coping with life in the new environment (Glazer & Moynihan, 1963; Light, 1984; Light & Gold, 2000; Zhou & Bankston, 1998). By noting the utility of skills, resources and social forms that immigrants bring with them, we can appreciate the potential for life-span development generated by immigration.

The effect of migration on human lives can thus be understood as the consequence of a combination of opportunities and costs that, in turn, shape life-span development. Benefits are created by taking advantage of new opportunities; costs involve losses imposed by moving, the need to relearn social knowledge, as well as the absence of expected options that become unavailable in the new context. In many cases, the relationship between the opportunities and costs associated with migration is quite complex. Moreover, subgroups of a given national or ethnic population experience distinct outcomes according to their social and demographic characteristics. For example, voluntary immigrants who are younger, have more skills and resources, and enter positive contexts of reception tend to enjoy the greatest advancement and encounter the fewest disadvantages. In contrast, refugees and other reluctant migrants, such as the elderly, as well as those with fewer skills and resources and those who enter hostile environments, often encounter difficulties, including status loss, downward mobility, discrimination, an inability to fulfill basic needs, and difficulties in communicating with members of the larger society. Thus, ready generalizations about "immigrant experiences" and their impact on life-span development are, in fact, hard to come by.

Focusing on U.S.-based migration (while also offering some relevant international examples), this chapter centers on the intersections between immigration and life span both according to interconnected key sociological variables (class factors, generation, gender and family, cross-cultural adaptation and interaction, political-institutional factors) and points in the life course. While individual personality or social roles do not evolve neatly through sequential age-linked stages, the age at the time of migration, the length of time since migration and the particular developmental tasks the immigrant is dealing with are all important (Berry, Phinney, Sam, & Vedder, 2006). Moreover, Stewart and Healy (1989) argue that historical events—and, we could add, life-altering events such as international migration—might affect individuals at different stages of development differently. Sociohistorical events happening during childhood are likely to influence a person's fundamental assumptions about life and the world, while those occurring during later adolescence (and early adulthood) will impact conscious identity. Conversely, social historical events that occur in the adult years will most likely have less impact on identity and values but will have an impact on available opportunities.

■ SOCIAL CLASS AND MIGRATION

We begin with a consideration of class and migration, since in the view of most sociologists, social class (defined in terms of income, wealth, education, and status) is among the most important determinants of life chances and, as it will become apparent throughout this chapter, it weaves into all other aspects of immigrant adaptation and development. Today's immigrants' class distribution follows an hourglass configuration, with a fraction being more educated than the U.S. population as a whole and another group being less educated (Bean & Stevens, 2003; Smith & Edmonston, 1997)—this distribution is significant in complicating the often one-sided perspectives of immigrant success, where examples of highly successful or down-trodden individuals and groups are portrayed.

A large fraction of working class migrants reside in segregated neighborhoods that affect them across the life span, beginning with poor schools, limited employment opportunities and low incomes, as well as separation from the more mainstream, native-born middle class. Many are active in the informal economy to make ends meet. This employment status denies them benefits and makes them subject to exploitation (Tienda & Raijman, 2000). The largest single immigrant nationality, Mexicans, are much less educated than most other immigrant groups or the U.S. population, with 70% of mid-1990s arrivals having less than a high school education (Portes & Rumbaut, 2006). While those who arrived as young children and those born in the Unites States do somewhat better than their parents, they still have relatively low levels of educational achievement and limited job prospects.

In contrast, highly educated, professional, and entrepreneurial immigrants often have access to the skills, resources, and legal status that allow them to join the native-born middle to upper class soon after arrival. [Many countries, including the United States, give skilled immigrants and investors special status (Marger & Hoffman, 1992)]. Such skills and resources also allow them to maintain ties in many countries simultaneously, including the country of origin. For example, Min Zhou's work shows how relatively affluent groups like Koreans and Chinese who own businesses and property and have political influence create ethnic enclaves (even if they don't live in them) and maintain ethnic and cultural associations, educational institutions, "cram schools"—that provide extra tutoring for their children—and the like. These pass class-based benefits on to the younger generation. In contrast, working-class immigrants generally lack the financial and cultural resources to do this, even as their communities are characterized by high population density (Bean & Stevens, 2003; Zhou, Lee, Agius Vallejo, Tafoya-Estrada, & Sao Xiong, 2008).

The social class environment into which immigrants settle determines the extent to which the adoption of host society social norms will foster or restrict mobility (Zhou, 1997a; Zhou & Bankston, 1998). From this perspective, a significant body of research has found that immigrant youth often adopt the cultural and economic orientation of their native-born, co-ethnic peers. As such, the effects of assimilation on economic mobility vary in terms of the class, racial, and ethnic context in which it occurs. Since a significant fraction of contemporary migrants are non-Whites, they are often steered into communities already occupied by people that, according to host society standards, share a common racial identity (Waters, 1999). Further, since race and class often overlap in the United States, racial sorting often means that migrants' phenotype determines the kind of neighborhood in which they settle: Black immigrants live among native Blacks; Latinos with Latinos; both in generally impoverished neighborhoods. Asians, who are somewhat less constrained by residential segregation and whose numbers include a larger middle-class component, reveal more diversity in their locations of settlement (Louie, 2004; Portes & Rumbaut, 2006). (For further discussion on this issue see the *Immigrant Youth* section.)

▦ FIRST, SECOND, AND 1.5 GENERATIONS AND MIGRATION

In addition to class standing, the concept of "generation" is essential to understanding immigrants' experiences. There are multiple ways to conceptualize this notion, with its meanings spanning both micro and macro levels of analysis. Most commonly, immigration sociologists have used it as a macrolevel, intrafamily, concept to examine how immigrants adapt, acculturate, and integrate over time and compare the first generation with their offspring. This interest was prompted by the children of post-1965 immigrants who are known as "the new second generation" and are examined in now-classic longitudinal studies, such as the Children of Immigrants Longitudinal Study whose impetus was that a new generation of Americans raised in immigrant families has been coming of age (Portes & Rumbaut, 2001).

The study thus followed the progress of over 5,000 teenagers representing 77 nationalities in two key settlement areas—Southern California and South Florida. The selected students were immigrant children, that is, U.S.-born youth with at least one foreign-born parent, or those who were themselves foreign-born and had immigrated before age 12. The sample represents the generational lines that sociologists employ—*first-generation* immigrants are born abroad, where they spend at least their childhoods and receive the foundations of their education and cultural exposure. Members of the *1.5 generation* are born abroad but arrive in their new country prior to the age of 12, thus being exposed to the new country's culture and formal schooling during their formative years. *Second-generation* youth are born in the new country to foreign-born parents. This study, and the later Longitudinal Immigrant Student Adaptation study that followed a comparatively smaller sample, attempted to understand the generational adaptation from multiple perspectives, including family situation, academic achievement and aspirations, language use and preferences, identity formation, and psychological and social adjustment. Generally, when making generational comparisons, the 1.5- and second-generation immigrants are best able to take full advantage of the opportunities available in the new country, regardless of initially pessimistic prognostications about second-generation decline. The first generation, benefits from a dual frame of reference, which involves the comparison of their current circumstances with those in the native country (Ogbu, 1991). For voluntary immigrants who purposefully left to seek a better life, optimism (Kao & Tienda, 1995) comes more easily in the new context even when conditions turn out to be less ideal than previously imagined. Data from the National Education Longitudinal Study also confirm that, even when controlling for structural and family background variables, immigrant and second-generation youth are more likely than their third (or later)-generation peers to complete secondary school and go on to postsecondary education (Glick & White, 2004). Nevertheless, newcomers often struggle more to learn English, an area in which the 1.5 and second-generation immigrants certainly have an advantage.

Also, sobering reports show that personal health, both psychological and physical, declines with length of residence in the host society. In what has been termed "the immigrant health paradox," researchers found that while immigrants are healthier than their native-born counterparts upon arrival, as they become more assimilated, their health declines even as their income and language skills increase (Suarez-Orozco, 2000).

The second generation and beyond lack access to benefits associated with a comparative frame of reference, but citizenship recognition, more consistent exposure to English (which often yields a positive effect on cognitive abilities), and easier identification with the new culture make their integration less difficult. All these variables, however, need to be analytically connected to the local contexts of reception where possible anti-immigrant sentiments, especially when reflected in different service-providing policies and language requirements, can cause resentment among migrants who wish for and have the right to be recognized justly as full members of the hostland.

A second conceptualization of generation at the macrolevel considers how common experiences in youth (often surrounding key historical events) can create shared frames of reference and affect worldview and political outlooks later in life (Eckstein & Barberia, 2002). This can explain why immigrants from common national origins can have very different experiences in the new country, depending on the time of migration, its correlation with larger sociopolitical contexts, and their own perspectives on the immigration process.

CULTURAL DIFFERENCES

The "culture shock" of migration has an impact on life-span development as country of origin norms often do not apply in the host society. Cultural changes are almost always a source of difficulty in varying degrees, even if less so for immigrants who are already familiar with the language, social practices, and economic life of the host society. Migrants competent in the host society culture are likely to have more positive experiences and do so sooner than those who must make significant adjustments. Research on immigrants and "social axioms"—the prevailing shared beliefs that generate a culture's scripts and guide individuals' behavior—has shown that a lack of knowledge of the new social axioms has a negative impact on social adaptation. More specifically, it has been found that knowing the new culture's prevailing social axioms contributes more to adaptation than do actual similarity between the newcomers' axioms and those of the majority culture (Kurman & Ronen-Eilon, 2004).

While groups' experiences will vary, some of the major areas of friction between new immigrants and the U.S. context of reception have to do with tensions between individualism and collectivism (Buki, Ma, Strom, & Strom, 2003; Kagitcibasi, 1996), family members' responsibilities, including those of the young toward parents (Phinney, Ong, & Madden, 2000), and perceptions of local attitudes that they regard as anti-family and anti-education. Moreover, what is considered to be an appropriate pace of maturation and acceptance of the responsibilities of adulthood varies considerably among different nationalities. When immigrant youth adopt the extended adolescence and delayed initiation of careers common in the United States, tensions between parents and children may be exacerbated due to clashing expectations about the life course.

Cross-cultural differences are doubtlessly crucial in considering immigrants' adaptation and overall well-being in the new context. However, assertions about the social influence of culture should be made with due caution for several reasons. First, culture is not static. To place two cultures in stark opposition often means overlooking evolving similarities that are products of a common context and intergroup inter-actions. The very presence of immigrants changes the face of communities and the norms that govern them (Ainslie, 1998; Alba & Nee, 1997). Second, cultural differences, as important as they are, can sometimes be emphasized to the extent that economic, political, and institutional factors, which shape immigrants' life chances, are ignored. One such formulation, the lingering "culture of poverty" thesis (Lewis, 1962), asserts that certain groups are guided by behavioral repertoires that preclude achievement and economic progress in favor of immediate gratification. Another—the Asian "model minority" thesis—contends that due to cultural heritage, Asian immigrants and their children are always successful. Such cultural arguments mask the diverse experi-ences of ethnically defined groups, while discouraging the creation of ameliorative social policies. Since success and failure are attributed to cultural inheritance rather than malleable contextual and environmental conditions, adherents of cultural deter-minism reject social reform as a futile project (Hernstein & Murray, 1994).

The contrast between Cubans and Puerto Ricans in the United States offers insight in how structural constraints can be obscured by cultural arguments. Cubans are often depicted as highly successful, while Puerto Ricans are seen as mired in poverty, even though culturally, the two groups are very similar in terms of language, religion, diet, and so on. Upon closer scrutiny, one realizes that structural differences among the groups may account for their contrasting fates in the United States, rather than culture. Key among these are class origins (earlier waves of Cuban immigrants were upper middle class, while Puerto Ricans are predominantly working class); points of settlement (Cubans in economically dynamic South Florida, Puerto Ricans in New York, where there are relatively few working class jobs), and race (many of the Cuban immigrants are White, while many of the Puerto Ricans are Black and hence subject to discrimination). These examples remind us that as we examine immigrants' development in their new society, culture and structural elements need to be maintained in balance.

FAMILY AND GENDER

Transformations associated with family and gender significantly affect life-span development, but the impacts are often complex, according to migrants' age, class, cul-tural background, and the residential location of family members. Early research on immigration focused on male labor migrants. Accordingly, the experience of migrant women and families received little analysis. More recently, however, issues of gender and family have become one of the major topics of investigation in migration studies. This is warranted because since the 1940s, the number of women migrants has been roughly equal to that of men (Pedraza, 1991; Zlotnick, 2003).

Research has shown that families make vital decision about migration and pro-vide members with resources and demands in both the country of origin and the point of resettlement. Funds are also exchanged between both locations. Accordingly, some scholars now argue that migration is better understood as a family process than one involving individuals, as has been the traditional focus of neoclassical economics (Kibria, 1993; Lauby & Stark, 1988; Massey et al., 1993; Taylor, 1999).

Despite the fact that immigration can be understood as familial activity, family relations are not always egalitarian and smoothly cooperative as some theorists have assumed. Instead, power, decision-making, work, and reward are often distributed differentially along the lines of gender, birth order, marital status, age, and generation. In a series of studies of Mexican immigrants in California, sociologist Pierrette Hondagneu-Sotelo (1992; 1994) has contributed to this knowledge by documenting the complex arrangements that complicate sometimes-romanticized notions of immigrant families: "Operating under the implicit assumption of the household model— that all resources, including social ones are shared equally among household and family members... [some] studies imply that married women automatically benefit from their husbands' social resources and expertise" (p. 396). However, research suggests that women—whether migrating alone or with families—often have very different resources, concerns, and reactions to migration than men, and accordingly, follow distinct adaptive strategies (Andezian, 1986; Dallalfar, 1994; DiLeonardo, 1984; Kibria, 1993; Min, 1998; Tenenbaum, 1993; Zhou & Logan, 1989). "Men and women in the same family may use different network resources, sometimes at cross purposes. These networks are significant for both migration processes and settlement outcomes" (Hondagneu-Sotelo, 1992, p. 396). It is thus essential that gender, as an analytic tool, be considered carefully in the intersections of migration and life-span development for both women and men.

Several studies assert that men's identity and positive sense of self are most strongly associated with paid employment, and especially with job-related earnings and prestige, while their work also offers them social networks. Women, in contrast, have multiple sources of identity, reflecting their concern with important relationships and income (Gabaccia, 1994; Hondagneu-Sotelo, 1992). Men and women may thus evaluate successful adaptation according to distinct criteria and the differentiation in their satisfaction sources, coupled with choices over division of labor, also reveals a paradox: women's desire for meaningful relationships as an adaptive strategy can also be a source of challenges, frustration, and isolation when they have less access to environments and networks outside the home. At the same time, women may also gain more power due to more egalitarian policies (including a prohibition on domestic violence), more demand for women's work and the ability to study, earn money, and travel outside the home, which is limited in many countries of origin (Grasmuck & Pessar, 1991; Kibria, 1993; Min, 1998; Smith, 2005).

Nevertheless, while women and girls often find increased opportunities, they must also conform to traditional expectations, and so perform a "second shift" of domestic work in addition to duties associated with work and education (Gabbacia, 1994; Min, 1998; Zhou & Bankston, 1998). Further, norms associated with sexual propriety and being chaste are enforced differentially according to the sexual double standard, yielding what Diane Wolf calls "transnational pressures." As a consequence, girls must conform to outlooks retained from the country of origin, while also earning money and achieving academically in a manner possible in the host society (Espiritu, 2003; Wolf, 1997). This range of duties is not imposed upon boys, who enjoy more leisure time and fewer constraints (Smith, 2005).

Among working class groups, women may want to remain in the host society to take advantage of increased power, enhanced freedom, and better life chances for their children. In contrast, their husbands may wish to return home, where discrimination is less and male privilege is greater (Grasmuck & Pessar, 1991). In middle-class groups, men sometimes use their greater earning power to control women, who are charged with completing domestic tasks and upholding traditional social practices in an unfamiliar environment without supportive friends and relatives (Dallalfar, 1994; Gold, 2002; Lev-Ari, 2008). In some of these cases, it is the women who wish to return home.

Scholars, activists, and resettlement staff often encourage immigrant women to take advantage of the greater degree of power available to women in the United States to "free" themselves from patriarchical constraints and oppression associated with their cultural origins (Ong, 2002). However, researchers who closely observe relations within immigrant families generally reject this strategy as simplistic. While accepting that immigrant women do encounter conflicts with co-ethnic men, Gabaccia (1994) argues that resources are also available to them in the ethnic family and community: "Immigrant women resembled women of America's racial minorities in viewing family ties as resources supporting female power and ethnic solidarity" (p. xv). Moreover, the fact that some ethnic traditions may stress unequal gender arrangements does not mean that ethnic families always maintain them. "Kinship also facilitated women's struggles against culturally specific traditions of misogyny" (Gabaccia, 1994, p. xv). Despite the importance of women's efforts to the achievement of economic survival, research suggests that family earnings are seldom shared equally. Several studies have argued that while women's labor makes ethnic families more affluent, the increased affluence and leisure time generated by female labor often accrue to men and that ethnic enclave employment is most exploitative of women (Gilbertson, 1995). However, this conclusion contrasts with other findings (see Dallalfar, 1994; Zhou, 1992). For example, in their study of earnings in New York's Chinatown, Zhou and Logan (1989) argued: "Viewed from an individualistic perspective, the enclave labor market appears exploitative of women. But we must remember that Chinese culture gives priority not to individual achievement but to the welfare of the family and community...female labor force participation is part of a family strategy" (p. 818). A similar sentiment is expressed in Fernández-Kelly and Garcia's quote from a Cuban woman who contributes to family coffers through home work in the garment industry: "It is foolish to give up your place as a mother and wife only to go take orders from men who aren't even part of your family. What's so liberated about that? It is better to see your husband succeed and to know you have supported one another" (Fernández-Kelly & García, 1990, p. 146).

Research reports a range of male reactions to migration. In contrast to their less-educated counterparts, highly skilled male immigrants tend to achieve impressive earnings (Bean & Stevens, 2003). However, despite the reality of male privilege, young men, too, encounter difficulties in adjusting to the United States. A fairly large body of work suggests that a combination of factors including greater availability of jobs and education for women, employer preferences, laws against domestic violence, a greater degree of gender equality than in countries of origin and more racial discrimination against young men of color yields greater marginality for less-skilled male migrants in the United States (Smith, 2005; Waldinger & Lichter, 2003). More difficult adaptation is especially challenging among racialized, undocumented and poor groups (Portes & Rumbaut, 2006; Smith, 2005; Zhou & Bankston, 1998).

Immigrant males are noted to be more often involved in oppositional culture than immigrant females (Zhou & Bankston, 1998). They are also regarded to be threatening by police, teachers, and employers and as such have lower rates of school graduation and higher rates of criminality and incarceration (Gans, 1992, Wilson, 1996). [One exception are Cambodian males who excel in schools despite their status as forced migrants, their lack of familiarity with Western culture and urban life and their attendance in poorly funded schools (Garcia Coll, Szalacha, & Palacios, 2005)]. On the other hand, some immigrant males are sometimes brutalized because they are not "tough enough." For example, in a study of immigrant youth in New York and Boston, Qin, Way, and Rana (2008) found that high-achieving Chinese immigrant males are singled out for hostile treatment by native-born students because of their small stature, studious attitudes, and behavioral styles that diverge from local forms of masculinity.

In sum, a considerable degree of the transformation of life-span development wrought by migration is a consequence of the complex ways by which moving to a new country alters the social expectations and resources associated with families, generations, and genders.

▨ CONTEXT OF RECEPTION: POLITICAL, INSTITUTIONAL, AND PERSONAL FACTORS

Immigrant adaptation cannot be attributed to immigrant characteristics alone. Institutions, both governmental and nongovernmental, facilitate the integration of immigrants through access to citizenship and its rights to benefits and to an equitable, bias-free life. Similarly, personal factors such as the presence of co-ethnic communities and the general response of the native-born population toward immigrants form the sociopolitic context of reception and thus affect immigrants' overall adaptation. Portes and Rumbaut (2006) refer to three contexts as crucial for determining the social and economic fate of migrant groups in the United States: the receiving government's immigration policies; the host society's labor market conditions (implicitly, the stereotypes through which locals view immigrants as workers) and the nature of the migrants' co-ethnic community. Each can have a neutral, positive, or negative impact on the immigrant population and its long-term prospects, both materially and psychologically, through the powerful symbols and actuality of recognition, prospects for advancement, belonging, and safety.

While there is a history of anti-immigrant movements in the United States, most research suggests that the social and economic impact of immigrants on American life has been highly positive (Fix & Passell, 1994). The popular imaginary in a nation generates different narratives about the place and reception deserved by immigrants (Bean & Stevens, 2003), often corresponding to the country's economic situation at particular times and with the socially constructed perceptions of what immigrants have to offer based on their origin, level of education and work training, and ethic. An overall welcoming environment may be troubled by concerns among native-born that the newly arrived members of their society cannot truly integrate because of their perceived vast cultural differences or because of their unwillingness to do so. However, both historical evidence and current studies show the contrary. For example, earlier waves of immigrants from countries different from those of the original settlers—such as the Irish or the South-Eastern Europeans—have become an integral part of American society despite the fact that they were originally considered incompatible with the standing and orientations of the country. At present, the large-scale studies of immigrant children conducted by Hernandez, Denton, and Macartney (2008) also highlight the immigrants' deep and permanent roots in the United States. Among immigrant children (those with at least one foreign-born parent), 64% have U.S.-citizen parents and 55% live in family-owned homes. This counters the popular fear that today's eligible immigrants do not naturalize and implicitly show reluctance toward integration.

In fact, the past 50 years have witnessed a tremendous growth in the number of persons choosing to become naturalized American citizens (Migration Policy Institute, 2008). While naturalization entails a fairly complex bureaucratic process that could present obstacles (North, 1987), current policy is more inclusive than in any time in the nation's history. Regardless of race, religion, or country of origin, lawful permanent residents older than age 18 are eligible for American citizenship through naturalization. While only children of immigrants born on U.S. territory automatically become citizens (and those born elsewhere do not automatically naturalize when their parents do), immigrant youth are eligible to apply themselves once they meet the age and residence requirements. Age also becomes a factor for older applicants for whom language requirements are waived if they are older than 55 years and have been living in United States as permanent residents for at least 15 years (or are older than 50 years, residing as permanent residents in the United States for 20 years). Moreover, changes implemented in the naturalization exam since 2008 have been presented as an attempt to further ensure the equity of the process through a more thorough standardization across the country's naturalization centers.

At the same time, however, these changes have raised questions about naturalization's accessibility to those of limited means (due to the increased application fee) and those with less education (due to the different nature of the civics questions). This is especially important since the state offers little integration support once immigrants are admitted (Bloemraad, 2002), does not foster the creation of local organizations that can assist newcomers and provides virtually no assistance to learn the language, acquire civics knowledge, and understand cultural norms. This lack of resources for the integration of voluntary newcomers exemplifies how governments can affect immigrants' well-being even in the absence of specific interventionist policy (and by limiting themselves to the implementation of protective policies such as anti-discrimination laws). Such support would be especially important for older immigrants who have not had the opportunity of sociocultural exposure and gradual integration.

The positive reception of immigrants, both at an institutional and personal level, is important because the groups that enjoy positive or at least neutral contexts of reception are likely to encounter very different experiences of life-span development—with more opportunities for work and education, the possibility of living in more desirable neighborhoods, more extensive chances to participate in the larger society and enhanced prospects for their children. In contrast, groups encountering a negative context of reception will have fewer advantages. Such differentiation in their life trajectories manifests itself not only in terms of the measurable quantities of economic integration, but also—and sometimes especially—in the more subjective aspects of belonging, identification with their context of reception, and overall psychological well-being over time.

▨ IMMIGRATION AT DIFFERENT POINTS IN THE LIFE SPAN: IMMIGRANT CHILDREN AND YOUTH

Systematic attention to the particular experiences of children and youth in the immigration process (rather than focusing on adults alone) is comparatively new, with interest growing in the last 15 years. As Mary Levitt's work in the *Students from Other Lands* project emphasizes, immigration has diverse ramifications across generations within the family system and it is important to look at the ways immigration is experienced differently by children and adults (Levitt, 2003). Attention to children is also crucial both because developmental and acculturative changes happen simultaneously, and because it coincides with demographic changes indicating that children in immigrant families are the fastest growing population of children. Indeed, 20% of children younger than age 18 in the United States are either immigrants themselves or the children of immigrants.

Although quick generalizations about the immigration experience should be avoided, processes of transition from a culture to another, and existing simultaneously in the home culture and that of the new country, afford these youth many similar challenges and possibilities. The focus is generally placed on challenges, in an effort to better serve these youth, especially since children are generally more stressed by the immigration experience than their parents (Levitt, 2003). However, it is also essential that they not be victimized. In fact, newer studies begin to reveal some counterintuitive findings about the adaptation of immigrant youth and the automatically negative impact of immigration on their adaptation and development.

For example, the *International Comparative Study of Ethnocultural Youth* suggests a great deal of variation in acculturation strategies and adaptation. Berry, Phinney, Sam, and Vedder (2006) report the findings of a large-scale study of 5000 adolescents in 13 countries that examined psychological and sociocultural adaptation. Findings suggest that, overall, immigrant youth showed slightly fewer psychological problems, behavior problems and better school adjustment, compared to national peers, but did not differ in self-esteem and life satisfaction. Interestingly, immigrants appeared to be better adapted socioculturally, but were similar to their native-born peers in psychological adaptation. Similarly, a large-scale study on a nationally representative sample of over 13,000 children found that even with greater socioeconomic disadvantages, children in recent immigrant families showed lower levels of emotional-behavioral problems and higher levels of academic performance (Georgiades, Boyle, & Duku, 2007).

The idea of the immigrant paradox thus emerged—the counterintuitive finding that immigrants could show better adaptation than native peers, even in light of the expectation that immigrants will inevitably face adaptation problems due to their bi-cultural living. The paradox also refers to the fact that adaptation seems to decline in the second generation, approaching the level of the native-born or tracking even lower. According to Berry and colleagues' findings, the immigrant paradox was supported in some cases and not in others, depending on the context of reception, as well. While some may be skeptical about the suggested ease involved in immigrant youth transitions, a key finding of this research is that while there did not appear to be big differences between the immigrants and the national samples, there were large variations within immigrant groups themselves. In turn, these differences depend on how the acculturation process takes place for each individual.

Indeed, negative outcomes for immigrant youth can be avoided (e.g., Berry & Sam, 1997), although there is a very high poverty rate among immigrant children. In 2002, 23% of the children of immigrants—and 29% of children who are immigrants themselves—lived in families with incomes below poverty. Recent studies across very long stretches of the lifetime (e.g., Laub & Sampson, 2003), albeit outside the realm of immigration, challenge the premise of trajectories set early in life and continuing relatively unaffected by external factors.

However, Mayer (2009) shows that in such areas as health, labor market behavior, affective relationships between parents and children, and learning motivation, early determinants appear more lasting. Moreover, there is also evidence that initial adaptation can deteriorate over time, increasing for example, school dropout rates (e.g., Garcia Coll et al., 2005; Perreira, Harris, & Lee, 2006). Therefore, since studies that look closely at the lives of immigrant youth show that negative outcomes and transition difficulties can and do occur, the focus of research is often placed on revealing these challenges.

That immigration is one of the most stressful human experiences is, informally exemplified by countless personal anecdotes and media coverage, as well as supported formally through extensive, cross-disciplinary research (e.g., Aronowitz, 1984; Choi, Meininger, & Roberts, 2006; Igoa, 1995; Suarez-Orozco & Suarez-Orozco, 2001; Zhou, 1997b). Focusing especially on immigrant children and youth, this accumulated work reveals specific stress-precipitating factors that span the youth's sociocultural domains in the new society. Attention to all these domains and how they interact in the developmental process is important since youth function in multiple overlapping contexts (Phelan, Davidson, & Yu, 1993) such as family, school, with peers, and in religious communities. Depending on the mode of migration, these patterns of adaptation begin even before the move itself and have long-lasting effects, especially in the case of forced migration, as refugees often experience violence-induced trauma leading to post traumatic stress disorder, anxiety, and depression (Craig, Sossou, Schnak, & Essex, 2008; Rothe et al., 2002; Volkan, 1993; Westermeyer & Wahmanholm, 1996). However, stress-inducing factors associated with immigration are not limited to refugees alone, but manifest themselves, albeit differently, in the case of voluntary migrants as well.

The role and place of children in the migration process was initially overlooked, but more recently, the many variables associated with their presence have made the subject of fairly large-scale research (e.g., Faulstich Orellana, Thorne, Chee, & Lam, 2001) and point out complex relational and adaptation dynamics. Separation occurs frequently in immigrant families, as parents leave children in the country of origin because of the cost of raising them abroad and in order to protect them from violence, gangs and alien cultural forms. Often parents leave one or more of the children in the care of extended family members or boarding schools (Hondagneu-Sotelo & Avila, 1997; Portes, Guarnizo, & Landolt, 1999) in hopes of later reunification. Of the 385 early adolescents in the bicoastal Longitudinal Immigrant Student Adaptation study, 85% experienced separation from one or both parents for extended periods of time (Suarez-Orozco, Todorova, & Louie, 2002). New ways of communication increase the possibility of maintaining transnational connection. Technology-facilitated relationships, however, and even the remittances parents send back to their homes cannot replace parental presence for the children. Meanwhile, the children become the connective tissue that maintains these transnational families.

Separation times can vary (sometimes amounting to years) and children often get attached to their temporary caretakers. Then, they have to experience new separation at the time when their own immigration is finally possible, only to find that family reunification can bring its own challenges (Falicov, 2002). They need to adapt to new family dynamics, as they often encounter new family members—siblings or parental figures—that have been added to the family in their absence. Moreover, youth who become reunited with their families but remain undocumented, naturally continue to experience fear of separation in case of apprehension, and such perpetual anxiety takes a high toll on their much-needed sense of stability and thus on their well-being.

Immigration transitions impact children's development in important ways, since these changes occur at the time when these children acquire the cognitive, affective, and communicative competencies characteristic of members of their culture, as well as the ability to manifest them in culturally appropriate ways. These sociocultural scripts undergo ruptures in the immigration process, as children and youth are thrust into new contexts where their previous scripts can no longer offer them the sense of predictability they usually offer the members of a culture. It is not surprising that those who immigrate as adolescents often experience a more difficult adaptation than younger immigrants (Beale Spenser & Dornbusch, 1990).

The norms of the family and those of the new society are often at odds—in fact, the reality of familial and intergenerational tensions that eventually occur between the members of immigrant families is one of the better-documented aspects of the immigration experience. Tensions arise as youth find they need to fulfill expected familial roles, while simultaneously being accepted into the larger culture by their peers and acquiring new cultural fluency (Garcia Coll & Magnuson, 1997). Their contact with the receiving culture most often happens at a higher rate than that of the parents, and they learn norms more rapidly (Portes & Rumbaut, 2001; Suarez-Orozco, Todorova, & Qin, 2006), as well as the language (e.g., Olsen, 2000; Qin, 2006; Wong Fillmore, 2005). This offers them skills, opportunities, and confidence and often turns them into cultural guides for other family members (Faulstich Orellana, 2003), because the parents often work with co-ethnics and as such are distant from mainstream American culture.

In recent years, children have been portrayed as producers—or at least as coproducers—of their own development, with an open direction of influence between socialization agents and children (Mayer, 2004). This is especially salient in the case of immigrant youth. Paradoxically, the role reversals children experience can deprive them of parental guidance in the new context. This may cause resentment among the older generation, as children may be increasingly socialized by the mass media, popular culture, and peer groups. In turn, this only distances them more from the advice that parents are able to give them according to the norms of their culture of origin.

How children negotiate these often conflicting expectations plays an important role in their adaptation and development, since parent–child relations are known to be strong predictors of child adjustment (Parke & Buriel, 2006; Steinberg, 2001). Caught in this reinforcing pattern, some take counterproductive and possibly self-destructive trajectories, especially if they are already exposed, as many of them are, to the negative contexts of segregated and impoverished neighborhoods, violence and gang activity. In fact, where immigrant families settle strongly shapes the experiences and adaptation of these youth, as those with few resources can easily end up isolated from the middle class, the cultural mainstream, and strong schools. Crosnoe (2005), for instance, showed that Mexican-origin young children were more likely to be overrepresented in problematic schools, even when family background differences were taken into account. Academically, this affected their mathematics achievement. In addition, mental health and interpersonal functioning were often at lower levels in such schools.

In contrast, other immigrant children fare much better, doing well academically and even outperforming their native-born peers. However, a disturbing trend that has emerged even among them is a discrepancy between academic performance and overall psychological well-being (Qin, 2008; Wolf, 1997). These youth struggle with inter-generational and inter-cultural tensions, as well as the pressures of functioning well in school environments that come with their own challenges—language barriers, cross-cultural conflicts, bullying, and even teachers who, although well-intentioned, often lack the resources and training to work with an increasingly diverse student body. Many immigrant youth have to perpetually cross the boundaries of often discontinuous sociocultural domains, as they connect home, peer, and school cultures to succeed. In building pathways across seemingly separate communities to prepare for college, Cooper, Dominguez, and Rosas (2005) have shown that the transition from childhood into adolescence is the critical time when the children's paths *toward* or *away from* a university education diverge. Therefore, this is the time when guidance, intervention and mentorship are necessary for positive outcomes.

In this bridging process, immigrant children also undergo a nuanced process of identity formation, which is described as the central developmental task in adolescence (Erickson, 1968). Close attention to identity formation and processes of social mirroring becomes essential, because too much cultural dissonance, negative messages from the context of reception and role confusion impact the youth's sense of self and adaptability (Suarez-Orozco, 2000). Depending on the sociocultural dynamics they experience, youth can, in general terms, become mostly attached to their ethnic group, show bicultural efficacy or forgo their ethnic identity. Social competence in both cultures has shown to be the healthier, more advantageous path for the youth who develop these flexible capacities. But being able to do so, and thus developing a fruitful sense of ethnic identity depends on the intersection of the individual's desire for an ethnic identification and the positive possibilities of recognition allowed by the larger context of reception (Phinney, Romero, Nava, & Huang, 2001).

Young Adult Immigrants

Young or "early adulthood" (Furstenberg, Cook, Sampson, & Slap, 2002) marks a time of continued individuation, separation from family, interacting within new contexts such as higher education, the work place, marriage, and parenthood. All of these generate additional roles and, with them, multiple relationships that need to be negotiated. These transitions apply regardless of one's native or immigrant status, but for young immigrants, coping with such situations can be indicative of successful adaptation. [In fact, ethnic/racial identity formation and acculturation, school and work, marriage and family, civic and political participation are among the categories investigated by Kasinitz, Mollenkopf, Waters, and Holdaway (2008) in their groundbreaking *Inheriting the City*, a large-scale study of the transitions to adulthood of post-1965 immigrants' children in New York.] While adolescence has typically been associated with identity formation and "coming into one's own," transitions into adulthood are culturally variable (Dasen & Mishra, 2000; Rogoff, 2003). Industrial societies increasingly foster an extended adolescence. Consequently, the age at which one is expected and considered capable of assuming adult roles has shifted and increased dramatically in the last century, in relation to the enhanced expectation and availability of schooling (Arnett, 2004).

In these new contexts, the gap between biological and social maturation can make for an especially difficult time. This disjuncture can be even greater in the case of immigrants (Ready, 2001) especially when their primary socialization in the family or ethnic community differs drastically from their secondary socialization in school and the work place. While most research on early adulthood has focused on White, native-born youth, especially in the middle class, scholars who have examined these transitions in the lives of immigrant youth (e.g., Kasinitz, Mollenkopf, Waters, & Holdaway, 2008; Ready, 2001; Smith, 2002, 2005;) reveal the importance of examining how immigration intersects with developmental and adaptation processes beyond adolescence. An understanding of immigrants' transitions to higher education or the workforce needs to consider how ethnicity, gender, and social class interact with the conditions of the labor market and schooling, as well as how immigrant families navigate and react to new means of adjusting to early adulthood.

For example, for the years K-12, public education is freely available to immigrant children regardless of their legal status. However, once they turn eighteen, undocumented status becomes a major obstacle. This is not only because they do not have access to financial resources required to pay tuition, which is generally charged at the out-of-state rate, but further because college attendance requires documentation of legal resident status. Therefore, even if undocumented immigrant youth do well academically, they soon reach an obstacle that severely frustrates their life plans in the new knowledge economy, and can leave them with complex feelings of resentment and resignation.

In terms of life trajectories, whether adolescents from immigrant families make a successful transition to adulthood depends on their educational achievement, their acquisition of employable skills and abilities, and their physical and mental health (Fuligni & Hardway, 2004). Educational outcomes are key to the social and economic mobility of young adult immigrants because today's segmented labor market can eventually limit opportunities for those with low levels of formal education (Gans, 1992; Portes & Zhou, 1993). Nevertheless, many immigrants who struggle academically leave school without the equipping they need to succeed in a highly competitive economy (Murnane, 1996).

Scholars who observed this pattern of differential opportunities for success, coupled with changes in the structure of opportunity developed the highly influential theory of "segmented assimilation" (Portes & Zhou, 1993; Zhou, 1999). The theory postulated that while earlier waves of immigrants assimilated progressively and irreversibly into the mainstream, many of the post-1965 immigrants would instead take different trajectories of integration available to them based on such factors as national origin, socioeconomic status, family resources, patterns of racial segregation and the way they are received in the United States. Accordingly, immigrants become part of different segments of society, and the perception of steady upward mobility across several generations was questioned for those with fewer resources, lower human capital and stigmatized racial characteristics (Borjas, 1999). It was replaced with notions of downward assimilation or second-generation decline (Gans, 1992) and socialization into oppositional identities by native minority youth in the impoverished areas where the poorer immigrants settle. At the same time, immigrant youth settling in middle-class areas with good schools encountered unprecedented levels of upward mobility, facilitated by the removal of discriminatory patterns in education and employment that were prevalent prior to the 1960s (Bean & Stevens, 2003; Kim, 2004; Portes & Rumbaut, 2006).

Despite initial prognostication regarding segmented assimilation and second-generation decline, there is more recent research that offers evidence of varied passages into adulthood and complicates predominantly grim prospects (Alba & Nee, 2003; Kasinitz et al., 2008). Nevertheless, there are continuing concerns regarding the experiences of second-generation young adults who are coming of age in contexts quite different from those under study (generally large a metropolis with a dynamic economy and more openness to immigrants, like New York). For example, the effects of post civil rights-era institutions helping minorities in school and work have aided children of immigrants to be upwardly mobile. Children of immigrants in the United States almost universally surpass their parents. In the *Inheriting the City* study, from educational and occupational achievement to earnings and labor force participation, each immigrant second-generation group studied was found to be upwardly mobile both in comparison to its first-generation parents and to its native-born reference group (Kasinitz et al., 2008).

Their "Second-Generation Advantage" theory posits that growing up, children of immigrant groups select and combine the best traits from their parents' ethnic culture and American culture to advance at school and work, thus providing the second generation a wider range of options than either immigrants or established members of the host society. Instead of descending into an urban underclass, these grown children of immigrants use immigrant advantages to avoid some of the obstacles that native minority groups cannot. Their speaking English and working in jobs that resemble those held by native New Yorkers their age show them as integrating into the mainstream with more ease than anticipated. Alternatively, when immigrant children assimilate into racialized "underclass" settings where schools are poor, job opportunities are limited and enthusiasm for schoolwork is berated as "selling out" or "acting white," retaining the mobility-oriented outlook and "adherence to traditional family values" associated with the immigrant culture may enhance life chances: "In such a situation, ethnicity itself can be a resource; indeed it may be the only resource available" (Zhou & Bankston, 1994, p. 843). For instance, in her research with West Indians, Waters (1999) found that those who had more resources purposefully maintained their accents and reminders of their non-native born identities, so that in the racialized structures of the new society, they would be less likely to encounter discrimination or be steered toward disadvantaged groups and contexts.

Also, other choices that may be associated with socialization in different networks—such as the time of marriage and child bearing—have an impact on life trajectories. While family formation is often attributed to a group's values [and the timing of this choice is one of the variables associated with the differential success of immigrant groups], scholars remind us that due to racial and economic characteristics, groups have differential access to neighborhoods, and thus to the kind of schools their children attend. In turn, the ability to attend better, more resourceful schools may contribute to higher educational attainment and postponement of family formation. It is important to maintain a broader view on the development of life trajectories as immigrants move through young adulthood and the complex interplay of forces in their lives.

Understanding how immigrant young adults undertake multiple memberships and make sense of their identity facilitates our understanding of how they draw on these affiliations in their adaptation processes to the new society. In addition to its other facets that accompany role transitions into adulthood, identity formation in the case of immigrants contains an important aspect of ethnic identity development whose negotiation is essential to their full member integration. Ethnic identities data collected through census categories appear static, and previous work on immigrants' ethnic identity showed the possibility of "reactive ethnicity"—the choice to identify to a greater extent with the country of origin and home culture as a means of symbolically (and even spatially, through ethnic enclaves) separate one's self from the hostility and denigration of the host society. However, more recent research, such as the in-depth interviews conducted by Kasinitz and his colleagues (2008) show that among second-generation young adults (at least those in an immigrant-friendly metropolitan area), identity choices are more fluid and contextual, with roots and consequences that go beyond subjectivity alone. Ethnic group membership also implies access to resources, settlement in different neighborhoods, and reliance on co-ethnic communities with different levels of institutional support. These factors can be both positive and negative, as they can both facilitate and restrict wider social membership as well as opportunities for socioeconomic mobility.

In considering these issues, it is best to avoid some of the extremes of the immigrant transition continuum, with immigrant youth being portrayed as either in despair or with rather glamorized, flexible identities that permit them to transcend social and economic obstacles. Although the resilience of immigrants is often celebrated, the admittedly difficult experiences of transition can also be rendered in terms that stigmatize the youth with too much emphasis on negative experiences. Psychological interpretations of these youth's development can do the same when the emphasis is on the ambivalence of multiple cultural menus or the diminished ties that "may result in an acute sense of alienation and impermanence" (Arnett, 2002, p. 778).

At the other end of the spectrum, immigrant youth in an era of globalization are often too easily depicted as bearing romanticized transcultural identities, or are allegedly part of "most people of the world now [because they] develop a bicultural identity" (Arnett, 2002, p. 778). Transnationalism, transculturalism, and global citizenship have become tempting labels in this age of intense movement, but under the surface of their appeal, lie the realities of economic and political structures, personal orientations and ways of human adaptation and sense-making, which are not always as glamorous. The realities of many immigrants' lives show, in fact, that "the notion of transnational identity or a transnational cultural space is quite exaggerated" (Waters, 1999). Even when they are possible, these patterns of cultural hybridity often pose specific problems that affect young and older immigrants alike.

Adult Immigrants

Developmentally, the adult years are filled with both the greatest achievement and the greatest stresses. For immigrants, the balance between them depends, once again, on many social factors. While life structures may have many, diverse components,

Levinson (1986) explains that only one or two components can occupy a central place in the structure. Family and occupation are most often the central components of adult life, with variations in their relative weight and in the importance of other components. This is especially evident in the case of immigrants, who often migrate for better socio-economic opportunities, family reunification and better life-chances for the young. Since the central components are those that have the greatest significance for the self and the evolving life course, they receive the largest share of the individual's time and energy. Thus in the case of adult immigrants, we will also focus on work, family and the connections between them.

Adult immigrants play central roles in making decisions about migration and, in most cases, they drive the family's process of migration. [A significant exception to this are so-called "parachute kids," those select foreign youth who come to study in the United States, maintaining transnational ties with their families, and often generating a micro-scale chain-migration through family reunification; see, e.g., Min, 1998; Zhou, 1998).] At least initially, single migrants often remain tied to their families back home, sending remittances and visiting often (Massey, Goldring, & Durand, 1994). Once established in the new location, they generally create border-spanning networks by bringing spouses, children, parents and other relatives, and friends to the point of settlement (Gold, 2005). They also establish links with co-ethnics and others persons in the host society. When this occurs, migrants' remittance-sending tends to reduce and with it, efforts devoted to maintaining a transnational existence.

However, families from diverse nationalities (Dominicans, Israelis, Trinidadians, Puerto-Ricans, Taiwanese, Indians, Haitians) still maintain transnational networks that shuttle members between the United States and the country of origin in order to maximize economic opportunities, expose children to multiple cultural environments, attend to economic holdings, stay connected to families and access an optimal mix of educational and health services. Nevertheless, with all its benefits, transnational responsibilities can also be a source of considerable financial and emotional drain on immigrant workers, especially those with less education and fewer economic means. (For more on transnational families see section on *Immigrant Children and Youth*.)

Trajectories across adulthood often are shaped by migrants' social characteristics – their educational level, gender, and family status—as well as conditions in the host society. Massey, Alarcon, Durand, & Gonzalez (1987), Piore (1979), and many others describe single males as the most common first-wave migrants, but young women also account for significant numbers of contemporary migrants (Gabaccia, 1994; Hondagneu-Sotelo, 1994; Pedraza, 1991), especially since some countries (e.g., the Philippines), produce far greater numbers of female than male emigrants (NSCB, 2007).

Immigrants with more financial and educational resources may use international educational programs as a means of travelling to and establishing ties with the host society. For these, permanent residence may be acquired through employers who sponsor their applications for a work visa. Regardless of their social class, immigrant adults sometimes become disillusioned because of family conflict, alienation from life in the host society or discrimination. Nevertheless, skilled, professional and entrepreneurial adults generally find migration to be less insecure and arduous and more financially rewarding than those with fewer skills and resources. In the new location, skilled migrants find enhanced economic opportunities, satisfying work, an improved standard of living, and improved conditions for their children and a welcome relief from social demands and conflicts associated with the country of origin (Borjas, 1990; Gold, 2003; Marger & Hoffman, 1992; Nonini & Ong, 1997). As a case in point, Soviet Jewish women interviewed by Gold (1995) in the 1990s generally found raising children to be easier in the United States than it was in their country of origin.

The tendency of immigrant parents to take calculated actions that benefit their children is revealed in economic research. Chiswick (1988) discovered that Jews, Chinese, Japanese, and Caribbeans who maintained behaviors involving low fertility, urban residence, relatively high education and low labor force participation rates by mothers when children are small, did especially well with regard to "schooling, earnings and rates of return from schooling" (p. 590) for offspring as compared to other ethnic groups not following these behaviors. This pattern reflects "parental investments (implicit and explicit) in the home-produced component of child quality" and appears to be an especially successful means for the intergenerational transfer of assets (Chiswick, 1988, p. 590).

At times, skilled migrants who received specialized training in the country of origin may be unable to pursue the same careers in the United States as their credentials are not officially recognized. Or, if they can, they often need to complete more extensive training and education to qualify for employment in the United States. Work and the ability to find both fulfillment and sustenance in it are intricately connected to people's sense of self in the adult years, and dealing with radical changes in these aspects of life of can be very difficult. Still, because of a combination of sociocultural factors, immigrants are less likely than natives to seek and receive counseling. For example, results from the National Latino and Asian American study showed that Asian immigrants used mental-health related services less than their American-born counterparts and overall, both Latinos and Asians demonstrated lower rates of use of any type of mental health-related service, compared to the general population (Abe-Kim et al., 2007). Some research suggests that this pattern is not due to less need, but rather because of the stigma associated with mental health problems in certain immigrant groups' cultures (Gold, 1995; Portes & Rumbaut, 2006).

Migrant parents will often sacrifice their own future for that of their kids—settling to work hard in dirty and undesirable "immigrant jobs," like light manufacturing, cab driver, janitor, domestic worker, laborer, and food service. They often struggle with language and cultural difficulties so that their offspring can obtain an education and a brighter future than that available in the country of origin (Dinnerstein, Nichols, & Riemers, 1990; Waters, 1999). Parents who were professionals prior to migration sometimes become shopkeepers or service workers in the point of settlement in order to earn a living (Gold, 1995; Lessinger, 1995; Min, 1996, 1998).

While immigrant entrepreneurs have traditionally relied on their children's labor to make their businesses succeed (Glazer & Moynihan, 1963; Goldscheidier & Kobrin, 1980), contemporary immigrant entrepreneurs often limit their children's involvement with businesses, hoping that higher education will lead to a more prestigious occupation (Gold, 1989; Kim, 2004; Song, 1999). In the short term, this makes for more work for the older generation and more time away from their children, but also allows youth to devote themselves to academic pursuits (Gold, 1995; Min, 1996). When parents have consciously decided to make sacrifices for their children, they can evaluate those choices and the access to enhanced opportunities associated with the new environment. In contrast, their children, who are the beneficiaries of such sacrifice, are forced to deal with the social transformations that their parents' actions yielded (Qin, 2008; Song, 1999) without having a fuller understanding of the larger picture. They often find adjustment to be quite challenging, yet are obliged to express only gratitude (Gold, 2003; Song, 1999) for the sacrifices that were made for their sake. This can cause both psychological difficulties for the young and enhance the level of tension and stress in family relationships.

At the same time, the pursuit of a higher education that the young have access to often benefits the adults as well. For example, several studies of the Korean-American community note how immigrants who grew up in the United States, and hence are familiar with the English language and American social practices, play vital roles in helping the entrepreneurially successful but inwardly directed first generation develop political resources that are essential for addressing conflicts with American customers, government officials, landlords, labor unions, wholesalers and the like (Chung, 2007; Min, 2008; Yoon, 1997). The losses and the gains of these choices then can often be balanced.

The often difficult choices made by immigrant adults to invest in the two major components of occupation and family reflect, in a sense, the selection-optimization-compensation model articulated by Freund and Baltes (2000). They argue that people, individually and collectively, master their lives through an orchestration of selection, optimization, and compensation, to maximize gains and minimize losses. Throughout the lifespan, opportunities and constraints specify a range of alternative domains of functioning.

From this large number of options, individuals, in collaboration with other forces, select a subset on which to focus their resources, find means to optimally set and reach goals, and invest resources into counteracting losses and compensate for them when they happen. As exemplified in the lives of immigrants, what means are best for optimization and compensation depends on individual situations as well as on the context in which these individuals are functioning.

Older Immigrants

As the balance between gains and losses changes during the life-course, old age is associated with more losses, both because of steady decline in physical and sometimes mental capacity, but also because of social norms in specific contexts and what is expected of the elderly and their roles. In a positive perspective, scholars have argued that aging is many times characterized simply by continuities in relationships, work, and commitments, rather than turning points or crises (Berger, 1994). Nevertheless, when older age and immigration intersect, challenges cannot always be cast in the positive light of personal growth, even if personal trajectories are not always grim. Aged immigrants do often encounter difficulty in their efforts to adapt to the host society, since they lose social contacts, have a hard time learning the new language, and experience difficulty in adjusting to the new social and cultural environment. In fact, relatively few elderly people choose to migrate on their own. Rather, they do so to accompany younger relatives over whom they often have less authority than in the country of origin (Foner, 1997; Gold, 1995). The largest groups of elderly migrants are associated with refugee populations like Soviet Jews (in the United States and Israel) and Cubans (in the United States) because their countries of origin required the exit of entire families (ORR, 1989).

Because of older migrants' difficulties in adjusting to the host society, they are frequently forced into early retirement. This is a problematic situation, given that paid work and formal volunteering reduce the rate mental health decline in later life (Hao, 2008). In contrast, being "continuously" retired is related to greater depressive symptoms among men (Kim & Moen, 2002). Such obstacles are encountered even by well-educated individuals. For example, while the young Soviet émigré adults that Gold (1995) interviewed did relatively well in the job market, older migrants described having a harder time. Because they received their education prior to the mid-1970s, when computers and other modern technology were first introduced in the USSR, their training was seen as outdated by U.S. employers. Finally, these refugees sometimes faced age discrimination and had problems with English. Despite their advanced degrees, many had to abandon their prior occupations and survive on meager refugee benefits or support themselves through undesirable and poorly paid jobs, such as factory worker or home-care attendant (Gold, 1995; Orleck, 1999). Alternatively, they can depend on their own adult children for support—especially Asian and Central and Southern Americans were found more likely to live in households in which their adult children provide most of the income (Glick & Van Hook, 2002)—and often feel isolated if co-ethnic groups are not easily accessible. One memorable example is of an elderly Russian man who complained to his daughter that his daily isolation in her condominium was as miserable an experience as that he endured in Stalin's camps during the 1930s (Gold, 1995).

Fortunately, the fate of elderly migrants is not universally dismal. Even those residing near few co-ethnics can adapt well, especially when they take advantage of services available to them, such as community English courses. There, they can connect with others in their situation, establish new friendships and thus maintain a sense of independence that is still vital for adaptive transitions into old age. When co-ethnic enclaves are available, elderly immigrants often remain attached to them so that they can socialize and consume services in a familiar cultural and linguistic environment. This can be isolating from the mainstream population, but many who settle in co-ethnic neighborhoods develop an active social life. In fact, the presence of numerous elderly Russian refugees who stroll daily in streets and parks in the communities where they settled is credited with making neighborhoods much safer in Brooklyn, Los Angeles, and other American cities. Accustomed to winters in Moscow and St. Petersburg, the hardy refugees remained undaunted by the U.S. climate, hence their salutary influence on public space was largely uninterrupted by seasonal changes (Markowitz, 1993; Orleck, 1999). Elderly immigrants also provide child care and other forms of assistance to their children and grandchildren. Their presence and ability to thus impact others can affect positively their sense of self-worth and the possibility to continue contributing to society and leave a worthy legacy for the next generation—aspects that are of high concern at this stage.

FUTURE DIRECTIONS IN THE STUDY OF MIGRATION AND LIFE-SPAN DEVELOPMENT

This review suggests that international migration's impact on life-span development is a very complex issue, yielding distinct outcomes for individuals and groups according to their own characteristics (age, educational level, gender, class, cultural background, racial identity, work experience) as well as the context of resettlement (economic conditions, integration and citizenship policies, presence of coethnic populations, discriminatory practices).

While there is clearly an important relationship between immigration and lifespan development, and recent research has focused on the experiences and coming of age of immigrant children, little if any research has been devoted to explicitly examining the impact of immigration across the lifespan. Accordingly, our major suggestion for future research is for scholars with expertise in these two areas to work together to explore how changing national settings alters human lives.

In many countries, immigrant children and the children of immigrants now account for a significant fraction of the entire population of young people. As a consequence, the experience of these children has become a central topic of investigation among sociologists and practitioners of related disciplines, including anthropology, psychology, education, history, and child development. Because this realm of study offers a promising venue for the exploration of the relationship between international migration and lifespan development, we encourage scholars involved in these studies of the new second generation to integrate these two fields of investigation. Through integrated studies, basic information about how immigrants with diverse social characteristics are making their way in a wide array of circumstances might be obtained. These findings could then be applied to develop a more refined understanding of the manner in which immigration shapes lifespan development and how receiving institutions may be better prepared to meet immigrants' needs over time.

▮ REFERENCES

Abe-Kim, J., Takeuchi, D. T., Hong, S., Zane, N., Sue, S., Spencer, M. S., et al. (2007). Use of mental health-related services among immigrant and U.S. born Asian Americans: Results from the National Latino and Asian American Study. *American Journal of Public Health, 97*, 91–98.

Ainslie, R. C. (1998). Cultural mourning, immigration, and engagement: Vignettes from the Mexican experience. In M. Suarez-Orozco (Ed.), *Crossings: Immigration and the socio-cultural remaking of the North American Space* (pp. 283–300). Cambridge, MA: Harvard University Press.

Alba, R., & Nee, V. (1997). Rethinking assimilation theory for a new era of immigration. *International Migration Review, 31*, 826–874.

Alba, R., & Nee, V. (2003). *Remaking the American mainstream: Assimilation and contemporary immigration.* Cambridge, MA: Harvard University Press.

Andezian, S. (1986). Women's roles in organizing symbolic life. In R. J. Simon & C. B. Brettell (Eds.), *International migration: The female experience* (pp. 254–265). Totowa, NJ: Rowman.

Arnett, J. J. (2002). The psychology of globalization. *American Psychologist, 57*, 774–783.

Arnett, J. J. (2004). *Emerging adulthood.* New York: Oxford University Press.

Aronowitz, M. (1984). The social and emotional adjustment of immigrant children: A review of the literature. *International Migration Review, 18*, 237–257.

Beale Spenser, M., & Dornbusch, S. M. (1990). Challenges in studying minority youths. In S. S. Feldman & G. R. Elliott (Eds.), *At the threshold: The developing adolescent* (pp. 123–146). Cambridge, MA: Harvard University Press.

Bean, F., & Stevens, G. (2003). *America's newcomers and the dynamics of diversity.* New York: Russell Sage Foundation.

Berger, K. S. (1994). *The developing person throughout the life span.* New York: Worth.

Berry, J., Phinney, J., Sam D., & Vedder, P. (2006) *Immigrant youth in cultural transition: acculturation, identity, and adaptation across national contexts.* New York: Routlege.

Berry, J., & Sam, D. (1997). Acculturation and adaptation. In J. Berry, M. Segall, & C. Kagitcibasi (Eds.), *Handbook of cross-cultural psychology, Volume 3: Social Behavior and applications* (pp. 291–326). Boston: Allyn & Bacon.

Bloemraad, I. (2002). The North American Naturalization Gap: An Institutional Approach to Citizenship Acquisition in the United States and Canada. *International Migration Review 36*, 193–228.

Borjas, G. (1990). *Friends or strangers: The impact of immigrants on the U.S. economy*. New York: Basic Books.

Borjas, G. (1999). *Heaven's door: Immigration policy and the American economy*. Princeton, NJ: Princeton University Press.

Buki, L., Ma, T. C., Strom, R., & Strom, S. K. (2003). Chinese immigrant mothers of adolescents: Self-perceptions of acculturation effects on parenting. *Cultural Diversity and Ethnic Minority Psychology, 9*, 127–140.

Chiswick, B. R. (1988). Differences in education and earnings across racial and ethnic groups: Tastes, discrimination, and investments in child quality. *Quarterly Journal of Economics, 103*, 590–591.

Choi, H., Meininger, J. C., & Roberts, R. E. (2006). Ethnic differences in adolescents' mental distress, social stress and resources. *Adolescence, 41*, 163–283.

Chung, A. Y. (2007). *Legacies of struggle: Conflict and cooperation in Korean American politics*. Stanford, CA: Stanford University Press.

Cooper, C. R., Dominguez, E., & Rosas, S. (2005). Soledad's dream: How immigrant children bridge their multiple words and build pathways to college. In C. R. Cooper, C. T. García Coll, W. T. Bartko, H. M. Davis, & C. Chatman (Eds.), *Developmental pathways through middle childhood: Rethinking context and diversity as resources* (pp. 235–260). Mahwah, NJ: Lawrence Erlbaum Associates.

Craig, B. D., Sossou, M. A., Schnak, M., & Essex, H. (2008). Complicated grief and its relationship to mental health and well-being among Bosnian refugees after resettlement in the United States: Implications for practice, policy, and research. *Traumatology, 14*, 103–115.

Crosnoe, R. (2005). Double disadvantage or signs of resilience?: The elementary school contexts of children from mexican immigrant families. *American Educational Research Journal 42*, 269–303.

Dallalfar, A. (1994). Iranian women as immigrant entrepreneurs. *Gender and Society, 8*, 541–561.

Dasen, P. R., & Mishra, R. C. (2000). Cross-cultural views on human development in the third millennium. *International Journal of Behavioral Development, 24*, 428–434.

Di Leonardo, M. (1984). *The varieties of ethnic experience*. Ithaca, NY: Cornell UP.

Dinnerstein, L., Nichols, R. L., & Riemers, D. M. (1990). *Natives and strangers: Blacks, Indians and immigrants in America* (2nd ed.). New York: Oxford University Press.

Eckstein, S., & Barberia, L. (2002). Grounding immigrant generations in history: Cuban Americans and their transnational ties. *International Migration Review, 36*, 799–837.

Erikson, E. H. (1968). *Identity: Youth and crisis*. New York: Norton.

Espiritu, Y. L. (2003). Gender and labor in Asian immigrant families. In P. Hondagneu-Sotelo (Ed.), *Gender and U.S. immigration: Contemporary trends* (pp. 81–100). Berkeley: University of California Press.

Falicov, C. J. (2002). Ambiguous loss: Risk and resilience in Latino immigrant families. In M. M. Suárez-Orozco & M. Páez (Eds.), *Latinos: Remaking America* (pp. 274–288). Berkeley, CA, and Cambridge, MA: University of California Press and David Rockefeller Center for Latin American Studies.

Faulstich Orellana, M., Thorne, B., Chee, A., & Lam, W. S. E. (2001). Transnational childhoods: The participation of children in processes of family migration. *Social Problems, 48*, 572–591.

Faulstich Orellana, M. (2003). Responsibilities of children in Latino immigrant homes. *New Directions for Youth Development*, 100, 25–39.

Fernández-Kelly, M. P., & García, A. M. (1990). Power surrendered, power restored: The politics of work and family among Hispanic garment workers in California and Florida. In L. A. Tilly & P. Gurin (Eds.), *Women, politics, and change* (pp. 130–152). New York: Russell Sage.

Fix, M., & Passel, J. S. (1994). *Immigration and immigrants: Setting the record straight*. Washington, D.C: The Urban Institute.

Foner, N. (1997). The immigrant family: Cultural legacies and cultural changes. *International Migration Review, 31*, 961–974.

Foner, N., Rumbaut, R. G., & Gold, S. J. (Eds.). (2000). Immigration and immigration research in the United States. In N. Foner, R. G. Rumbaut, & S. J. Gold (Eds.), *Immigration Research for a New Century: Multidisciplinary Perspectives* (pp. 1–19). New York: Russell Sage Foundation.

Freund, A. M., & Baltes, P. B. (2000). The orchestration of selection, optimization, and compensation: An action-theoretical conceptualization of a theory of developmental regulation. In W. J. Perrig

& A. Grob (Eds.), *Control of human behavior, mental processes, and consciousness* (pp. 35–58). Mahwah, NJ: Erlbaum.

Fuligni, A. J., & Hardway, C. (2004). Preparing diverse adolescents for the transition to adulthood. *The Future of Children, 14*(2) 99–119.

Furstenberg, F., Cook, T. Sampson, R., & Slap, G. (2002). Preface. Early adulthood in cross- national perspective. *Annals of the American Academy of Political and Social Science, 580,* 6–15.

Gabaccia, D. (1994). *From the other side: Women, gender, and immigrant life in the U.S., 1820–1990.* Bloomington, IN: Indiana University Press.

Gans, H. (1992). Second generation decline: Scenarios for the economic and ethnic futures of the post-1965 American immigrants. *Ethnic and Racial Studies, 15,* 173–192.

Garcia Coll, C., & Magnuson, K. (1997). The psychological experience of immigration: A developmental perspective. In A. Booth, A. C. Crouter, & N. Landale (Eds.), *Immigration and the family: Research and policy on U.S. immigrants* (pp. 91–132). Mahwah, NJ: Lawrence Erlbaum Associates.

Garcia Coll, C. T., Szalacha, L. A., & Palacios, N. (2005). Children of Dominican, Portuguese, and Cambodian immigrant families: Academic attitudes and pathways during middle childhood. In C. R. Cooper, C. T. Garcia Coll, W. T. Bartko, H. D., & C. Chatman (Eds.), *Developmental pathways through middle childhood: Rethinking contexts and diversity as resources* (pp. 207–235). Mahwah, NJ: Lawrence Erlbaum Associates.

Georgiades, K., Boyle, M. H., & Duku, E. (2007). Contextual influences on children's mental health and school performance: The moderating effects of family immigrant status. *Child Development, 78,* 1572–1591.

Gilbertson, G. A. (1995). Women's labor and enclave employment: The case of Dominican and Colombian women in NYC. *International Migration Review, 29,* 657–670.

Glazer, N., & Moynihan, D. P. (1963). *Beyond the melting pot.* Cambridge, MA: The MIT Press.

Glick, J. E., & Van Hook, J. (2002). Parents' coresidence with adult children: Can immigration explain racial and ethnic variation? *Journal of Marriage and the Family, 64,* 240–253.

Glick, J. E., & White, M. J. (2004). Post-secondary school participation of immigrant and native youth: The role of familial resources and educational expectations. *Social Science Research, 33,* 272–299.

Gold, S. J. (1989). Differential adjustment among new immigrant family members. *Journal of Contemporary Ethnography, 17,* 408–434.

Gold, S. J. (1995). *From the workers' state to the golden state: Jews from the former Soviet Union in California.* Boston: Allyn and Bacon.

Gold, S. J. (2002). *The Israeli diaspora.* Seattle, WA: University of Washington Press/Routledge.

Gold, S. J. (2003). Israeli and Russian Jews: Gendered perspectives on settlement and return migration. In P. Hondagneu-Sotelo (Ed.), *Gender and U.S. immigration: Contemporary trends* (pp. 127–147). Berkeley, CA: University of California Press.

Gold, S. J. (2005). Migrant networks: A summary and critique of relational approaches to international migration, In M. Romero & E. Margolis (Eds.), *The Blackwell Companion to Social Inequalities* (pp. 257–285). Malden, MA: Blackwell.

Goldscheider, C., & Kobrin, F. E. (1980). Ethnic continuity and the process of self-employment. *Ethnicity, 7,* 256–278.

Gordon, M. (1964). *Assimilation in American life.* New York: Oxford.

Grasmuck, S., & Pessar, P. (1991). *Between Two Islands: Dominican International Migration.* Berkeley, CA: University of California Press.

Hao, Y. (2008). Productive activities and psychological well-being among alder adults. *The Journals of Gerontology Series B: Psychological Sciences and Social Sciences, 63,* 64–72.

Hernandez, D. J., Denton, N. A., & Macartney, S. E. (2008). Children in immigrant families: Looking to America's future. *Social Policy Report: Giving Child and Youth Development Knowledge Away, 13,* 3–22.

Hernstein, R. J., & Murray, C. (1994). *The bell curve.* New York: The Free Press.

Hondagneu-Sotelo, P. (1992). Overcoming patriarchal constraints: The reconstruction of gender relations among Mexican immigrant women and men. *Gender & Society, 6,* 393–415.

Hondagneu-Sotelo, P. (1994). *Gendered transitions: Mexican experiences of immigration.* Berkeley, CA: University of California Press.

Hondagneu-Sotelo, P., & Avila, E. (1997). 'I'm here, but I'm there:' The meanings of transnational motherhood. *Gender and Society, 11,* 548–571.

Igoa, C. (1995). *Inner world of the immigrant child.* New York: St. Martin's.

Kagitcibasi, C. (1996). *Family and human development across cultures*. Mahwah, NJ: Erlbaum.

Kao, G., & Tienda, M. (1995). Optimism and achievement: The educational performance of immigrant youth. *Social Science Quarterly, 76*, 1–19.

Kasinitz, P., Mollenkopf, J., Waters, M., & Holdaway, J. (2008). *Inheriting the city: The second generation comes of age*. New York: Russell Sage Foundation.

Kibria, N. (1993). Family tightrope: *The changing lives of Vietnamese Americans*. Princeton, NJ: Princeton University Press.

Kim, D. Y. (2004). Leaving the ethnic economy: The rapid integration of second-generation Korean Americans in New York. In P. Kasinitz, J. H. Mollenkopf, & M. C. Waters (Eds.), *Becoming New Yorkers: Ethnographies of the new second generation*. New York: Russell Sage Foundation.

Kim J. E., & Moen, P. (2002). Retirement transitions, gender, and psychological well-being: A life-course, ecological model. *The Journals of Gerontology Series B: Psychological Sciences and Social Sciences, 57*, 212–222.

Kurman, J., & Ronen-Eilon, C. (2004). Lack of knowledge of a culture's social axioms and adaptation difficulties among immigrants. *Journal of Cross-Cultural Psychology 35*, 192–208.

Laub, J. H., & Sampson R. J. (2003). *Shared beginnings, divergent lives: Delinquent boys to age 70*. Cambridge, MA: Harvard University Press.

Lauby, J., & Stark, O. (1988). Individual migration as a family strategy: Young women in the Philippines. *Population Studies: A Journal of Demography, 42*, 473–486.

Lessinger, J. (1995). *From the Ganges to the Hudson: Indian immigrants in New York City*. Boston: Allyn & Bacon.

Lev-Ari, L. (2008). *The American dream—For men only? Gender, immigration, and the assimilation of Israelis in the United States*. San Antonio, TX: LFB Publishers.

Levinson, D. J. (1986). A conception of adult development. *American Psychologist, 41*, 3–13.

Levitt, M. (2003). Newly immigrant children and adolescents: Child and parent adjustment in the first post-migration year. Paper presented at the meeting of the Society for the Study of Human Development, Boston.

Lewis, O. (1962). *Five Families; Mexican Case Studies in the Culture of Poverty*. New York: Wiley.

Light, I. (1984). Immigrant and ethnic enterprise in North America. *Ethnic and Racial Studies, 17*, 195–216.

Light, I., & Gold, G. (2000). *Ethnic Economies*. San Diego, CA: Academic Press

Louie, V. (2004). Compelled to excel: Immigration, education and opportunity among Chinese Americans. Palo Alto, CA: Stanford University Press.

Marger, M., & Hoffman, C. (1992). Ethnic enterprise in Ontario: Immigrant participation in the small business sector. *International Migration Review, 26*, 968–981.

Markowitz, F. (1993). *A community in spite of itself: Soviet Jewish émigrés in New York*. Washington, DC: Smithsonian.

Massey, D. S., Arango, J., Hugo, G., Kouaouci, A, Pellegrino, A., & Taylor, J. E. (1993). Theories of international migration: A review and appraisal. *Population and Development Review, 19*, 431–466.

Massey, D. S., Goldring, L., & Durand, J. (1994). Continuities in transnational migration: An analysis of nineteen Mexican communities. *American Journal of Sociology, 99*, 1492–1533.

Massey, D. S., Alarcon, R., Durand, J., & Gonzalez, H. (1987). *Return to Aztlan*. Berkeley, CA: University of California Press.

Mayer, K. U. (2004). Whose lives? How history, societies and institutions define and shape life courses. *Research in Human Development, 1*, 161–187.

Mayer, K. U. (2009). New directions in life course research. *Annual Review of Sociology, 35*, 413–433.

Migration Policy Institute. (2008). High stakes, more meaning: An overview of the process of redesigning the US citizenship test. *Immigration Backgrounder, 6*, 1–18.

Min, P. G. (1996). *Caught in the middle: Korean communities in New York and Los Angeles*. Berkeley, CA: University of California Press.

Min, P. G. (1998). *Changes and conflicts: Korean immigrant families in New York*. Boston: Allyn and Bacon.

Min, P. G. (2008). *Ethnic solidarity for economic survival*. New York: Russell Sage Foundation.

Murnane, R. (1996). *Teaching the New Basic Skills: Principles for Educating Children to Thrive in a Changing Economy*. New York: Martin Kessler Books/Free Press.

National Statistical Coordination Board. (2007). Filipino Emigrants to New Zealand Increase Four-Fold in 2006. Retrieved March 28, 2009 from http://www.nscb.gov.ph/factsheet/pdf07/FS-200708-NS1-04.asp.

Nonini, D., & Ong, A. (1997). Introduction: Chinese transnationalism as an alternative modernity. In A. Ong & D. Nonini (Eds.), *Ungrounded empires: The cultural politics of modern Chinese transnationalism* (pp. 3–33). New York: Routledge.

North, D. S. (1987). The long grey welcome: A study of the American naturalization program. *International Migration Review, 21,* 311–326.

Office of Refugee Resettlement (ORR). (1989). Report to Congress. Refugee resettlement program.

Ogbu, J. (1991). Immigrant and involuntary minorities in comparative perspective. In M. A. Gibson & J. U. Ogbu (Eds.), *Minority status and schooling: A comparative study of immigrant and involuntary minorities* (pp. 3–36). New York: Garland Press.

Olsen, L. (2000). Learning English and learning America: Immigrants in the center of a storm. *Theory into Practice, 39,* 196–202.

Ong, A. (2002). *Buddha is Hiding Refugees, Citizenship, The New America.* Berkeley and Los Angeles: University of California Press.

Orleck, A. (1999). *The Soviet Jewish Americans.* Westport, CT: Greenwood.

Park, R. (1950). *Race and culture.* Glencoe, IL: The Free Press.

Parke, R., & Buriel, R. (2006). Socialization in the family: Ethnic, ecological perspectives. In N. Eisenberg (Ed.), *The handbook of child psychology.* New York: Wiley.

Pedraza, S. (1991). Women and migration: The social consequences of gender. *Annual Review of Sociology,* 17, 303–325.

Perreira, K. M., Harris, K. M., & Lee, D. (2006). Making it in America: High school completion by immigrant and native youth. *Demography, 43,* 511–536.

Phelan, P., Davidson, L. D., & Yu, H. C. (1993). Students' multiple worlds: Navigating the borders of family, peer and school cultures. In P. Phelan & L. D. Davidson (Eds.), *Renegotiating cultural diversity in American school.* (pp. 52–88). New York: Teachers College Press.

Phinney, J., Ong, A., & Madden, T. (2000). Cultural values and intergenerational value discrepancies in immigrant and non immigrant families. *Child Development, 71,* 528–539.

Phinney, J. S., Romero, I., Nava, M., & Huang, D. (2001). The role of language, parents, and peers in ethnic identity among adolescents in immigrant families. *Journal of Youth and Adolescence, 30,* 135–153.

Piore, M. J. (1979). *Birds of passage.* New York: Cambridge University Press.

Portes, A., Guarnizo, L. E., Landolt, P. (1999). Introduction: Pitfalls and promise of an emergent research field. *Ethnic and Racial Studies, 22,* 217–327.

Portes, A., & Rumbaut, R. (2001). *Legacies: The story of the second generation.* Berkeley, CA: University of California Press.

Portes, A., & Rumbaut, R. (2006). *Immigrant America: A portrait* (3rd ed.). Berkeley, CA: University of California Press.

Portes, A., & Zhou, M. (1993). The new second generation: Segmented assimilation and its variants. *Annals of the American Academy of Political and Social Sciences, 530,* 74–96.

Qin, D. B. (2006). Our child doesn't talk to us anymore: Alienation in immigrant Chinese families. *Anthropology and Education Quarterly, 37,* 162–179.

Qin, D. B. (2008). Doing well vs. feeling well: Understanding family dynamics and the psychological adjustment of Chinese immigrant adolescents. *Journal of Youth and Adolescence, 37,* 22–35.

Qin, D. B., Way, N., & Rana, M. (2008). The "model minority" and their discontent: Examining peer discrimination and harassment of Chinese American immigrant youth. *New directions for child and adolescent development, 121,* 27–42.

Ready, T. (2001). *Latino immigrant youth: Passages from adolescence to adulthood.* New York: Taylor and Francis.

Rogoff, B. (2003). *The cultural nature of human development.* New York: Oxford University Press.

Rothe, E. M., Lewis, J., Castillo-Matos, H., Martinez, O., Busquets, R., & Martinez, I. (2002). Posttraumatic stress disorder among Cuban children and adolescents after release from a refugee camp. *Psychiatric Services, 53,* 970–976.

Sigelman, C. K., & Shaffer, D. R. (1995). *Life-span human development (2nd ed.).* Belmont, CA: Brooks/Cole.

Smith, J. P., & Edmonston, B. (Eds.). (1997). *The New Americans: Economic, demographic, and fiscal effects of immigration.* Washing, DC: National Academy Press.

Smith, R. C. (2002). Social location, generation and life course as social processes shaping second generation transnational life. In P. Levitt & M. Waters (Eds.), *The changing face of home* (pp. 145–168). New York: Russell Sage Foundation.

Smith, R. C. (2005). *Mexican New York: Transnational worlds of new immigrants.* Berkeley, CA: University of California Press.

Song, M. (1999). *Helping out: Children's labor in ethnic businesses.* Philadelphia: Temple University Press.

Steinberg, L. (2001). We know some things: Parent-adolescent relationships in retrospect and prospect. *Journal of Research on Adolescence, 11,* 1–19.

Stewart, A. J., & Healy, J. M. (1989). Linking individual development and social changes. *American Psychologist, 44,* 30–42.

Suárez-Orozco, C. (2000). Identities under siege: Immigration stress and social mirroring among the children of immigrants. In A. Robben & M. Suárez-Orozco (Eds.), *Cultures under siege: Social violence and trauma.* (pp. 194–226). Cambridge: Cambridge University Press.

Suarez-Orozco, M. (2000). Everything you ever wanted to know about assimilation but were afraid to ask. *Daedalus Journal of the American Academy of Arts and Sciences, 129,* 1–30.

Suarez-Orozco, C., & Suarez-Orozco, M. (2001). *Children of immigration.* Cambridge, MA: Harvard University Press.

Suárez-Orozco, C., Todorova, I. L. G., & Louie, J. (2002). Making up for lost time: The experience of separation and reunification among immigrant families. *Family Process, 41,* 625–643.

Suarez-Orozco, C., Todorova, I., & Qin, D. B. (2006). The well-being of immigrant adolescents: A longitudinal perspective on risk and protective factors. In F. Villarruel & T. Luster (Eds.), *The crisis in youth mental health: Critical issues and effective program. Vol. 2* (pp. 53–84). Westport, CT: Praeger.

Taylor, J. E. (1999). The new economics of labor migration and the role of remittances in the migration process. *International Migration, 37,* 63–88.

Tenenbaum, S. (1993) *A credit to their community.* Detroit, MI: Wayne State University Press.

Tienda, M., & Raijman, R. (2000). Immigrants' income packaging and invisible labor force activity. *Social Science Quarterly, 81,* 291–311.

Volkan, V. D. (1993). Immigration and refugees: A psychodynamic perspective. *Mind and Human Interaction, 4,* 63–69.

Waldinger, R., & Lichter, M. I. (2003). *How the other half works: Immigration and the social organization of labor.* Berkeley: University of California Press.

Waters, M. C. (1999). *Black identities: West Indian immigrant dreams and American realities.* Cambridge, MA: Harvard University Press.

Westermeyer, J., & Wahmanholm, K. (1996). Refugee children. In R. J. Apfel & B. Simon (Eds.), *Minefields in their hearts: The mental health of children in war and communal violence* (pp. 75–103). New Haven, CT: Yale University Press.

Wilson, W. J. (1996). *When work disappears: The world of the new urban poor.* New York: Knopf.

Wolf, D. L. (1997). Family secrets: Transnational struggles among children of Filipino immigrants. *Sociological Perspectives, 40,* 457–482.

Wong Fillmore, L. (2005). When learning a second language means losing the first. In M. M. Suárez-Orozco, C. Suárez-Orozco, & D. B. Qin (Eds.), *The new immigration: An interdisciplinary reader* (pp. 289–308). New York: Routledge.

Yoon, I. J. (1997). *On my own: Korean businesses and race relations in America.* Chicago: University of Chicago Press.

Zhou, M. (1992). *Chinatown: The socioeconomic potential of an urban enclave.* Philadelphia: Temple University Press.

Zhou, M. (1997a). Segmented assimilation: Issues, controversies, and recent research on the new second generation. *International Migration Review, 31,* 825–858.

Zhou, M. (1997b). Growing up American: The challenge confronting immigrant children and children of immigrants. *Annual Review of Sociology, 23,* 63–95.

Zhou, M. (1998). "Parachute kids" in Southern California: The educational experience of Chinese children in transnational families. *Educational Policy, 12,* 682–704.

Zhou, M., & Bankston, C. L. III. (1994). Social capital and the adaptation of the second generation: The case of Vietnamese youth in New Orleans. *International Migration Review, 28,* 821–845.

Zhou, M., & Bankston, C. III. (1998). *Growing up American: How Vietnamese children adapt to life in the United States.* New York: Russell Sage Foundation.

Zhou, M., & Logan, J. R. (1989). Returns on human capital in ethnic enclaves. *American Sociological Review, 54,* 809–820.

Zhou, M. (1999). Segmented assimilation: Issues, controversies, and recent research on the new second generation. In C. Hirschman, P. Kasinitz, & J. DeWind (Eds.), *The Handbook of International Migration: The American Experience* (pp. 196-211). New York: Russell Sage Foundation.

Zhou, M., Lee, J., Agius Vallejo, J., Tafoya-Estrada, R., & Sao Xiong, Y. (2008). Success attained, deterred and denied: Divergent pathways to social mobility in Los Angeles's new second generation. *The Annals, 620,* 37–61.

Zlotnick, H. (2003). *The global dimensions of female migration.* Washington, DC: Migration Policy Institute.

HOW DO NEIGHBORHOODS MATTER ACROSS THE LIFE SPAN?

31

Jondou J. Chen, Kimberly S. Howard, and Jeanne Brooks-Gunn

Neighborhood residents, academic researchers, and policy makers have often struggled over and disagreed about how to name or bound their own and others' neighborhoods (Coulton, Korbin, Chan, & Su, 2001). Similarly, perceptions and beliefs about neighborhood values also have been found to vary (Sastry, Pebley, & Zonta, 2002). Yet residents of the same neighborhood are more likely to agree about what their neighborhood is and how it is to live there than residents living in other neighborhoods (Bass & Lambert, 2004). Residents view neighborhoods as the place where community values are established and taught (Anderson, 1978), where residents move about to live their daily lives (Moudon et al., 2006), and where people age and grow closer together (Oh, 2003a, 2003b). In the end, people's earnest disagreements over how to define their own neighborhoods reflect the same sentiment as the breadth of research on these geographically bounded communities of residents: neighborhoods matter.

Children, adolescents, and adults live and develop in a number of contexts including relationships, physical space, time, and history. Over the past decade, research on the potential influences of neighborhoods on life-span development has been rapidly growing. Even as individual- and family-level predictors remain the best determinants of developmental outcomes, a number of factors have fueled research on this more distal layer of Bronfenbrenner's (1979) ecological model.

First, conditions such as poverty and poor environment clearly can exist at both the family and neighborhood levels, each with potentially unique contributions to development (e.g., Klebanov, Brooks-Gunn, McCarton, & McCormick, 1998). Second, researchers have continued to use novel research designs and statistical methods to model how neighborhood processes are associated with individuals' development (Sampson, Morenoff, & Gannon-Rowley, 2002). Third, in response to critics who argue that neighborhood influences are simply an amalgamation of personal and family characteristics (Oakes, 2004), neighborhood researchers have sought to control for individual- and family-level variables and have also considered that both direct and indirect pathways through neighborhoods might make a difference for residents (e.g., Xue, Leventhal, Brooks-Gunn, & Earls, 2005). Fourth, the residential instability of participants, long a threat to longitudinal neighborhood research, is now emerging as a research target in and of itself (Buu et al., 2007; 2009). Fifth, even as much of psychological research increasingly focuses on the role of genes on individual development, it has also become clear that gene expression depends on environmental context (e.g., Eley et al., 2004; Suomi, Higley, & Lesch, 2005). Finally, the increased links between developmental research and policy (Shonkoff & Phillips, 2000) make it clear that neighborhoods must be included to understand development across the life span and to create effective preventative and ameliorative interventions.

Our premise is that neighborhoods do matter in the development of children, youth, and adults, both as individuals and in families; the question is how much, in what circumstances, and through which processes. We build upon previous reviews (Duncan & Raudenbush, 1999; Jencks & Mayer, 1990; Leventhal & Brooks-Gunn, 2000, 2003a; Sampson et al., 2002). Our goal is to establish a theoretical basis for how neighborhood characteristics and processes might influence development across the life span; understand the benefits and challenges of existing research designs for measuring neighborhood "effects"; discuss findings from quantitative neighborhood-level research with a focus on findings from the past decade; and argue for a continued multifaceted research agenda to understand the role of neighborhoods in human development. A caveat is in order: although the term "neighborhood effects" is used commonly even in research circles, this article shall instead use the terms "association," "influence," or "link" to describe how neighborhoods potentially shape life-span development due to the numerous challenges regarding attribution of causality.

Typically, associations between neighborhood-level conditions and a number of health-related, cognitive, emotional, and economic individual outcomes are examined. Neighborhood variables include economic and demographic characteristics (e.g., concentrated affluence, concentrated disadvantage), which are typically drawn from U.S. Census data regarding median household income, single-parent households, percent of families living in poverty, unemployment, parental educational attainment, and occupational status. Other variables represent dynamic processes (e.g., neighborhood collective efficacy, which is defined as social cohesion and informal enforcement of neighborhood norms), which must be collected through observation or resident-report. Still others concentrate on the built environment (parks, fast-food restaurants) or consider social disorganization (e.g., crime, vandalized buildings). Another line of research examines neighborhood-based interventions (e.g., moves out of high-rise public housing, moves from poor to nonpoor neighborhoods, demolition and reconstruction of public housing). Debates about the findings, and implications of these findings, are ongoing (Clampet-Lundquist & Massey, 2008; Sampson, 2008).

▨ WHY STUDY NEIGHBORHOODS?

We now turn to the rationale behind studying neighborhoods, which can be understood in several ways. At the macro level, developmentalists have come to understand neighborhoods as part of the ecology and an extension of family process models. Sociologists have long framed neighborhoods, and in particular poorer ones, from a disorganization perspective. Because of the increased focus in recent decades on the relationship between poverty and families and neighborhoods, researchers have synthesized both of these perspectives into a number of more specific theoretical frameworks, which we describe in our conclusion to this section.

Much of neighborhood research on human development has emerged from the synthesis of developmental psychology's ecological systems theory and sociology's social disorganization theory. Developmentalists generally ground neighborhood research in the ecological systems theory of Bronfenbrenner (1979; 1986). This theory describes individuals as nested within a series of contextual shells from the most proximate infant–parent relationship to the more distal influences of neighborhoods and institutions. Linking concepts from developmental and social psychology, Bronfenbrenner derived this model joining Vygotsky's (1978) dyadic theory of parents influencing children's rate of development with Lewin's (1936) bidirectional relationship between human experience and psychological environment. Taken together, environmental contexts not only shape the developing individual, but individuals also have the potential to shape their own environment (Aber, Gephart, Brooks-Gunn, Connell, & Spencer, 1997).

Bronfenbrenner's model, while typically used by those studying children and family, is also applicable across the life span. It has been invoked in the development of models examining family processes, two of which could be applied to neighborhood research (although typically are not). The first has to do with family stress, especially as influenced by material hardship (Conger & Donnellan, 2007; McLoyd, 1998). Material hardship is usually thought of as a family-level variable, but also can be a neighborhood-level one, with parenting processes potentially influenced by both (Klebanov, Brooks-Gunn, & Duncan, 1994). Even among older adults who are no longer parenting, similar family stress processes (affected by neighborhood and family hardship) may influence their well-being (Aneshensel et al., 2007; Lang et al., 2008; Loukaitou-Sideris, 2006). The second is the human capital or resource model, which is derived from the family economic and sociological literature; here, parental human capital is typically examined (Magnuson, 2007); again, neighborhoods also may be characterized in terms of human capital and economic resources, which may influence parents' behavior toward their children (Klebanov et al., 1994, 1998). We mention these two well-researched aspects of family life to highlight the point that many of the processes studied at the family level are also relevant at the neighborhood level and may in fact interact to influence children's development (e.g., Browning, Gardner, Maimon, & Brooks-Gunn, 2009; Maimon, Browning, & Brooks-Gunn, 2010).

At the neighborhood level, the family stress model bears a marked resemblance to Shaw and McKay's (1942) classic theory of social disorganization. Rather than following individuals or families, however, social disorganization theory considers neighborhoods to be the unit of analysis in understanding how factors such as social and economic capital, racial/ethnic composition, residential stability, and family disruption predict negative neighborhood outcomes such as crime and delinquency (Sampson & Groves, 1989). And similar to family environments undergoing periodic transitions (e.g., birth, deaths, and income fluctuations), neighborhoods also change over time as families move and local economies evolve (Massey & Denton, 1993; Wilson, 1987; 1996).

Although some of these shifts have been sudden, as in the case of the Great Depression (Elder, 1999), others have been more gradual, as seen in the case of rural families (Conger & Conger, 2002) and in urban centers (Furstenberg, Brooks-Gunn, & Morgan, 1987; Werner & Smith, 1989; Wilson, 1987; 1996). In the year 2000, more than 18.1 million people in the United States (or 6.4% of the total population) lived in severely distressed neighborhoods where at least three of the following four characteristics were met: 27.4% or more of families lived below the federal poverty line; 37.1% or more of households were female-headed; at least 34.0% or more of working-age males were unemployed; and 23% or more of adults were high school dropouts (O'Hare & Mather, 2003). Children are more likely to live in severely distressed neighborhoods, with 5.6 million children representing 7.7% of the child population living in these conditions. Like children, older adults are also at a higher risk for living in poorer neighborhoods (Lang et al., 2008). Both children and the elderly are also at increased risk as income disparities between poor and wealthier families has continued to grow into the new millennium even as absolute poverty rates declined slightly during the 1990s (Sawhill & McLanahan, 2006). Presently, the great recession is characterized by large increases in unemployed or underemployed among adults, with results still forthcoming regarding the impact on families and children.

Furthermore, associations between poverty and race are evident at the neighborhood as well as the family level, with Black children 20 times more likely than their White counterparts to live in neighborhoods with poverty rates above 40% (Duncan, Brooks-Gunn, & Klebanov, 1994). In a 1980 sample of Black and White U.S. children, almost 50% of Black children but fewer than 10% of White children who did not live in poor families still lived in neighborhoods with poverty levels in excess of 20%. And although half of White children never lived in either a poor family or neighborhood during the 6-year study, only 1 in 20 Black children avoided poverty in both the family and neighborhood context (Duncan et al., 1994).

From the life-course perspective then, individuals begin life largely in the context of their families, but over time increasingly emerge from the family to socialize in schools and neighborhoods, eventually developing their own sense of emotional, cognitive, sexual, and perhaps economic and residential independence (Halfon & Hochstein, 2002). Individuals can be seen being exposed to numerous neighborhood resources such as parks and schools as well as risk factors such as violence and social disorder (Blaine, 1999; Wadsworth, 1999).

Allowing for a more agentic perspective of neighborhoods, Mayer and Jencks (1989; Jencks & Mayer, 1990) described six theoretical taxonomies to account for how neighborhood characteristics and processes might shape individual development and interpersonal dynamics. These include contagion theories, relative deprivation theories, scarce resource theories, collective socialization theories, institutional theories, and counterfactual theories that consider neighborhoods simply as the aggregation of independent individuals. *Contagion* (or *epidemic*) *theories* posit that risky behaviors, which are more common in low socioeconomic status (SES) neighborhoods, will influence community members who might not see these same behaviors or factors in their own households (Crane, 1991). *Relative deprivation theories* suggest that neighborhood residents experiencing or cognizant of relative, rather than absolute, disparities compared with neighbors or other neighborhoods will respond negatively (Hipp, 2007; Turley, 2002), and potentially seek to create a counterculture of risky behavior and risk factors (Curtis, 1975). *Scarce resource/competition theories* view neighborhood residents and groups as competing over limited resources (Venkatesh, 2006), with successful emergence dependent on individual agency (Mayer & Jencks, 1989). *Collective socialization/social control* theories describe how neighborhood residents modeling positive behaviors and enforcing against delinquency might influence resident behavior controlling for, and perhaps in spite of, socialization in their own households (Furstenberg, 1993; Kornhauser, 1978; Wilson, 1987). *Institutional/ environmental resource* theories suggest that beyond the actions of residents, the provision and maintenance of institutions such as schools, parks, and police departments can influence positive development (Reisig & Parks, 2004; Takano, Nakamura, & Watanabe, 2002; Xu, Fiedler, & Flaming, 2005) whereas other environmental factors such as toxins and pollutants present risk factors (Jerrett et al., 2005). Furthermore, evidence also exists for higher frequencies of certain businesses in certain neighborhoods over others (e.g., liquor stores or fast-food restaurants in neighborhoods that have more African American or poor residents; Block, Scribner, & DeSalvo, 2004; LaVeist & Wallace, 2000). The increased presence of such risk factors represents potential mediators for how neighborhoods influence outcomes such as obesity (Kumanyika & Grier, 2006). Finally, Jencks and Mayer (1990) acknowledge that the absence of any neighborhood influence on individual action and development might comprise a sixth model—the counterfactual to any neighborhood influences.

Jencks and Mayer (1990) cautioned, however, that the connection between neighborhoods theory and actual research remains complicated because of the multilevel and non-laboratory nature of neighborhoods. Theories and influences rarely, if ever, operate in isolation, and a single significant finding can be explained by multiple theories (Entwisle, 2007). For instance, controlling for individual SES, neighborhood, and school SES have been associated with higher academic achievement and aspirations (reviewed by Jencks & Mayer, 1990). This association could be caused by students having higher performing peers, living in neighborhoods where adults socialize children to work harder in school, living in neighborhoods with better libraries, or students having positive self-esteem because of being relatively wealthy in contrast to nearby neighborhoods. Leventhal and Brooks-Gunn (2000) extended the breadth of research reviewed to include research on neighborhood dynamics in addition to neighborhood characteristics. They also described more recent research initiatives that have sought to better understand neighborhood links as well as to evidence causality.

This movement from theory to research has required interdisciplinary collaboration to encapsulate concepts and methods from a number of fields including developmental psychology, sociology, public health, measurement, and economics. Whereas the initial wave of neighborhood research (e.g., Brooks-Gunn, Duncan, Klebanov, & Sealand, 1993; Crane, 1991) tied neighborhood demographic descriptors to individual outcomes, a second wave of research has sought to identify processes within neighborhoods (e.g., Gardner & Brooks-Gunn, 2009; Sampson, Raudenbush, & Earls, 1997). Presently a third wave of research is emerging involving contingent effects whereby neighborhood influences emerge at specific tipping points for family or individual-level variables (e.g., Browning et al., 2009; Gardner & Brooks-Gunn, 2009) which evidence nonlinear associations. Such findings also lead us to consider interactions between family-level and neighborhood-level processes as well as doing work on clusters of neighborhoods (i.e., whether it is worse if one lives in a highly concentrated poor neighborhood surrounded by others that are similar than if adjoined to more affluent neighborhoods; Morenoff, 2003) and in-migration and out-migration patterns (Lyons, 2008).

▓ HOW HAVE NEIGHBORHOODS BEEN STUDIED?

In this section, we will discuss various methods for studying neighborhood effects on development and continue with a brief discussion of the ongoing methodological challenges to studying neighborhoods. In our ecological consideration of neighborhoods, neighborhoods do not exist as the most proximal context in which individuals develop. That is, although census and other local data sources provide useful measures of central tendency on a number of variables (e.g., median household income), studies using these data as a proxy for family-level variables are not considered in this chapter. First, those studies that have added neighborhood-level variables above and beyond (and controlled for) individual- and family-level data are examined. Although not designed for the study of neighborhoods, large-scale datasets (national or regional) have been matched with U.S. Census data to derive neighborhood-level variables. Second, studies intentionally designed to study both neighborhood characteristics and processes are discussed. Third, experiments involving housing are considered. Other studies use geographically linked data over time to examine what happens to health outcomes when an environmental condition is changed (i.e., reduction of lead levels in gasoline). This literature is not reviewed here (see Fauth & Brooks-Gunn, 2007).

National and Regional Longitudinal Studies

Partnerships with city or regionally based institutions such as school districts or police departments often simplify data collection (Xu et al., 2005). In these cases, the data are only as representative of the population as these partner organizations are with potential for age bias (e.g., in studies of children in schools) or socioeconomic bias (e.g., in studies of poverty and families receiving government assistance).

National or multisite studies are ideal for both generalizability and assessing individual development over time. Such size is also advantageous in statistical analyses where individual and family-level variables are controlled and multi-way interactions are tested. For instance, the Panel Study of Income Dynamics (PSID; Survey Research Center, 1984) is a nationally representative dataset that originally included approximately 5,000 families in 1968 and included over 7,400 families by 2001 (Duncan et al., 1994; Vartanian, 1997, 1999a, 1999b). In 1968, approximately 10% of the heads of households in PSID families were younger than 25 years, 45% were between 25 and 44 years of age, 35% were between 45 and 64 years of age, and 10% were older than 65 years. Researchers then linked individual data to neighborhood values using U.S. Census data. These factors include the poverty rate and the percentage of households receiving public assistance, with findings published regarding child development, adult health, and family functioning. Another study, the Infant Health and Development Program (IHDP), studied low-birth-weight and premature infants born in eight U.S. cities and followed initially for 3 years during a random assignment treatment and then re-interviewed after 5 and 8 years (IHDP, 1990; Klebanov et al., 1994, 1998). Once again, U.S. Census data provided values for neighborhood-level variables to supplement individual participant information. Finally, the 1979 cohort of the National Longitudinal Survey of Youth (NLSY) followed a sample of almost 700 children born in 1979, whose data were combined with U.S. Census data (Chase-Lansdale, Mott, Brooks-Gunn, & Phillips, 1991; Chase-Lansdale & Gordon, 1996; Chase-Lansdale, Gordon, Brooks-Gunn, & Klebanov, 1997).

Neighborhood-Based Studies Using Clustered Designs

Intentionally seeking to study not only neighborhood demographic indicators but also neighborhood dynamics, researchers from developmental psychology, public health, sociology, and statistics designed the Project on Human Development in

Chicago Neighborhoods (PHDCN) to examine development in the urban context across neighborhoods with a wide racial and economic range (Sampson et al., 1997). PHDCN data include individual-level and family-level data for 6,000 children from ages 0 through 18 years who were seen three times during a 7-year period (with parental reports, child assessments, home observations, and youth reports). These families were clustered in 80 neighborhoods, which were chosen by random draw to represent all 343 neighborhoods in Chicago in 1994. Neighborhoods were classified in 21 groups based on SES (three categories) and racial/ethnic composition (seven categories); all but 3 of the 21 "cells" are represented (there were no lowest SES neighborhoods which were primarily White and no highest SES neighborhoods which were primarily Hispanic). Families were identified in each neighborhood through door-to-door canvassing (40,000 households) with approximately 8,000 families recruited to participate and over 6,000 families agreeing to participate. With approximately 80 families per neighborhood cluster, estimates of between and within neighborhood effects are possible. Children were drawn from multiple cohorts—birth to 1-, 3-, 6-, 9-, 12-, 15-, and 18-year groups. Multiple children from each household could be included if they fell into one of the cohort groups.

A separate community sample was also drawn. The almost 8,000 adults (mean age 43) represented all 343 neighborhood clusters in Chicago. Responses of adults within neighborhoods were summed to get neighborhood-level information. A key construct from PHDCN was the development of a measure for *collective efficacy*, to potentially assess whether community members exerting informal control and building social cohesion might counter the effects of social disadvantage. Sample items include, "People around here can be trusted," "People in this neighborhood do not share the same values," and "If a child were showing disrespect to an adult, how likely is it that people in your neighborhood would scold that child?" (Earls, Brooks-Gunn, Raudenbush, & Sampson, 1997). Other measures assessed in the community survey included perceived physical and social disorder, legal cynicism, community organizations, social capital, and family/friends network.

Another clustered neighborhood design was used in the Los Angeles Families and Neighborhoods Study (Sastry, Ghosh-Dastidar, Adams, & Pebley, 2006). Data from 65 census tracts were combined with two waves of resident data collected 6 to 7 years apart to investigate potential neighborhood influences on development ranging from self-reported health for adults with chronic conditions (Brown, Ang, & Pebley, 2007) to adolescent substance use (Musick, Seltzer, & Schwartz, 2008) to maternal depression (Lara-Cinisomo & Griffin, 2007). In each household, data were collected from one randomly selected adult (18 years of age or older, with a mean age of 43 years) and one randomly selected child (9–17 years of age, with a mean age of 15 years), if there were any children residing in the selected households.

The clustered neighborhood design provides better estimates of neighborhood associations, because it compares between and within neighborhood estimates, and uses nested models to account for the clustering of individuals and families within neighborhoods. Both studies are longitudinal, which allows for an examination of change over time in both individuals and in neighborhoods, the addition of controls for prior behavior, and the use of fixed effects models. These studies, although subject to selection bias, are a vast improvement on the earlier work (Sampson, Morenoff, & Earls, 1999; Sampson et al., 2002; Sampson & Raudenbush, 1999). These studies, of course, only represent two large cities (Villarreal & Silva, 2006); whether results would generalize to other settings is not known. Some scholars have argued that the neighborhood estimates are not precise enough (Gault & Silver, 2008); however, even the experiments, to be discussed later, have problems with selection (Heckman & Smith, 2004).

Experimental and Quasi-Experimental Methods

Selection bias is a concern of all neighborhood research, that is, to what degree do neighborhood residents select their neighborhoods and how much agency do residents have in moving to "better" neighborhoods? (Tienda, 1991). Experiments are one solution (although they raise other concerns, given selection into the experiment itself, the characteristics of individuals chosen to participate, and the actual take-up rate in the experiment). Housing mobility programs have been subject to random assignment. In these programs, participants eligible for government housing assistance and often already living in public housing were randomly assigned to a variety of conditions. In some, individuals were given vouchers to move (either regular Section 8 vouchers or special vouchers only to be used in low-poverty neighborhoods). In others, individuals were assigned to new, scattered-site housing in low-poverty neighborhoods. In yet others, individuals were moved into new housing when old public housing was demolished.

A 1976 Supreme Court decision against the U.S. Department of Housing and Urban Development resulted in a move of families from public housing in Chicago into private housing in the suburbs or elsewhere in Chicago. This program, labeled Gautreaux after the plaintiff, has since moved more than 7,100 families from the highly concentrated disadvantage of Chicago public housing to private housing either in the city of Chicago or the surrounding suburbs (Rosenbaum, 1995). Approximately 1,500 of these families were followed, using a quasi-experimental design (Rosenbaum, 1995).

In 1994, following the stated successes of Gautreaux, Moving to Opportunity for Fair Housing (MTO) served as the U.S. Department of Housing and Urban Development's 10-year program demonstration in five cities involving 4,610 families (mean age for adults was 35 years and the mean number of children per household was 2.5; Feins, Holin, & Phipps, 1996; Goering et al., 1999). Three groups were formed via random assignment. The two treatment groups were given either a housing voucher only or a voucher and assistance to move into private housing in non-poor neighborhoods (less than 10% of the residents could be poor); the control group remained in public housing. As expected, given the requirements, the voucher and assistance group moved to less poor neighborhoods than the voucher only group (60% vs. 48%, Goering et al., 1999). Follow-up surveys were done at each site about 2 years after random assignment and a national follow-up of all families in all five cities was done 5 years later (Katz, Kling, & Liebman, 2001; Leventhal & Brooks-Gunn, 2003b).

Another housing mobility program, beginning in 1988, presented itself when a court decision required the city of Yonkers, NY, to desegregate its public housing (Briggs, 1998; Fauth, Leventhal, & Brooks-Gunn, 2004; 2005; 2007; 2008). Whereas previously all Yonkers public housing had been concentrated in the southwest quadrant of the city, one third of all housing units were required by the court order to be placed in the remainder of the city. These new housing units were built in areas that were middle class and consisted of predominantly low-rise apartments and row homes, whereas the original housing projects were high-rise towers in areas highly concentrated with social disadvantage. Data were collected 1 year, 3 years, 5 years, and 7 years after the initial move beginning in 1992 with approximately 100 families that moved and 100 families that stayed.

The federally funded Housing Opportunities for People Everywhere (HOPE) VI projects are relevant (but not really natural experiments) as families were moved out of soon-to-be-demolished housing projects. Some of these families have been re-settled in other poorer neighborhoods, but others have been re-settled in their original neighborhoods and sometimes within the housing constructed over the original projects. Although much of the research on the Hope VI projects has been qualitative (Clampet-Lundquist, 2004; Salama, 1999), more large-scale quantitative analyses are underway, assessing changes in the original neighborhoods after HOPE VI and assessing changes for the HOPE VI residents who moved (Popkin et al., 2004).

■ WHAT ARE THE CHALLENGES IN STUDYING NEIGHBORHOODS?

As previously discussed, the study of neighborhood influences on development can rarely make causal claims because of selection. Social scientists cannot randomly assign participants to different neighborhoods or control for in-migration and out-migration (Tienda, 1991). And, neighborhood choice is not random as it is often constrained for individuals by cost, knowledge, availability of housing stock and mortgages, and discrimination. Even housing experiments are subject to selection; they target one group—families living in public housing who choose to move (uptake is often around 50% in mobility experiments). And, these families often move again, after the re-assignment (Clampet-Lundquist & Massey, 2008; Sampson, 2008).

Furthermore, some outcomes may not have the same meaning across contexts. For instance in the Gautreaux study, a number of students on the honor roll in urban Chicago schools were tested as 2 years behind grade level, but this was not true of students in the suburban schools, suggesting that standards for honor roll were quite different standards within schools (Rosenbaum, 1995). Likewise school discipline codes and social promotion policies might differ across settings (Leventhal & Brooks-Gunn, 2003a).

In other instances, contexts assumed to be different may not be so different. In a meta-analysis of MTO sites, the difference in school quality between treatment and control group children was minimal, with children in the control group attending schools placing at the 15th percentile nationally, and children in the treatment group attending schools placing in the 19th percentile nationally (Sanbonmatsu, Kling, Duncan, & Brooks-Gunn, 2006). Such a small difference in school quality leads one to question if the treatment really qualifies as a treatment at all (Clampet-Lundquist & Massey, 2008). Differences between neighborhoods were more pronounced than schools, however, leading to possible contamination of neighborhood effects by a lack of differences in schools attended (Katz et al., 2001; Leventhal & Brooks-Gunn, 2004). As these neighborhood researchers pointed out, MTO was not looking at school change but at neighborhood change, with a change in latter but not the former is unlikely to alter students' school achievement.

Most studies have examined linear associations, rather than nonlinear associations. A few (e.g., Crane, 1991; Hogan & Kitagawa, 1985) have found that factors such as SES and racial composition of neighborhoods operate more similarly to discrete measures involving cutoff points rather than continuous influences. Gladwell (2002) popularized the term "tipping point" to describe these cutoff points, which identify nonlinear effects. Some of these threats have been addressed by creating threshold measures (such as concentrated poverty or affluence; Brooks-Gunn et al., 1993; Sampson, et al. 1997).

Another challenge arises from the attribution of variance in modeling neighborhood influences. In general, after controlling for individual- and family-level variables, neighborhood effect sizes tend to appear small relative to individual or family-level predictors. Duncan and Raudenbush (1999) attribute this in part to the direct association between many family- and neighborhood-level variables (e.g., one's family income is a factor in calculating and highly correlated with median neighborhood income). Once the more immediate context (family) is controlled for, neighborhood effect sizes will appear much smaller. Yet if one considers that families and neighborhoods might serve as mediators for various processes, it is possible for neighborhoods to exert both small direct effects and larger indirect effects on developmental outcomes (Duncan & Raudenbush, 1999). Considering these indirect pathways resolves the challenge of whether or not to model certain neighborhood variables as exogenous (independent of individual/family characteristics) or not (endogenous) (Duncan, Magnuson, & Ludwig, 2004). For example, not only are family and neighborhood SES partially dependent on one another (the latter being an aggregation of the former). It is safest (and most conservative) to consider neighborhood variables to be endogenous and control for family-level variables, tending to render neighborhood effect sizes quite small. Virtually all of the non-experimental data reported in this chapter have taken this approach.

With these challenges in mind, we turn now to findings from neighborhood research, focusing in particular on research reported over the past decade. We understand many of these studies to be only descriptive or prospective, and we also posit that these findings, which have used increasingly stringent controls, serve as an ample foundation upon which additional research is both merited and necessary.

WHAT NEIGHBORHOOD ASSOCIATIONS EXIST?

Across the life span, neighborhood characteristics and processes have been associated with a number of developmental outcomes. Research on these outcomes has varied by life phase, both as certain outcomes are more phase specific (e.g., parenting to adults and onset of sexual activity to adolescence), and as different paths can be used to explain development at each phase (e.g., schools and public housing for families). In this section, we review what is known about neighborhood influences upon the well-being of five age groups—preschool children, school-aged children, adolescents, younger adults, and older adults. Three general domains of well-being are reviewed—cognitive, linguistic, and achievement outcomes; emotional, social, and behavioral outcomes; and physical health-related outcomes. Unless otherwise noted, all results are significant at $p < .05$ or better.

Preschool Children

Although preschool children's (birth to age 6) development is largely nested within the family context, neighborhood influences have been shown to occur, over and above family-level influences. Perhaps the most researched area has to do with income characteristics of neighborhoods (with less done on neighborhood processes to date). Poverty as well as low social support and higher levels of environmental toxins have been associated with infant mortality, low birth-weight, and early childhood hospitalization. By age 3, children growing up in poor neighborhoods are more likely to exhibit internalizing and externalizing behavior symptoms, and children growing up in affluent neighborhoods are more likely to do better on cognitive and language tests associated with school-readiness.

Physical Health

Changes in air pollution have been associated with decreases in infant mortality in an analysis of national data (Chay & Greenstone, 2003) as well as California state data (Currie & Neidell, 2005). Although these studies were based on changes over time, Lleras-Muney (2005) found that variation in ozone levels across communities was associated with hospitalization rates for children aged 2 to 5 years from military families. Neighborhood poverty, independent of family income, was also associated with higher rates of emergency department visits in a sample of premature low-birth-weight children aged 0 to 3 years (Brooks-Gunn, McCormick, Klebanov, & McCarton, 1998).

Neighborhood dynamics such as social support (Buka, Brennan, Rich-Edwards, Raudenbush, & Earls, 2003) have been associated with likelihood of infants being born with low birth-weight, with links to not only the mother's neighborhood, but those adjoining neighborhoods as well (Morenoff, 2003). It should also be noted that, although certain negative health outcomes have been linked with neighborhood variables, many children living in poverty receive some health protection through government-funded children's health insurance, which in many states covers children living in families making up to 200% of the federal poverty line (Fauth & Brooks-Gunn, 2008).

Cognitive Outcomes

Cognitive outcomes include intelligence tests, language tests, and early letter-word recognition and math skills. Appending census tract data to the IHDP, the NLSY, and the Canadian NLSY data revealed remarkable consistency. Neighborhood affluence, defined as 30% or more of residents making more than $30,000 in 1980, was positively associated with higher cognitive test scores for young children, controlling for family income (Brooks-Gunn et al., 1993; Chase-Lansdale & Gordon, 1996; Chase-Lansdale et al., 1997; Duncan et al., 1994; Klebanov et al., 1998; Kohen, Brooks-Gunn, Leventhal, & Hertzman, 2002). Although no neighborhood effects were found on child IQ at ages 1 and 2 years (Klebanov et al., 1998), significant differences in child IQ and language appeared at age 3 (Brooks-Gunn et al., 1993; Kohen et al., 2002). At ages 5 to 6 years, similar associations have been found with regard to reading achievement and receptive language in the NLSY sample (Chase-Lansdale & Gordon, 1996; Chase-Lansdale et al., 1997) and in the IHDP sample (Brooks-Gunn et al., 1993; Chase-Lansdale et al., 1997; Duncan et al., 1994). Kohen and colleagues (2002) also found in their Canadian sample that perceived social cohesion was associated with cognitive scores, controlling for family and neighborhood SES, a finding replicated in a sample of immigrant children from PHDCN (Leventhal, Xue, & Brooks-Gunn, 2006).

An analysis of family-level variables in the same sample of Black and White 5-year-old children found that controlling for family and neighborhood income as well as home environment essentially eliminated the one standard deviation gap in cognitive scores between White and Black children (Brooks-Gunn, Klebanov, & Duncan, 1996). Given the previously discussed differences in the experience of poverty between White and Black families (Duncan et al., 1994), these results suggest the importance of designing interventions to address the dual risk factors of family and neighborhood poverty which are more likely to be simultaneously faced by Black children than White children.

One possible mechanism for these findings has to do with the quality of child care (Campbell, Ramey, Pungello, Sparling, & Miller-Johnson, 2002). Controlling for family income, neighborhood SES is also significantly associated with the quality of childcare centers (Burchinal, Nelson, Carlson, & Brooks-Gunn, 2009). Federally funded early education centers, which primarily serve more disadvantaged populations, however, were associated with improved quality of child care centers (Burchinal et al., 2009).

Emotional and Behavioral Well-Being

Mothers report that children at age 3 and living in neighborhoods where fewer adults hold managerial or professional jobs are more likely to have externalizing and internalizing behavior problems (Brooks-Gunn et al., 1993). In a sample of children born prematurely with low birth-weight, and controlling for family-level characteristics, children at age 5 who lived in low-SES neighborhoods (with a family income under $10,000 in 1985) were more likely to manifest externalizing behavior problems such as temper tantrums or destroying things, as reported by mothers (Chase-Lansdale et al., 1997; Duncan et al., 1994).

School-Aged Children

Neighborhood associations exist for school-aged children's (age 7–12) well-being. Schools represent a potential institutional, environmental, and social influence on children, as school-aged children are spending increasing amounts of time outside of the home. As children leave their homes to attend schools, children are exposed to environmental factors such as fast-food restaurants that are associated with obesity. The previously discussed associations between affluence and cognitive outcomes as well as poverty and emotional and behavioral well-being continue. It should also be noted that most research has been unable to disentangle the influence of neighborhood and school.

Physical Health

Children (age 6–15) who had recently moved out of public housing were almost half as likely (5.9% compared with 10.5%) to require emergency medical attention as children who had remained in public housing (Katz et al., 2001). Several studies have also associated living in poverty with obesity. Children attending schools in poorer neighborhoods and neighborhoods with more African American and Latino residents are more likely to pass by more fast-food restaurants and stores that sell liquor and tobacco (Sturm, 2008; Zenk & Powell, 2008) which has in turn been associated with higher rates of obesity (Sallis & Glanz, 2006), which in turn has been associated with lower cognitive scores (Florence, Asbridge, & Veugelers, 2008).

Cognitive Outcomes

In their early review of research in which family SES was controlled, Jencks and Mayer (1990) found that attending elementary school with students with higher SES was associated with higher student test scores by one sixth of a standard deviation. These associations were especially strong for low-SES boys, and increased in size as children aged (Myers, 1985). As previously discussed, these findings were more recently replicated using data from Chicago (Leventhal et al., 2006).

Findings from Gautreaux support these results: after initial drops in parent-reported school performance, children from families who moved to the suburbs performed better than children who stayed in the cities. A more recent analysis using PSID data also found that neighborhood affluence, above and beyond family SES, predicted increased participation in after-school lessons, programs, and summer camps, explaining 11–46% of the benefits associated with these activities (Dearing et al., 2009). Interestingly, neighborhood affluence negatively predicted church attendance, a variable not typically included in studies of after-school programs, perhaps reflecting differences in the availability of out-of-school programming for children and the prevalence of churches in poorer neighborhoods. In analysis of data from Chicago, lower levels of anxious and depressive symptoms were associated with participation in community-based organized activities only in violent neighborhoods, whereas lower levels of substance use were associated with participation in church groups only in nonviolent neighborhoods (Fauth, Roth, & Brooks-Gunn, 2007).

In terms of housing experiments, there were generally no effects on school achievement or test scores in the MTO sample (Sanbonmatsu et al., 2006). Although children (age 6–20) from the experimental group were more likely to attend schools with higher attendance rates, higher scores on state-standards exams, fewer students of color, and fewer students eligible for free or reduced price lunch, these differences were not large. Compared with national data, however, children from the experimental group did not attend schools with smaller class-sizes, and child-reported data indicated little difference in school quality. This finding is not surprising given that children who moved attended schools that were only marginally better (19th percentile nationally vs. 15th percentile) and still not even close to average (Sanbonmatsu et al., 2006).

At no age/grade was there a significant effect size for performance on the nationally standardized Woodcock-Johnson Revised tests for reading and math (Sanbonmatsu et al., 2006; Woodcock & Johnson, 1989, 1990). A significant effect existed for African American children, placing them slightly above the sample mean. Sanbonmatsu and colleagues (2006) replicated an earlier finding for cognitive gains in primary school for MTO youth in Baltimore (Ludwig, Ladd, & Duncan, 2001), but also found that associations for the original age groups sampled by Ludwig and colleagues had faded out by secondary school. Positive links to improved reading scores were also found in both Baltimore and Chicago for African American children who moved (Sanbonmatsu et al., 2006). These two sites were also the most racially homogenous and African American of the five cities. Other structural factors or processes such as school differences might explain the positive effects for children in Baltimore and Chicago, or else these differences might have resulted by chance. The lack of MTO impacts could also be due to the fact that achievement has been linked to residence in affluent neighborhoods compared with poor and middle-income neighborhoods. MTO families, however, did not move to affluent neighborhoods, moving instead to suburbs just outside the inner city, which were less poor than the city neighborhoods but not affluent.

Emotional and Behavioral Well-Being

Among MTO families who moved out of public housing in New York City, children (age 8–13) from families given the opportunity to move reported significantly fewer anxious/depressive (39%) and dependence (29%) problems than children who were not given the same opportunity to move, with larger differences for older male children (Leventhal & Brooks-Gunn, 2003b) and similar findings were observed among families in Boston (Katz et al., 2001). Across all MTO sites, depressive symptoms were lower for girls in the experimental group and the effect size was substantial (Kling, Liebman, & Katz, 2007).

Using data from Chicago on older children and early adolescents, Browning and colleagues (2009) found externalizing behavior to be negatively associated with residential stability and also found that internalizing and externalizing symptoms increased for youth exposed to lethal violence, especially in neighborhoods with lower collective efficacy. Combining seven behavior problems (trouble with teacher, associating with troublemakers, bullying other children, inability to sit still, disobedience at home, disobedience at school, and depression) drawn from the National Health Interview Survey and the NLSY Children's Supplement, parents reported that boys (age 6–15) in the experimental group were significantly less likely to exhibit behavior problems (24% compared with 33%) and girls (age 6–15) were significantly less likely to have a close friend exhibit behavior problems than the control group (Katz et al., 2001).

For youth aged 8 to 9 years in Yonkers, Fauth and colleagues (2005) found that movers experienced not only fewer behavior problems and less delinquency, but also lower rates of victimization, disorder, and access to illegal substances relative to those who remained in high-poverty neighborhoods, potentially offering fewer stressors and risk factors to which children would have to respond.

Adolescents (13–19)

Adolescence continues children's progression through schools and toward more independence. Physically, adolescence marks the beginning of sexual maturation, and for many youth, the onset of sexual behavior. Increasingly, adolescent cognitive outcomes are measured in terms of school grades and test scores. Adolescence also represents an age where individuals can begin to self-report their own psychological and emotional well-being. It can also be seen that a number of outcomes lie in multiple domains. For example, a student's emotional well-being might influence his or her graduation from high school, and the externalizing behavior of several youth engaged in physical altercations could potentially result in physical harm.

Physical Health

Controlling for family characteristics, Black adolescents in lower SES neighborhoods were more likely to be pregnant than both White adolescents in the same neighborhoods and Black adolescents in higher SES neighborhoods (Crane, 1991; Hogan & Kitagawa, 1985). Black 15- and 16-year-olds in predominantly (more than 80%) Black classes were 27% more likely to have had sexual intercourse than Black students in non-predominantly Black classes (c.f. Brooks-Gunn & Paikoff, 1993; Furstenberg, Morgan, Moore, & Peterson, 1987).

Using PHDCN data, differences in age of onset of sexual behavior for African American youth was reduced to being nonsignificant when neighborhood poverty was included and other family-level characteristics were controlled for in a sample of 11- to 16-year-old Chicago youth (Browning, Leventhal, & Brooks-Gunn, 2004). Also, a two standard deviation increase in neighborhood-level collective efficacy was associated with a 27% reduction in likelihood of onset of sexual behavior by age 16.

In the same sample, among adolescents with low levels of parental monitoring (place monitoring; from the HOME, Caldwell & Bradley, 1984; Leventhal, Selner-O'Hagan, Brooks-Gunn, Bingenheimer, & Earls, 2004) and family attachment and support (from Turner, Frankel, & Levin, 1983), collective efficacy was associated with delays in onset of sexual activity (Browning, Leventhal, & Brooks-Gunn, 2005). A one standard deviation increase in collective efficacy for unmonitored adolescents resulted in a 33% reduction in odds of onset of sexual activity by age 16. Evidence was also found for a large peer influence on delayed onset of sexual behavior for female adolescents but not for male adolescents, with no significant difference in parental monitoring between male and female adolescents. Finally, in examining number of sexual partners, neighborhood collective efficacy was associated with having only one sexual partner versus having two or more sexual partners for these adolescents in Chicago (Browning, Burrington, Leventhal, & Brooks-Gunn, 2008).

Cognitive Outcomes

In adolescence, cognitive outcomes are commonly measured using school achievement and attainment. Mayer and Jencks' (1989) early review of neighborhood links for adolescents found no significant effects for mean school SES on educational attainment through high school and aspirations regarding college, after controlling for previous academic performance and family SES. Similarly, Crane (1991) found that racial differences were rendered nonsignificant when controlling for family and neighborhood-level factors, except in neighborhoods where less than 5% of the workers were employed in white-collar or managerial positions, in which case White students were slightly more likely to not drop out of school. A more recent study of college aspirations found that neighborhood physical disorder negatively predicted college aspirations in a sample of over 700 Black adolescents from Georgia and Iowa (Stewart, Stewart, & Simons, 2007).

For adolescents in the quasi-experimental designed Gautreaux, those who moved from public housing to the suburbs were less likely to drop out of school (5% vs. 20%) and significantly less likely to be paid minimum wage (9% vs. 43%) compared with adolescents who moved from public housing but stayed in the city (Rosenbaum & Kaufman, 1991). These adolescent movers were also significantly more likely to attend college (54% vs. 21%), and if not in college, they were more likely to work in better paying jobs (21% vs. 5%) with benefits (55% vs. 23%). These academic and employment outcomes are especially telling because high school grades did not differ significantly between suburban and urban adolescents in this sample.

Using the Woodcock-Johnson cognitive battery, however, as previously mentioned, Sanbonmatsu and colleagues (2006) found no significant differences by grade or by city across the MTO sites. As previously discussed, these findings raise the question of whether the results are the product of school culture or program failure (Kain, 1968; Schuman & Bobo, 1988) or the fact that it is affluence rather than a lack of poverty that predicts neighborhood links with cognition (Sanbonmatsu et al., 2006). Using another cognitive assessment, the Maryland Functional Test in reading, MTO adolescents in Baltimore middle and high schools were almost twice (37% vs. 19%) as likely to pass compared with the control group (Ludwig et al., 2001). Moreover, adolescents who were given the opportunity to move were significantly more likely to be retained and marginally more likely to drop out than adolescents in the control group.

Similarly, male and female adolescents (age 14–20) in the experimental voucher and assistance group reported lower school grades and engagement relative to the control groups who remained in highly concentrated-poverty neighborhoods in New York city (Leventhal, Fauth, & Brooks-Gunn, 2005). These findings were replicated in a 7-year follow-up for adolescent movers in Yonkers, NY, who also reported lower school performance than adolescents who stayed in public housing with highly concentrated social disadvantage (Fauth et al., 2007).

Emotional and Behavioral Well-Being

Across all five MTO sites, only one consistent difference emerged: female (but not male) adolescent movers experienced lower levels of distress, depression, and anxiety (Kling et al., 2007). Adolescents who moved in Baltimore were marginally more likely to be suspended or expelled from school (Ludwig, Duncan, & Hirschfield, 2001), whereas there appeared to be no significant reductions in male delinquency for MTO adolescents in New York (Kling, Ludwig, & Katz, 2005; Leventhal & Brooks-Gunn, 2003b). Ludwig and colleagues (2001) hypothesized that suspension and expulsion rates might vary because of differences in school discipline culture resulting in a confound potentially nullifying any MTO effect. In a meta-analysis of all five sites, adolescents in the experimental mover group were significantly more likely to have behavior problems at school from ages 11 to 14 according to parent reports (Sanbonmatsu et al., 2006).

In a non-school-related analysis of all five MTO sites, Kling and colleagues (2005) reported that the number of self-reported lifetime arrests for violent crimes was significantly lower (15%) for adolescents and young adults aged 15 to 25 years from families that received a housing voucher and assistance. These results replicated similar analyses and results found in Baltimore (Ludwig et al., 2001). Women in the experimental group were approximately one third less likely to be arrested for violent and property crimes, but men were more likely to be arrested for property crimes, especially in the 3 to 4 years following random assignment to the experimental group. Analyses of sibling arrest records reveal similar gender and crime-type effects. Variance across time in effects for juvenile and adult arrest rates for males seem to suggest that housing mobility/neighborhood effects are more robust for women than for men.

Findings from Yonkers suggest that similar increases in adolescent delinquency might be tied to lower levels of parental monitoring and potentially increased parenting employment (Fauth et al., 2007; 2008). Significant differences in behavior problems were especially strong for adolescents from the ages of 16 to 18 years (Fauth et al., 2005). At the same time, the same researchers found harsher parenting for mothers who moved in the MTO sample relative to those who stayed, a finding not necessarily contradicting the Yonkers results (Leventhal & Brooks-Gunn, 2005). Another possible pathway was discussed in an analysis of data from adolescent males in Chicago, suggesting that nonviolent delinquency is predicted by associations with deviant peers, informal socializing, and prior externalizing behavior problems (Gardner & Brooks-Gunn, 2009). An older analysis of adolescents in Chicago and Denver found that neighborhood disadvantage negatively predicted informal social control, number of friends (both prosocial and delinquent), and prosocial behavior for adolescents aged 10 to 18 years (Elliott et al., 1996). These deficits, in turn, were associated with poorer social integration in the Denver sample and more behavior problems reported in the Chicago sample.

Regarding findings for housing mobility programs, Jencks and Mayer (1990) argued that such trends might suggest that youth, and especially adolescent males, whose families relocated to less disadvantaged neighborhoods, would still return to their old neighborhoods. Fauth and colleagues (2005, 2007, & 2008) found no significant differences, however, in arrest patterns for adolescents with pretreatment records of antisocial behavior in the Yonkers study. Two other mechanisms seem more plausible. First, females in the experimental group were marginally more likely to have three or more adults to confide in, and believe that they will complete college, and less likely to have as many days absent from school than either their male counterparts or females from the control group. It is also possible that male adolescents in the experimental group responded to the relative achievement gap in their new schools by taking additional risks (Sanbonmatsu et al., 2006).

Adding credibility to this possibility are findings from Aneshensel and Sucoff's (1996) study of 877 adolescents in Los Angeles. Here, adolescents' perceived sense of neighborhood hazard (crime, violence, drug use, and graffiti) was associated with higher levels of depression, anxiety, oppositional defiant disorder symptoms, and conduct disorder symptoms. Similar to the more well-known findings by Sampson and colleagues (1997), Aneshensel and Sucoff (1996) found residential stability to be negatively associated with hazard and positively with adolescents' social cohesion, which served as a protective factor with regard to depression. Neighborhood hazard framed in terms of lower social capital and social disorder has also been associated with increased alcohol and drug use, independent of individual and family-level variables, in a sample of 38,000 adolescents (age 12–17; Winstanley et al., 2008).

Rather than testing theories based on deprivation models, Rosenbaum's (1995) study in Gautreaux examined experiences with overt racism on a smaller sample of approximately 90 adolescents. Black adolescents who had moved from public housing to the predominantly White suburbs did not experience significantly more name-calling and were not more likely to be threatened or harmed than Black adolescents who remained in the city. There were no significant differences between the groups with regard to being part of an in-group, being seen as popular, being socially active, or feeling like they did not fit in. Suburban Black youth were also more likely to have more White friends, and feel more positive about White friends, on average, than urban Black youth, while having no significant differences in the number of or relational quality of Black friendships.

Other more proximal mechanisms have also been considered as pathways of neighborhood influences on adolescents. Externalizing behavior has been associated with higher neighborhood residential instability (PHDCN: Browning et al., 2009; Child Development Project [CDP]: Beyers, Bates, Pettit, & Dodge, 2003). This negative influence was lower for the CDP study, however, in families with higher levels of parental monitoring (Beyers et al., 2003). Higher neighborhood disadvantage was associated with stronger negative influences of adolescents' attitudes and behaviors on younger siblings with regard to symptoms of conduct disorder in a non-inner-city sample of African American families (Brody, Ge, Conger, et al., 2003; Brody, Ge, Kim, et al.,2003).

Negative peer influences were also summative with neighborhood disadvantage in both Brody, Ge, Kim, et al.'s (2003b) non-inner-city sample of African Americans and in a sample of Midwestern 10th grade males (Cantillon, 2006; Cantillon, Davidson, & Schweitzer, 2003). By "summative," we refer to the additive nature of multiple risks on the outcome variable of interest. That is, risk factors at the neighborhood level (e.g., poverty/concentrated disadvantage or exposure to violence) add to the influence of risk factors faced at the individual or family levels. In these latter studies, sense of community and informal community social control served as protective factors for the influence of perceived disadvantage on delinquency (Cantillon, 2006; Cantillon et al., 2003). De Coster, Heimer, and Wittrock (2006) created a new measure of neighborhood milieu including peer delinquency as well as accessibility of guns, exposure to violence, and criminally violent victimization within the neighborhood. This new variable was aggregated at the neighborhood level and not only highly associated with more traditional measures of neighborhood disadvantage, but also served as a better predictor of participating adolescents committing crimes themselves (De Coster, Heimer, & Wittrock, 2006).

In one of the only studies focusing on neighborhoods and female adolescents, an interaction was found between pubertal timing and neighborhood disadvantage for adolescent females in Chicago (Obeidallah, Brennan, Brooks-Gunn, & Earls, 2004). That is, early pubertal maturation was associated with a threefold increase in violent behavior when the adolescent girls lived in neighborhoods with high levels of disadvantage compared with when girls lived in neighborhoods with lower levels of disadvantage.

Adults (18–50)

Neighborhood research on adults considers the previously considered domains: physical health and emotional and behavioral well-being, but considers employment and parenting in addition. Although cognitive outcomes are still relevant to those pursuing higher education, such outcomes are no longer nearly as universal as at earlier life stages. In a number of studies, poverty and concentrated disadvantage at the neighborhood level have been linked to deficits in the previously mentioned domains. Given the link between adult well-being and child development, a picture of the cyclical consequences of disadvantage begins to develop in this life phase.

Physical Health

In a five-city sample of adults aged 45 to 64 years, neighborhood disadvantage was associated with increased likelihood of having coronary heart disease and increased levels of risk factors such as smoking and cholesterol (Diez-Roux et al., 1997). Movers in Yonkers did feel significantly better in terms of physical health (Fauth et al., 2008), which matches results from families moving out of public housing in Boston (Katz et al., 2001). This improvement might be explained by reductions in exposure to violence as head of household reports showed significant treatment reductions in self-reports of seeing someone with a weapon, hearing gunfire, witnessing drug use or sales, and property crimes along with a significant increase in overall report of feeling safe (Katz et al., 2001). These findings did not hold across any of the other MTO sites, however, perhaps suggesting something unique about the Boston program in its earlier stages (Kling et al., 2007).

Physical activity, and walking in particular, serves as another potential mediator for the association between neighborhood disadvantage and poor health outcomes (Michael, Beard, Choi, Farquhar, & Carlson, 2006). Assessing neighborhood walkability for adult residents in 12 Boston-area housing projects, Bennett and colleagues (2007) found that perceived nighttime safety, but not daytime safety, was associated with a 26% increase in steps walked by women in the top tertile versus the lowest tertile with regard to perceived neighborhood safety. Given that a recent review of neighborhoods and obesity suggests that physical activity accounts for more of the variability in neighborhoods than the availability of healthy foods (Black & Macinko, 2008), perceived neighborhood safety is more important for residents' health than for Bennett and colleagues' sample group, where participants on average were obese (mean BMI = 30) and walking less than half the daily-recommended 10,000 steps.

Emotional and Behavioral Well-Being

Across all five sites, adults in the MTO experimental group reported better mental health (lower distress and worry, fewer depressive symptoms, increased calmness, and more sleep) than adults in the control group (Kling et al., 2007). Mover adults in Yonkers, however, reported no significant differences in mental health (Fauth et al., 2008).

Higher levels of drug use have been posited as both an emotional and physical response and risk factor (Boardman, Finch, Ellison, Williams, & Jackson, 2001). Such use then serves as one potential mediator for negative health outcomes associated with neighborhood disadvantage controlling for individual income.

Employment

Rosenbaum and Popkin (1991) have reported that housing voucher recipients in Gautreaux who moved to the suburbs were significantly more likely to be employed than those who remained in the city (64–51%), but those who worked did not receive higher wages or work more hours. Participants in the suburbs felt that there were more jobs available there, and that the suburbs provided enough safety for children so that parents could afford to work. In a 7-year follow-up of Yonkers families who relocated, mover adults were more likely to work and less likely to receive welfare than those families that stayed in areas with highly concentrated social disadvantage (Fauth et al., 2008). These findings were not replicated in MTO, however, where no significance evidence was found for improved economic self-sufficiency (Ludwig et al., 2008). Analysis of potential mediators from Yonkers suggest that mover adults felt their neighborhoods were safer for children and had higher levels of collective efficacy at both the 3- and 7-year follow-up, allowing adults to work and leave children at home (Fauth et al., 2004; 2008). Some fade-out effects were seen in Yonkers, however, as after 7 years adults no longer reported significant differences with regard to being satisfied with neighborhood resources and housing quality or regarding using alcohol and socializing with neighbors.

Parenting

The percentage of neighborhood families earning less than $10,000 (in 1985) was associated with poorer home physical environment (e.g., play environment does not appear safe; poor lighting) and decreased maternal warmth (e.g., less kissing or cuddling), even after controlling for family-level variables in a multisite study of premature, low-birth-weight babies (Klebanov et al., 1994). Parents who moved out of public housing in NYC reported significantly less (20%) distress than parents who remained in high-poverty neighborhoods 3 years after moving from highly concentrated to less-concentrated poor neighborhoods using the Hopkins Symptom Checklist (Leventhal & Brooks-Gunn, 2003b; Rickels, Garcia, Lipman, Derogatis, & Fisher, 1976).

Studies of neighborhood processes show that neighborhood dynamics such as social disorder, how often people witnessed people loitering, using substances, or behaving in a hostile manner in public, predict childcare and early childhood education decisions made by parents with variation by race (Burchinal et al., 2009). Children in neighborhoods with higher levels of inter-resident interaction were less likely to receive care from unrelated adults. In comparison, children in neighborhoods with higher levels of social cohesion and informal control were more likely to be cared for by unrelated adults. The previously mentioned association between neighborhood disadvantage and lower quality childcare centers grew when mothers had received less education (Burchinal et al., 2009). That is, there was a summative effect of family and neighborhood risk factors where, in poorer neighborhoods, less educated mothers were more likely to select even poorer quality centers than their fellow residents.

An analysis of data from the National Study of Children found that neighborhood disadvantage had an amplifying effect on the association between exposure to violence and negative family dynamics such as parental use of physical discipline and coercion and decreased parental monitoring (Hay, Fortson, Hollist, Altheimer, & Schaible, 2006). Findings from the National Longitudinal Study of Adolescent Health also suggest a weakened protective role for strong parent–child relationships in neighborhoods with fewer social resources (Wickrama & Bryant, 2003). Using longitudinal data, Kotchick, Dorsey, and Heller (2005) found that higher neighborhood stress had a negative influence on positive parenting 15 months later for mothers, a result that increased for mothers with fewer social supports. Similarly, Brody, Ge, Conger, et al., (2003) and Brody, Ge, Kim, et al. (2003) found that associations between harsh parenting and children's conduct disorder symptoms were larger in the most disadvantaged neighborhoods, in a sample of rural African American families.

In contrast, Cleveland, Gibbons, Gerrard, Pomery, and Brody's (2005) analysis of that same sample found that positive parenting (monitoring, communication regarding substance use, and parental warmth) when children were 10 years old served to protect against alcohol, tobacco, and marijuana use at age 15. Also, as previously discussed, increased parental monitoring was found to be a protective factor against early adolescent externalizing behavior in neighborhoods with higher residential instability (Beyers et al., 2003). Another positive parenting technique, use of inductive reasoning with children, served as a protective factor against depressive symptoms among youth aged 11–13 years in disadvantaged neighborhoods (Beyers et al., 2003).

Finally, one contrary study by Stewart, Simons, and Conger (2002) suggests that family-level variables (e.g., associating with violent peers, parental use of violence) is associated with neighborhood affluence rather than poverty in negatively predicting childhood violence in a sample of 867 rural African American youth. Further research is needed to bridge this present paradox: studies with more representative participant samples tend to find associations with affluence, whereas studies targeted disadvantage populations have tended to find differences associated with poverty.

Older Adults (50+)

A growing population in much of the developed world, older adults typically have fewer childcare responsibilities and typically rely on some sort of pre-established income (i.e., retirement or government benefits). At the same time, older adults tend to be at risk, on average, of living in neighborhoods with lower education levels in the United States (Wight et al., 2006) and in neighborhood with lower SES (Lang et al., 2008). Much research on older adults, then, focuses on rates of aging in physical health and cognitive outcomes, with concentrated disadvantage being associated with steeper rates of decline.

Physical Health

Studies in both rural and urban areas have showed proximity to and frequency of safe walking areas in neighborhoods are associated with increased exercise for older adults (Shores, West, Theriault, & Davison, 2009; Takano et al., 2002). Community support of physical activity also predicted exercise in the sample of rural older adults (Shores et al., 2009), and King (2008) found that perceived social cohesion and safety outweighed neighborhood physical conditions as predictors of older adults walking in a city-level study of Denver neighborhoods, a finding supported by the negative association between car traffic and amount of time spent walking in a sample of older adults in Portland, Oregon (Nagel, Carlson, Bosworth, & Michael, 2008). In a review of research on the association between perceived neighborhood safety on physical activity, Loukaitou-Sideris (2006) found age, and in particular being older, to be a key determinant in significant associations between neighborhood condition and physical activity as well as being overweight.

In an analysis of a nationally representative sample of adults older than 70 years in 1993, associations with neighborhood poverty and racial/ethnic composition became nonsignificant once individual-level variables were controlled (Aneshensel et al., 2007). Analyzing the same sample of 2,000 older adults in New Haven reported earlier, Subramanian, Kubzansky, Berkman, Fay, and Kawachi (2006) found neighborhood poverty to be associated with lower self-rated health, with the percentage of elderly adults in the neighborhood serving as a protective factor. In an analysis of observed versus perceived neighborhood conditions in a sample of older adults (50–67 years old) in Chicago, the influence of Census-measured physical and institutional environments was reduced to nonsignificance when including individual-level variables (Wen, Hawkley, & Capioppo, 2006). Perceived neighborhood social environment, based on social cohesion and participatory opportunities, however, was positively associated with self-reported health even after controlling for individual-level variables.

During an atypically long heat wave in Chicago in 1995, commercial decline (defined as presence of burned out, abandoned, or boarded up commercial buildings, liquor stores or advertising, bars, pool halls, or video game parlors) was associated with higher neighborhood mortality rates for adults older than 60 years (Browning, Wallace, Feinberg, & Cagney, 2006). Although collective efficacy was not associated with neighborhood mortality rates during this period, it was significantly associated with lower neighborhood mortality rates during more typical summer periods in the years preceding and following the heat wave.

In another study of Chicago residents, it was found that neighborhood affluence interacted with individual income for post-hospitalization mortality in a sample of 10,000 Medicaid patients (Wen & Christakis, 2005). That is, neighborhood affluence was generally associated with higher likelihood of survival, especially in cases involving myocardial infarctions, and was associated with even higher survival rates for wealthier individuals post-hospitalization but was detrimental for the poorer residents in those same neighborhoods. Wen and Christakis (2005) have argued that this evidences a relative deprivation effect derived from lower level of perceived social standing. Residential instability, in turn, has been associated with increased likelihood of ischemic heart disease following a myocardial infarction, with higher mean neighborhood income serving as a protective factor in a sample of 56- to 70-year-old Swedish adults (Chaix, Rosvall, & Merlo, 2007).

Cognitive Outcomes

A few studies suggest that neighborhood factors are associated with differential rates of cognitive decline for the elderly. The English Longitudinal Study of Aging conducted a battery of cognitive assessments testing time orientation, verbal fluency, working memory, attention, and mental speed on 7,000 adults older than 50 years (Lang et al., 2008). Controlling for individual education and SES, a combined measure of neighborhood deprivation (poverty, unemployment, fewer educational and health care services, inadequate housing, physical and social disorder), accounted for differences in cognitive functioning for adults both between 50 and 70 years old and 70 years old and older (Lang et al., 2008). The difference between individuals living in the least deprived neighborhoods (top quintile) and those living in the most deprived neighborhoods (bottom quintile) was 0.26 of one standard deviation, with significant differences for all women and for men younger than 70 years. This finding has been replicated in a sample of older adults in San Antonio (Espino, Lichtenstein, Palmer, & Hazuda, 2001). Wight and colleagues (2006) also found that neighborhood education level, above and beyond individual-level education, predicted cognitive functioning in a national sample of 3,400 older adults.

Emotional and Behavioral Well-Being

The concentration of poverty has been associated with the manifestation of depressive symptoms in a sample of adults older than 65 years in New Haven, Connecticut (Kubzansky et al., 2005). At the same time, the concentration of elderly people in this same sample had a protective effect, although this finding should be interpreted with caution because the data were collected in 1982 and serve simply to partially offset the finding regarding poverty.

FUTURE DIRECTIONS IN THE STUDY OF NEIGHBORHOODS AND LIFE-SPAN DEVELOPMENT

In general, the descriptive and longitudinal findings from IHDP, PSID, and PHDCN suggest that neighborhood characteristics and dynamics are associated with a number of developmental outcomes. Attempts to show causal relationships through housing mobility programs reveal few consistent findings. The most consistently positive study seems to be at the original site, Gautreaux. Rosenbaum (1995) has explained that Gautreaux was a narrowly tailored program that excluded families that had large debts, had more than four children, or were deemed to have poor housekeeping practices and only included families that were in the process of moving. Neighborhoods that families moved into were carefully screened to avoid White flight or racist groups (e.g., the Ku Klux Klan had active groups in two of the Chicago suburbs considered) and also to avoid re-segregating Black families in predominantly Black suburbs. The rate of movement of Black families into predominantly White suburbs was carefully monitored to prevent "White flight" from neighborhoods as previously researched by Farley, Bianchi, and Colasanto (1979), who also noted possible shifts in U.S. racial attitudes from region to region (Farley & Frey, 1994). Most importantly perhaps, though, was that positive effects from Gautreaux were not found until several years after families had moved. Finally, unlike the other mobility experiments, Gautreaux families moved to the suburbs, which were affluent and had high quality schools. MTO and Yonkers, in contrast, had families who moved from poor to middle-income or working-class inner ring suburbs or within the city. Another explanation for variation in the findings is the role of welfare reform that was enacted after Gautreaux and before MTO had begun resulting in many more mothers entering the work force with potential effects on child development.

What is also needed is the use of qualitative in addition to quantitative studies such as ethnographic reviews of underground economies and partnering with lower tier social institutions (Venkatesh, 1997; 1999). Although not discussed here, much qualitative research has already informed research findings such as why girls but not boys were influenced in certain domains in certain interventions or why the

MTO intervention was weak to begin with (Turney, Clampet-Lundquist, Edin, Kling, & Duncan, 2006). The continued use of natural experiments is also recommended (Oakes, 2004), with perhaps novel attempts to understand how treatments beyond housing can be considered (e.g., Costello, Compton, Keeler, & Angold, 2003) as new studies have questioned the previously unquestioned condemnation of public housing as a whole (Currie & Yelowitz, 2000; Venkatesh, 2002).

As research on neighborhood influences on development continues to become more intentional and experimentally designed, findings continue to suggest associations between neighborhood characteristics and dynamics and development across the life span. In particular, neighborhood factors have been linked to small to moderate changes in physical health, cognitive development, behavioral self-regulation, and family processes. Although these direct effect sizes are generally smaller than would be found for individual or family-level variables, the extant research also points to numerous examples of indirect influences through these individual and family-level variables. Future research should seek to replicate existing findings as well as explore ways to manipulate variables in a more experimentally controlled fashion. Current neighborhood research, and especially longitudinal programs, must also consider further research on older adults, who are increasingly becoming segregated residentially from the rest of the population (Glymour & Manly, 2008). Research on the interaction between culture and SES is especially needed in our rapidly globalizing and modernizing world.

ACKNOWLEDGMENT

We would like to thank our colleagues at the National Center for Children and Families, Teachers College, Columbia University, as well as the following federal government agencies: NICHD, NSF, NIMH, NIJ, HUD; and also the Spencer Foundation, the Russell Sage Foundation, March of Dimes, and the John D. and Catherine T. MacArthur Foundation, for funding our center's research on neighborhoods.

REFERENCES

Aber, J. L., Gephart, M., Brooks-Gunn, J., Connell, J., & Spencer, M. B. (1997). Neighborhood, family and individual processes as they influence child and adolescent outcomes. In J. Brooks-Gunn, G. J. Duncan, & J. L. Aber (Eds.), *Neighborhood poverty: Volume 1. Context and consequences for children* (pp. 44–61). New York: Russell Sage Foundation.

Anderson, E. (1978). *A place on the corner.* Chicago: University of Chicago Press.

Aneshensel, C. S., & Sucoff, C.A. (1996). The neighborhood context of adolescent mental health. *Journal of Health and Social Behavior, 37,* 293–310.

Aneshensel, C. S., Wight, R. G., Miller-Martinez, D., Botticello, A. L., Karlamangla, A. S., & Seeman, T. E. (2007). Urban neighborhoods and depressive symptoms among older adults. *Journal of Gerontology, 62B*(1), S52–59.

Bass, J. K., & Lambert, S.F. (2004). Urban adolescents' perceptions of their neighborhoods: An examination of spatial dependence. *Journal of Community Psychology, 32*(3), 277.

Bennett, G. G., McNeill, L. H., Wolin, K. Y., Duncan, D. T., Puleo, E., & Emmons, K. M. (2007). Safe to walk? Neighborhood safety and physical activity among public housing residents. *PLoS Medicine, 4*(10), 1599–1607.

Beyers, J. M., Bates, J. E., Pettit, G. S., & Dodge, K. A. (2003). Neighborhood structure, parenting processes, and the development of youths' externalizing behaviors: A multilevel analysis. *American Journal of Community Psychology, 31*(1–2), 35–53.

Black, J. L., & Macinko, J. (2008). Neighborhoods and obesity. *Nutrition Review, 66*(1), 2–20.

Blain, D. (1999). The life course, the social gradient, and health. In R. G. Wilkinson & M. Marmot (Eds.), *Social determinants of health* (pp. 64–80). New York: Oxford University Press.

Block, J. P., Scribner, R. A., & DeSalvo, K. B. (2004). Fast food, race/ethnicity, and income: A geographic analysis. *American Journal of Preventative Medicine, 27*(3), 211–217.

Boardman, J. D., Finch, B. K., Ellison, C. G., Williams, D. R., & Jackson, J. S. (2001). Neighborhood disadvantage, stress, and drug use among adults. *Journal of Health and Social Behavior, 42*(2), 151–165.

Briggs, X. D. (1998). Brown kids in white suburbs: Housing mobility and the many faces of social capital. *Housing Policy Debate, 9*(1), 177–221.

Brody, G. H., Ge, X., Conger, R., Gibbons, F. X., Murry, V. M., Gerrard, M., et al. (2003).The influence of neighborhood disadvantage, collective socialization, and parenting on African American children's affiliation with deviant peers. *Child Development, 72*, 1231–1246.

Brody, G. H., Ge, X., Kim, S. Y., Murry, V. M., Simons, R. L., Gibbons, F. X., et al. (2003). Neighborhood disadvantage moderates associations of parenting and older sibling problem attitudes and behavior with conduct disorder in African American children. *Journal of Consulting and Clinical Psychology, 71*(2), 211–222.

Bronfenbrenner, U. (1979). *The ecology of human development.* Cambridge, MA: Harvard University Press.

Bronfenbrenner, U. (1986). Ecology of the family as a context for human development: Research perspectives. *Developmental Psychology, 22*, 723–742.

Brooks-Gunn, J., Duncan, G. J., Klebanov, P. K., & Sealand, N. (1993). Do neighborhoods influence child and adolescent development? *American Journal of Sociology, 99*(2), 353–395.

Brooks-Gunn, J., Klebanov, P. K., & Duncan, G. J. (1996). Ethnic differences in children's intelligence test scores: Role of economic deprivation, home environment, and maternal characteristics. *Child Development, 67*(2), 396–408.

Brooks-Gunn, J., McCormick, M. C., Klebanov, P. K., & McCarton, C. (1998). Health care use of 3-year-old low birth weight premature children: Effects of family and neighborhood poverty. *Journal of Pediatrics, 132*(6), 971–975.

Brooks-Gunn, J., & Paikoff, R. (1993). "Sex is a gamble, kissing is a game": Adolescent sexuality and health promotion. In S. G. Millstein, A. C. Peterson, & E. O. Nightingale (Eds.), *Promoting the health of adolescents: New directions for the 21st century* (pp. 180–208). New York: Oxford University Press.

Brown, A. F., Ang, A., & Pebley, A. R. (2007). The relationship between neighborhood characteristics and self-rated health for adults with chronic conditions. *American Journal of Public Health, 97*(5), 926–932.

Browning, C. R., Burrington, L. A., Leventhal, T., & Brooks-Gunn, J. (2008). Neighborhood structural inequality, collective efficacy, and sexual risk behavior among urban youth. *Journal of Health and Social Behavior, 49*(3), 269–285.

Browning, C. R., Gardner, M., Maimon, D., & Brooks-Gunn, J. (2009). *Collective efficacy and the contingent consequences of exposure to lethal violence.* Unpublished manuscript.

Browning, C. R., Leventhal, T., & Brooks-Gunn, J. (2004). Neighborhood context and racial differences in early adolescent sexual activity. *Demography, 41*(4), 697–720.

Browning, C. R., Leventhal, T., & Brooks-Gunn, J. (2005). Sexual initiation in early adolescence: The nexus of parental and community control. *American Sociological Review, 70*(5), 758–778.

Browning, C. R., Wallace, D., Feinberg, S. L., & Cagney, K. A. (2006). Neighborhood social processes, physical conditions, and disaster-related mortality: The case of the 1995 Chicago Heat Wave. *American Sociological Review, 71*, 661–678.

Buka, S. L., Brennan, R. T., Rich-Edwards, J. W., Raudenbush, S. W., & Earls, F. J. (2003). Neighborhood support and the birth weight of urban infants. *American Journal of Epidemiology, 157*(1), 1–8.

Burchinal, M., Nelson, L., Carlson, M., & Brooks-Gunn. (2009). Neighborhood characteristics, and child care type and quality. *Early Education and Development, 19*(5), 702–725.

Buu, A., DiPiazza, C., Wang, J., Puttler, L. I., Fitzgerald, H. E., & Zucker, R. A. (2009). Parent, family and neighborhood effects on the development of child substance use and other psychopathology from preschool to the start of adulthood. *Journal of Studies on Alcohol and Drugs, 70*(4), 489–498.

Buu, A., Mansour, M., Wang, J., Refior, S. K., Fitzgerald, H. E., & Zucker, R. A. (2007). Alcoholism effects on social migration and neighborhood effects on alcoholism over the course of 12 years. *Alcoholism: Clinical and Experimental Research, 31*(9), 1545–1551.

Caldwell, B. M., & Bradley, R. H. (1984). *Home observation for measurement of the environment.* Little Rock, AR: University of Arkansas Press.

Campbell, F. A., Ramey, C. T., Pungello, E., Sparling, J., & Miller-Johnson, S. (2002). Early childhood education: Young adult outcomes from the Abecedarian Project. *Applied Developmental Science, 6*(1), 42–57.

Cantillon, D. (2006). Community social organization, parents, and peers as mediators of perceived neighborhood block characteristics on delinquent and prosocial activities. *American Journal of Community Psychology, 37*(1–2), 111–127.

Cantillon, D., Davidson, W. S., & Schweitzer, J. H. (2003). Measuring community social organization: Sense of community as a mediator in social disorganization theory. *Journal of Criminal Justice, 31*, 321–339.

Chaix, B., Rosvall, M., & Merlo, J. (2007). Neighborhood socioeconomic deprivation and residential instability: Effects on incidence of ischemic heart disease and survival after myocardial infarction. *Epidemiology, 18*(1), 104–111.

Chase-Lansdale, L. P., & Gordon, R. A. (1996). Economic hardship and the development of five- and six-year-olds: Neighborhood and regional perspectives. *Child Development, 67*, 3338–3367.

Chase-Lansdale, P. L., Gordon, R. A., Brooks-Gunn, J., & Klebanov, P. K. (1997).Neighborhood and family influences on the intellectual and behavioral competence of preschool and early school-age children. In J. Brooks-Gunn, G. J. Duncan, & J. L. Aber (Eds.), *Neighborhood poverty: Vol. I. Context and consequences for children* (pp. 79–118). New York: Russell Sage Foundation.

Chase-Lansdale, P. L., Mott, F. L., Brooks-Gunn, J., & Phillips, D. A. (1991). Children of the National Longitudinal Survey of Youth: A unique research opportunity. *Developmental Psychology, 27*(6), 918–931.

Chay, K. Y., & Greenstone, M. (2003). The impact of air pollution on infant mortality: Evidence from geographic variation in pollution shocks induced by a recession. *Quarterly Journal of Economics, 118*(3), 1121–1167.

Clampet-Lundquist, S. (2004). HOPE VI relocation: Moving to new neighborhoods and building new ties. *Housing Policy Debate, 15*(2), 415–447.

Clampet-Lundquist, S., & Massey, D. S. (2008). Neighborhood effects on economic self-sufficiency: A reconsideration of the moving to opportunity experiment. *American Journal of Sociology, 114*(1), 107–143.

Cleveland, M. J., Gibbons, F. X., Gerrard, M., Pomery, E. A., & Brody, G. H. (2005). The impact of parenting on risk cognitions and risk behavior: A study of mediation and moderation in a panel of African American adolescents. *Child Development, 76*, 900–916.

Conger, R. D., & Conger, K. J. (2002). Resilience in Midwestern families: Selected findings from the first decade of a prospective, longitudinal study. *Journal of Marriage and Family, 64*(2), 361–373.

Conger, R. D., & Donnellan, M. B. (2007). An interactionist perspective on the socioeconomic context of human development. *Annual Review of Psychology, 58*, 175–199.

Costello, E. J., Compton, S. N., Keeler, G., & Angold, A. (2003). Relationships between poverty and psychopathology: A natural experiment. *Journal of the American Medical Association, 290*(15), 2023–2029.

Coulton, C. J., Korbin, J., Chan, T., & Su, M. (2001). Mapping residents' perceptions of neighborhood boundaries: A methodological note. *American Journal of Community Psychology, 29*(2), 371–383.

Crane, J. (1991). The epidemic theory of ghettos and neighborhood effects on dropping out and teenage childbearing. *American Journal of Sociology, 96*(5), 1226–1259.

Currie, J., & Neidell, M. (2005). Air pollution and infant health: What can we learn from California's recent experience. *Quarterly Journal of Economics, 120*(3), 1003–1030.

Currie, J., & Yelowitz, A. (2000). Are public housing projects good for kids? *Journal of Public Economics, 112*, 99–124.

Curtis, L. (1975). *Violence, race, and culture.* Lexington, MA: Heath.

Dearing, E., Wimer, C., Simpkins, S. D., Lund, T., Bouffard, S. M., Caronongan, P., et al. (2009). Do neighborhood and home contexts help explain why low-income children miss opportunities to participate in activities outside of school?. *Developmental Psychology, 45*, 1545–1562.

De Coster, S., Heimer, K., & Wittrock, S. M. (2006). Neighborhood disadvantage, social capital, street context, and youth violence. *The Sociological Quarterly, 47*(4), 723–753.

Diez Roux, A. V., Nieto, F. J., Muntaner, C., Tyroler, H. A., Comstock, G. W., Shahar, E., et al. (1997). Neighborhood environments and coronary heart disease: A multilevel analysis. *American Journal of Epidemiology, 146*(1), 48–63.

Duncan, G. J., Brooks-Gunn, J., & Klebanov, P. K. (1994). Economic deprivation and early-childhood development. *Child Development, 65*(2), 296–318.

Duncan, G. J., Magnuson, K. A., & Ludwig, J. (2004). The endogeneity problem in developmental studies. *Research in Human Development, 1*(1–2), 59–80.

Duncan, G. J., & Raudenbush, S. W. (1999). Assessing the effects of context in studies of child and youth development. *Educational Psychologist, 34*(1), 29–41.

Earls, F. J., Brooks-Gunn, J., Raudenbush, S. W., & Sampson, S. J. (1997). *Project on Human Development in Chicago Neighborhoods, Community Survey, 1994–1995.* Boston: Harvard Medical School.

Elder, G. H. (1999). *Children of the great depression (25th anniversary ed.).* Boulder, CO: Westview Press.

Eley, T. C., Sugden, K., Corsico, A., Gregory, A. M., Sham, P., McGuffin, P., et al. (2004). Gene-environment interaction analysis of serotonin system markers with adolescent depression. *Molecular Psychiatry, 9*(10), 908–915.

Elliott, D. S., Wilson, W. J., Huizinga, D., Sampson, R. J., Elliott, A., & Rankin, B. (1996).The effects of neighborhood disadvantage on adolescent development. *Journal of Research in Crime and Delinquency, 33*(4), 389–426.

Entwisle, B. (2007). Putting people into place. *Demography, 44*(4), 687–703.

Espino, D. V., Lichtenstein, M. J., Palmer, R. F., & Hazuda, H. P. (2001). Ethnic differences in Mini-Mental State Examination (MMSE) scores: Where you live makes a difference. *Journal of the American Geriatrics Society, 49*(5), 538–548.

Farley, R., Bianchi, S., & Colasanto, D. (1979). Barriers to the racial integration of neighborhoods: The Detroit case. *Annals of the American Academy of Political and Social Science, 411*, 97–113.

Farley, R., & Frey, W. H. (1994). Changes in the segregation of whites from blacks during the 1980s: Small steps toward a more integrated society. *American Sociological Review, 59*(1), 23–45.

Fauth, R. C., & Brooks-Gunn, J. (2007). Are some neighborhoods better for child health than others? In R. F. Schoeni, J. S. House, G. A. Kaplan, & H. Pollack (Eds.), *Making Americans healthier: Social and economic policy as health policy* (pp. 344–376). New York: Russell Sage Foundation.

Fauth, R. C., & Brooks-Gunn, J. (2008). Are some neighborhoods better for child health than others? In R. F. Schoeni, J. S. House, G. A. Kalpan, & H. Pollack (Eds.), *Making Americans healthier: Social and economic policy as health policy* (pp. 344–376). New York: Russell Sage Foundation.

Fauth, R. C., Leventhal, T., & Brooks-Gunn, J. (2004). Short-term effects of moving from public housing in poor to middle-class neighborhoods on low-income, minority adults' outcomes. *Social Science & Medicine, 59*(11), 2271–2284.

Fauth, R. C., Leventhal, T., & Brooks-Gunn, J. (2005). Early impacts of moving from poor to middle-class neighborhoods on low-income youth. *Journal of Applied Developmental Psychology, 26*(4), 415–439.

Fauth, R. C., Leventhal, T., & Brooks-Gunn, J. (2007). Welcome to the neighborhood? Long-term impacts of moving to low-poverty neighborhoods on poor children's and adolescents' outcomes. *Journal of Research on Adolescence, 17*(2), 249–284.

Fauth, R. C., Leventhal, T., & Brooks-Gunn, J. (2008). Seven years later: Effects of a neighborhood mobility program on poor black and Latino adults' well-being. *Journal of Health and Social Behavior, 49*(2), 119–130.

Fauth, R. C., Roth, J. L., & Brooks-Gunn, J. (2007). Does the neighborhood context alter the link between youth's after-school time activities and developmental outcomes? A multilevel analysis. *Developmental Psychology, 43*(3), 760–777.

Feins, J. D., Holin, M. J., & Phipps, A. (1996). *Moving to opportunity for fair housing program operations manual.* Cambridge, MA: Abt Associates.

Florence, M. D., Asbridge, M., & Veugelers, P. J. (2008). Diet quality and academic performance. *Journal of School Health, 78*(4), 209–215.

Furstenberg, F. F. (1993). How families manage risk and opportunity in dangerous neighborhoods. In W. J. Wilson (Ed.), *Sociology and the public agenda* (pp. 231–258). Newbury Park, CA: Sage.

Furstenberg, F. F., Brooks-Gunn, J., & Morgan, S. P. (1987). *Adolescent mothers in later life.* New York: Cambridge University Press.

Furstenberg, F. F., Morgan, S. P., Moore, K. A., & Peterson, J. (1987). Race differences in the timing of adolescent intercourse. *American Sociological Review, 52*, 511–518.

Gardner, M., & Brooks-Gunn, J. (2009). Adolescents' exposure to community violence: Are neighborhood youth organizations protective? *Journal of Community Psychology, 37*(4), 505–525.

Gault, M., & Silver, E. (2008). Spuriousness or mediation? Broken windows according to Sampson and Raudenbush (1999). *Journal of Criminal Justice, 36*(3), 240–243.

Gladwell, M. (2002). *The tipping point: How little things can make a big difference.* New York: Little, Brown & Company.

Glymour, M. M., & Manly, J. J. (2008). Lifecourse social conditions and racial and ethnic patterns of cognitive aging. *Neuropsychological Review, 18*(3), 223–254.

Goering, J., Kraft, J., Feins, J. D., McInnis, D., Holin, M. J., & Elhassan, H. (1999). *Moving to opportunity for fair housing demonstration program: Current status and initial findings.* Washington, DC: US Department of Housing and Urban Development.

Halfon, N., & Hochstein, M. (2002). Life course health development: An integrated framework for developing health, policy, and research. *The Milbank Quarterly, 80*(3), 433–479.

Hay, C., Fortson, E. N., Hollist, D. R., Altheimer, I., & Schaible, L. M. (2006). The impact of community disadvantage on the relationship between the family and juvenile crime. *Journal of Research in Crime and Delinquency, 43*(4), 326–356.

Heckman, J. J., & Smith, J. A. (2004). The determinants of participation in a social program: Evidence from a prototypical job training program. *Journal of Labor Economics, 22*(2), 243–298.

Hipp, J. R. (2007). Income inequality, race, and place: Does the distribution of race and class within neighborhoods affect crime rates? *Criminology, 45*(3), 665–697.

Hogan, D. P., & Kitagawa, E. M. (1985). The impact of social status, family structure, and neighborhood on the fertility of black adolescents. *American Journal of Sociology, 90*, 825–855.

Infant Health and Development Program. (1990). The Infant Health and Development Program, Enhancing the outcomes of low-birth-weight, premature infants: A multisite, randomized trial, *Journal of the American Medical Association, 263*, 3035–3042.

Jencks, C., & Mayer, S. (1990). The social consequences of grow up in a poor neighborhood. In L. E. Lynn & M. F. H. McGeary (Eds.), *Inner-city poverty in the United States* (pp. 111–186). Washington, DC; National Academy Press.

Jerrett, M., Burnett, R. T., Ma, R., Pope, C. A., III, Krewski, D., Newbold, K. B., et al. (2005). Spatial analysis of air pollution and mortality in Los Angeles. *Epidemiology, 16*(6), 727–736.

Kain, J. F. (1968). Housing segregation, Negro employment, and metropolitan decentralization. *Quarterly Journal of Economics, 87*(2), 175–197.

Katz, L. F., Kling, J. R., & Liebman, J. B. (2001). Moving to Opportunity in Boston: Early results of a randomized mobility experiment. *Quarterly Journal of Economics,* 116(2), 607–654.

King, D. (2008). Neighborhood and individual factors in activity in older adults: Results from the neighborhood and senior health study. *Journal of Aging and Physical Activity, 16*(2), 144–170.

Klebanov, P. K., Brooks-Gunn, J., & Duncan, G. J. (1994). Does neighborhood and family poverty affect mothers parenting, mental-health, and social support. *Journal of Marriage and the Family, 56*(2), 441–455.

Klebanov, P. K., Brooks-Gunn, J., McCarton, C., & McCormick, M. C. (1998). The contribution of neighborhood and family income to developmental test scores over the first three years of life. *Child Development,* 69(5), 1420–1436.

Kling, J. R., Liebman, J. B., & Katz, L. F. (2007). Experimental analysis of neighborhood effects. *Econometrica, 75*(1), 83–119.

Kling, J. R., Ludwig, J., & Katz, L. F. (2005). Neighborhood effects on crime for female and male youth: Evidence from a randomized housing voucher experiment. *The Quarterly Journal of Economics, 120*(1), 87–130.

Kohen, D. E., Brooks-Gunn, J., Leventhal, T., & Hertzman, C. (2002). Neighborhood income and physical and social disorder in Canada: Associations with young children's competencies. *Child Development,* 73(6), 1844–1860.

Kornhauser, R. R. (1978). *Social sources of delinquency: An appraisal of analytic models.* Chicago: University of Chicago Press.

Kotchick, B. A., Dorsey, S., & Heller, L. (2005). Predictors of parenting among African American single mothers: Personal and contextual factors. *Journal of Marriage and Family, 67*(2), 448–460.

Kubzansky, L. D., Subramanian, S. V., Kawachi, I., Fay, M. E., Soobader, M. J., & Berkman, L. F. (2005). Neighborhood contextual influences on depressive symptoms in the elderly. *American Journal of Epidemiology, 162*(3), 253–260.

Kumanyika, S., & Grier, S. (2006). Targeting interventions for ethnic minority and low-income populations. *The Future of Children, 16*(1), 187–207.

Lang, I. A., Llewellyn, D. J., Langa, K. M., Wallace, R. B., Huppert, F. A., & Melzer, D. (2008). Neighborhood deprivation, individual socioeconomic status, and cognitive function in older people: Analyses from the English Longitudinal Study of Ageing. *Journal of the American Geriatric Society, 56*(2), 191–198.

Lara-Cinisomo, S., & Griffin, B. A. (2007). Factors associated with major depression among mothers in Los Angeles. *Women's Health Issues, 17*(5), 316–324.

LaVeist, T. A., & Wallace, J. M., Jr. (2000). Health risk and inequitable distribution of liquor stores in African-American neighborhood. *Social Science & Medicine, 51*(4), 613–617.

Leventhal, T., & Brooks-Gunn, J. (2000). The neighborhoods they live in: The effects of neighborhood residence on child and adolescent outcomes. *Psychological Bulletin, 126*(2), 309–337.

Leventhal, T., & Brooks-Gunn, J. (2003a). Children and youth in neighborhood contexts. *Current Directions in Psychological Science, 12*(1), 27–31.

Leventhal, T., & Brooks-Gunn, J. (2003b). Moving to opportunity: An experimental study of neighborhood effects on mental health. *American Journal of Public Health, 93*(9), 1576–1582.

Leventhal, T., & Brooks-Gunn, J. (2004). A randomized study of neighborhood effects on low-income children's educational outcomes. *Developmental Psychology, 40*(4), 488–507.

Leventhal, T., & Brooks-Gunn, J. (2005). Neighborhood and gender effects on family processes: Results from the moving to opportunity program. *Family Relations, 54*(5), 633–643.

Leventhal, T., Fauth, R. C., & Brooks-Gunn, J. (2005). Neighborhood poverty and public policy: A 5-year follow-up of children's educational outcomes in the New York City moving to opportunity demonstration. *Developmental Psychology, 41*(6), 933–952.

Leventhal, T., Selner-O'Hagan, M. B., Brooks-Gunn, J., Bingenheimer, J. B., & Earls, F. J. (2004). The homelife interview from the project on human development in Chicago neighborhoods: Assessment of parenting and home environment for 3- to 15-year olds. *Parenting: Science and Practice, 4*, 211–241.

Leventhal, T., Xue, Y., & Brooks-Gunn, J. (2006). Immigrant differences in school-age children's verbal trajectories: A look at four racial/ethnic groups. *Child Development, 77*(5), 1359–1374.

Lewin, K. (1936). *Principles of topological psychology.* (F. Heider & G. M. Heider, Trans.) New York: McGraw-Hill.

Lleras-Muney, A. (2005.) The needs of the army: Using compulsory relocation in the military to estimate the effects of air pollutants on children's health. Unpublished working paper, Princeton University.

Loukaitou-Sideris, A. (2006). Is it safe to walk? Neighborhood safety and security considerations and their effects on walking. *Journal of Planning Literature, 20*(3), 219–232.

Ludwig, J., Duncan, G. J., & Hirschfield, P. (2001). Urban poverty and juvenile crime: Evidence from a randomized housing mobility experiment. *Quarterly Journal of Economics, 116*(2), 655–679.

Ludwig, J., Ladd, H. F., & Duncan, G. J. (2001). Urban poverty and educational outcomes. *Brookings-Wharton Papers on Urban Affairs, 21*, 147–201.

Ludwig, J., Liebman, J. B., Kling, J. R., Duncan, G. J., Katz, L. F., Kessler, R. C., et al. (2008). What can we learn about neighborhood effects from the moving to opportunity experiment? *American Journal of Sociology, 114*(1), 144–188.

Lyons, C. J. (2008). Defending turf: Racial demographics and hate crimes against blacks and whites. *Social Forces, 87*(1), 357–385.

Magnuson, K. (2007). Maternal education and children's academic achievement during middle childhood. *Developmental Psychology, 43*(6), 1497–1512.

Maimon, D., Browning, C. R., & Brooks-Gunn, J. (2010). *Collective efficacy, family attachment, and urban adolescent suicide attempts.* Unpublished manuscript.

Massey, D., & Denton, N. (1993). *American apartheid: Segregation and the making of the American underclass.* Cambridge, MA: Harvard University Press.

Mayer, S., & Jencks, C. (1989). Growing up in poor neighborhoods: How much does it really matter? *Science, 243*(4897), 1441–1445.

McLoyd, V. C. (1998). Socioeconomic disadvantage and child development. *American Psychologist, 53*, 185–204.

Michael, Y., Beard, T., Choi, D. S., Farquhar, S., & Carlson, N. (2006). Measuring the influence of built neighborhood environments on walking in older adults. *Journal of Aging and Physical Activity, 14*(3), 302–312.

Morenoff, J. D. (2003). Neighborhood mechanisms and the spatial dynamics of birthweight. *American Journal of Sociology, 108*(5), 976–1017.

Moudon, A. V., Lee, C., Cheadle, A. D., Garvin, C., Johnson, D., Schmid, T. L., et al. (2006). Operational definitions of walkable neighborhoods: Theoretical and empirical insights. *Journal of Physical Activity and Health, 3*(Suppl 1), S99–S117.

Musick, K., Seltzer, J. A., & Schwartz, C. R. (2008). Neighborhood norms and substance use among teens. *Social Science Research, 37*(1), 138–155.

Myers, D. E. (1985). The relationship between school poverty concentration and students' reading and math achievement and learning. In M. Kennedy, R. Jung, & M. Orland (Eds.) *Poverty, achievement and the distribution of compensatory education services* (D17–D60).Washington, DC: U.S. Department of Education, Office of Educational Research and Improvement.

Nagel, C. L., Carlson, N. E., Bosworth, M., & Michael, Y. L. (2008). The relation between neighborhood built environment and walking activity among older adults. *American Journal of Epidemiology, 168*(4), 461–468.

O'Hare, W., & Mather, M. (2003). *The growing number of kids in severely distressed neighborhoods: Evidence from the 2000 Census*. Washington, DC: Anne E. Casey Foundation.

Oakes, J. M. (2004). The (mis)estimation of neighborhood effects: Causal inference for a practicable social epidemiology. *Social Science Medicine, 58*(10), 1929–1952.

Oh, J. H. (2003a). Social bonds and the migration intentions of elderly urban residents: The mediating effect of residential satisfaction. *Population Research and Policy Review, 22*(2), 127–146.

Oh, J. H. (2003b). Assessing the social bonds of elderly neighbors: The roles of length of residence, crime victimization, and perceived disorder. *Sociological Inquiry, 73*(4), 490–510.

Obeidallah, D., Brennan, R. T., Brooks-Gunn, J., & Earls, F. (2004). Links between pubertal timing and neighborhood contexts: Implications for girls' violent behavior. *Journal of the American Academy of Child and Adolescent Psychiatry, 43*(12), 1460–1468.

Popkin, S. J., Katz, B., Cunningham, M. K., Brown, K. D, Gustafson, J., & Turner, M. A. (2004). *A decade of HOPE VI: Research findings and policy challenges*. Washington, DC: Urban Institute.

Reisig, M. D., & Parks, R. B. (2004). Can community policing help the truly disadvantaged? *Crime & Delinquency, 50*(2), 139–167.

Rickels, K., Garcia, C. R., Lipman, R. S., Derogatis, L. R., & Fisher, E. L. (1976). The Hopkins Symptom Checklist: Assessing emotional distress in obstetric gynecological practice. *Primary Care; 3*, 751–764.

Rosenbaum, J. E. (1995). Changing the geography of opportunity by expanding residential choice: Lessons from the Gautreaux Program. *Housing Policy Debate, 6*(1), 231–269.

Rosenbaum, J. E., & Kaufman, J. E. (1991). Educational and occupational achievements of low-income black youth in white suburbs. Paper read at the *Annual Meeting of the American Sociological Association*, Cincinnati, OH: ASA.

Rosenbaum, J. E., & Popkin, S. J. (1991). Employment and earnings of low-income blacks who move to middle-class suburbs. In C. Jencks & P.E. Peterson (Eds.), *The urban underclass* (pp. 342–356). Washington, DC: The Brookings Institution.

Salama, J. J. (1999). The redevelopment of distressed public housing: Early results from Hope VI projects in Atlanta, Chicago, and San Antonio. *Housing Policy Debate, 10*(1), 95–142.

Sallis, J. F., & Glanz, K. (2006). The role of built environments in physical activity, eating, and obesity in childhood. *Future of Children, 16*(1), 89–108.

Sampson, R. J. (2008). Moving to inequality: Neighborhood effects and experiments meet social structure. *American Journal of Sociology, 114*(1), 189–231.

Sampson, R. J., Groves, W. B. (1989). Community structure and crime: Testing social-disorganization theory. *American Journal of Sociology, 94*(4), 774–802.

Sampson, R. J., Morenoff, J. D., & Earls, F. (1999). Beyond social capital: Spatial dynamics of collective efficacy for children. *American Sociological Review, 64*(5), 633–660.

Sampson, R. J., Morenoff, J. D., & Gannon-Rowley, T. (2002). Assessing 'neighborhood effects': Social processes and new directions in research. *Annual Review of Sociology, 28*, 443–478.

Sampson, R. J., & Raudenbush, S. W. (1999). Systematic social observation of public spaces. A new look at disorder in urban neighborhoods. *American Journal of Sociology, 105*(3), 603–651.

Sampson, R. J., Raudenbush, S. W., & Earls, F. (1997). Neighborhoods and violent crime: A multilevel study of collective efficacy. *Science, 277*, 918–924.

Sanbonmatsu, L., Kling, J. R., Duncan, G. J., & Brooks-Gunn, J. (2006). Neighborhoods and academic achievement. *Journal of Human Resources, 41*(4), 649–691.

Sastry, N., Ghosh-Dastidar, B., Adams, J., & Pebley, A. R. (2006). The design of a multilevel survey of children, families, and communities: The Los Angeles Family and Neighborhood Survey. *Social Science Research, 35*(4), 1000–1024.

Sastry, N., Pebley, A., & Zonta, M. (2002). *Neighborhood definitions and the spatial dimension of daily life in Los Angeles*. Los Angeles: California Center for Population Research.

Sawhill, I., & McLanahan, S. (2006). Opportunity in America: Introducing the issue. *The Future of Children, 16*(2), 3–17.

Schuman, H., & Bobo, L. (1988). Survey-based experiments on white racial attitudes toward residential integration. *American Journal of Sociology, 94*(2), 273–299.

Shaw, C. R., & McKay, H. D. (1942.) *Juvenile delinquency and urban areas.* Chicago: University of Chicago Press.

Shonkoff, J. P., & Phillips, D. A. (Eds.). (2000). *From neurons to neighborhoods: The science of early childhood development.* Washington, DC: National Academy Press.

Shores, K. A., West, S. T., Theriault, D. S., & Davison, E. A. (2009). Extra-individual correlates of physical activity attainment in rural older adults. *Journal of Rural Health, 25*(2), 211–218.

Stewart, E. A., Simons, R. L., & Conger, R. D. (2002). Assessing neighborhood and social psychological influences on childhood violence in an African-American sample. *Criminology, 40*(4), 801–830.

Stewart, E. B., Stewart, E. A., & Simons, R. L. (2007). The effect of neighborhood context on the college aspirations of African American adolescents. *American Educational Research Journal, 44*(4), 896–919.

Sturm, R. (2008). Disparities in the food environment surrounding US middle and high schools. *Public Health, 122*(7), 681–690.

Subramanian, S. V., Kubzansky, L., Berkman, L., Fay, M., & Kawachi, I. (2006). Neighborhood effects on the self-rated health of elders: Uncovering the relative importance of structural and service-related neighborhood environments. *Journal of Gerontology, 61B*(3), S153–S160.

Suomi, S. J., Higley, J. D., & Lesch, K. P. (2005). Monoamine oxidase A gene promoter variation and rearing experience influences aggressive behavior in rhesus monkeys. *Biological Psychiatry, 57*(2), 167–172.

Survey Research Center. (1984). *User guide to the Panel Study of Income Dynamics.* Ann Arbor, MI: Inter-University Consortium for Political and Social Research.

Takano, T., Nakamura, K., & Watanabe, M. (2002). Urban residential environments and senior citizens' longevity in megacity areas: The importance of walkable green spaces. *Journal of Epidemiology and Community Health, 56*(12), 913–918.

Tienda, M. (1991). Poor people, poor places: Deciphering neighborhood effects on poverty outcomes. In J. Huber (Ed.), *Macro-micro linkages in sociology* (pp. 244–262). Newbury Park, CA: Sage Publications.

Turley, R. N. L. (2002). Is relative deprivation beneficial? The effects of richer and poorer neighbors on children's outcomes. *Journal of Community Psychology, 30*(6), 671–686.

Turner, R. J., Frankel, B. G., & Levin, D. (1983). Social support: conceptualization, measurement, and implications for mental health. *Research in Community and Mental Health, 3,* 67–111.

Turney, K., Clampet-Lundquist, S., Edin, K., Kling, J. R., & Duncan, G.J. (2006). Neighborhood effects on barriers to employment: Results from a randomized housing mobility experiment in Baltimore. In G. Burtless & J.R. Pack (Eds.) *Brookings-Wharton Papers on Urban Affairs* (pp. 137–187). Washington, D.C.: Brookings Institution Press.

Vartanian, T. P. (1997). Neighborhood effects on AFDC exits: Examining the social isolation, relative deprivation, and epidemic theories. *Social Service Review, 71*(4), 548–573.

Vartanian, T. P. (1999a). Childhood conditions and adult welfare use: Examining neighborhood and family factors. *Journal of Marriage and the Family, 61*(1), 225–237.

Vartanian, T. P. (1999b). Adolescent neighborhood effects on labor market and economic outcomes. *Social Service Review, 73*(2), 142–167.

Venkatesh, S. A. (1997). The social organization of street gang activity in an urban ghetto. *American Journal of Sociology, 103*(1), 82–111.

Venkatesh, S. A. (1999). Community-based interventions into street gang activity. *Journal of Community Psychology, 27*(5), 551–567.

Venkatesh, S. A. (2002). *American project: The rise and fall of a modern ghetto.* Cambridge, MA: Harvard University Press.

Venkatesh, S. A. (2006). *Off the books: The underground economy of the urban poor.* Cambridge, MA: Harvard University Press.

Villarreal, A., & Silva, B. F. (2006) Social cohesion, criminal victimization and perceived risk of crime in Brazilian neighborhoods. *Social Forces, 84,*1725–1753.

Vygotsky, L. S. (1978). *Mind and society: The development of higher psychological processes.* Cambridge, MA: Harvard University Press.

Wadsworth, M. E. J. (1999). Early life. In M. Marmot & R.G. Wilkinson (Eds.), *Social determinants of health* (pp. 44–63). New York: Oxford University Press.

Wen, M., & Christakis, N. A. (2005). Neighborhood effects on posthospitalization mortality: A population based cohort study of the elderly in Chicago. *Health Services Research, 40*(4), 1108–1127.

Wen, M., Hawkley, L. C., & Capioppo, J. T. (2006). Objective and perceived neighborhood environment, individual SES and psychosocial factors, and self-rated health: An analysis of older adults in Cook County, Illinois. *Social Science & Medicine, 63*(10), 2575–2590.

Werner, E. E., & Smith, R. S. (1989). *Vulnerable but invincible: A longitudinal study of resilient children and youth.* New York: Adams, Bannister, Cox.

Wickrama, K. A. S., & Bryant, C. M. (2003). Community context of social resources and adolescent mental health. *Journal of Marriage and Family, 65*(4), 850.

Wight, R. G., Aneshensel, C. S., Miller-Martinez, D., Botticello, A. L., Cummings, J. R., Karlamangla, A. S., et al. (2006). Urban neighborhood context, educational attainment, and cognitive function among older adults. *American Journal of Epidemiology, 163*(12), 1071–1078.

Wilson, W. J. (1987). *The truly disadvantaged: The inner city, the underclass, and public policy.* Chicago: University of Chicago Press.

Wilson, W. J. (1996). *When work disappears: The world of the new urban poor.* New York: Knopf.

Winstanley, E. L., Steinwachs, D. M., Ensminger, M. E., Latkin, C. A., Stitzer, M. L. & Olsen, Y. (2008). The association of self-reported neighborhood disorganization and social capital with adolescent alcohol and drug use, dependence, and access to treatment. *Drug & Alcohol Dependency, 92*(1–3), 173–182.

Woodcock, R. W., & Johnson, M. B. (1989, 1990). *Woodcock-Johnson psycho-educational battery-Revised.* Itasca, IL: Riverside Publishing.

Xu, Y., Fiedler, M. L., & Flaming, K. H. (2005). Discovering the impact of community policing: The broken windows thesis, collective efficacy, and citizens' judgment. *Journal of Research in Crime and Delinquency, 42*(2), 147–186.

Xue, Y. G., Leventhal, T., Brooks-Gunn, J., & Earls, F. J. (2005). Neighborhood residence and mental health problems of 5-to 11-year-olds. *Archives of General Psychiatry, 62*(5), 554–563.

Zenk, S. N., & Powell, L. M. (2008). US secondary schools and food outlets. *Health & Place, 14*(2), 336–346.

CONTEXTS AND CONTENTS OF SOCIALIZATION: A LIFE-SPAN PERSPECTIVE

32

Marc H. Bornstein, Robert H. Bradley, Karen Lutfey,
Jeylan T. Mortimer, and Amy Pennar

INTRODUCTION

Life-span socialization is interested in the status quo of individual characteristics (constructs, structures, functions, and processes) at each stage in the life course as well as their development. Stage-specific socialization, the orientation we adopt here, assumes that individuals progress from one life stage to the next and experience socialization contexts and contents specific to each stage. In a companion chapter (Bornstein, Mortimer, Lutfey, & Bradley, Chapter 2), we distinguished between consistency within individuals (stability) and consistency in a group (continuity). Continuity and stability reflect theoretically and statistically different realms of development, and individual consistency and mean consistency are independent and orthogonal constructs (Bornstein, Brown, & Slater, 1996; Hartmann, Pelzel, & Abbott, 2011; McCall, 1981; Wohlwill, 1973). Questions about stability and continuity of characteristics are embedded in conceptions of life-span socialization. Discontinuities appear to be prevalent and pervasive in socialization, and apply more to socialization stages, contexts, and contents than to socialization processes. Social science has identified only a small universe of possible mechanisms of socialization, and socializees appear to be socialized by processes that are equally applicable across stages, contexts, and contents. Discontinuity permeates context as childhood socialization in the family gives way to socialization in the peer group; later school functions as a major force in socialization of older children and adolescents; afterward the work setting assumes priority in socialization; finally, perhaps, assisted living circumstances prevail in old age socialization. The contents of socialization follow these changing contexts and so change as well.

In the same companion chapter, we defined socialization and reviewed several considerations pertinent to individual variation and transaction, contexts and contents, processes, and continuity and stability in socialization (Bornstein et al., Chapter 2). With these in mind, here we discuss the contexts and contents of socialization in four unequal but traditional and psychologically distinct phases of development over the life span. The four are infancy and early childhood, middle childhood and adolescence, adulthood, and old age. Of course, other divisions of the life course are possible and defensible. However, these four align with common perspectives in life-span developmental science (Steinberg, Bornstein, Vandell, & Rook, 2010). The contexts and contents of socialization are powerfully moderated by social class, culture, and time; as the scope of this chapter is necessarily circumscribed, we dwell on socialization in 21st century middle-class Western society. Moreover, because this exposition travels across diverse terrain, and marshals myriad examples, we appeal to a common forum of socialization—gender—as a unifying leitmotif. We do not, however, intend that socialization contexts and contents, as we describe and explicate them, are in any way limited to the domain of gender but extend across the broad array of features of human psychology.

CONTEXTS AND CONTENTS OF SOCIALIZATION IN INFANCY AND EARLY CHILDHOOD: PARENTS, FAMILY, DAYCARE

From an evolutionary perspective, several characteristics of the human species render the socialization contexts and contents in infancy and early childhood unique. The plastic nature of human beings from birth, their protracted period of dependence and the tendency to create strong emotional ties with caregivers, robust learning capabilities, and the gradual specialization and adaptation of cognition and behavior to local circumstances ensure that infancy and early childhood are marked by extensive adaptation that is organized and channeled by people who already know much of what the young need to learn and who are invested in the young physically, cognitively, emotionally, and socially (Bjorklund & Pellegrini, 2002). Parents, caregivers, siblings, peers, and other members of the community all function as agents of early socialization. In their interactions with infants and young children, they communicate the expectations and goals of society. Whatever the local context, infants and young children have the same biological needs and must meet and succeed at the same basic developmental tasks and challenges, and their socializers share the same responsibilities to guide offspring to survival and adaptation to their physical environment and social culture. It is the continuing task of caregivers to prepare infants and young children for the physical, psychosocial, economic, and educational situations that are characteristic of the contexts in which the young are to survive and to thrive.

Fundamental needs of infants and young children are for nourishment, security, and protection, and parents are uniquely positioned to meet these needs. Indeed, the necessity for protection forms a basis for the development of a strong relationship between parent and child (Ainsworth, Blehar, Waters, & Wall, 1978; Bowlby, 1969). The quality of the socializee–socializer relationship is of major significance in ensuring the success of socialization. The social bias that is evident in early perceptual capacity, for example, directs children's attention in ways that optimize learning about the world from other people from the earliest years of life (Gauvain, 2001; Johnson, 2011). Moreover, the parent–child relationship is more fixed and less mutable than most other relationships. In addition to being constrained by legal and social definitions, this relationship entails long histories of emotional interaction and close consistent exchanges that foster shared values and expectations (Bugental & Grusec, 2006).

Agents of socialization operate along many convergent lines to produce socializees who fit into their cultural milieu. Historically, theorists looked to parents as those thought to influence infants and young children the most, although in many societies early childhood socialization is acknowledged to involve a variety of other individuals and to take place in a variety of contexts: families, peer groups, daycare centers, fields, and classrooms. Many theoretical accounts for how socialization of infants and young children takes place have been proposed. For most, however, it is primarily through parenting that adult culture is first passed down to each successive generation of children. Parents are the primary agents who set the agenda for what young children learn and who administer the rewards and punishments that strengthen desired characteristics and weaken undesired ones in children. Parents constitute initial influences on the socialization of children.

Consider gender socialization. Parents appear to succumb to a strong tendency to socialize children differently by gender. Classic "Baby X" studies (where the gender of the infant is not known to study participants) have shown that parents (and other adults as well) conceive of, and behave toward, infants differently depending on whether they think they are interacting with a girl or a boy (Seavey, Katz, & Zalk, 1975; Sidorowicz & Lunney, 1980). Even before birth (Sweeney & Bradbard, 1989), parents purchase gender-stereotyped toys for their children—prior to when children could express gender-typed toy preferences themselves (Pomerleau, Bolduc, Malcuit, & Cossette, 1990). Parents tend not only to give their children gender-typed toys but also to encourage gender-typed play (Eisenberg, Wolchik, Hernandez, & Pasternack, 1985; Fisher-Thompson, 1993; Pomerleau et al., 1990; Rheingold & Cook, 1975; Robinson & Morris, 1986). As children grow, socialization strategies change accordingly, as when parents assign household chores along gender-stereotyped lines that have societal implications beyond children's learning of particular skills (Antill, Goodnow, Russell, & Cotton, 1996).

Family contexts are essential to the successful primary socialization of children; it is normally in families that infants and young children develop physically, cognitively, emotionally, and socially and acquire the sense of self and skills that are required for interaction with others and for effective adaptation to future roles (Corsaro & Eder, 1995; Gecas, 1981). Thus, it is through family socialization that children learn about other roles they will assume later in life. The absence of this basic socialization, as with feral children, for example, profoundly disadvantages the young (Gecas, 2000). The basis of successful socialization is the creation of a positive relationship with parents or other agents of socialization that in turn fosters a willingness and desire to be receptive to their directives. Child socializees are responsive to socialization because of positive aspects of the relationship they have with their adult socializers.

Extensive research on families as contexts for socialization indicates that parents exert robust influences on infants and young children, extending through adolescence and into adulthood. Although parents typically play the major role in socializing their young, highlighting relationships involving children and their parents' disguises the roles of significant others and the extent to which child–parent relationships themselves are embedded in broader socialization contexts. Siblings, peers, and other adult caregivers also function as important agents in early childhood socialization (Clarke-Stewart & Allhusen, 2002, 2005; Rubin & Burgess, 2002; Zukow-Goldring, 2002). In turn, the family shapes, and is shaped by, component relationships within it (e.g., the relationship between the parents) as well as by the communities in which it is embedded.

In the view of family systems theory, what transpires between a parent and a child is governed not only by the characteristics of each individual but also by patterns of transaction between them and others (Bornstein & Sawyer, 2005; Cox & Paley, 2003). Parent and child develop in a system composed of subsystems that include them as well as other individuals and relationships among those individuals. Each subsystem within the family both affects, and is affected by, the others, and a change in any one subsystem can lead to changes in others. How responsive a mother or father may be to their infant at any given moment is determined not only by a parent's characteristic warmth and the child's characteristic temperament but also by patterns the parents have created jointly between them. For example, parents behave one way when each interacts one-on-one with a young child and another when the whole family is together (Deal, Hagan, Bass, Hetherington, & Clingempeel, 1999). Parenting thus occurs in the context of all relationships within the family, and it occurs between the family and its many larger social contexts (such as culture).

Parents and Parenting in the Socialization of Infants and Young Children

How do we know that parents actually socialize infants and young children? Of course, parents contribute directly to the genetic makeup of their offspring by passing on biological characteristics. Behavior genetics seeks to elucidate endowed biological sources of variation in human characteristics. It assumes that sources of variation in a characteristic can be separated into independent genetic and environmental components that together (with error) account for all of the variance in a characteristic. By studying individuals of varying genetic relatedness (identical and fraternal twins, biological and adopted siblings who live or do not live in the same households), behavioral geneticists attempt to estimate the amount of variation (heritability) in characteristics that may be explained by genetic factors. Modern behavior genetics asserts that characteristics of offspring in a host of different realms—height and weight, intelligence and personality—reflect inheritance in some degree (Knafo & Plomin, 2006). Normally, genetic transmission is not subsumed under socialization. Perhaps not as the term is commonly used; however, it is an important mode of influence and affects socialization through shared parent and child traits.

Behavior genetic designs also prove parental socialization effects (Baird & Bergeman, Chapter 27). In (ideal) natural experiments of adoption, one child shares genes but not environment with biological parents, and another child shares environment but not genes with adoptive parents. In France, children were located who had been given up in infancy by their low–socioeconomic status (SES) parents and adopted by upper-middle-SES parents. These children all had biological siblings or half-siblings who remained with their biological mother and were reared by her in impoverished circumstances. No other selective factors systematically differentiated the groups. When tested in middle childhood, adopted children's IQs averaged significantly higher than those of their natural siblings, and the children who remained with their biological mothers were more likely to exhibit failures in school performance (Duyme, Dumaret, & Stanislaw, 1999; Schiff, Duyme, Dumaret, & Tomkiewicz, 1982). O'Connor, Deater-Deckard, Fulker, Rutter, and Plomin (1998) identified two groups of adoptees: one at genetic risk for antisocial behavior (i.e., a history of antisocial behavior in the biological mother) and the other not at risk. At several points during the adoptees' childhood, the investigators assessed both the children's characteristics and the adoptive parents' childrearing methods. Children carrying a genetic risk for antisocial behavior were more likely to receive negative socialization inputs from their adoptive parents, but parental negative socialization contributed independently to children's externalizing behavior, over and above children's genetic predispositions.

Heredity accounts for only a portion of variance in human development, rarely as much as half (McCartney, Harris, & Bernieri, 1990). Moreover, evidence for heritability neither negates nor even diminishes evidence for direct (and indirect) effects of socialization. Parents directly shape their infants' and young children's socialization. The strongest deductions that could be made about parenting socialization effects would be based on experiments or interventions in which parents are assigned randomly to treatment/intervention versus control groups, with resulting changes in the behaviors of both the parents and their otherwise untreated children in the treatment group. Such experiments show that interventions alter parenting in treatment groups, even in the absence of changes in comparison groups, and that changes in the mediating mechanisms in parents effect changes in children. Van den Boom (1989, 1994) demonstrated that an intervention to train mothers to respond sensitively to their young children modified both mothers' negative responses to child irrationality and reduced the extent of avoidant attachment in their distress-prone children.

In the natural course of things, these two main sorts of direct effects are confounded: Parents who endow their child with their biology also socialize their children. Nonshared environmental effects refer to the influence of events specific to an individual's life, which are not shared by other family members. Even within the same family and home setting, parents (and other factors) help to create distinctive and effective nonshared environments for different children (Stoolmiller, 1999; Turkheimer & Waldron, 2000). Even sharing 50% of their genes, siblings turn out different from one another.

Parents directly socialize through their beliefs and by their behaviors (Bornstein, 2006; Collins, Maccoby, Steinberg, Hetherington, & Bornstein, 2000). Early in life, socialization is a foundation for an intricate system of communication and interpersonal interaction. From a practical perspective, the prolonged period of dependency and close contact between parent and child also motivate parents to instill appropriate and desirable behaviors in young children. Close and frequent contact between parent and child affords opportunities for parents to monitor children and to come to understand and anticipate their attitudes and actions, conditions that foster successful socialization. Adults too are responsible for the overall physical dimensions of children's experiences, including the number, variety, and composition of inanimate objects (toys, books, tools) available to the child, the level of ambient stimulation, the situations and locales where children find themselves, and limits on their physical freedom. The amount of time young children spend interacting with their parent-provided inanimate surroundings rivals or exceeds the time children spend in direct social interaction with parents or others. Parents also mediate and monitor their children's social relationships with others, such as peers (Ladd & Pettit, 2002; Rubin, Bukowski, & Parker, 1998; Stattin & Kerr, 2000).

Different cultures distribute the responsibilities of caregiving in different ways, but in the minds of many observers mother is the principal caregiver, the role of mother being universal and unique (Barnard & Solchany, 2002; Georgas, Berry, Kağitçibaşi, Poortinga, & van de Vijver, 2006). Cross-cultural surveys attest to the primacy of biological mothers' caregiving (Leiderman, Tulkin, & Rosenfeld, 1977; Weisner & Gallimore, 1977), even if in different times and places fathers' social and legal claims and responsibilities for children have been pre-eminent (French,

2002). The maternal role in socialization is normally better articulated and defined than is the paternal role, and mothers generally have more opportunities to acquire and practice socialization skills that are central to childrearing than do fathers. But fathers are hardly inept or uninterested in socialization. Fathers hold a diversity of socialization cognitions as do mothers and engage children in the same range of socialization practices. Traditionally, mothers and fathers interacted with and cared for children in complementary ways; that is, they tended to divide the labors of socialization and engage children by emphasizing different and mutually corroborating types of interactions.

Contemporary families grant fathers more responsibility and opportunity for parenting. For example, dual-worker families often share parenting. Many parents of young children manage to work nonoverlapping shifts so one or the other parent can always be with the child (Gottfried, Gottfried, & Bathurst, 2002). The increasing percentage of families where mothers are primary breadwinners has set the stage for more equitable family tasks, including child care. As society has become more tolerant and flexible regarding adult gender roles, a small but growing number of fathers choose to stay at home with their children while mothers work. Coparenting broadly refers to ways that parents (or parental figures) relate to each other in the role of parent (McHale et al., 2002). Erel and Burman (1995) documented changes in children's physiology, cognitions, and emotions in response to marital conflict, for example. Supported mothers are less harried and less overwhelmed, have fewer competing demands on their time, and, as a consequence, are more available to their young children.

Parents socialize not only through their direct interactions with infants and young children but also as managers of infants' and young children's social lives (Furstenberg, Cook, Eccles, Elder, & Sameroff, 1999; Parke et al., 2003). Parents make choices about neighborhoods and preschools as well as the formal and informal activities in which their infants and young children participate, which include access to, and interaction with, peers; these decisions in turn dramatically influence the course of children's early socialization (Ladd & Pettit, 2002). Through their own social networks, parents provide opportunities for their children's social contacts (Parke et al., 2002). They also cocoon their children or protect them from undesirable events and people (e.g., restricting exposure to certain forms of media or particular peers) as well as prearm them by warning them of temptations and providing them with ways of avoiding temptations (e.g., Miller & Sperry, 1988; Thornton, Chatters, Taylor, & Allen, 1990; Watson-Gegeo, 1992).

The conception of parenting *qua* a set of socialization functions expands the focus of discussion beyond biological parents; other related and nonrelated caregivers are also centrally engaged in socialization (Leon, 2002). Mothers and fathers share parenting responsibilities, although siblings, grandparents, and various other nonparental figures also socialize infants and young children. A dynamic family systems perspective acknowledges that multiple family and community members—mothers, fathers, siblings, and other kin and nonkin community members—play interrelated roles in socializing infants and young children. Although each of these agents has a distinctive part—one that may be prescribed by societal values—they tend to operate in concert to influence socialization. Thus, dyadic relationships, such as child–parent or child–sibling, constitute one level of organization within the family along with triadic (child–mother–father, father–sibling–sibling) and extended family (grandparents–parents–siblings) and community (child–parent–preschool teacher) levels.

Siblings' Roles in the Socialization of Infants and Young Children

Many infants and young children spend significant amounts of time with siblings, and older siblings play salient roles in younger siblings' socialization. Experiences interacting with other children foster the development of a more sophisticated and flexible repertoire of skills by exposing children to different individuals who have varying behavioral styles. In some cultures, children spend relatively little time playing with siblings; patterns of sibling interaction in New England families suggest that formal responsibilities by siblings may not be as common in American culture as in other cultures (Edwards & Whiting, 1993). When siblings enter the socialization picture, most of their interactions involve caregiving or protection. Siblings of non-Western, nonindustrialized socializees often assume much more diverse socialization responsibilities (Zukow-Goldring, 2002). These sibling relationships incorporate features of both the child–adult and child–peer systems. On the one hand, child–sibling dyads share common interests and have more similar behavioral repertoires than do child–adult dyads. On the other hand, sibling pairs resemble child–adult pairs to the extent that they differ in experience and levels of both cognitive and social ability. Siblings contribute to infants' and young children's socialization in their roles as playmates (Larson & Richards, 1994). Play with siblings provides a context for expressing a range of positive social behaviors as well as experiences with conflictual encounters and their resolution (Dunn, 1993). Zukow-Goldring (2002) described the ways in which Mexican older siblings not only care for younger siblings but also, through play, teach skills (how to make tortillas) their younger siblings will need to succeed in society. In African, Polynesian, and Latin cultures, children, especially girls, become involved in sibling caregiving at a relatively early age (Weisner, 1993). Older siblings tend to lead interactions; they engage in more dominant, assertive, and directing behaviors than their younger siblings. Reciprocally, younger siblings appear inordinately interested in what their older siblings are doing; they follow them around, attempting to imitate or explore toys just abandoned by older children, for example. This strategy maximizes sibling learning from an older child.

Through their interactions with siblings, infants and young children develop interaction patterns and acquire social skills that may generalize to relationships with other children (Rubin, Coplan, Chen, Bowker, & McDonald, 2010). Older siblings may be important socialization agents in their own right, shaping both prosocial and aggressive behavior in younger siblings. Older siblings influence the cognitive and social skills of infants and young children through combinations of teaching and modeling (Zajonc, 1983; Zukow-Goldring, 2002).

Peers' Parts in the Socialization of Infants and Young Children

By 2 years of age, children are receptive to rules of group life, that is, to the "proper" ways of eating, dressing, cleanliness, politeness, and other conventional routines (Dunn & Munn, 1985; Emde, Biringen, Clyman, & Oppenheim, 1991; Smetana, Kochanska, & Chuang, 2000). By this age, children also show self-aware emotions (e.g., shame, guilt), and the possibility now opens for self-regulation to occur in response to group norms. Peers can serve as the primary socializers of group rules. Lewin (1947) theorized that we change when we participate in peer group inter-action, and Harris (1995, 1998) elaborated on this view to assert that experience out-side the home, and especially within the peer group, constitutes the major source of socialization. According to Harris, group socialization affects a range of children's behavior, from language and cognition to emotions and social interaction. Peers thus play increasingly significant and formative roles as socializers as children develop (and we discuss more about peers in the next section on middle childhood and adolescence). However, parents and peers exert joint socialization influences on the developing child. Children are not randomly assigned to peer groups; rather, parents and parent–child relationships influence which peers children are exposed to and engage.

Institutions and the Socialization of Infants and Young Children

Institutions too are charged with helping infants and young children acquire knowledge, skills, and attitudes they will later need as competent adults. The majority of children in the United States are now cared for by some adult other than a parent, and this situation exerts a variety of effects on their socialization. The National Institute of Child Health and Human Development (NICHD) Early Child Care Research Network (1997) found that the vast majority of children (81%) in a U.S. national study experienced regular nonmaternal child care during their first 12 months of life, with most starting prior to 4 months of age and enrolled for nearly 30 hours per week. Because so many children are placed in out-of-home care, extensive efforts have been made to conceptualize and measure child care and criteria established to ensure high-quality care (Fenichel, Lurie-Hurvitz, & Griffin, 1999). Measures of socialization quality typically fall into two types: structure (group size, teacher–child ratios, and teacher training) assesses broad markers of the environments that bear a straightforward relation to children's interactions in the setting, and process (experiences, caregivers' interactional competence with children, and the breadth and diversity of the learning curricu-lum) assesses the quality of care experienced by children (Lamb & Ahnert, 2006). Structural measures are associated with process measures: Higher staff-to-child ratios and better training correlate with quality of caregiver–child interaction and the frequency of parent–caregiver communication (Helburn, 1995; NICHD Early Child Care Research Network, 1996).

Childcare structure and process are linked to children's early socialization (Clarke-Stewart & Allhusen, 2005). Infants and young children in child care facil-ities are not only exposed regularly to sets of experiences additional to the home, but also have socialization experiences at home that differ from those experienced by peers who do not receive regular nonparental care. For example, parents interact more intensely with children who attend child care centers as if attempting to make up for the time they are apart (Booth, Clarke-Stewart, Vandell, McCartney, & Owen, 2002). Relationships with care providers also affect infants' and young children's socialization. The security of child–mother and child–careprovider attachments is independent, and both are correlated with the level of children's competence evident when playing with adults as well as with peers (Howes & Hamilton, 1993; Howes, Matheson, & Hamilton, 1994).

Schools are, by definition, critical contexts for socialization (Eccles & Roeser, 2011). It is in schools that children's academic performance is evaluated and labeled, which contributes to their developing self-concept. As in family contexts, children in school settings are not mere passive recipients of socialization, but are differentially sensitive and responsive to these environments. School as a context for socialization accomplishes more than teaching socializees specific skills and knowledge but builds on children's primary socialization at home in communicating social messages and providing opportunities.

Evidence of "neighborhood effects" across a range of developmental outcomes is abundant in infancy and early childhood, but these effects tend to be modest after taking family effects into account (Elliot et al., 2006; Leventhal & Brooks-Gunn, 2000). That is, effects of neighborhoods on infants and young children tend to be mediated by parenting practices such as supervision and monitoring. For example, when parents perceive their neighborhoods as dangerous and low in social control, they place more restrictions on their young children's activities (O'Neil, Parke, & McDowell, 2001). In the United States, parents choose the type and quality of infant daycare and pre- and elementary schools that young children attend and the neighborhoods where their children grow. These choices make a difference to young children's socialization experiences and subsequent development.

In overview, there is initially asymmetry in parent and child contributions to socialization. Responsibility for socialization at the start—whether it be nurturing, promoting physical growth, fostering sociability, teaching language and other cultural constituents, and material provisions—appears to lie more unambiguously with parents and other (often more mature) socialization agents. As childhood progresses, children play more active and anticipatory roles in their socialization. A complex developmental system of primary socialization includes infants' and young children's own capacities and proclivities, children's and parents' multiple social relationships (with one another and with siblings, peers, teachers, and neighbors) embedded in multiple developmental contexts (homes, schools, neighborhoods, socioeconomic class, culture, and time).

■ CONTEXTS AND CONTENTS OF SOCIALIZATION IN MIDDLE CHILDHOOD AND ADOLESCENCE: PEERS, SCHOOL, WORK

As children move from early childhood through middle childhood and into adolescence, they enter new arenas of socialization and become ever more conscious actors in their socialization. With age and experience, youth gain domain-specific knowledge and are increasingly capable of more complex social interactions (Crick & Dodge, 1994). For example, children in middle childhood are more likely than kindergarteners to engage in problem-solving behaviors rather than aggression during a peer conflict. Around age 4 or 5, the majority of children enter more formal social settings (e.g., schools) where their socialization experiences expand to include new peers and adults with whom they have less intimate ties and where the settings themselves impose more exacting requirements. As the environment changes, youth adapt social goals and behaviors to fit within the new context. At roughly the same period, children achieve levels of cognitive competence and social understanding such that they become more effective self-socializers, and they begin to more consciously select people, activities, and places where they wish to spend time. As a consequence children learn different things about how they should act in social situations, and they learn them in somewhat different ways (Ladd, 2007). In this section, we turn our attention to peers, school, and work as contexts for socialization, with a focus on youth from around entry into school through adolescence. We consider the affordances of these major contexts as purveyors of socialization experiences and the effects of socialization experiences on children's behavior and development.

Peers as Socializers in Middle Childhood and Adolescence

As children enter formal care environments, be it child care or school settings, they routinely encounter other children. Preschool-age children learn to cooperatively interact with peers while competing for limited resources such as classroom supplies or time for individual interactions with teachers (Ladd, Herald, & Kochel, 2006). Experiences with peers help shape children's social understanding, behavior, and interpersonal interactions. Children whose goals and ways of interacting do not mature as their peer interactions become increasingly complex may have difficulty gaining acceptance in peer groups (Ladd, 2005).

Peer socialization is a normative, bidirectional, and interactive developmental process that lays the social foundation for future interpersonal relationships (Bell, 1968; Sameroff, 1975). Peer interactions provide a forum for acquiring social knowledge about oneself and others (Ladd, 2003, 2007). Peer socialization involves the acquisition of social skills, social understanding, and emotional maturity to interact with others in dyads or groups (Maccoby, 2007). Children socialize one another through modeling, talk, and social reinforcement (Hartup, 1999). That said, what children actually do to socialize and influence one another is not well documented.

Principles of social learning theory help explain how experiences with peers contribute to social competence and patterns of social behavior. Specifically, through observation, children learn to imitate behaviors, both positive and negative, enacting them with peers (Bandura, 1977), and by evaluating their effectiveness, children develop social skills and become more socially competent in the peer environment (Ladd, 2007). What this means is that children's long-term success in social situations depends on whom they observe and imitate. Children who observe and imitate unsuccessful peers have a propensity to form fewer adaptive social skills (Ladd, 2005).

Modeling is not the only means through which peers socialize school-age children. Children also reward and punish peer behavior during interpersonal interactions thereby shaping future social behaviors (Baer & Wolf, 1970). Children who engage in desirable (most often prosocial and socially acceptable) behavior are more likely to form positive relationships with their peers; conversely, children punish undesirable peer behaviors that violate group norms (Bukowski, Brendgen, & Vitaro, 2007). For example, reward and punishment are often used to inculcate gender-appropriate play (Lamb, Easterbrooks, & Holden, 1980).

Social information processing theory (Dodge, 1986) posits that children learn not merely through observation and reinforcement, but by processing information obtained during interactions. Children perceive, encode, and interpret social and situational cues during encounters with peers. School-age children evaluate situations with respect to the social affordances present and their personal goals (Crick & Dodge, 1994). They cognitively search for and evaluate potential responses, then select a response and enact it. Peer interactions provide youth with opportunities to engage one another, learn new skills, and build their repertoire of behaviors. Peer relationships are discussed under several rubrics: dyadic friendships, peer groups, and aggressor–victim relationships (Ladd, Herald, & Andrews, 2006).

Friendships are dyadic relationships between children that are voluntary and amenable to termination (Hartup, 2005; Ladd, 1988), with children exercising ever more deliberate choices about friends as they move through middle childhood and into adolescence (Hartup & Stevens, 1999; Price & Ladd, 1986). The role and function of friendships change from childhood to adolescence (Parker & Gottman, 1989). In early childhood, friendships facilitate opportunities for play and to explore new behaviors, modify existing behaviors, and solidify behavioral responses that elicit positive peer responses. Friendships in middle childhood allow children to refine the skills necessary for self-presentation and are resources of social acceptance and support. In adolescence, friendships become increasingly complex and aid in identity development and self-exploration. That said, the specific ways friends influence children's behavior depend on characteristics of the friends and the quality of the friendships (Hartup, 1996).

Successful relationships with peers can be instrumental in determining the opportunities children have and their emotional well-being. For example, friends can serve to buffer the child against bullying or teasing by other children (Schwartz, Dodge, Pettit, & Bates, 2000; Smith, Shu, & Madsen, 2001). As a general rule, children show reduced levels of stress when with a preferred friend (Field et al., 1992). Likewise, friends can be a means of helping children accomplish things they could not do on their own.

The quality of a child's friendships and the density of a child's peer social network help determine what socialization experiences a child has and the degree to which those experiences promote social competence. Over time social competence and peer status become more entwined, suggesting that, as children gain social knowledge and competence from successful peer interactions, they also gain peer status (Ladd & Price, 1986). Socially competent children, who exhibit more prosocial and socially acceptable behaviors, have more positive peer interactions. Children who exhibit few prosocial behaviors, and more aggressive behaviors, have fewer positive interactions and are deemed socially incompetent. Social competence requires that children have the capacity to think about themselves, their peers, and what social situations afford by way of demands and opportunities. It also requires the capacity to regulate one's emotions. Children who are able to regulate their emotions, and those who display more positive emotions during peer interactions, are more accepted by peers than those who exhibit negative emotions (Eisenberg et al., 1995; Hubbard, 2001).

Over time, socially maladjusted children are excluded from peer groups and friendships. This reduces future interpersonal opportunities to interact with peers, thereby inhibiting further social learning and placing rejected children at risk for lower self-esteem and self-efficacy (Coie, Dodge, & Coppotelli, 1982). Children who experience prolonged peer rejection are more likely to be socially incompetent and exhibit adjustment problems (Burks, Dodge, & Price, 1995; Kochenderfer & Ladd, 1996; Ladd & Burgess, 2001; Ladd & Troop-Gordon, 2003; Panak & Garber, 1992).

Schools as a Context of Socialization in Middle Childhood and Adolescence

Schools have long been recognized as a vehicle through which children are indoctrinated into the ways of society as well as a means of preparing children to function well as members of society (Durkheim, 1956). Dreeben (1968) argued that schools provide youth with four key values that facilitate their successful adaptation to their future roles in society: independence (the ability to do one's own work), achievement (social acceptance is conditional on performance), universalism (the treatment of individuals as members of general categories), and specificity (the interest in specific attributes individuals possess rather than the "whole person"). Jackson (1968) promulgated the idea that schools promote such values and norms both overtly and covertly. Brint (1998) refined Jackson's notions stipulating that there are three "zones" of socialization within classrooms. The core (school rules and embedded practices) largely directed by teachers is aimed at adaptive functioning within the classroom and adult society. The inner ring (explicit moral instruction) and outer ring (implicit moral instruction) are the joint province of both teachers and peers, with teachers focusing on cultural conformity (mostly within the classroom) and peers focusing on moral conformity (both in the classroom and on the playground).

Wentzel and Looney (2007) stipulated that the value systems and affordances of school settings concentrate on a relatively small set of competencies and proclivities, some of which are connected to lifelong functioning (e.g., the requirements of citizenship, family maintenance, and productive employment) and some to daily functioning within the school setting itself (e.g., goal-directedness, planfulness, capacities for self-monitoring, self-control, and the regulation of emotions, being socially responsive to group goals, acting in a socially responsible manner, acting in prosocial and cooperative ways with peers). The structures and activities of social contexts provide resources and opportunities to promote certain capacities and proclivities. These include, for example, the physical arrangements of people and objects (including displays that convey particular social messages), school/classroom routines, and standards of comparison used when evaluating performance (objective standards, prior performance, accomplishment of others). Much has been said in the professional and popular literature about these arrangements, but relatively little has been documented in terms of their socialization of children. There is anecdotal evidence that schools vary considerably in regard to such physical, organizational, and social affordances. By implication these variations should move youth toward different social beliefs, competencies, and patterns of behavior. For example, cooperative learning tasks tend to promote goals such as sharing and being helpful to others (Solomon, Watson, Battistich, Schaps, & Delucchi, 1992) and to facilitate the development of specific problem-solving skills (Wentzel & Watkins, 2002). In effect, for outcomes considered highly salient for either classroom functioning or long-term adult functioning, the principle of equifinality suggests that some of the same outcomes may be achieved by different patterns of socialization experience within schools.

Ongoing social interactions teach youth what they need to do to function in a competent and socially acceptable way—this leads to values and behavioral tendencies. Teachers tend to communicate expectations regarding behavior in the classroom (e.g., impulse control, attending to task assignments, involvement in class activities, proper conduct relative to classmates and the teacher, and personal responsibility). Teachers also convey different expectations for academic behavior and performance to different youth or similar expectations in different ways (Weinstein, 2002). Consequently, youth are moved toward a diverse array of different social and performance goals, and they are moved toward similar goals at different rates and with different intensity.

Peers also communicate expectations regarding involvement in learning, being cooperative and sociable, following the teacher's directions, engaging in play, and the like (Wentzel, Looney, & Battle, 2006). For example, peer expectations play a substantial role in adolescents' prosocial tendencies at school (Wentzel, Filisetti, & Looney, 2007). Socialization messages from peers at school may take the form of modeling, providing information or assistance, and giving reinforcement—points elaborated earlier (Bandura, 1986; Cooper, Ayers-Lopez, & Marquis, 1982; Fabes, Hanish, & Martin, 2003; Price & Dodge, 1989; Wentzel et al., 2006). The impact of these efforts on a child's behavior depends on the degree to which the child identifies with, and feels connected to, a particular peer or peer group (Berndt & Perry, 1986; Buhs & Ladd, 2001; Hartup, 2005; Pettit, 2004; Wentzel, 1994, 2003).

The quality of social relationships provides motivational significance. When children are in a responsive nurturant environment, they are moved to accept and endorse the expectations and styles of behavior promulgated by valued others, be they peers or teachers (Birch & Ladd, 1998; Davis, 2001; Hamre & Pianta, 2001; Harter, 1996; Pianta, Hamre, & Stuhlman, 2003; Roeser, Midgley, & Urdan, 1996; Skinner & Belmont, 1993; Wentzel, 2002). The quality of the student–teacher relationship, and consequently its power to direct youth along certain paths, is not solely a function of what the teacher does to support the relationship. The importance of relationships with teachers also tends to vary with age. Most elementary school children value relationships with their teachers; but relationships with particular teachers tend to be of lesser importance to adolescents (Lempers & Clark-Lempers, 1992; Reid, Landesman, Treder, & Jaccard, 1989). However, this expressed decline in level of importance accorded to teacher–student relationships may at least partially reflect the structure of secondary schools and the reduced opportunity for youth to spend time with any individual teacher. For example, secondary school students feel less supported, and a significant number tend to disengage from school activities and deep involvement in learning (Felner et al., 1995; Seidman, Allen, Aber, Mitchell, & Feinman, 1994).

Relationships with peers also seem to affect how children respond to the school environment. Children who have friends, and especially those with high-quality friendships, view themselves more positively, are more agentic as regards social relationships, show more adaptive behavior, and achieve more. Victimization leads to loneliness and maladaptive behavior (Ladd, 2007). Peer group rejection predicts both classroom participation and achievement (Ladd, Birch, & Buhs, 1999), and peer acceptance promotes social inclusion in the classroom and increased student involvement in learning activities (Buhs & Ladd, 2001).

Despite the importance accorded to schools as a context for socialization, very little is documented regarding socialization at school. Teachers teach or make reference to social rules very infrequently (Pianta, La Paro, Payne, Cox, & Bradley, 2002). When one considers values connected to work performance, values connected to interaction between self and others, traditional values—honesty, fairness, responsibility, considerateness, reliability, courage, and modern values—cultural diversity, appreciation of one's own culture, appreciation of individual uniqueness, appreciation of choice and variety, far and away the most frequent message in primary grade classrooms is about orderliness (71%), followed by academic effort (13%); messages about self-regulation and relationships with others are next (11%); less than 5% of messages pertain to traditional values, and less than 2% pertain to modern values (Brint, Contreras, & Matthews, 2001). Content analysis of books used in classrooms indicates that about 75% of text material in Language Arts and Social Studies activities have value-relevant messages, and these include both traditional and modern values. As regards classroom practices that potentially carry a socialization message, frequent use is made of rewards to increase desired behavior and not just commands for obedience, the use of group as well as individual projects, reliance on activity centers for instruction, and even rotation to specialized classrooms rather than exclusive reliance on a single teacher. Socialization messages in schools come in many forms, and different kinds of messages tend to predominate at different levels of school organization.

Successful functioning in school, and the likelihood schools will successfully socialize children for school tasks and lifelong adaptive functioning, depend on how well children are socialized to function in school prior to school entry (Ladd, Herald, & Kochel, 2006). That is, children must come prepared to engage in tasks that typically occur in formal school settings and to connect to peers and teachers/adults in ways that are productive. The rules, structures, social encounters, and other affordances present in elementary classrooms tend to vary somewhat from those present in home environments, child care, and preschool. Consequently, lack of proper socialization for what happens in elementary school environments decreases the likelihood that children will function well during elementary school or benefit sufficiently from the socialization presses encountered there. In effect, children best enter kindergarten socially competent and emotionally mature as well as task-oriented and self-directed (Wesley & Buysse, 2003).

Because most of young children's socialization experiences occur at home or in child care (as we described earlier), the degree of continuity between home and school, or between child care and school, can loom large in how successfully children transition to school. The ethos that pervades most American schools is one that reflects modern middle-class values. Accordingly, the adjustment can be more difficult for children from low-SES, immigrant, and cultural minority families. Language socialization can be particularly important given that language is the principal means by which instruction occurs in classrooms. When children have not been schooled in the verbal and nonverbal communication patterns typically used in middle-class English-speaking American families, the discontinuity between home and school communication patterns renders the transition to school difficult (Lovelace & Wheeler, 2006).

The management of one's emotions in school is critical for school success and long-term adaptive functioning. Youth must be able to cope with the (social and instructional) stresses connected with school, and they need to mobilize positive emotions if they are to benefit maximally from what schools have to offer (Ladd, Herald, & Kochel, 2006). At present, substantially more is known about how parenting is implicated in the socialization of emotions than is known about how schooling is. An observational study in child care centers serving children aged 3–5 indicated that teacher discussions of emotions helped children identify emotion-related words, understand the causes of emotion, and deal with their emotions positively

(Ahn & Stifter, 2006). Most often, teachers simply talked to children about emotions, but about one third also used book reading as a forum to discuss emotions. Teachers expressed a preference for children's expression of positive emotion using verbal reinforcement. They encouraged children's smiles and laughter, and they responded positively when children expressed empathy toward others. They often commented affirmatively when children expressed empathy toward each other. Teachers were also observed directly instructing children how to express emotions in constructive ways. In a later study, preschool teachers responded differently to children depending on whether a child expressed positive or negative emotions (Ahn & Stifter, 2006). The teacher's response to positive emotion was positive 56% of the time and discouraging only 34% of the time. By contrast, when children manifested negative emotions, teachers ignored them 11% of the time, provided physical comfort 11%, responded negatively 9%, provided a constructive alternative 15%, showed empathy 5%, and tried to distract the child 5%. The most common response was to intervene to address the cause of the negative emotional response (38%). Detailed coding of preschool teachers' responses to children's expressions of affect showed that teachers responded to 59% of children's affective displays, more often to displays of negative than positive affect, and teachers more often responded to displays of sadness (88%) than anger (65%). They labeled children's behavioral expressions of emotion (81%) more frequently than they labeled children's feelings per se (33%). In 42% of observed instances, teachers' responses entailed a discussion of the causes and consequences of children's expressions. In 35% of instances, teachers conveyed to children which expressions of emotions were desirable and appropriate, and in 43% of instances they made clear how emotions should be expressed. Teachers rarely encouraged children to express emotions, positive or negative, and teachers more often responded to boys than girls, younger than older children, and children perceived to be less than more socially competent (Reimer, 1996).

Work as a Socialization Context in Adolescence

Despite the near universal character of adolescent work in the United States, the workplace has received little attention as a context for adolescent socialization. Still, the fact that most adolescents work means that the workplace is a widely available context for vocational socialization. Moreover, what is learned in that context may have important implications for socialization and adaptation in educational and other occupational settings. Research on this topic highlights a consistent theme of this chapter: The adolescent socializee is an active agent in socialization.

Most U.S. parents believe that paid employment will foster independence in their children, a sense of responsibility, interpersonal skills, and knowledge of the world of work. In fact, when parents are asked to describe how their jobs, as teenagers, influenced their own development, they describe the very same benefits (Aronson, Mortimer, Zierman, & Hacker, 1996). Employment in the adolescent years may have deleterious consequences too because working may lead teens to disengage from school, get lower grades, encourage "adult-like" vices and problem behaviors, and subject them to work stressors for which they are not yet ready to cope (Steinberg & Cauffman, 1995; Steinberg & Dornbusch, 1991). Youth who work might be exposed to older, delinquent coworkers who socialize them in ways that foster delinquency, substance use, and other deviant behaviors.

The vast majority of research on teen employment has focused on the effects of work intensity on academic outcomes and problem behavior (Bachman & Schulenberg, 1993; Mihalic & Elliott, 1997; Mortimer, Finch, Ryu, & Shanahan, 1996; Steinberg & Dornbusch, 1991). Studies with more rigorous controls for selection bias and unobserved sources of heterogeneity report nonsignificant effects of work intensity on grade point average (Schoenhals, Tienda, & Schneider, 1998; Warren, LePore, & Mare, 2000) or problem behavior (Apel, Paternoster, Bushway, & Brame, 2006; Apel et al., 2007; Paternoster, Bushway, Brame, & Apel, 2003). The effects of working on school dropout appear to be complicated, however, conditional on characteristics of students as well as their situations (Lee & Staff, 2007; Staff, Messersmith, & Schulenberg, 2009; Warren & Lee, 2003). Here we address the implications of adolescent work for vocational socialization, educational achievement, and career development (Mortimer & Zimmer-Gembeck, 2007; Stone & Mortimer, 1998).

Although adolescent work is more restricted than that of adults, adolescents assume many of the same kinds of responsibilities, and are subject to the same types of rules and constraints, as adult workers. They learn the importance of being on time, following directions, and how to behave vis-à-vis supervisors, coworkers, and customers. They usually start their work careers with informal types of employment—not surprisingly babysitting for girls and yard work for boys—and later come to work more formally for particular employers or firms, for example, the service sector (Committee on the Health and Safety Implications of Child Labor, 1998). As they move through high school, their jobs tend to involve more hours, more training, more complexity, and greater supervisory responsibility (Mortimer, 2003).

Vocational development begins in childhood, but intensifies during adolescence with more focused exploration of career interests, work values, and preferences (Blustein, 1992; Meeus, Iedema, Helsen, & Vollebergh, 1999). The increasingly prolonged transition to adulthood, prompted by the growing prevalence of higher education, has extended vocational exploration to older ages (Mortimer, Zimmer-Gembeck, Holmes, & Shanahan, 2002). Still, adolescents must make critical decisions toward the end of high school that have important implications for career development, including whether to pursue postsecondary education, what kind of school or college to attend, or whether to move directly into the full-time labor market. Work experiences during high school have the potential to influence all of these considerations.

Work experiences provide adolescents with opportunities to learn about employment and themselves. They afford occasion to think about the kinds of work they would like to have and the educational credentials needed to acquire more "adult" and "career-like" jobs. Adolescent workers begin to set forth future vocational goals in response to their experiences in the workplace (Mortimer, Zimmer-Gembeck, et al., 2002; Zimmer-Gembeck & Mortimer, 2007). When asked to reflect on their work experiences (Mortimer, 2003), some adolescents emphasize that their early jobs taught them about what kinds of jobs they wanted to avoid in the future; others point out that they learned, very early on, about the generic types of work experiences that were most appealing to them (e.g., working with people).

The work environment also provides opportunities for adolescents to develop work-related competencies and identities (Mortimer, Harley, & Staff, 2002). Working during adolescence brings adolescents into contact with adults with more diverse characteristics than those they are likely to come across in their families, neighborhoods, and schools. Such experience contributes to the development of mature interpersonal skills (Mortimer, 2003). Moreover, working provides opportunities for relationships with responsible adults (other than teachers and parents) who can mentor and act as positive role models (Blustein, 1997; Flouri & Buchanan, 2002).

Adolescents move in and out of employment, changing jobs frequently as they move in and out of school (they are more likely to work, and they work longer hours during the summers than during the school year) and as their circumstances permit.

Adolescent motivations, goals, and anticipations about the future, measured on entry to high school, lead to higher or lower levels of investment in work and distinct work experiences (Mortimer, 2003). As a result of their lesser interest and engagement in school, lower academic performance, and greater problem behavior, some adolescents face greater obstacles and disadvantages in pursuing higher education. These youth invest more strongly in employment during high school, acquiring experiences that foster human capital development and prepare them for entry to the full-time adult workforce (Mortimer, 2003). The "most invested" adolescent workers tend to go on to vocational schools and community colleges and move relatively rapidly toward self-identified "careers" (Mortimer, Vuolo, Staff, Wakefield, & Xie, 2008). In contrast, adolescents with greater academic promise, who may expect to have greater returns for investment in school, restrict their work hours so as to be able to enact the full range of activities characteristic of "well-rounded" individuals, including homework and extracurricular interests. "Steady" workers go on to 4-year colleges and universities and are especially likely to attain degrees (Staff & Mortimer, 2007). Each pattern thus moves youth toward an outcome that is consistent with their earlier goals, resources, and motivations.

When adolescents report higher-quality work experiences, they also tend to have more positive leadership or other interpersonal skills, stronger work motivation, higher vocational self-efficacy, and greater success in the job market following high school. Adolescents also report greater career maturity when they have more work-related skills and a career role model. In contrast, the lack of opportunity to use skills, and having work schedules that conflict with school, are linked to greater cynicism toward work, and adolescents report lower career maturity when they report greater career pressure (Mortimer & Zimmer-Gembeck, 2007).

Evaluative judgments about the various rewards that work has to offer are of special relevance for vocational development. With growing vocational maturity, youth learn that employment can be the source of manifold rewards, both intrinsic and extrinsic. The particular emphases or mixes of these values have been found to have important consequences for occupational choice, job satisfaction, and career development (Johnson, 2001a, 2001b, 2002). Finding congruence between values and work experiences is a central goal in occupational choice. There is evidence from the youth development study that both intrinsic and extrinsic work values are heightened when adolescents have salutary experiences at work that foster learning opportunities (Mortimer, 2003; Mortimer, Pimentel, Ryu, Shanahan, & Call, 1996). Furthermore, adolescents who are able to crystallize their occupational values and formulate career goals, albeit tentatively, have more positive vocational outcomes. Youth who make occupational choices during high school or in their early to mid-20s are more likely to complete college by their mid-20s than youth who show greater indecision or vacillation in their career goals (Zimmer-Gembeck & Mortimer, 2007).

Support from supervisors at work heightens adolescents' self-efficacy, or anticipations of success in future life domains, including work, family, and health (Cunnien, MartinRogers, & Mortimer, 2009). This is an example of how successful experiences and validation of one's role as an effective worker (e.g., through the belief that one is paid well) foster self-efficacy (Finch, Shanahan, Mortimer, & Ryu, 1991; Grabowski, Call, & Mortimer, 2001). Stressors at work such as overload, role conflict, and exposure to noxious work conditions reduce self-esteem and self-efficacy (Mortimer, Harley, et al., 2002; Shanahan, Finch, Mortimer, & Ryu, 1991). Such experiences, however, may have long-term benefits. Although stressors may induce feelings of psychological distress and strain in the short term, the resultant growth and increase in adaptive capacities may enhance adaptation and problem solving in the longer term (Shanahan & Mortimer, 1996). Those who experienced such work problems for the first time in their early 20s suffer diminished self-efficacy and self-esteem, and greater depressed mood; their counterparts who confronted such challenges during high school show a high degree of resilience as they cope better subsequently (Mortimer & Staff, 2004).

In overview, as youth move from early childhood through middle childhood and into adolescence, they encounter numerous new socialization experiences with peers and in school and at work. These experiences combine with experiences in an expanding array of other settings to shape more mature social understanding, social expectations, motivations, and competencies. At this point, research has only begun to document the interplay of these processes and how they converge to influence socialization in the balance of the life span. In adolescence, when there is less parental control and monitoring, peers, school experiences, and technology and media use play increasingly larger roles in socialization; however, family values, norms, and beliefs continue to shape socialization toward maturity.

CONTEXTS AND CONTENTS OF SOCIALIZATION IN ADULTHOOD: FAMILY AND WORK

Socialization continues throughout life as individuals enter new contexts and adapt to new social situations, roles, and challenges. Moreover, as the pace of change accelerates in contemporary societies, the character of contexts cannot be anticipated by youth through observation of their elders or adequately prepared for in educational settings. Models of socialization are often static, failing to address the dynamic and sometimes turbulent character of postmodern society (Lutfey & Mortimer, 2003). Some occupational roles enacted by contemporary adults did not exist when they were children (e.g., Web designer). Under conditions of rapid change, the outcomes of effective socialization are likely to be the capacity to learn and to react quickly and effectively to changing circumstances (Orrange, 2003). This dynamic argues that adult socialization is becoming increasingly important.

Much prior work is devoted to understanding the early period of adulthood, when individuals are adapting to new family and work roles and forming new identities (Hartmann & Swartz, 2007; Shanahan, Porfeli, Mortimer, & Erickson, 2005). Defining the time of entry to adulthood, however, is complicated by the prolonged character of the transition to adult roles; Arnett (2007) called the run-up "emerging adulthood." Adult socialization refers, here, to what occurs in graduate, professional, and vocational training after the completion of general education, and in family, work, and other roles throughout emerging adult and adult life.

The literature on socialization in adulthood (Mortimer & Simmons, 1978) is scattered over a wide variety of disciplines, and subdisciplines, including professional education (Finlay, Mutran, Zeitler, & Randall, 1991; Hafferty, 1991) and training (Hodson, Hooks, & Rieble, 1992; Hull & Zacher, 2007), work (Hermanowicz, 2009; Johnson, 2001a, 2001b), organizations (Wanous, Reichers, & Malik, 1984), the family (Shapiro & Cooney, 2007; Wethington & Kamp Dush, 2007), volunteer settings (Omoto & Snyder 1995), and the broad field of consumption, media use, and leisure (Ritzer, 2001). Research in this area has been energized by scholarly interest in life-span development in psychology (Lerner, Easterbrooks, & Mistry, 2004) and the life course in sociology (Mortimer & Shanahan, 2003). It is increasingly recognized that new learning occurs each time individuals enter new age-graded social roles, including cognitive shifts in attitudes and values, alterations in self-concept and identity, behavioral accommodations to enact new skills, and new ways of relating to others. The ways socialization contexts are structured have much to do with the effectiveness of socialization, whether gauged by the quality of performance in new roles, satisfaction, or mental health.

Differences Between Socialization in Adulthood and in Earlier Phases of the Life Span

As previous sections of this chapter show, preadult socialization involves general self-regulation, the forging of attachments that serve as templates for later social relationships, and the development of fundamental values, self-concepts, and identities. In adulthood, more specific norms and behaviors needed to enact particular adult roles must be learned. Adult socialization is also more likely to involve the replacement of what is already learned with new ways of thinking and behaving; these are referred to in various literatures as a "destructive" phase of socialization, "culture shedding" (Berry, 2007), or "disengagement" from prior roles.

The socialization settings of young children and adolescents are more likely to be mandatory and selected by adults; by contrast, adult socialization is more often self-initiated and voluntary. Adults have greater freedom to select roles and contexts that are congruent with their already-formed interests, abilities, values, and identities (Heinz, 2002). For example, adults pick contexts for their professional socialization and training, work (Zimmer-Gembeck & Mortimer, 2007), volunteerism (Clary et al., 1998), and marriage (Alwin, Cohen, & Newcomb, 1991; Bulcroft, 2000). In the work sphere, adults make occupational choices on the basis of intrinsic and extrinsic work values, and adult socialization within the occupational setting reinforces those same judgments about work (Johnson, 2001a, 2001b; Mortimer & Lorence, 1979). Preexisting political orientations are also reinforced in selected work environments (Lorence & Mortimer, 1979).

Furthermore, adults have more resources than infants, young children, and adolescents to disrupt and challenge their socializers' attempts to alter their identities and behavior (Hull & Zacher, 2007); they can also utilize their accumulated capacities to act collectively to change socialization contexts that are not to their liking (Jermier, Knights, & Nord, 1994). Likewise, adults are abler and more likely to exit socialization contexts at will.

Preadult socialization often takes place in contexts (as we have seen) that place the socializee in the status of neophyte or learner in institutions, such as the family or school whose societally designated function is to perform that activity. Adult socialization occurs more often in contexts where socializees are already incumbents of the social roles that they are attempting to learn. As a result, they have full responsibility, for example, as a parent, worker, or member of a community organization. Their mistakes and false starts are therefore likely to have more severe consequences. Because preadult socialization is detached from the typical constraints and pressures of actual situations, it is sometimes characterized as more "idealistic," whereas adult socialization is necessarily more "realistic," as the neophyte attempts to "learn the ropes" (Karp & Yoels, 1981) in everyday situations.

Adult socialization also differs from socialization that occurs previously in the extent of diversity among socializees' life histories. Past experiences may significantly alter the character and outcomes of socialization in adulthood (Lutfey & Mortimer, 2003). With increasing diversity and unpredictability in early life-span trajectories (Shanahan, 2000), adults come to the same new socialization contexts at markedly different ages and with distinct prior and concurrent experiences. Instead of stable progressions from one life stage to another, delays, reversals, and turning points are common. Divergent psychological orientations, economic resources, and social supports, linked to diverse social locations and prior life experiences, influence adult socializees' capacities to learn and engage in socialization.

In the family realm, individuals may become parents for the first time in their teens, 20s, 30s, and, facilitated by new assisted reproduction technologies, even 40s (Bornstein & Putnick, 2007; Bornstein, Putnick, Suwalsky, & Gini, 2006; Golombok, 2002). Socialization to parenthood is a very different, and likely more difficult and less predictable, process for the new parent who has not yet finished schooling, is unmarried, and not employed in comparison to one who, even if the same chronological age, has achieved all of these familial and occupational markers of adulthood. Those who are propelled by technological and economic changes to seek new occupational knowledge and skills by returning to school may vary in age as well as in work and life experience. Such biographical differences produce variation in temporal orientations and opportunities—for example, adults who lose their jobs at age 55 may have more difficulty in "retooling" for a new career than those in the same circumstances at age 30.

Unique to adulthood is the possibility of resocialization, such as occurs after immigration, in psychotherapeutic settings, the military, or in correctional institutions. Because of the wholesale movement of populations across national boundaries, attention has recently been directed to the resocialization (acculturation) of adult immigrants (Berry, 2007; Jasso, 2003). Economic and social revolutions likewise require resocialization. For example, the shift from a centrally controlled to a competitive market economy in the previous Soviet block states placed a premium on new entrepreneurial orientations and behaviors, which would have been impossible to anticipate in childhood and adolescence (Diewald, 2006; Pinquart & Silbereisen, 2009). Adult socialization in settings such as these might be considered transformative, as old habits, ways of thinking, and identities are replaced. During periods of rapid change, both socializees and socializers may be uncertain as to what kinds of learning or adaptation would be most useful and what socializing experiences are in order. Ambiguity in the process of socialization can foster strain, confusion, and disorganization, but also provides opportunity for socializees to create their own definitions of the situation and alter the goals of socializers in a manner corresponding to their own interests.

Features of Contexts That Influence Socialization in Adulthood

Adult socialization contexts differ in the extent to which they allow advance preparation or anticipatory socialization, which facilitates adjustment to the new role (Gage & Christensen, 1991). Adult roles may be more or less visible to children and adolescents. For example, many occupational roles are invisible to outsiders or represented inaccurately, as in the media. Some youth may choose to enter police work after seeing only the most dramatic and exciting aspects of this occupation featured in television and the movies. Prior to adulthood, individuals may or may not have access to models who successfully enact the adult roles to be entered (Aronson, 2007). As more children and adolescents grow up in single-parent families, they have less opportunity to observe models who effectively perform both spousal roles. As parenting while cohabiting becomes more common, children are more often exposed to adult relational models in possibly less stable, and more conflictual, cohabiting unions.

Individuals are motivated to engage in preadult anticipatory socialization to the extent that new roles are expected. Most youth presume to marry, to become parents, and to enter full-time work. Many adults, however, must adapt to other, unexpected roles and challenges, including separation and divorce, unemployment, chronic illness, and disability. Under these circumstances, there may be little prior preparation (e.g., the recently widowed woman who has no knowledge of family finances) and few resources to draw on to facilitate resocialization.

Aside from factors that affect anticipatory socialization, some features of adult socialization contexts influence the character and outcomes of the process. Of fundamental importance is whether socialization occurs within, or outside, the role that is being prepared for. Large discrepancies may exist between the content of what is learned in the socialization context and the knowledge, skills, and attitudes needed in the new role. For example, technical colleges, and even professional education, are often criticized because the educators' own training is outdated, as are the techniques and equipment used in socialization (Hodson et al., 1992). Socializees learn the role as it was once performed, rather than the role that they will be expected to enact in the future. At other times, educators may be imbued with new theories and knowledge that have not yet become widely dispersed in practice. In either case, socialization may be out of step with contemporary circumstances and challenges.

A dramatic illustration of discrepancy between the role of socializee and the new role that is being prepared for occurs in correctional institutions (Uggen & Wakefield, 2005). Inmates are socialized to the role of prisoner, while attempts at rehabilitation are directed to an entirely different role as a free, conforming, and productive member of society. Complete separation from that outside world may engender unrealistic and idealistic expectations of life "on the outside" in the family, workplace, and community, which often are not supported after release by social relationships and resources that foster enactment and consolidation of the new desired roles and identities (Uggen, Manza, & Behrens, 2004). Becker's (1964) concept of "situational adjustment" is pertinent to this circumstance and many others like it that are not so extreme; socializees have the dual task of accommodating to their roles as learner at the same time that they have to prepare and "readjust" to new sets of circumstances when they enter a new role.

Adult socialization contexts also differ in the extent to which there are socializers who can guide the socializee. When the adult socializee must act as a full incumbent of the role that is being learned, as in some work settings, at times there are no socializers designated to instruct the newcomer. Informal relationships with mentors may be differentially available to workers, depending on their ethnicity, gender, or other characteristics (Cox & Nkomo, 1991). A relevant consideration is whether other workers experience gains or losses for devoting their time and energy to instruct the socializee.

Adult socialization contexts vary in the number of people who are being socialized at the same time and the duration of their involvement in the setting. The socializee may be solitary (a client undergoing psychoanalysis) or one of a class of learners (as in a professional school). For serial cohorts, more senior socializees may teach newcomers, and their own role-relevant knowledge, values, and orientations are strengthened in the process. Teachers or supervisors may teach the formal contents of a role, and peers establish informal norms regarding effort and what is actually learned (Becker, Geer, Hughes, & Strauss, 1961).

Also relevant are characteristics of the context that affect the motivation of people to be engaged and to continue participation despite initial failures and other obstacles. What are the rewards for successful socialization? Individuals are motivated to assume the roles of spouse, parent, and full-time worker because these are markers of a desired "adult" status that convey many other privileges, autonomy and independence, and responsibilities. This is unlike roles associated with widowhood, divorce, chronic illness, and, perhaps to a lesser extent, retirement. In the latter circumstances, people may not only fail to engage in anticipatory socialization but also resist new identities and behaviors that would facilitate adaptation to new, undesired social locations.

Etzioni (1961) detailed a typology of rewards available to motivate socialization of participants in organizations. When organizations can provide rewards that confer prestige or symbolize normative approval, morale and commitment are greatest, as in professional schools or seminaries. Other organizations make use of economic incentives, such as at work that sanction performance through salaries and bonuses, or if performance is inadequate, lack of career advancement. Organizations that do not have access to either economic or normative rewards must rely on physical coercion and force. Prisons are an example. Socializing organizations may be unsuccessful, not because they do not incorporate the best methods of teaching or other socialization techniques, but because they have little control over outcomes that could motivate socializees either within the organization or outside it in the future (Hull & Zacher, 2007).

Adult Socialization in Family Contexts

Whereas socialization in family contexts has often been viewed as mainly one way—from parents to children—a consideration of adult socialization reinforces our contention (discussed earlier) that familial socialization processes are reciprocal as family members continually socialize one another. Newlyweds socialize each other into new marital roles in ways that often reinforce cultural norms and suppress deviant behavior (Arnett, 2007; Sampson & Laub, 1993). Children, even at a very young age, exert influence on how their parents enact the parental role (Lerner, Lewin-Bizan, & Warren, 2010). Moreover, when children arrive, the couple's own parents are inducted, and socialized, into grandparent roles largely by their adult children and grandchildren (Smith & Drew, 2002). Thus, a good deal of adult socialization occurs in the family setting.

Research on socialization to marriage highlights the significance of spousal biographies. By selecting newly married couples, Tallman, Gray, Kullberg, and Henderson (1999) illuminated the dynamics through which husbands and wives socialize one another. Couples from intact, divorced/separated, or mixed (one parent from each type) families were asked to discuss a topic on which they disagreed. Individuals from similar backgrounds behaved in ways that were remarkably consistent with what would be expected based on their prior experience, having been exposed to either positive models of communication and marital stability or more negative models of conflict and turmoil. Newly married couples from intact families readily exhibited compromise, accommodation, and trust toward their spouse despite their disagreements; those whose parents divorced showed less sympathy and trust toward their partners. Whereas young adults from intact families reacted more positively and constructively, interactions were more divisive and hostile among couples from nonintact families. In mixed couples, the spouses came into the marriage with different expectations and response sets, providing greater potential for change. The spouse from the intact family was found to have greater impact, moving the couple toward a more conciliatory and constructive stance and a more gratifying and effective mode of conflict resolution over time.

Socialization occurs throughout the family life cycle in response to changing needs and circumstances. When children arrive, new parents are socialized into the parental role. They may look to their own parents and friends for guidance. When families split apart, resocialization to new statuses of divorce must occur, involving many behavioral adaptations as well as shifts in identity (Vaughan, 1986). Remarriage brings even more resocialization, as individuals adapt to new marriage partners, stepchildren, and an array of new relatives (Cherlin & Furstenberg, 1994; Wethington & Kamp Dush, 2007).

Parents and children may be considered ever-changing convoys of social support (Kahn & Antonucci, 1980), with need for resocialization as their relative resources, power, authority, and exchange patterns change over time and as they encounter new circumstances, such as parental or adult child divorce (Swartz, 2009). Parents who experience less conventional states or transitions, such as cohabitation, divorce, and remarriage, appear to have less positive relationships with their children, and more ambivalent attitudes toward them, perhaps as a result of the lack of normative structure and social support surrounding these new circumstances (Shapiro & Cooney, 2007; Wethington & Kamp Dush, 2007).

Adult Socialization to Work

Research on adult socialization in work settings has proceeded along two paths. The first focuses on specific occupations, often by means of ethnographic observation of workers as they are being socialized. The second path examines the impacts of dimensions of work contexts that cross-cut occupations, usually by means of surveys of large representative samples of the working population.

The first approach highlights what adults need in the way of new knowledge, skills, and attitudes to effectively perform a specific occupational role (Mortimer & Simmons, 1978). Socializees learn the values associated with their occupational subcultures, the manner in which performance is graded and rewarded in the occupational setting, and customary orientations toward coworkers, customers, and clients. There are case studies of socialization to the role of physician (Becker et al., 1961), medical technologist (Blau, 1999), psychiatrist (Light, 1980), auditor (Morrison, 2002), mortician (Cahill, 1999), policeman (Hopper, 1977), factory worker (Burawoy, 1979), clergyman (Schoenherr & Greeley, 1974), and sociologist (Wright, 1967), among others. This literature emphasizes the difficulty, and importance, of the earliest phases of socialization during which inaccurate images formed during anticipatory socialization are challenged by the reality of the new role. Newcomers may be surprised, even shocked, to learn about the unattractive features of the role, such as the amount of paperwork and other routine activities, or about threats to the prestige or autonomy of the practitioner. They may become demoralized as they realize that they may not be able to acquire the occupational roles that they prepared for because of deficiencies in their training or the scarcity of open positions (Hull & Zacher, 2007).

When high levels of commitment and engagement are necessary to learn a new role, socializees may be isolated to lessen the power of alternative reference groups (e.g., medical and graduate schools where students spend all their time in the early years). Such isolation fosters disengagement from old roles and reference groups and reengagement with new ones, as well as solidarity among peers who are being socialized collectively.

Counternormative experiences that may attend this kind of socialization are largely hidden from outsiders. To lessen commitment to prior ways of thinking and identities, newcomers may be hazed by established peers, insulted by supervisors, and debased, even mortified, in other ways. These experiences increase anxiety and are sometimes thought to heighten cohesion in the subject socializee cohort and enhance identification later with the occupational group. Classic studies of medical school students (Becker et al., 1961; Fox, 1957) highlight the intense anxiety that comes about when students are confronted with voluminous material to learn and myriad uncertainties, including those related to diagnostic knowledge, their own inadequacies in mastering the extant knowledge base, and the unpredictable character of the course of illness and recovery.

It is important for new recruits to experience challenge and mastery of tasks in the early phases of incumbency of a new role, which may engender spiraling success as confidence is gained and new opportunities for demonstrating effective performance are seized. In contrast, spiraling failure may ensue when initial tasks are either not challenging enough or too challenging. If initial effectiveness in the new role cannot be demonstrated, the individual may become discouraged, withhold effort, and retreat from opportunities that could build skills and enhance competence.

Adult socialization at work is a dynamic as "new work contexts" are characterized by rapid change, threats of obsolescence, and increasing job insecurity at all levels (Heinz, 2003). The new economy is characterized by nonstandard and often short-term employment contracts, temp work, freelancing, and other arrangements that reduce the commitment of the employer to the employee and reduce the employee's expectation of long-term employment with any one firm (Fullerton & Wallace, 2007). Even career ladders in large bureaucratic organizations are being dismantled as highly specialized managerial and professional work is outsourced (Skaggs & Leicht, 2005). In these circumstances, companies are less likely to invest in worker training, and workers may be less likely to want to invest their own energies in the acquisition of firm-specific knowledge, skills, and attitudes. To the extent that these conditions undermine worker commitment and engagement with employers, the effectiveness of socialization and training attempts can be expected to diminish.

The study of adult socialization mainly considers socialization to adult roles serially, but it is important to acknowledge that people are socialized to new roles in concert, and different roles may be more or less compatible. For example, the transition to parenthood is the occasion for resocialization with respect to both work and family roles whose requirements largely contradict. Whereas the emphasis on the male breadwinner role makes family and work more compatible for men than for women, increasingly men also feel strain resulting from simultaneous commitments to their families and their jobs, and they are taking a more active role in fathering (Bianchi, Robinson, & Milkie, 2006). Workers in higher social class positions have more access to institutional supports to alleviate difficulties in coordinating family and work roles (e.g., access to flex-time, family leave policies, and so forth) than those in working-class positions (Ammons & Kelly, 2008), but even they are unlikely to be prepared for these challenges through prior socialization.

To adjust to their new circumstances, new parents realign their roles, often falling back on more gender-typical arrangements (with mothers exiting the labor force or "scaling back" their involvement) and men emphasizing their breadwinner role (Moen & Roehling, 2005). Other couples try to maintain equal labor force participation by finding appropriate day care, sharing child care and housework, and making other adaptations that honor their dual commitments to family and work. There are many studies of time use that compare hours spent in work, child care, and household tasks (Bianchi et al., 2006), but little is known about the dynamics of adult socialization that engender different outcomes.

In overview, adulthood brings with it changing responsibilities and shifting roles in socialization. The main contexts of socialization in adulthood are family and work, and adulthood is supposedly the fulfillment of past socialization processes directed to productive and responsible community participation as well as the socialization of the succeeding generation. In the past, adulthood would have constituted socialization's culmination and end stage. Today, however, socialization does not conclude in adulthood. Rather, contemporary biological and social forces have influenced longevity to render old age new period of life-span socialization.

◼ CONTEXTS AND CONTENTS OF SOCIALIZATION IN OLD AGE: SOCIAL NETWORK, RETIREMENT, HEALTH CARE

In this section, we discuss three substantive arenas of socialization in late life: social networks, work and retirement, and health and health care. Despite some exceptions (Fingerman & Pitzer, 2007), theoretical and empirical research on socialization in old age remains scant relative to socialization at earlier stages in the life span, and therefore we also identify key issues for moving this line of inquiry forward in ways that capitalize on unique features of late life. Specifically, we consider ways in which critical perspectives on aging contribute to socialization studies—in particular, the relevance of gender to socialization in later life; and, finally, changes in the social landscape that are relevant to understanding socialization in old age.

Social Networks and Socialization in Old Age

As adults approaching old age transition out of some relationships and into new ones, their changing social networks provide major contexts of socialization. Research on social networks consistently shows that social ties positively affect health and mortality in late life (Berkman, 2000; Charles & Mavandadi, 2004; Cohen & Janicki-Deverts 2009). Furthermore, extensive research suggests that the quality of relationships improves with age as older adults report better marriages, more supportive friendships, and less conflict than their younger counterparts (Fingerman, Hay, & Birditt, 2004). Older adults report more positive feelings and fewer problems in their relationships than do younger adults (Fingerman & Charles, 2010). For example, older adults report feeling "very close to 5–10 social partners," whereas younger adults report having a higher number of contacts in their social networks but feeling less close to them (Antonucci et al., 2002; Fingerman & Pitzer, 2007). It has been suggested that older adults maximize investment in their most meaningful relationships as they approach the latter stage of their lives (Carstensen, Isaacowitz, & Charles, 1999), and social partners of elderly adults may act to minimize tensions to facilitate positive emotional experiences. In terms of socialization, the long-term relationships and the elderly may provide reinforcing effects over time so that less contact is required to acquire the same benefit. Furthermore, relationships lasting long periods of time may also allow for reference to earlier stages of life and therefore greater continuity over time in terms of reinforcing notions of self and identity—expanding potentially to include deceased members of a social network as well. Together, social networks constitute one component in a broader set of socializing agents that extend beyond individuals in one's social circles. In the case of socialization in old age, the interactions among parts of a social network over time, as well as interactions between the network and institutional or structural aspects of social life, are more prominent as compared with socialization to earlier life stages, when changes over time are less significant, the agents of socialization are fewer, and less reciprocal socialization occurs.

Work and Retirement in Socialization in Old Age

The transition away from formal labor markets and into retirement is another major life change associated with entry into old age, and an extensive body of research has developed around this topic (Gall & Evans, 2000; Kim & Moen, 2002; Moen, Kim, & Hofmeister, 2001; Moen, Sweet, & Swisher, 2005; Pinquart & Schindler, 2007; Quick & Moen, 1998). As part of extended life expectancy, people are living with increased amounts of chronic illness and often require more sustained care once they are not able to care for themselves independently. At the same time, earlier stages of old age are more likely to be characterized by good health and physical activity, so that periods of retirement that were once associated with disengagements across multiple life domains are now marked by disengagement with work but continued activity in terms of leisure and physical recreation. In terms of socialization, these changes affect anticipatory ideas about the length of old age, the proportion of the life span spent in old age, and the types of activity associated with late life, including sources of instrumental and emotional support available in the event that an elderly person can no longer live independently.

Beyond basic demographic shifts, the postwar era in the United States has witnessed major changes in the organization of family life, including not only family formation but also geographic mobility. Compared to 1960, people marry later (Goodwin, McGill, & Chandra, 2009), delay parenthood (Mathews & Hamilton, 2009), and divorce at higher rates (Registration of Methods Branch Division of Vital Statistics, 1964; Tejada-Vera & Sutton, 2009). At the same time, women have entered the formal labor force at increased rates and also taken on a second shift (Hochschild, 1989) as they continue to shoulder a disproportionate share of household and childrearing work at home. Geographic mobility has also increased, so that families and individuals move house more frequently, and multiple generations of families are less likely to live in close proximity. All of these changes are critical to socialization in old age as they lead to a new and potentially more diverse set of scenarios for how people will experience later segments of the life course—where, with whom, with what responsibilities, with what kind of social interaction, and how such arrangements may facilitate continuity of existing identities and roles or lead to their dissolution.

As a result, the meaning of retirement has changed significantly, and therefore the decades leading to the transition to retirement are increasingly in flux as new pathways to, and configurations of, retirement emerge. The early 20th-century model of (mostly white men) working for long periods with one employer, contributing over decades to a pension, and moving in "lock-step" toward a full retirement at age 65 has altered significantly (Moen et al., 2005). Much of the infrastructure that historically supported this life course transition has been rendered obsolete by globalization, changing gender composition of the work force, increased longevity, shortened tenures with single employers, the disappearance of traditional pensions, and, most recently, a large-scale economic downturn that destabilized savings and retirement planning just as large demographic groups were approaching retirement age. These factors underscore how a single model of retirement is inadequate to the task of understanding socialization processes. Moen et al. (2005) outlined a series of factors relevant to retirement planning and the transition away from formal work roles.

To begin, research points to the existence of gendered pathways through the transition to retirement (Kim & Moen, 2002; Moen, 1996; Pinquart & Schindler, 2007; Smith & Moen, 2004; Talaga & Beehr, 1995). Quick and Moen (1998) found that men report modestly greater retirement satisfaction, but the sources of satisfaction are different for the two sexes: for women retirement satisfaction is associated with good health, having had a continuous career, and good postretirement income, but for men retirement satisfaction is associated with good health, having enjoyed the preretirement job, and retiring for internally motivated reasons. Additional work on this topic shows retirement transitions affect multiple aspects of well-being, including decreased marital quality for husbands and wives (Moen et al., 2001).

Finally, Moen et al. (2005) observed real differences in financial versus lifestyle planning for retirement, with the former occurring more extensively (see also Petkoska & Earl, 2009). However, for male respondents, Gall and Evans (2000) found that preretirement expectations significantly predicted quality of life measures

6–7 years following retirement. Particularly in light of the social changes surrounding the midcentury pension-based model of retirement, an emphasis on financial planning at the expense of lifestyle preparation may be significantly associated with differential satisfaction postretirement (by gender and other demographics). Given the diverse trajectories preceding and following retirement, in addition to the variation in ways that the transition itself can be managed (e.g., age, phased retirement, planned postretirement activity, or whether retirement is coordinated with a spouse), well-rounded planning for social and lifestyle aspects of transitions are increasingly important for old age health and marital well-being. Residents of continuing care retirement communities perceive transitions as both disempowering and final (Shippee, 2009).

As with various aspects of old age socialization outlined earlier, the transition to retirement would also benefit from attention to the diversity of ways men and women disengage from formal work roles and the implications that change has for multiple domains of their lives. Similar gender differences pervade social relations and resource deficits in France, Germany, Japan, and the United States in the sense that women are more likely than men to experience widowhood, illness, and financial strain in all these places (Antonucci et al., 2002). As a function of their differential longevity, older men and women have different life contexts and sociostructural opportunities over the life course. Smith and Baltes (1998) examined women and men between the ages of 70 and 103 years in the Berlin aging study. They observed significant gender differences in more than half of personality factors, social relationship measures, everyday activity patterns, and reported well-being. The relative risk of a less desirable profile was 1.6 times higher for women than for men. For older adults, gender carries differences in physical frailty and life conditions that likely have consequences for psychological functioning.

Health and Health Care and Socialization in Old Age

Earlier, we emphasized how critical perspectives on health and aging illustrate how social and economic factors in aging ultimately have significance for health outcomes. At the same time, we recognize the importance of physiological factors in aging and specifically how physical changes interact with social conditions and institutional resources in the health care system. In overlap with demographic changes is the emergence of a medical-industrial complex (Ehrenreich & Ehrenreich, 1971; Estes, Harrington, & Pellow, 2000; Relman, 1980) and an aging enterprise (Estes, 1979), both of which are characterized by a "commodification of health that transformed health care and the needs of the elderly and others in society into commodities for specific economic markets" (Estes, 2001, p. 12). These developments are particularly insidious in combination. First, they contribute to the medicalization of old age by making social problems into profit-generating medical problems, which increases individuals' reliance on medical systems for assistance. Second, they promote treatment of age-related problems through individual-level and privatized outlets, thereby undermining the notion that problems of aging are social structural issues or concerns of the state. As a result, people are increasingly pressured to rely on privatized medical care for assistance rather than state-level provision of wage or housing support that could mitigate the negative social effects of aging. This shift in focus to medical rather than social strategies for problems associated with aging is particularly problematic vis-à-vis the gendered (and ethnic and socioeconomic) aspects of aging discussed previously, as medicalized approaches have no capacity for addressing these differences and rather exacerbate them because women are likely to depend on their spouses for insurance. The new medical-industrial complex has profound implications for old age socialization as it provides large-scale redefinitions of what the central problems are of old age and how they should be addressed (and paid for). Furthermore, these changes put the health care system and its workers in key positions as agents of socialization, for the elderly themselves and also their family members and caregivers.

Beyond large-scale structural changes surrounding aging, health in old age and interaction with the health care system are critical contexts for socialization, with potential to significantly influence trajectories of people once they reach later life. They do so in ways that build on, as well as undermine, earlier life experiences. For example, Fingerman, Hay, Kamp Dush, Cichy, and Hosterman (2007) found that elderly parents and their offspring report worse relationships when the parent had a functional disability or disease, even if the offspring was not required to provide care. In this sense, health during old age mediates other relationships and has the potential to affect social networks, even before accounting for functional impairment or variations in caregiving circumstances.

Interactions with the health care system mitigate or amplify these health effects. Experimental research on clinical decision making has demonstrated a "gendered ageism" effect wherein physicians are significantly less likely to provide appropriate care for, say, coronary heart disease for women (Arber et al., 2006). The complex intersection of physical and mental health treatment adds an important layer for understanding socialization into old age. Increasing medicalization of sadness (Horwitz & Wakefield, 2007) may compound problems for the elderly as normal sadness associated with life changes typical of old age (e.g., death of a spouse, loss of social roles, potential loss of independence) is medicalized and treated with pharmaceuticals, thereby intensifying reliance on the health care system. Indeed, rates of depression diagnosis for the elderly more than doubled in the 1990s, with about two thirds of those diagnosed receiving treatment (Crystal, Sambamoorthi, Walkup, & Akincigil, 2003).

At the same time, however, prevalence rates for mental disorders may be underestimated in elderly populations, in part because mental health problems that present comorbid with physical health problems or cognitive deficits are difficult to diagnose, and also because mentally ill elderly may be left out of community-based samples because they are disproportionately likely to be living in institutions (Krause, 1999). These mixed results suggest that people in late life may simultaneously be at risk for unnecessary medicalization of normatively sad events while also being at risk for underdiagnosis and treatment of more serious mental problems. In a factorial study of coronary heart disease, qualitative data showed how physicians often missed a diagnosis with female patients because they interpreted standardized signs and symptoms of coronary heart disease as evidence of depression (Lutfey & McKinlay, 2009). This type of interaction between physical and mental illness in the elderly— whether it be risk of over- or underdiagnosis and treatment—further contributes to the multifaceted nature of health and health care for the aged.

These health and health care factors alter how age-related problems are to be defined and, by extension, how they are to be solved. Together, these exposures

shape socializers and socializees, their ideologies about old age, their instrumental resources, and their priorities as they navigate (as opposed to just prepare for)
later life.

Key Issues in Old Age Socialization

In addition to the socialization arenas outlined earlier, serious consideration of
socialization processes in old age introduces a series of theoretical, conceptual, and
empirical issues that are distinct from earlier stages of the life span. Socialization of
younger people and even adults is often framed in terms of preparation for future roles
by people who already have experience with those roles (e.g., parenting or mentoring
in school and work settings), but much socialization around old age occurs through
agents who have not already experienced that life stage themselves. Furthermore,
there is a wide range of agents involved in socialization around old age, as contributors both to anticipatory and concurrent socialization to "successful aging."

These individual-level processes are contextualized in broader historical, economic, and political environments that have the potential to significantly influence
individual experiences over the course of several decades of life. Contacts with
macrolevel influences such as the health care system, governmental programs and
policies, political ideologies around aging, and media and cultural portrayals of older
people, all play unique roles in late-life socialization. As life expectancies continue
to increase, the potential for these macrolevel influences to shape the experiences of
old age are even greater as there is time for policy changes to be implemented and
absorbed into social and economic contexts.

At the same time, elderly socializees have extensive life experience prior to
arriving at old age. People are socialized in various ways to old age throughout the
life span, such that even very young children have (if rudimentary) ideas about what
it means to be old. Over time, these expectations evolve in tandem with varied life
experiences, life choices, normative and non-normative life events, planful competence, and the accumulation of roles and identities from other earlier stages of life,
some of which continue and some of which are phased out by later life. In this way,
socialization contexts around old age implicate all the domains of socialization that
have come previously (see Levy, Chung and Canavan Chapter 17; Levy, 2009).

Aging research has proliferated across a range of fields related to biology, clinical
medicine and psychiatry, and the social and behavioral sciences. Critical perspectives on health and aging include political economy, feminist theory, and humanistic gerontology, all of which challenge mainstream assumptions about aging and
thereby "reveal underlying ideological justifications of existing structural arrangements and resource distributions that affect health and aging" (Estes & Linkins,
2000, p. 154). Lessons learned from these fields about instrumental and ideological
expectations surrounding late life are relevant to understanding socialization processes, particularly aspects of socialization that are relatively unique to late life. A
unifying theme among these critical perspectives is that aging is primarily a socially
constructed, rather than a singularly biological, process, so that conceptions of aging,
and the problems faced by the elderly, are a product of social processes occurring at
the macro- and microlevels.

This contemporary constructivist stance stands in contrast to earlier aging
theories such as disengagement theory (Cumming & Henry, 1961), which

suggested that old age is a period in which individuals and society are in a process of mutual separation, or later perspectives, such as continuity theory (Costa & McCrae, 1980) and successful aging (Baltes & Baltes, 1990; Rowe & Kahn, 1987), which emphasized role continuity from earlier life stages into old age. Estes and Linkins (2000) noted that, if these latter theories countered stereotypes that old age is characterized by protracted, inevitable, and unidirectional decline, they did not account for the influence of structural factors on individual actions or the diversity of experiences that occur within the elderly population. More recent discussions around "normal," "usual," and "successful" aging also do not account for the diversity of life experiences leading into old age as emphasized in a life-span perspective (Schulz & Heckhausen, 1996). Following from our earlier discussion, these theoretical distinctions resonate with some of the differences observed between socialization in old age compared with earlier life stages and the particular importance of accounting for multilevel influences in old age socialization as well as the cumulative import of diversity in trajectories over the course of a lifetime.

Later studies in the areas of health and aging, including life-span perspectives, have emphasized the contributions of social and environmental factors to health outcomes (Estes, 2003; House, Kessler, & Herzog, 1990). Although this body of work tends to focus on morbidity and mortality, and socialization research is concerned with a broader range of issues, the general points remain informative. For today's elderly in the United States, the role of the state in supporting its citizens in old age has changed dramatically within their lifetimes. The implementation of the Social Security Act, followed by Medicare and Medicaid, provided unprecedented resources for later life and also contributed to social ideologies about later life and how responsibilities for assistance should be jointly managed by individuals and the public. These influences interact with gender such that older women tend to have fewer financial resources by old age. For example, many aspects of social and health policy in the United States reward married women compared to their unmarried counterparts, as is the case for retirement benefits through social security or the provision of private health insurance through employment, which are based on breadwinner models and women's dependence on their husbands for economic security (Estes, 2001; Estes & Linkins, 2000). To effectively attend to factors such as the wide range of socializing agents relevant to old age, the importance of long-term anticipatory socialization, the role of reciprocal socialization between socializees and socializers, and the diversity of individual experiences, socialization research must give serious consideration to micro–macro linkages that are specific to elderly groups and prominent in their resource calculations.

In overview, socialization extends beyond maturity, the period normatively conceived of as the culmination of socialization and the home of responsibility for future intergenerational socialization. Today, socialization stretches into old age, where the contents and contexts tend to focus on social networks, quality of life, and health care. Previous work on socialization in the life span focused on earlier stages, specific agents of socialization, and key transitions, such as the transition to adulthood. Socialization to old age has, by comparison, received less attention. Socialization processes in old age have several qualities that distinguish them from other points in the life course, including more agents from more domains of life that occur over a longer period of time. Also, anticipatory socialization occurs over a longer period leading up to old age as people develop a sense of the meaning and identities associated with that life stage over many decades.

▨ FUTURE ISSUES IN THE STUDY OF LIFE-SPAN CONTEXTS OF SOCIALIZATION

Socialization is a lifelong process. However, the different roles that people assume in socialization, the manners in which they contribute to socialization, and the contexts in which they find themselves being socialized and socializing vary substantially. In early childhood, parents (mostly) are children's primary socializers and special influences on their development. When children are young and still at home, parents model, reinforce, and scaffold beliefs or behaviors in their children as well as construct most of their children's formative opportunities and experiences. For instance, child–parent play introduces children to the values and routine adult activities of their context, which are critical components of socialization. As children develop, however, socialization influences beyond the family begin to rival parents for sway over socialization. Two forces, interpersonal (peers) and institutional (school, work), play increasingly central parts in socialization as socializees later develop. Parents were once seen primarily as trainers or transmitters of society, and children as empty vessels who were gradually filled up with the necessary social repertoires; today, socializees of all ages are conceived of as active participants in their own socialization. Early socialization theory and research consisted largely of a search for direct connections between parental practices and child outcomes, whereas current work focuses on family systems and reciprocal processes. Indirect effects, such as how paternal efforts at socialization may partially be directed through what mothers do, are also increasingly acknowledged. Parents do not relinquish their responsibilities or authority entirely, of course, and good parent–child relationships maintain parent input lifelong; even in adolescence and adulthood, values, norms, and beliefs of the family of origin continue to shape socialization. In this chapter on life-span socialization, we adopted a multiagent multisetting view of four broad stages of life-span socialization, and we adhered to a developmental contextual perspective.

Socialization intersects with three dimensions of time—past, present, and future. In this exposition, we have implicitly emphasized how socialization constitutes preparation for the future. It is also situated in the present, however, as individuals at each point in the life span are socialized to adapt to current as well as future roles and situations and to the role of socializee (e.g., from preschool student to doctoral candidate). Socialization is intimately connected to the past as well. The socializee's history, especially socialization during prior developmental periods, is thought individually or cumulatively to affect socialization at succeeding periods. The quality of earlier parenting affects school adaptation, and parent–child relationships and parenting practices can influence whether young children are popular with, rejected from, or victimized by peers. Earlier experiences in the family with parents and siblings come to shape emerging ideas and behaviors that carry over into adolescence (e.g., intimate relationships with teen boyfriends/girlfriends) and adulthood (intimacy in cohabiting and marital relationships). By organizing our exposition on life-span socialization according to developmental stages, we do not intend to underestimate essential connective or cumulative processes of socialization across the human life span. They constitute a significant arena for future work.

At the same time, research on socialization in old age especially constitutes a new frontier that would benefit from increased attention to theoretical concepts that have figured prominently in work on other life stages. For example, increased attention to the diversity of life trajectories would contribute to a reconceptualization of old age from being a unidirectional deterioration or disengagement from various life roles to a more multifacted phenomenon. This diversity is critical for understanding how people approach old age, the choices they make about how to configure their lives as they age, and the ways they engage with various institutions and life course domains over time. Because old age is a product of all that has come before, including individual-level experiences, dispositions, and decisions as well as more macro, economic, historical, and policy influences, it poses unique and complex challenges for understanding life-span socialization.

ACKNOWLEDGMENT

We thank G. Ladd for helpful thoughts on peer and school socialization, M. Sandoval, and T. Taylor. Supported by the Intramural Research Program of the NIH, NICHD.

REFERENCES

Ahn, H. J., & Stifter, C. (2006). Child care teachers' response to children's emotional expression. *Early Education and Development, 17,* 253–270.

Ainsworth, M. S., Blehar, M. C., Waters, E., & Wall, S. (1978). *Patterns of attachment: A psychological study of the strange situation.* Hillsdale, NJ: Erlbaum.

Alwin, D. F., Cohen, R. L., & Newcomb, T. M. (1991). *Political attitudes over the life span: The Bennington women after fifty years.* Madison, WI: University of Wisconsin Press.

Ammons, S. K., & Kelly, E. L. (2008). Social class and the experience of work-family conflict during the transition to adulthood. *New Directions for Child and Adolescent Development, 119,* 71–84.

Antill, J. K., Goodnow, J. J., Russell, G., & Cotton, S. (1996). The influence of parents and family context on children's involvement in household tasks. *Sex Roles, 34,* 215–236.

Antonucci, T. C., Lansford, J. E., Akiyama, H., Smith, J., Baltes, M. M., Takahashi, K., et al. (2002). Differences between men and women in social relations, resource deficits, and depressive symptomatology during later life in four nations. *Journal of Social Issues, 58,* 767–783.

Apel, R., Bushway, S., Brame, R., Haviland, A. M., Nagin, D. S., & Paternoster, R. (2007). Unpacking the relationship between adolescent employment and antisocial behavior: A matched samples comparison. *Criminology, 45,* 67–97.

Apel, R., Paternoster, R., Bushway, S. D., & Brame, R. (2006). A job isn't just a job: The differential impact of formal versus informal work on adolescent problem behavior. *Crime and Delinquency, 52,* 333–369.

Arber, S., McKinlay, J., Adams, A., Marceau, L., Link, C., & O'Donnell, A. (2006). Patient characteristics and inequalities in doctors' diagnostic and management strategies relating to CHD: A video-simulation experiment. *Social Science and Medicine, 62,* 103–115.

Arnett, J. J. (2007). Socialization in emerging adulthood: From the family to the wider world, from socialization to self-socialization. In J. E. Grusec & P. D. Hastings (Eds.), *Handbook of socialization: Theory and research* (pp. 208–231). New York: Guilford Press.

Aronson, P. (2007). Growing up alone: The absence of young women's positive life models. In R. MacMillan (Ed.), *Advances in life course research: Vol. 11. Constructing adulthood: Agency and subjectivity in adolescence and adulthood* (pp. 69–95). New York: Elsevier.

Aronson, P. J., Mortimer, J. T., Zierman, C., & Hacker, M. (1996). Generational differences in early work experiences and evaluations. In J. T. Mortimer & M. D. Finch (Eds.), *Adolescents, work, and family: An intergenerational developmental analysis. Understanding families* (Vol. 6, pp. 25–62). Thousand Oaks, CA: Sage.

Bachman, J. G., & Schulenberg, J. (1993). How part-time work intensity relates to drug use, problem behavior, time use, and satisfaction among high school seniors: Are these consequences or merely correlates? *Developmental Psychology, 29*, 220–235.

Baer, D. B., & Wolf, M. M. (1970). Recent examples of behavior modification in preschool settings. In C. Neuringer & J. L. Michael (Eds.), *Behavior modification in clinical psychology* (pp. 10–25). New York: Appleton-Century-Crofts.

Baltes, P. B., & Baltes, M. M. (1990). Psychological perspectives on successful aging: The model of selective optimization with compensation. In P. B. Baltes & M. M. Baltes (Eds.), *Successful aging: Perspectives from the behavioral sciences* (pp. 1–34). New York: Cambridge University Press.

Bandura, A. (1977). *Social learning theory.* Englewood Cliffs, NJ: Prentice Hall.

Bandura, A. (1986). *Social foundations of thought and action: A social cognitive theory.* Englewood Cliffs, NJ: Prentice Hall.

Barnard, K. E., & Solchany, J. E. (2002). Mothering. In M. H. Bornstein (Ed.), *Handbook of parenting: Vol. 3. Being and becoming a parent* (2nd ed., pp. 3–26). Mahwah, NJ: Erlbaum.

Becker, H. S. (1964). Personal change in adult life. *Sociometry, 27*, 40–53.

Becker, H. S., Geer, B., Hughes, E. C., & Strauss, A. L. (1961). *Boys in white: Student culture in medical school.* Chicago, IL: University of Chicago Press.

Bell, R. Q. (1968). A reinterpretation of the direction of effects in studies of socialization. *Psychological Review, 75*, 81–95.

Berkman, L. F. (2000). Which influences cognitive function: Living alone or being alone? *The Lancet, 355*, 1291–1292.

Berndt, T. J., & Perry, T. B. (1986). Children's perceptions of friendships as supportive relationships. *Developmental Psychology, 22*, 640–648.

Berry, J. W. (2007). Acculturation. In J. E. Grusec & P. D. Hastings (Eds.), *Handbook of socialization: Theory and research* (pp. 543–558). New York: Guilford Press.

Bianchi, S. M., Robinson, J. P., & Milkie, M. A. (2006). *Changing rhythms of American family life.* New York: Russell Sage Foundation.

Birch, S. H., & Ladd, G. W. (1998). Children's interpersonal behaviors and the teacher-child relationship. *Developmental Psychology, 34*, 934–946.

Bjorklund, D. F., & Pellegrini, A. D. (2002). *The origins of human nature: Evolutionary developmental psychology.* Washington, DC: American Psychological Association.

Blau, G. (1999). Early-career job factors influencing the professional commitment of medical technologists. *Academy of Management Journal, 42*, 687–695.

Blustein, D. L. (1992). Applying current theory and research in career exploration to practice. *Career Development Quarterly, 41*, 174–184.

Blustein, D. L. (1997). The role of work in adolescent development. *Career Development Quarterly, 45*, 381–389.

Booth, C. L., Clarke-Stewart, K. A., Vandell, D. L., McCartney, K., & Owen, M. T. (2002). Child-care usage and mother-infant "quality time." *Journal of Marriage and Family, 64*, 16–26.

Bornstein, M. H. (2006). Parenting science and practice. In K. A. Renninger & I. E. Sigel (Volume Eds.) and W. Damon & R. M. Lerner (Eds.), *Handbook of child psychology: Vol. 4. Child psychology in practice* (6th ed., pp. 893–949). Hoboken, NJ: John Wiley & Sons.

Bornstein, M. H., Brown, E., & Slater, A. (1996). Patterns of stability and continuity in attention across early infancy. *Journal of Reproductive and Infant Psychology, 14*, 195–206.

Bornstein, M. H., & Putnam, D. L. (2007). Chronological age, cognitions, and practices in European American mothers: A multivariate study of parenting. *Developmental Psychology, 43*, 850–864.

Bornstein, M. H., Putnick, D. L., Suwalsky, J. T. D., & Gini, M. (2006). Maternal chronological age, prenatal and perinatal history, social support, and parenting of infants. *Child Development, 77*, 875–892.

Bornstein, M. H., & Sawyer, J. (2005). Family systems. In K. McCartney & D. Phillips (Eds.), *Blackwell handbook on early childhood development* (pp. 381–398). Malden, MA: Blackwell.

Bowlby, J. (1969). *Attachment and loss: Vol. I. Attachment.* New York: Basic Books.

Brint, S. (1998). *Schools and societies.* Thousand Oaks, CA: Pine Forge Press.

Brint, S., Contreras, M. F., & Matthews, M. T. (2001). Socialization messages in primary schools: An organizational analysis. *Sociology of Education, 74*, 157–180.

Bugental, D. B., & Grusec, J. E. (2006). Socialization processes. In N. Eisenberg (Vol. Ed.), W. Damon, & R. M. Lerner (Series Eds.), *Handbook of child psychology: Vol. 3. Social, emotional, and personality development* (6th ed., pp. 366–428). Hoboken, NJ: John Wiley & Sons.

Buhs, E. S., & Ladd, G. W. (2001). Peer rejection as antecedent of young children's school adjustment: An examination of mediating processes. *Developmental Psychology, 37,* 550–560.

Bukowski, W. M., Brendgen, M., & Vitaro, F. (2007). Peers and socialization: Effects on externalizing and internalizing problems. In J. E. Grusec & P. D. Hastings (Eds.), *Handbook of socialization: Theory and research* (pp. 355–381). New York: Guilford Press.

Bulcroft, K. (2000). Mate selection theories. In E. F. Borgatta & R. J. V. Montgomery (Eds.), *Encyclopedia of sociology* (2nd ed., pp. 1774–1780). New York: Macmillan Reference.

Burawoy, M. (1979). *Manufacturing consent: Changes in the labor process under monopoly capitalism.* Chicago, IL: University of Chicago Press.

Burks, V. S., Dodge, K. A., & Price, J. M. (1995). Models of internalizing outcomes of early rejection. *Development and Psychopathology, 7,* 683–695.

Cahill, S. E. (1999). Emotional capital and professional socialization: The case of mortuary science students (and me). *Social Psychology Quarterly, 62,* 101–116.

Carstensen, L. L., Isaacowitz, D. M., & Charles, S. T. (1999). Taking time seriously: A theory of socioemotional selectivity. *American Psychologist, 54,* 165–181.

Charles, S. T., & Mavandadi, S. (2004). Social support and physical health across the life span: Socioemotional influences. In F. R. Lang & K. L. Fingerman (Eds.), *Growing together: Personal relationships across the lifespan* (pp. 240–267). Cambridge: Cambridge University Press.

Cherlin, A. J., & Furstenberg, F. F., Jr. (1994). Stepfamilies in the United States: reconsideration. *Annual Review of Sociology, 20,* 359–381.

Clarke-Stewart, K. A., & Allhusen, V. D. (2002). Nonparental caregiving. In M. H. Bornstein (Ed.), *Handbook of parenting Vol. 3 Status and social conditions of parenting* (2nd ed., pp. 215–252). Mahwah, NJ: Erlbaum.

Clarke-Stewart, K. A., & Allhusen, V. D. (2005). *What we know about childcare.* Cambridge, MA: Harvard University Press.

Clary, E. G., Snyder, M., Ridge, R. D., Copeland, J., Stukas, A. A., Haugen, J., et al. (1998). Understanding and assessing the motivations of volunteers: A functional approach. *Journal of Personality and Social Psychology, 74,* 1516–1530.

Cohen, S., & Janicki-Deverts, D. (2009). Can we improve our physical health by altering our social networks? *Perspectives on Psychological Science, 4,* 375–378.

Coie, J. D., Dodge, K. A., & Coppotelli, H. (1982). Dimensions and types of social status: A cross-age perspective. *Developmental Psychology, 18,* 557–570.

Collins, W. A., Maccoby, E. E., Steinberg, L., Hetherington, E. M., & Bornstein, M. H. (2000). Contemporary research on parenting: The case for nature and nurture. *American Psychologist, 55,* 218–232.

Committee on the Health and Safety Implications of Child Labor. (1998). *Protecting youth at work: Health, safety, and development of working children and adolescents in the United States.* Washington, DC: National Academy Press.

Cooper, C. R., Ayers-Lopez, S., & Marquis, A. (1982). Children's discourse during peer learning in experimental and naturalistic situations. *Discourse Processes, 5,* 177–191.

Corsaro, W. A., & Eder, D. (1995). The development and socialization of children and adolescents. In K. S. Cook, G. A. Fine, & J. S. House (Eds.), *Sociological perspectives on social psychology* (pp. 421–451). Boston: Allyn & Bacon.

Costa, P. T., & McCrae, R. R. (1980). Still stable after all these years: Personality as a year to some issues in aging. In P. B. Baltes & O. G. Brim (Eds.), *Lifespan development and behavior* (Vol. 3, pp. 65–102). New York: Academic Press.

Cox, M. J., & Paley, B. (2003). Understanding families as systems. *Current Directions in Psychological Science, 12,* 193–196.

Cox, T. H., & Nkomo, S. M. (1991). A race and gender-group analysis of the early career experience of MBA's. *Work and Occupations, 18,* 431–446.

Crick, N. R., & Dodge, K. A. (1994). A review and reformulation of social information-processing mechanisms in children's social adjustment. *Psychological Bulletin, 115,* 74–101.

Crystal, S., Sambamoorthi, U., Walkup, J. T., & Akincigil, A. (2003). Diagnosis and treatment of depression in the elderly Medicare population: Predictors, disparities, and trends. *Journal of the American Geriatric Society, 51,* 1718–1728.

Cumming, E., & Henry, W. E. (1961). *Growing old: The process of disengagement.* New York: Basic Books.

Cunnien, K. A., MartinRogers, N., & Mortimer, J. T. (2009). Adolescent work experience and self-efficacy. *International Journal of Sociology and Social Policy, 29,* 164–175.

Davis, H. A. (2001). The quality and impact of relationships between elementary school students and teachers. *Contemporary Educational Psychology, 26*, 431–453.

Deal, J. E., Hagan, M. S., Bass, B., Hetherington, E. M., & Clingempeel, G. (1999). Marital interaction in dyadic and triadic contexts: Continuities and discontinuities. *Family Process, 38*, 105–115.

Diewald, M. (2006). Spirals of success and failure? The interplay of control beliefs and working lives in the transition from planned to market economy. In M. Diewald, A. Goedicke, & K. U. Mayer (Eds.), *After the fall of the wall: Life courses in the transformation of East Germany* (pp. 214–236). Stanford: Stanford University Press.

Dodge, K. A. (1986). A social information processing model of social competence in children. In M. Perlmutter (Ed.), *Cognitive perspectives on children's social and behavioral development. The Minnesota Symposia on Child Psychology* (Vol. 18, pp. 77–125). Hillsdale, NJ: Erlbaum.

Dreeben, R. (1968). *On what is learned in school.* Reading, MA: Addison-Wesley.

Dunn, J. (1993). *Young children's close relationships: Beyond attachment.* Newbury Park, CA: Sage.

Dunn, J., & Munn, P. (1985). Becoming a family member: Family conflict and the development of social understanding in the second year. *Child Development, 56*, 480–492.

Durkheim, E. (1956). *Education and sociology.* Glencoe, IL: Free Press.

Duyme, M., Dumaret, A.-C., & Stanislaw, T. (1999). How can we boost IQs of "dull children"?: A late adoption study. *Proceedings of the National Academy of Sciences, 96*, 8790–8794.

Eccles, J. S., & Roeser, R. W. (2011). School and community influences on human development. In M. H. Bornstein & M. E. Lamb (Eds.), *Developmental science: An advanced textbook* (6th ed., pp. 566–638). New York: Taylor & Francis Group.

Edwards, C. P., & Whiting, B. B. (1993). "Mother, older sibling and me": The overlapping roles of caregivers and companions in the social world of two- to three-year-olds in Ngeca, Kenya. In K. MacDonald (Ed.), *Parent-child play: Descriptions and implications* (pp. 305–329). Albany, NY: State University of New York Press.

Ehrenreich, B., & Ehrenreich, J. (1971). *The American health empire: Power, profits, and politics* (Report for the Health Policy Advisory Center). New York: Vintage.

Eisenberg, N., Fabes, R. A., Murphy, B., Maszk, P., Smith, M., & Karbon, M. (1995). The role of emotionality and regulation in children's social functioning: A longitudinal study. *Child Development, 66*, 1360–1384.

Eisenberg, N., Wolchik, S. A., Hernandez, R., & Pasternack, J. F. (1985). Parental socialization of young children's play: A short-term longitudinal study. *Child Development, 56*, 1506–1513.

Elliot, D. B., Menard, S., Rankin, B., Elliot, A., Huizinga, D., & Wilson, W. J. (2006). *Good kids from bad neighborhoods: Successful development in social context.* New York: Cambridge University Press.

Emde, R. N., Biringen, Z., Clyman, R. B., & Oppenheim, D. (1991). The moral self of infancy: Affective core and procedural knowledge. *Developmental Review, 11*, 251–270.

Erel, O., & Burman, B. (1995). Interrelatedness of marital relations and parent-child relations: A meta-analytic review. *Psychological Bulletin, 118*, 108–132.

Estes, C. L. (1979). *The aging enterprise: A critical examination of social policies and services for the aged.* San Francisco, CA: Jossey-Bass.

Estes, C. L. (2001). *Social policy & aging: A critical perspective.* Thousand Oaks, CA: Sage.

Estes, C. L. (2003). Theoretical perspectives on old age policy: A critique and a proposal. In S. Biggs, A. Lowenstein, & J. Hendricks (Eds.), *The need for theory: Critical approaches to social gerontology* (pp. 219–244). Amityville, NY: Baywood.

Estes, C. L., Harrington, C., & Pellow, D. N. (2000). The medical industrial complex. In E. F. Borgatta & R. J. V. Montgomery (Eds.), *Encyclopedia of sociology* (Vol. 3, 2nd ed., pp. 1243–1254). New York: MacMillan Reference.

Estes, C. L., & Linkins, K. W. (2000). Critical perspectives on health and aging. In G. L. Albrecht, R. Fitzpatrick, & S. C. Scrimshaw (Eds.), *The handbook of social studies in health & medicine* (pp. 154–172). London: Sage.

Etzioni, A. (1961). *A comparative analysis of complex organizations.* New York: Free Press.

Fabes, R. A., Hanish, L. D., & Martin, C. L. (2003). Children at play: The role of peers in understanding the effects of child care. *Child Development, 74*, 1039–1043.

Felner, R. D., Brand, S., DuBois, D. L., Adan, A. M., Mulhall, P. F., & Evans, E. G. (1995). Socioeconomic disadvantage, proximal environmental experiences, and socioemotional and academic adjustment in early adolescence: Investigation of a mediated effects model. *Child Development, 66*, 774–792.

Fenichel, E., Lurie-Hurvitz, E., & Griffin, A. (1999). Seizing the moment to build momentum for quality infant/toddler child care: Highlights of the Child Care Bureau and Head Start Bureau's national leadership forum on quality care for infants and toddlers. *Zero to Three, 19*, 3–17.

Field, T., Greenwald, P., Morrow, C., Healy, B., Foster, T., Guthertz, M., et al. (1992). Behavior state matching during interactions of preadolescent friends versus acquaintances. *Developmental Psychology, 28,* 242–250.

Finch, M. D., Shanahan, M. J., Mortimer, J. T., & Ryu, S. (1991). Work experience and control orientation in adolescence. *American Sociological Review, 56,* 597–611.

Fingerman, K. L., & Charles, S. T. (2010). It takes two to tango: Why older people have the best relationships. *Current Directions in Psychological Science, 19*(3), 172–176.

Fingerman, K. L., Hay, E. L., & Birditt, K. S. (2004). The best of ties, the worst of ties: Close, problematic, and ambivalent relationships across the lifespan. *Journal of Marriage and Family, 66,* 792–808.

Fingerman, K. L., Hay, E. L., Kamp Dush, C. M., Cichy, K. E., & Hosterman, S. J. (2007). Parents' and offspring's perceptions of change and continuity when parents experience the transition to old age. In T. J. Owens & J. J. Suitor (Eds.), *Advances in life course research: Vol. 12. Interpersonal relations across the life course* (pp. 275–306). New York: Elsevier.

Fingerman, K. L., & Pitzer, L. (2007). Socialization in old age. In J. E. Grusec & P. D. Hastings (Eds.), *Handbook of socialization: Theory and research* (pp. 232–255). New York: Guilford Press.

Finlay, W., Mutran, E. J., Zeitler, R. R., & Randall, C. S. (1991). Experience, attitudes, and plans: Determinants of the productivity of medical residents in a primary care clinic. *Work and Occupations, 18,* 447–458.

Fisher-Thompson, D. (1993). Adult toy purchase for children: Factors affecting sex-typed toy selection. *Journal of Applied Developmental Psychology, 14,* 385–406.

Flouri, E., & Buchanan, A. (2002). The role of work-related skills and career role models in adolescent career maturity. *The Career Development Quarterly, 51,* 36–43.

Fox, R. C. (1957). Training for uncertainty. In R. K. Merton, G. C. Reader, & P. L. Kendall (Eds.), *The student physician: Introductory studies in the sociology of medical education* (pp. 207–241). Cambridge, MA: Harvard University Press.

French, V. (2002). History of parenting: The ancient Mediterranean world. In M. H. Bornstein (Ed.), *Handbook of parenting: Vol. 2. Biology and ecology of parenting* (2nd ed., pp. 345–376). Mahwah, NJ: Erlbaum.

Fullerton, A. S., & Wallace, M. (2007). Traversing the flexible turn: U.S. workers' perceptions of job security, 1997–2002. *Social Science Research, 36,* 201–221.

Furstenberg, F. F., Jr., Cook, T. D., Eccles, J., Elder, G. H., Jr., & Sameroff, A. (1999). *Managing to make it: Urban families and adolescent success.* Chicago, IL: University of Chicago Press.

Gage, M. G., & Christensen, D. H. (1991). Parental role socialization and the transition to adulthood. *Family Relations, 40,* 332–337.

Gall, T. L., & Evans, D. R. (2000). Preretirement expectations and the quality of life of male retirees in later retirement. *Canadian Journal of Behavioural Science, 32,* 187–197.

Gauvain, M. (2001). *The social context of cognitive development.* New York: Guilford.

Gecas, V. (1981). Contexts of socialization. In M. Rosenberg & R. H. Turner (Eds.), *Social psychology: Sociological perspectives* (pp. 165–199). New York: Basic Books.

Gecas, V. (2000). Socialization. In E. F. Borgatta (Ed.), *Encyclopedia of sociology* (pp. 2855–2864). Detroit, MI: Macmillan.

Georgas, J., Berry, J. W., Kağitçibaşi, Ç., Poortinga, Y. H., & van de Vijver, F. (2006). *Family structure and function in 30 nations: A psychological study.* Cambridge: Cambridge University Press.

Golombok, S. (2002). Parenting and contemporary reproductive technologies. In M. H. Bornstein (Ed.), *Handbook of parenting Vol. 3 Status and social conditions of parenting* (2nd ed., pp. 339–360). Mahwah, NJ: Erlbaum.

Goodwin, P., McGill, B., & Chandra, A. (2009). *Who marries and when? Age at first marriage in the United States: 2002* (NCHS Data Brief 19). Hyattsville, MD: National Center for Health Statistics, Center for Disease Control.

Gottfried, A. E., Gottfried, A. W., & Bathurst, K. (2002). Maternal and dual-earner employment status and parenting. In M. H. Bornstein (Ed.), *Handbook of parenting Vol. 2 Biology and ecology of parenting* (2nd ed., pp. 207–229). Mahwah, NJ: Erlbaum.

Grabowski, L. S., Call, K. T., & Mortimer, J. T. (2001). Global and economic self efficacy in the educational attainment process. *Social Psychology Quarterly, 64,* 164–179.

Hafferty, F. (1991). *Into the valley: Death and the socialization of medical students.* New Haven, CT: Yale University Press.

Hamre, B. K., & Pianta, R. C. (2001). Early teacher-child relationships and the trajectory of children's school outcomes through eighth grade. *Child Development, 72,* 625–638.

Harris, J. R. (1995). Where is the child's environment? A group socialization theory of development. *Psychological Review, 102,* 458–489.

Harris, J. R. (1998). *The nurture assumption.* New York: Free Press.

Harter, S. (1996). Teacher and classmate influences on scholastic motivation, self-esteem, and level of voice in adolescents. In J. Juvonen & K. R. Wentzel (Eds.), *Social motivation: Understanding children's school adjustment* (pp. 11–42). Cambridge: Cambridge University Press.

Hartmann, D., & Swartz, T. T. (2007). The new adulthood? The transition to adulthood from the perspective of transitioning young adults. In R. MacMillan (Ed.), *Advances in life course research: Vol. 11. Constructing adulthood: Agency and subjectivity in adolescence and adulthood* (pp. 253–286). New York: Elsevier.

Hartmann, D. P., Pelzel, K. E., & Abbott, C. B. (2011). Design, measurement, and analysis in developmental research. In M. H. Bornstein & M. E. Lamb (Eds.), *Developmental science: An advanced textbook* (6th ed., pp. 107–195). New York: Taylor & Francis Group.

Hartup, W. W. (1996). The company they keep: Friendships and their developmental significance. *Child Development, 67,* 1–13.

Hartup, W. W. (1999). Constraints on peer socialization: Let me count the ways. *Merrill-Palmer Quarterly, 45,* 172–183.

Hartup, W. W. (2005). Peer interaction: What causes what? *Journal of Abnormal Child Psychology, 33,* 387–394.

Hartup, W. W., & Stevens, N. (1999). Friendships and adaptation across the life span. *Current Directions in Psychological Science, 8,* 76–79.

Heinz, W. R. (2002). Self-socialization and post-traditional society. In R. A. Settersten & T. J. Owens (Eds.), *Advances in life course research: Vol. 7: New frontiers in socialization* (pp. 41–64). New York: Elsevier.

Heinz, W. R. (2003). From work trajectories to negotiated careers: The contingent work life course. In J. T. Mortimer & M. J. Shanahan (Eds.), *Handbook of the life course* (pp. 185–904). New York: Kluwer/Academic Plenum.

Helburn, S. W. (Ed.). (1995). *Cost, quality, and child outcomes in child care centers: Technical report.* Denver, CO: Department of Economics, Center for Research in Economic and Social Policy, University of Colorado at Denver.

Hermanowicz, J. C. (2009). *Lives in science: How institutions affect academic careers.* Chicago, IL: University of Chicago Press.

Hochschild, A. (with Machung, A.). (1989). *The second shift: Working parents and the revolution at home.* New York: Viking.

Hodson, R., Hooks, G., & Rieble, A. (1992). Customized training in the workplace. *Work and Occupations, 19,* 272–292.

Hopper, M. (1977). Becoming a policeman: Socialization of cadets in a police academy. *Urban Life, 6,* 149–170.

Horwitz, A. V., & Wakefield, J. C. (2007). *The loss of sadness: How psychiatry transformed normal sorrow into Depressive Disorder.* New York: Oxford University Press.

House, J. S., Kessler, R. C., & Herzog, A. R. (1990). Age, socioeconomic status, and health. *Milbank Quarterly, 68,* 383–411.

Howes, C., & Hamilton, C. E. (1993). The changing experience of child care: Changes in teachers and in teacher-child relationships and children's social competence with peers. *Early Childhood Research Quarterly, 8,* 15–32.

Howes, C., Matheson, C. C., & Hamilton, C. E. (1994). Maternal, teacher, and child care history correlates of children's relationships with peers. *Child Development, 65,* 264–273.

Hubbard, J. A. (2001). Emotion expression processes in children's peer interaction: The role of peer rejection, aggression, and gender. *Child Development, 72,* 1426–1438.

Hull, G. A., & Zacher, J. (2007). Enacting identities: An ethnography of a job training program. *Identity, 7,* 71–102.

Jackson, P. W. (1968). *Life in classrooms.* New York: Holt, Rinehart, and Winston.

Jasso, G. (2003). Migration, human development, and the life course. In J. T. Mortimer & M. J. Shanahan (Eds.), *Handbook of the life course* (pp. 331–364). New York: Kluwer/Academic Plenum.

Jermier, J. M., Knights, D., & Nord, W. R. (Eds.). (1994). *Resistance and power in organizations: Agency, subjectivity, and the labor process.* London: Routledge.

Johnson, M. H. (2011). Developmental neuroscience, psychophysiology, and genetics. In M. H. Bornstein & M. E. Lamb (Eds.), *Developmental science: An advanced textbook* (6th ed., pp. 199–237). New York: Taylor & Francis Group.

Johnson, M. K. (2001a). Change in job values during the transition to adulthood. *Work and Occupations, 28,* 315–345.

Johnson, M. K. (2001b). Job values in the young adult transition: Stability and change with age. *Social Psychology Quarterly, 64,* 297–317.

Johnson, M. K. (2002). Social origins, adolescent experiences, and work value trajectories during the transition to adulthood. *Social Forces, 80,* 1307–1341.

Kahn, R. L., & Antonucci, T. (1980). Convoys over the life course: Attachment, roles and social support. In P. Baltes & O. G. Brim (Eds.), *Lifespan development and behavior* (pp. 253–286). New York: Academic Press.

Karp, D. A., & Yoels, W. C. (1981). Work, careers, and aging. *Qualitative Sociology, 4,* 145–166.

Kim, J. E., & Moen, P. (2002). Retirement transitions, gender, and psychological well-being: A life-course, ecological model. *Journal of Gerontology, 57B,* 212–222.

Knafo, A., & Plomin, R. (2006). Prosocial behavior from early to middle childhood: Genetic and environmental influences on stability and change. *Developmental Psychology, 42,* 771–786.

Kochenderfer, B. J., & Ladd, G. W. (1996). Peer victimization: Cause or consequence of school maladjustment? *Child Development, 67,* 1305–1317.

Krause, N. (1999). Mental disorder in late life: Exploring the influence of stress and socioeconomic status. In C. S. Aneshensel & J. C. Phelan (Eds.), *Handbook of the sociology of mental health* (pp. 183–208). New York: Kluwer Academic/Plenum Publishers.

Ladd, G. W. (1988). Friendship patterns and peer status during early and middle childhood. *Journal of Developmental and Behavioral Pediatrics, 9,* 229–238.

Ladd, G. W. (2003). Probing the adaptive significance of children's behavior and relationships in the school context: A child by environment perspective. *Advances in Child Development and Behavior, 31,* 43–104.

Ladd, G. W. (2005). *Children's peer relations and social competence: A century of progress.* New Haven, CT: Yale University Press.

Ladd, G. W. (2007). Social learning in the peer context. In O. N. Saracho & B. Spodek (Eds.), *Contemporary perspectives on socialization and social development in early childhood education* (pp. 133–164). Charlotte, NC: Information Age.

Ladd, G. W., Birch, S. H., & Buhs, E. S. (1999). Children's social and scholastic lives in kindergarten: Related spheres of influence? *Child Development, 70,* 1373–1400.

Ladd, G. W., & Burgess, K. B. (2001). Do relational risks and protective factors moderate the linkages between childhood aggression and early psychological and school adjustment? *Child Development, 72,* 1579–1601.

Ladd, G. W., Herald, S. L., & Andrews, R. K. (2006). Young children's peer relations and social competence. In B. Spodek & O. N. Saracho (Eds.), *Handbook of research on the education of young children* (Vol. 2, pp. 23–54). Mahwah, NJ: Erlbaum.

Ladd, G. W., Herald, S. L., & Kochel, K. P. (2006). School readiness: Are there social prerequisites? *Early Education and Development, 17,* 115–150.

Ladd, G. W., & Pettit, G. S. (2002). Parenting and the development of children's peer relationships. In M. H. Bornstein (Ed.), *Handbook of parenting: Vol. 5. Practical issues in parenting* (2nd ed., pp. 269–309). Mahwah, NJ: Erlbaum.

Ladd, G. W., & Price, J. M. (1986). Promoting children's cognitive and social competence: The relation between parents' perceptions of task difficulty and children's perceived and actual competence. *Child Development, 57,* 446–460.

Ladd, G. W., & Troop-Gordon, W. (2003). The role of chronic peer difficulties in the development of children's psychological adjustment problems. *Child Development, 74,* 1344–1367.

Lamb, M. E., & Ahnert, L. (2006). Nonparental child care: Context, concepts, correlates, and consequences. In K. A. Renninger & I. E. Sigel (Vol. Eds.), W. Damon & R. M. Lerner (Series Eds.), *Handbook of child psychology: Vol. 4. Child psychology in practice* (6th ed., pp. 950–1016). New York: Wiley.

Lamb, M. E., Easterbrooks, M. A., & Holden, G. W. (1980). Reinforcement and punishment among preschoolers: Characteristics, effects, and correlates. *Child Development, 51,* 1230–1236.

Larson, R., & Richards, M. H. (1994). *Divergent realities: The emotional lives of mothers, fathers, and adolescents.* New York: Basic Books.

Lee, J. C., & Staff, J. (2007). When work matters: The varying impact of adolescent work intensity on high school drop-out. *Sociology of Education, 80,* 158–178.

Leiderman, P. H., Tulkin, S. R., & Rosenfeld, A. (Eds.). (1977). *Culture and infancy: Variations in the human experience.* New York: Academic Press.

Lempers, J. D., & Clark-Lempers, D. S. (1992). Young, middle, and late adolescents' comparisons of the functional importance of five significant relationships. *Journal of Youth and Adolescence, 21,* 53–96.

Leon, I. G. (2002). Adoption losses: Naturally occurring or socially constructed? *Child Development, 73,* 652–663.

Lerner, R. M., Easterbrooks, A., & Mistry, J. (Eds.). (2004). *Handbook of psychology: Vol. 6. Developmental psychology.* New York: Wiley.

Lerner, R. M., Lewin-Bizan, S., & Warren, A. E. A. (2011). Concepts and theories of human development. In M. H. Bornstein & M. E. Lamb (Eds.), *Developmental science: An advanced textbook* (6th ed., pp. 3–49). New York: Taylor & Francis Group.

Leventhal, T., & Brooks-Gunn, J. (2000). The neighborhoods they live in: The effects of neighborhood residence on child and adolescent outcomes. *Psychological Bulletin, 126,* 309–337.

Levy, B. (2009). Stereotype embodiment. *Current Directions in Psychological Science, 18,* 332–336.

Lewin, K. (1947). Group decision and social change. In T. Newcomb & E. Hartley (Eds.), *Readings in social psychology* (pp. 330–344). New York: Holt, Rinehart and Winston.

Light, D. (1980). *Becoming psychiatrists: The professional transformation of the self.* New York: W. W. Norton.

Lorence, J., & Mortimer, J. T. (1979). Work experience and political orientation: A panel study. *Social Forces, 58,* 651–676.

Lovelace, S., & Wheeler, T. R. (2006). Cultural discontinuity between home and school language socialization patterns: Implications for teachers. *Education, 127,* 303–309.

Lutfey, K. E., & McKinlay, J. B. (2009). What happens along the diagnostic pathway to CHD treatment? Qualitative results concerning cognitive processes. *Sociology of Health and Illness, 31,* 1077–1092.

Lutfey, K. E., & Mortimer, J. T. (2003). Development and socialization through the adult life course. In J. DeLamater (Ed.), *Handbook of social psychology* (pp. 183–202). New York: Plenum.

Maccoby, E. E. (2007). Historical overview of socialization research and theory. In J. E. Grusec & P.D. Hastings (eds.), *Handbook of socialization: Theory and research* (pp. 13–41). New York: Guilford Press.

Mathews, T. J., & Hamilton, B. E. (2009). *Delayed childbearing: More women are having their first child later in life* (NCHS Data Brief 21). Hyattsville, MD: National Center for Health Statistics, Center for Disease Control.

McCall, R. B. (1981). Nature-nurture and the two realms of development: A proposed integration with respect to mental development. *Child Development, 52,* 1–12.

McCartney, K., Harris, M. J., & Bernieri, F. (1990). Growing up and growing apart: A developmental meta-analysis of twin studies. *Psychological Bulletin, 107,* 226–237.

McHale, J., Khazan, I., Erera, P., Rotman, T., DeCourcey, W., & McConnell, M. (2002). Co-parenting in diverse family systems. In M. H. Bornstein (Ed.), *Handbook of parenting: Vol. 3. Status and social conditions of parenting* (2nd ed., pp. 75–107). Mahwah, NJ: Erlbaum.

Meeus, W., Iedema, J., Helsen, M., & Vollebergh, W. (1999). Patterns of adolescent identity development: Review of literature and longitudinal analysis. *Developmental Review, 19,* 419–461.

Mihalic, S. W., & Elliott, D. (1997). Short and long term consequences of adolescent work. *Youth and Society, 28,* 464–498.

Miller, P. J., & Sperry, L. L. (1988). Early talk about the past: The origins of conversational stories of personal experience. *Journal of Child Language, 15,* 293–315.

Moen, P. (1996). A life course perspective on retirement, gender, and well-being. *Journal of Occupational Health Psychology, 1,* 131–144.

Moen, P., Kim, J. E., & Hofmeister, H. (2001). Couples' work/retirement transitions, gender, and marital quality. *Social Psychology Quarterly, 64,* 55–71.

Moen, P., & Roehling, P. (2005). *The career mystique: Cracks in the American dream.* Lanham, MD: Rowman and Littlefield.

Moen, P., Sweet, S., & Swisher, R. (2005). Embedded career clocks: The case of retirement planning. In R. Macmillan (Ed.), *Advances in life course research series: Vol. 9. The structure of the life course: Standardized? Individualized? Differentiated?* (pp. 237–265). New York: Elsevier.

Morrison, E. W. (2002). Newcomers' relationships: The role of social network ties during socialization. *Academy of Management Journal, 45,* 1149–1160.

Mortimer, J. T. (2003). *Working and growing up in America.* Cambridge, MA: Harvard University Press.

Mortimer, J. T., Finch, M., Ryu, S., & Shanahan, M. (1996). The effects of work intensity on adolescent mental health, achievement, and behavioral adjustment: New evidence from a prospective study. *Child Development, 67,* 1243–1261.

Mortimer, J. T., Harley, C., & Staff, J. (2002). The quality of part-time work and youth mental health. *Work and Occupations, 29,* 166–197.

Mortimer, J. T., & Lorence, J. (1979). Work experience and occupational value socialization: A longitudinal study. *American Journal of Sociology, 84,* 1361–1385.

Mortimer, J. T., Pimentel, E., Ryu, S., Shanahan, M., & Call, K. T. (1996). The effects of work intensity on adolescent mental health, achievement, and behavioral adjustment: New evidence from a prospective study. *Child Development, 67,* 1243–1261.

Mortimer, J. T., & Shanahan, M. J. (Eds.) (2003). *Handbook of the life course.* New York: Kluwer Academic/Plenum.

Mortimer, J. T., & Simmons, R. G. (1978). Adult socialization. *Annual Review of Sociology, 4,* 421–454.

Mortimer, J. T., & Staff, J. (2004). Early work as a source of developmental discontinuity during the transition to adulthood. *Development and Psychopathology, 16,* 1047–1070.

Mortimer, J. T., Vuolo, M., Staff, J., Wakefield, S., & Xie, W. (2008). Tracing the timing of 'career' acquisition in a contemporary youth cohort. *Work and Occupations, 35,* 44–84.

Mortimer, J. T., & Zimmer-Gembeck, M. J. (2007). Adolescent paid work and career development. In V. Skorikov & W. Patton (Eds.), *Career development in childhood and adolescence* (pp. 255–275). Rotterdam, The Netherlands: Sense.

Mortimer, J. T., Zimmer-Gembeck, M. J., Holmes, M., & Shanahan, M. J. (2002). The process of occupational decision-making: Patterns during the transition to adulthood. *Journal of Vocational Behavior, 61,* 439–465.

National Institute of Child Health and Human Development Early Child Care Research Network. (1996). Characteristics of infant child care: Factors contributing to positive caregiving. *Early Childhood Research Quarterly, 11,* 269–306.

National Institute of Child Health and Human Development Early Child Care Research Network. (1997). Child care in the first year of life. *Merrill-Palmer Quarterly, 43,* 340–360.

O'Connor, T. G., Deater-Deckard, K., Fulker, D., Rutter, M., & Plomin, R. (1998). Genotype-environment correlations in late childhood and early adolescence: Antisocial behavior problems and coercive parenting. *Developmental Psychology, 34,* 970–981.

Omoto, A. M., & Snyder, M. (1995). Sustained helping without obligation: Motivation, longevity of service, and perceptual attitude change among AIDS volunteers. *Journal of Personality and Social Psychology, 68,* 671–686.

O'Neil, R., Parke, R. D., & McDowell, D. J. (2001). Objective and subjective features of children's neighborhoods: Relations to parental regulatory strategies and children's social competence. *Journal of Applied Developmental Psychology, 22,* 135–155.

Orrange, R. (2003). The emerging mutable self: Gender dynamics and creative adaptations in defining work, family, and the future. *Social Forces, 82,* 1–34.

Panak, W. F., & Garber, J. (1992). Role of aggression, rejection, and attributions in the prediction of depression in children. *Development and Psychopathology, 4,* 145–165.

Parke, R. D., Killian, C. M., Dennis, J., Flyr, M. V., McDowell, D. J., Simpkins, S., et al. (2003). Managing the external environment: The parent and child as active agents in the system. In L. Kuczynski (Ed.), *Handbook of dynamics in parent-child relations* (pp. 247–270). Thousand Oaks, CA: Sage.

Parke, R. D., Simpkins, S. D., McDowell, D. J., Kim, M., Killian, C., Dennis, J., et al. (2002). Relative contributions of families and peers to children's social development. In P. K. Smith & C. H. Craig (Eds.), *Blackwell handbook of childhood social development* (pp. 156–177). Malden, MA: Blackwell.

Parker, J. G., & Gottman, J. M. (1989). Social and emotional development in a relational context: Friendship interaction from early childhood to adolescence. In T. J. Berndt & G. W. Ladd (Eds.), *Peer relationships in child development* (pp. 95–131). New York: John Wiley & Sons.

Paternoster, R., Bushway, S., Brame, R., & Apel, R. (2003). The effect of teenage employment on delinquency and problem behaviors. *Social Forces, 82,* 297–336.

Petkoska, J., & Earl, J. K. (2009). Understanding the influence of demographic and psychological variables in retirement planning. *Psychology and Aging, 24,* 245–251.

Pettit, G. S. (2004). Violent children in developmental perspective: Risk and protective factors and the mechanisms through which they (may) operate. *Current Directions in Psychological Science, 13,* 194–197.

Pianta, R. C., Hamre, B., & Stuhlman, M. (2003). Relationships between teachers and children. In W. M. Reynolds & G. E. Miller (Vol. Eds.), & I. B. Weiner (Series Ed.), *Handbook of psychology: Vol. 7. Educational psychology* (pp. 199–234). New York: John Wiley and Sons.

Pianta, R. C., La Paro, K. M., Payne, C., Cox, M. J., & Bradley, R. (2002). The relation of kindergarten classroom environment to teacher, family, and school characteristics and child outcomes. *The Elementary School Journal, 102,* 225–238.

Pinquart, M., & Schindler, I. (2007). Changes of life satisfaction in the transition to retirement: A latent-class approach. *Psychology and Aging, 22,* 442–455.

Pinquart, M., & Silbereisen, R. K. (2009). European Union. In M. H. Bornstein (Ed.), *The handbook of cultural developmental science. Part 2. Development in different places on earth* (pp. 341–357). New York: Taylor & Francis Group.

Pomerleau, A., Bolduc, D., Malcuit, G., & Cossette, L. (1990). Pink or blue: Environmental gender stereotypes in the first two years of life. *Sex Roles, 22,* 359–367.

Price, J. M., & Dodge, K. A. (1989). Reactive and proactive aggression in childhood: Relations to peer status and social context dimensions. *Journal of Abnormal Child Psychology, 17,* 455–471.

Price, J. M., & Ladd, G. W. (1986). Assessment of children's friendships: Implications for social competence and social adjustment. In R. Prinz (Ed.), *Advances in behavioral assessment of children and families* (Vol. 2, pp. 121–149). Greenwich, CT: JAI Press.

Quick, H. E., & Moen P. (1998). Gender, employment, and retirement quality: A life course approach to the differential experiences of men and women. *Journal of Occupational Health Psychology, 3,* 44–64.

Registration of Methods Branch Division of Vital Statistics. (1964). *Vital statistics of the United States: Volume III—Marriage and divorce.* Washington, DC: U.S. Department of Health, Education and Welfare.

Reid, M., Landesman, S., Treder, R., & Jaccard, J. (1989). "My family and friends": Six- to twelve-year-old children's perceptions of social support. *Child Development, 60,* 896–910.

Reimer, K. J. (1996). Emotion socialization and children's emotional expressiveness in the preschool context (emotional expression). *Dissertation Abstracts International, 57*(07A), 0010.

Relman, A. S. (1980). The new medical-industrial complex. *New England Journal of Medicine, 303,* 963–970.

Rheingold, H. L., & Cook, K. V. (1975). The contents of boys' and girls' rooms as an index of parents' behavior. *Child Development, 46,* 445–463.

Ritzer, G. (2001). *Explorations in the sociology of consumption: Fast food, credit cards, and casinos.* Thousand Oaks, CA: Sage.

Robinson, C. C., & Morris, J. T. (1986). The gender-stereotyped nature of Christmas toys received by 36-, 48-, and 60- month-old children: A comparison between nonrequested vs. requested toys. *Sex Roles, 15,* 21–32.

Roeser, R. W., Midgley, C., & Urdan, T. C. (1996). Perceptions of the school psychological environment and early adolescents' psychological and behavioral functioning in school: Mediating the role of goals and belonging. *Journal of Educational Psychology, 88,* 408–422.

Rowe, J. W., & Kahn, R. L. (1987). Human aging. *Science, 237,* 143–149.

Rubin, K. H., Bukowski, W., & Parker, J. G. (1998). Peer interactions, relationships, and groups. In N. Eisenberg & W. Damon (Eds.), *Handbook of child psychology: Vol. 3. Social, emotional, and personality development* (5th ed., pp. 619–700). New York: Wiley.

Rubin, K. H., & Burgess, K. B. (2002). Parents of aggressive and withdrawn children. In M. H. Bornstein (Ed.), *Handbook of parenting Vol. 1 Children and parenting* (2nd ed., pp. 383–418). Mahwah, NJ: Erlbaum.

Rubin, K. H., Coplan, R., Chen, X., Bowker, J., & McDonald, K. L. (2011). The role of parent-child relationships in child development. In M. H. Bornstein & M. E. Lamb (Eds.), *Developmental science: An advanced textbook* (6th ed., pp. 519–570). New York: Taylor & Francis Group.

Sameroff, A. (1975). Transactional models of early social relations. *Human Development, 18,* 65–79.

Sampson, R. J., & Laub, J. H. (1993). *Crime in the making: Pathways and turning points through life.* Cambridge, MA: Harvard University Press.

Schiff, M., Duyme, M., Dumaret, A., & Tomkiewicz, S. (1982). How much could we boost scholastic achievement and IQ scores? A direct answer from a French adoption study. *Cognition, 12,* 165–196.

Schoenhals, M., Tienda, M., & Schneider, B. (1998). The educational and personal consequences of adolescent employment. *Social Forces, 77,* 723–748.

Schoenherr, R. A., & Greeley, A. M. (1974). Role commitment processes and the American Catholic priesthood. *American Sociological Review, 39,* 407–426.

Schulz, R., & Heckhausen, J. (1996). A life span model of successful aging. *American Psychologist, 51,* 702–714.

Schwartz, D., Dodge, K. A., Pettit, G. S., & Bates, J. E. (2000). Friendship as a moderating factor in the pathway between early harsh home environment and later victimization in the peer group. *Developmental Psychology, 36,* 646–662.

Seavey, C. A., Katz, P. A., & Zalk, S. R. (1975). Baby X: The effect of gender labels on adult responses to infants. *Sex Roles, 1,* 103–110.

Seidman, E., Allen, L., Aber, J. L., Mitchell, C., & Feinman, J. (1994). The impact of school transitions in early adolescence on the self-system and perceived social context of poor urban youth. *Child Development, 65,* 507–522.

Shanahan, M. J. (2000). Pathways to adulthood in changing societies: Variability and mechanisms in life course perspective. *Annual Review of Sociology, 26,* 667–692.

Shanahan, M. J., Finch, M. D., Mortimer, J. T., & Ryu, S. (1991). Adolescent work experience and depressive affect. *Social Psychology Quarterly, 54,* 299–317.

Shanahan, M. J., & Mortimer, J. T. (1996). Understanding the positive consequences of psychosocial stress. *Advances in Group Processes, 13,* 189–209.

Shanahan, M. J., Porfeli, E., Mortimer, J. T., & Erickson, L. (2005). Subjective age identity and the transition to adulthood: When does one become an adult? In R. A. Settersten, Jr., F. F. Furstenberg, Jr., & R. G. Rumbaut (Eds.), *On the frontier of adulthood: Theory, research, and public policy* (pp. 225–255). Chicago, IL: University of Chicago Press.

Shapiro, A., & Cooney, T. M. (2007). Divorce and intergenerational relations across the life course. In T. J. Owens & J. J. Suitor (Eds.), *Advances in life course research: Vol. 12: Interpersonal relations across the life course* (pp. 191–219). New York: Elsevier.

Shippee, T. P. (2009). But I am not moving: Residents' perspectives on transitions within a continuing care retirement community. *The Gerontologist, 49,* 418–427.

Sidorowicz, L. S., & Lunney, G. S. (1980). Baby X revisited. *Sex Roles, 6,* 67–73.

Skaggs, B. C., & Leicht, K. T. (2005). Management paradigm change in the United States: A professional autonomy prospective. *Research in the Sociology of Work, 15,* 123–149.

Skinner, E. A., & Belmont, M. J. (1993). Motivation in the classroom: Reciprocal effects of teacher behavior and student engagement across the school year. *Journal of Educational Psychology, 85,* 571–581.

Smetana, J. G., Kochanska, G., & Chuang, S. (2000). Mothers' conceptions of everyday rules for young toddlers: A longitudinal investigation. *Merrill-Palmer Quarterly, 46,* 391–416.

Smith, D., & Moen, P. (2004). Retirement satisfaction for retirees and their spouses: Do gender and the retirement decision-making process matter? *Journal of Family Issues, 25,* 262–285.

Smith, J., & Baltes, M. M. (1998). The role of gender in very old age: Profiles of functioning and everyday life patterns. *Psychology and Aging, 13,* 676–695.

Smith, P. K., & Drew, L. M. (2002). Grandparenthood. In M. H. Bornstein (Ed.), *Handbook of parenting: Vol. 3. Status and social conditions of parenting* (2nd ed., pp. 141–172). Mahwah, NJ: Erlbaum.

Smith, P. K., Shu, S., & Madsen, K. (2001). Characteristics of victims of school bullying: Developmental changes in coping strategies and skills. In J. Juvonen & S. Graham (Eds.), *Peer harassment in school: The plight of the vulnerable and victimized* (pp. 332–351). New York: Guilford Press.

Solomon, D., Watson, M., Battistich, V., Schaps, E., & Delucchi, K. (1992). Creating a caring community: Educational practices that promote children's prosocial development. In F. Oser, D. Andreas, & J. Patry (Eds.), *Effective and responsible teaching: The new synthesis* (pp. 383–395). San Francisco, CA: Jossey-Bass.

Staff, J., Messersmith, E. E., & Schulenberg, J. E. (2009). Adolescents and the world of work. In R. Lerner & L. Steinberg (Eds.), *Handbook of adolescent psychology* (3rd ed., pp. 270–313). New York: John Wiley and Sons.

Staff, J., & Mortimer, J. T. (2007). Educational and work strategies from adolescence to early adulthood: Consequences for educational attainment. *Social Forces, 85,* 1169–1194.

Stattin, H., & Kerr, M. (2000). Parental monitoring: A reinterpretation. *Child Development, 71,* 1072–1085.

Steinberg, L., Bornstein, M. H., Vandell, D. L., & Rook, K. S. (2010). *Lifespan development.* Belmont, CA: Wadsworth.

Steinberg, L., & Cauffman, E. (1995). The impact of employment on adolescent development. *Annals of Child Development, 11,* 131–166.

Steinberg, L., & Dornbusch, S. M. (1991). Negative correlates of part-time employment during adolescence: Replication and elaboration. *Developmental Psychology, 27,* 304–313.

Stone, J. R., & Mortimer, J. T. (1998). The effect of adolescent employment on vocational development: Public and educational policy implications. *Journal of Vocational Behavior, 53,* 184–214.

Stoolmiller, M. (1999). Implications of the restricted range of family environments for estimates of heritability and nonshared environment in behavior genetic adoption studies. *Psychological Bulletin, 125,* 392–409.

Swartz, T. T. (2009). Intergenerational family relations in adulthood: Patterns, variations, and implications in the contemporary United States. *Annual Review of Sociology, 35,* 191–212.

Sweeney, J., & Bradbard, M. R. (1989). Mothers' and fathers' changing perceptions of their male and female infants over the course of pregnancy. *Journal of Genetic Psychology, 149,* 393–404.

Talaga, J. A., & Beehr, T. A. (1995). Are there gender differences in predicting retirement decisions? *Journal of Applied Psychology, 80,* 16–28.

Tallman, I., Gray, L. N., Kullberg, V., & Henderson, D. (1999). The intergenerational transmission of marital conflict: Testing a process model. *Social Psychology Quarterly, 62,* 219–239.

Tejada-Vera, B., & Sutton, P. D. (2009). *Births, marriages, divorces, and deaths: Provisional data for 2008* (National Vital Statistics Report 57). Hyattsville, MD: National Center for Health Statistics, Center for Disease Control.

Thornton, M. C., Chatters, L. M., Taylor, R. J., & Allen, W. R. (1990). Sociodemographic and environmental correlates of racial socialization by Black parents. *Child Development, 61,* 401–409.

Turkheimer, E., & Waldron, M. (2000). Nonshared environment: A theoretical, methodological, and quantitative review. *Psychological Bulletin, 126,* 78–108.

Uggen, C., Manza, J., & Behrens, A. (2004). "Less than the average citizen": Stigma, role transition, and the civic reintegration of convicted felons. In S. Maruna & R. Immarigeon (Eds.), *After crime and punishments: Pathways to offender reintegration* (pp. 258–290). Cullompton, Devon: Willan.

Uggen, C., & Wakefield, S. (2005). Young adults reentering the community from the criminal justice system: The challenge of becoming an adult. In D. W. Osgood, E. M. Foster, C. Flanagan, & G. R. Ruth (Eds.), *On your own without a net: The transition to adulthood for vulnerable populations* (pp. 114–144). Chicago, IL: University of Chicago Press.

Van den Boom, D. C. (1989). Neonatal irritability and the development of attachment. In G. A. Kohnstamm & J. E. Bates (Eds.), *Temperament in childhood* (pp. 299–318). Oxford: Wiley.

Van den Boom, D. C. (1994). The influence of temperament and mothering on attachment and exploration: An experimental manipulation of sensitive responsiveness among lower-class mothers with irritable infants. *Child Development, 65,* 1457–1477.

Vaughan, D. (1986). *Uncoupling: Turning points in intimate relationships.* New York: Oxford University Press.

Wanous, J. P., Reichers, A. E., & Malik, S. D. (1984). Organizational socialization and group development: Toward an integrative perspective. *Academy of Management Review, 9,* 670–683.

Warren, J. R., & Lee, J. C. (2003). The impact of adolescent employment on high school dropout: Differences by individual and labor-market characteristics. *Social Science Research, 32,* 98–128.

Warren, J. R., LePore, P. C., & Mare, R. D. (2000). Employment during high school: Consequences for students' grades in academic courses. *American Educational Research Journal, 37,* 943–969.

Watson-Gegeo, K. A. (1992). Thick explanation in the ethnographic study of child socialization: A longitudinal study of the problem of schooling for Kwara'ae (Solomon Islands) children. In W. A. Corsaro & P. J. Miller (Eds.), *The Jossey-Bass education series: No. 58. Interpretive approaches to children's socialization. New directions for child development* (pp. 51–66). San Francisco, CA: Jossey-Bass.

Weinstein, R. S. (2002). *Reaching higher: The power of expectations in schooling.* Cambridge, MA: Harvard University Press.

Weisner, T. S. (1993). Overview: Sibling similarity and difference in different cultures. In C. W. Nuckolls (Ed.), *Siblings in south Asia: Brothers and sisters in cultural context* (pp. 1–17). New York: Guilford Press.

Weisner, T. S., & Gallimore, R. (1977). My brother's keeper: Child and sibling caretaking. *Current Anthropology, 18,* 169–190.

Wentzel, K. R. (1994). Relations of social goal pursuit to social acceptance, classroom behavior, and perceived social support. *Journal of Educational Psychology, 86,* 173–182.

Wentzel, K. R. (2002). Are effective teachers like good parents? Teaching styles and student adjustment in early adolescence. *Child Development, 73,* 287–301.

Wentzel, K. R. (2003). Sociometric status and adjustment in middle school: A longitudinal study. *Journal of Early Adolescence, 23,* 5–28.

Wentzel, K. R., Filisetti, L., & Looney, L. (2007). Adolescent prosocial behavior: The role of self-processes and contextual cues. *Child Development, 78,* 895–910.

Wentzel, K. R., & Looney, L. (2007). Socialization in school settings. In J. E. Grusec & P. D. Hastings (Eds.), *Handbook of socialization: Theory and research* (pp. 382–403). New York: Guilford Press.

Wentzel, K. R., Looney, L., & Battle, A. (2006). *Teacher and peer contributions to classroom climate in middle school and high school.* Unpublished manuscript, University of Maryland, College Park.

Wentzel, K. R., & Watkins, D. E. (2002). Peer relationships and collaborative learning as contexts for academic enablers. *School Psychology Review, 31,* 366–377.

Wesley, P. W., & Buysse, V. (2003). Making meaning of school readiness in schools and communities. *Early Childhood Research Quarterly, 18,* 351–375.

Wethington, E., & Kamp Dush, C. M. (2007). Assessments of parenting quality and experiences across the life course. In T. J. Owens & J. J. Suitor (Eds.), *Advances in life course research: Vol. 12: Interpersonal relations across the life course* (pp. 123–152). New York: Elsevier.

Wohlwill, J. F. (1973). *The study of behavioral development.* Oxford: Academic Press.

Wright, C. R. (1967). Changes in the occupational commitment of graduate sociology students. *Sociological Inquiry, 37,* 55–62.

Zajonc, R. B. (1983). Validating the confluence model. *Psychological Bulletin, 95,* 457–465.

Zimmer-Gembeck, M. J., & Mortimer, J. T. (2007). Selection processes and vocational development: A multi-method approach. In R. MacMillan (Ed.), *Advances in life course research: Vol. 11: Constructing adulthood: Agency and subjectivity in adolescence and adulthood* (pp. 121–148). New York: Elsevier.

Zukow-Goldring, P. (2002). Sibling caregiving. In M. H. Bornstein (Ed.), *Handbook of parenting: Vol. 3. Status and social conditions of parenting* (2nd ed., pp. 253–286). Mahwah, NJ: Erlbaum.

INDEX

Note: Page references followed by "*f*" and "*t*" denote figures and tables, respectively.